Features for Students

MyStatLab provides students with a personalized, interactive environment where they can learn at their own pace and measure their progress.

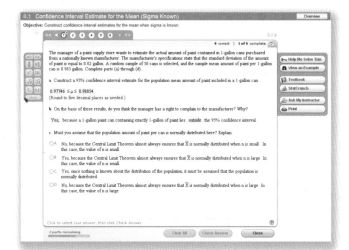

◀ Interactive tutorial exercises

MyStatLab's homework and practice exercises, correlated to the exercises in the textbook, are generated algorithmically, giving students unlimited opportunity for practice and mastery. Exercises include guided solutions, sample problems, and learning aids for extra help at point-of-use, and they offer helpful feedback when students enter incorrect answers.

StatCrunch ▶

StatCrunch offers both numerical and data analysis and uses interactive graphics to illustrate the connection between objects selected in a graph and the underlying data. In most MyStatLab courses, all data sets from the textbook are pre-loaded in StatCrunch, and StatCrunch is also available as a tool from all online homework and practice exercises.

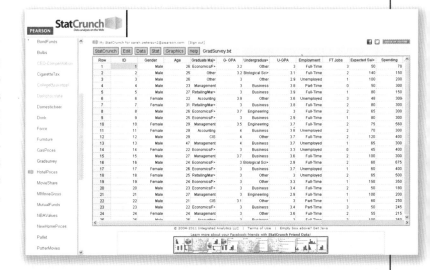

Student Purchasing Options

There are many ways for students to sign up for MyStatLab:

• Use the access kit bundled with a new textbook

• Purchase a stand-alone access kit from the bookstore

• Register online through **pearsonmylabandmastering.com**

PEARSON

Business ninth edition
Statistics
A Decision-Making Approach

ninth edition

Business
Statistics
A Decision-Making Approach

DAVID F. GROEBNER
Boise State University, Professor Emeritus of Production Management

PATRICK W. SHANNON
Boise State University, Dean of the College of Business and Economics

PHILLIP C. FRY
Boise State University, Professor, ITSCM Department Chair

PEARSON

Boston   Columbus   Indianapolis   New York   San Francisco   Upper Saddle River
Amsterdam   Cape Town   Dubai   London   Madrid   Milan   Munich   Paris   Montreal   Toronto
Delhi   Mexico City   Sao Paulo   Sydney   Hong Kong   Seoul   Singapore   Taipei   Tokyo

Editor in Chief: Donna Battista
Senior Project Manager: Mary Kate Murray
Editorial Assistant: Ashlee Bradbury
Director of Marketing: Maggie Moylan
Marketing Manager: Jami Minard
Marketing Assistant: Gianna Sandri
Senior Managing Editor: Judy Leale
Operations Specialist: Cathleen Petersen
Creative Director: Blair Brown
Art Director: Steve Frim
Cover Designer: Joseph DePinho
Manager, Rights and Permissions: Brooks Hill-Whilton
Image Permission Coordinator: Jason Perkins
Manager, Cover Visual Research & Permissions: Karen Sanatar
Media Producer: Sarah Peterson
Media Project Manager: John Cassar
Full-Service Project Management: Tammy Haskins
Composition: PreMediaGlobal, Inc.
Printer/Binder: Courier / Kendallville
Cover Printer: Lehigh-Phoenix Color / Hagerstown
Text Font: 10/12 Times

Credits and acknowledgments borrowed from other sources and reproduced, with permission, in this textbook appear on appropriate page within text.

Microsoft and/or its respective suppliers make no representations about the suitability of the information contained in the documents and related graphics published as part of the services for any purpose. All such documents and related graphics are provided "as is" without warranty of any kind. Microsoft and/or its respective suppliers hereby disclaim all warranties and conditions with regard to this information, including all warranties and conditions of merchantability, whether express, implied or statutory, fitness for a particular purpose, title and non-infringement. In no event shall Microsoft and/or its respective suppliers be liable for any special, indirect or consequential damages or any damages whatsoever resulting from loss of use, data or profits, whether in an action of contract, negligence or other tortious action, arising out of or in connection with the use or performance of information available from the services.

The documents and related graphics contained herein could include technical inaccuracies or typographical errors. Changes are periodically added to the information herein. Microsoft and/or its respective suppliers may make improvements and/or changes in the product(s) and/or the program(s) described herein at any time. Partial screen shots may be viewed in full within the software version specified.

Microsoft® and Windows® are registered trademarks of the Microsoft Corporation in the U.S.A. and other countries. This book is not sponsored or endorsed by or affiliated with the Microsoft Corporation.

Many of the designations by manufacturers and seller to distinguish their products are claimed as trademarks. Where those designations appear in this book, and the publisher was aware of a trademark claim, the designations have been printed in initial caps or all caps.

Library of Congress Cataloging-in-Publication Data
Business statistics : a decision-making approach / David F. Groebner . . . [et al.]. — 9th ed.
   p. cm.
  ISBN 978-0-13-302184-4 (hbk.)
  1. Commercial statistics. 2. Statistical decision. I. Groebner, David F.
  HF1017.G73 2014
  519.5—dc23

                       2012041149

10 9 8 7 6 5 4 3 2 1

ISBN-10:   0-13-302184-X
ISBN-13: 978-0-13-302184-4

To Jane and my family, who survived the process one more time.

David F. Groebner

To Kathy, my wife and best friend; to our children, Jackie and Jason.

Patrick W. Shannon

To my wonderful family: Susan, Alex, Allie, Candace, and Courtney.

Phillip C. Fry

About the **Authors**

David F. Groebner is Professor Emeritus of Production Management in the College of Business and Economics at Boise State University. He has bachelor's and master's degrees in engineering and a Ph.D. in business administration. After working as an engineer, he has taught statistics and related subjects for 27 years. In addition to writing textbooks and academic papers, he has worked extensively with both small and large organizations, including Hewlett-Packard, Boise Cascade, Albertson's, and Ore-Ida. He has worked with numerous government agencies, including Boise City and the U.S. Air Force.

Patrick W. Shannon, Ph.D. is Dean and Professor of Supply Chain Operations Management in the College of Business and Economics at Boise State University. In addition to his administrative responsibilities, he has taught graduate and undergraduate courses in business statistics, quality management, and production and operations management. In addition, Dr. Shannon has lectured and consulted in the statistical analysis and quality management areas for more than 20 years. Among his consulting clients are Boise Cascade Corporation, Hewlett-Packard, PowerBar, Inc., Potlatch Corporation, Woodgrain Millwork, Inc., J.R. Simplot Company, Zilog Corporation, and numerous other public- and private-sector organizations. Professor Shannon has co-authored several university-level textbooks and has published numerous articles in such journals as *Business Horizons, Interfaces, Journal of Simulation, Journal of Production and Inventory Control, Quality Progress,* and *Journal of Marketing Research.* He obtained B.S. and M.S. degrees from the University of Montana and a Ph.D. in statistics and quantitative methods from the University of Oregon.

Phillip C. Fry is a professor in the College of Business and Economics at Boise State University, where he has taught since 1988. Phil received his B.A. and M.B.A. degrees from the University of Arkansas and his M.S. and Ph.D. degrees from Louisiana State University. His teaching and research interests are in the areas of business statistics, production management, and quantitative business modeling. In addition to his academic responsibilities, Phil has consulted with and provided training to small and large organizations, including Boise Cascade Corporation, Hewlett-Packard Corporation, the J.R. Simplot Company, United Water of Idaho, Woodgrain Millwork, Inc., Boise City, and Micron Electronics. Phil spends most of his free time with his wife, Susan, and his four children, Phillip Alexander, Alejandra Johanna, and twins Courtney Rene and Candace Marie.

Brief **Contents**

Chapter 1   The Where, Why, and How of Data Collection   1

Chapter 2   Graphs, Charts, and Tables—Describing Your Data   31

Chapter 3   Describing Data Using Numerical Measures   81

Chapters 1–3   Special Review Section   133

Chapter 4   Introduction to Probability   140

Chapter 5   Discrete Probability Distributions   182

Chapter 6   Introduction to Continuous Probability Distributions   224

Chapter 7   Introduction to Sampling Distributions   255

Chapter 8   Estimating Single Population Parameters   295

Chapter 9   Introduction to Hypothesis Testing   336

Chapter 10   Estimation and Hypothesis Testing for Two Population Parameters   386

Chapter 11   Hypothesis Tests and Estimation for Population Variances   435

Chapter 12   Analysis of Variance   462

Chapters 8–12   Special Review Section   514

Chapter 13   Goodness-of-Fit Tests and Contingency Analysis   530

Chapter 14   Introduction to Linear Regression and Correlation Analysis   559

Chapter 15   Multiple Regression Analysis and Model Building   612

Chapter 16   Analyzing and Forecasting Time-Series Data   683

Chapter 17   Introduction to Nonparametric Statistics   743

Chapter 18   Introduction to Quality and Statistical Process Control   774

APPENDIX *A*   Random Numbers Table   802

APPENDIX *B*   Cumulative Binomial Distribution Table   803

APPENDIX *C*   Cumulative Poisson Probability Distribution Table   816

APPENDIX *D*   Standard Normal Distribution Table   821

APPENDIX *E*   Exponential Distribution Table   822

APPENDIX *F*   Values of t for Selected Probabilities   823

APPENDIX *G*   Values of χ^2 for Selected Probabilities   824

APPENDIX *H* F-Distribution Table   825

APPENDIX *I*   Distribution of the Studentized Range (q-values)   831

APPENDIX *J*   Critical Values of r in the Runs Test   833

APPENDIX *K*   Mann-Whitney U Test Probabilities ($n < 9$)   834

APPENDIX *L*   Mann-Whitney U Test Critical Values ($9 \leq n \leq 20$)   836

APPENDIX *M*   Critical Values of T in the Wilcoxon Matched-Pairs Signed-Ranks Test ($n \leq 25$)   838

APPENDIX *N*   Critical Values d_L and d_U of the Durbin-Watson Statistic D 839

APPENDIX *O*   Lower and Upper Critical Values W of Wilcoxon Signed-Ranks Test   841

APPENDIX *P*   Control Chart Factors   842

ix

Contents

Preface   xxi

Chapter 1   The Where, Why, and How of Data Collection   1

What Is Business Statistics?   2

Descriptive Statistics   2
Charts and Graphs   3

Inferential Procedures   5
Estimation   5
Hypothesis Testing   5

Procedures for Collecting Data   7

Data Collection Methods   7
Written Questionnaires and Surveys   9
Direct Observation and Personal Interviews   11

Other Data Collection Methods   11

Data Collection Issues   12
Data Accuracy   12
Interviewer Bias   12
Nonresponse Bias   12
Selection Bias   12
Observer Bias   12
Measurement Error   13
Internal Validity   13
External Validity   13

Populations, Samples, and Sampling Techniques   14

Populations and Samples   14
Parameters and Statistics   15

Sampling Techniques   15
Statistical Sampling   16

Data Types and Data Measurement Levels   20

Quantitative and Qualitative Data   20

Time-Series Data and Cross-Sectional Data   21

Data Measurement Levels   21
Nominal Data   21
Ordinal Data   22
Interval Data   22
Ratio Data   22

A Brief Introduction to Data Mining   25

Data Mining—Finding the Important, Hidden Relationships in Data   25
Visual Summary   27 • Key Terms   29 • Chapter Exercises   29

Video Case 1: Statistical Data Collection @ McDonald's   30

Chapter 2   Graphs, Charts, and Tables—Describing Your Data   31

Frequency Distributions and Histograms   32

Frequency Distribution   33

Grouped Data Frequency Distributions   37
Steps for Grouping Data into Classes   38

Histograms   41
Issues with Excel   43

Relative Frequency Histograms and Ogives   45

Joint Frequency Distributions   46

Bar Charts, Pie Charts, and Stem and Leaf Diagrams   53

Bar Charts   53

Pie Charts   57

Stem and Leaf Diagrams   59

Line Charts and Scatter Diagrams   63

Line Charts   63

Scatter Diagrams   66

Descriptive Statistics and Data Mining   69

Pareto Charts   69

Scatter Diagrams   70

Visual Summary   74 • Equations   75 • Key Terms   75 • Chapter Exercises   75

Video Case 2: Drive-Thru Service Times @ McDonald's   78

Case 2.1: Server Downtime   79

Case 2.2: Hudson Valley Apples, Inc.   79

Case 2.3: Welco Lumber Company—Part A   80

Chapter 3   Describing Data Using Numerical Measures   81

Measures of Center and Location   81

Parameters and Statistics   82

Population Mean   82

Sample Mean   85

The Impact of Extreme Values on the Mean   86

Median   87

Skewed and Symmetric Distributions   88

Mode   89

Applying the Measures of Central Tendency   90

Issues with Excel   91

Other Measures of Location   92

Weighted Mean   92

Percentiles   93

Quartiles   95

Issues with Excel   95

Box and Whisker Plots   95

Data-Level Issues   97

Measures of Variation   102

Range   103

Interquartile Range   103

Population Variance and Standard Deviation   104

Sample Variance and Standard Deviation   107

Using the Mean and Standard Deviation Together   113

Coefficient of Variation   113

The Empirical Rule   115

Tchebysheff's Theorem   116

Standardized Data Values   117

Visual Summary   123 • Equations   124 • Key Terms   125 • Chapter Exercises   125

Video Case 3: Drive-Thru Service Times @ McDonald's   129

Case 3.1: WGI—Human Resources   130

Case 3.2: National Call Center   131

Case 3.3: Welco Lumber Company—Part B   131

Case 3.4: AJ's Fitness Center   132

Chapters 1–3   Special Review Section   133

Chapters 1–3   133

Exercises   136

Review Case 1: State Department of Insurance   138

Term Project Assignments   138

Chapter 4   Introduction to Probability   140

The Basics of Probability   141

   Important Probability Terms   141

      Events and Sample Space   141

      Using Tree Diagrams   142

      Mutually Exclusive Events   144

      Independent and Dependent Events   145

   Methods of Assigning Probability   145

      Classical Probability Assessment   146

      Relative Frequency Assessment   147

      Subjective Probability Assessment   149

The Rules of Probability   153

   Measuring Probabilities   153

      Possible Values and the Summation of Possible Values   153

      Addition Rule for Individual Outcomes   153

      Complement Rule   156

      Addition Rule for Any Two Events   157

      Addition Rule for Mutually Exclusive Events   160

   Conditional Probability   160

      Tree Diagrams   163

      Conditional Probability for Independent Events   163

   Multiplication Rule   165

      Multiplication Rule for Two Events   165

      Using a Tree Diagram   166

      Multiplication Rule for Independent Events   166

   Bayes' Theorem   168

Visual Summary   176 • Equations   177 • Key Terms   177 • Chapter Exercises   177

Case 4.1: Great Air Commuter Service   180

Case 4.2: Let's Make a Deal   181

Chapter 5   Discrete Probability Distributions   182

Introduction to Discrete Probability Distributions   183

   Random Variables   183

      Displaying Discrete Probability Distributions Graphically   183

   Mean and Standard Deviation of Discrete Distributions   184

      Calculating the Mean   184

      Calculating the Standard Deviation   185

The Binomial Probability Distribution   190

   The Binomial Distribution   190

   Characteristics of the Binomial Distribution   191

      Combinations   192

      Binomial Formula   194

      Using the Binomial Distribution Table   195

      Mean and Standard Deviation of the Binomial Distribution   196

      Additional Information about the Binomial Distribution   199

Other Discrete Probability Distributions   204

   The Poisson Distribution   204

      Characteristics of the Poisson Distribution   204

      Poisson Probability Distribution Table   206

      The Mean and Standard Deviation of the Poisson Distribution   208

   The Hypergeometric Distribution   209

      The Hypergeometric Distribution with More Than Two Possible Outcomes per Trial   213

Visual Summary   217 • Equations   218 • Key Terms   218 • Chapter Exercises   218

Case 5.1: SaveMor Pharmacies   221

Case 5.2: Arrowmark Vending   222

Case 5.3: Boise Cascade Corporation   222

Chapter 6   Introduction to Continuous Probability Distributions   224

The Normal Probability Distribution   225

The Normal Distribution   225

The Standard Normal Distribution   226

Using the Standard Normal Table   228

Approximate Areas under the Normal Curve   236

Other Continuous Probability Distributions   240

Uniform Probability Distribution   240

The Exponential Probability Distribution   242

Visual Summary   248 • Equations   249 • Key Terms   249 •
Chapter Exercises   249

Case 6.1: State Entitlement Programs   253

Case 6.2: Credit Data, Inc.   253

Case 6.3: American Oil Company   254

Chapter 7   Introduction to Sampling Distributions   255

Sampling Error: What It Is and Why It Happens   256

Calculating Sampling Error   256

The Role of Sample Size in Sampling Error   259

Sampling Distribution of the Mean   264

Simulating the Sampling Distribution for $\bar{x}$ 265

Sampling from Normal Populations   267

The Central Limit Theorem   272

Sampling Distribution of a Proportion   279

Working with Proportions   279

Sampling Distribution of $\bar{p}$ 282

Visual Summary   289 • Equations   290 • Key Terms   290 •
Chapter Exercises   290

Case 7.1: Carpita Bottling Company   294

Case 7.2: Truck Safety Inspection   294

Chapter 8   Estimating Single Population Parameters   295

Point and Confidence Interval Estimates for a Population Mean   296

Point Estimates and Confidence Intervals   296

Confidence Interval Estimate for the Population Mean, σ Known   297

Confidence Interval Calculation   299

Impact of the Confidence Level on the Interval Estimate   301

Impact of the Sample Size on the Interval Estimate   304

Confidence Interval Estimates for the Population Mean, σ Unknown   304

Student's t-Distribution   304

Estimation with Larger Sample Sizes   310

Determining the Required Sample Size for Estimating a Population Mean   314

Determining the Required Sample Size for Estimating μ, σ Known   315

Determining the Required Sample Size for Estimating μ, σ Unknown   316

Estimating a Population Proportion   321

Confidence Interval Estimate for a Population Proportion   321

Determining the Required Sample Size for Estimating a Population Proportion   323

Visual Summary   329 • Equations   330 • Key Terms   330 •
Chapter Exercises   331

Video Case 4: New Product Introductions @ McDonald's   333

Case 8.1: Management Solutions, Inc.   334

Case 8.2: Federal Aviation Administration   334

Case 8.3: Cell Phone Use   334

Chapter 9   Introduction to Hypothesis Testing   336

Hypothesis Tests for Means   337

Formulating the Hypotheses   337
Null and Alternative Hypotheses   337
Testing the Status Quo   337
Testing a Research Hypothesis   338
Testing a Claim about the Population   338
Types of Statistical Errors   340

Significance Level and Critical Value   341

Hypothesis Test for μ, σ Known   342
Calculating Critical Values   342
Decision Rules and Test Statistics   344
p-Value Approach   347

Types of Hypothesis Tests   348

p-Value for Two-Tailed Tests   349

Hypothesis Test for μ, σ Unknown   351

Hypothesis Tests for a Proportion   358

Testing a Hypothesis about a Single Population Proportion   358

Type II Errors   365

Calculating Beta   365

Controlling Alpha and Beta   367

Power of the Test   371

Visual Summary   376 • Equations   377 • Key Terms   378 •
Chapter Exercises   378

Video Case 4: New Product Introductions @ McDonald's   383

Case 9.1: Campbell Brewery, Inc.—Part 1   383

Case 9.2: Wings of Fire   384

Chapter 10   Estimation and Hypothesis Testing for Two Population Parameters   386

Estimation for Two Population Means Using Independent Samples   387

Estimating the Difference between Two Population Means When σ_1 and σ_2 Are Known, Using Independent Samples   387
Estimating the Difference between Two Means When σ_1 and σ_2 Are Unknown, Using Independent Samples   389
What If the Population Variances Are Not Equal?   393

Hypothesis Tests for Two Population Means Using Independent Samples   398

Testing for $\mu_1 - \mu_2$ When σ_1 and σ_2 Are Known, Using Independent Samples   398
Using p-Values   400

Testing $\mu_1 - \mu_2$ When σ_1 and σ_2 Are Unknown, Using Independent Samples   400
What If the Population Variances Are Not Equal?   407

Interval Estimation and Hypothesis Tests for Paired Samples   411

Why Use Paired Samples?   411

Hypothesis Testing for Paired Samples   414

Estimation and Hypothesis Tests for Two Population Proportions   419

Estimating the Difference between Two Population Proportions   419

Hypothesis Tests for the Difference between Two Population Proportions   420

Visual Summary   427 • Equations   428 • Key Terms   429 •
Chapter Exercises   429

Case 10.1: Motive Power Company—Part 1   432

Case 10.2: Hamilton Marketing Services   433

Case 10.3: Green Valley Assembly Company   433

Case 10.4: U-Need-It Rental Agency   434

Chapter 11   Hypothesis Tests and Estimation for Population Variances   435

Hypothesis Tests and Estimation for a Single Population Variance   435

Chi-Square Test for One Population Variance   436

Interval Estimation for a Population Variance   441

Hypothesis Tests for Two Population Variances   445

F-Test for Two Population Variances   445

Additional F-Test Considerations   453

Visual Summary   457 • Equations   458 • Key Terms   458 •
Chapter Exercises   458

Case 11.1: Motive Power Company—Part 2   460

Chapter 12   Analysis of Variance   462

One-Way Analysis of Variance   463

Introduction to One-Way ANOVA   463

Partitioning the Sum of Squares   464

The ANOVA Assumptions   465

Applying One-Way ANOVA   467

The Tukey-Kramer Procedure for Multiple Comparisons   473

Fixed Effects Versus Random Effects in Analysis of Variance   478

Randomized Complete Block Analysis of Variance   483

Randomized Complete Block ANOVA   483

Was Blocking Necessary?   487

Fisher's Least Significant Difference Test   490

Two-Factor Analysis of Variance with Replication   494

Two-Factor ANOVA with Replications   495

Interaction Explained   498

A Caution about Interaction   501

Visual Summary   505 • Equations   506 • Key Terms   506 •
Chapter Exercises   506

Video Case 3: Drive-Thru Service Times @ McDonald's   509

Case 12.1: Agency for New Americans   510

Case 12.2: McLaughlin Salmon Works   511

Case 12.3: NW Pulp and Paper   511

Case 12.4: Quinn Restoration   512

Business Statistics Capstone Project   512

Chapters 8–12   Special Review Section   514

Chapters 8–12   514

Using the Flow Diagrams   526

Exercises   527

Term Project Assignments   529

Business Statistics Capstone Project   529

Chapter 13   Goodness-of-Fit Tests and Contingency Analysis   530

Introduction to Goodness-of-Fit Tests   530

Chi-Square Goodness-of-Fit Test   531

Introduction to Contingency Analysis   544

2×2 Contingency Tables   544

$r \times c$ Contingency Tables   548

Chi-Square Test Limitations   550

Visual Summary   554 • Equations   555 • Key Term   555 •
Chapter Exercises   555

Case 13.1: American Oil Company   557

Case 13.2: Bentford Electronics—Part 1   558

Chapter 14   **Introduction to Linear Regression and Correlation Analysis   559**

Scatter Plots and Correlation   560

The Correlation Coefficient   560

Significance Test for the Correlation   562

Cause-and-Effect Interpretations   566

Simple Linear Regression Analysis   570

The Regression Model and Assumptions   570

Meaning of the Regression Coefficients   571

Least Squares Regression Properties   576

Significance Tests in Regression Analysis   580

The Coefficient of Determination, R^2 580

Significance of the Slope Coefficient   583

Uses for Regression Analysis   592

Regression Analysis for Description   592

Regression Analysis for Prediction   595

Confidence Interval for the Average y, Given x 595

Prediction Interval for a Particular y, Given x 596

Common Problems Using Regression Analysis   598

Visual Summary   604 • Equations   605 • Key Terms   606 • Chapter Exercises   606

Case 14.1: A & A Industrial Products   609

Case 14.2: Sapphire Coffee—Part 1   610

Case 14.3: Alamar Industries   610

Case 14.4: Continental Trucking   611

Chapter 15   **Multiple Regression Analysis and Model Building   612**

Introduction to Multiple Regression Analysis   613

Basic Model-Building Concepts   615

Model Specification   615

Model Building   616

Model Diagnosis   616

Computing the Regression Equation   619

The Coefficient of Determination   620

Model Diagnosis   620

Is the Model Significant?   621

Are the Individual Variables Significant?   622

Is the Standard Deviation of the Regression Model Too Large?   623

Is Multicollinearity a Problem?   625

Confidence Interval Estimation for Regression Coefficients   626

Using Qualitative Independent Variables   631

Possible Improvements to the First City Appraisal Model   635

Working with Nonlinear Relationships   639

Analyzing Interaction Effects   643

The Partial-F Test   647

Stepwise Regression   654

Forward Selection   654

Backward Elimination   655

Standard Stepwise Regression   658

Best Subsets Regression   659

Determining the Aptness of the Model   664

Analysis of Residuals   664

Checking for Linearity   664
Do the Residuals Have Equal Variances at all Levels of Each *x* Variable?   667
Are the Residuals Independent?   667
Checking for Normally Distributed Error Terms   668

Corrective Actions   672

Visual Summary   675 • Equations   676 • Key Terms   676 •
Chapter Exercises   676

Case 15.1: Dynamic Scales, Inc.   680

Case 15.2: Glaser Machine Works   681

Case 15.3: Hawlins Manufacturing   681

Case 15.4: Sapphire Coffee—Part 2   682

Case 15.5: Wendell Motors   682

Chapter 16   Analyzing and Forecasting Time-Series Data   683

Introduction to Forecasting, Time-Series Data, and Index Numbers   683

General Forecasting Issues   684

Components of a Time Series   684
Trend Component   685
Seasonal Component   685
Cyclical Component   687
Random Component   687

Introduction to Index Numbers   687

Aggregate Price Indexes   689

Weighted Aggregate Price Indexes   690
The Paasche Index   691
The Laspeyres Index   692

Commonly Used Index Numbers   693
Consumer Price Index   693
Producer Price Index   694

Stock Market Indexes   694

Using Index Numbers to Deflate a Time Series   694

Trend-Based Forecasting Techniques   697

Developing a Trend-Based Forecasting Model   697

Comparing the Forecast Values to the Actual Data   700
Autocorrelation   702
True Forecasts   706

Nonlinear Trend Forecasting   708
Some Words of Caution   712

Adjusting for Seasonality   712
Computing Seasonal Indexes   713
The Need to Normalize the Indexes   716
Deseasonalizing   716
Using Dummy Variables to Represent Seasonality   718

Forecasting Using Smoothing Methods   723

Exponential Smoothing   724
Single Exponential Smoothing   724
Double Exponential Smoothing   728

Visual Summary   734 • Equations   735 • Key Terms   735 •
Chapter Exercises   736

Video Case 2: Restaurant Location and Re-imaging Decisions @ McDonald's   739

Case 16.1: Park Falls Chamber of Commerce   740

Case 16.2: The St. Louis Companies   741

Case 16.3: Wagner Machine Works   741

Chapter 17   Introduction to Nonparametric Statistics   743

The Wilcoxon Signed Rank Test for One Population Median   743

The Wilcoxon Signed Rank Test—Single Population   744

Nonparametric Tests for Two Population Medians   749

The Mann–Whitney U-Test   749

Mann–Whitney U-Test—Large Samples   752

The Wilcoxon Matched-Pairs Signed Rank Test   754
Ties in the Data   756
Large-Sample Wilcoxon Test   756

Kruskal–Wallis One-Way Analysis of Variance   761

Limitations and Other Considerations   765

Visual Summary   768 • Equations   769 • Chapter Exercises   770

Case 17.1: Bentford Electronics—Part 2   773

Chapter 18   Introduction to Quality and Statistical Process Control   774

Introduction to Statistical Process Control Charts   774

The Existence of Variation   775

Sources of Variation   775
Types of Variation   776
The Predictability of Variation: Understanding the Normal Distribution   776
The Concept of Stability   776

Introducing Statistical Process Control Charts   777

$\bar{x}$ Chart and R-Chart   778

Using the Control Charts   782
p-Charts   786
Using the p-Chart   789
c-Charts   789
Other Control Charts   792

Visual Summary   796 • Equations   797 • Chapter Exercises   798

Case 18.1: Izbar Precision Casters, Inc.   799

Appendices   801

APPENDIX **A**   Random Numbers Table   802
APPENDIX **B**   Cumulative Binomial Distribution Table   803
APPENDIX **C**   Cumulative Poisson Probability Distribution Table   816
APPENDIX **D**   Standard Normal Distribution Table   821
APPENDIX **E**   Exponential Distribution Table   822
APPENDIX **F**   Values of t for Selected Probabilities   823
APPENDIX **G**   Values of χ^2 for Selected Probabilities   824
APPENDIX **H** F-Distribution Table   825
APPENDIX **I**   Distribution of the Studentized Range (q-values)   831
APPENDIX **J**   Critical Values of r in the Runs Test   833
APPENDIX **K**   Mann-Whitney U Test Probabilities ($n < 9$)   834
APPENDIX **L**   Mann-Whitney U Test Critical Values ($9 \leq n \leq 20$)   836
APPENDIX **M**   Critical Values of T in the Wilcoxon Matched-Pairs Signed-Ranks Test ($n \leq 25$)   838
APPENDIX **N**   Critical Values d_L and d_U of the Durbin-Watson Statistic D 839
APPENDIX **O**   Lower and Upper Critical Values W of Wilcoxon Signed-Ranks Test   841
APPENDIX **P**   Control Chart Factors   842

Answers to Selected Odd-Numbered Problems   843

References   863

Glossary   867

Index   873

Preface

In today's workplace, students can have an immediate competitive edge over both new graduates and experienced employees if they know how to apply statistical analysis skills to real-world decision-making problems.

Our intent in writing *Business Statistics: A Decision-Making Approach* is to provide an introductory business statistics text for students who do not necessarily have an extensive mathematics background but who need to understand how statistical tools and techniques are applied in business decision making.

This text differs from its competitors in three key ways:

1. Use of a direct approach and concepts and techniques consistently presented in a systematic and ordered way

2. Presentation of the content at a level that makes it accessible to students of all levels of mathematical maturity. The text features clear, step-by-step explanations that make learning business statistics straightforward.

3. Engaging examples, drawn from our years of experience as authors, educators, and consultants, to show the relevance of the statistical techniques in realistic business decision situations.

Regardless of how accessible or engaging a textbook is, we recognize that many students do not read the chapters from front to back. Instead, they use the text "backward." That is, they go to the assigned exercises and try them, and if they get stuck, they turn to the text to look for examples to help them. Thus, this text features clearly marked, step-by-step examples that students can follow. Each detailed example is linked to a section exercise, which students can use to build specific skills needed to work exercises in the section.

Each chapter begins with a clear set of specific chapter outcomes. The examples and practice exercises are designed to reinforce the objectives and lead students toward the desired outcomes. The exercises are ordered from easy to more difficult and are divided into categories: Conceptual, Skill Development, Business Applications, and Database Exercises.

Another difference is the importance this text places on data and how data are obtained. Many business statistics texts assume that data have already been collected. We have decided to underscore a more modern theme: Data are the starting point. We believe that effective decision making relies on a good understanding of the different types of data and the different data collection options that exist. To highlight our theme, we begin a discussion of data and collecting data in Chapter 1 before any discussion of data analysis is presented. In Chapters 2 and 3, where the important descriptive statistical techniques are introduced, we tie these statistical techniques to the type and level of data for which they are best suited.

Although we know that the role of the computer is important in applying business statistics, it can be overdone at the beginning level to the point where instructors are required to spend too much time teaching the software and too little time teaching statistical concepts. This text features Excel but limits the inclusion of software output to those areas where it is of particular advantage to beginning students.

New to This Edition

- **Textual examples:** Many new business examples throughout the text provide step-by-step details, enabling students to follow solution techniques easily. These examples are provided in addition to the vast array of business applications to give students a real-world, competitive edge. Featured companies in these new examples include Dove Shampoo and Soap, the Frito-Lay Company, Goodyear Tire Company, Lockheed Martin Corporation, the National Federation of Independent Business, Oakland Raiders NFL Football, Southwest Airlines, and Whole Foods Grocery.
- **New Test Manual:** A new test manual has been prepared with well-thought-out test question that correspond directly to this new edition.
- **MyStatLab:** The latest version of this proven student learning tool provides text-specific online homework and assessment opportunities and offers a wide set of course materials, featuring free-response exercises that are algorithmically generated for

unlimited practice and mastery. Students can also use a variety of online tools to independently improve their understanding and performance in the course. Instructors can use MyStatLab's homework and test manager to select and assign their own online exercises and can import TestGen tests for added flexibility.

- **More Excel Focus:** This edition features Excel 2010, with Excel 2010 screen captures used extensively throughout the text to illustrate how this highly regarded software is used as an aid to statistical analysis. While Minitab screen captures have been removed from this edition to improve the flow and readability, detailed Excel 2010 and Minitab instructions are included.

- **New Business Applications:** Numerous new business applications have been included in this edition to provide students current examples showing how the statistical techniques introduced in this text are actually used by real companies. The new applications involve familiar companies and products. These applications help students understand the relevance of statistics and are motivational. These applications cover all business areas from accounting and finance to supply chain management.

- **New Exercises and Data Files:** New exercises have been included throughout the text, and other exercises have been revised and updated. Many new data files have been added to correspond to the new Computer Database exercises, and other data files have been updated with current data.

- **Improved Notation:** The notation associated with population and sample proportions has been revised and improved to be consistent with the general approach taken by most faculty who teach the course.

Key Pedagogical Features

- **Business applications:** One of the strengths of the previous editions of this textbook has been the emphasis on business applications and decision making. This feature is expanded even more in the ninth edition. Many new applications are included, and all applications are highlighted in the text with special icons, making them easier for students to locate as they use the text.

- **Quick prep links:** Each chapter begins with a list that provides several ways to get ready for the topics discussed in the chapter.

- **Chapter outcomes:** At the beginning of each chapter, outcomes, which identify what is to be gained from completing the chapter, are linked to the corresponding main headings. Throughout the text, the chapter outcomes are recalled at the appropriate main headings to remind students of the objectives.

- **Step-by-step approach:** This edition provides continued and improved emphasis on providing concise, step-by-step details to reinforce chapter material.
  - **How to Do It** lists are provided throughout each chapter to summarize major techniques and reinforce fundamental concepts.
  - **Textual examples** throughout the text provide step-by-step details, enabling students to follow solution techniques easily. Students can then apply the methodology from each example to solve other problems. These examples are provided in addition to the vast array of business applications to give students a real-world, competitive edge.

- **Real-world application:** The chapters and cases feature real companies, actual applications, and rich data sets, allowing the authors to concentrate their efforts on addressing how students apply this statistical knowledge to the decision-making process.
  - **McDonald's Corporation video cases**—The authors' relationship with McDonald's provides students with real-world statistical data and integrated video case series.
  - **Chapter cases**—Cases provided in nearly every chapter are designed to give students the opportunity to apply statistical tools. Each case challenges students to define a problem, determine the appropriate tool to use, apply it, and then write a summary report.

- **Special review sections:** For Chapters 1 to 3 and Chapters 8 to 12, special review sections provide a summary and review of the key issues and statistical techniques. Highly effective flow diagrams help students sort out which statistical technique is appropriate to use in a given problem or exercise. These flow diagrams serve as a mini-decision support system that takes the emphasis off memorization and encourages students to seek a higher level of understanding and learning. Integrative questions and exercises ask students to demonstrate their comprehension of the topics covered in these sections.

- **Problems and exercises:** This edition includes an extensive revision of exercise sections, featuring more than 250 new problems. The exercise sets are broken down into three categories for ease of use and assignment purposes:
  1. **Skill Development**—These problems help students build and expand upon statistical methods learned in the chapter.
  2. **Business Applications**—These problems involve realistic situations in which students apply decision-making techniques.
  3. **Computer Applications**—In addition to the problems that may be worked out manually, many problems have associated data files and can be solved using Excel, Minitab, or other statistical software.

- **Virtual office hours:** The authors appear in three- to five-minute video clips in which they work examples taken directly from the book. Now students can watch and listen to the instructor walk through an example and obtain even greater clarity with respect to how the example is worked and how the results are interpreted.

- **Computer integration:** The text seamlessly integrates computer applications with textual examples and figures, always focusing on interpreting the output. The goal is for students to be able to know which tools to use, how to apply the tools, and how to analyze their results for making decisions.
  - **Microsoft Excel 2010** integration instructs students in how to use the Excel 2010 user interface for statistical applications.
  - **PHStat** is the Pearson Education add-in for Microsoft Excel that simplifies the task of operating Excel. PHStat creates *real* Excel worksheets that use in-worksheet calculations. The version of PHStat included with this book requires no setup other than unzipping files from the download zip archive. PHStat consists of the following files:
    - **PHStat.xlam** The actual add-in workbook itself. (This file is compatible with current Microsoft Windows and OS X versions of Microsoft Excel.)
    - **PHStat readme.pdf** The readme file, in PDF format, that you should download and read before using PHStat.
    - **PHStatHelp.chm** The help system that provides context-sensitive help for users of Microsoft Windows Excel. Context-sensitive help is not available for OS X Excel users. OS X users can use this file as a stand-alone help system by downloading a free CHM reader from the Mac Apps store online.
    - **PHStatHelp.pdf** The help system in the form of a PDF file that users of Microsoft Windows and OS X Excel versions can both use.
  - **MyStatLab** is a proven book-specific online homework and assessment tool that provides a rich and flexible set of course materials, featuring free-response exercises that are algorithmically generated for unlimited practice and mastery. Students can also use a variety of online tools to independently improve their understanding and performance in the course. Instructors can use MyStatLab's homework and test manager to select and assign their own online exercises and import TestGen tests for added flexibility.

Student Resources

Student Solutions Manual

The Student Solutions Manual contains worked-out solutions to odd-numbered problems in the text. It displays the detailed process that students should use to work through the problems. The manual also provides interpretation of the answers and serves as a valuable learning tool for students. Students can purchase this solutions manual by visiting www.mypearsonstore.com and searching for ISBN 0-13-302246-3.

MyStatLab

MyStatLab provides students with direct access to the online resources as well as the following exclusive online features and tools:

- **Interactive tutorial exercises:** A comprehensive set of exercises—correlated to your textbook at the objective level—is algorithmically generated for unlimited practice and mastery. Most exercises are free-response exercises and provide guided solutions, sample problems, and learning aids for extra help at point of use.
- **Personalized study plan:** When a student completes a test or quiz in MyStatLab, the program generates a personalized study plan for that student, indicating which topics have been mastered and linking students directly to tutorial exercises for topics they need to study and retest.
- **Statistics tools:** MyStatLab includes built-in tools for statistics, including statistical software called StatCrunch. Students also have access to statistics animations and applets that illustrate key ideas for the course. For those who use technology in their course, technology manual PDFs are included.
- **StatCrunch:** This powerful online tool provides an interactive environment for doing statistics. You can use StatCrunch for both numerical and graphical data analysis, taking advantage of interactive graphics to help you see the connection between objects selected in a graph and the underlying data. In MyStatLab, the data sets from your textbook are preloaded into StatCrunch. StatCrunch is also available as a tool from the online homework and practice exercises in MyStatLab and in MathXL for Statistics. Also available is Statcrunch.com, Web-based software that allows students to perform complex statistical analysis in a simple manner.
- **Pearson Tutor Center** (www.pearsontutorservices.com)**:** Access to the Pearson Tutor Center is automatically included with MyStatLab. The Tutor Center is staffed by qualified mathematics instructors who provide textbook-specific tutoring for students via toll-free phone, fax, email, and interactive Web sessions.
- **Integration with Pearson eTexts:** iPad users can download a free app at www.apple.com/ipad/apps-for-ipad/ and then sign in using their MyStatLab account to access a bookshelf of all their Pearson eTexts. The iPad app also allows access to the Do Homework, Take a Test, and Study Plan pages of their MyStatLab course.

MyStatLab is powered by CourseCompass™, Pearson Education's online teaching and learning environment, and by MathXL®, an online homework, tutorial, and assessment system. For more information about MyStatLab, visit www.mystatlab.com.

Student Videos

Student videos—located at MyStatLab only—feature McDonald's video cases and the virtual office hours videos.

Student Online Resources

Valuable online resources for both students and professors can be downloaded for free from www.pearsonhighered.com/groebner; these include the following:

- **Online chapter—Introduction to Decision Analysis:** This chapter discusses the analytic methods used to deal with the wide variety of decision situations a student might encounter.
- **Data files:** The text provides an extensive number of data files for examples, cases, and exercises. These files are also located at MyStatLab.
- **Excel tutorials:** Customized PowerPoint tutorials for Excel use data sets from text examples. Separate tutorials for Excel 2003 and Excel 2007 are provided. Students who need additional instruction in Excel can access the menu-driven tutorial, which shows exactly the steps needed to replicate all computer examples in the text. These tutorials are also located at MyStatLab.

- **Excel simulations:** Several interactive simulations illustrate key statistical topics and allow students to do "what-if" scenarios. These simulations are also located at MyStatLab.
- **PHStat:** PHStat is the Pearson Education add-in for Microsoft Excel that simplifies the task of operating Excel. PHStat creates *real* Excel worksheets that use in-worksheet calculations. This tool is located at www.pearsonhighered.com/groebner and MyStatLab.

Instructor Resources

Instructor Resource Center: The Instructor Resource Center contains the electronic files for the complete Instructor's Solutions Manual, the Test Item File, and Lecture PowerPoint presentations (www.pearsonhighered.com/groebner).

- **Register, Redeem, Login:** At www.pearsonhighered.com/irc, instructors can access a variety of print, media, and presentation resources that are available with this text in downloadable, digital format.
- **Need help?** Our dedicated technical support team is ready to assist instructors with questions about the media supplements that accompany this text. Visit http://247pearsoned.com/ for answers to frequently asked questions and toll-free user-support phone numbers.

Instructor's Solutions Manual

The Instructor's Solutions Manual, created by the authors and accuracy checked by Annie Puciloski, contains worked-out solutions to all the problems and cases in the text.

Lecture PowerPoint Presentations

A PowerPoint presentation, created by Roman Erenshteyn, is available for each chapter. The PowerPoint slides provide instructors with individual lecture outlines to accompany the text. The slides include many of the figures and tables from the text. Instructors can use these lecture notes as is or can easily modify the notes to reflect specific presentation needs.

Test Item File

The Test Item File, by Tariq Mughal of the University of Utah, contains a variety of true/false, multiple-choice, and short-answer questions for each chapter.

TestGen

Pearson Education's test-generating software is available from www.pearsonhighered.com/irc. The software is PC/Mac compatible and preloaded with all of the Test Item File questions. You can manually or randomly view test questions and drag and drop to create a test. You can add or modify test-bank questions as needed. Conversions of TestGens for use in BlackBoard and WebCT are available. Conversions to D2L or Angel can be requested through your local Pearson sales representative.

MyStatLab

- **MathXL® for Statistics:** This powerful online homework, tutorial, and assessment system accompanies Pearson Education textbooks in statistics. With MathXL for Statistics, instructors can create, edit, and assign online homework and tests, using algorithmically generated exercises correlated at the objective level to the textbook. They can also create and assign their own online exercises and import TestGen tests for added flexibility. All student work is tracked in MathXL's online gradebook. Students can take chapter tests in MathXL and receive personalized study plans based on their test results. The study plan diagnoses weaknesses and links students directly to tutorial exercises for the objectives they need to study and retest. Students can also access supplemental animations and video clips directly from selected exercises. MathXL for Statistics is available to qualified adopters. For more information, visit www.mathxl.com or contact your sales representative.

- **MyStatLab™:** Part of the MyMathLab® and MathXL® product family, MyStatLab™ is a text-specific, easily customizable online course that integrates interactive multimedia instruction with textbook content. MyStatLab gives you the tools you need to deliver all or a portion of your course online, whether your students are in a lab setting or working from home.
- **Assessment Manager:** An easy-to-use assessment manager lets instructors create online homework, quizzes, and tests that are automatically graded and correlated directly to the textbook. Assignments can be created using a mix of questions from the MyStatLab exercise bank, instructor-created custom exercises, and/or TestGen test items.
- **Grade book:** Designed specifically for mathematics and statistics, the MyStatLab grade book automatically tracks students' results and gives you control over how to calculate final grades. You can also add offline (paper-and-pencil) grades to the gradebook.
- **MathXL Exercise Builder:** You can use the MathXL Exercise Builder to create static and algorithmic exercises for your online assignments. A library of sample exercises provides an easy starting point for creating questions, and you can also create questions from scratch.
  - **eText-MathXL for Statistics Full Integration:** Students using appropriate mobile devices can use your eText annotations and highlights for each course, and iPad users can download a free app that allows them access to the Do Homework, Take a Test, and Study Plan pages of their course.
  - **"Ask the Publisher" Link in "Ask My Instructor" Email:** You can easily notify the content team of any irregularities with specific questions by using the "Ask the Publisher" functionality in the "Ask My Instructor" emails you receive from students.
  - **Tracking Time Spent on Media:** Because the latest version of MyStatLab requires students to explicitly click a "Submit" button after viewing the media for their assignments, you will be able to track how long students are spending on each media file.

CourseSmart

CourseSmart eTextbooks were developed for students looking to save on required or recommended textbooks. Students simply select their eText by title or author and purchase immediate access to the content for the duration of the course using any major credit card. With a CourseSmart eText, students can search for specific keywords or page numbers, take notes online, print out reading assignments that incorporate lecture notes, and bookmark important passages for later review. For more information or to purchase a CourseSmart eTextbook, visit www.coursesmart.com.

Acknowledgments

Publishing this ninth edition of *Business Statistics: A Decision-Making Approach* has been a team effort involving the contributions of many people. At the risk of overlooking someone, we express our sincere appreciation to the many key contributors. Throughout the two years we have worked on this revision, many of our colleagues from colleges and universities around the country have taken time from their busy schedules to provide valuable input and suggestions for improvement. We would like to thank the following people:

Huaite Chao, *Kutztown University*

Alan Chow, *University of South Alabama*

Chun Jin, *Central Connecticut State University*

Tariq Mughal, *University of Utah*

Mike Petroski, *Lynn University*

Mohammad Oskoorouchi, *California State University, San Marcos*

Michael Slagel, *College of Southern Idaho*

We also wish to thank Roman Erenshteyn, who designed and developed the PowerPoint slides that accompany this text. Thanks also to David Stephen for his expert work in developing the PHStat add-ins for Excel that accompany the text.

Thanks, too, to Annie Puciloski, who error checked the manuscript and the solutions to every exercise. This is a very time-consuming but extremely important role, and we greatly appreciate her efforts. In addition, we wish to thank Tariq Mughal of the University of Utah for developing the test manual. This, too, requires a huge commitment of time and effort, and we appreciate Dr. Mughal's contributions to the package of materials that accompany the text. Howard Flomberg at the Metropolitan State College of Denver contributed his skills and creative abilities to develop the Excel tutorials that are so useful to students, and we thank him for all his contributions.

Finally, we wish to give our utmost thanks and appreciation to the Prentice Hall publishing team that has assisted us in every way possible to make this ninth edition a reality. Sarah Peterson oversaw all the media products that accompany this text. Mary Kate Murray, project manager, in her role as editorial project manager, served as our day-to-day contact and expertly facilitated the project in every way imaginable and, in her role as production project manager, guided the development of the book from its initial design all the way through to final printing. And finally, we wish to give the highest thanks possible to Donna Battista, the Editor in Chief, who has provided valuable guidance, motivation, and leadership from beginning to end on this project. It has been a great pleasure to work with Donna and her team at Prentice Hall.

—David F. Groebner

—Patrick W. Shannon

—Phillip C. Fry

Chapter 1 Quick Prep Links

- **Locate** a recent copy of a business periodical, such as *Fortune* or *Business Week*, and take note of the graphs, charts, and tables that are used in the articles and advertisements.

- **Recall** any recent experiences you have had in which you were asked to complete a written survey or respond to a telephone survey.

- **Make sure** that you have access to Excel software. Open Excel and familiarize yourself with the software.

The Where, Why, and How of Data Collection

1.1 What Is Business Statistics?
(pg. 2–6)

1.2 Procedures for Collecting Data (pg. 7–14) ← **Outcome 1.** Know the key data collection methods.

1.3 Populations, Samples, and Sampling Techniques (pg. 14–20) ← **Outcome 2.** Know the difference between a population and a sample.

Outcome 3. Understand the similarities and differences between different sampling methods.

1.4 Data Types and Data Measurement Levels (pg. 20–25) ← **Outcome 4.** Understand how to categorize data by type and level of measurement.

1.5 A Brief Introduction to Data Mining (pg. 25–26) ← **Outcome 5.** Become familiar with the concept of data mining and some of its applications.

Why you need to know

A transformation is taking place in many organizations involving how managers are using data to help improve their decision making. Because of the recent advances in software and database systems, managers are able to analyze data in more depth than ever before. A new discipline called **data mining** is growing, and one of the fastest-growing career areas is referred to as **business intelligence**. Data mining or knowledge discovery is an interdisciplinary field involving primarily computer science and statistics. While many data mining statistical techniques are beyond the scope of this text, most are based on topics covered in this course. People working in this field are referred to as "data scientists." Doing an Internet search on data mining will yield a large number of sites talking about the field.

In today's workplace, you can have an immediate competitive edge over other new employees, and even those with more experience, by applying statistical analysis skills to real-world decision making. The purpose of this text is to assist in your learning process and to complement your instructor's efforts in conveying how to apply a variety of important statistical procedures.

The major automakers such as GM, Ford, and Toyota maintain databases with information on production, quality, customer satisfaction, safety records, and much more. Walmart, the world's largest retail chain, collects and manages massive amounts of data related to the operation of its stores throughout the world. Its highly sophisticated database systems contain sales data, detailed customer data, employee satisfaction data, and much more. Governmental agencies amass extensive data on such things as unemployment, interest rates, incomes, and education. However, access to data is not limited to large companies. The relatively low cost of computer hard drives with 100-gigabyte or larger capacities

Data Mining
The application of statistical techniques and algorithms to the analysis of large data sets.

Business Intelligence
The application of tools and technologies for gathering, storing, retrieving, and analyzing data that businesses collect and use.

Anton Foltin/Shutterstock

makes it possible for small firms and even individuals to store vast amounts of data on desktop computers. But without some way to transform the data into useful information, the data these companies have gathered are of little value.

Transforming data into information is where business statistics comes in—the statistical procedures introduced in this text are those that are used to help transform data into information. This text focuses on the practical application of statistics; we do not develop the theory you would find in a mathematical statistics course. Will you need to use math in this course? Yes, but mainly the concepts covered in your college algebra course.

Statistics does have its own terminology. You will need to learn various terms that have special statistical meaning. You will also learn certain dos and don'ts related to statistics. But most importantly, you will learn specific methods to effectively convert data into information. Don't try to memorize the concepts; rather, go to the next level of learning called *understanding*. Once you understand the underlying concepts, you will be able to *think statistically*.

Because data are the starting point for any statistical analysis, Chapter 1 is devoted to discussing various aspects of data, from how to collect data to the different types of data that you will be analyzing. You need to gain an understanding of the where, why, and how of data and data collection, because the remaining chapters deal with the techniques for transforming data into useful information.

1.1 What Is Business Statistics?

Articles in your local newspaper, news stories on television, and national publications such as the *Wall Street Journal* and *Fortune* discuss stock prices, crime rates, government-agency budgets, and company sales and profit figures. These values are statistics, but they are just a small part of the discipline called **business statistics**, which provides a wide variety of methods to assist in data analysis and decision making.

Business Statistics

A collection of procedures and techniques that are used to convert data into meaningful information in a business environment.

Descriptive Statistics

Business statistics can be segmented into two general categories. The first category involves the procedures and techniques designed to *describe data*, such as charts, graphs, and numerical measures. The second category includes tools and techniques that help decision makers *draw inferences* from a set of data. Inferential procedures include estimation and hypothesis testing. A brief discussion of these techniques follows.

BUSINESS APPLICATION **DESCRIBING DATA**

INDEPENDENT TEXTBOOK PUBLISHING, INC. Independent Textbook Publishing, Inc. publishes 15 college-level texts in the business and social sciences areas. Figure 1.1 shows an Excel spreadsheet containing data for each of these 15 textbooks. Each column

FIGURE 1.1

Excel 2010 Spreadsheet of Independent Textbook Publishing, Inc.

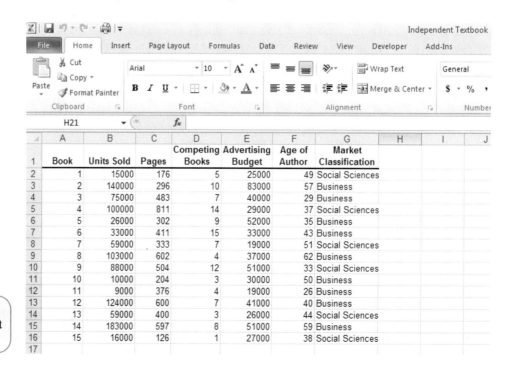

Excel 2010 Instructions:
1. Open File: **Independent Textbook.xlsx**.

Book	Units Sold	Pages	Competing Books	Advertising Budget	Age of Author	Market Classification
1	15000	176	5	25000	49	Social Sciences
2	140000	296	10	83000	57	Business
3	75000	483	7	40000	29	Business
4	100000	811	14	29000	37	Social Sciences
5	26000	302	9	52000	35	Business
6	33000	411	15	33000	43	Business
7	59000	333	7	19000	51	Social Sciences
8	103000	602	4	37000	62	Business
9	88000	504	12	51000	33	Social Sciences
10	10000	204	3	30000	50	Business
11	9000	376	4	19000	26	Business
12	124000	600	7	41000	40	Business
13	59000	400	3	26000	44	Social Sciences
14	183000	597	8	51000	59	Business
15	16000	126	1	27000	38	Social Sciences

FIGURE 1.2

Histogram Showing the
Copies Sold Distribution

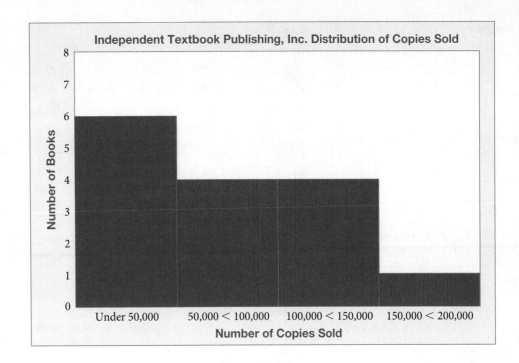

in the spreadsheet corresponds to a different factor for which data were collected. Each row corresponds to a different textbook. Many statistical procedures might help the owners describe these textbook data, including descriptive techniques such as *charts*, *graphs*, and *numerical measures*.

Charts and Graphs Chapter 2 will discuss many different charts and graphs—such as the one shown in Figure 1.2, called a *histogram*. This graph displays the shape and spread of the distribution of number of copies sold. The *bar chart* shown in Figure 1.3 shows the total number of textbooks sold broken down by the two markets, business and social sciences.

Bar charts and histograms are only two of the techniques that could be used to graphically analyze the data for the textbook publisher. In Chapter 2, you will learn more about these and other techniques.

BUSINESS APPLICATION **DESCRIBING DATA**

CROWN INVESTMENTS At Crown Investments, a senior analyst is preparing to present data to upper management on the 100 fastest-growing companies on the Hong Kong Stock Exchange. Figure 1.4 shows an Excel worksheet containing a subset of the data. The columns correspond to the different items of interest (growth percentage, sales, and so on). The data for each company are in a single row. The entire data are in a file called **Fast100**.

FIGURE 1.3

Bar Chart Showing Copies
Sold by Sales Category

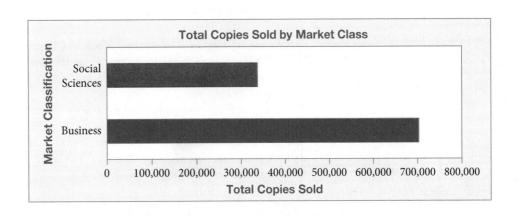

FIGURE 1.4

Crown Investment Example

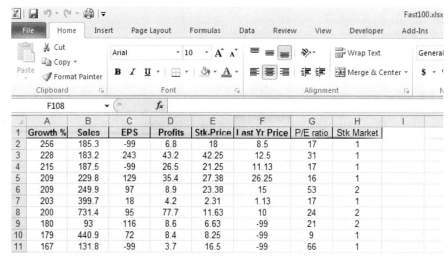

* –99 indicates missing data

Arithmetic Mean or Average
The sum of all values divided by the number of values.

In addition to preparing appropriate graphs, the analyst will compute important numerical measures. One of the most basic and most useful measures in business statistics is one with which you are already familiar: the **arithmetic mean** or **average**.

Average

The sum of all the values divided by the number of values. In equation form:

$$\text{Average} = \frac{\sum_{i=1}^{N} x_i}{N} = \frac{\text{Sum of all data values}}{\text{Number of data values}} \tag{1.1}$$

where:

$$N = \text{Number of data values}$$
$$x_i = i\text{th data value}$$

The analyst may be interested in the average profit (that is, the average of the column labeled "Profits") for the 100 companies. The total profit for the 100 companies is $3,193.60, but profits are given in millions of dollars, so the total profit amount is actually $3,193,600,000. The average is found by dividing this total by the number of companies:

$$\text{Average} = \frac{\$3,193,600,000}{100} = \$31,936,000, \text{ or } \$31.936 \text{ million}$$

As we will discuss in greater depth in Chapter 3, the average, or mean, is a measure of the center of the data. In this case, the analyst may use the average profit as an indicator—firms with above-average profits are rated higher than firms with below-average profits.

The graphical and numerical measures illustrated here are only some of the many descriptive procedures that will be introduced in Chapters 2 and 3. The key to remember is that the purpose of any descriptive procedure is to describe data. Your task will be to select the procedure that best accomplishes this. As Figure 1.5 reminds you, the role of statistics is to convert data into meaningful information.

FIGURE 1.5

The Role of Business
Statistics

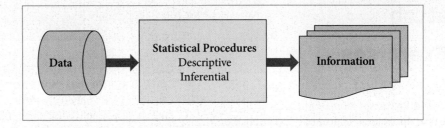

Inferential Procedures

Advertisers pay for television ads based on the audience level, so knowing how many viewers watch a particular program is important; millions of dollars are at stake. Clearly, the networks don't check with everyone in the country to see if they watch a particular program. Instead, they pay a fee to the Nielsen company (http://www.nielsen.com/), which uses **statistical inference procedures** to *estimate* the number of viewers who watch a particular television program.

There are two primary categories of statistical inference procedures: *estimation* and *hypothesis testing*. These procedures are closely related but serve very different purposes.

Statistical Inference Procedures

Procedures that allow a decision maker to reach a conclusion about a set of data based on a subset of that data.

Estimation   In situations in which we would like to know about all the data in a large data set but it is impractical to work with all the data, decision makers can use techniques to estimate what the larger data set looks like. The estimates are formed by looking closely at a subset of the larger data set.

BUSINESS APPLICATION   **STATISTICAL INFERENCE**

NEW PRODUCT INTRODUCTION   Energy-boosting drinks such as Red Bull, Go Girl, Monster, and Full Throttle have become very popular among college students and young professionals. But how do the companies that make these products determine whether they will sell enough to warrant the product introduction? A typical approach is to do market research by introducing the product into one or more test markets. People in the targeted age, income, and educational categories (*target market*) are asked to sample the product and indicate the likelihood that they would purchase the product. The percentage of people who say that they will buy forms the basis for an *estimate* of the true percentage of *all* people in the target market who will buy. If that estimate is high enough, the company will introduce the product.

In Chapter 8, we will discuss the estimating techniques that companies use in new product development and many other applications.

Hypothesis Testing   Television advertising is full of product claims. For example, we might hear that "Goodyear tires will last at least 60,000 miles" or that "more doctors recommend Bayer Aspirin than any other brand." Other claims might include statements like "General Electric light bulbs last longer than any other brand" or "customers prefer McDonald's over Burger King." Are these just idle boasts, or are they based on actual data? Probably some of both! However, consumer research organizations such as Consumers Union, publisher of *Consumer Reports*, regularly test these types of claims. For example, in the hamburger case, *Consumer Reports* might select a sample of customers who would be asked to blind taste test Burger King's and McDonald's hamburgers, under the hypothesis that there is no difference in customer preferences between the two restaurants. If the sample data show a substantial difference in preferences, then the hypothesis of no difference would be rejected. If only a slight difference in preferences was detected, then *Consumer Reports* could not reject the hypothesis. Chapters 9 and 10 introduce basic hypothesis-testing techniques that are used to test claims about products and services using information taken from samples.

MyStatLab

1-1: **Exercises**

Skill Development

1-1. For the following situation, indicate whether the statistical application is primarily descriptive or inferential.

> "The manager of Anna's Fabric Shop has collected data for 10 years on the quantity of each type of dress fabric that has been sold at the store. She is interested in making a presentation that will illustrate these data effectively."

1-2. Consider the following graph that appeared in a company annual report. What type of graph is this? Explain.

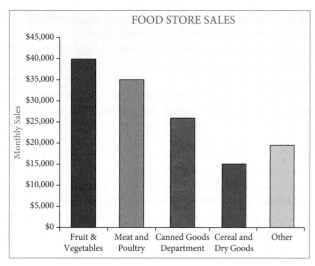

1-3. Review Figures 1.2 and 1.3 and discuss any differences you see between the histogram and the bar chart.

1-4. Think of yourself as working for an advertising firm. Provide an example of how hypothesis testing can be used to evaluate a product claim.

1-5. Define what is meant by hypothesis testing. Provide an example in which you personally have tested a hypothesis (even if you didn't use formal statistical techniques to do so).

1-6. In what situations might a decision maker need to use statistical inference procedures?

1-7. Explain under what circumstances you would use hypothesis testing as opposed to an estimation procedure.

1-8. Discuss any advantages a graph showing a whole set of data has over a single measure, such as an average.

1-9. Discuss any advantages a single measure, such as an average, has over a table showing a whole set of data.

Business Applications

1-10. Describe how statistics could be used by a business to determine if the dishwasher parts it produces last longer than a competitor's brand.

1-11. Locate a business periodical such as *Fortune* or *Forbes* or a business newspaper such as *The Wall Street*

Journal. Find three examples of the use of a graph to display data. For each graph,
   a. Give the name, date, and page number of the periodical in which the graph appeared.
   b. Describe the main point made by the graph.
   c. Analyze the effectiveness of the graphs.

1-12. The human resources manager of an automotive supply store has collected the following data showing the number of employees in each of five categories by the number of days missed due to illness or injury during the past year.

Missed Days	0–2 days	3–5 days	6–8 days	8–10 days
Employees	159	67	32	10

Construct the appropriate chart for these data. Be sure to use labels and to add a title to your chart.

1-13. Suppose *Fortune* would like to determine the average age and income of its subscribers. How could statistics be of use in determining these values?

1-14. Locate an example from a business periodical or newspaper in which estimation has been used.
   a. What specifically was estimated?
   b. What conclusion was reached using the estimation?
   c. Describe how the data were extracted and how they were used to produce the estimation.
   d. Keeping in mind the goal of the estimation, discuss whether you believe that the estimation was successful and why.
   e. Describe what inferences were drawn as a result of the estimation.

1-15. Locate one of the online job Web sites and pick several job listings. For each job type, discuss one or more situations in which statistical analyses would be used. Base your answer on research (Internet, business periodicals, personal interviews, etc.). Indicate whether the situations you are describing involve descriptive statistics or inferential statistics or a combination of both.

1-16. Suppose Super-Value, a major retail food company, is thinking of introducing a new product line into a market area. It is important to know the age characteristics of the people in the market area.
   a. If the executives wish to calculate a number that would characterize the "center" of the age data, what statistical technique would you suggest? Explain your answer.
   b. The executives need to know the percentage of people in the market area that are senior citizens. Name the basic category of statistical procedure they would use to determine this information.
   c. Describe a hypothesis the executives might wish to test concerning the percentage of senior citizens in the market area.

Chapter Outcome 1. → **1.2** **Procedures for Collecting Data**

We have defined business statistics as a set of procedures that are used to transform data into information. Before you learn how to use statistical procedures, it is important that you become familiar with different types of data collection methods.

Data Collection Methods

There are many methods and procedures available for collecting data. The following are considered some of the most useful and frequently used data collection methods:

- Experiments
- Telephone surveys
- Written questionnaires and surveys
- Direct observation and personal interviews

BUSINESS APPLICATION **EXPERIMENTS**

FOOD PROCESSING A company often must conduct a specific experiment or set of experiments to get the data managers need to make informed decisions. For example, Lamb Weston, McCain and the J. R. Simplot Company are the primary suppliers of french fries to McDonald's in North America. At its Caldwell, Idaho, factory, the J. R. Simplot Company has a test center that, among other things, houses a mini french fry plant used to conduct experiments on its potato manufacturing process. McDonald's has strict standards on the quality of the french fries it buys. One important attribute is the color of the fries after cooking. They should be uniformly "golden brown"—not too light or too dark.

French fries are made from potatoes that are peeled, sliced into strips, blanched, partially cooked, and then freeze-dried—not a simple process. Because potatoes differ in many ways (such as sugar content and moisture), blanching time, cooking temperature, and other factors vary from batch to batch.

Simplot employees start their **experiments** by grouping the raw potatoes into batches with similar characteristics. They run some of the potatoes through the line with blanch time and temperature settings set at specific levels defined by an **experimental design**. After measuring one or more output variables for that run, employees change the settings and run another batch, again measuring the output variables.

Figure 1.6 shows a typical data collection form. The output variable (for example, percentage of fries without dark spots) for each combination of potato category, blanch time, and temperature is recorded in the appropriate cell in the table. Chapter 12 introduces the fundamental concepts related to experimental design and analysis.

Experiment

A process that produces a single outcome whose result cannot be predicted with certainty.

Experimental Design

A plan for performing an experiment in which the variable of interest is defined. One or more factors are identified to be manipulated, changed, or observed so that the impact (or influence) on the variable of interest can be measured or observed.

FIGURE 1.6

Data Layout for the French Fry Experiment

Blanch Time	Blanch Temperature	Potato Category 1	2	3	4
10 minutes	100 110 120				
15 minutes	100 110 120				
20 minutes	100 110 120				
25 minutes	100 110 120				

PUBLIC ISSUES Chances are that you have been on the receiving end of a telephone call that begins something like: "Hello. My name is Mary Jane and I represent the XYZ organization. I am conducting a survey on …" Political groups use telephone surveys to poll people about candidates and issues. Marketing research companies use phone surveys to learn likes and dislikes of potential customers.

Telephone surveys are a relatively inexpensive and efficient data collection procedure. Of course, some people will refuse to respond to a survey, others are not home when the calls come, and some people do not have home phones—only have a cell phone—or cannot be reached by phone for one reason or another. Figure 1.7 shows the major steps in conducting a telephone survey. This example survey was run a few years ago by a Seattle television station to determine public support for using tax dollars to build a new football stadium for the National Football League's Seattle Seahawks. The survey was aimed at property tax payers only.

Because most people will not stay on the line very long, the phone survey must be short—usually one to three minutes. The questions are generally what are called **closed-end questions**. For example, a closed-end question might be, "To which political party do you belong? Republican? Democrat? Or other?"

The survey instrument should have a short statement at the beginning explaining the purpose of the survey and reassuring the respondent that his or her responses will remain confidential. The initial section of the survey should contain questions relating to the central issue of the survey. The last part of the survey should contain **demographic questions** (such as gender, income level, education level) that will allow you to break down the responses and look deeper into the survey results.

Closed-End Questions

Questions that require the respondent to select from a short list of defined choices.

Demographic Questions

Questions relating to the respondents' characteristics, backgrounds, and attributes.

FIGURE 1.7 |

Major Steps for a Telephone Survey

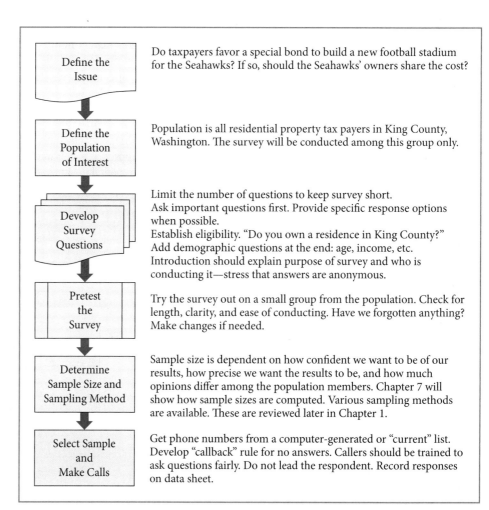

Define the Issue	Do taxpayers favor a special bond to build a new football stadium for the Seahawks? If so, should the Seahawks' owners share the cost?
Define the Population of Interest	Population is all residential property tax payers in King County, Washington. The survey will be conducted among this group only.
Develop Survey Questions	Limit the number of questions to keep survey short. Ask important questions first. Provide specific response options when possible. Establish eligibility. "Do you own a residence in King County?" Add demographic questions at the end: age, income, etc. Introduction should explain purpose of survey and who is conducting it—stress that answers are anonymous.
Pretest the Survey	Try the survey out on a small group from the population. Check for length, clarity, and ease of conducting. Have we forgotten anything? Make changes if needed.
Determine Sample Size and Sampling Method	Sample size is dependent on how confident we want to be of our results, how precise we want the results to be, and how much opinions differ among the population members. Chapter 7 will show how sample sizes are computed. Various sampling methods are available. These are reviewed later in Chapter 1.
Select Sample and Make Calls	Get phone numbers from a computer-generated or "current" list. Develop "callback" rule for no answers. Callers should be trained to ask questions fairly. Do not lead the respondent. Record responses on data sheet.

A survey budget must be considered. For example, if you have $3,000 to spend on calls and each call costs $10 to make, you obviously are limited to making 300 calls. However, keep in mind that 300 calls may not result in 300 usable responses.

The phone survey should be conducted in a short time period. Typically, the prime calling time for a voter survey is between 7:00 P.M. and 9:00 P.M. However, some people are not home in the evening and will be excluded from the survey unless there is a plan for conducting callbacks.

Written Questionnaires and Surveys The most frequently used method to collect opinions and factual data from people is a written questionnaire. In some instances, the questionnaires are mailed to the respondent. In others, they are administered directly to the potential respondents. Written questionnaires are generally the least expensive means of collecting survey data. If they are mailed, the major costs include postage to and from the respondents, questionnaire development and printing costs, and data analysis. Figure 1.8 shows the major steps in conducting a written survey. Note how written surveys are similar to telephone surveys; however, written surveys can be slightly more involved and, therefore, take more time to complete than those used for a telephone survey. However, you must be careful to construct a questionnaire that can be easily completed without requiring too much time.

Open-End Questions

Questions that allow respondents the freedom to respond with any value, words, or statements of their own choosing.

A written survey can contain both closed-end and **open-end questions**. Open-end questions provide the respondent with greater flexibility in answering a question; however, the responses can be difficult to analyze. Note that telephone surveys can use open-end questions, too. However, the caller may have to transcribe a potentially long response, and there is risk that the interviewees' comments may be misinterpreted.

Written surveys also should be formatted to make it easy for the respondent to provide accurate and reliable data. This means that proper space must be provided for the responses,

FIGURE 1.8 |

Written Survey Steps

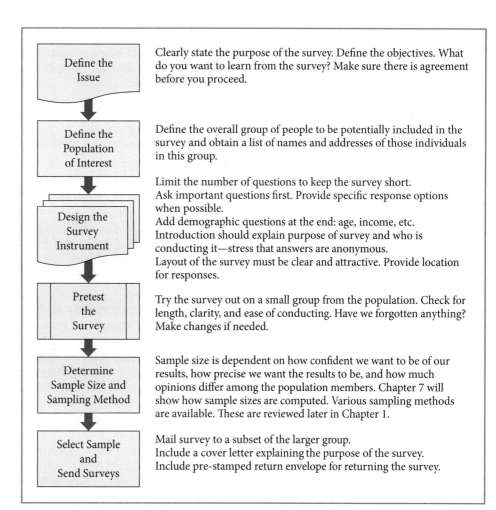

Define the Issue	Clearly state the purpose of the survey. Define the objectives. What do you want to learn from the survey? Make sure there is agreement before you proceed.
Define the Population of Interest	Define the overall group of people to be potentially included in the survey and obtain a list of names and addresses of those individuals in this group.
Design the Survey Instrument	Limit the number of questions to keep the survey short. Ask important questions first. Provide specific response options when possible. Add demographic questions at the end: age, income, etc. Introduction should explain purpose of survey and who is conducting it—stress that answers are anonymous. Layout of the survey must be clear and attractive. Provide location for responses.
Pretest the Survey	Try the survey out on a small group from the population. Check for length, clarity, and ease of conducting. Have we forgotten anything? Make changes if needed.
Determine Sample Size and Sampling Method	Sample size is dependent on how confident we want to be of our results, how precise we want the results to be, and how much opinions differ among the population members. Chapter 7 will show how sample sizes are computed. Various sampling methods are available. These are reviewed later in Chapter 1.
Select Sample and Send Surveys	Mail survey to a subset of the larger group. Include a cover letter explaining the purpose of the survey. Include pre-stamped return envelope for returning the survey.

and the directions must be clear about how the survey is to be completed. A written survey needs to be pleasing to the eye. How it looks will affect the response rate, so it must look professional.

You also must decide whether to manually enter or scan the data gathered from your written survey. The survey design will be affected by the approach you take. If you are administering a large number of surveys, scanning is preferred. It cuts down on data entry errors and speeds up the data gathering process. However, you may be limited in the form of responses that are possible if you use scanning.

If the survey is administered directly to the desired respondents, you can expect a high response rate. For example, you probably have been on the receiving end of a written survey many times in your college career, when you were asked to fill out a course evaluation form at the end of the term. Most students will complete the form. On the other hand, if a survey is administered through the mail, you can expect a low response rate—typically 5% to 20%. Therefore, if you want 200 responses, you should mail out 1,000 to 4,000 questionnaires.

Overall, written surveys can be a low-cost, effective means of collecting data if you can overcome the problems of low response. Be careful to pretest the survey and spend extra time on the format and look of the survey instrument.

Developing a good written questionnaire or telephone survey instrument is a major challenge. Among the potential problems are the following:

- Leading questions
    Example: "Do you agree with most other reasonably minded people that the city should spend more money on neighborhood parks?"
        Issue: In this case, the phrase "Do you agree" may suggest that you should agree. Also, by suggesting that "most reasonably minded people" already agree, the respondent might be compelled to agree so that he or she can also be considered "reasonably minded."
        Improvement: "In your opinion, should the city increase spending on neighborhood parks?"
    Example: "To what extent would you support paying a small increase in your property taxes if it would allow poor and disadvantaged children to have food and shelter?"
        Issue: The question is ripe with emotional feeling and may imply that if you don't support additional taxes, you don't care about poor children.
        Improvement: "Should property taxes be increased to provide additional funding for social services?"
- Poorly worded questions
    Example: "How much money do you make at your current job?"
        Issue: The responses are likely to be inconsistent. When answering, does the respondent state the answer as an hourly figure or as a weekly or monthly total? Also, many people refuse to answer questions regarding their income.
        Improvement: "Which of the following categories best reflects your weekly income from your current job?
        _____ Under $500   _____ $500–$1,000
        _____ Over $1,000"
    Example: "After trying the new product, please provide a rating from 1 to 10 to indicate how you like its taste and freshness."
        Issue: First, is a low number or a high number on the rating scale considered a positive response? Second, the respondent is being asked to rate two factors, taste and freshness, in a single rating. What if the product is fresh but does not taste good?
        Improvement: "After trying the new product, please rate its taste on a 1 to 10 scale with 1 being best. Also rate the product's freshness using the same 1 to 10 scale.
        _____ Taste   _____ Freshness"

The way a question is worded can influence the responses. Consider an example that occurred in September 2008 during the financial crisis that resulted from the sub-prime mortgage crisis and bursting of the real estate bubble. Three surveys were conducted on the same basic issue. The following questions were asked:

"Do you approve or disapprove of the steps the Federal Reserve and Treasury Department have taken to try to deal with the current situation involving the stock market and major financial institutions?" (*ABC News/Washington Post*) 44% Approve — 42% Disapprove — 14% Unsure

"Do you think the government should use taxpayers' dollars to rescue ailing private financial firms whose collapse could have adverse effects on the economy and market, or is it not the government's responsibility to bail out private companies with taxpayer dollars?" (*LA Times*/Bloomberg) 31% Use Tax Payers' Dollars — 55% Not Government's Responsibility — 14% Unsure

"As you may know, the government is potentially investing billions to try and keep financial institutions and markets secure. Do you think this is the right thing or the wrong thing for the government to be doing?" (Pew Research Center) 57% Right Thing — 30% Wrong Thing — 13% Unsure

Note the responses to each of these questions. The way the question is worded can affect the responses.

Direct Observation and Personal Interviews *Direct observation* is another procedure that is often used to collect data. As implied by the name, this technique requires the process from which the data are being collected to be physically observed and the data recorded based on what takes place in the process.

Possibly the most basic way to gather data on human behavior is to watch people. If you are trying to decide whether a new method of displaying your product at the supermarket will be more pleasing to customers, change a few displays and watch customers' reactions. If, as a member of a state's transportation department, you want to determine how well motorists are complying with the state's seat belt laws, place observers at key spots throughout the state to monitor people's seat belt habits. A movie producer, seeking information on whether a new movie will be a success, holds a preview showing and observes the reactions and comments of the movie patrons as they exit the screening. The major constraints when collecting observations are the amount of time and money required. For observations to be effective, trained observers must be used, which increases the cost. Personal observation is also time-consuming. Finally, personal perception is subjective. There is no guarantee that different observers will see a situation in the same way, much less report it the same way.

Personal interviews are often used to gather data from people. Interviews can be either **structured** or **unstructured**, depending on the objectives, and they can utilize either open-end or closed-end questions.

Regardless of the procedure used for data collection, care must be taken that the data collected are accurate and reliable and that they are the right data for the purpose at hand.

Other Data Collection Methods

Data collection methods that take advantage of new technologies are becoming more prevalent all the time. For example, many people believe that Walmart is one of the best companies in the world at collecting and using data about the buying habits of its customers. Most of the data are collected automatically as checkout clerks scan the UPC bar codes on the products customers purchase. Not only are Walmart's inventory records automatically updated, but information about the buying habits of customers is also recorded. This allows Walmart to use *analytics* and *data mining* to drill deep into the data to help with its decision making about many things, including how to organize its stores to increase sales. For instance, Walmart apparently decided to locate beer and disposable diapers close together when it discovered that many male customers also purchase beer when they are sent to the store for diapers.

Bar code scanning is used in many different data collection applications. In a DRAM (dynamic random-access memory) wafer fabrication plant, batches of silicon wafers have bar codes. As the batch travels through the plant's workstations, its progress and quality are tracked through the data that are automatically obtained by scanning.

Structured Interview
Interviews in which the questions are scripted.

Unstructured Interview
Interviews that begin with one or more broadly stated questions, with further questions being based on the responses.

Every time you use your credit card, data are automatically collected by the retailer and the bank. Computer information systems are developed to store the data and to provide decision makers with procedures to access the data.

In many instances, your data collection method will require you to use *physical measurement*. For example, the Andersen Window Company has quality analysts physically measure the width and height of its windows to assure that they meet customer specifications, and a state Department of Weights and Measures will physically test meat and produce scales to determine that customers are being properly charged for their purchases.

Data Collection Issues

Data Accuracy When you need data to make a decision, we suggest that you first see if appropriate data have already been collected, because it is usually faster and less expensive to use existing data than to collect data yourself. However, before you rely on data that were collected by someone else for another purpose, you need to check out the source to make sure that the data were collected and recorded properly.

Such organizations as *Bloomberg*, *Value Line*, and *Fortune* have built their reputations on providing quality data. Although data errors are occasionally encountered, they are few and far between. You really need to be concerned with data that come from sources with which you are not familiar. This is an issue for many sources on the World Wide Web. Any organization or any individual can post data to the Web. Just because the data are there doesn't mean they are accurate. Be careful.

Interviewer Bias There are other general issues associated with data collection. One of these is the potential for **bias** in the data collection. There are many types of bias. For example, in a personal interview, the interviewer can interject bias (either accidentally or on purpose) by the way she asks the questions, by the tone of her voice, or by the way she looks at the subject being interviewed. We recently allowed ourselves to be interviewed at a trade show. The interviewer began by telling us that he would only get credit for the interview if we answered all of the questions. Next, he asked us to indicate our satisfaction with a particular display. He wasn't satisfied with our less-than-enthusiastic rating and kept asking us if we really meant what we said. He even asked us if we would consider upgrading our rating! How reliable do you think these data will be?

Nonresponse Bias Another source of bias that can be interjected into a survey data collection process is called *nonresponse bias*. We stated earlier that mail surveys suffer from a high percentage of unreturned surveys. Phone calls don't always get through, or people refuse to answer. Subjects of personal interviews may refuse to be interviewed. There is a potential problem with nonresponse. Those who respond may provide data that are quite different from the data that would be supplied by those who choose not to respond. If you aren't careful, the responses may be heavily weighted by people who feel strongly one way or another on an issue.

Selection Bias Bias can be interjected through the way subjects are selected for data collection. This is referred to as *selection bias*. A study on the virtues of increasing the student athletic fee at your university might not be best served by collecting data from students attending a football game. Sometimes, the problem is more subtle. If we do a telephone survey during the evening hours, we will miss all of the people who work nights. Do they share the same views, income, education levels, and so on as people who work days? If not, the data are biased.

Written and phone surveys and personal interviews can also yield flawed data if the interviewees *lie* in response to questions. For example, people commonly give inaccurate data about such sensitive matters as income. Lying is also an increasing problem with *exit polls* in which voters are asked who they voted for immediately after casting their vote. Sometimes, the data errors are not due to lies. The respondents may not know or have accurate information to provide the correct answer.

Observer Bias Data collection through personal observation is also subject to problems. People tend to view the same event or item differently. This is referred to as *observer bias*.

Bias

An effect that alters a statistical result by systematically distorting it; different from a random error, which may distort on any one occasion but balances out on the average.

One area in which this can easily occur is in safety check programs in companies. An important part of behavioral-based safety programs is the safety observation. Trained data collectors periodically conduct a safety observation on a worker to determine what, if any, unsafe acts might be taking place. We have seen situations in which two observers will conduct an observation on the same worker at the same time, yet record different safety data. This is especially true in areas in which judgment is required on the part of the observer, such as the distance a worker is from an exposed gear mechanism. People judge distance differently.

Measurement Error A few years ago, we were working with a wood window manufacturer. The company was having a quality problem with one of its saws. A study was developed to measure the width of boards that had been cut by the saw. Two people were trained to use digital calipers and record the data. This caliper is a U-shaped tool that measures distance (in inches) to three decimal places. The caliper was placed around the board and squeezed tightly against the sides. The width was indicated on the display. Each person measured 500 boards during an 8-hour day. When the data were analyzed, it looked like the widths were coming from two different saws; one set showed considerably narrower widths than the other. Upon investigation, we learned that the person with the narrower width measurements was pressing on the calipers much more firmly. The soft wood reacted to the pressure and gave narrower readings. Fortunately, we had separated the data from the two data collectors. Had they been merged, the measurement error might have gone undetected.

Internal Validity When data are collected through experimentation, you need to make sure that proper controls have been put in place. For instance, suppose a drug company such as Pfizer is conducting tests on a drug that it hopes will reduce cholesterol. One group of test participants is given the new drug while a second group (a control group) is given a placebo. Suppose that after several months, the group using the drug saw significant cholesterol reduction. For the results to have **internal validity**, the drug company would have had to make sure the two groups were controlled for the many other factors that might affect cholesterol, such as smoking, diet, weight, gender, race, and exercise habits. Issues of internal validity are generally addressed by randomly assigning subjects to the test and control groups. However, if the extraneous factors are not controlled, there could be no assurance that the drug was the factor influencing reduced cholesterol. For data to have internal validity, the extraneous factors must be controlled.

> **Internal Validity**
> A characteristic of an experiment in which data are collected in such a way as to eliminate the effects of variables within the experimental environment that are not of interest to the researcher.

External Validity Even if experiments are internally valid, you will always need to be concerned that the results can be generalized beyond the test environment. For example, if the cholesterol drug test had been performed in Europe, would the same basic results occur for people in North America, South America, or elsewhere? For that matter, the drug company would also be interested in knowing whether the results could be replicated if other subjects are used in a similar experiment. If the results of an experiment can be replicated for groups different from the original population, then there is evidence the results of the experiment have **external validity**.

> **External Validity**
> A characteristic of an experiment whose results can be generalized beyond the test environment so that the outcomes can be replicated when the experiment is repeated.

An extensive discussion of how to measure the magnitude of bias and how to reduce bias and other data collection problems is beyond the scope of this text. However, you should be aware that data may be biased or otherwise flawed. Always pose questions about the potential for bias and determine what steps have been taken to reduce its effect.

MyStatLab

1-2: Exercises

Skill Development

1-17. If a pet store wishes to determine the level of customer satisfaction with its services, would it be appropriate to conduct an experiment? Explain.

1-18. Define what is meant by a leading question. Provide an example.

1-19. Briefly explain what is meant by an experiment and an experimental design.

1-20. Refer to the three questions discussed in this section involving the financial crises of 2008 and 2009 and possible government intervention. Note that the questions elicited different responses. Discuss the way the questions were worded and why they might have produced such different results.

1-21. Suppose a survey is conducted using a telephone survey method. The survey is conducted from 9 A.M. to 11 A.M. on Tuesday. Indicate what potential problems the data collectors might encounter.

1-22. For each of the following situations, indicate what type of data collection method you would recommend and discuss why you have made that recommendation:
   a. collecting data on the percentage of bike riders who wear helmets
   b. collecting data on the price of regular unleaded gasoline at gas stations in your state
   c. collecting data on customer satisfaction with the service provided by a major U.S. airline

1-23. Assume you have received a class assignment to determine the attitude of students in your school toward the school's registration process. What are the validity issues you should be concerned with?

Business Applications

1-24. According to a report issued by the U.S. Department of Agriculture (USDA), the agency estimates that Southern fire ants spread at a rate of 4 to 5 miles a year. What data collection method do you think was used to collect this data? Explain your answer.

1-25. Suppose you are asked to survey students at your university to determine if they are satisfied with the food service choices on campus. What types of biases must you guard against in collecting your data?

1-26. Briefly describe how new technologies can assist businesses in their data collection efforts.

1-27. Assume you have used an online service such as Orbitz or Travelocity to make an airline reservation. The following day, you receive an e-mail containing a questionnaire asking you to rate the quality of the experience. Discuss both the advantages and disadvantages of using this form of questionnaire delivery.

1-28. In your capacity as assistant sales manager for a large office products retailer, you have been assigned the task of interviewing purchasing managers for medium and large companies in the San Francisco Bay area. The objective of the interview is to determine the office product buying plans of the company in the coming year. Develop a personal interview form that asks both issue-related questions as well as demographic questions.

1-29. The regional manager for Macy's is experimenting with two new end-of-aisle displays of the same product. An end-of-aisle display is a common method retail stores use to promote new products. You have been hired to determine which is more effective. Two measures you have decided to track are which display causes the highest percentage of people to stop and, for those who stop, which causes people to view the display the longest. Discuss how you would gather such data.

1-30. In your position as general manager for United Fitness Center, you have been asked to survey the customers of your location to determine whether they want to convert the racquetball courts to an aerobic exercise space. The plan calls for a written survey to be handed out to customers when they arrive at the fitness center. Your task is to develop a short questionnaire with at least three "issue" questions and at least three demographic questions. You also need to provide the finished layout design for the questionnaire.

1-31. According to a national CNN/USA/Gallup survey of 1,025 adults, conducted March 14–16, 2008, 63% say they have experienced a hardship because of rising gasoline prices. How do you believe the survey was conducted and what types of bias could occur in the data collection process?

END EXERCISES 1-2

Chapter Outcome 2. → **1.3** # Populations, Samples, and Sampling Techniques

Populations and Samples

Two of the most important terms in statistics are **population** and **sample**.

   The list of all objects or individuals in the population is referred to as the *frame*. Each object or individual in the frame is known as a sampling unit. The choice of the frame depends on what objects or individuals you wish to study and on the availability of the list of these objects or individuals. Once the frame is defined, it forms the list of sampling units. The next example illustrates this concept.

Population
The set of all objects or individuals of interest or the measurements obtained from all objects or individuals of interest.

Sample
A subset of the population.

BUSINESS APPLICATION   **POPULATIONS AND SAMPLES**

U.S. BANK We can use U.S. Bank to illustrate the difference between a population and a sample. U.S. Bank is very concerned about the time customers spend waiting in the drive-up teller line. At a particular U.S. Bank, on a given day, 347 cars arrived at the drive-up.

Census

An enumeration of the entire set of measurements taken from the whole population.

A population includes measurements made on all the items of interest to the data gatherer. In our example, the U.S. Bank manager would define the population as the waiting time for all 347 cars. The list of these cars, possibly by license number, forms the frame. If she examines the entire population, she is taking a **census**. But suppose 347 cars are too many to track. The U.S. Bank manager could instead select a subset of these cars, called a *sample*. The manager could use the sample results to make statements about the population. For example, she might calculate the average waiting time for the sample of cars and then use that to conclude what the average waiting time is for the population. How this is done will be discussed in later chapters.

There are trade-offs between taking a census and taking a sample. Usually the main trade-off is whether the information gathered in a census is worth the extra cost. In organizations in which data are stored on computer files, the additional time and effort of taking a census may not be substantial. However, if there are many accounts that must be manually checked, a census may be impractical.

Another consideration is that the measurement error in census data may be greater than in sample data. A person obtaining data from fewer sources tends to be more complete and thorough in both gathering and tabulating the data. As a result, with a sample there are likely to be fewer human errors.

Parameters and Statistics Descriptive numerical measures, such as an average or a proportion, that are computed from an entire population are called *parameters*. Corresponding measures for a sample are called *statistics*. Suppose in the previous example, the U.S. Bank manager timed every car that arrived at the drive-up teller on a particular day and calculated the average. This population average waiting time would be a parameter. However, if she selected a sample of cars from the population, the average waiting time for the sampled cars would be a statistic. These concepts are more fully discussed in Chapters 3 and 7.

Sampling Techniques

Statistical Sampling Techniques

Those sampling methods that use selection techniques based on chance selection.

Nonstatistical Sampling Techniques

Those methods of selecting samples using convenience, judgment, or other nonchance processes.

Once a manager decides to gather information by sampling, he or she can use a sampling technique that falls into one of two categories: **statistical** or **nonstatistical**.

Both nonstatistical and statistical sampling techniques are commonly used by decision makers. Regardless of which technique is used, the decision maker has the same objective—to obtain a sample that is a close representative of the population. There are some advantages to using a statistical sampling technique, as we will discuss many times throughout this text. However, in many cases, nonstatistical sampling represents the only feasible way to sample, as illustrated in the following example.

BUSINESS APPLICATION   **NONSTATISTICAL SAMPLING**

SUN-CITRUS ORCHARDS Sun-Citrus Orchards owns and operates a large fruit orchard and fruit-packing plant in Florida. During harvest time in the orange grove, pickers load 20-pound sacks with oranges, which are then transported to the packing plant. At the packing plant, the oranges are graded and boxed for shipping nationally and internationally. Because of the volume of oranges involved, it is impossible to assign a quality grade to each individual orange. Instead, as each sack moves up the conveyor into the packing plant, a quality manager selects an orange sack every so often, grades the individual oranges in the sack as to size, color, and so forth, and then assigns an overall quality grade to the entire shipment from which the sample was selected.

Convenience Sampling

A sampling technique that selects the items from the population based on accessibility and ease of selection.

Because of the volume of oranges, the quality manager at Sun-Citrus uses a nonstatistical sampling method called **convenience sampling**. In doing so, the quality manager is willing to assume that orange quality (size, color, etc.) is evenly spread throughout the many sacks of oranges in the shipment. That is, the oranges in the sacks selected are of the same quality as those that were not inspected.

There are other nonstatistical sampling methods, such as *judgment sampling* and *ratio sampling*, which are not discussed here. Instead, the most frequently used statistical sampling techniques will now be discussed.

Statistical Sampling *Statistical sampling* methods (also called *probability sampling*) allow every item in the population to have a known or calculable chance of being included in the sample. The fundamental statistical sample is called a *simple random sample*. Other types of statistical sampling discussed in this text include *stratified random sampling*, *systematic sampling*, and *cluster sampling*.

Chapter Outcome 3. →   **BUSINESS APPLICATION**   **SIMPLE RANDOM SAMPLING**

CABLE-ONE A salesperson at Cable-One wishes to estimate the percentage of people in a local subdivision who have satellite television service (such as Direct TV). The result would indicate the extent to which the satellite industry has made inroads into Cable-One's market. The population of interest consists of all families living in the subdivision.

For this example, we simplify the situation by saying that there are only five families in the subdivision: James, Sanchez, Lui, White, and Fitzpatrick. We will let N represent the population size and n the sample size. From the five families ($N = 5$), we select three ($n = 3$) for the sample. There are 10 possible samples of size 3 that could be selected.

{James, Sanchez, Lui}	{James, Sanchez, White}	{James, Sanchez, Fitzpatrick}
{James, Lui, White}	{James, Lui, Fitzpatrick}	{James, White, Fitzpatrick}
{Sanchez, Lui, White}	{Sanchez, Lui, Fitzpatrick}	{Sanchez, White, Fitzpatrick}
{Lui, White, Fitzpatrick}		

Note that no family is selected more than once in a given sample. This method is called *sampling without replacement* and is the most commonly used method. If the families could be selected more than once, the method would be called *sampling with replacement*.

Simple random sampling is the method most people think of when they think of random sampling. In a correctly performed simple random sample, each of these samples would have an equal chance of being selected. For the Cable-One example, a simplified way of selecting a simple random sample would be to put each sample of three names on a piece of paper in a bowl and then blindly reach in and select one piece of paper. However, this method would be difficult if the number of possible samples were large. For example, if $N = 50$ and a sample of size $n = 10$ is to be selected, there are more than 10 billion possible samples. Try finding a bowl big enough to hold those!

Simple random samples can be obtained in a variety of ways. We present two examples to illustrate how simple random samples are selected in practice.

Simple Random Sampling
A method of selecting items from a population such that every possible sample of a specified size has an equal chance of being selected.

BUSINESS APPLICATION   **RANDOM NUMBERS**

STATE SOCIAL SERVICES Suppose the state director for a Midwestern state's social services system is considering changing the timing on food stamp distribution from once a month to once every two weeks. Before making any decisions, he wants to survey a sample of 100 citizens who are on food stamps in a particular county from the 300 total food stamp recipients in that county. He first assigns recipients a number (001 to 300). He can then use the random number function in Excel to determine which recipients to include in the sample. Figure 1.9 shows the results when Excel chooses 10 random numbers. The first recipient sampled is number 115, followed by 31, and so forth. The important thing to remember is that assigning each recipient a number and then randomly selecting a sample from those numbers gives each possible sample an equal chance of being selected.

Excel Tutorial

RANDOM NUMBERS TABLE If you don't have access to computer software such as Excel, the items in the population to be sampled can be determined by using the *random numbers table* in Appendix A. Begin by selecting a starting point in the random numbers table (row and digit). Suppose we use row 5, digit 8 as the starting point. Go down 5 rows and over 8 digits. Verify that the digit in this location is 1. Ignoring the blanks between columns that are there only to make the table more readable, the first three-digit number is 149. Recipient number 149 is the first one selected in the sample. Each subsequent random number is obtained from the random numbers in the next row down. For instance, the second number is 127. The procedure continues selecting numbers from top to bottom in each subsequent column. Numbers exceeding 300 and duplicate numbers are skipped. When enough numbers

FIGURE 1.9

Excel 2010 Output of Random Numbers for State Social Services Example

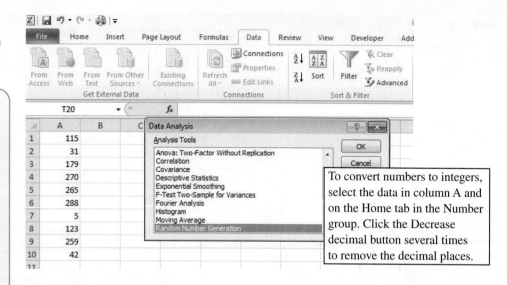

Excel 2010 Instructions:
1. On the **Data** tab, click **Data Analysis**.
2. Select **Random Number Generation** option.
3. Set the **Number of Random Numbers** to 10.
4. Select **Uniform** as the distribution.
5. Define range as between 1 and 300.
6. Indicate that the results are to go in cell A1.
7. Click **OK**.

To convert numbers to integers, select the data in column A and on the Home tab in the Number group. Click the Decrease decimal button several times to remove the decimal places.

	A
1	115
2	31
3	179
4	270
5	265
6	288
7	5
8	123
9	259
10	42

are found for the desired sample size, the process is completed. Food-stamp recipients whose numbers are chosen are then surveyed.

BUSINESS APPLICATION **STRATIFIED RANDOM SAMPLING**

Stratified Random Sampling

A statistical sampling method in which the population is divided into subgroups called *strata* so that each population item belongs to only one stratum. The objective is to form strata such that the population values of interest within each stratum are as much alike as possible. Sample items are selected from each stratum using the simple random sampling method.

FEDERAL RESERVE BANK Sometimes, the sample size required to obtain a needed level of information from a simple random sampling may be greater than our budget permits. At other times, it may take more time to collect than is available. **Stratified random sampling** is an alternative method that has the potential to provide the desired information with a smaller sample size. The following example illustrates how stratified sampling is performed.

Each year, the Federal Reserve Board asks its staff to estimate the total cash holdings of U.S. financial institutions as of July 1. The staff must base the estimate on a sample. Note that not all financial institutions (banks, credit unions, and the like) are the same size. A majority are small, some are medium sized, and only a few are large. However, the few large institutions have a substantial percentage of the total cash on hand. To make sure that a simple random sample includes an appropriate number of small, medium, and large institutions, the sample size might have to be quite large.

As an alternative to the simple random sample, the Federal Reserve staff could divide the institutions into three groups called *strata*: small, medium, and large. Staff members could then select a simple random sample of institutions from each stratum and estimate the total cash on hand for all institutions from this combined sample. Figure 1.10 shows the stratified random sampling concept. Note that the combined sample size ($n_1 + n_2 + n_3$) is the sum of the simple random samples taken from each stratum.

The key behind stratified sampling is to develop a stratum for each characteristic of interest (such as cash on hand) that has items that are quite *homogeneous*. In this example, the size of the financial institution may be a good factor to use in stratifying. Here the combined sample size ($n_1 + n_2 + n_3$) will be less than the sample size that would have been required if no stratification had occurred. Because sample size is directly related to cost (in both time and money), a stratified sample can be more cost effective than a simple random sample.

Multiple layers of stratification can further reduce the overall sample size. For example, the Federal Reserve might break the three strata in Figure 1.10 into *substrata* based on type of institution: state bank, interstate bank, credit union, and so on.

Most large-scale market research studies use stratified random sampling. The well-known political polls, such as the Gallup and Harris polls, use this technique also. For instance, the Gallup poll typically samples between 1,800 and 2,500 people nationwide to estimate how more than 60 million people will vote in a presidential election. We encourage you to go to the Web site http://www.gallup.com/poll/101872/how-does-gallup-polling-work.aspx to read a very good discussion about how the Gallup polls are conducted. The Web site discusses how samples are selected and many other interesting issues associated with polling.

FIGURE 1.10

Stratified Sampling Example

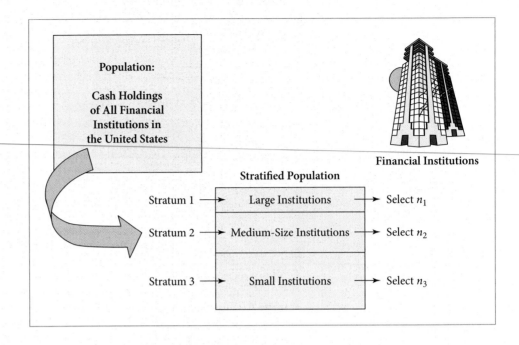

Systematic Random Sampling

A statistical sampling technique that involves selecting every *k*th item in the population after a randomly selected starting point between 1 and *k*. The value of *k* is determined as the ratio of the population size over the desired sample size.

BUSINESS APPLICATION SYSTEMATIC RANDOM SAMPLING

STATE UNIVERSITY ASSOCIATED STUDENTS A few years ago, elected student council officers at mid-sized state university in the Northeast decided to survey fellow students on the issue of the legality of carrying firearms on campus. To determine the opinion of its 20,000 students, a questionnaire was sent to a sample of 500 students. Although simple random sampling could have been used, an alternative method called **systematic random sampling** was chosen.

The university's systematic random sampling plan called for it to send the questionnaire to every 40th student ($20,000/500 = 40$) from an alphabetic list of all students. The process could begin by using Excel to generate a single random number in the range 1 to 40. Suppose this value was 25. The 25th student in the alphabetic list would be selected. After that, every 40th students would be selected (25, 65, 105, 145, . . .) until there were 500 students selected.

Systematic sampling is frequently used in business applications. Use it as an alternative to simple random sampling only when you can assume the population is randomly ordered with respect to the measurement being addressed in the survey. In this case, students' views on firearms on campus are likely unrelated to the spelling of their last name.

BUSINESS APPLICATION CLUSTER SAMPLING

OAKLAND RAIDERS FOOTBALL TEAM The Oakland Raiders of the National Football League plays its home games at O.co (formerly Overstock.com) Coliseum in Oakland, California. Despite its struggles to win in recent years, the team has a passionate fan base. Recently, an outside marketing group was retained by the Raiders to interview season ticket holders about the potential for changing how season ticket pricing is structured. The Oakland Raiders Web site http://www.raiders.com/tickets/seating-price-map.html shows the layout of the O.co Coliseum.

The marketing firm plans to interview season ticket holders just prior to home games during the current season. One sampling technique is to select a simple random sample of size *n* from the population of all season ticket holders. Unfortunately, this technique would likely require that interviewer(s) go to each section in the stadium. This would prove to be an expensive and time-consuming process. A systematic or stratified sampling procedure also would probably require visiting each section in the stadium. The geographical spread of those being interviewed in this case causes problems.

A sampling technique that overcomes the geographical spread problem is **cluster sampling**. The stadium sections would be the clusters. Ideally, the clusters would each have the same characteristics as the population as a whole.

Cluster Sampling

A method by which the population is divided into groups, or clusters, that are each intended to be mini-populations. A simple random sample of *m* clusters is selected. The items chosen from a cluster can be selected using any probability sampling technique.

After the clusters have been defined, a sample of *m* clusters is selected at random from the list of possible clusters. The number of clusters to select depends on various factors, including our survey budget. Suppose the marketing firm randomly selects eight clusters:

$$104 - 142 - 147 - 218 - 228 - 235 - 307 - 327$$

These are the *primary clusters*. Next, the marketing company can either survey all the ticketholders in each cluster or select a simple random sample of ticketholders from each cluster, depending on time and budget considerations.

MyStatLab

1-3: Exercises

Skill Development

1-32. Indicate which sampling method would most likely be used in each of the following situations:
   a. an interview conducted with mayors of a sample of cities in Florida
   b. a poll of voters regarding a referendum calling for a national value-added tax
   c. a survey of customers entering a shopping mall in Minneapolis

1-33. A company has 18,000 employees. The file containing the names is ordered by employee number from 1 to 18,000. If a sample of 100 employees is to be selected from the 18,000 using systematic random sampling, within what range of employee numbers will the first employee selected come from?

1-34. Describe the difference between a statistic and a parameter.

1-35. Why is convenience sampling considered to be a nonstatistical sampling method?

1-36. Describe how systematic random sampling could be used to select a random sample of 1,000 customers who have a certificate of deposit at a commercial bank. Assume that the bank has 25,000 customers who own a certificate of deposit.

1-37. Explain why a census does not necessarily have to involve a population of people. Use an example to illustrate.

1-38. If the manager at First City Bank surveys a sample of 100 customers to determine how many miles they live from the bank, is the mean travel distance for this sample considered a parameter or a statistic? Explain.

1-39. Explain the difference between stratified random sampling and cluster sampling.

1-40. Use Excel to generate five random numbers between 1 and 900.

Business Applications

1-41. According to the U.S. Bureau of Labor Statistics, the annual percentage increase in U.S. college tuition and fees in 1995 was 6.0%, in 1999 it was 4.0%, in 2004 it was 9.5%, and in 2011 it was 5.4%. Are these percentages statistics or parameters? Explain.

1-42. According to an article in the *Idaho Statesman*, a poll taken the day before elections in Germany showed Chancellor Gerhard Schroeder behind his challenger, Angela Merkel, by 6 to 8 percentage points. Is this a statistic or a parameter? Explain.

1-43. Give the name of the kind of sampling that was most likely used in each of the following cases:
   a. a *Wall Street Journal* poll of 2,000 people to determine the president's approval rating
   b. a poll taken of each of the General Motors (GM) dealerships in Ohio in December to determine an estimate of the average number of Chevrolets not yet sold by GM dealerships in the United States
   c. a quality-assurance procedure within a Frito-Lay manufacturing plant that tests every 1,000th bag of Fritos Corn Chips produced to make sure the bag is sealed properly
   d. a sampling technique in which a random sample from each of the tax brackets is obtained by the Internal Revenue Service to audit tax returns

1-44. Your manager has given you an Excel file that contains the names of the company's 500 employees and has asked you to sample 50 employees from the list. You decide to take your sample as follows. First, you assign a random number to each employee using Excel's random number function **Rand**(). Because the random number is volatile (it recalculates itself whenever you modify the file), you freeze the random numbers using the Copy—Paste Special—Values feature. You then sort by the random numbers in ascending order. Finally, you take the first 50 sorted employees as your sample. Does this approach constitute a statistical or a nonstatistical sample?

Computer Applications

1-45. Sysco Foods is a statewide food distributor to restaurants, universities, and other establishments that prepare and sell food. The company has a very large warehouse in which the food is stored until it is pulled from the shelves to be delivered to the customers. The warehouse has 64 storage racks numbered 1–64. Each rack is three shelves high, labeled A, B, and C, and each shelf is divided into 80 sections, numbered 1–80.

Products are located by rack number, shelf letter, and section number. For example, breakfast cereal is located at 43-A-52 (rack 43, shelf A, section 52).

Each week, employees perform an inventory for a sample of products. Certain products are selected and counted. The *actual count* is compared to the *book count* (the quantity in the records that should be in stock). To simplify things, assume that the company has selected breakfast cereals to inventory. Also for simplicity's sake, suppose the cereals occupy racks 1 through 5.

a. Assume that you plan to use simple random sampling to select the sample. Use Excel to determine the sections on each of the five racks to be sampled.
b. Assume that you wish to use cluster random sampling to select the sample. Discuss the steps you would take to carry out the sampling.
c. In this case, why might cluster sampling be preferred over simple random sampling? Discuss.

1-46. United Airlines established a discount airline named Ted. The managers were interested in determining how flyers using Ted rate the airline service. They plan to question a random sample of flyers from the November 12 flights between Denver and Fort Lauderdale. A total of 578 people were on the flights that day. United has a list of the travelers together with their mailing addresses. Each traveler is given an identification number (here, from 001 to 578). Use Excel to generate a list of 40 flyer identification numbers so that those identified can be surveyed.

1-47. The National Park Service has started charging a user fee to park at selected trailheads and cross-country ski lots. Some users object to this fee, claiming they already pay taxes for these areas. The agency has decided to randomly question selected users at fee areas in Colorado to assess the level of concern.

a. Define the population of interest.
b. Assume a sample of 250 is required. Describe the technique you would use to select a sample from the population. Which sampling technique did you suggest?
c. Assume the population of users is 4,000. Use Excel to generate a list of users to be selected for the sample.

1-48. Mount Hillsdale Hospital has more than 4,000 patient files listed alphabetically in its computer system. The office manager wants to survey a statistical sample of these patients to determine how satisfied they were with service provided by the hospital. She plans to use a telephone survey of 100 patients.

a. Describe how you would attach identification numbers to the patient files; for example, how many digits (and which digits) would you use to indicate the first patient file?
b. Describe how the first random number would be obtained to begin a simple random sample method.
c. How many random digits would you need for each random number you selected?
d. Use Excel to generate the list of patients to be surveyed.

END EXERCISES 1-3

Chapter Outcome 4. →

1.4 Data Types and Data Measurement Levels

Chapters 2 and 3 will introduce a variety of techniques for describing data and transforming the data into information. As you will see in those chapters, the statistical techniques deal with different types of data. The level of measurement may vary greatly from application to application. In general, there are four types of data: *quantitative, qualitative, time-series,* and *cross-sectional*. A discussion of each follows.

Quantitative and Qualitative Data

Quantitative Data
Measurements whose values are inherently numerical.

In some cases, data values are best expressed in purely numerical, or **quantitative**, terms, such as in dollars, pounds, inches, or percentages. As an example, a cell phone provider might collect data on the number of outgoing calls placed during a month by its customers. In another case, a sports bar could collect data on the number of pitchers of beer sold weekly.

In other situations, the observation may signify only the category to which an item belongs. Categorical data are referred to as **qualitative** data.

Qualitative Data
Data whose measurement scale is inherently categorical.

For example, a bank might conduct a study of its outstanding real estate loans and keep track of the marital status of the loan customer—*single, married, divorced,* or *other.* The same study also might examine the credit status of the customer—*excellent, good, fair,* or *poor.* Still another part of the study might ask the customers to rate the service by the bank on a 1 to 5 scale with 1 = very poor, 2 = poor, 3 = neutral, 4 = good, and 5 = very good. Note, although the customers are asked to record a number (1 to 5) to indicate the service quality, the data would still be considered qualitative because the numbers are just codes for the categories.

Time-Series Data and Cross-Sectional Data

Time-Series Data
A set of consecutive data values observed at successive points in time.

Cross-Sectional Data
A set of data values observed at a fixed point in time.

Data may also be classified as being either **time-series** or **cross-sectional**.

The data collected by the bank about its loan customers would be cross-sectional because the data from each customer relates to a fixed point in time. In another case, if we sampled 100 stocks from the stock market and determined the closing stock price on March 15, the data would be considered cross-sectional because all measurements corresponded to one point in time.

On the other hand, Ford Motor Company tracks the sales of its F-150 pickup trucks on a monthly basis. Data values observed at intervals over time are referred to as time-series data. If we determined the closing stock price for a particular stock on a daily basis for a year, the stock prices would be time-series data.

Data Measurement Levels

Data can also be identified by their *level of measurement*. This is important because the higher the data level, the more sophisticated the analysis that can be performed. This will be clear when you study the material in the remaining chapters of this text.

We shall discuss and give examples of four levels of data measurements: *nominal, ordinal, interval,* and *ratio.* Figure 1.11 illustrates the hierarchy among these data levels, with nominal data being the lowest level.

Nominal Data *Nominal data* are the lowest form of data, yet you will encounter this type of data many times. Assigning codes to categories generates nominal data. For example, a survey question that asks for marital status provides the following responses:

  1. Married 2. Single 3. Divorced 4. Other

For each person, a code of 1, 2, 3, or 4 would be recorded. These codes are nominal data. Note that the values of the code numbers have no specific meaning, because the order of the categories is arbitrary. We might have shown it this way:

  1. Single 2. Divorced 3. Married 4. Other

With nominal data, we also have complete control over what codes are used. For example, we could have used

  88. Single 11. Divorced 33. Married 55. Other

All that matters is that you know which code stands for which category. Recognize also that the codes need not be numeric. We might use

  S = Single D = Divorced M = Married O = Other

FIGURE 1.11

Data Level Hierarchy

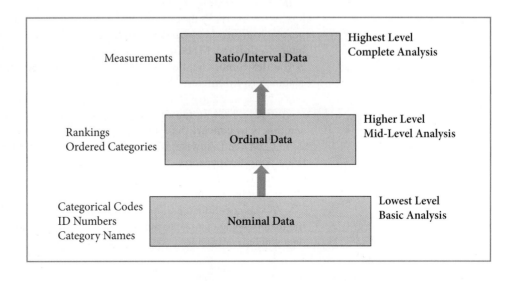

Ordinal Data *Ordinal* or *rank data* are one notch above nominal data on the measurement hierarchy. At this level, the data elements can be rank-ordered on the basis of some relationship among them, with the assigned values indicating this order. For example, a typical market research technique is to offer potential customers the chance to use two unidentified brands of a product. The customers are then asked to indicate which brand they prefer. The brand eventually offered to the general public depends on how often it was the preferred test brand. The fact that an ordering of items took place makes this an ordinal measure.

Bank loan applicants are asked to indicate the category corresponding to their household incomes:

_____ Under $20,000	_____ $20,000 to $40,000	_____ over $40,000
(1)	(2)	(3)

The codes 1, 2, and 3 refer to the particular income categories, with higher codes assigned to higher incomes.

Ordinal measurement allows decision makers to equate two or more observations or to rank-order the observations. In contrast, nominal data can be compared only for equality. You cannot order nominal measurements. Thus, a primary difference between ordinal and nominal data is that ordinal data can have both an equality ($=$) and a greater than ($>$) or a less than ($<$) relationship, whereas nominal data can have only an equality ($=$) relationship.

Interval Data If the distance between two data items can be measured on some scale and the data have ordinal properties ($>$, $<$, or $=$) the data are said to be *interval data*. The best example of interval data is the temperature scale. Both the Fahrenheit and Celsius temperature scales have ordinal properties of ">" or "<" and "=" In addition, the distances between equally spaced points are preserved. For example, $32°F > 30°F$, and $80°C > 78°C$. The difference between $32°F$ and $30°F$ is the same as the difference between $80°F$ and $78°F$, two degrees in each case. Thus, interval data allow us to precisely measure the difference between any two values. With ordinal data this is not possible, because all we can say is that one value is larger than another.

Ratio Data Data that have all the characteristics of interval data but also have a true zero point (at which zero means "none") are called *ratio data*. Ratio measurement is the highest level of measurement.

Packagers of frozen foods encounter ratio measures when they pack their products by weight. Weight, whether measured in pounds or grams, is a ratio measurement because it has a unique zero point—zero meaning no weight. Many other types of data encountered in business environments involve ratio measurements, for example, distance, money, and time.

The difference between interval and ratio measurements can be confusing because it involves the definition of a true zero. If you have $5 and your brother has $10, he has twice as much money as you. If you convert the dollars to pounds, euros, yen, or pesos, your brother will still have twice as much. If your money is lost or stolen, you have no dollars. Money has a true zero. Likewise, if you travel 100 miles today and 200 miles tomorrow, the ratio of distance traveled will be 2/1, even if you convert the distance to kilometers. If on the third day you rest, you have traveled no miles. Distance has a true zero. Conversely, if today's temperature is $35°F$ ($1.67°C$) and tomorrow's is $70°F$ ($21.11°C$), is tomorrow twice as warm as today? The answer is no. One way to see this is to convert the Fahrenheit temperature to Celsius: The ratio will no longer be 2/1 ($12.64/1$). Likewise, if the temperature reads $0°F$ ($-17.59°C$) this does not imply that there is no temperature. It's simply colder than $10°F$ ($-12.22°C$) Also, $0°C$ ($32°F$) is not the same temperature as $0°F$. Thus, temperature, measured with either the Fahrenheit or Celsius scale (an interval-level variable), does not have a true zero.

As was mentioned earlier, a major reason for categorizing data by level and type is that the methods you can use to analyze the data are partially dependent on the level and type of data you have available.

EXAMPLE 1-1   **CATEGORIZING DATA**

Joe Gough/Shutterstock

For many years, *U.S. News and World Report* has published annual rankings based on various data collected from U.S. colleges and universities. Figure 1.12 shows a portion of the data in the file named **Colleges and Universities**. Each column corresponds to a different variable for which data were collected. Before doing any statistical analyses with these data, *U.S. News and World Report* employees need to determine the type and level for each of the factors. Limiting the effort to only those factors that are shown in Figure 1.12, this is done using the following steps:

Step 1   **Identify each factor in the data set.**

The factors (or variables) in the data set shown in Figure 1.12 are

College Name	State	Public (1) Private (2)	Math SAT	Verbal SAT	# appli. rec'd.	# appli. accepted.	# new stud. enrolled	# FT under-grad	# PT under-grad

Each of the 10 columns represents a different factor. Data might be missing for some colleges and universities.

Step 2   **Determine whether the data are time-series or cross-sectional.**

Because each row represents a different college or university and the data are for the same year, the data are cross-sectional. Time-series data are measured over time—say, over a period of years.

Step 3   **Determine which factors are quantitative data and which are qualitative data.**

Qualitative data are codes or numerical values that represent categories. Quantitative data are those that are purely numerical. In this case, the data for the following factors are qualitative:

    College Name

    State

    Code for Public or Private College or University

Data for the following factors are considered quantitative:

Math SAT	Verbal SAT	# new stud. enrolled
# appl. rec'd.	# appl. accepted	
# PT undergrad	# FT undergrad	

FIGURE 1.12

Data for U.S. Colleges and Universities

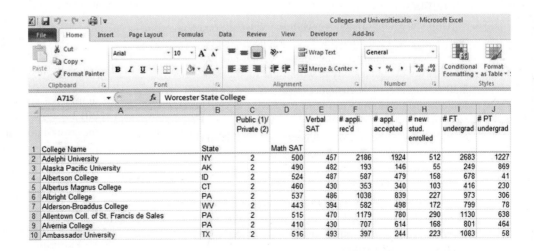

Step 4 **Determine the level of data measurement for each factor.**

The four levels of data are nominal, ordinal, interval, and ratio. This data set has only nominal- and ratio-level data. The three nominal-level factors are

College Name

State

Code for Public or Private College or University

The others are all ratio-level data.

>> END EXAMPLE

MyStatLab

1-4: Exercises

Skill Development

1-49. For each of the following, indicate whether the data are cross-sectional or time-series:
a. quarterly unemployment rates
b. unemployment rates by state
c. monthly sales
d. employment satisfaction data for a company

1-50. What is the difference between qualitative and quantitative data?

1-51. For each of the following variables, indicate the level of data measurement:
a. product rating {1 = excellent, 2 = good, 3 = fair, 4 = poor, 5 = very poor}
b. home ownership {own, rent, other}
c. college grade point average
d. marital status {single, married, divorced, other}

1-52. What is the difference between ordinal and nominal data?

1-53. *Consumer Reports*, in its rating of cars, indicates repair history with circles. The circles are either white, black, or half and half. To which level of data does this correspond? Discuss.

Business Applications

1-54. Verizon has a support center customers can call to get questions answered about their cell phone accounts. The manager in charge of the support center has recently conducted a study in which she surveyed 2,300 customers. The customers who called the support center were transferred to a third party, who asked the customers a series of questions.
a. Indicate whether the data generated from this study will be considered cross-sectional or time-series. Explain why.
b. One of the questions asked customers was approximately how many minutes they had been on hold waiting to get through to a support person. What level of data measurement is obtained from this question? Explain.

c. Another question asked the customer to rate the service on a scale of 1–7, with 1 being the worst possible service and 7 being the best possible service. What level of data measurement is achieved from this question? Will the data be quantitative or qualitative? Explain.

1-55. The following information can be found in the Murphy Oil Corporation Annual Report to Shareholders. For each variable, indicate the level of data measurement.
a. List of Principal Offices (e.g., El Dorado, Calgary, Houston)
b. Income (in millions of dollars) from Continuing Operations
c. List of Principal Subsidiaries (e.g., Murphy Oil USA, Inc., Murphy Exploration & Production Company)
d. Number of branded retail outlets
e. Petroleum products sold, in barrels per day
f. Major Exploration and Production Areas (e.g., Malaysia, Congo, Ecuador)
g. Capital Expenditures measured in millions of dollars

1-56. You have collected the following information on 15 different real estate investment trusts (REITs). Identify whether the data are cross-sectional or time-series.
a. income distribution by region in 2012
b. per share (diluted) funds from operations (FFO) for the years 2006 to 2012
c. number of properties owned as of December 31, 2012
d. the overall percentage of leased space for the 119 properties in service as of December 31, 2012
e. dividends per share for the years 2006–2012

1-57. A loan manager for Bank of the Cascades has the responsibility for approving automobile loans. To assist her in this matter, she has compiled data on 428 cars and trucks. These data are in the file called **2004-Automobiles**.

Indicate the level of data measurement for each of the variables in this data file.

1-58. Recently, the manager of the call center for a large Internet bank asked his staff to collect data on a random sample of the bank's customers. Data on the following variables were collected and placed in a file called **Bank Call Center**:

Column A	Column B	Column C	Column D	Column E	Column F
Account Number	Caller Gender	Account Holder Gender	Past Due Amount	Current Amount Due	Was This a Billing Question?
Unique Tracking #	1 = Male 2 = Female	1 = Male 2 = Female	Numerical Value	Numerical Value	3 = Yes 4 = No

A small portion of the data is as follows:

Account Number	Caller Gender	Account Holder Gender	Past Due Amount	Current Amount Due	Was This a Billing Question?
4348291	2	2	40.35	82.85	3
6008516	1	1	0	−129.67	4
17476479	1	2	0	76.38	4
13846306	2	2	0	99.24	4
21393711	1	1	0	37.98	3

a. Would you classify these data as time-series or cross-sectional? Explain.
b. Which of the variables are quantitative and which are qualitative?
c. For each of the six variables, indicate the level of data measurement.

END EXERCISES 1-4

Chapter Outcome 5. → **1.5 A Brief Introduction to Data Mining**

Data Mining—Finding the Important, Hidden Relationships in Data

What food products have an increased demand during hurricanes? How do you win baseball games without star players? Is my best friend the one to help me find a job? What color car is least likely to be a "lemon"? These and other interesting questions can and have been answered using data mining. Data mining consists of applying sophisticated statistical techniques and algorithms to the analysis of big data (i.e., the wealth of new data that organizations collect in many and varied forms). Through the application of data mining, decisions can now be made on the basis of statistical analysis rather than on only managerial intuition and experience. The statistical techniques introduced in this text provide the basis for the more sophisticated statistical tools that are used by data mining analysts.

Wal-Mart, the nation's largest retailer, uses data mining to help it tailor product selection based on the sales, demographic, and weather information it collects. While Wal-Mart managers might not be surprised that the demand for flashlights, batteries, and bottled water increased with hurricane warnings, they were surprised to find that there was also an increase in the demand for strawberry Pop-Tarts before hurricanes hit. This knowledge allowed Wal-Mart to increase the availability of Pop-Tarts at selected stores affected by the hurricane alerts. The McKinsey Global Institute estimates that the full application of data mining to retailing could result in a potential increase in operating margins by as much as 60%. (Source: McKinsey Global Institute: *Big Data: The Next Frontier for Innovation, Competition, and Productivity*, May 2011 by *James Manyika, Michael Chui, Brad Brown, Jacques Bughin, Richard Dobbs, Charles Roxburgh, Angela Hung Byers*.)

Data are everywhere, and businesses are collecting more each day. Accounting and sales data are now captured and streamed instantly when transactions occur. Digital sensors in industrial equipment and automobiles can record and report data on vibration, temperature, physical location, and the chemical composition of the surrounding air. But data are now more than numbers. Much of the data being collected today consists of words from Internet search engines such as Google searches and from pictures from social media postings on such platforms as Facebook. Together with the traditional numbers comprising quantitative data, the availability of new unstructured, qualitative data has led to a data explosion. IDC, a technology research firm, estimates that data are growing at a rate of 50 percent a year. All of these data—referred to as big data—have created a need not only for highly skilled data scientists who can mine and analyze it but also for managers who can make decisions using it. McKinsey Global Institute, a consultancy firm, believes that big data offer an opportunity for organizations to create competitive advantages for themselves if they can understand and use the information to its full potential. They report that the use of big data "will become a key basis of competition and growth for individual firms." This will create a need for highly trained data scientists and managers who can use data to support their decision making. Unfortunately, McKinsey predicts that by 2018, there could be a shortage in the United States of 140,000 to 190,000 people with deep analytical skills as well as 1.5 million managers and analysts with the know-how needed to use big data to make meaningful and effective decisions. (Source: McKinsey Global Institute: *Big Data: The Next Frontier for Innovation, Competition, and Productivity*, May 2011 by James Manyika, Michael Chui, Brad Brown, Jacques Bughin, Richard Dobbs, Charles Roxburgh, Angela Hung Byers.) The statistical tools you will learn in this course will provide you with a good first step toward preparing yourself for a career in data mining and business analytics.

Visual Summary

Chapter 1: Business statistics is a collection of procedures and techniques used by decision-makers to transform data into useful information. Chapter 1 introduces the subject of business statistics and lays the groundwork for the remaining chapters in the text. Included is a discussion of the different types of data and data collection methods. Chapter 1 also describes the difference between populations and samples.

 1.1 What Is Business Statistics? (pg. 2–6)

Summary

The two areas of statistics, **descriptive statistics** and **inferential statistics**, are introduced to set the stage for what is coming in subsequent chapters. Descriptive statistics includes **visual tools** such as charts and graphs and also the **numerical measures** such as the arithmetic average. The role of descriptive statistics is to describe data and help transform data into usable information. Inferential techniques are those that allow decision-makers to draw conclusions about a large body of data by examining a smaller subset of those data. Two areas of inference, **estimation** and **hypothesis testing**, are described.

 1.2 Procedures for Collecting Data (pg. 7–14)

Summary

Before data can be analyzed using business statistics techniques, the data must be collected. The types of data collection reviewed are: **experiments**, **telephone surveys**, **written questionnaires** and **direct observation** and **personal interviews**. Data collection issues such as **interviewer bias**, **nonresponse bias**, **selection bias**, **observer bias**, and **measurement error** are covered. The concepts of **internal validity** and **external validity** are defined.

Outcome 1. Know the key data collection methods.

1.3 Populations, Samples, and Sampling Techniques (pg. 14–20)

Summary

The important concepts of **population** and **sample** are defined and examples of each are provided. Because many statistical applications involve samples, emphasis is placed on how to select samples. Two main sampling categories are presented, **nonstatistical sampling** and **statistical sampling**. The focus is on statistical sampling and four statistical sampling methods are discussed: **simple random sampling**, **stratified random sampling**, **cluster sampling**, and **systematic random sampling**.

Outcome 2. Know the difference between a population and a sample.

Outcome 3. Understand the similarities and differences between different sampling methods.

 Conclusion

Statistical analysis begins with data. You need to know how to collect data, how to select samples from a population, and the type and level of data you are using. **Figure 1.13** summarizes the different sampling techniques presented in this chapter. **Figure 1.14** gives a synopsis of the different data collection procedures and **Figure 1.15** shows the different data types and measurement levels.

 1.5 A Brief Introduction to Data Mining (pg. 25–26)

Summary

Because electronic data storage is so inexpensive, organizations are collecting and storing greater volumes of data that ever before. As a result, a relatively new field of study called **data mining** has emerged. Data mining involves the art and science of delving into the data to identify patterns and conclusions that are not immediately evident in the data. This section briefly introduces the subject and discusses a few of the applications. Although data mining is not covered in depth in this text, the concepts presented throughout the text form the basis for this important discipline.

Outcome 5. Become familiar with the concept of data mining and some of its applications.

  1.4 Data Types and Data Measurement Levels (pg. 20–25)

Summary

This section discusses various ways in which data are classified. For example, data can be classified as being either **quantitative** or **qualitative**. Data can also be **cross-sectional** or **time-series**. Another way to classify data is by the level of measurement. There are four levels from lowest to highest: **nominal**, **ordinal**, **interval**, and **ratio**. Knowing the type of data you have is very important as you will see in Chapters 2 and 3 because the data type influences the type of statistical procedures you can use.

Outcome 4. Understand how to categorize data by type and level of measurement.

FIGURE 1.13

Sampling Techniques

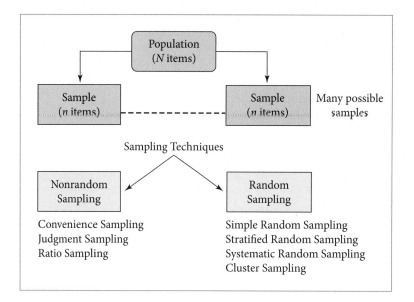

FIGURE 1.14

Data Collection Techniques

Data Collection Method	Advantages	Disadvantages
Experiments	Provide controls Preplanned objectives	Costly Time-consuming Requires planning
Telephone Surveys	Timely Relatively inexpensive	Poor reputation Limited scope and length
Mail Questionnaires Written Surveys	Inexpensive Can expand length Can use open-end questions	Low response rate Requires exceptional clarity
Direct Observation Personal Interview	Expands analysis opportunities No respondent bias	Potential observer bias Costly

FIGURE 1.15

Data Classification

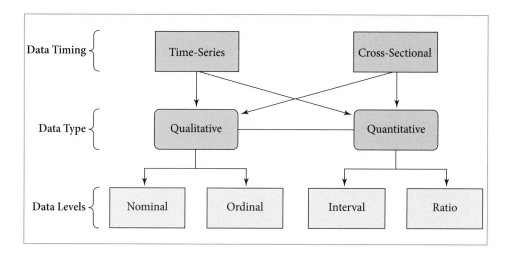

Key Terms

Arithmetic mean, or average pg. 4
Bias pg. 12
Business intelligence pg. 1
Business statistics pg. 2
Census pg. 15
Closed-end questions pg. 8
Cluster sampling pg. 18
Convenience sampling pg. 15
Cross-sectional data pg. 21
Data Mining pg. 1

Demographic questions pg. 8
Experiment pg. 7
Experimental design pg. 7
External validity pg. 13
Internal validity pg. 13
Nonstatistical sampling techniques pg. 15
Open-end questions pg. 9
Population pg. 14
Qualitative data pg. 20
Quantitative data pg. 20

Sample pg. 14
Simple random sampling pg. 16
Statistical inference procedures
  pg. 5
Statistical sampling techniques pg. 15
Stratified random sampling pg. 17
Structured interview pg. 11
Systematic random sampling pg. 18
Time-series data pg. 21
Unstructured interview pg. 11

Chapter Exercises

MyStatLab

Conceptual Questions

1-59. Several organizations publish the results of presidential approval polls. Movements in these polls are seen as an indication of how the general public views presidential performance. Comment on these polls within the context of what was covered in this chapter.

1-60. With what level of data is a bar chart most appropriately used?

1-61. With what level of data is a histogram most appropriately used?

1-62. Two people see the same movie; one says it was average and the other says it was exceptional. What level of data are they using in these ratings? Discuss how the same movie could receive different reviews.

1-63. The University of Michigan publishes a monthly measure of consumer confidence. This is taken as a possible indicator of future economic performance. Comment on this process within the context of what was covered in this chapter.

Business Applications

1-64. In a business publication such as *The Wall Street Journal* or *Business Week*, find a graph or chart representing time-series data. Discuss how the data were gathered and the purpose of the graph or chart.

1-65. In a business publication such as *The Wall Street Journal* or *Business Week*, find a graph or chart representing cross-sectional data. Discuss how the data were gathered and the purpose of the graph or chart.

1-66. *The Oregonian* newspaper has asked readers to e-mail and respond to the question, "Do you believe police officers are using too much force in routine traffic stops?"

  a. Would the results of this survey be considered a random sample?

  b. What type of bias might be associated with a data collection system such as this? Discuss what options might be used to reduce this bias potential.

1-67. The makers of Mama's Home-Made Salsa are concerned about the quality of their product. The particular trait of concern is the thickness of the salsa in each jar.

  a. Discuss a plan by which the managers might determine the percentage of jars of salsa believed to have an unacceptable thickness by potential purchasers. (1) Define the sampling procedure to be used, (2) the randomization method to be used to select the sample, and (3) the measurement to be obtained.

  b. Explain why it would or wouldn't be feasible (or, perhaps, possible) to take a census to address this issue.

1-68. A maker of energy drinks is considering abandoning can containers and going exclusively to bottles because the sales manager believes customers prefer drinking from bottles. However, the vice president in charge of marketing is not convinced the sales manager is correct.

  a. Indicate the data collection method you would use.

  b. Indicate what procedures you would follow to apply this technique in this setting.

  c. State which level of data measurement applies to the data you would collect. Justify your answer.

  d. Are the data qualitative or quantitative? Explain.

Video Case 1

Statistical Data Collection @ McDonald's

Think of any well-known, successful business in your community. What do you think has been its secret? Competitive products or services? Talented managers with vision? Dedicated employees with great skills? There's no question these all play an important part in its success. But there's more, lots more. It's "data." That's right, data.

The data collected by a business in the course of running its daily operations form the foundation of every decision made. Those data are analyzed using a variety of statistical techniques to provide decision makers with a succinct and clear picture of the company's activities. The resulting statistical information then plays a key role in decision making, whether those decisions are made by an accountant, marketing manager, or operations specialist. To better understand just what types of business statistics organizations employ, let's take a look at one of the world's most well-respected companies: McDonald's.

McDonald's operates more than 30,000 restaurants in more than 118 countries around the world. Total annual revenues recently surpassed the $20 billion mark. Wade Thomas, vice president of U.S. Menu Management for McDonalds, helps drive those sales but couldn't do it without statistics.

"When you're as large as we are, we can't run the business on simple gut instinct. We rely heavily on all kinds of statistical data to help us determine whether our products are meeting customer expectations, when products need to be updated, and much more," says Wade. "The cost of making an educated guess is simply too great a risk."

McDonald's restaurant owner/operators and managers also know the competitiveness of their individual restaurants depends on the data they collect and the statistical techniques used to analyze the data into meaningful information. Each restaurant has a sophisticated cash register system that collects data such as individual customer orders, service times, and methods of payment, to name a few. Periodically, each U.S.–based restaurant undergoes a restaurant operations improvement process, or ROIP, study. A special team of reviewers monitors restaurant activity over a period of several days, collecting data about everything from front-counter service and kitchen efficiency to drive-thru service times. The data are analyzed by McDonald's U.S. Consumer and Business Insights group at McDonald's headquarters near Chicago to help the restaurant owner/operator and managers better understand what they're doing well and where they have opportunities to grow.

Steve Levigne, vice president of Consumer and Business Insights, manages the team that supports the company's decision-making efforts. Both qualitative and quantitative data are collected and analyzed all the way down to the individual store level. "Depending on the audience, the results may be rolled up to an aggregate picture of operations," says Steve. Software packages such as Microsoft Excel, SAS, and SPSS do most of the number crunching and are useful for preparing the graphical representations of the information so decision makers can quickly see the results.

Not all companies have an entire department staffed with specialists in statistical analysis, however. That's where you come in. The more you know about the procedures for collecting and analyzing data, and how to use them, the better decision maker you'll be, regardless of your career aspirations. So it would seem there's a strong relationship here—knowledge of statistics and your success.

Discussion Questions:

1. You will recall that McDonald's vice president of U.S. Menu Management, Wade Thomas, indicated that McDonald's relied heavily on statistical data to determine, in part, if its products were meeting customer expectations. The narrative indicated that two important sources of data were the sophisticated register system and the restaurant operations improvement process, ROIP. Describe the types of data that could be generated by these two methods and discuss how these data could be used to determine if McDonald's products were meeting customer expectations.

2. One of McDonald's uses of statistical data is to determine when products need to be updated. Discuss the kinds of data McDonald's would require to make this determination. Also provide how these types of data would be used to determine when a product needed to be updated.

3. This video case presents the types of data collected and used by McDonald's in the course of running its daily operations. For a moment, imagine that McDonald's did not collect these data. Attempt to describe how it might make a decision concerning, for instance, how much its annual advertising budget would be.

4. Visit a McDonald's in your area. While there, take note of the different types of data that could be collected using observation only. For each variable you identify, determine the level of data measurement. Select three different variables from your list and outline the specific steps you would use to collect the data. Discuss how each of the variables could be used to help McDonald's manage the restaurant.

- **Review** the definitions for nominal, ordinal, interval, and ratio data in Sections 1–4.
- **Examine** the statistical software, such as Excel, that you will be using during this course to make sure you are aware of the procedures for constructing graphs and tables. For instance, in Excel, look at the Charts group on the Insert tab and the *Pivot Table* feature on the Insert tab.
- **Look at** popular newspapers such as *USA Today* and business periodicals such as *Fortune, Business Week*, or *The Wall Street Journal* for instances in which charts, graphs, or tables are used to convey information.

chapter **2**

Graphs, Charts, and Tables— Describing Your Data

2.1	Frequency Distributions and Histograms (pg. 32–53)	**Outcome 1.** Construct frequency distributions both manually and with your computer.
		Outcome 2. Construct and interpret a frequency histogram.
		Outcome 3. Develop and interpret joint frequency distributions.
2.2	Bar Charts, Pie Charts, and Stem and Leaf Diagrams (pg. 53–63)	**Outcome 4.** Construct and interpret various types of bar charts.
		Outcome 5. Build a stem and leaf diagram.
2.3	Line Charts and Scatter Diagrams (pg. 63–73)	**Outcome 6.** Create a line chart and interpret the trend in the data.
		Outcome 7. Construct a scatter diagram and interpret it.

Why you need to know

We live in an age in which presentations and reports are expected to include high-quality graphs and charts that effectively transform data into information. Although the written word is still vital, words become even more powerful when coupled with an effective visual illustration of data. The adage that a picture is worth a thousand words is particularly relevant in business decision making. We are constantly bombarded with visual images and stimuli. Much of our time is spent watching television, playing video games, or working at a computer. These technologies are advancing rapidly, making the images sharper and more attractive to our eyes. Flat-panel, high-definition televisions and high-resolution monitors represent significant improvements over the original technologies they replaced. However, this phenomenon is not limited to video technology but has also become an important part of the way businesses communicate with customers, employees, suppliers, and other constituents.

When you graduate, you will find yourself on both ends of the data analysis spectrum. On the one hand, regardless of what you end up doing for a career, you will almost certainly be involved in preparing reports and making presentations that require using visual descriptive statistical tools presented in this chapter. You will be on the "do it" end of the data analysis process. Thus, you need to know how to use these statistical tools.

On the other hand, you will also find yourself reading reports or listening to presentations that others have made. In many instances, you will be required to make important decisions or to reach conclusions based on the information in those reports or presentations. Thus, you will be on the "use it" end of the data analysis process. You need to be knowledgeable about these tools to effectively screen and critique the work that others do for you.

Charts and graphs are not just tools used internally by businesses. Business periodicals such as *Fortune* and *Business Week* use graphs and charts extensively in articles to help readers better understand key concepts. Many advertisements will even use graphs and charts effectively to convey their messages. Virtually every issue of *The Wall Street Journal* contains different graphs, charts, or tables that display data in an informative way.

MishAl/Shutterstock

Thus, you will find yourself to be both a producer and a consumer of the descriptive statistical techniques known as graphs, charts, and tables. You will create a competitive advantage for yourself through-out your career if you obtain a solid understanding of the techniques introduced in Chapter 2. This chapter introduces some of the most frequently used tools and techniques for describing data with graphs, charts, and tables. Although this analysis can be done manually, we will provide output from Excel software showing that software can be used to perform the analysis easily, quickly, and with a finished quality that once required a graphic artist.

2.1 Frequency Distributions and Histograms

In today's business climate, companies collect massive amounts of data they hope will be useful for making decisions. Every time a customer makes a purchase at a store like Macy's or the Gap, data from that transaction is updated to the store's database. Major retail stores like Walmart capture the number of different product categories included in each "market basket" of items purchased. Table 2.1 shows these data for all customer transactions for a single day at one Walmart store in Dallas. A total of 450 customers made purchases on the day in question. The first value in Table 2.1, 4, indicates that the customer's purchase included four different product categories (for example food, sporting goods, photography supplies, and dry goods).

TABLE 2.1 | **Product Categories per Customer at the Dallas Walmart**

4	2	5	8	8	10	1	4	8	3	4	1	1	3	4
1	4	4	5	4	4	4	9	5	4	4	10	7	11	4
10	2	6	7	10	5	4	6	4	6	2	3	2	4	5
5	4	11	1	4	1	9	2	4	6	6	7	6	2	3
6	5	3	4	5	6	5	3	10	6	5	7	7	4	3
8	2	2	6	5	11	9	9	5	5	6	5	3	1	7
6	6	5	3	8	4	3	3	4	4	4	7	6	4	9
1	6	5	5	4	4	7	5	6	6	9	5	6	10	4
7	5	8	4	4	7	4	6	6	4	4	2	10	4	5
4	11	8	7	9	5	6	4	2	8	4	2	6	6	6
6	4	6	5	7	1	6	9	1	5	9	10	5	5	10
5	4	7	5	7	6	9	5	3	2	1	5	5	5	5
5	9	5	3	2	5	7	2	4	6	4	4	4	4	4
6	5	8	5	5	5	5	5	2	5	5	6	4	6	5
5	7	10	2	2	6	8	3	1	3	5	6	3	3	6
5	4	5	3	3	7	9	4	4	5	10	6	10	5	9
4	3	8	7	1	8	4	3	1	3	6	7	5	5	5
4	7	4	11	6	6	3	7	9	4	4	2	9	7	5
1	6	6	8	3	8	4	4	1	9	3	9	3	4	2
9	5	5	7	10	5	3	4	7	7	6	2	2	4	4
4	7	3	5	4	9	2	3	4	3	2	1	6	4	6
1	8	1	4	3	5	5	10	4	4	4	6	9	2	7
9	4	5	3	6	5	5	3	4	6	5	7	3	6	8
3	6	1	5	7	7	5	4	6	6	6	3	6	9	5
4	5	10	1	5	5	7	8	9	1	6	5	6	6	4
10	6	5	5	5	1	6	5	6	4	7	9	10	2	6
4	4	6	11	9	5	4	4	3	5	4	6	2	6	7
3	5	6	7	4	5	4	6	9	4	3	3	6	9	4
3	7	5	6	11	4	4	8	4	2	8	2	4	2	3
6	5	1	10	5	9	5	4	5	1	4	9	5	4	4

Although the data in Table 2.1 are easy to capture with the technology of today's cash registers, in this form, the data provide little or no information that managers could use to determine the buying habits of their customers. However, these data can be converted into useful information through descriptive statistical analysis.

Chapter Outcome 1. → # Frequency Distribution

Frequency Distribution

A summary of a set of data that displays the number of observations in each of the distribution's distinct categories or classes.

Discrete Data

Data that can take on a countable number of possible values.

One of the first steps would be to construct a **frequency distribution**.

The product data in Table 2.1 take on only a few possible values (1, 2, 3, . . . , 11). The minimum number of product categories is 1 and the maximum number of categories in these data is 11. These data are called **discrete data**.

When you encounter discrete data, where the variable of interest can take on only a reasonably small number of possible values, a frequency distribution is constructed by counting the number of times each possible value occurs in the data set. We organize these counts into a *frequency distribution table*, as shown in Table 2.2. Now, from this frequency distribution we are able to see how the data values are spread over the different number of possible product categories. For instance, you can see that the most frequently occurring number of product categories in a customer's "market basket" is 4, which occurred 92 times. You can also see that the three most common numbers of product categories are 4, 5, and 6. Only a very few times do customers purchase 10 or 11 product categories in their trip to the store.

Consider another example in which a consulting firm surveyed random samples of residents in two cities, Philadelphia and Knoxville. The firm is investigating the labor markets in these two communities for a client that is thinking of relocating its corporate offices to one of the two locations. Education level of the workforce in the two cities is a key factor in making the relocation decision. The consulting firm surveyed 160 randomly selected adults in Philadelphia and 330 adults in Knoxville and recorded the number of years of college attended. The responses ranged from zero to eight years. Table 2.3 shows the frequency distributions for each city.

Relative Frequency

The proportion of total observations that are in a given category. Relative frequency is computed by dividing the frequency in a category by the total number of observations. The relative frequencies can be converted to percentages by multiplying by 100.

Suppose now we wished to compare the distribution for years of college for Philadelphia and Knoxville. How do the two cities' distributions compare? Do you see any difficulties in making this comparison? Because the surveys contained different numbers of people, it is difficult to compare the frequency distributions directly. When the number of total observations differs, comparisons are aided if **relative frequencies** are computed. Equation 2.1 is used to compute the relative frequencies.

Table 2.4 shows the relative frequencies for each city's distribution. This makes a comparison of the two much easier. We see that Knoxville has relatively more people without any college (56.7%) or with one year of college (18.8%) than Philadelphia (21.9%

TABLE 2.2 | **Dallas Walmart Product Categories Frequency Distribution**

Number of Product Catagories	Frequency
1	25
2	29
3	42
4	92
5	83
6	71
7	35
8	19
9	29
10	18
11	7
	Total = 450

TABLE 2.3 | **Frequency Distributions of Years of College Education**

Philadelphia		Knoxville	
Years of College	Frequency	Years of College	Frequency
0	35	0	187
1	21	1	62
2	24	2	34
3	22	3	19
4	31	4	14
5	13	5	7
6	6	6	3
7	5	7	4
8	3	8	0
	Total = 160		Total = 330

Relative Frequency

$$\text{Relative frequency} = \frac{f_i}{n} \tag{2.1}$$

where:

f_i = Frequency of the ith value of the discrete variable

$n = \sum_{i=1}^{k} f_i = $ Total number of observations

k = The number of different values for the discrete variable

---

and 13.1%). At all other levels of education, Philadelphia has relatively more people than Knoxville.

The frequency distributions shown in Table 2.2 and Table 2.3 were developed from *quantitative data*. That is, the variable of interest was numerical (number of product categories or number of years of college). However, a frequency distribution can also be developed

TABLE 2.4 | **Relative Frequency Distributions of Years of College**

Years of College	Philadelphia		Knoxville	
	Frequency	Relative Frequency	Frequency	Relative Frequency
0	35	35/160 = 0.219	187	187/330 = 0.567
1	21	21/160 = 0.131	62	62/330 = 0.188
2	24	24/160 = 0.150	34	34/330 = 0.103
3	22	22/160 = 0.138	19	19/330 = 0.058
4	31	31/160 = 0.194	14	14/330 = 0.042
5	13	13/160 = 0.081	7	7/330 = 0.021
6	6	6/160 = 0.038	3	3/330 = 0.009
7	5	5/160 = 0.031	4	4/330 = 0.012
8	3	3/160 = 0.019	0	0/330 = 0.000
Total	160		330	

TABLE 2.5 | **TV Source Frequency Distribution**

TV Source	Frequency
DISH	80
Direct-TV	90
Cable	20
Other	10
Total =	200

How to do it (Example 2-1)

Developing Frequency and Relative Frequency Distributions for Discrete Data

To develop a discrete data frequency distribution, perform the following steps:

1. List all possible values of the variable. If the variable is ordinal level or higher, order the possible values from low to high.

2. Count the number of occurrences at each value of the variable and place this value in a column labeled "frequency."

To develop a relative frequency distribution, do the following:

3. Use Equation 2.1 and divide each frequency count by the total number of observations and place in a column headed "relative frequency."

when the data are *qualitative data*, or nonnumerical data. For instance, if a survey asked homeowners how they get their TV signal, the possible responses in this region are:

DISH   DirectTV   Cable   Other

Table 2.5 shows the frequency distribution from a survey of 200 homeowners.

EXAMPLE 2-1   **FREQUENCY AND RELATIVE FREQUENCY DISTRIBUTIONS**

Real Estate Transactions In late 2008, the United States experienced a major economic decline thought to be due in part to the sub-prime loans that many lending institutions made during the previous few years. When the housing bubble burst, many institutions experienced severe problems. As a result, lenders became much more conservative in granting home loans, which in turn made buying and selling homes more challenging. To demonstrate the magnitude of the problem in Kansas City, the Association of Real Estate Brokers conducted a survey of 16 real estate agencies and collected data on the number of real estate transactions closed in December 2008. The following data were observed:

3	0	0	1
1	2	2	0
0	2	1	0
2	1	4	2

The real estate analysts can use the following steps to construct a frequency distribution and a relative frequency distribution for the number of real estate transactions.

Step 1 **List the possible values.**
The possible values for the discrete variable, listed in order, are 0, 1, 2, 3, 4.

Step 2 **Count the number of occurrences at each value.**
The frequency distribution follows:

Transactions	Frequency	Relative Frequency
0	5	5/16 = 0.3125
1	4	4/16 = 0.2500
2	5	5/16 = 0.3125
3	1	1/16 = 0.0625
4	1	1/16 = 0.0625
Total = 16		1.0000

Step 3 **Determine the relative frequencies.**
The relative frequencies are determined by dividing each frequency by 16, as shown in the right-hand column above. Thus, just over 31% of those responding reported no transactions during December 2008.

>> **END EXAMPLE**

TRY PROBLEM 2-1 (pg. 49)

EXAMPLE 2-2   **FREQUENCY DISTRIBUTION FOR QUALITATIVE DATA**

Automobile Accidents State Farm Insurance recently surveyed a sample of the records for 15 policy holders to determine the make of the vehicle driven by the eldest member in the household. The following data reflect the results for 15 of the respondents:

Ford	Dodge	Toyota	Ford	Buick
Chevy	Toyota	Nissan	Ford	Chevy
Ford	Toyota	Chevy	BMW	Honda

The frequency distribution for this qualitative variable is found as follows:

Step 1 List the possible values.

For these sample data, the possible values for the variable are BMW, Buick, Chevy, Dodge, Ford, Honda, Nissan, Toyota.

Step 2 Count the number of occurrences at each value.

The frequency distribution is

Car Company	Frequency
BMW	1
Buick	1
Chevy	3
Dodge	1
Ford	4
Honda	1
Nissan	1
Toyota	3
Total =	15

>> **END EXAMPLE**

TRY PROBLEM 2-8 (pg. 50)

BUSINESS APPLICATION **FREQUENCY DISTRIBUTIONS**

Excel Tutorial

ATHLETIC SHOE SURVEY In recent years, a status symbol for many students has been the brand and style of athletic shoes they wear. Companies such as Nike and Adidas compete for the top position in the sport shoe market. A survey was recently conducted in which 100 college students at a southern state school were asked a number of questions, including how many pairs of Nike shoes they currently own. The data are in a file called **SportsShoes**.

The variable *Number of Nike* is a discrete quantitative variable. Figure 2.1 shows the frequency distribution (output from Excel) for the number of Nike shoes owned by those

FIGURE 2.1

Excel 2010 Output—Nike Shoes Frequency Distribution

Excel 2010 Instructions:
1. Open File: **SportsShoes.xlsx**.
2. Enter the Possible Values for the Variable; i.e., 0, 1, 2, 3, 4, etc.
3. Select the cells to contain the Frequency values.
4. Select the **Formulas** tab.
5. Click on the f_x button.
6. Select the **Statistics— FREQUENCY** function.
7. Enter the range of data and the bin range (the cells containing the possible number of shoes).
8. Press **Ctrl-Shift-Enter** to determine the frequency values.

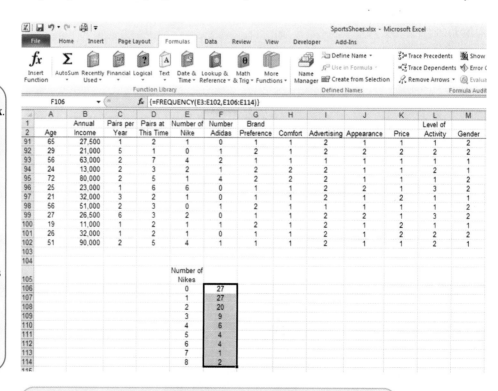

Minitab Instructions (for similar results):
1. Open file: **SportsShoes.MTW**.
2. Choose **Stat > Tables > Tally Individual Variables**.
3. In **Variables**, enter data column.
4. Under **Display**, check **Counts**.
5. Click **OK**.

surveyed. These frequency distributions show that, although a few people own more than six pairs of Nike shoes, the bulk of those surveyed own two or fewer pairs.

Chapter Outcome 1. →

Grouped Data Frequency Distributions

In the previous examples, the variable of interest was a discrete variable and the number of possible values for the variable was limited to only a few. However, there are many instances in which the variable of interest will be either **continuous** (e.g., weight, time, length) or discrete and will have many possible outcomes (e.g., age, income, stock prices), yet you want to describe the variable using a frequency distribution.

Continuous Data

Data whose possible values are uncountable and that may assume any value in an interval.

BUSINESS APPLICATION **GROUPED DATA FREQUENCY DISTRIBUTIONS**

NETFLIX Netflix is one of the largest video rental companies in the United States. It rents movies that are sent to customers by mail and also provides a video streaming service via the Internet. Recently, a distribution manager for Netflix conducted a survey of customers. Among the questions asked on the written survey was "How many DVD movies do you own?" A total of 230 people completed the survey; Table 2.6 shows the responses to the DVD ownership question. These data are discrete, quantitative data. The values range from 0 to 30.

The manager is interested in transforming these data into useful information by constructing a frequency distribution. Table 2.7 shows one approach in which the possible values for the number of DVD movies owned is listed from 0 to 30. Although this frequency distribution is a step forward in transforming the data into information, because of the large number of possible values for DVD movies owned, the 230 observations are spread over a large range, making analysis difficult. In this case, the manager might consider forming a *grouped data frequency distribution* by organizing the possible number of DVD movies owned into discrete categories or *classes*.

To begin constructing a grouped frequency distribution, sort the quantitative data from low to high. The sorted data is called a *data array*. Now, define the classes for the variable of interest. Care needs to be taken when constructing these classes to ensure each data point is put into one, and only one, possible class. Therefore, the classes should meet four criteria.

TABLE 2.6 | **DVD Movies Owned: Netflix Survey**

9	4	13	10	5	10	13	14	10	19
0	10	16	9	11	14	8	15	7	15
10	11	9	7	6	12	12	14	15	16
15	14	10	13	9	12	12	10	10	11
15	14	9	19	3	9	16	19	15	9
4	2	4	5	6	2	3	4	7	5
6	2	2	0	0	8	3	4	3	2
2	5	2	5	2	2	6	2	5	6
5	2	7	3	5	1	6	4	3	6
3	7	7	1	6	2	7	1	3	2
4	0	2	2	4	6	2	5	3	7
4	16	9	10	11	7	10	9	10	11
11	12	9	8	9	7	9	17	8	13
14	13	10	6	12	5	14	7	13	12
9	6	10	15	7	7	9	9	13	10
9	3	17	5	11	9	6	9	15	8
11	13	4	16	13	9	11	5	12	13
0	3	3	3	2	1	4	0	2	0
3	7	1	5	2	2	3	2	1	3
2	3	3	3	0	3	3	3	1	1
13	24	24	17	17	15	25	20	15	20
21	23	25	17	13	22	18	17	30	21
18	21	17	16	25	14	15	24	21	15

TABLE 2.7 | **Frequency Distribution of DVD Movies Owned**

DVD Movies Owned	Frequency
0	8
1	8
2	22
3	22
4	11
5	13
6	12
7	14
8	5
9	19
10	14
11	9
12	8
13	12
14	8
15	12
16	6
17	7
18	2
19	3
20	2
21	4
22	1
23	1
24	3
25	3
26	0
27	0
28	0
29	0
30	1
	Total = 230

Mutually Exclusive Classes
Classes that do not overlap so that a data value can be placed in only one class.

All-Inclusive Classes
A set of classes that contains all the possible data values.

Equal-Width Classes
The distance between the lowest possible value and the highest possible value in each class is equal for all classes.

First, they must be **mutually exclusive**.

Second, they must be **all-inclusive**.

Third, if at all possible, they should be of **equal width**.

Fourth, avoid empty classes if possible.

Equal-width classes make analyzing and interpreting the frequency distribution easier. However, there are some instances in which the presence of extreme high or low values makes it necessary to have an open-ended class. For example, annual family incomes in the United States are mostly between $15,000 and $200,000. However, there are some families with much higher family incomes. To best accommodate these high incomes, you might consider having the highest income class be "over $200,000" or "$200,000 and over" as a catchall for the high-income families.

Empty classes are those for which there are no data values. If this occurs, it may be because you have set up classes that are too narrow.

Steps for Grouping Data into Classes   There are four steps for grouping data, such as that found in Table 2.6, into classes.

Step 1   **Determine the number of groups or classes to use.**
Although there is no absolute right or wrong number of classes, one rule of thumb is to have *between 5 and 20 classes*. Another guideline for helping you determine how many classes to use is the $2^k \geq n$ rule, where $k =$ the number

of classes and is defined to be the smallest integer so that $2^k \geq n$, where n is the number of data values. For example, for $n = 230$, the $2^k \geq n$ rule would suggest $k = 8$ classes ($2^8 = 256 \geq 230$ while $2^7 = 128 < 230$). This latter method was chosen for our example. Our preliminary step, as specified previously, is to produce a frequency distribution from the data array as in Table 2.7. This will enhance our ability to envision the data structure and the classes.

Remember, these are only guidelines for the number of classes. There is no specific right or wrong number. In general, use fewer classes for smaller data sets; more classes for larger data sets. However, using too few classes tends to condense data too much, and information can be lost. Using too many classes spreads out the data so much that little advantage is gained over the original raw data.

Class Width

The distance between the lowest possible value and the highest possible value for a frequency class.

Step 2 Establish the class width.

The minimum **class width** is determined by Equation 2.2.

$$W = \frac{\text{Largest value} - \text{Smallest value}}{\text{Number of classes}} \qquad \textbf{(2.2)}$$

For the Netflix data using eight classes, we get

$$W = \frac{\text{Largest value} - \text{Smallest value}}{\text{Number of classes}} = \frac{30 - 0}{8} = 3.75$$

This means we could construct eight classes that are each 3.75 units wide to provide mutually exclusive and all-inclusive classes. However, because our purpose is to make the data more understandable, we suggest that you *round up to a more convenient class width*, such as 4.0. If you do round the class width, always round up.

Step 3 Determine the class boundaries for each class.

Class Boundaries

The upper and lower values of each class.

The **class boundaries** determine the lowest possible value and the highest possible value for each class. In the Netflix example, if we start the first class at 0, we get the class boundaries shown in the first column of the following table. Notice the classes have been formed to be *mutually exclusive* and *all-inclusive*.

Step 4 Determine the class frequency for each class.

The count for each class is known as a class frequency. As an example, the number of observations in the first class is 60.

DVD Movies Owned (Classes)	Frequency
0–3	60
4–7	50
8–11	47
12–15	40
16–19	18
20–23	8
24–27	6
28–31	1
	Total = 230

Cumulative Frequency Distribution

A summary of a set of data that displays the number of observations with values less than or equal to the upper limit of each of its classes.

Cumulative Relative Frequency Distribution

A summary of a set of data that displays the proportion of observations with values less than or equal to the upper limit of each of its classes.

Another step we can take to help analyze the Netflix data is to construct a relative frequency distribution, a **cumulative frequency distribution**, and a **cumulative relative frequency distribution**.

DVD Movies	Frequency	Relative Frequency	Cumulative Frequency	Cumulative Relative Frequency
0–3	60	0.261	60	0.261
4–7	50	0.217	110	0.478
8–11	47	0.204	157	0.683
12–15	40	0.174	197	0.857
16–19	18	0.078	215	0.935
20–23	8	0.035	223	0.970
24–27	6	0.026	229	0.996
28–31	1	0.004	230	1.000
Total = 230				

The cumulative frequency distribution is shown in the "Cumulative Frequency" column. We can then form the cumulative relative frequency distribution as shown in the "Cumulative Relative Frequency" column. The cumulative relative frequency distribution indicates, as an example, that 85.7% of the sample own fewer than 16 DVD movies.

How to do it (Example 2-3)

Developing Frequency Distributions for Continuous Variables

To develop a continuous data frequency distribution, perform the following steps:

1. Determine the desired number of classes or groups. One rule of thumb is to use 5 to 20 classes. The $2^k \geq n$ rule can also be used.

2. Determine the minimum class width using

$$W = \frac{\text{Largest Value} - \text{Smallest Value}}{\text{Number of classes}}$$

Round the class width up to a more convenient value.

3. Define the class boundaries, making sure that the classes that are formed are *mutually exclusive* and *all-inclusive*. Ideally, the classes should have equal widths and should all contain at least one observation.

4. Determine the class frequency for each class.

EXAMPLE 2-3 **FREQUENCY DISTRIBUTION FOR CONTINUOUS VARIABLES**

Emergency Response Communication Links One of the major efforts of the United States Office of Homeland Security has been to improve the communication between emergency responders, like the police and fire departments. The communications have been hampered by problems involving linking divergent radio and computer systems, as well as communication protocols. While most cities have recognized the problem and made efforts to solve it, Homeland Security recently funded practice exercises in 72 cities of different sizes throughout the United States. The resulting data, already sorted but representing seconds before the systems were linked, are as follows:

35	339	650	864	1,025	1,261
38	340	655	883	1,028	1,280
48	395	669	883	1,036	1,290
53	457	703	890	1,044	1,312
70	478	730	934	1,087	1,341
99	501	763	951	1,091	1,355
138	521	788	969	1,126	1,357
164	556	789	985	1,176	1,360
220	583	789	993	1,199	1,414
265	595	802	997	1,199	1,436
272	596	822	999	1,237	1,479
312	604	851	1,018	1,242	1,492

Homeland Security wishes to construct a frequency distribution showing the times until the communication systems are linked. The frequency distribution is determined as follows:

Step 1 Group the data into classes.
The number of classes is arbitrary but typically will be between 5 and 20, depending on the volume of data. In this example, we have $n = 72$ data items. A common method of determining the number of classes is to use the $2^k \geq n$ guideline. We get $k = 7$ classes since $2^7 = 128 \geq 72$ and $2^6 = 64 < 72$.

Step 2 Determine the class width.

$$W = \frac{\text{Largest value} - \text{Smallest value}}{\text{Number of classes}} = \frac{1,492 - 35}{7} = 208.1429 \Rightarrow 225$$

Note, we have rounded the class width up from the minimum required value of 208.1429 to the more convenient value of 225.

Step 3 Define the class boundaries.

0	and under	225
225	and under	450
450	and under	675
675	and under	900
900	and under	1,125
1,125	and under	1,350
1,350	and under	1,575

These classes are mutually exclusive, all-inclusive, and have equal widths.

Step 4 Determine the class frequency for each class.

Time to Link Systems (in seconds)	Frequency
0 and under 225	9
225 and under 450	6
450 and under 675	12
675 and under 900	13
900 and under 1,125	14
1,125 and under 1,350	11
1,350 and under 1,575	7

This frequency distribution shows that most cities took between 450 and 1,350 seconds (7.5 and 22.5 minutes) to link their communications systems.

>> **END EXAMPLE**

TRY PROBLEM 2-5 (pg. 49)

Chapter Outcome 2. → # Histograms

Although frequency distributions are useful for analyzing large sets of data, they are presented in table format and may not be as visually informative as a graph. If a frequency distribution has been developed from a quantitative variable, a **frequency histogram** can be constructed directly from the frequency distribution. In many cases, the histogram offers a superior format for transforming the data into useful information. (Note: Histograms cannot be constructed from a frequency distribution in which the variable of interest is qualitative. However, a similar graph, called a *bar chart*, discussed later in this chapter, is used when qualitative data are involved.)

A histogram shows three general types of information:

1. It provides a visual indication of where the approximate center of the data is. Look for the center point along the horizontal axes in the histograms in Figure 2.2. Even though the shapes of the histograms are the same, there is a clear difference in where the data are centered.
2. We can gain an understanding of the degree of spread (or variation) in the data. The more the data cluster around the center, the smaller the variation in the data. If the data are spread out from the center, the data exhibit greater variation. The examples in Figure 2.3 all have the same center but are different in terms of spread.
3. We can observe the shape of the distribution. Is it reasonably flat, is it weighted to one side or the other, is it balanced around the center, or is it bell shaped?

Frequency Histogram

A graph of a frequency distribution with the horizontal axis showing the classes, the vertical axis showing the frequency count, and (for equal class widths) the rectangles having a height equal to the frequency in each class.

BUSINESS APPLICATION   **CONSTRUCTING HISTOGRAMS**

CAPITAL CREDIT UNION   Even for applications with small amounts of data, such as the Netflix example, constructing grouped data frequency distributions and histograms is a time-consuming process. Decision makers may hesitate to try different numbers of classes and different class limits because of the effort involved and because the "best" presentation of the data may be missed.

We showed earlier that Excel provides the capability of constructing frequency distributions. It is also quite capable of generating grouped data frequency distributions and histograms.

Excel

tutorials

Excel Tutorial

FIGURE 2.2

Histograms Showing Different Centers

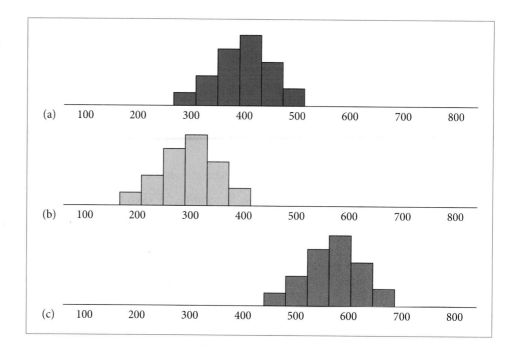

Consider Capital Credit Union (CCU) in Mobile, Alabama, which recently began issuing a new credit card. Managers at CCU have been wondering how customers use the card, so a sample of 300 customers was selected. Data on the current credit card balance (rounded to the nearest dollar) and the genders of the cardholders appear in the file **Capital**.

As with the manual process, the first step in Excel is to determine the number of classes. Recall that the rule of thumb is to use between 5 and 20 classes, depending on the amount of data. Suppose we decide to use 10 classes.

Next, we determine the class width using Equation 2.2. The highest account balance in the sample is $1,493.00. The minimum is $99.00. Thus, the class width is

$$W = \frac{1,493.00 - 99.00}{10} = 139.40$$

which we round up to $150.00.

FIGURE 2.3

Histograms—Same Center, Different Spread

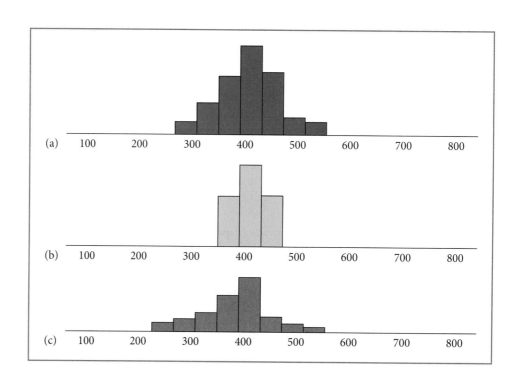

Our classes will be

$90–$239.99
$240–$389.99
$390–$539.99

etc.

The resulting histogram in Figure 2.4 shows that the data are centered in the class from $690 to $839.99. The customers vary considerably in their credit card balances, but the distribution is quite symmetrical and somewhat bell shaped. CCU managers must decide whether the usage rate for the credit card is sufficient to warrant the cost of maintaining the credit card accounts.

Issues with Excel If you use Excel to construct a histogram as indicated in the instructions in Figure 2.4, the initial graph will have gaps between the bars. Because histograms illustrate the distribution of data across the range of all possible values for the quantitative variable, *histograms do not have gaps*. Therefore, to get the proper histogram format, you need to close these gaps by setting the gap width to zero, as indicated in the Excel instructions shown in Figure 2.4.

FIGURE 2.4

Excel 2010 Histogram of Credit Card Balances

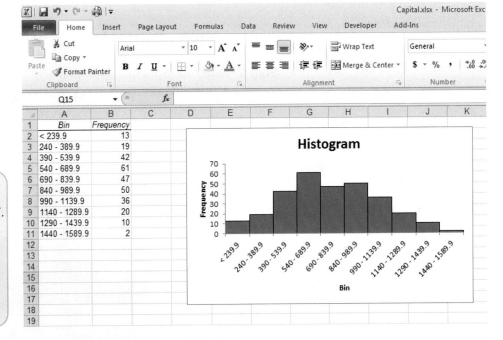

Minitab Instructions (for similar results):
1. Open file: **Capital.MTW**.
2. Choose **Graph > Histogram**.
3. Click **Simple**.
4. Click **OK**.
5. In **Graph variables**, enter data column.
6. Click **OK**.

Excel 2010 Instructions:
1. Open file: **Capital.xlsx**.
2. Set up an area on the worksheet for the bins defined as 239.99, 389.99, etc. up to 1589.99. Be sure to include a label such as "Bins."
3. On the **Data** tab, click **Data Analysis**.
4. Select **Histogram**.
5. Input Range specifies the actual data values as the **Credit Card Account Balance** column and the bin range as the area defined in Step 2.
6. Put on a new worksheet ply and include the Chart Output.
7. Right mouse click on the bars and use the **Format Data Series Options** to set gap width to zero and add lines to the bars.
8. Convert the bins to actual class labels by typing labels in Column A. Note: The bin 239.99 is labeled 0–239.99.

How to do it (Example 2-4)

Constructing Frequency Histograms

To construct a frequency histogram, perform the following steps:

1–4. Follow the steps for constructing a frequency distribution (see Example 2-3).

5. Use the horizontal axis to represent classes for the variable of interest. Use the vertical axis to represent the frequency in each class.

6. Draw vertical bars for each class or data value so that the heights of the bars correspond to the frequencies. Make sure there are no gaps between the bars. (Note, if the classes do not have equal widths, the bar height should be adjusted to make the area of the bar proportional to the frequency.)

7. Label the histogram appropriately.

EXAMPLE 2-4   FREQUENCY HISTOGRAMS

Emergency Response Times The Paris, France, director of Emergency Medical Response, is interested in analyzing the time needed for response teams to reach their destinations in emergency situations after leaving their stations. She has acquired the response times for 1,220 calls last month. To develop the frequency histogram, perform the following steps:

Steps 1–4   Construct a frequency distribution.
Because response time is a continuous variable measured in seconds, the data should be broken down into classes, and the steps given in Example 2-3 should be used. The following frequency distribution with 10 classes was developed:

Response Time	Frequency	Response Time	Frequency
0 and under 30	36	180 and under 210	145
30 and under 60	68	210 and under 240	80
60 and under 90	195	240 and under 270	43
90 and under 120	180	270 and under 300	31
120 and under 150	260		Total = 1,220
150 and under 180	182		

Step 5   Construct the axes for the histogram.
The horizontal axis will be response time and the vertical axis will be frequency.

Step 6   Construct bars with heights corresponding to the frequency of each class.

Step 7   Label the histogram appropriately.
This is shown as follows:

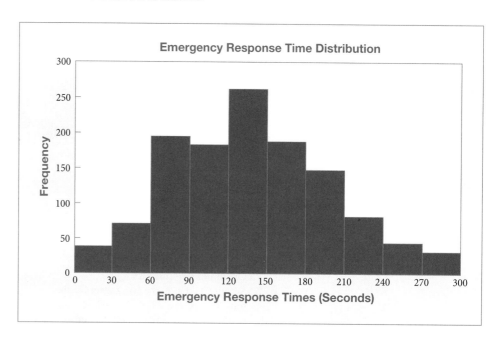

This histogram indicates that the response times vary considerably. The center is somewhere in the range of 120 to 180 seconds.

>> **END EXAMPLE**

TRY PROBLEM 2-10 (pg. 50)

Relative Frequency Histograms and Ogives

Ogive

The graphical representation of the cumulative relative frequency. A line is connected to points plotted above the upper limit of each class at a height corresponding to the cumulative relative frequency.

Histograms can also be used to display relative frequency distributions and cumulative relative frequency distributions. A relative frequency histogram is formed in the same manner as a frequency histogram, but relative frequencies, rather than frequencies, are used on the vertical axis. The cumulative relative frequency is presented using a graph called an **ogive**. Example 2-5 illustrates each of these graphical tools.

EXAMPLE 2-5   **RELATIVE FREQUENCY HISTOGRAMS AND OGIVES**

Emergency Response Times (*Continued*) Example 2-4 introduced the situation facing the emergency response manager in Paris. In that example, she formed a frequency distribution for a sample of 1,220 response times. She is now interested in graphing the relative frequencies and the ogive. To do so, use the following steps:

Step 1   Convert the frequency distribution into relative frequencies and cumulative relative frequencies.

Response Time	Frequency	Relative Frequency	Cumulative Relative Frequency
0 and under 30	36	36/1220 = 0.0295	0.0295
30 and under 60	68	68/1220 = 0.0557	0.0852
60 and under 90	195	195/1220 = 0.1598	0.2451
90 and under 120	180	180/1220 = 0.1475	0.3926
120 and under 150	260	260/1220 = 0.2131	0.6057
150 and under 180	182	182/1220 = 0.1492	0.7549
180 and under 210	145	145/1220 = 0.1189	0.8738
210 and under 240	80	80/1220 = 0.0656	0.9393
240 and under 270	43	43/1220 = 0.0352	0.9746
270 and under 300	31	31/1220 = 0.0254	1.0000
	1,220	1.0000	

Step 2   Construct the relative frequency histogram.
Place the quantitative variable on the horizontal axis and the relative frequencies on the vertical axis. The vertical bars are drawn to heights corresponding to the relative frequencies of the classes.

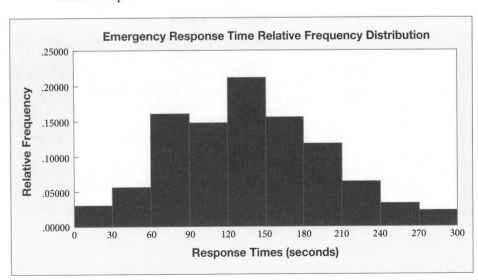

Note the relative frequency histogram has exactly the same shape as the frequency histogram. However, the vertical axis has a different scale.

Step 3 Construct the ogive.

Place a point above the *upper limit* of each class at a height corresponding to the cumulative relative frequency. Complete the ogive by drawing a line connecting these points.

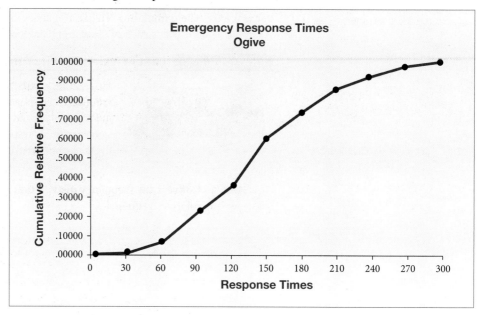

>> **END EXAMPLE**

TRY PROBLEM 2-16 (pg. 52)

Chapter Outcome 3. → # Joint Frequency Distributions

Frequency distributions are effective tools for describing data. Thus far, we have discussed how to develop grouped and ungrouped frequency distributions for one variable at a time. For instance, in the Capital Credit Union example, we were interested in customer credit card balances for all customers. We constructed a frequency distribution and histogram for that variable. However, often we need to examine data that are characterized by more than one variable. This may involve constructing a *joint frequency distribution* for two variables. Joint frequency distributions can be constructed for qualitative or quantitative variables.

EXAMPLE 2-6   **JOINT FREQUENCY DISTRIBUTION**

Miami City Parking Parking is typically an issue in many large cities like Miami, Florida. Problems seem to occur for customers and employees both in locating a parking spot and in being able to quickly exit a lot at busy times. The parking manager for Miami City Parking has received complaints about the time required to exit garages in the downtown sector. To start analyzing the situation, she has collected a small sample of data from 12 customers showing the type of payment (cash or charge) and the garage number (Garage Number 1, 2, or 3). One possibility is that using credit card payments increases exit times at the parking lots. The manager wishes to develop a joint frequency distribution to better understand the paying habits of those using her garages. To do this, she can use the following steps:

Step 1 Obtain the data.

The paired data for the two variables for a sample of 12 customers are obtained.

Customer	Payment Method	Parking Garage
1	Charge	2
2	Charge	1
3	Cash	2
4	Charge	2
5	Charge	1

Customer	Payment Method	Parking Garage
6	Cash	1
7	Cash	3
8	Charge	1
9	Charge	3
10	Cash	2
11	Cash	1
12	Charge	1

How to do it (Example 2-6)

Constructing Joint Frequency Distributions

A joint frequency distribution is constructed using the following steps:

1. Obtain a set of data consisting of paired responses for two variables. The responses can be qualitative or quantitative. If the responses are quantitative, they can be discrete or continuous.

2. Construct a table with *r* rows and *c* columns, in which the number of rows represents the number of categories (or numeric classes) of one variable and the number of columns corresponds to the number of categories (or numeric classes) of the second variable.

3. Count the number of joint occurrences at each row level and each column level for all combinations of row and column values and place these frequencies in the appropriate cells.

4. Compute the row and column totals, which are called the *marginal frequencies*.

5. If a joint relative frequency distribution is desired, divide each cell frequency by the total number of paired observations.

Step 2 Construct the rows and columns of the joint frequency table.
The row variable will be the payment method, and two rows will be used, corresponding to the two payment methods. The column variable is parking garage number, and it will have three levels, because the data for this variable contain only the values 1, 2, and 3. (Note, if a variable is continuous, classes should be formed using the methods discussed in Example 2-3.)

	Parking Garage		
	1	2	3
Payment			
Cash			

Step 3 Count the number of joint occurrences at each row level and each column level for all combinations of row and column values and place these frequencies in the appropriate cells.

	Parking Garage			
	1	2	3	Total
Charge	4	2	1	7
Cash	2	2	1	5
Total	6	4	2	12

Step 4 Calculate the row and column totals (see Step 3).
The manager can now see that for this sample, most people charged their parking fee (seven people), and Garage number 1 was used by most people in the sample used (six people). Likewise, four people used Garage number 1 and charged their parking fee.

>> **END EXAMPLE**

TRY PROBLEM 2-12 (pg. 51)

Excel Tutorial

BUSINESS APPLICATION   JOINT FREQUENCY DISTRIBUTION

CAPITAL CREDIT UNION (CONTINUED) Recall that the Capital Credit Union discussed earlier was interested in evaluating the success of its new credit card. Figure 2.4 showed the frequency distribution and histogram for a sample of customer credit card balances. Although this information is useful, the managers would like to know more. Specifically, what does the credit card balance distribution look like for male versus female cardholders?

One way to approach this is to sort the data by the gender variable and develop frequency distributions and histograms for males and females separately. You could then make a visual comparison of the two to determine what, if any, difference exists between males and females. However, an alternative approach is to jointly analyze the two variables: gender and credit card balance.

Excel provides a means for analyzing two variables jointly. In Figure 2.4, we constructed the frequency distribution for the 300 credit card balances using 10 classes. The class width

FIGURE 2.5 | Excel 2010 Joint Frequency Distribution for Capital Credit Union

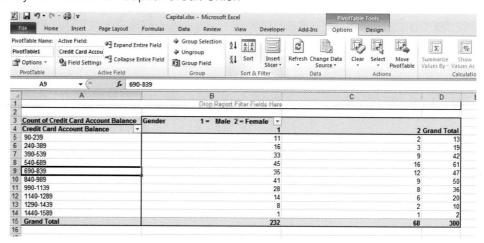

Excel 2010 Instructions:
1. Open file: **Capital.xlsx**.
2. Place cursor anywhere in the data.
3. On the **Insert** tab, click on **PivotTable** and click **OK**.
4. On the **Options** tab, select **Options** in the PivotTable group. Select the **Display** tab and check **Classic PivotTable** layout. Click **OK**.
5. Drag **Credit Card Account Balance** to "*Drop Row Fields Here*" area.
6. Right-click in **Credit Card Account Balance** numbers and click **Group**.
7. Change **Start at** to 90. Change **End** to 1589. Change **By** to 150.
8. Drag **Gender** to "*Drop Column Fields Here*" area.
9. Drag **Credit Card Account Balance** to "*Drop Value Fields Here*" area.
10. Place cursor in the *Data Item* area, right click, and select **Summarize Values By** and select **Count**.

Minitab Instructions (for similar results):
1. Open file: **Capital.MTW**.
2. Click on **Data > Code > Numeric to Text**.
3. Under **Code data from columns,** select data column.
4. Under **Into columns**, specify destination column: *Classes*.
5. In **Original values**, define each data class range.
6. In **New**, specify code for each class.
7. Click **OK**.
8. Click on **Stat > Tables > Cross Tabulation and Chi-Square**.
9. Under **Categorical Variables For rows** enter *Classes* column and **For columns** enter *Gender* column.
10. Under **Display** check **Counts**.
11. Click **OK**.

was set at $150. Figure 2.5 shows a table that is called a *joint frequency distribution*. This type of table is also called a *cross-tabulation* table.[1]

The Capital Credit Union managers can use a joint frequency table to analyze the credit card balances for males versus females. For instance, for the 42 customers with balances of $390 to $539, Figure 2.5 shows that 33 were males and 9 were females. Previously, we discussed the concept of relative frequency (proportions, which Excel converts to percentages) as a useful tool for making comparisons between two data sets. In this example, comparisons between males and females would be easier if the frequencies were converted to proportions (or percentages). The result is the *joint relative frequency table* shown in Figure 2.6. Notice that the percentages in each cell are percentages of the total 300 people in the survey. For example, the $540-to-$689 class had 20.33% (61) of the 300 customers. The male customers with balances in the $540-to-$689 range constituted 15% (45) of the 300 customers, whereas females with that balance level made up 5.33% (16) of all 300 customers. On the surface, this result seems to indicate a big difference between males and females at this credit balance level.

Suppose we really wanted to focus on the male versus female issue and control for the fact that there are far more male customers than female. We could compute the percentages differently. Rather than using a base of 300 (the entire sample size), we might instead be interested in the percentages of the males who have balances at each level, and the same measure for females.[2]

There are many options for transferring data into useful information. Thus far, we have introduced frequency distributions, joint frequency tables, and histograms. In the next section, we discuss one of the most useful graphical tools: the bar chart.

---

[1] In Excel, the joint frequency distribution is developed using a tool called Pivot tables.
[2] Such distributions are known as *marginal distributions*.

FIGURE 2.6

Excel 2010 Joint Relative
Frequencies for Capital
Credit Union

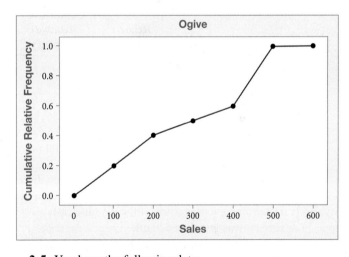

Excel 2010 Instructions:
1. Place cursor in the **Gender** numbers of the PivotTable.
2. Right-click and select **Value Field Settings**.
3. On the **Show values as** tab, click on the down arrow and select **% of Grand Total**.
4. Click **OK**.

In Figure 2.6, we have used the Data Field Settings in the Excel PivotTable to represent the data as percentages.

Count of Credit Card Account Balance	Gender	1 = Male 2 = Female		
Credit Card Account Balance		1	2	Grand Total
90-239		3.67%	0.67%	4.33%
240-389		5.33%	1.00%	6.33%
390-539		11.00%	3.00%	14.00%
540-689		15.00%	5.33%	20.33%
690-839		11.67%	4.00%	15.67%
840-989		13.67%	3.00%	16.67%
990-1139		9.33%	2.67%	12.00%
1140-1289		4.67%	2.00%	6.67%
1290-1439		2.67%	0.67%	3.33%
1440-1589		0.33%	0.33%	0.67%
Grand Total		77.33%	22.67%	100.00%

Minitab Instructions (for similar results):
1. Open file: **Capital.MTW**.
2. Steps 2–7 as in Figure 2.6.
3. Click on **Stat > Tables > Cross Tabulation and Chi-square**.
4. Under **Categorical variables For rows** enter *Classes* column and **For columns** enter *Gender* column.
5. Under **Display**, check **Total Percents**.
6. Click **OK**.

MyStatLab

2-1: Exercises

Skill Development

2-1. Given the following data, develop a frequency distribution:

5	3	2	6	6
7	3	3	6	7
7	9	7	5	3
12	6	10	7	2
6	8	0	7	4

2-2. Assuming you have data for a variable with 2,000 values, using the $2^k \geq n$ guideline, what is the smallest number of groups that should be used in developing a grouped data frequency distribution?

2-3. A study is being conducted in which a variable of interest has 1,000 observations. The minimum value in the data set is 300 points and the maximum is 2,900 points.
   a. Use the $2^k \geq n$ guideline to determine the minimum number of classes to use in developing a grouped data frequency distribution.
   b. Based on the answer to part a, determine the class width that should be used (round up to the nearest 100 points).

2-4. Produce the relative frequency distribution from a sample size of 50 that gave rise to the following ogive:

[Ogive chart: Cumulative Relative Frequency (y-axis, 0.0 to 1.0) vs Sales (x-axis, 0 to 600). Points approximately at (0, 0.0), (100, 0.2), (200, 0.4), (300, 0.5), (400, 0.6), (500, 1.0), (600, 1.0).]

2-5. You have the following data:

8	6	11	14	10
11	9	7	2	8
9	5	5	5	12
7	8	4	17	8
12	7	8	8	7
10	8	6	9	9
11	16	2	7	4
8	4	4	5	5
9	9	6	6	7
7	9	5	4	5
14	2	9	0	6
1	1	12	11	4

a. Construct a frequency distribution for these data. Use the $2^k \geq n$ guideline to determine the number of classes to use.
b. Develop a relative frequency distribution using the classes you constructed in part a.
c. Develop a cumulative frequency distribution and a cumulative relative frequency distribution using the classes you constructed in part a.
d. Develop a histogram based on the frequency distribution you constructed in part a.

2-6. Fill in the missing components of the following frequency distribution constructed for a sample size of 50:

Class	Frequency	Relative Frequency	Cumulative Relative Frequency
7.85 – < _____	_____	_____	0.12
_____ – < 8.05	_____	_____	0.48
8.05 – < _____	4	_____	_____
_____ – < 8.25	_____	0.10	_____
8.25 – < _____	_____	_____	_____

2-7. The following cumulative relative frequency distribution summarizes data obtained in a study of the ending overages (in dollars) for the cash register balance at a business:

Class	Frequency	Relative Frequency	Cumulative Relative Frequency
−60.00 – < −40.00	2	0.04	0.04
−40.00 – < −20.00	2	0.04	0.08
−20.00 – < −00.00	8	0.16	0.24
00.00 – < 20.00	16	0.32	0.56
20.00 – < 40.00	20	0.40	0.96
40.00 – < 60.00	2	0.04	1.00

a. Determine the proportion of the days in which there were no shortages.
b. Determine the proportion of the days the cash register was less than $20 off.
c. Determine the proportion of the days the cash register was less than $40 over or at most $20 short.

2-8. You are given the following data:

6	10	6	4	9	5
5	5	5	7	6	2
5	5	5	4	5	7
6	7	8	6	8	4
7	5	5	5	5	7
8	7	6	7	5	4
6	4	4	7	4	6
6	7	8	6	7	6
7	8	5	6	5	7
3	6	4	7	4	4

a. Construct a frequency distribution for these data.
b. Based on the frequency distribution, develop a histogram.

c. Construct a relative frequency distribution.
d. Develop a relative frequency histogram.
e. Compare the two histograms. Why do they look alike?

2-9. Using the data from Problem 2-8,
a. Construct a grouped data relative frequency distribution of the data. Use the $2^k \geq n$ guideline to determine the number of classes.
b. Construct a cumulative frequency distribution of the data.
c. Construct a relative frequency histogram.
d. Construct an ogive.

Business Applications

2-10. Burger King is one of the largest fast-food franchise operations in the world. Recently, the district manager for Burger King in Las Vegas conducted a study in which she selected a random sample of sales receipts. She was interested in the number of line items on the receipts. For instance, if a customer ordered two 1/4-pound hamburgers, one side of fries, and two soft drinks, the number of line items would be five. The following data were observed:

7	5	7	6	5	5	4	8	6	5
8	7	6	5	6	2	9	4	4	5
8	4	9	6	6	5	8	9	9	1
6	5	10	6	7	6	5	5	5	6
8	7	6	8	6	6	9	6	12	7
5	6	7	11	4	4	3	4	1	4
11	2	5	5	8	2	3	4	9	6
6	5	8	6	3	6	4	5	8	10

a. Develop a frequency distribution for these data. Discuss briefly what the frequency distribution tells you about these sample data.
b. Based on the results in part a, construct a frequency histogram for these sample data.

2-11. In a survey conducted by AIG, investors were asked to rate how knowledgeable they felt they were as investors. Both online and traditional investors were included in the survey. The survey resulted in the following data:

Of the online investors, 8%, 55%, and 37% responded they were "savvy," "experienced," and "novice," respectively.

Of the traditional investors, the percentages were 4%, 29%, and 67%, respectively.

Of the 600 investors surveyed, 200 were traditional investors.

a. Use the information to construct a joint frequency distribution.
b. Use the information to construct a joint relative frequency distribution.
c. Determine the proportion of investors who were both online investors and rated themselves experienced.
d. Calculate the proportion of investors who were online investors.

2-12. The sales manager for the Fox News TV station affiliate in a southern Florida city recently surveyed 20 advertisers and asked each one to rate the service of the station on the following scale:

Very Good	Good	Fair	Poor	Very Poor
1	2	3	4	5

He also tracked the general time slot when the advertiser's commercials were shown on the station. The following codes were used:

1 = morning   2 = afternoon

3 = evening   4 = various times

The following sample data were observed:

Rating	Time Slot	Rating	Time Slot
2	1	4	3
1	1	2	2
3	3	3	3
2	1	3	3
1	1	2	1
4	4	1	1
2	2	1	1
1	1	5	3
2	1	2	4
2	2	3	4

a. Construct separate relative frequency distributions for each of the two variables.
b. Construct a joint frequency distribution for these two variables.
c. Construct a joint relative frequency distribution for these two variables. Write a short paragraph describing what the data imply.

2-13. A St. Louis–based shipping company recently selected a random sample of 49 airplane weight slips for crates shipped from an automobile parts supplier. The weights, measured in pounds, for the sampled crates are as follows:

89	83	97	101	86	89	86
91	84	89	87	93	86	90
86	92	92	88	88	92	86
93	80	93	77	98	94	95
94	88	95	87	99	98	90
91	87	89	89	96	88	94
95	79	94	86	92	94	85

a. Create a data array of the weights.
b. Develop a frequency distribution using five classes having equal widths.
c. Develop a histogram from the frequency distribution you created in part b.
d. Develop a relative frequency and a cumulative relative frequency distribution for the weights using the same five classes created in part b. What percent of the sampled crates have weights greater than 96 pounds?

2-14. The bubble in U.S. housing prices burst in 2008, causing sales of houses to decline in almost every part of the country. Many homes were foreclosed because the owners could not make the payments. Below is a sample of 100 residential properties and the total balance on the mortgage at the time of foreclosure.

$172,229	$211,021	$159,205	$247,697	$247,469
$176,736	$240,815	$195,056	$315,097	$257,150
$129,779	$207,451	$165,225	$178,970	$319,101
$ 87,429	$219,808	$242,761	$277,389	$213,803
$153,468	$205,696	$210,447	$179,029	$241,331
$117,808	$188,909	$376,644	$185,523	$168,145
$158,094	$135,461	$131,457	$263,232	$256,262
$240,034	$289,973	$302,341	$178,684	$226,998
$176,440	$268,106	$181,507	$118,752	$251,009
$196,457	$195,249	$195,986	$201,680	$233,182
$271,552	$123,262	$212,411	$246,462	$177,673
$103,699	$252,375	$192,335	$265,992	$232,247
$320,004	$213,020	$192,546	$295,660	$211,876
$265,787	$207,443	$203,043	$133,014	$289,645
$251,560	$302,054	$185,381	$284,345	$184,869
$237,485	$282,506	$278,783	$335,920	$199,630
$248,272	$232,234	$188,833	$168,905	$357,612
$241,894	$186,956	$114,601	$301,728	$251,865
$207,040	$221,614	$318,154	$156,611	$219,730
$201,473	$174,840	$196,622	$263,686	$159,029

a. Using the $2^k \geq n$ guideline, what is the minimum number of classes that should be used to display these data in a grouped data frequency distribution?
b. Referring to part a, what should the class width be, assuming you round the width up to nearest $1,000?
c. Referring to parts a and b, develop a grouped data frequency distribution for these mortgage balance data.
d. Based on your answer to part c, construct and interpret a frequency histogram for the mortgage balance data.

2-15. Wageweb exhibits salary data obtained from surveys. It provides compensation information on more than 170 benchmark positions, including finance positions. It recently reported that salaries of chief finance officers (CFOs) ranged from $127,735 to $209,981 (before bonuses). Suppose the following data represent a sample of the annual salaries for 25 CFOs. Assume that data are in thousands of dollars.

173.1	171.2	141.9	112.6	211.1	156.5	145.4	134.0
192.0	185.8	168.3	131.0	214.4	155.2	164.9	123.9
161.9	162.7	178.8	161.3	182.0	165.8	213.1	177.4
159.3							

a. Using 11 classes, construct a cumulative frequency distribution.
b. Determine the proportion of CFO salaries that are at least $175,000.
c. Determine the proportion of CFO salaries that are less than $205,000 and at least $135,000.

2-16. One effect of the great recession was to lower the interest rate on fixed-rate mortgages. A sample of 30-year fixed-rate mortgage rates taken from financial institutions in the Pacific Northwest resulted in the following:

3.79	4.03	3.92	3.87	3.86
3.93	3.87	3.69	3.99	3.88
3.91	3.81	3.85	3.81	3.65
4.15	3.98	3.82	4.08	3.84
3.95	4.03	3.96	3.69	3.97
4.08	3.86	3.82	3.83	4.19
3.49	3.49	3.75	3.46	3.92
3.67	3.63	3.81	3.86	4.15
3.85	4.01	3.93	4.02	4.09

a. Construct a histogram with eight classes beginning at 3.46.

b. Determine the proportion of 30-year fixed mortgage rates that are at least 3.76%.

c. Produce an ogive for the data.

Computer Database **Exercises**

2-17. J.D. Power and Associates' annual customer-satisfaction survey, the Automotive Performance, Execution and Layout (APEAL) Study[SM], in its 13th year, was released on September 22, 2008. The study measures owners' satisfaction with the design, content, layout, and performance of their new vehicles. A file titled **APEAL2** contains the satisfaction ratings for 2008 for each make of car.

a. Construct a histogram that starts at 710 and has class widths of 20 for the APEAL ratings.

b. The past industry average APEAL rating was 866 for 2005. What does the 2008 data suggest in terms of the relative satisfaction with the 2008 models?

2-18. The Franklin Tire Company is interested in demonstrating the durability of its steel-belted radial tires. To do this, the managers have decided to put four tires on 100 different sport utility vehicles and drive them throughout Alaska. The data collected indicate the number of miles (rounded to the nearest 1,000 miles) that each of the SUVs traveled before one of the tires on the vehicle did not meet minimum federal standards for tread thickness. The data file is called **Franklin**.

a. Construct a frequency distribution and histogram using eight classes. Use 51 as the lower limit of the first class.

b. The marketing department wishes to know the tread life of at least 50% of the tires, the 10% that had the longest tread life, and the longest tread life of these tires. Provide this information to the marketing department. Also provide any other significant items that point out the desirability of this line of steel-belted tires.

c. Construct a frequency distribution and histogram using 12 classes, using 51 as the lower limit of the first class. Compare your results with those in parts a and b. Which distribution gives the best information about the desirability of this line of steel-belted tires? Discuss.

2-19. The California Golf Association recently conducted a survey of its members. Among other questions, the members were asked to indicate the number of 18-hole rounds that they played last year. Data for a sample of 294 members are provided in the data file called **Golf Survey**.

a. Using the $2^k \geq n$ guideline, what is the minimum number of classes that should be used to display these data in a grouped data frequency distribution?

b. Referring to part a, what should the class width be, assuming you round the width up to the nearest integer?

c. Referring to parts a and b, develop a grouped data frequency distribution for these golf data.

d. Based on your answer to part c, construct and interpret a frequency histogram for the data.

2-20. *Ars Technia* LLD published a news release (Eric Bangeman, "Dell Still King of Market Share") that presented the results of a study concerning the world market share for the major manufacturers of personal computers. It indicated that Dell held 17.9% of this market. The file titled **PCMarket** contains a sample of the market shares alluded to in the article.

a. Construct a histogram from this set of data and identify the sample shares for each of the listed manufacturers.

b. Excluding the data referred to as "other," determine the total share of the sample for manufacturers that have headquarters in the United States.

2-21. Orlando, Florida, is a well-known, popular vacation destination visited by tourists from around the world. Consequently, the Orlando International Airport is busy throughout the year. Among the variety of data collected by the Greater Orlando Airport Authority is the number of passengers by airline. The file **Orlando Airport** contains passenger data for December 2011. Suppose the airport manager is interested in analyzing the column labeled "Total" for this data.

a. Using the $2^k \geq n$ guideline, what is the minimum number of classes that should be used to display the data in the "Total" column in a grouped data frequency distribution?

b. Referring to part a, what should the class width be, assuming you round the width up to the nearest 1,000 passengers?

c. Referring to parts a and b, develop a grouped data frequency distribution for these airport data.

d. Based on your answer to part c, construct and interpret a frequency histogram for the data.

2-22. The manager of AJ's Fitness Center, a full-service health and exercise club, recently conducted a survey of 1,214 members. The objective of the survey was to determine the satisfaction level of his club's customers. In addition, the survey asked for several demographic factors such as age and gender. The data from the survey are in a file called **AJFitness**.

a. One of the key variables is "Overall Customer Satisfaction." This variable is measured on an ordinal scale as follows:

5 = very satisfied 4 = satisfied 3 = neutral
2 = dissatisfied 1 = very dissatisfied

Develop a frequency distribution for this variable and discuss the results.

b. Develop a joint relative frequency distribution for the variables "Overall Customer Satisfaction" and "Typical Visits Per Week." Discuss the results.

2-23. The file **Danish Coffee** contains data on individual coffee consumption (in kg) for 144 randomly selected Danish coffee drinkers.

a. Construct a data array of the coffee consumption data.

b. Construct a frequency distribution of the coffee consumption data. Within what class do more of the observations fall?

c. Construct a histogram of the coffee consumption data. Briefly comment on what the histogram reveals concerning the data.

d. Develop a relative frequency distribution and a cumulative relative frequency distribution of the coffee data. What percentage of the coffee drinkers sampled consume 8.0 kg or more annually?

END EXERCISES 2-1

2.2 Bar Charts, Pie Charts, and Stem and Leaf Diagrams

Chapter Outcome 4. → **Bar Charts**

Bar Chart

A graphical representation of a categorical data set in which a rectangle or bar is drawn over each category or class. The length or height of each bar represents the frequency or percentage of observations or some other measure associated with the category. The bars may be vertical or horizontal. The bars may all be the same color or they may be different colors depicting different categories. Additionally, multiple variables can be graphed on the same bar chart.

Section 2-1 introduced some of the basic tools for describing numerical variables, both discrete and continuous, when the data are in their raw form. However, in many instances, you will be working with categorical data or data that have already been summarized to some extent. In these cases, an effective presentation tool is often a **bar chart**.

| BUSINESS APPLICATION | DEVELOPING BAR CHARTS |

NEW CAR SALES The automobile industry is a significant part of the U.S economy. When car sales are up, the economy is up, and vice versa. Table 2.8 displays data showing the total number of cars sold in January 2012 by the eight largest automobile companies in the world. Although the table format is informative, a graphical presentation is often desirable. Because the car sales data are characterized by car company, a bar chart would work well in this instance. The bars on a bar chart can be vertical (called a *column bar chart*) or horizontal (called a *horizontal bar chart*). Figure 2.7 illustrates an example of a column bar chart. The height of the bars corresponds to the number of cars sold by each company. This gives you an idea of the sales advantage held by General Motors in January 2012.

One strength of the bar chart is its capability of displaying multiple variables on the same chart. For instance, a bar chart can conveniently compare new car sales data for January 2012 and

TABLE 2.8 | **January 2012 New Car Sales for the Top Eight Automobile Companies (United States)**

Car Company	January 2012 Sales
General Motors	167,900
Ford	136,300
Chrysler	101,150
Toyota	125,500
Honda	83,000
Nissan	79,300
Hyundai	42,700
Mazda	24,000

Source: Wall Street Journal, Online, February 1, 2012.

FIGURE 2.7

Bar Chart Showing January
2012 New Car Sales

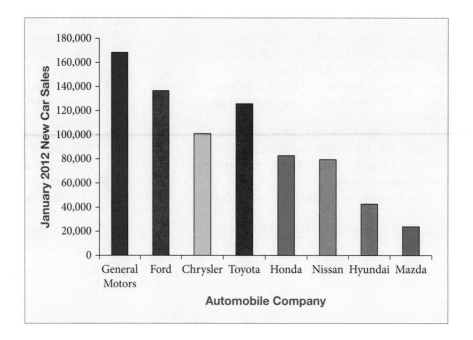

sales for the same month the previous year. Figure 2.8 is a horizontal bar chart that does just that. Notice that only General Motors had lower sales in January 2012 than in the previous January.

People sometimes confuse histograms and bar charts. Although there are some similarities, they are two very different graphical tools. Histograms are used to represent a frequency distribution associated with a single quantitative (ratio- or interval-level) variable. Refer to the histogram illustrations in Section 2-1. In every case, the variable on the horizontal axis was numerical, with values moving from low to high. The vertical axis shows the frequency count,

FIGURE 2.8

Bar Chart Comparing January
2011 and January 2012
New Cars Sold

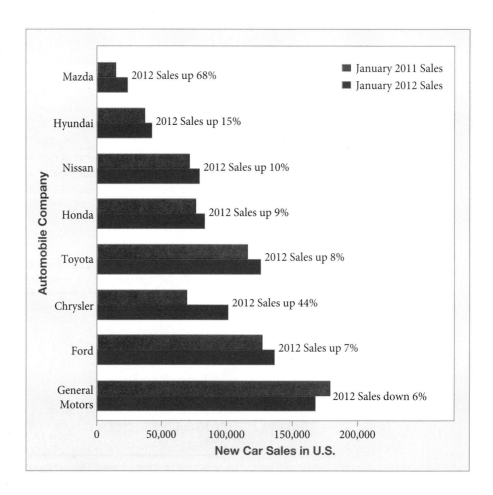

or relative frequency, for each numerical value or range of values. There are no gaps between the histogram bars. On the other hand, bar charts are used when one or more variables of interest are categorical, as in this case in which the category is "car company."

How to do it (Example 2-7)

Constructing Bar Charts

A bar chart is constructed using the following steps:

1. Define the categories for the variable of interest.

2. For each category, determine the appropriate measure or value.

3. For a column bar chart, locate the categories on the horizontal axis. The vertical axis is set to a scale corresponding to the values in the categories. For a horizontal bar chart, place the categories on the vertical axis and set the scale of the horizontal axis in accordance with the values in the categories. Then construct bars, either vertical or horizontal, for each category such that the length or height corresponds to the value for the category.

EXAMPLE 2-7   BAR CHARTS

Investment Recommendations *Fortune* contained an article by David Stires called "The Best Stocks to Buy Now." The article identified 40 companies as good investment opportunities. These companies were divided into five categories: Growth and Income, Bargain Growth, Deep Value, Small Wonders, and Foreign Value. For each company, data for several key variables were reported, including the price/earnings (PE) ratio based on the previous 12 months' reported earnings. We are interested in constructing a bar chart of the PE ratios for the eight companies classified as Growth and Income.

Step 1   Define the categories.
Data for stock price and PE ratio for each of eight companies is shown as follows:

Company (Ticker Symbol)	PE Ratio	Stock Price
Abbott Labs (ABT)	21	$49
Altria Group (MO)	14	$65
Coca-Cola (KO)	21	$42
Colgate-Palmolive (CL)	20	$51
General Mills (GIS)	17	$51
Pfizer (PFE)	13	$29
Procter & Gamble (PG)	21	$53
Wyeth (WYE)	15	$43

The category to be displayed is the company.

Step 2   Determine the appropriate measure to be displayed.
The measure of interest is the PE ratio.

Step 3   Develop the bar chart.
A column bar chart is developed by placing the eight companies on the horizontal axis and constructing bars whose heights correspond to the value of the company's PE ratio. Each company is assigned a different-colored bar. The resulting bar chart is

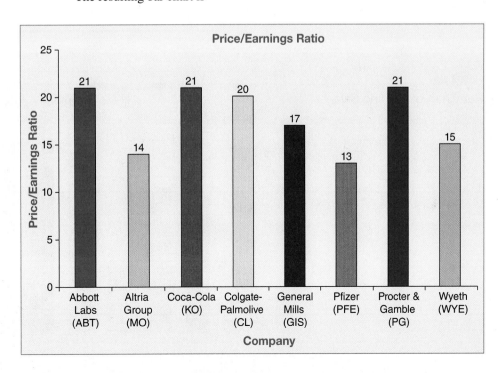

Step 4 Interpret the results.

The bar chart shows three companies with especially low PE ratios. These are Altria Group, Pfizer, and Wyeth. Thus, of the eight recommended companies in the Growth and Income group, these three have the lowest PE ratios.

>> **END EXAMPLE**

TRY PROBLEM 2-27 (pg. 60)

Excel Tutorial

BUSINESS APPLICATION **CONSTRUCTING BAR CHARTS**

BACH, LOMBARD, & WILSON One of the most useful features of bar charts is that they can display multiple issues. Consider Bach, Lombard, & Wilson, a New England law firm. Recently, the firm handled a case in which a woman was suing her employer, a major electronics firm, claiming the company gave higher starting salaries to men than to women. Consequently, she stated, even though the company tended to give equal-percentage raises to women and men, the gap between the two groups widened.

Attorneys at Bach, Lombard, & Wilson had their staff assemble massive amounts of data. Table 2.9 provides an example of the type of data they collected. A bar chart is a more effective way to convey this information, as Figure 2.9 shows. From this graph we can quickly see that in all years except 2009, the starting salaries for males did exceed those for females. The bar chart also illustrates that the general trend in starting salaries for both groups has been increasing, though with a slight downturn in 2011. Do you think the information in Figure 2.9 alone is sufficient to rule in favor of the claimant in this lawsuit? Bar charts like the one in Figure 2.9 that display two or more variables are referred to as *cluster bar charts*.

TABLE 2.9	Salary Data for Bach, Lombard, & Wilson
Year	Males: Average Starting Salaries	Females: Average Starting Salaries
2006	$44,456	$41,789
2007	$47,286	$46,478
2008	$56,234	$53,854
2009	$57,890	$58,600
2010	$63,467	$59,070
2011	$61,090	$55,321
2012	$67,543	$64,506

FIGURE 2.9

Bar Chart of Starting Salaries

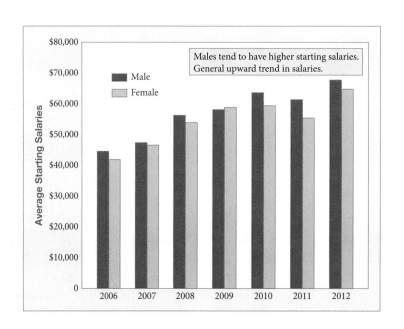

Pie Chart

A graph in the shape of a circle. The circle is divided into "slices" corresponding to the categories or classes to be displayed. The size of each slice is proportional to the magnitude of the displayed variable associated with each category or class.

How to do it (Example 2-8)

Constructing Pie Charts
A pie chart is constructed using the following steps:

1. Define the categories for the variable of interest.

2. For each category, determine the appropriate measure or value. The value assigned to each category is the proportion the category is to the total for all categories.

3. Construct the pie chart by displaying one slice for each category that is proportional in size to the proportion the category value is to the total of all categories.

Pie Charts

Another graphical tool that can be used to transform data into information is the **pie chart**.

EXAMPLE 2-8   PIE CHARTS

Golf Equipment A survey was recently conducted of 300 golfers that asked questions about the impact of new technology on the game. One question asked the golfers to indicate which area of golf equipment is most responsible for improving an amateur golfer's game. The following data were obtained:

Equipment	Frequency
Golf ball	81
Club head material	66
Shaft material	63
Club head size	63
Shaft length	3
Don't know	24

To display these data in pie chart form, use the following steps:

Step 1   Define the categories.
The categories are the six equipment-response categories.

Step 2   Determine the appropriate measure.
The appropriate measure is the proportion of the golfers surveyed. The proportion for each category is determined by dividing the number of golfers in a category by the total sample size. For example, for the category "golf ball," the percentage is $81/300 = 0.27 = 27\%$.

Step 3   Construct the pie chart.
The pie chart is constructed by dividing a circle into six slices (one for each category) such that each slice is proportional to the percentage of golfers in the category.

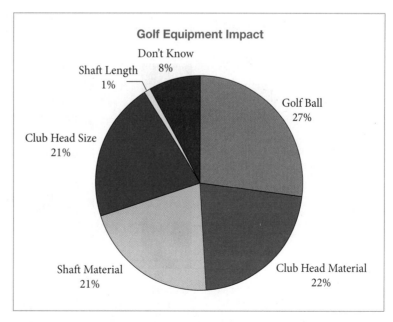

Golf Equipment Impact

Don't Know 8%
Shaft Length 1%
Golf Ball 27%
Club Head Size 21%
Shaft Material 21%
Club Head Material 22%

>> **END EXAMPLE**

TRY PROBLEM 2-28 (pg. 60)

FIGURE 2.10

Pie Chart: Per-Student
Funding for Universities

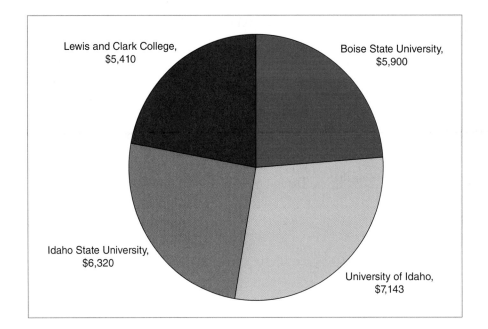

Pie charts are sometimes mistakenly used when a bar chart would be more appropriate. For example, a few years ago the student leaders at Boise State University wanted to draw attention to the funding inequities among the four public universities in Idaho. To do so, they rented a large billboard adjacent to a major thoroughfare through downtown Boise. The billboard contained a large pie chart like the one shown in Figure 2.10, where each slice indicated the funding per student at a given university. However, for a pie chart to be appropriate, the slices of the pie should represent parts of a total. But in the case of the billboard, that was not the case. The amounts merely represented the dollars of state money spent per student at each university. The sum of the four dollar amounts on the pie chart was a meaningless number. In this case, a bar chart like that shown in Figure 2.11 would have been more appropriate.

FIGURE 2.11

Bar Chart: Per-Student
Funding for Universities

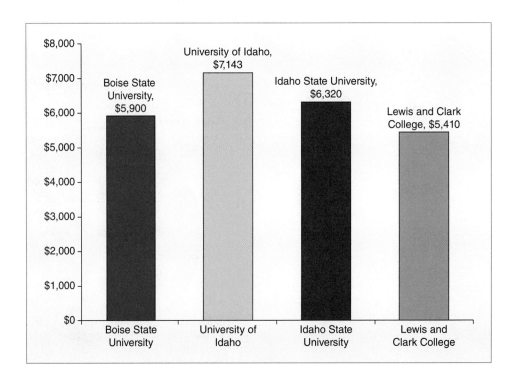

Chapter Outcome 5. → # Stem and Leaf Diagrams

Another graphical technique useful for doing an exploratory analysis of quantitative data is called the *stem and leaf diagram*. The stem and leaf diagram is similar to the histogram introduced in Section 2-1 in that it displays the distribution for the quantitative variable. However, unlike the histogram, in which the individual values of the data are lost if the variable of interest is broken into classes, the stem and leaf diagram shows the individual data values.

Although Excel does not have a stem and leaf procedure, the PHStat add-ins to Excel do have a stem and leaf procedure.

How to do it (Example 2-9)

Constructing Stem and Leaf Diagrams

To construct the stem and leaf diagram for a quantitative variable, use the following steps:

1. Sort the data from low to high.

2. Analyze the data for the variable of interest to determine how you wish to split the values into a stem and a leaf.

3. List all possible stems in a single column between the lowest and highest values in the data.

4. For each stem, list all leaves associated with the stem.

EXAMPLE 2-9   STEM AND LEAF DIAGRAMS

Walk-In Health Clinic The administrator for the Walk-In Health Clinic in Sydney, Australia, is interested in performing an analysis of the number of patients who enter the clinic daily. One method for analyzing the data for a sample of 200 days is the stem and leaf diagram. The following data represent the number of patients on each of the 200 days:

113	112	63	127	110	129	142	115	192	94
165	121	105	140	85	93	105	140	93	126
183	118	67	104	162	110	76	109	91	132
88	96	132	80	144	112	57	139	123	124
172	149	198	114	88	111	133	117	138	134
53	147	108	109	153	89	159	99	130	93
161	118	115	117	128	98	125	184	134	132
117	127	166	72	122	109	124	92	82	69
110	128	151	67	142	177	135	121	143	89
160	115	138	79	104	76	89	110	44	140
117	103	59	109	145	117	162	108	141	139
148	175	107	117	87	87	150	152	80	168
88	127	131	85	143	101	137	111	128	147
110	81	111	149	154	90	150	117	101	116
153	176	112	147	87	177	190	66	62	154
143	122	176	153	97	106	86	62	146	98
134	135	127	118	109	143	146	152	140	95
102	137	158	69	122	135	136	129	91	136
135	86	131	154	132	59	136	85	142	137
155	190	120	154	102	109	97	157	144	149

The stem and leaf diagram is constructed using the following steps:

Step 1 **Sort the data from low to high.**
The lowest value is 44 patients and the highest value is 198 patients.

Step 2 **Split the values into a stem and leaf.**

Stem = tens place   leaf = units place

For example, for the value 113, the stem is 11 and the leaf is 3. We are keeping one digit for the leaf.

Step 3 **List all possible stems from lowest to highest.**

Step 4 **Itemize the leaves from lowest to highest and place next to the appropriate stems.**

4	4
5	3 7 9 9
6	2 2 3 6 7 7 9 9
7	2 6 6 9
8	0 0 1 2 5 5 5 6 6 7 7 7 8 8 8 9 9 9
9	0 1 1 2 3 3 3 4 5 6 7 7 8 8 9
10	1 1 2 2 3 4 4 5 5 6 7 8 8 9 9 9 9 9 9
11	0 0 0 0 0 1 1 1 2 2 2 3 4 5 5 5 6 7 7 7 7 7 7 7 7 8 8 8
12	0 1 1 2 2 2 3 4 4 5 6 7 7 7 7 8 8 8 9 9
13	0 1 1 2 2 2 2 3 4 4 4 4 5 5 5 5 6 6 6 7 7 7 8 8 9 9
14	0 0 0 0 1 2 2 2 3 3 3 3 4 4 5 6 6 7 7 7 8 9 9 9
15	0 0 1 2 2 3 3 3 4 4 4 4 5 7 8 9
16	0 1 2 2 5 6 8
17	2 5 6 6 7 7
18	3 4
19	0 0 2 8

The stem and leaf diagram shows that most days have between 80 and 160 patients, with the most frequent value in the 110- to 120-patient range.

>> **END EXAMPLE**

TRY PROBLEM 2-25 (pg. 60)

MyStatLab

2-2: Exercises

Skill Development

2-24. The following data reflect the percentages of employees with different levels of education:

Education Level	Percentage
Less than high school graduate	18
High school graduate	34
Some college	14
College graduate	30
Graduate degree	4
	Total = 100

a. Develop a pie chart to illustrate these data.
b. Develop a horizontal bar chart to illustrate these data.

2-25. Given the following data, construct a stem and leaf diagram:

0.7	1.7	2.8	3.8
0.8	1.8	3.3	4.3
1.0	2.0	4.4	5.4
1.1	2.1	5.3	6.3
1.4	2.4	5.4	6.4
2.0	3.0		

2-26. A university has the following number of students at each grade level.

Freshman	3,450
Sophomore	3,190
Junior	2,780
Senior	1,980
Graduate	750

a. Construct a bar chart that effectively displays these data.
b. Construct a pie chart to display these data.
c. Referring to the graphs constructed in parts a and b, indicate which you would favor as the most effective way of presenting these data. Discuss.

2-27. Given the following sales data for product category and sales region, construct at least two different bar charts that display the data effectively:

		Region			
		East	West	North	South
	XJ-6 Model	200	300	50	170
Product	X-15-Y Model	100	200	20	100
Type	Craftsman	80	400	60	200
	Generic	100	150	40	50

2-28. The 2010 Annual Report of Murphy Oil Corporation reports the following refinery yields, in barrels per day, by product category for the United States and the United Kingdom.

United States 2010	
Product Category	Refinery Yields— barrels per day
Gasoline	61,128
Kerosene	11,068
Diesel and Home Heating Oils	41,305
Residuals	18,082
Asphalt, LPG, and other	14,802
Fuel and Loss	834

United Kingdom 2010

Product Category	Refinery Yields—barrels per day
Gasoline	20,889
Kerosene	11,374
Diesel and Home Heating Oils	25,995
Residuals	8,296
Asphalt, LPG, and other	14,799
Fuel and Loss	2,810

a. Construct a pie chart to display United States refinery yields by product per day. Display the refinery yields data for each product category as a percentage of total refinery yields for all product categories.

b. Construct a pie chart to display United Kingdom refinery yields by product per day. Display the refinery yields data for each product category as a percentage of total refinery yields for all product categories.

c. Construct a bar chart that effectively compares United States and United Kingdom refinery yields by product category.

2-29. Boston Properties is a real estate investment trust (REIT) that owns first-class office properties in selected markets. According to its 2010 annual report, its percentage of net operating income distribution by region (as a percent of total income) for the year ended December 31, 2010, was

Region	2010 Income Distribution
New York	41%
Washington, D.C.	23%
Boston	21%
San Francisco	12%
Princeton	3%

a. Construct a pie chart to display the percentage of net operating income distribution by region for 2010.

b. Construct a bar chart to display the net operating income distribution by region for 2010.

c. Briefly comment on which of the two charts you believe better summarizes and displays the data.

2-30. Hileman Services Company recently released the following data concerning its operating profits (in $billions) for the five years:

Year	2004	2005	2006	2007	2008
Profit	0.5	0.1	0.7	0.5	0.2

a. Construct a bar chart to graphically display these data.

b. Construct a pie chart to graphically display these data.

c. Select the display that most effectively displays the data and provide reasons for your choice.

2-31. DaimlerChrysler recently sold its Chrysler division to a private equity firm. Before the sale, it reported its first-half revenues (in $billions) as follows:

Division	Mercedes	Chrysler	Commercial Vehicles	Financial Services	Total
Revenues	27.7	30.5	23.2	8.9	90.3

a. Produce a bar chart for these data.

b. Determine the proportion of first-half revenues accounted for by its vehicle divisions.

Business Applications

2-32. At the March meeting of the board of directors for the Graystone Services Company, one of the regional managers put the following data on the overhead projector to illustrate the ratio of the number of units manufactured to the number of employees at each of Graystone's five manufacturing plants:

Plant Location	Units Manufactured/Employees
Bismarck, ND	14.5
Boulder, CO	9.8
Omaha, NE	13.0
Harrisburg, PA	17.6
Portland, ME	5.9

a. Discuss whether a pie chart or a bar chart would be most appropriate to present these data graphically.

b. Construct the chart you recommended in part a.

2-33. The first few years after the turn of the century saw a rapid increase in housing values, followed by a rapid decline due in part to the sub-prime crisis. The following table indicates the increase in the number of homes valued at more than one million dollars before 2005.

Year	Number of $1 Million Homes
2000	394,878
2001	495,600
2002	595,441
2003	714,467
2004	1,034,386

Develop a horizontal bar chart to represent these data in graphical form.

2-34. The pharmaceutical industry is a very fast-growing segment of the U.S. and international economies. Recently, there has been controversy over how studies are done to show that drugs are both safe and effective. One drug product, Cymbalta, which is an antidepressant, was purported in a published abstract of an article in a medical journal to be superior to other competing products. Yet the article itself stated that no studies had actually been done to show such comparisons between Cymbalta and other competing products. In an August 2005 report in an article titled "Reading Fine Print, Insurers Question Drug Studies" in *The Wall Street Journal*, the following data were presented showing the U.S. sales of antidepressant drugs by major brand. The sales data for the first half of 2005 are shown in the following table.

Antidepressant Drug	Sales (First Half 2005 in Billions)
Effexor XR	$1.29
Lexapro	$1.03
Zoloft	$1.55
Cymbalta	$0.27
Other	$0.97

Construct an appropriate graph to display these data.

2-35. The number of branded retail outlets in the United States and the United Kingdom for Murphy Oil Corporation as of December 31 of each year from 2001 to 2010 is shown below:

Branded Retail Outlets	2001	2002	2003	2004	2005	2006	2007	2008	2009	2010
United States (total)	815	914	994	1,127	1,201	1,164	1,126	1,154	1,169	1,215
United Kingdom	411	416	384	358	412	402	389	454	453	451

Develop a chart that effectively compares the number of branded retail outlets in North America with the number in the United Kingdom.

2-36. The 2011 Annual Report of the Procter & Gamble Company reported the following net sales information for its six global business segments:

Global Segment	2011 Net Sales ($Millions)
Beauty	20,157
Grooming	8,025
Health Care	12,033
Snacks and Pet Care	3,156
Fabric Care and Home Care	24,837
Baby Care and Family Care	15,606

a. Construct a bar chart that displays this information by global business segment for 2011.
b. Construct a pie chart that displays each global business segment's net sales as a percentage of total global segment net sales for 2011.

2-37. A fast-food restaurant monitors its drive-thru service times electronically to ensure that its speed of service is meeting the company's goals. A sample of 28 drive-thru times was recently taken and is shown here.

Speed of Service (Time in Seconds)			
83	138	145	147
130	79	156	156
90	85	68	93
178	76	73	119
92	146	88	103
116	134	162	71
181	110	105	74

a. Construct a stem and leaf diagram of the speed of service times.
b. What range of time might the restaurant say is the most frequent speed of service?

2-38. A random sample of 30 customer records for a physician's office showed the following time (in days) to collect insurance payments:

Number of Days to Collect Payment				
34	55	36	39	36
32	35	30	47	31
60	66	48	43	33
24	37	38	65	35
22	45	33	29	41
38	35	28	56	56

a. Construct a stem and leaf diagram of these data.
b. Within what range of days are most payments collected?

2-39. *USA Today* presented data to show that major airlines accounting for more than half of capacity were expected to be in bankruptcy court. The total seat capacity of major airlines was 858 billion at the time. For airlines expected to be in bankruptcy court, the following data were presented:

Airline Seat Capacity (in Billions)					
Airline	United	Delta	Northwest	U.S. Airways	ATA
Capacity	145	130	92	54	21

a. Construct a bar graph representing the contribution to the total seat capacity of the major airlines for the five airlines indicated.
b. Produce a pie chart exhibiting the percentage of the total seat capacity for the five major airlines expected to be in bankruptcy court and the combined capacity of all others.
c. Calculate the percentage of the total capacity of the airlines expected to be in bankruptcy court. Was *USA Today* correct in the percentage stated?

2-40. Many of the world's most successful companies rely on The NPD Group to provide global sales and marketing information that helps clients make more informed, fact-based decisions to optimize their businesses. These customers need NPD help for insight on what is selling, where, and why so that they can understand and leverage the latest trends. They recently (July 2009) released the following results of a survey intended to determine the market share distribution for the major corporations that make digital music devices:

Corporation	Apple	SanDisk	Creative Technology	iRiver	Samsung
Market Share	74%	6.4%	3.9%	3.6%	2.6%

a. Generate a bar chart to display these data.
b. Generate a pie chart to display these data.
c. Which of the two displays most effectively presents the data? Explain your answer.

Computer Database **Exercises**

2-41. The Honda Ridgeline was among the highest-ranked compact pickups in J.D. Power and Associates' annual customer-satisfaction survey. The study also found that models with high ratings have a tendency to stay on dealers' lots a shorter period of time. As an example, the Honda Ridgeline had stayed on dealers' lots an average of 24 days. The file titled **Honda** contains 50 lengths of stay on dealers' lots for Ridgeline trucks.
   a. Construct a stem and leaf display for these data.
   b. Determine the average length of stay on dealers' lots for the Honda Ridgeline. Does this agree with the average obtained by J.D. Power and Associates? Explain the difference.

2-42. The manager for Capital Educators Federal Credit Union has selected a random sample of 300 of the credit union's credit card customers. The data are in a file called **Capital**. The manager is interested in graphically displaying the percentage of card holders of each gender.
   a. Determine the appropriate type of graph to use in this application.
   b. Construct the graph and interpret it.

2-43. Recently, a study was conducted in which a random sample of hospitals was selected from each of four categories of hospitals: university related, religious related, community owned, and privately owned. At issue is the hospital charges associated with outpatient gall bladder surgery. The following data are in the file called **Hospitals**:

University Related	Religious Affiliated	Municipally Owned	Privately Held
$6,120	$4,010	$4,320	$5,100
$5,960	$3,770	$4,650	$4,920
$6,300	$3,960	$4,575	$5,200
$6,500	$3,620	$4,440	$5,345
$6,250	$3,280	$4,900	$4,875
$6,695	$3,680	$4,560	$5,330

University Related	Religious Affiliated	Municipally Owned	Privately Held
$6,475	$3,350	$4,610	$5,415
$6,250	$3,250	$4,850	$5,150
$6,880	$3,400		$5,380
$6,550			

a. Compute the average charge for each hospital category.
b. Construct a bar chart showing the averages by hospital category.
c. Discuss why a pie chart would not in this case be an appropriate graphical tool.

2-44. Amazon.com has become one of the success stories of the Internet age. Its growth can be seen by examining its increasing sales volume (in $billions) and the net income/loss during Amazon's operations. A file titled **Amazon** contains these data for its first 13 years.
   a. Construct one bar graph illustrating the relationship between sales and income for each separate year of Amazon's existence.
   b. Describe the type of relationship that exists between the years in business and Amazon's sales volume.
   c. Amazon's sales rose sharply. However, its net income yielded losses, which increased during the first few years. In which year did this situation reverse itself and show improvement in the net income balance sheet?

2-45. In your capacity as assistant to the administrator at Freedom Hospital, you have been asked to develop a graphical presentation that focuses on the insurance carried by the geriatric patients at the hospital. The data file **Patients** contains data for a sample of geriatric patients. In developing your presentation, please do the following:
   a. Construct a pie chart that shows the percentage of patients with each health insurance payer.
   b. Develop a bar chart that shows total charges for patients by insurance payer.
   c. Develop a stem and leaf diagram for the length-of-stay variable.
   d. Develop a bar chart that shows the number of males and females by insurance carrier.

END EXERCISES 2-2

2.3 Line Charts and Scatter Diagrams

Chapter Outcome 6. → ## Line Charts

Line Chart

A two-dimensional chart showing time on the horizontal axis and the variable of interest on the vertical axis.

Most of the examples that have been presented thus far have involved *cross-sectional data*, or data gathered from many observations, all taken at the same time. However, if you have *time-series* data that are measured over time (e.g., monthly, quarterly, annually), an effective tool for presenting such data is a **line chart**.

Excel Tutorial

BUSINESS APPLICATION   **CONSTRUCTING LINE CHARTS**

MCGREGOR VINEYARDS McGregor Vineyards owns and operates a winery in the Sonoma Valley in northern California. At a recent company meeting, the financial manager

FIGURE 2.12

Excel 2010 Output Showing McGregor Line Charts for Sales and Profits

Minitab Instructions (for similar results):
1. Open file: **McGregor.MTW**.
2. Choose **Graph > Times Series Plot**.
3. Select **Simple**.
4. Click **OK**.
5. In Series enter *Sales* and *Profit* columns.
6. Select **Multiple Graphs**.
7. Under **Show Graph Variables**, select **In separate panels of the same graph**.
8. Click **OK**. **OK**.

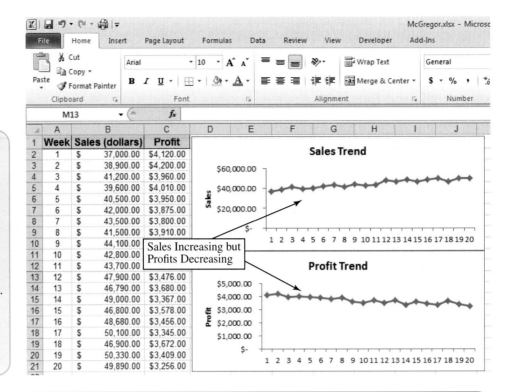

Excel 2010 Instructions:
1. Open file: **McGregor.xlsx**.
2. Select the **Sales (dollars)** data to be graphed.
3. On the **Insert** tab, click the **Line** chart.
4. Click the **Line with Markers** option.
5. Use the **Layout** tab in the **Chart Tools** to remove the Legend, change the Chart Title, add the Axis Titles, and remove the grid lines.
6. Repeat Steps 2–5 for the **Profit** data.

FIGURE 2.13

Excel 2010 Line Chart of McGregor Profit and Sales Using a Single Vertical Axis

Minitab Instructions (for similar results):
1. Open file: **McGregor.MTW**.
2. Choose **Graph > Times Series Plot**.
3. Select **Multiple**.
4. Click **OK**.
5. In Series enter *Sales* and *Profit* columns.
6. Select **Multiple Graphs**.
7. Under **Show Graph Variables**, select **Overlaid on the same graph**.
8. Click **OK**. **OK**.

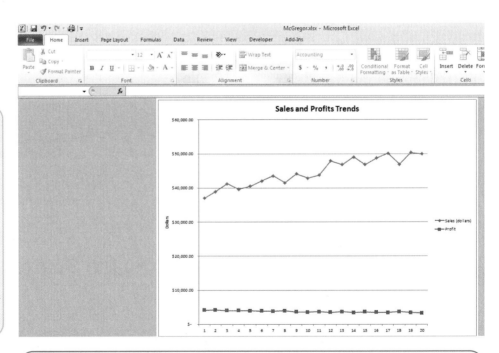

Excel 2010 Instructions:
1. Open file: **McGregor.xlsx**.
2. Select the two variables, **Sales (dollars)** and **Profit**, to be graphed.
3. On the **Insert** tab, click the **Line** chart.
4. Click the **Line with Markers** option.
5. Use the **Layout** tab in the **Chart Tools** to change the Chart Title, add the Axis Titles, remove the border, and remove the grid lines.

FIGURE 2.14

Excel 2010 Line Chart for Sales and Profits Using Two Vertical Axes and Different Scales

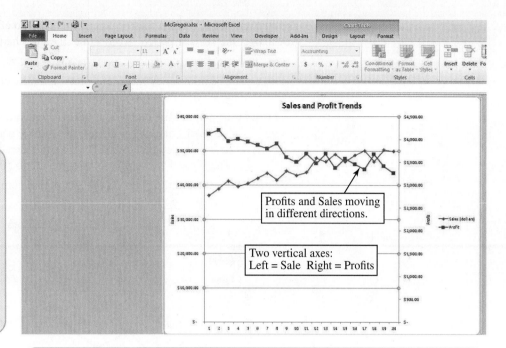

**Minitab Instructions
(for similar results):**
1. Open file:
   McGregor.MTW.
2. Choose **Graph > Times Series Plot**.
3. Select **Multiple**.
4. Click **OK**.
5. In **Series**, enter *Sales* and *Profit* columns.
6. Select **Multiple Graphs**.
8. Click **OK**.

Excel 2010 Instructions:

1. Open file: **McGregor.xlsx**.
2. Select data from the profit and sales column.
3. Click on **Insert**.
4. Click on **Line Chart**.
5. Move graph to separate page.
6. Select Profit Line on graph and rick click.
7. Click on the **Format Data Series**.
8. Click on **Secondary Axis**.
9. Click on **Layout** and add titles as desired.

expressed concern about the company's profit trend over the past 20 weeks. He presented weekly profit and sales data to McGregor management personnel. The data are in the file **McGregor**.

Initially, the financial manager developed two separate line charts for this data: one for sales, the other for profits. These are displayed in Figure 2.12. These line charts provide an indication that, although sales have been increasing, the profit trend is downward. But to fit both Excel graphs on one page, he had to compress the size of the graphs. This "flattened" the lines somewhat, masking the magnitude of the problem.

What the financial manager needed is one graph with both profits and sales. Figure 2.13 shows his first attempt. This is better, but there still is a problem: The sales and profit variables are of different magnitudes. This results in the profit line being flattened out to almost a straight line. The profit trend is hidden.

To overcome this problem, the financial manager needed to construct his graph using two scales, one for each variable. Figure 2.14 shows the improved graph. We can now clearly see that although sales are moving steadily higher, profits are headed downhill. For some reason, costs are rising faster than revenues, and this graph should motivate McGregor Vineyards to look into the problem.

How to do it (Example 2-10)

Constructing Line Charts

A line chart, also commonly called a *trend chart*, is developed using the following steps:

1. Identify the time-series variable of interest and determine the maximum value and the range of time periods covered in the data.

2. Construct the horizontal axis for the time periods using equal spacing between time periods. Construct the vertical axis with a scale appropriate for the range of values of the time-series variable.

3. Plot the points on the graph and connect the points with straight lines.

EXAMPLE 2-10   LINE CHARTS

Grogan Builders Grogan Builders produces mobile homes in Alberta, Canada. The owners are planning to expand the manufacturing facilities. To do so requires additional financing. In preparation for the meeting with the bankers, the owners have assembled data on total annual sales for the past 10 years. These data are shown as follows:

2003	2004	2005	2006	2007	2008	2009	2010	2011	2012
1,426	1,678	2,591	2,105	2,744	3,068	2,755	3,689	4,003	3,997

The owners wish to present these data in a line chart to effectively show the company's sales growth over the 10-year period. To construct the line chart, the following steps are used:

Step 1 Identify the time-series variable.
The time-series variable is units sold measured over 10 years, with a maximum value of 4,003.

Step 2 Construct the horizontal and vertical axes.
The horizontal axis will have the 10 time periods equally spaced. The vertical axis will start at zero and go to a value exceeding 4,003. We will use 4,500. The vertical axis will also be divided into 500-unit increments.

Step 3 Plot the data values on the graph and connect the points with straight lines.

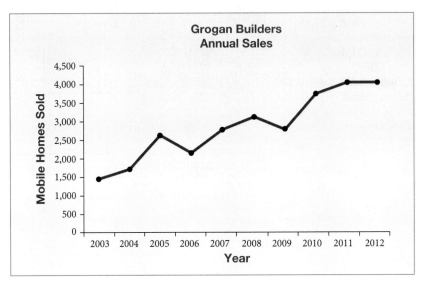

>> **END EXAMPLE**

TRY PROBLEM 2-47 (pg. 70)

Chapter Outcome 7. → # Scatter Diagrams

In Section 2.1, we introduced a set of statistical procedures known as joint frequency distributions that allow the decision maker to examine two variables at the same time. Another procedure used to study two quantitative variables simultaneously is the **scatter diagram**, or the **scatter plot**.

There are many situations in which we are interested in understanding the *bivariate* relationship between two *quantitative* variables. For example, a company would like to know the relationship between sales and advertising. A bank might be interested in the relationship between savings account balances and credit card balances for its customers. A real estate agent might wish to know the relationship between the selling price of houses and the number of days that the houses have been on the market. The list of possibilities is almost limitless.

Regardless of the variables involved, there are several key relationships we are looking for when we develop a scatter diagram. Figure 2.15 shows scatter diagrams representing some key bivariate relationships that might exist between two quantitative variables.

Chapters 14 and 15 make extensive use of scatter diagrams. They introduce a statistical technique called *regression analysis* that focuses on the relationship between two variables. These variables are known as **dependent** and **independent variables**.

Scatter Diagram, or Scatter Plot
A two-dimensional graph of plotted points in which the vertical axis represents values of one quantitative variable and the horizontal axis represents values of the other quantitative variable. Each plotted point has coordinates whose values are obtained from the respective variables.

Dependent Variable
A variable whose values are thought to be a function of, or dependent on, the values of another variable called the *independent variable*. On a scatter plot, the dependent variable is placed on the *y* axis and is often called the response variable.

Independent Variable
A variable whose values are thought to impact the values of the *dependent variable*. The independent variable, or explanatory variable, is often within the direct control of the decision maker. On a scatter plot, the independent variable, or explanatory variable, is graphed on the *x* axis.

BUSINESS APPLICATION **CREATING SCATTER DIAGRAMS**

PERSONAL COMPUTERS Can you think of any product that has increased in quality and capability as rapidly as personal computers? Not that many years ago, an 8-MB RAM system with a 486 processor and a 640-KB hard drive sold in the mid-$2,500 range. Now the same money would buy a 3.0 GHz or faster machine with a 100+ GB hard drive and 512-MB RAM or more!

A few years ago, we examined various Web sites looking for the best prices on personal computers. The data file called **Personal Computers** contains data on several characteristics,

FIGURE 2.15

Scatter Diagrams Showing Relationships Between *x* and *y*

Excel Tutorial

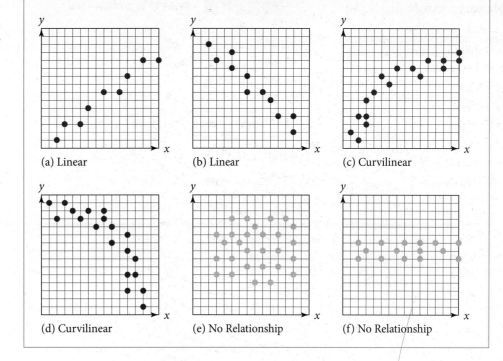

including processor speed, hard drive capacity, RAM, whether a monitor is included, and price for 13 personal computers. Of particular interest is the relationship between the computer price and processing speed. Our objective is to develop a scatter diagram to graphically depict what, if any, relationship exists between these two variables. The dependent variable is price and the independent variable is processor speed. Figure 2.16 shows the Excel scatter diagram output. The relationship between processor speed and price is somewhat curvilinear and positive.

FIGURE 2.16

Excel 2010 Scatter Diagrams for Personal Computer Data

Minitab Instructions (for similar results):

1. Open file: **Personal Computers.MTW**.
2. Choose **Graph > Scatterplot**.
3. Select **Simple**.
4. Click **OK**.
5. In **Y**, enter *Price* column. In **X**, enter *Processor Speed* column.
6. Click **OK**.

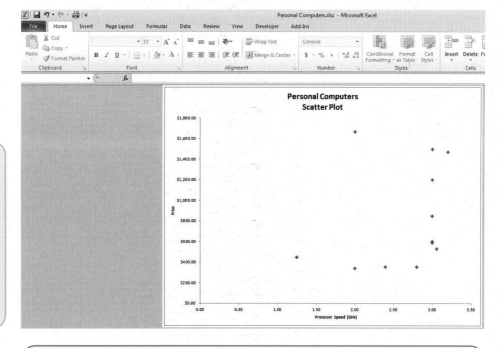

Excel 2010 Instructions:

1. Open file: **Personal Computers.xlsx**.
2. Select data for chart (Processor GHz and Price). Hint: Use Crtl key to select just the two desired columns.
3. On **Insert** tab, click **Scatter**, and then click **Scatter with only Markers** option.
4. Move chart to separate page.
5. Use the **Layout** tab of the **Chart Tools** to add titles and remove grid lines.

How to do it (Example 2-11)

Constructing Scatter Diagrams
A scatter diagram is a two-dimensional graph showing the joint values for two quantitative variables. It is constructed using the following steps:

1. Identify the two quantitative variables and collect paired responses for the two variables.

2. Determine which variable will be placed on the vertical axis and which variable will be placed on the horizontal axis. Often the vertical axis can be considered the dependent variable (y) and the horizontal axis can be considered the independent variable (x).

3. Define the range of values for each variable and define the appropriate scale for the x and y axes.

4. Plot the joint values for the two variables by placing a point in the x,y space. Do not connect the points.

EXAMPLE 2-11   **SCATTER DIAGRAMS**

Fortune's Best Eight Companies Each year, *Fortune* magazine surveys employees regarding job satisfaction to try to determine which companies are the "best" companies to work for in the United States. *Fortune* also collects a variety of data associated with these companies. For example, the table here shows data for the top eight companies on three variables: number of U.S. employees; number of training hours per year per employee; and total revenue in millions of dollars.

Company	U.S. Employees	Training Hr/Yr	Revenues ($Millions)
Southwest Airlines	24,757	15	$3,400
Kingston Technology	552	100	$1,300
SAS Institute	3,154	32	$ 653
Fel-Pro	2,577	60	$ 450
TD Industries	976	40	$ 127
MBNA	18,050	48	$3,300
W.L. Gore	4,118	27	$1,200
Microsoft	14,936	8	$8,700

To better understand these companies, we might be interested in the relationship between number of U.S. employees and revenue and between training hours and U.S. employees. To construct these scatter diagrams, we can use the following steps:

Step 1 **Identify the two variables of interest**.
In the first case, one variable is U.S. employees and the second is revenue. In the second case, one variable is training hours and the other is U.S. employees.

Step 2 **Identify the dependent and independent variables**.
In each case, think of U.S. employees as the independent (x) variable. Thus,

Case 1: y = revenue (vertical axis) x = U.S. employees (horizontal axis)

Case 2: y = training hours (vertical axis) x = U.S. employees (horizontal axis)

Step 3 **Establish the scales for the vertical and horizontal axes**.
The maximum value for each variable is

revenue = $8,700   U.S.employees = 24,757   training hours = 100

Step 4 **Plot the joint values for the two variables by placing a point in the x, y space**.

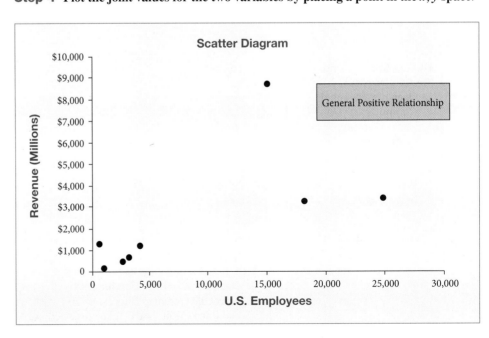

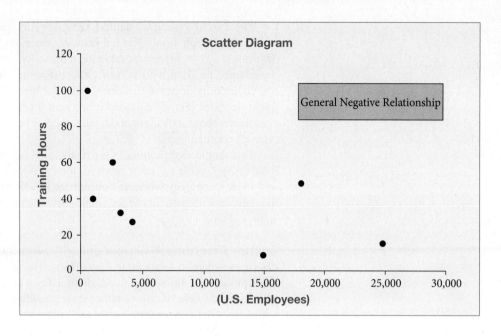

>> **END EXAMPLE**

TRY PROBLEM 2-46 (pg. 70)

Descriptive Statistics and Data Mining

The purpose of data mining and the descriptive statistics techniques discussed in the chapter are essentially the same—that is, to take large amounts of data and arrange it so some underlying pattern is more easily identifiable to the decision maker. In fact, several of the tools are the same, only under different names. A few examples should suffice.

Pareto Charts We once had the CEO of a Fortune 500 company tell us most companies don't get serious about quality until they face a crisis. The crisis his company faced was running out of money. Pareto charts are a commonly used tool of quality, but they are just histograms with a different name.

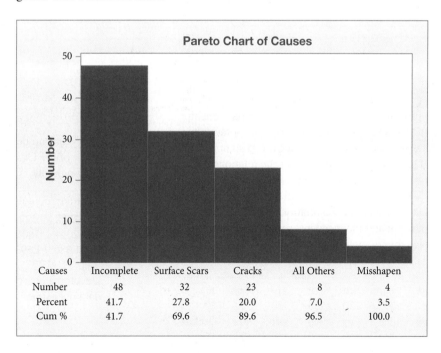

Causes	Incomplete	Surface Scars	Cracks	All Others	Misshapen
Number	48	32	23	8	4
Percent	41.7	27.8	20.0	7.0	3.5
Cum %	41.7	69.6	89.6	96.5	100.0

The Pareto Principle, named after Alfredo Pareto but identified in quality circumstances by Joseph Juran, has led business decision makers to realize the majority of sick days taken by employees are taken by a minority of employees, or the majority of customer complaints are filed by a minority of customers, or a majority of quality problems arise from a minority of possible causes. Consider the previous Pareto chart taken from a popular quality-control text. The example involves a company trying to determine the reason for complaints about its shipments to customers. The company was able to identify 20 possible types of complaints.

This should look familiar. It is a histogram, although it is called a Pareto Chart, and shows 3 out of 20 possible causes account for almost 90% of the complaints. This form of histogram will show a company where to concentrate its efforts to reduce customer complaints. Charts like this are also easier to use for employees who are not comfortable using more complicated statistical tools.

Scatter Diagrams Numerous police departments use a version of scatter diagrams to determine where to concentrate their efforts. The area of the diagram is a map of the city and the locations of crimes are plotted, often using a color code to identify the type of crime. By identifying clusters of crimes rather than spreading their efforts equally throughout the city, police are able to concentrate patrol and reduction efforts where the plots indicate clusters are happening. Numerous cities, such as San Francisco, have found such scatter diagrams to be effective tools in combating crime.

MyStatLab

2-3: **Exercises**

Skill **Development**

2-46. The following data represent 11 observations of two quantitative variables:

x = contact hours with client,
y = profit generated from client.

x	y	x	y	x	y	x	y
45	2,345	54	3,811	34	−700	24	1,975
56	4,200	24	2,406	45	3,457	32	206
26	278	23	3,250	47	2,478		

a. Construct a scatter plot of the data. Indicate whether the plot suggests a linear or nonlinear relationship between the dependent and independent variables.

b. Determine how much influence one data point will have on your perception of the relationship between the independent and dependent variables by deleting the data point with the smallest x value. What appears to be the relationship between the dependent and independent variables?

2-47. You have the following sales data for the past 12 months. Develop a line graph for these data.

Month	Jan	Feb	Mar	Apr	May	Jun
Sales	200	230	210	300	320	290
Month	Jul	Aug	Sep	Oct	Nov	Dec
Sales	300	360	400	410	390	450

2-48. The following data have been selected for two variables, y and x. Construct a scatter plot for these two variables and indicate what type of relationship, if any, appears to be present.

y	x
100	23.5
250	17.8
70	28.6
130	19.3
190	15.9
250	19.1
40	35.3

2-49. The year-end dollar value (in millions) of deposits for Bank of the Ozarks, Inc., for the years 1997–2010 are shown below

Year	1997	1998	1999	2000	2001	2002	2003
Deposits	296	529	596	678	678	790	1,062
Year	2004	2005	2006	2007	2008	2009	2010
Deposits	1,380	1,592	2,045	2,057	2,341	2,029	2,541

Develop a chart that effectively displays the deposit data over time.

2-50. VanAuker Properties' controller collected the following data on annual sales and the years of experience of members of his sales staff:

Sales $K:	200	191	135	236	305	183	50	192	184	73
Years:	10	4	5	9	12	6	2	7	6	2

a. Construct a scatter plot representing these data.
b. Determine the kind of relationship that exists (if any) between years of experience and sales.
c. Approximate the increase in sales that accrues with each additional year of experience for a member of the sales force.

Business Applications

2-51. Amazon.com celebrated its 13th anniversary in July 2007. Its growth can be seen by examining its increasing sales volume (in $billions) as reported by Hoovers Inc.

Sales	0.0005	0.0157	0.1477	0.6098	1.6398
Year	1995	1996	1997	1998	1999
Sales	2.7619	3.1229	3.9329	5.2637	6.9211
Year	2000	2001	2002	2003	2004
Sales	8.490	10.711	14.835		
Year	2005	2006	2007		

a. Construct a line plot for Amazon's sales.
b. Describe the type of relationship that exists between the years in business and Amazon's sales volume.
c. In which year does it appear that Amazon had the sharpest increase in sales?

2-52. In July 2005, Greg Sandoval of the Associated Press authored a study of the video game industry that focused on the efforts of the industry to interest women in the games. In that study, he cited another report by the Entertainments Software Association that indicated that the percentage of women who played video games in 2004 was 43%, whereas only 12.5% of the software developers were female. Sandoval also presented the following data showing the U.S. computer/video game sales:

Year	Sales (Billions)
1996	$3.80
1997	$4.30
1998	$5.70
1999	$6.10
2000	$6.00
2001	$6.30
2002	$6.95
2003	$7.00
2004	$7.30

Construct a line chart showing these computer/video game sales data. Write a short statement describing the graph.

2-53. The recent performance of U.S. equity markets has increased the popularity of dividend-paying stocks for some investors. Shown below are the diluted net earnings per common share and the dividends per common share for the Procter & Gamble Company (P&G) for the years 1996–2011.

Year	Diluted Net Earnings per Common Share	Dividends per Common Share
1996	$1.00	$0.40
1997	$1.14	$0.45
1998	$1.28	$0.51
1999	$1.29	$0.57
2000	$1.23	$0.64
2001	$1.03	$0.70
2002	$1.54	$0.76
2003	$1.85	$0.82
2004	$2.32	$0.93
2005	$2.66	$1.03
2006	$2.64	$1.15
2007	$3.04	$1.28
2008	$3.64	$1.45
2009	$4.26	$1.64
2010	$4.11	$1.80
2011	$3.93	$1.97

a. Construct a line chart of diluted net earnings per common share for the years shown.
b. Construct a line chart of dividends per common share for the years shown.
c. Construct the appropriate chart for determining whether there is a relationship between diluted net earnings per common share and dividends per common share for the years shown. Briefly comment on the nature of any relationship you believe your chart reveals.

2-54. *Business Week* (Reed, Stanley, et al., "Open Season on Big Oil," September 26, 2005) reported on data provided by A. G. Edwards & Sons concerning the profits ($billions) for 10 of the largest integrated oil and gas companies over the period from 1999 to 2005.

Year	1999	2000	2001	2002	2003	2004	2005
Profit ($Billions)	33.3	62.5	58.3	41.7	66.7	91.7	118.0

a. Produce a line plot of the profit versus the year.
b. Describe the types of relationships that exist between years and profits during the specified time period.
c. Which of the relationships would you use to project the companies' profits in the year 2006? Explain your answer.

Computer Database **Exercises**

2-55. Major League Baseball (MLB) is played in 30 North American cities, including Toronto, Canada. Having a team in a city is generally considered to provide an economic boost to the community. Although winning is the stated goal for all teams, the business side of baseball has to do with attendance. The data file **MLB Attendance-2008** contains data for both home and road game attendance for all 30 MLB teams for 2008. Of interest is the relationship between average home attendance and average road attendance. Using the 2008 attendance data, construct the appropriate graph to help determine the relationship between these two variables and discuss the implications of the graph.

2-56. In the October 17, 2005, issue of *Fortune*, a special advertising section focused on private jets. Included in the section was an article about "fractional" jet ownership, in which wealthy individuals and companies share ownership in private jets. The idea is that the expensive airplanes can be better utilized if more than one individual or company has an ownership stake. AvData, Inc., provided data showing the number of fractional ownerships since 1986. These data are in the file called **JetOwnership**. Using these data, develop a line chart that displays the trend in fractional ownership between 1986 and 2004. Discuss.

2-57. Starting in 2005, a chain of events, including the war in Iraq, Hurricane Katrina, and the expanding economies in India and China, lead to a sharp increase in fuel costs. As a result, the U.S. airline industry has been hit hard financially, with many airlines declaring bankruptcy. Some airlines are substituting smaller planes on certain routes in an attempt to reduce fuel costs. As an analyst for one of the major airlines, you have been asked to analyze the relationship between passenger capacity and fuel consumption per hour. Data for 19 commonly flown planes is presented in the file called **Airplanes**. Develop the appropriate graph to illustrate the relationship between fuel consumption per hour and passenger capacity. Discuss.

2-58. Japolli Bakery tracks sales of its different bread products on a daily basis. The data at the bottom of this page show sales for 22 consecutive days at one of its retail outlets in Nashville. Develop a line chart that displays these data. The data are also located in a data file called **Japolli Bakery**. Discuss what, if any, conclusions you might be able to reach from the line chart.

2-59. Energy prices have been a major source of economic and political debate in the United States and around the world. Consumers have recently seen gasoline prices both rise and fall rapidly, and the impact of fuel prices has been blamed for economic problems in the United States at different points in time. Although no longer doing so, for years the California Energy Commission published yearly gasoline prices. The data (found in the file called **Gasoline Prices**) reflect the average price of regular unleaded gasoline in the state of California for the years between 1970 and 2005. The first price column is the actual average price of gasoline during each of

Japolli Bakery

Day of Week	White	Wheat	Multigrain	Black	Cinnamon Raisin	Sourdough French	Light Oat
Friday	436	456	417	311	95	96	224
Saturday	653	571	557	416	129	140	224
Sunday	496	490	403	351	114	108	228
Monday	786	611	570	473	165	148	304
Tuesday	547	474	424	365	144	104	256
Wednesday	513	443	380	317	100	92	180
Thursday	817	669	622	518	181	152	308
Friday	375	390	299	256	124	88	172
Saturday	700	678	564	463	173	136	248
Sunday	597	502	457	383	140	144	312
Monday	536	530	428	360	135	112	356
Tuesday	875	703	605	549	201	188	356
Wednesday	421	433	336	312	100	104	224
Thursday	667	576	541	438	152	144	304
Friday	506	461	406	342	135	116	264
Saturday	470	352	377	266	84	92	172
Sunday	748	643	599	425	153	148	316
Monday	376	367	310	279	128	104	208
Tuesday	704	646	586	426	174	160	264
Wednesday	591	504	408	349	140	120	276
Thursday	564	497	415	348	107	120	212
Friday	817	673	644	492	200	180	348

those years. The second column is the average price adjusted for inflation, with 2005 being the base year.

a. Construct an appropriate chart showing the actual average price of gasoline in California over the years between 1970 and 2005.

b. Add to the graph developed in part a the data for the adjusted gasoline prices.

c. Based on the graph from part b, what conclusions might be reached about the price of gasoline over the years between 1970 and 2005?

2-60. Federal flood insurance underwritten by the federal government was initiated in 1968. This federal flood insurance coverage has, according to *USA Today* ("How You Pay for People to Build in Flood Zones," September 21, 2005), more than tripled in the past 15 years. A file titled **Flood** contains the amount of federal flood insurance coverage for each of the years from 1990 to 2004.

a. Produce a line plot for these data.

b. Describe the type of relationship between the year and the amount of federal flood insurance.

c. Determine the average increase per year in federal flood insurance.

2-61. The Office of Management and Budget keeps data on many facets of corporations. One item that has become a matter of concern is the number of applications for patents submitted compared to the backlog of

applications that have not been processed by the end of the year. A file titled **Patent** provides data extracted from a *USA Today* article that addresses the problem.

a. Construct the two line plots on the same axes.

b. Determine the types of relationships that exist between the years and the two patent-related variables.

c. During which year(s) did the backlog of applications at the end of the year equal approximately the same number of patent applications?

2-62. The sub-prime mortgage crisis that hit the world economy also impacted the real estate market. Both new and existing home sales were affected. A file titled **EHSales** contains the number of existing homes sold (in millions) from September of 2007 to September 2008.

a. Construct a line plot for these data.

b. The data file also contains data concerning the median selling price ($thousands). Construct a graph containing the line plot for both the number of sales (*tens* of thousands) and the median ($thousands) price of these sales for the indicated time period.

c. Describe the relationship between the two line plots constructed in part b.

END EXERCISES 2-3

Visual Summary

Chapter 2: The old adage states that a picture is worth a thousand words. In many ways this applies to descriptive statistics. The use of graphs, charts, and tables to display data in a way that helps decision-makers better understand the data is one of the major applications of business statistics. This chapter has introduced many of the most frequently used graphical techniques using examples and business applications.

2.1 Frequency Distributions and Histograms (pg. 32–53)

Summary

A **frequency distribution** is used to determine the number of occurrences in your data that fall at each possible data value or within defined ranges of possible values. It represents a good summary of the data and from a frequency distribution, you can form a graph called a **histogram**. This histogram gives a visual picture showing how the data are distributed. You can use the histogram to see where the data's center is and how spread out the data are. It is often helpful to convert the frequencies in a frequency distribution to **relative frequencies** and to construct a **relative frequency distribution** and a relative frequency histogram. Another option is to convert the frequency distribution to a **cumulative frequency distribution** and then a graph called an ogive. Finally, if you are analyzing two variables simultaneously, you may want to construct a **joint frequency distribution**.

> **Outcome 1.** Construct frequency distributions both manually and with your computer.
> **Outcome 2.** Construct and interpret a frequency histogram.
> **Outcome 3.** Develop and interpret joint frequency distributions.

2.2 Bar Charts, Pie Charts and Stem and Leaf Diagrams (pg. 53–63)

Summary

If your data are **discrete**, or are **nominal** or **ordinal level**, three charts introduced in this section are often considered. These are **bar charts**, **pie charts**, and **stem and leaf diagrams**. A bar chart can be arranged with the bars **vertical** or **horizontal**. A single bar chart can be used to describe two or more variables. In situations where you wish to show how the parts making up a total are distributed, a **pie chart** is often used. The "slices" of the pie are many times depicted as the percentage of the total. A lesser used graphical tool that provides a quick view of how the data are distributed is the **stem and leaf diagram**.

> **Outcome 4.** Construct and interpret various types of bar charts.
> **Outcome 5.** Build a stem and leaf diagram.

2.3 Line Charts and Scatter Diagrams (pg. 63–73)

Summary

When you are working with **time-series** data and you are interested in displaying the pattern in the data over time, the chart that is used is called a **line chart**. The vertical axis displays the value of the time-series variable while the horizontal axis contains the time increments. The points are plotted and are usually connected by straight lines. In other cases you may be interested in the relationship between two **quantitative** variables; the graphical tool that is used is called a **scatter diagram**. The variable judged to be the **dependent variable** is placed on the vertical axis and **independent variable** goes on the horizontal axis. The joint values are plotted as points in the two-dimensional space. Do not connect the points with lines.

> **Outcome 6.** Create a line chart and interpret the trend in the data.
> **Outcome 7.** Create a scatter plot and interpret it.

Conclusion

There are many types of charts, graphs, and tables that can be used to display data. The technique that is used often depends on the type and level of data you have. In cases where multiple graphs or charts can apply, you should select the one that most effectively displays the data for your application. **Figure 2.17** summarizes the different graphical options that are presented in chapter 2.

FIGURE 2.17 |

Summary: Descriptive
Statistical Techniques

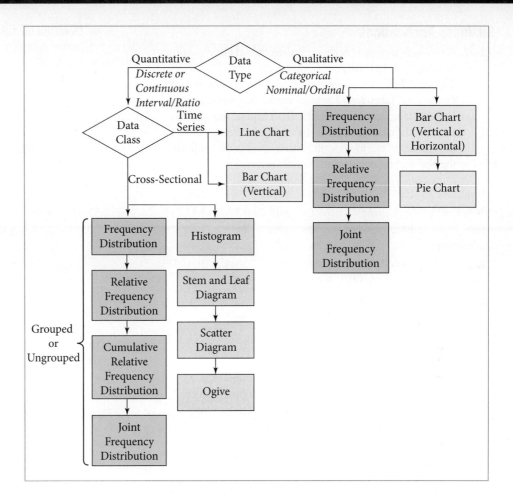

Equations

(2.1) Relative Frequency pg. 34

$$\text{Relative frequency} = \frac{f_i}{n}$$

(2.2) Class Width pg. 39

$$W = \frac{\text{Largest value} - \text{Smallest value}}{\text{Number of classes}}$$

Key Terms

All-inclusive classes pg. 38
Bar chart pg. 53
Class boundaries pg. 39
Class width pg. 39
Continuous data pg. 37
Cumulative frequency distribution pg. 39
Cumulative relative frequency distribution pg. 39

Dependent variable pg. 66
Discrete data pg. 33
Equal-width classes pg. 38
Frequency distribution pg. 33
Frequency histogram pg. 41
Independent variable pg. 66
Line chart pg. 63

Mutually exclusive classes pg. 38
Ogive pg. 45
Pie chart pg. 57
Relative frequency pg. 33
Scatter diagram or scatter plot pg. 66

Chapter Exercises   MyStatLab

Conceptual Questions

2-63. Discuss the advantages of constructing a relative frequency distribution as opposed to a frequency distribution.

2-64. What are the characteristics of a data set that would lead you to construct a bar chart?

2-65. What are the characteristics of a data set that would lead you to construct a pie chart?

2-66. Discuss the differences in data that would lead you to construct a line chart as opposed to a scatter plot.

Business Applications

2-67. *USA Today* reported (Anthony Breznican and Gary Strauss, "Where Have All the Moviegoers Gone?" June 23, 2005) that in the summer of 2005, ticket sales to movie theaters had fallen for 17 straight weeks, the industry's longest losing streak since 1985. To determine the long-term trends in ticket sales, the following data representing the number of admissions (in billions) were obtained from the National Association of Theatre Owners:

Year	1987	1988	1989	1990	1991	1992
Admissions	1.09	1.08	1.26	1.19	1.14	1.17
Year	1993	1994	1995	1996	1997	1998
Admissions	1.24	1.28	1.26	1.34	1.39	1.48
Year	1999	2000	2001	2002	2003	2004
Admissions	1.47	1.42	1.49	1.63	1.57	1.53
Year	2005	2006	2007			
Admissions	1.38	1.41	1.40			

   a. Produce a line plot of the data.
   b. Describe any trends that you detect.

2-68. The following data represent the commuting distances for employees of the Pay-and-Carry Department store.
   a. The personnel manager for Pay-and-Carry would like you to develop a frequency distribution and histogram for these data.
   b. Develop a stem and leaf diagram for these data.
   c. Break the data into three groups (under 3 miles, 3 and under 6 miles, and 6 and over). Construct a pie chart to illustrate the proportion of employees in each category.

		Commuting Distance (miles)					
3.5	2.0	4.0	2.5	0.3	1.0	12.0	17.5
3.0	3.5	6.5	9.0	3.0	4.0	9.0	16.0
3.5	0.5	2.5	1.0	0.7	1.5	1.4	12.0
9.2	8.3	1.0	3.0	7.5	3.2	2.0	1.0
3.5	3.6	1.9	2.0	3.0	1.5	0.4	6.4
11.0	2.5	2.4	2.7	4.0	2.0	2.0	3.0

   d. Referring to part c, construct a bar chart to depict the proportion of employees in each category.

2-69. Anyone attending college realizes tuition costs have increased rapidly. In fact, tuition had risen at a faster pace than inflation for more than two decades. Data showing costs for both private and public colleges, for selected years, are shown below.

Year	1984	1989	1994	1999	2004
Private College Tuition	$9,202	$12,146	$13,844	$16,454	$19,710
Public College Tuition	$2,074	$ 2,395	$ 3,188	$ 3,632	$ 4,694

   a. Construct one bar graph illustrating the relationship between private and public university tuition for the displayed years.

   b. Describe the tuition trend for both private and public college tuition.

2-70. A recent article in *USA Today* used the following data to illustrate the decline in the percentage of men who receive college and advanced degrees:

	Bachelor			**Doctorate**		
	1989	2003	2014*	1989	2003	2014*
Men	47	43	40	64	57	49
Women	53	57	60	36	43	51

*Education Department projection.

   a. Use one graph that contains two bar charts, each of which represents the kind of degree received, to display the relationship between the percentages of men and women receiving each type of degree.
   b. Describe any trends that might be evident.

2-71. The Minnesota State Fishing Bureau has contracted with a university biologist to study the length of walleyes (fish) caught in Minnesota lakes. The biologist collected data on a sample of 1,000 fish caught and developed the following relative frequency distribution:

Class Length (inches)	Relative Frequency f_i
8 to less than 10	0.22
10 to less than 12	0.15
12 to less than 14	0.25
14 to less than 16	0.24
16 to less than 18	0.06
18 to less than 20	0.05
20 to less than 22	0.03

   a. Construct a frequency distribution from this relative frequency distribution and then produce a histogram based on the frequency distribution.
   b. Construct a pie chart from the relative frequency distribution. Discuss which of the two graphs, the pie chart or the histogram, you think is more effective in presenting the fish length data.

2-72. A computer software company has been looking at the amount of time customers spend on hold after their call is answered by the central switchboard. The company would like to have at most 2% of the callers wait two minutes or more. The company's calling service has provided the following data showing how long each of last month's callers spent on hold:

Class	Number
Less than 15 seconds	456
15 to less than 30 seconds	718
30 to less than 45 seconds	891
45 to less than 60 seconds	823
60 to less than 75 seconds	610
75 to less than 90 seconds	449
90 to less than 105 seconds	385
105 to less than 120 seconds	221

(Continued)

Class	Number
120 to less than 150 seconds	158
150 to less than 180 seconds	124
180 to less than 240 seconds	87
More than 240 seconds	153

a. Develop a relative frequency distribution and ogive for these data.

b. The company estimates it loses an average of $30 in business from callers who must wait two minutes or more before receiving assistance. The company thinks that last month's distribution of waiting times is typical. Estimate how much money the company is losing in business per month because people have to wait too long before receiving assistance.

2-73. The regional sales manager for American Toys, Inc., recently collected data on weekly sales (in dollars) for the 15 stores in his region. He also collected data on the number of salesclerk work hours during the week for each of the stores. The data are as follows:

Store	Sales	Hours
1	23,300	120
2	25,600	135
3	19,200	96
4	10,211	102
5	19,330	240
6	35,789	190
7	12,540	108
8	43,150	234
9	27,886	140
10	54,156	300
11	34,080	254
12	25,900	180
13	36,400	270
14	25,760	175
15	31,500	256

a. Develop a scatter plot of these data. Determine which variable should be the dependent variable and which should be the independent variable.

b. Based on the scatter plot, what, if any, conclusions might the sales manager reach with respect to the relationship between sales and number of clerk hours worked? Do any stores stand out as being different? Discuss.

Computer Database Exercises

2-74. The Energy Information Administration published a press release on September 26, 2005 (Paula Weir and Pedro Saavedra, "Two Multi-Phase Surveys That Combine Overlapping Sample Cycles at Phase I"). The file titled **Diesel$** contains the average on-highway diesel prices for each of 53 weeks from September 27, 2004, to September 26, 2005. It also contains equivalent information for the state of California, recognized as having the highest national prices.

a. Construct a chart containing line plots for both the national average and California's diesel prices. Describe the relationship between the diesel prices in California and the national average.

b. In what week did the California average diesel price surpass $3.00 a gallon?

c. Determine the smallest and largest price paid in California for a gallon of diesel. At what weeks did these occur? Use this information to project when California gas prices might exceed $4.00, assuming a linear trend between California diesel prices and the weeks in which they occurred.

2-75. A recent article in *USA Today* reported that Apple had 74% of the digital music device market, according to researcher The NPD Group. The NPD Group provides global sales and marketing information that helps clients make more informed, fact-based decisions to optimize their businesses. The data in the file titled **Digital** provide the brand of digital devices owned by a sample of consumers that would produce the market shares alluded to in the article. Produce a pie chart that represents the market shares obtained from the referenced sample. Indicate the market shares and the identity of those manufacturers in the pie chart.

2-76. The file **Home-Prices** contains information about single-family housing prices in 100 metropolitan areas in the United States.

a. Construct a frequency distribution and histogram of 1997 median single-family home prices. Use the $2^k \geq n$ guideline to determine the appropriate number of classes.

b. Construct a cumulative relative frequency distribution and ogive for 1997 median single-family home prices.

c. Repeat parts a and b but this time use 1.5 times as many class intervals as recommended by the $2^k \geq n$ guideline. What was the impact of using more class intervals?

2-77. Elliel's Department Store tracks its inventory on a monthly basis. Monthly data for the years 2008–2012 are in the file called **Elliels**.

a. Construct a line chart showing the monthly inventory over the five years. Discuss what this graph implies about inventory.

b. Sum the monthly inventory figures for each year. Then present the sums in bar chart form. Discuss whether you think this is an appropriate graph to describe the inventory situation at Elliels.

2-78. The Energy Information Administration (EIA) surveys the price of diesel fuel. The EIA-888 is a survey of diesel fuel outlet prices from truck stops and service stations across the country. It produces estimates of national and regional prices. The diesel fuel prices that are released are used by the trucking industry to make rate adjustments in hauling contracts. The file titled **Diesel$** contains the average on-highway diesel prices for each of 53 weeks from September 27, 2004, to September 26, 2005.

a. Construct a histogram with 11 classes beginning at $1.85.

b. Are there any data points that are unusually larger than the rest of the data? In which classes do these points occur? What is the interpretation of this phenomenon?

Video Case 2

Drive-Thru Service Times @ McDonald's

When you're on the go and looking for a quick meal, where do you go? If you're like millions of people every day, you make a stop at McDonald's. Known as "quick service restaurants" in the industry (not "fast food"), companies such as McDonald's invest heavily to determine the most efficient and effective ways to provide fast, high-quality service in all phases of their business.

Drive-thru operations play a vital role. It's not surprising that attention is focused on the drive-thru process. After all, more than 60% of individual restaurant revenues in the United States come from the drive-thru experience. Yet understanding the process is more complex than just counting cars. Marla King, professor at the company's international training center Hamburger University, got her start 25 years ago working at a McDonald's drive-thru. She now coaches new restaurant owners and managers. "Our stated drive-thru service time is 90 seconds or less. We train every manager and team member to understand that a quality customer experience at the drive-thru depends on them," says Marla. Some of the factors that affect customers' ability to complete their purchases within 90 seconds include restaurant staffing, equipment layout in the restaurant, training, efficiency of the grill team, and frequency of customer arrivals, to name a few. Also, customer order patterns also play a role. Some customers will just order drinks, whereas others seem to need enough food to feed an entire soccer team. And then there are the special orders. Obviously, there is plenty of room for variability here.

Yet that doesn't stop the company from using statistical techniques to better understand the drive-thru action. In particular, McDonald's uses graphical techniques to display data and to help transform the data into useful information. For restaurant managers to achieve the goal in their own restaurants, they need training in proper restaurant and drive-thru operations. Hamburger University, McDonald's training center located near Chicago, Illinois, satisfies that need. In the mock-up restaurant service lab, managers go through a "before and after" training scenario. In the "before" scenario, they run the restaurant for 30 minutes as if they were back in their home restaurants. Managers in the training class are assigned to be crew, customers, drive-thru cars, special-needs guests (such as hearing impaired, indecisive, clumsy), or observers. Statistical data about the operations, revenues, and service times are collected and analyzed. Without the right training, the restaurant's operations usually start breaking down after 10−15 minutes. After debriefing and analyzing the data collected, the managers make suggestions for adjustments and head back to the service lab to try again. This time, the results usually come in well within standards. "When presented with the quantitative results, managers are pretty quick to make the connections

between better operations, higher revenues, and happier customers," Marla states.

When managers return to their respective restaurants, the training results and techniques are shared with staff who are charged with implementing the ideas locally. The results of the training eventually are measured when McDonald's conducts a restaurant operations improvement process study, or ROIP. The goal is simple: improved operations. When the ROIP review is completed, statistical analyses are performed and managers are given their results. Depending on the results, decisions might be made that require additional financial resources, building construction, staff training, or reconfiguring layouts. Yet one thing is clear: Statistics drive the decisions behind McDonald's drive-through service operations.

Discussion Questions:

1. After returning from the training session at Hamburger University, a McDonald's store owner selected a random sample of 362 drive-thru customers and carefully measured the time it took from when a customer entered the McDonald's property until the customer received the order at the drive-thru window. These data are in the file called **McDonald's Drive-Thru Waiting Times**. Note, the owner selected some customers during the breakfast period, others during lunch, and others during dinner. Construct any appropriate graphs and charts that will effectively display these drive-thru data. Prepare a short discussion indicating the conclusions that this store owner might reach after reviewing the graphs and charts you have prepared.

2. Referring to question 1, suppose the manager comes away with the conclusion that his store is not meeting the 90-second customer service goal. As a result, he plans to dig deeper into the problem by collecting more data from the drive-thru process. Discuss what other measures you would suggest the manager collect. Discuss how these data could be of potential value in helping the store owner understand his problem.

3. Visit a local McDonald's that has a drive-thru facility. Randomly sample 20 drive-thru customers and collect the following data:

a. the total time from arrival on the property to departure from the drive-thru window

b. the time from when customers place the order until they receive their order and exit the drive-thru process

c. the number of cars in the line when the sampled vehicle enters the drive-thru process

d. Using the data that you have collected, construct appropriate graphs and charts to describe these data. Write a short report discussing the data

Case 2.1

Server Downtime

After getting outstanding grades in high school and scoring very high on his ACT and SAT tests, Clayton Haney had his choice of colleges but wanted to follow his parents' legacy and enrolled at Northwestern University. Clayton soon learned that there is a big difference between getting high grades in high school and being a good student. Although he was recognized as being quite bright and very quick to pick up on things, he had never learned how to study. As a result, after slightly more than two years at Northwestern, Clayton was asked to try his luck at another university. To the chagrin of his parents, Clayton decided that college was not for him.

After short stints working for a computer manufacturer and as a manager for a Blockbuster video store, Clayton landed a job working for EDS. EDS contracts to support information technology implementation and application for companies in the United States and throughout the world. Clayton had to train himself in virtually all aspects of personal computers and local area networks and was assigned to work for a client in the Chicago area.

Clayton's first assignment was to research the downtime on one of the client's primary network servers. He was asked to study the downtime data for the month of April and to make a short presentation to the company's management. The downtime data are in a file called **Server Downtime**. These data are also shown in Table C-2.1-A. Although Clayton is very good at solving computer problems, he has had no training or experience in analyzing data, so he is going to need some help.

Required Tasks:

1. Construct a frequency distribution showing the number of times during the month that the server was down for each downtime cause category.
2. Develop a bar chart that displays the data from the frequency distribution in part a.
3. Develop a histogram that displays the downtime data.

TABLE C-2.1-A

Date	Problem Experienced	Downtime Minutes
04/01	Lockups	25
04/02	Lockups	35
04/05	Memory Errors	10
04/07	Lockups	40
04/09	Weekly Virus Scan	60
04/09	Lockups	30
04/09	Memory Errors	35
04/09	Memory Errors	20
04/12	Slow Startup	45
04/12	Weekly Virus Scan	60
04/13	Memory Errors	30
04/14	Memory Errors	10
04/19	Manual Re-start	20
04/20	Memory Errors	35
04/20	Weekly Virus Scan	60
04/20	Lockups	25
04/21	Memory Errors	35
04/22	Memory Errors	20
04/27	Memory Errors	40
04/28	Weekly Virus Scan	60
04/28	Memory Errors	15
04/28	Lockups	25

4. Develop a pie chart that breaks down the percentage of total downtime that is attributed to each downtime cause during the month.
5. Prepare a short written report that discusses the downtime data. Make sure you include the graphs and charts in the report.

Case 2.2

Hudson Valley Apples, Inc.

As a rule, Stacey Fredrick preferred to work in the field rather than do "office" work in her capacity as a midlevel manager with Hudson Valley Apples, Inc., a large grower and processor of apples in the state of New York. However, after just leaving a staff meeting at which she was asked to prepare a report of apple consumption in the United States, Stacey was actually looking forward to spending some time at her computer "crunching some numbers." Arden Golchein, senior marketing manager, indicated that he would e-mail her a data file that contained apple consumption data from 1970 through 2009 and told her that he wanted a very nice report using graphs, charts, and tables to describe apple consumption.

When she got to her desk, the e-mail was waiting, and she saved the file under the name **Hudson Valley Apples**. Stacey had done quite a bit of descriptive analysis in her previous job with the New York State Department of Agriculture, so she had several

ideas for types of graphs and tables that she might construct. She began by creating a list of the tasks that she thought would be needed.

Required Tasks:

1. Construct a line chart showing the total annual availability of apples.
2. Construct one line chart that shows two things: the annual availability of fresh apples and the annual availability of processed apples.
3. Construct a line chart that shows the annual availability for each type of processed apples.
4. Construct a histogram for the total annual availability of apples.
5. Write a short report that discusses the historical pattern of apple availability. The report will include all pertinent charts and graphs.

Case 2.3

Welco Lumber Company—Part A

Gene Denning wears several hats at the Welco Lumber Company, including process improvement team leader, shipping manager, and assistant human resources manager. Welco Lumber makes cedar fencing materials at its Naples, Idaho, facility, employing about 160 people.

More than 75% of the cost of the finished cedar fence boards is in the cedar logs that the company buys on the open market. Therefore, it is very important that the company get as much finished product as possible from each log. One of the most important steps in the manufacturing process is referred to as the head rig. The head rig is a large saw that breaks down the logs into slabs and cants. Figure C-2.3-A shows the concept. From small logs with diameters of 12 inches or less, one cant and four or fewer usable slabs are obtained. From larger logs, multiple cants and four slabs are obtained. Finished fence boards can be produced from both the slabs and the cants.

At some companies, the head rig cutting operation is automated and the cuts are made based on a scanner system and computer algorithms. However, at Welco Lumber, the head rig is operated manually by operators who must look at a log as it arrives and determine how best to break the log down to get the most finished product. In addition, the operators are responsible for making sure that the cants are "centered" so that maximum product can be gained from them.

Recently, Gene Denning headed up a study in which he video-taped 365 logs being broken down by the head rig. All three operators, April, Sid, and Jim, were involved. Each log was marked as to its true diameter. Then Gene observed the way the log was broken

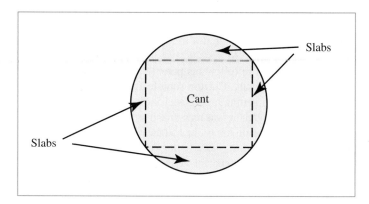

FIGURE C-2.3-A | Log Breakdown at the Head Rig

down and the degree to which the cants were properly centered. He then determined the projected value of the finished product from each log given the way it was actually cut. In addition, he also determined what the value would have been had the log been cut in the optimal way. Data for this study is in a file called **Welco Lumber**. A portion of the data is shown in Table C-2.3-A.

You have been asked to assist Gene by analyzing these data using graphs, charts, and tables as appropriate. He wishes to focus on the lost profit to the company and whether there are differences among the operators. Also, do the operators tend to do a better job on small logs than on large logs? In general, he is hoping to learn as much as possible from this study and needs your help with the analysis.

TABLE C-2.3-A | Head Rig Data—Welco Lumber Company

5-Nov-06	Through	21-Nov-06 Head Rig Log Study			Baseline			
Log #	Operator	Log Size	Large/Small Log	Correct Cut (Yes or No)	Error Category	Actual Value	Potential Value	Potential Gain
1	Sid	15	Large	No	Excessive Log Breakdown	$59.00	$65.97	$6.97
2	Sid	17	Large	No	Excessive Log Breakdown	$79.27	$85.33	$6.06
3	Sid	11	Small	Yes	No Error	$35.40	$35.40	$0.00
4	Sid	11	Small	No	Off Center Cant	$31.61	$35.40	$3.79
5	Sid	14	Large	No	Reduced Value Cut	$47.67	$58.86	$11.19
6	Sid	17	Large	Yes	No Error	$85.33	$85.33	$0.00
7	Sid	8	Small	Yes	No Error	$16.22	$16.22	$0.00
8	Sid	11	Small	Yes	No Error	$35.40	$35.40	$0.00
9	Sid	9	Small	Yes	No Error	$21.54	$21.54	$0.00
10	Sid	9	Small	No	Off Center Cant	$18.92	$21.54	$2.62
11	Sid	10	Small	Yes	No Error	$21.54	$21.54	$0.00
12	Sid	8	Small	Yes	No Error	$16.22	$16.22	$0.00
13	Sid	10	Small	No	Off Center Cant	$25.71	$28.97	$3.26
14	Sid	12	Small	Yes	No Error	$41.79	$41.79	$0.00
15	Sid	11	Small	Yes	No Error	$35.40	$35.40	$0.00

- **Review** the definitions for nominal, ordinal, interval, and ratio data in Section 1.4.
- **Examine** the statistical software, such as Excel used during this course to identify

the tools for computing descriptive measures. For instance, in Excel, look at the function wizard and the descriptive statistics tools on the Data tab under Data Analysis.

- **Review** the material on frequency histograms in Section 2.1, paying special attention to how histograms help determine where the data are centered and how the data are spread around the center.

Describing Data Using Numerical Measures

3.1 Measures of Center and Location (pg. 81–102) ⟵

Outcome 1. Compute the mean, median, mode, and weighted mean for a set of data and understand what these values represent.

Outcome 2. Construct a box and whisker graph and interpret it.

3.2 Measures of Variation (pg. 102–113) ⟵

Outcome 3. Compute the range, interquartile range, variance, and standard deviation and know what these values mean.

3.3 Using the Mean and Standard Deviation Together (pg. 113–122) ⟵

Outcome 4. Compute a z score and the coefficient of variation and understand how they are applied in decision-making situations.

Outcome 5. Understand the Empirical Rule and Tchebysheff's Theorem

Why you need to know

Suppose you are the advertising manager for a major airline and you want to develop an ad campaign touting how much cheaper your fares are than the competition's. You must be careful that your claims are valid. First, the Federal Trade Commission (FTC) is charged with regulating advertising and requires that advertising be truthful. Second, customers who can show that they were misled by an incorrect claim about prices could sue your company. You need to use statistical procedures to determine the validity of any claim you might want to make about your prices. Graphs and charts provide effective tools for transforming data into information; however, they are only a starting point. Graphs and charts do not reveal all the information contained in a set of data. To make your descriptive toolkit complete, you need to become familiar with key descriptive measures that are widely used in fully describing data.

You might start by sampling travel routes from your company and from the competition. You could then determine the price of a round-trip flight for each route for your airline and your competitors. You might graph the data for each company as a histogram, but a clear comparison using only this graph might be difficult. Instead, you could compute the summary flight price measures for the various airlines and show these values side by side, perhaps in a bar chart. Thus, to effectively describe data, you will need to combine the graphical tools discussed in Chapter 2 with the numerical measures introduced in this chapter.

3.1 Measures of Center and Location

You learned in Chapter 2 that frequency histograms are an effective way of converting quantitative data into useful information. The histogram provides a visual indication of where data are centered and how much spread

Okea/Fotolia LLC

there is in the data around the center. However, to fully describe a quantitative variable, we also need to compute measures of its center and spread. These measures can then be coupled with the histogram to give a clear picture of the variable's distribution. This section focuses on measures of the center of data. Section 3.2 introduces measures of the spread of data.

Parameters and Statistics

Depending on whether we are working with a population or a sample, a numerical measure is known as either a **parameter** or a **statistic**.

Population Mean

There are three important measures of the center of a set of data. The first of these is the **mean**, or average, of the data. To find the mean, we sum the values and divide the sum by the number of data values, as shown in Equation 3.1.

Parameter

A measure computed from the entire population. As long as the population does not change, the value of the parameter will not change.

Statistic

A measure computed from a sample that has been selected from a population. The value of the statistic will depend on which sample is selected.

Mean

A numerical measure of the center of a set of quantitative measures computed by dividing the sum of the values by the number of values in the data.

Population Mean

$$\mu = \frac{\sum_{i=1}^{N} x_i}{N}$$ (3.1)

where:

μ = Population mean (mu)
N = Population size
x_i = ith individual value of variable x

Population Mean

The average for all values in the population computed by dividing the sum of all values by the population size.

The **population mean** is represented by the Greek symbol μ, pronounced "mu." The formal notation in the numerator for the sum of the x values reads

$$\sum_{i=1}^{N} x_i \rightarrow \text{Sum all } x_i \text{ values where } i \text{ goes from } 1 \text{ to } N$$

In other words, we are summing all N values in the population.

Because you almost always sum all the data values, to simplify notation in this text, we generally will drop the subscripts after the first time we introduce a formula. Thus, the formula for the population mean will be written as

$$\mu = \frac{\sum x}{N}$$

Chapter Outcome 1. → **BUSINESS APPLICATION**   **POPULATION MEAN**

FOSTER CITY HOTEL The manager of a small hotel in Foster City, California, was asked by the corporate vice president to analyze the Sunday night registration information for the past eight weeks. Data on three variables were collected:

x_1 = Total number of rooms rented

x_2 = Total dollar revenue from the room rentals

x_3 = Number of customer complaints that came from guests each Sunday

These data are shown in Table 3.1. They are a population because they include all data that interest the vice president.

Figure 3.1 shows the frequency histogram for the number of rooms rented. If the manager wants to describe the data further, she can locate the center of the data by finding the balance point for the histogram. Think of the horizontal axis as a plank and the histogram bars as weights proportional to their area. The center of the data would be the point at which the plank would balance. As shown in Figure 3.1, the balance point seems to be about 15 rooms.

TABLE 3.1 | **Foster City Hotel Data**

Week	Rooms Rented	Revenue	Complaints
1	22	$1,870	0
2	13	$1,590	2
3	10	$1,760	1
4	16	$2,345	0
5	23	$4,563	2
6	13	$1,630	1
7	11	$2,156	0
8	13	$1,756	0

Eyeing the histogram might yield a reasonable approximation of the center. However, computing a numerical measure of the center directly from the data is preferable. The most frequently used measure of the center is the mean. The population mean for number of rooms rented is computed using Equation 3.1 as follows:

$$\mu = \frac{\Sigma x}{N} = \frac{22 + 13 + 10 + 16 + 23 + 13 + 11 + 13}{8}$$

$$= \frac{121}{8}$$

$$\mu = 15.125$$

Thus, the average number of rooms rented on Sunday for the past eight weeks is 15.125. This is the true balance point for the data. Take a look at Table 3.2, where we calculate what is called a *deviation* $(x_i - \mu)$ by subtracting the mean from each value, x_i.

FIGURE 3.1

Balance Point, Rooms Rented at Foster City Hotel

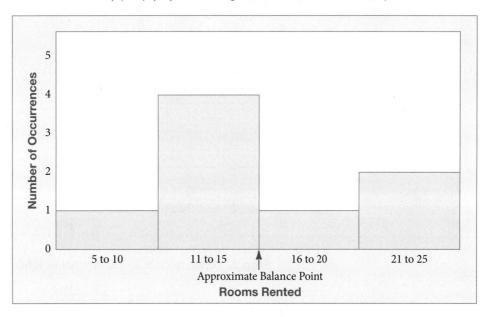

TABLE 3.2 | **Centering Concept of the Mean Using Hotel Data**

x	(x−μ) = Deviation
22	22 − 15.125 = 6.875
13	13 − 15.125 = −2.125
10	10 − 15.125 = −5.125
16	16 − 15.125 = 0.875
23	23 − 15.125 = 7.875
13	13 − 15.125 = −2.125
11	11 − 15.125 = −4.125
13	13 − 15.125 = −2.125
	$\Sigma (x-\mu) =$ 0.000 ← Sum of deviations equals zero.

Note that the sum of the deviations of the data from the mean is zero. This is not a coincidence. *For any set of data, the sum of the deviations around the mean will be zero.*

How to do it (Example 3-1)

Computing the Population Mean

When the available data constitute the population of interest, the population mean is computed using the following steps:

1. Collect the data for the variable of interest for all items in the population. The data must be quantitative.

2. Sum all values in the population (Σx_i).

3. Divide the sum (Σx_i). by the number of values (N) in the population to get the population mean. The formula for the population mean is

$$\mu = \frac{\Sigma x}{N}$$

EXAMPLE 3-1 **COMPUTING THE POPULATION MEAN**

Bruce Leibowitz/Shutterstock

United Airlines As the airline industry becomes increasingly competitive, in an effort to increase profits, many airlines are reducing flights. Therefore the supply of idled airplanes has increased. United Airlines, headquartered in Chicago, has decided to expand its fleet. Suppose United selects additional planes from a list of 17 possible planes, including such models as the Boeing 747-400, the Air Bus 300-B4, and the DC 9-10. At a recent meeting, the chief operating officer asked a member of his staff to determine the mean fuel consumption rate per hour of operation for the population of 17 planes.

Step 1 Collect data for the quantitative variable of interest.

The staff member was able to determine, for each of the 17 planes, the hourly fuel consumption in gallons for a flight between Chicago and New York City. These data are recorded as follows:

Airplane	Fuel Consumption (gal/hr)
B747-400	3,529
L-1011-100/200	2,215
DC-10-10	2,174
A300-B4	1,482
A310-300	1,574
B767-300	1,503
B767-200	1,377
B757-200	985
B727-200	1,249
MD-80	882
B737-300	732
DC-9-50	848
B727-100	806
B737-100/200	1,104
F-100	631
DC-9-30-11	804
DC-9-10	764

Step 2 Add the data values.

$$\Sigma x = 3,529 + 2,215 + 2,174 + \cdots + 764 = 22,659$$

Step 3 Divide the sum by the number of values in the population using Equation 3.1.

$$\mu = \frac{\Sigma x}{N} = \frac{22,659}{17} = 1,332.9$$

The mean number of gallons of fuel consumed per hour on these 17 planes is 1,332.9.

>> **END EXAMPLE**

BUSINESS APPLICATION **POPULATION MEAN**

FOSTER CITY HOTEL (*CONTINUED*) In addition to collecting data on the number of rooms rented on Sunday nights, the Foster City Hotel manager also collected data on the room-rental revenue generated and the number of complaints on Sunday nights. Excel can quite easily be used to calculate numerical measures such as the mean. Because these data are the population of all nights of interest to the hotel manager, she can compute the population mean,

Excel 2010 Instructions:
1. Open file: **Foster.xlsx**.
2. Select the **Data** tab.
3. Click on **Data Analysis
   > Descriptive Statistics**.
4. Define data range for
   the desired variables.
5. Check **Summary
   Statistics**.
6. Name new Output Sheet.
7. On **Home** tab, adjust
   decimal places as
   desired.

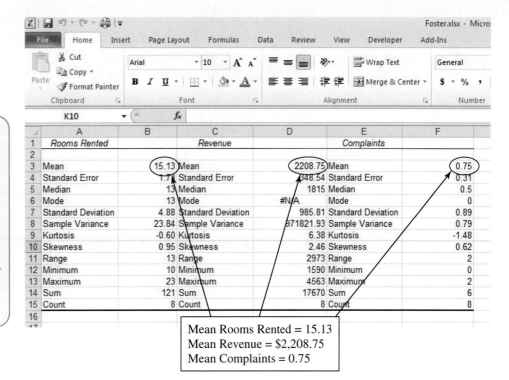

Mean Rooms Rented = 15.13
Mean Revenue = $2,208.75
Mean Complaints = 0.75

Minitab Instructions (for similar results):
1. Open file: **Foster.MTW**.
2. Choose **Stat > Basic Statistics > Display
   Descriptive Statistics**.
3. In **Variables**, enter columns *Rooms
   Rented, Revenue,* and *Complaints*.
4. Click **Statistics**.
5. Check required statistics.
6. Click **OK. OK.**

μ, revenue per night. The population mean is $\mu = \$2,208.75$, as shown in the Excel output in Figure 3.2. Likewise, the mean number of complaints is $\mu = 0.75$ per night. (Note, there are other measures shown in the figures. We will discuss several of these later in the chapter.)

Now, for these eight Sunday nights, the manager can report to the corporate vice president that the mean number of rooms rented is 15.13. This level of business generated a mean nightly revenue of $2,208.75. The number of complaints averaged 0.75 (less than 1) per night. These values are the true means for the population and are, therefore, called parameters.

Chapter Outcome 1. ➞ ## Sample Mean

The data for the Foster City Hotel constituted the population of interest. Thus, $\mu = 15.13$ rooms rented is the parameter measure. However, if the data constitute a sample rather than a population, the mean for the sample (**sample mean**) is computed using Equation 3.2.

Sample Mean
The average for all values in the sample computed by dividing the sum of all sample values by the sample size.

Sample Mean

$$\bar{x} = \frac{\sum_{i=1}^{n} x_i}{n} \tag{3.2}$$

where:

$\bar{x}$ = Sample mean (pronounced "x-bar")
n = Sample size

Notice, Equation 3.2 is the same as Equation 3.1 *except* that we sum the sample values, not the population values, and divide by the sample size, not the population size.

The notation for the sample mean is $\bar{x}$. Sample descriptors (statistics) are usually assigned a Roman character. (Recall that population values usually are assigned a Greek character.)

EXAMPLE 3-2   COMPUTING A SAMPLE MEAN

Professor Salaries A newspaper reporter in Wisconsin collected a sample of seven university professors and determined their annual salaries. As part of her story, she wished to be able to report the mean salary. The following steps are used to calculate the sample mean salaries for professors in Wisconsin.

Step 1 Collect the sample data.

$$\{x_i\} = \{\text{Professor Salaries}\} = \{\$144,000; \$98,000; \$204,000;$$
$$\$177,000; \$155,000; \$316,000; \$100,000\}$$

Step 2 Add the values in the sample.

$$\Sigma x = \$144,000 + \$98,000 + \$204,000 + \$177,000 + \$155,000$$
$$+ \$316,000 + \$100,000 = \$1,194,000$$

Step 3 Divide the sum by the sample size (Equation 3.2).

$$\bar{x} = \frac{\Sigma x}{n} = \frac{\$1,194,000}{7} = \$170,571.43$$

Therefore, the mean salary for the sample of seven professors is $170,571.43.

>> END EXAMPLE

The Impact of Extreme Values on the Mean

The mean (population or sample) is the balance point for data, so using the mean as a measure of the center generally makes sense. However, the mean does have a potential disadvantage: *The mean can be affected by extreme values.* There are many instances in business when this may occur. For example, in a population or sample of income data, there likely will be extremes on the high end that will pull the mean upward from the center. Example 3-3 illustrates how an extreme value can affect the mean. In these situations, a second measure called the *median* may be more appropriate.

EXAMPLE 3-3   IMPACT OF EXTREME VALUES

Professor Salaries Suppose the sample of professor salaries (see Example 3-2) had been slightly different. If the salary recorded as $316,000 had actually been $1,000,000 (must also be the college's football coach!), how would the mean be affected? We can see the impact as follows:

Step 1 Collect the sample data.

$$\{x_i\} = \{\text{Professor Salaries}\} = \{\$144,000; \$98,000; \$204,000;$$
$$\$177,000; \$155,000; \$1,000,000; \$100,000\}$$

extreme value

Step 2 Add the values.

$$\Sigma x = \$144,000 + 98,000 + 204,000 + 177,000 + 155,000 + 1,000,000 + 100,000$$
$$= \$1,878,000$$

Step 3 Divide the sum by the number of values in the sample.

$$\bar{x} = \frac{\Sigma x}{n} = \frac{\$1,878,000}{7} = \$268,285.71$$

Recall, in Example 3-2, the sample mean was $170,571.43.

With only one value in the sample changed, the mean is now substantially higher than before. Because the mean is affected by extreme values, it may be a misleading measure of the data's center. In this case, the mean is larger than all but one of the starting salaries.

>> **END EXAMPLE**

TRY PROBLEM 3-15 (pg. 100)

Chapter Outcome 1. → # Median

Median

The median is a center value that divides a data array into two halves. We use $\tilde{u}$ to denote the population median and M_d to denote the sample median.

Data Array

Data that have been arranged in numerical order.

Another measure of the center is called the **median**.

The median is found by first arranging data in numerical order from smallest to largest. Data that are sorted in order are referred to as a **data array**.

Equation 3.3 is used to find the index point corresponding to the median value for a set of data placed in numerical order from low to high.

Median Index

$$i = \frac{1}{2}n \qquad\qquad (3.3)$$

where:

i = The index of the point in the data array corresponding to the median value
n = Sample size

If i is not an integer, round its value up to the next highest integer. This next highest integer then is the position of the median in the data array.

If i is an integer, the median is the average of the values in position i and position $i + 1$.

For instance, suppose a personnel manager has hired 10 new employees. The ages of each of these employees sorted from low to high is listed as follows:

23   25   25   34   35   45   46   47   52   54

Using Equation 3.3 to find the median index, we get

$$i = \frac{1}{2}n = \frac{1}{2}(10) = 5$$

Since the index is an integer, the median value will be the average of the 5th and 6th values in the data set. Thus, the median is

$$M_d = \frac{35 + 45}{2} = 40$$

Consider another case in which customers at a restaurant are asked to rate the service they received on a scale of 1 to 100. A total of 15 customers were asked to provide the ratings. The data, sorted from low to high, are presented as follows:

60   68   75   77   80   80   80   85   88   90   95   95   95   95   99

Using Equation 3.3, we get the median index:

$$i = \frac{1}{2}n = \frac{1}{2}(15) = 7.5$$

Since the index is not an integer, we round 7.5 up to 8. Thus, the median (M_d) is the 8th data value from either end. In this case,

$$M_d = 85$$

EXAMPLE 3-4   **COMPUTING THE MEDIAN**

Professor Salaries Consider again the example involving the news reporter in Wisconsin and the sample salary data in Example 3-2. The median for these data is computed using the following steps:

Step 1 **Collect the sample data.**

$$\{x_i\} = \{ \text{Professor Salaries} \} = \{ \$144{,}000; \$98{,}000; \$204{,}000; \$177{,}000; \\ \$155{,}000; \$316{,}000; \$100{,}000 \}$$

Step 2 **Sort the data from smallest to largest, forming a data array.**

$$\{x_i\} = \{ \$98{,}000; \$100{,}000; \$144{,}000; \$155{,}000; \$177{,}000; \$204{,}000; \$316{,}000 \}$$

Step 3 **Calculate the median index.**
Using Equation 3.3, we get $i = \frac{1}{2}(7) = 3.5$. Rounding up, the median is the fourth value from either end of the data array.

Step 4 **Find the median.**

$$\{x_i\} = \{ \$98{,}000; \$100{,}000; \$144{,}000; \$155{,}000; \$177{,}000; \$204{,}000; \$316{,}000 \}$$

fourth value $= M_d$

The median salary is $155,000. The notation for the sample median is M_d.

Note, if the number of data values in a sample or population is an even number, the median is the average of the two middle values.

>> **END EXAMPLE**

TRY PROBLEM 3-2 (pg. 98)

Symmetric Data

Data sets whose values are evenly spread around the center. For symmetric data, the mean and median are equal.

Skewed Data

Data sets that are not symmetric. For skewed data, the mean will be larger or smaller than the median.

Right-Skewed Data

A data distribution is right skewed if the mean for the data is larger than the median.

Left-Skewed Data

A data distribution is left skewed if the mean for the data is smaller than the median.

Skewed and Symmetric Distributions

Data in a population or sample can be either **symmetric** or **skewed**, depending on how the data are distributed around the center.

In the original professor salary example (Example 3-2), the mean for the sample of seven managers was $170,571.43. In Example 3-4, the median salary was $155,000. Thus, for these data the mean and the median are not equal. This sample data set is **right skewed**, because $\bar{x} = \$170{,}571.43 > M_d = \$155{,}000$.

Figure 3.3 illustrates examples of right-skewed, **left-skewed**, and symmetric distributions. The greater the difference between the mean and the median, the more skewed the distribution. *Example 3-5 shows that an advantage of the median over the mean is that the median is not affected by extreme values.* Thus, the median is particularly useful as a measure of the center when the data are highly skewed.[1]

FIGURE 3.3

Skewed and Symmetric Distributions

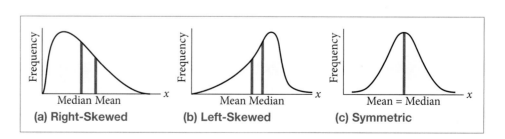

(a) Right-Skewed   (b) Left-Skewed   (c) Symmetric

---

[1]Excel can be used to calculate a skewness statistic. The sign on the skewness statistic implies the direction of skewness. The higher the absolute value, the more the data are skewed.

| **EXAMPLE 3-5** | **IMPACT OF EXTREME VALUES ON THE MEDIAN** |

Professor Salaries (*Continued*) In Example 3-3, when we substituted a $1,000,000 salary for the professor who had a salary of $316,000, the sample mean salary increased from $170,571.43 to $268,285.71. What will happen to the median? The median is determined using the following steps:

Step 1 Collect the sample data.

The sample salary data (including the extremely high salary) are

$$\{x_i\} = \{\text{Professor Salary}\} = \{\$144,000; \$98,000; \$204,000; \$177,000;$$
$$\$155,000; \$1,000,000; \$100,000\}$$

Step 2 Sort the data from smallest to largest, forming a data array.

$$\{x_i\} = \{\$98,000; \$100,000; \$144,000; \$155,000; \$177,000; \$204,000; \$1,000,000\}$$

Step 3 Calculate the median index.

Using Equation 3.3, we get $i = \frac{1}{2}(7) = 3.5$. Rounding up, the median is the fourth value from either end of the data array.

Step 4 Find the median.

$$\{x_i\} = \{\$98,000; \$100,000; \$144,000; \$155,000; \$177,000; \$204,000; \$1,000,000\}$$

$$\text{fourth value} = M_d$$

The median professor salary is $155,000, the same value as in Example 3-4, when the high salary was not included in the data. Thus, the median is not affected by the extreme values in the data.

>> **END EXAMPLE**

TRY PROBLEM 3-2 (pg. 98)

Chapter Outcome 1. → ## Mode

Mode

The mode is the value in a data set that occurs most frequently.

The mean is the most commonly used measure of central location, followed closely by the median. However, the **mode** is another measure that is occasionally used as a measure of central location.

A data set may have more than one mode if two or more values tie for the most frequently occurring value. Example 3-6 illustrates this concept and shows how the mode is determined.

| **EXAMPLE 3-6** | **DETERMINING THE MODE** |

Beth Van Trees/Shutterstock

Smoky Mountain Pizza The owners of Smoky Mountain Pizza are planning to expand their restaurant to include an open-air patio. Before finalizing the design, the managers want to know what the most frequently occurring group size is so they can organize the seating arrangements to best meet demand. They wish to know the mode, which can be calculated using the following steps:

Step 1 Collect the sample data.

A sample of 20 groups was selected at random. These data are

$$\{x_i\} = \{\text{people}\} = \{2, 4, 1, 2, 3, 2, 4, 2, 3, 6, 8, 4, 2, 1, 7, 4, 2, 4, 4, 3\}$$

Step 2 Organize the data into a frequency distribution.

x_i	Frequency
1	2
2	6
3	3
4	6

x_i	Frequency
5	0
6	1
7	1
8	1
	Total = 20

Step 3 Determine the value(s) that occurs (occur) most frequently.
In this case, there are two modes, because the values 2 and 4 each occurred six times. Thus the modes are 2 and 4.

>> **END EXAMPLE**

TRY PROBLEM 3-2 (pg. 98)

A common mistake is to state the mode as being the frequency of the most frequently occurring value. In Example 3-6, you might be tempted to say that the mode = 6 because that was the highest frequency. Instead, there were two modes, 2 and 4, each of which occurred six times.

If no value occurs more frequently than any other, the data set is said to not have a mode. The mode might be particularly useful in describing the central location value for clothes sizes. For example, shoes come in full and half sizes. Consider the following sample data that have been sorted from low to high:

$$\{x\} = \{7.5, 8.0, 8.5, 9.0, 9.0, 10.0, 10.0, 10.0, 10.5, 10.5, 11.0, 11.5\}$$

The mean for these sample data is

$$\bar{x} = \frac{\sum x}{n} = \frac{7.5 + 8.0 + \cdots + 11.5}{12} = \frac{115.50}{12} = 9.63$$

Although 9.63 is the numerical average, the mode is 10, because more people wore that size shoe than any other. In making purchasing decisions, a shoe store manager would order more shoes at the modal size than at any other size. The mean isn't of any particular use in her purchasing decision.

Applying the Measures of Central Tendency

Excel

tutorials

Excel Tutorial

The cost of tuition is an important factor that most students and their families consider when deciding where to attend college. The data file **Colleges and Universities** contains data for a sample of 718 colleges and universities in the United States. The cost of out-of-state tuition is one of the variables in the data file. Suppose a guidance counselor who will be advising students about college choices wishes to conduct a descriptive analysis for this quantitative variable.

Figure 3.4 shows a frequency histogram generated using Excel. This histogram is a good place to begin the descriptive analysis since it allows the analyst to get a good indication of the center value, the spread around the center, and the general shape of the distribution of out-of-state tuition for these colleges and universities. Given that the file contains 718 colleges and universities, using the $2^k \geq n$ rule introduced in Chapter 2, the guidance counselor used $k = 10$ classes. The least expensive school in the file is CUNY–Medgar Evers College in New York at \$2,600 and the most expensive is Franklin and Marshall in Pennsylvania at \$24,940. Based on this histogram in Figure 3.4, what would you conclude about the distribution of college tuition? Is it skewed right or left?

The analysis can be extended by computing appropriate descriptive measures for the out-of-state tuition variable. Specifically, we want to look at measures of central location. Figure 3.5 shows the Excel output with descriptive measures for out-of-state tuition. First, focus on the primary measures of central location: mean and median. These are

Mean = \$9,933.38   Median = \$9,433

These statistics provide measures of the center of the out-of-state tuition variable. The mean tuition value was \$9,933.38, whereas the median was \$9,433. Because the mean exceeds the

FIGURE 3.4

Excel 2010 Frequency Histogram of College Tuition Prices

Excel 2010 Instructions:

1. Open file **Colleges and Universities.xlsx**.
2. Set up an area in the worksheet for the bins (upper limit of each class) as 4750, 7000, etc. Be sure to label the column of upper limits as "Bins."
3. On the **Data** tab, click **Data Analysis > Histogram**.
4. Input Range specifies the actual data values as the *out-of-state tuition*.
5. Put on a new worksheet and include **Chart Output**.
6. Right click on the bars and use the **Format Data Series Options** to set gap width to zero and add lines to bars.
7. Convert the bins in column A of the histogram output sheet to actual class labels. Note the bin labeled 4750 is changed to "under $4,750."
8. Click on **Layout** and set titles as desired.

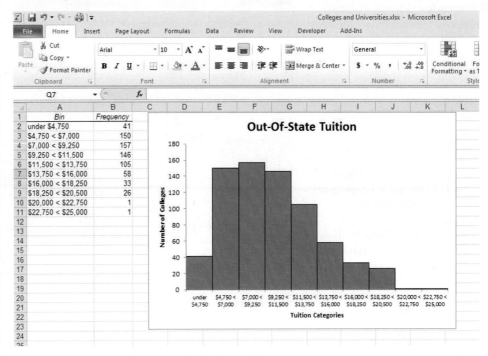

Minitab Instructions (for similar results):

1. Open file: **Colleges and Universities.MTW**.
2. Choose **Graph > Histogram**.
3. Click **Simple**.
4. Click **OK**.
5. In **Graph variables**, enter data column *out-of-state tuition*.
6. Click **OK**.

median, we conclude that the data are right skewed—the same conclusion you should have reached by looking at the histogram in Figure 3.4.

Issues with Excel In many instances, data files will have "missing values." That is, the values for one or more variables may not be available for some of the observations. The data may have been lost, or they were not measured when the data were collected. Many times when you receive data like this, the missing values will be coded in a special way. For example, the code "N/A" might be used or a "−99" might be entered to signify that the datum for that observation is missing.

Statistical software packages typically have flexible procedures for dealing with missing data. *However, Excel does not contain a missing-value option.* If you attempt to use certain data analysis options in Excel, such as Descriptive Statistics, in the presence of nonnumeric ("N/A") data, you will get an error message. When that happens you must clear the missing values, generally by deleting all rows with missing values. In some instances, you can save the good data in the row by using **Edit-Clear-All** for the cell in question. However, a bigger problem exists when the missing value has been coded as an arbitrary numeric value (−99). In this case, unless you go into the data and clear these values, Excel will use the −99 values in the computations as if they are real values. The result will be incorrect calculations.

Also, if a data set contains more than one mode, Excel's Descriptive Statistics tool will only show the first mode in the list of modes and will not warn you that multiple modes exist. For instance, if you look at Figure 3.5, Excel has computed a mode = $6,550. If you examine these data, you will see that a tuition of $6,550 occurred 14 times. This is the most frequently occurring value. However, had other tuition values occurred 14 times too, Excel's Descriptive Statistics tool would not have so indicated. Excel 2010, does, however have a function MODE.MULT that will display multiple modes when they exist.

FIGURE 3.5

Excel 2010 Descriptive
Statistics for College Tuition
Data

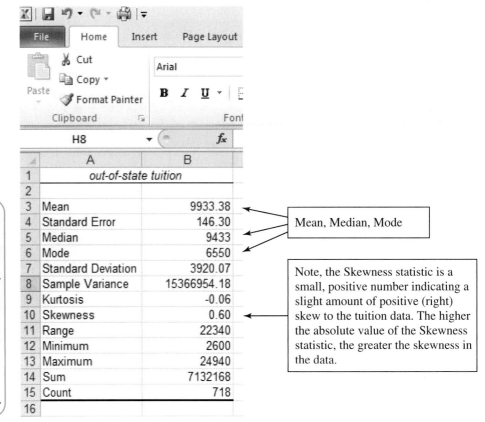

Excel 2010 Instructions:
1. Open file: **Colleges and Universities.xlsx**.
2. Select the **Data** tab.
3. Click on **Data Analysis > Descriptive Statistics**.
4. Define data range for the desired variables.
5. Check **Summary Statistics**.
6. Name new Output Sheet.
7. On **Home** tab, adjust decimal places as desired.

	out-of-state tuition
Mean	9933.38
Standard Error	146.30
Median	9433
Mode	6550
Standard Deviation	3920.07
Sample Variance	15366954.18
Kurtosis	-0.06
Skewness	0.60
Range	22340
Minimum	2600
Maximum	24940
Sum	7132168
Count	718

Mean, Median, Mode

Note, the Skewness statistic is a small, positive number indicating a slight amount of positive (right) skew to the tuition data. The higher the absolute value of the Skewness statistic, the greater the skewness in the data.

Minitab Instructions (for similar results):
1. Open file: **Colleges and Universities.MTW**.
2. Choose **Stat > Basic Statistics > Display Descriptive Statistics**.
3. In **Variables**, enter column *out-of-state tuition*.
4. Click **Statistics**.
5. Check required statistics.
6. Click **OK. OK**.

Chapter Outcome 1. → # Other Measures of Location

Weighted Mean   The arithmetic mean is the most frequently used measure of central location. Equations 3.1 and 3.2 are used when you have either a population or a sample. For instance, the sample mean is computed using

$$\bar{x} = \frac{\sum x}{n} = \frac{x_1 + x_2 + x_3 + \cdots + x_n}{n}$$

In this case, each x value is given an equal weight in the computation of the mean. However, in some applications there is reason to weight the data values differently. In those cases, we need to compute a **weighted mean**.

Equations 3.4 and 3.5 are used to find the weighted mean (or weighted average) for a population and for a sample, respectively.

Weighted Mean

The mean value of data values that have been weighted according to their relative importance.

Weighted Mean for a Population

$$\mu_w = \frac{\sum w_i x_i}{\sum w_i}$$

(3.4)

> **Weighted Mean for a Sample**
>
> $$\bar{x}_w = \frac{\sum w_i x_i}{\sum w_i}$$ (3.5)
>
> where:
>
> w_i = The weight of the ith data value
> x_i = The ith data value

EXAMPLE 3-7   CALCULATING A WEIGHTED POPULATION MEAN

Myers & Associates Recently, the law firm of Myers & Associates was involved in litigating a discrimination suit concerning ski instructors at a ski resort in Colorado. One ski instructor from Germany had sued the operator of the ski resort, claiming he had not received equitable pay compared with the other ski instructors from Norway and the United States. In preparing a defense, the Myers attorneys planned to compute the mean annual income for all seven Norwegian ski instructors at the resort. However, because these instructors worked different numbers of days during the ski season, a weighted mean needed to be computed. This was done using the following steps:

Step 1 **Collect the desired data and determine the weight to be assigned to each data value.**

In this case, the variable of interest was the income of the ski instructors. The population consisted of seven Norwegian instructors. The weights were the number of days that the instructors worked. The following data and weights were determined:

x_i = Income:	$7,600	$3,900	$5,300	$4,000	$7,200	$2,300	$5,100
w_i = Days:	50	30	40	25	60	15	50

Step 2 **Multiply each weight by the data value and sum these.**

$$\sum w_i x_i = (50)(\$7,600) + (30)(\$3,900) + \cdots + (50)(\$5,100) = \$1,530,500$$

Step 3 **Sum the weights for all values (the weights are the days).**

$$\sum w_i = 50 + 30 + 40 + 25 + 60 + 15 + 50 = 270$$

Step 4 **Compute the weighted mean.**

Divide the weighted sum by the sum of the weights. Because we are working with the population, the result will be the population weighted mean.

$$\mu_W = \frac{\sum w_i x_i}{\sum w_i} = \frac{\$1,530,500}{270} = \$5,668.52$$

Thus, taking into account the number of days worked, the Norwegian ski instructors had a mean income of $5,668.52.

>> **END EXAMPLE**

TRY PROBLEM 3-8 (pg. 99)

One weighted-mean example that you are probably very familiar with is your college grade point average (GPA). At most schools, A = 4 points, B = 3 points, and so forth. Each course has a certain number of credits (usually 1 to 5). The credits are the weights. Your GPA is computed by summing the product of points earned in a course and the credits for the course, and then dividing this sum by the total number of credits earned.

Percentiles
The pth percentile in a data array is a value that divides the data set into two parts. The lower segment contains at least $p\%$ and the upper segment contains at least $(100 - p)\%$ of the data. The 50th percentile is the median.

Percentiles In some applications, we might wish to describe the location of the data in terms other than the center of the data. For example, prior to enrolling at your university, you took the SAT or ACT test and received a **percentile** score in math and verbal skills.

If you received word that your standardized exam score was at the 90th percentile, it means that you scored as high as or higher than 90% of the other students who took the exam. The score at the 50th percentile would indicate that you were at the median, where at least 50% scored at or below and at least 50% scored at or above your score.[2]

To illustrate how to manually approximate a percentile value, consider a situation in which you have 309 customers enter a bank during the course of a day. The time (rounded to the nearest minute) that each customer spends in the bank is recorded. If we wish to approximate the 10th percentile, we would begin by first sorting the data in order from low to high, then assign each data value a location index from 1 to 309, and next determine the location index that corresponds to the 10th percentile using Equation 3.6.

Percentile Location Index

$$i = \frac{p}{100}(n)$$

(3.6)

where:

p = Desired percent

n = Number of values in the data set

If i is not an integer, round up to the next highest integer. The next integer greater than i corresponds to the position of the pth percentile in the data set.

If i is an integer, the pth percentile is the average of the values in position i and position $i + 1$.

Thus, the index value associated with the 10th percentile is

$$i = \frac{p}{100}(n) = \frac{10}{100}(309) = 30.90$$

Because $i = 30.90$ is not an integer, we round to the next highest integer, which is 31. The 10th percentile corresponds to the value in the 31st position from the low end of the sorted data.

How to do it (Example 3-8)

Calculating Percentiles

To calculate a specific percentile for a set of quantitative data, you can use the following steps:

1. Sort the data in order from the lowest to highest value.

2. Determine the percentile location index, i, using Equation 3.6.

$$i = \frac{p}{100}(n)$$

where

p = Desired percent

n = Number of values in the data set

3. If i is not an integer, then round to next highest integer. The pth percentile is located at the rounded index position. If i is an integer, the pth percentile is the average of the values at location index positions i and $i + 1$.

| EXAMPLE 3-8 | CALCULATING PERCENTILES |

Gilles Lougassi/Shutterstock

Henson Trucking The Henson Trucking Company is a small company in the business of moving people from one home to another within the Dallas, Texas, area. Historically, the owners have charged the customers on an hourly basis, regardless of the distance of the move within the Dallas city limits. However, they are now considering adding a surcharge for moves over a certain distance. They have decided to base this charge on the 80th percentile. They have a sample of travel-distance data for 30 moves. These data are as follows:

13.5	8.6	16.2	21.4	21.0	23.7	4.1	13.8	20.5	9.6
11.5	6.5	5.8	10.1	11.1	4.4	12.2	13.0	15.7	13.2
13.4	13.1	21.7	14.6	14.1	12.4	24.9	19.3	26.9	11.7

The 80th percentile can be computed using these steps.

Step 1 Sort the data from lowest to highest

4.1	4.4	5.8	6.5	8.6	9.6	10.1	11.1	11.5	11.7
12.2	12.4	13.0	13.1	13.2	13.4	13.5	13.8	14.1	14.6
15.7	16.2	19.3	20.5	21.0	21.4	21.7	23.7	24.9	26.9

---

[2]More rigorously, the percentile is that value (or set of values) such that at least $p\%$ of the data is as small or smaller than that value and at least $(100 - p)\%$ of the data is at least as large as that value. For introductory courses, a convention has been adopted to average the largest and smallest values that qualify as a certain percentile. This is why the median was defined as it was earlier for data sets with an even number of data values.

Step 2 Determine percentile location index, i, using Equation 3.6.
The 80th percentile location index is

$$i = \frac{p}{100}(n) = \frac{80}{100}(30) = 24$$

Step 3 Locate the appropriate percentile.
Because $i = 24$ is an integer value, the 80th percentile is found by averaging the values in the 24th and 25th positions. These are 20.5 and 21.0. Thus, the 80th percentile is $(20.5 + 21.0)/2 = 20.75$; therefore, any distance exceeding 20.75 miles will be subject to a surcharge.

>> **END EXAMPLE**

TRY PROBLEM 3-7 (pg. 99)

Quartiles

Quartiles in a data array are those values that divide the data set into four equal-sized groups. The median corresponds to the second quartile.

Quartiles Another location measure that can be used to describe data is **quartiles**.

The first quartile corresponds to the 25th percentile. That is, it is the value at or below which there is at least 25% (one quarter) of the data and at or above which there is at least 75% of the data. The third quartile is also the 75th percentile. It is the value at or below which there is at least 75% of the data and at or above which there is at least 25% of the data. The second quartile is the 50th percentile and is also the median.

A quartile value can be approximated manually using the same method as for percentiles using Equation 3.6. For the 309 bank customer-service times mentioned earlier, the location of the first-quartile (25th percentile) index is found, after sorting the data, as

$$i = \frac{p}{100}(n) = \frac{25}{100}(309) = 77.25$$

Because 77.25 is not an integer value, we round up to 78. The first quartile is the 78th value from the low end of the sorted data.

Issues with Excel The procedure that Excel uses to compute quartiles *is not standard*. Therefore, the quartile and percentile values from Excel will be slightly different from those we find manually using Equation 3-6. For example, referring to Example 3-8, when Excel is used to compute the 80th percentile for the moving distances, the value returned is 20.60 miles. This is slightly different from the 20.75 we found in Example 3-8. Equation 3-6 is generally accepted by statisticians to be correct. However, Excel will give reasonably close percentile and quartile values.

Chapter Outcome 2. ⟶ ## Box and Whisker Plots

Box and Whisker Plot

A graph that is composed of two parts: a box and the whiskers. The box has a width that ranges from the first quartile (Q_1) to the third quartile (Q_3). A vertical line through the box is placed at the median. Limits are located at a value that is 1.5 times the difference between Q_1 and Q_3 below Q_1 and above Q_3. The whiskers extend to the left to the lowest value within the limits and to the right to the highest value within the limits.

A descriptive tool that many decision makers like to use is called a **box and whisker plot** (or a box plot). The box and whisker plot incorporates the median and the quartiles to graphically display quantitative data. It is also used to identify *outliers* that are unusually small or large data values that lie mostly by themselves.

EXAMPLE 3-9   **CONSTRUCTING A BOX AND WHISKER PLOT**

Laura Gangi Pond/Shutterstock

Chevron Corporation A demand analyst for Chevron Corporation has recently performed a study at one of the company's stores in which he asked customers to set their trip odometer to zero when they filled up. Then, when the customers returned for their next fill-up, he recorded the miles that had been driven and wishes to construct a box and whisker plot as part of a presentation to describe the driving patterns of Chevron customers between fill-ups. The sorted sample data showing the miles between fill-ups is as follows:

231	236	241	242	242	243	243	243	248
248	249	250	251	251	252	252	254	255
255	256	256	257	259	260	260	260	260
262	262	264	265	265	265	266	268	268
270	276	277	277	280	286	300	324	345

How to do it (Example 3-9)

Constructing a Box and Whisker Plot

A box and whisker plot is a graphical summary of a quantitative variable. It is constructed using the following steps:

1. Sort the data values from low to high.

2. Use Equation 3.6 to find the 25th percentile (Q_1 = first quartile), the 50th percentile (Q_2 = median), and the 75th percentile (Q_3 = third quartile).

3. Draw a box so that the ends of the box are at Q_1 and Q_3. This box will contain the middle 50% of the data values in the population or sample.

4. Draw a vertical line through the box at the median. Half the data values in the box will be on either side of the median.

5. Calculate the *interquartile range* ($IQR = Q_3 - Q_1$). (The interquartile range will be discussed more fully in Section 3.2.) Compute the lower limit for the box and whisker plot as $Q_1 - 1.5(Q_3 - Q_1)$. The upper limit is $Q_3 + 1.5(Q_3 - Q_1)$. Any data values outside these limits are referred to as outliers.

6. Extend dashed lines (called the whiskers) from each end of the box to the lowest and highest value within the limits.

7. Any value outside the limits (outlier) found in step 5 is marked with an asterisk (*).

The box and whisker plot is computed using the following steps:

Step 1   Sort the data from low to high.

Step 2   Calculate the 25th percentile (Q_1), the 50th percentile (median), and the 75th percentile (Q_3).
The location index for Q_1 is

$$i = \frac{p}{100}(n) = \frac{25}{100}(45) = 11.25$$

Thus, Q_1 will be the 12th value, which is 250 miles.
The median location is

$$i = \frac{p}{100}(n) = \frac{50}{100}(45) = 22.5$$

In the sorted data, the median is the 23rd value, which is 259 miles. The third-quartile location is

$$i = \frac{p}{100}(n) = \frac{75}{100}(45) = 33.75$$

Thus, Q_3 is the 34th data value. This is 266 miles.

Step 3   Draw the box so the ends correspond to Q_1 and Q_3.

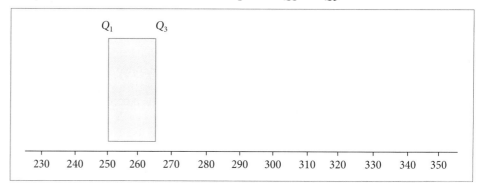

Step 4   Draw a vertical line through the box at the median.

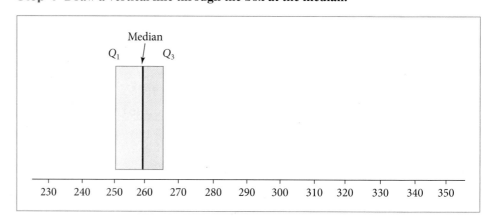

Step 5   Compute the upper and lower limits.
The lower limit is computed as $Q_1 - 1.5(Q_3 - Q_1)$. This is

$$\text{Lower Limit} = 250 - 1.5(266 - 250) = 226$$

The upper limit is $Q_3 + 1.5(Q_3 - Q_1)$. This is

$$\text{Upper Limit} = 266 + 1.5(266 - 250) = 290$$

Any value outside these limits is identified as an outlier.

Step 6 Draw the whiskers.
The whiskers are drawn to the smallest and largest values within the limits.

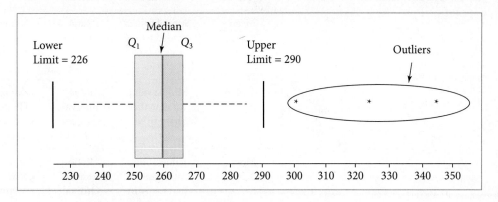

Step 7 Plot the outliers.
The outliers are plotted as values outside the limits.

>> **END EXAMPLE**

TRY PROBLEM 3-5 (pg. 99)

Data-Level Issues

You need to be very aware of the level of data you are working with before computing the numerical measures introduced in this chapter. A common mistake is to compute means on nominal-level data. For example, a major electronics manufacturer recently surveyed a sample of customers to determine whether they preferred black, white, or colored stereo cases. The data were coded as follows:

$$1 = black$$
$$2 = white$$
$$3 = colored$$

A few of the responses are

$$Color code = \{1, 1, 3, 2, 1, 2, 2, 2, 3, 1, 1, 1, 3, 2, 2, 1, 2\}$$

Using these codes, the sample mean is

$$\bar{x} = \frac{\sum x}{n}$$
$$= \frac{30}{17} = 1.765$$

As you can see, reporting that customers prefer a color somewhere between black and white but closer to white would be meaningless. The mean should not be used with nominal data. This type of mistake tends to happen when people use computer software to perform their calculations. Asking Excel or other statistical software to compute the mean, median, and so on for all the variables in the data set is very easy. Then a table is created and, before long, the meaningless measures creep into your report. Don't let that happen.

There is also some disagreement about whether means should be computed on ordinal data. For example, in market research, a 5- or 7-point scale is often used to measure customers' attitudes about products or TV commercials. For example, we might set up the following scale:

$$1 = Strongly\ agree$$
$$2 = Agree$$
$$3 = Neutral$$
$$4 = Disagree$$
$$5 = Strongly\ disagree$$

Customer responses to a particular question are obtained on this scale from 1 to 5. For a sample of $n = 10$ people, we might get the following responses to a question:

$$Response = \{2, 2, 1, 3, 3, 1, 5, 2, 1, 3\}$$

FIGURE 3.6

Descriptive Measures of the Center

Descriptive Measure	Computation Method	Data Level	Advantages/ Disadvantages
Mean	Sum of values divided by the number of values	Ratio Interval	• Numerical center of the data • Sum of deviations from the mean is zero • Sensitive to extreme values
Median	Middle value for data that have been sorted	Ratio Interval Ordinal	• Not sensitive to extreme values • Computed only from the center values • Does not use information from all the data
Mode	Value(s) that occur most frequently in the data	Ratio Interval Ordinal Nominal	• May not reflect the center • May not exist • Might have multiple modes

The mean rating is 2.3. We could then compute the mean for a second issue and compare the means. However, what exactly do we have? First, when we compute a mean for a scaled variable, we are making two basic assumptions:

1. We are assuming the distance between a rating of 1 and 2 is the same as the distance between 2 and 3. We are also saying these distances are exactly the same for the second issue's variable to which you wish to compare it. Although from a numerical standpoint this is true, in terms of what the scale is measuring, is the difference between strongly agree and agree the same as the difference between agree and neutral? If not, is the mean really a meaningful measure?

2. We are also assuming people who respond to the survey have the same definition of what "strongly agree" means or what "disagree" means. When you mark a 4 (disagree) on your survey, are you applying the same criteria as someone else who also marks a 4 on the same issue? If not, then the mean might be misleading.

Although these difficulties exist with ordinal data, we see many examples in which means are computed and used for decision purposes. In fact, we once had a dean who focused on one particular question on the course evaluation survey that was administered in every class each semester. This question was "Considering all factors of importance to you, how would you rate this instructor?"

1 = Excellent   2 = Good   3 = Average   4 = Poor   5 = Very poor

The dean then had his staff compute means for each class and for each professor. He then listed classes and faculty in order based on the mean values, and he based a major part of the performance evaluation on where a faculty member stood with respect to mean score on this one question. By the way, he carried the calculations for the mean out to three decimal places!

In general, the median is the preferred measure of central location for ordinal data instead of the mean.

Figure 3.6 summarizes the three measures of the center that have been discussed in this section.

MyStatLab

3-1: **Exercises**

Skill **Development**

3-1. A random sample of 15 articles in *Fortune* revealed the following word counts per article:

5,176	6,005	5,052	5,310	4,188
4,132	5,736	5,381	4,983	4,423
5,002	4,573	4,209	5,611	4,568

Compute the mean, median, first quartile, and third quartile for these sample data.

3-2. The following data reflect the number of defects produced on an assembly line at the Dearfield Electronics Company for the past 8 days.

3	0	2	0	1	3	5	2
5	1	3	0	0	1	3	3
4	3	1	8	4	2	4	0

a. Compute the mean number of defects for this population of days.

b. Compute the median number of defects produced for this population of days.

c. Determine if there is a mode number of defects and, if so, indicate the mode value.

3-3. A European cereal maker recently sampled 20 of its medium-size oat cereal packages to determine the weights of the cereal in each package. These sample data, measured in ounces, are as follows:

| 14.7 | 16.3 | 14.3 | 14.2 | 18.7 | 13.2 | 13.1 | 14.4 | 16.2 | 12.8 |
| 13.6 | 17.1 | 14.4 | 11.5 | 15.5 | 15.9 | 13.8 | 14.2 | 15.1 | 13.5 |

Calculate the first and third quartiles for these sample data.

3-4. The time (in seconds) that it took for each of 16 vehicles to exit a parking lot in downtown Cincinnati is

106	153	169	116
135	78	51	129
100	141	72	101
130	125	128	139

Compute the mean, median, first quartile, and third quartile for the sample data.

3-5. A random sample of the miles driven by 20 rental car customers is shown as follows:

90	85	100	150
125	75	50	100
75	60	35	90
100	125	75	85
50	100	50	80

Develop a box and whisker plot for the sample data.

3-6. Examine the following data:

| 23 | 65 | 45 | 19 | 35 | 28 | 39 | 100 | 50 | 26 | 25 | 27 |
| 24 | 17 | 12 | 106 | 23 | 19 | 39 | 70 | 20 | 18 | 44 | 31 |

a. Compute the quartiles.

b. Calculate the 90th percentile.

c. Develop a box and whisker plot.

d. Calculate the 20th and the 30th percentiles.

3-7. Consider the following data that represent the commute distances for students who attend Emory University:

| 3.1 | 4.7 | 8.4 | 11.6 | 12.1 | 13.0 | 13.4 | 16.1 | 17.3 | 20.8 |
| 22.8 | 24.3 | 26.2 | 26.6 | 26.7 | 31.2 | 32.2 | 35.8 | 35.8 | 39.8 |

a. Determine the 80th percentile.

b. Determine numbers that are the 25th and 75th percentiles.

c. Determine a number that qualifies as a median for these data.

3-8. A professor wishes to develop a numerical method for giving grades. He intends to base the grade on homework, two midterms, a project, and a final examination. He wishes the final exam to have the largest influence on the grade. He wants the project to have 10%, each midterm to have 20%, and the

homework to have 10% of the influence of the semester grade.

a. Determine the weights the professor should use to produce a weighted average for grading purposes.

b. For a student with the following grades during the quarter, calculate a weighted average for the course:

Instrument	Final	Project	Midterm 1	Midterm 2	Homework
Percentage Grade	64	98	67	63	89

c. Calculate an (unweighted) average of these five scores and discuss why the weighted average would be preferable here.

Business Applications

3-9. The manager for the Jiffy Lube in Saratoga, Florida, has collected data on the number of customers who agreed to purchase an air filter when they were also having their oil changed. The sample data are shown as follows:

| 21 | 19 | 21 | 19 | 19 | 20 | 18 | 12 | 20 | 19 | 17 | 14 |
| 21 | 22 | 25 | 21 | 22 | 23 | 10 | 19 | 25 | 14 | 17 | 18 |

a. Compute the mean, median, and mode for these data.

b. Indicate whether the data are skewed or symmetrical.

c. Construct a box and whisker plot for these data. Referring to your answer in part b, does the box plot support your conclusion about skewness? Discuss.

3-10. During the past few years, there has been a lot of discussion about the price of university textbooks. The complaints have come from many places, including students, faculty, parents, and even government officials. The publishing companies have been called on to explain why textbooks cost so much. Recently, one of the major publishing companies was asked to testify before a congressional panel in Washington, D.C. As part of the presentation, the president of the company organized his talk around four main areas: production costs, author royalties, marketing costs, and bookstore markup. He used one of his company's business statistics texts as an example when he pointed out the production costs—including editing, proofing, printing, binding, inventory holding, and distribution—come to about $32 per book sold. Authors receive $12 per copy for the hundreds of hours of creative work in writing the book and supplementary materials. Marketing costs are pegged at about $5 per copy sold and go to pay for the book sales force and examination copies sent to professors. The book is then sold to bookstores for $70 per copy, a markup on costs of about 40% to cover overhead and the publishing costs associated with many upper-division, low-market texts that lose money for the company. Once university bookstores purchase the book, they mark it up, place it on the shelf, and sell it to the student. If books go unsold, they are returned to the publisher for a full refund. The following data reflect the dollar markup on the business statistics text for a sample of 20 college bookstores:

$33	$32	$42	$31	$31
$37	$37	$34	$47	$31
$42	$29	$36	$32	$25
$29	$47	$26	$32	$40

a. Compute the mean markup on the business statistics text by university bookstores in the sample.
b. Compute the median markup.
c. Determine the mode markup.
d. Write a short paragraph discussing the statistics computed in parts a–c.

3-11. The Xang Corporation operates five clothing suppliers in China to provide merchandise for Nike. Nike recently sought information from the five plants. One variable for which data were collected was the total money (in U.S. dollars) the company spent on medical support for its employees in the first three months of the year. Data on number of employees at the plants are also shown. These data are as follows:

Medical	$7,400	$14,400	$12,300	$6,200	$3,100
Employees	123	402	256	109	67

a. Compute the weighted mean medical payments for these five plants using number of employees as the weights.
b. Explain why Nike would desire that a weighted average be computed in this situation rather than a simple numeric average.

3-12. The Tru-Green Lawn Company provides yard care services for customers throughout the Denver area. The company owner recently tracked the time his field employees spent at a sample of customer locations. He was hoping to use these data to help him with his scheduling and to establish billing rates. The following sample data, in minutes, were recorded:

31	27	29	22	24	30	28	21	29	26
22	17	17	20	38	10	38	25	27	23
23	13	17	34	25	29	22	22	14	11
29	26	29	29	37	32	27	26	18	22

Describe the central tendency of these data by computing the mean, median, and mode. Based on these measures, can you conclude that the distribution of time spent at customer locations is skewed or symmetric?

3-13. Eastern States Bank and Trust monitors its drive-thru service times electronically to ensure that its speed of service is meeting the company's goals. A sample of 28 drive-thru times was recently taken and is shown here.

Speed of Service (time in seconds)			
83	138	145	147
130	79	156	156
90	85	68	93
178	76	73	119
92	146	88	103
116	134	162	71
181	110	105	74

a. Compute the mean, median, and mode for these sample data.
b. Indicate whether the data are symmetrical or skewed.
c. Construct a box and whisker plot for the sample data. Does the box and whisker plot support your conclusions in part b concerning the symmetry or skewness of these data?

3-14. Todd Lindsey & Associates, a commercial real estate company located in Boston, owns six office buildings in the Boston area that it leases to businesses. The lease price per square foot differs by building due to location and building amenities. Currently, all six buildings are fully leased at the prices shown here.

	Price per Square Foot	Number of Square Feet
Building 1	$ 75	125,000
Building 2	$ 85	37,500
Building 3	$ 90	77,500
Building 4	$ 45	35,000
Building 5	$ 55	60,000
Building 6	$110	130,000

a. Compute the weighted average (mean) price per square foot for these buildings.
b. Why is the weighted average price per square foot preferred to a simple average price per square foot in this case?

3-15. *Business Week* recently reported that L. G. Philips LCD Co. would complete a new factory in Paju, South Korea. It will be the world's largest maker of liquid-crystal display panels. The arrival of the plant means that flat-panel LCD televisions would become increasingly affordable. The average retail cost of a 20″ LCD television in 2000 was $5,139. To obtain what the average retail cost of a 37″ LCD was in 2008, a survey yielded the following data (in $U.S.):

606.70	558.12	625.82	533.70	464.37
511.15	400.56	538.20	531.64	632.14
474.86	567.46	588.39	528.78	610.32
564.71	912.68	475.87	545.25	589.15

a. Calculate the mean cost for these data.
b. Examine the data presented. Choose an appropriate measure of the center of the data, justify the choice, and calculate the measure.

c. The influence an observation has on a statistic may be calculated by deleting the observation and calculating the difference between the original statistic and the statistic with the data point removed. The larger the difference, the more influential the data point. Identify the data points that have the most and the least influence in the calculation of the sample mean.

3-16. The following table exhibits base salary data obtained from a survey of over 170 benchmark positions, including finance positions. It reports the salaries of a sample of 25 chief finance officers for mid-sized firms. Assume the data are in thousands of dollars.

173.1	171.2	141.9	112.6	211.1	156.5	145.4	134.0	192.0
185.8	168.3	131.0	214.4	155.2	164.9	123.9	161.9	162.7
178.8	161.3	182.0	165.8	213.1	177.4	159.3		

a. Calculate the mean salary of the CFOs.
b. Based on measures of the center of the data, determine if the CFO salary data are skewed.
c. Construct a box and whisker plot and summarize the characteristics of the CFO salaries that it reveals.

3-17. The Federal Deposit Insurance Corporation (FDIC) insures deposits in banks and thrift institutions for up to $250,000. Before the banking crisis of late 2008, there were 8,885 FDIC–insured institutions, with deposits of $6,826,804,000,000; there were 7,436 in late 2011 with deposits of 7,966,700,000,000.

a. Calculate the average deposits per bank for FDIC–insured institutions during both time periods.
b. Describe the relationship between the two averages calculated in part a. Can you provide a reason for the difference?
c. Would the two averages be considered to be parameters or statistics? Explain.

Computer **Database Exercises**

3-18. Each year, *Business Week* publishes information and rankings of master of business administration (MBA) programs. The data file **MBA Analysis** contains data on several variables for eight reputable MBA programs. The variables include pre– and post–MBA salary, percentage salary increase, undergraduate GPA, average Graduate Management Admission Test (GMAT) score, annual tuition, and expected annual student cost. Compute the mean and median for each of the variables in the database and write a short report that summarizes the data. Include any appropriate charts or graphs to assist in your report.

3-19. Dynamic random-access memory (DRAM) memory chips are made from silicon wafers in manufacturing facilities through a very complex process called wafer fabs. The wafers are routed through the fab machines in an order that is referred to as a recipe. The wafers may go through the same machine several times as the chip is created. The data file **DRAM Chips** contains a sample of processing times, measured in fractions

of hours, at a particular machine center for one chip recipe.

a. Compute the mean processing time.
b. Compute the median processing time.
c. Determine what the mode processing time is.
d. Calculate the 80th percentile for processing time.

3-20. Japolli Bakery tracks sales of its different bread products on a daily basis. The data for 22 consecutive days at one of its retail outlets in Nashville are in a file called **Japolli Bakery**. Calculate the mean, mode, and median sales for each of the bread categories and write a short report that describes these data. Use any charts or graphs that may be helpful in more fully describing the data.

3-21. Before the sub-prime loan crisis and the end of the "housing bubble" in 2008, the value of houses was escalating rapidly, as much as 40% a year in some areas. In an effort to track housing prices, the National Association of Realtors developed the Pending Home Sales Index (PHSI), a new leading indicator for the housing market. An index of 100 is equal to the average level of contract activity during 2001, the first year to be analyzed. The index is based on a large national sample representing about 20% of home sales. The file titled **Pending** contains the PHSI from December 2010 to December 2011.

a. Determine the mean and median for the PHSI from December 2010 through December 2011. Specify the shape of the PHSI's distribution.
b. The PHSI was at 91.5 in December 2010 and it was at 100.1 in November of 2011. Determine the average monthly increase in the PHSI for this period.
c. Using your answer to part b, suggest a weighting scheme to calculate the weighted mean for the months between December 2010 and November 2011. Use the scheme to produce the weighted average of the PHSI in this time period.
d. Does the weighted average seem more appropriate here? Explain.

3-22. Homeowners and businesses pay taxes on the assessed value of their property. As a result, property taxes can be a problem for elderly homeowners who are on a fixed retirement income. Whereas these retirement incomes remain basically constant, because of rising real estate prices, the property taxes in many areas of the country have risen dramatically. In some cases, homeowners are required to sell their homes because they can't afford the taxes. In Phoenix, Arizona, government officials are considering giving certain elderly homeowners a property tax reduction based on income. One proposal calls for all homeowners over the age of 65 with incomes at or below the 20th percentile to get a reduction in property taxes. A random sample of 50 people over the age of 65 was selected, and the household income (as reported on the most current federal tax return) was recorded. These data are also in the file called **Property Tax Incomes**.

Use these data to establish the income cutoff point to qualify for the property tax cut.

$35,303	$56,855	$ 7,928	$26,006	$28,278
$54,215	$38,850	$15,733	$29,786	$65,878
$46,658	$62,874	$49,427	$19,017	$46,007
$32,367	$31,904	$35,534	$66,668	$37,986
$10,669	$54,337	$ 8,858	$45,263	$37,746
$14,550	$ 8,748	$58,075	$23,381	$11,725
$45,044	$55,807	$54,211	$42,961	$62,682
$32,939	$38,698	$11,632	$66,714	$31,869
$57,530	$59,233	$14,136	$ 8,824	$42,183
$58,443	$34,553	$26,805	$16,133	$61,785

3-23. Suppose a random sample of 137 households in Detroit was taken as part of a study on annual household spending for food at home. The sample data are contained in the file **Detroit Eats**.
   a. For the sample data, compute the mean and the median and construct a box and whisker plot.

   b. Are the data skewed or symmetric?
   c. Approximately what percent of the data values are between $2,900 and $3,250?

3-24. *USA Today* reported a survey made by Nationwide Mutual Insurance that indicated the average amount of time spent to resolve identity theft cases was slightly more than 88 hours. The file titled **Theft** contains data that would produce this statistic.
   a. Construct a stem and leaf display. Indicate the shape of data displayed by the stem and leaf display.
   b. Use measures that indicate the shape of the distribution. Do these measures give results that agree with the shape shown in part a?
   c. Considering your answers to part a and b, indicate which measure you would recommend using to indicate the center of the data.

END EXERCISES 3-1

3.2 Measures of Variation

BUSINESS APPLICATION MEASURING VARIATION USING THE RANGE

FLEETWOOD MOBILE HOMES Consider the situation involving two manufacturing facilities for Fleetwood Mobile Homes. The division vice president asked the two plant managers to record the number of mobile homes produced weekly over a five-week period. The resulting sample data are shown in Table 3.3.

Instead of reporting these raw data, the managers reported only the mean and median for their data. The following are the computed statistics for the two plants:

TABLE 3.3 | **Manufacturing Output for Fleetwood Mobile Homes**

Plant A	Plant B
15 units	23 units
25 units	26 units
35 units	25 units
20 units	24 units
30 units	27 units

Plant A	Plant B
$\bar{x} = 25$ units	$\bar{x} = 25$ units
$M_d = 25$ units	$M_d = 25$ units

The division vice president looked at these statistics and concluded the following:

1. Average production is 25 units per week at both plants.
2. The median production is 25 units per week at both plants.
3. Because the mean and median are equal, the distribution of production output at the two plants is symmetrical.
4. Based on these statistics, there is no reason to believe that the two plants are different in terms of their production output.

However, if he had taken a closer look at the raw data, he would have seen there is a very big difference between the two plants. The difference is the production **variation** from week to week. Plant B is very stable, producing almost the same number of units every week. Plant A varies considerably, with some high-output weeks and some low-output weeks. Thus, looking at only measures of the data's central location can be misleading. To fully describe a set of data, we need a measure of variation or spread.

There is variation in everything that is made by humans or that occurs in nature. The variation may be small, but it is there. Given a fine enough measuring instrument, we can detect the variation. Variation is either a natural part of a process (or inherent to a product) or can be attributed to a special cause that is not considered random.

Several different measures of variation are used in business decision making. In this section, we introduce four of these measures: range, interquartile range, variance, and standard deviation.

Variation

A set of data exhibits variation if all the data are not the same value.

Chapter Outcome 3. → # Range

Range
The range is a measure of variation that is computed by finding the difference between the maximum and minimum values in a data set.

The simplest measure of variation is the **range**. It is both easy to compute and easy to understand.

The range is computed using Equation 3.7.

Range

$$R = \text{Maximum Value} - \text{Minimum Value} \tag{3.7}$$

BUSINESS APPLICATION   **CALCULATING THE RANGE**

FLEETWOOD MOBILE HOMES (*CONTINUED*) Table 3.3 showed the production-volume data for the two Fleetwood Mobile Home plants. The range in production for each plant is determined using Equation 3.7 as follows:

Plant A	Plant B
$R = \text{Maximum} - \text{Minimum}$	$R = \text{Maximum} - \text{Minimum}$
$R = 35 - 15$	$R = 27 - 23$
$R = 20$	$R = 4$

We see Plant A has a range that is five times as great as Plant B.

Although the range is quick and easy to compute, it does have some limitations. First, because we use only the high and low values to compute the range, it is very sensitive to extreme values in the data. Second, regardless of how many values are in the sample or population, the range is computed from only two of these values. For these reasons, it is considered a weak measure of variation.

Chapter Outcome 3. → # Interquartile Range

Interquartile Range
The interquartile range is a measure of variation that is determined by computing the difference between the third and first quartiles.

A measure of variation that tends to overcome the range's susceptibility to extreme values is called the **interquartile range**.

Equation 3.8 is used to compute the interquartile range.

Interquartile Range

$$\text{Interquartile Range} = \text{Third Quartile} - \text{First Quartile} \tag{3.8}$$

EXAMPLE 3-10   **COMPUTING THE INTERQUARTILE RANGE**

Verizon Wireless A systems capacity manager for Verizon Wireless is interested in better understanding Verizon customer text messaging use. To do this, she has collected a random sample of 100 customers under the age of 25 and recorded the number of text messages sent in a one-week period. She wishes to analyze the variation in these data by computing the range and the interquartile range. She could use the following steps to do so:

Step 1 Sort the data into a data array from lowest to highest.
The 100 sorted values are as follows:

33	164	173	184	190	197	207	216	224	237
53	164	175	186	191	197	207	217	225	240
150	164	175	186	191	198	208	217	225	240
152	166	175	186	192	200	208	217	229	240
157	166	178	187	193	200	208	219	231	250
160	168	178	188	193	201	210	222	231	251
161	169	179	188	194	202	211	223	234	259
162	171	180	188	194	204	212	223	234	270
162	171	182	190	196	205	213	223	235	379
163	172	183	190	196	205	216	224	236	479

Step 2   Compute the range using Equation 3.7.

$$R = \text{Maximum value} - \text{Minimum value}$$
$$R = 479 - 33 = 446$$

Note, the range is sensitive to extreme values. The small value of 33 and the high value of 479 cause the range value to be very large.

Step 3   Compute the first and third quartiles.

Equation 3.6 can be used to find the location of the third quartile (75th percentile) and the first quartile (25th percentile).

For Q_3 the location $i = \frac{75}{100}(100) = 75$. Thus, Q_3 is halfway between the 75th and 76th data values, which is found as follows:

$$Q_3 = (219 + 222)/2 = 220.50$$

For Q_1, the location is $i = \frac{25}{100}(100) = 25$. Then Q_1 is halfway between the 25th and 26th data values.

$$Q_1 = (178 + 178)/2 = 178$$

Step 4   Compute the interquartile range.

The interquartile range overcomes the range's problem of sensitivity to extreme values. It is computed using Equation 3.8:

$$\text{Interquartile range} = Q_3 - Q_1$$
$$= 220.50 - 178 = 42.50$$

Note, the interquartile range would be unchanged even if the values on the high or low end of the distribution were even more extreme than those shown in these sample data.

>> **END EXAMPLE**

TRY PROBLEM 3-30 (pg. 111)

Chapter Outcome 3. ➞ # Population Variance and Standard Deviation

Although the range is easy to compute and understand and the interquartile range is designed to overcome the range's sensitivity to extreme values, neither measure uses all the available data in its computation. Thus, both measures ignore potentially valuable information in data.

Variance

The population variance is the average of the squared distances of the data values from the mean.

Standard Deviation

The standard deviation is the positive square root of the variance.

Two measures of variation that incorporate all the values in a data set are the **variance** and the **standard deviation**.

These two measures are closely related. The standard deviation is the positive square root of the variance. The standard deviation is in the original units (dollars, pounds, etc.), whereas the units of measure in the variance are squared. Because dealing with original units is easier than dealing with the square of the units, we usually use the standard deviation to measure variation in a population or sample.

BUSINESS APPLICATION   **CALCULATING THE VARIANCE AND STANDARD DEVIATION**

FLEETWOOD MOBILE HOMES (*CONTINUED*) Recall the Fleetwood Mobile Home application, in which we compared the weekly production output for two of the company's plants. Table 3.3 showed the data, which are considered a population for our purposes here.

Previously, we examined the variability in the output from these two plants by computing the ranges. Although those results gave us some sense of how much more variable Plant A is than Plant B, we also pointed out some of the deficiencies of the range. The variance and standard deviation offer alternatives to the range for measuring variation in data.

Equation 3.9 is the formula for the population variance. Like the population mean, the population variance and standard deviation are assigned Greek symbols.

Population Variance

$$\sigma^2 = \frac{\displaystyle\sum_{i=1}^{N}(x_i - \mu)^2}{N} \tag{3.9}$$

where:

μ = Population mean
N = Population size
σ^2 = Population variance (sigma squared)

We begin by computing the variance for the output data from Plant A. The first step in manually calculating the variance is to find the mean using Equation 3.1.

$$\mu = \frac{\sum x}{N} = \frac{15 + 25 + 35 + 20 + 30}{5} = \frac{125}{5} = 25$$

Next, subtract the mean from each value, as shown in Table 3.4. Notice the sum of the deviations from the mean is 0. Recall from Section 3.1 that this will be true for any set of data. The positive differences are cancelled out by the negative differences. To overcome this fact when computing the variance, we square each of the differences and then sum the squared differences. These calculations are also shown in Table 3.4.

The final step in computing the population variance is to divide the sum of the squared differences by the population size, $N = 5$.

$$\sigma^2 = \frac{\sum(x - \mu)^2}{N} = \frac{250}{5} = 50$$

The population variance is 50 *mobile homes squared*.

Manual calculations for the population variance may be easier if you use an alternative formula for σ^2 that is the algebraic equivalent. This is shown as Equation 3.10.

Population Variance Shortcut

$$\sigma^2 = \frac{\sum x^2 - \dfrac{(\sum x)^2}{N}}{N} \tag{3.10}$$

Example 3-11 will illustrate using Equation 3.10 to find a population variance.

Because we squared the deviations to keep the positive values and negative values from canceling, the units of measure were also squared, but the term *mobile homes squared* doesn't have a meaning. To get back to the original units of measure, take the square root of the

TABLE 3.4 | **Computing the Population Variance: Squaring the Deviations**

x_i	$(x_i - \mu)$	$(x_i - \mu)^2$
15	$15 - 25 = -10$	100
25	$25 - 25 = 0$	0
35	$35 - 25 = 10$	100
20	$20 - 25 = -5$	25
30	$30 - 25 = 5$	25
	$\sum(x_i - \mu) = 0$	$\sum(x_i - \mu)^2 = 250$

variance. The result is the standard deviation. Equation 3.11 shows the formula for the population standard deviation.

Population Standard Deviation

$$\sigma = \sqrt{\sigma^2} = \sqrt{\dfrac{\displaystyle\sum_{i=1}^{N}(x_i - \mu)^2}{N}} \qquad\qquad (3.11)$$

Therefore, the population standard deviation of Plant A's production output is

$$\sigma = \sqrt{50}$$
$$\sigma = 7.07 \text{ mobile homes}$$

The population standard deviation is a parameter and will not change unless the population values change.

We could repeat this process using the data for Plant B, which also had a mean output of 25 mobile homes. You should verify that the population variance is

$$\sigma^2 = \frac{\Sigma(x - \mu)^2}{N} = \frac{10}{5} = 2 \text{ mobile homes squared}$$

The standard deviation is found by taking the square root of the variance.

$$\sigma = \sqrt{2}$$
$$\sigma = 1.414 \text{ mobile homes}$$

Thus, Plant A has an output standard deviation that is five times larger than Plant B's. The fact that Plant A's range was also five times larger than the range for Plant B is merely a coincidence.

How to do it (Example 3-11)

Computing the Population Variance and Standard Deviation

The population variance and standard deviation are computed using the following steps:

1. Collect quantitative data for the variable of interest for the entire population.

2. Use either Equation 3.9 or Equation 3.10 to compute the variance.

3. If Equation 3.10 is used, find the sum of the x-values (Σx^2) and then square this sum $(\Sigma x)^2$.

4. Square each x value and sum these squared values (Σx^2).

5. Compute the variance using

$$\sigma^2 = \frac{\Sigma x^2 - \dfrac{(\Sigma x)^2}{N}}{N}$$

6. Compute the standard deviation by taking the positive square root of the variance:

$$\sigma = \sqrt{\sigma^2}$$

EXAMPLE 3-11   **COMPUTING A POPULATION VARIANCE AND STANDARD DEVIATION**

Svitlana Kataieva/Shutterstock

Boydson Shipping Company Boydson Shipping Company owns and operates a fleet of tanker ships that carry commodities between the countries of the world. In the past six months, the company has had seven contracts that called for shipments between Vancouver, Canada, and London, England. For many reasons, the travel time varies between these two locations. The scheduling manager is interested in knowing the variance and standard deviation in shipping times for these seven shipments. To find these values, he can follow these steps:

Step 1 Collect the data for the population.
The shipping times are shown as follows:

$$x = \text{shipping weeks}$$
$$= \{5, 7, 5, 9, 7, 4, 6\}$$

Step 2 Select Equation 3.10 to find the population variance.

$$\sigma^2 = \frac{\Sigma x^2 - \dfrac{(\Sigma x)^2}{N}}{N}$$

Step 3 Add the x values and square the sum.

$$\Sigma x = 5 + 7 + 5 + 9 + 7 + 4 + 6 = 43$$
$$(\Sigma x^2) = (43)^2 = 1{,}849$$

Step 4 **Square each of the x values and sum these squares.**

$$\Sigma x^2 = 5^2 + 7^2 + 5^2 + 9^2 + 7^2 + 4^2 + 6^2 = 281$$

Step 5 **Compute the population variance.**

$$\sigma^2 = \frac{\Sigma x^2 - \dfrac{(\Sigma x)^2}{N}}{N} = \frac{281 - \dfrac{1,849}{7}}{7} = 2.4082$$

The variance is in units squared, so in this example the population variance is 2.4082 weeks squared.

Step 6 **Calculate the standard deviation as the square root of the variance.**

$$\sigma = \sqrt{\sigma^2} = \sqrt{2.4082} = 1.5518 \text{ weeks}$$

Thus, the standard deviation for the number of shipping weeks between Vancouver and London for the seven shipments is 1.5518 weeks.

>> **END EXAMPLE**

TRY PROBLEM 3-27 (pg. 110)

Sample Variance and Standard Deviation

Equations 3.9, 3.10, and 3.11 are the equations for the population variance and standard deviation. Any time you are working with a population, these are the equations that are used. However, in most instances, you will be describing sample data that have been selected from the population. In addition to using different notations for the sample variance and sample standard deviation, the equations are also slightly different. Equations 3.12 and 3.13 can be used to find the sample variance. Note that Equation 3.13 is considered the shortcut formula for manual computations.

Sample Variance

$$s^2 = \frac{\displaystyle\sum_{i=1}^{n} (x_i - \bar{x})^2}{n - 1} \tag{3.12}$$

Sample Variance Shortcut

$$s^2 = \frac{\Sigma x^2 - \dfrac{(\Sigma x)^2}{n}}{n - 1} \tag{3.13}$$

where:

$$n = \text{Sample size}$$
$$\bar{x} = \text{Sample mean}$$
$$s^2 = \text{Sample variance}$$

The sample standard deviation is found by taking the square root of the sample variance, as shown in Equation 3.14.

Sample Standard Deviation

$$s = \sqrt{s^2} = \sqrt{\frac{\displaystyle\sum_{i=1}^{n} (x_i - \bar{x})^2}{n - 1}} \tag{3.14}$$

Take note in Equations 3.12, 3.13, and 3.14 that the denominator is $n - 1$ (sample size minus 1). This may seem strange, given that the denominator for the population variance and the standard deviation is simply N, the population size. The mathematical justification for the $n - 1$ divisor is outside the scope of this text. However, the general reason for this is that we want the average sample variance to equal the population variance. If we were to select all possible samples of size n from a given population and for each sample we computed the sample variance using Equation 3.12 or Equation 3.13, the average of all the sample variances would equal σ^2 (the population variance), provided we used $n - 1$ as the divisor. Using n instead of $n - 1$ in the denominator would produce an average sample variance that would be smaller than σ^2, the population variance. Because we want an estimator on average to equal the population variance, we use $n - 1$ in the denominator of s^2.

| **EXAMPLE 3-12** | **COMPUTING A SAMPLE VARIANCE AND STANDARD DEVIATION** |

Balco Industries The internal auditor for Balco Industries, a manufacturer of equipment used in the food processing business, recently examined the transaction records related to 10 of the company's customers. For each client, the auditor counted the number of incorrectly recorded entries (i.e "defects"). The ten customers' accounts can be considered to be samples of all possible Balco customers that could be analyzed. To fully analyze the data, the auditor can calculate the sample variance and sample standard deviation using the following steps:

Step 1 **Select the sample and record the data for the variable of interest.**

Client	Defects = x	Client	Defects = x
1	4	6	0
2	7	7	3
3	1	8	2
4	0	9	6
5	5	10	2

Step 2 **Select either Equation 3.12 or Equation 3.13 to compute the sample variance.**
If we use Equation 3.12,

$$s^2 = \frac{\Sigma(x - \overline{x})^2}{n - 1}$$

Step 3 **Compute $\overline{x}$.**
The sample mean number of defectives is

$$\overline{x} = \frac{\Sigma x}{n} = \frac{30}{10} = 3.0$$

Step 4 **Determine the sum of the squared deviations of each x value from $\overline{x}$.**

Client	Defectives = x	$(x - \overline{x})$	$(x - \overline{x})^2$
1	4	1	1
2	7	4	16
3	1	−2	4
4	0	−3	9
5	5	2	4
6	0	−3	9
7	3	0	0
8	2	−1	1

Client	Defectives = x	$(x - \bar{x})$	$(x - \bar{x})^2$
9	6	3	9
10	2	−1	1
	$\Sigma = 30$	$\Sigma = 0$	$\Sigma = 54$

Step 5 **Compute the sample variance using Equation 3.12.**

$$s^2 = \frac{\Sigma(x - \bar{x})^2}{n - 1} = \frac{54}{9} = 6$$

The sample variance is measured in squared units. Thus, the variance in this example is 6 defectives squared.

Step 6 **Compute the sample standard deviation by taking the square root of the variance (see Equation 3.14).**

$$s = \sqrt{\frac{\Sigma(x - \bar{x})^2}{n - 1}} = \sqrt{\frac{54}{9}} = \sqrt{6}$$
$$s = 2.4495 \text{ defects}$$

This sample standard deviation measures the variation in the sample data for the number of incorrectly recorded entries.

>> **END EXAMPLE**

TRY PROBLEM 3-25 (pg. 110)

BUSINESS APPLICATION   **CALCULATING MEASURES OF VARIATION USING EXCEL**

COLLEGES AND UNIVERSITIES (CONTINUED) In Section 3.1, the guidance counselor was interested in describing the data representing the cost of out-of-state tuition for a large number of colleges and universities in the United States. The data for 718 schools are in the file called **Colleges and Universities**. Previously, we determined the following descriptive measures of the center for the variable, out-of-state tuition:

Mean = $9,933.38

Median = $9,433.00

Mode = $6,550

Excel Tutorial

Next, the analyst will turn her attention to measures of variability. The range (maximum − minimum) is one measure of variability. Excel can be used to compute the range and the standard deviation of tuition, which is a more powerful measure of variation than the range. Figure 3.7 shows the Excel descriptive statistics results. We find the following measures of variation:

Range = $22,340.00

Standard Deviation = $3,920.07

These values are measures of the spread in the data. You should know that outlier values in a data set will increase both the range and standard deviation. One guideline for identifying outliers is the ±3 standard deviation rule. That is, if a value falls outside ±3 standard deviations from the mean, it is considered an outlier. Also, as shown in Section 3.1, outliers can be identified using box and whisker plots.

FIGURE 3.7 |

Excel 2010 Descriptive
Statistics for Colleges and
Universities Data

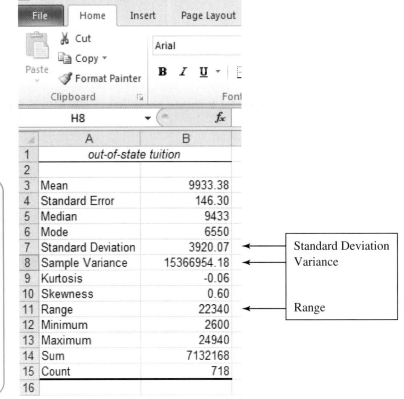

Excel 2010 Instructions:
1. Open file: **Colleges and Universities.xlsx**.
2. Select the **Data** tab.
3. Click on **Data Analysis > Descriptive Statistics**.
4. Define data range for the desired variables.
5. Check **Summary Statistics**.
6. Name new Output Sheet.
7. On **Home** tab, adjust decimal places as desired.

Minitab Instructions (for similar results):
1. Open file: **Colleges and Universities.MTW**.
2. Choose **Stat > Basic Statistics > Display Descriptive Statistics**.
3. In **Variables**, enter column *out-of-state tuition*.
4. Click **Statistics**.
5. Check required statistics.
6. Click **OK. OK**.

MyStatLab

3-2: Exercises

Skill Development

3-25. Google is noted for its generous employee benefits. The following data reflect the number of vacation days that a sample of employees at Google have left to take before the end of the year:

3	0	2	0	1	3	5	2
5	1	3	0	0	1	3	3
4	3	1	8	4	2	4	0

a. Compute the range for these sample data.
b. Compute the variance for these sample data.
c. Compute the standard deviation for these sample data.

3-26. The following data reflect the number of times a population of business executives flew on business during the previous month:

4   6   9   4   5   7

a. Compute the range for these data.
b. Compute the variance and standard deviation.
c. Assuming that these data represent a sample rather than a population, compute the variance and standard deviation. Discuss the difference between the values computed here and in part b.

3-27. The following data are the population of ages of students who have recently purchased a sports video game:

16	15	17	15	15	15
14	9	16	15	13	10
8	18	20	17	17	17
18	23	7	15	20	10
14	14	12	12	24	21

a. Compute the population variance.
b. Compute the population standard deviation.

3-28. A county library in Minnesota reported the following number of books checked out in 15 randomly selected months:

5,176	6,005	5,052	5,310	4,188
4,132	5,736	5,381	4,983	4,423
5,002	4,573	4,209	5,611	4,568

Determine the range, variance, and standard deviation for the sample data.

3-29. The following data show the number of hours spent watching television for 12 randomly selected freshmen attending a liberal arts college in the Midwest:

Hours of Television Viewed Weekly			
7.5	11.5	14.4	7.8
13.0	10.3	5.4	12.0
12.2	8.9	8.5	6.6

Calculate the range, variance, standard deviation, and interquartile range for the sample data.

3-30. Consider the following two separate samples:

27	27	25	12	15	10	20	37	31	35

and

1	3	2	16	18	16	16	4	16	118

a. Calculate the range, variance, standard deviation, and interquartile range for each data set.
b. Which data set is most spread out based on these statistics?
c. Now remove the largest number from each data set and repeat the calculations called for in part a.
d. Compare the results of parts a and c. Which statistic seems to be most affected by outliers?

3-31. The following set of data shows the number of alcoholic drinks that students at a Kansas university reported they had consumed in the past month:

24	16	23	26	30	21	15	9
18	27	14	6	14	10	12	

a. Assume the data set is a sample. Calculate the range, variance, standard deviation, and interquartile range for the data set.
b. Assume the data set is a population. Calculate the range, variance, standard deviation, and interquartile range for the data set.
c. Indicate the relationship between the statistics and the respective parameters calculated in parts a and b.

Business Applications

3-32. Easy Connect, Inc., provides access to computers for business uses. The manager monitors computer use to make sure that the number of computers is sufficient to meet the needs of the customers. Recently, the manager collected data on a sample of customers and tracked the time the customers started working at a computer until they were finished. The elapsed times, in minutes, are shown as follows:

40	42	18	32	43	35	11	39	36	37
8	34	34	50	20	39	31	75	33	17

Compute appropriate measures of the center and variation to describe the time customers spend on the computer.

3-33. A random sample of 20 pledges to a public radio fund-raiser revealed the following dollar pledges:

90	85	100	150
125	75	50	100
75	60	35	90
100	125	75	85
50	100	50	80

a. Compute the range, variance, standard deviation, and interquartile range for these sample data.
b. Briefly explain the difference between the range and the interquartile range as a measure of dispersion.

3-34. Gold's Gym selected a random sample of 10 customers and monitored the number of times each customer used the workout facility in a one-month period. The following data were collected:

10	19	17	19	12	20	20	15	16	13

Gold's managers are considering a promotion in which they reward frequent users with a small gift. They have decided that they will only give gifts to those customers whose number of visits in a one-month period is 1 standard deviation above the mean. Find the minimum number of visits required to receive a gift.

3-35. The registrar at Whitworth College has been asked to prepare a report about the graduate students. Among other things, she wants to analyze the ages of the students. She has taken a sample of 10 graduate students and has found the following ages:

32	22	24	27	27	33	28	23	24	21

a. Compute the range, interquartile range, and standard deviation for these data.
b. An earlier study showed that the mean age of graduate students in U.S. colleges and universities is 37.8 years. Based on your calculations in part a, what might you conclude about the age of students in Whitworth's programs?

3-36. The branch manager for the D. L. Evens Bank has been asked to prepare a presentation for next week's board meeting. At the presentation, she will discuss the status of her branch's loans issued for recreation vehicles (RVs). In particular, she will analyze the loan balances for a sample of 10 RV loans. The following data were collected:

$11,509	$8,088	$13,415	$17,028	$16,754
$18,626	$4,917	$11,740	$16,393	$ 8,757

a. Compute the mean loan balance.
b. Compute the loan balance standard deviation.
c. Write a one-paragraph statement that uses the statistics computed in parts a and b to describe the RV loan data at the branch.

3-37. A parking garage in Memphis monitors the time it takes customers to exit the parking structure from the time they get in their car until they are on the streets. A sample of 28 exits was recently taken and is shown here.

Garage Exit (time in seconds)			
83	138	145	147
130	79	156	156
90	85	68	93
178	76	73	119
92	146	88	103
116	134	162	71
181	110	105	74

a. Calculate the range, interquartile range, variance, and standard deviation for these sample data.
b. If the minimum time and the maximum time in the sample data are both increased by 10 seconds, would this affect the value for the interquartile range that you calculated in part a? Why or why not?
c. Suppose the clock that electronically recorded the times was not working properly when the sample was taken and each of the sampled times needs to be increased by 10 seconds. How would adding 10 seconds to each of the sampled speed of service times change the sample variance of the data?

3-38. Nielsen Monitor-Plus, a service of Nielsen Media Research, is one of the leaders in advertising information services in the United States, providing advertising activity for 16 media, including television tracking, in all 210 Designated Market Areas (DMAs). One of the issues it has researched is the increasing amount of "clutter"—nonprogramming minutes in an hour of prime time—including network and local commercials and advertisements for other shows. Recently it found the average nonprogramming minutes in an hour of prime-time broadcasting for network television was 15:48 minutes. For cable television, the average was 14:55 minutes.
a. Calculate the difference in the average clutter between network and cable television.
b. Suppose the standard deviation in the amount of clutter for both the network and cable television was either 5 minutes or 15 seconds. Which standard deviation would lead you to conclude that there was a major difference in the two clutter averages? Comment.

3-39. The Bureau of Labor Statistics, in its *Monthly Labor Review,* published the "over-the-month" percent change in the price index for imports from December 2010 to December 2011. These data are reproduced next.

Month	Change in Index
Jan	0.1
Feb	0.2
Mar	1.3
Apr	−0.4
May	−2.5
Jun	−0.7
Jul	0.7
Aug	−0.5
Sep	0.3
Oct	−0.3
Nov	1.2
Dec	−0.9

a. Calculate the mean, standard deviation, and interquartile range for these data.
b. Consider the mean calculated in part a. What does this value indicate about the price index?
c. What does the standard deviation indicate about the price index?

3-40. The U.S. Government Accountability Office recently indicated the price of college textbooks has been rising an average of 6% annually since the late 1980s. The report estimated that the average cost of books and supplies for first-time, full-time students at four-year public universities for the academic year had reached $898. A data set that would produce this average follows:

537.51	1032.52	1119.17	877.27	856.87	739.91	963.79
847.92	1393.81	524.68	1012.91	1176.46	944.60	708.26
1074.35	778.87	967.91	562.55	789.50	1051.65	

a. Calculate the mean and standard deviation.
b. Determine the number of standard deviations the most extreme cost is away from the mean. If you were to advise a prospective student concerning the money the student should save to afford the cost of books and supplies for at least 90% of the colleges, determine the amount you would suggest. (*Hint:* Don't forget the yearly inflation of the cost of books and supplies.)

Computer Database **Exercises**

3-41. The manager of a phone kiosk in the Valley Mall recently collected data on a sample of 50 customers who purchased a cell phone and a monthly call plan. The data she recorded are in the data file called **Phone Survey**.
a. The manager is interested in describing the difference between male and female customers with respect to the price of the phone purchased. She wants to compute mean and standard deviation of phone purchase price for each group of customers.

b. The manager is also interested in an analysis of the phone purchase price based on whether the use will be for home or business. Again, she wants to compute mean and standard deviation of phone purchase price for each group of customers.

3-42. Each year, *Business Week* publishes information and rankings of MBA programs. The data file **MBA Analysis** contains data on several variables for eight reputable MBA programs. The variables include pre– and post–MBA salary, percentage salary increase, undergraduate GPA, average GMAT score, annual tuition, and expected annual student cost. Compute the mean, median, range, variance, and standard deviation for each of the variables in the database and write a short report that summarizes the data using these measures. Include any appropriate charts or graphs to assist in your report.

3-43. The First City Real Estate Company lists and sells residential real estate property in and around Yuma, Arizona. At a recent company meeting, the managing partner asked the office administrator to provide a descriptive analysis of the asking prices of the homes the company currently has listed. This list includes 319 homes; the price data, along with other home characteristics, are included in the data file called **First City Real Estate**. These data constitute a population.
 a. Compute the mean listing price.
 b. Compute the median listing price.
 c. Compute the range in listing prices.
 d. Compute the standard deviation in listing prices.
 e. Write a short report using the statistics computed in parts a–d to describe the prices of the homes currently listed by First City Real Estate.

3-44. Suppose there is an investigation to determine whether the increased availability of generic drugs, Internet drug purchases, and cost controls have reduced out-of-pocket drug expenses. As a part of the investigation, a random sample of 196 privately insured adults with incomes above 200% of the poverty level was taken,

and their 2005 out-of-pocket medical expenses for prescription drugs were collected. The data are in the file **Drug Expenses**.
 a. Calculate the mean and median for the sample data.
 b. Calculate the range, variance, standard deviation, and interquartile range for the sample data.
 c. Construct a box and whisker plot for the sample data.
 d. Write a short report that describes out-of-pocket drug expenses for privately insured adults whose incomes are greater than 200% of the poverty level.

3-45. Executive MBA programs have become increasingly popular. In an article titled "The Best Executive MBAs," *Business Week* provided data concerning the top 25 executive MBA programs for one specific year. The tuition for each of the schools selected was given. A file titled **EMBA** contains this data.
 a. Calculate the 20th, 40th, 60th, and 80th percentile among the ranks.
 b. Calculate the mean and standard deviation of the tuition for the five subgroups defined by the rank percentiles in part a. (*Hint*: For this purpose, are the data subgroups samples or populations?)
 c. Do the various subgroups' descriptive statistics echo their standing among the listed programs? Comment.

3-46. When PricewaterhouseCoopers Saratoga released its Human Capital Index Report, it indicated that the average hiring cost for an American company to fill a job vacancy was $3,270. Sample data for recent job hires is in a file titled **Hired**.
 a. Calculate the variance and standard deviation for the sample data.
 b. Construct a box and whisker plot. Does this plot indicate that extreme values (outliers) may be inflating the measures of spread calculated in part a?
 c. Suggest and calculate a measure of spread that is not affected by outliers.

END EXERCISES 3-2

3.3 Using the Mean and Standard Deviation Together

In the previous sections, we introduced several important descriptive measures that are useful for transforming data into meaningful information. Two of the most important of these measures are the mean and the standard deviation. In this section, we discuss several statistical tools that combine these two.

Chapter Outcome 4. → ## Coefficient of Variation

The standard deviation measures the variation in a set of data. For decision makers, the standard deviation indicates how spread out a distribution is. For distributions having the same mean, the distribution with the largest standard deviation has the greatest relative spread. When two or more distributions have different means, the relative spread cannot be determined by merely comparing standard deviations.

Coefficient of Variation

The ratio of the standard deviation to the mean expressed as a percentage. The coefficient of variation is used to measure variation relative to the mean.

 The **coefficient of variation** (*CV*) is used to measure the relative variation for distributions with different means.

The coefficient of variation for a population is computed using Equation 3.15, whereas Equation 3.16 is used for sample data.

Population Coefficient of Variation

$$CV = \frac{\sigma}{\mu}(100)\%$$ (3.15)

Sample Coefficient of Variation

$$CV = \frac{s}{\bar{x}}(100)\%$$ (3.16)

When the coefficients of variation for two or more distributions are compared, the distribution with the largest CV is said to have the greatest relative spread.

In finance, the CV measures the relative risk of a stock portfolio. Assume portfolio A has a collection of stocks that average a 12% return with a standard deviation of 3% and portfolio B has an average return of 6% with a standard deviation of 2%. We can compute the CV values for each as follows:

$$CV(A) = \frac{3}{12}(100)\% = 25\%$$

and

$$CV(B) = \frac{2}{6}(100)\% = 33\%$$

Even though portfolio B has a lower standard deviation, it would be considered more risky than portfolio A because B's CV is 33% and A's CV is 25%.

EXAMPLE 3-13   **COMPUTING THE COEFFICIENT OF VARIATION**

Agra-Tech Industries Agra-Tech Industries has recently introduced feed supplements for both cattle and hogs that will increase the rate at which the animals gain weight. Three years of feedlot tests indicate that steers fed the supplement will weigh an average of 125 pounds more than those not fed the supplement. However, not every steer on the supplement has the same weight gain; results vary. The standard deviation in weight-gain advantage for the steers in the three-year study has been 10 pounds.

Similar tests with hogs indicate those fed the supplement average 40 additional pounds compared with hogs not given the supplement. The standard deviation for the hogs was also 10 pounds. Even though the standard deviation is the same for both cattle and hogs, the mean weight gains differ. Therefore, the coefficient of variation is needed to compare relative variability. The coefficient of variation for each is computed using the following steps:

Step 1 **Collect the sample (or population) data for the variable of interest.**
In this case, we have two samples: weight gain for cattle and weight gain for hogs.

Step 2 **Compute the mean and the standard deviation.**
For the two samples in this example, we get
Cattle: $\bar{x} = 125$ lb and $s = 10$ lb
Hogs: $\bar{x} = 40$ lb and $s = 10$ lb

Step 3 **Compute the coefficient of variation using Equation 3.15 (for populations) or Equation 3.16 (for samples).**
Because the data in this example are from samples, the CV is computed using

$$CV = \frac{s}{\bar{x}}(100)\%$$

For each data set, we get

$$CV(\text{cattle}) = \frac{10}{125}(100)\% = 8\%$$

$$CV(\text{hogs}) = \frac{10}{40}(100)\% = 25\%$$

These results indicate that hogs exhibit much greater relative variability in weight gain compared with cattle.

>> **END EXAMPLE**

TRY PROBLEM 3-50 (pg. 119)

Chapter Outcome 5. →

The Empirical Rule A tool that is helpful in describing data in certain circumstances is called the **Empirical Rule**. For the Empirical Rule to be used, the frequency distribution must be bell-shaped, such as the one shown in Figure 3.8.

Empirical Rule

If the data distribution is bell shaped, then the interval

$\mu \pm 1\sigma$ contains approximately 68% of the values

$\mu \pm 2\sigma$ contains approximately 95% of the values

$\mu \pm 3\sigma$ contains virtually all of the data values

Dan Peretz/Shutterstock

BUSINESS APPLICATION **EMPIRICAL RULE**

BURGER N' BREW The standard deviation can be thought of as a measure of distance from the mean. Consider the Phoenix Burger n' Brew restaurant chain, which records the number of each hamburger option it sells each day at each location. The numbers of chili burgers sold each day for the past 365 days are in the file called **BurgerNBrew**. Figure 3.9 shows the frequency histogram for those data. The distribution is nearly *symmetrical* and is approximately *bell-shaped*. The mean number of chili burgers sold was 15.1, with a standard deviation of 3.1.

The Empirical Rule is a very useful statistical concept for helping us understand the data in a bell-shaped distribution. In the Burger N' Brew example, with $\bar{x} = 15.1$ and $s = 3.1$, if we move 1 standard deviation in each direction from the mean, approximately 68% of the data should lie within the following range:

$$15.1 \pm 1(3.1)$$
$$12.0 \text{ -------------------------- } 18.2$$

Excel Tutorial

FIGURE 3.8

Illustrating the Empirical Rule for the Bell-Shaped Distribution

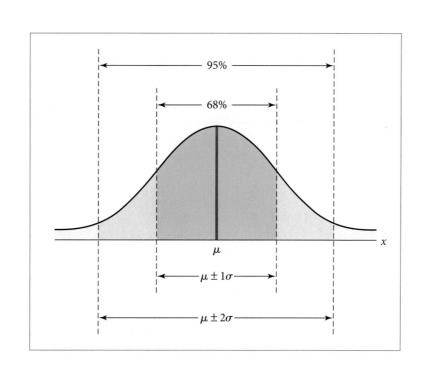

FIGURE 3.9

Excel 2010 Histogram for
Burger n' Brew Data

Excel 2010 Instructions:
1. Open file
   BurgerNBrew.xlsx.
2. Set up an area in the
   worksheet for the bins
   (upper limit of each class)
   as 7, 9, etc. Be sure to
   label the column of upper
   limits as "Bins."
3. On the **Data** tab, click
   **Data Analysis >
   Histogram**.
4. Input Range specifies the
   actual data values.
5. Put on a new worksheet
   and include **Chart
   Output**.
6. Right click on the bars
   and use the **Format Data
   Series Options** to set gap
   width to zero and add
   lines to bars.
7. Convert the bins in
   column A of the histogram
   output sheet to actual
   class labels. Note the bin
   labeled 7 is changed to
   "6 - 7".
8. Click on **Layout** and set
   titles as desired.

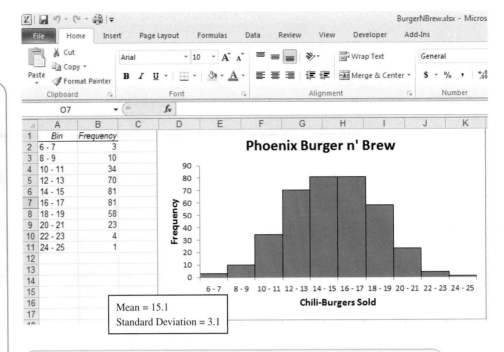

Minitab Instructions (for similar results):
1. Open file: **BurgerNBrew.MTW**.
2. Choose **Graph > Histogram**.
3. Click **Simple**.
4. Click **OK**.
5. In **Graph variables**, enter
   data column *Chili-Burgers Sold*.
6. Click **OK**.

The actual number of days Burger n' Brew sold between 12 and 18 chili burgers is 263. Thus, out of 365 days, on 72% of the days, Burger n' Brew sold between 12 and 18 chili burgers. (The reason that we didn't get exactly 68% is that the distribution in Figure 3.9 is not perfectly bell-shaped.)

If we look at the interval 2 standard deviations from either side of the mean, we would expect approximately 95% of the data. The interval is

$$15.1 \pm 2(3.1)$$
$$15.1 \pm 6.2$$
$$8.9 \text{ -------------------------- } 21.30$$

Counting the values between these limits, we find 353 of the 365 values, or 97%. Again this is close to what the Empirical Rule predicted. Finally, according to the Empirical Rule, we would expect almost all of the data to fall within 3 standard deviations. The interval is

$$15.1 \pm 3(3.1)$$
$$15.1 \pm 9.3$$
$$5.80 \text{ ------------------------- } 24.40$$

Looking at the data in Figure 3.9, we find that in fact, all the data do fall within this interval. Therefore, if we know only the mean and the standard deviation for a set of data, the Empirical Rule gives us a tool for describing how the data are distributed if the distribution is bell-shaped.

Tchebysheff's Theorem

Regardless of how data are distributed, *at least* $(1 - 1/k^2)$ of the values will fall within k standard deviations of the mean. For example:

At least $\left(1 - \dfrac{1}{1^2}\right) = 0 = 0\%$ of the values will fall within $k = 1$ standard deviation of the mean.

At least $\left(1 - \dfrac{1}{2^2}\right) = \dfrac{3}{4} = 75\%$ of the values will lie within $k = 2$ standard deviations of the mean.

At least $\left(1 - \dfrac{1}{3^2}\right) = \dfrac{8}{9} = 89\%$ of the values will lie within $k = 3$ standard deviations of the mean.

Chapter Outcome 5. → # Tchebysheff's Theorem

The Empirical Rule applies when a distribution is bell-shaped. But what about the many situations in which a distribution is skewed and not bell-shaped? In these cases, we can use **Tchebysheff's theorem**.

Tchebysheff's theorem is conservative. It tells us nothing about the data within 1 standard deviation of the mean. Tchebysheff indicates that *at least* 75% of the data will fall within 2 standard deviations—it could be more. If we applied Tchebysheff's theorem to bell-shaped distributions, the percentage estimates are very low. The thing to remember is that Tchebysheff's theorem applies to *any distribution*. This gives it great flexibility.

Chapter Outcome 4. →

Standardized Data Values

When you are dealing with quantitative data, you will sometimes want to convert the measures to a form called **standardized data values**. This is especially useful when we wish to compare data from two or more distributions when the data scales for the two distributions are substantially different.

Standardized Data Values

The number of standard deviations a value is from the mean. Standardized data values are sometimes referred to as *z* scores.

BUSINESS APPLICATION   **STANDARDIZING DATA**

HUMAN RESOURCES Consider a company that uses placement exams as part of its hiring process. The company currently will accept scores from either of two tests: AIMS Hiring and BHS-Screen. The problem is that the AIMS Hiring test has an average score of 2,000 and a standard deviation of 200, whereas the BHS-Screen test has an average score of 80 with a standard deviation of 12. (These means and standard deviations were developed from a large number of people who have taken the two tests.) How can the company compare applicants when the average scores and measures of spread are so different for the two tests? One approach is to *standardize* the test scores.

Suppose the company is considering two applicants, John and Mary. John took the AIMS Hiring test and scored 2,344, whereas Mary took the BHS-Screen and scored 95. Their scores can be standardized using Equation 3.17.

Standardized Population Data

$$z = \frac{x - \mu}{\sigma}$$

(3.17)

where:

x = Original data value
μ = Population mean
σ = Population standard deviation
z = Standard score (number of standard deviation x is from μ)

If you are working with sample data rather than a population, Equation 3.18 can be used to standardize the values.

Standardized Sample Data

$$z = \frac{x - \bar{x}}{s}$$

(3.18)

where:

x = Original data value
$\bar{x}$ = Sample mean
s = Sample standard deviation
z = The standard score

We can standardize the test scores for John and Mary using

$$z = \frac{x - \mu}{\sigma}$$

For the AIMS Hiring test, the mean, μ, is 2,000 and the standard deviation, σ, equals 200. John's score of 2,344 converts to

$$z = \frac{2,344 - 2,000}{200}$$
$$z = 1.72$$

The BHS-Screen's $\mu = 80$ and $\sigma = 12$. Mary's score of 95 converts to

$$z = \frac{95 - 80}{12}$$
$$z = 1.25$$

Compared to the average score on the AIMS Hiring test, John's score is 1.72 standard deviations higher. Mary's score is only 1.25 standard deviations higher than the average score on the BHS-Screen test. Therefore, even though the two tests used different scales, standardizing the data allows us to conclude John scored relatively better on his test than Mary did on her test.

How to do it (Example 3.14)

Converting Data to Standardized Values

For a set of quantitative data, each data value can be converted to a corresponding standardized value by determining how many standard deviations the value is from the mean. Here are the steps to do this.

1. Collect the population or sample values for the quantitative variable of interest.

2. Compute the population mean and standard deviation or the sample mean and standard deviation.

3. Convert the values to standardized z-values using Equation 3.17 or Equation 3.18. For populations,

$$z = \frac{x - \mu}{\sigma}$$

For samples,

$$z = \frac{x - \bar{x}}{s}$$

EXAMPLE 3-14   CONVERTING DATA TO STANDARDIZED VALUES

SAT and ACT Exams Many colleges and universities require students to submit either SAT or ACT scores or both. One eastern university requires both exam scores. However, in assessing whether to admit a student, the university uses whichever exam score favors the student among all the applicants. Suppose the school receives 4,000 applications for admission. To determine which exam will be used for each student, the school will standardize the exam scores from both tests. To do this, it can use the following steps:

Step 1   Collect data.
The university will collect the data for the 4,000 SAT scores and the 4,000 ACT scores for those students who applied for admission.

Step 2   Compute the mean and standard deviation.
Assuming that these data reflect the population of interest for the university, the population mean is computed using

$$\text{SAT:} \quad \mu = \frac{\Sigma x}{N} = 1,255 \qquad \text{ACT:} \quad \mu = \frac{\Sigma x}{N} = 28.3$$

The standard deviation is computed using

$$\text{SAT:} \quad \sigma = \sqrt{\frac{\Sigma(x - \mu)^2}{N}} = 72 \qquad \text{ACT:} \quad \sigma = \sqrt{\frac{\Sigma(x - \mu)^2}{N}} = 2.4$$

Step 3   Standardize the data.
Convert the x values to z values using

$$z = \frac{x - \mu}{\sigma}$$

Suppose a particular applicant has an SAT score of 1,228 and an ACT score of 27. These test scores can be converted to standardized scores.

$$\text{SAT:} \quad z = \frac{x - \mu}{\sigma} = \frac{1,228 - 1,255}{72} = -0.375$$

$$\text{ACT:} \quad z = \frac{x - \mu}{\sigma} = \frac{27 - 28.3}{2.4} = -0.542$$

The negative z values indicate that this student is below the mean on both the SAT and ACT exams. Because the university wishes to use the score that most favors the student, it will use the SAT score. The student is only 0.375 standard deviations below the SAT mean, compared with 0.542 standard deviations below the ACT mean.

>> END EXAMPLE

TRY PROBLEM 3-52 (pg. 119)

MyStatLab

3-3: Exercises

Skill Development

3-47. A population of unknown shape has a mean of 3,000 and a standard deviation of 200.
  a. Find the minimum proportion of observations in the population that are in the range 2,600 to 3,400.
  b. Determine the maximum proportion of the observations that are above 3,600.
  c. What statement could you make concerning the proportion of observations that are smaller than 2,400?

3-48. The mean time that a certain model of light bulb will last is 400 hours, with a standard deviation equal to 50 hours.
  a. Calculate the standardized value for a light bulb that lasts 500 hours.
  b. Assuming that the distribution of hours that light bulbs last is bell-shaped, what percentage of bulbs could be expected to last longer than 500 hours?

3-49. Consider the following set of sample data:

78	121	143	88	110	107	62	122	130	95	78	139	89	125

  a. Compute the mean and standard deviation for these sample data.
  b. Calculate the coefficient of variation for these sample data and interpret its meaning.
  c. Using Tchebysheff's theorem, determine the range of values that should include at least 89% of the data. Count the number of data values that fall into this range and comment on whether your interval range was conservative.

3-50. You are given the following parameters for two populations:

Population 1	Population 2
$\mu = 700$	$\mu = 29,000$
$\sigma = 50$	$\sigma = 5,000$

  a. Compute the coefficient of variation for each population.
  b. Based on the answers to part a, which population has data values that are more variable relative to the size of the population mean?

3-51. Two distributions of data are being analyzed. Distribution A has a mean of 500 and a standard deviation equal to 100. Distribution B has a mean of 10 and a standard deviation equal to 4.0. Based on this information, use the coefficient of variation to determine which distribution has greater relative variation.

3-52. Given two distributions with the following characteristics:

Distribution A	Distribution B
$\mu = 45,600$	$\mu = 33.40$
$\sigma = 6,333$	$\sigma = 4.05$

If a value from distribution A is 50,000 and a value from distribution B is 40.0, convert each value to a standardized z value and indicate which one is relatively closer to its respective mean.

3-53. If a sample mean is 1,000 and the sample standard deviation is 250, determine the standardized value for
  a. $x = 800$
  b. $x = 1,200$
  c. $x = 1,000$

3-54. The following data represent random samples taken from two different populations, A and B:

A	31	10	69	25	62	61	46	74	57
B	1,030	1,111	1,155	978	943	983	932	1,067	1,013

  a. Compute the mean and standard deviation for the sample data randomly selected from population A.
  b. Compute the mean and standard deviation for the sample data randomly selected from population B.
  c. Which sample has the greater spread when measured by the standard deviation?
  d. Compute the coefficient of variation for the sample data selected from population A and from population B. Which sample exhibits the greater relative variation?

3-55. Consider the following sample:

22	46	25	37	35	84	33	54	80	37
76	34	48	86	41	13	49	45	62	47
72	70	91	51	91	43	56	25	12	65

  a. Calculate the mean and standard deviation for this data.
  b. Determine the percentage of data values that fall in each of the following intervals: $\bar{x} \pm s, \bar{x} \pm 2s, \bar{x} \pm 3s$.
  c. Compare these with the percentages that should be expected from a bell-shaped distribution. Does it seem plausible that these data came from a bell-shaped population? Explain.

3-56. Consider the following population:

71	89	65	97	46	52	99	41	62	88
73	50	91	71	52	86	92	60	70	91
73	98	56	80	70	63	55	61	40	95

　　a. Determine the mean and variance.
　　b. Determine the percentage of data values that fall in each of the following intervals: $\bar{x} \pm 2s, \bar{x} \pm 3s, \bar{x} \pm 4s$.
　　c. Compare these with the percentages specified by Tchebysheff's theorem.

Business Applications

3-57. Pfizer, Inc., a major U.S. pharmaceutical company, is developing a new drug aimed at reducing the pain associated with migraine headaches. Two drugs are currently under development. One consideration in the evaluation of the medication is how long the pain-killing effects of the drugs last. A random sample of 12 tests for each drug revealed the following times (in minutes) until the effects of the drug were neutralized. The random samples are as follows:

Drug A	258	214	243	227	235	222	240	245	245	234	243	211
Drug B	219	283	291	277	258	273	289	260	286	265	284	266

　　a. Calculate the mean and standard deviation for each of the two drugs.
　　b. Based on the sample means calculated in part a, which drug appears to be effective longer?
　　c. Based on the sample standard deviations calculated in part a, which drug appears to have the greater variability in effect time?
　　d. Calculate the sample coefficient of variation for the two drugs. Based on the coefficient of variation, which drug has the greater variability in its time until the effect is neutralized?

3-58. Wells Fargo Bank's call center has representatives that speak both English and Spanish. A random sample of 11 calls to English-speaking service representatives and a random sample of 14 calls to Spanish-speaking service representatives was taken and the time to complete the calls was measured. The results (in seconds) are as follows:

Time to Complete the Call (in seconds)	
English-Speaking	131 80 140 118 79 94 103 145 113 100 122
Spanish-Speaking	170 177 150 208 151 127 147 140 109 184 119 149 129 152

　　a. Compute the mean and standard deviation for the time to complete calls to English-speaking service representatives.
　　b. Compute the mean and standard deviation for the time to complete calls to Spanish-speaking service representatives.
　　c. Compute the coefficient of variation for the time to complete calls to English-speaking and Spanish-speaking service representatives. Which group has the greater relative variability in the time to complete calls?
　　d. Construct box and whisker plots for the time required to complete the two types of calls and briefly discuss.

3-59. Lockheed Martin is a supplier for the aerospace industry. Recently, the company was considering switching to Cirus Systems, Inc., a new supplier for one of the component parts it needs for an assembly. At issue is the variability of the components supplied by Cirus Systems, Inc., compared to that of the existing supplier. The existing supplier makes the desired part with a mean diameter of 3.75 inches and a standard deviation of 0.078 inches. Unfortunately, Lockheed Martin does not have any of the exact same parts from the new supplier. Instead, the new supplier has sent a sample of 20 parts of a different size that it claims are representative of the type of work it can do. These sample data are shown here and in the data file called **Cirus**.

Diameters (in inches)					
18.018	17.856	18.095	17.992	18.086	17.812
17.988	17.996	18.129	18.003	18.214	18.313
17.983	18.153	17.996	17.908		
17.948	18.219	18.079	17.799		

　　Prepare a short letter to Lockheed-Martin indicating which supplier you would recommend based on relative variability.

3-60. A recent article in *The Washington Post Weekly Edition* indicated that about 80% of the estimated $200 billion of federal housing subsidies consists of tax breaks (mainly deductions for mortgage interest payments and preferential treatment for profits on home sales). Federal housing benefits average $8,268 for those with incomes between $50,000 and $200,000 and $365 for those with income of $40,000 to $50,000. Suppose the standard deviations of the housing benefits in these two categories were equal to $2,750 and $120, respectively.
　　a. Examine the two standard deviations. What do these indicate about the range of benefits enjoyed by the two groups?
　　b. Repeat part a using the coefficient of variation as the measure of relative variation.

3-61. Anaheim Human Resources, Inc., performs employment screening for large companies in southern California. It usually follows a two-step process. First, potential applicants are given a test that covers basic knowledge and intelligence. If applicants score within a certain range, they are called in for an interview. If they score below a certain point, they are sent a rejection letter. If applicants score above a certain point, they are sent directly to the client's human resources office without the interview. Recently, Anaheim Human Resources began working with a new client and formulated a new test just for this company. Thirty people were given the test, which is supposed to produce scores that are distributed according to a bell-shaped distribution. The following data reflect the scores of those 30 people:

76	75	74	56	61	76
62	96	68	62	78	76

84	67	60	96	77	59
67	81	66	71	69	65
58	77	82	75	76	67

Anaheim Human Resources has in the past issued a rejection letter with no interview to the lower 16% taking the test. They also send the upper 2.5% directly to the company without an interview. Everyone else is interviewed. Based on the data and the assumption of a bell-shaped distribution, what score should be used for the two cutoffs?

3-62. The College Board's Annual Survey of Colleges provides up-to-date information on tuition and other expenses associated with attending public and private nonprofit institutions of postsecondary education in the United States. Each fall, the College Board releases the survey results on how much colleges and universities are charging undergraduate students in the new academic year. The survey indicated that the average published tuition and fees for 2005–2006 were $8,244 at public four-year colleges and universities and $28,500 at private, nonprofit four-year colleges and universities. The standard deviation was approximately $4,500 at public four-year colleges and universities and approximately $12,000 for private colleges and universities.

   a. Do the private, nonprofit four-year colleges and universities have the larger relative variability? Provide statistical evidence to support your answer.

   b. If the data on published tuition and fees were bell shaped, determine the largest and smallest amount paid at the four-year private, nonprofit colleges and universities.

   c. Based on your answer to part b, do you believe that the data are bell shaped? Support your answer using statistical reasoning.

Computer Database **Exercises**

3-63. April 15 of every year is a day that most adults in the United States can relate to—the day that federal and state income taxes are due. Although there have been several attempts by Congress and the Internal Revenue Service over the past few years to simplify the income tax process, many people still have a difficult time completing their tax returns properly. To draw attention to this problem, a West Coast newspaper has asked 50 certified public accountant (CPA) firms to complete the same tax return for a hypothetical head of household. The CPA firms have their tax experts complete the return with the objective of determining the total federal income tax liability. The data in the file **Taxes** show the taxes owed as figured by each of the 50 CPA firms. Theoretically, they should all come up with the same taxes owed.

Based on these data, write a short article for the paper that describes the results of this experiment.

Include in your article such descriptive statistics as the mean, median, and standard deviation. You might consider using percentiles, the coefficient of variation, and Tchebysheff's theorem to help describe the data.

3-64. Nike ONE Black is one of the golf balls Nike, Inc., produces. It must meet the specifications of the United States Golf Association (USGA). The USGA mandates that the diameter of the ball shall not be less than 1.682 inches (42.67 mm). To verify that this specification is met, sample golf balls are taken from the production line and measured. These data are found in the file titled **Diameter**.

   a. Calculate the mean and standard deviation of this sample.

   b. Examine the specification for the diameter of the golf ball again. Does it seem that the data could possibly be bell shaped? Explain.

   c. Determine the proportion of diameters in the following intervals: $\bar{x} \pm 2s, \bar{x} \pm 3s, \bar{x} \pm 4s$. Compare these with the percentages specified by Tchebysheff's theorem.

3-65. The Centers for Disease Control and Prevention (CDC) started the Vessel Sanitation Program (VSP) in the early 1970s because of several disease outbreaks on cruise ships. The VSP was established to protect the health of passengers and crew by minimizing the risk of gastrointestinal illness on cruise ships. Inspections are scored on a point system of maximum 100, and cruise ships earn a score based on the criteria. Ships that score an 86 or higher have a satisfactory sanitation level. Data from a recent inspection are contained in a file titled **Cruiscore**.

   a. Calculate the mean, standard deviation, median, and interquartile range. Which of these measures would seem most appropriate to characterize this data set?

   b. Produce a box and whisker plot of the data. Would the Empirical Rule or Tchebysheff's theorem be appropriate for describing this data set? Explain.

   c. If you wished to travel only on those ships that are at the 90th percentile or above in terms of sanitation, what would be the lowest sanitation score you would find acceptable?

3-66. Airfare prices were collected for a round trip from Los Angeles (LAX) to Salt Lake City (SLC). Airfare prices were also collected for a round trip from Los Angeles (LAX) to Barcelona, Spain (BCN). Airfares were obtained for the designated and nearby airports during high travel months. The passenger was to fly coach class round-trip, staying seven days. The data are contained in a file titled **Airfare**.

   a. Calculate the mean and standard deviation for each of the flights.

   b. Calculate an appropriate measure of the relative variability of these two flights.

   c. A British friend of yours is currently in Barcelona and wishes to fly to Los Angeles. If the flight fares are the same but priced in English pounds, determine his mean, standard deviation, and measure of relative dispersion for that data. (*Note*: $1 = 0.566$ GBP.)

3-67. Doing business internationally is no longer something reserved for the largest companies. In fact, medium-size and, in some cases, even small companies are finding themselves with the opportunity to do business internationally. One factor that will be important for world trade is the growth rate of the population of the world's countries. The data file **Country Growth** contains the most recent United Nations data on the population and the growth rate for the last decade for 231 countries throughout the world. Based on these data, which countries had growth rates that exceeded 2 standard deviations higher than the mean growth rate? Which countries had growth rates more than 2 standard deviations below the mean growth rate?

Visual Summary

Chapter 3: To fully describe your data, not only do you need to use the graphs, charts, and tables introduced in Chapter 2, you need to provide the measures of the center and measures of variations in the data that are presented in this chapter. Together, the numeric measures and the graphs and charts can paint a complete picture of the data that transform it from just data to useful information for decision-making purposes.

3.1 Measures of Center and Location (pg. 81-102)

Summary

The three numerical measures of the center for a set of data are the **mean**, **median** and the **mode**. The mean is the **arithmetic average** and is the most frequently used measure. However, if the data are **skewed** or are **ordinal** level, the median is suggested. Unlike the mean which is sensitive to extreme values in the data, the median is unaffected by extremes. The mode is less frequently used as a measure of the center since it is simply the value in the data that occurs most frequently. When one of these measures is computed from a **population**, the measure is said to be a **parameter**, but if the measure is computed from **sample** data, the measure is called a **statistic**. Other measures of location that are commonly used are **percentiles** and **quartiles**. Finally, many decision makers prefer to construct a **box and whisker plot** which uses a box to display the range of the middle 50 percent of the data. The limits of whiskers are calculated based on the numerical distance between the first and third quartiles.

Outcome 1. Compute the mean, median, mode and weighted average for a set of data and understand what these values represent.

Outcome 2. Construct a box and whisker graph and interpret it.

3.2 Measures of Variation (pg. 102-113)

Summary

One of the major issues that business decision makers face every day is the **variation** that exists in their operations, processes, and people. Because virtually all data exhibit variation, it is important to measure it. The simplest measure of variation is the **range** which is the difference between the highest value and the lowest value in the data. An alternative to the range that ignores the extremes in the data is the **interquartile range** which measures the numerical distance between the 3rd and 1st quartiles. But the two most frequently used measures of variation are the **variance** and the **standard deviation**. The equations for these two measures differ slightly depending on whether you are working with a population or a sample. The standard deviation is measured in the same units as the variable of interest and is a measure of the average deviation of the individual data items around the mean.

Outcome 3. Compute the range, variance, and standard deviation and know what these values mean.

3.3 Using the Mean and Standard Deviation Together (pg. 113-122)

Summary

The real power of statistical measures of the center and variation come when they are used together to fully describe the data. One particular measure that is used a great deal in business, especially in financial analysis, is the **coefficient of variation**. When comparing two or more data sets, the larger the coefficient of variation, the greater the relative variation of the data. Another very important way in which the mean and standard deviation are used together is evident in the **empirical rule** which allows decision makers to better understand the data from a **bell-shaped** distribution. In cases where the data are not bell-shaped, the data can be described using **Tchebysheff's Theorem**. The final way discussed in this chapter in which the mean and standard deviation are used together is the **z-value**. Z-values for each individual data point measure the number of standard deviations a data value is from the mean.

Outcome 4. Compute a z score and the coefficient of variation and understand how they are applied in decision-making situations.

Outcome 5. Understand the Empirical Rule and Tchebysheff's Theorem

Conclusion

A very important part of the descriptive tools in statistics is the collection of numerical measures that can be computed. When these measures of the center and variation in the data are combined with charts and graphs, you can fully describe the data. **Figure 3.10** presents a summary of the key numerical measures that are discussed in Chapter 3. Remember, measures computed from a population are called parameters while measures computed from a sample are called statistics.

FIGURE 3.10

Summary of Numerical
Statistical Measures

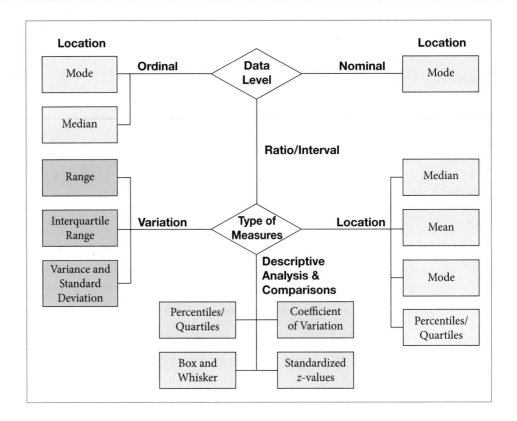

Equations

(3.1) Population Mean pg. 82

$$\mu = \frac{\sum_{i=1}^{N} x_i}{N}$$

(3.2) Sample Mean pg. 85

$$\bar{x} = \frac{\sum_{i=1}^{n} x_i}{n}$$

(3.3) Median Index pg. 87

$$i = \frac{1}{2} n$$

(3.4) Weighted Mean for a Population pg. 92

$$\mu_w = \frac{\sum w_i x_i}{\sum w_i}$$

(3.5) Weighted Mean for a Sample pg. 93

$$\bar{x}_w = \frac{\sum w_i x_i}{\sum w_i}$$

(3.6) Percentile Location Index pg. 94

$$i = \frac{p}{100}(n)$$

(3.7) Range pg. 103

$$R = \text{Maximum value} - \text{Minimum value}$$

(3.8) Interquartile Range pg. 103

$$\text{Interquartile range} = \text{Third quartile} - \text{First quartile}$$

(3.9) Population Variance pg. 105

$$\sigma^2 = \frac{\sum_{i=1}^{N} (x_i - \mu)^2}{N}$$

(3.10) Population Variance Shortcut pg. 105

$$\sigma^2 = \frac{\sum x^2 - \frac{(\sum x)^2}{N}}{N}$$

(3.11) Population Standard Deviation pg. 106

$$\sigma = \sqrt{\sigma^2} = \sqrt{\frac{\sum_{i=1}^{N} (x_i - \mu)^2}{N}}$$

(3.12) Sample Variance pg. 107

$$s^2 = \frac{\sum\limits_{i=1}^{n}(x_i - \bar{x})^2}{n-1}$$

(3.13) Sample Variance Shortcut pg. 107

$$s^2 = \frac{\sum x^2 - \dfrac{(\sum x)^2}{n}}{n-1}$$

(3.14) Sample Standard Deviation pg. 107

$$s = \sqrt{s^2} = \sqrt{\frac{\sum\limits_{i=1}^{n}(x_i - \bar{x})^2}{n-1}}$$

(3.15) Population Coefficient of Variation pg. 114

$$CV = \frac{\sigma}{\mu}(100)\%$$

(3.16) Sample Coefficient of Variation pg. 114

$$CV = \frac{s}{\bar{x}}(100)\%$$

(3.17) Standardized Population Data pg. 117

$$z = \frac{x - \mu}{\sigma}$$

(3.18) Standardized Sample Data pg. 117

$$z = \frac{x - \bar{x}}{s}$$

Key Terms

Box and whisker plot pg. 95
Coefficient of variation pg. 113
Data array pg. 87
Empirical Rule pg. 115
Interquartile range pg. 103
Left-skewed data pg. 88
Mean pg. 82
Median pg. 87
Mode pg. 89

Parameter pg. 82
Percentiles pg. 93
Population mean pg. 82
Quartiles pg. 95
Range pg. 103
Right-skewed data pg. 88
Sample mean pg. 85
Skewed data pg. 88

Standard deviation pg. 104
Standardized data values pg. 117
Statistic pg. 82
Symmetric data pg. 88
Tchebysheff's theorem pg. 116
Variance pg. 104
Variation pg. 102
Weighted mean pg. 92

Chapter Exercises   MyStatLab

Conceptual Questions

3-68. Consider the following questions concerning the sample variance:
  a. Is it possible for a variance to be negative? Explain.
  b. What is the smallest value a variance can be? Under what conditions does the variance equal this smallest value?
  c. Under what conditions is the sample variance smaller than the corresponding sample standard deviation?

3-69. For a continuous variable that has a bell-shaped distribution, determine the percentiles associated with the endpoints of the intervals specified in the Empirical Rule.

3-70. Consider that the Empirical Rule stipulates that virtually all of the data values are within the interval $\mu \pm 3\sigma$. Use this stipulation to determine an approximation for the standard deviation involving the range.

3-71. At almost every university in the United States, the university computes student grade point averages (GPAs). The following scale is typically used by universities:

A = 4 points	B = 3 points	C = 2 points
D = 1 point	F = 0 points	

Discuss what, if any, problems might exist when GPAs for two students are compared. What about comparing GPAs for students from two different universities?

3-72. Since the standard deviation of a set of data requires more effort to compute than the range does, what advantages does the standard deviation have when discussing the spread in a set of data?

3-73. The mode seems like a very simple measure of the location of a distribution. When would the mode be preferred over the median or the mean?

Business Applications

3-74. Home Pros sells supplies to "do-it-yourselfers." One of the things the company prides itself on is fast service. It uses a number system and takes customers in the order they arrive at the store. Recently, the assistant manager tracked the time customers spent in the store from the time they took a number until they left. A sample of 16 customers was selected and the following data (measured in minutes) were recorded:

15	14	16	14	14	14	13	8
12	9	7	17	10	15	16	16

a. Compute the mean, median, mode, range, interquartile range, and standard deviation.

b. Develop a box and whisker plot for these data.

3-75. More than 272 million computer and video games were sold in 2010—more than two games for every U.S. household. Gamers spend an average of 3 to 4 hours playing games online every day. The average age of players is 28. Video games and gamers have even created a new form of marketing—called "advergaming." "Advergaming is taking games—something that people do for recreation—and inserting a message," said Julie Roehm, director of marketing communications for the Chrysler Group, which sells Chrysler, Jeep, and Dodge brand vehicles. "It's important we go to all the places our consumers are." Suppose it is possible to assume the standard deviation of the ages of video game users is 9 years and that the distribution is bell shaped. To assist the marketing department in obtaining demographics to increase sales, determine the proportion of players who are

a. between 19 and 28

b. between 28 and 37

c. older than 37

3-76. Travelers are facing increased costs for both driving and flying to chosen destinations. With rising costs for both modes of transportation, what really weighs on the decision to drive or to fly? To gain a better understanding of the "fly or drive" decision, a recent study compared the costs for trips between Los Angeles and Denver, 1,016 miles one way. Los Angeles to Denver round-trip costs $218 by car and $159.00 by plane. Cost flexibility is greater with the flying trips because of greater airfare choices. The driving trip costs, except for the on-road lunches, are pretty much set in place. Assume the standard deviation for the cost of flying trips is approximately $54.

a. If a flight to Denver from Los Angeles was chosen at random, determine the proportion of the time that the cost would be smaller than $164. Assume the flight costs are bell-shaped.

b. Determine a flight cost that would qualify as the 25th percentile.

c. If nothing can be assumed about the distribution of the flight costs, determine the largest percentile that could be attributed to an airfare of $128.

3-77. With the ups and downs in the economy since 2008, many discount airline fares are available if a customer knows how to obtain the discount. Many travelers complain that they get a different price every time they call. The American Consumer Institute recently priced tickets between Spokane, Washington, and St. Louis, Missouri. The passenger was to fly coach class round-trip, staying seven days. Calls were made directly to airlines and to travel agents with the following results. Note that the data reflect round-trip airfare.

| $229.00 | $345.00 | $599.00 | $229.00 | $429.00 | $605.00 |
| $339.00 | $339.00 | $229.00 | $279.00 | $344.00 | $407.00 |

a. Compute the mean quoted airfare.

b. Compute the variance and standard deviation in airfares quoted. Treat the data as a sample.

3-78. The manager of the Cottonwood Grille recently selected a random sample of 18 customers and kept track of how long the customers were required to wait from the time they arrived at the restaurant until they were actually served dinner. This study resulted from several complaints the manager had received from customers saying that their wait time was unduly long and that it appeared that the objective was to keep people waiting in the lounge for as long as possible to increase the lounge business. The following data were recorded, with time measured in minutes:

| 34 | 24 | 43 | 56 | 74 | 20 | 19 | 33 | 55 |
| 43 | 54 | 34 | 27 | 34 | 36 | 24 | 54 | 39 |

a. Compute the mean waiting time for this sample of customers.

b. Compute the median waiting time for this sample of customers.

c. Compute the variance and standard deviation of waiting time for this sample of customers.

d. Develop a frequency distribution using six classes, each with a class width of 10. Make the lower limit of the first class 15.

e. Develop a frequency histogram for the frequency distribution.

f. Construct a box and whisker plot of these data.

g. The manager is considering giving a complementary drink to customers whose waiting time is longer than the third quartile. Determine the minimum number of minutes a customer would have to wait in order to receive a complementary drink.

3-79. Simplot Agri-Chemical has decided to implement a new incentive system for the managers of its three plants. The plan calls for a bonus to be paid next month to the manager whose plant has the greatest relative improvement over the average monthly production volume. The following data reflect the historical production volumes at the three plants:

Plant 1	Plant 2	Plant 3
$\mu = 700$	$\mu = 2,300$	$\mu = 1,200$
$\sigma = 200$	$\sigma = 350$	$\sigma = 30$

At the close of next month, the monthly output for the three plants was

| Plant 1 = 810 | Plant 2 = 2,600 | Plant 3 = 1,320 |

Suppose the division manager has awarded the bonus to the manager of Plant 2 since her plant increased its production by 300 units over the mean, more than that for any of the other managers. Do you agree with the award of the bonus for this month? Explain, using the appropriate statistical measures to support your position.

3-80. According to the annual report issued by Wilson & Associates, an investment firm in Bowling Green, the stocks in its Growth Fund have generated an average return of 8% with a standard deviation of 2%. The stocks in the Specialized Fund have generated an average return of 18% with a standard deviation of 6%.

   a. Based on the data provided, which of these funds has exhibited greater relative variability? Use the proper statistical measure to make your determination.

   b. Suppose an investor who is very risk averse is interested in one of these two funds. Based strictly on relative variability, which fund would you recommend? Discuss.

   c. Suppose the distributions for the two stock funds had a bell-shaped distribution with the means and standard deviations previously indicated. Which fund appears to be the best investment, assuming future returns will mimic past returns? Explain.

3-81. The Dakota Farm Cooperative owns and leases prime farmland in the upper Midwest. Most of its 34,000 acres are planted in grain. The cooperative performs a substantial amount of testing to determine what seed types produce the greatest yields. Recently, the cooperative tested three types of corn seed on test plots. The following values were observed after the first test year:

	Seed Type A	Seed Type B	Seed Type C
Mean Bushels/Acre	88	56	100
Standard Deviation	25	15	16

   a. Based on the results of this testing, which seed seems to produce the greatest average yield per acre? Comment on the type of testing controls that should have been used to make this study valid.

   b. Suppose the company is interested in consistency. Which seed type shows the least relative variability?

   c. Assuming the Empirical Rule applies, describe the production distribution for each of the three seed types.

   d. Suppose you were a farmer and had to obtain at least 135 bushels per acre to escape bankruptcy. Which seed type would you plant? Explain your choice.

   e. Rework your answer to part d assuming the farmer needed 115 bushels per acre instead.

3-82. The Hillcrest Golf and Country Club manager selected a random sample of the members and recorded the number of rounds of golf they played last season. The reason for his interest in this data is that the club is thinking of applying a discount to members who golf more than a specified number of rounds per year. The sample of eight people produced the following number of rounds played:

13	32	12	9	16	17	16	12

   a. Compute the mean for these sample data.
   b. Compute the median for these sample data.
   c. Compute the mode for these sample data.
   d. Calculate the variance and standard deviation for these sample data.
   e. Note that one person in the sample played 32 rounds. What effect, if any, does this large value have on each of the three measures of location? Discuss.
   f. For these sample data, which measure of location provides the best measure of the center of the data? Discuss.
   g. Given this sample data, suppose the manager wishes to give discounts to golfers in the top quartile. What should the minimum number of rounds played be to receive a discount?

3-83. Stock investors often look to beat the performance of the S&P 500 Index, which generally serves as a yardstick for the market as a whole. The following table shows a comparison of the five-year cumulative total shareholder returns for IDACORP common stock, the S&P 500 Index, and the Edison Electric Institute (EEI) Electric Utilities Index. The data assume that $100 was invested on December 31, 2002, with beginning-of-period weighting of the peer group indices (based on market capitalization) and monthly compounding of returns (*Source:* IDACORP 2007 Annual Report).

Year	IDACORP ($)	S&P 500 ($)	EEI Electric Utilities Index ($)
2002	100.00	100.00	100.00
2003	128.86	128.67	123.48
2004	137.11	142.65	151.68
2005	136.92	149.66	176.02
2006	186.71	173.27	212.56
2007	176.26	182.78	247.76

Using the information provided, construct appropriate statistical measures that illustrate the performance of the three investments. How well has IDACORP performed over the time periods compared to the S&P 500? How well has it performed relative to its industry as measured by the returns of the EEI Electric Utilities Index?

3-84. The Zagat Survey®, a leading provider of leisure-based survey results, released its San Francisco Restaurants Survey involving participants who dined out an average of 3.2 times per week. The report showed the average price per meal falling from the previous year from $34.07 to $33.75.

a. If the standard deviation of the price of meals in San Francisco was $10, determine the largest proportion of meal prices that could be larger than $50.

b. If the checks were paid in Chinese currency ($1 USD = 8.0916 Chinese Yuan), determine the mean and standard deviation of meal prices in San Francisco. How would this change of currency affect your answer to part a?

Computer Database **Exercises**

3-85. The data in the file named **Fast100** were collected by D. L. Green & Associates, a regional investment management company that specializes in working with clients who wish to invest in smaller companies with high growth potential. To aid the investment firm in locating appropriate investments for its clients, Sandra Williams, an assistant client manager, put together a database on 100 fast-growing companies. The database consists of data on eight variables for each of the 100 companies. Note that in some cases data are not available. A code of –99 has been used to signify missing data. These data will have to be omitted from any calculations.

a. Select the variable Sales. Develop a frequency distribution and histogram for Sales.

b. Compute the mean, median, and standard deviation for the Sales variable.

c. Determine the interquartile range for the Sales variable.

d. Construct a box and whisker plot for the Sales variable. Identify any outliers. Discard the outliers and recalculate the measures in part b.

e. Each year, a goal is set for sales. Next year's goal will be to have average sales that are at this year's 65th percentile. Identify next year's sales goal.

3-86. The Environmental Protection Agency (EPA) tests all new cars and provides a mileage rating for both city and highway driving conditions. Thirty cars were tested and are contained in the data file **Automobiles**. The file contains data on several variables. In this problem, focus on the city and highway mileage data.

a. Calculate the sample mean miles per gallon (mpg) for both city and highway driving for the 30 cars. Also calculate the sample standard deviation for the two mileage variables. Do the data tend to support the premise that cars get better mileage on the highway than around town? Discuss.

b. Referring to part a, what can the EPA conclude about the relative variability between car models for highway versus city driving? (*Hint*: Compute the appropriate measure to compare relative variability.)

c. Assume that mileage ratings are approximately bell shaped. Approximately what proportion of cars gets at least as good mileage in city driving conditions as the mean mileage for highway driving for all cars?

3-87. American Express estimates current Halloween spending to be about $53 per person. Much of the spending was expected to come from young adults. A file titled **Halloween** contains sample data on Halloween spending.

a. Calculate the mean and standard deviation of these data.

b. Determine the following intervals for this data set: $\bar{x} \pm 1s, \bar{x} \pm 2s, \bar{x} \pm 3s$.

c. Suppose your responsibility as an assistant manager was to determine the price of costumes to be sold. The manager has informed you to set the price of one costume so that it was beyond the budget of only 2.5% of the customers. Assume that the data set has a bell-shaped distribution.

3-88. PayScale is a source of online compensation information, providing access to accurate compensation data for both employees and employers. PayScale allows users to obtain compensation information providing a snapshot of the job market. Recently, it published statistics for the salaries of MBA graduates. The file titled **Payscale** contains data with the same characteristics as those obtained by PayScale for California and Florida.

a. Calculate the standard deviations of the salaries for both states' MBA graduates. Which state seems to have the widest spectrum of salaries for MBA graduates?

b. Calculate the average and median salary for each state's MBA graduates.

c. Examining the averages calculated in part b, determine which state's MBA graduates have the largest relative dispersion.

3-89. *Yahoo! Finance* makes available historical stock prices. It lists the opening, high, and low stock prices for each stock available on NYSE and NASDAQ. A file titled **GEstock** gives this data for General Electric (GE) for a recent 99-day period.

a. Calculate the difference between the opening and closing stock prices for GE over this time period. Then calculate the mean, median, and standard deviation of these differences.

b. Indicate what the mean in part a indicates about the relative prices of the opening and closing stock prices for GE.

c. Compare the dispersion of the opening stock prices with the difference between the opening and closing stock prices.

3-90. Zepolle's Bakery makes a variety of bread types that it sells to supermarket chains in the area. One of Zepolle's problems is that the number of loaves of each type of bread sold each day by the chain stores varies considerably, making it difficult to know how many loaves to bake. A sample of daily demand data is contained in the file **Bakery**.

  a. Which bread type has the highest average daily demand?

  b. Develop a frequency distribution for each bread type.

  c. Which bread type has the highest standard deviation in demand?

  d. Which bread type has the greatest relative variability? Which type has the lowest relative variability?

  e. Assuming that these sample data are representative of demand during the year, determine how many loaves of each type of bread should be made such that demand would be met on at least 75% of the days during the year.

  f. Create a new variable called Total Loaves Sold. On which day of the week is the average for total loaves sold the highest?

3-91. The Internal Revenue Service (IRS) has come under a great deal of criticism in recent years for various actions it is purported to have taken against U.S. citizens related to collecting federal income taxes. The IRS is also criticized for the complexity of the tax code, although the tax laws are actually written by congressional staff and passed by Congress. For the past few years, one of the country's biggest tax-preparing companies has sponsored an event in which 50 certified public accountants from all sizes of CPA firms are asked to determine the tax owed for a fictitious citizen. The IRS is also asked to determine the "correct" tax owed. Last year, the "correct" figure stated by the IRS was $11,560. The file **Taxes** contains the data for the 50 accountants.

  a. Compute a new variable that is the difference between the IRS number and the number determined by each accountant.

  b. For this new variable computed in part a, develop a frequency distribution.

  c. For the new variable computed in part a, determine the mean, median, and standard deviation.

  d. Determine the percentile that would correspond to the "correct" tax figure if the IRS figure were one of the CPA firms' estimated tax figures. Describe what this implies about the agreement between the IRS and consultants' calculated tax.

3-92. The Cozine Corporation operates a garbage hauling business. Up to this point, the company has been charged a flat fee for each of the garbage trucks that enters the county landfill. The flat fee is based on the assumed truck weight of 45,000 pounds. In two weeks, the company is required to appear before the county commissioners to discuss a rate adjustment. In preparation for this meeting, Cozine has hired an independent company to weigh a sample of Cozine's garbage trucks just prior to their entering the landfill. The data file **Cozine** contains the data the company has collected.

  a. Based on the sample data, what percentile does the 45,000-pound weight fall closest to?

  b. Compute appropriate measures of central location for the data.

  c. Construct a frequency histogram based on the sample data. Use the $2^k \geq n$ guideline (see Chapter 2) to determine the number of classes. Also, construct a box and whisker plot for these data. Discuss the relative advantages of histograms and box and whisker plots for presenting these data.

  d. Use the information determined in parts a–c to develop a presentation to the county commissioners. Make sure the presentation attempts to answer the question of whether Cozine deserves a rate reduction.

video Video Case 3

Drive-Thru Service Times @ McDonald's

When you're on the go and looking for a quick meal, where do you go? If you're like millions of people every day, you make a stop at McDonald's. Known as "quick service restaurants" in the industry (not "fast food"), companies such as McDonald's invest heavily to determine the most efficient and effective ways to provide fast, high-quality service in all phases of their business.

    Drive-thru operations play a vital role. It's not surprising that attention is focused on the drive-thru process. After all, more than 60% of individual restaurant revenues in the United States come from the drive-thru experience. Yet understanding the process is more complex than just counting cars. Marla King, professor at

the company's international training center, Hamburger University, got her start 25 years ago working at a McDonald's drive-thru. She now coaches new restaurant owners and managers. "Our stated drive-thru service time is 90 seconds or less. We train every manager and team member to understand that a quality customer experience at the drive-thru depends on them," says Marla. Some of the factors that affect customers' ability to complete their purchases within 90 seconds include restaurant staffing, equipment layout in the restaurant, training, efficiency of the grill team, and frequency of customer arrivals, to name a few. Also, customer order patterns play a role. Some customers will just order drinks, whereas others seem to need enough food to feed an entire soccer team. And then there are the special orders. Obviously, there is plenty of room for variability here.

Yet that doesn't stop the company from using statistical techniques to better understand the drive-thru action. In particular, McDonald's utilizes numerical measures of the center and spread in the data to help transform the data into useful information. For restaurant managers to achieve the goal in their own restaurants, they need training in proper restaurant and drive-thru operations. Hamburger University, McDonald's training center located near Chicago, Illinois, satisfies that need. In the mock-up restaurant service lab, managers go through a "before and after" training scenario. In the "before" scenario, they run the restaurant for 30 minutes as if they were back in their home restaurants. Managers in the training class are assigned to be crew, customers, drive-thru cars, special-needs guests (such as hearing impaired, indecisive, clumsy), or observers. Statistical data about the operations, revenues, and service times are collected and analyzed. Without the right training, the restaurant's operations usually start breaking down after 10 to 15 minutes. After debriefing and analyzing the data collected, the managers make suggestions for adjustments and head back to the service lab to try again. This time, the results usually come in well within standards. "When presented with the quantitative results, managers are pretty quick to make the connections between better operations, higher revenues, and happier customers," Marla states.

When managers return to their respective restaurants, the training results and techniques are shared with staff charged with implementing the ideas locally. The results of the training eventually are measured when McDonald's conducts a restaurant operations improvement process study, or ROIP. The goal is simple: improved operations. When the ROIP review is completed, statistical analyses are performed and managers are given their results. Depending on the results, decisions might be made that require additional financial resources, building construction, staff training, or layout reconfiguration. Yet one thing is clear: Statistics drive the decisions behind McDonald's drive-thru service operations.

Discussion Questions:

1. After returning from the training session at Hamburger University, a McDonald's store owner selected a random sample of 362 drive-thru customers and carefully measured the time it took from when a customer entered the McDonald's property until the customer had received the order at the drive-thru window. These data are in the file called **McDonald's Drive-Thru Waiting Times**. Note, the owner selected some customers during the breakfast period, others during lunch, and others during dinner. For the overall sample, compute the key measures of central tendency. Based on these measures, what conclusion might the owner reach with respect to how well his store is doing in meeting the 90-second customer service goal? Discuss.

2. Referring to question 1, compute the key measures of central tendency for drive-thru times broken down by breakfast, lunch, and dinner time periods. Based on these calculations, does it appear that the store is doing better at one of these time periods than the others in providing shorter drive-thru waiting times? Discuss.

3. Referring to questions 1 and 2, compute the range and standard deviation for drive-thru times for the overall sample and for the three different times of the day. Also calculate the appropriate measure of relative variability for each time period. Discuss these measures of variability and what they might imply about what customers can expect at this McDonald's drive-thru.

4. Determine the 1st and 3rd quartiles for drive-thru times and develop a box and whisker diagram for the overall sample data. Are there any outliers identified in these sample data? Discuss.

Case 3.1

WGI—Human Resources

WGI is a large international construction company with operations in 43 countries. The company has been a major player in the reconstruction efforts in Iraq, with a number of subcontracts under the major contractor, Haliburton, Inc. However, the company is also involved in many small projects both in the United States and around the world. One of these is a sewer line installation project in Madison, Wisconsin. The contract is what is called a "cost plus" contract, meaning that the city of Madison will pay for all direct costs, including materials and labor, of the project plus an additional fee to WGI. Roberta Bernhart is the human resources (HR) manager for the Madison project and is responsible for overseeing all aspects of employee compensation and HR issues.

WGI is required to produce a variety of reports to the Madison city council on an annual basis. Recently, the council asked WGI to prepare a report showing the current hourly rates for the nonsalaried work crew on the project. Specifically, the council is interested in any proposed pay increases to the work crew that will ultimately be passed along to the city of Madison. In response to the city's request, Roberta put together a data file for all 19 nonsalaried work crew members, called **WGI**, which shows their current hourly pay rate and the proposed increase to take place the first of next month. These data are as follows:

Name	Current Rate	New Rate
Jody	$20.55	$22.55
Tim	$22.15	$23.81
Thomas	$14.18	$15.60
Shari	$14.18	$15.60
John	$18.80	$20.20
Jared	$18.98	$20.20
Loren	$25.24	$26.42
Mike	$18.36	$19.28
Patrick	$17.20	$18.06
Sharon	$16.99	$17.84
Sam	$16.45	$17.27
Susan	$18.90	$19.66
Chris	$18.30	$19.02
Steve F	$27.45	$28.12
Kevin	$16.00	$16.64
Larry	$17.47	$18.00
MaryAnn	$23.99	$24.47
Mark	$22.62	$23.08
Aaron	$15.00	$15.40

The city council expects the report to contain both graphic and numerical descriptive analyses. Roberta has outlined the following tasks and has asked you to help her.

Required Tasks:

1. Develop and interpret histograms showing the distributions of current hourly rates and proposed new hourly rates for the crew members.
2. Compute and interpret key measures of central tendency and variation for the current and new hourly rates. Determine the coefficient of variation for each.

3. Compute a new variable called Pay Increase that reflects the difference between the proposed new pay rate and the current rate. Develop a histogram for this variable, and then compute key measures of the center and variation for the new variable.
4. Compute a new variable that is the percentage increase in hourly pay rate. Prepare a graphical and numerical description of this new variable.
5. Prepare a report to the city council that contains the results from tasks 1–4.

Case 3.2

National Call Center

Candice Worthy and Philip Hanson are day shift supervisors at National Call Center's Austin, Texas, facility. National provides contract call center services for a number of companies, including banks and major retail companies. Candice and Philip have both been with the company for slightly more than five years, having joined National right after graduating with bachelor's degrees from the University of Texas. As they walked down the hall together after the weekly staff meeting, the two friends were discussing the assignment they were just handed by Mark Gonzales, the division manager. The assignment came out of a discussion at the meeting in which one of National's clients wanted a report describing the calls being handled for them by National. Mark had asked Candice and Philip to describe the data in a file called **National Call Center** and produce a report that would both graphically and numerically analyze the data. The data are for a sample of 57 calls and for the following variables:

Account Number

Caller Gender

Account Holder Gender

Past Due Amount

Current Account Balance

Nature of Call (Billing Question or Other)

By the time they reached their office, Candice and Philip had outlined some of the key tasks that they needed to do.

Required Tasks:

1. Develop bar charts showing the mean and median current account balance by gender of the caller.
2. Develop bar charts showing the mean and median current account balance by gender of the account holder.
3. Construct a scatter diagram showing current balance on the horizontal axis and past due amount on the vertical axis.
4. Compute the key descriptive statistics for the center and for the variation in current account balance broken down by gender of the caller, gender of the account holder, and by the nature of the call.
5. Repeat task 4 but compute the statistics for the past due balances.
6. Compute the coefficient of variation for current account balances for male and female account holders.
7. Develop frequency and relative frequency distributions for the gender of callers, gender of account holders, and nature of the calls.
8. Develop joint frequency and joint relative frequency distributions for the account holder gender by whether or not the account has a past due balance.
9. Write a report to National's client that contains the results for tasks 1–8 along with a discussion of these statistics and graphs.

Case 3.3

Welco Lumber Company—Part B

Case 2.3 in Chapter 2 introduced you to the Welco Lumber Company and to Gene Denning, Welco Lumber Company's process improvement team leader. Welco Lumber makes cedar fencing materials at its Naples, Idaho, facility, employing about 160 people.

In Case 2.3 you were asked to help Gene develop a graphical descriptive analysis for data collected from the head rig. The head rig is a large saw that breaks down the logs into slabs and cants. Refer to Case 2.3 for more details involving a study that Gene recently conducted in which he videotaped 365 logs

being broken down by the head rig. All three operators, April, Sid, and Jim, were involved. Each log was marked as to its true diameter. Then Gene observed the way the log was broken down and the degree to which the cants were properly centered. He then determined the projected value of the finished product from each log given the way it was actually cut. In addition, he also determined what the value would have been had the log been cut in the optimal way. Data for this study are in a file called **Welco Lumber**.

In addition to the graphical analysis that you helped Gene perform in Case 2.3, you have been asked to assist Gene by analyzing these data using appropriate measures of the center and variation. He wishes to focus on the lost profit to the company and whether there are differences among the operators. Also, do the operators tend to perform better on small logs than on large logs? In general, he is hoping to learn as much as possible from this study and needs your help with the analysis.

Case 3.4

AJ's Fitness Center

When A. J. Reeser signed papers to take ownership of the fitness center previously known as the Park Center Club, he realized that he had just taken the biggest financial step in his life. Every asset he could pull together had been pledged against the mortgage. If the new AJ's Fitness Center didn't succeed, he would be in really bad shape financially. But A. J. didn't plan on failing. After all, he had never failed at anything.

As a high school football All-American, A. J. had been heavily recruited by major colleges around the country. Although he loved football, he and his family had always put academics ahead of sports. Thus, he surprised almost everyone other than those who knew him best when he chose to attend an Ivy League university not particularly noted for its football success. Although he excelled at football and was a member of two winning teams, he also succeeded in the classroom and graduated in four years. He spent six years working for McKinsey & Company, a major consulting firm, at which he gained significant experience in a broad range of business situations.

He was hired away from McKinsey & Company by the Dryden Group, a management services company that specializes in running health and fitness operations and recreational resorts throughout the world. After eight years of leading the Fitness Center section at Dryden, A. J. found that earning a high salary and the perks associated with corporate life were not satisfying him. Besides, the travel was getting old now that he had married and had two young children. When the opportunity to purchase the Park Center Club came, he decided that the time was right to control his own destiny.

A key aspect of the deal was that AJ's Fitness Club would keep its existing clientele, consisting of 1,833 memberships. One of the things A. J. was very concerned about was whether these members would stay with the club after the sale or move on to other fitness clubs in the area. He knew that keeping existing customers is a lot less expensive than attracting new customers.

Within days of assuming ownership, A. J. developed a survey that was mailed to all 1,833 members. The letter that accompanied the survey discussed A. J.'s philosophy and asked several key questions regarding the current level of satisfaction. Survey respondents were eligible to win a free lifetime membership in a drawing—an inducement that was no doubt responsible for the 1,214 usable responses.

To get help with the analysis of the survey data, A. J. approached the college of business at a local university with the idea of having a senior student serve as an intern at AJ's Fitness Center. In addition to an hourly wage, the intern would get free use of the fitness facilities for the rest of the academic year.

The intern's first task was to key the data from the survey into a file that could be analyzed using a spreadsheet or a statistical software package. The survey contained eight questions that were keyed into eight columns, as follows:

Column 1:   Satisfaction with the club's weight- and exercise-equipment facilities

Column 2:   Satisfaction with the club's staff

Column 3:   Satisfaction with the club's exercise programs (aerobics, etc.)

Column 4:   Satisfaction with the club's overall service

Note, columns 1 through 4 were coded on an ordinal scale as follows:

1	2	3	4	5
Very unsatisfied	Unsatisfied	Neutral	Satisfied	Very satisfied

Column 5:   Number of years that the respondent had been a member at this club

Column 6:   Gender (1 = Male, 2 = Female)

Column 7:   Typical number of visits to the club per week

Column 8:   Age

The data, saved in the file **AJFitness**, were clearly too much for anyone to comprehend in raw form. At yesterday's meeting, A. J. asked the intern to "make some sense of the data." When the intern asked for some direction, A. J.'s response was, "That's what I'm paying you the big bucks for. I just want you to develop a descriptive analysis of these data. Use whatever charts, graphs, and tables that will help us understand our customers. Also, use any pertinent numerical measures that will help in the analysis. For right now, give me a report that discusses the data. Why don't we set a time to get together next week to review your report?"

Special Review Section

Chapter 1   The Where, Why, and How of Data Collection

Chapter 2   Graphs, Charts, and Tables—Describing Your Data

Chapter 3   Describing Data Using Numerical Measures

This is the first of two special review sections in this text. The material in these sections, which is presented using block diagrams and flowcharts, is intended to help you tie together the material from several key chapters. These sections are not a substitute for reading and studying the chapters covered by the review. However, you can use this review material to add to your understanding of the individual topics in the chapters.

Chapters 1–3

Chapters 1 to 3 introduce data, data collection, and statistical tools for describing data. The steps needed to gather "good" statistical data, transform it to usable information, and present the information in a manner that allows good decisions are outlined in the following figures.

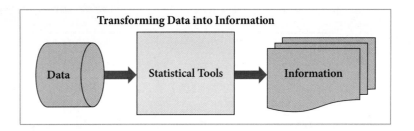

A Typical Application Sequence

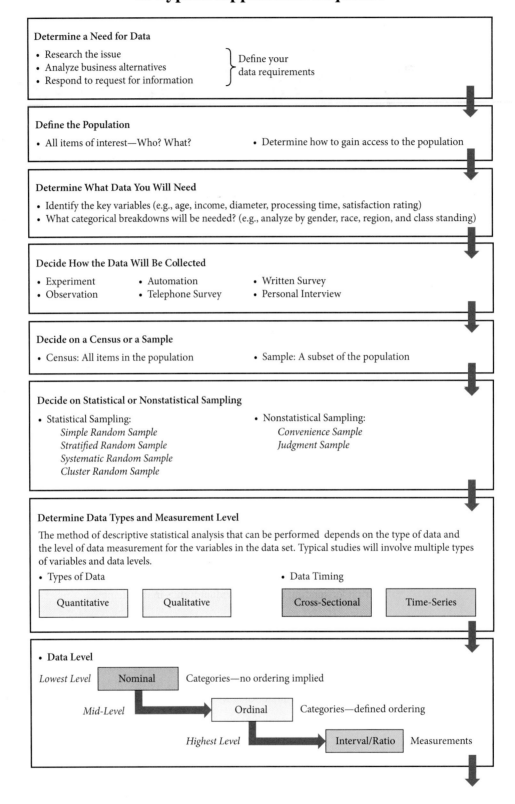

Determine a Need for Data

- Research the issue
- Analyze business alternatives
- Respond to request for information

} Define your data requirements

Define the Population

- All items of interest—Who? What?
- Determine how to gain access to the population

Determine What Data You Will Need

- Identify the key variables (e.g., age, income, diameter, processing time, satisfaction rating)
- What categorical breakdowns will be needed? (e.g., analyze by gender, race, region, and class standing)

Decide How the Data Will Be Collected

- Experiment
- Observation
- Automation
- Telephone Survey
- Written Survey
- Personal Interview

Decide on a Census or a Sample

- Census: All items in the population
- Sample: A subset of the population

Decide on Statistical or Nonstatistical Sampling

- Statistical Sampling:
  Simple Random Sample
  Stratified Random Sample
  Systematic Random Sample
  Cluster Random Sample

- Nonstatistical Sampling:
  Convenience Sample
  Judgment Sample

Determine Data Types and Measurement Level

The method of descriptive statistical analysis that can be performed depends on the type of data and the level of data measurement for the variables in the data set. Typical studies will involve multiple types of variables and data levels.

- Types of Data

  Quantitative   Qualitative

- Data Timing

  Cross-Sectional   Time-Series

- Data Level

  Lowest Level   Nominal   Categories—no ordering implied

  Mid-Level   Ordinal   Categories—defined ordering

  Highest Level   Interval/Ratio   Measurements

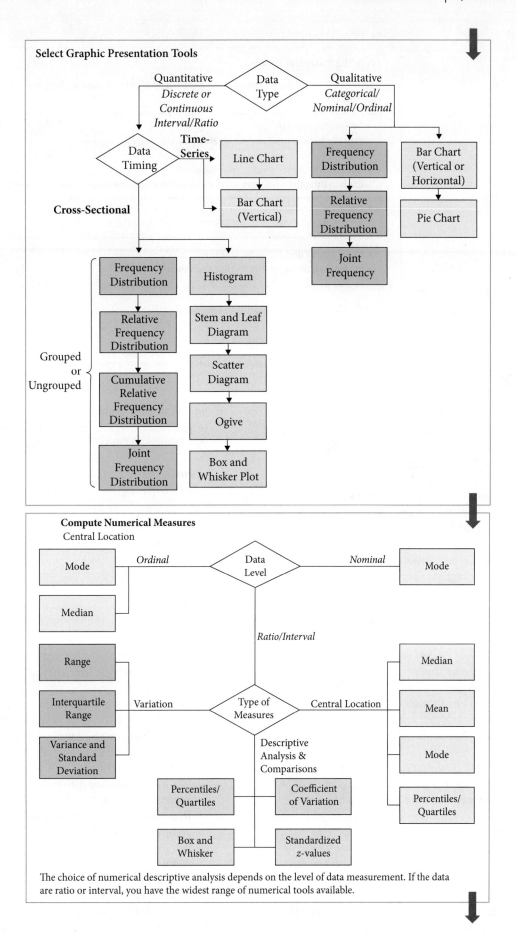

The choice of numerical descriptive analysis depends on the level of data measurement. If the data are ratio or interval, you have the widest range of numerical tools available.

Write the Statistical Report

There is no one set format for writing a statistical report. However, there are a few suggestions you may find useful.

- *Lay the foundation*:
  Provide background and motivation for the analysis.

- *Describe the data collection methodology*:
  Explain how the data were gathered and the sampling techniques were used.

- *Use a logical sequence*:
  Follow a systematic plan for presenting your findings and analysis.

- *Label figures and tables by number*:
  Employ a consistent numbering and labeling format.

MyStatLab

Exercises

Integrative **Application Exercises**

Chapters 1 to 3 have introduced you to the basics of descriptive statistics. Many of the business application problems, advanced business application problems, and cases in these chapters will give you practice in performing descriptive statistical analysis. However, too often you are told which procedure you should use, or you can surmise which to use by the location of the exercise. It is important that you learn to identify the appropriate procedure on your own in order to solve problems for test purposes. But more important, this ability is essential throughout your career when you are required to select procedures for the tasks you will undertake. The following exercises will provide you with identification practice.

SR.1. Go to your university library and obtain the *Statistical Abstract of the United States*.
  a. Construct a frequency distribution for unemployment rate by state for the most current year available.
  b. Justify your choice of class limits and number of classes.
  c. Locate the unemployment rate for the state in which you are attending college. (1) What proportion of the unemployment rates are below that of your state? (2) Describe the distribution's shape with respect to symmetry. (3) If you were planning to build a new manufacturing plant, what state would you choose in which to build? Justify your answer. (4) Are there any unusual features of this distribution? Describe them.

SR.2. The State Industrial Development Council is currently working on a financial services brochure to send to out-of-state companies. It is hoped that the brochure will be helpful in attracting companies to relocate to your state. You are given the following frequency distribution on banks in your state:

Deposit Size (in millions)	Number of Banks	Total Deposits (in millions)
Less than 5	2	7.2
5 to less than 10	7	52.1
10 to less than 25	6	111.5
25 to less than 50	3	95.4
50 to less than 100	2	166.6
100 to less than 500	2	529.8
Over 500	2	1663.0

  a. Does this frequency distribution violate any of the rules of construction for frequency distributions? If so, reconstruct the frequency distribution to remedy this violation.
  b. The Council wishes to target companies that would require financial support from banks that have at least $25 million in deposits. Reconstruct the frequency distribution to attract such companies to relocate to your state. Do this by considering different classes that would accomplish such a goal.
  c. Reconstruct the frequency distribution to attract companies that require financial support from banks that have between $5 million and $25 million in deposits.
  d. Present an eye-catching, two-paragraph summary of what the data would mean to a company that is considering moving to the state. Your boss has said you need to include relative frequencies in this presentation.

SR.3. As an intern for Intel Corporation, suppose you have been asked to help the vice president prepare a newsletter to the shareholders. You have been given access to the data in a file called **Intel** that contains Intel Corporation financial data for the years 1987 through 1996. Go to the Internet or to Intel's annual report and update the file to include the same variables for the years 1997 to the present. Then use graphs to effectively present the data in a format that would be usable for the vice president's newsletter. Write a short article that discusses the information shown in your graphs.

SR.4. The Woodmill Company makes windows and door trim products. The first step in the process is to rip dimension (2 × 8, 2 × 10, etc.) lumber into narrower pieces. Currently, the company uses a manual process in which an experienced operator quickly looks at a board and determines what rip widths to use. The decision is based on the knots and defects in the wood.

A company in Oregon has developed an optical scanner that can be used to determine the rip widths. The scanner is programmed to recognize defects and to determine rip widths that will optimize the value of the board. A test run of 100 boards was put through the scanner and the rip widths were identified. However, the boards were not actually ripped. A lumber grader determined the resulting values for each of the 100 boards assuming that the rips determined by the scanner had been made. Next, the same 100 boards were manually ripped using the normal process. The grader then determined the value for each board after the manual rip process was completed. The resulting data, in the file **Woodmill**, consist of manual rip values and scanner rip values for each of the 100 boards.

a. Develop a frequency distribution for the board values for the scanner and the manual process.

b. Compute appropriate descriptive statistics for both manual and scanner values. Use these data along with the frequency distribution developed in part a to prepare a written report that describes the results of the test. Be sure to include in your report a conclusion regarding whether the scanner outperforms the manual process.

c. Which process, scanner or manual, generated the most values that were more than 2 standard deviations from the mean?

d. Which of the two processes has the least relative variability?

SR.5. The commercial banking industry is undergoing rapid changes due to advances in technology and competitive pressures in the financial services sector. The data file **Banks** contains selected information tabulated by *Fortune* concerning the revenues, profitability, and number of employees for the 51 largest U.S. commercial banks in terms of revenues. Use the information in this file to complete the following:

a. Compute the mean, median, and standard deviation for the three variables revenues, profits, and number of employees.

b. Convert the data for each variable to a z value. Consider Mellon Bank Corporation headquartered in Pittsburgh. How does it compare to the average bank in the study on the three variables? Discuss.

c. As you can see by examining the data and by looking at the statistics computed in part a, not all banks had the same revenue, same profit, or the same number of employees. Which variable had the greatest relative variation among the banks in the study?

d. Calculate a new variable: profits per employee. Develop a frequency distribution and a histogram for this new variable. Also compute the mean, median, and standard deviation for the new variable. Write a short report that describes the profits per employee for the banks.

e. Referring to part d, how many banks had a profit-per-employee ratio that exceeded 2 standard deviations from the mean?

Here is an integrative case study designed to give you more experience. In addition, we have included several term project assignments that require you to collect and analyze data.

Review Case 1

State Department of Insurance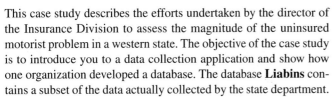

This case study describes the efforts undertaken by the director of the Insurance Division to assess the magnitude of the uninsured motorist problem in a western state. The objective of the case study is to introduce you to a data collection application and show how one organization developed a database. The database **Liabins** contains a subset of the data actually collected by the state department.

The impetus for the case came from the legislative transportation committee, which heard much testimony during the recent legislative session about the problems that occur when an uninsured motorist is involved in a traffic accident in which damages to individuals and property occur. The state's law enforcement officers also testified that a large number of vehicles are not covered by liability insurance.

Because of both political pressure and a sense of duty to do what is right, the legislative committee spent many hours wrestling with what to do about drivers who do not carry the mandatory liability insurance. Because the actual magnitude of the problem was unknown, the committee finally arrived at a compromise plan, which required the state Insurance Division to perform random audits of vehicles to determine whether the vehicle was covered by liability insurance. The audits are to be performed on approximately 1% of the state's 1 million registered vehicles each month. If a vehicle is found not to have liability insurance, the vehicle license and the owner's driver's license will be revoked for three months and a $250 fine will be imposed.

However, before actually implementing the audit process, which is projected to cost $1.5 million per year, Herb Kriner, director of the Insurance Division, was told to conduct a preliminary study of the uninsured motorists' problem in the state and to report back to the legislative committee in six months.

The Study

A random sample of 12 counties in the state was selected in a manner that gave the counties with higher numbers of registered vehicles proportionally higher chances of being selected. Two locations

were selected in each county, and the state police set up roadblocks on a randomly selected day. Vehicles with in-state license plates were stopped at random until approximately 100 vehicles had been stopped at each location. The target total was about 2,400 vehicles statewide.

The issue of primary interest was whether the vehicle was insured. This was determined by observing whether the vehicle was carrying the required certificate of insurance. If so, the officer took down the insurance company name and address and the policy number. If the certificate was not in the car, but the owner stated that insurance was carried, the owner was given a postcard to return within five days supplying the required information. A vehicle was determined to be uninsured if no postcard was returned or if, subsequently, the insurance company reported that the policy was not valid on the day of the survey.

In addition to the issue of insurance coverage, Herb Kriner wanted to collect other information about the vehicle and the owner. This was done using a personal interview during which the police officer asked a series of questions and observed certain things such as seat belt usage and driver's and vehicle license expiration status. Also, the owners' driving records were obtained through the Transportation Department's computer division and added to the information gathered by the state police.

The Data

The data are contained in the file **Liabins**. The sheet titled "Description" contains an explanation of the data set and the variables.

Issues to Address

Herb Kriner has two weeks before making a presentation to the legislative subcommittee that has been dealing with the liability insurance issue. As Herb's chief analyst, your job is to perform a comprehensive analysis of the data and to prepare the report that Herb will deliver to the legislature. Remember, this report will go a long way in determining whether the state should spend the $1.5 million to implement a full liability insurance audit system.

Term Project Assignments

For the project selected, you are to devise a sampling plan, collect appropriate data, and carry out a full descriptive analysis aimed at shedding light on the key issues for the project. The finished project will include a written report of a length and format specified by your professor.

- Day or evening
- Morning or afternoon
- One-day, two-day, or three-day schedules
- Weekend
- Location (on or off campus)

Project A

Issue: Your College of Business and Economics seeks input from business majors regarding class scheduling. Some potential issues are

Project B

Issue: Intercollegiate athletics is a part of most major universities. Revenue from attendance at major sporting events is one key to financing the athletic program. Investigate the drivers of attendance at your university's men's basketball and football games. Some potential issues:

- Game times
- Game days (basketball)
- Ticket prices
- Athletic booster club memberships
- Competition for entertainment dollars

Project C

Issue: The department of your major is interested in surveying department alumni. Some potential issues are

- Satisfaction with degree
- Employment status
- Job satisfaction
- Suggestions for improving course content

Capstone Project

Project Objective

The objective of this business statistics capstone project is to provide you with an opportunity to integrate the statistical tools and concepts that you have learned thus far in your business statistics course. Like all real-world applications, completing this project will not require you to utilize every statistical technique covered in the first three chapters. Rather, an objective of the assignment is for you to determine which of the statistical tools and techniques are appropriate for the situation you have selected.

Project Description

Assume that you are working as an intern for a financial management company. Your employer has a large number of clients who trust the company managers to invest their funds. In your position, you are responsible for producing reports for clients when they request information. Your company has two large data files with financial information for a large number of U.S. companies. The first is called **US Companies 2003**, which contains financial information for the companies' 2001 or 2002 fiscal year-end. The second file is called **US Companies 2005**, which has data for the fiscal 2003 or 2004 year-end. The 2003 file has data for 7,098 companies. The 2005 file has data for 6,992 companies. Thus,

many companies are listed in both files, but some are just in one or the other.

The two files have many of the same variables, but the 2003 file has a larger range of financial variables than the 2005 file. For some companies, the data for certain variables are not available, and a code of NA is used to so indicate. The 2003 file has a special worksheet that contains the description of each variable. These descriptions apply to the 2005 data file as well.

You have been given access to these two data files for use in preparing your reports. Your role will be to perform certain statistical analyses that can be used to help convert these data into useful information in order to respond to the clients' questions.

This morning, one of the partners of your company received a call from a client who asked for a report that would compare companies in the financial services industry (SIC codes in the 6000s) to companies in production-oriented businesses (SIC codes in the 2000s and 3000s). There are no firm guidelines on what the report should entail, but the partner has suggested the following:

- Start with the 2005 data file. Pull the data for all companies with the desired SIC codes into a new worksheet.
- Prepare a complete descriptive analysis of key financial variables using appropriate charts and graphs to help compare the two types of businesses.
- Determine whether there are differences between the two classes of companies in terms of key financial measures.
- Using data from the 2003 file for companies that have these SIC codes and that are also in the 2005 file, develop a comparison that shows the changes over the time span both within SIC code grouping and between SIC code groupings.

Project Deliverables

To successfully complete this capstone project, you are required to deliver a management report that addresses the partner's requests (listed above) and also contains at least one other substantial type of analysis not mentioned by the partner. This latter work should be set off in a special section of the report.

The final report should be presented in a professional format using the style or format suggested by your instructor.

Chapter 4 Quick Prep Links

- **Review** the discussion of statistical sampling in Section 1.3.

- **Examine** recent business periodicals and newspapers looking for examples in which probability concepts are discussed.

- **Think about** how you determine what decision to make in situations in which you are uncertain about your choices.

Introduction to Probability

4.1 The Basics of Probability
(pg. 141–153)

Outcome 1. Understand the three approaches to assessing probabilities.

4.2 The Rules of Probability
(pg. 153–175)

Outcome 2. Be able to apply the Addition Rule.

Outcome 3. Know how to use the Multiplication Rule.

Outcome 4. Know how to use Bayes' Theorem for applications involving conditional probabilities.

Why you need to know

Recently the Powerball lottery raised the cost of buying a ticket from $1 to $2. With the higher ticket prices, lottery officials expect the jackpot prize value to increase more rapidly and thereby entice even greater ticket sales. Most people recognize when buying a lottery ticket that there is a very small *probability* of winning and that whether they win or lose is based on chance alone. In case you are not familiar with the Powerball lottery system, a drum contains 59 balls, numbered 1 to 59. The player must choose (or have a computer choose) five numbers between 1 and 59. The player also chooses a 6th number called the power ball. On the night of the drawing, five balls are *randomly* selected and then placed in numerical order. Lastly, a sixth ball (the power ball) is randomly selected. To win the jackpot, the player must match all five numbers plus the power ball. The odds of winning are shown on the Powerball website to be 1 in 175,223,510 or about 0.00000000571. Later in the chapter, you will learn the method for computing probabilities like this. One analogy might put this in perspective. Suppose we take a college football field and cover it with 175,223,510 tiny red ants. One of these ants has a yellow dot on it. If you were blindfolded, your chances of picking the one ant with the yellow dot from the millions of ants on the football field would be the same as winning the Powerball jackpot! We suggest you come up with a different retirement strategy.

In business decision making, in many instances, chance is involved in determining the outcome of a decision. For instance, when a TV manufacturer establishes a warranty on its television sets, there is a certain probability that any given TV will last less than the warranty life and customers will have to be compensated. Accountants perform audits on the financial statements of a client and sign off on the statements as accurate while realizing there is a chance that problems exist that were not uncovered by the audit. A food processor manufacturer recognizes that there is a chance that one or more of its products will be substandard and dissatisfy the customer. Airlines overbook flights to make sure that the seats on the plane are as full as possible because they know there is a certain probability that customers will not show for their flight. Professional poker players base their decisions to fold or play a hand based on their assessment of the chances that their hand beats those of their opponents.

Photo_Ma/Fotolia

If we always knew what the result of our decisions would be, our life as decision makers would be a lot less stressful. However, in most instances, uncertainty exists. To deal with this uncertainty, we need to know how to incorporate probability concepts into the decision process. Chapter 4 takes the first step in teaching you how to do this by introducing the basic concepts and rules of probability. You need to have a solid understanding of these basics before moving on to the more practical probability applications that you will encounter in business.

4.1 The Basics of Probability

The mathematical study of probability originated more than 300 years ago. The Chevalier de Méré, a French nobleman (who today would probably own a gaming house in Monte Carlo), began asking questions about games of chance. He was mostly interested in the probability of observing various outcomes when dice were repeatedly rolled. The French mathematician Blaise Pascal (you may remember studying Pascal's triangle in a mathematics class), with the help of his friend Pierre de Fermat, was able to answer de Méré's questions. Of course, Pascal began asking more and more complicated questions of himself and his colleagues, and the formal study of probability began.

Important Probability Terms

Several explanations of what probability is have come out of this mathematical study. However, the definition of **probability** is quite basic.

Probability

The chance that a particular event will occur. The probability value will be in the range 0 to 1. A value of 0 means the event will not occur. A probability of 1 means the event will occur. Anything between 0 and 1 reflects the uncertainty of the event occurring. The definition given is for a countable number of events.

For instance, if we look out the window and see rain, we can say the probability of rain today is 1 since we know for sure that it will rain. If an airplane has a top speed of 450 mph, and the distance between city A and city B is 900 miles, we can say the probability the plane will make the trip in 1.5 hours is zero—it can't happen. These examples involve situations in which we are *certain* of the outcome, and our 1 and 0 probabilities reflect this.

However, in most business situations, we do not have certainty but instead are uncertain. For instance, if a real estate investor has the option to purchase a small shopping mall, determining rate of return on this investment involves uncertainty. The investor does not know with certainty whether she will make a profit, break even, or lose money. After looking closely at the situation, she might say the chance of making a profit is 0.30. This value between 0 and 1 reflects her uncertainty about whether she will make a profit from purchasing the shopping mall.

Events and Sample Space   As discussed in Chapter 1, data come in many forms and are gathered in many ways. In probability language, the process that produces the outcomes is an **experiment**.

Experiment

A process that produces a single outcome whose result cannot be predicted with certainty.

For instance, a very simple experiment might involve flipping a coin one time. When this experiment is performed, two possible experimental outcomes can occur: head and tail. If the coin-tossing experiment is expanded to involve two flips of the coin, the experimental outcomes are

Head on first flip and head on second flip, denoted by (H,H)

Head on first flip and tail on second flip, denoted by (H,T)

Tail on first flip and head on second flip, denoted by (T,H)

Tail on first flip and tail on second flip, denoted by (T,T)

In business situations, the experiment can be things like an investment decision, a personnel decision, or a choice of warehouse location.

The collection of possible experimental outcomes is called the **sample space**.

Sample Space

The collection of all outcomes that can result from a selection, decision, or experiment.

EXAMPLE 4-1	**DEFINING THE SAMPLE SPACE**

ExQuisine/Fotolia

Five Guys Hamburgers   The sales manager for the Five Guys Hamburger chain is interested in analyzing the sales of its three best-selling hamburgers. As part of this analysis, he might be interested in determining the sample space (possible outcomes) for two randomly selected customers. To do this, he can use the following steps.

Step 1 Define the experiment.

The experiment is the sale. The item of interest is the product sold.

Step 2 Define the outcomes for one trial of the experiment.

The manager can define the outcomes to be

$$e_1 = \text{Hamburger}$$

$$e_2 = \text{Cheeseburger}$$

$$e_3 = \text{Bacon Burger}$$

Step 3 Define the sample space.

The sample space (SS) for an experiment involving a single sale is

$$SS = \{e_1, e_2, e_3\}$$

If the experiment is expanded to include two sales, the sample space is

$$SS = \{e_1, e_2, e_3, e_4, e_5, e_6, e_7, e_8, e_9\}$$

where the outcomes include what happens on both sales and are defined as

Outcome	Sale 1	Sale 2
e_1	Hamburger	Hamburger
e_2	Hamburger	Cheeseburger
e_3	Hamburger	Bacon Burger
e_4	Cheeseburger	Hamburger
e_5	Cheeseburger	Cheeseburger
e_6	Cheeseburger	Bacon Burger
e_7	Bacon Burger	Hamburger
e_8	Bacon Burger	Cheeseburger
e_9	Bacon Burger	Bacon Burger

>> **END EXAMPLE**

TRY PROBLEM 4-3 (pg. 150)

Using Tree Diagrams A tree diagram is often a useful way to define the sample space for an experiment that helps ensure no outcomes are omitted or repeated. Example 4-2 illustrates how a tree diagram is used.

EXAMPLE 4-2   **USING A TREE DIAGRAM TO DEFINE THE SAMPLE SPACE**

Clearwater Marketing Research Clearwater Marketing Research is involved in a project in which television viewers were asked whether they objected to hard-liquor advertisements being shown on television. The analyst is interested in listing the sample space, using a tree diagram as an aid, when three viewers are interviewed. The following steps can be used:

Step 1 Define the experiment.

Three people are interviewed and asked, "Would you object to hard-liquor advertisements on television?" Thus, the experiment consists of three trials.

Step 2 Define the outcomes for a single trial of the experiment.

The possible outcomes when one person is interviewed are

no
yes

Step 3 Define the sample space for three trials using a tree diagram.

Begin by determining the outcomes for a single trial. Illustrate these with tree branches beginning on the left side of the page:

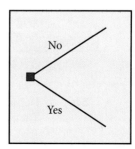

For each of these branches, add branches depicting the outcomes for a second trial. Continue until the tree has the number of sets of branches corresponding to the number of trials.

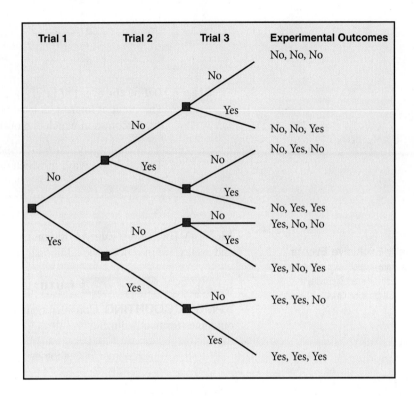

>> **END EXAMPLE**

TRY PROBLEM 4-4 (pg. 150)

Event

A collection of experimental outcomes.

A collection of possible outcomes is called an **event**. An example will help clarify these terms.

EXAMPLE 4-3   **DEFINING AN EVENT OF INTEREST**

KPMG Accounting The KPMG Accounting firm is interested in the sample space for an audit experiment in which the outcome of interest is the audit's completion status. The sample space is the list of all possible outcomes from the experiment. The accounting firm is also interested in specifying the outcomes that make up an event of interest. This can be done using the following steps:

Step 1 Define the experiment.
The experiment consists of two randomly chosen audits.

Step 2 List the outcomes associated with one trial of the experiment.
For a single audit, the following completion-status possibilities exist:

Audit done early

Audit done on time

Audit done late

Step 3 Define the sample space.
For two audits (two trials), we define the sample space as follows:

Experimental Outcome		Audit 1	Audit 2
e_1	=	Early	Early
e_2	=	Early	On time

Experimental Outcome		Audit 1	Audit 2
e_3	=	Early	Late
e_4	=	On time	Early
e_5	=	On time	On time
e_6	=	On time	Late
e_7	=	Late	Early
e_8	=	Late	On time
e_9	=	Late	Late

Step 4 Define the event of interest.

The event of interest, at least one audit is completed late, is composed of all the outcomes in which one or more audits are late. This event (E) is

$$E = \{ e_3, e_6, e_7, e_8, e_9 \}$$

There are five ways in which one or more audits are completed late.

>> **END EXAMPLE**

TRY PROBLEM 4-11 (pg. 151)

Mutually Exclusive Events Keeping in mind the definitions for *experiment, sample space,* and *events,* we introduce two additional concepts. The first is **mutually exclusive events**.

Mutually Exclusive Events

Two events are mutually exclusive if the occurrence of one event precludes the occurrence of the other event.

BUSINESS APPLICATION **MUTUALLY EXCLUSIVE EVENTS**

KPMG ACCOUNTING Consider again the KPMG Accounting firm example. The possible outcomes for two audits are

Experimental Outcomes		Audit 1	Audit 2
e_1	=	Early	Early
e_2	=	Early	On time
e_3	=	Early	Late
e_4	=	On time	Early
e_5	=	On time	On time
e_6	=	On time	Late
e_7	=	Late	Early
e_8	=	Late	On time
e_9	=	Late	Late

Suppose we define one event as consisting of the outcomes in which at least one of the two audits is late.

$$E_1 = \{ e_3, e_6, e_7, e_8, e_9 \}$$

Further, suppose we define a second event as follows:

$$E_2 = \text{Neither audit is late} = \{ e_1, e_2, e_4, e_5 \}$$

Events E_1 and E_2 are mutually exclusive: If E_1 occurs, E_2 cannot occur; if E_2 occurs, E_1 cannot occur. That is, if at least one audit is late, then it is not possible for neither audit to be late. We can verify this fact by observing that no outcomes in E_1 appear in E_2. This observation provides another way of defining mutually exclusive events: Two events are mutually exclusive if they have no common outcomes.

EXAMPLE 4-4 **MUTUALLY EXCLUSIVE EVENTS**

Tech-Works, Inc. Tech-Works, Inc. located in Dublin, Ireland, does contract assembly work for companies such as Hewlett-Packard. Each item produced on the assembly line can be thought of as an experimental trial. The managers at this facility can analyze their process to determine whether the events of interest are mutually exclusive using the following steps:

Step 1 Define the experiment.

The experiment is producing a part on an assembly line.

Step 2 Define the outcomes for a single trial of the experiment.

On each trial, the outcome is either a *good* or a *defective* item.

Step 3 Define the sample space.

If two products are produced (two trials), the following sample space is defined:

Experimental Outcomes	
Product 1	Product 2
e_1 = Good	Good
e_2 = Good	Defective
e_3 = Defective	Good
e_4 = Defective	Defective

Step 4 Determine whether the events are mutually exclusive.

Let event E_1 be defined as both products produced are good, and let event E_2 be defined as at least one product is defective:

$$E_1 = \text{Both good} = \{e_1\}$$
$$E_2 = \text{At least one defective} = \{e_2, e_3, e_4\}$$

Then events E_1 and E_2 are determined to be mutually exclusive because the two events have no outcomes in common. Having two good items and at the same time having at least one defective item is not possible.

>> END EXAMPLE

TRY PROBLEM 4-9 (pg. 150)

Independent Events

Two events are independent if the occurrence of one event in no way influences the probability of the occurrence of the other event.

Dependent Events

Two events are dependent if the occurrence of one event impacts the probability of the other event occurring.

Independent and Dependent Events A second probability concept is that of **independent** versus **dependent events**.

BUSINESS APPLICATION **INDEPENDENT AND DEPENDENT EVENTS**

PETROGLYPH Petroglyph is a subsidiary of the Intermountain Gas Company and is responsible for natural gas exploration in the western U.S. and Canada. During the exploration phase, seismic surveys are conducted that provide information about the Earth's underground formations. Based on history, the company knows that if the seismic readings are favorable, gas will more likely be discovered than if the seismic readings are not favorable. However, the readings are not perfect indicators. Suppose the company currently is exploring in eastern Colorado. The possible outcomes for the seismic survey are defined as

$$e_1 = \text{Favorable}$$
$$e_2 = \text{Unfavorable}$$

If the company decides to drill, the outcomes are defined as

$$e_3 = \text{Strike gas}$$
$$e_4 = \text{Dry hole}$$

If we let the event E_1 be that the seismic survey is favorable and event E_2 be that the hole is dry, we can say that the events A and B are not mutually exclusive, because one event's occurrence does not preclude the other event from occurring. We can also say that the two events are dependent because the probability of a dry hole depends on whether the seismic survey is favorable or unfavorable. If the result of drilling was not related to the seismic survey, the events would be independent.

Chapter Outcome 1. ➞ # Methods of Assigning Probability

Part of the confusion surrounding probability may be due to the fact that probability can be assigned to outcomes in more than one way. There are three common ways to assign probability to outcomes: *classical probability assessment, relative frequency assessment,* and *subjective probability assessment.* The following notation is used when we refer to the probability of an event:

$$P(E_i) = \text{Probability of event } E_i \text{ occurring}$$

Classical Probability Assessment The first method of probability assessment involves **classical probability**.

You are probably already familiar with classical probability. It had its beginning with games of chance and is still most often discussed in those terms.

Consider again the experiment of flipping a coin one time. There are two possible outcomes: head and tail. Each of these is equally likely. Thus, using the classical assessment method, the probability of a head is the ratio of the number of ways a head can occur (1 way) to the total number of ways any outcome can occur (2 ways). Thus we get

$$P(\text{Head}) = \frac{1 \text{ way}}{2 \text{ ways}} = \frac{1}{2} = 0.50$$

The chance of a head occurring is 1 out of 2, or 0.50.

In those situations in which all possible outcomes are *equally likely,* the classical probability measurement is defined in Equation 4.1.

Classical Probability Assessment

The method of determining probability based on the ratio of the number of ways an outcome or event of interest can occur to the number of ways *any* outcome or event can occur when the individual outcomes are equally likely.

Classical Probability Assessment

$$P(E_i) = \frac{\text{Number of ways } E_i \text{ can occur}}{\text{Total number of possible outcomes}}$$

(4.1)

EXAMPLE 4-5   **CLASSICAL PROBABILITY ASSESSMENT**

Michael Flippo/Fotolia

Active Sporting Goods, Inc. The managers at Active Sporting Goods plan to hold a special promotion over Labor Day Weekend. Each customer making a purchase exceeding $100 will qualify to select an envelope from a large drum. Inside the envelope are coupons for percentage discounts off the purchase total. At the beginning of the weekend, there were 500 coupons. Four hundred of these were for a 10% discount, 50 were for 20%, 45 were for 30%, and 5 were for 50%. The probability of getting a particular discount amount can be determined using classical assessment with the following steps:

Step 1 Define the experiment.
An envelope is selected from a large drum.

Step 2 Determine whether the possible outcomes are equally likely.
In this case, the envelopes with the different discount amounts are unmarked from the outside and are thoroughly mixed in the drum. Thus, any one envelope has the same probability of being selected as any other envelope. The outcomes are equally likely.

Step 3 Determine the total number of outcomes.
There are 500 envelopes in the drum.

Step 4 Define the event of interest.
We might be interested in assessing the probability that the first customer will get a 20% discount.

Step 5 Determine the number of outcomes associated with the event of interest.
There are 50 coupons with a discount of 20% marked on them.

Step 6 Compute the classical probability using Equation 4.1:

$$P(E_i) = \frac{\text{Number of ways } E_i \text{ can occur}}{\text{Total number of possible outcomes}}$$

$$P(20\% \text{ discount}) = \frac{\text{Number of ways } 20\% \text{ can occur}}{\text{Total number of possible outcomes}} = \frac{50}{500} = 0.10$$

Note: After the first customer selects an envelope from the drum, the probability that the next customer will get a particular discount will change, because the values in the denominator and possibly the numerator will change.

>> **END EXAMPLE**

TRY PROBLEM 4-10 (pg. 151)

As you can see, the classical approach to probability measurement is fairly straightforward. Many games of chance are based on classical probability assessment. However, classical probability assessment does not apply in many business situations. Rarely are the individual outcomes equally likely. For instance, you might be thinking of starting a business. The sample space is

$$SS = \{\text{Succeed, Fail}\}$$

Would it be reasonable to use classical assessment to determine the probability that your business will succeed? If so, we would make the following assessment:

$$P(\text{Succeed}) = \frac{1}{2}$$

If this were true, then the chance of any business succeeding would be 0.50. Of course, this is not true. Many factors go into determining the success or failure of a business. The possible outcomes (Succeed, Fail) are not equally likely. Instead, we need another method of probability assessment in these situations.

Relative Frequency Assessment The **relative frequency assessment** approach is based on actual observations.

Equation 4.2 shows how the relative frequency assessment method is used to assess probabilities.

Relative Frequency Assessment
The method that defines probability as the number of times an event occurs divided by the total number of times an experiment is performed in a large number of trials.

Relative Frequency Assessment

$$P(E_i) = \frac{\text{Number of times } E_i \text{ occurs}}{N} \qquad (4.2)$$

where:

E_i = The event of interest
N = Number of trials

BUSINESS APPLICATION **RELATIVE FREQUENCY ASSESSMENT**

HATHAWAY HEATING & AIR CONDITIONING The sales manager at Hathaway Heating & Air Conditioning has recently developed the customer profile shown in Table 4.1. The profile is based on a random sample of 500 customers. As a promotion for the company, the sales manager plans to randomly select a customer once a month and perform a free service on the customer's system. What is the probability that the first customer selected is a residential customer? What is the probability that the first customer has a Hathaway heating system?

TABLE 4.1 | **Hathaway Heating & Air Conditioning Co.**

		Customer Category		Total
		E_1 Commercial	E_2 Residential	
E_3	Heating Systems	55	145	200
E_4	Air-Conditioning Systems	45	255	300
	Total	100	400	500

To determine the probability that the customer selected is residential, we determine from Table 4.1 the number of residential customers and divide by the total number of customers, both residential and commercial. We then apply Equation 4.2:

$$P(E_2) = P(\text{Residential}) = \frac{400}{500} = 0.80$$

Thus, there is an 80% chance the customer selected will be a residential customer.

The probability that the customer selected has a Hathaway heating system is determined by the ratio of the number of customers with heating systems to the number of total customers.

$$P(E_3) = P(\text{Heating}) = \frac{200}{500} = 0.40$$

There is a 40% chance the randomly selected customer will have a Hathaway heating system.

The sales manager hopes the customer selected is a residential customer with a Hathaway heating system. Because there are 145 customers in this category, the relative frequency method assesses the probability of this event occurring as follows:

$$P(E_2 \text{ and } E_3) = P(\text{Residential with heating}) = \frac{145}{500} = 0.29$$

There is a 29% chance the customer selected will be a residential customer with a Hathaway heating system.

EXAMPLE 4-6   **RELATIVE FREQUENCY PROBABILITY ASSESSMENT**

Starbucks Coffee The international coffee chain, Starbucks, has a store in a busy mall in Pittsburgh, Pennsylvania. Starbucks sells caffeinated and decaffeinated drinks. One of the difficulties in this business is determining how much of a given product to prepare for the day. The manager is interested in determining the probability that a customer will select a decaf versus a caffeinated drink. She has maintained records of customer purchases for the past three weeks. The probability can be assessed using relative frequency with the following steps:

Step 1 Define the experiment.
A randomly chosen customer will select between decaf and caffeinated.

Step 2 Define the events of interest.
The manager is interested in the event E_1 customer selects caffeinated.

Step 3 Determine the total number of occurrences.
In this case, the manager has observed 2,250 sales of decaf and caffeinated in the past week. Thus, $N = 2{,}250$.

Step 4 For the event of interest, determine the number of occurrences.
In the past week, 1,570 sales were for caffeinated drinks.

Step 5 Use Equation 4.2 to determine the probability assessment.

$$P(E_1) = \frac{\text{Number of times } E_1 \text{ occurs}}{N} = \frac{1{,}570}{2{,}250} = 0.6978$$

Thus, based on past history, the chance that a customer will purchase a caffeinated drink is just under 0.70.

>> **END EXAMPLE**

TRY PROBLEM 4-9 (pg. 150)

POTENTIAL ISSUES WITH THE RELATIVE FREQUENCY ASSESSMENT METHOD There are a couple of concerns that you should be aware of before applying the relative frequency assessment method. First, for this method to be useful, all of the observed frequencies must be comparable. For instance, consider again the case in which you are interested in starting a small business. Two outcomes can occur: business succeeds or business fails. If we are interested in the probability that the business will succeed, we might be tempted to study a sample of, say, 200 small businesses that have been started in the past and determine the number of those that have succeeded—say, 50. Using Equation 4.2 for the relative frequency method, we get

$$P(\text{Succeed}) = \frac{50}{200} = 0.25$$

However, before we can conclude the chance your small business will succeed is 0.25, you must be sure that the conditions of each of the 200 businesses match your conditions (that is, location, type of business, management expertise and experience, financial standing, and so on). If not, then the relative frequency method should not be used.

Another issue involves the size of the denominator in Equation 4.2. If the number of possible occurrences is quite small, the probability assessment may be unreliable. For instance, suppose a basketball player took five free throws during the first ten games of the season and missed them all. The relative frequency method would determine the probability that he will make the next free throw to be

$$P(\text{Make}) = \frac{0 \text{ made}}{5 \text{ shots}} = \frac{0}{5} = 0.0$$

But do you think that there is a zero chance that he will make his next free throw? No, even the notoriously poor free-throw shooter, Shaquille O'Neal, former National Basketball Association (NBA) star player, made some of his free throws. The problem is that the base of five free throws is too small to provide a reliable probability assessment.

Subjective Probability Assessment Unfortunately, even though managers may have some experience to guide their decision making, new factors will always be affecting each decision, making that experience only an approximate guide to the future. In other cases, managers may have little or no experience and, therefore, may not be able to use a relative frequency as even a starting point in assessing the desired probability. When experience is not available, decision makers must make a **subjective probability assessment**. A subjective probability is a measure of a personal conviction that an outcome will occur. Therefore, in this instance, probability represents a person's belief that an event will occur.

Subjective Probability Assessment

The method that defines probability of an event as reflecting a decision maker's state of mind regarding the chances that the particular event will occur.

BUSINESS APPLICATION   **SUBJECTIVE PROBABILITY ASSESSMENT**

BECHTEL CORPORATION The Bechtel Corporation is preparing a bid for a major infrastructure construction project. The company's engineers are very good at defining all the elements of the projects (labor, materials, and so on) and know the costs of these with a great deal of certainty. In finalizing the bid amount, the managers add a profit markup to the projected costs. The problem is how much markup to add. If they add too much, they won't be the low bidder and may lose the contract. If they don't mark the bid up enough, they may get the project and make less profit than they might have made had they used a higher markup. The managers are considering four possible markup values, stated as percentages of base costs:

10%   12%   15%   20%

To make their decision, the managers need to assess the probability of winning the contract at each of these markup levels. Because they have never done a project exactly like this one, they can't rely on relative frequency assessment. Instead, they must subjectively assess the probability based on whatever information they currently have available, such as who the other bidders are, the rapport Bechtel has with the potential client, and so forth.

After considering these values, the Bechtel managers make the following assessments:

$$
\begin{aligned}
P(\text{Win at } 10\%) &= 0.30 \\
P(\text{Win at } 12\%) &= 0.25 \\
P(\text{Win at } 15\%) &= 0.15 \\
P(\text{Win at } 20\%) &= 0.05
\end{aligned}
$$

These assessments indicate the managers' state of mind regarding the chances of winning the contract. If new information (for example, a competitor drops out of the bidding) becomes available before the bid is submitted, these assessments could change.

Each of the three methods by which probabilities are assessed has specific advantages and specific applications. Regardless of how decision makers arrive at a probability assessment, the rules by which people use these probabilities in decision making are the same. These rules will be introduced in Section 4.2.

MyStatLab

4-1: Exercises

Skill Development

4-1. A special roulette wheel, which has an equal number of red and black spots, has come up red four times in a row. Assuming that the roulette wheel is fair, what concept allows a player to know that the probability the next spin of the wheel will come up black is 0.5?

4-2. In a survey, respondents were asked to indicate their favorite brand of cereal (Post or Kellogg's). They were allowed only one choice. What is the probability concept that implies it is not possible for a single respondent to state both Post and Kellogg's to be the favorite cereal?

4-3. If two customers are asked to list their choice of ice cream flavor from among vanilla, chocolate, and strawberry, list the sample space showing the possible outcomes.

4-4. Use a tree diagram to list the sample space for the number of movies rented by three customers at a video store where customers are allowed to rent one, two, or three movies (assuming that each customer rents at least one movie).

4-5. In each of the following, indicate what method of probability assessment would most likely be used to assess the probability.
   a. What is the probability that a major earthquake will occur in California in the next three years?
   b. What is the probability that a customer will return a purchase for a refund?
   c. An inventory of appliances contains four white washers and one black washer. If a customer selects one at random, what is the probability that the black washer will be selected?

4-6. Long-time friends Pat and Tom agree on many things, but not the outcome of the American League pennant race and the World Series. Pat is originally from Boston, and Tom is from New York. They have a steak dinner bet on next year's race, with Pat betting on the Red Sox and Tom on the Yankees. Both are convinced they will win.
   a. What probability assessment technique is being used by the two friends?
   b. Why would the relative frequency technique not be appropriate in this situation?

4-7. Students who live on campus and purchase a meal plan are randomly assigned to one of three dining halls: the Commons, Northeast, and Frazier. What is the probability that the next student to purchase a meal plan will be assigned to the Commons?

4-8. The results of a census of 2,500 employees of a mid-sized company with 401(k) retirement accounts are as follows:

Account Balance (to nearest $)	Male	Female
<$25,000	635	495
$25,000 − $49,999	185	210
$50,000 − $99,999	515	260
>$100,000	155	45

Suppose researchers are going to sample employees from the company for further study.
   a. Based on the relative frequency assessment method, what is the probability that a randomly selected employee will be a female?
   b. Based on the relative frequency assessment method, what is the probability that a randomly selected employee will have a 401(k) account balance of between $25,000 and $49,999?
   c. Compute the probability that a randomly selected employee will be a female with an account balance between $50,000 and $99,999.

4-9. Cross County Bicycles makes two mountain bike models, the **XB-50** and the **YZ-99**, in three distinct colors. The following table shows the production volumes for last week:

Model	Color		
	Blue	Brown	White
XB-50	302	105	200
YZ-99	40	205	130

   a. Based on the relative frequency assessment method, what is the probability that a mountain bike is brown?
   b. What is the probability that the mountain bike is a YZ-99?

c. What is the joint probability that a randomly selected mountain bike is a YZ-99 and brown?

d. Suppose a mountain bike is chosen at random. Consider the following two events: the event that model YZ-99 is chosen and the event that a white product is chosen. Are these two events mutually exclusive? Explain.

4-10. Cyber-Plastics, Inc., is in search of a CEO and a CFO. The company has a short list of candidates for each position. The CEO candidates graduated from Chicago (C) and three Ivy League universities: Harvard (H), Princeton (P), and Yale (Y). The four CFO candidates graduated from MIT (M), Northwestern (N), and two Ivy League universities: Dartmouth (D) and Brown (B). One candidate from each of the respective lists will be chosen randomly to fill the positions. The event of interest is that both positions are filled with candidates from the Ivy League.

a. Determine whether the outcomes are equally likely.

b. Determine the number of equally likely outcomes.

c. Define the event of interest.

d. Determine the number of outcomes associated with the event of interest.

e. Compute the classical probability of the event of interest using Equation 4.1.

4-11. Three consumers go to a Best Buy to shop for high-definition televisions (HDTVs). Let *B* indicate that one of the consumers buys an HDTV. Let *D* be that the consumer doesn't buy an HDTV. Assume these events are equally likely. Consider the following: (1) only two consumers buy an HDTV, (2) at most two consumers buy HDTVs, and (3) at least two consumers buy HDTVs.

a. Determine whether the outcomes 1, 2, and 3 are equally likely.

b. Determine the total number of equally likely outcomes for the three shoppers.

c. Define the events of interest in each of 1, 2, and 3.

To define the events of interest, list the possible outcomes in each of the following events:

- only two consumers buy an HDTV (E_1)

- at most two consumers buy HDTVs (E_2)

- at least two consumers buy HDTVs (E_3)

d. Determine the number of outcomes associated with each of the events of interest. Use the classical probability assessment approach to assign probabilities to each of the possible outcomes and calculate the probabilities of the events.

e. Compute the classical probabilities of each of the events in part d by using Equation 4.1.

Business Applications

4-12. Cyber Communications, Inc., has a new cell phone product under development in the research and development (R&D) lab. It will increase the megapixel capability of cell phone cameras to the 6+ range. The head of R&D made a presentation to the company

CEO stating that the probability the company will earn a profit in excess of $20 million next year is 80%. Comment on this probability assessment.

4-13. Five doctors work at the Evergreen Medical Clinic. The plan is to staff Saturdays with three doctors. The office manager has decided to make up Saturday schedules in such a way that no set of three doctors will be in the office together more than once. How many weeks can be covered by this schedule? (*Hint*: Use a tree diagram to list the sample space.)

4-14. Prince Windows, Inc. makes high-quality windows for the residential home market. Recently, three marketing managers were asked to assess the probability that sales for next year will be more than 15% higher than the current year. One manager stated that the probability of this happening was 0.40. The second manager assessed the probability to be 0.60, and the third manager stated the probability to be 0.90.

a. What method of probability assessment are the three managers using?

b. Which manager is expressing the least uncertainty in the probability assessment?

c. Why is it that the three managers did not provide the same probability assessment?

4-15. The marketing manager for the *Charlotte Times* newspaper has commissioned a study of the advertisements in the classified section. The results for the Wednesday edition showed that 204 are help-wanted ads, 520 are real estate ads, and 306 are other ads.

a. If the newspaper plans to select an ad at random each week to be published free, what is the probability that the ad for a specific week will be a help-wanted ad?

b. What method of probability assessment is used to determine the probability in part a?

c. Are the events that a help-wanted ad is chosen and that an ad for other types of products or services is chosen for this promotion on a specific week mutually exclusive? Explain.

4-16. Before passing away in 2009, Larry Miller owned the Utah Jazz basketball team of the NBA and several automobile dealerships in Utah and Idaho. One of the dealerships sells Buick, Cadillac, and Pontiac automobiles. It also sells used cars that it gets as trade-ins on new car purchases. Supposing two cars are sold on Tuesday by the dealership, what is the sample space for the type of cars that might be sold?

4-17. The Pacific Northwest has a substantial volume of cedar forests and cedar product manufacturing companies. Welco Lumber manufactures cedar fencing material in Marysville, Washington. The company's quality manager inspected 5,900 boards and found that 4,100 could be rated as a #1 grade.

a. If the manager wanted to assess the probability that a board being produced will be a #1 grade, what method of assessment would he likely use?

b. Referring to your answer in part a, what would you assess the probability of a #1 grade board to be?

4-18. The results of Fortune Personnel Consultants' survey of 405 workers was reported in *USA Today*. One of the questions in the survey asked, "Do you feel it's OK for your company to monitor your Internet use?" The possible responses were: (1) Only after informing me, (2) Does not need to inform me, (3) Only when company believes I am misusing, (4) Company does not have right, and (5) Only if I have previously misused. The following table contains the results for the 405 respondents:

Response	1	2	3	4	5
Number of Respondents	223	130	32	14	6

  a. Calculate the probability that a randomly chosen respondent would indicate that there should be some restriction concerning the company's right to monitor Internet use.

  b. Indicate the method of probability assessment used to determine the probability in part a.

  c. Are the events that a randomly selected respondent chose response 1 and that another randomly selected respondent chose response 2 independent, mutually exclusive, or dependent events? Explain.

4-19. Famous Dave's is a successful barbeque chain and sells its beef, pork, and chicken items to three kinds of customers: dine-in, delivery, and carry-out. Last year's sales showed that 12,753 orders were dine-in, 5,893 were delivery orders, and 3,122 orders were carry-out. Suppose an audit of last year's sales is being conducted.

  a. If a customer order is selected at random, what is the probability it will be a carry-out order?

  b. What method of probability assessment was used to determine the probability in part a?

  c. If two customer orders are selected at random, list the sample space indicating the type of order for both customers.

4-20. VERCOR provides merger and acquisition consultants to assist corporations when an owner decides to offer the business for sale. One of their news releases, "Tax Audit Frequency Is Rising," written by David L. Perkins Jr., a VERCOR partner, originally appeared in *The Business Owner*. Perkins indicated that audits of the largest businesses, those corporations with assets of $10 million and over climbed to 9,560 in the previous year. That was up from a low of 7,125 a year earlier. He indicated one in six large corporations was being audited.

  a. Designate the type of probability assessment method that Perkins used to assess the probability of large corporations being audited.

  b. Determine the number of large corporations that filed tax returns for the previous fiscal year.

  c. Determine the probability that a large corporation was not audited using the relative frequency probability assessment method.

Computer **Database Exercises**

4-21. According to a September 2005 article on the Womensenews.org Web site, "Caesarean sections, in which a baby is delivered by abdominal surgery, have increased fivefold in the past 30 years, prompting concern among health advocates . . ." The data in the file called **Babies** indicate whether the past 50 babies delivered at a local hospital were delivered using the Caesarean method.

  a. Based on these data, what is the probability that a baby born in this hospital will be born using the Caesarean method?

  b. What concerns might you have about using these data to assess the probability of a Caesarean birth? Discuss.

4-22. Recently, a large state university conducted a survey of undergraduate students regarding their use of computers. The results of the survey are contained in the data file **ComputerUse**.

  a. Based on the data from the survey, what is the probability that undergraduate students at this university will have a major that requires them to use a computer on a daily basis?

  b. Based on the data from this survey, if a student is a business major, what is the probability of the student believing that the computer lab facilities are very adequate?

4-23. A company produces scooters used by small businesses, such as pizza parlors, that find them convenient for making short deliveries. The company is notified whenever a scooter breaks down, and the problem is classified as being either mechanical or electrical. The company then matches the scooter to the plant where it was assembled. The file **Scooters** contains a random sample of 200 breakdowns. Use the data in the file and the relative frequency assessment method to find the following probabilities:

  a. What is the probability a scooter was assembled at the Tyler plant?

  b. What is the probability that a scooter breakdown was due to a mechanical problem?

  c. What is the probability that a scooter was assembled at the Lincoln plant and had an electrical problem?

4-24. A Harris survey on cell phone use asked, in part, what was the most important reason that people give for not using a wireless phone exclusively. The responses were: (1) Like the safety of traditional phone, (2) Need line for Internet access, (3) Pricing not attractive enough, (4) Weak or unreliable cell signal at home, (5) Coverage not good enough, and (6) Other. The file titled **Wireless** contains the responses for the 1,088 respondents.

  a. Calculate the probability that a randomly chosen respondent would not use a wireless phone exclusively because of some type of difficulty in placing and receiving calls with a wireless phone.

  b. Calculate the probability that a randomly chosen person would not use a wireless phone exclusively because of some type of difficulty in placing and receiving calls with a wireless phone and is over the age of 55.

c. Determine the probability that a randomly chosen person would not use a wireless phone exclusively because of a perceived need for Internet access and the safety of a traditional phone.

d. Of those respondents under 36, determine the probability that an individual in this age group would not use a wireless phone exclusively because of some type of difficulty in placing and receiving calls with a wireless phone.

4-25. CNN staff writer Pariia Bhatnagar reported ("Coke, Pepsi Losing the Fizz," March 8, 2005) that Atlanta-based Coke saw its domestic market share drop to 43.1% in 2004. New York-based PepsiCo had used its "Pepsi Challenge" advertising approach to increase its market share, which stood at 31.7% in 2004. A selection of soft-drink users is asked to taste the two disguised soft drinks and indicate which they prefer. The file titled **Challenge** contains the results of a simulated Pepsi Challenge on a college campus.

a. Determine the probability that a randomly chosen student prefers Pepsi.

b. Determine the probability that one of the students prefers Pepsi and is less than 20 years old.

c. Of those students who are less than 20 years old, calculate the probability that a randomly chosen student prefers (1) Pepsi and (2) Coke.

d. Of those students who are at least 20 years old, calculate the probability that a randomly chosen student prefers (1) Pepsi and (2) Coke.

END EXERCISES 4-1

4.2 The Rules of Probability

Measuring Probabilities

The probability attached to an event represents the likelihood the event will occur on a specified trial of an experiment. This probability also measures the perceived uncertainty about whether the event will occur.

Possible Values and the Summation of Possible Values If we are certain about the outcome of an event, we will assign the event a probability of 0 or 1, where $P(E_i) = 0$ indicates the event E_i will not occur and $P(E_i) = 1$ means that E_i will definitely occur.[1] If we are uncertain about the result of an experiment, we measure this uncertainty by assigning a probability between 0 and 1. Probability Rule 1 shows that the probability of an event occurring is always between 0 and 1.

Probability Rule 1

For any event E_i,

$$0 \leq P(E_i) \leq 1 \quad \text{for all } i \qquad (4.3)$$

All possible outcomes associated with an experiment form the sample space. Therefore, the sum of the probabilities of all possible outcomes is 1, as shown by Probability Rule 2.

Probability Rule 2

$$\sum_{i=1}^{k} P(e_i) = 1 \qquad (4.4)$$

where:

$$k = \text{Number of outcomes in the sample}$$
$$e_i = i\text{th outcome}$$

Chapter Outcome 2. → **Addition Rule for Individual Outcomes** If a single event is composed of two or more individual outcomes, then the probability of the event is found by summing the probabilities of the individual outcomes. This is illustrated by Probability Rule 3.

---

[1]These statements are true only if the number of outcomes of an experiment is countable. They do not apply when the number of outcomes is infinitely uncountable. This will be discussed when continuous probability distributions are discussed in Chapter 6.

Probability Rule 3: Addition Rule for Individual Outcomes

The probability of an event E_i is equal to the *sum* of the probabilities of the individual outcomes forming E_i. For example, if

$$E_i = \{e_1, e_2, e_3\}$$

then

$$P(E_i) = P(e_1) + P(e_2) + P(e_3) \qquad \textbf{(4.5)}$$

BUSINESS APPLICATION **ADDITION RULE**

GOOGLE Google has become synonymous with Web searches and is clearly the market leader in the search engine marketplace. Officials at the northern California headquarters have recently performed a survey of computer users to determine how many Internet searches individuals do daily using Google. Table 4.2 shows the results of the survey of Internet users.

The sample space for the experiment for each respondent is

$$SS = \{e_1, e_2, e_3, e_4\}$$

where the possible outcomes are

$$e_1 = \text{at least 10 searches}$$
$$e_2 = \text{3 to 9 searches}$$
$$e_3 = \text{1 to 2 searches}$$
$$e_4 = \text{0 searches}$$

Using the relative frequency assessment approach, we assign the following probabilities.

$$P(e_1) = \quad 400/5{,}000 = 0.08$$
$$P(e_2) = 1{,}900/5{,}000 = 0.38$$
$$P(e_3) = 1{,}500/5{,}000 = 0.30$$
$$P(e_4) = 1{,}200/5{,}000 = 0.24$$
$$\Sigma = 1.00$$

Assume we are interested in the event *respondent performs 1 to 9 searches per month.*

$$E = \text{Internet User Performs 1 to 9 searches per day}$$

The outcomes that make up E are

$$E = \{e_2, e_3\}$$

We can find the probability, $P(E)$, by using Probability Rule 3 (Equation 4.5), as follows:

$$P(E) = P(e_2) + P(e_3)$$
$$= 0.38 + 0.30$$
$$= 0.68$$

TABLE 4.2 | **Google's Survey Results**

Searches Per Day	Frequency	Relative Frequency
at least 10	400	0.08
3 to 9	1,900	0.38
1 to 2	1,500	0.30
0	1,200	0.24
Total	5,000	1.00

| EXAMPLE 4-7 | THE ADDITION RULE FOR INDIVIDUAL OUTCOMES |

KFI 640 Radio The KFI 640 radio station in Los Angeles is a combination news/talk and "oldies" station. During a 24-hour day, a listener can tune in and hear any of the following four programs being broadcast:

"Oldies" music

News stories

Talk programming

Commercials

Recently, the station has been having trouble with its transmitter. Each day, the station's signal goes dead for a few seconds; it seems that these outages are equally likely to occur at any time during the 24-hour broadcast day. There seems to be no pattern regarding what is playing at the time the transmitter problem occurs. The station manager is concerned about the probability that these problems will occur during either a news story or a talk program.

Step 1 Define the experiment.

The station conducts its broadcast starting at 12:00 midnight, extending until a transmitter outage is observed.

Step 2 Define the possible outcomes.

The possible outcomes are the type of programming that is playing when the transmitter outage occurs. There are four possible outcomes:

$$e_1 = \text{Oldies}$$
$$e_2 = \text{News}$$
$$e_3 = \text{Talk programs}$$
$$e_4 = \text{Commercials}$$

Step 3 Determine the probability of each possible outcome.

The station manager has determined that out of the 1,440 minutes per day, 540 minutes are oldies, 240 minutes are news, 540 minutes are talk programs, and 120 minutes are commercials. Therefore, the probability of each type of programming being on at the moment the outage occurs is assessed as follows:

Outcome $= e_i$	$P(e_i)$
$e_1 = $ Oldies	$P(e_1) = \dfrac{540}{1,440} = 0.375$
$e_2 = $ News	$P(e_2) = \dfrac{240}{1,440} = 0.167$
$e_3 = $ Talk programs	$P(e_3) = \dfrac{540}{1,440} = 0.375$
$e_4 = $ Commercials	$P(e_4) = \dfrac{120}{1,440} = 0.083$
	$\sum = 1.000$

Note, based on Equation 4.4 (Probability Rule 2), the sum of the probabilities of the individual possible outcomes is 1.0.

Step 4 Define the event of interest.

The event of interest is a transmitter problem occurring during a news or talk program. This is

$$E = \{e_2, e_3\}$$

Step 5 Use Probability Rule 3 (Equation 4.5) to compute the desired probability.

$$P(E) = P(e_2) + P(e_3)$$
$$P(E) = 0.167 + 0.375$$
$$P(E) = 0.542$$

Thus, there is slightly higher than a 0.5 probability that when a transmitter problem occurs, it will happen during either a news or talk program.

>> **END EXAMPLE**

TRY PROBLEM 4-26 (pg. 171)

Complement

The complement of an event *F* is the collection of all possible outcomes not contained in event *E*.

Complement Rule Closely connected with Probability Rules 1 and 2 is the **complement** of an event. The complement of event E is represented by $\overline{E}$. The Complement Rule is a corollary to Probability Rules 1 and 2.

Complement Rule

$$P(\overline{E}) = 1 - P(E) \qquad\qquad (4.6)$$

That is, the probability of the complement of event E is 1 minus the probability of event E.

EXAMPLE 4-8   **THE COMPLEMENT RULE**

Capital Consulting The managing partner for Capital Consulting is working on a proposal for a consulting project with a client in Sydney, Australia. The manager lists four possible net profits from the consulting engagement and his subjectively assessed probabilities related to each profit level.

Outcome	P(Outcome)
$ 0	0.70
$ 2,000	0.20
$15,000	0.07
$50,000	0.03
	$\Sigma = \overline{1.00}$

Note that each probability is between 0 and 1 and that the sum of the probabilities is 1, as required by Rules 1 and 2.

The manager plans to submit the proposal if the consulting engagement will have a positive profit, so he is interested in knowing the probability of an outcome greater than $0. This probability can be found using the Complement Rule with the following steps:

Step 1 Determine the probabilities for the outcomes.

$$P(\$0) = 0.70$$
$$P(\$2,000) = 0.20$$
$$P(\$15,000) = 0.07$$
$$P(\$50,000) = 0.03$$

Step 2 Find the desired probability.

Let E be the consulting outcome event $= \$0$. The probability of the zero outcome is

$$P(E) = 0.70$$

The complement, $\overline{E}$, is all investment outcomes greater than $0. Using the Complement Rule, the probability of profit greater than $0 is

$$P(\text{Profit} > \$0) = 1 - P(\text{Profit} = \$0)$$
$$P(\text{Profit} > \$0) = 1 - 0.70$$
$$P(\text{Profit} > \$0) = 0.30$$

Based on his subjective probability assessment, there is a 30% chance the consulting project will have a positive profit.

>> **END EXAMPLE**

TRY PROBLEM 4-32 (pg. 172)

Chapter Outcome 2. → Addition Rule for Any Two Events

BUSINESS APPLICATION **ADDITION RULE**

GOOGLE (CONTINUED) Suppose the staff who conducted the survey for Google discussed earlier also asked questions about the computer users' ages. The Google managers consider age important in designing their search engine methodologies. Table 4.3 shows the breakdown of the sample by age group and by the number of times a user performs a search each day.

Table 4.3 shows that there are seven events defined. For instance, E_1 is the event that a computer user performs 10 or more searches per day. This event is composed of three individual outcomes associated with the three age categories. These are

$$E_1 = \{e_1, e_2, e_3\}$$

In another case, event E_5 corresponds to a survey respondent being younger than 30 years of age. It is composed of four individual outcomes associated with the four levels of search activity. These are

$$E_5 = \{e_1, e_4, e_7, e_{10}\}$$

Table 4.3 illustrates two important concepts in data analysis: *joint frequencies* and *marginal frequencies*. Joint frequencies, which were discussed in Chapter 2, are the values inside the table. They provide information on age group and search activity jointly. Marginal frequencies are the row and column totals. These values give information on only the age group or only Google search activity.

For example, 2,100 people in the survey are in the 30- to 50-year age group. This column total is a marginal frequency for the age group 30 to 50 years, which is represented by E_6. Now notice that 600 respondents are younger than 30 years old and perform three to nine searches a day. The 600 is a joint frequency whose outcome is represented by e_4. The joint frequencies are the number of times their associated outcomes occur.

Table 4.4 shows the relative frequencies for the data in Table 4.3. These values are the probabilities of the events and outcomes.

Suppose we wish to find the probability of E_4 (0 searches) **or** E_6 (being in the 30-to-50 age group). That is,

$$P(E_4 \text{ or } E_6) = ?$$

TABLE 4.3 | **Google Search Study**

	Age Group			
Searches Per Day	E_5 Less than 30	E_6 30 to 50	E_7 Over 50	Total
$E_1 \geq$ 10 Searches	e_1 200	e_2 100	e_3 100	400
E_2 3 to 9 Searches	e_4 600	e_5 900	e_6 400	1,900
E_3 1 to 2 Searches	e_7 400	e_8 600	e_9 500	1,500
E_4 0 Searches	e_{10} 700	e_{11} 500	e_{12} 0	1,200
Total	1,900	2,100	1,000	5,000

TABLE 4.4 | **Google—Joint Probability Table**

	Age Group			
Searches per Day	E_5 Less than 30	E_6 30 to 50	E_7 Over 50	Total
$E_1 \geq$ 10 Searches	e_1 200/5,000 = 0.04	e_2 100/5,000 = 0.02	e_3 100/5,000 = 0.02	400/5,000 = 0.08
E_2 3 to 9 Searches	e_4 600/5,000 = 0.12	e_5 900/5,000 = 0.18	e_6 400/5,000 = 0.08	1,900/5,000 = 0.38
E_3 1 to 2 Searches	e_7 400/5,000 = 0.08	e_8 600/5,000 = 0.12	e_9 500/5,000 = 0.10	1,500/5,000 = 0.30
E_4 0 Searches	e_{10} 700/5,000 = 0.14	e_{11} 500/5,000 = 0.10	e_{12} 0/5,000 = 0.00	1,200/5,000 = 0.24
Total	1,900/5,000 = 0.38	2,100/5,000 = 0.42	1,000/5,000 = 0.20	5,000/5,000 = 1.00

FIGURE 4.1

Venn Diagram—Addition Rule
for Any Two Events

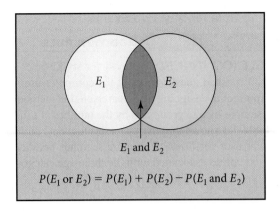

$$P(E_1 \text{ or } E_2) = P(E_1) + P(E_2) - P(E_1 \text{ and } E_2)$$

To find this probability, we must use Probability Rule 4.

Probability Rule 4: Addition Rule for Any Two Events, E_1 and E_2

$$P(E_1 \text{ or } E_2) = P(E_1) + P(E_2) - P(E_1 \text{ and } E_2) \qquad \textbf{(4.7)}$$

The key word in knowing when to use Rule 4 is *or*. The word *or* indicates addition. [You may have covered this concept as a *union* in a math class. $P(E_1 \text{ or } E_2) = P(E_1 \cup E_2)$.] Figure 4.1 is a Venn diagram that illustrates the application of the Addition Rule for Any Two Events. Notice that the probabilities of the outcomes in the overlap between the two events, E_1 and E_2, are double-counted when the probabilities of the outcomes in E_1 are added to those of E_2. Thus, the probabilities of the outcomes in the overlap, which is E_1 *and* E_2, need to be subtracted to avoid the double counting.

Referring to the Google situation, the probability of E_4 (0 searches) *or* E_6 (being in the 30-to-50 age group) is

$$P(E_4 \text{ or } E_6) = ?$$

Table 4.5 shows the relative frequencies with the events of interest shaded. The overlap corresponds to the *joint occurrence* (intersection) of conducting 0 searches *and* being in the 30-to-50 age group. The probability of the outcomes in the overlap is represented by $P(E_4 \text{ and } E_6)$ and must be subtracted. This is done to avoid double-counting the probabilities of the outcomes that are in both E_4 and E_6 when calculating the $P(E_4 \text{ or } E_6)$. Thus,

$$P(E_4 \text{ or } E_6) = P(E_4) + P(E_6) - P(E_4 \text{ and } E_6)$$
$$= 0.24 + 0.42 - 0.10$$
$$= 0.56$$

Therefore, the probability that a respondent will either be in the 30-to-50 age group or perform zero searches on a given day is 0.56.

TABLE 4.5 | **Google Searches—Addition Rule Example**

Searches Per Day	Age Group			
	E_5 Less than 30	E_6 30 to 50	E_7 Over 50	Total
$E_1 \geq$ **10 Searches**	e_1 200/5,000 = 0.04	e_2 100/5,000 = 0.02	e_3 100/5,000 = 0.02	400/5,000 = 0.08
E_2 **3 to 9 Searches**	e_4 600/5,000 = 0.12	e_5 900/5,000 = 0.18	e_6 400/5,000 = 0.08	1,900/5,000 = 0.38
E_3 **1 to 2 Searches**	e_7 400/5,000 = 0.08	e_8 600/5,000 = 0.12	e_9 500/5,000 = 0.10	1,500/5,000 = 0.30
E_4 **0 Searches**	e_{10} 700/5,000 = 0.14	e_{11} 500/5,000 = 0.10	e_{12} 0/5,000 = 0.00	1,200/5,000 = 0.24
Total	1,900/5,000 = 0.38	2,100/5,000 = 0.42	1,000/5,000 = 0.20	5,000/5,000 = 1.00

TABLE 4.6 | **Google—Addition Rule Example**

	Age Group			
Searches Per Day	E_5 Less than 30	E_6 30 to 50	E_7 Over 50	Total
$E_1 \geq 10$ Searches	e_1 200/5,000 = 0.04	e_2 100/5,000 = 0.02	e_3 100/5,000 = 0.02	400/5,000 = 0.08
E_2 3 to 9 Searches	e_4 600/5,000 = 0.12	e_5 100/5,000 = 0.18	e_6 400/5,000 = 0.08	1,900/5,000 = 0.38
E_3 1 to 2 Searches	e_7 400/5,000 = 0.08	e_8 600/5,000 = 0.12	e_9 500/5,000 = 0.10	1,500/5,000 = 0.30
E_4 0 Searches	e_{10} 700/5,000 = 0.14	e_{11} 500/5,000 = 0.10	e_{12} 0/5,000 = 0.00	1,200/5,000 = 0.24
Total	1,900/5,000 = 0.38	2,100/5,000 = 0.42	1,000/5,000 = 0.20	5,000/5,000 = 1.00

What is the probability a respondent will perform 1 to 2 searches *or* be in the over-50 age group? Again, we can use Rule 4:

$$P(E_3 \text{ or } E_7) = P(E_3) + P(E_7) - P(E_3 \text{ and } E_7)$$

Table 4.6 shows the relative frequencies for these events. We have

$$P(E_3 \text{ or } E_7) = 0.30 + 0.20 - 0.10 = 0.40$$

Thus, there is a 0.40 chance that a respondent will perform 1−2 searches **or** be in the "over 50" age group.

EXAMPLE 4-9   **ADDITION RULE FOR ANY TWO EVENTS**

British Columbia Forest Products British Columbia Forest Products manufactures lumber for large material supply centers like Home Depot and Lowe's in the U.S. and Canada. A representative from Home Depot is due to arrive at the BC plant for a meeting to discuss lumber quality. When the Home Depot representative arrives, he will ask BC's managers to randomly select one board from the finished goods inventory for a quality check. Boards of three dimensions and three lengths are in the inventory. The following chart shows the number of boards of each size and length.

	Dimension			
Length	E_4 2″ × 4″	E_5 2″ × 6″	E_6 2″ × 8″	Total
$E_1 = 8$ feet	1,400	1,500	1,100	4,000
$E_2 = 10$ feet	2,000	3,500	2,500	8,000
$E_3 = 12$ feet	1,600	2,000	2,400	6,000
Total	5,000	7,000	6,000	18,000

The BC manager will be selecting one board at random from the inventory to show the Home Depot representative. Suppose he is interested in the probability that the board selected will be 8 feet long or a 2″ × 6″. To find this probability, he can use the following steps:

Step 1   **Define the experiment.**
One board is selected from the inventory and its dimensions are obtained.

Step 2   **Define the events of interest.**
The manager is interested in boards that are 8 feet long.

$$E_1 = 8 \text{ foot boards}$$

He is also interested in the 2″ × 6″ dimension, so

$$E_5 = 2″ × 6″ \text{ boards}$$

Step 3   **Determine the probability for each event.**
There are 18,000 boards in inventory, and 4,000 of these are 8 feet long, so

$$P(E_1) = \frac{4,000}{18,000} = 0.2222$$

Of the 18,000 boards, 7,000 are 2″ × 6″, so the probability is

$$P(E_5) = \frac{7,000}{18,000} = 0.3889$$

Step 4 **Determine whether the two events overlap, and if so, compute the joint probability.**

Of the 18,000 total boards, 1,500 are 8 feet long and 2″ × 6″. Thus the joint probability is

$$P(E_1 \text{ and } E_5) = \frac{1,500}{18,000} = 0.0833$$

Step 5 **Compute the desired probability using Probability Rule 4.**

$$P(E_1 \text{ or } E_5) = P(E_1) + P(E_5) - P(E_1 \text{ and } E_5)$$
$$P(E_1 \text{ or } E_5) = 0.2222 + 0.3889 - 0.0833$$
$$= 0.5278$$

The chance of selecting an 8-foot board or a 2″ × 6″ board is just under 0.53.

>> **END EXAMPLE**

TRY PROBLEM 4-31 (pg. 172)

Addition Rule for Mutually Exclusive Events We indicated previously that when two events are mutually exclusive, both events cannot occur at the same time. Thus, for mutually exclusive events,

$$P(E_1 \text{ and } E_2) = 0$$

Therefore, when you are dealing with mutually exclusive events, the Addition Rule assumes a different form, shown as Rule 5.

Probability Rule 5: Addition Rule for Mutually Exclusive Events

For two mutually exclusive events E_1 and E_2,

$$P(E_1 \text{ or } E_2) = P(E_1) + P(E_2) \tag{4.8}$$

Figure 4.2 is a Venn diagram illustrating the application of the Addition Rule for Mutually Exclusive Events.

Conditional Probability

In dealing with probabilities, you will often need to determine the chances of two or more events occurring either at the same time or in succession. For example, a quality control manager for a manufacturing company may be interested in the probability of selecting two successive defective products from an assembly line. If the probability of this event is low, the quality control manager will be surprised when it occurs and might readjust the production process. In other instances, the decision maker might know that an event has occurred and may then want to know the probability of a second event occurring. For instance, suppose that an oil company geologist who believes oil will be found at a certain drilling site makes a favorable report. Because oil is not always found at locations with a favorable report, the oil

FIGURE 4.2

Venn Diagram—Addition Rule for Two Mutually Exclusive Events

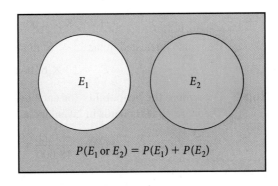

$P(E_1 \text{ or } E_2) = P(E_1) + P(E_2)$

company's exploration vice president might well be interested in the probability of finding oil, given the favorable report.

Conditional Probability

The probability that an event will occur *given* that some other event has already happened.

Situations such as this refer to a probability concept known as **conditional probability**.

Probability Rule 6 offers a general rule for conditional probability. The notation $P(E_1|E_2)$ reads "probability of event E_1 *given* event E_2 has occurred." Thus, the probability of one event is conditional upon a second event having occurred.

Probability Rule 6: Conditional Probability for Any Two Events

For any two events E_1, E_2,

$$P(E_1|E_2) = \frac{P(E_1 \text{ and } E_2)}{P(E_2)} \qquad (4.9)$$

where:

$$P(E_2) > 0$$

Rule 6 uses a *joint probability*, $P(E_1 \text{ and } E_2)$, and a *marginal probability*, $P(E_2)$, to calculate the conditional probability $P(E_1|E_2)$. Note that to find a conditional probability, we find the ratio of how frequently E_1 occurs to the total number of observations, given that we restrict our observations to only those cases in which E_2 has occurred.

BUSINESS APPLICATION   **CONDITIONAL PROBABILITY**

SYRINGA NETWORKS Syringa Networks is an Internet service provider to rural areas in the western United States. The company has studied its customers' Internet habits. Among the information collected are the data shown in Table 4.7.

The company is focusing on high-volume users, and one of the factors that will influence Syringa Networks' marketing strategy is whether time spent using the Internet is related to a customer's gender. For example, suppose the company knows a user is female and wants to know the chances this woman will spend between 20 and 40 hours a month on the Internet. Let

$$E_2 = \{e_3, e_4\} = \text{Event: Person uses services 20 to 40 hours per month}$$

$$E_4 = \{e_1, e_3, e_5\} = \text{Event: User is female}$$

A marketing analyst needs to know the probability of E_2 given E_4.

One way to find the desired probability is as follows:

1. We know E_4 has occurred (customer is female). There are 850 females in the survey.
2. Of the 850 females, 300 use Internet services 20 to 40 hours per month.
3. Then,

$$P(E_2|E_4) = \frac{300}{850}$$

$$= 0.35$$

However, we can also apply Rule 6, as follows:

$$P(E_2|E_4) = \frac{P(E_2 \text{ and } E_4)}{P(E_4)}$$

TABLE 4.7 | **Joint Frequency Distribution for Syringa Network**

Hours per Month	Gender		Total
	E_4 Female	E_5 Male	
$E_1 < 20$	e_1 450	e_2 500	950
E_2 20 to 40	e_3 300	e_4 800	1,100
$E_3 > 40$	e_5 100	e_6 350	450
Total	850	1,650	2,500

TABLE 4.8 | **Joint Relative Frequency Distribution for Syringa Networks**

Hours per Month	Gender		Total
	E_4 Female	E_5 Male	
$E_1 < 20$	$e_1\ 450/2{,}500 = 0.18$	$e_2\ 500/2{,}500 = 0.20$	$950/2{,}500 = 0.38$
E_2 20 to 40	$e_3\ 300/2{,}500 = 0.12$	$e_4\ 800/2{,}500 = 0.14$	$1{,}100/2{,}500 = 0.44$
$E_3 > 40$	$e_5\ 100/2{,}500 = 0.14$	$e_6\ 350/2{,}500 = 0.14$	$450/2{,}500 = 0.18$
Total	$850/2{,}500 = 0.34$	$1{,}650/2{,}500 = 0.66$	$2{,}500/2{,}500 = 1.00$

Table 4.8 shows the relative frequencies of interest. From Table 4.8, we get the joint probability $P(E_2 \text{ and } E_4) = 0.12$
and

$$P(E_4) = 0.34$$

Then applying Rule 6,

$$P(E_2 | E_4) = \frac{0.12}{0.34} = 0.35$$

EXAMPLE 4-10   **COMPUTING CONDITIONAL PROBABILITIES**

Retirement Planning Most financial publications suggest that the older the investor is, the more conservative his or her investment strategy should be. For example, younger investors might hold more in stocks, while older investors might hold more in bonds. A recent survey conducted by a major financial publication yielded the following table, which shows the number of people in the study by age group and percentage of retirement funds in the stock market.

	Age of Investor	Percentage of Retirement Investments in the Stock Market					Total
		E_5 <5%	E_6 5% < 10%	E_7 10% < 30%	E_8 30% < 50%	E_9 50% or more	
E_1	< 30 years	70	240	270	80	55	715
E_2	30 < 50 years	90	300	630	1,120	1,420	3,560
E_3	50 < 65 years	110	305	780	530	480	2,205
E_4	65+ years	200	170	370	260	65	1,065
	Total	470	1,015	2,050	1,990	2,020	7,545

The publication's editors are interested in knowing the probability that someone 65 or older will have 50% or more of retirement funds invested in the stock market. Assuming the data collected in this study reflect the population of investors, the editors can find this conditional probability using the following steps:

Step 1 Define the experiment.
A randomly selected person age 65 or older has his or her portfolio analyzed for percentage of retirement funds in the stock market.

Step 2 Define the events of interest.
In this case, we are interested in two events:

$$E_4 = \text{At least 65 years old}$$
$$E_9 = \text{50\% or more in stocks}$$

Step 3 Define the probability statement of interest.
The editors are interested in

$$P(E_9 | E_4) = \text{Probability of 50\% or more stocks } given \text{ at least 65 years}$$

Step 4 Convert the data to probabilities using the relative frequency assessment method.
We begin with the event that is given to have occurred (E_4). A total of 1,065 people in the study were at least 65 years of age. Of the 1,065 people, 65 had 50% or more of their retirement funds in the stock market.

$$P(E_9 | E_4) = \frac{65}{1,065} = 0.061$$

Thus, the conditional probability that someone at least 65 will have 50% or more of retirement assets in the stock market is 0.061. This value can be found using Step 5 as well.

Step 5 Use Probability Rule 6 to find the conditional probability.

$$P(E_9 | E_4) = \frac{P(E_9 \text{ and } E_4)}{P(E_4)}$$

The necessary probabilities are found using the relative frequency assessment method:

$$P(E_4) = \frac{1,065}{7,545} = 0.1412$$

and the joint probability is

$$P(E_9 \text{ and } E_4) = \frac{65}{7,545} = 0.0086$$

Then, using Probability Rule 6, we get

$$P(E_9 | E_4) = \frac{P(E_9 \text{ and } E_4)}{P(E_4)} = \frac{0.0086}{0.1412} = 0.061$$

>> **END EXAMPLE**

TRY PROBLEM 4-34 (pg. 172)

Tree Diagrams Another way of organizing the events of an experiment that aids in the calculation of probabilities is the *tree diagram*.

| BUSINESS APPLICATION | **USING TREE DIAGRAMS** |

SYRINGA NETWORKS (*CONTINUED*) Figure 4.3 illustrates the tree diagram for Syringa Networks, the Internet service provider discussed earlier. Note that the branches at each node in the tree diagram represent mutually exclusive events. Moving from left to right, the first two branches indicate the two customer types (male and female—mutually exclusive events). Three branches grow from each of these original branches, representing the three possible categories for Internet use. The probabilities for the events male and female are shown on the first two branches. The probabilities shown on the right of the tree are the joint probabilities for each combination of gender and hours of use. These figures are found using Table 4.8, which was shown earlier. The probabilities on the branches following the male and female branches showing hours of use are conditional probabilities. For example, we can find the probability that a male customer (E_5) will spend more than 40 hours on the Internet (E_3) by

$$P(E_3 | E_5) = \frac{P(E_3 \text{ and } E_5)}{P(E_5)} = \frac{0.14}{0.66} = 0.2121$$

Conditional Probability for Independent Events We previously discussed that two events are independent if the occurrence of one event has no bearing on the probability that the second event occurs. Therefore, when two events are independent, the rule for conditional probability takes a different form, as indicated in Probability Rule 7.

Probability Rule 7: Conditional Probability for Independent Events

For independent events E_1, E_2

$$P(E_1 | E_2) = P(E_1) \qquad P(E_2) > 0 \qquad\qquad (4.10)$$

and

$$P(E_2 | E_1) = P(E_2) \qquad P(E_1) > 0$$

FIGURE 4.3

Tree Diagram for Syringa Networks

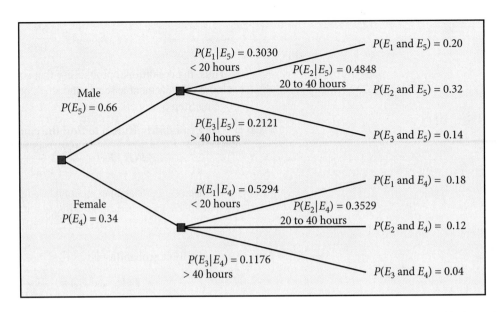

As Rule 7 shows, the conditional probability of one event occurring, given a second independent event has already occurred, is simply the probability of the event occurring.

EXAMPLE 4-11   **CHECKING FOR INDEPENDENCE**

British Columbia Forest Products In Example 4-9, the manager at the British Columbia Forest Products Company reported the following data on the boards in inventory:

	Dimension			
Length	E_4 2″ × 4″	E_5 2″ × 6″	E_6 2″ × 8″	Total
E_1 = 8 feet	1,400	1,500	1,100	4,000
E_2 = 10 feet	2,000	3,500	2,500	8,000
E_3 = 12 feet	1,600	2,000	2,400	6,000
Total	5,000	7,000	6,000	18,000

He will be selecting one board at random from the inventory to show a visiting customer. Of interest is whether the length of the board is independent of the dimension. This can be determined using the following steps:

Step 1 **Define the experiment.**
A board is randomly selected and its dimensions determined.

Step 2 **Define one event for length and one event for dimension.**
Let E_2 = Event that the board is 10 feet long and E_5 = Event that the board is a 2″ × 6″ dimension.

Step 3 **Determine the probability for each event.**

$$P(E_2) = \frac{8,000}{18,000} = 0.4444 \quad \text{and} \quad P(E_5) = \frac{7,000}{18,000} = 0.3889$$

Step 4 **Assess the joint probability of the two events occurring.**

$$P(E_2 \text{ and } E_5) = \frac{3,500}{18,000} = 0.1944$$

Step 5 **Compute the conditional probability of one event given the other using Probability Rule 6.**

$$P(E_2|E_5) = \frac{P(E_2 \text{ and } E_5)}{P(E_5)} = \frac{0.1944}{0.3889} = 0.50$$

Step 6 Check for independence using Probability Rule 7.

Because $P(E_2|E_5) = 0.50 > P(E_2) = 0.4444$, the two events, board length and board dimension, are not independent.

>> **END EXAMPLE**

TRY PROBLEM 4-42 (pg. 173)

Chapter Outcome 3. → # Multiplication Rule

We needed to find the joint probability of two events in the discussion on addition of two events and in the discussion on conditional probability. We were able to find $P(E_1 \text{ and } E_2)$ simply by examining the joint relative frequency tables. However, we often need to find $P(E_1 \text{ and } E_2)$ when we do not know the joint relative frequencies. When this is the case, we can use the multiplication rule for two events.

Multiplication Rule for Two Events

Probability Rule 8: Multiplication Rule for Any Two Events

For two events, E_1 and E_2,

$$P(E_1 \text{ and } E_2) = P(E_1)P(E_2|E_1) \qquad \text{(4.11)}$$

BUSINESS APPLICATION   MULTIPLICATION RULE

HONG KONG FIREWORKS To illustrate how to find a joint probability, consider an example involving the Hong Kong Fireworks company, a manufacturer of fireworks used by cities, fairs, and other commercial establishments for large-scale fireworks displays. The company uses two suppliers of material used in making a particular product. The materials from the two suppliers are intermingled on the manufacturing process. When a case of fireworks is being made, the material is pulled randomly from inventory without regard to which company made it. Recently, a customer ordered two products. At the time of assembly, the material inventory contained 30 units of MATX and 50 units of Quinex. What is the probability that both fireworks products ordered by this customer will have MATX material?

To answer this question, we must recognize that two events are required to form the desired outcome. Therefore, let

$$E_1 = \text{Event: MATX Material in first product}$$

$$E_2 = \text{Event: MATX Material in second product}$$

The probability that both fireworks products contain MATX material is written as $P(E_1 \text{ and } E_2)$. The key word here is *and*, as contrasted with the Addition Rule, in which the key word is *or*. The *and* signifies that we are interested in the joint probability of two events, as noted by $P(E_1 \text{ and } E_2)$. To find this probability, we employ Probability Rule 8.

$$P(E_1 \text{ and } E_2) = P(E_1)P(E_2|E_1)$$

We start by assuming that each unit of material in the inventory has the same chance of being selected for assembly. For the first fireworks product,

$$P(E_1) = \frac{\text{Number of MATX units}}{\text{Number of Firework Materials in inventory}}$$

$$= \frac{30}{80} = 0.375$$

Then, because we are not replacing the first firework material, we find $P(E_2|E_1)$ by

$$P(E_2|E_1) = \frac{\text{Number of remaining MATX units}}{\text{Number of remaining Firework Materials units}}$$

$$= \frac{29}{79} = 0.3671$$

Now, by Rule 8,

$$P(E_1 \text{ and } E_2) = P(E_1)P(E_2|E_1) = (0.375)(0.3671)$$
$$= 0.1377$$

Therefore, there is a 13.77% chance the two fireworks products will contain the MATX material

Using a Tree Diagram

BUSINESS APPLICATION   **MULTIPLICATION RULE**

HONG KONG FIREWORKS (CONTINUED) A tree diagram can be used to display the situation facing Hong Kong Fireworks. The company uses material from two suppliers, which is intermingled in the inventory. Recently a customer ordered two products and found that both contained the MATX material. Assuming that the inventory contains 30 MATX and 50 Quinex units, to determine the probability of both products containing the MATX material you can use a tree diagram. The two branches on the left side of the tree in Figure 4.4 show the possible material options for the first product. The two branches coming from each of the first branches show the possible material options for the second product. The probabilities at the far right are the joint probabilities for the material options for the two products. As we determined previously, the probability that both products will contain a MATX unit is 0.1377, as shown on the top right on the tree diagram.

We can use the Multiplication Rule and the Addition Rule in one application when we determine the probability that two products will have different materials. Looking at Figure 4.4, we see there are two ways this can happen.

$$P[(\text{MATX } and \text{ Quinex}) \text{ or } (\text{Quinex } and \text{ MATX})] = ?$$

If the first product is a MATX and the second one is a Quinex, then the first cannot be a Quinex and the second a MATX. These two events are mutually exclusive and, therefore, Rule 5 can be used to calculate the required probability. The joint probabilities (generated from the Multiplication Rule) are shown on the right side of the tree. To find the desired probability, using Rule 5, we can add the two joint probabilities:

$$P[(\text{ MATX } and \text{ Quinex}) \text{ or } (\text{Quinex } and \text{ MATX})] =$$
$$0.2373 \quad + \quad 0.2373 \quad = 0.4746$$

The chance that a customer buying two products will get two different materials is 47.46%.

Multiplication Rule for Independent Events When we determined the probability that two products would have MATX material, we used the general multiplication rule (Rule 8). The general multiplication rule requires that conditional probability be used because the

FIGURE 4.4

Tree Diagram for the
Fireworks Product Example

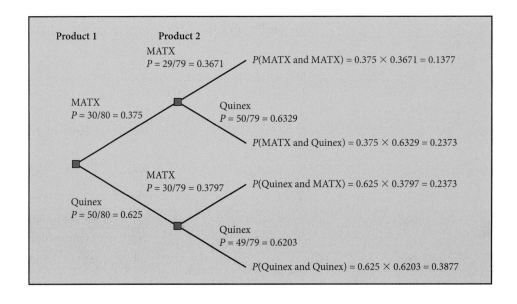

probability associated with the second product depends on the material selected for the first product. The chance of obtaining a MATX was lowered from 30/80 to 29/79, given the first material was a MATX.

However, if the two events of interest are *independent,* the imposed condition does not alter the probability, and the Multiplication Rule takes the form shown in Probability Rule 9.

Probability Rule 9: Multiplication Rule for Independent Events

For independent events $E_1, E_2,$

$$P(E_1 \text{ and } E_2) = P(E_1)P(E_2) \tag{4.12}$$

The joint probability of two independent events is simply the product of the probabilities of the two events. Rule 9 is the primary way that you can determine whether any two events are independent. If the product of the probabilities of the two events equals the joint probability, then the events are independent.

EXAMPLE 4-12   **USING THE MULTIPLICATION RULE AND THE ADDITION RULE**

Christiansen Accounting Christiansen Accounting prepares tax returns for individuals and companies. Over the years, the firm has tracked its clients and has discovered that 12% of the individual returns have been selected for audit by the Internal Revenue Service. On one particular day, the firm signed two new individual tax clients. The firm is interested in the probability that at least one of these clients will be audited. This probability can be found using the following steps:

Step 1 **Define the experiment.**
The IRS randomly selects a tax return to audit.

Step 2 **Define the possible outcomes.**
For a single client, the following outcomes are defined:

$$A = \text{Audit}$$
$$N = \text{No audit}$$

For each of the clients, we define the outcomes as

Client 1: A_1; N_1
Client 2: A_2; N_2

Step 3 **Define the overall event of interest.**
The event that Christiansen Accounting is interested in is

$$E = \text{At least one client is audited}$$

Step 4 **List the outcomes for the events of interest.**
The possible outcomes for which at least one client will be audited are as follows:

E_1:	A_1	A_2	both are audited
E_2:	A_1	N_2	only one client is audited
E_3:	N_1	A_2	

Step 5 **Compute the probabilities for the events of interest.**
Assuming the chances of the clients being audited are independent of each other, probabilities for the events are determined using Probability Rule 9 for independent events:

$$P(E_1) = P(A_1 \text{ and } A_2) = 0.12 \times 0.12 = 0.0144$$
$$P(E_2) = P(A_1 \text{ and } N_2) = 0.12 \times 0.88 = 0.1056$$
$$P(E_3) = P(N_1 \text{ and } A_2) = 0.88 \times 0.12 = 0.1056$$

Step 6 **Determine the probability for the overall event of interest.**
Because events E_1, E_2, and E_3 are mutually exclusive, compute the probability of at least one client being audited using Rule 5, the Addition Rule for Mutually Exclusive Events:

$$
\begin{aligned}
P(E_1 \text{ or } E_2 \text{ or } E_3) &= P(E_1) + P(E_2) + P(E_3) \\
&= 0.0144 + 0.1056 + 0.1056 \\
&= 0.2256
\end{aligned}
$$

The chance of one or both of the clients being audited is 0.2256.

>> **END EXAMPLE**

TRY PROBLEM 4-30 (pg. 171)

Chapter Outcome 4. → # Bayes' Theorem

As decision makers, you will often encounter situations that require you to assess probabilities for events of interest. Your assessment may be based on relative frequency or subjectivity. However, you may then come across new information that causes you to revise the probability assessment. For example, a human resources manager who has interviewed a person for a sales job might assess a low probability that the person will succeed in sales. However, after seeing the person's very high score on the company's sales aptitude test, the manager might revise her assessment upward. A medical doctor might assign an 80% chance that a patient has a particular disease. However, after seeing positive results from a lab test, he might increase his assessment to 95%.

In these situations, you will need a way to formally incorporate the new information. One very useful tool for doing this is called *Bayes' Theorem*, which is named for the Reverend Thomas Bayes, who developed the special application of conditional probability in the 1700s. Letting event B be an event that is given to have occurred, the conditional probability of event E_i occurring can be computed as shown earlier using Equation 4.9:

$$
P(E_i | B) = \frac{P(E_i \text{ and } B)}{P(B)}
$$

The numerator can be reformulated using the Multiplication Rule (Equation 4.11) as

$$
P(E_i \text{ and } B) = P(E_i) P(B | E_i)
$$

The conditional probability is then

$$
P(E_i | B) = \frac{P(E_i) P(B | E_i)}{P(B)}
$$

The denominator, $P(B)$, can be found by adding the probability of the k possible ways that event B can occur. This is

$$
P(B) = P(E_1) P(B | E_1) + P(E_2) P(B | E_2) + \cdots + P(E_k) P(B | E_k)
$$

Then, Bayes' Theorem is formulated as Equation 4.13.

Bayes' Theorem

$$
P(E_i | B) = \frac{P(E_i) P(B | E_i)}{P(E_1) P(B | E_1) + P(E_2) P(B | E_2) + \cdots + P(E_k) P(B | E_k)}
\tag{4.13}
$$

where:

$$
\begin{aligned}
E_i &= i\text{th event of interest of the } k \text{ possible events} \\
B &= \text{Event that has occurred that might impact } P(E_i)
\end{aligned}
$$

Events E_1 to E_k are mutually exclusive and collectively exhaustive.

BUSINESS APPLICATION **BAYES' THEOREM**

severija kirilovaite/Fotolia

TILE PRODUCTION The Glerum Tile and Flooring Company has two production facilities, one in Ohio and one in Virginia. The company makes the same type of tile at both facilities. The Ohio plant makes 60% of the company's total tile output and the Virginia plant 40%. All tiles from the two facilities are sent to regional warehouses, where they are intermingled. After extensive study, the quality assurance manager has determined that 5% of the tiles produced in Ohio and 10% of the tiles produced in Virginia are unusable due to quality problems. When the company sells a defective tile, it incurs not only the cost of replacing the item but also the loss of goodwill. The vice president for production would like to allocate these costs fairly between the two plants. To do so, he knows he must first determine the probability that a defective tile was produced by a particular production line. Specifically, he needs to answer these questions:

1. What is the probability that the tile was produced at the Ohio plant, given that the tile is defective?
2. What is the probability that the tile was produced at the Virginia plant, given that the tile is defective?

In notation form, with D representing the event that an item is defective, what the manager wants to know is

$$P(\text{Ohio}|D) = ?$$
$$P(\text{Virginia}|D) = ?$$

We can use Bayes' Theorem (Equation 4.13) to determine these probabilities, as follows:

$$P(\text{Ohio}|D) = \frac{P(\text{Ohio})P(D|\text{Ohio})}{P(D)}$$

We know that event D(Defective tile) can happen if it is made in either Ohio or Virginia. Thus,

$$P(D) = P(\text{Ohio and Defective}) + P(\text{Virginia and Defective})$$
$$P(D) = P(\text{Ohio})P(D|\text{Ohio}) + P(\text{Virginia})P(D|\text{Virginia})$$

We already know that 60% of the tiles come from Ohio and 40% from Virginia. So, $P(\text{Ohio}) = 0.60$ and $P(\text{Virginia}) = 0.40$. These are called the *prior* probabilities. Without Bayes' Theorem, we would likely allocate the total cost of defects in a 60/40 split between Ohio and Virginia, based on total production. However, the new information about the quality from each line is

$$P(D|\text{Ohio}) = 0.05 \quad \text{and} \quad P(D|\text{Virginia}) = 0.10$$

which can be used to properly allocate the cost of defects. This is done using Bayes' Theorem.

$$P(\text{Ohio}|D) = \frac{P(\text{Ohio})P(D|\text{Ohio})}{P(\text{Ohio})P(D|\text{Ohio}) + P(\text{Virginia})P(D|\text{Virginia})}$$

then,

$$P(\text{Ohio}|D) = \frac{(0.60)(0.05)}{(0.60)(0.05) + (0.40)(0.10)} = 0.4286$$

and

$$P(\text{Virginia}|D) = \frac{P(\text{Virginia})P(D|\text{Virginia})}{P(\text{Virginia})P(D|\text{Virginia}) + P(\text{Ohio})P(D|\text{Ohio})}$$

$$P(\text{Virginia}|D) = \frac{(0.40)(0.10)}{(0.40)(0.10) + (0.60)(0.05)} = 0.5714$$

These probabilities are *revised* probabilities. The prior probabilities have been revised given the new quality information. We now see that 42.86% of the cost of defects should be allocated to the Ohio plant, and 57.14% should be allocated to the Virginia plant.

TABLE 4.9 | **Bayes' Theorem Calculations for Glerum Tile and Flooring**

Events	Prior Probabilities	Conditional Probabilities	Joint Probabilities	Revised Probabilities
Ohio	0.60	0.05	$(0.60)(0.05) = 0.03$	$0.03/0.07 = 0.4286$
Virginia	0.40	0.10	$(0.40)(0.10) = \underline{0.04}$	$0.04/0.07 = \underline{0.5714}$
			0.07	1.0000

Note, the denominator $P(D)$ is the overall probability of a defective tile. This probability is

$$P(D) = P(\text{Ohio})P(D|\text{Ohio}) + P(\text{Virginia})P(D|\text{Virginia})$$
$$= (0.60)(0.05) + (0.40)(0.10)$$
$$= 0.03 + 0.04$$
$$= 0.07$$

Thus, 7% of all the tiles made by Glerum are defective.

You might prefer to use a tabular approach like that shown in Table 4.9 when you apply Bayes' Theorem.

EXAMPLE 4-13   BAYES' THEOREM

Techtronics Equipment Corporation The Techtronics Equipment Corporation has developed a new electronic device that it would like to sell to the U.S. military for use in fighter aircraft. The sales manager believes there is a 0.60 chance that the military will place an order. However, after making an initial sales presentation, military officials will often ask for a second presentation to other military decision makers. Historically, 70% of successful companies are asked to make a second presentation, whereas 50% of unsuccessful companies are asked back a second time. Suppose Techtronics Equipment has just been asked to make a second presentation; what is the revised probability that the company will make the sale? This probability can be determined using the following steps:

Step 1   Define the events.
In this case, there are two events:

$$S = \text{Sale} \quad N = \text{No sale}$$

Step 2   Determine the prior probabilities for the events.
The probability of the events prior to knowing whether a second presentation will be requested are

$$P(S) = 0.60 \quad P(N) = 0.40$$

Step 3   Define an event that if it occurs could alter the prior probabilities.
In this case, the altering event is the invitation to make a second presentation. We label this event as SP.

Step 4   Determine the conditional probabilities.
The conditional probabilities are associated with being invited to make a second presentation:

$$P(SP|S) = 0.70 \quad P(SP|N) = 0.50$$

Step 5   Use the tabular approach for Bayes' Theorem to determine the *revised probabilities*.
These correspond to

$$P(S|SP) \text{ and } P(N|SP)$$

Event	Prior Probabilities	Conditional Probabilities	Joint Probabilities	Revised Probabilities
S = Sale	0.60	$P(SP\|S) = 0.70$	$P(S)P(SP\|S) = (0.60)(0.70) = 0.42$	$0.42/0.62 = 0.6774$
N = No sale	0.40	$P(SP\|N) = 0.50$	$P(N)P(SP\|N) = (0.40)(0.50) = \underline{0.20}$	$0.20/0.62 = \underline{0.3226}$
			0.62	1.0000

Thus, using Bayes' Theorem, if Techtronics Equipment gets a second presentation opportunity, the probability of making the sale is revised upward from 0.60 to 0.6774.

>> **END EXAMPLE**

TRY PROBLEM 4-33 (pg. 172)

MyStatLab

4-2: Exercises

Skill Development

4-26. Based on weather data collected in Racine, Wisconsin, on Christmas Day, the weather had the following distribution:

Event	Relative Frequency
Clear & dry	0.20
Cloudy & dry	0.30
Rain	0.40
Snow	0.10

  a. Based on these data, what is the probability that next Christmas will be dry?
  b. Based on the data, what is the probability that next Christmas will be rainy or cloudy and dry?
  c. Supposing next Christmas is dry, determine the probability that it will also be cloudy.

4-27. The Jack In The Box franchise in Bangor, Maine, has determined that the chance a customer will order a soft drink is 0.90. The probability that a customer will order a hamburger is 0.60. The probability that a customer will order french fries is 0.50.

  a. If a customer places an order, what is the probability that the order will include a soft drink and no fries if these two events are independent?
  b. The restaurant has also determined that if a customer orders a hamburger, the probability the customer will also order fries is 0.80. Determine the probability that the order will include a hamburger and fries.

4-28. Ponderosa Paint and Glass carries three brands of paint. A customer wants to buy another gallon of paint to match paint she purchased at the store previously. She can't recall the brand name and does not wish to return home to find the old can of paint. So she selects two of the three brands of paint at random and buys them.

  a. What is the probability that she matched the paint brand?
  b. Her husband also goes to the paint store and fails to remember what brand to buy. So he also purchases two of the three brands of paint at random. Determine the probability that both the woman and her husband fail to get the correct brand of paint. (*Hint*: Are the husband's selections independent of his wife's selections?)

4-29. The college basketball team at West Texas State University has 10 players; 5 are seniors, 2 are juniors, and 3 are sophomores. Two players are randomly selected to serve as captains for the next game. What is the probability that both players selected are seniors?

4-30. Micron Technology has sales offices located in four cities: Dallas, Seattle, Boston, and Los Angeles. An analysis of the company's accounts receivables reveals the number of overdue invoices by days, as shown here.

Days Overdue	Dallas	Seattle	Boston	Los Angeles
Under 30 days	137	122	198	287
30–60 days	85	46	76	109
61–90 days	33	27	55	48
Over 90 days	18	32	45	66

Assume the invoices are stored and managed from a central database.

  a. What is the probability that a randomly selected invoice from the database is from the Boston sales office?
  b. What is the probability that a randomly selected invoice from the database is between 30 and 90 days overdue?
  c. What is the probability that a randomly selected invoice from the database is over 90 days old and from the Seattle office?

d. If a randomly selected invoice is from the Los Angeles office, what is the probability that it is 60 or fewer days overdue?

4-31. Three events occur with probabilities $P(E_1) = 0.35, P(E_2) = 0.15, P(E_3) = 0.40$. If the event B occurs, the probability becomes $P(E_1|B) = 0.25, P(B) = 0.30$.
   a. Calculate $P(E_1 \text{ and } B)$
   b. Compute $P(E_1 \text{ or } B)$
   c. Assume that E_1, E_2, and E_3 are independent events. Calculate $P(E_1 \text{ and } E_2 \text{ and } E_3)$.

4-32. The URS construction company has submitted two bids, one to build a large hotel in London and the other to build a commercial office building in New York City. The company believes it has a 40% chance of winning the hotel bid and a 25% chance of winning the office building bid. The company also believes that winning the hotel bid is independent of winning the office building bid.
   a. What is the probability the company will win both contracts?
   b. What is the probability the company will win at least one contract?
   c. What is the probability the company will lose both contracts?

4-33. Suppose a quality manager for Dell Computers has collected the following data on the quality status of disk drives by supplier. She inspected a total of 700 disk drives.

	Drive Status	
Supplier	**Working**	**Defective**
Company A	120	10
Company B	180	15
Company C	50	5
Company D	300	20

   a. Based on these inspection data, what is the probability of randomly selecting a disk drive from company B?
   b. What is the probability of a defective disk drive being received by the computer company?
   c. What is the probability of a defect given that company B supplied the disk drive?

4-34. Three events occur with probabilities of $P(E_1) = 0.35$, $P(E_2) = 0.25, P(E_3) = 0.40$. Other probabilities are: $P(B|E_1) = 0.25, P(B|E_2) = 0.15, P(B|E_3) = 0.60$.
   a. Compute $P(E_1|B)$.
   b. Compute $P(E_2|B)$.
   c. Compute $P(E_3|B)$.

4-35. Men have a reputation for not wanting to ask for directions. A Harris study conducted for Lincoln Mercury indicated that 42% of men and 61% of women would stop and ask for directions. The U.S. Census Bureau's 2007 population estimate was that

for individuals 18 or over, 48.2% were men and 51.8% were women. This exercise addresses this age group.
   a. A randomly chosen driver gets lost on a road trip. Determine the probability that the driver is a woman and stops to ask for directions.
   b. Calculate the probability that the driver stops to ask for directions.
   c. Given that a driver stops to ask for directions, determine the probability that the driver was a man.

Business Applications

4-36. A local FedEx/Kinkos has three black-and-white copy machines and two color copiers. Based on historical data, the chance that each black-and-white copier will be down for repairs is 0.10. The color copiers are more of a problem and are down 20% of the time each.
   a. Based on this information, what is the probability that if a customer needs a color copy, both color machines will be down for repairs?
   b. If a customer wants both a color copy and a black-and-white copy, what is the probability that the necessary machines will be available? (Assume that the color copier can also be used to make a black-and-white copy if needed.)
   c. If the manager wants to have at least a 99% chance of being able to furnish a black-and-white copy on demand, is the present configuration sufficient? (Assume that the color copier can also be used to make a black-and-white copy if needed.) Back up your answer with appropriate probability computations.
   d. What is the probability that all five copiers will be up and running at the same time? Suppose the manager added a fourth black-and-white copier; how would the probability of all copiers being ready at any one time be affected?

4-37. Suppose the managers at FedEx/Kinkos wish to meet the increasing demand for color photocopies and to have more reliable service. (Refer to Problem 4-36.) As a goal, they would like to have at least a 99.9% chance of being able to furnish a black-and-white copy or a color copy on demand. They also wish to purchase only four copiers. They have asked for your advice regarding the mix of black-and-white and color copiers. Supply them with your advice. Provide calculations and reasons to support your advice.

4-38. The Snappy Service gas station manager is thinking about a promotion that she hopes will bring in more business to the full-service island. She is considering the option that when a customer requests a fill-up, if the pump stops with the dollar amount at $19.99, the customer will get the gasoline free. Previous studies show that 70% of the customers require more than $20.00 when they fill up, so would not be eligible for the free gas. What is the probability that a customer will get free gas at this station if the promotion is implemented?

4-39. Suppose the manager in Problem 4-38 is concerned about alienating customers who buy more than $20.00, since they would not be eligible to win the free gas under the original concept. To overcome this, she is thinking about changing the contest. The customer will get free gas if any of the following happens:

$21.11, $22.22, $23.33, $24.44, $25.55, $26.66, $27.77, $28.88, $29.99

Past data show that only 5% of all customers require $30.00 or more. If one of these big-volume customers arrives, he will get to blindly draw a ball from a box containing 100 balls (99 red, 1 white). If the white ball is picked, the customer gets his gas free. Considering this new promotion, what is the probability that a customer will get free gas?

4-40. Hubble Construction Company has submitted a bid on a state government project that is to be funded by the federal government's stimulus money in Arizona. The price of the bid was predetermined in the bid specifications. The contract is to be awarded on the basis of a blind drawing from those who have bid. Five other companies have also submitted bids.

a. What is the probability of the Hubble Construction Company winning the bid?

b. Suppose that there are two contracts to be awarded by a blind draw. What is the probability of Hubble winning both contracts? Assume sampling with replacement.

c. Referring to part b, what is the probability of Hubble not winning either contract?

d. Referring to part b, what is the probability of Hubble winning exactly one contract?

4-41. Drake Marketing and Promotions has randomly surveyed 200 men who watch professional sports. The men were separated according to their educational level (college degree or not) and whether they preferred the NBA or the National Football League (NFL). The results of the survey are shown:

Sports Preference	College Degree	No College Degree
NBA	40	55
NFL	10	95

a. What is the probability that a randomly selected survey participant prefers the NFL?

b. What is the probability that a randomly selected survey participant has a college degree and prefers the NBA?

c. Suppose a survey participant is randomly selected and you are told that he has a college degree. What is the probability that this man prefers the NFL?

d. Is a survey participant's preference for the NBA independent of having a college degree?

4-42. Until the summer of 2008, the real estate market in Fresno, California, had been booming, with prices skyrocketing. Recently, a study showed the sales patterns in Fresno for single-family homes. One chart presented in the commission's report is reproduced here. It shows the number of homes sold by price range and number of days the home was on the market.

| Price Range ($000) | Days on the Market | | |
	1–7	8–30	Over 30
Under $200	125	15	30
$200–$500	200	150	100
$501–$1,000	400	525	175
Over $1,000	125	140	35

a. Using the relative frequency approach to probability assessment, what is the probability that a house will be on the market more than 7 days?

b. Is the event 1–7 *days on the market* independent of the price $200–$500?

c. Suppose a home has just sold in Fresno and was on the market less than 8 days, what is the most likely price range for that home?

4-43. Vegetables from the summer harvest are currently being processed at Skone and Conners Foods, Inc. The manager has found a case of cans that have not been properly sealed. There are three lines that processed cans of this type, and the manager wants to know which line is most likely to be responsible for this mistake. Provide the manager this information.

Line	Contribution to Total	Proportion Defective
1	0.40	0.05
2	0.35	0.10
3	0.25	0.07

4-44. A corporation has 11 manufacturing plants. Of these, seven are domestic and four are outside the United States. Each year a performance evaluation is conducted for four randomly selected plants. What is the probability that a performance evaluation will include at least one plant outside the United States? (*Hint*: Begin by finding the probability that only domestic plants are selected.)

4-45. Parts and materials for the skis made by the Downhill Adventures Company are supplied by two suppliers. Supplier A's materials make up 30% of what is used, with Supplier B providing the rest. Past records indicate that 15% of Supplier A's materials are defective and 10% of B's are defective. Since it is impossible to tell which supplier the materials came from once they are in inventory, the manager wants to know which supplier more likely supplied the defective materials the foreman has brought to his attention. Provide the manager this information.

4-46. A major electronics manufacturer has determined that when one of its televisions is sold, there is 0.08 chance that the set will need service before the warranty period expires. It has also assessed a 0.05 chance that a DVD player will need service prior to the expiration of the warranty.

a. Suppose a customer purchases one of the company's televisions and one of the DVD players. What is the probability that at least one of the products will require service prior to the warranty expiring?

b. Suppose a retailer sells four televisions on a particular Saturday. What is the probability that none of the four will need service prior to the warranty expiring?

c. Suppose a retailer sells four televisions on a particular Saturday. What is the probability that at least one will need repair?

4-47. The Committee for the Study of the American Electorate indicated that 60.7% of the voting-age voters cast ballots in the 2004 presidential election. It also indicated that 85.3% of registered voters voted in the election. The percentage of those who voted for President Bush was 50.8%.

a. Determine the proportion of voting-age voters who voted for President Bush.

b. Determine the proportion of voting-age voters who were registered to vote.

4-48. A distributor of outdoor yard lights has four suppliers. This past season, she purchased 40% of the lights from Franklin Lighting, 30% from Wilson & Sons, 20% from Evergreen Supply, and the rest from A. L. Scott. In prior years, 3% of Franklin's lights were defective, 6% of the Wilson lights were defective, 2% of Evergreen's were defective, and 8% of the Scott lights were defective. When the lights arrive at the distributor, she puts them in inventory without identifying the supplier. Suppose that a defective light string has been pulled from inventory; what is the probability that it was supplied by Franklin Lighting?

4-49. *USA Today* reported ("Study Finds Better Survival Rates at 'High-Volume' Hospitals") that "high-volume" hospitals performed at least 77% of bladder removal surgeries; "low-volume" hospitals performed at most 23%. Assume the percentages are 77% and 23%. In the first two weeks after surgery, 3.1% of patients at low-volume centers died, compared to 0.7% at the high-volume hospitals.

a. Calculate the probability that a randomly chosen bladder-cancer patient had surgery at a high-volume hospital and survived the first two weeks after surgery.

b. Calculate the probability that a randomly chosen bladder-cancer patient survived the first two weeks after surgery.

c. If two bladder-cancer patients were chosen randomly, determine the probability that only one would survive the first two weeks after surgery.

d. If two bladder-cancer patients were chosen randomly, determine the probability that at least one would survive the first two weeks after surgery.

4-50. Suppose an auditor has 18 tax returns, 12 of which are for physicians. If three of the 18 tax returns are randomly selected, then what is the probability that at least one of the three selected will be a physician's tax return?

4-51. A box of 50 remote control devices contains 3 that have a defective power button. If devices are randomly sampled from the box and inspected one at a time, determine

a. The probability that the first control device is defective.

b. The probability that the first control device is good and the second control device is defective.

c. The probability that the first three sampled devices are all good.

Computer Database **Exercises**

4-52. The data file **Colleges** contains data on more than 1,300 colleges and universities in the United States. Suppose a company is planning to award a significant grant to a randomly selected college or university. Using the relative frequency method for assessing probabilities and the rules of probability, respond to the following questions. (If data are missing for a needed variable, reduce the number of colleges in the study appropriately.)

a. What is the probability that the grant will go to a private college or university?

b. What is the probability that the grant will go to a college or university that has a student/faculty ratio over 20?

c. What is the probability that the grant will go to a college or university that is both private and has a student/faculty ratio over 20?

d. If the company decides to split the grant into two grants, what is the probability that both grants will go to California colleges and universities? What might you conclude if this did happen?

4-53. A Courtyard Hotel by Marriott conducted a survey of its guests. Sixty-two surveys were completed. Based on the data from the survey, found in the file **CourtyardSurvey**, determine the following probabilities using the relative frequency assessment method.

a. Of two customers selected, what is the probability that both will be on a business trip?

b. What is the probability that a customer will be on a business trip or will experience a hotel problem during a stay at the Courtyard?

c. What is the probability that a customer on business has an in-state area code phone number?

d. Based on the data in the survey, can the Courtyard manager conclude that a customer's rating regarding staff attentiveness is independent of whether he or she is traveling on business, pleasure, or both? Use the rules of probability to make this determination.

4-54. Continuing with the Marriott survey done by the managers of a Marriott Courtyard Hotel, based on the data from the survey, found in the file **CourtyardSurvey**, determine the following probabilities using the relative frequency assessment method.

a. Of two customers selected, what is the probability that neither will be on a business trip?

b. What is the probability that a customer will be on a business trip or will not experience a hotel problem during a stay at the Courtyard?

c. What is the probability that a customer on a pleasure trip has an in-state area code phone number?

4-55. A Harris survey asked, in part, what the most important reason was that people give for not using a wireless phone exclusively. The responses were: (1) Like the safety of traditional phone, (2) Need line for Internet access, (3) Pricing not attractive enough, (4) Weak or unreliable cell signal at home, (5) Coverage not good enough, and (6) Other. The file titled **Wireless** contains the responses for the 1,088 respondents.

a. Of those respondents 36 or older, determine the probability that an individual in this age group would not use a wireless phone exclusively because of some type of difficulty in placing and receiving calls with a wireless phone.

b. If three respondents were selected at random from those respondents younger than 36, calculate the probability that at least one of the respondents stated the most important reason for not using a wireless exclusively was that they need a line for Internet access.

4-56. A recent news release published by *Ars Technica, LLD* presented the results of a study concerning the world and domestic market share for the major manufacturers of personal computers (PCs). The file titled **PCMarket** contains a sample that would produce the market shares alluded to in the article and the highest academic degrees achieved by the owners of those PCs.

a. Determine the probability that the person had achieved at least a bachelor's degree and owns a Dell PC.

b. If a randomly selected person owned a Dell PC, determine the probability that the person had achieved at least a bachelor's degree.

c. Consider these two events: (1) At least a bachelor's degree and (2) Owns a Dell PC. Are these events independent, dependent, or mutually exclusive? Explain.

4-57. PricewaterhouseCoopers Saratoga, in its 2005/2006 Human Capital Index Report, indicated the average number of days it took for an American company to fill a job vacancy in 2004 was 48 days. Sample data similar to those used in the study are in a file titled **Hired**. Categories for the days and hire cost are provided under the headings "Time" and "Cost," respectively.

a. Calculate the probability that a company vacancy took at most 100 days or cost at most $4,000 to fill.

b. Of the vacancies that took at most 100 days to fill, calculate the probability that the cost was at most $4,000.

c. If three of the vacancies were chosen at random, calculate the probability that two of the vacancies cost at most $4,000 to fill.

4-58. A company produces scooters used by small businesses, such as pizza parlors, that find them convenient for making short deliveries. The company is notified whenever a scooter breaks down, and the problem is classified as being either mechanical or electrical. The company then matches the scooter to the plant where it was assembled. The file **Scooters** contains a random sample of 200 breakdowns. Use the data in the file to find the following probabilities.

a. If a scooter was assembled in the Tyler plant, what is the probability its breakdown was due to an electrical problem?

b. Is the probability of a scooter having a mechanical problem independent of the scooter being assembled at the Lincoln plant

c. If mechanical problems are assigned a cost of $75 and electrical problems are assigned a cost of $100, how much cost would be budgeted for the Lincoln and Tyler plants next year if a total of 500 scooters were expected to be returned for repair?

END EXERCISES 4-2

Visual Summary

Chapter 4: Probability is used in our everyday lives and in business decision-making all the time. You might base your decision to call ahead for dinner reservations based on your assessment of the probability of having to wait for seating. A company may decide to switch suppliers based on their assessment of the probability that the new supplier will provide higher quality products or services. Probability is the way we measure our uncertainty about events. However, in order to properly use probability you need to know the probability rules and the terms associated with probability.

4.1 The Basics of Probability (pg. 141–153)

Summary

In order to effectively use probability it is important to understand key concepts and terminology. Some of the most important of these are discussed in section 4.1 including **sample space**, **dependent** and **independent events**, and **mutually exclusive events**. Probabilities are assessed in three main ways, **classical assessment**, **relative frequency assessment**, and **subjective assessment**.

> **Outcome 1.** Understand the three approaches to assessing probabilities.

4.2 The Rules of Probability (pg. 153–175)

Summary

To effectively work with probability, it is important to know the probability rules. Section 4.2 introduces nine rules including three **addition rules**, and two **multiplication rules**. Rules for **conditional probability** and the **complement rule** are also very useful. **Bayes' Theorem** is used to calculate conditional probabilities in situations where the probability of the given event is not provided and must be calculated.

> **Outcome 2.** Be able to apply the Addition Rule.
> **Outcome 3.** Know how to use the Multiplication Rule.
> **Outcome 4.** Know how to use Bayes' Theorem for applications involving conditional probabilities

Conclusion

Probability is how we measure our uncertainty about whether an outcome will occur. The closer the probability assessment is to 1.0 or 0.0, the more certain we are that event will or will not occur. Assessing probabilities and then using those probabilities to help make decisions is a central part of what business decision-makers do on a regular basis. This chapter has introduced the fundamentals of probability and the rules that are used when working with probability. These rules and the general probability concepts will be used throughout the remainder of this text.

Equations

(4.1) Classical Probability Assessment pg. 146

$$P(E_i) = \frac{\text{Number of ways } E_i \text{ can occur}}{\text{Total number of possible outcomes}}$$

(4.2) Relative Frequency Assessment pg. 147

$$P(E_i) = \frac{\text{Number of times } E_i \text{ occurs}}{N}$$

(4.3) Probability Rule 1 pg. 153

$$0 \leq P(E_i) \leq 1 \text{ for all } i$$

(4.4) Probability Rule 2 pg. 153

$$\sum_{i=1}^{k} P(e_i) = 1$$

(4.5) Probability Rule 3 pg. 154

Addition rule for individual outcomes:

The probability of an event E_i is equal to the *sum* of the probabilities of the possible outcomes forming E_i. For example, if

$$E_i = \{e_1, e_2, e_3\}$$

then

$$P(E_i) = P(e_1) + P(e_2) + P(e_3)$$

(4.6) Complement Rule pg. 156

$$P(\overline{E}) = 1 - P(E)$$

(4.7) Probability Rule 4 pg. 158

Addition rule for any two events E_1 and E_2:

$$P(E_1 \text{ or } E_2) = P(E_1) + P(E_2) - P(E_1 \text{ and } E_2)$$

(4.8) Probability Rule 5 pg. 160

Addition rule for mutually exclusive events E_1, E_2:

$$P(E_1 \text{ or } E_2) = P(E_1) + P(E_2)$$

(4.9) Probability Rule 6 pg. 161

Conditional probability for any two events E_1, E_2:

$$P(E_1 | E_2) = \frac{P(E_1 \text{ and } E_2)}{P(E_2)}$$

(4.10) Probability Rule 7 pg. 163

Conditional probability for independent events E_1, E_2:

$$P(E_1 | E_2) = P(E_1) \qquad P(E_2) > 0$$

and

$$P(E_2 | E_1) = P(E_2) \qquad P(E_1) > 0$$

(4.11) Probability Rule 8 pg. 165

Multiplication rule for any two events, E_1 and E_2:

$$P(E_1 \text{ and } E_2) = P(E_1)P(E_2 | E_1)$$

(4.12) Probability Rule 9 pg. 167

Multiplication rule for independent events E_1, E_2:

$$P(E_1 \text{ and } E_2) = P(E_1)P(E_2)$$

(4.13) Bayes' Theorem pg. 168

$$P(E_i | B) = \frac{P(E_i)P(B | E_i)}{P(E_1)P(B | E_1) + P(E_2)P(B | E_2) + \cdots + P(E_k)P(B | E_k)}$$

Key Terms

Classical probability assessment pg. 146
Complement pg. 156
Conditional probability pg. 161
Dependent events pg. 145

Event pg. 143
Experiment pg. 141
Independent events pg. 145
Mutually exclusive events pg. 144

Probability pg. 141
Relative frequency assessment pg. 147
Sample space pg. 141
Subjective probability assessment pg. 149

Chapter Exercises   MyStatLab

Conceptual Questions

4-59. Discuss what is meant by *classical probability assessment* and indicate why classical assessment is not often used in business applications.

4-60. Discuss what is meant by the *relative frequency assessment approach* to probability assessment. Provide a business-related example, other than the one given in the text, in which this method of probability assessment might be used.

4-61. Discuss what is meant by *subjective probability*. Provide a business-related example in which subjective probability assessment would likely be used. Also,

provide an example of when you have personally used subjective probability assessment.

4-62. Examine the relationship between independent, dependent, and mutually exclusive events. Consider two events A and B that are mutually exclusive such that $P(A) \neq 0$.

a. Calculate $P(A|B)$.

b. What does your answer to part a say about whether two mutually exclusive events are dependent or independent?

c. Consider two events C and D such that $P(C) = 0.4$ and $P(C|D) = 0.15$. (1) Are events

C and D mutually exclusive? (2) Are events C and D independent or dependent? Are dependent events necessarily mutually exclusive events?

4-63. Consider the following table:

	A	$\overline{A}$	Totals
B	800	200	1,000
$\overline{B}$	600	400	1,000
Totals	1,400	600	2,000

Explore the complements of conditional events:

a. Calculate the following probabilities: $P(A|B)$,

$$P(\overline{A}|\overline{B}), P(\overline{A}|B), P(A|\overline{B}).$$

b. Now determine which pair of events are complements of each other. (*Hint*: Use the probabilities calculated in part a and the Complement Rule.)

4-64. Examine the following table:

	A	$\overline{A}$	Totals
B	200	800	1,000
$\overline{B}$	300	700	1,000
Totals	500	1,500	2,000

a. Calculate the following probabilities: $P(A), P(\overline{A})$,

$P(A|B), P(\overline{A}|B), P(A|\overline{B}),$ and $P(\overline{A}|\overline{B})$.

b. Show that (1) A and B, (2) A and $\overline{B}$ (3) $\overline{A}$ and B, (4) $\overline{A}$ and $\overline{B}$ are dependent events.

Business Applications

4-65. An accounting professor at a state university in Vermont recently gave a three-question multiple-choice quiz. Each question had four optional answers.

a. What is the probability of getting a perfect score if you were forced to guess at each question?

b. Suppose it takes at least two correct answers out of three to pass the test. What is the probability of passing if you are forced to guess at each question? What does this indicate about studying for such an exam?

c. Suppose through some late-night studying you are able to correctly eliminate two answers on each question. Now answer parts a and b.

4-66. Simmons Market Research conducted a national consumer study of 13,787 respondents. A subset of the respondents was asked to indicate the primary source of the vitamins or mineral supplements they consume. Six out of 10 U.S. adults take vitamins or mineral supplements. Of those who do, 58% indicated a multiple formula was their choice.

a. Calculate the probability that a randomly chosen U.S. adult takes a multiple formula as her or his primary source.

b. Calculate the probability that a randomly chosen U.S. adult does not take a multiple formula.

c. If three U.S. adults were chosen at random, compute the probability that only two of them take a multiple formula as their primary source.

4-67. *USA Today* reported the IRS audited 1 in 63 wealthy individuals and families, about 1 of every 107 individuals, 20% of corporations in general, and 44% of the largest corporations with assets of at least $250 million.

a. Calculate the probability that at least 1 wealthy individual in a sample of 10 would be audited.

b. Compute the probability that at least 1 from a sample of 10 corporations with assets of at least $250 million would be audited.

c. Calculate the probability that a randomly chosen wealthy CEO of a corporation with assets of $300 million would be audited or that the corporation would be audited.

4-68. Simmons Furniture Company is considering changing its starting hour from 8:00 A.M. to 7:30 A.M. A census of the company's 1,200 office and production workers shows 370 of its 750 production workers favor the change and a total of 715 workers favor the change. To further assess worker opinion, the region manager decides to talk with random workers.

a. What is the probability a randomly selected worker will be in favor of the change?

b. What is the probability a randomly selected worker will be against the change *and* be an office worker?

c. Are the events *job type* and *opinion* independent? Explain.

4-69. A survey released by the National Association of Convenience Stores (NACS) indicated that 70% of gas purchases paid for at the pump were made with a credit or debit card.

a. Indicate the type of probability assessment method that NACS would use to assess this probability.

b. In one local store, 10 randomly chosen customers were observed. All 10 of these customers used a credit or a debit card. If the NACS statistic applies to this area, determine the probability that 10 out of 10 customers would use a credit or debit card.

c. If 90% of gas purchases paid for at the pump were made with a credit or debit card, determine the probability that 10 out of 10 customers would use a credit or debit card.

d. Based on your answers to parts b and c, does it appear that a larger percentage of local individuals use credit or debit cards than is true for the nation as a whole? Explain.

4-70. Ponderosa Paint and Glass makes paint at three plants. It then ships the unmarked paint cans to a central warehouse. Plant A supplies 50% of the paint, and past records indicate that the paint is incorrectly mixed 10% of the time. Plant B contributes 30%, with paint mixed incorrectly 5% of the time. Plant C supplies 20%, with paint mixed incorrectly 20% of the time. If Ponderosa guarantees its product and spent $10,000 replacing improperly mixed paint last year, how should the cost be distributed among the three plants?

4-71. Recently, several long-time customers at the Sweet Haven Chocolate Company have complained about the quality of the chocolates. It seems there are several partially covered chocolates being found in boxes. The defective chocolates should have been caught when the boxes were packed. The manager is wondering which of the three packers is not doing the job properly. Clerk 1 packs 40% of the boxes and usually has a 2% defective rate. Clerk 2 packs 30%, with a 2.5% defective rate. Clerk 3 boxes 30% of the chocolates, and her defective rate is 1.5%. Which clerk is most likely responsible for the boxes that raised the complaints?

4-72. Tamarack Resorts and Properties is considering opening a skiing area near McCall, Idaho. It is trying to decide whether to open an area catering to family skiers or to some other group. To help make its decision, it gathers the following information. Let

A_1 = Family will ski
A_2 = Family will not ski
B_1 = Family has children but none in the 8–16 age group
B_2 = Family has children in the 8–16 age group
B_3 = Family has no children

then, for this location,

$$P(A_1) = 0.40$$
$$P(B_2) = 0.35$$
$$P(B_1) = 0.25$$
$$P(A_1|B_2) = 0.70$$
$$P(A_1|B_1) = 0.30$$

a. Use the probabilities given to construct a joint probability distribution table.

b. What is the probability a family will ski *and* have children who are not in the 8–16 age group? How do you write this probability?

c. What is the probability a family with children in the 8–16 age group will not ski?

d. Are the categories *skiing* and *family composition* independent?

4-73. Fifty chief executive officers of small to medium-sized companies were classified according to their gender and functional background as shown in the table below:

Functional Background	Male	Female	Total
Marketing	4	10	14
Finance	11	5	16
Operations	17	3	20
Total	32	18	50

a. If a chief executive is randomly selected from this group what is the probability that the executive is a female?

b. What is the probability that a randomly selected executive from this group is a male whose functional background is marketing?

c. Assume that an executive is selected and you are told that the executive's functional background was in operations. What is the probability that this executive is a female?

d. Assume that an executive is selected and you are told that the executive is a female. What is the probability the executive's functional area is marketing?

e. Are gender and functional background independent for this set of executives?

4-74. A manufacturing firm has two suppliers for an electrical component used in its process: one in Mexico and one in China. The supplier in Mexico ships 82% of all the electrical components used by the firm and has a defect rate of 4%. The Chinese supplier ships 18% of the electrical components used by the firm and has a defect rate of 6%.

a. Calculate the probability that an electrical component is defective.

b. Suppose an electrical component is defective. What is the probability that component was shipped from Mexico? (Hint: Use Bayes' theorem.)

Computer Database **Exercises**

4-75. A survey of 300 CEOs was conducted in which the CEOs were to list their corporation's geographical location: Northeast (NE), Southeast (SE), Midwest (MW), Southwest (SW), and West (W). They were also requested to indicate their company's industrial type: Communication (C), Electronics (E), Finance (F), and Manufacturing (M). The file titled **CEOInfo** contains sample data similar to that used in this study.

a. Determine the probability that a randomly chosen CEO would have a corporation in the West.

b. Compute the probability that a randomly chosen CEO would have a corporation in the West and head an electronics corporation.

c. Calculate the probability that a randomly chosen CEO would have a corporation in the East or head a communications corporation.

d. Of the corporations located in the East, calculate the probability that a randomly selected CEO would head a communications corporation.

4-76. The ECCO company makes backup alarms for machinery like forklifts and commercial trucks. When a customer returns one of the alarms under warranty, the quality manager logs data on the product. From the data available in the file named **Ecco,** use relative frequency to find the following probabilities.

a. What is the probability the product was made at the Salt Lake City plant?

b. What is the probability the reason for the return was a wiring problem?

c. What is the joint probability the returned item was from the Salt Lake City plant and had a wiring-related problem?

d. What is the probability that a returned item was made on the day shift at the Salt Lake plant and had a cracked lens problem?

e. If an item was returned, what is the most likely profile for the item, including plant location, shift, and cause of problem?

4-77. Continuing with the ECCO company from Problem 4-76, when a customer returns one of the alarms under warranty, the quality manager logs data on the product. From the data available in the **Ecco** file, use relative frequency to find the following probabilities.

a. If a part was made in the Salt Lake plant, what is the probability the cause of the returned part was wiring?

b. If the company incurs a $30 cost for each returned alarm, what percentage of the cost should be assigned to each plant if it is known that 70% of all production is done in Boise, 20% in Salt Lake, and the rest in Toronto?

4-78. The Employee Benefit Research Institute (EBRI) issued a news release ("Saving in America: Three Key Sets of Figures") on October 25, 2005. In 2005, about 69% of workers said they have saved for retirement. The file titled **Retirement** contains sample data similar to those used in this study.

a. Construct a frequency distribution of the total savings and investments using the intervals (1) Less than $25,000, (2) $25,000–$49,999, (3) $50,000–$99,999, (4) $100,000–$249,999, and (5) $250,000 or more.

b. Determine the probability that an individual who has saved for retirement has saved less than $50,000. Use relative frequencies.

c. Determine the probability that a randomly chosen individual has saved less than $50,000 toward retirement.

d. Calculate the probability that at least two of four individuals have saved less than $50,000 toward retirement.

4-79. *USA Today* reported on the impact of Generation Y on the workforce. The workforce is comprised of (1) Silent generation (born before 1946), 7.5%; (2) Baby boomers (1946–1964), 42%; (3) Generation X (1965–1976), 29.5%; and (4) Generation Y (1977–1989), 21%. Ways of communication are changing. Randstad Holding, an international supplier of services to businesses and institutions, examined the different methods of communication preferred by the different elements of the workforce. The file titled **Communication** contains sample data comparable to those found in this study.

a. Construct a frequency distribution for each of the generations. Use the communication categories (1) Gp Meeting, (2) Face-to-Face, (3) E-mail, and (4) Other.

b. Calculate the probability that a randomly chosen member of the workforce prefers communicating face to face.

c. Given that an individual in the workforce prefers to communicate face to face, determine the generation of which the individual is most likely a member.

Case 4.1

Great Air Commuter Service

The Great Air Commuter Service Company started in 1984 to provide efficient and inexpensive commuter travel between Boston and New York City. People in the airline industry know Peter Wilson, the principal owner and operating manager of the company, as "a real promoter." Before founding Great Air, Peter operated a small regional airline in the Rocky Mountains with varying success. When Cascade Airlines offered to buy his company, Peter decided to sell and return to the East.

Peter arrived at his office near Fenway Park in Boston a little later than usual this morning. He had stopped to have a business breakfast with Aaron Little, his long-time friend and sometime partner in various business deals. Peter needed some advice and through the years has learned to rely on Aaron as a ready source, no matter what the subject.

Peter explained to Aaron that his commuter service needed a promotional gimmick to improve its visibility in the business communities in Boston and New York. Peter was thinking of running a contest on each flight and awarding the winner a prize. The idea would be that travelers who commute between Boston and New York might just as well have fun on the way and have a chance to win a nice prize.

As Aaron listened to Peter outlining his contest plans, his mind raced through contest ideas. Aaron thought that a large variety of contests would be needed, because many of the passengers would likely be repeat customers and might tire of the same old thing. In addition, some of the contests should be chance-type contests, whereas others should be skill based.

"Well, what do you think?" asked Peter. Aaron finished his scrambled eggs before responding. When he did, it was completely in character. "I think it will fly," Aaron said, and proceeded to offer a variety of suggestions.

Peter felt good about the enthusiastic response Aaron had given to the idea and thought that the ideas discussed at breakfast presented a good basis for the promotional effort. Now back at the office, Peter does have some concerns with one part of the plan. Aaron thought that in addition to the regular in-flight contests for prizes (such as free flights, dictation equipment, and business periodical subscriptions), each month on a randomly selected day a major prize should be offered on all Great Air flights. This would encourage regular business fliers to fly Great Air all the time. Aaron proposed that the prize could be a trip to the Virgin Islands or somewhere similar, or the cash equivalent.

Great Air has three flights daily to New York and three flights returning to Boston, for a total of six flights. Peter is concerned that the cost of funding six prizes of this size each month plus six daily smaller prizes might be excessive. He also believes that it might be better to increase the size of the large prize to something such as a new car but use a contest that will not guarantee a winner.

But what kind of a contest can be used? Just as he is about to dial Aaron's number, Margaret Runyon, Great Air's marketing manager, enters Peter's office. He has been waiting for her to return from a meeting so he can run the contest idea past her and get her input.

Margaret's response is not as upbeat as Aaron's, but she does think the idea is worth exploring. She offers an idea for the large-prize contest that she thinks might be workable. She outlines the contest as follows.

On the first of each month, she and Peter will randomly select a day for that month on which the major contest will be run. That date will not be disclosed to the public. Then, on each flight that day, the flight attendant will have passengers write down their birthdays (month and day). If any two people on the plane have the same birthday, they will place their names in a hat and one name will be selected to receive the grand prize.

Margaret explains that because the capacity of each flight is 40 passengers plus the crew, there is a very low chance of a birthday match and, therefore, the chance of giving away a grand prize on any one flight is small. Peter likes the idea, but when he asks Margaret what the probability is that a match will occur, her response does not sound quite right. She believes the probability for a match will be 40/365 for a full plane and less than that when there are fewer than 40 passengers aboard.

After Margaret leaves, Peter decides that it would be useful to know the probability of one or more birthday matches on flights with 20, 30, and 40 passengers. He realizes that he will need some help from someone with knowledge of statistics.

Required Tasks:

1. Assume that there are 365 days in a year (in other words, there is no leap year). Also assume there is an equal probability of a passenger's birthday falling on any one of the 365 days. Calculate the probability that there will be at least one birthday match for a flight containing exactly 20 passengers. (*Hint*: This calculation is made easier if you will first calculate the probability that there are no birthday matches for a flight containing 20 passengers.)

2. Repeat (1) above for a flight containing 30 passengers and a flight containing 40 passengers. Again, it will be easier to compute the probabilities of one or more matches if you first compute the probability of no birthday matches.

3. Assuming that each of the six daily flights carries 20 passengers, calculate the probability that the airline will have to award two or more major prizes that month. (Hint: It will be easier to calculate the probability of interest by first calculating the probability that the airline will award one or fewer prizes in a month).

Case 4.2

Let's Make a Deal

Quite a few years ago, a popular show called *Let's Make a Deal* appeared on network television. Contestants were selected from the audience. Each contestant would bring some silly item that he or she would trade for a cash prize or a prize behind one of three doors.

Suppose that you have been selected as a contestant on the show. You are given a choice of three doors. Behind one door is a new sports car. Behind the other doors are a pig and a chicken—booby prizes to be sure! Let's suppose that you pick door number one. Before opening that door, the host, who knows what is behind each door, opens door two to show you the chicken. He then asks you, "Would you be willing to trade door one for door three?" What should you do?

Required Tasks:

1. Given that there are three doors, one of which hides a sports car, calculate the probability that your initial choice is the door that hides the sports car. What is the probability that you have not selected the correct door?

2. Given that the host knows where the sports car is, and has opened door 2, which revealed a booby prize, does this affect the probability that your initial choice is the correct one?

3. Given that there are now only two doors remaining and that the sports car is behind one of them, is it to your advantage to switch your choice to door 3? (*Hint*: Eliminate door 2 from consideration. The probability that door 1 is the correct door has not changed from your initial choice. Calculate the probability that the prize must be behind door 3. This problem was discussed in the movie *21* starring Jim Sturgess, Kate Bosworth, and Kevin Spacey.)

Chapter 5 Quick Prep Links

- **Review** the concepts of simple random sampling discussed in Chapter 1.

- **Review** the discussion of weighted averages in Chapter 3.

- **Review** the basic rules of probability in Chapter 4, including the Addition and Multiplication Rules.

Discrete Probability Distributions

5.1 Introduction to Discrete ⟵──── Probability Distributions (pg. 183–190)

Outcome 1. Be able to calculate and interpret the expected value of a discrete random variable.

5.2 The Binomial Probability ⟵──── Distribution (pg. 190–204)

Outcome 2. Be able to apply the binomial distribution to business decision-making situations.

5.3 Other Discrete Probability ⟵──── Distributions (pg. 204–216)

Outcome 3. Be able to compute probabilities for the Poisson and hypergeometric distributions and apply these distributions to decision-making situations.

Why you need to know

Pak-Sense, a manufacturer of temperature sensor equipment for the food industry, receives component parts for its sensors weekly from suppliers. When a batch of parts arrives, the quality-assurance section randomly samples a fixed number of parts and tests them to see if any are defective. Suppose in one such test, a sample of 50 parts is selected from a supplier whose contract calls for at most 2% defective parts. How many defective parts in the sample of 50 should Pak-Sense expect if the contract is being satisfied? What should be concluded if the sample contains three defects? Answers to these questions require calculations based on a probability distribution known as the *binomial distribution*.

How many toll stations should be constructed when a new toll bridge is built in California? If there are four toll stations, will drivers have to wait too long, or will there be too many toll stations and excess employees? To help answer these questions, decision makers use a probability distribution known as the *Poisson distribution*.

A personnel manager has a chance to promote 3 people from 10 equally qualified candidates. Suppose none of six women are selected by the manager. Is this evidence of gender bias, or would we expect to see this type of result? A distribution known as the *hypergeometric distribution* would be very helpful in addressing this issue.

The *binomial, Poisson,* and *hypergeometric* distributions are three *discrete* probability distributions used in business decision making. This chapter introduces discrete probability distributions and shows how they are used in business settings. As you learned in Chapter 4, probability is the way decision makers express their uncertainty about outcomes and events. Through the use of well-established discrete probability distributions like those introduced in Chapter 5, you will be better prepared for making decisions in an uncertain environment.

Cobalt Creative/Shutterstock

5.1 Introduction to Discrete Probability Distributions

Random Variables

As discussed in Chapter 4, when a random experiment is performed, some outcome must occur. When the experiment has a quantitative characteristic, we can associate a number with each outcome. For example, an inspector who examines three plasma flat-panel televisions can judge each television as "acceptable" or "unacceptable." The outcome of the experiment defines the specific number of acceptable televisions. The possible outcomes are

$$x = \{0, 1, 2, 3\}$$

Random Variable

A variable that takes on different numerical values based on chance.

The value x is called a **random variable**, since the numerical values it takes on are random and vary from trial to trial. Although the inspector knows these are the possible values for the variable before she samples, she does not know which value will occur in any given trial. Further, the value of the random variable may be different each time three plasma televisions are inspected.

Discrete Random Variable

A random variable that can only assume a finite number of values or an infinite sequence of values such as 0, 1, 2....

Two classes of random variables exist: **discrete random variables** and **continuous random variables**. For instance, if a bank auditor randomly examines 15 accounts to verify the accuracy of the balances, the number of inaccurate account balances can be represented by a discrete random variable with the following values:

$$x = \{0, 1, \ldots, 15\}$$

Continuous Random Variables

Random variables that can assume an uncountably infinite number of values.

In another situation, 10 employees were recently hired by a major electronics company. The number of females in that group can be described as a discrete random variable with possible values equal to

$$x = \{0, 1, 2, 3, \ldots, 10\}$$

Notice that the value for a discrete random variable is often determined by counting. In the bank auditing example, the value of variable x is determined by counting the number of accounts with errors. In the hiring example, the value of variable x is determined by counting the number of females hired.

In other situations, the random variable is said to be continuous. For example, the exact time it takes a city bus to complete its route may be any value between two points, say 30 minutes to 35 minutes. If x is the time required, then x is continuous because, if measured precisely enough, the possible values, x, can be any value in the interval 30 to 35 minutes. Other examples of continuous variables include measures of distance and measures of weight when measured precisely. A continuous random variable is generally defined by measuring, which is contrasted with a discrete random variable, whose value is typically determined by counting. Chapter 6 focuses on some important probability distributions for continuous random variables.

Displaying Discrete Probability Distributions Graphically The probability distribution for a discrete random variable is composed of the values the variable can assume and the probabilities for each of the possible values. For example, if three parts are tested to determine if they are defective, the probability distribution for the number of defectives might be

x = Number of Defectives	P(x)
0	0.10
1	0.30
2	0.40
3	0.20
	$\Sigma = 1.00$

Graphically, the discrete probability distribution associated with these defectives can be represented by the areas of rectangles in which the base of each rectangle is one unit wide and the height corresponds to the probability. The areas of the rectangles sum to 1. Figure 5.1 illustrates two examples of discrete probability distributions. Figure 5.1(a) shows a discrete

FIGURE 5.1

Discrete Probability
Distributions

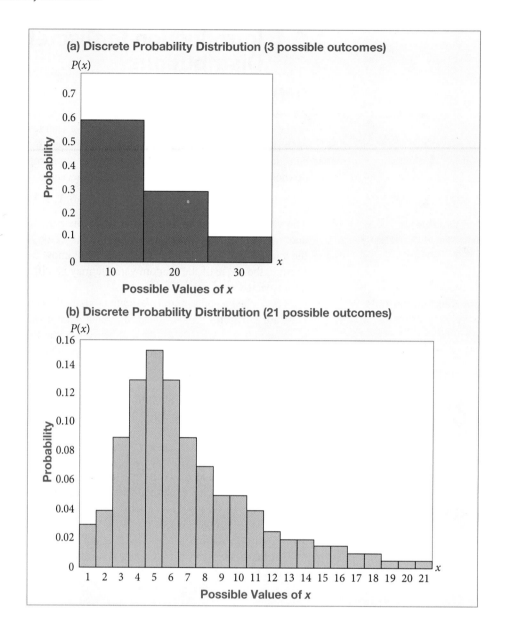

(a) **Discrete Probability Distribution (3 possible outcomes)**

(b) **Discrete Probability Distribution (21 possible outcomes)**

random variable with only three possible outcomes. Figure 5.1(b) shows the probability distribution for a discrete variable that has 21 possible outcomes. Note, as the number of possible outcomes increases, the distribution becomes smoother and the individual probability of any particular value tends to be reduced. In all cases, the sum of the probabilities is 1.

Discrete probability distributions have many applications in business decision-making situations. In the remainder of this section, we discuss several important issues that are of particular importance to discrete probability distributions.

Mean and Standard Deviation of Discrete Distributions

A probability distribution, like a frequency distribution, can be only partially described by a graph. To aid in a decision situation, you may need to calculate the distribution's *mean* and *standard deviation*. These values measure the central location and spread, respectively, of the probability distribution.

Expected Value

The mean of a probability distribution. The average value when the experiment that generates values for the random variable is repeated over the long run.

Chapter Outcome 1. ⟶ **Calculating the Mean** The mean of a discrete probability distribution is also called the **expected value** of the random variable from an experiment. The expected value is actually a *weighted average* of the random variable values in which the weights are the probabilities assigned to the values. The expected value is given in Equation 5.1.

Expected Value of a Discrete Probability Distribution

$$E(x) = \sum xP(x) \qquad \text{(5.1)}$$

where:

$E(x)$ = Expected value of x
x = Values of the random variable
$P(x)$ = probability of the random variable taking on the value x

Calculating the Standard Deviation The standard deviation measures the spread, or dispersion, in a set of data. The standard deviation also measures the spread in the values of a random variable. To calculate the standard deviation for a discrete probability distribution, use Equation 5.2.

Standard Deviation of a Discrete Probability Distribution

$$\sigma_x = \sqrt{\sum [x - E(x)]^2\, P(x)} \qquad \text{(5.2)}$$

where:

x = Values of the random variable
$E(x)$ = Expected value of x
$P(x)$ = Probability of the random variable taking on the value x

Equation 5.2 is different in form than the previous equations given for standard deviation, Equations 3.9 and 3.12. This is because we are now dealing with a discrete probability distribution rather than population or sample values.

| **EXAMPLE 5-1** | **COMPUTING THE MEAN AND STANDARD DEVIATION OF A DISCRETE RANDOM VARIABLE** |

Swenson Security Sales Swenson Security Sales is a company that sells and installs home security systems throughout the eastern United States. Each week, the company's quality managers examine one randomly selected security installation in all 21 states where the company operates to see whether the installers made errors. The discrete random variable, x, is the number of errors discovered on each installation examined, ranging from 0 to 3. The following frequency distribution was developed:

x	Frequency
0	150
1	110
2	50
3	90
	$\Sigma = 400$

Assuming that these data reflect typical performance by the installers, the company leadership wishes to develop a discrete probability distribution for the number of install errors and compute the mean and standard deviation for the distribution. This can be done using the following steps:

Step 1 **Convert the frequency distribution into a probability distribution using the relative frequency assessment method.**

x	Frequency
0	$150/400 = 0.375$
1	$110/400 = 0.275$

x	Frequency
2	$50/400 = 0.125$
3	$90/400 = \underline{0.225}$
	$\Sigma = 1.000$

Step 2 **Compute the expected value using Equation 5.1.**

$$E(x) = \Sigma x P(x)$$

$$E(x) = (0)(0.375) + (1)(0.275) + (2)(0.125) + (3)(0.225)$$

$$E(x) = 1.20$$

The expected value is 1.20 errors per install. Thus, assuming the distribution of the number of errors is representative of that of each individual installation, the long-run average number of errors per installation will be 1.20.

Step 3 **Compute the standard deviation using Equation 5.2.**

$$\sigma_x = \sqrt{\Sigma[x - E(x)]^2 P(x)}$$

x	$P(x)$	$[x - E(x)]$	$[x - E(x)]^2$	$[x - E(x)]^2 P(x)$
0	0.375	$0 - 1.2 = -1.20$	1.44	0.540
1	0.275	$1 - 1.2 = -0.20$	0.04	0.011
2	0.125	$2 - 1.2 = 0.80$	0.64	0.080
3	0.225	$3 - 1.2 = 1.80$	3.24	$\underline{0.729}$
				$\Sigma = 1.360$

$$\sigma_x = \sqrt{1.36} = 1.17$$

The standard deviation of the discrete probability distribution is 1.17 errors per security system installed.

>> **END EXAMPLE**

TRY PROBLEM 5-4 (pg. 187)

BUSINESS APPLICATION **EXPECTED VALUES**

TABLE 5.1 | **Probability Distribution—Defect Rate for Supplier B**

Defect Rate x	Probability $P(x)$
0.01	0.3
0.05	0.4
0.10	0.2
0.15	0.1

BENSON LIGHT FIXTURES Benson Light Fixtures imports fixtures from Taiwan and other Far East countries for distribution in France and Spain. For one particular product line, Benson currently has two suppliers. Both suppliers have poor records when it comes to quality. Benson is planning to purchase 100,000 of a particular light fixture and wants to use the least-cost supplier for the entire purchase. Supplier A is less expensive by $1.20 per fixture and has an ongoing record of supplying 10% defects. Supplier B is more expensive but may be a higher-quality supplier. Benson records indicate that the rate of defects from supplier B varies. Table 5.1 shows the probability distributions for the defect percentages for supplier B. Each defect is thought to cost the company $9.50.

Looking first at supplier A, at a defect rate of 0.10, out of 100,000 units the number of defects is expected to be 10,000. The cost of these is $9.50 × 10,000 = $95,000. For supplier B, the expected defect rate is found using Equation 5.1 as follows:

$$E(\text{Defect rate}) = \Sigma x P(x)$$
$$E(\text{Defect rate}) = (0.01)(0.3) + (0.05)(0.4) + (0.10)(0.2) + (0.15)(0.1)$$
$$E(\text{Defect rate}) = 0.058$$

Thus, supplier B is expected to supply 5.8% defects, or 5,800 out of the 100,000 units ordered, for an expected cost of $9.50 × 5,800 = $55,100. Based on defect cost alone, supplier B is less expensive ($55,100 versus $95,000). However, recall that supplier B's product sells for $1.20 per unit more. Thus, on a 100,000-unit order, supplier B costs an extra $1.20 × 100,000 = $120,000 more than supplier A. The relative costs are

Supplier A = $95,000   Supplier B = $55,100 + $120,000 = $175,100

Therefore, based on expected costs, supplier A should be selected to supply the 100,000 light fixtures.

MyStatLab

5-1: Exercises

Skill Development

5-1. An economics quiz contains six multiple-choice questions. Let x represent the number of questions a student answers correctly.
  a. Is x a continuous or discrete random variable?
  b. What are the possible values of x?

5-2. Two numbers are randomly drawn without replacement from a list of five. If the five numbers are 2, 2, 4, 6, 8, what is the probability distribution of the sum of the two numbers selected? Show the probability distribution graphically.

5-3. If the Prudential Insurance Company surveys its customers to determine the number of children under age 22 living in each household,
  a. What is the random variable for this survey?
  b. Is the random variable discrete or continuous?

5-4. Given the following discrete probability distribution,

x	$P(x)$
50	0.375
65	0.15
70	0.225
75	0.05
90	0.20

  a. Calculate the expected value of x.
  b. Calculate the variance of x.
  c. Calculate the standard deviation of x.

5-5. Because of bad weather, the number of days next week that the captain of a charter fishing boat can leave port is uncertain. Let x = number of days that the boat is able to leave port per week. The following probability distribution for the variable, x, was determined based on historical data when the weather was poor:

x	$P(x)$
0	0.05
1	0.10
2	0.10
3	0.20
4	0.20
5	0.15
6	0.15
7	0.05

Based on the probability distribution, what is the expected number of days per week the captain can leave port?

5-6. Consider the following discrete probability distribution:

x	$P(x)$
3	0.13
6	0.12
9	0.15
12	0.60

  a. Calculate the variance and standard deviation of the random variable.
  b. Let $y = x + 7$. Calculate the variance and standard deviation of the random variable y.
  c. Let $z = 7x$. Calculate the variance and standard deviation of the random variable z.
  d. From your calculations in part a and part b, indicate the effect that adding a constant to a random variable has on its variance and standard deviation.
  e. From your calculations in part a and part c, indicate the effect that multiplying a random variable with a constant has on the variance and the standard deviation of the random variable.

5-7. Given the following discrete probability distribution,

x	$P(x)$
100	0.25
125	0.30
150	0.45

  a. Calculate the expected value of x.
  b. Calculate the variance of x.
  c. Calculate the standard deviation of x.

5-8. The roll of a pair of dice has the following probability distribution, where the random variable x is the sum of the values produced by each die:

x	$P(x)$
2	1/36
3	2/36
4	3/36
5	4/36
6	5/36
7	6/36
8	5/36
9	4/36
10	3/36
11	2/36
12	1/36

a. Calculate the expected value of x.
b. Calculate the variance of x.
c. Calculate the standard deviation of x.

5-9. Consider the following discrete probability distribution:

x	$P(x)$
5	0.10
10	0.15
15	0.25
20	0.50

a. Calculate the expected value of the random variable.
b. Let $y = x + 5$. Calculate the expected value of the new random variable y.
c. Let $z = 5x$. Calculate the expected value of the new random variable z.
d. From your calculations in part a and part b, indicate the effect that adding a constant to a random variable has on the expected value of the random variable.
e. From your calculations in part a and part c, indicate the effect that multiplying a random variable by a constant has on the expected value of the random variable.

5-10. Examine the following probability distribution:

x	5	10	15	20	25	30	35	40	45	50
$P(x)$	0.01	0.05	0.14	0.20	0.30	0.15	0.05	0.04	0.01	0.05

a. Calculate the expected value and standard deviation for this random variable.
b. Denote the expected value as μ. Calculate $\mu - \sigma$ and $\mu + \sigma$.
c. Determine the proportion of the distribution that is contained within the interval $\mu \pm \sigma$.
d. Repeat part c for (1) $\mu \pm 2\sigma$ and (2) $\mu \pm 3\sigma$.

Business **Applications**

5-11. The U.S. Census Bureau (Annual Social & Economic Supplement) collects demographics concerning the number of people in families per household. Assume the distribution of the number of people per household is shown in the following table:

x	$P(x)$
2	0.27
3	0.25
4	0.28
5	0.13
6	0.04
7	0.03

a. Calculate the expected number of people in families per household in the United States.
b. Compute the variance and standard deviation of the number of people in families per household.

5-12. Jennings Assembly in Hartford, Connecticut, uses a component supplied by a company in Brazil. The component is expensive to carry in inventory and consequently is not always available in stock when requested. Furthermore, shipping schedules are such that the lead time for transportation of the component is not a constant. Using historical records, the manufacturing firm has developed the following probability distribution for the product's lead time. The distribution is shown here, where the random variable x is the number of days between the placement of the replenishment order and the receipt of the item.

x	$P(x)$
2	0.15
3	0.45
4	0.30
5	0.075
6	0.025

a. What is the average lead time for the component?
b. What is the coefficient of variation for delivery lead time?
c. How might the manufacturing firm in the United States use this information?

5-13. Marque Electronics is a family-owned electronics repair business in Kansas City. The owner has read an advertisement from a local competitor that guarantees all high-definition television (HDTV) repairs within four days. Based on his company's experience, he wants to know if he can offer a similar guarantee. His past service records are used to determine the following probability distribution:

Number of Days	Probability
1	0.15
2	0.25
3	0.30
4	0.18
5	0.12

a. Calculate the mean number of days his customers wait for an HDTV repair.
b. Also calculate the variance and standard deviation.
c. Based on the calculations in parts a and b, what conclusion should the manager reach regarding his company's repair times?

5-14. Cramer's Bar and Grille in Dallas can seat 130 people at a time. The manager has been gathering data on the number of minutes a party of four spends in the restaurant from the moment they are seated to when they pay the check. What is the mean number of minutes for a dinner party of four? What is the variance and standard deviation?

Number of Minutes	Probability
60	0.05
70	0.15

Number of Minutes	Probability
80	0.20
90	0.45
100	0.10
110	0.05

5-15. Rossmore Brothers, Inc., sells plumbing supplies for commercial and residential applications. The company currently has only one supplier for a particular type of faucet. Based on historical data that the company has maintained, the company has assessed the following probability distribution for the proportion of defective faucets that it receives from this supplier:

Proportion Defective	Probability
0.01	0.4
0.02	0.3
0.05	0.2
0.10	0.1

This supplier charges Rossmore Brothers, Inc., $29.00 per unit for this faucet. Although the supplier will replace any defects free of charge, Rossmore managers figure the cost of dealing with the defects is about $5.00 each.

a. Assuming that Rossmore Brothers is planning to purchase 2,000 of these faucets from the supplier, what is the total expected cost to Rossmore Brothers for the deal?

b. Suppose that Rossmore Brothers has an opportunity to buy the same faucets from another supplier at a cost of $28.50 per unit. However, based on its investigations, Rossmore Brothers has assessed the following probability distribution for the proportion of defective faucets that will be delivered by the new supplier:

Proportion Defective x	Probability $P(x)$
0.01	0.1
0.02	0.1
0.05	0.7
0.10	0.1

Assuming that the defect cost is still $5.00 each and based on total expected cost for an order of 2,000 faucets, should Rossmore buy from the new supplier or stick with its original supplier?

5-16. Radio Shack stocks four alarm clock radios. If it has fewer than four clock radios available at the end of a week, the store restocks the item to bring the in-stock level up to four. If weekly demand is greater than the four units in stock, the store loses the sale. The radio sells for $25 and costs the store $15. The Radio Shack manager estimates that the probability distribution of weekly demand for the radio is as follows:

x (Weekly Demand)	$P(x)$
0	0.05
1	0.05
2	0.10
3	0.20
4	0.40
5	0.10
6	0.05
7	0.05

a. What is the expected weekly demand for the alarm clock radio?

b. What is the probability that weekly demand will be greater than the number of available radios?

c. What is the expected weekly profit from the sale of the alarm clock radio? (Remember: There are only four clock radios available in any week to meet demand.)

d. On average, how much profit is lost each week because the radio is not available when demanded?

5-17. Fiero Products, LTD, of Bologna, Italy, makes a variety of footwear, including indoor slippers, children's shoes, and flip-flops. To keep up with increasing demand, it is considering three expansion plans: (1) a small factory with yearly costs of $150,000 that will increase the production of flip-flops to 400,000; (2) a mid-sized factory with yearly costs of $250,000 that will increase the production of flip-flops by 600,000; and (3) a large factory with yearly costs of $350,000 that will increase the production of flip-flops by 900,000. The profit per flip-flop is projected to be $0.75. The probability distribution of demand for flip-flops is considered to be

Demand	300,000	700,000	900,000
Probability	0.2	0.5	0.3

a. Compute the expected profit for each of the expansion plans.

b. Calculate the standard deviation for each of the expansion plans.

c. Which expansion plan would you suggest? Provide the statistical reasoning behind your selection.

5-18. A large corporation in search of a CEO and a CFO has narrowed the fields for each position to a short list. The CEO candidates graduated from Chicago (C) and three Ivy League universities: Harvard (H), Princeton (P), and Yale (Y). The four CFO candidates graduated from MIT (M), Northwestern (N), and two Ivy League universities, Dartmouth (D) and Brown (B). The personnel director wishes to determine the distribution of the number of Ivy League graduates who could fill these positions.

a. Assume the selections were made randomly. Construct the probability distribution of the number of Ivy League graduates who could fill these positions.

b. Would it be surprising if both positions were filled with Ivy League graduates?

c. Calculate the expected value and standard deviation of the number of Ivy League graduates who could fill these positions.

Computer Database **Exercises**

5-19. Starbucks has entered into an agreement with a publisher to begin selling a food and beverage magazine on a trial basis. The magazine retails for $3.95 in other stores. Starbucks bought it for $1.95 and sold it for $3.49. During the trial period, Starbucks placed 10 copies of the magazine in each of 150 stores throughout the country. The file titled **Sold** contains the number of magazines sold in each of the stores.

a. Produce a frequency distribution for these data. Convert the frequency distribution into a probability distribution using the relative frequency assessment method.

b. Calculate the expected profit from the sale of these 10 magazines.

c. Starbucks is negotiating returning all unsold magazines for a salvage price. Determine the salvage price Starbucks will need to obtain to yield a positive expected profit from selling 10 magazines.

5-20. Pfizer Inc. is the manufacturer of Revolution (Selamectin), a topical parasiticide used for the treatment, control, and prevention of flea infestation, heartworm, and ear mites for dogs and cats. One of its selling points is that it provides protection for an entire month. Such claims are made on the basis of research and statistical studies. The file titled **Fleafree** contains data similar to those obtained in Pfizer's research.

It presents the number of days Revolution could remain effective when applied to mature cats.

a. Produce a frequency distribution for these data. Convert the frequency distribution into a probability distribution using the relative frequency assessment method.

b. Calculate the expected value and standard deviation for the number of days Revolution could remain effective.

c. If the marketing department wished to advertise the number of days that 90% of the cats remain protected while using Revolution, what would this number of days be?

5-21. Fiber Systems makes boat tops for a number of boat manufacturers. Its fabric has a limited two-year warranty. Periodic testing is done to determine if the warranty policy should be changed. One such study may have examined those covers that became unserviceable while still under warranty. Data that could be produced by such a study are contained in the file titled **Covers**. The data represent assessment of the number of months a cover was used until it became unserviceable.

a. Produce a frequency distribution for these data. Convert the frequency distribution into a probability distribution using the relative frequency assessment method.

b. Calculate the expected value and standard deviation for the time until the covers became unserviceable.

c. The quality-control department thinks that among those covers that do become unserviceable while still under warranty, the majority last longer than 19 months. Produce the relevant statistic to verify this assumption.

END EXERCISES 5-1

Chapter Outcome 2. → ## 5.2 The Binomial Probability Distribution

In Section 5.1, you learned that random variables can be classified as either *discrete* or *continuous*. In most instances, the value of a discrete random variable is determined by counting. For instance, the number of customers who arrive at a store each day is a discrete variable. Its value is determined by counting the customers.

Several theoretical discrete distributions have extensive application in business decision making. A probability distribution is called *theoretical* when the mathematical properties of its random variable are used to produce its probabilities. Such distributions are different from the distributions that are obtained subjectively or from observation. Sections 5.2 and 5.3 focus on theoretical discrete probability distributions. Chapter 6 will introduce important theoretical continuous probability distributions.

The Binomial Distribution

The first theoretical probability distribution we will consider is the **binomial distribution** that describes processes whose trials have only two possible outcomes. The physical events described by this type of process are widespread. For instance, a quality-control system in a manufacturing plant labels each tested item as either defective or acceptable. A firm bidding for a contract either will or will not get the contract. A marketing research firm may receive responses to a questionnaire in the form of "Yes, I will buy" or "No, I will not buy." The personnel manager in an organization is faced with two possible outcomes each time he offers a job—the applicant either accepts the offer or rejects it.

Binomial Probability Distribution Characteristics

A distribution that gives the probability of x successes in n trials in a process that meets the following conditions:

1. A trial has only two possible outcomes: a success or a failure.
2. There is a fixed number, n, of identical trials.
3. The trials of the experiment are independent of each other. This means that if one outcome is a success, this does not influence the chance of another outcome being a success.
4. The process must be consistent in generating successes and failures. That is, the probability, p, associated with a success remains constant from trial to trial.
5. If p represents the probability of a success, then $(1 - p) = q$ is the probability of a failure.

Characteristics of the Binomial Distribution

The binomial distribution requires that the experiment's trials be independent. This can be assured if the sampling is performed with replacement from a finite population. This means that an item is sampled from a population and returned to the population, after its characteristic(s) have been recorded, before the next item is sampled. However, sampling with replacement is the exception rather than the rule in business applications. Most often, the sampling is performed without replacement. Strictly speaking, when sampling is performed without replacement, the conditions for the binomial distribution cannot be satisfied. However, the conditions are approximately satisfied if the sample selected is quite small relative to the size of the population from which the sample is selected. A commonly used rule of thumb is that the binomial distribution can be applied if the sample size is at most 5% of the population size.

BUSINESS APPLICATION **USING THE BINOMIAL DISTRIBUTION**

LAKE CITY AUTOMOTIVE Lake City Automotive performs 300 automobile transmission repairs every week. Transmission repair work is not an exact science, and a percentage of the work done must be reworked. Lake City shop managers have determined that even when the mechanics perform the work in a proper manner, 10% of the time the car will have to be worked on again to fix a problem. The binomial distribution applies to this situation because the following conditions exist:

1. There are only two possible outcomes when a car is repaired: It either needs rework or it doesn't. We are interested in the cars that need rework, so we will consider a reworked car to be a "success." A success occurs when we observe the outcome of interest.
2. All repair jobs are considered to be equivalent in the work required.
3. The outcome of a repair (rework or no rework) is independent of whether the preceding repair required rework or not.
4. The probability of rework being needed, $p = 0.10$, remains constant from car to car.
5. The probability of a car not needing rework, $q = 1 - p = 0.90$, remains constant from car to car.

To determine whether the Lake City mechanics are continuing to function at the standard level of performance, the shop foreman randomly selects four cars from the week's list of repaired vehicles and tracks those to see whether they need rework or not (note, the need for rework is known within a few hours of the work being completed). Because the sample size is small ($4/300 = 0.0133$ or 1.33%) relative to the size of the population (300 units per week), the conditions of independence and constant probability will be approximately satisfied because the sample is less than 5% of the population.

We let the number of reworked cars be the random variable of interest. The number of reworked units is limited to discrete values, $x = 0, 1, 2, 3,$ or 4. We can determine the probability that the random variable will have any of the discrete values. One way is to list the sample space, as shown in Table 5.2. We can find the probability of zero cars needing rework, for instance, by employing the Multiplication Rule for Independent Events.

$$P(x = 0 \text{ reworks}) = P(G \text{ and } G \text{ and } G \text{ and } G)$$

where:

$$G = \text{Car does not require rework}$$

Here,

$$P(G) = 0.90$$

and we have assumed the repair jobs are independent. Using the Multiplication Rule for Independent Events introduced in Chapter 4 (Rule 9),

$$P(G \text{ and } G \text{ and } G \text{ and } G) = P(G)P(G)P(G)P(G) = (0.90)(0.90)(0.90)(0.90)$$
$$= 0.90^4$$
$$= 0.6561$$

TABLE 5.2 | **Sample Space for Lake City Automotive**

Results	No. of Reworked Cars	No. of Ways
G,G,G,G	0	1
G,G,G,D	1	
G,G,D,G	1	4
G,D,G,G	1	
D,G,G,G	1	
G,G,D,D	2	
G,D,G,D	2	
D,G,G,D	2	6
G,D,D,G	2	
D,G,D,G	2	
D,D,G,G	2	
D,D,D,G	3	
D,D,G,D	3	4
D,G,D,D	3	
G,D,D,D	3	
D,D,D,D	4	1

We can also find the probability of exactly one reworked car in a sample of four. This is accomplished using both the Multiplication Rule for Independent Events and the Addition Rule for Mutually Exclusive Events, which was also introduced in Chapter 4 (Rule 5):

$$D = \text{car needs rework}$$

$$
\begin{aligned}
P(x = 1 \text{ rework}) = {} & P(G \text{ and } G \text{ and } G \text{ and } D) + P(G \text{ and } G \text{ and } D \text{ and } G) \\
& + P(G \text{ and } D \text{ and } G \text{ and } G) + P(D \text{ and } G \text{ and } G \text{ and } G)
\end{aligned}
$$

where:

$$
\begin{aligned}
P(G \text{ and } G \text{ and } G \text{ and } D) &= P(G)P(G)P(G)P(D) = (0.90)(0.90)(0.90)(0.10) \\
&= (0.90^3)(0.10)
\end{aligned}
$$

Likewise:

$$
\begin{aligned}
P(G \text{ and } G \text{ and } D \text{ and } G) &= (0.90^3)(0.10) \\
P(G \text{ and } D \text{ and } G \text{ and } G) &= (0.90^3)(0.10) \\
P(D \text{ and } G \text{ and } G \text{ and } G) &= (0.90^3)(0.10)
\end{aligned}
$$

Then:

$$
\begin{aligned}
P(1 \text{ rework}) &= (0.90^3)(0.10) + (0.90^3)(0.10) + (0.90^3)(0.10) + (0.90^3)(0.10) \\
&= (4)(0.90^3)(0.10) \\
&= 0.2916
\end{aligned}
$$

Note that each of the four possible ways of finding one rework car has the same probability $[(0.90^3)(0.10)]$. We determine the probability of one of the ways to obtain one rework car and multiply this value by the number of ways (four) of obtaining one reworked car. This produces the overall probability of one reworked car.

Combinations In this relatively simple application, we can fairly easily list the sample space and from that count the number of ways that each possible number of reworked cars can occur. However, for examples with larger sample sizes, this approach is inefficient. A more effective method exists for counting the number of ways binomial events can occur. This method is called the **counting rule for combinations**. This rule is used to find the number of outcomes from an experiment in which x objects are to be selected from a group of n objects. Equation 5.3 is used to find the combinations.

Counting Rule for Combinations

$$C_x^n = \frac{n!}{x!(n-x)!}$$

(5.3)

where:

C_x^n = Number of combinations of x objects selected from n objects

$n!$ = $n(n-1)(n-2)\ldots(2)(1)$

$0!$ = 1 by definition

Using Equation 5.3, we find the number of ways that $x = 2$ reworked cars can occur in a sample of $n = 4$ as

$$C_x^n = \frac{n!}{x!(n-x)!} = \frac{4!}{2!(4-2)!} = \frac{(4)(3)(2)(1)}{(2)(1)(2)(1)} = \frac{24}{4} = 6 \text{ ways}$$

Refer to Table 5.2 to see that this is the same value for two reworked cars in a sample of four that was obtained by listing the sample space.

Now we can find the probabilities of two reworked cars.

$$P(2 \text{ reworks}) = (6)(0.90^2)(0.10^2)$$
$$= 0.0486$$

Use this method to verify the following:

$$P(3 \text{ reworks}) = (4)(0.90)(0.10^3)$$
$$= 0.0036$$
$$P(4 \text{ reworks}) = (1)(0.10^4)$$
$$= 0.0001$$

TABLE 5.3 | **Binomial Distribution for Lake City Automotive:** $n = 4, p = 0.10$

x = # of Reworks	$P(x)$
0	0.6561
1	0.2916
2	0.0486
3	0.0036
4	0.0001
	$\Sigma = \overline{1.0000}$

The key to developing the probability distribution for a binomial process is first to determine the probability of any one way the event of interest can occur and then to multiply this probability by the number of ways that event can occur. Table 5.3 shows the binomial probability distribution for the number of reworked cars in a sample size of four when the probability of any individual car requiring rework is 0.10. The probability distribution is graphed in Figure 5.2. Most samples would contain zero or one reworked car when the mechanics at Lake City are performing the work to standard.

FIGURE 5.2 |

Binomial Distribution for Lake City Automotive

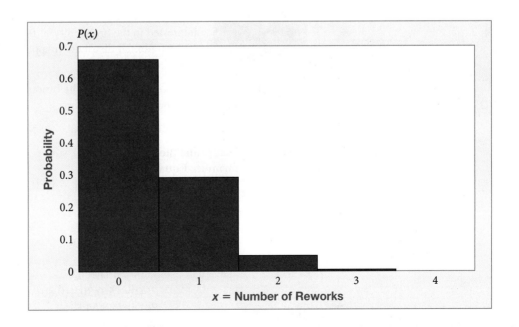

Binomial Formula   The steps that we have taken to develop this binomial probability distribution can be summarized through a formula called the *binomial formula*, shown as Equation 5.4. Note, this formula is composed of two parts: the combinations of *x* items selected from *n* items and the probability that *x* items can occur.

Binomial Formula

$$P(x) = \frac{n!}{x!(n-x)!} p^x q^{n-x}$$ (5.4)

where:

n = Random sample size

x = Number of successes (when a success is defined as what we are looking for)

$n - x$ = Number of failures

p = Probability of a success

$q = 1 - p$ = Probability of a failure

$n! = n(n-1)(n-2)(n-3) \ldots (2)(1)$

$0! = 1$ by definition

Applying Equation 5.4 to the Lake City Automotive example for $n = 4, p = 0.10$, and $x = 2$ reworked cars, we get

$$P(x) = \frac{n!}{x!(n-x)!} p^x q^{n-x}$$

$$P(2) = \frac{4!}{2!2!}(0.10^2)(0.90^2) = 6(0.10^2)(0.90^2) = 0.0486$$

This is the same value we calculated earlier when we listed out the sample space above.

EXAMPLE 5-2   **USING THE BINOMIAL FORMULA**

Creative Style and Cut Creative Style and Cut, an upscale beauty salon in San Francisco, offers a full refund to anyone who is not satisfied with the way his or her hair looks after it has been cut and styled. The owners believe the hairstyle satisfaction from customer to customer is independent and that the probability a customer will ask for a refund is 0.20. Suppose a random sample of six customers is observed. In four instances, the customer has asked for a refund. The owners might be interested in the probability of four refund requests from six customers. If the binomial distribution applies, the probability can be found using the following steps:

Step 1   Define the characteristics of the binomial distribution.
In this case, the characteristics are

$$n = 6, \qquad p = 0.20, \qquad q = 1 - p = 0.80$$

Step 2   Determine the probability of *x* successes in *n* trials using the binomial formula, Equation 5.4.
In this case, $n = 6, p = 0.20, q = 0.80$, and we are interested in the probability of $x = 4$ successes.

$$P(x) = \frac{n!}{x!(n-x)!} p^x q^{n-x}$$

$$P(4) = \frac{6!}{4!(6-4)!}(0.20^4)(0.80^{6-4})$$

$$P(4) = 15(0.20^4)(0.80^2)$$

$$P(4) = 0.0154$$

There is only a 0.0154 chance that exactly four customers will want a refund in a sample of six if the chance that any one of the customers will want a refund is 0.20.

>> **END EXAMPLE**

TRY PROBLEM 5-24 (pg. 200)

Using the Binomial Distribution Table Using Equation 5.4 to develop the binomial distribution is not difficult, but it can be time consuming. To make binomial probabilities easier to find, you can use the binomial table in Appendix B. This table is constructed to give *cumulative* probabilities for different sample sizes and probabilities of success. Each column is headed by a probability, *p*, which is the probability associated with a success. The column headings correspond to probabilities of success ranging from 0.01 to 1.00. Down the left side of the table are integer values that correspond to the number of successes, *x*, for the specified sample size, *n*. The values in the body of the table are the cumulative probabilities of *x* or fewer successes in a random sample of size *n*.

BUSINESS APPLICATION   **BINOMIAL DISTRIBUTION TABLE**

BIG O TIRE COMPANY Big O Tire Company operates tire and repair stores throughout the western United States. Upper management is considering offering a money-back warranty if one of their tires blows out in the first 20,000 miles of use. The managers are willing to make this warranty if 2% or fewer of the tires they sell blow out within the 20,000-mile limit.

The company plans to test 10 randomly selected tires over 20,000 miles of use in test conditions. The number of possible blowouts will be $x = 0, 1, 2, \ldots 10$. We can use the binomial table in Appendix B to develop the probability distribution. This table is called a *cumulative* probability table. Go to the table for $n = 10$ and the column for $p = 0.02$. The values of *x* are listed down the left side of the table. For example, the cumulative probability of $x \leq 2$ occurrences is 0.9991. This means that it is extremely likely that 2 or fewer tires in a sample of 10 would blow out in the first 20,000 miles of use if the overall fraction of tires that will blow out is 0.02. The probability of 3 or more blowouts in the sample of $n = 10$ is

$$P(x \geq 3) = 1 - P(x \leq 2) = 1 - 0.9991 = 0.0009$$

There are about 9 chances in 10,000 that we would find 3 or more tires in a sample of 10 that will blow out if the probability of it happening for any one tire is $p = 0.02$. If the test did show that 3 tires blew out, the true rate of tire blowouts *likely* exceeds 2%, and the company should have serious doubts about making the warranty. Note, the decision about this will depend on which sample outcome occurs.

EXAMPLE 5-3   **USING THE BINOMIAL TABLE**

Ronen/Shutterstock

Nielsen Television Ratings The Nielsen Media Group is the best-known television ratings company. On Monday, February 6, 2012, the day after the 2012 Super Bowl between the Giants and the Patriots, Nielsen reported that the game was the most-watched program in history, with just over 40% of all televisions in the United States tuned to the game on Sunday. Assuming that the 40% rating is correct, what is the probability that in a random sample of 20 television sets, 2 or fewer would have been tuned to the Super Bowl? This question can be answered, assuming that the binomial distribution applies, using the following steps:

Step 1 Define the characteristics of the binomial distribution.
In this case, the characteristics are

$$n = 20, \qquad p = 0.40 \qquad q = 1 - p = 0.60$$

Step 2 Define the event of interest.
We are interested in knowing

$$P(x \leq 2) = P(0) + P(1) + P(2)$$

Step 3 **Go to the binomial table in Appendix B to find the desired probability.**

In this case, we locate the section of the table corresponding to sample size equal to $n = 20$ and go to the column headed $p = 0.40$ and the row labeled $x = 2$. The cumulative, $P(x \leq 2)$, listed in the table is 0.0036.

Thus, there is only a 0.0036 chance that 2 or fewer sets in a random sample of 20 were tuned to the Super Bowl. Thus, it is unlikely that 2 or fewer sets in a sample of 20 TV sets would have been tuned to the Super Bowl in 2012.

>> **END EXAMPLE**

TRY PROBLEM 5-28 (pg. 200)

EXAMPLE 5-4 **USING THE BINOMIAL DISTRIBUTION**

Clearwater Research Clearwater Research is a full-service marketing research consulting firm. Recently it was retained to do a project for a major U.S. airline. The airline was considering changing from an assigned-seating reservation system to one in which fliers would be able to take any seat they wished on a first-come, first-served basis. The airline believes that 80% of its fliers would like this change if it was accompanied with a reduction in ticket prices. Clearwater Research will survey a large number of customers on this issue, but prior to conducting the full research, it has selected a random sample of 20 customers and determined that 12 like the proposed change. What is the probability of finding 12 or fewer who like the change if the probability is 0.80 that a customer will like the change?

If we assume the binomial distribution applies, we can use the following steps to answer this question:

Step 1 **Define the characteristics of the binomial distribution.**

In this case, the characteristics are

$$n = 20, \quad p = 0.80, \quad q = 1 - p = 0.20$$

Step 2 **Define the event of interest.**

We are interested in knowing

$$P(x \leq 12)$$

Step 3 **Go to the binomial table in Appendix B to find the desired probability.**

Locate the table for the sample size, n. Locate the column for $p = 0.80$. Go to the row corresponding to $x = 12$ and the column for $p = 0.80$ in the section of the table for $n = 20$ to get

$$P(x \leq 12) = 0.0321$$

Thus, it is quite unlikely that if 80% of customers like the new seating plan, 12 or fewer in a sample of 20 would like it. The airline may want to rethink its plan.

>> **END EXAMPLE**

TRY PROBLEM 5-29 (pg. 200)

Mean and Standard Deviation of the Binomial Distribution In Section 5.1, we stated the mean of a discrete probability distribution is also referred to as the *expected value*. The expected value of a discrete random variable, x, is found using Equation 5.1.

$$\mu_x = E(x) = \Sigma x P(x)$$

MEAN OF A BINOMIAL DISTRIBUTION This equation for the expected value can be used with any discrete probability distribution, including the binomial. However, if we are working with a binomial distribution, the expected value can be found more easily by using Equation 5.5.

Expected Value of a Binomial Distribution

$$\mu_x = E(x) = np \tag{5.5}$$

where:

n = Sample size

p = Probability of a success

Excel Tutorial

BUSINESS APPLICATION **BINOMIAL DISTRIBUTION**

CATALOG SALES Catalog sales have been a part of the U.S. economy for many years, and companies such as Lands' End, L.L. Bean, and Eddie Bauer have enjoyed increased business. One feature that has made mail-order buying so popular is the ease with which customers can return merchandise. Nevertheless, one mail-order catalog has the goal of no more than 11% of all purchased items returned.

The binomial distribution can describe the number of items returned. For instance, in a given hour, the company shipped 300 items. If the probability of an item being returned is $p = 0.11$, the expected number of items (mean) to be returned is

$$\mu_x = E(x) = np$$

$$\mu_x = E(x) = (300)(0.11) = 33$$

Thus, the average number of returned items for each 300 items shipped is 33.

Suppose the company sales manager wants to know if the return rate is stable at 11%. To test this, she monitors a random sample of 300 items and finds that 44 have been returned. This return rate exceeds the mean of 33 units, which concerns her. However, before reaching a conclusion, she will be interested in the probability of observing 44 or more returns in a sample of 300.

$$P(x \geq 44) = 1 - P(x \leq 43)$$

The binomial table in Appendix B does not contain sample sizes as large as 300. Instead, we can use Excel's BINOM.DIST function to find the probability. The Excel output in Figure 5.3 shows the cumulative probability of 43 or fewer is equal to

$$P(x \leq 43) = 0.97$$

Then the probability of 44 or more returns is

$$P(x \geq 44) = 1 - 0.97 = 0.03$$

There is only a 3% chance of 44 or more items being returned if the 11% return rate is still in effect. This low probability suggests that the return rate may have increased above 11%, because we would not expect to see 44 returned items. The probability is very small.

FIGURE 5.3 |

Excel 2010 Binomial
Distribution Output for
Catalog Sales

Excel 2010 Instructions:
1. Open blank worksheet.
2. Click on f_x (function wizard).
3. Select **Statistical** category.
4. Select the **BINOM.DIST** function.
5. Fill in the requested information in the template.
6. **True** indicates cumulative probabilities.

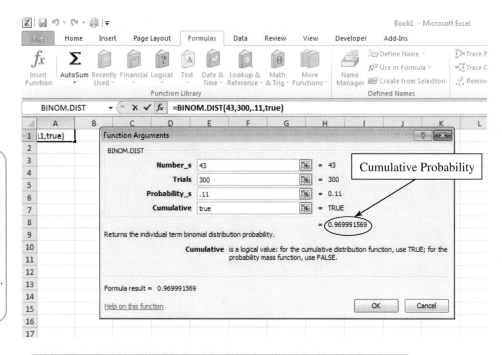

Minitab Instructions (for similar results):
1. Choose **Calc > Probability Distribution > Binomial**.
2. Choose **Cumulative probability**.
3. In **Number of trials** enter sample size.
4. In **Probability of success** enter *p*.
5. In **Input constant** enter the number of successes: *x*.
6. Click **OK**.

EXAMPLE 5-5   FINDING THE MEAN OF THE BINOMIAL DISTRIBUTION

Clearwater Research In Example 5-4, Clearwater Research had been hired to do a study for a major airline that is planning to change from a designated-seat assignment plan to an open-seating system. The company believes that 80% of its customers approve of the idea. Clearwater Research interviewed a sample of $n = 20$ and found 12 who like the proposed change. If the airline is correct in its assessment of the probability, what is the expected number of people in a sample of $n = 20$ who will like the change? We can find this using the following steps:

Step 1 Define the characteristics of the binomial distribution.
In this case, the characteristics are

$$n = 20, \qquad p = 0.80, \qquad q = 1 - p = 0.20$$

Step 2 Use Equation 5.5 to find the expected value.

$$\mu_x = E(x) = np$$
$$E(x) = 20(0.80) = 16$$

The average number who would say they like the proposed change is 16 in a sample of 20.

>> **END EXAMPLE**

TRY PROBLEM 5-33a (pg. 201)

STANDARD DEVIATION OF A BINOMIAL DISTRIBUTION The standard deviation for any discrete probability distribution can be calculated using Equation 5.2. We show this again as

$$\sigma_x = \sqrt{\sum[x - E(x)]^2 P(x)}$$

If a discrete probability distribution meets the binomial distribution conditions, the standard deviation is more easily computed by Equation 5.6.

Standard Deviation of the Binomial Distribution

$$\sigma = \sqrt{npq} \tag{5.6}$$

where:

n = Sample size
p = Probability of a success
$q = 1 - p$ = Probability of a failure

| **EXAMPLE 5-6** | **FINDING THE STANDARD DEVIATION OF A BINOMIAL DISTRIBUTION** |

Clearwater Research Refer to Examples 5-4 and 5-5, in which Clearwater Research surveyed a sample of $n = 20$ airline customers about changing the way seats are assigned on flights. The airline believes that 80% of its customers approve of the proposed change. Example 5-5 showed that if the airline is correct in its assessment, the expected number in a sample of 20 who would like the change is 16. However, there are other possible outcomes if 20 customers are surveyed. What is the standard deviation of the random variable, x, in this case? We can find the standard deviation for the binomial distribution using the following steps:

Step 1 Define the characteristics of the binomial distribution.
In this case, the characteristics are

$$n = 20, \qquad p = 0.80, \qquad q = 1 - p = 0.20$$

Step 2 Use Equation 5.6 to calculate the standard deviation.

$$\sigma = \sqrt{npq} = \sqrt{20(0.80)(0.20)} = 1.7889$$

>> **END EXAMPLE**

TRY PROBLEM 5-33b (pg. 201)

Additional Information about the Binomial Distribution At this point, several comments about the binomial distribution are worth making. If p, the probability of a success, is 0.50, the binomial distribution is *symmetrical* and bell-shaped, regardless of the sample size. This is illustrated in Figure 5.4, which shows frequency histograms for samples of $n = 5, n = 10$, and $n = 50$. Notice that all three distributions are centered at the expected value, $E(x) = np$.

When the value of p differs from 0.50 in either direction, the binomial distribution is skewed. The skewness will be most pronounced when n is small and p approaches 0 or 1. However, the binomial distribution becomes more bell shaped as n increases. The frequency histograms shown in Figure 5.5 bear this out.

FIGURE 5.4

The Binomial Distribution with Varying Sample Sizes ($p = 0.50$)

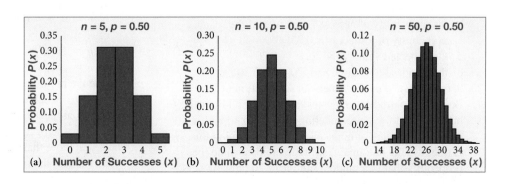

FIGURE 5.5

The Binomial Distribution
with Varying Sample Sizes
($p = 0.05$)

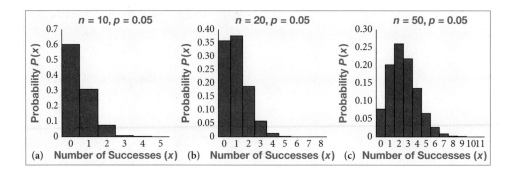

MyStatLab

5-2: Exercises

Skill Development

5-22. The manager for State Bank and Trust has recently examined the credit card account balances for the customers of her bank and found that 20% have an outstanding balance at the credit card limit. Suppose the manager randomly selects 15 customers and finds 4 that have balances at the limit. Assume that the properties of the binomial distribution apply.

   a. What is the probability of finding 4 customers in a sample of 15 who have "maxed out" their credit cards?

   b. What is the probability that 4 or fewer customers in the sample will have balances at the limit of the credit card?

5-23. For a binomial distribution with a sample size equal to 10 and a probability of a success equal to 0.30, what is the probability that the sample will contain exactly three successes? Use the binomial formula to determine the probability.

5-24. Use the binomial formula to calculate the following probabilities for an experiment in which $n = 5$ and $p = 0.4$:

   a. the probability that x is at most 1

   b. the probability that x is at least 4

   c. the probability that x is less than 1

5-25. If a binomial distribution applies with a sample size of $n = 20$, find

   a. the probability of 5 successes if the probability of a success is 0.40

   b. the probability of at least 7 successes if the probability of a success is 0.25

   c. the expected value, $n = 20, p = 0.20$

   d. the standard deviation, $n = 20, p = 0.20$

5-26. A report issued by the American Association of Building Contractors indicates that 40% of all home buyers will do some remodeling to their home within the first five years of home ownership. Assuming this is true, use the binomial distribution to determine the probability that in a random sample of 20 homeowners, 2 or fewer will remodel their homes. Use the binomial table.

5-27. Find the probability of exactly 5 successes in a sample of $n = 10$ when the probability of a success is 0.70.

5-28. Assuming the binomial distribution applies with a sample size of $n = 15$, find

   a. the probability of 5 or more successes if the probability of a success is 0.30

   b. the probability of fewer than 4 successes if the probability of a success is 0.75

   c. the expected value of the random variable if the probability of success is 0.40

   d. the standard deviation of the random variable if the probability of success is 0.40

5-29. A random variable follows a binomial distribution with a probability of success equal to 0.65. For a sample size of $n = 7$, find

   a. the probability of exactly 3 successes

   b. the probability of 4 or more successes

   c. the probability of exactly 7 successes

   d. the expected value of the random variable

5-30. A random variable follows a binomial distribution with a probability of success equal to 0.45. For $n = 11$, find

   a. the probability of exactly 1 success

   b. the probability of 4 or fewer successes

   c. the probability of at least 8 successes

5-31. Use the binomial distribution table to determine the following probabilities:

   a. $n = 6, p = 0.08$; find $P(x = 2)$

   b. $n = 9, p = 0.80$; determine $P(x < 4)$

   c. $n = 11, p = 0.65$; calculate $P(2 < x \leq 5)$

   d. $n = 14, p = 0.95$; find $P(x \geq 13)$

   e. $n = 20, p = 0.50$; compute $P(x > 3)$

5-32. Use the binomial distribution in which $n = 6$ and $p = 0.3$ to calculate the following probabilities:

   a. x is at most 1.

   b. x is at least 2.

   c. x is more than 5.

   d. x is less than 6.

5-33. Given a binomial distribution with $n = 8$ and $p = 0.40$, obtain the following:
   a. the mean
   b. the standard deviation
   c. the probability that the number of successes is larger than the mean
   d. the probability that the number of successes is within ± 2 standard deviations of the mean

Business Applications

5-34. Magic Valley Memorial Hospital administrators have recently received an internal audit report that indicates that 15% of all patient bills contain an error of one form or another. After spending considerable effort to improve the hospital's billing process, the administrators are convinced that things have improved. They believe that the new error rate is somewhere closer to 0.05.
   a. Suppose that recently the hospital randomly sampled 10 patient bills and conducted a thorough study to determine whether an error exists. It found 3 bills with errors. Assuming that managers are correct that they have improved the error rate to 0.05, what is the probability that they would find 3 or more errors in a sample of 10 bills?
   b. Referring to part a, what conclusion would you reach based on the probability of finding 3 or more errors in the sample of 10 bills?

5-35. The Center for the Study of the American Electorate indicated that 64% of the voting-age voters cast ballots in the 2008 presidential election. It also indicated in the west, 34.6% of voting-age voters voted for a Democrat as a Representative, an increase from 30.8 % in 2004. A start-up company in San Jose, California, has 10 employees.
   a. How many of the employees would you expect to have voted for a Democrat as a Representative?
   b. All of the employees indicated that they voted in the 2008 presidential election. Determine the probability of this assuming they followed the national trend.
   c. Eight of the employees voted for a Democratic Representative. Determine the probability that at least 8 of the employees would vote for the Democrat if they followed the national trend.
   d. Based on your calculations in parts b and c, do the employees reflect the national trend? Support your answer with statistical calculations and reasoning.

5-36. Dell Computers receives large shipments of microprocessors from Intel Corp. It must try to ensure the proportion of microprocessors that are defective is small. Suppose Dell decides to test five microprocessors out of a shipment of thousands of these microprocessors. Suppose that if at least one of the microprocessors is defective, the shipment is returned.
   a. If Intel Corp.'s shipment contains 10% defective microprocessors, calculate the probability the entire shipment will be returned.
   b. If Intel and Dell agree that Intel will not provide more than 5% defective chips, calculate the probability that the entire shipment will be returned even though only 5% are defective.
   c. Calculate the probability that the entire shipment will be kept by Dell even though the shipment has 10% defective microprocessors.

5-37. In his article titled "Acceptance Sampling Solves Drilling Issues: A Case Study," published in *Woodworking Magazine*, author Ken Wong discusses a problem faced by furniture manufacturing companies dealing with the quality of the drilling of dowel holes. Wong states, "Incorrect sizing and distances with respect to dowel holes can cause many problems for the rest of the process especially when drilling is conducted early in the production process."

   Consider the case of Dragon Wood Furniture in Bismarck, North Dakota, which believes that when the drilling process is operating at an acceptable rate, the upper limit on the percentage of incorrectly drilled dowel holes is 4%. To monitor its drilling process, Dragon Wood Furniture randomly samples 20 products each hour and determines if the dowel hole in each product is correctly drilled or not. If, in the sample of 20 holes, 1 or more incorrectly drilled holes is discovered, the production process is stopped and the drilling process is recalibrated.
   a. If the process is really operating correctly $(p = 0.04)$, what is the probability that the sampling effort will produce $x = 0$ defective holes and thus the process will properly be left to continue running?
   b. Suppose the true defect rate has risen to 0.10. What is the probability the sample will produce results that properly tell the managers to halt production to recalibrate the drilling machine?
   c. Prepare a short letter to the manufacturing manager at Dragon Wood Furniture discussing the effectiveness of the sampling process that her company is using. Base your response on the results to parts a and b.

5-38. Mooney, Hileman & Jones, a marketing agency located in Cleveland, has created an advertising campaign for a major retail chain, which the agency's executives believe is a winner. For an ad campaign to be successful, at least 80% of those seeing a television commercial must be able to recall the name of the company featured in the commercial one hour after viewing the commercial. Before distributing the ad campaign nationally, the company plans to show the commercial to a random sample of 20 people. It will also show the same people two additional commercials for different products or businesses.
   a. Assuming that the advertisement will be successful (80% will be able to recall the name of the company

in the ad), what is the expected number of people in the sample who will recall the company featured in the Mooney, Hileman & Jones commercial one hour after viewing the three commercials?

b. Suppose that in the sample of 20 people, 11 were able to recall the name of the company in the Mooney, Hileman & Jones commercial one hour after viewing. Based on the premise that the advertising campaign will be successful, what is the probability of 11 or fewer people being able to recall the company name?

c. Based on your responses to parts a and b, what conclusion might Mooney, Hileman & Jones executives make about this particular advertising campaign?

5-39. A survey by KRC Research for *U.S. News* reported that 37% of people plan to spend more on eating out after they retire. If eight people are randomly selected, then determine the

a. expected number of people who plan to spend more on eating out after they retire

b. standard deviation of the individuals who plan to spend more on eating out after they retire

c. probability that two or fewer in the sample indicate that they actually plan to spend more on eating out after retirement

5-40. Nielsen is the major media measurement company and conducts surveys to determine household viewing choices. The following table shows the top 10 broadcast television programs for the week of January 23, 2012.

Rank*	Program	Network	HH Rating**	Viewers***
1	*American Idol—Wednesday*	FOX	11.1	19.671
2	*American Idol—Thursday*	FOX	10.0	17.141
3	*Big Bang Theory*	CBS	9.7	16.130
4	*CSI*	CBS	9.0	14.257
5	*Criminal Minds*	CBS	8.7	13.815
6	*NCIS*	CBS	8.1	12.548
7	*Undercover Boss*	CBS	7.9	13.151
8	*AFC-NFC Pro-Bowl*	NBC	7.3	12.498
9	*The Good Wife*	CBS	7.2	11.083
10	*60 Minutes*	CBS	7.1	11.188

Rank is based on U.S. Household Rating % from Nielsen's National People Meter Sample.

**A household rating is the estimate of the size of a television audience relative to the total universe, expressed as a percentage. As of August 27, 2012, there are an estimated 114,200,000 television households in the United States. A single national household ratings point represents 1%, or 1,142,000 households.*

***Measured in millions; includes all persons over the age of two.*

Source: www.nielsenmedia.com

a. Suppose that the producers of *NCIS* commissioned a study that called for the consultants to randomly call 25 people immediately after the *NCIS* time slot and interview those who said that they had just watched *NCIS*. Suppose the consultant submits a report saying that it found no one in the sample of 25 homes who claimed to have watched the program and therefore did not do any surveys. What is the probability of this happening, assuming that the Nielsen ratings for the show are accurate?

b. Assume the producers for *The Big Bang Theory* planned to survey 1,000 people on the day following the broadcast of the program. The purpose of the survey was to determine what the reaction would be if one of the leading characters was retired from the show. Based on the Nielsen ratings, what would be the expected number of people who would end up being included in the analysis, assuming that all 1,000 people could be reached?

5-41. A small hotel in a popular resort area has 20 rooms. The hotel manager estimates that 15% of all confirmed reservations are "no-shows." Consequently, the hotel accepts confirmed reservations for as many as 25 rooms. If more confirmed reservations arrive than there are rooms, the overbooked guests are sent to another hotel and given a complementary dinner. If the hotel currently has 25 confirmed reservations, find

a. the probability that no customers will be sent to another hotel

b. the probability that exactly 2 guests will be sent to another hotel

c. the probability that 3 or more guests will be sent to another hotel

5-42. A manufacturing firm produces a product that has a ceramic coating. The coating is baked on to the product, and the baking process is known to produce 15% defective items (for example, cracked or chipped finishes). Every hour, 20 products from the thousands that are baked hourly are sampled from the ceramic-coating process and inspected.

a. What is the probability that 5 defective items will be found in the next sample of 20?

b. On average, how many defective items would be expected to occur in each sample of 20?

c. How likely is it that 15 or more nondefective (good) items would occur in a sample due to chance alone?

5-43. The Employee Benefit Research Institute reports that 69% of workers reported that they and/or their spouse had saved some money for retirement.

a. If a random sample of 30 workers is taken, what is the probability that fewer than 17 workers and/or their spouses have saved some money for retirement?

b. If a random sample of 50 workers is taken, what is the probability that more than 40 workers and/or their spouses have saved some money for retirement?

5-44. Radio frequency identification (RFID) is an electronic scanning technology that can be used to identify items in a number of ways. One advantage of RFID is that it can eliminate the need to manually count inventory, which can help improve inventory management. The technology is not infallible, however, and sometimes errors occur when items are scanned. If the probability that a scanning error occurs is 0.0065, use either Excel or Minitab to find

a. the probability that exactly 20 items will be scanned incorrectly from the next 5,000 items scanned

b. the probability that more than 20 items will be scanned incorrectly from the next 5,000 items scanned

c. the probability that the number of items scanned incorrectly is between 10 and 25 from the next 5,000 items scanned

d. the expected number of items scanned incorrectly from the next 5,000 items scanned

5-45. Peter S. Kastner, director of the consulting firm Vericours Inc., reported that 40% of all rebates are not redeemed because consumers either fail to apply for them or their applications are rejected. TCA Fulfillment Services published its redemption rates: 50% for a $30 rebate on a $100 product, 10% for a $10 rebate on a $100 product, and 35% for a $50 rebate on a $200 product.

a. Calculate the weighted average proportion of redemption rates for TCA Fulfillment using the size of the rebate to establish the weights. Does it appear that TCA Fulfillment has a lower rebate rate than that indicated by Vericours? Explain.

b. To more accurately answer the question posed in part a, a random sample of 20 individuals who purchased an item accompanied by a rebate could be asked if they submitted their rebate. Suppose four of the questioned individuals said they did redeem their rebate. If Vericours' estimate of the redemption rate is correct, determine the expected number of rebates that would be redeemed. Does it appear that Vericours' estimate may be too high?

c. Determine the likelihood that such an extreme sample result as indicated in part b or something more extreme would occur if the weighted average proportion provides the actual rebate rate.

d. Repeat the calculations of part c assuming that Vericours' estimate of the redemption rate is correct.

e. Are you convinced that the redemption rate is smaller than that indicated by Vericours? Explain.

5-46. *Business Week* reported that business executives want to break down the obstacles that keep them from communicating directly with stock owners. Ms. Borrus reports that 80% of shareholders hold stock in "street names," which are registered with their bank or brokerage. If the brokerage doesn't furnish these names to the corporations, executives cannot communicate with their shareholders. To determine if

the percent reported by Ms. Borrus is correct, a sample of 20 shareholders was asked if they held their stock in "street names." Seventeen responded that they did.

a. Supposing the true proportion of shareholders that hold stock under street names is 0.80, calculate the probability that 17 or more of the sampled individuals hold their stock under street names.

b. Repeat the calculation in part a using proportions of 0.70 and 0.90.

c. Based on your calculations in parts a and b, which proportion do you think is most likely true? Support your answer.

Computer Database **Exercises**

5-47. *USA Today* has reported on the gender gap that exists between married spouses. One of the measures is the number of women who outearn their husbands. According to a study conducted by the Bureau of Labor Statistics, 32.5% of female spouses outearn their male counterparts. The file titled **Gendergap** contains the incomes of 150 married couples in Utah.

a. Determine the number of families in which the female outearns her husband.

b. Calculate the expected number of female spouses who outearn their male counterparts in the sample of 150 married couples based on the Bureau of Labor Statistics study.

c. If the percentage of married women in Utah who outearn their male spouses is the same as that indicated by the Bureau of Labor Statistics, determine the probability that at least the number found in part a would occur.

d. Based on your calculation in part c, does the Bureau of Labor Statistics' percentage seem plausible if Utah is not different from the rest of the United States?

5-48. Tony Hsieh is CEO of e-tailer Zappos.com. His company sells shoes online. It differentiates itself by its selection of shoes and a devotion to customer service. It offers free shipping and free return shipping. An area in which costs could be cut back is the shipping charges for return shipping, specifically those that result from the wrong size of shoes being sent. Zappos may try to keep the percentage of returns due to incorrect size to no more than 5%. The file titled **Shoesize** contains a sample of 125 shoe sizes that were sent to customers and the sizes that were actually ordered.

a. Determine the number of pairs of wrong-size shoes that were delivered to customers.

b. Calculate the probability of obtaining at least that many pairs of wrong-sized shoes delivered to customers if the proportion of incorrect sizes is actually 0.05.

c. On the basis of your calculation, determine whether Zappos has kept the percentage of returns due to incorrect size to no more than 5%. Support your answer with statistical reasoning.

d. If Zappos sells 5 million pairs of shoes in one year and it costs an average of $4.75 a pair to return them, calculate the expected cost associated with wrong-sized shoes being returned using the probability calculated from the sample data.

5-49. International Data Corp. (IDC) has shown that the average return on business analytics projects was almost four-and-a-half times the initial investment. Analytics consists of tools and applications that present better metrics to the user and to the probable future outcome of an event. IDC looked at how long it takes a typical company to recoup its investment in analytics. It determined that 29% of the U.S. corporations that adopted analytics took six months or less to recoup

their investment. The file titled **Analytics** contains a sample of the time it might have taken 35 corporations to recoup their investment in analytics.

a. Determine the number of corporations that recovered their investment in analytics in six months or less.

b. Calculate the probability of obtaining at most the number of corporations that you determined in part a if the percent of those recovering their investment is as indicated by IDC.

c. Determine the 70th percentile of the number of the 35 corporations that recovered their investment in analytics in six months or less. (*Hint*: Recall and use the definition of percentiles from Section 3.1.)

END EXERCISES 5-2

5.3 Other Discrete Probability Distributions

The binomial distribution is very useful in many business situations, as indicated by the examples and applications presented in the previous section. However, as we pointed out, there are several requirements that must hold before we can use the binomial distribution to determine probabilities. If those conditions are not satisfied, there may be other theoretical probability distributions that could be employed. In this section, we introduce two other very useful discrete probability distributions: the Poisson distribution and the hypergeometric distribution.

Chapter Outcome 3. → ## The Poisson Distribution

To use the binomial distribution, we must be able to count the number of successes and the number of failures. Although in many situations you may be able to count the number of successes, you often cannot count the number of failures. For example, suppose a company builds freeways in Vermont. The company could count the number of potholes that develop per mile (here a pothole is referred to as a success because it is what we are looking for), but how could it count the number of nonpotholes? Or what about a hospital supplying emergency medical services in Los Angeles? It could easily count the number of emergencies its units respond to in one hour, but how could it determine how many calls it did not receive? Obviously, in these cases, the number of possible outcomes of (successes + failures) is difficult, if not impossible, to determine. If the total number of possible outcomes cannot be determined, the binomial distribution cannot be applied. In these cases you may be able to use the Poisson distribution.

Poisson Distribution

The Poisson distribution describes a process that extends over space, time, or any well-defined interval or unit of inspection in which the outcomes of interest occur at random and the number of outcomes that occur in any given interval are counted. The Poisson distribution, rather than the binomial distribution, is used when the total number of possible outcomes cannot be determined.

Characteristics of the Poisson Distribution The **Poisson distribution**[1] describes a process that extends over time, space, or any well-defined unit of inspection. The outcomes of interest, such as emergency calls or potholes, occur at random, and we count the number of outcomes that occur in a given segment of time or space. We might count the number of emergency calls in a one-hour period or the number of potholes in a two-mile stretch of freeway. As we did with the binomial distribution, we will call these outcomes *successes* even though (like potholes) they might be undesirable.

The possible counts are the integers 0, 1, 2, . . . , and we would like to know the probability of each of these values. For example, what is the chance of getting exactly four emergency calls in a particular hour? What is the chance that a chosen two-mile stretch of freeway will contain zero potholes?

---

[1]The Poisson distribution can be derived as the limiting distribution of the binomial distribution as the number of trials; n tends to infinity and the probability of success decreases to zero. It serves as a good approximation to the binomial when n is large.

We can use the Poisson probability distribution to answer these questions if we make the following assumptions:

1. We know λ, the average number of successes in one segment. For example, we know that there is an average of 8 emergency calls per hour ($\lambda = 8$) or an average of 15 potholes per mile of freeway ($\lambda = 15$).
2. The probability of x successes in a segment is the same for all segments of the same size. For example, the probability distribution of emergency calls is the same for any one-hour period of time at the hospital.
3. What happens in one segment has no influence on any nonoverlapping segment. For example, the number of calls arriving between 9:30 P.M. and 10:30 P.M. has no influence on the number of calls between 11:00 P.M. and 12:00 midnight.
4. We imagine dividing time or space into tiny subsegments. Then the chance of *more* than one success in a subsegment is negligible and the chance of exactly one success in a tiny subsegment of length t is λt. For example, the chance of two emergency calls in the same second is essentially 0, and if $\lambda = 8$ calls per hour, the chance of a call in any given second is $(8)(1/3,600) \approx 0.0022$.

Once λ has been determined, we can calculate the average occurrence rate for any number of segments (t). This is λt. Note that λ and t must be in compatible units. If we have $\lambda = 20$ arrivals per hour, the segments must be in hours or fractional parts of an hour. That is, if we have $\lambda = 20$ per hour and we wish to work with half-hour time periods, the segment would be

$$t = \frac{1}{2} \text{hour}$$

not $t = 30$ minutes.

Although the Poisson distribution is often used to describe situations such as the number of customers who arrive at a hospital emergency room per hour or the number of calls the Hewlett-Packard LaserJet printer service center receives in a 30-minute period, the segments need not be time intervals. Poisson distributions are also used to describe such random variables as the number of knots in a sheet of plywood or the number of contaminants in a gallon of lake water. The segments would be the sheet of plywood and the gallon of water.

Another important point is that λt, the average number in t segments, is not necessarily the number we will see if we observe the process for t segments. We might expect an average of 20 people to arrive at a checkout stand in any given hour, but we do not expect to find exactly that number arriving every hour. The actual arrivals will form a distribution with an expected value, or mean, equal to λt. So, for the Poisson distribution,

$$E[x] = \mu_x = \lambda t$$

Once λ and t have been specified, the probability for any discrete value in the Poisson distribution can be found using Equation 5.7.

Poisson Probability Distribution

$$P(x) = \frac{(\lambda t)^x e^{-\lambda t}}{x!} \tag{5.7}$$

where:

t = Number of segments of interest
x = Number of successes in t segments
λ = Expected number of successes in one segment
e = Base of the natural logarithm system ($2.71828 \ldots$)

BUSINESS APPLICATION   **POISSON DISTRIBUTION**

WHOLE FOODS GROCERY A study conducted at Whole Foods Grocery shows that the average number of arrivals to the checkout section of the store per hour is 16. Further, the distribution for the number of arrivals is considered to be Poisson distributed. Figure 5.6 shows

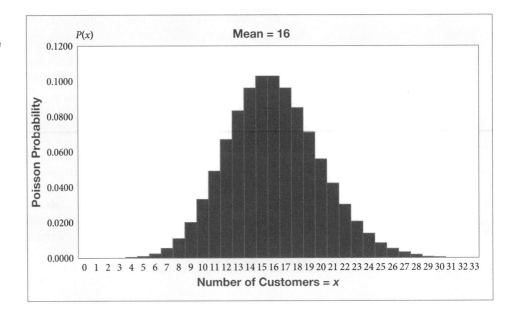

the shape of the Poisson distribution for $\lambda = 16$. The probability of each possible number of customers arriving can be computed using Equation 5.7. For example, we can find the probability of $x = 12$ customers in one hour ($t = 1$) as follows:

$$P(x = 12) = \frac{(\lambda t)^x \, e^{-\lambda t}}{x!} = \frac{16^{12} e^{-16}}{12!} = 0.0661$$

Poisson Probability Distribution Table   As was the case with the binomial distribution, a table of probabilities exists for the Poisson distribution. (The Poisson table appears in Appendix C.) The Poisson table shows the cumulative probabilities for x or fewer occurrences for different λt values. We can use the following business application to illustrate how to use the Poisson table.

BUSINESS APPLICATION   **USING THE POISSON DISTRIBUTION TABLE**

WHOLE FOODS GROCERY (CONTINUED)   At Whole Foods Grocery, customers are thought to arrive at the checkout section according to a Poisson distribution with $\lambda = 16$ customers per hour. (See Figure 5.6.) Based on previous studies, the store manager believes that the service time for each customer is quite constant at six minutes. Suppose, during each six-minute time period, the store has three checkers available. This means that three customers can be served during each six-minute segment. The manager is interested in the probability that one or more customers will have to wait for service during a six-minute period.

To determine this probability, you will need to convert the mean arrivals from $\lambda = 16$ customers per hour to a new average for a six-minute segment. Six minutes corresponds to 0.10 hours, so you will change the segment size, $t = 0.10$. Then the mean number of arrivals in six minutes is $\lambda t = 16(0.10) = 1.6$ customers.

Now, because there are three checkers, any time four or more customers arrive in a six-minute period, at least one customer will have to wait for service. Thus,

$$P(\text{1 or more customers wait}) = P(4) + P(5) + P(6) + \ldots$$

or you can use the *Complement Rule*, discussed in Chapter 4, as follows:

$$P(\text{1 or more customers wait}) = 1 - P(x \leq 3)$$

The Poisson table in Appendix C can be used to find the necessary probabilities. To use the table, first go across the top of the table until you find the desired value of λt. In this case, look for $\lambda t = 1.6$. Next, go down the left-hand side to find the value of x corresponding to the number of occurrences of interest. For example, consider $x = 3$ customer arrivals. Because

Appendix C is a cumulative Poisson table, the probabilities are for x or fewer occurrences. This, the probability of $x \leq 3$ is given in the table as 0.9212. Thus,

$$P(x \leq 3) = 0.9212$$

Then the probability of four or more customers arriving is

$$P(4 \text{ or more customers}) = 1 - P(x \leq 3)$$
$$P(4 \text{ or more customers}) = 1 - 0.9212 = 0.0788$$

Given the store's capacity to serve three customers in a six-minute period, the probability of one or more customers having to wait is 0.0778.

Suppose that when the store manager sees this probability, she is somewhat concerned. She states that she wants enough checkout stands open so that the chance of a customer waiting does not exceed 0.05. To determine the appropriate number of checkers, you can use the Poisson table to find the following:

$$P(4 \text{ or more customers}) = 1 - P(x \leq ?) \leq 0.05$$

In other words, a customer will have to wait if more customers arrive than there are checkers. As long as the number of arrivals, x, is less than or equal to the number of checkers, no one will wait. Then what value of x will provide the following?

$$1 - P(x \leq ?) \leq 0.05$$

Therefore, you want

$$P(x \leq ?) \geq 0.95$$

You can go to the table for $\lambda t = 1.6$ and scan down the column starting with $P(x = 0) = 0.2019$ until the cumulative probability listed is 0.95 or higher. When you reach $x = 4$, the cumulative probability, $P(x \leq 4) \geq 0.9763$. Then,

$$P(4 \text{ or more customers}) = 1 - P(x \leq 4) = 1 - 0.9763 = 0.0237$$

Because 0.0237 is less than or equal to the 0.05 limit imposed by the manager, she would have to schedule four checkers.

How to do it (Example 5-7)

Using the Poisson Distribution
The following steps are used to find probabilities using the Poisson distribution:

1. Define the segment units.
   The segment units are usually blocks of time, areas of space, or volume.

2. Determine the mean of the random variable.
   The mean is the parameter that defines the Poisson distribution and is referred to as λ. It is the average number of successes in a segment of unit size.

3. Determine t, the number of the segments to be considered, and then calculate λt.

4. Define the event of interest and use the Poisson formula or the Poisson table to find the probability.

EXAMPLE 5-7   **USING THE POISSON DISTRIBUTION**

Fashion Leather Products Fashion Leather Products, headquartered in Argentina, makes leather clothing for export to many other countries around the world. Before shipping, quality managers perform tests on the leather products. The industry standards call for the average number of defects per square meter of leather to not exceed five. During a recent test, the inspector selected 3 square meters, finding 18 defects. To determine the probability of this event occurring if the leather meets the industry standards, assuming that the Poisson distribution applies, the company can perform the following steps:

Step 1 Define the segment unit.
Because the mean was stated as five defects per square meter, the segment unit in this case is one meter.

Step 2 Determine the mean of the random variable.
In this case, if the company meets the industry standards, the mean will be

$$\lambda = 5$$

Step 3 Determine the segment size t.
The company quality inspectors analyzed 3 square meters, which is equal to 3 units. So $t = 3.0$ Then,

$$\lambda t = (5)(3.0) = 15.0$$

When looking at 3 square meters, the company would expect to find at most 15.0 defects if the industry standards are being met.

Step 4 Define the event of interest and use the Poisson formula or the Poisson tables to find the probability.

In this case, 18 defects were observed. Because 18 exceeds the expected number $(\lambda t = 15.0)$ the company would want to find,

$$P(x \geq 18) = P(x = 18) + P(x = 19) + \ldots$$

The Poisson table in Appendix C is used to determine these probabilities. Locate the desired probability under the column headed $\lambda t = 15.0$ Then find the values of x down the left-hand column.

$$P(x \geq 18) = 1 - P(x \leq 17)$$
$$= 1 - 0.7489$$
$$= 0.2511$$

There is about a 0.25 chance of finding 18 or more defects in 3 square meters of leather products made by Fashion Leather if they are meeting the quality standard.

>> **END EXAMPLE**

TRY PROBLEM 5-50 (pg. 214)

The Mean and Standard Deviation of the Poisson Distribution The mean of the Poisson distribution is λt. This is the value we use to specify which Poisson distribution we are using. We must know the mean before we can find probabilities for a Poisson distribution.

Figure 5.6 illustrated that the outcome of a Poisson distributed variable is subject to variation. Like any other discrete probability distribution, the standard deviation for the Poisson can be computed using Equation 5.2:

$$\sigma_x = \sqrt{\sum [x - E(x)]^2 \, P(x)}$$

However, for a Poisson distribution, the standard deviation also can be found using Equation 5.8.

Standard Deviation of the Poisson Distribution

$$\sigma = \sqrt{\lambda t} \qquad\qquad (5.8)$$

The standard deviation of the Poisson distribution is simply the square root of the mean. Therefore, if you are working with a Poisson process, reducing the mean will reduce the variability also.

BUSINESS APPLICATION   **THE POISSON PROBABILITY DISTRIBUTION**

Excel Tutorial

HERITAGE TILE To illustrate the importance of the relationship between the mean and standard deviation of the Poisson distribution, consider Heritage Tile in New York City. The company makes ceramic tile for kitchens and bathrooms. The quality standards call for the number of imperfections in a tile to average 3 or fewer. The distribution of imperfections is thought to be Poisson. Many software packages, including Excel will generate Poisson probabilities in much the same way as for the binomial distribution, which was discussed in Section 5.2. If we assume that the company is meeting the standard, Figure 5.7 shows the Poisson probability distribution generated using Excel when $\lambda t = 3.0$. Even though the average number of defects is 3, the manager is concerned about the high probabilities associated with the number of imperfections equal to 4, 5, 6, or more on a tile. The variability is too great. Using Equation 5.5, the standard deviation for this distribution is

$$\sigma = \sqrt{3.0} = 1.732$$

This large standard deviation means that although some tiles will have few if any imperfections, others will have several, causing problems for installers and unhappy customers.

FIGURE 5.7 |

Excel 2010 Output for
Heritage Tile Example

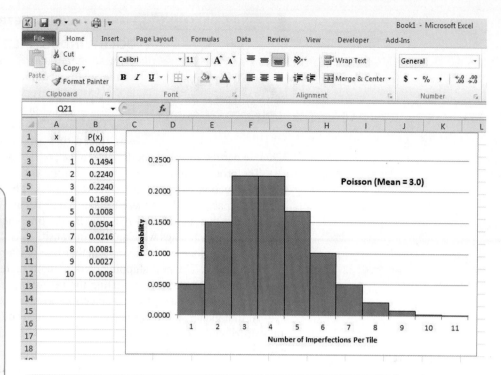

Excel 2010 Instructions:
1. Enter values for *x* ranging from 0 to 10.
2. Place the cursor in the first blank cell in the next column.
3. Click on *fx* (*function wizard*) and then select the **Statistical** category.
4. Select the **POISSON. DIST** function.
5. Reference the cell with the desired *x* value and enter the mean. Enter **False** to choose noncumulative probabilities.
6. Copy function down for all values of *x*.
7. Graph using **Insert > Column**. Remove gaps and add lines to the bars. Label axes and add titles.

Minitab Instructions (for similar results):
1. Create column *Number* with integers from 0 to 10.
2. Choose **Calc > Probability Distributions > Poisson**.
3. Select **Probability**.
4. In **Mean**, enter 3.
5. Select **Input column**.
6. In **Input column**, enter the column of integers.
7. In **Optional storage**, enter column *Probability*.
8. Click **OK**.
9. Choose **Graph > Bar Chart**.
10. In **Bars represent**, select **Values from a Table**, select **Simple**.
11. Click **OK**.
12. In **Graph variables**, Insert *Probability*.
13. In **Categorical variable**, insert *Number*.
14. Click **OK**.

A quality-improvement effort directed at reducing the average number of imperfections to 2.0 would also reduce the standard deviation to

$$\sigma = \sqrt{2.0} = 1.414$$

Further reductions in the average would also reduce variation in the number of imperfections between tiles. This would mean more consistency for installers and higher customer satisfaction.

Chapter Outcome 3. ➔ ## The Hypergeometric Distribution

Although the binomial and Poisson distributions are very useful in many business decision-making situations, they both require that the trials be independent. For instance, in binomial applications, the probability of a success in one trial must be the same as the probability of a success in any other trial. Although there are certainly times when this assumption can be satisfied, or at least approximated, in instances in which the population is fairly small and we are sampling without replacement, the condition of independence will not hold. In these cases, a discrete probability distribution referred to as the *hypergeometric distribution* can be useful.

Discovod/Fotolia

DOLBY INDUSTRIES Dolby Industries contracts with a Chinese manufacturer to make women's handbags. Because of the intense competition in the marketplace for handbags, Dolby has made every attempt to provide high-quality products. However, a recent production run of 20 handbags of a particular model contained 2 units that tested out as defective. The problem was traced to a shipment of defective latches that Dolby's Chinese partner received shortly before the production run started.

The production manager ordered that the entire batch of 20 handbags be isolated from other production output until further testing could be completed. Unfortunately, a new shipping clerk packaged 10 of these isolated handbags and shipped them to a California retailer to fill an order that was already overdue. By the time the production manager noticed what had happened, the handbags were already in transit.

The immediate concern was whether one or more of the defectives had been included in the shipment. The new shipping clerk thought there was a good chance that no defectives were included. Short of reinspecting the remaining handbags, how might Dolby Industries determine the probability that no defectives were actually shipped?

At first glance, it might seem that the question could be answered by employing the binomial distribution with $n = 10, p = 2/20 = 0.10$, and $x = 0$. Using the binomial distribution table in Appendix B, we get

$$P(x = 0) = 0.3487$$

There is a 0.3487 chance that no defectives were shipped, assuming the selection process satisfied the requirements of a binomial distribution. However, for the binomial distribution to be applicable, the trials must be independent, and the probability of a success, p, must remain constant from trial to trial. In order for this to occur when the sampling is from a "small," *finite* population as is the case here, the sampling must be performed with *replacement*. This means that after each item is selected, it is returned to the population and, therefore, may be selected again later in the sampling.

In the Dolby example, the sampling was performed without replacement because each handbag could only be shipped one time. Also, the population of handbags is finite with size $N = 20$, which is a "small" population. Thus, p, the probability of a defective handbag, does not remain equal to 0.10 on each trial. The value of p on any particular trial depends on what has already been selected on previous trials.

The event of interest is

$$G\ G\ G\ G\ G\ G\ G\ G\ G\ G$$

The probability that the first item selected for shipment would be good would be 18/20, because there were 18 good handbags in the batch of 20. Now, assuming the first unit selected was good, the probability the second unit was good is 17/19, because we then had only 19 handbags to select from and 17 of those would be good. The probability that all 10 items selected were good is

$$\frac{18}{20} \times \frac{17}{19} \times \frac{16}{18} \times \frac{15}{17} \times \frac{14}{16} \times \frac{13}{15} \times \frac{12}{14} \times \frac{11}{13} \times \frac{10}{12} \times \frac{9}{11} = 0.2368$$

This value is not the same as the 0.3847 probability we got when the binomial distribution was used. This demonstrates that when sampling is performed without replacement from finite populations, the binomial distribution produces inaccurate probabilities. To protect against large inaccuracies, the binomial distribution should only be used when the sample is small relative to the size of the population. Under that circumstance, the value of p will not change very much as the sample is selected, and the binomial distribution will be a reasonable approximation to the actual probability distribution.

In cases in which the sample is large relative to the size of the population, a discrete probability distribution, called the **hypergeometric distribution**, is the correct distribution for computing probabilities for the random variable of interest.

Hypergeometric Distribution

The hypergeometric distribution is formed by the ratio of the number of ways an event of interest can occur over the total number of ways any event can occur.

We use combinations (see Section 5.2) to form the equation for computing probabilities for the hypergeometric distribution. When each trial has two possible outcomes (success and failure), hypergeometric probabilities are computed using Equation 5.9.

Hypergeometric Distribution (Two Possible Outcomes per Trial)

$$P(x) = \frac{C_{n-x}^{N-X} \cdot C_x^X}{C_n^N}$$

(5.9)

where:

N = Population size
X = Number of successes in the population
n = Sample size
x = Number of successes in the sample
$n - x$ = Number of failures in the sample

Notice that the numerator of Equation 5.9 is the product of the number of ways you can select x successes in a random sample out of the X successes in the population and the number of ways you can select $n - x$ failures in a sample from the $N - X$ failures in the population. The denominator in the equation is the number of ways the sample can be selected from the population.

In the earlier Dolby Industries example, the probability of zero defectives being shipped $(x = 0)$ is

$$P(x = 0) = \frac{C_{10-0}^{20-2} \cdot C_0^2}{C_{10}^{20}}$$

$$P(x = 0) = \frac{C_{10}^{18} \cdot C_0^2}{C_{10}^{20}}$$

Carrying out the arithmetic, we get

$$P(x = 0) = \frac{(43,758)(1)}{184,756} = 0.2368$$

As we found before, the probability that zero defectives were included in the shipment is 0.2368, or approximately 24%.

The probabilities of $x = 1$ and $x = 2$ defectives can also be found by using Equation 5.9, as follows:

$$P(x = 1) = \frac{C_{10-1}^{20-2} \cdot C_1^2}{C_{10}^{20}} = 0.5264$$

and

$$P(x = 2) = \frac{C_{10-2}^{20-2} \cdot C_2^2}{C_{10}^{20}} = 0.2368$$

Thus, the hypergeometric probability distribution for the number of defective handbags in a random selection of 10 is

x	$P(x)$
0	0.2368
1	0.5264
2	0.2368
	$\Sigma P(x) = 1.0000$

Recall that when we introduced the hypergeometric distribution, we said that it is used in situations when we are sampling without replacement from a finite population. However, when the population size is large relative to the sample size, decision makers typically use the binomial distribution as an approximation of the hypergeometric. This eases the computational burden and provides useful approximations in those cases. Although there is no exact rule for when the binomial approximation can be used, we suggest that the sample should be less than 5% of the population size. Otherwise, use the hypergeometric distribution when sampling is done without replacement from the finite population.

> **EXAMPLE 5-8**   **THE HYPERGEOMETRIC DISTRIBUTION (ONE OF TWO POSSIBLE OUTCOMES PER TRIAL)**

Gender Equity One of the biggest changes in U.S. business practice in the past few decades has been the inclusion of women in the management ranks of companies. Tom Peters, management consultant and author of such books as *In Search of Excellence,* has stated that one of the reasons the Middle Eastern countries have suffered economically compared with countries such as the United States is that they have not included women in their economic system. However, there are still issues in U.S. business. Consider a situation in which a Maryland company needed to downsize one department having 30 people—12 women and 18 men. Ten people were laid off, and upper management said the layoffs were done randomly. By chance alone, 40% (12/30) of the layoffs would be women. However, of the 10 laid off, 8 were women. This is 80%, not the 40% due to chance. A labor attorney is interested in the probability of eight or more women being laid off by chance alone. This can be determined using the following steps:

Step 1   **Determine the population size and the combined sample size.**
The population size and sample size are

$$N = 30 \quad \text{and} \quad n = 10$$

Step 2   **Define the event of interest.**
The attorney is interested in the event:

$$P(x \geq 8) = ?$$

What are the chances that eight or more women would be selected?

Step 3   **Determine the number of successes in the population and the number of successes in the sample.**
In this situation, a success is the event that a woman is selected. There are $X = 12$ women in the population and $x \geq 8$ in the sample. We will break this down as $x = 8, x = 9, x = 10$.

Step 4   **Compute the desired probabilities using Equation 5.9.**

$$P(x) = \frac{C_{n-x}^{N-X} \cdot C_x^X}{C_n^N}$$

We want:[2]

$$P(x \geq 8) = P(x = 8) + P(x = 9) + P(x = 10)$$

$$P(x = 8) = \frac{C_{10-8}^{30-12} \cdot C_8^{12}}{C_{10}^{30}} = \frac{C_2^{18} \cdot C_8^{12}}{C_{10}^{30}} = 0.0025$$

$$P(x = 9) = \frac{C_1^{18} \cdot C_9^{12}}{C_{10}^{30}} = 0.0001$$

$$P(x = 10) = \frac{C_0^{18} \cdot C_{10}^{12}}{C_{10}^{30}} \approx 0.0000$$

Therefore, $P(x \geq 8) = 0.0025 + 0.0001 + 0.0000 = 0.0026$

The chances that 8 or more women would have been selected among the 10 people chosen for layoff strictly due to chance is 0.0026. The attorney will likely wish to challenge the layoffs based on this extremely low probability.

>> **END EXAMPLE**

TRY PROBLEM 5-53 (pg. 214)

---

[2]Note, you can use Excel's HYPGEOM.DIST function to compute these probabilities.

The Hypergeometric Distribution with More Than Two Possible Outcomes per Trial Equation 5.9 assumes that on any given sample selection or trial, only one of two possible outcomes will occur. However, the hypergeometric distribution can easily be extended to consider any number of possible categories of outcomes on a given trial by employing Equation 5.10.

Hypergeometric Distribution (*k* Possible Outcomes per Trial)

$$P(x_1, x_2, \ldots, x_k) = \frac{C_{x_1}^{X_1} \cdot C_{x_2}^{X_2} \cdot C_{x_3}^{X_3} \cdot \ldots \cdot C_{x_k}^{X_K}}{C_n^N} \tag{5.10}$$

where:

$$\sum_{i=1}^{k} X_i = N$$

$$\sum_{i=1}^{k} x_i = n$$

N = Population size
n = Total sample size
X_i = Number of items in the population with outcome i
x_i = Number of items in the sample with outcome i

EXAMPLE 5-9	**THE HYPERGEOMETRIC DISTRIBUTION FOR MULTIPLE OUTCOMES**

Breakfast Cereal Preferences Consider a marketing study that involves placing breakfast cereal made by four different companies in a basket at the exit to a food store. A sign on the basket invites customers to take one box of cereal free of charge. At the beginning of the study, the basket contains the following:

5 brand A
4 brand B
6 brand C
4 brand D

The researchers were interested in the brand selection patterns for customers who could select without regard to price. Suppose six customers were observed and three selected brand B, two selected brand D, and one selected brand C. No one selected brand A. The probability of this selection mix, assuming the customers were selecting entirely at random without replacement from a finite population, can be found using the following steps:

Step 1 **Determine the population size and the combined sample size.**
The population size and sample size are
$$N = 19 \quad \text{and} \quad n = 6$$

Step 2 **Define the event of interest.**
The event of interest is
$$P(x_1 = 0; x_2 = 3; x_3 = 1; x_4 = 2) = ?$$

Step 3 **Determine the number in each category in the population and the number in each category in the sample.**

$X_1 =$	5	(brand A)	$x_1 = 0$
$X_2 =$	4	(brand B)	$x_2 = 3$
$X_3 =$	6	(brand C)	$x_3 = 1$
$X_4 =$	4	(brand D)	$x_4 = 2$
$N = 19$			$n = 6$

Step 4 Compute the desired probability using Equation 5.10

$$P(x_1, x_2, x_3, \ldots, x_k) = \frac{C_{x_1}^{X_1} \cdot C_{x_2}^{X_2} \cdot C_{x_3}^{X_3} \cdot \ldots \cdot C_{x_k}^{X_k}}{C_n^N}$$

$$P(0,3,1,2) = \frac{C_0^5 \cdot C_3^4 \cdot C_1^6 \cdot C_2^4}{C_6^{19}}$$

$$= \frac{(1)(4)(6)(6)}{27,132} = \frac{144}{27,132}$$

$$= 0.0053$$

There are slightly more than 5 chances in 1,000 of this exact selection occurring by random chance.

>> **END EXAMPLE**

TRY PROBLEM 5-52 (pg. 214)

MyStatLab

5-3: **Exercises**

Skill **Development**

5-50. The mean number of errors per page made by a member of the word-processing pool for a large company is thought to be 1.5, with the number of errors distributed according to a Poisson distribution. If three pages are examined, what is the probability that more than three errors will be observed?

5-51. Arrivals to a bank automated teller machine (ATM) are distributed according to a Poisson distribution with a mean equal to three per 15 minutes.
   a. Determine the probability that in a given 15-minute segment, no customers will arrive at the ATM.
   b. What is the probability that fewer than four customers will arrive in a 30-minute segment?

5-52. Consider a situation in which a used-car lot contains five Fords, four General Motors (GM) cars, and five Toyotas. If five cars are selected at random to be placed on a special sale, what is the probability that three are Fords and two are GMs?

5-53. A population of 10 items contains 3 that are red and 7 that are green. What is the probability that in a random sample of 3 items selected without replacement, 2 red and 1 green items are selected?

5-54. If a random variable follows a Poisson distribution with $\lambda = 20$ and $t = \frac{1}{2}$, find the
   a. expected value, variance, and standard deviation of this Poisson distribution
   b. probability of exactly 8 successes

5-55. A corporation has 11 manufacturing plants. Of these, seven are domestic and four are located outside the United States. Each year, a performance evaluation is conducted for 4 randomly selected plants.
   a. What is the probability that a performance evaluation will include exactly 1 plant outside the United States?
   b. What is the probability that a performance evaluation will contain 3 plants from the United States?
   c. What is the probability that a performance evaluation will include 2 or more plants from outside the United States?

5-56. Determine the following values associated with a Poisson distribution with λt equal to 3:
   a. $P(x \leq 3)$
   b. $P(x > 3)$
   c. $P(2 < x \leq 5)$
   d. Find the smallest x' so that $P(x \leq x') > 0.50$.

5-57. A random variable, x, has a hypergeometric distribution with $N = 10$, $X = 7$, and $n = 4$. Calculate the following quantities:
   a. $P(x = 3)$
   b. $P(x = 5)$
   c. $P(x \geq 4)$
   d. Find the largest x' so that $P(x > x') > 0.25$.

Business **Applications**

5-58. A new phone-answering system installed by the Ohio Power Company is capable of handling five calls every 10 minutes. Prior to installing the new system, company analysts determined that the incoming calls to the system are Poisson distributed with a mean equal to two every 10 minutes. If this incoming call distribution is what the analysts think it is, what is the probability that in a 10-minute period more calls will arrive than the system can handle? Based on this probability, comment on the adequacy of the new answering system.

5-59. The Weyerhauser Lumber Company headquartered in Tacoma, Washington, is one of the largest timber- and wood-product companies in the world. Weyerhauser manufactures plywood at one of its Oregon plants. Plywood contains minor imperfections that can be repaired with small "plugs." One customer will accept plywood with a maximum of 3.5 plugs per sheet on average. Suppose a shipment was sent to this customer, and when the customer inspected two sheets at random, 10 plugged defects were counted. What is the probability of observing 10 or more plugged defects if in fact the 3.5 average per sheet is being satisfied? Comment on what this probability implies about whether you think the company is meeting the 3.5 per sheet defect rate.

5-60. When things are operating properly, E-Bank United, an Internet bank, can process a maximum of 25 electronic transfers every minute during the busiest periods of the day. If it receives more transfer requests than this, then the bank's computer system will become so overburdened that it will slow to the point that no electronic transfers can be handled. If during the busiest periods of the day requests for electronic transfers arrive at the rate of 170 per 10-minute period on average, what is the probability that the system will be overwhelmed by requests? Assume that the process can be described using a Poisson distribution.

5-61. A stock portfolio contains 20 stocks. Of these stocks, 10 are considered "large-cap" stocks, 5 are "mid cap," and 5 are "small cap." The portfolio manager has been asked by his client to develop a report that highlights 7 randomly selected stocks. When she presents her report to the client, all 7 of the stocks are large-cap stocks. The client is very suspicious that the manager has not randomly selected the stocks. She believes that the chances of all 7 of the stocks being large cap must be very low. Compute the probability of all 7 being large cap and comment on the concerns of the client.

5-62. College-Pro Painting does home interior and exterior painting. The company uses inexperienced painters that do not always do a high-quality job. It believes that its painting process can be described by a Poisson distribution with an average of 4.8 defects per 400 square feet of painting.
   a. What is the probability that a 400-square-foot painted section will have fewer than 6 blemishes?
   b. What is the probability that six randomly sampled sections of size 400 square feet will each have 7 or fewer blemishes?

5-63. Masters-at-Work was founded by two brothers in Atlanta to provide in-home computer and electronic installation services as well as tech support to solve hardware, software, or computer peripheral crises. Masters-at-Work became highly successful with branches throughout the South and was purchased by Best Buy but continued to operate under the Masters-at-Work name. A shipment of 20 Intel® Pentium® 4 processors was sent to Masters-at-Work. Four of them were defective. One of the Masters-at-Work technicians selected 5 of the processors to put in his parts inventory, and went on three service calls.
   a. Determine the probability that only 1 of the 5 processors is defective.
   b. Determine the probability that 3 of the 5 processors are not defective.
   c. Determine the probability that the technician will have enough processors to replace 3 defective processors at the repair sites.

5-64. John Thurgood founded a company that translates Chinese books into English. His company is currently testing a computer-based translation service. Since Chinese symbols are difficult to translate, John assumes the computer program will make some errors, but then so do human translators. The computer error rate is supposed to be an average of 3 per 400 words of translation. Suppose John randomly selects a 1,200-word passage. Assuming that the Poisson distribution applies, if the computer error rate is actually 3 errors per 400 words,
   a. determine the probability that no errors will be found.
   b. calculate the probability that more than 14 errors will be found.
   c. find the probability that fewer than 9 errors will be found.
   d. If 15 errors are found in the 1,200-word passage, what would you conclude about the computer company's claim? Why?

5-65. Beacon Hill Trees & Shrubs currently has an inventory of 10 fruit trees, 8 pine trees, and 14 maple trees. It plans to give 4 trees away at next Saturday's lawn and garden show in the city park. The 4 winners can select which type of tree they want. Assume they select randomly.
   a. What is the probability that all 4 winners will select the same type of tree?
   b. What is the probability that 3 winners will select pine trees and the other tree will be a maple?
   c. What is the probability that no fruit trees and 2 of each of the others will be selected?

5-66. Fasteners used in a manufacturing process are shipped by the supplier to the manufacturer in boxes that contain 20 fasteners. Because the fasteners are critical to the production process, their failure will cause the product to fail. The manufacturing firm and the supplier have agreed that a random sample of 4 fasteners will be selected from every box and tested to see if the fasteners meet the manufacturer's specifications. The nature of the testing process is such that tested fasteners become unusable and must be discarded. The supplier and the manufacturer have agreed that if 2 or more fasteners fail the test, the entire box will be rejected as being defective. Assume that a new box has just been received for inspection. If the box has 5 defective fasteners, what is the probability that a random sample of 4 will have 2 or more defective fasteners? What is the probability the box will be accepted?

5-67. Lucky Dogs sells spicy hot dogs from a pushcart. The owner of Lucky Dogs is open every day between 11:00 A.M. and 1:00 P.M. Assume the demand for spicy hot dogs follows a Poisson distribution with a mean of 50 per hour.

a. What is the probability the owner will run out of spicy dogs over the two-hour period if he stocks his cart with 115 spicy dogs every day?

b. How many spicy hot dogs should the owner stock if he wants to limit the probability of being out of stock to less than 2.5%?
(*Hint*: to solve this problem use Excel's Formulas **Statistics** > POISSON.DIST function or Minitab's **Calc** > **Probability Distributions** > **Poisson** option.)

5-68. *USA Today* recently reported that about one-third of eligible workers haven't enrolled in their employers' 401(k) plans. Costco has been contemplating new incentives to encourage more participation from its employees. Of the 12 employees in one of Costco's automotive departments, 5 have enrolled in Costco's 401(k) plan. The store manager has randomly selected 7 of the automotive department employees to receive investment training.

a. Calculate the probability that all of the employees currently enrolled in the 401(k) program are selected for the investment training.

b. Calculate the probability that none of the employees currently enrolled in the 401(k) program is selected for the investment training.

c. Compute the probability that more than half of the employees currently enrolled in the 401(k) program are selected for the investment training.

5-69. The Small Business Administration's Center for Women's Business Research indicated 30% of private firms had female owners, 52% had male owners, and 18% had male and female co-owners. In one community, there are 50 privately owned firms. Ten privately owned firms are selected to receive assistance in marketing their products. Assume the percentages indicated by the Small Business Administration apply to this community.

a. Calculate the probability that one-half of the firms selected will be solely owned by a woman, 3 owned by men, and the rest co-owned by women and men.

b. Calculate the probability that all of the firms selected will be solely owned by women.

c. Calculate the probability that 6 will be owned by a woman and the rest co-owned.

Computer Database **Exercises**

5-70. The National Federation of Independent Business (NFIB) survey contacted 130 small firms. One of the many inquiries was to determine the number of employees the firms had. The file titled **Employees** contains the responses by the firms. The number of employees was grouped into the following categories: (1) fewer than 20; (2) 20–99; (3) 100–499; and (4) 500 or more.

a. Determine the number of firms in each of these categories.

b. If the NFIB contacts 25 of these firms to gather more information, determine the probability that it will choose the following number of firms in each category: (1) 22, (2) 2, (3) 1, and (4) 0.

c. Calculate the probability that it will choose all of the firms from those businesses with fewer than 20 workers.

5-71. Cliff Summey is the quality-assurance engineer for Sticks and Stones Billiard Supply, a manufacturer of billiard supplies. One of the items that Sticks and Stones produces is sets of pocket billiard balls. Cliff has been monitoring the finish of the pocket billiard balls. He is concerned that sets of billiard balls have been shipped with an increasing number of scratches. The company's goal is to have no more than an average of one scratch per set of pocket billiard balls. A set contains 16 balls. Over the last week, Cliff selected a sample of 48 billiard balls and inspected them to determine the number of scratches. The data collected by Cliff are displayed in the file called **Poolball**.

a. Determine the number of scratches in the sample.

b. Calculate the average number of scratches for 48 pocket billiard balls if Sticks and Stones has met its goal.

c. Determine the probability that there would be at least as many scratches observed per set of pocket billiard balls if Sticks and Stones has met its goal.

d. Based on the sample evidence, does it appear that Sticks and Stones has met its goal? Provide statistical reasons for your conclusion.

Visual Summary

Chapter 5: A **random variable** can take on values that are either discrete or continuous. This chapter has focused on discrete random variables where the potential values are usually integer values. Examples of discrete random variables include the number of defects in a sample of twenty parts, the number of customers who purchase Coca-Cola rather than Pepsi when 100 customers are observed, the number of days late a shipment will be when the product is shipped from India to the United States, or the number of female managers who are promoted from a pool of 30 females and 60 males at a Fortune 500 company. The probabilities associated with the individual values of a random variable form the probability distribution. The most frequently used discrete probability distributions are the **binomial distribution** and the **Poisson distribution**.

5.1 Introduction to Discrete Probability Distributions (pg. 183–190)

Summary

A **discrete random** variable can assume only a finite number of values or an infinite sequence of values such as 0, 1, 2,.... The mean of a discrete random variable is called the **expected value** and represents the long-run average value for the random variable. The graph of a discrete random variable looks like a histogram with the values of the random variable presented on the horizontal axis and the bars above the values having heights corresponding to the probability of the outcome occurring. The sum of the individual probabilities sum to one.

> **Outcome 1.** Be able to calculate and interpret the expected value of a discrete random variable

5.2 The Binomial Probability Distribution (pg. 190–204)

Summary

The **binomial distribution** applies when an experimental trial has only two possible outcomes called *success* and *failure*, the probability of success remains constant from trial to trial, the trials are **independent**, and there are a fixed number of identical trials being considered. The probabilities for a binomial distribution can be calculated using **Equation 5.4**, derived from the **binomial table** in the appendix, or found using Excel or Minitab. The expected value of the binomial distribution is found by multiplying n, the number of trials, by p, the probability of a success on any one trial. The shape of a binomial distribution depends on the sample size (number of trials) and p, the probability of a success. When p is close to .50, the binomial distribution will be fairly symmetric and bell shaped. Even when p is near 0 or 1, if n, the sample size, is large, the binomial distribution will still be fairly symmetric and bell shaped.

> **Outcome 2.** Be able to apply the binomial distribution to business decision-making situations

5.3 Other Discrete Probability Distributions (pg. 204–216)

Summary

Although the **binomial distribution** may be the most often applied discrete distribution for business decision makers, the **Poisson distribution** and the **hypergeometric distribution** are also frequently employed. The Poisson distribution is used in situations where the value of the random variable is found by counting the number of occurrences within a defined segment of time or space. If you know the mean number of occurrences per segment, you can use the Poisson formula, the Poisson tables in the appendix, or software such as Excel or Minitab to find the probability of any specific number of occurrences within the segment. The Poisson distribution is often used to describe the number of customers who arrive at a service facility in a specific amount of time. The **hypergeometric** distribution is used in situations where the sample size is large relative to the size of the population and the sampling is done without replacement.

> **Outcome 3.** Be able to compute probabilities for the Poisson and hypergeometric distributions and apply these distributions to decision-making situations

Conclusion

Business applications involving discrete random variables are very common in business situations. The probabilities for each possible outcome of the discrete random variable form the discrete probability distribution. The expected value of a discrete probability distribution is the mean and represents the long-run average value of the random variable. Chapter 5 has introduced three specific discrete random variables that are frequently used in business situations: binomial distribution, Poisson distribution, and the hypergeometric distribution.

Equations

(5.1) Expected Value of a Discrete Probability Distribution pg. 185

$$E(x) = \Sigma x P(x)$$

(5.2) Standard Deviation of a Discrete Probability Distribution pg. 185

$$\sigma_x = \sqrt{\Sigma[x - E(x)]^2 P(x)}$$

(5.3) Counting Rule for Combinations pg. 193

$$C_x^n = \frac{n!}{x!(n-x)!}$$

(5.4) Binomial Formula pg. 194

$$P(x) = \frac{n!}{x!(n-x)!} p^x q^{n-x}$$

(5.5) Expected Value of a Binomial Distribution pg. 197

$$\mu_x = E(x) = np$$

(5.6) Standard Deviation of the Binomial Distribution pg. 199

$$\sigma = \sqrt{npq}$$

(5.7) Poisson Probability Distribution pg. 205

$$P(x) = \frac{(\lambda t)^x e^{-\lambda t}}{x!}$$

(5.8) Standard Deviation of the Poisson Distribution pg. 208

$$\sigma = \sqrt{\lambda t}$$

(5.9) Hypergeometric Distribution (Two Possible Outcomes per Trial) pg. 211

$$P(x) = \frac{C_{n-x}^{N-X} \cdot C_x^X}{C_n^N}$$

(5.10) Hypergeometric Distribution (k Possible Outcomes per Trial) pg. 213

$$P(x_1, x_2, \ldots, x_k) = \frac{C_{x_1}^{X_1} \cdot C_{x_2}^{X_2} \cdot C_{x_3}^{X_3} \cdot \ldots \cdot C_{x_k}^{X_K}}{C_n^N}$$

Key Terms

Binomial Probability Distribution
  Characteristics pg. 190
Continuous random variable pg. 183

Counting rule for combinations pg. 192
Discrete random variable pg. 183
Expected value pg. 184

Hypergeometric distribution pg. 210
Random variable pg. 183
Poisson distribution pg. 204

Chapter Exercises   MyStatLab

Conceptual Questions

5-72. Three discrete distributions were discussed in this chapter. Each was defined by a random variable that measured the number of successes. To apply these distributions, you must know which one to use. Describe the distinguishing characteristics for each distribution.

5-73. How is the shape of the binomial distribution changed for a given value of p as the sample size is increased? Discuss.

5-74. Discuss the basic differences and similarities between the binomial distribution and the Poisson distribution.

5-75. Beginning statistics students are often puzzled by two characteristics of distributions in this chapter: (1) The trials are independent, and (2) the probability of a success remains constant from trial to trial. Students often think these two characteristics are the same. The questions in this exercise point out the difference. Consider a hypergeometric distribution where $N = 3, X = 2$, and $n = 2$.
  a. Mathematically demonstrate that the trials for this experiment are dependent by calculating the probability of obtaining a success on the second

trial if the first trial resulted in a success. Repeat this calculation if the first trial was a failure. Use these two probabilities to prove that the trials are dependent.
  b. Now calculate the probability that a success is obtained on each of the three respective trials and, therefore, demonstrate that the trials are dependent but that the probability of a success is constant from trial to trial.

5-76. Consider an experiment in which a sample of size $n = 5$ is taken from a binomial distribution.
  a. Calculate the probability of each value of the random variable for the probability of a success equal to (1) 0.1, (2) 0.25, (3) 0.50, (4) 0.75, and (5) 0.9.
  b. Which probabilities produced a right-skewed distribution? Why?
  c. Which probability of a success yielded a symmetric distribution? Why?
  d. Which probabilities produced a left-skewed distribution? Discuss why.

Business Applications

5-77. The McMillan Newspaper Company sometimes makes printing errors in its advertising and is forced to provide corrected advertising in the next issue of the paper. The managing editor has done a study of this problem and found the following data:

No. of Errors x	Relative Frequency
0	0.56
1	0.21
2	0.13
3	0.07
4	0.03

a. Using the relative frequencies as probabilities, what is the expected number of errors? Interpret what this value means to the managing editor.

b. Compute the variance and standard deviation for the number of errors and explain what these values measure.

5-78. The Ziteck Corporation buys parts from international suppliers. One part is currently being purchased from a Malaysian supplier under a contract that calls for at most 5% of the 10,000 parts to be defective. When a shipment arrives, Ziteck randomly samples 10 parts. If it finds 2 or fewer defectives in the sample, it keeps the shipment; otherwise, it returns the entire shipment to the supplier.

a. Assuming that the conditions for the binomial distribution are satisfied, what is the probability that the sample will lead Ziteck to keep the shipment if the defect rate is actually 0.05?

b. Suppose the supplier is actually sending Ziteck 10% defects. What is the probability that the sample will lead Ziteck to accept the shipment anyway?

c. Comment on this sampling plan (sample size and accept/reject point). Do you think it favors either Ziteck or the supplier? Discuss.

5-79. California-based Wagner Foods, Inc., has a process that inserts fruit juice into 24-ounce containers. When the process is in control, half the cans actually contain more than 24 ounces and half contain less. Suppose a quality inspector has just randomly sampled nine cans and found that all nine had more than 24 ounces. Calculate the probability that this result would occur if the filling process was actually still in control. Based on this probability, what conclusion might be reached? Discuss.

5-80. Your company president has told you that the company experiences product returns at the rate of two per month with the number of product returns distributed as a Poisson random variable. Determine the probability that next month there will be

a. no returns

b. one return

c. two returns

d. more than two returns

e. In the last three months your company has had only one month in which the number of returns was at most two. Calculate the probability of this event occurring. What will you tell the president of your

company concerning the return rate? Make sure you support your statement with something other than opinion.

5-81. The Defense Department has recently advertised for bids for producing a new night-vision binocular. Vista Optical has decided to submit a bid for the contract. The first step was to supply a sample of binoculars for the army to test at its Kentucky development grounds. Vista makes a superior night-vision binocular. However, the 4 sent to the army for testing were taken from a development-lab project of 20 units that contained 4 defectives. The army has indicated it will reject any manufacturer that submits 1 or more defective binoculars. What is the probability that this mistake has cost Vista any chance for the contract?

5-82. VERCOR provides merger and acquisition consultants to assist corporations when owners decide to offer their business for sale. One of its news releases, "Tax Audit Frequency Is Rising," written by David L. Perkins Jr., a VERCOR partner, and which originally appeared in *The Business Owner,* indicated that the proportion of the largest businesses, those corporations with assets of $10 million and over, that were audited was 0.17.

a. One member of VERCOR's board of directors is on the board of directors of four other large corporations. Calculate the expected number of these five corporations that should get audited, assuming selection is random.

b. Three of the five corporations were actually audited. Determine the probability that at least three of the five corporations would be audited if 17% of large corporations are audited. (Assume random selection.)

c. The board member is concerned that the corporations have been singled out to be audited by the Internal Revenue Service (IRS). Respond to these thoughts using probability and statistical logic.

5-83. Stafford Production, Inc., is concerned with the quality of the parts it purchases that will be used in the end items it assembles. Part number 34-78D is used in the company's new laser printer. The parts are sensitive to dust and can easily be damaged in shipment even if they are acceptable when they leave the vendor's plant. In a shipment of four parts, the purchasing agent has assessed the following probability distribution for the number of defective products:

x	$P(x)$
0	0.20
1	0.20
2	0.20
3	0.20
4	0.20

a. What is the expected number of defectives in a shipment of four parts? Discuss what this value really means to Stafford Production, Inc.

b. Compute and interpret the standard deviation of the number of defective parts in a shipment of four.

c. Examine the probabilities as assessed and indicate why this probability distribution might be called a uniform distribution. Provide some reasons why the probabilities might all be equal, as they are in this case.

5-84. Bach Photographs takes school pictures and charges only $0.99 for a sitting, which consists of six poses. The company then makes up three packages that are offered to the parents, who have a choice of buying 0, 1, 2, or all 3 of the packages. Based on his experience in the business, Bill Bach has assessed the following probabilities of the number of packages that might be purchased by a parent:

No. of Packages x	P(x)
0	0.30
1	0.40
2	0.20
3	0.10

a. What is the expected number of packages to be purchased by each parent?

b. What is the standard deviation for the random variable, x?

c. Suppose all of the picture packages are to be priced at the same level. How much should they be priced if Bach Photographs wants to break even? Assume that the production costs are $3.00 per package. Remember that the sitting charge is $0.99.

5-85. The managing partner for Westwood One Investment Managers, Inc., gave a public seminar in which she discussed a number of issues, including investment risk analysis. In that seminar, she reminded people that the coefficient of variation often can be used as a measure of risk of an investment. (See Chapter 3 for a review of the coefficient of variation.) To demonstrate her point, she used two hypothetical stocks as examples. She let x equal the change in assets for a $1,000.00 investment in stock 1 and y reflect the change in assets for a $1,000.00 investment in stock 2. She showed the seminar participants the following probability distributions:

x	P(x)	Y	P(y)
−$1,000.00	0.10	−$1,000.00	0.20
0.00	0.10	0.00	0.40
500.00	0.30	500.00	0.30
1,000.00	0.30	1,000.00	0.05
2,000.00	0.20	2,000.00	0.05

a. Compute the expected values for random variables x and y.

b. Compute the standard deviations for random variables x and y.

c. Recalling that the coefficient of variation is determined by the ratio of the standard deviation over the mean, compute the coefficient of variation for each random variable.

d. Referring to part c, suppose the seminar director said that the first stock was riskier since its standard deviation was greater than the standard deviation of the second stock. How would you respond? (*Hint*: What do the coefficients of variation imply?)

5-86. Simmons Market Research conducted a national consumer study of 13,787 respondents. The respondents were asked to indicate the primary source of the vitamins or mineral supplements they consume. Thirty-five percent indicated a multiple formula was their choice. A subset of 20 respondents who used multiple vitamins was selected for further questioning. Half of them used a One A Day vitamin; the rest used generic brands. Of this subset, 4 were asked to fill out a more complete health survey.

a. Calculate the probability that the final selection of 4 subset members were all One A Day multiple vitamin users.

b. Compute the number of One A Day users expected to be selected.

c. Calculate the probability that fewer than half of the final selection were One A Day users.

5-87. The 700-room Westin Charlotte offers a premiere uptown location in the heart of the city's financial district. On a busy weekend, the hotel has 20 rooms that are not occupied. Suppose that smoking is allowed in 8 of the rooms. A small tour group arrives, which has four smokers and six nonsmokers. The desk clerk randomly selects 10 rooms and gives the keys to the tour guide to distribute to the travelers.

a. Compute the probability that the tour guide will have the correct mix of rooms so that all members of the tour group will receive a room that accommodates their smoking preferences.

b. Determine the probability that the tour guide will have to assign at least one nonsmoker to a smoking room.

c. Determine the probability that the tour guide will have to assign at least one smoker to a nonsmoking room.

Computer Database **Exercises**

5-88. A 23-mile stretch of a two-lane highway east of Paso Robles, California, was once considered a "death trap" by residents of San Luis Obispo County. Formerly known as "Blood Alley," Highway 46 gained notoriety for the number of fatalities (29) and crashes over a 240-week period. More than two-thirds involved head-on collisions. The file titled **Crashes** contains the simulated number of fatal crashes during this time period.

a. Determine the average number of crashes in the 240 weeks.

b. Calculate the probability that at least 19 crashes would occur over the 240-week period if the average number of crashes per week was as calculated in part a.

c. Calculate the probability that at least 19 crashes would occur over a five-year period if the average number of crashes per week was as calculated in part a.

d. A coalition of state, local, and private organizations devised a coordinated and innovative approach to dramatically reduce deaths and injuries on this road. During the 16 months before and after completion of the project, fatal crashes were reduced to zero. Calculate the probability that there would be no fatal crashes if the mean number of fatal crashes was not changed by the coalition. Does it appear that the average number of fatal accidents has indeed decreased?

5-89. American Household, SM Inc., produces a wide array of home safety and security products. One of its products is the First Alert SA302 Dual Sensor Remote Control Smoke Alarm. As part of its quality control program, it constantly tests to assure that the alarms work. A change in the manufacturing process requires the company to determine the proportion of alarms that fail the quality control tests. Each day, 20 smoke alarms are taken from the production line and tested, and the number of defectives is recorded. A file titled **Smokeless** contains the possible results from the last 90 days of testing.

a. Compute the proportion of defective smoke alarms.

b. Calculate the expected number and the standard deviation of defectives for each day's testing. Assume the proportion of defectives is what was computed in part a. (*Hint*: Recall the formulas for the mean and the standard deviation for a binomial distribution.)

c. To make sure that the proportion of defectives does not change, the quality control manager wants to establish control limits that are 3 standard deviations above the mean and 3 standard deviations below the mean. Calculate these limits.

d. Determine the probability that a randomly chosen set of 20 smoke alarms would have a number of defectives that was beyond the control limits established in part c.

5-90. Covercraft manufactures covers to protect automobile interiors and finishes. Its Block-It 200 Series fabric has a limited two-year warranty. Periodic testing is done to determine if the warranty policy should be changed. One such study examined those covers that became unserviceable while still under warranty. Data that could be produced by such a study are contained in the file titled **Covers**. The data represent the number of months a cover was used until it became unserviceable. Covercraft might want to examine more carefully the covers that became unserviceable while still under warranty. Specifically, it wants to examine those that became unserviceable before they had been in use one year.

a. Determine the number of covers that became unserviceable before they had been in use less than a year and a half.

b. If Covercraft quality-control staff selects 20 of the covers at random, determine the probability that none of them will have failed before they had been in service a year and a half.

c. If Covercraft quality control staff needs to examine at least 5 of the failed covers, determine the probability that they will obtain this many.

Case 5.1

SaveMor Pharmacies

A common practice now is for large retail pharmacies to buy the customer base from smaller, independent pharmacies. The way this works is that the buyer requests to see the customer list along with the buying history. The buyer then makes an offer based on its projection of how many of the seller's customers will move their business to the buyer's pharmacy and on how many dollars of new business will come to the buyer as a result of the purchase. Once the deal is made, the buyer and seller usually send out a joint letter to the seller's customers explaining the transaction and informing them that their prescription files have been transferred to the purchasing company.

The problem is that there is no guarantee regarding what proportion of the existing customers will make the switch to the buying company. That is the issue facing Heidi Fendenand, acquisitions manager for SaveMor Pharmacies. SaveMor has the opportunity to purchase the 6,780-person customer base from Hubbard Pharmacy in San Jose, California. Based on previous acquisitions,

Heidi believes that if 70% or more of the customers will make the switch, then the deal is favorable to SaveMor. However, if 60% or less make the move to SaveMor, then the deal will be a bad one and she would recommend against it.

Quincy Kregthorpe, a research analyst who works for Heidi, has suggested that SaveMor take a new approach to this acquisition decision. He has suggested that SaveMor contact a random sample of 20 Hubbard customers telling them of the proposed sale and asking them if they will be willing to switch their business to SaveMor. Quincy has suggested that if 15 or more of the 20 customers indicate that they would make the switch, then SaveMor should go ahead with the purchase. Otherwise, it should decline the deal or negotiate a lower purchase price.

Heidi liked this idea and contacted Cal Hubbard, Hubbard's owner, to discuss the idea of surveying 20 randomly selected customers. Cal was agreeable as long as only these 20 customers would be told about the potential sale.

Before taking the next step, Heidi met with Quincy to discuss the plan one more time. She was concerned that the proposed sampling plan might have too high a probability of rejecting the purchase deal even if it was a positive one from SaveMor's viewpoint. On the other hand, she was concerned that the plan might also have a high probability of accepting the purchase deal when in fact it would be unfavorable to SaveMor. After discussing these concerns for over an hour, Quincy finally offered to perform an evaluation of the sampling plan.

Required Tasks:

1. Compute the probability that the sampling plan will provide a result that suggests that SaveMor should reject the deal

even if the true proportion of all customers who would switch is actually 0.70.

2. Compute the probability that the sampling plan will provide a result that suggests that SaveMor should accept the deal even if the true proportion of all customers who would switch is actually only 0.60.

3. Write a short report to Heidi outlining the sampling plan, the assumptions on which the evaluation of the sampling plan has been based, and the conclusions regarding the potential effectiveness of the sampling plan. The report should make a recommendation about whether Heidi should go through with the idea of using the sampling plan.

Case 5.2

Arrowmark Vending

Arrowmark Vending has the contract to supply pizza at all home football games for a university in the Big 12 athletic conference. It is a constant challenge at each game to determine how many pizzas to have available at the games. Tom Kealey, operations manager for Arrowmark, has determined that his fixed cost of providing pizzas, whether he sells 1 pizza or 4,000 pizzas, is $1,000. This cost includes hiring employees to work at the concession booths, hiring extra employees to cook the pizzas the day of the game, delivering

them to the game, and advertising during the game. He believes that this cost should be equally allocated between two types of pizzas.

Tom has determined that he will supply only two types of pizzas: plain cheese and pepperoni-and-cheese combo. His cost to make a plain cheese pizza is $4.50 each, and his cost to make pepperoni-and-cheese combo is $5.00 each. Both pizzas will sell for $9.00 at the game. Unsold pizzas have no value and are donated to a local shelter for the homeless.

Experience has shown the following demand distributions for the two types of pizza at home games:

Plain Cheese Demand	Probability	Pepperoni-and-Cheese Demand	Probability
200	0.10	300	0.10
300	0.15	400	0.20
400	0.15	500	0.25
500	0.20	600	0.25
600	0.20	700	0.15
700	0.10	800	0.05
800	0.05		
900	0.05		

Required Tasks:

1. For each type of pizza, determine the profit (or loss) associated with producing at each possible demand level. For instance, determine the profit if 200 plain cheese pizzas are produced and 200 are demanded. What is the profit if 200 plain cheese pizzas are produced but 300 were demanded, and so on?

2. Compute the expected profit associated with each possible production level (assuming Tom will only produce at one of the possible demand levels) for each type of pizza.

3. Prepare a short report that provides Tom with the information regarding how many of each type of pizza he should produce if he wants to achieve the highest expected profit from pizza sales at the game.

Case 5.3

Boise Cascade Corporation

At the Boise Cascade Corporation, lumber mill logs arrive by truck and are scaled (measured to determine the number of board feet) before they are dumped into a log pond. Figure C-5.3 illustrates the basic flow. The mill manager must determine how many

scale stations to have open during various times of the day. If he has too many stations open, the scalers will have excessive idle time and the cost of scaling will be unnecessarily high. On the other hand, if too few scale stations are open, some log trucks will have to wait.

FIGURE C-5.3

Truck Flow for Boise Cascade
Mill Example

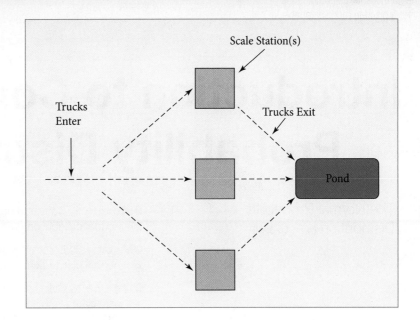

The manager has studied the truck arrival patterns and has determined that during the first open hour (7:00 A.M.–8:00 A.M.), the trucks randomly arrive at 12 per hour on average. Each scale station can scale 6 trucks per hour (10 minutes each). If the manager knew how many trucks would arrive during the hour, he would know how many scale stations to have open.

| 0 to 6 trucks: | open 1 scale station |
| 7 to 12 trucks: | open 2 scale stations etc. |

However, the number of trucks is a random variable and is uncertain. Your task is to provide guidance for the decision.

chapter 6

Chapter 6 Quick Prep Links

- **Review** the methods for determining the probability for a discrete random variable in Chapter 5.

- **Review** the discussion of the mean and standard deviation in Sections 3.1 and 3.2.

- **Review** the concept of z-scores outlined in Section 3.3.

Introduction to Continuous Probability Distributions

6.1 The Normal Probability Distribution (pg. 225–240)

← **Outcome 1.** Convert a normal distribution to a standard normal distribution.

Outcome 2. Determine probabilities using the standard normal distribution.

Outcome 3. Calculate values of the random variable associated with specified probabilities from a normal distribution.

6.2 Other Continuous Probability Distributions (pg. 240–247)

← **Outcome 4.** Calculate probabilities associated with a uniformly distributed random variable.

Outcome 5. Determine probabilities using an exponential probability distribution.

Why you need to know

You will encounter many business situations in which the random variable of interest is discrete and in which probability distributions such as the binomial, the Poisson, or the hypergeometric will be useful for analyzing decision situations. Chapter 5 introduced these distributions and provided many examples and applications. But there will also be many situations in which the random variable of interest is *continuous* rather than discrete. For instance, the managers at Harley Davidson might be interested in a measure called throughput time, which is the time it takes from when a motorcycle is started on the manufacturing line until it is completed. Lots of factors can affect the throughput time, including breakdowns, need for rework, the type of accessories added to the motorcycle, and worker productivity. The managers might be interested in determining the probability that the throughput time will be between 3.5 and 5.0 hours. In this case, time is the random variable of interest and is continuous.

A pharmaceutical company may be interested in the probability that a new drug will reduce blood pressure by more than 20 points for patients. Blood pressure is the continuous random variable of interest. The Kellogg's Cereal company could be interested in the probability that cereal boxes labeled as containing 16 ounces will actually contain at least that much cereal. Here, the variable of interest is weight, which can be measured on a continuous scale.

In each of these examples, the value of the variable of interest is determined by measuring (measuring the time required to make a motorcycle, measuring the blood pressure reading, measuring the weight of cereal in a box). In every instance, the number of possible values for the variable is limited only by the capacity of the measuring device. The constraints imposed by the measuring devices produce a finite number of outcomes. In these and similar situations, a continuous probability distribution can be used to approximate the distribution of possible outcomes for the random variables. The approximation is appropriate when the number of possible outcomes is large. Chapter 6 introduces three specific continuous probability distributions of particular importance for decision making and the study of business statistics. The first of these, the *normal distribution*, is by far the most important because a great many applications involve random variables that possess the characteristics of the normal distribution. In addition, many of the topics in the remaining chapters of this textbook dealing with statistical estimation and hypothesis testing are based on the normal distribution.

Rafa Irusta/Shutterstock

In addition to the normal distribution, you will be introduced to the uniform distribution and the exponential distribution. Both are important continuous probability distributions and have many applications in business decision making. You need to have a firm understanding and working knowledge of all three continuous probability distributions introduced in this chapter.

6.1 The Normal Probability Distribution

A Pepsi-Cola can is supposed to contain 12 ounces, but it might actually contain any amount between 11.90 and 12.10 ounces, such as 11.9853 ounces. When the variable of interest, such as the volume of soda in a can, is approximately continuous, the probability distribution associated with the random variable is called a *continuous probability distribution*.

One important difference between discrete and continuous probability distributions involves the calculation of probabilities associated with specific values of the random variable. For instance, in a market research example in which 100 people are surveyed and asked whether they have a positive view of a product, we could use the binomial distribution introduced in Chapter 5 to find the probability of any specific number of positive reviews, such as $P(x = 75)$ or $P(x = 76)$. Although these individual probabilities may be small values, they can be computed because the random variable is discrete. However, if the random variable is continuous, as in the Pepsi-Cola example, there is an uncountable infinite number of possible outcomes for the random variable. Theoretically, the probability of any one of these individual outcomes is zero. That is, $P(x = 11.92) = 0$ or $P(x = 12.05) = 0$. Thus, when you are working with continuous distributions, you will need to find the probability for a range of possible values such as $P(x \leq 11.92)$ or $P(11.92 \leq x \leq 12.0)$. You can also conclude that

$$P(x \leq 11.92) = P(x < 11.92)$$

because we assume that $P(x = 11.92) = 0$.

There are many different continuous probability distributions, but the most important of these is the *normal distribution*.

Normal Distribution

The normal distribution is a bell-shaped distribution with the following properties:

1. It is *unimodal*; that is, the normal distribution peaks at a single value.
2. It is *symmetrical*; this means that the two areas under the curve between the mean and any two points equidistant on either side of the mean are identical. One side of the distribution is the mirror image of the other side.
3. The mean, median, and mode are equal.
4. The normal approaches the horizontal axis on either side of the mean toward plus and minus infinity (∞). In more formal terms, the normal distribution is *asymptotic* to the *x* axis.
5. The amount of variation in the random variable determines the height and spread of the normal distribution.

The Normal Distribution[1]

Figure 6.1 illustrates a typical normal distribution and highlights the normal distribution's characteristics. All normal distributions have the same general shape as the one shown in Figure 6.1. However, they can differ in their mean value and their variation, depending on the situation being considered. The process being represented determines the scale of the horizontal axis. It may be pounds, inches, dollars, or any other attribute

FIGURE 6.1 |

Characteristics of the Normal Distribution

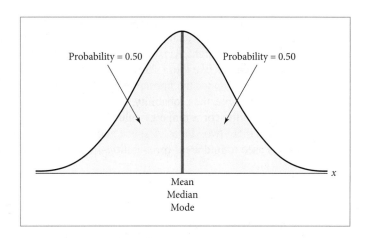

---

[1]It is common to refer to the very large family of normal distributions as "*the* normal distribution."

FIGURE 6.2

Difference between Normal
Distributions

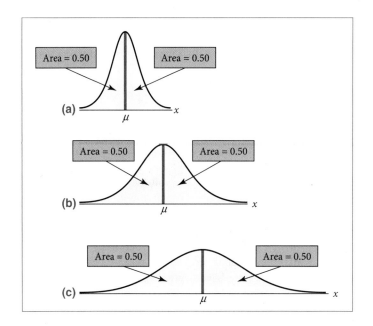

with a continuous measurement. Figure 6.2 shows several normal distributions with different centers and different spreads. Note that the total area (probability) under each normal curve equals 1.

The normal distribution is described by the rather complicated-looking probability density function, shown in Equation 6.1.

Normal Probability Density Function

$$f(x) = \frac{1}{\sigma\sqrt{2\pi}} e^{-(x-\mu)^2/2\sigma^2}$$

(6.1)

where:

x = Any value of the continuous random variable
σ = Population standard deviation
π = 3.14159
e = Base of the natural log = 2.71828
μ = Population mean

To graph the normal distribution, we need to know the mean, μ, and the standard deviation, σ. Placing μ, σ, and a value of the variable, x, into the probability density function, we can calculate a height, $f(x)$, of the density function. If we could try enough x values, we could construct curves like those shown in Figures 6.1 and 6.2.

The area under the normal curve corresponds to probability. Because x is a continuous random variable, the probability, $P(x)$, is equal to 0 for any particular x. However, we can find the probability for a range of values between x_1 and x_2 by finding the area under the curve between these two values. A special normal distribution called the *standard normal distribution* is used to find areas (probabilities) for all normal distributions.

Chapter Outcome 1.

Standard Normal Distribution

A normal distribution that has a mean = 0.0 and a standard deviation = 1.0 The horizontal axis is scaled in z-values that measure the number of standard deviations a point is from the mean. Values above the mean have positive z-values. Values below the mean have negative z-values.

The Standard Normal Distribution

The trick to finding probabilities for a normal distribution is to convert the normal distribution to a **standard normal distribution**.

To convert a normal distribution to a standard normal distribution, the values (x) of the random variable are standardized as outlined previously in Chapter 3. The conversion formula is shown as Equation 6.2.

Standardized Normal z-Value

$$z = \frac{x - \mu}{\sigma}$$ **(6.2)**

where:

z = Scaled value (the number of standard deviations a point x is from the mean)
x = Any point on the horizontal axis
μ = Mean of the specific normal distribution
σ = Standard deviation of the specific normal distribution

Equation 6.2 *scales* any normal distribution axis from its true units (time, weight, dollars, volume, and so forth) to the standard measure referred to as a *z-value*. Thus, any value of the normally distributed continuous random variable can be represented by a unique *z*-value. Positive *z*-values represent corresponding values of the random variable, *x*, that are higher than the population mean. Values of *x* that are less than the population mean will have corresponding *z*-values that are negative.

BUSINESS APPLICATION   **STANDARD NORMAL DISTRIBUTION**

FRUIT PRODUCTION Fruit growers in California and Florida strive for consistency in their products in terms of quality and size. For example, a grower in Florida that specializes in grapefruit has determined that in one orchard, the mean weight of his "King" brand grapefruit is 16 ounces. Suppose after careful analysis, he has determined the grapefruit weight distribution is approximated by a normal distribution with a standard deviation of 4 ounces. Figure 6.3 shows this normal distribution with $\mu = 16$ and $\sigma = 4$.

Three grapefruit were selected from a case in the grower's cold storage. The weights of these three grapefruit were

Grapefruit 1: $x = 16$ ounces

Grapefruit 2: $x = 18.5$ ounces

Grapefruit 3: $x = 9$ ounces

Equation 6.2 is used to convert these values from a normally distributed population with $\mu = 16$ and $\sigma = 4$ to corresponding *z*-values in a standard normal distribution. For Grapefruit 1, we get

$$z = \frac{x - \mu}{\sigma} = \frac{16 - 16}{4} = 0$$

Note, Grapefruit 1 weighed 16 ounces, which happens to be equal to the population mean for all grapefruit. The standardized *z*-value corresponding to the population mean is zero. This indicates that the population mean is 0 standard deviations from itself.

FIGURE 6.3

Distribution of Grapefruit Weights

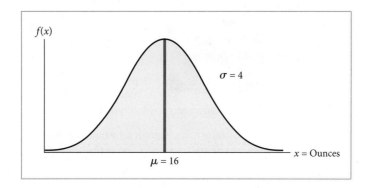

FIGURE 6.4

Standard Normal Distribution

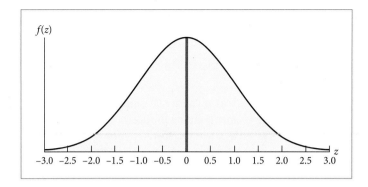

For Grapefruit 2, we get

$$z = \frac{x - \mu}{\sigma} = \frac{18.5 - 16}{4} = 0.63$$

Thus, a grapefruit that weighs 18 ounces is 0.63 standard deviations heavier than the mean for all grapefruit. The standardized z-value for Grapefruit 3 is

$$z = \frac{x - \mu}{\sigma} = \frac{9 - 16}{4} = -1.75$$

This means a grapefruit that weighs only 9 ounces is 1.75 standard deviations below the population mean. Note, a negative z-value always indicates the x-value is less than the mean, μ.

The z-value represents the number of standard deviations a point is above or below the population mean. Equation 6.2 can be used to convert any specified value, x, from the population distribution to a corresponding z-value. If the population distribution is normally distributed as shown in Figure 6.3, then the distribution of z-values will also be normally distributed and is called the *standard normal distribution*. Figure 6.4 shows a standard normal distribution where the horizontal axis represents *z-values*.

You can convert the normal distribution to a standard normal distribution and use the standard normal table to find the desired probability. Example 6-1 shows the steps required to do this.

Using the Standard Normal Table The *standard normal table* in Appendix D provides probabilities (or areas under the normal curve) associated with many different z-values. The standard normal table is constructed so that the probabilities provided represent the chance of a value being between a positive z-value and its population mean, 0.

The standard normal table is also reproduced in Table 6.1. This table provides probabilities for z-values between $z = 0.00$ and $z = 3.09$. Note, because the normal distribution is symmetric, the probability of a value being between a positive z-value and its population mean, 0, is the same as that of a value being between a negative z-value and its population mean, 0. So we can use one standard normal table for both positive and negative z-values.

Chapter Outcome 2.

How to do it (Example 6-1)

Using the Normal Distribution

If a continuous random variable is distributed as a normal distribution, the distribution is symmetrically distributed around the mean and is described by the mean and standard deviation. To find probabilities associated with a normally distributed random variable, use the following steps:

1. Determine the mean, μ, and the standard deviation, σ.

2. Define the event of interest, such as $P(x \geq x_1)$.

3. Convert the normal distribution to the standard normal distribution using Equation 6.2:

$$z = \frac{x - \mu}{\sigma}$$

4. Use the standard normal distribution table to find the probability associated with the calculated z-value. The table gives the probability between the z-value and the mean.

5. Determine the desired probability using the knowledge that the probability of a value being on either side of the mean is 0.50 and the total probability under the normal distribution is 1.0.

EXAMPLE 6-1	**USING THE STANDARD NORMAL TABLE**

claudiozacc / Fotolia

Airline Passenger Loading Times After completing a study, the Chicago O'Hare Airport managers have concluded that the time needed to get passengers loaded onto an airplane is normally distributed with a mean equal to 15 minutes and a standard deviation equal to 3.5 minutes. Recently one airplane required 22 minutes to get passengers on board and ready for takeoff. To find the probability that a flight will take 22 or more minutes to get passengers loaded, you can use the following steps:

Step 1 Determine the mean and standard deviation for the random variable.

The parameters of the probability distribution are

$$\mu = 15 \quad \text{and} \quad \sigma = 3.5$$

Step 2   Define the event of interest.

The flight load time is 22 minutes. We wish to find

$$P(x \geq 22) = ?$$

Step 3   Convert the random variable to a standardized value using Equation 6.2.

$$z = \frac{x - \mu}{\sigma} = \frac{22 - 15}{3.5} = 2.00$$

Step 4   Find the probability associated with the z-value in the standard normal distribution table (Table 6.1 or Appendix D).

To find the probability associated with $z = 2.00$, [i.e., $P(0 \leq z \leq 2.00)$], do the following:

1. Go down the left-hand column of the table to $z = 2.0$.
2. Go across the top row of the table to the column 0.00 for the second decimal place in $z = 2.00$.
3. Find the value where the row and column intersect.

The value, 0.4772, is the probability that a value in a normal distribution will lie between the mean and 2.00 standard deviations above the mean.

Step 5   Determine the probability for the event of interest.

$$P(x \geq 22) = ?$$

We know that the area on each side of the mean under the normal distribution is equal to 0.50. In Step 4, we computed the probability associated with $z = 2.00$ to be 0.4772, which is the probability of a value falling between the mean and 2.00 standard deviations above the mean. Then, the probability we are looking for is

$$P(x \geq 22) = P(z \geq 2.00) = 0.5000 - 0.4772 = 0.0228$$

>> **END EXAMPLE**

TRY PROBLEM 6-2 (pg. 236)

BUSINESS APPLICATION   **THE NORMAL DISTRIBUTION**

FRUIT PRODUCTION (*CONTINUED*) Earlier, we discussed the situation involving the fruit grower in Florida. The grapefruit for this grower's orchard have a mean weight of 16 ounces. We assumed the distribution for grapefruit weight was normally distributed with $\mu = 16$ and $\sigma = 4$. A local television station that runs a consumer advocacy program reported that a grapefruit from this grower was selected and weighed only 14 ounces. The reporter said she thought it should have been heavier if the mean weight is supposed to be 16 ounces. The grower, when interviewed, said that he thought the probability was quite high that a grapefruit would weigh 14 or more ounces. To check his statement out, we want to find

$$P(x \geq 14) = ?$$

This probability corresponds to the area under a normal distribution to the right of $x = 14$ ounces. This will be the sum of the area between $x = 14$ and $\mu = 16$ plus the area to the right of $\mu = 16$. Refer to Figure 6.5.

TABLE 6.1 | **Standard Normal Distribution Table**

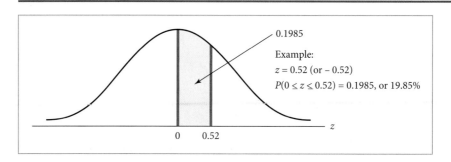

z	.00	.01	.02	.03	.04	.05	.06	.07	.08	.09
0.0	.0000	.0040	.0080	.0120	.0160	.0199	.0239	.0279	.0319	.0359
0.1	.0398	.0438	.0478	.0517	.0557	.0596	.0636	.0675	.0714	.0753
0.2	.0793	.0832	.0871	.0910	.0948	.0987	.1026	.1064	.1103	.1141
0.3	.1179	.1217	.1255	.1293	.1331	.1368	.1406	.1443	.1480	.1517
0.4	.1554	.1591	.1628	.1664	.1700	.1736	.1772	.1808	.1844	.1879
0.5	.1915	.1950	.1985	.2019	.2054	.2088	.2123	.2157	.2190	.2224
0.6	.2257	.2291	.2324	.2357	.2389	.2422	.2454	.2486	.2517	.2549
0.7	.2580	.2611	.2642	.2673	.2704	.2734	.2764	.2794	.2823	.2852
0.8	.2881	.2910	.2939	.2967	.2995	.3023	.3051	.3078	.3106	.3133
0.9	.3159	.3186	.3212	.3238	.3264	.3289	.3315	.3340	.3365	.3389
1.0	.3413	.3438	.3461	.3485	.3508	.3531	.3554	.3577	.3599	.3621
1.1	.3643	.3665	.3686	.3708	.3729	.3749	.3770	.3790	.3810	.3830
1.2	.3849	.3869	.3888	.3907	.3925	.3944	.3962	.3980	.3997	.4015
1.3	.4032	.4049	.4066	.4082	.4099	.4115	.4131	.4147	.4162	.4177
1.4	.4192	.4207	.4222	.4236	.4251	.4265	.4279	.4292	.4306	.4319
1.5	.4332	.4345	.4357	.4370	.4382	.4394	.4406	.4418	.4429	.4441
1.6	.4452	.4463	.4474	.4484	.4495	.4505	.4515	.4525	.4535	.4545
1.7	.4554	.4564	.4573	.4582	.4591	.4599	.4608	.4616	.4625	.4633
1.8	.4641	.4649	.4656	.4664	.4671	.4678	.4686	.4693	.4699	.4706
1.9	.4713	.4719	.4726	.4732	.4738	.4744	.4750	.4756	.4761	.4767
2.0	.4772	.4778	.4783	.4788	.4793	.4798	.4803	.4808	.4812	.4817
2.1	.4821	.4826	.4830	.4834	.4838	.4842	.4846	.4850	.4854	.4857
2.2	.4861	.4864	.4868	.4871	.4875	.4878	.4881	.4884	.4887	.4890
2.3	.4893	.4896	.4898	.4901	.4904	.4906	.4909	.4911	.4913	.4916
2.4	.4918	.4920	.4922	.4925	.4927	.4929	.4931	.4932	.4934	.4936
2.5	.4938	.4940	.4941	.4943	.4945	.4946	.4948	.4949	.4951	.4952
2.6	.4953	.4955	.4956	.4957	.4959	.4960	.4961	.4962	.4963	.4964
2.7	.4965	.4966	.4967	.4968	.4969	.4970	.4971	.4972	.4973	.4974
2.8	.4974	.4975	.4976	.4977	.4977	.4978	.4979	.4979	.4980	.4981
2.9	.4981	.4982	.4982	.4983	.4984	.4984	.4985	.4985	.4986	.4986
3.0	.4987	.4987	.4987	.4988	.4988	.4989	.4989	.4989	.4990	.4990

To illustrate: 19.85% of the area under a normal curve lies between the mean, μ, and a point 0.52 standard deviation units away.

FIGURE 6.5 |

Probabilities from the Normal
Curve for Fruit Production

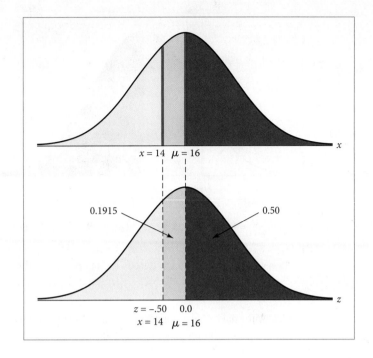

To find this probability, you first convert $x = 14$ ounces to its corresponding z-value. This is equivalent to determining the number of standard deviations $x = 14$ is from the population mean of $\mu = 16$. Equation 6.2 is used to do this as follows:

$$z = \frac{x - \mu}{\sigma} = \frac{14 - 16}{4} = -0.50$$

Because the normal distribution is symmetrical, even though the z-value is –0.50, we find the desired probability by going to the standard normal distribution table for a positive $z = 0.50$. The probability in the table for $z = 0.50$ corresponds to the probability of a z-value occurring between $z = 0.50$ and $z = 0.00$. This is the same as the probability of a z-value falling between $z = -0.50$ and $z = 0.00$. Thus, from the standard normal table (Table 6.1 or Appendix D), we get

$$P(-0.50 \leq z \leq 0.00) = 0.1915$$

This is the area between $x = 14$ and $\mu = 16$ in Figure 6.5. We now add 0.1915 to 0.5000 $[P(x > 16 = 0.5000)]$. Therefore, the probability that a grapefruit will weigh 14 or more ounces is

$$P(x \geq 14) = 0.1915 + 0.5000 = 0.6915$$

This is illustrated in Figure 6.5. Thus, there is nearly a 70% chance that a grapefruit will weigh at least 14 ounces.

BUSINESS APPLICATION   **USING THE NORMAL DISTRIBUTION**

GENERAL ELECTRIC COMPANY Several states, including California, have passed legislation requiring automakers to sell a certain percentage of zero-emissions cars within their borders. One current alternative is battery-powered cars. The major problem with battery-operated cars is the limited time they can be driven before the batteries must be recharged. Suppose that General Electric (GE) has developed a Longlife battery pack it claims will power a car at a sustained speed of 45 miles per hour for an average of 8 hours. But of course there will be variations: Some battery packs will last longer and some less than 8 hours. Current data indicate that the standard deviation of battery operation time before a charge is needed is 0.4 hours. Data show a normal distribution of uptime on these battery

FIGURE 6.6

Longlife Battery

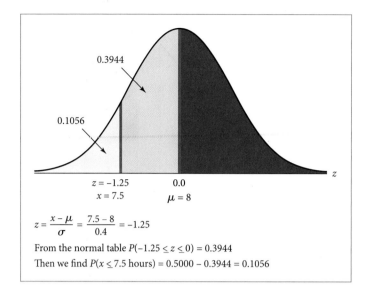

$$z = \frac{x - \mu}{\sigma} = \frac{7.5 - 8}{0.4} = -1.25$$

From the normal table $P(-1.25 \leq z \leq 0) = 0.3944$

Then we find $P(x \leq 7.5 \text{ hours}) = 0.5000 - 0.3944 = 0.1056$

packs. Automakers are concerned that batteries may run short. For example, drivers might find an "8-hour" battery that lasts 7.5 hours or less unacceptable. What are the chances of this happening with the Longlife battery pack?

To calculate the probability the batteries will last 7.5 hours or less, find the appropriate area under the normal curve shown in Figure 6.6. There is approximately 1 chance in 10 that a battery will last 7.5 hours or less when the vehicle is driven at 45 miles per hour.

Suppose this level of reliability is unacceptable to the automakers. Instead of a 10% chance of an "8-hour" battery lasting 7.5 hours or less, the automakers will accept no more than a 2% chance. GE managers ask what the mean uptime would have to be to meet the 2% requirement.

Assuming that uptime is normally distributed, we can answer this question by using the standard normal distribution. However, instead of using the standard normal table to find a probability, we use it in reverse to find the z-value that corresponds to a known probability. Figure 6.7 shows the uptime distribution for the battery packs. Note, the 2% probability is shown in the left tail of the distribution. This is the allowable chance of a battery lasting 7.5 hours or less. We must solve for μ, the mean uptime that will meet this requirement.

1. Go to the body of the standard normal table, where the probabilities are located, and find the probability as close to 0.48 as possible. This is 0.4798.
2. Determine the z-value associated with 0.4798. This is $z = 2.05$. Because we are below the mean, the z is negative. Thus, $z = -2.05$.

FIGURE 6.7

Longlife Battery, Solving for the Mean

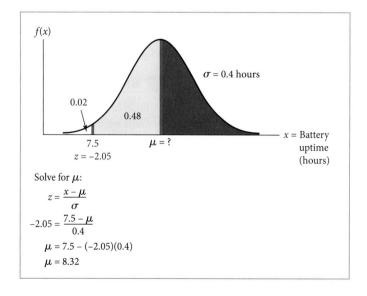

Solve for μ:

$$z = \frac{x - \mu}{\sigma}$$

$$-2.05 = \frac{7.5 - \mu}{0.4}$$

$$\mu = 7.5 - (-2.05)(0.4)$$

$$\mu = 8.32$$

3. The formula for z is

$$z = \frac{x - \mu}{\sigma}$$

4. Substituting the known values, we get

$$-2.05 = \frac{7.5 - \mu}{0.4}$$

5. Solve for μ:

$$\mu = 7.5 - (-2.05)(0.4) = 8.32 \text{ hours}$$

General Electric will need to increase the mean life of the battery pack to 8.32 hours to meet the automakers' requirement that no more than 2% of the batteries fail in 7.5 hours or less.

Chapter Outcome 3. → **BUSINESS APPLICATION** **USING THE NORMAL DISTRIBUTION**

Excel Tutorial

STATE BANK AND TRUST The director of operations for the State Bank and Trust recently performed a study of the time bank customers spent from when they walk into the bank until they complete their banking. The data file **State Bank** contains the data for a sample of 1,045 customers randomly observed over a four-week period. The customers in the survey were limited to those who were there for basic bank business, such as making a deposit or a withdrawal or cashing a check. The histogram in Figure 6.8 shows that the banking times are distributed as an approximate normal distribution.[2]

FIGURE 6.8

Excel 2010 Output for State Bank and Trust Service Times

Excel 2010 Instructions:
1. Open file: **State Bank.xlsx**.
2. Create bins (upper limit of each class).
3. Select **Data > Data Analysis**.
4. Select **Histogram**.
5. Define data and bin ranges.
6. Check **Chart Output**.
7. Define Output Location and click **OK**.
8. Select the chart and right click.
9. Click on **Format Data Series** and set gap width to zero. Add lines to the bars and label axes and title appropriately.

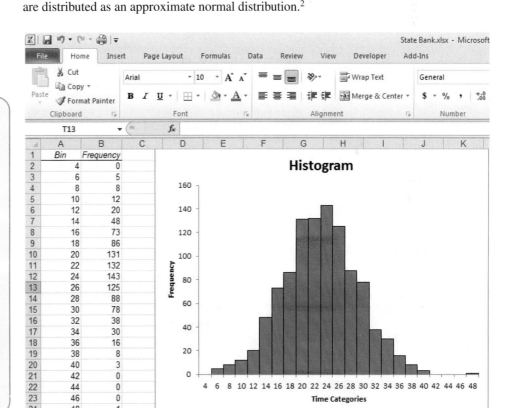

Minitab Instructions (for similar results):
1. Open file: **State Bank**. MTW.
2. Choose **Graph > Histogram**.
3. Click **Simple**.
4. Click **OK**.

5. In **Graph Variables**, enter data column *Service Time*.
6. Click **OK**.

---

[2]A statistical technique known as the chi-square goodness-of-fit test, introduced in Chapter 13, can be used to determine statistically whether the data follow a normal distribution.

FIGURE 6.9

Normal Distribution for the
State Bank and Trust Example

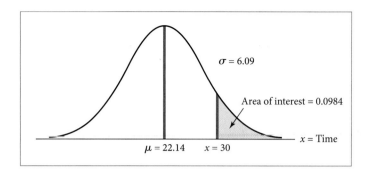

The mean service time for the 1,045 customers was 22.14 minutes, with a standard deviation equal to 6.09 minutes. On the basis of these data, the manager assumes that the service times are normally distributed with $\mu = 22.14$ and $\sigma = 6.09$. Given these assumptions, the manager is considering providing a gift certificate to a local restaurant to any customer who is required to spend more than 30 minutes to complete basic bank business. Before doing this, she is interested in the probability of having to pay off on this offer.

Figure 6.9 shows the theoretical distribution, with the area of interest identified. The manager is interested in finding

$$P(x > 30 \text{ minutes})$$

This can be done manually or with Excel. Figure 6.10 shows the computer output for Excel. The cumulative probability is

$$P(x \leq 30) = 0.9016$$

Then to find the probability of interest, we subtract this value from 1.0, giving

$$P(x \leq 30 \text{ minutes}) = 1.0 - 0.9016 = 0.0984$$

FIGURE 6.10

Excel 2010 Output for State
Bank and Trust

Excel 2010 Instructions:
1. Open a blank worksheet.
2. Select **Formulas**.
3. Click on f_x (*function wizard*).
4. Select the **Statistical** category.
5. Select the **NORM.DIST** function.
6. Fill in the requested information in the template.
7. **True** indicates cumulative probabilities.
8. Click **OK**.

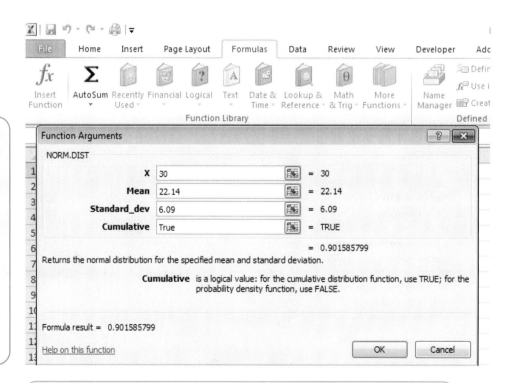

Minitab Instructions (for similar results):
1. Choose **Calc > Probability Distribution > Normal**.
2. Choose **Cumulative probability**.
3. In **Mean**, enter μ.
4. In **Standard deviation**, enter σ.
5. In **Input constant**, enter x.
6. Click **OK**.

Thus, there are just under 10 chances in 100 that the bank would have to give out a gift certificate. Suppose the manager believes this policy is too liberal. She wants to set the time limit so that the chance of giving out the gift is at most only 5%. You can use the standard normal table or the NORM.INV function in Excel to find the new limit.[3] To use the table, we first consider that the manager wants a 5% area in the upper tail of the normal distribution. This will leave

$$0.50 - 0.05 = 0.45$$

between the new time limit and the mean. Now go to the body of the standard normal table, where the probabilities are, and locate the value as close to 0.45 as possible (0.4495 or 0.4505). Next, determine the z-value that corresponds to this probability. Because 0.45 lies midway between 0.4495 and 0.4505, we interpolate halfway between $z = 1.64$ and $z = 1.65$ to get

$$z = 1.645$$

Now, we know

$$z = \frac{x - \mu}{\sigma}$$

We then substitute the known values and solve for x:

$$1.645 = \frac{x - 22.14}{6.09}$$
$$x = 22.14 + 1.645(6.09)$$
$$x = 32.158 \text{ minutes}$$

Therefore, any customer required to spend more than 32.158 minutes will receive the gift. This should result in no more than 5% of the customers getting the restaurant certificate. Obviously, the bank will work to reduce the average service time or standard deviation so even fewer customers will have to be in the bank for more than 32 minutes.

EXAMPLE 6-2   **USING THE NORMAL DISTRIBUTION**

Lockheed Martin Lockheed Martin, the defense contractor, has a project underway involving the design and construction of communication satellite systems to be used by the U.S. military. Because of the very high cost (more than $1 billion each), the company performs numerous tests on every component. These tests tend to extend the component assembly time. The time required to construct and test (called build time) a particular component part is thought to be normally distributed, with a mean equal to 30 hours and a standard deviation equal to 4.7 hours. To keep the assembly flow moving on schedule, this component needs to have a build time of between 26 to 35 hours. To determine the probability of this happening, use the following steps:

Step 1 **Determine the mean, μ, and the standard deviation, σ.**
The mean build time for this step in the process is thought to be 30 hours, and the standard deviation is thought to be 4.7 hours.

Step 2 **Define the event of interest.**
We are interested in determining the following:

$$P(26 \leq x \leq 35) = ?$$

Step 3 **Convert values of the specified normal distribution to corresponding values of the standard normal distribution using Equation 6.2:**

$$z = \frac{x - \mu}{\sigma}$$

---

[3]The function is = NORM.INV (probability, mean, standard deviation). For this example NORM.INV (.95,22.14,6.09) = 32.157.

We need to find the z-value corresponding to $x = 26$ and to $x = 35$.

$$z = \frac{x - \mu}{\sigma} = \frac{26 - 30}{4.7} = -0.85 \quad \text{and} \quad z = \frac{35 - 30}{4.7} = 1.06$$

Step 4   **Use the standard normal table to find the probabilities associated with each z value.**

For $z = -0.85$, the probability is 0.3023.

For $z = 1.06$, the probability is 0.3554.

Step 5   **Determine the desired probability for the event of interest.**

$$P(26 \leq x \leq 35) = 0.3023 + 0.3554 = 0.6577$$

Thus, there is a 0.6577 chance that the build time will be such that assembly will stay on schedule. Using Excel's NORM.DIST function we find NORM.DIST(35,30,4.7,true) − NORM.DIST(26,30,4.7,true) = 0.6589. The difference in the two probabilities is due to rounding of the calculated z-values when done using the table.

>> **END EXAMPLE**

TRY PROBLEM 6-13 (pg. 237)

Approximate Areas under the Normal Curve In Chapter 3 we introduced the Empirical Rule for probabilities with bell-shaped distributions. For the normal distribution we can make this rule more precise. Knowing the area under the normal curve between $\pm 1\sigma$, $\pm 2\sigma$, and $\pm 3\sigma$ provides a useful benchmark for estimating probabilities and checking reasonableness of results. Figure 6.11 shows these benchmark areas for any normal distribution.

FIGURE 6.11

Approximate Areas under the Normal Curve

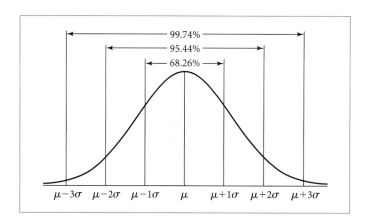

MyStatLab

6-1: **Exercises**

Skill **Development**

6-1. For a normally distributed population with $\mu = 200$ and $\sigma = 20$, determine the standardized z-value for each of the following:
a. $x = 225$
b. $x = 190$
c. $x = 240$

6-2. For a standardized normal distribution, calculate the following probabilities:

a. $P(z < 1.5)$
b. $P(z \geq 0.85)$
c. $P(-1.28 < z < 1.75)$

6-3. For a standardized normal distribution, calculate the following probabilities:
a. $P(0.00 < z \leq 2.33)$
b. $P(-1.00 < z \leq 1.00)$
c. $P(1.78 < z < 2.34)$

6-4. For a standardized normal distribution, determine a value, say z_0, so that
   a. $P(0 < z < z_0) = 0.4772$
   b. $P(-z_0 \le z < 0) = 0.45$
   c. $P(-z_0 \le z \le z_0) = 0.95$
   d. $P(z > z_0) = 0.025$
   e. $P(z \le z_0) = 0.01$

6-5. Consider a random variable, z, that has a standardized normal distribution. Determine the following probabilities:
   a. $P(0 < z < 1.96)$
   b. $P(z > 1.645)$
   c. $P(1.28 < z \le 2.33)$
   d. $P(-2 \le z \le 3)$
   e. $P(z > -1)$

6-6. A random variable, x, has a normal distribution with $\mu = 13.6$ and $\sigma = 2.90$. Determine a value, x_0, so that
   a. $P(x > x_0) = 0.05$.
   b. $P(x \le x_0) = 0.975$.
   c. $P(\mu - x_0 \le x \le \mu + x_0) = 0.95$.

6-7. For the following normal distributions with parameters as specified, calculate the required probabilities:
   a. $\mu = 5, \sigma = 2$; calculate $P(0 < x < 8)$.
   b. $\mu = 5, \sigma = 4$; calculate $P(0 < x < 8)$.
   c. $\mu = 3, \sigma = 2$; calculate $P(0 < x < 8)$.
   d. $\mu = 4, \sigma = 3$; calculate $P(x > 1)$.
   e. $\mu = 0, \sigma = 3$; calculate $P(x > 1)$.

6-8. A population is normally distributed with $\mu = 100$ and $\sigma = 20$.
   a. Find the probability that a value randomly selected from this population will have a value greater than 130.
   b. Find the probability that a value randomly selected from this population will have a value less than 90.
   c. Find the probability that a value randomly selected from this population will have a value between 90 and 130.

6-9. A random variable is known to be normally distributed with the following parameters:

$$\mu = 5.5 \quad \text{and} \quad \sigma = 0.50$$

   a. Determine the value of x such that the probability of a value from this distribution exceeding x is at most 0.10.
   b. Referring to your answer in part a, what must the population mean be changed to if the probability of exceeding the value of x found in part a is reduced from 0.10 to 0.05?

6-10. A randomly selected value from a normal distribution is found to be 2.1 standard deviations above its mean.
   a. What is the probability that a randomly selected value from the distribution will be greater than 2.1 standard deviations above the mean?
   b. What is the probability that a randomly selected value from the distribution will be less than 2.1 standard deviations from the mean?

6-11. Assume that a random variable is normally distributed with a mean of 1,500 and a variance of 324.

   a. What is the probability that a randomly selected value will be greater than 1,550?
   b. What is the probability that a randomly selected value will be less than 1,485?
   c. What is the probability that a randomly selected value will be either less than 1,475 or greater than 1,535?

6-12. A random variable is normally distributed with a mean of 25 and a standard deviation of 5. If an observation is randomly selected from the distribution,
   a. What value will be exceeded 10% of the time?
   b. What value will be exceeded 85% of the time?
   c. Determine two values of which the smallest has 25% of the values below it and the largest has 25% of the values above it.
   d. What value will 15% of the observations be below?

6-13. A random variable is normally distributed with a mean of 60 and a standard deviation of 9.
   a. What is the probability that a randomly selected value from the distribution will be less than 46.5?
   b. What is the probability that a randomly selected value from the distribution will be greater than 78?
   c. What is the probability that a randomly selected value will be between 51 and 73.5?

Business Applications

6-14. A global financial institution transfers a large data file every evening from offices around the world to its London headquarters. Once the file is received, it must be cleaned and partitioned before being stored in the company's data warehouse. Each file is the same size and the time required to transfer, clean, and partition a file is normally distributed, with a mean of 1.5 hours and a standard deviation of 15 minutes.
   a. If one file is selected at random, what is the probability that it will take longer than 1 hour and 55 minutes to transfer, clean, and partition the file?
   b. If a manager must be present until 85% of the files are transferred, cleaned, and partitioned, how long will the manager need to be there?
   c. What percentage of the data files will take between 63 minutes and 110 minutes to be transferred, cleaned, and partitioned?

6-15. Doggie Nuggets Inc. (DNI) sells large bags of dog food to warehouse clubs. DNI uses an automatic filling process to fill the bags. Weights of the filled bags are approximately normally distributed with a mean of 50 kilograms and a standard deviation of 1.25 kilograms.
   a. What is the probability that a filled bag will weigh less than 49.5 kilograms?
   b. What is the probability that a randomly sampled filled bag will weigh between 48.5 and 51 kilograms?
   c. What is the minimum weight a bag of dog food could be and remain in the top 15% of all bags filled?
   d. DNI is unable to adjust the mean of the filling process. However, it is able to adjust the standard

deviation of the filling process. What would the standard deviation need to be so that no more than 2% of all filled bags weigh more than 52 kilograms?

6-16. LaCrosse Technology is one of many manufacturers of atomic clocks. It makes an atomic digital watch that is radio controlled and that maintains its accuracy by reading a radio signal from a WWVB radio signal from Colorado. It neither loses nor gains a second in 20 million years. It is powered by a 3-volt lithium battery expected to last three years. Suppose the life of the battery has a standard deviation of 0.3 years and is normally distributed.

   a. Determine the probability that the watch's battery will last longer than 3.5 years.
   b. Calculate the probability that the watch's battery will last more than 2.75 years.
   c. Compute the length-of-life value for which 10% of the watch's batteries last longer.

6-17. The average number of acres burned by forest and range fires in a large Wyoming county is 4,300 acres per year, with a standard deviation of 750 acres. The distribution of the number of acres burned is normal.

   a. Compute the probability that more than 5,000 acres will be burned in any year.
   b. Determine the probability that fewer then 4,000 acres will be burned in any year.
   c. What is the probability that between 2,500 and 4,200 acres will be burned?
   d. In those years when more than 5,500 acres are burned, help is needed from eastern-region fire teams. Determine the probability help will be needed in any year.

6-18. An Internet retailer stocks a popular electronic toy at a central warehouse that supplies the eastern United States. Every week, the retailer makes a decision about how many units of the toy to stock. Suppose that weekly demand for the toy is approximately normally distributed with a mean of 2,500 units and a standard deviation of 300 units.

   a. If the retailer wants to limit the probability of being out of stock of the electronic toy to no more than 2.5% in a week, how many units should the central warehouse stock?
   b. If the retailer has 2,750 units on hand at the start of the week, what is the probability that weekly demand will be greater than inventory?
   c. If the standard deviation of weekly demand for the toy increases from 300 units to 500 units, how many more toys would have to be stocked to ensure that the probability of weekly demand exceeding inventory is no more than 2.5%?

6-19. F&G Industries manufactures a wash-down motor that is used in the food processing industry. The motor is marketed with a warranty that guarantees it will be replaced free of charge if it fails within the first 13,000 hours of operation. On average, F&G wash-down motors operate for 15,000 hours with a standard deviation of 1,250 hours before failing. The number

of operating hours before failure is approximately normally distributed.

   a. What is the probability that a wash-down motor will have to be replaced free of charge?
   b. What percentage of F&G wash-down motors can be expected to operate for more than 17,500 hours?
   c. If F&G wants to design a wash-down motor so that no more than 1% are replaced free of charge, what would the average hours of operation before failure have to be if the standard deviation remains at 1,250 hours?

6-20. A private equity firm is evaluating two alternative investments. Although the returns are random, each investment's return can be described using a normal distribution. The first investment has a mean return of $2,000,000 with a standard deviation of $125,000. The second investment has a mean return of $2,275,000 with a standard deviation of $500,000.

   a. How likely is it that the first investment will return $1,900,000 or less?
   b. How likely is it that the second investment will return $1,900,000 or less?
   c. If the firm would like to limit the probability of a return being less than $1,750,000, which investment should it make?

6-21. L.J. Raney & Associates is a financial planning group in Kansas City, Missouri. The company specializes in financial planning for schoolteachers in the Kansas City area. As such, it administers a 403(b) tax shelter annuity program in which public schoolteachers can participate. The teachers can contribute up to $20,000 per year on a pretax basis to the 403(b) account. Very few teachers have incomes sufficient to allow them to make the maximum contribution. The lead analyst at L.J. Raney & Associates has recently analyzed the company's 403(b) clients and determined that the annual contribution is approximately normally distributed with a mean equal to $6,400. Further, he has determined that the probability a customer will contribute more than $13,000 is 0.025. Based on this information, what is the standard deviation of contributions to the 403(b) program?

6-22. No Leak Plumbing and Repair provides customers with firm quotes for a plumbing repair job before actually starting the job. To be able to do this, No Leak has been very careful to maintain time records over the years. For example, it has determined that the time it takes to remove a broken sink disposal and to install a new unit is normally distributed with a mean equal to 47 minutes and a standard deviation equal to 12 minutes. The company bills at $75.00 for the first 30 minutes and $2.00 per minute for anything beyond 30 minutes.

   Suppose the going rate for this procedure by other plumbing shops in the area is $85.00, not including the cost of the new equipment. If No Leak bids the disposal job at $85, on what percentage of such jobs will the actual time required exceed the time for which it will be getting paid?

6-23. According to *Business Week*, Maternity Chic, a purveyor of designer maternity wear, sells dresses and pants priced around $150 each for an average total sale of $1,200. The total sale has a normal distribution with a standard deviation of $350.

a. Calculate the probability that a randomly selected customer will have a total sale of more than $1,500.

b. Compute the probability that the total sale will be within ±2 standard deviations of the mean total sales.

c. Determine the median total sale.

6-24. The Aberdeen Coca-Cola Bottling plant located in Aberdeen, North Carolina, is the bottler and distributor for Coca-Cola products in the Aberdeen area. The company's product line includes 12-ounce cans of Coke products. The cans are filled by an automated filling process that can be adjusted to any mean fill volume and that will fill cans according to a normal distribution. However, not all cans will contain the same volume due to variation in the filling process. Historical records show that regardless of what the mean is set at, the standard deviation in fill will be 0.035 ounces. Operations managers at the plant know that if they put too much Coke in a can, the company loses money. If too little is put in the can, customers are short changed, and the North Carolina Department of Weights and Measures may fine the company.

a. Suppose the industry standards for fill volume call for each 12-ounce can to contain between 11.98 and 12.02 ounces. Assuming that the Aberdeen manager sets the mean fill at 12 ounces, what is the probability that a can will contain a volume of Coke product that falls in the desired range?

b. Assume that the Aberdeen manager is focused on an upcoming audit by the North Carolina Department of Weights and Measures. She knows the process is to select one Coke can at random and that if it contains less than 11.97 ounces, the company will be reprimanded and potentially fined. Assuming that the manager wants at most a 5% chance of this happening, at what level should she set the mean fill level? Comment on the ramifications of this step, assuming that the company fills tens of thousands of cans each week.

6-25. MP-3 players, and most notably the Apple iPod, have become an industry standard for people who want to have access to their favorite music and videos in a portable format. The iPod can store massive numbers of songs and videos with its 120-GB hard drive. Although owners of the iPod have the potential to store lots of data, a recent study showed that the actual disk storage being used is normally distributed with a mean equal to 1.95 GB and a standard deviation of 0.48 GB. Suppose a competitor to Apple is thinking of entering the market with a low-cost iPod clone that has only 1.0 GB of storage. The marketing slogan will be "Why Pay for Storage Capacity that You Don't Need?"

Based on the data from the study of iPod owners, what percentage of owners, based on their current usage, would have enough capacity with the new 1-GB player?

6-26. According to the Federal Reserve Board, the average credit card debt per U.S. household was $8,565 in 2008. Assume that the distribution of credit card debt per household has a normal distribution with a standard deviation of $3,000.

a. Determine the percentage of households that have a credit card debt of more than $13,000.

b. One household has a credit card debt that is at the 95th percentile. Determine its credit card debt.

c. If four households were selected at random, determine the probability that at least half of them would have credit card debt of more than $13,000.

6-27. Georgia-Pacific is a major forest products company in the United States. In addition to timberlands, the company owns and operates numerous manufacturing plants that make lumber and paper products. At one of their plywood plants, the operations manager has been struggling to make sure that the plywood thickness meets quality standards. Specifically, all sheets of their 3/4-inch plywood must fall within the range 0.747 to 0.753 inches in thickness. Studies have shown that the current process produces plywood that has thicknesses that are normally distributed with a mean of 0.751 inches and a standard deviation equal to 0.004 inches.

a. Use Excel to determine the proportion of plywood sheets that will meet quality specifications (0.747 to 0.753), given how the current process is performing.

b. Referring to part a, suppose the manager is unhappy with the proportion of product meeting specifications. Assuming that he can get the mean adjusted to 0.75 inches, what must the standard deviation be if he is going to have 98% of his product meet specifications?

6-28. A senior loan officer for Whitney National Bank has recently studied the bank's real estate loan portfolio and found that the distribution of loan balances is approximately normally distributed with a mean of $155,600 and a standard deviation equal to $33,050. As part of an internal audit, bank auditors recently randomly selected 100 real estate loans from the portfolio of all loans and found that 80 of these loans had balances below $170,000. The senior loan officer is concerned that the sample selected by the auditors is not representative of the overall portfolio. In particular, he is interested in knowing the expected proportion of loans in the portfolio that would have balances below $170,000. You are asked to conduct an appropriate analysis and write a short report to the senior loan officers with your conclusion about the sample.

Computer Database **Exercises**

6-29. The PricewaterhouseCoopers Human Capital Index Report indicated that the average cost for an American company to fill a job vacancy during the study period was $3,270. Sample data similar to those used in the study are in a file titled **Hired**.

a. Produce a relative frequency histogram for these data. Does it seem plausible the data were sampled from a normally distributed population?

b. Calculate the mean and standard deviation of the cost of filling a job vacancy.

c. Determine the probability that the cost of filling a job vacancy would be between $2,000 and $3,000.

d. Given that the cost of filling a job vacancy was between $2,000 and $3,000, determine the probability that the cost would be more than $2,500.

6-30. A recent article in *USA Today* discussed prices for the 200 brand-name drugs most commonly used by Americans over age 50. Atrovent, a treatment for lung conditions such as emphysema, was one of the drugs. The file titled **Drug$** contains daily cost data similar to those obtained in the research.

a. Produce a relative frequency histogram for these data. Does it seem plausible the data were sampled from a population that was normally distributed?

b. Compute the mean and standard deviation for the sample data in the file **Drug$**.

c. Assuming the sample came from a normally distributed population and the sample standard deviation is a good approximation for the population standard deviation, determine the probability that a randomly chosen transaction would yield a price of $2.12 or smaller even though the population mean was $2.51.

6-31. *USA Today*'s annual survey of public flagship universities (Arienne Thompson and Breanne Gilpatrick, "Double-Digit Hikes Are Down," October 5, 2005) indicates that the median increase in in-state tuition was 7% for the 2005–2006 academic year. A file titled **Tuition** contains the percentage change for the 67 flagship universities.

a. Produce a relative frequency histogram for these data. Does it seem plausible that the data are from a population that has a normal distribution?

b. Suppose the decimal point of the three largest numbers had inadvertently been moved one place to the right in the data. Move the decimal point one place to the left and reconstruct the relative frequency histogram. Now does it seem plausible that the data have an approximate normal distribution?

c. Use the normal distribution of part b to approximate the proportion of universities that raised their in-state tuition more than 10%. Use the appropriate parameters obtained from this population.

d. Use the normal distribution of part b to approximate the fifth percentile for the percent of tuition increase.

END EXERCISES 6-1

6.2 Other Continuous Probability Distributions

This section introduces two additional continuous probability distributions that are used in business decision making: the uniform distribution and the exponential distribution.

Chapter Outcome 4. → ## Uniform Probability Distribution

The *uniform distribution* is sometimes referred to as the *distribution of little information*, because the probability over any interval of the continuous random variable is the same as for any other interval of the same width.

Equation 6.3 defines the *continuous uniform density function*.

Continuous Uniform Density Function

$$f(x) = \begin{cases} \dfrac{1}{b-a} & \text{if } a \leq x \leq b \\ 0 & \text{otherwise} \end{cases} \tag{6.3}$$

where:
$f(x)$ = Value of the density function at any x-value
a = The smallest value assumed by the uniform random variable of interest
b = The largest value assumed by the uniform random variable of interest

---

FIGURE 6.12

Uniform Distributions

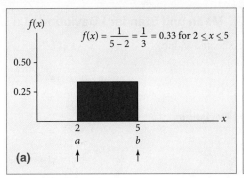
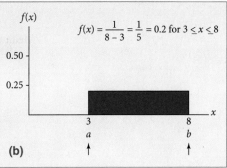

Figure 6.12 illustrates two examples of uniform probability distributions with different a to b intervals. Note the height of the probability density function is the same for all values of x between a and b for a given distribution. The graph of the uniform distribution is a rectangle.

EXAMPLE 6-3   USING THE UNIFORM DISTRIBUTION

Georgia Pacific The Georgia Pacific Company owns and operates several tree farms in different parts of the United States and South America. The lead botanist for the company has stated that pine trees on one parcel of land will increase in diameter between one and four inches per year according to a uniform distribution. Suppose the company is interested in the probability that a given tree will have an increased diameter of more than 2 inches. The probability can be determined using the following steps:

Step 1 **Define the density function.**

The height of the probability rectangle, $f(x)$, for the tree growth interval of one to four inches is determined using Equation 6.3, as follows:

$$f(x) = \frac{1}{b-a}$$

$$f(x) = \frac{1}{4-1} = \frac{1}{3} = 0.33$$

Step 2 **Define the event of interest.**

The botanist is specifically interested in a tree that has increased by more than two inches in diameter. This event of interest is $x > 2.0$.

Step 3 **Calculate the required probability.**

We determine the probability as follows:

$$
\begin{aligned}
P(x > 2.0) &= 1 - P(x \le 2.0) \\
&= 1 - f(x)(2.0 - 1.0) \\
&= 1 - 0.33(1.0) \\
&= 1 - 0.33 \\
&= 0.67
\end{aligned}
$$

Thus, there is a 0.67 probability that a tree will increase by more than two inches in diameter.

>> **END EXAMPLE**

TRY PROBLEM 6-32 (pg. 245)

Like the normal distribution, the uniform distribution can be further described by specifying the mean and the standard deviation. These values are computed using Equations 6.4 and 6.5.

Mean and Standard Deviation of a Uniform Distribution

Mean (Expected Value):

$$E(x) = \mu = \frac{a+b}{2}$$ (6.4)

Standard Deviation:

$$\sigma = \sqrt{\frac{(b-a)^2}{12}}$$ (6.5)

where:

a = The smallest value assumed by the uniform random variable of interest
b = The largest value assumed by the uniform random variable of interest

EXAMPLE 6-4 **THE MEAN AND STANDARD DEVIATION OF A UNIFORM DISTRIBUTION**

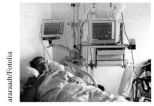

Surgery Recovery The chief administrator of a San Francisco–area surgical center has analyzed data from a large number of shoulder surgeries conducted by her center and others in a medical association in California. The analysis shows that the recovery time for shoulder surgery ranges between 15 and 45 weeks. Without any further information, the administrator will apply a uniform distribution to surgery times. Based on this, she can determine the mean and standard deviation for the recovery duration using the following steps:

Step 1 **Define the density function.**

Equation 6.3 can be used to define the distribution:

$$f(x) = \frac{1}{b-a} = \frac{1}{45-15} = \frac{1}{30} = 0.0333$$

Step 2 **Compute the mean of the probability distribution using Equation 6.4.**

$$\mu = \frac{a+b}{2} = \frac{15+45}{2} = 30$$

Thus, the mean recovery time is 30 weeks.

Step 3 **Compute the standard deviation using Equation 6.5.**

$$\sigma = \sqrt{\frac{(b-a)^2}{12}} = \sqrt{\frac{(45-15)^2}{12}} = \sqrt{75} = 8.66$$

The standard deviation is 8.66 weeks.

>> **END EXAMPLE**

TRY PROBLEM 6-34 (pg. 245)

Chapter Outcome 5. ➡ **The Exponential Probability Distribution**

Another continuous probability distribution frequently used in business situations is the *exponential distribution*. The exponential distribution is used to measure the time that elapses between two occurrences of an event, such as the time between "hits" on an Internet home page. The exponential distribution might also be used to describe the time between arrivals of customers at a bank drive-in teller window or the time between failures of an electronic component. Equation 6.6 shows the probability density function for the exponential distribution.

Exponential Density Function

A continuous random variable that is exponentially distributed has the probability density function given by

$$f(x) = \lambda e^{-\lambda x}, \qquad x \geq 0 \qquad\qquad \textbf{(6.6)}$$

where:

$$e = 2.71828\ldots$$
$$1/\lambda = \text{The mean time between events}\,(\lambda > 0)$$

Note, the parameter that defines the exponential distribution is λ (lambda). You should recall from Chapter 5 that λ is the mean value for the Poisson distribution. If the number of occurrences per time period is known to be Poisson distributed with a mean of λ then the time between occurrences will be exponentially distributed with a mean time of $1/\lambda$.

If we select a value for λ, we can graph the exponential distribution by substituting λ and different values for x into Equation 6.6. For instance, Figure 6.13 shows exponential density functions for $\lambda = 0.5, \lambda = 1.0, \lambda = 2.0$, and $\lambda = 3.0$. Note in Figure 6.13 that for any exponential density function, $f(x)$, $f(0) = \lambda$, as x increases, $f(x)$ approaches zero. It can also be shown that *the standard deviation of any exponential distribution is equal to the mean,* $1/\lambda$.

As with any continuous probability distribution, the probability that a value will fall within an interval is the area under the graph between the two points defining the interval. Equation 6.7 is used to find the probability that a value will be equal to or less than a particular value for an exponential distribution.

Exponential Probability

$$P(0 \leq x \leq a) = 1 - e^{-\lambda a} \qquad\qquad \textbf{(6.7)}$$

where:

$$a = \text{the value of interest}$$
$$1/\lambda = \text{Mean}$$
$$e = \text{Base of natural log; 2.71828}$$

FIGURE 6.13 |

Exponential Distributions

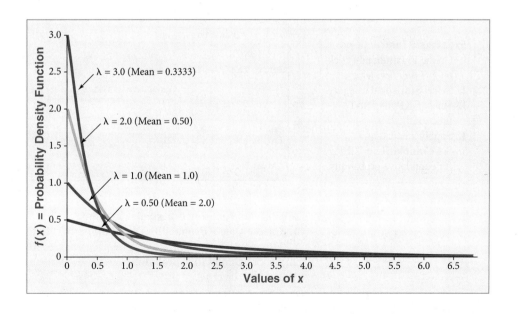

Appendix E contains a table of $e^{-\lambda a}$ values for different values of λa. You can use this table and Equation 6.7 to find the probabilities when the λa of interest is contained in the table. You can also use Excel to find exponential probabilities, as the following application illustrates.

Excel Tutorial

BUSINESS APPLICATION **USING EXCEL TO CALCULATE EXPONENTIAL PROBABILITIES**

HAINES INTERNET SERVICES The Haines Internet Services Company has determined that the number of customers who attempt to connect to the Internet per hour is Poisson distributed with $\lambda = 30$ per hour. The time between connect requests is exponentially distributed with a mean time between requests of 2.0 minutes, computed as follows:

$$\lambda = 30 \text{ attempts per 60 minutes} = 0.50 \text{ attempts per minute}$$

The mean time between attempted connects, then, is

$$1/\lambda = \frac{1}{0.50} = 2.0 \text{ minutes}$$

Because of the system that Haines uses, if customer requests are too close together—45 seconds (0.75 minutes) or less—the connection will fail. The managers at Haines are analyzing whether they should purchase new equipment that will eliminate this problem. They need to know the probability that a customer will fail to connect. Thus, they want

$$P(x \le 0.75 \text{ minutes}) = ?$$

FIGURE 6.14

Excel 2010 Exponential Probability Output for Haines Internet Services

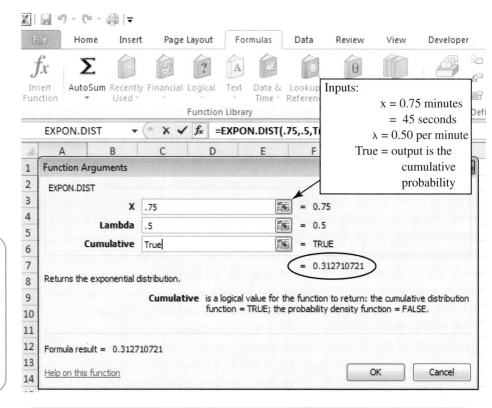

Excel 2010 Instructions:
1. On the **Formula** tab, click on f_x (*function wizard*).
2. Select **Statistical** category.
3. Select **EXPON.DIST** function.
4. Supply x and λ.
5. Set **Cumulative = TRUE** for cumulative probability.

Minitab Instructions (for similar results):
1. Choose **Calc > Probability Distributions > Exponential**.
2. Choose **Cumulative probability**.
3. In **Scale**, enter μ.
4. In **Input constant,** enter value for x.
5. Click **OK**.

To find this probability using a calculator, we need to first determine λa. In this example, $\lambda = 0.50$ and $a = 0.75$. Then,

$$\lambda a = (0.50)(0.75) = 0.3750$$

We find that the desired probability is

$$1 - e^{-\lambda a} = 1 - e^{-0.3750}$$
$$= 0.3127$$

The managers can also use the EXPON.DIST function in Excel to compute the precise value for the desired probability.[4] Using Excel, Figure 6.14 shows that the chance of failing to connect is 0.3127. This means that nearly one third of the customers will experience a problem with the current system.

_____
[4]The Excel EXPON.DIST function requires that λ be inputted rather than $1/\lambda$.

MyStatLab

6-2: Exercises

Skill Development

6-32. A continuous random variable is uniformly distributed between 100 and 150.
   a. What is the probability a randomly selected value will be greater than 135?
   b. What is the probability a randomly selected value will be less than 115?
   c. What is the probability a randomly selected value will be between 115 and 135?

6-33. Determine the following:
   a. the probability that a uniform random variable whose range is between 10 and 30 assumes a value in the interval (10 to 20) or (15 to 25)
   b. the quartiles for a uniform random variable whose range is from 4 to 20
   c. the mean time between events for an exponential random variable that has a median equal to 10
   d. the 90th percentile for an exponential random variable that has the mean time between events equal to 0.4.

6-34. Suppose a random variable, x, has a uniform distribution with $a = 5$ and $b = 9$.
   a. Calculate $P(5.5 \leq x \leq 8)$.
   b. Determine $P(x > 7)$.
   c. Compute the mean, μ, and standard deviation, σ, of this random variable.
   d. Determine the probability that x is in the interval $(\mu \pm 2\sigma)$.

6-35. Let x be an exponential random variable with $\lambda = 0.5$. Calculate the following probabilities:
   a. $P(x < 5)$
   b. $P(x > 6)$
   c. $P(5 \leq x \leq 6)$
   d. $P(x \geq 2)$
   e. the probability that x is at most 6

6-36. The useful life of an electrical component is exponentially distributed with a mean of 2,500 hours.

   a. What is the probability the circuit will last more than 3,000 hours?
   b. What is the probability the circuit will last between 2,500 and 2,750 hours?
   c. What is the probability the circuit will fail within the first 2,000 hours?

6-37. The time between telephone calls to a cable television payment processing center follows an exponential distribution with a mean of 1.5 minutes.
   a. What is the probability that the time between the next two calls will be 45 seconds or less?
   b. What is the probability that the time between the next two calls will be greater than 112.5 seconds?

Business Applications

6-38. Suppose you are traveling on business to a foreign country for the first time. You do not have a bus schedule or a watch with you. However, you have been told that buses stop in front of your hotel every 20 minutes throughout the day. If you show up at the bus stop at a random moment during the day, determine the probability that
   a. you will have to wait for more than 10 minutes
   b. you will only have to wait for 6 minutes or less
   c. you will have to wait between 8 and 15 minutes

6-39. When only the value-added time is considered, the time it takes to build a laser printer is thought to be uniformly distributed between 8 and 15 hours.
   a. What are the chances that it will take more than 10 value-added hours to build a printer?
   b. How likely is it that a printer will require less than 9 value-added hours?
   c. Suppose a single customer orders two printers. Determine the probability that the first and second printer each will require less than 9 value-added hours to complete.

6-40. The time required to prepare a dry cappuccino using whole milk at the Daily Grind Coffee House is uniformly distributed between 25 and 35 seconds. Assuming a customer has just ordered a whole-milk dry cappuccino,

a. What is the probability that the preparation time will be more than 29 seconds?

b. What is the probability that the preparation time will be between 28 and 33 seconds?

c. What percentage of whole-milk dry cappuccinos will be prepared within 31 seconds?

d. What is the standard deviation of preparation times for a dry cappuccino using whole milk at the Daily Grind Coffee House?

6-41. The time to failure for a power supply unit used in a particular brand of personal computer (PC) is thought to be exponentially distributed with a mean of 4,000 hours as per the contract between the vendor and the PC maker. The PC manufacturer has just had a warranty return from a customer who had the power supply fail after 2,100 hours of use.

a. What is the probability that the power supply would fail at 2,100 hours or less? Based on this probability, do you feel the PC maker has a right to require that the power supply maker refund the money on this unit?

b. Assuming that the PC maker has sold 100,000 computers with this power supply, approximately how many should be returned due to failure at 2,100 hours or less?

6-42. A delicatessen located in the heart of the business district of a large city serves a variety of customers. The delicatessen is open 24 hours a day every day of the week. In an effort to speed up take-out orders, the deli accepts orders by fax. If, on the average, 20 orders are received by fax every two hours throughout the day, find the

a. probability that a faxed order will arrive within the next 9 minutes

b. probability that the time between two faxed orders will be between 3 and 6 minutes

c. probability that 12 or more minutes will elapse between faxed orders

6-43. Dennis Cauchon and Julie Appleby reported in *USA Today* that the average patient cost per stay in American hospitals was $8,166. Assume that this cost is exponentially distributed.

a. Determine the probability that a randomly selected patient's stay in an American hospital will cost more than $10,000.

b. Calculate the probability that a randomly selected patient's stay in an American hospital will cost less than $5,000.

c. Compute the probability that a randomly selected patient's stay in an American hospital will cost between $8,000 and $12,000.

6-44. During the busiest time of the day, customers arrive at the Daily Grind Coffee House at an average of 15 customers per 20-minute period.

a. What is the probability that a customer will arrive within the next 3 minutes?

b. What is the probability that the time between the arrivals of customers is 12 minutes or more?

c. What is the probability that the next customer will arrive within 4 and 6 minutes?

6-45. The average amount spent on electronics each year in U.S. households is $1,250, according to an article in *USA Today* (Michelle Kessler, "Gadget Makers Make Mad Dash to Market," January 4, 2006). Assume that the amount spent on electronics each year has an exponential distribution.

a. Calculate the probability that a randomly chosen U.S. household would spend more than $5,000 on electronics.

b. Compute the probability that a randomly chosen U.S. household would spend more than the average amount spent by U.S. households.

c. Determine the probability that a randomly chosen U.S. household would spend more than 1 standard deviation below the average amount spent by U.S. households.

6-46. Charter Southeast Airlines states that the flight between Fort Lauderdale, Florida, and Los Angeles takes 5 hours and 37 minutes. Assume that the actual flight times are uniformly distributed between 5 hours and 20 minutes and 5 hours and 50 minutes.

a. Determine the probability that the flight will be more than 10 minutes late.

b. Calculate the probability that the flight will be more than 5 minutes early.

c. Compute the average flight time between these two cities.

d. Determine the variance in the flight times between these two cities.

6-47. A corrugated container company is testing whether a computer decision model will improve the uptime of its box production line. Currently, knives used in the production process are checked manually and replaced when the operator believes the knives are dull. Knives are expensive, so operators are encouraged not to change the knives early. Unfortunately, if knives are left running for too long, the cuts are not made properly, which can jam the machines and require that the entire process be shut down for unscheduled maintenance. Shutting down the entire line is costly in terms of lost production and repair work, so the company would like to reduce the number of shutdowns that occur daily. Currently, the company experiences an average of 0.75 knife-related shutdowns per shift, exponentially distributed. In testing, the computer decision model reduced the frequency of knife-related shutdowns to an average of 0.20 per shift, exponentially distributed. The decision model is expensive, but the company will install it if it can help achieve the target of four consecutive shifts without a knife-related shutdown.

a. Under the current system, what is the probability that the plant would run four or more consecutive shifts without a knife-related shutdown?

b. Using the computer decision model, what is the probability that the plant could run four or more consecutive shifts without a knife-related shutdown? Has the decision model helped the company achieve its goal?

c. What would be the maximum average number of shutdowns allowed per day such that the probability of experiencing four or more consecutive shifts without a knife-related shutdown is greater than or equal to 0.70?

Computer Database **Exercises**

6-48. Rolls-Royce PLC provides forecasts for the business jet market and covers the regional and major aircraft markets. In a recent release, Rolls Royce indicated that in both North America and Europe, the number of delayed departures has declined since a peak in 1999/2000. This is partly due to a reduction in the number of flights at major airports and the younger aircraft fleets, but it also results from improvements in air traffic management capacity, especially in Europe. Comparing January–April 2003 with the same period in 2001 (for similar traffic levels), the average en route delay per flight was reduced by 65%, from 2.2 minutes to 0.7 minutes. The file titled **Delays** contains a possible sample of the en route delay times in minutes for 200 flights.

a. Produce a relative frequency histogram for this data. Does it seem plausible the data come from a population that has an exponential distribution?

b. Calculate the mean and standard deviation of the en route delays.

c. Determine the probability that this exponential random variable will be smaller than its mean.

d. Determine the median time in minutes for the en route delays assuming they have an exponential distribution with a mean equal to that obtained in part b.

e. Using only the information obtained in parts c and d, describe the shape of this distribution. Does this agree with the findings in part a?

6-49. Although some financial institutions do not charge fees for using ATMs, many do. A recent study found the average fee charged by banks to process an ATM transaction was $2.91. The file titled **ATM Fees** contains a list of ATM fees that might be required by banks.

a. Produce a relative frequency histogram for these data. Does it seem plausible the data came from a population that has an exponential distribution?

b. Calculate the mean and standard deviation of the ATM fees.

c. Assume that the distribution of ATM fees is exponentially distributed with the same mean as that of the sample. Determine the probability that a randomly chosen bank's ATM fee would be greater than $3.00.

6-50. The San Luis Obispo, California, Transit Program provides daily fixed-route transit service to the general public within the city limits and to Cal Poly State University's staff and students. The most heavily traveled route schedules a city bus to arrive at Cal Poly at 8:54 A.M. The file titled **Late** lists plausible differences between the actual and scheduled time of arrival rounded to the nearest minute for this route.

a. Produce a relative frequency histogram for these data. Does it seem plausible the data came from a population that has a uniform distribution?

b. Provide the density for this uniform distribution.

c. Classes start 10 minutes after the hour and classes are a 5-minute walk from the drop-off point. Determine the probability that a randomly chosen bus on this route would cause the students on board to be late for class. Assume the differences form a continuous uniform distribution with a range the same as the sample.

d. Determine the median difference between the actual and scheduled arrival times.

END EXERCISES 6-2

Visual Summary

Chapter 6: A **random variable** can take on values that are either discrete or continuous. This chapter has focused on continuous random variables where the potential values of the variable can be any value on a continuum. Examples of continuous random variables include the time it takes a worker to assemble a part, the weight of a potato, the distance it takes to stop a car once the brakes have been applied, and the volume of waste water emitted from a food processing facility. Values of a continuous random variable are generally determined by measuring. One of the most frequently used continuous probability distributions is called the **normal distribution**.

6.1 The Normal Probability Distribution (pg. 225–240)

Summary

The **normal distribution** is a symmetric, bell-shaped probability distribution. Half the probability lies to the right and half lies to the left of the mean. To find probabilities associated with a normal distribution, you will want to convert to a **standard normal distribution** by first converting values of the random variables to **standardized z-values**. The probabilities associated with a range of values for the random variable are found using the **normal distribution table** in the Appendix or by using Excel.

Outcome 1. Convert a normal distribution to a standard normal distribution.
Outcome 2. Determine probabilities using the standard normal distribution.
Outcome 3. Calculate values of the random variable associated with specified probabilities from a normal distribution.

6.2 Other Continuous Probability Distributions (pg. 240–247)

Summary

Although the normal distribution is by far the most frequently used continuous probability distribution, two other continuous distributions are introduced in this section. These are the *uniform distribution* and the **exponential distribution**. With the uniform distribution, the probability over any interval is the same as any other interval of the same width. The probabilities for the uniform distribution are computed using Equation 6.3. The exponential distribution is based on a single parameter, lambda, and is often used to describe random service times or the time between customer arrivals in waiting line applications. The probability over a range of values for an exponential distribution can be computed using Equation 6.7 or by using the exponential table in the Appendix. Also, Excel and Minitab have functions for calculating the exponential probabilities.

Outcome 4. Calculate probabilities associated with a uniformly distributed random variable.
Outcome 5. Determine probabilities for an exponential probability distribution.

Conclusion

The normal distribution has wide application throughout the study of business statistics. You will be making use of the normal distribution in subsequent chapters. The normal distribution has very special properties. It is a symmetric, bell-shaped distribution. To find probabilities for a normal distribution, you will first standardize the distribution by converting values of the random variable to standardized z-values. Other continuous distributions introduced in this chapter are the exponential distribution and the uniform distribution. **Figure 6.15** summarizes the discrete probability distributions introduced in Chapter 5 and the continuous probability distributions introduced in this chapter.

FIGURE 6.15

Probability Distribution
Summary

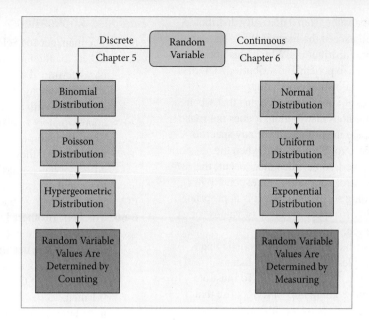

Equations

(6.1) Normal Probability Density Function pg. 226

$$f(x) = \frac{1}{\sigma\sqrt{2\pi}} e^{-(x-\mu)^2/2\sigma^2}$$

(6.2) Standardized Normal z-Value pg. 227

$$z = \frac{x - \mu}{\sigma}$$

(6.3) Continuous Uniform Density Function pg. 240

$$f(x) = \begin{cases} \dfrac{1}{b-a} & \text{if } a \le x \le b \\ 0 & \text{otherwise} \end{cases}$$

(6.4) Mean of the Uniform Distribution pg. 242

$$E(x) = \mu = \frac{a+b}{2}$$

(6.5) Standard Deviation of the Uniform Distribution pg. 242

$$\sigma = \sqrt{\frac{(b-a)^2}{12}}$$

(6.6) Exponential Density Function pg. 243

$$f(x) = \lambda e^{-\lambda x}, \quad x \ge 0$$

(6.7) Exponential Probability pg. 243

$$P(0 \le x \le a) = 1 - e^{-\lambda a}$$

Key Terms

Normal distribution pg. 225

Standard normal distribution pg. 226

Chapter Exercises   MyStatLab

Conceptual Questions

6-51. Discuss the difference between discrete and continuous probability distributions. Discuss two situations in which a variable of interest may be considered either continuous or discrete.

6-52. Recall the Empirical Rule from Chapter 3. It states that if the data distribution is bell shaped, then the interval $\mu \pm \sigma$ contains approximately 68% of the values, $\mu \pm 2\sigma$ contains approximately 95%, and $\mu \pm 3\sigma$ contains virtually all of the data values.

The bell-shaped distribution referenced is the normal distribution.

a. Verify that a standard normal distribution contains approximately 68% of the values in the interval $\mu \pm \sigma$.

b. Verify that a standard normal distribution contains approximately 95% of the values in the interval $\mu \pm 2\sigma$.

c. Verify that a standard normal distribution contains virtually all of the data in the interval $\mu \pm 3\sigma$.

6-53. The probability that a value from a normally distributed random variable will exceed the mean is 0.50. The same is true for the uniform distribution. Why is this not necessarily true for the exponential distribution? Discuss and show examples to illustrate your point.

6-54. Suppose you tell one of your fellow students that when working with a continuous distribution, it does not make sense to try to compute the probability of any specific value since it will be zero. She says that when the experiment is performed, some value must occur; the probability can't be zero. Your task is to respond to her statement and, in doing so, explain why it is appropriate to find the probability for specific ranges of values for a continuous distribution.

6-55. The exponential distribution has a characteristic that is called the "memoryless" property. This means $P(X > x) = P(X > x + x_0 | X > x_0)$. To illustrate this, consider the calls coming into 911. Suppose that the distribution of the time between occurrences has an exponential distribution with a mean of one half hour $(=0.5)$.
  a. Calculate the probability that no calls come in during the first hour.
  b. Now suppose that you are monitoring the call frequency, and you note that a call does not come in during the first two hours. Determine the probability that no calls will come in during the next hour.

6-56. Revisit Problem 6-55, but examine whether it would matter when you started monitoring the 911 calls if the time between occurrences had a uniform distribution with a mean of 2 and a range of 4.
  a. Calculate the probability that no call comes in during the first hour.
  b. Now suppose that you are monitoring the call frequency, and you note that no call comes in during the first two hours. Determine the probability that no calls will arrive during the next hour.

6-57. Suppose that, on average, 20 customers arrive every hour at a twenty-four-hour coffee shop. Assume that the time between customer arrivals is exponentially distributed. Determine
  a. The probability that a customer arrives within the next 2 minutes.
  b. The probability that the time between two arriving customers will be between 1 and 4 minutes.
  c. The probability that 5 or more minutes will pass between customer arrivals.

6-58. Assume that the time required to receive a confirmation that an electronic transfer has occurred is uniformly distributed between 30 and 90 seconds.
  a. What is the probability that a randomly selected transfer will take between 30 and 45 seconds?
  b. What is the probability that a randomly selected transfer will take between 50 and 90 seconds?
  c. What proportion of transfers will take between 40 and 75 seconds?

Business Applications

6-59. The manager for Select-a-Seat, a company that sells tickets to athletic games, concerts, and other events, has determined that the number of people arriving at the Broadway location on a typical day is Poisson distributed with a mean of 12 per hour. It takes approximately four minutes to process a ticket request. Thus, if customers arrive in intervals that are less than four minutes, they will have to wait. Assuming that a customer has just arrived and the ticket agent is starting to serve that customer, what is the probability that the next customer who arrives will have to wait in line?

6-60. The Four Brothers Lumber Company is considering buying a machine that planes lumber to the correct thickness. The machine is advertised to produce "6-inch lumber" having a thickness that is normally distributed, with a mean of 6 inches and a standard deviation of 0.1 inch.
  a. If building standards in the industry require a 99% chance of a board being between 5.85 and 6.15 inches, should Four Brothers purchase this machine? Why or why not?
  b. To what level would the company that manufactures the machine have to reduce the standard deviation for the machine to conform to industry standards?

6-61. Two automatic dispensing machines are being considered for use in a fast-food chain. The first dispenses an amount of liquid that has a normal distribution with a mean of 11.9 ounces and a standard deviation of 0.07 ounces. The second dispenses an amount of liquid that has a normal distribution with a mean of 12.0 ounces and a standard deviation of 0.05 ounces. Acceptable amounts of dispensed liquid are between 11.9 and 12.0 ounces. Calculate the relevant probabilities and determine which machine should be selected.

6-62. A small private ambulance service in Kentucky has determined that the time between emergency calls is exponentially distributed with a mean of 41 minutes. When a unit goes on call, it is out of service for 60 minutes. If a unit is busy when an emergency call is received, the call is immediately routed to another service. The company is considering buying a second ambulance. However, before doing so, the owners are interested in determining the probability that a call will come in before the ambulance is back in service. Without knowing the costs involved in this situation, does this probability tend to support the need for a second ambulance? Discuss.

6-63. Assume that after the first 12 hours, the average remaining useful life of a particular battery (before recharging is required) is 9 hours and that the remaining time is exponentially distributed. What is the probability that a randomly sampled battery of this type will last between 15 and 17 hours?

6-64. An online article (http://beauty.about.com) by Julyne Derrick, "Shelf Lives: How Long Can You Keep Makeup," suggests that eye shadow and eyeliner each have a shelf life of up to three years. Suppose the shelf lives of these two products are exponentially distributed with an average shelf life of one year.

a. Calculate the probability that the shelf life of eye shadow will be longer than three years.

b. Determine the probability that at least one of these products will have a shelf life of more than three years.

c. Determine the probability that a purchased eyeliner that is useful after one year will be useful after three years.

6-65. The Shadow Mountain Golf Course is preparing for a major LPGA golf tournament. Since parking near the course is extremely limited (room for only 500 cars), the course officials have contracted with the local community to provide parking and a bus shuttle service. Sunday, the final day of the tournament, will have the largest crowd, and the officials estimate there will be between 8,000 and 12,000 cars needing parking spaces but think no value is more likely than another. The tournament committee is discussing how many parking spots to contract from the city. If they want to limit the chance of not having enough provided parking to 10%, how many spaces do they need from the city on Sunday?

6-66. One of the products of Pittsburg Plate Glass Industries (PPG) is laminated safety glass. It is made up of two pieces of glass 0.125 inch thick, with a thin layer of vinyl sandwiched between them. The average thickness of the laminated safety glass is 0.25 inch. The thickness of the glass does not vary from the mean by more than 0.10 inch. Assume the thickness of the glass has a uniform distribution.

a. Provide the density for this uniform distribution.

b. If the glass has a thickness that is more than 0.05 inch below the mean, it must be discarded for safety considerations. Determine the probability that a randomly selected automobile glass is discarded due to safety considerations.

c. If the glass is more than 0.075 above the mean, it will create installation problems and must be discarded. Calculate the probability that a randomly selected automobile glass will be rejected due to installation concerns.

d. Given that a randomly selected automobile glass is not rejected for safety considerations, determine the probability that it will be rejected for installation concerns.

6-67. A traffic control camera at a busy intersection records, on average, 5 traffic violations per hour. Assume that the random variable number of recorded traffic violations follow a Poisson distribution.

a. What is the probability that the next recorded violation will occur within 5 minutes?

b. How likely is it that no traffic violations will be recorded within the next 7 minutes?

6-68. The St. Maries plywood plant is part of the Potlatch Corporation's Northwest Division. The plywood superintendent organized a study of the tree diameters that are being shipped to the mill. After collecting a large amount of data on diameters, he concluded that the distribution is approximately normally distributed with a mean of 14.25 inches and a standard deviation of 2.92 inches. Because of the way plywood is made, there is a certain amount of waste on each log because the peeling process leaves a core that is approximately 3 inches thick. For this reason, he feels that any log less than 10 inches in diameter is not profitable for making plywood.

a. Based on the data the superintendent has collected, what is the probability that a log will be unprofitable?

b. An alternative is to peel the log and then sell the core as "peeler logs." These peeler logs are sold as fence posts and for various landscape projects. There is not as much profit in these peeler logs, however. The superintendent has determined that he can make a profit if the peeler log's diameter is not more than 32% of the diameter of the log. Using this additional information, calculate the proportion of logs that will be unprofitable.

6-69. The personnel manager for a large company is interested in the distribution of sick-leave hours for employees of her company. A recent study revealed the distribution to be approximately normal, with a mean of 58 hours per year and a standard deviation of 14 hours.

An office manager in one division has reason to believe that during the past year, two of his employees have taken excessive sick leave relative to everyone else. The first employee used 74 hours of sick leave, and the second used 90 hours. What would you conclude about the office manager's claim and why?

6-70. If the number of hours between servicing required for a particular snowmobile engine is exponentially distributed with an average of 118 hours, determine the probability that a randomly selected engine

a. Will run at least 145 hours before servicing is needed.

b. Will run at most 161 hours before servicing is needed.

6-71. Assume that the amount of time (in minutes) for eighth graders to compete an assessment examination is 78 minutes with a standard deviation of 12 minutes.

a. What proportion of eighth graders completes the assessment examination in 72 minutes or less?

b. What proportion of eighth graders completes the assessment examination in 82 minutes or more?

c. For what number of minutes would 90% of all eighth graders complete the assessment examination?

Computer Database **Exercises**

6-72. The Cozine Corporation runs the landfill operation outside Little Rock, Arkansas. Each day, each of the company's trucks makes several trips from the city to the landfill. On each entry, the truck is weighed. The data file **Cozine** contains a sample of 200 truck weights. Determine the mean and standard deviation for the garbage truck weights. Assuming that these sample values are representative of the population of all Cozine garbage trucks, and assuming that the distribution is normally distributed,

   a. Determine the probability that a truck will arrive at the landfill weighing in excess of 46,000 pounds.

   b. Compare the probability in part a to the proportion of trucks in the sample that weighed more than 46,000 pounds. What does this imply to you?

   c. Suppose the managers are concerned that trucks are returning to the landfill before they are fully loaded. If they have set a minimum weight of 38,000 pounds before the truck returns to the landfill, what is the probability that a truck will fail to meet the minimum standard?

6-73. The Hydronics Company is in the business of developing health supplements. Recently, the company's research and development department came up with two weight-loss products that included products produced by Hydronics. To determine whether these products are effective, the company has conducted a test. A total of 300 people who were 30 pounds or more overweight were recruited to participate in the study. Of these, 100 people were given a placebo supplement, 100 people were given product 1, and 100 people were given product 2. As might be expected, some people dropped out of the study before the four-week study period was completed. The weight loss (or gain) for each individual is listed in the data file called **Hydronics**. Note, positive values indicate that the individual actually gained weight during the study period.

   a. Develop a frequency histogram for the weight loss (or gain) for those people on product 1. Does it appear from this graph that weight loss is approximately normally distributed?

   b. Referring to part a, assuming that a normal distribution does apply, compute the mean and standard deviation weight loss for the product 1 subjects.

   c. Referring to parts a and b, assume that the weight-change distribution for product 1 users is normally distributed and that the sample mean and standard deviation are used to directly represent the population mean and standard deviation. What is the probability that a plan 1 user will lose over 12 pounds in a four-week period?

   d. Referring to your answer in part c, would it be appropriate for the company to claim that plan 1 users can expect to lose as much as 12 pounds in four weeks? Discuss.

6-74. Midwest Fan Manufacturing Inc. was established in 1986 as a manufacturer and distributor of quality ventilation equipment. Midwest Fan's products include the AXC range hood exhaust fans. The file titled **Fan Life** contains the length of life of 125 randomly chosen AXC fans that were used in an accelerated life-testing experiment.

   a. Produce a relative frequency histogram for the data. Does it seem plausible the data came from a population that has an exponential distribution?

   b. Calculate the mean and standard deviation of the fans' length of life.

   c. Calculate the median length of life of the fans.

   d. Determine the probability that a randomly chosen fan will have a life of more than 25,000 hours.

6-75. Team Marketing Report (TMR) produces the Fan Cost Index™ (FCI) survey, now in its 16th year, which tracks the cost of attendance for a family of four at National Football League (NFL) games. The FCI includes four average-price tickets, four small soft drinks, two small beers, four hot dogs, two game programs, parking, and two adult-size caps. The league's average FCI in 2008 was $396.36. The file titled **NFL Price** is a sample of 175 randomly chosen fans' FCIs.

   a. Produce a relative frequency histogram for these data. Does it seem plausible the data were sampled from a population that was normally distributed?

   b. Calculate the mean and standard deviation of the league's FCI.

   c. Calculate the 90th percentile of the league's fans' FCI.

   d. The San Francisco 49ers had an FCI of $376.71. Determine the percentile of the FCI of a randomly chosen family whose FCI is the same as that of the 49ers' average FCI.

6-76. The Future-Vision Cable TV Company recently surveyed its customers. A total of 548 responses were received. Among other things, the respondents were asked to indicate their household income. The data from the survey are found in a file named **Future-Vision**.

   a. Develop a frequency histogram for the income variable. Does it appear from the graph that income is approximately normally distributed? Discuss.

   b. Compute the mean and standard deviation for the income variable.

   c. Referring to parts a and b and assuming that income is normally distributed and the sample mean and standard deviation are good substitutes for the population values, what is the probability that a Future-Vision customer will have an income exceeding $40,000?

   d. Suppose that Future-Vision managers are thinking about offering a monthly discount to customers who have a household income below a certain level.

If the management wants to grant discounts to no more than 7% of the customers, what income level should be used for the cutoff?

6-77. Championship Billiards, owned by D & R Industries, in Lincolnwood, Illinois, provides some of the finest billiard fabrics, cushion rubber, and component parts in the industry. It sells billiard cloth in bolts and half-bolts. A half-bolt of billiard cloth has an average length of 35 yards with widths of either 62 or 66 inches. The file titled **Half Bolts** contains the lengths of 120 randomly selected half-bolts.

a. Produce a relative frequency histogram for these data. Does it seem plausible the data came from a population that has a uniform distribution?
b. Provide the density, $f(x)$, for this uniform distribution.
c. A billiard retailer, Sticks & Stones Billiard Supply, is going to recover the pool tables in the local college pool hall, which has eight tables. It takes approximately 3.8 yards per table. If Championship ships a randomly chosen half-bolt, determine the probability that it will contain enough cloth to recover the eight tables.

Case 6.1

State Entitlement Programs

Franklin Joiner, director of health, education, and welfare, had just left a meeting with the state's newly elected governor and several of the other recently appointed department heads. One of the governor's campaign promises was to try to halt the rising cost of a certain state entitlement program. In several speeches, the governor indicated the state of Idaho should allocate funds only to those individuals ranked in the bottom 10% of the state's income distribution. Now the governor wants to know how much one could earn before being disqualified from the program, and he also wants to know the range of incomes for the middle 95% of the state's income distribution.

Frank had mentioned in the meeting that he thought incomes in the state could be approximated by a normal distribution and that mean per capita income was about $33,000 with a standard deviation of nearly $9,000. The governor was expecting a memo in his office by 3:00 P.M. that afternoon with answers to his questions.

Required Tasks:

1. Assuming that incomes can be approximated using a normal distribution with the specified mean and standard deviation, calculate the income that cut off the bottom 10% of incomes.
2. Assuming that incomes can be approximated using a normal distribution with the specified mean and standard deviation, calculate the middle 95% of incomes. *Hint*: This requires calculating two values.
3. Write a short memo describing your results and how they were obtained. Your memo should clearly state the income that would disqualify people from the program, as well as the range of incomes in the middle 95% of the state's income distribution.

Case 6.2

Credit Data, Inc.

Credit Data, Inc., has been monitoring the amount of time its bill collectors spend on calls that produce contacts with consumers. Management is interested in the distribution of time a collector spends on each call in which he or she initiates contact, informs a consumer about an outstanding debt, discusses a payment plan, and receives payments by phone. Credit Data is mostly interested in how quickly a collector can initiate and end a conversation to move on to the next call. For employees of Credit Data, time is money in the sense that one account may require one call and 2 minutes to collect, whereas another account may take five calls and 10 minutes per call to collect. The company has discovered that the time collectors spend talking to consumers about accounts is approximated by a normal distribution with a mean of 8 minutes and a standard deviation of 2.5 minutes. The managers believe that the mean is too high and should be reduced by more efficient phone call methods. Specifically, they wish to have no more than 10% of all calls require more than 10.5 minutes.

Required Tasks:

1. Assuming that training can affect the average time but not the standard deviation, the managers are interested in knowing to what level the mean call time needs to be reduced in order to meet the 10% requirement.
2. Assuming that the standard deviation can be affected by training but the mean time will remain at 8 minutes, to what level must the standard deviation be reduced in order to meet the 10% requirement?
3. If nothing is done, what percent of all calls can be expected to require more than 10.5 minutes?

Case 6.3

American Oil Company

Chad Williams, field geologist for the American Oil Company, settled into his first class seat on the Sun-Air flight between Los Angeles and Oakland, California. Earlier that afternoon, he had attended a meeting with the design engineering group at the Los Angeles New Product Division. He was now on his way to the home office in Oakland. He was looking forward to the one-hour flight because it would give him a chance to reflect on a problem that surfaced during the meeting. It would also give him a chance to think about the exciting opportunities that lay ahead in Australia.

Chad works with a small group of highly trained people at American Oil who literally walk the earth looking for new sources of oil. They make use of the latest in electronic equipment to take a wide range of measurements from many thousands of feet below the earth's surface. It is one of these electronic machines that is the source of Chad's current problem. Engineers in Los Angeles have designed a sophisticated enhancement that will greatly improve the equipment's ability to detect oil. The enhancement requires 800 capacitors, which must operate within ±0.50 microns from the specified standard of 12 microns.

The problem is that the supplier can provide capacitors that operate according to a normal distribution, with a mean of 12 microns and a standard deviation of 1 micron. Thus, Chad knows that not all capacitors will meet the specifications required by the new piece of exploration equipment. This will mean that to have at least 800 usable capacitors, American Oil will have to order more than 800 from the supplier. However, these items are very expensive, so he wants to order as few as possible to meet their needs. At the meeting, the group agreed that they wanted a 98% chance that any order of capacitors would contain the sufficient number of usable items. If the project is to remain on schedule, Chad must place the order by tomorrow. He wants the new equipment ready to go by the time he leaves for an exploration trip in Australia. As he reclined in his seat, sipping a cool lemonade, he wondered whether a basic statistical technique could be used to help determine how many capacitors to order.

Chapter 7 Quick Prep Links

- **Review** the discussion of random sampling in Chapter 1.
- **Review** the steps for computing means and standard deviations in Chapter 3.
- **Make sure** you are familiar with the normal distribution and how to compute standardized *z*-values as introduced in Chapter 6.
- **Review** the concepts associated with finding probabilities with a standard normal distribution as discussed in Chapter 6.

chapter **7**

Introduction to Sampling Distributions

7.1   Sampling Error: What It Is and Why It Happens (pg. 256–264) ←——— **Outcome 1.** Understand the concept of sampling error.

7.2   Sampling Distribution of the Mean (pg. 264–279) ←——— **Outcome 2.** Determine the mean and standard deviation for the sampling distribution of the sample mean $\bar{x}$.

Outcome 3. Understand the importance of the Central Limit Theorem.

7.3   Sampling Distribution of a Proportion (pg. 279–288) ←——— **Outcome 4.** Determine the mean and standard deviation for the sampling distribution of the sample proportion, $\bar{p}$.

Why you need to know

The Jamaica Director of Tourism has recently conducted a study that shows that the mean daily expenditure for adult visitors to the country is $318.69. The mean value is based on a statistical sample of 780 adult visitors to Jamaica. The $318.69 is a *statistic*, not a *parameter*, because it is based on a sample rather than an entire population. If you were this official, you might have several questions:

- Is the actual population mean equal to $318.69?
- If the population mean is not $318.69, how close is $318.69 to the true population mean?
- Is a sample of 780 taken from a population of almost 2 million annual visitors to the country sufficient to provide a "good" estimate of the population mean?

A furniture manufacturer that makes made-to-assemble furniture kits selects a random sample of kits boxed and ready for shipment to customers. These kits are unboxed and inspected to see whether what is in the box matches exactly what is supposed to be in the box. This past week, 150 kits were sampled and 15 had one or more discrepancies. This is a 10% defect rate. Should the quality engineer conclude that exactly 10% of the 6,900 furniture kits made since the first of the year reached the customer with one or more order discrepancies? Is the actual percentage higher or lower than 10% and, if so, by how much? Should the quality engineer request that more furniture kits be sampled?

The questions facing the tourism director and the furniture quality engineer are common to those faced by people in business everywhere. You will almost assuredly find yourself in a similar situation many times in the future. To help answer these questions, you need to have an understanding of *sampling distributions*. Whenever decisions are based on samples rather than an entire

gdvcom/Shutterstock

population, questions about the sample results exist. Anytime we sample from a population, there are many, many possible samples that could have been selected. Each sample will contain different items. Because of this, the sample means for each possible sample can be different, or the sample percentages can be different. The sampling distribution describes the distribution of possible sample outcomes. Knowing what this distribution looks like will help you understand the specific result you obtained from the one sample you selected.

This chapter introduces you to the important concepts of sampling error and sampling distributions and discusses how you can use this knowledge to help answer the questions facing the tourism director and the quality engineer. The information presented here provides an essential building block to understanding statistical estimation and hypothesis testing, which will be covered in upcoming chapters.

7.1 Sampling Error: What It Is and Why It Happens

As discussed in previous chapters, you will encounter many situations in business in which a sample will be taken from a population and you will be required to analyze the sample data. Chapter 1 introduced several different statistical sampling techniques, including random sampling. The objective of random sampling is to gather data that accurately represent a population. Then when analysis is performed on the sample data, the results will be as though we had worked with all the population data.

Chapter Outcome 1. → ## Calculating Sampling Error

Regardless of how careful we are in using random sampling methods, the sample may not be a perfect representation of the population. For example, a *statistic* such as $\bar{x}$ might be computed for sample data. Unless the sample is a perfect replication of the population, the statistic will likely not equal the *parameter*, μ. In this case, the difference between the sample mean and the population mean is called **sampling error**. In the case in which we are interested in the mean value, the sampling error is computed using Equation 7.1.

Sampling Error

The difference between a measure computed from a sample (a statistic) and the corresponding measure computed from the population (a parameter).

Sampling Error of the Sample Mean

$$\text{Sampling error} = \bar{x} - \mu \qquad \textbf{(7.1)}$$

where:

$\bar{x} = \text{Sample mean}$
$\mu = \text{Population mean}$

BUSINESS APPLICATION **SAMPLING ERROR**

HUMMEL DEVELOPMENT CORPORATION The Hummel Development Corporation has built 12 office complexes. Table 7.1 shows a list of the 12 projects and the total square footage of each project.

Because these 12 projects are all the office complexes the company has worked on, the square-feet area for all 12 projects, shown in Table 7.1, is a population. Equation 7.2 is used to compute the mean square feet in the population of projects.

TABLE 7.1 | **Square Feet for Office Complex Projects**

Complex	Square Feet
1	114,560
2	202,300
3	78,600
4	156,700
5	134,600
6	88,200
7	177,300
8	155,300
9	214,200
10	303,800
11	125,200
12	156,900

Population Mean

$$\mu = \frac{\sum x}{N} \qquad \textbf{(7.2)}$$

where:

$\mu = \text{Population mean}$
$x = \text{Values in the population}$
$N = \text{Population size}$

The mean square feet for the 12 office complexes is

$$\mu = \frac{114{,}560 + 202{,}300 + \cdots + 125{,}200 + 156{,}900}{12}$$

$$\mu = 158{,}972 \text{ square feet}$$

Parameter

A measure computed from the entire population. As long as the population does not change, the value of the parameter will not change.

Simple Random Sample

A sample selected in such a manner that each possible sample of a given size has an equal chance of being selected.

The average square footage of the offices built by the firm is 158,972 square feet. This value is a **parameter**. No matter how many times we compute the value, assuming no arithmetic mistakes, we will get the same value for the population mean.

Hummel is a finalist to be the developer of a new office building in Madison, Wisconsin. The client who will hire the firm plans to select a **simple random sample** of $n = 5$ projects from those the finalists have completed. The client plans to travel to these office buildings to see the quality of the construction and to interview owners and occupants. (You may want to refer to Chapter 1 to review the material on simple random samples.)

Referring to the office complex data in Table 7.1, suppose the client randomly selects the following five Hummel projects from the population:

Complex	Square Feet
5	134,600
4	156,700
1	114,560
8	155,300
9	214,200

Key in the selection process is the finalists' past performance on large projects, so the client might be interested in the mean size of the office buildings that the Hummel Development Company has built. Equation 7.3 is used to compute the sample mean.

Sample Mean

$$\bar{x} = \frac{\sum x}{n} \qquad (7.3)$$

where:

$\bar{x}$ = Sample mean
x = Sample values selected from the population
n = Sample size

The sample mean is

$$\bar{x} = \frac{134{,}600 + 156{,}700 + 114{,}560 + 155{,}300 + 214{,}200}{5} = \frac{775{,}360}{5} = 155{,}072$$

The average number of square feet in the random sample of five Hummel office buildings selected by the client is 155,072. This value is a *statistic* based on the sample.

Recall the mean for the population:

$$\mu = 158{,}972 \text{ square feet}$$

The sample mean is

$$\bar{x} = 155{,}072 \text{ square feet}$$

As you can see, the sample mean does not equal the population mean. This difference is called the *sampling error*. Using Equation 7.1, we compute the sampling error as follows.

$$\text{Sampling error} = \bar{x} - \mu$$
$$= 155{,}072 - 158{,}972 = -3{,}900 \text{ square feet}$$

The sample mean for the random sample of $n = 5$ office buildings is 3,900 square feet less than the population mean. Regardless of how carefully you construct your sampling plan, you can expect to see sampling error. A random sample will almost never be a perfect representation of its population. The sample value and the population value will most likely be different.

Suppose the client who selected the random sample throws these five projects back into the stack and selects a second random sample of five as follows:

Complex	Square Feet
9	214,200
6	88,200
5	134,600
12	156,900
10	303,800

The mean for this sample is

$$\bar{x} = \frac{214,200 + 88,200 + 134,600 + 156,900 + 303,800}{5} = \frac{897,700}{5} = 179,540 \text{ square feet}$$

This time, the sample mean is larger than the population mean. This time the sampling error is

$$\bar{x} - \mu = 179,540 - 158,972$$
$$= 20,568 \text{ square feet}$$

This illustrates some useful fundamental concepts:

- The size of the sampling error depends on which sample is selected.
- The sampling error may be positive or negative.
- There is potentially a different $\bar{x}$ for each possible sample.

If the client wanted to use these sample means to estimate the population mean, in one case they would be 3,900 square feet too small, and in the other they would be 20,568 square feet too large.

EXAMPLE 7-1   **COMPUTING THE SAMPLING ERROR**

nexusseven/Fotolia

High-Definition Televisions The website for a major seller of consumer electronics has 10 different brands of HD televisions available. The stated prices for the 46-inch size for the 10 brands are listed as follows:

$479	$569	$599	$649	$649	$699	$699	$749	$799	$799

Suppose a competitor who is monitoring this company has randomly sampled $n = 4$ HD brands and recorded the prices from the population of $N = 10$. The selected HD prices were

$569	$649	$799	$799

The sampling error can be computed using the following steps:

Step 1 Determine the population mean using Equation 7.2.

$$\mu = \frac{\Sigma x}{N} = \frac{479 + 569 + 599 + \cdots + 799 + 799}{10} = \frac{6,690}{10} = \$669$$

Step 2 Compute the sample mean using Equation 7.3.

$$\bar{x} = \frac{\Sigma x}{n} = \frac{569 + 649 + 799 + 799}{4} = \frac{2,816}{4} = \$704$$

Step 3 Compute the sampling error using Equation 7.1.

$$\bar{x} - \mu = 704 - 669 = \$35$$

This sample of four has a sampling error of $35. The sample of TV prices has a slightly larger mean price than the mean for the population.

>> **END EXAMPLE**

TRY PROBLEM 7-1 (pg. 261)

The Role of Sample Size in Sampling Error

BUSINESS APPLICATION   **SAMPLING ERROR**

HUMMEL DEVELOPMENT CORPORATION (*CONTINUED*) Previously, we selected random samples of 5 office complexes from the 12 projects Hummel Development Corporation has built. We then computed the resulting sampling error. There are actually 792 possible samples of size 5 taken from 12 projects. This value is found using the counting rule for combinations, which was discussed in Chapter 5.[1]

In actual situations, only one sample is selected, and the decision maker uses the sample measure to estimate the population measure. A "small" sampling error may be acceptable. However, if the sampling error is too "large," conclusions about the population could be misleading.

We can look at the extremes on either end to evaluate the potential for extreme sampling error. The population of square feet for the 12 projects is

Complex	Square Feet	Complex	Square Feet
1	114,560	7	177,300
2	202,300	8	155,300
3	78,600	9	214,200
4	156,700	10	303,800
5	134,600	11	125,200
6	88,200	12	156,900

Suppose, by chance, the developers ended up with the five smallest office complexes in their sample. These would be

Complex	Square Feet
3	78,600
6	88,200
1	114,560
11	125,200
5	134,600

The mean of this sample is

$$\bar{x} = 108,232 \text{ square feet}$$

Of all the possible random samples of five, this one provides the smallest sample mean. The sampling error is

$$\bar{x} - \mu = 108,232 - 158,972 = -50,740 \text{ square feet}$$

On the other extreme, suppose the sample contained the five largest office complexes, as follows:

Complex	Square Feet
10	303,800
9	214,200
2	202,300
7	177,300
12	156,900

---

[1]The number of combinations of items from a sample of is $\dfrac{n!}{x!\,(n-x)!}$

TABLE 7.2 | **Hummel Office Building Example for *n* = 3 (Extreme Samples)**

Smallest Office Buildings		Largest Office Buildings	
Complex	Square Feet	Complex	Square Feet
3	78,600	10	303,800
6	88,200	9	214,200
1	114,560	2	202,300
$x = 93,786.67$ sq. feet		$\bar{x} = 240,100$ sq. feet	
Sampling Error:		Sampling Error:	
$93,786.67 - 158,972 = -65,185.33$ square feet		$240,100 - 158,972 = 81,128$ square feet	

The mean for this sample is $\bar{x} = 210,900$. This is the largest possible sample mean from all the possible samples of five complexes. The sampling error in this case would be

$$\bar{x} - \mu = 210,900 - 158,972 = 51,928 \text{ square feet}$$

The potential for extreme sampling error ranges from

$$-50,740 \text{ to } +51,928 \text{ square feet}$$

The remaining possible random samples of five will provide sampling errors between these limits.

What happens if the size of the sample selected is larger or smaller? Suppose the client scales back his sample size to $n = 3$ office complexes. Table 7.2 shows the extremes.

By reducing the sample size from five to three, the range of potential sampling error has increased from

$$(-50,740 \text{ to } +51,928 \text{ square feet})$$

to

$$(-65,185.33 \text{ to } +81,128 \text{ square feet})$$

This illustrates that the potential for extreme sampling error is greater when smaller-sized samples are used. Likewise, larger sample sizes will reduce the range of potential sampling error.

Although larger sample sizes reduce the potential for extreme sampling error, there is no guarantee that a larger sample size will always give a smaller sampling error. For example, Table 7.3 shows two further applications of the office complex data. As illustrated, this random sample of three has a sampling error of $-2,672$ square feet, whereas the larger random sample of size five has a sampling error of 16,540 square feet. In this case, the smaller sample was

TABLE 7.3 | **Hummel Office Building Example with Different Sample Sizes**

n = 5		*n* = 3	
Complex	Square Feet	Complex	Square Feet
4	156,700	12	156,900
1	114,560	8	155,300
7	177,300	4	156,700
11	125,200		
10	303,800		
$\bar{x} = 175,512$ sq. feet		$\bar{x} = 156,300$ sq. feet	
Sampling Error:		Sampling Error:	
$175,512 - 158,972 = 16,540$ square feet		$156,300 - 158,972 = -2,672$ square feet	

"better" than the larger sample. However, in Section 7.2, you will learn that, on average, the sampling error produced by large samples will be less than the sampling error from small samples.

MyStatLab

7-1: Exercises

Skill Development

7-1. A population has a mean of 125. If a random sample of 8 items from the population results in the following sampled values, what is the sampling error for the sample?

103	123	99	107	121	100	100	99

7-2. The following data are the 16 values in a population:

10	5	19	20	10	8	10	2
14	18	7	8	14	2	3	10

a. Compute the population mean.
b. Suppose a simple random sample of 5 values from the population is selected with the following results:

5	10	20	2	3

Compute the mean of this sample.
c. Based on the results for parts a and b, compute the sampling error for the sample mean.

7-3. The following population is provided:

17	15	8	12	9	7	9	11
12	14	16	9	5	10	14	13
12	12	11	9	14	8	14	12

Further, a simple random sample from this population gives the following values:

12	9	5	10	14	11

Compute the sampling error for the sample mean in this situation.

7-4. Consider the following population:

18	26	32	17	34	17	17	22
29	24	24	35	13	29	38	

The following sample was drawn from this population:

35	18	24	17	24	32	17	29

a. Determine the sampling error for the sample mean.
b. Determine the largest possible sampling error for this sample of $n = 8$.

7-5. Assume that the following represent a population of $N = 24$ values:

10	14	32	9	34	19	31	24
33	11	14	30	6	27	33	32
28	30	10	31	19	13	6	35

a. If a random sample of $n = 10$ items includes the following values, compute the sampling error for the sample mean:

32	19	6	11	10
19	28	9	13	33

b. For a sample of size $n = 6$, compute the range for the possible sampling error. (*Hint*: Find the sampling error for the 6 smallest sample values and the 6 largest sample values.)
c. For a sample of size $n = 12$, compute the range for the possible sampling error. How does sample size affect the potential for extreme sampling error?

7-6. Assume that the following represent a population of $N = 16$ values.

25	12	21	13	19	17	15	18
23	16	18	15	22	14	23	17

a. Compute the population mean.
b. If a random sample of $n = 9$ includes the following values,

12	18	13	17	23	14	16	25	15

compute the sample mean and calculate the sampling error for this sample.
c. Determine the range of extreme sampling error for a sample of size $n = 4$. (*Hint*: Calculate the lowest possible sample mean and highest possible sample mean.)

7-7. Consider the following population:

3	6	9

a. Calculate the population mean.
b. Select, with replacement, and list each possible sample of size 2. Also, calculate the sample mean for each sample.

c. Calculate the sampling error associated with each sample mean.

d. Assuming that each sample is equally likely, produce the distribution of the sampling errors.

Business Applications

7-8. Hillman Management Services manages apartment complexes in Tulsa, Oklahoma. They currently have 30 units available for rent. The monthly rental prices (in dollars) for this population of 30 units are

455	690	450	495	550	780	800	395	500	405
675	550	490	495	700	995	650	550	400	750
600	780	650	905	415	600	600	780	575	750

a. What is the range of possible sampling error if a random sample of size $n = 6$ is selected from the population?

b. What is the range of possible sampling error if a random sample of size $n = 10$ is selected? Compare your answers to parts a and b and explain why the difference exists.

7-9. A previous report from the Centers for Disease Control and Prevention (CDC) indicates that smokers, on average, miss 6.16 days of work per year due to sickness (including smoking-related acute and chronic conditions). Nonsmokers miss an average of 3.86 days of work per year. If two years later the CDC believes that the average days of work missed by smokers has not changed, it could confirm this by sampling. Consider the following sample:

13	4	4	5	12	8	9	11	1	5
6	9	14	6	3	5	10	7	0	14
6	15	0	2	5	3	10	8	6	7
0	0	15	14	6	2	2	1	4	15
10	12	3	0	14	10	0	1	9	14

Determine the sampling error of this sample, assuming that the CDC supposition is correct.

7-10. An Internet service provider states that the average number of hours its customers are online each day is 3.75. Suppose a random sample of 14 of the company's customers is selected and the average number of hours that they are online each day is measured. The sample results are

3.11	1.97	3.52	4.56	7.19	3.89	7.71
2.12	4.68	6.78	5.02	4.28	3.23	1.29

Based on the sample of 14 customers, how much sampling error exists? Would you expect the sampling error to increase or decrease if the sample size was increased to 40?

7-11. The Anasazi Real Estate Company has 20 listings for homes in Santa Fe, New Mexico. The number of days each house has been on the market without selling is as follows:

26	45	16	77	33	50	19	23	55	107
88	15	7	19	30	60	80	66	31	17

a. Considering these 20 values to be the population of interest, what is the mean of the population?

b. The company is making a sales brochure and wishes to feature 5 homes selected at random from the list. The number of days the 5 sampled homes have been on the market is

77	60	15	31	23

If these 5 houses were used to estimate the mean for all 20, what would the sampling error be?

c. What is the range of possible sampling error if 5 homes are selected at random from the population?

7-12. The administrator at Saint Frances Hospital is concerned about the amount of overtime the nursing staff is incurring and wonders whether so much overtime is really necessary. The hospital employs 60 nurses. Following is the number of hours of overtime reported by each nurse last week. These data are the population of interest.

Nurse	Overtime	Nurse	Overtime	Nurse	Overtime
1	2	21	4	41	3
2	1	22	2	42	3
3	7	23	3	43	2
4	0	24	5	44	1
5	4	25	5	45	3
6	2	26	6	46	3
7	6	27	2	47	3
8	4	28	2	48	3
9	2	29	7	49	4
10	5	30	4	50	6
11	5	31	4	51	0
12	4	32	3	52	3
13	5	33	3	53	4
14	0	34	4	54	6
15	6	35	5	55	0
16	0	36	5	56	3
17	2	37	0	57	3
18	4	38	0	58	7
19	2	39	4	59	5
20	5	40	3	60	7

Using the random numbers table in Appendix A with a starting point in column (digit) 14 and row 10, select a random sample of 6 nurses. Go down the table from the starting point. Determine the mean hours of overtime for these 6 nurses and calculate the sampling error associated with this particular sample mean.

7-13. Princess Cruises recently offered a 16-day voyage from Beijing to Bangkok during the time period from May to August. The announced price, excluding airfare, for a room with an ocean view or a balcony was listed as $3,475. Cruise fares usually are quite variable due to discounting by the cruise line and travel agents. A sample of 20 passengers who purchased this cruise paid the following amounts (in dollars):

3,559	3,005	3,389	3,505	3,605	3,545	3,529	3,709	3,229	3,419
3,439	3,375	3,349	3,559	3,419	3,569	3,559	3,575	3,449	3,119

a. Calculate the sample mean cruise fare.
b. Determine the sampling error for this sample.
c. Would the results obtained in part b indicate that the average cruise fare during this period for this cruise is different from the listed price? Explain your answer from a statistical point of view.

7-14. An investment advisor has worked with 24 clients for the past five years. Following are the percentage rates of average five-year returns that these 24 clients experienced over this time frame on their investments:

11.2	11.2	15.9	2.7	4.6	7.6	15.6	1.3	3.3	4.8	12.8	14.9
10.1	10.9	4.9	−2.1	12.5	3.7	7.6	4.9	10.2	0.4	9.6	−0.5

This investment advisor plans to introduce a new investment program to a sample of his customers this year. Because this is experimental, he plans to randomly select 5 of the customers to be part of the program. However, he would like those selected to have a mean return rate close to the population mean for the 24 clients. Suppose the following 5 values represent the average five-year annual return for the clients that were selected in the random sample:

11.2	−2.1	12.5	1.3	3.3

Calculate the sampling error associated with the mean of this random sample. What would you tell this advisor regarding the sample he has selected?

7-15. A computer lab at a small college has 25 computers. Twice during the day, a full scan for viruses is performed on each computer. Because of differences in the configuration of the computers, the times required to complete the scan are different for each machine. Records for the scans are kept and indicate that the time (in seconds) required to perform the scan for each machine is as shown here.

Time in Seconds to Complete Scan

1,500	1,347	1,552	1,453	1,371
1,362	1,447	1,362	1,216	1,378
1,647	1,093	1,350	1,834	1,480
1,522	1,410	1,446	1,291	1,601
1,365	1,575	1,134	1,532	1,534

a. What is the mean time required to scan all 25 computers?
b. Suppose a random sample of 5 computers is taken and the scan times for each are as follows: 1,534, 1,447, 1,371, 1,410, and 1,834. If these 5 randomly sampled computers are used to estimate the mean scan time for all 25 computers, what would the sampling error be?

c. What is the range of possible sampling error if a random sample size of 7 computers is taken to estimate the mean scan time for all 25 machines?

Computer Database **Exercises**

7-16. *USA Today* reports salaries for National Football League (NFL) teams. The file **Jaguars** contains the salaries for the 2011 Jacksonville Jaguars.
a. Calculate the average total salary for the Jacksonville Jaguars for 2011.
b. Calculate the smallest sample mean for total salary and the largest sample mean for total salary using a sample size of 10. Calculate the sampling error for each sample mean.
c. Repeat the calculations in part b for samples of size 5 and 2.
d. What effect does a change in the sample size appear to have on the dispersion of the sampling errors?

7-17. The file titled **Clothing** contains the monthly retail sales ($millions) of U.S. women's clothing stores for 70 months. A sample taken from this population to estimate the average sales in this time period follows:

2,942	2,574	2,760	2,939	2,642	2,905	2,568
2,677	2,572	3,119	2,697	2,884	2,632	2,742
2,671	2,884	2,946	2,825	2,987	2,729	2,676
2,846	3,112	2,924	2,676			

a. Calculate the population mean.
b. Calculate the sample mean.
c. How much sampling error is present in this sample?
d. Determine the range of possible sampling error if 25 sales figures are sampled at random from this population.

7-18. The Dow-Jones Industrial Average (DJIA) Index is a well-known stock index. The index was originally developed in 1884 and has been in place ever since as a gauge of how the U.S. stock market is performing. The file **Dow Jones** contains date, open, high, low, close, and volume for the DJIA for almost eight years of the trading days.
a. Assuming that the data in the file **Dow Jones** constitute the population of interest, what is the population mean closing value for the DJIA?
b. Using Excel, select a random sample of 10 days' closing values (make certain not to include duplicate days) and calculate the sample mean and the sampling error for the sample.
c. Repeat part b with a sample size of 50 days' closing values.
d. Repeat part b with a sample size of 100 days' closing values.
e. Write a short statement describing your results. Were they as expected? Explain.

7-19. Welco Lumber Company is based in Shelton, Washington, and is a privately held company that makes cedar siding, cedar lumber, and cedar fencing products for sale and distribution throughout North America. The major cost of production is the cedar logs that are the raw material necessary to make the finished cedar products. Thus, it is very important to the company to get the maximum yield from each log. Of course, the dollar value to be achieved from a log depends initially on the diameter of the log. Each log is 8 feet long when it reaches the mill. The file called **Welco** contains a random sample of logs of various diameters and the potential value of the finished products that could be developed from the log if it is made into fence boards.

a. Calculate the sample mean potential value for each diameter of logs in the sample.

b. Discuss whether there is a way to determine how much sampling error exists for a given diameter log based on the sample. Can you determine whether the sampling error will be positive or negative? Discuss.

7-20. Maher, Barney, and White LLC is a legal firm with 40 employees. All of the firm's employees are eligible to participate in the company's 401(k) plan, and the firm is proud of its 100% participation rate. The file **MBW 401** contains the most recent year-end 401(k) account balance for each of the firm's 40 employees.

a. Compute the population mean and population standard deviation for the most recent year-end 401(k) account balances at Maher, Barney, and White.

b. Suppose that an audit of the firm's 401(k) plan is being conducted and 12 randomly selected employee account balances are to be examined. If the following employees (indicated by employee number) are randomly selected to be included in the study, what is the estimate for the most recent

year-end mean 401(k) account balance? How much sampling error is present in this estimate?

Employee #											
26	8	31	3	38	30	17	9	21	39	18	11

c. Calculate the range of possible sampling error if a random sample of 15 employees is used to estimate the most recent year-end mean 401(k) account balance.

7-21. The Badke Foundation was set up by the Fred Badke family following his death in 2001. Fred had been a very successful heart surgeon and real estate investor in San Diego, and the family wanted to set up an organization that could be used to help less fortunate people. However, one of the concepts behind the Badke Foundation is to use the Badke money as seed money for gathering contributions from middle-class families. To help in the solicitation of contributions, the foundation was considering the idea of hiring a consulting company that specialized in this activity. Leaders of the consulting company maintained in their presentation that the mean contribution from families who actually contribute after receiving a specially prepared letter would be $20.00.

Before actually hiring the company, the Badke Foundation sent out the letter and request materials to many people in the San Diego area. They received contributions from 166 families. The contribution amounts are in the data file called **Badke**.

a. Assuming that these data reflect a random sample of the population of contributions that would be received, compute the sampling error based on the claim made by the consulting firm.

b. Comment on any issues you have with the assumption that the data represent a random sample. Does the calculation of the sampling error matter if the sample is not a random sample? Discuss.

END EXERCISES 7-1

7.2 Sampling Distribution of the Mean

Section 7.1 introduced the concept of sampling error. A random sample selected from a population will not perfectly match the population. Thus, the sample statistic likely will not equal the population parameter. If this difference arises because the random sample is not a perfect representation of the population, it is called sampling error.

In business applications, decision makers select a single random sample from a population. They compute a sample measure and use it to make decisions about the entire population. For example, Nielsen Media Research takes a single random sample of television viewers to determine the percentage of the population who are watching a particular program during a particular week. Of course, the sample selected is only one of many possible samples that could have been selected from the same population. The sampling error will differ depending on which sample is selected. If, in theory, you were to select all possible random samples of a given size and compute the sample means for each one, these means would vary above and below the true population mean. If we graphed these values as a histogram, the graph would be the **sampling distribution**.

Sampling Distribution

The distribution of all possible values of a statistic for a given sample size that has been randomly selected from a population.

In this section, we introduce the basic concepts of sampling distributions. We will use an Excel tool to select repeated samples from the same population for demonstration purposes only.

Chapter Outcome 2. → # Simulating the Sampling Distribution for $\bar{x}$

Excel Tutorial

BUSINESS APPLICATION   **SAMPLING DISTRIBUTIONS**

AIMS INVESTMENT COMPANY Aims Investment Company handles employee retirement funds, primarily for small companies. The file named **AIMS** contains data on the number of mutual funds in each client's portfolio. The file contains data for all 200 Aims customers, so it is considered a population. Figure 7.1 shows a histogram for the population.

The mean number of mutual funds in a portfolio is 2.505 funds. The standard deviation is 1.507 funds. The graph in Figure 7.1 indicates that the population is spread between zero and six funds, with more customers owning two funds than any other number.

Suppose the controller at Aims plans to select a random sample of 10 accounts. In Excel, we can use the Sampling tool to generate the random sample.[2] Figure 7.2 shows the number of mutual funds owned for a random sample of 10 clients. The sample mean of 2.1 is also shown. To illustrate the concept of a sampling distribution, we repeat this process 500 times, generating 500 different random samples of 10. For each sample, we compute the sample mean. Figure 7.3 shows the frequency histogram for these sample means. Note that the horizontal axis represents the $\bar{x}$-values. The graph in Figure 7.3 is not a complete sampling distribution because it is based on only 500 samples out of the many possible samples that could be selected. However, this simulation gives us an idea of what the sampling distribution looks like.

Look again at the population distribution in Figure 7.1 and compare it with the shape of the frequency histogram in Figure 7.3. Although the population distribution is somewhat skewed, the distribution of sample means is taking the shape of a normal distribution.

Note also the population mean number of mutual funds owned by the 200 Aims Investment customers in the population is 2.505. If we average the 500 sample means in Figure 7.3, we get 2.41. This value is the *mean of the 500 sample means*. It is reasonably close to the population mean.

FIGURE 7.1

Distribution of Mutual Funds for the Aims Investment Company

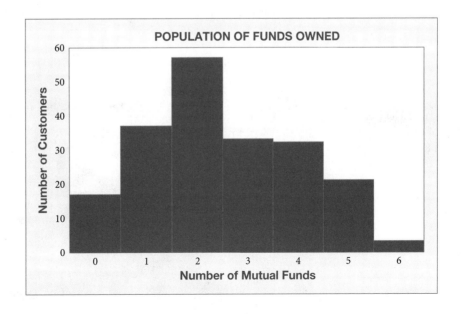

---

[2]The same thing can be achieved in Minitab by using the Sample from Columns option under the Calc > Probability Data command.

FIGURE 7.2

Excel 2010 Output for the Aims Investment Company First Sample Size $n = 10$

Excel 2010 Instructions:
1. Open file: **Aims.xlsx**.
2. Select **Data > Data Analysis**.
3. Select **Sampling**.
4. Define the population data range {B2:B201}.
5. Select **Random, Number of Samples: 10**.
6. Select **Output Range**: D2.
7. Compute sample mean using Excel **=Average** function, using the range (D2:D11).

	A	B	C	D
2	19100	4		0
3	5034	4		1
4	29824	1		2
5	44955	0		2
6	44230	5		2
7	47923	5		2
8	725	2		1
9	20371	3		5
10	43162	4		1
11	6929	1		5
12	12252	4	Mean =	2.1
13	2274	2		
14	1619	0		
15	8206	4		

L23 | f_x

Minitab Instructions (for similar results):
1. Open file: **AIMS.MTW**.
2. Choose **Calc > Random Data > Sample From Columns.**
3. In **Number of rows to Sample,** enter the sample size.
4. In box following **From column(s),** enter data column: *Number of Mutual Fund Accounts.*
5. In **Store Samples in,** enter sample's storage column.
6. Click **OK**.
7. Choose **Calc > Calculator.**
8. In **Store Result in Variable** enter column to store mean.
9. Choose **Mean** from **Functions. Expression: Mean (Sample Column).**
10. Repeat steps 3–10 to form sample.
11. Click **OK**.

FIGURE 7.3

Aims Investment Company, Histogram of 500 Sample Means from Sample Size $n = 10$

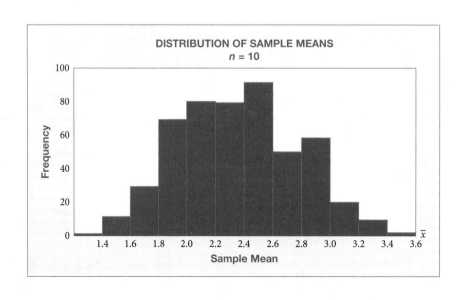

DISTRIBUTION OF SAMPLE MEANS
$n = 10$

Had we selected all possible random samples of size 10 from the population and computed all possible sample means, the average of all the possible sample means would be equal to the population mean. This concept is expressed as Theorem 1.

Theorem 1

For any population, the average value of all possible sample means computed from all possible random samples of a given size from the population will equal the population mean. This is expressed as

$$\mu_{\bar{x}} = \mu$$

Unbiased Estimator

A characteristic of certain statistics in which the average of all possible values of the sample statistic equals a parameter, no matter the value of the parameter.

When the average of all possible values of the sample statistic equals the corresponding parameter, no matter the value of the parameter, we call that statistic an **unbiased estimator** of the parameter.

Also, the population standard deviation is 1.507 mutual funds. This measures the variation in the number of mutual funds between individual customers. When we compute the standard deviation of the 500 sample means, we get 0.421, which is considerably smaller than the population standard deviation. If all possible random samples of size n are selected from the population, the distribution of possible sample means will have a standard deviation that is equal to the population standard deviation divided by the square root of the sample size, as Theorem 2 states.

Theorem 2

For any population, the standard deviation of the possible sample means computed from all possible random samples of size n is equal to the population standard deviation divided by the square root of the sample size. This is shown as

$$\sigma_{\bar{x}} = \frac{\sigma}{\sqrt{n}}$$

Recall the population standard deviation is $\sigma = 1.507$. Then, based on Theorem 2, had we selected all possible random samples of size $n = 10$ rather than only 500 samples, the standard deviation for the possible sample means would be

$$\sigma_{\bar{x}} = \frac{\sigma}{\sqrt{n}} = \frac{1.507}{\sqrt{10}} = 0.477$$

Our simulated value of 0.421 is fairly close to 0.477.

The standard deviation of the sampling distribution will be less than the population standard deviation. To further illustrate, suppose we increased the sample size from $n = 10$ to $n = 20$ and selected 500 new samples of size 20. Figure 7.4 shows the distribution of the 500 different sample means.

The distribution in Figure 7.4 is even closer to a normal distribution than what we observed in Figure 7.3. As sample size increases, the distribution of sample means will become shaped more like a normal distribution. The average sample mean for these 500 samples is 2.53, and the standard deviation of the different sample means is 0.376. Based on Theorems 1 and 2, for a sample size of 20, we would expect the following:

$$\mu_{\bar{x}} = \mu = 2.505 \quad \text{and} \quad \sigma_{\bar{x}} = \frac{\sigma}{\sqrt{n}} = \frac{1.507}{\sqrt{20}} = 0.337$$

Thus, our simulated values are quite close to the theoretical values we would expect had we selected all possible random samples of size 20.

Sampling from Normal Populations The previous discussion began with the population of mutual funds shown in Figure 7.1. The population was not normally distributed, but as we increased the sample size, the sampling distribution of possible sample means began to approach a normal distribution. We will return to this situation shortly, but what happens if the population itself is normally distributed? To help answer this question, Theorem 3 can be applied.

FIGURE 7.4

Aims Investment Company,
Histogram of Sample Means
from Sample Size $n = 20$

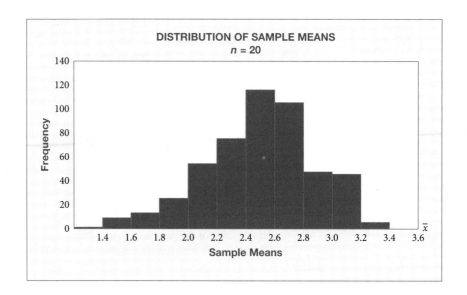

Theorem 3

If a population is normally distributed, with mean μ and a standard deviation σ, the sampling distribution of the sample mean $\bar{x}$ is also normally distributed with a mean equal to the population mean $(\mu_{\bar{x}} = \mu)$ and a standard deviation equal to the population standard deviation divided by the square root of the sample size $(\sigma_{\bar{x}} = \sigma/\sqrt{n})$.

In Theorem 3, the quantity $(\sigma_{\bar{x}} = \sigma/\sqrt{n})$ is the *standard deviation of the sampling distribution*. Another term that is given to this is the *standard error of $\bar{x}$*, because it is the measure of the standard deviation of the potential sampling error.

We can again use simulation to demonstrate Theorem 3. We begin by using Excel to generate a normally distributed population.[3] Figure 7.5 shows a simulated population that is approximately normally distributed with a mean equal to 1,000 and a standard deviation equal to 200. The data range is from 250 to 1,800.

Next, we simulate the selection of 2,000 random samples of size $n = 10$ from the normally distributed population and compute the sample mean for each sample. These sample means can then be graphed as a frequency histogram, as shown in Figure 7.6. This histogram represents the sampling distribution. Note that it, too, is approximately normally distributed.

FIGURE 7.5

Simulated Normal Population
Distribution

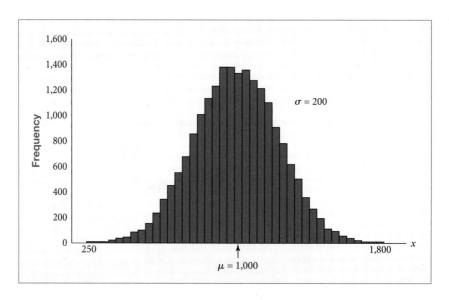

---

[3]The same task can be performed in Minitab using the Calc. > Random Data command. However, you will have to generate each sample individually, which will take time.

FIGURE 7.6

Approximated Sampling
Distribution (*n* = 10)

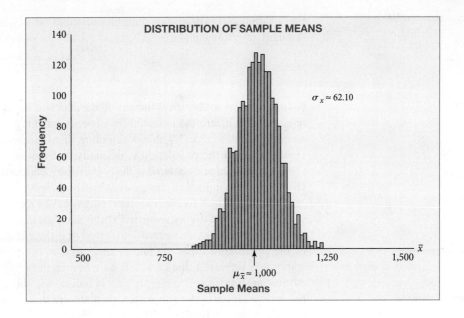

We next compute the average of the 2,000 sample means and use it to approximate $\mu_{\bar{x}}$, as follows:

$$\mu_{\bar{x}} \approx \frac{\sum \bar{x}}{2,000} = \frac{2,000,178}{2,000} \approx 1,000$$

The mean of these sample means is approximately 1,000. This is the same value as the population mean.

We also approximate the standard deviation of the sample means as follows:

$$\sigma_{\bar{x}} \approx \sqrt{\frac{\sum (\bar{x} - \mu_{\bar{x}})^2}{2,000}} = 62.10$$

We see the standard deviation of the sample means is 62.10. This is much smaller than the population standard deviation, which is 200. The largest sample mean was just more than 1,212, and the smallest sample mean was just less than 775. Recall, however, that the population ranged from 250 to 1,800. The variation in the sample means always will be less than the variation for the population as a whole. Using Theorem 3, we would expect the sample means to have a standard deviation equal to

$$\sigma_{\bar{x}} = \frac{\sigma}{\sqrt{n}} = \frac{200}{\sqrt{10}} = 63.25$$

Our simulated standard deviation of 62.10 is fairly close to the theoretical value of 63.25.

Suppose we again use the simulated population shown in Figure 7.5, with $\mu = 1,000$ and $\sigma = 200$. We are interested in seeing what the sampling distribution will look like for different size samples. For a sample size of 5, Theorem 3 indicates that the sampling distribution will be normally distributed and have a mean equal to 1,000 and a standard deviation equal to

$$\sigma_{\bar{x}} = \frac{200}{\sqrt{5}} = 89.44$$

If we were to take a random sample of 10 (as simulated earlier), Theorem 3 indicates the sampling distribution would be normal, with a mean equal to 1,000 and a standard deviation equal to

$$\sigma_{\bar{x}} = \frac{200}{\sqrt{10}} = 63.25$$

For a sample size of 20, the sampling distribution will be centered at $\mu_{\bar{x}} = 1,000$, with a standard deviation equal to

$$\sigma_{\bar{x}} = \frac{200}{\sqrt{20}} = 44.72$$

Notice, as the sample size is increased, the standard deviation of the sampling distribution is reduced. This means the potential for extreme sampling error is reduced when larger sample sizes are used. Figure 7.7 shows sampling distributions for sample sizes of 5, 10, and 20. However, when the population is normally distributed, the sampling distribution of $\bar{x}$ will always be normal and centered at the population mean. Only the spread in the distribution will change as the sample size changes.

This illustrates a very important statistical concept referred to as *consistency*. Earlier we defined a statistic as *unbiased* if the average value of the statistic equals the parameter to be estimated. Theorem 1 asserted that the sample mean is an *unbiased* estimator of the population mean no matter the value of the parameter. However, just because a statistic is unbiased does not tell us whether the statistic will be close in value to the parameter. But if, as the sample size is increased, we can expect the value of the statistic to become closer to the parameter, then we say that the statistic is a **consistent estimator** of the parameter. Figure 7.7 illustrates that the sample mean is a consistent estimator of the population mean.

The sampling distribution is composed of all possible sample means of the same size. Half the sample means will lie above the center of the sampling distribution and half will lie below. The relative distance that a given sample mean is from the center can be determined by *standardizing* the sampling distribution. As discussed in Chapter 6, a standardized value is determined by converting the value from its original units into a z-value. A z-value measures the number of standard deviations a value is from the mean. This same concept can be used when working with a sampling distribution. Equation 7.4 shows how the z-values are computed.

Consistent Estimator

An unbiased estimator is said to be a consistent estimator if the difference between the estimator and the parameter tends to become smaller as the sample size becomes larger.

FIGURE 7.7

Theorem 3 Examples

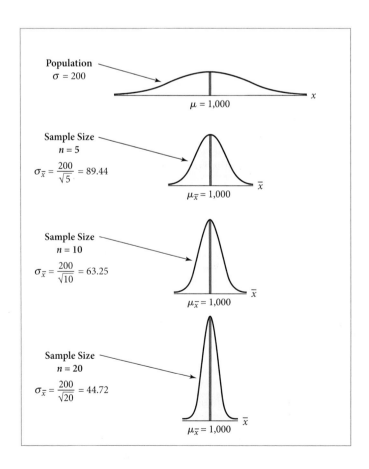

z-Value for Sampling Distribution of $\bar{x}$

$$z = \frac{\bar{x} - \mu}{\frac{\sigma}{\sqrt{n}}}$$

(7.4)

where:

$\bar{x}$ = Sample mean
μ = Population mean
σ = Population standard deviation
n = Sample size

Note, if the sample being selected is large relative to the size of the population (greater than 5% of the population size), of if the sampling is being done without replacement, we need to modify how we compute the standard deviation of the sampling distribution and z-value using what is known as the *finite population correction factor*, as shown in Equation 7.5.

z-Value Adjusted for the Finite Population Correction Factor

$$z = \frac{\bar{x} - \mu}{\frac{\sigma}{\sqrt{n}} \sqrt{\frac{N-n}{N-1}}}$$

(7.5)

where:

N = Population size
n = Sample size
$\sqrt{\dfrac{N-n}{N-1}}$ = Finite population correction factor

The finite population correction factor is used to calculate the standard deviation of the sampling distribution when the sampling is performed without replacement or when the sample size is greater than 5% of the population size.

EXAMPLE 7-2   **FINDING THE PROBABILITY THAT $\bar{x}$ IS IN A GIVEN RANGE**

Wollwerth Imagery/Fotolia

Scribner Products Scribner Products manufactures flooring materials for the residential and commercial construction industries. One item they make is a mosaic tile for bathrooms and showers. When the production process is operating according to specifications, the diagonal dimension of a tile used for decorative purposes is normally distributed with a mean equal to 1.5 inches and a standard deviation of 0.05 inches. Before shipping a large batch of these tiles, Scribner quality analysts have selected a random sample of eight tiles with the following diameters:

| 1.57 | 1.59 | 1.48 | 1.60 | 1.59 | 1.62 | 1.55 | 1.52 |

The analysts want to use these measurements to determine if the process is no longer operating within the specifications. The following steps can be used:

Step 1 Determine the mean for this sample.

$$\bar{x} = \frac{\sum x}{n} = \frac{12.52}{8} = 1.565 \text{ inches}$$

Step 2 Define the sampling distribution for $\bar{x}$ using Theorem 3.

Theorem 3 indicates that if the population is normally distributed, the sampling distribution for $\bar{x}$ will also be normally distributed, with

$$\mu_{\bar{x}} = \mu \quad \text{and} \quad \sigma_{\bar{x}} = \frac{\sigma}{\sqrt{n}}$$

Thus, in this case, the mean of the sampling distribution should be 1.50 inches, and the standard deviation should be $0.05/\sqrt{8} = 0.0177$ inches.

Step 3 Define the probability statement of interest.

Because the sample mean is $\bar{x} = 1.565$, which is greater than the mean of the sampling distribution, we want to find

$$P(\bar{x} \geq 1.565 \text{ inches}) = ?$$

Step 4 Convert the sample mean to a standardized z-value, using Equation 7.4.

$$z = \frac{\bar{x} - \mu}{\dfrac{\sigma}{\sqrt{n}}} = \frac{1.565 - 1.50}{\dfrac{0.05}{\sqrt{8}}} = \frac{0.065}{0.0177} = 3.67$$

Step 5 Use the standard normal distribution table to determine the desired probability.

$$P(z \geq 3.67) = ?$$

The standard normal distribution table in Appendix D does not show z-values as high as 3.67. This implies that $P(z \geq 3.67) \approx 0.00$. So, if the production process is working properly, there is virtually no chance that a random sample of eight tiles will have a mean diameter of 1.565 inches or greater. Because the analysts at Scribner Products did find this sample result, there is a very good chance that something is wrong with the process.

>> **END EXAMPLE**

TRY PROBLEM 7-26 (pg. 277)

Chapter Outcome 3. ➞ # The Central Limit Theorem

Theorem 3 applies when the population is normally distributed. Although there are many situations in business in which this will be the case, there are also many situations in which the population is not normal. For example, incomes in a region tend to be right skewed. Some distributions, such as people's weight, are bimodal (a peak weight group for males and another peak weight group for females).

What does the sampling distribution of $\bar{x}$ look like when a population is not normally distributed? The answer is . . . it depends. It depends on what the shape of the population is and what size sample is selected. To illustrate, suppose we have a U-shaped population, such as the one in Figure 7.8, with mean = 14.00 and standard deviation = 3.00. Now, we

FIGURE 7.8

Simulated Nonnormal Population

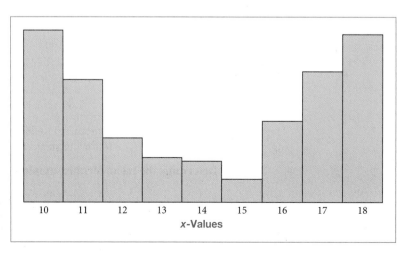

FIGURE 7.9

Frequency Histogram of
$\bar{x}(n = 3)$

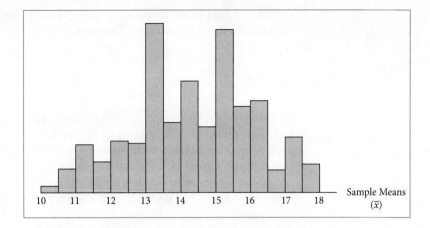

select 3,000 simple random samples of size 3 and compute the mean for each sample. These $\bar{x}$-values are graphed in the histogram shown in Figure 7.9.

The average of these 3,000 sample means is

$$\frac{\sum \bar{x}}{3,000} \approx \mu_{\bar{x}} = 14.02$$

Notice this value is approximately equal to the population mean of 14.00, as Theorem 1 would suggest.[4]

Next we compute the standard deviation as

$$\sigma_{\bar{x}} \approx \sqrt{\frac{\sum (\bar{x} - \mu_{\bar{x}})^2}{3,000}} = 1.82$$

The standard deviation of the sampling distribution is less than the standard deviation for the population, which was 3.00. This will always be the case.

The frequency histogram of $\bar{x}$-values for the 3,000 samples of 3 looks different from the population distribution, which is U-shaped. Suppose we increase the sample size to 10 and take 3,000 samples from the same U-shaped population. The resulting frequency histogram of $\bar{x}$-values is shown in Figure 7.10. Now the frequency distribution looks much like a normal distribution. The average of the sample means is still equal to 14.02, which is virtually equal to the population mean. The standard deviation for this sampling distribution is now reduced to 0.97.

FIGURE 7.10

Frequency Histogram of
$\bar{x}(n = 10)$

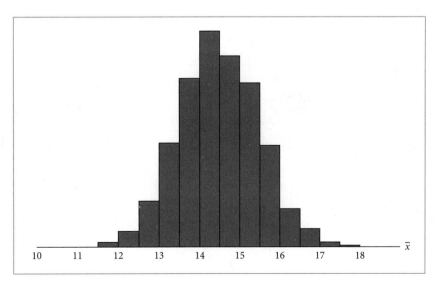

14.02 = Average of sample means

0.97 = Standard deviation of sample means

---

[4]Note, if we had selected all possible samples of three, the average of the samples means would have been equal to the population mean.

This example is not a special case. Instead, it illustrates a very important statistical concept called the **Central Limit Theorem**.

> ### Theorem 4: The Central Limit Theorem
>
> For simple random samples of n observations taken from a population with mean μ and standard deviation σ, regardless of the population's distribution, provided the sample size is sufficiently large, the distribution of the sample means, $\bar{x}$, will be approximately normal with a mean equal to the population mean $(\mu_{\bar{x}} = \mu)$ and a standard deviation equal to the population standard deviation divided by the square root of the sample size $(\sigma_{\bar{x}} = \sigma / \sqrt{n})$. The larger the sample size, the better the approximation to the normal distribution.

The Central Limit Theorem is very important because with it, we know the shape of the sampling distribution even though we may not know the shape of the population distribution. The one catch is that the sample size must be "sufficiently large." What is a sufficiently large sample size?

The answer depends on the shape of the population. If the population is quite symmetric, then sample sizes as small as 2 or 3 can provide a normally distributed sampling distribution. If the population is highly skewed or otherwise irregularly shaped, the required sample size will be larger. Recall the example of the U-shaped population. The frequency distribution obtained from samples of 3 was shaped differently than the population, but not like a normal distribution. However, for samples of 10, the frequency distribution was a very close approximation to a normal distribution. Figures 7.11, 7.12, and 7.13 show some examples of the Central Limit Theorem concept. Simulation studies indicate that even for very strange-looking populations, samples of 25 to 30 produce sampling distributions that are approximately normal. Thus, *a conservative definition of a sufficiently large sample size is $n \geq 30$.* The Central Limit Theorem is illustrated in the following example.

FIGURE 7.11

Central Limit Theorem
With Uniform Population
Distribution

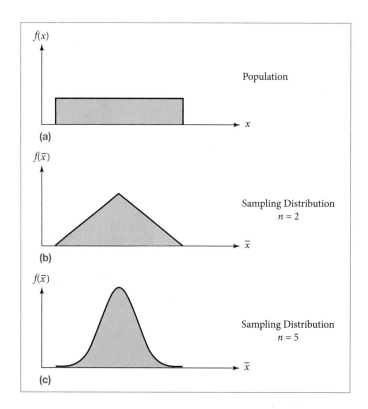

FIGURE 7.12 |

Central Limit Theorem With
Triangular Population

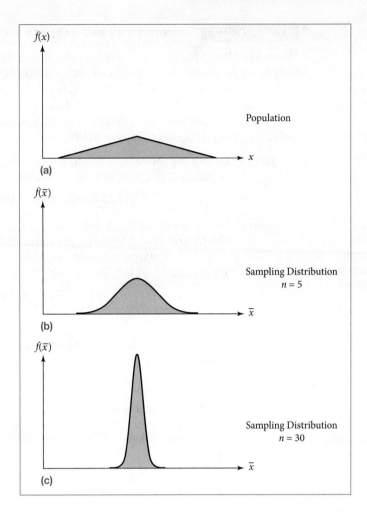

FIGURE 7.13 |

Central Limit Theorem With a
Skewed Population

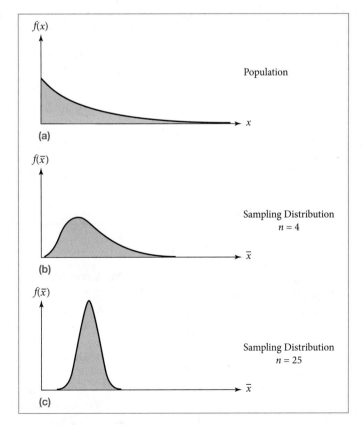

How to do it (Example 7-3)

Sampling Distribution of $\bar{x}$

To find probabilities associated with a sampling distribution of $\bar{x}$ for samples of size n from a population with mean μ and standard deviation σ, use the following steps.

1. Compute the sample mean using

$$\bar{x} = \frac{\sum x}{n}$$

2. Define the sampling distribution.

If the population is normally distributed, the sampling distribution also will be normally distributed for any size sample. If the population is not normally distributed but the sample size is sufficiently large, the sampling distribution will be approximately normal. In either case, the sampling distribution will have

$$\mu_{\bar{x}} = \mu \quad \text{and} \quad \sigma_{\bar{x}} = \frac{\sigma}{\sqrt{n}}$$

3. Define the probability statement of interest.

We are interested in finding the probability of some range of sample means, such as

$$P(\bar{x} \geq 25) = ?$$

4. Use the standard normal distribution to find the probability of interest, using Equation 7.4 or 7.5 to convert the sample mean to a corresponding z-value.

$$z = \frac{\bar{x} - \mu}{\frac{\sigma}{\sqrt{n}}} \quad \text{or} \quad z = \frac{\bar{x} - \mu}{\frac{\sigma}{\sqrt{n}} \sqrt{\frac{N-n}{N-1}}}$$

Then use the standard normal table to find the probability associated with the calculated z-value.

EXAMPLE 7-3   **FINDING THE PROBABILITY THAT $\bar{X}$ IS IN A GIVEN RANGE**

Westside Drive-In. Past sales records indicate that the dollar value of lunch orders at the State Street restaurant are right skewed, with a population mean of $12.50 per customer and a standard deviation of $5.50. The Westside Drive-In manager has selected a random sample of 100 lunch receipts. She is interested in determining the probability that the mean lunch order for this sample from this population will fall between $12.25 and $13.00. To find this probability, she can use the following steps.

Step 1   Determine the sample mean.

In this case, two sample means are being considered:

$$\bar{x} = \$12.25 \quad \text{and} \quad \bar{x} = \$13.00$$

Step 2   Define the sampling distribution.

The Central Limit Theorem can be used because the sample size is large enough $(n = 100)$ to determine that the sampling distribution will be approximately normal (even though the population is right skewed), with

$$\mu_{\bar{x}} = \$12.50 \quad \text{and} \quad \sigma_{\bar{x}} = \frac{\$5.50}{\sqrt{100}} = \$0.55$$

Step 3   Define the probability statement of interest.

The manager is interested in

$$P(\$12.25 \leq \bar{x} \leq \$13.00) = ?$$

Step 4   Use the standard normal distribution to find the probability of interest.

Assuming the population of lunch receipts is quite large, we use Equation 7.4 to convert the sample means to corresponding z-values.

$$z = \frac{\bar{x} - \mu}{\frac{\sigma}{\sqrt{n}}} = \frac{12.25 - 12.50}{\frac{5.50}{\sqrt{100}}} = -0.46 \quad \text{and} \quad z = \frac{\bar{x} - \mu}{\frac{\sigma}{\sqrt{n}}} = \frac{13.00 - 12.50}{\frac{5.50}{\sqrt{100}}} = 0.91$$

From the standard normal table in Appendix D, the probability associated with $z = -0.46$ is 0.1772, and the probability for $z = 0.91$ is 0.3186. Therefore,

$$P(\$12.25 \leq \bar{x} \leq \$13.00) = P(-0.46 \leq z \leq 0.91) = 0.1772 + 0.3186 = 0.4958$$

There is nearly a 0.50 chance that the sample mean will fall in the range $12.25 to $13.00.

>> **END EXAMPLE**

TRY PROBLEM 7-30 (pg. 277)

MyStatLab

7-2: Exercises

Skill Development

7-22. A population with a mean of 1,250 and a standard deviation of 400 is known to be highly skewed to the right. If a random sample of 64 items is selected from the population, what is the probability that the sample mean will be less than 1,325?

7-23. Suppose that a population is known to be normally distributed with $\mu = 2,000$ and $\sigma = 230$. If a random sample of size $n = 8$ is selected, calculate the probability that the sample mean will exceed 2,100.

7-24. A normally distributed population has a mean of 500 and a standard deviation of 60.
   a. Determine the probability that a random sample of size 16 selected from this population will have a sample mean less than 475.
   b. Determine the probability that a random sample of size 25 selected from the population will have a sample mean greater than or equal to 515.

7-25. If a population is known to be normally distributed with $\mu = 250$ and $\sigma = 40$, what will be the characteristics of the sampling distribution for $\bar{x}$ based on a random sample of size 25 selected from the population?

7-26. Suppose nine items are randomly sampled from a normally distributed population with a mean of 100 and a standard deviation of 20. The nine randomly sampled values are

125	95	66	116	99
91	102	51	110	

Calculate the probability of getting a sample mean that is smaller than the sample mean for these nine sampled values.

7-27. A random sample of 100 items is selected from a population of size 350. What is the probability that the sample mean will exceed 200 if the population mean is 195 and the population standard deviation equals 20? (*Hint*: Use the finite population correction factor since the sample size is more than 5% of the population size.)

7-28. Given a distribution that has a mean of 40 and a standard deviation of 13, calculate the probability that a sample of 49 has a sample mean that is
  a. greater than 37
  b. at most 43
  c. between 37 and 43
  d. between 43 and 45
  e. no more than 35

7-29. Consider a normal distribution with mean = 12 and standard deviation = 90. Calculate $P(\bar{x} > 36)$ for each of the following sample sizes:
  a. $n = 1$
  b. $n = 9$
  c. $n = 16$
  d. $n = 25$

Business Applications

7-30. SeeClear Windows makes windows for use in homes and commercial buildings. The standards for glass thickness call for the glass to average 0.375 inches with a standard deviation equal to 0.050 inches. Suppose a random sample of $n = 50$ windows yields a sample mean of 0.392 inches.
  a. What is the probability of $\bar{x} \geq 0.392$ if the windows meet the standards?
  b. Based on your answer to part a, what would you conclude about the population of windows? Is it meeting the standards?

7-31. Many Happy Returns is a tax preparation service with offices located throughout the western United States. Suppose the average number of returns processed by employees of Many Happy Returns during tax season is 12 per day with a standard deviation of 3 per day. A random sample of 36 employees taken during tax season revealed the following number of returns processed daily:

11	17	13	9	13	13	13	12	15
15	13	15	10	15	13	13	15	13
9	9	9	15	13	14	9	14	11
11	17	16	9	8	10	15	12	11

  a. What is the probability of having a sample mean equal to or smaller than the sample mean for this sample if the population mean is 12 processed returns daily with a standard deviation of 3 returns per day?
  b. What is the probability of having a sample mean larger than the one obtained from this sample if the population mean is 12 processed returns daily with a standard deviation of 3 returns per day?
  c. Explain how it is possible to answer parts a and b when the population distribution of daily tax returns at Many Happy Returns is not known.

7-32. SeaFair Fashions relies on its sales force of 220 to do an initial screening of all new fashions. The company is currently bringing out a new line of swimwear and has invited 40 salespeople to its Orlando home office. An issue of constant concern to the SeaFair sales office is the volume of orders generated by each salesperson. Last year, the overall company average was $417,330 with a standard deviation of $45,285. (*Hint*: The finite population correction factor, Equation 7.5, is required.)
  a. Determine the probability the sample of 40 will have a sales average less than $400,000.
  b. What shape do you think the distribution of all possible sample means of 40 will have? Discuss.
  c. Determine the value of the standard deviation of the distribution of the sample mean of all possible samples of size 40.
  d. How would the answers to parts a, b, and c change if the home office brought 60 salespeople to Orlando? Provide the respective answers for this sample size.
  e. Each year SeaFair invites the sales personnel with sales above the 85th percentile to enjoy a complementary vacation in Hawaii. Determine the smallest average salary for the sales personnel that were in Hawaii last year. (Assume the distribution of sales was normally distributed last year.)

7-33. Suppose the life of a particular brand of calculator battery is approximately normally distributed with a mean of 75 hours and a standard deviation of 10 hours.
  a. What is the probability that a single battery randomly selected from the population will have a life between 70 and 80 hours?
  b. What is the probability that 16 randomly sampled batteries from the population will have a sample mean life of between 70 and 80 hours?
  c. If the manufacturer of the battery is able to reduce the standard deviation of battery life from 10 to 9 hours, what would be the probability that 16 batteries randomly sampled from the population will have a sample mean life of between 70 and 80 hours?

7-34. Sands, Inc., makes particleboard for the building industry. Particleboard is built by mixing wood chips and resins together and pressing the sheets under extreme heat and pressure to form a 4-feet × 8-feet sheet that is used as a substitute for plywood. The strength of the particleboards is tied to the board's weight. Boards that are too light are brittle and do not meet the quality standard for strength. Boards that are too heavy are strong but are difficult for customers to handle. The company knows that there will be variation in the boards' weight. Product specifications call for the weight per sheet to average 10 pounds with a standard deviation of 1.75 pounds. During each shift, Sands employees select and weigh a random sample of 25 boards. The boards are thought to have a normally distributed weight distribution.

If the average of the sample slips below 9.60 pounds, an adjustment is made to the process to add more moisture and resins to increase the weight (and, Sands hopes, the strength).

a. Assuming that the process is operating correctly according to specifications, what is the probability that a sample will indicate that an adjustment is needed?

b. Assume the population mean weight per sheet slips to 9 pounds. Determine the probability that the sample will indicate an adjustment is not needed.

c. Assuming that 10 pounds is the mean weight, what should the cutoff be if the company wants no more than a 5% chance that a sample of 25 boards will have an average weight less than 9.6 lbs?

7-35. The branch manager for United Savings and Loan in Seaside, Virginia, has worked with her employees in an effort to reduce the waiting time for customers at the bank. Recently, she and the team concluded that average waiting time is now down to 3.5 minutes with a standard deviation equal to 1.0 minute. However, before making a statement at a managers' meeting, this branch manager wanted to double-check that the process was working as thought. To make this check, she randomly sampled 25 customers and recorded the time they had to wait. She discovered that mean wait time for this sample of customers was 4.2 minutes. Based on the team's claims about waiting time, what is the probability that a sample mean for $n = 25$ people would be as large or larger than 4.2 minutes? What should the manager conclude based on these data?

7-36. Mileage ratings for cars and trucks generally come with a qualifier stating actual mileage will depend on driving conditions and habits. Ford is stating the Ecoboost F-150 pickup truck will get 19 miles per gallon with combined town and country driving. Assume the mean stated by Ford is the actual average, and the distribution has a standard deviation of 3 mpg.

a. Given the above mean and standard deviation, what is the probability that 100 drivers will get more than 19.2 miles per gallon average?

b. Suppose 1,000 drivers were randomly selected. What is the probability the average obtained by these drivers would exceed 19.2 mpg?

7-37. Airlines have recently toughened their standards for the weight of checked baggage, limiting the weight of a bag to 50 pounds on domestic U.S. flights. Heavier bags will be carried, but at an additional fee. Suppose that one major airline has stated in an internal memo to employees that the mean weight for bags checked last year on the

airline was 34.3 pounds with a standard deviation of 5.7 pounds. Further, it stated that the distribution of weights was approximately normally distributed. This memo was leaked to a consumers' group in Atlanta. This group had selected and weighed a random sample of 14 bags to be checked on a flight departing from Atlanta. The following data (pounds) were recorded:

29	27	40	34	30	30	35
44	33	28	36	33	30	40

What is the probability that a sample mean as small or smaller than the one for this sample would occur if the airline's claims about the population of baggage weight is accurate? Comment on the results.

7-38. ACNielsen is a New York–based corporation and a member of the modern marketing research industry. One of the items that ACNielsen tracks is the expenditure on over-the-counter (OTC) cough medicines. ACNielsen recently indicated that consumers spent $620 million on OTC cough medicines in the United States. The article also indicated that nearly 30 million visits for coughs were made to doctors' offices in the United States.

a. Determine the average cost of OTC cough medicines per doctor's office visit based on 30 million purchases.

b. Assuming that the average cost indicated in part a is the true average cost of OTC cough medicines per doctor's visit and the standard deviation is $10, determine the probability that the average cost for a random selection of 30 individuals will result in an average expenditure of more than $25 in OTC cough medicines.

c. Determine the 90th percentile for the average cost of OTC cough medicines for a sample of 36 individuals, all of whom have visited a doctor's office for cough symptoms.

Computer Database **Exercises**

7-39. One of the top-selling video games continues to be *Madden NFL 12*. While prices vary widely depending on store or website, the suggested retail price for this video game is $59.95. The file titled **Madden** contains a random sample of the retail prices paid for *Madden NFL 12*.

a. Calculate the sample mean and standard deviation of retail prices paid for *Madden NFL 12*.

b. To determine if the average retail price has fallen, assume the population mean is $59.95, calculate the probability that a sample of size 200 would result in a sample mean no larger than the one calculated in part a. Assume that the sample standard deviation is representative of the population standard deviation.

c. In part b, you used $59.95 as the population mean. Calculate the probability required in part b assuming that the population mean is $59.50.

d. On the basis of your calculations in parts b and c, does it seem likely that the average retail price for *Madden NFL 12* has decreased? Explain.

7-40. Acee Bottling and Distributing bottles and markets Pepsi-Cola products in southwestern Montana. The average fill volume for Pepsi cans is supposed to be 12 ounces. The filling machine has a known standard deviation of 0.05 ounces. Each week, the company selects a simple random sample of 60 cans and carefully measures the volume in each can. The results of the latest sample are shown in the file called **Acee Bottling**. Based on the data in the sample, what would you conclude about whether the filling process is working as expected? Base your answer on the probability of observing the sample mean you compute for these sample data.

7-41. Bruce Leichtman is president of Leichtman Research Group, Inc. (LRG), which specializes in research and consulting on broadband, media, and entertainment industries. In a recent survey, the company determined the cost of extra high-definition (HD) gear needed to watch television in HD. The costs ranged from $5 a month for a set-top box to $200 for a new satellite. The file titled **HDCosts** contains a sample of the cost of the extras whose purchase was required to watch television in HD. Assume that the population average cost is $150 and the standard deviation is $50.

   a. Create a box and whisker plot and use it and the sample average to determine if the population from which this sample was obtained could be normally distributed.

   b. Determine the probability that the mean of a random sample of size 150 costs for HD extras would be more than $5 away from the mean of the sample described above.

   c. Given your response to part a, do you believe the results obtained in part b are valid? Explain.

7-42. CEO pay has been a controversial subject for several years, and even came up in the 2012 presidential election. The file **CEO Compensation** contains data on the 100 top paid CEOs in either 2010 or 2011, depending on when the information was made available.

   a. Treating the data in the file as the population of interest, compute the population mean and standard deviation for CEO compensation.

   b. Use Excel to select a simple random sample of 30 executive compensation amounts. Compute the sample mean for this sample. Find the probability of getting a sample mean as extreme or more extreme than the one you got. (*Hint*: Use the finite population correction factor because the sample is large relative to the size of the population.)

7-43. The data file called **CEO Compensation** contains data for the most highly paid CEOs in the nation. Separate the values into those from 2010 and those from 2011. Treat the values found for 2010 data as population values. Assume the value found for the mean of the 2011 data is a sample from the 2010 population. What is the probability of finding a value this large or larger?

7-44. The file **Salaries** contains the annual salary for all faculty at a small state college in the Midwest. Assume that these faculty salaries represent the population of interest.

   a. Compute the population mean and population standard deviation.

   b. Develop a frequency distribution of these data using 10 classes. Do the population data appear to be normally distributed?

   c. What is the probability that a random sample of 16 faculty selected from the population would have a sample mean annual salary greater than or equal to $56,650?

   d. Suppose the following 25 faculty were randomly sampled from the population and used to estimate the population mean annual salary:

Faculty ID Number				
137	040	054	005	064
134	013	199	168	027
095	065	193	059	192
084	176	029	143	182
009	033	152	068	044

What would the sampling error be?

   e. Referring to part d, what is the probability of obtaining a sample mean smaller than the one obtained from this sample?

END EXERCISES 7-2

7.3 Sampling Distribution of a Proportion

Working with Proportions

In many instances, the objective of sampling is to estimate a population proportion. For instance, an accountant may be interested in determining the proportion of accounts payable balances that are correct. A production supervisor may wish to determine the percentage of product that is defect-free. A marketing research department might want to know the proportion of potential customers who will purchase a particular product. In all these instances, the decision makers could select a sample, compute the sample proportion, and make their decision based on the sample results.

   Sample proportions are subject to sampling error, just as are sample means. The concept of sampling distributions provides us a way to assess the potential magnitude of the sampling error for proportions in given situations.

Population Proportion

The fraction of values in a population that have a specific attribute.

FLORIDA POWER AND LIGHT Customer service managers at Florida Power and Light surveyed every customer who had new power service installed in a suburb of Tampa during the month of September last year. The key question in the survey was "Are you satisfied with the service received?"

The population size was 80 customers. The number of customers who answered "Yes" to the question was 72. The value of interest in this example is the **population proportion**. Equation 7.6 is used to compute a population proportion.

Population Proportion

$$p = \frac{X}{N}$$

(7.6)

where:

p = Population proportion
X = Number of items in the population having the attribute of interest
N = Population size

The proportion of customers in the population who are satisfied with the service by Florida Power and Light is

$$p = \frac{72}{80} = 0.90$$

Therefore, 90% of the population responded "Yes" to the survey question. This is the *parameter*. It is a measurement taken from the population. It is the "true value."

Now, suppose that Florida Power and Light wishes to do a follow-up survey for a simple random sample of $n = 20$ of the same 80 customers. What fraction of this sample will be people who had previously responded "Yes" to the satisfaction question?

The answer depends on which sample is selected. There are many (3.5353×10^{18} to be precise) possible random samples of 20 that could be selected from 80 people. However, the company will select only one of these possible samples. At one extreme, suppose the 20 people selected for the sample included all 8 who answered "No" to the satisfaction question and 12 others who answered "Yes." The **sample proportion** is computed using Equation 7.7.

Sample Proportion

The fraction of items in a sample that have the attribute of interest.

Sample Proportion

$$\bar{p} = \frac{x}{n}$$

(7.7)

where:

$\bar{p}$ = Sample proportion
x = Number of items in the sample with the attribute of interest
n = Sample size

For the Florida Power and Light example, the sample proportion of "Yes" responses is

$$\bar{p} = \frac{12}{20} = 0.60$$

The sample proportion of "Yes" responses is 0.60, whereas the population proportion is 0.90. The difference between the sample value and the population value is sampling error. Equation 7.8 is used to compute the sampling error involving a single proportion.

Single-Proportion Sampling Error

$$\text{Sampling error} = \bar{p} - p \qquad\qquad (7.8)$$

where:

$$p = \text{Population proportion}$$
$$\bar{p} = \text{Sample proportion}$$

Then for this extreme situation we get

$$\text{Sampling error} = 0.60 - 0.90 = -0.30$$

If a sample on the other extreme had been selected and all 20 people came from the original list of 72 who had responded "Yes," the sample proportion would be

$$\bar{p} = \frac{20}{20} = 1.00$$

For this sample, the sampling error is

$$\text{Sampling error} = 1.00 - 0.90 = 0.10$$

Thus, the range of sampling error in this example is from -0.30 to 0.10. As with any sampling situation, you can expect some sampling error. The sample proportion will probably not equal the population proportion because the sample selected will not be a perfect replica of the population.

EXAMPLE 7-4 | **SAMPLING ERROR FOR A PROPORTION**

Tatiana Popova/Shutterstock

Hewlett-Packard–Compaq Merger In 2002, a proxy fight took place between the management of Hewlett-Packard (HP) and Walter Hewlett, the son of one of HP's founders, over whether the merger between HP and Compaq should be approved. Each outstanding share of common stock was allocated one vote. After the vote in March 2002, the initial tally showed that the proportion of shares in the approval column was 0.51. After the vote, a lawsuit was filed by a group led by Walter Hewlett, which claimed improprieties by the HP management team. Suppose the attorneys for the Hewlett faction randomly selected 40 shares from the millions of total shares. The intent was to interview the owners of these shares to determine whether they had voted for the merger. Of the shares in the sample, 26 carried an "Approval" vote. The attorneys can use the following steps to assess the sampling error:

Step 1 **Determine the population proportion.**
In this case, the proportion of votes cast in favor of the merger is

$$p = 0.51$$

This is the number of approval votes divided by the total number of shares.

Step 2 **Compute the sample proportion using Equation 7.7.**
The sample proportion is

$$\bar{p} = \frac{x}{n} = \frac{26}{40} = 0.65$$

Step 3 **Compute the sampling error using Equation 7.8.**

$$\text{Sampling error} = \bar{p} - p = 0.65 - 0.51 = 0.14$$

The proportion of "Approval" votes from the shares in this sample exceeds the population proportion by 0.14.

>> **END EXAMPLE**

TRY PROBLEM 7-47 (pg. 285)

Chapter Outcome 4. → # Sampling Distribution of $\bar{p}$

In many applications, you will be interested in determining the proportion p of all items in a population that possess a particular attribute. The best estimate of this population proportion will be $\bar{p}$, the sample proportion. However, any inference about how close your estimate is to the true population value will be based on the distribution of this sample proportion, $\bar{p}$, whose underlying distribution is the binomial. However, if the sample size is sufficiently large such that

$$np \geq 5 \quad \text{and} \quad n(1-p) \geq 5$$

then the normal distribution can be used as a reasonable approximation to the discrete binomial distribution.[5] Providing we have a large enough sample size, the distribution of all possible sample proportions will be approximately normally distributed. In addition to being normally distributed, the sampling distribution will have a mean and standard error as indicated in Equations 7.9 and 7.10.

Mean and Standard Error of the Sampling Distribution of $\bar{p}$

$$\text{Mean} = \mu_{\bar{p}} = p \qquad \qquad (7.9)$$

and

$$\text{Standard error} = \sigma_{\bar{p}} = \sqrt{\frac{p(1-p)}{n}} \qquad \qquad (7.10)$$

where:

$$p = \text{Population proportion}$$
$$n = \text{Sample size}$$
$$\bar{p} = \text{Sample proportion}$$

In Section 7.2, we introduced Theorem 4, the Central Limit Theorem, which indicates that regardless of the shape of the population distribution, the distribution of possible sample means will be approximately normal as long as the sample size is sufficiently large. Theorem 5 is similar but pertains to the sampling distribution for the sample proportion.

Theorem 5: Sampling Distribution of $\bar{p}$

Regardless of the value of the population proportion, p, (with the obvious exceptions of $p = 0$ and $p = 1$), the sampling distribution for the sample proportion, $\bar{p}$, will be approximately normally distributed with $\mu_{\bar{p}} = p$ and

$$\sigma_{\bar{p}} = \sqrt{\frac{p(1-p)}{n}},$$

providing $np \geq 5$ and $n(1-p) \geq 5$. The approximation to the normal distribution improves as the sample size increases and p approaches 0.50.

BUSINESS APPLICATION   **SAMPLING DISTRIBUTION FOR PROPORTIONS**

ON-LINE COUPONS, INC. On-Line Coupons, Inc. is one of the many companies that have entered the market to sell discount coupons online. Buyers get discounts at local retail and service establishments. The On-Line Coupon marketing managers have analyzed coupon

---

[5]An application of the Central Limit Theorem provides the rationale for this statement. Recall that $\bar{p} = x/n$, where x is the sum of random variables (x_i) whose values are 0 and 1. Therefore, $\bar{p}$ is in reality just a sample mean. Each of these x_i can be thought of as binomial random variables from a sample of size $n = 1$. Thus, they each have a mean of $\mu = np = p$ and a variance of $\sigma^2 = np(1-p) = p(1-p)$. As we have seen from the Central Limit Theorem, the sample mean has an expected value of μ and a variance of σ^2/n. Thus, the sample proportion has an expected value of $\mu = p$ and a variance of $\sigma^2 = \dfrac{p(1-p)}{n}$.

redemption patterns and have determined that 15% of coupons purchased go unused by the buyer. There appears to be no particular pattern to the lack of coupon use, and one coupon going unused seems independent of whether any other coupon is not used.

Suppose that the company recently received an e-mail from a retailer who says that 18% of the 500 coupons sold were not used by the expiration date. Assume the nonuse rate for the population of all coupons sold is

$$p = 0.15$$

How likely is it that a sample of

$$n = 500$$

coupons sold will have 18% or more unused? To answer this question, we first check to determine if the sample size is sufficiently large. Because both

$$n(p) = 500(0.15) = 75 \geq 5 \quad \text{and} \quad n(1-p) = 500(0.85) = 425 \geq 5$$

we can safely conclude that the sampling distribution of sample proportions will be approximately normal. Using Equations 7.9 and 7.10, we can compute the mean and standard error for the sampling distribution as follows:

$$\mu_{\bar{p}} = 0.15$$

and

$$\sigma_{\bar{p}} = \sqrt{\frac{(0.15)(0.85)}{500}} = 0.016$$

Equation 7.11 is used to convert the sample proportion to a standardized z-value.

---

z-Value for Sampling Distribution of $\bar{p}$

$$z = \frac{\bar{p} - p}{\sigma_{\bar{p}}} \qquad\qquad \textbf{(7.11)}$$

where:

z = Number of standard errors $\bar{p}$ is from p

$\bar{p}$ = Sample proportion

$\sigma_{\bar{p}} = \sqrt{\dfrac{p(1-p)}{n}}$ = Standard error of the sampling distribution[6]

p = Population proportion

From Equation 7.11, we get

$$z = \frac{\bar{p} - p}{\sigma_{\bar{p}}} = \frac{0.18 - 0.15}{\sqrt{\dfrac{(0.15)(0.85)}{500}}} = 1.88$$

Therefore, the 0.18 nonredemption rate reported by the retailer is 1.88 standard errors above the population proportion of 0.15. Figure 7.14 illustrates that the chances of a defect rate of 0.18 or more is

$$P(\bar{p} \geq 0.18) = 0.0301$$

Because this is a low probability, the On-Line Coupons, Inc. managers might want to see if there was something unusual about this coupon offering.

---

[6]If the sample size n is greater than 5% of the population size, the standard error of the sampling distribution should be computed using the finite population correction factor as $\sigma_{\bar{p}} = \sqrt{\dfrac{p(1-p)}{n}} \sqrt{\dfrac{N-n}{N-1}}$.

FIGURE 7.14

Standard Normal Distribution
for On-Line Coupons, Inc.

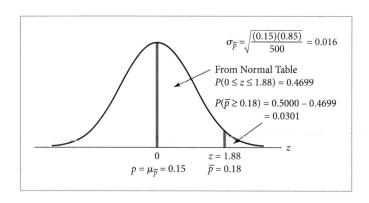

$$\sigma_{\bar{p}} = \sqrt{\frac{(0.15)(0.85)}{500}} = 0.016$$

From Normal Table
$P(0 \leq z \leq 1.88) = 0.4699$

$P(\bar{p} \geq 0.18) = 0.5000 - 0.4699$
$= 0.0301$

$z = 1.88$
z

0
$p = \mu_{\bar{p}} = 0.15$
$\bar{p} = 0.18$

How to do it (Example 7-5)

Sampling Distribution of $\bar{p}$
To find probabilities associated with a sampling distribution for a single-population proportion, the following steps can be used.

1. Determine the population proportion, p, using

$$p = \frac{X}{N}$$

2. Calculate the sample proportion using

$$\bar{p} = \frac{x}{n}$$

3. Determine the mean and standard deviation of the sampling distribution using

$$\mu_{\bar{p}} = p \quad \text{and} \quad \sigma_{\bar{p}} = \sqrt{\frac{p(1-p)}{n}}$$

4. Define the event of interest. For example:

$$P(\bar{p} \geq 0.30) = ?$$

5. If np and $n(1-p)$ are both ≥ 5, then convert $\bar{p}$ to a standardized z-value using

$$z = \frac{\bar{p} - p}{\sigma_{\bar{p}}}$$

6. Use the standard normal distribution table in Appendix D to determine the required probability.

EXAMPLE 7-5   FINDING THE PROBABILITY THAT $\bar{p}$ IS IN A GIVEN RANGE

Craig's List An analysis is performed of whether "apartment for rent" ads placed online result in a rental within two weeks is 0.80 or higher. As part of a story being written for a national publication about these types of services, the author wishes to make the claim that the proportion of apartments rented within two weeks using Craig's List is 0.80. Before doing this, she has selected a simple random sample of 100 "apartment for rent" ads and tracked down the rental result for each. Of these, 73 resulted in a rental within the two-week period. To determine the probability of this result or something more extreme, she can use the following steps:

Step 1   Determine the population proportion, p.
The population proportion is believed to be $p = 0.80$ based on the analysis.

Step 2   Calculate the sample proportion.
In this case, a random sample of $n = 100$ ads was selected, with 73 having the attribute of interest (rented within two weeks). Thus,

$$\bar{p} = \frac{x}{n} = \frac{73}{100} = 0.73$$

Step 3   Determine the mean and standard deviation of the sampling distribution.
The mean of the sampling distribution is equal to $\bar{p}$, the population proportion. So

$$\mu_{\bar{p}} = p = 0.80$$

The standard deviation of the sampling distribution for $\bar{p}$ is computed using

$$\sigma_{\bar{p}} = \sqrt{\frac{p(1-p)}{n}} = \sqrt{\frac{0.80(1-0.80)}{100}} = 0.04$$

Step 4   Define the event of interest.
In this case, because 0.73 is less than 0.80, we are interested in

$$P(\bar{p} \leq 0.73) = ?$$

Step 5   If np and $n(1-p)$ are both ≥ 5, then convert $\bar{p}$ to a standardized z-value.
Checking, we get

$$np = 100(0.80) = 80 \geq 5 \quad \text{and} \quad n(1-p) = 100(0.20) = 20 \geq 5$$

Then we convert to a standardized z-value using

$$z = \frac{\bar{p} - p}{\sigma_{\bar{p}}} = \frac{0.73 - 0.80}{\sqrt{\frac{0.80(1-0.80)}{100}}} = -1.75$$

Step 6 **Use the standard normal distribution table in Appendix D to determine the probability for the event of interest.**
We want

$$P(\bar{p} \leq 0.73) \quad \text{or} \quad P(z \leq -1.75)$$

From the normal distribution table for $z = -1.75$, we get 0.4599, which corresponds to the probability of a z-value between -1.75 and 0.0. To get the probability of interest, we subtract 0.4599 from 0.5000, giving 0.0401. There is only a 4% chance that a random sample of $n = 100$ apartments would produce a sample proportion of $\bar{p} \leq 0.73$ that are rented within two week if the true population proportion is 0.80. The author might want to use caution before making this claim.

>> **END EXAMPLE**

TRY PROBLEM 7-45 (pg. 285)

MyStatLab

7-3: Exercises

Skill Development

7-45. A population has a proportion equal to 0.30. Calculate the following probabilities with $n = 100$:
   a. $P(\bar{p} \leq 0.35)$
   b. $P(\bar{p} > 0.40)$
   c. $P(0.25 < \bar{p} \leq 0.40)$
   d. $P(\bar{p} \geq 0.27)$.

7-46. If a random sample of 200 items is taken from a population in which the proportion of items having a desired attribute is $p = 0.30$, what is the probability that the proportion of successes in the sample will be less than or equal to 0.27?

7-47. The proportion of items in a population that possess a specific attribute is known to be 0.70.
   a. If a simple random sample of size $n = 100$ is selected and the proportion of items in the sample that contain the attribute of interest is 0.65, what is the sampling error?
   b. Referring to part a, what is the probability that a sample of size 100 would have a sample proportion of 0.65 or less if the population proportion is 0.70?

7-48. Given a population in which the proportion of items with a desired attribute is $p = 0.25$, if a sample of 400 is taken,
   a. What is the standard deviation of the sampling distribution of $\bar{p}$?
   b. What is the probability the proportion of successes in the sample will be greater than 0.22?

7-49. Given a population in which the probability of success is $p = 0.20$, if a sample of 500 items is taken, then
   a. Calculate the probability the proportion of successes in the sample will be between 0.18 and 0.23.

   b. Calculate the probability the proportion of successes in the sample will be between 0.18 and 0.23 if the sample size is 200.

7-50. Given a population in which the proportion of items with a desired attribute is $p = 0.50$, if a sample of 200 is taken,
   a. Find the probability the proportion of successes in the sample will be between 0.47 and 0.51.
   b. Referring to part a, what would the probability be if the sample size were 100?

7-51. Given a population in which the probability of a success is $p = 0.40$, if a sample of 1,000 is taken,
   a. Calculate the probability the proportion of successes in the sample will be less than 0.42.
   b. What is the probability the proportion of successes in the sample will be greater than 0.44?

7-52. A random sample of size 100 is to be taken from a population that has a proportion equal to 0.35. The sample proportion will be used to estimate the population proportion.
   a. Calculate the probability that the sample proportion will be within ± 0.05 of the population proportion.
   b. Calculate the probability that the sample proportion will be within ± 1 standard error of the population proportion.
   c. Calculate the probability that the sample proportion will be within ± 0.10 of the population proportion.

7-53. A survey is conducted from a population of people of whom 40% have a college degree. The following sample data were recorded for a question asked of each person sampled, "Do you have a college degree?"

YES	NO	NO	YES	YES
YES	YES	YES	YES	YES
YES	NO	NO	NO	YES
NO	YES	YES	NO	NO
NO	YES	YES	YES	NO
YES	NO	YES	NO	NO
YES	NO	NO	NO	YES
YES	NO	NO	NO	NO
NO	NO	YES	NO	NO
NO	YES	NO	YES	YES
NO	NO	NO	YES	NO
NO	NO	NO	YES	YES

a. Calculate the sample proportion of respondents who have a college degree.

b. What is the probability of getting a sample proportion as extreme or more extreme than the one observed in part a if the population has 40% with college degrees?

Business Applications

7-54. United Manufacturing and Supply makes sprinkler valves for use in residential sprinkler systems. United supplies these valves to major companies such as Rain Bird and Nelson, who in turn sell sprinkler products to retailers. United recently entered into a contract to supply 40,000 sprinkler valves. The contract called for at least 97% of the valves to be free of defects. Before shipping the valves, United managers tested 200 randomly selected valves and found 190 defect-free valves in the sample. The managers wish to know the probability of finding 190 or fewer defect-free valves if in fact the population of 40,000 valves is 97% defect-free. Discuss how they could use this information to determine whether to ship the valves to the customer.

7-55. The J R Simplot Company is one of the world's largest privately held agricultural companies, employing more than 10,000 people in the United States, Canada, China, Mexico, and Australia. More information can be found at the company's website: www.Simplot.com. One of its major products is french fries that are sold primarily on the commercial market to customers such as McDonald's and Burger King. French fries have numerous quality attributes that are important to customers. One of these is called "dark ends," which are the dark-colored ends that can occur when the fries are cooked. Suppose a major customer will accept no more than 0.06 of the fries having dark ends.

Recently, the customer called the Simplot Company saying that a recent random sample of 300 fries was tested from a shipment and 27 fries had dark ends. Assuming that the population does meet the 0.06 standard, what is the probability of getting a sample of 300 with 27 or more dark ends? Comment on this result.

7-56. The National Association of Realtors released a survey indicating that a surprising 43% of first-time home buyers purchased their homes with no-money-down loans during the time before the housing bubble collapsed. Many house prices declined, leaving homeowners owing more than their homes are worth. Even today, some forecasters estimate there exists a 50% risk that prices will decline within two years in major metro areas such as San Diego, Boston, Long Island, New York City, Los Angeles, and San Francisco.

a. A survey taken by realtors in the San Francisco area found that 12 out of the 20 first time home buyers sampled purchased their home with no-money-down loans. Calculate the probability that at least 12 in a sample of 20 first-time buyers would take out no-money-down loans if San Francisco's proportion is the same as the nationwide proportion of no-money-down loans.

b. Determine the probability requested in part a if the nationwide proportion is 0.53.

c. Determine the probability that between 8 and 12 of a sample of 20 first-time home buyers would take out no-money-down loans if the 43% value applies.

7-57. According to the most recent Labor Department data, 10.5% of engineers (electrical, mechanical, civil, and industrial) were women. Suppose a random sample of 50 engineers is selected.

a. How likely is it that the random sample of 50 engineers will contain 8 or more women in these positions?

b. How likely is it that the random sample will contain fewer than 5 women in these positions?

c. If the random sample included 200 engineers, how would this change your answer to part b?

7-58. The federal government is currently trying to devise plans to help homeowners who owe more on their mortgages than their houses are worth. A new survey estimates that 33% or those holding "underwater" mortgages would be helped by the current plan.

a. In samples of mortgages of size 75, what proportion of the samples would you expect to produce sample proportions equal to or larger than 0.25?

b. If a sample of size 75 produced a sample proportion of 0.45, what would you infer that the population proportion of mortgages "underwater" really is?

c. In a sample of 90 mortgages, what would the probability be that the number of mortgages "underwater" would be between 25 and 35?

7-59. Airgistics provides air consolidation and freight-forwarding services for companies that ship their products internationally. As a part of its commitment to continuous process improvement, Airgistics monitors the performance of its partner carriers to ensure that high standards of on-time delivery are met. Airgistics currently believes that it achieves a 96% on-time performance for its customers. Recently, a random sample of 200 customer shipments was selected for study, and 188 of them were found to have met the on-time delivery promise.

a. What is the probability that a random sample of 200 customer shipments would contain 188 or fewer on-time deliveries if the true population of on-time deliveries is 96%?

b. Would you be surprised if the random sample of 200 customer shipments had 197 on-time deliveries?

c. Suppose the random sample of 200 customer shipments revealed that 178 were on time. Would such a finding cause you to question Airgistics's claim that its on-time performance is 96%? Support your answer with a probability calculation.

Computer Database **Exercises**

7-60. Procter & Gamble (P&G) merged with Gillette in 2005. One of the concerns the new, larger company has is the increasing burden of retirement expenditures. An effort is being made to encourage employees to participate in 401(k) accounts. Nationwide, 66% of eligible workers participate in these accounts. The file titled **Gillette** contains responses of 200 P&G workers when asked if they were currently participating in a 401(k) account.

a. Determine the sample proportion of P&G workers who participate in 401(k) accounts.

b. Determine the sampling error if in reality P&G workers have the same proportion of participants in 401(k) accounts as does the rest of the nation.

c. Determine the probability that a sample proportion at least as large as that obtained in the sample would be obtained if P&G workers have the same proportion of participants in 401(k) accounts as does the rest of the nation.

d. Does it appear that a larger proportion of P&G workers participate in 401(k) accounts than do the workers of the nation as a whole? Support your response.

7-61. The Bureau of Transportation Statistics releases information concerning the monthly percentage of U.S. airline flights that land no later than 15 minutes after scheduled arrival. The average of these percentages for the 12 months in 2010 was 78.5%. These data become available as soon as feasible. However, the airlines can provide preliminary results by obtaining a sample. The file titled **Ontime** contains the sample data indicating the number of minutes after scheduled arrival time that the aircraft arrived. Note that a negative entry indicates the minutes earlier than the scheduled arrival time that the aircraft arrived.

a. Calculate the proportion of sampled airline flights that landed within 15 minutes of scheduled arrival.

b. Calculate the probability that a sample proportion of on-time flights would be within ±0.06 of a population proportion equal to 0.785.

c. If the airlines' goal was to attain the same proportion of on-time arrivals as in 2010, do the preliminary results indicate that they have met this goal? Support your assertions.

7-62. The Bureau of Labor Statistics, U.S. Office of Personnel Management, indicated that the average hourly compensation (salary plus benefits) for federal workers (not including military or postal service employees) was $44.82. The rates for private industry and state and local government workers are believed to be considerably less than that. The file titled **Paychecks** contains a random sample of the hourly amounts paid to state and local government workers.

a. If the hourly compensation for federal workers was normally distributed, determine the median hourly compensation.

b. Calculate the sample proportion of the state and local government workers whose hourly compensation is less than $44.82.

c. If a sample of size 150 was obtained from a population whose population proportion was equal to your answer to part a, determine the probability that the sample proportion would be equal to or greater than the answer obtained in part b.

d. On the basis of your work in parts a, b, and c, would you conclude that the proportion of state and local workers whose hourly compensation is less than $44.82 is the same as that of the federal workers? Explain.

7-63. *Driven*, a recently released magazine targeted to young professionals, states that 65% of its subscribers have an annual income greater than $100,000. The sales staff at *Driven* uses this high proportion of subscribers earning more than $100,000 as a selling point when trying to get companies to place advertisements with the magazine. *Driven* is currently trying to sell a large amount of advertising to Meuscher, an upscale chocolatier, for a special year-end issue on fine foods and wines. Before committing to advertise in *Driven*, Meuscher's market research staff has decided to randomly sample 201 of *Driven*'s subscribers to verify *Driven*'s claim that 65% of its subscribers earn more than $100,000 annually.

a. The file **Driven** contains the responses of 196 randomly sampled subscribers of the magazine. The responses are coded "Yes" if the subscriber earns more than $100,000 annually and "No" if the subscriber does not earn more than $100,000 annually. Open the file **Driven** and create a new variable that has a value of 1 for "yes" and 0 for "no."

b. Calculate the sample proportion of subscribers who have annual incomes greater than $100,000.

c. How likely is it that a sample proportion greater than the one calculated in part b would be obtained if the population proportion of subscribers earning more than $100,000 annually is 65%?

d. Based on the probability you calculated in part c, should Meuscher advertise in *Driven*?

7-64. A study conducted by Watson Wyatt Worldwide, a human resources consulting firm, revealed that 13% of Fortune 1000 companies either terminated or froze their defined-benefit pension plans. As part of a study to evaluate how well its benefits package compares to other Fortune 1000 companies, a retail firm randomly samples 36 Fortune 1000 companies in odd-numbered years and asks them to complete a benefits questionnaire. One question asked is whether the company has changed its defined-benefits pension plan by either freezing it or terminating it during the survey year. The results of the survey are contained in the file **Pension Survey**.

a. Open the file **Pension Survey**. Create a new variable that has a value equal to 1 if the firm has either terminated or frozen its defined-benefits pension plan and equal to 0 if the firm has not significantly altered its pension plan.

b. Determine the sample proportion of companies that either terminated or froze their defined-benefits pension plan.

c. How likely is it that a sample proportion greater than or equal to the one found in the survey would occur if the true population of firms who have terminated or frozen their defined-benefits pension plan is as reported by Watson Wyatt Worldwide?

END EXERCISES 7-3

Visual Summary

Chapter 7: Many business situations require that a sample be taken from a population and an analysis performed on the sample data. The objective of random sampling is to select data that mirror the population. Then when the sampled data are analyzed the results will be as if we had worked with all the population data. Whenever decisions are based on samples rather than a population, questions about the sample results exist. Chapter 7 introduces the important concepts associated with making decisions based on samples. Included is a discussion of sampling error, as well as the sampling distribution of the mean and the sampling distribution of a proportion.

 7.1 Sampling Error: What It Is and Why It Happens (pg. 256–264)

Summary

Regardless of how careful we are in selecting a random sample the sample may not perfectly represent the population. In such cases the sample statistic will likely not equal the population parameter. If this difference arises because the random sample is not a perfect representation of the population, it is called **sampling error**. **Sampling error** refers to the difference between a measure computed from a sample (**a statistic**) and the corresponding measure computed from the population (**a parameter**). Some fundamental concepts associated with sampling errors include the following:

The size of the sampling error depends on which sample is selected.
The sampling error may be positive or negative.
There is potentially a different statistic for each sample selected.

Outcome 1. Understand the concept of sampling error.

 7.2 Sampling Distribution of the Mean (pg. 264–279)

Summary

In business applications, decision makers select a single random sample from a population. A sample measure is then computed from the sample and used to make decisions about the population. The selected sample is, of course, only one of many that could have been drawn from the population. If all possible random samples of a given sample size were selected and the sample mean was computed for each sample taken, the sample means would vary above and below the true population mean. If these values were graphed as a histogram, the graph would be a **sampling distribution**. Therefore, the **sampling distribution** is the distribution of all possible values of a statistic for a given sample size that has been randomly selected from a population. When the average of all possible values of the sample statistic equals the corresponding parameter, the statistic is said to be an **unbiased estimator** of the parameter. An unbiased estimator is **consistent** if the difference between the estimator and the parameter tends to become smaller as the sample size becomes larger. An important statistical concept called the **Central Limit Theorem** tells us that for a sufficiently large sample size the distribution of the sample means will be approximately normal with a mean equal to the population mean and a standard deviation equal to the population standard deviation divided by the square root of the sample size. The larger the sample size the better the approximation to the normal distribution.

Outcome 2. Determine the mean and standard deviation for the sampling distribution of the sample mean $\bar{x}$.
Outcome 3. Understand the importance of the Central Limit Theorem.

 7.3 Sampling Distribution of a Proportion (pg. 279–288)

Summary

In many situations the objective of sampling will be to estimate a **population proportion**. Sample proportions are subject to sampling error, just as sample means. Again, the concept of sampling distributions provides a way to assess the potential magnitude of the sampling error for proportions in a given situation.

In those situations where you are interested in determining the proportion of all items that possess a particular attribute, the sample proportion will be the best estimate of the true population proportion. The distribution of the sample proportion is binomial; however, if the sample size is sufficiently large then the **Central Limit Theorem** tells us that normal distribution can be used as an approximation.

Outcome 4. Determine the mean and standard deviation for the sampling distribution of the sample proportion $\bar{p}$.

Conclusion

When a sample is taken it is one of many that could have been chosen. Consequently, the sample statistic is only one of many that could have been calculated. There is no reason to believe that the sample statistic will equal the population parameter. The difference between the two is called sampling error. Because sampling error exists, decision makers must be aware of how sample statistics are distributed in order to understand the potential for extreme sampling error. The **Central Limit Theorem** tells us that no matter how the population is distributed, if the sample size is large enough then the sampling distribution will be approximately normally distributed.

Equations

(7.1) **Sampling Error of the Sample Mean** pg. 256

$$\text{Sampling error} = \bar{x} - \mu$$

(7.2) **Population Mean** pg. 256

$$\mu = \frac{\sum x}{N}$$

(7.3) **Sample Mean** pg. 257

$$\bar{x} = \frac{\sum x}{n}$$

(7.4) **z-Value for Sampling Distribution of $\bar{x}$** pg. 271

$$z = \frac{\bar{x} - \mu}{\frac{\sigma}{\sqrt{n}}}$$

(7.5) **z-Value Adjusted for the Finite Population Correction Factor** pg. 271

$$z = \frac{\bar{x} - \mu}{\frac{\sigma}{\sqrt{n}}\sqrt{\frac{N-n}{N-1}}}$$

(7.6) **Population Proportion** pg. 280

$$p = \frac{X}{N}$$

(7.7) **Sample Proportion** pg. 280

$$\bar{p} = \frac{x}{n}$$

(7.8) **Single-Proportion Sampling Error** pg. 281

$$\text{Sampling error} = \bar{p} - p$$

(7.9) **Mean of the Sampling Distribution of $\bar{p}$** pg. 282

$$\text{Mean} = \mu_{\bar{p}} = p$$

(7.10) **Standard Error of the Sampling Distribution of $\bar{p}$** pg. 282

$$\text{Standard error} = \sigma_{\bar{p}} = \sqrt{\frac{p(1-p)}{n}}$$

(7.11) **z-Value for Sampling Distribution of $\bar{p}$** pg. 283

$$z = \frac{\bar{p} - p}{\sigma_{\bar{p}}}$$

Key Terms

Central Limit Theorem pg. 274
Consistent estimator pg. 270
Parameter pg. 257

Population proportion pg. 280
Sample proportion pg. 280
Sampling distribution pg. 264

Sampling error pg. 256
Simple random sample pg. 257
Unbiased estimator pg. 267

Chapter Exercises
MyStatLab

Conceptual **Questions**

7-65. Under what conditions should the finite population correction factor be used in determining the standard error of a sampling distribution?

7-66. A sample of size 30 is obtained from a population that has a proportion of 0.34. Determine the range of sampling errors possible when the sample proportion is used to estimate the population proportion. (*Hint*: Review the Empirical Rule.)

7-67. Discuss why the sampling distribution will be less variable than the population distribution. Give a short example to illustrate your answer.

7-68. Discuss the similarities and differences between a standard deviation and a standard error.

7-69. A researcher has collected all possible samples of a size of 150 from a population and listed the sample means for each of these samples.

a. If the average of the sample means is 450.55, what would be the numerical value of the true population mean? Discuss.

b. If the standard deviation of the sample means is 12.25, determine the standard deviation of the model from which the samples came. To perform this calculation, assume the population has a size of 1,250.

7-70. Consider the standard error of a sample proportion obtained from a sample of size 100.

a. Determine the standard error obtained from a population with $p = 0.1$.

b. Repeat part a for a population proportion equal to (1) 0.5 and (2) 0.9.

c. Which population proportion results in the largest standard error?

d. Given your responses to parts a, b, and c, which value of a population proportion would produce the largest sampling error?

7-71. If a population is known to be normally distributed, what size sample is required to ensure that the sampling distribution of $\bar{x}$ is normally distributed?

7-72. Suppose we are told the sampling distribution developed from a sample of size 400 has a mean of 56.78 and a standard error of 9.6. If the population is known to be normally distributed, what are the population mean and population standard deviation? Discuss how these values relate to the values for the sampling distribution.

Business Applications

7-73. The Baily Hill Bicycle Shop sells mountain bikes and offers a maintenance program to its customers. The manager has found the average repair bill during the maintenance program's first year to be $15.30 with a standard deviation of $7.00.
   a. What is the probability a random sample of 40 customers will have a mean repair cost exceeding $16.00?
   b. What is the probability the mean repair cost for a sample of 100 customers will be between $15.10 and $15.80?
   c. The manager has decided to offer a spring special. He is aware of the mean and standard deviation for repair bills last year. Therefore, he has decided to randomly select and repair the first 50 bicycles for $14.00 each. He notes this is not even 1 standard deviation below the mean price to make such repairs. He asks your advice. Is this a risky thing to do? Based upon the probability of a repair bill being $14.00 or less, what would you recommend? Discuss.

7-74. When its ovens are working properly, the time required to bake fruit pies at Ellardo Bakeries is normally distributed with a mean of 45 minutes and a standard deviation of 5 minutes. Yesterday, a random sample of 16 pies had an average baking time of 50 minutes.
   a. If Ellardo's ovens are working correctly, how likely is it that a sample of 16 pies would have an average baking time of 50 minutes or more?
   b. Would you recommend that Ellardo inspect its ovens to see if they are working properly? Justify your answer.

7-75. An analysis performed by Hewitt Associates indicated the median amount saved in a 401(k) plan by people 50 to 59 years old was $53,440. The average saved is $115,260 for that age group. Assume the standard deviation is $75,000.
   a. Examining these statements, would it be possible to use a normal distribution to determine the proportion of workers who have saved more than $115,260? Support your assertions.
   b. If it is possible to determine the probability that a sample of size 5 has an average amount saved in a 401(k) plan that is more than $115,260, do so. If not, explain why you are unable to do so.
   c. Repeat the instructions in part b with a sample size of 35.

7-76. Suppose at your university, some administrators believe that the proportion of students preferring to take classes at night exceeds 0.30. The president is skeptical and so has an assistant take a simple random sample of 200 students. Of these, 66 indicate that they prefer night classes. What is the probability of finding a sample proportion equal to or greater than that found if the president's skepticism is justified? Assume $n \leq 5$ percent of N.

7-77. A year-old study found that the service time for all drive-thru customers at the Stardust Coffee Shop is uniformly distributed between 3 and 6 minutes. Assuming the service time distribution has not changed, a random sample of 49 customers is taken and the service time for each is recorded.
   a. Calculate the mean and standard deviation of service times for all drive-thru customers at the Stardust Coffee Shop. (*Hint*: Review the uniform distribution from Chapter 6.)
   b. What is the probability that a sample of 49 customers would have a sample mean of 4.25 minutes or more if the true population mean and standard deviation for service times are as calculated in part a?
   c. How can the probability in part b be determined when the population of service times is not normally distributed?

7-78. The time it takes a mechanic to tune an engine is known to be normally distributed with a mean of 45 minutes and a standard deviation of 14 minutes.
   a. Determine the mean and standard error of a sampling distribution for a sample size of 20 tune-ups. Draw a picture of the sampling distribution.
   b. Calculate the largest sampling error you would expect to make in estimating the population mean with the sample size of 20 tune-ups.

7-79. Frito-Lay is one of the world's largest makers of snack foods. One of the final steps in making products like Cheetos and Doritos is to package the product in sacks or other containers. Suppose Frito-Lay managers set the fill volume on Cheetos to an average volume of 16 ounces. The filling machine is known to fill with a standard deviation of 0.25 ounces with a normal distribution around the mean fill level.
   a. What is the probability that a single bag of Cheetos will have a fill volume that exceeds 16.10 ounces?
   b. What is the probability that a random sample of 12 bags of Cheetos will have a mean fill volume that exceeds 16.10 ounces?
   c. Compare your answers to parts a and b and discuss why they are different.

7-80. Frank N. Magid Associates conducted a telephone survey of 1,109 consumers to obtain the number of cell phones in houses. The survey obtained the following results:

Cell phones	0	1	2	3	≥4
Percent	19	26	33	13	9

a. Determine the sample proportion of households that own two or more cell phones.

b. If the proportion of households that own two or more cell phones is equal to 0.50, determine the probability that in a sample of 1,109 consumers at least 599 would own two or more cell phones.

c. The margin of error of the survey was ±3 percentage points. This means that the sample proportion would be within 3 percentage points of the population proportion. If the population proportion of households that had two or more cell phones was 0.50, determine the probability that the margin of error would be ±3 percentage points.

7-81. The Bendbo Corporation has a total of 300 employees in its two manufacturing locations and the headquarters office. A study conducted five years ago showed the average commuting distance to work for Bendbo employees was 6.2 miles with a standard deviation of 3 miles. Recently, a follow-up study based on a random sample of 100 employees indicated an average travel distance of 5.9 miles.

a. Assuming that the mean and standard deviation of the original study hold, what is the probability of obtaining a sample mean of 5.9 miles or less?

b. Based on this probability, do you think the average travel distance may have decreased?

c. A second random sample of 40 was selected. This sample produced a mean travel distance of 5.9 miles. If the mean for all employees is 6.2 miles and the standard deviation is 3 miles, what is the probability of observing a sample mean of 5.9 miles or less?

d. Discuss why the probabilities differ even though the sample results were the same in each case.

7-82. MPC makes personal computers that are then sold directly over the phone and over the Internet. One of the most critical factors in the success of PC makers is how fast they can turn their inventory of parts. Faster inventory turns mean lower average inventory cost. Recently at a meeting, the vice president (VP) of manufacturing said that there is no reason to continue offering hard disk drives that have less than a 250-GB storage capacity since only 10% of MPC customers ask for the smaller hard disks. After much discussion and debate about the accuracy of the VP's figure, it was decided to sample 100 orders from the past week's sales. This sample revealed 14 requests for drives with less than 250-GB capacity.

a. Determine the probability of finding 14 or more requests like this if the VP's assertion is correct. Do you believe that the proportion of customers requesting hard drives with storage capacity is as small as 0.10? Explain.

b. Suppose a second sample of 100 customers was selected. This sample again yielded 14 requests for a hard drive with less than 250 GB of storage.

Combining this sample information with that found in part a, what conclusion would you now reach regarding the VP's 10% claim? Base your answer on probability.

7-83. The economic downturn after the financial crisis early in the current century affected all salaried employees, certainly starting MBA employees. While the average starting salary varies depending on the source of the study and field of emphasis, one respected source shows an average annual starting base salary of $88,626. The high starting salary was set in 2001 at approximately $92,500 after adjusting for inflation.

a. Assuming that the standard deviation of the salary and bonus for new MBAs was $20,000, calculate the probability that a randomly selected sample of size 5,829 graduates would yield a sample mean of at most $88,626 if the population mean equaled $92,500.

b. Assuming the distribution of salaries was normal with a mean of $92,500, determine the probability that at least half of 5 MBA graduates would get annual base salaries of at least $92,500.

7-84. A major video rental chain recently decided to allow customers to rent movies for three nights rather than one. The marketing team that made this decision reasoned that at least 70% of the customers would return the movie by the second night anyway. A sample of 500 customers found 68% returned the movie prior to the third night.

a. Given the marketing team's estimate, what would be the probability of a sample result with 68% or fewer returns prior to the third night?

b. Based on your calculations, would you recommend the adoption of the new rental policy? Support your answer with statistical reasoning and calculations.

Computer Database **Exercises**

7-85. The **Patients** file contains information for a random sample of geriatric patients. During a meeting, one hospital administrator indicated that 70% of the geriatric patients are males.

a. Based on the data contained in the **Patients** file, would you conclude the administrator's assertion concerning the proportion of male geriatric patients is correct? Justify your answer.

b. The administrator also believes 80% of all geriatric patients are covered by Medicare (Code = CARE). Again, based on the data contained in the file, what conclusion should the hospital administrator reach concerning the proportion of geriatric patients covered by Medicare? Discuss.

7-86. *USA Today* reported the results of a survey conducted by HarrisInteractive to determine the percentage of adults who use a computer to access the Internet (from work, home, or other locations). The newspaper indicated the survey revealed that 74% of adults use a computer to access the Internet. The file titled **Online** produces a representative sample of the data collected by *USA Today*.

a. Calculate the sample proportion of adults who connect to the Internet using a computer.

b. If the Harris poll's estimate of the proportion of adults using the Internet is correct, determine the sampling error for the sample in the **Online** file.

c. Determine the probability that a sample proportion would be at most as far away as the **Online** sample if the Harris poll's estimate was correct.

d. The Harris poll indicated that its sample had a margin of error of $\pm 2\%$. The sample size used by the Harris poll was 2,022. Calculate the probability that the sample proportion from a sample size of 2,022 would be at most as far away from the population proportion as suggested by the margin of error.

7-87. The file **High Desert Banking** contains information regarding consumer, real estate, and small commercial loans made last year by the bank. Use your computer software to do the following:

a. Construct a frequency histogram using eight classes for dollar value of loans made last year. Does the population distribution appear to be normally distributed?

b. Compute the population mean for all loans made last year.

c. Compute the population standard deviation for all loans made last year.

d. Select a simple random sample of 36 loans. Compute the sample mean. By how much does the sample mean differ from the population mean? Use the Central Limit Theorem to determine the probability that you would have a sample mean this small or smaller and the probability that you would have a sample mean this large or larger.

7-88. Analysis by American Express found high fuel prices and airline losses resulted in increasing fares for business travelers. The average fare paid for business travel rose during the second quarter of 2008 to $260, up from $236 in the second quarter of 2007. However, fuel prices started declining in the fall of 2008. The file titled **Busfares** contains sample prices paid by business travelers in the first quarter of 2009.

a. Determine the sample average fare for business travelers in the first quarter of 2009.

b. If the average has not changed since the second quarter of 2008, determine the sampling error.

c. If these data were normally distributed, determine the probability that the sample mean would be as far away from the population mean or more if $\sigma = \$25$.

d. Does it appear that the average business traveler's fare has changed since 2008's second quarter? Explain.

7-89. Covercraft manufactures covers to protect automobile interiors and finishes. Its Block-It 200 Series fabric has a limited two-year warranty. Periodic testing is done to determine if the warranty policy should be changed. One such study may have examined those covers that became unserviceable while still under warranty. Data that could be produced by such a study are contained in the file titled **Covers**. The data represent the number of months a cover was used until it became unserviceable. Covercraft might want to examine more carefully the covers that became unserviceable while still under warranty. Specifically, it wants to examine those that became unserviceable before they had been in use one year.

a. Covercraft has begun to think that it should lower its warranty period to perhaps 20 months. It believes that in doing this, 20% of the covers that now fail before the warranty is up will have surpassed the 20-month warranty rate. Calculate the proportion of the sample that became unserviceable after 20 months of service.

b. Determine the probability of obtaining a sample proportion at least as large as that calculated in part a if the true proportion was equal to 0.20.

c. Based on your calculation in part b, should Covercraft lower its warranty period to 20 months? Support your answer.

7-90. The data file **Trucks** contains data on a sample of 200 trucks that were weighed on two scales. The WIM (weigh-in-motion) scale weighs the trucks as they drive down the highway. The POE scale weighs the trucks while they are stopped at the port-of-entry station. The maker of the WIM scale believes that its scale will weigh heavier than the POE scale 60% of the time when gross weight is considered.

a. Create a new variable that has a value $= 1$ when the WIM gross weight $>$ POE gross weight, and 0 otherwise.

b. Determine the sample proportion of times the WIM gross weight exceeds POE gross weight.

c. Based on this sample, what is the probability of finding a proportion less than that found in part b? For this calculation, assume the WIM maker's assertion is correct.

d. Based on the probability found in part c, what should the WIM maker conclude? Is his 60% figure reasonable?

Case 7.1

Carpita Bottling Company

Don Carpita owns and operates Carpita Bottling Company in Lakeland, Wisconsin. The company bottles soda and beer and distributes the products in the counties surrounding Lakeland.

The company has four bottling machines, which can be adjusted to fill bottles at any mean fill level between 2 ounces and 72 ounces. The machines exhibit some variation in actual fill from the mean setting. For instance, if the mean setting is 16 ounces, the actual fill may be slightly more or less than that amount.

Three of the four filling machines are relatively new, and their fill variation is not as great as that of the older machine. Don has observed that the standard deviation in fill for the three new machines is about 1% of the mean fill level when the mean fill is set at 16 ounces or less, and it is 0.5% of the mean at settings exceeding 16 ounces. The older machine has a standard deviation of about 1.5% of the mean setting regardless of the mean fill setting. However, the older machine tends to underfill bottles more than overfill, so the older machine is set at a mean fill slightly in excess of the desired mean to compensate for the propensity to underfill. For example, when 16-ounce bottles are to be filled, the machine is set at a mean fill level of 16.05 ounces.

The company can simultaneously fill bottles with two brands of soda using two machines, and it can use the other two machines to bottle beer. Although each filling machine has its own warehouse and the products are loaded from the warehouse directly onto a truck, products from two or more filling machines may be loaded on the same truck. However, an individual store almost always receives bottles on a particular day from just one machine.

On Saturday morning, Don received a call at home from the J. R. Summers grocery store manager. She was very upset because the shipment of 16-ounce bottles of beer received yesterday contained several bottles that were not adequately filled. The manager wanted Don to replace the entire shipment at once.

Don gulped down his coffee and prepared to head to the store to check out the problem. He started thinking how he could determine which machine was responsible for the problem. If he could at least determine whether it was the old machine or one of the new ones, he could save his maintenance people a lot of time and effort checking all the machines.

His plan was to select a sample of 64 bottles of beer from the store and measure the contents. Don figured that he might be able to determine, on the basis of the average contents, whether it was more likely that the beer was bottled by a new machine or by the old one.

The results of the sampling showed an average of 15.993 ounces. Now Don needs some help in determining whether a sample mean of 15.993 ounces or less is more likely to come from the new machines or the older machine.

Case 7.2

Truck Safety Inspection

The Idaho Department of Law Enforcement, in conjunction with the federal government, recently began a truck inspection program in Idaho. The current inspection effort is limited to an inspection of only those trucks that visually appear to have some defect when they stop at one of the weigh stations in the state. The proposed inspection program will not be limited to the trucks with visible defects, but will potentially subject all trucks to a comprehensive safety inspection.

Jane Lund of the Department of Law Enforcement is in charge of the new program. She has stated that the ultimate objective of the new truck inspection program is to reduce the number of trucks with safety defects operating in Idaho. Ideally, all trucks passing through or operating within Idaho would be inspected once a month, and substantial penalties would be applied to operators if safety defects were discovered. Ms. Lund is confident that such an inspection program would, without fail, reduce the number of defective trucks operating on Idaho's highways. However, each safety inspection takes about an hour, and because of limited money to hire inspectors, she realizes that all trucks cannot be inspected. She also knows it is unrealistic to have trucks wait to be inspected until trucks ahead of them have been checked. Such delays would cause problems with the drivers.

In meetings with her staff, Jane has suggested that before the inspection program begins, the number of defective trucks currently operating in Idaho should be estimated. This estimate can be compared with later estimates to see if the inspection program has been effective. To arrive at this initial estimate, Jane thinks that some sort of sampling plan to select representative trucks from the population for all trucks in the state must be developed. She has suggested that this sampling be done at the eight weigh stations near Idaho's borders, but she is unsure how to establish a statistically sound sampling plan that is practical to implement.

- **Review** material on calculating and interpreting sample means and standard deviations in Chapter 3.

- **Review** the normal distribution in Section 6.1.

- **Make sure** you understand the concepts associated with sampling distributions for $\bar{x}$ and $\bar{p}$ by reviewing Sections 7.1, 7.2, and 7.3.

Estimating Single Population Parameters

8.1 Point and Confidence ⟵ Interval Estimates for a Population Mean (pg. 296–314)

Outcome 1. Distinguish between a point estimate and a confidence interval estimate.

Outcome 2. Construct and interpret a confidence interval estimate for a single population mean using both the standard normal and t distributions.

8.2 Determining the Required ⟵ Sample Size for Estimating a Population Mean (pg. 314–320)

Outcome 3. Determine the required sample size for estimating a single population mean.

8.3 Estimating a Population ⟵ Proportion (pg. 321–328)

Outcome 4. Establish and interpret a confidence interval estimate for a single population proportion.

Outcome 5. Determine the required sample size for estimating a single population proportion.

Why you need to know

Chapter 1 discussed various sampling techniques, including statistical and non-statistical methods. Chapter 7 introduced the concepts of sampling error and sampling distributions. Chapter 8 builds on these concepts and introduces the steps needed to develop and interpret statistical estimations of various population values. The concepts introduced here will be very useful. You will undoubtedly need to estimate population parameters as a regular part of your managerial decision-making activities. In addition, you will receive estimates that other people have developed that you will need to evaluate before relying on them as inputs to your decision-making process. Was the sample size large enough to provide valid estimates of the population parameter? How confident can you be that the estimate matches the population parameter of interest? These and similar questions can all be answered using the concepts and procedures presented in this chapter.

dwphotos/Shutterstock

8.1 Point and Confidence Interval Estimates for a Population Mean

Chapter Outcome 1. → **Point Estimates and Confidence Intervals**

Every election year, political parties and news agencies conduct polls. These polls attempt to determine the percentage of voters who will favor a particular candidate or a particular issue. For example, suppose a poll indicates that 82% of the people older than 18 in your state favor banning texting while driving a motor vehicle. The pollsters have not contacted every person in the state; rather, they have sampled only a relatively few people to arrive at the 82% figure. In statistical terminology, the 82% is the **point estimate** of the true population percentage of people who favor a ban on texting and driving.

The Environmental Protection Agency (EPA) tests the mileage of automobiles sold in the United States. The resulting EPA mileage rating is actually a point estimate for the true average mileage of all cars of a given model.

Production managers study their companies' manufacturing processes to determine product costs. They typically select a sample of items and follow each sampled item through a complete production process. The costs at each step in the process are measured and summed to determine the total cost. They then divide the sum by the sample size to get the mean cost. This figure is the point estimate for the true mean cost of all the items produced. The point estimate is used in assigning a selling price to the finished product.

Which point estimator the decision maker uses depends on the population characteristic the decision maker wishes to estimate. However, regardless of the population value being estimated, we always expect **sampling error**.

Chapter 7 discussed sampling error. You cannot eliminate sampling error, but you can deal with it in your decision process. For example, when production managers use $\bar{x}$, the average cost of a sample of items, to establish the average cost of production, the point estimate, $\bar{x}$, will most likely not equal the population mean, μ. In fact, the probability of $\bar{x} = \mu$ is essentially zero. With $\bar{x}$ as their only information, the cost accountants will have no way of determining exactly how far $\bar{x}$ is from μ.

To overcome this problem with point estimates, the most common procedure is to calculate an interval estimate known as a **confidence interval**.

An application will help to make this definition clear.

Point Estimate

A single statistic, determined from a sample, that is used to estimate the corresponding population parameter.

Sampling Error

The difference between a measure (a statistic) computed from a sample and the corresponding measure (a parameter) computed from the population.

Confidence Interval

An interval developed from sample values such that if all possible intervals of a given width were constructed, a percentage of these intervals, known as the confidence level, would include the true population parameter.

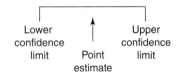

Excel Tutorial

BUSINESS APPLICATION CALCULATING A CONFIDENCE INTERVAL ESTIMATE

FIVE STAR ENERGY DRINK The Five Star Energy Drink Company makes and markets a popular energy-enhancing drink. The company has recently installed a new machine that automatically fills the energy drink bottles. The machine allows the operator to adjust the mean fill quantity. However, no matter what the mean setting, the actual volume of the energy drink liquid will vary from bottle to bottle. The machine has been carefully tested and is known to fill bottles with an amount of liquid that has a standard deviation of $\sigma = 0.2$ ounce.

The filling machine has been adjusted to fill cans at an average of 12 ounces. After running the machine for several hours, a simple random sample of 100 bottles is selected, and the volume of liquid in each bottle is measured in the company's quality lab. Figure 8.1 shows the frequency histogram of the sample data. (The data are in a file called **Five Star Energy**.) Notice that the distribution seems to be centered at a point larger than 12 ounces. The manager wishes to use the sample data to estimate the mean fill amount for all bottles filled by this machine.

The sample mean computed from 100 bottles is $\bar{x} = 12.09$ ounces. This is the *point estimate* of the population mean, μ. Because of the potential for sampling error, the manager should not expect a particular $\bar{x}$ to equal μ. However, as discussed in Chapter 7, the Central Limit Theorem indicates that the distribution of all possible sample means for samples of size $n = 100$ will be approximately normally distributed around the population mean with its spread measured by $\sigma / \sqrt{n}$, as illustrated in Figure 8.2.

Although the sample mean is 12.09 ounces, the manager knows the true population mean may be larger or smaller than this number. To account for the potential for sampling error, the

FIGURE 8.1

Excel 2010 Histogram for
Five Star Energy Drink

Excel 2010 Instructions:
1. Open File: **Five Star Energy.xlsx**.
2. Create bins (upper limit for each class).
3. Select **Data > Data Analysis**.
4. Select **Histogram**.
5. Define data and bin ranges.
6. Check **Chart Output**.
7. Modify bin definitions.
8. Select chart and right click.
9. Click **Format Data Series** and close gap width to zero.
10. Label Axes using **Layout > Axis Titles**.

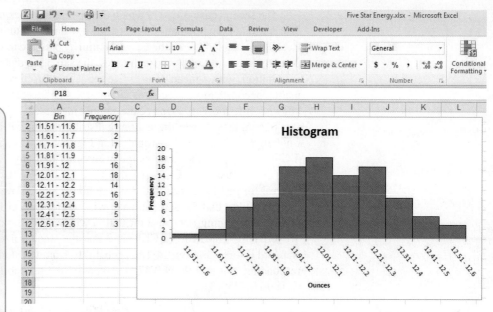

Minitab Instructions (for similar results):
1. Open file: **Five Star Energy.MTW**.
2. Choose **Graph > Histogram**.
3. Click **Simple**.
4. Click **OK**.
5. In **Graph** variables, enter data Column: *Ounces*.
6. Click **OK**.

manager can develop a *confidence interval estimate* for μ. This estimate will take the following form:

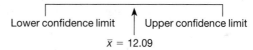

Lower confidence limit   Upper confidence limit

$\bar{x} = 12.09$

The key is to determine the upper and lower limits of the interval. The specific method for computing these values depends on whether the population standard deviation, σ, is known or unknown. We first take up the case in which σ is known.

Confidence Interval Estimate for the Population Mean, σ Known

There are two cases that must be considered. The first is the case in which the simple random sample is drawn from a normal distribution. Given a population mean of μ and a population standard deviation of σ, the sampling distribution of the sample mean is a normal distribution with a mean of $\mu_{\bar{x}} = \mu$ and a standard deviation (or **standard error**) of $\sigma_{\bar{x}} = \sigma/\sqrt{n}$. This is true for any sample size.

Standard Error

A value that measures the spread of the sample means around the population mean. The standard error is reduced when the sample size is increased.

FIGURE 8.2

Sampling Distribution of $\bar{x}$

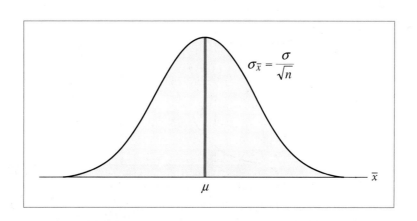

The second case is one in which the population does not have a normal distribution or the distribution of the population is not known. Chapter 7 addressed these specific circumstances. Recall that in such cases, the Central Limit Theorem can be invoked if the sample size is sufficiently large $(n \geq 30)$. In such cases, the sampling distribution is an approximately normal distribution, with a mean of $\mu_{\bar{x}} = \mu$ and a standard deviation of $\sigma_{\bar{x}} = \sigma/\sqrt{n}$. The approximation becomes more precise as the sample size increases. The standard deviation, $\sigma/\sqrt{n}$, is known as the *standard error* of the sample mean.

In both these cases, the sampling distribution for $\bar{x}$ is assumed to be normally distributed. Looking at the sampling distribution in Figure 8.2, it is apparent that the probability that any $\bar{x}$ will exceed μ is the same as the probability that any $\bar{x}$ will be less than μ. We also know from our discussion in Chapter 7 that we can calculate the percentage of sample means in the interval formed by a specified distance above and below μ. This percentage corresponds to the probability that the sample mean will be in the specified interval. For example, the probability of obtaining a value for $\bar{x}$ that is within 1.96 standard errors either side of μ is 0.95. To verify this, recall from Chapter 7 that the standardized z-value measures the number of standard errors $\bar{x}$ is from μ. The probability from the standard normal distribution table corresponding to $z = 1.96$ is 0.4750. Likewise, the probability corresponding to $z = -1.96$ is equal to 0.4750. Therefore,

$$P(-1.96 \leq z \leq 1.96) = 0.4750 + 0.4750 = 0.95$$

This is illustrated in Figure 8.3.

Because the standard error is $\sigma/\sqrt{n}$, then 95% of all sample means will fall in the range

$$\mu - 1.96\frac{\sigma}{\sqrt{n}} \text{ ——— } \mu + 1.96\frac{\sigma}{\sqrt{n}}$$

This is illustrated in Figure 8.4.

In a like manner, we can determine that 80% of all sample means will fall in the range

$$\mu - 1.28\frac{\sigma}{\sqrt{n}} \text{ ——— } \mu + 1.28\frac{\sigma}{\sqrt{n}}$$

Also, we can determine that 90% of all sample means will fall in the range

$$\mu - 1.645\frac{\sigma}{\sqrt{n}} \text{ ——— } \mu + 1.645\frac{\sigma}{\sqrt{n}}$$

This concept can be generalized to any probability by substituting the appropriate z-value from the standard normal distribution.

Now, given that our objective is to estimate μ based on a random sample of size n, if we form an interval estimate using

$$\bar{x} \pm z\frac{\sigma}{\sqrt{n}}$$

the proportion of all possible intervals containing μ will equal the probability associated with the specified z-value. In estimation terminology, the z-value is referred to as the *critical value*.

FIGURE 8.3

Critical Value for a 95% Confidence Interval

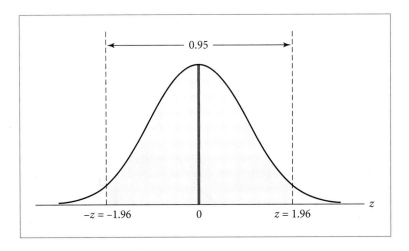

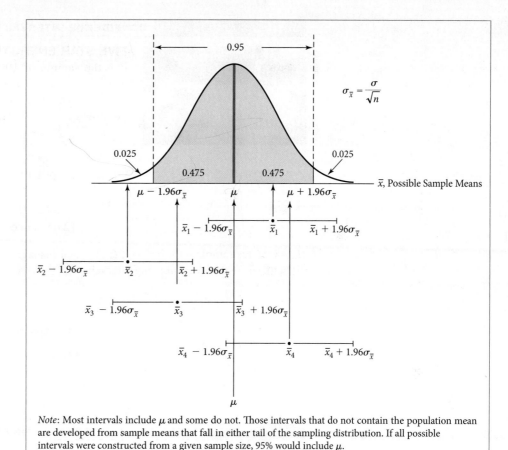

FIGURE 8.4 |

95% Confidence Intervals from Selected Random Samples

Note: Most intervals include μ and some do not. Those intervals that do not contain the population mean are developed from sample means that fall in either tail of the sampling distribution. If all possible intervals were constructed from a given sample size, 95% would include μ.

Chapter Outcome 2. → Confidence Interval Calculation Confidence interval estimates can be constructed using the general format shown in Equation 8.1.

Confidence Interval General Format

$$\text{Point estimate} \pm (\text{Critical value})(\text{Standard error}) \qquad \textbf{(8.1)}$$

Confidence Level

The percentage of all possible confidence intervals that will contain the true population parameter.

The first step in developing a confidence interval estimate is to specify the **confidence level** that is needed to determine the critical value.

Once you decide on the confidence level, the next step is to determine the critical value. If the population standard deviation is known and either the population is normally distributed, or if the sample size is large enough to comply with the Central Limit Theorem requirements, the critical value is a z-value from the standard normal table. Table 8.1 shows several of the most frequently used critical values.

The next step is to compute the standard error for the sampling distribution, shown in Chapter 7 and also earlier in this chapter to be $\sigma_{\bar{x}} = \sigma/\sqrt{n}$. Then, Equation 8.2 is used to compute the confidence interval estimate for μ.

TABLE 8.1 | Critical Values for Commonly Used Confidence Levels

Confidence Level	Critical Value
80%	$z = 1.28$
90%	$z = 1.645$
95%	$z = 1.96$
99%	$z = 2.575$

Note: Instead of using the standard normal table, you can also find the critical z-value using Excel's NORM.S.INV function.

Confidence Interval Estimate for μ, σ Known

$$\bar{x} \pm z\frac{\sigma}{\sqrt{n}} \qquad \textbf{(8.2)}$$

---

where:

z = Critical value from the standard normal table for a specified confidence level
σ = Population standard deviation
n = Sample size

BUSINESS APPLICATION CONFIDENCE INTERVAL ESTIMATE FOR μ

FIVE STAR ENERGY DRINK (CONTINUED) Recall that the sample of 100 energy drink bottles produced a sample mean of $\bar{x} = 12.09$ ounces and the Five Star manager knows that $\sigma = 0.2$ ounce. Thus, the 95% confidence interval estimate for the population mean is

$$\bar{x} \pm z \frac{\sigma}{\sqrt{n}}$$

$$12.09 \pm 1.96 \frac{0.2}{\sqrt{100}}$$

$$12.09 \pm 0.04$$

12.05 ounces ————— 12.13 ounces

Based on this sample information, the Five Star manager believes that the true mean fill for all bottles is within the following interval:

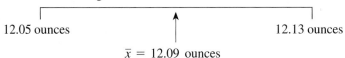

12.05 ounces   12.13 ounces

$$\bar{x} = 12.09 \text{ ounces}$$

Because this interval does not contain the target mean of 12 ounces, the manager should conclude that the filling equipment is out of adjustment and is putting in too much energy drink, on average.

How to do it (Example 8-1)

Confidence Interval Estimate for μ with σ Known
Use the following steps to compute a confidence interval estimate for the population mean when the population standard deviation is assumed known and either the population distribution is normal or the sample size n is $\geq$ 30.

1. Define the population of interest and select a simple random sample of size n.

2. Specify the confidence level.

3. Compute the sample mean using

$$\bar{x} = \frac{\sum x}{n}$$

4. Determine the standard error of the sampling distribution using

$$\sigma_{\bar{x}} = \frac{\sigma}{\sqrt{n}}$$

5. Determine the critical value, z, from the standard normal table.

6. Compute the confidence interval estimate using

$$\bar{x} \pm z \frac{\sigma}{\sqrt{n}}$$

EXAMPLE 8-1 CONFIDENCE INTERVAL ESTIMATE FOR μ, σ KNOWN

Medical Expenses Department of Health and Welfare officials in Portland, Maine, wish to know the mean amount of dollars that senior citizens spend per year on medical care. To estimate this value, they could use the following steps:

Step 1 **Define the population of interest and select a simple random sample of size n.**
The population is the amount of dollars spent per year by senior citizens for health care. A simple random sample of 200 senior citizens will be selected, and the annual amount spent on health care will be recorded.

Step 2 **Specify the confidence level.**
The officials want to develop a 90% confidence interval estimate. Thus, 90% of all possible interval estimates will contain the population mean.

Step 3 **Compute the sample mean.**
After the sample has been selected and the dollars spent on health care have been recorded for each of the 200 people sampled, the sample mean is computed using

$$\bar{x} = \frac{\sum x}{n}$$

Assume the sample mean is $5,230.

Step 4 **Determine the standard error of the sampling distribution.**
Suppose past studies have indicated that the population standard deviation for senior citizen health care spending in Portland, Maine, is

$$\sigma = \$500$$

Then the standard error of the sampling distribution is computed using

$$\sigma_{\bar{x}} = \frac{\sigma}{\sqrt{n}} = \frac{\$500}{\sqrt{200}} = \$35.36$$

Step 5 **Determine the critical value, z, from the standard normal table.**
Because the sample size is large, the Central Limit Theorem applies. The sampling distribution will be normally distributed, and the critical value will

be a z-value from the standard normal distribution. The officials want a 90% confidence level, so the z-value is 1.645.

Step 6 Compute the confidence interval estimate.
The 90% confidence interval estimate for the population mean is

$$\bar{x} \pm z \frac{\sigma}{\sqrt{n}}$$

$$\$5,230 \pm 1.645 \frac{500}{\sqrt{200}}$$

$$\$5,230 \pm \$58.16$$

$$\$5,171.84 \underline{\hspace{1.5cm}} \$5,288.16$$

Thus, based on the sample results, with 90% confidence, the Health and Welfare officials in Portland, Maine, believe that the true population mean annual dollars spent on health care is between \$5,171.84 and \$5,288.16.

>> **END EXAMPLE**

TRY PROBLEM 8-1 (pg. 310)

Special Message about Interpreting Confidence Intervals

There is a subtle distinction to be made here. Beginning students often wonder if it is permissible to say, "There is a 0.90 probability that the population mean is between \$5,171.84 and \$5,288.16." This may seem to be the logical consequence of constructing a confidence interval. However, we must be very careful to attribute probability only to random events or variables. Because the population mean is a fixed value, there can be no probability statement about the population mean. The confidence interval we have computed either will contain the population mean or it will not. If you were to produce all the possible 90% confidence intervals using the mean of each possible sample of a given size from the population, then 90% of these intervals would contain the population mean.

Impact of the Confidence Level on the Interval Estimate

BUSINESS APPLICATION **MARGIN OF ERROR**

Mikheyev Viktor/Shutterstock

FIVE STAR ENERGY DRINK (CONTINUED) In the Five Star Energy Drink example, the manager specified a 95% confidence level. The resulting confidence interval estimate for the population mean was

$$\bar{x} \pm z \frac{\sigma}{\sqrt{n}}$$

$$12.09 \pm 1.96 \frac{0.2}{\sqrt{100}}$$

$$12.09 \pm 0.04$$

$$12.05 \text{ ounces} \underline{\hspace{1.5cm}} 12.13 \text{ ounces}$$

Margin of Error

The amount that is added and subtracted to the point estimate to determine the endpoints of the confidence interval. Also, a measure of how close we expect the point estimate to be to the population parameter with the specified level of confidence.

The quantity, 0.04, on the right of the $\pm$ sign is called the **margin of error**. This is illustrated in Equation 8.3. The margin of error defines the relationship between the sample mean and the population mean.

Margin of Error for Estimating μ, σ Known

$$e = z \frac{\sigma}{\sqrt{n}} \tag{8.3}$$

where:

$$e = \text{Margin of error}$$
$$z = \text{Critical value}$$
$$\frac{\sigma}{\sqrt{n}} = \text{Standard error of the sampling distibution}$$

Now suppose the manager at Five Star is willing to settle for 80% confidence. This will impact the critical value. To determine the new value, divide 0.80 by 2, giving 0.40. Go to the standard normal table and locate a probability value (area under the curve) that is as close to 0.40 as possible. The corresponding z-value is 1.28.[1] The 80% confidence interval estimate is

$$\bar{x} \pm z \frac{\sigma}{\sqrt{n}}$$

$$12.09 \pm (1.28)\frac{0.2}{\sqrt{100}}$$

$$12.09 \pm 0.03$$

$$12.06 \text{ ounces} \text{ --------- } 12.12 \text{ ounces}$$

Based on this sample information and the 80% confidence interval, we believe that the true average fill level is between 12.06 ounces and 12.12 ounces.

By lowering the confidence level, we are less likely to obtain an interval that contains the population mean. However, on the positive side, the margin of error has been reduced from ± 0.04 ounces to ± 0.03 ounces. For equivalent samples from a population:

1. If the confidence level is decreased, the margin of error is reduced.
2. If the confidence level is increased, the margin of error is increased.

The Five Star Energy Drink manager will need to decide which is more important, a higher confidence level or a lower margin of error.

EXAMPLE 8-2   IMPACT OF CHANGING THE CONFIDENCE LEVEL

National Recycling National Recycling operates a garbage hauling company in a southern Maine city. Each year, the company must apply for a new contract with the state. The contract is in part based on the pounds of recycled materials collected. Part of the analysis that goes into contract development is an estimate of the mean pounds of recycled material submitted by each customer in the city on a quarterly basis. The city has asked for both 99% and 90% confidence interval estimates for the mean. If, after the contract has been signed, the actual mean pounds deviates from the estimate over time, an adjustment will be made (up or down) in the amount National Recycling receives. The steps used to generate these estimates follow.

Step 1 Define the population of interest and select a simple random sample of size *n*.

The population is the collection of all of National Recycling's customers, and a simple random sample of $n = 100$ customers is selected.

Step 2 Specify the confidence level.

The city requires 99% and 90% confidence interval estimates.

Step 3 Compute the sample mean.

After the sample has been selected and the pounds of recycled materials have been determined for each of the 100 customers sampled, the sample mean is computed using

$$\bar{x} = \frac{\sum x}{n}$$

Suppose the sample mean is 40.78 pounds.

---

[1]You can use Excel 2010 to compute the critical z-value using the NORM.S.INV function. This function requires one input: the probability in the left tail of the distribution. For this example we want an 80% confidence interval. The probability for the lower tail is 0.1. For the upper-tail value, the probability is 0.9. Note these probabilities "cut off" the required 0.1 area in each tail needed to give us the 80% confidence interval. The function's input and the corresponding critical values are NORM.S.INV (0.1) $= -1.2816$, which is the lower-tail z-value, and NORM.S.INV(0.9) $= 1.2816$, which is the upper-tail critical value.

Step 4 Determine the standard error of the sampling distribution.

Suppose, from past years, the population standard deviation is known to be $\sigma = 12.6$ pounds. Then the standard error of the sampling distribution is computed using

$$\sigma_{\bar{x}} = \frac{\sigma}{\sqrt{n}} = \frac{12.6}{\sqrt{100}} = 1.26 \text{ pounds}$$

Step 5 Determine the critical value, z, from the standard normal table.

First, the state wants a 99% confidence interval estimate, so the z-value is determined by finding a probability in Appendix D corresponding to $0.99/2 = 0.495$. The correct z-value is between $z = 2.57$ and $z = 2.58$. We split the difference to get the critical value: $z = 2.575$. For 90% confidence, the critical z is determined to be 1.645.

Step 6 Compute the confidence interval estimate.

The 99% confidence interval estimate for the population mean is

$$\bar{x} \pm z \frac{\sigma}{\sqrt{n}}$$

$$40.78 \pm 2.575 \frac{12.6}{\sqrt{100}}$$

$$40.78 \pm 3.24$$

$$37.54 \text{ pounds} \text{ —————— } 44.02 \text{ pounds}$$

The margin of error at 99% confidence is ± 3.24 pounds.
The 90% confidence interval estimate for the population mean is

$$\bar{x} \pm z \frac{\sigma}{\sqrt{n}}$$

$$40.78 \pm 1.645 \frac{12.6}{\sqrt{100}}$$

$$40.78 \pm 2.07$$

$$38.71 \text{ pounds} \text{ —————— } 42.85 \text{ pounds}$$

The margin of error is only 2.07 pounds when the confidence level is reduced from 99% to 90%. The margin of error will be smaller when the confidence level is smaller.

>> **END EXAMPLE**

TRY PROBLEM 8-5 (pg. 310)

Lowering the confidence level is one way to reduce the margin of error. However, by examining Equation 8.3, you will note there are two other values that affect the margin of error. One of these is the population standard deviation. The more the population's standard deviation, σ, can be reduced, the smaller the margin of error will be. In a business environment, large standard deviations for measurements related to the quality of a product are not desired. In fact, corporations spend considerable effort to decrease the variation in their products either by changing their process or by controlling variables that cause the variation. Typically, all avenues for reducing the standard deviation should be pursued before thoughts of reducing the confidence level are entertained.

Unfortunately, there are many situations in which reducing the population standard deviation is not possible. In these cases, another step that can be taken to reduce the margin of error is to increase the sample size. As you learned in Chapter 7, an increase in sample size reduces the standard error of the sampling distribution. This can be the most direct way of reducing the margin of error as long as obtaining an increased sample is not prohibitively costly or unattainable for other reasons.

Impact of the Sample Size on the Interval Estimate

BUSINESS APPLICATION   UNDERSTANDING THE VALUE OF A LARGER SAMPLE SIZE

FIVE STAR ENERGY DRINK (*CONTINUED*) Suppose the Five Star Energy Drink production manager decided to increase the sample to 400 bottles. This is a four-fold increase over the original sample size. We learned in Chapter 7 that an increase in sample size reduces the standard error of the sampling distribution because the standard error is computed as $\sigma/\sqrt{n}$, Thus, without adversely affecting his confidence level, the manager can reduce the margin of error by increasing his sample size.

Assume that the sample mean for the larger sample size also happens to be $\bar{x} = 12.09$ ounces. The new 95% confidence interval estimate is

$$12.09 \pm 1.96 \frac{0.2}{\sqrt{400}}$$
$$12.09 \pm 0.02$$
$$12.07 \text{ ounces} \text{ ——— } 12.11 \text{ ounces}$$

Notice that by increasing the sample size to 400 bottles, the margin of error is reduced from the original 0.04 ounces to 0.02 ounces. The production manager now believes that his sample mean is within ± 0.02 ounces of the true population mean.

The production manager was able to reduce the margin of error without reducing the confidence level. However, the downside is that sampling 400 bottles instead of 100 bottles will cost more money and take more time. That's the trade-off. Absent the possibility of reducing the population standard deviation, if he wants to reduce the margin of error, he must either reduce the confidence level or increase the sample size, or some combination of each. If he is unwilling to do so, he will have to accept the larger margin of error.

Confidence Interval Estimates for the Population Mean, σ Unknown

In the Five Star Energy Drink application, the manager was dealing with a filling machine that had a known standard deviation in fill volume. You may encounter situations in which the standard deviation is known. However, in most cases, if you do not know the population mean, you also will not know the population standard deviation. When this occurs, you need to make a minor, but important, modification to the confidence interval estimation process.

Student's *t*-Distribution

When the population standard deviation is known, the sampling distribution of the mean has only one unknown parameter: its mean, μ. This is estimated by $\bar{x}$. However, when the population standard deviation is unknown, there are two unknown parameters, μ and σ, which can be estimated by $\bar{x}$ and s, respectively. This estimation doesn't affect the general format for a confidence interval, as shown earlier in Equation 8.1:

$$\text{Point estimate} \pm \text{(Critical value)(Standard error)}$$

However, not knowing the population standard deviation does affect the critical value. Recall that when σ is known and the population is normally distributed or the Central Limit Theorem applies, the critical value is a z-value taken from the standard normal table. But when σ is not known, the critical value is a t-value taken from a family of distributions called the **Student's *t*-distributions**.

Because the specific t-distribution chosen is based on its *degrees of freedom*, it is important to understand what *degrees of freedom* means. Recall that the sample standard deviation is an estimate of the population's standard deviation and is defined as

$$s = \sqrt{\frac{\sum(x - \bar{x})^2}{n-1}}$$

Student's *t*-Distributions

A family of distributions that is bell shaped and symmetrical like the standard normal distribution but with greater area in the tails. Each distribution in the *t*-family is defined by its degrees of freedom. As the degrees of freedom increase, the *t*-distribution approaches the normal distribution.

Therefore, if we wish to estimate the population standard deviation, we must first calculate the sample mean. The sample mean is itself an estimator of a parameter, namely, the population mean. The sample mean is obtained from a sample of n randomly and independently chosen data values. Once the sample mean has been obtained, there are only $n - 1$ independent pieces of data information left in the sample.

To illustrate, examine a sample of size $n = 3$ in which the sample mean is calculated to be 12. This implies that the sum of the three data values equals $36\,(3 \times 12)$. If you know that the first two data values are 10 and 8, respectively, then the third data value is determined to be 18. Similarly, if you know that the first two data values are 18 and 7, respectively, the third data value must be 11. You are free to choose any two of the three data values. In general, if you must estimate k parameters before you are able to estimate the population's standard deviation from a sample of n data values, you have the freedom to choose any $n - k$ data values before the remaining k-values are determined. This value, $n - k$, is called the **degrees of freedom**.

When the population is normally distributed, the t-value represents the number of standard errors $\bar{x}$ is from μ, as shown in Equation 8.4. Appendix F contains a table of standardized t-values that correspond to specified tail areas and different degrees of freedom. The t-table is used to determine the critical value when we do not know the population standard deviation. The t-table is reproduced on the inside back endsheet of your text and also in Table 8.2. Note, in Equation 8.4, we use the sample standard deviation, s, to estimate the population standard deviation, σ. The fact that we are estimating σ is the reason the t-distribution is more spread out (i.e., has a larger standard deviation) than the normal distribution (see Figure 8.5). By estimating σ, we are introducing more uncertainty into the estimation process; therefore, achieving the same level of confidence requires a t-value larger than the z-value for the same confidence level. As the sample size increases, our estimate of σ becomes better and the t-distribution converges to the z-distribution.

Degrees of Freedom

The number of independent data values available to estimate the population's standard deviation. If k parameters must be estimated before the population's standard deviation can be calculated from a sample of size n, the degrees of freedom are equal to $n-k$

---

t-Value for $\bar{x}$

$$t = \frac{\bar{x} - \mu}{\dfrac{s}{\sqrt{n}}}$$

(8.4)

where:

$\bar{x}$ = Sample mean
μ = Population mean
s = Sample standard deviation
n = Sample size

Assumption

The t-distribution is based on the assumption that the population is normally distributed. Although beyond the scope of this text, it can be shown that as long as the population is reasonably symmetric, the t-distribution can be used.

FIGURE 8.5

t-Distribution and Normal Distribution

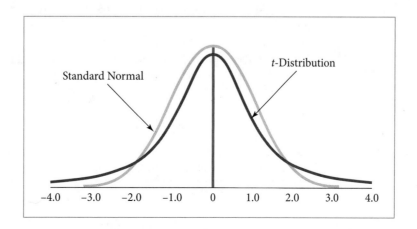

TABLE 8.2 | **Values of *t* for Selected Probabilities**

	Probabilities (or Areas under *t*-Distribution Curve)								
Conf. Level	0.1	0.3	0.5	0.7	0.8	0.9	0.95	0.98	0.99
One Tail	0.45	0.35	0.25	0.15	0.1	0.05	0.025	0.01	0.005
Two Tails	0.9	0.7	0.5	0.3	0.2	0.1	0.05	0.02	0.01
d.f.					*Values of t*				
1	0.1584	0.5095	1.0000	1.9626	3.0777	6.3137	12.7062	31.8210	63.6559
2	0.1421	0.4447	0.8165	1.3862	1.8856	2.9200	4.3027	6.9645	9.9250
3	0.1366	0.4242	0.7649	1.2498	1.6377	2.3534	3.1824	4.5407	5.8408
4	0.1338	0.4142	0.7407	1.1896	1.5332	2.1318	2.7765	3.7469	4.6041
5	0.1322	0.4082	0.7267	1.1558	1.4759	2.0150	2.5706	3.3649	4.0321
6	0.1311	0.4043	0.7176	1.1342	1.4398	1.9432	2.4469	3.1427	3.7074
7	0.1303	0.4015	0.7111	1.1192	1.4149	1.8946	2.3646	2.9979	3.4995
8	0.1297	0.3995	0.7064	1.1081	1.3968	1.8595	2.3060	2.8965	3.3554
9	0.1293	0.3979	0.7027	1.0997	1.3830	1.8331	2.2622	2.8214	3.2498
10	0.1289	0.3966	0.6998	1.0931	1.3722	1.8125	2.2281	2.7638	3.1693
11	0.1286	0.3956	0.6974	1.0877	1.3634	1.7959	2.2010	2.7181	3.1058
12	0.1283	0.3947	0.6955	1.0832	1.3562	1.7823	2.1788	2.6810	3.0545
13	0.1281	0.3940	0.6938	1.0795	1.3502	1.7709	2.1604	2.6503	3.0123
14	0.1280	0.3933	0.6924	1.0763	1.3450	1.7613	2.1448	2.6245	2.9768
15	0.1278	0.3928	0.6912	1.0735	1.3406	1.7531	2.1315	2.6025	2.9467
16	0.1277	0.3923	0.6901	1.0711	1.3368	1.7459	2.1199	2.5835	2.9208
17	0.1276	0.3919	0.6892	1.0690	1.3334	1.7396	2.1098	2.5669	2.8982
18	0.1274	0.3915	0.6884	1.0672	1.3304	1.7341	2.1009	2.5524	2.8784
19	0.1274	0.3912	0.6876	1.0655	1.3277	1.7291	2.0930	2.5395	2.8609
20	0.1273	0.3909	0.6870	1.0640	1.3253	1.7247	2.0860	2.5280	2.8453
21	0.1272	0.3906	0.6864	1.0627	1.3232	1.7207	2.0796	2.5176	2.8314
22	0.1271	0.3904	0.6858	1.0614	1.3212	1.7171	2.0739	2.5083	2.8188
23	0.1271	0.3902	0.6853	1.0603	1.3195	1.7139	2.0687	2.4999	2.8073
24	0.1270	0.3900	0.6848	1.0593	1.3178	1.7109	2.0639	2.4922	2.7970
25	0.1269	0.3898	0.6844	1.0584	1.3163	1.7081	2.0595	2.4851	2.7874
26	0.1269	0.3896	0.6840	1.0575	1.3150	1.7056	2.0555	2.4786	2.7787
27	0.1268	0.3894	0.6837	1.0567	1.3137	1.7033	2.0518	2.4727	2.7707
28	0.1268	0.3893	0.6834	1.0560	1.3125	1.7011	2.0484	2.4671	2.7633
29	0.1268	0.3892	0.6830	1.0553	1.3114	1.6991	2.0452	2.4620	2.7564
30	0.1267	0.3890	0.6828	1.0547	1.3104	1.6973	2.0423	2.4573	2.7500
40	0.1265	0.3881	0.6807	1.0500	1.3031	1.6839	2.0211	2.4233	2.7045
50	0.1263	0.3875	0.6794	1.0473	1.2987	1.6759	2.0086	2.4033	2.6778
60	0.1262	0.3872	0.6786	1.0455	1.2958	1.6706	2.0003	2.3901	2.6603
70	0.1261	0.3869	0.6780	1.0442	1.2938	1.6669	1.9944	2.3808	2.6479
80	0.1261	0.3867	0.6776	1.0432	1.2922	1.6641	1.9901	2.3739	2.6387
90	0.1260	0.3866	0.6772	1.0424	1.2910	1.6620	1.9867	2.3685	2.6316
100	0.1260	0.3864	0.6770	1.0418	1.2901	1.6602	1.9840	2.3642	2.6259
250	0.1258	0.3858	0.6755	1.0386	1.2849	1.6510	1.9695	2.3414	2.5956
500	0.1257	0.3855	0.6750	1.0375	1.2832	1.6479	1.9647	2.3338	2.5857
∞	0.1257	0.3853	0.6745	1.0364	1.2816	1.6449	1.9600	2.3264	2.5758

Excel Tutorial

tutorials

USING THE *t*-DISTRIBUTION

HERITAGE SOFTWARE Heritage Software, a maker of educational and business software, operates a service center in Tulsa, Oklahoma, where employees respond to customer calls about questions and problems with the company's software packages. Recently, a team of Heritage employees was asked to study the average length of time service representatives spend with customers. The team decided that a simple random sample of 25 calls would be collected and the population mean call time would be estimated based on the sample data. Not only did the team not know the average length of time, μ, but it also didn't know the standard deviation of length of the service time, σ.

Table 8.3 shows the sample data for 25 calls. (These data are in a file called **Heritage**.) The managers at Heritage Software are willing to assume the population of call times is approximately normal.[2]

Heritage's sample mean and standard deviation are

$$\bar{x} = 7.088 \text{ minutes}$$
$$s = 4.64 \text{ minutes}$$

If the managers need a single-valued estimate of the population mean, they would use the point estimate, $\bar{x} = 7.088$ minutes. However, they should realize that this point estimate is subject to sampling error. To take the sampling error into account, the managers can construct a confidence interval estimate. Equation 8.5 shows the formula for the confidence interval estimate for the population mean when the population standard deviation is unknown.

TABLE 8.3 | **Sample Call Times for Heritage Software**

7.1	11.6	12.4	8.5	0.4
13.6	1.7	11.0	6.1	11.0
1.4	16.9	3.7	3.3	0.8
3.6	2.6	14.6	6.1	6.4
1.9	7.7	8.8	6.9	9.1

Chapter Outcome 2. →

Confidence Interval Estimate for μ, σ Unknown

$$\bar{x} \pm t \frac{s}{\sqrt{n}} \tag{8.5}$$

where:

$\bar{x} = $ Sample mean
$t = $ Critical value from the *t*-distribution with $n - 1$ degrees of freedom for the desired confidence level
$s = $ Sample standard deviation
$n = $ Sample size

The first step is to specify the desired confidence level. For example, suppose the Heritage team specifies a 95% confidence level. To get the critical *t*-value from the *t*-table in Appendix F, go to the top of the table to the row labeled "Conf. Level." Locate the column headed "0.95." Next, go to the row corresponding to

$$n - 1 = 25 - 1 = 24 \text{ degrees of freedom}$$

The critical *t*-value for 95% confidence and 24 degrees of freedom is

$$t = 2.0639*$$

---

[2]Chapter 13 introduces a statistical technique called the goodness-of-fit test that can be used to test whether the sample data could have come from a normally distributed population. PHStat, an add-in to Excel contains box and whisker plot feature, and you could also use Excel to construct a histogram.
*You can use Excel 2010 to compute the critical *t*-value using the T.INV function. This function requires two inputs: the probability in the left tail of the distribution and the degrees of freedom. For this example, we want a 95% confidence interval. The probability for the lower tail is 0.025. For the upper-tail value, the probability is 0.975. Note these probabilities "cut off" the required 0.025 area in each tail needed to give us the 95% confidence interval. The function's inputs and the corresponding critical values are T.INV (0.025, 24) = −2.0639, which is the lower-tail *t*-value, and T.INV (0.975,24) = 2.0639, which is the upper-tail critical value.

FIGURE 8.6

Excel 2010 Output for the
Heritage Example

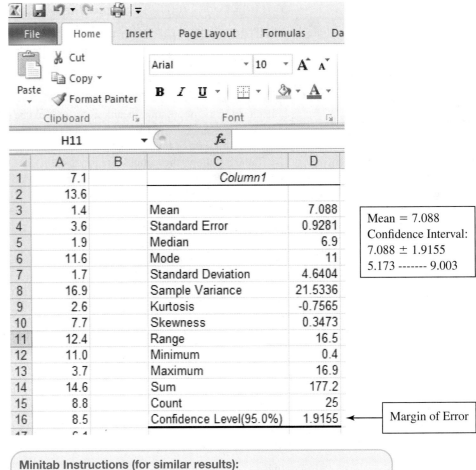

Excel 2010 Instructions:
1. Open file: **Heritage.xlsx**.
2. Select **Data** tab.
3. Select **Data Analysis** >
   Descriptive Statistics.
4. Specify data range.
5. Define **Output Location**.
6. Check **Summary
   Statistics**.
7. Check **Confidence Level
   for Mean:** 95%.
8. Click **OK**.

Minitab Instructions (for similar results):
1. Open file: **Heritage.MTW**.
2. Choose **Stat > Basic Statistics >
   1– sample t**.
3. In **Samples in column**, enter data
   column.
4. Click **Options**.
5. In **Confidence level**,
   enter confidence level.
6. Click **OK. OK**.

The Heritage team can now compute the 95% confidence interval estimate using Equation 8.5 as follows:

$$\bar{x} \pm t \frac{s}{\sqrt{n}}$$

$$7.088 \pm 2.0639 \frac{4.64}{\sqrt{25}}$$

$$7.088 \pm 1.915$$

$$5.173 \, min. \text{ ——— } 9.003 \, min.$$

Therefore, based on the random sample of 25 calls and the 95% confidence interval, the Heritage Software team has estimated the true average time per call to be between 5.173 minutes and 9.003 minutes.

Excel has a procedure for computing the confidence interval estimate of the population mean. The Excel output is shown in Figure 8.6. Note, the margin of error is printed. You will have to use it and the sample mean to compute the upper and lower limits.

EXAMPLE 8-3 **CONFIDENCE INTERVAL ESTIMATE FOR μ, σ UNKNOWN**

State Tax Commission The chairman of the audit department for the Illinois State Tax Commission is interested in estimating the mean tax collected per transaction at a home improvement center. The team he put together to conduct an audit for the home improvement

How to do it (Example 8-3)

Confidence Interval Estimates for a Single Population Mean

A confidence interval estimate for a single population mean can be developed using the following steps.

1. Define the population of interest and the variable for which you wish to estimate the population mean.

2. Determine the sample size and select a simple random sample.

3. Compute the confidence interval as follows, depending on the conditions that exist:

- If σ is known, and the population is normally distributed, use

$$\bar{x} \pm z\frac{\sigma}{\sqrt{n}}$$

- If σ is unknown and we can assume that the population distribution is approximately normal, use

$$\bar{x} \pm t\frac{s}{\sqrt{n}}$$

center wished to develop an estimate for the mean tax collected per transaction. The department wishes to develop a 90% confidence interval estimate for the population mean. To do so, it can use the following steps:

Step 1 Define the population and select a simple random sample of size n from the population.
In this case, the population consists of the individual sales tax payments made by customers at the home improvement center in a given week. A simple random sample of $n = 20$ transactions is selected, with the following data.

$0.00	$1.20	$0.43	$1.00	$1.47	$0.83	$0.50	$3.34	$1.58	$1.46
−$0.36	−$1.10	$2.60	$0.00	$0.00	−$1.70	$0.83	$1.99	$0.00	$1.34

Step 2 Specify the confidence level.
A 90% confidence interval estimate is desired.

Step 3 Compute the sample mean and sample standard deviation.
After the sample has been selected and the tax amounts have been determined for each of the 20 customers sampled, the sample mean is computed using

$$\bar{x} = \frac{\sum x}{n} = \frac{\$15.41}{20} = \$0.77$$

The sample standard deviation is computed using

$$s = \sqrt{\frac{\sum(x-\bar{x})^2}{n-1}} = \sqrt{\frac{(0.00-0.77)^2 + (1.20-0.77)^2 + \cdots + (1.34-0.77)^2}{20-1}} = \$1.19$$

Step 4 Determine the standard error of the sampling distribution.
Because the population standard deviation is unknown, the standard error of the sampling distribution is estimated using

$$\sigma_{\bar{x}} = \frac{s}{\sqrt{n}} = \frac{\$1.19}{\sqrt{20}} = \$0.27$$

Step 5 Determine the critical value for the desired level of confidence.
Because we do not know the population standard deviation and the sample size is reasonably small, the critical value will come from the t-distribution, providing we can assume that the population is normally distributed. A box and whisker plot can give some insight about how the population might look.

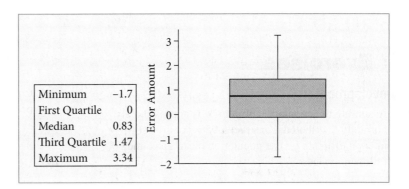

Minimum	−1.7
First Quartile	0
Median	0.83
Third Quartile	1.47
Maximum	3.34

This diagram does not indicate that there is any serious skewness or other abnormality in the data, so we will continue with the normal distribution assumption.

The critical value for 90% confidence and $20 - 1 = 19$ degrees of freedom is found in the t-distribution table as $t = 1.7291$.

Step 6 Compute the confidence interval estimate.

The 90% confidence interval estimate for the population mean is

$$\bar{x} \pm t\frac{s}{\sqrt{n}}$$

$$0.77 \pm 1.7291\frac{1.19}{\sqrt{20}}$$

$$0.77 \pm 0.46$$

$$\$0.31 \longrightarrow \$1.23$$

Thus, based on the sample data, with 90% confidence, the auditors can conclude that the population mean tax collected per transaction is between $0.31 and $1.23.

>> **END EXAMPLE**

TRY PROBLEM 8-7 (pg. 311)

Estimation with Larger Sample Sizes We saw earlier that a change in sample size can affect the margin of error in a statistical estimation situation when the population standard deviation is known. This is also true in applications in which the standard deviation is not known. In fact, the effect of a change is compounded because the change in sample size affects both the calculation of the standard error and the critical value from the t-distribution.

The t-distribution table in Appendix F shows degrees of freedom up to 30 and then incrementally to 500. Observe that for any confidence level, as the degrees of freedom increase, the t-value gets smaller as it approaches a limit equal to the z-value from the standard normal table in Appendix D for the same confidence level. If you need to estimate the population mean with a sample size that is not listed in the t-table, you can use the Excel **T.INV** function to get the critical t-value for any specified degrees of freedom and then use Equation 8.5.

You should have noticed that the format for confidence interval estimates for μ is essentially the same, regardless of whether the population standard deviation is known. The basic format is

$$\text{Point estimate} \pm (\text{Critical value})(\text{Standard error})$$

Later in this chapter, we introduce estimation examples in which the population value of interest is p the population proportion. The same confidence interval format is used. In addition, the trade-offs between margin of error, confidence level, and sample size that were discussed in this section also apply to every other estimation situation.

MyStatLab

8-1: **Exercises**

Skill **Development**

8-1. Assuming the population of interest is approximately normally distributed, construct a 95% confidence interval estimate for the population mean given the following values:

$$\bar{x} = 18.4 \quad s = 4.2 \quad n = 13$$

8-2. Construct a 90% confidence interval estimate for the population mean given the following values:

$$\bar{x} = 70 \quad \sigma = 15 \quad n = 65$$

8-3. Construct a 95% confidence interval estimate for the population mean given the following values:

$$\bar{x} = 300 \quad \sigma = 55 \quad n = 250$$

8-4. Construct a 98% confidence interval estimate for the population mean given the following values:

$$\bar{x} = 120 \quad \sigma = 20 \quad n = 50$$

8-5. Determine the 90% confidence interval estimate for the population mean of a normal distribution given $n = 100, \sigma = 121$, and $\bar{x} = 1,200$.

8-6. Determine the margin of error for a confidence interval estimate for the population mean of a normal distribution given the following information:

a. confidence level = 0.98, $n = 13, s = 15.68$

b. confidence level = 0.99, $n = 25, \sigma = 3.47$

c. confidence level = 0.98, standard error = 2.356

8-7. The following sample data have been collected based on a simple random sample from a normally distributed population:

2	8	0	2	3
5	3	1	4	2

a. Compute a 90% confidence interval estimate for the population mean.
b. Show what the impact would be if the confidence level is increased to 95%. Discuss why this occurs.

8-8. A random sample of size 20 yields $\bar{x} = 3.13$ and $s^2 = 1.45$. Calculate a confidence interval for the population mean whose confidence level is as follows:
a. 0.99
b. 0.98
c. 0.95
d. 0.90
e. 0.80
f. What assumptions were necessary to establish the validity of the confidence intervals calculated in parts a through e?

8-9. A random sample of $n = 12$ values taken from a normally distributed population resulted in the following sample values:

107	109	99	91	103	105
105	94	107	94	97	113

Use the sample information to construct a 95% confidence interval estimate for the population mean.

8-10. A random sample of $n = 9$ values taken from a normally distributed population with a population variance of 25 resulted in the following sample values:

53	46	55	45	44	52	46	60	49

Use the sample values to construct a 90% confidence interval estimate for the population mean.

8-11. A random sample was selected from a population having a normal distribution. Calculate a 90% confidence interval estimate for μ for each of the following situations:
a. $\Sigma x = 134, n = 10, s = 3.1$
b. $\Sigma x = 3,744, n = 120, s = 8.2$
c. $\Sigma x = 40.5, n = 9, \sigma = 2.9$
d. $\Sigma x = 585.9, \Sigma x^2 = 15,472.37, n = 27$ (*Hint:* Refer to Equation 3.13.)

Business Applications

8-12. Allante Pizza delivers pizzas throughout its local market area at no charge to the customer. However, customers often tip the driver. The owner is interested in estimating the mean tip income per delivery. To do this, she has selected a simple random sample of 12 deliveries and has recorded the tips that were received by the drivers. These data are

$2.25	$2.50	$2.25	$2.00	$2.00	$1.50
$0.00	$2.00	$1.50	$2.00	$3.00	$1.50

a. Based on these sample data, what is the best point estimate to use as an estimate of the true mean tip per delivery?
b. Suppose the owner is interested in developing a 90% confidence interval estimate. Given the fact that the population standard deviation is unknown, what distribution will be used to obtain the critical value?
c. Referring to part b, what assumption is required to use the specified distribution to obtain the critical value? Develop a box and whisker plot to illustrate whether this assumption seems to be reasonably satisfied.
d. Referring to parts b and c, construct and interpret the 90% confidence interval estimate for the population mean.

8-13. The BelSante Company operates retail pharmacies in 10 eastern states. Recently, the company's internal audit department selected a random sample of 300 prescriptions issued throughout the system. The objective of the sampling was to estimate the average dollar value of all prescriptions issued by the company. The following data were collected:

$$\bar{x} = \$14.23$$
$$s = 3.00$$

a. Determine the 90% confidence interval estimate for the true average sales value for prescriptions issued by the company. Interpret the interval estimate.
b. One of its retail outlets recently reported that it had monthly revenue of $7,392 from 528 prescriptions. Are such results to be expected? Do you believe that the retail outlet should be audited? Support your answer with calculations and logic.

8-14. Even before the record gas prices during the summer of 2008, an article written by Will Lester of the Associated Press reported on a poll in which 80% of those surveyed say that Americans who currently own a SUV (sport utility vehicle) should switch to a more fuel-efficient vehicle to ease America's dependency on foreign oil. This study was conducted by the Pew Research Center for the People & the Press. As a follow-up to this report, a consumer group conducted a study of SUV owners to estimate the mean mileage for their vehicles. A simple random sample of 91 SUV owners was selected, and the owners were asked to report their highway mileage. The following results were summarized from the sample data:

$$\bar{x} = 18.2 \text{ mpg}$$
$$s = 6.3 \text{ mpg}$$

Based on these sample data, compute and interpret a 90% confidence interval estimate for the mean highway mileage for SUVs.

8-15. According to *USA Today*, customers are not settling for automobiles straight off the production lines. As an example, those who purchase a $355,000 Rolls Royce typically add $25,000 in accessories. One of the affordable automobiles to receive additions is BMW's

Mini Cooper. A sample of 179 recent Mini purchasers yielded a sample mean of $5,000 above the $20,200 base sticker price. Suppose the cost of accessories purchased for all Mini Coopers has a standard deviation of $1,500.

a. Calculate a 95% confidence interval for the average cost of accessories on Mini Coopers.

b. Determine the margin of error in estimating the average cost of accessories on Mini Coopers.

c. What sample size would be required to reduce the margin of error by 50%?

8-16. XtraNet, an Internet service provider (ISP), has experienced rapid growth in the past five years. As a part of its marketing strategy, XtraNet promises fast connections and dependable service. To achieve its objectives, XtraNet constantly evaluates the capacity of its servers. One component of its evaluation is an analysis of the average amount of time a customer is connected and using the Internet daily. A random sample of 12 customer records shows the following daily usage times, in minutes:

| 268 | 336 | 296 | 311 | 306 | 335 |
| 301 | 278 | 290 | 393 | 373 | 329 |

a. Using the sample data, compute the best point estimate of the population mean for daily usage times for XtraNet's customers.

b. The managers of XtraNet's marketing department would like to develop a 99% confidence interval estimate for the population mean daily customer usage time. Because the population standard deviation of daily customer usage time is unknown and the sample size is small, what assumption must the marketing managers make concerning the population of daily customer usage times?

c. Construct and interpret a 99% confidence interval for the mean daily usage time for XtraNet's customers.

d. Assume that before the sample was taken, XtraNet's marketing staff believed that mean daily usage for its customers was 267 minutes. Does their assumption concerning mean daily usage seem reasonable based on the confidence interval developed in part c?

8-17. In a study conducted by American Express, corporate clients were surveyed to determine the extent to which hotel room rates quoted by central reservation systems differ from the rates negotiated by the companies. The study found that the mean overcharge by hotels was $11.35 per night. Suppose a follow-up study was done in which a random sample of 30 corporate hotel bookings was analyzed. Only those cases in which an error occurred were included in the study. The following data show the amounts by which the quoted rate differs from the negotiated rate. Positive values indicate an overcharge and negative values indicate an undercharge.

$15.45	$24.81	$6.02	$14.00	$25.60	$8.29
−$17.34	−$5.72	$11.61	$3.48	$18.91	$7.14
$6.64	$12.48	$6.31	−$4.85	$5.72	$12.72
$5.23	$4.57	$15.84	$2.09	−$4.56	$3.00
$23.60	$30.86	$9.25	$0.93	$20.73	$12.45

a. Compute a 95% confidence interval estimate for the mean error in hotel charges. Interpret the confidence interval estimate.

b. Based on the interval computed in part a, do these sample data tend to support the results of the American Express study? Explain.

8-18. A regional U.S. commercial bank issues both Visa credit cards and MasterCard credit cards. As a part of its annual review of the profitability of each type of credit card, the bank randomly samples 36 customers to measure the average annual charges per card. It has completed its analysis of the Visa card accounts and is now focused on its MasterCard customers. A random sample of 36 MasterCard accounts shows the following annual spending per account (rounded to the nearest dollar):

$2,869	$3,770	$2,854	$2,750	$2,574	$2,972
$2,549	$3,267	$3,013	$2,707	$2,794	$1,189
$2,230	$2,178	$3,032	$3,485	$2,679	$2,010
$1,994	$2,768	$3,853	$2,064	$3,244	$2,738
$2,807	$2,395	$3,405	$3,006	$3,368	$2,691
$1,996	$3,008	$2,730	$2,518	$2,710	$3,719

a. Based on these randomly sampled accounts, what is the best point estimate of the true mean annual spending for MasterCard account holders?

b. If the bank is interested in developing a 95% confidence interval estimate of mean annual spending, what distribution will be used to determine the critical value?

c. Determine the standard error of the sampling distribution.

d. Construct the 95% confidence interval estimate for the population mean of annual MasterCard spending for the bank's customers.

e. If the bank desires to have a higher level of confidence in its interval estimate, what will happen to the margin of error?

8-19. Nielsen Media Research reported that the average American home watched more television in 2007 than in any previous season. From September 2006 to September 2007 (the official start and end of television season in the United States), the average time spent by U.S. households tuned into television was 8 hours and 14 minutes per day. This is 13.85% higher than 10 years ago, and the highest levels ever reported since television viewing was first measured by Nielsen Media Research in the 1950s. To determine if television viewing has changed in 2008, a sample (in minutes) similar to the following would be used:

494	533	597	530	577	514	466	416	403	625
562	448	592	567	564	537	370	627	416	511
750	661	570	579	494	533	549	583	610	423

a. Calculate the sample standard deviation and mean number of minutes spent viewing television.

b. Calculate a 95% confidence interval for the average number of minutes spent viewing television in 2008.

c. Would the results obtained in part b indicate that households viewed more television in 2008 than in 2007?

8-20. The concession managers for the Arkansas Travelers (a minor league baseball team located in Little Rock) are interested in estimating the average amount spent on food by fans attending the team's Friday night home games. Suppose a random sample of 36 receipts for food orders was taken from last year's receipts for Friday night home games with the following food expenditures recorded:

$30.50	$10.63	$3.77	$21.90	$21.95	$9.65
$14.31	$11.39	$25.36	$15.79	$30.88	$12.20
$8.48	$20.70	$28.54	$9.13	$15.54	$14.95
$11.96	$11.91	$8.28	$12.87	$24.26	$21.04
$20.08	$10.08	$25.37	$12.02	$11.61	$11.22
$25.36	$28.07	$17.71	$23.00	$31.79	$17.70

a. Based on the sampled receipts, what is the best point estimate for the mean food expenditures for Friday night home games?

b. Use the sample information to construct a 95% confidence interval estimate for the true mean expenditures for Friday night home games.

c. Before the sample was taken, the food concessions manager stated that mean food expenditures were about $19.00 per order. Does his statement seem consistent with the results obtained in part b?

Computer Database **Exercises**

8-21. Suppose a study of 196 randomly sampled privately insured adults with incomes more than 200% of the current poverty level is to be used to measure out-of-pocket medical expenses for prescription drugs for this income class. The sample data are in the file **Drug Expenses**.

a. Based on the sample data, construct a 95% confidence interval estimate for the mean annual out-of-pocket expenditures on prescription drugs for this income class. Interpret this interval.

b. The study's authors hope to use the information to make recommendations concerning insurance reimbursement guidelines and patient copayment recommendations. If the margin of error calculated in part a is considered to be too large for this purpose, what options are available to the study's authors?

8-22. One of the reasons for multiple car accidents on highways is thought to be poor visibility. Recently, the National Transportation Agency (NTA) of the federal government sponsored a study of one rural section of highway in Idaho that had been the scene of several multiple-car accidents. Two visibility sensors were located near the site for the purposes of recording the number of miles of visibility each time the visibility reading is performed. The two visibility sensors are made by different companies, Scorpion and Vanguard. The NTA would like to develop 95% confidence interval estimates of the mean visibility at this location as recorded by both visibility sensors. The random sample data are in a file called **Visibility**. Also, comment on whether there appears to be a difference between the two sensors in terms of average visibility readings.

8-23. The file **Danish Coffee** contains a random sample of 144 Danish coffee drinkers and measures the annual coffee consumption in kilograms for each sampled coffee drinker. A marketing research firm wants to use this information to develop an advertising campaign to increase Danish coffee consumption.

a. Based on the sample's results, what is the best point estimate of average annual coffee consumption for Danish coffee drinkers?

b. Develop and interpret a 90% confidence interval estimate for the mean annual coffee consumption of Danish coffee drinkers.

8-24. The manager at a new tire and repair shop in Hartford, Connecticut, wants to establish guidelines for the time it should take to put new brakes on vehicles. In particular, he is interested in estimating the mean installation time for brakes for passenger cars and SUVs made by three different manufacturers. To help with this process, he set up an experiment in his shop in which five brake jobs were performed for each manufacturer and each class of vehicle. He recorded the number of minutes that it took to complete the jobs. These data are in a file called **Brake-test** and are also shown as follows:

| | **Manufacturer** | | |
	Company A	Company B	Company C
Passenger Car	55	68	80
	58	49	67
	66	78	70
	44	60	77
	78	72	90
SUV	102	89	119
	89	90	102
	127	88	98
	78	95	80
	90	101	106

a. Use software such as Excel to compute the point estimate for the population mean installation time for each category.

b. Use software such as Excel to compute the necessary sample statistics needed to construct 95% confidence interval estimates for the population mean installation times. What assumption is required?

c. Based on the results from part b, what conclusions might you reach about the three companies in terms of the time it takes to install their brakes for passenger cars and for SUVs? Discuss.

8-25. The Transportation Security Administration (TSA) has examined the possibility of a Registered Traveler program. This program is intended to be a way to shorten security lines for "trusted travelers." In a study run at Orlando International Airport, 13,000 people paid an annual $80 fee to participate in the program. They spent an average of four seconds in security lines at Orlando according to Verified Identity Pass, the company that ran the program. For comparison purposes, a sample was obtained of the time it took the other passengers to pass through security at Orlando. The file titled **PASSTIME** contains these data. Assume the distribution of time required to pass through security at Orlando International Airport for those flyers in the Registered Traveler program is normally distributed.

a. Calculate the sample mean and the sample standard deviation for this sample of passenger times.

b. Assume that the distribution of time required to pass through security at Orlando International Airport is normally distributed. Use the sample data to construct a 95% confidence interval for the average time required to pass through security.

c. What is the margin of error for the confidence interval constructed in b?

8-26. The per capita consumption of chicken has risen from 28 pounds in 1960 to 90.6 pounds in 2007$ according to the U.S. Department of Agriculture. That constitutes an average increase of approximately 1.33 pounds per capita per year. To determine if this trend has continued, in 2008 a random sample of 200 individuals was selected to determine the amount of chicken they consumed in 2008. A file titled **Chickwt** contains the data.

a. Calculate the mean and standard deviation of the amount of chicken consumed by the individuals in the sample.

b. Calculate a 99% confidence interval for the 2008 per capita consumption of chicken in the United States.

c. Based on your calculation in part b, determine if the specified trend has continued.

END EXERCISES 8-1

Chapter Outcome 3. → **8.2** Determining the Required Sample Size for Estimating a Population Mean

We have discussed the basic trade-offs that are present in all statistical estimations: the desire is to have a high confidence level, a low margin of error, and a small sample size. The problem is these three objectives conflict. For a given sample size, a high confidence level will tend to generate a large margin of error. For a given confidence level, a small sample size will result in an increased margin of error. Reducing the margin of error requires either reducing the confidence level or increasing the sample size, or both.

A common question from business decision makers who are planning an estimation application is, "How large a sample size do I really need?" To answer this question, we usually begin by asking a couple of questions of our own:

1. How much money do you have budgeted to do the sampling?
2. How much will it cost to select each item in the sample?

The answers to these questions provide the upper limit on the sample size that can be selected. For instance, if the decision maker indicates that she has a $2,000 budget for selecting the sample and the cost will be about $10 per unit to collect the sample, the sample size's upper limit is $2,000 ÷ $10 = 200 units.

Keeping in mind the estimation trade-offs discussed earlier, the issue should be fully discussed with the decision maker. For instance, is a sample of 200 sufficient to give the desired margin of error at a specified confidence level? Is 200 more than is needed, or not enough, to achieve the desired margin of error?

Therefore, before we can give a definite answer about what sample size is needed, the decision maker must specify her confidence level and a desired margin of error. Then the required sample size can be computed.

Determining the Required Sample Size for Estimating μ, σ Known

BUSINESS APPLICATION **CALCULATING THE REQUIRED SAMPLE SIZE**

FEDERAL TRANSPORTATION ADMINISTRATION The Federal Transportation Administration is interested in knowing the mean number of miles that male adults in San Diego commute to and from work on a weekly basis. Because of the size of the population of interest, the only way to get this number is to select a random sample of adult males and develop a statistical estimation of the mean. Officials at the Transportation Administration have specified that the estimate must be based on a 95% confidence level. Further, the margin of error for the population mean must not exceed ± 30 miles. Given these requirements, what size sample is needed?

To answer this question, if the population standard deviation is known, we start with Equation 8.3, the equation for calculating the margin of error.

$$e = z\frac{\sigma}{\sqrt{n}}$$

We next substitute into this equation the values we know. For example, the margin of error was specified to be

$$e = 30 \text{ miles}$$

The confidence level was specified to be 95%. The z-value for 95% is 1.96. (Refer to the standard normal table in Appendix D.) This gives us

$$30 = 1.96\frac{\sigma}{\sqrt{n}}$$

We need to know the population standard deviation. The Transportation Administration officials might know this value from other studies that it has conducted in the past. Assume for this example that σ, the population standard deviation, is 200 miles. We can now substitute

$$\sigma = 200$$

into the equation for e, as follows:

$$30 = 1.96\frac{200}{\sqrt{n}}$$

We now have a single equation with one unknown, n, the sample size. Doing the algebra to solve for n, we get

$$n = \left(\frac{1.96(200)}{30}\right)^2 = 170.73 \approx 171 \text{ adult males}$$

Thus, to meet the requirements of the Federal Transportation Agency, a sample of $n = 171$ adult males should be selected. Equation 8.6 is used to determine the required sample size for estimating a single population mean when σ is known.

Sample Size Requirement for Estimating μ, σ Known

$$n = \left(\frac{z\sigma}{e}\right)^2 = \frac{z^2\sigma^2}{e^2} \tag{8.6}$$

where:

z = Critical value for the specified confidence level
e = Desired margin of error
σ = Population standard deviation

If the officials conducting this study feel that the cost of sampling 171 adult males will be too high, it might allow for a higher margin of error or a lower confidence level. For example, if the confidence level is lowered to 90%, the z-value is lowered to 1.645, as found in the standard normal table.[3]

We can now use Equation 8.6 to determine the revised sample-size requirement.

$$n = \frac{1.645^2 (200)^2}{30^2} = 120.27 = 121$$

The Agency will need to sample only 121 (120.27 rounded up) adult males for a confidence level of 90% rather than 95%.

EXAMPLE 8-4   **DETERMINING THE REQUIRED SAMPLE SIZE, σ KNOWN**

United Meat Producers The general manager for United Meat Producers is interested in estimating the mean pounds of hamburger that are purchased per month by households in the Honolulu, Hawaii, area. He would like his estimate to be within plus or minus 0.50 pounds per month, and he would like the estimate to be at the 99% confidence level. Past studies have shown that the standard deviation for hamburger purchase amount is 4.0 pounds. To determine the required sample size, he can use the following steps:

Step 1   Specify the desired margin of error.
The manager wishes to have his estimate be within ± 0.50 pounds, so the margin of error is

$$e = 0.50 \text{ pounds}$$

Step 2   Determine the population standard deviation.
Based on other studies, the manager is willing to conclude that the population standard deviation is known. Thus,

$$\sigma = 4.0$$

Step 3   Determine the critical value for the desired level of confidence.
The critical value will be a z-value from the standard normal table for 99% confidence. This is

$$z = 2.575$$

Step 4   Compute the required sample size using Equation 8.6.
The required sample size is

$$n = \frac{z^2 \sigma^2}{e^2} = \frac{2.575^2 4.0^2}{0.50^2} = 424.36 \approx 425 \text{ households}$$

Note: The sample size is always rounded up to the next integer value.

>> **END EXAMPLE**

TRY PROBLEM 8-27 (pg. 318)

Determining the Required Sample Size for Estimating μ, σ Unknown

Equation 8.6 assumes you know the population standard deviation. Although this may be the case in some situations, most likely we won't know the population standard deviation. To get around this problem, we can use three approaches. One is to use a value for σ that is considered to be at least as large as the true σ. This will provide a conservatively large sample size.

The second option is to select a **pilot sample**, a sample from the population that is used explicitly to estimate σ.

Pilot Sample
A sample taken from the population of interest of a size smaller than the anticipated sample size that is used to provide an estimate for the population standard deviation.

---

[3]You can also use the Excel function, NORM.S.INV, to determine the z-value or Minitab's Calc > Probability Distributions > Normal command.

The third option is to use the range of the population to estimate the population's standard deviation. Recall the Empirical Rule in Chapter 3 and the examination in Chapter 6 of the normal distribution. Both sources suggest that $\mu \pm 3\sigma$ contains virtually all of the data values of a normal distribution. If this were the case, then $\mu - 3\sigma$ would be approximately the smallest number and $\mu + 3\sigma$ would be approximately the largest number. Remember that the Range $= R =$ Maximum value $-$ Minimum value. So, $R \approx (\mu + 3\sigma) - (\mu - 3\sigma) = 6\sigma$. We can, therefore, obtain an estimate of the standard deviation as

$$\sigma \approx \frac{R}{6}$$

We can also use a procedure that produces a larger estimate of the standard deviation, which will lead to a larger, more conservative sample size. This involves dividing the range by 4 instead of 6.

We seldom know the standard deviation of the population. However, very often we have a very good idea about the largest and smallest value of the population. Therefore, this third method can be used in many instances in which you do not wish to, or cannot, obtain a pilot sample or you are unable to offer a conjecture concerning a conservatively large value of the standard deviation.

EXAMPLE 8-5 **DETERMINING THE REQUIRED SAMPLE SIZE, σ UNKNOWN**

Sandor Jackal/Fotolia

Oceanside Petroleum Consider a situation in which the regional manager for Oceanside Petroleum in Oregon wishes to know the mean gallons of gasoline purchased by customers each time they fill up their cars. Not only does he not know μ, he also does not know the population standard deviation. He wants a 90% confidence level and is willing to have a margin of error of 0.50 gallons in estimating the true mean gallons purchased. The required sample size can be determined using the following steps.

Step 1 Specify the desired margin of error.
The manager wants the estimate to be within ± 0.50 gallons of the true mean. Thus,

$$e = 0.50$$

Step 2 Determine an estimate for the population standard deviation.
The manager will select a pilot sample of $n = 20$ fill-ups and record the number of gallons for each. These values are

18.9	22.4	24.6	25.7	26.3	28.4	21.7	31.0	19.0	31.7
17.4	25.5	20.1	34.3	25.9	20.3	21.6	25.8	31.6	28.8

The estimate for the population standard deviation is the sample standard deviation for the pilot sample. This is computed using

$$s = \sqrt{\frac{\Sigma(x - \bar{x})^2}{n - 1}} = \sqrt{\frac{(18.9 - 25.05)^2 + (22.4 - 25.05)^2 + \cdots + (28.8 - 25.05)^2}{20 - 1}} = 4.85$$

We will use

$$\sigma \approx 4.85$$

Step 3 Determine the critical value for the desired level of confidence.
The critical value will be a z-value from the standard normal table. The 90% confidence level gives

$$z = 1.645$$

Step 4 **Calculate the required sample size using Equation 8.6.**

Using the pilot sample's standard deviation the required sample size is

$$n = \frac{z^2\sigma^2}{e^2} = \frac{(1.645^2)(4.85^2)}{0.50^2} = 254.61 = 255$$

The required sample size is 255 fill-ups, but we can use the pilot sample as part of this total. Thus, the net required sample size in this case is $255 - 20 = 235$.

>> **END EXAMPLE**

TRY PROBLEM 8-34 (pg. 318)

MyStatLab

8-2: **Exercises**

Skill **Development**

8-27. What sample size is needed to estimate a population mean within ± 50 of the true mean value using a confidence level of 95%, if the true population variance is known to be 122,500?

8-28. An advertising company wishes to estimate the mean household income for all single working professionals who own a foreign automobile. If the advertising company wants a 90% confidence interval estimate with a margin of error of $\pm \$2,500$, what sample size is needed if the population standard deviation is known to be $27,500?

8-29. A manager wishes to estimate a population mean using a 95% confidence interval estimate that has a margin of error of ± 44.0. If the population standard deviation is thought to be 680, what is the required sample size?

8-30. A sample size must be determined for estimating a population mean given that the confidence level is 90% and the desired margin of error is 0.30. The largest value in the population is thought to be 15 and the smallest value is thought to be 5.

   a. Calculate the sample size required to estimate the population using a generously large sample size. (*Hint*: Use the range/4 option.)

   b. If a conservatively small sample size is desired, calculate the required sample size. (*Hint*: Use the range/6 option.) Discuss why the answers in parts a and b are different.

8-31. Suppose a study estimated the population mean for a variable of interest using a 99% confidence interval. If the width of the estimated confidence interval (the difference between the upper limit and the lower limit) is 600 and the sample size used in estimating the mean is 1,000, what is the population standard deviation?

8-32. Determine the smallest sample size required to estimate the population mean under the following specifications:

   a. $e = 2.4$, confidence level $= 80\%$, data between 50 and 150

   b. $e = 2.4$, confidence level $= 90\%$, data between 50 and 150

   c. $e = 1.2$, confidence level $= 90\%$, data between 50 and 150

   d. $e = 1.2$ confidence level $= 90\%$, data between 25 and 175

8-33. Calculate the smallest sample size required to estimate the population mean under the following specifications:

   a. confidence level 95%, $\sigma = 16$, and $e = 4$

   b. confidence level 90%, $\sigma = 23$, and $e = 0.5$

   c. confidence level 99%, $\sigma = 0.5$, and $e = 1$

   d. confidence level 98%, $\sigma = 1.5$, and $e = 0.2$

   e. confidence level 95%, $\sigma = 6$, and $e = 2$

8-34. A decision maker is interested in estimating the mean of a population based on a random sample. She wants the confidence level to be 90% and the margin of error to be ± 0.30. She does not know what the population standard deviation is, so she has selected the following pilot sample:

8.80	4.89	10.98	15.11	14.79
16.93	1.27	9.06	14.38	5.65
7.24	3.24	2.61	6.09	6.91

Based on this pilot sample, how many more items must be sampled so that the decision maker can make the desired confidence interval estimate?

Business **Applications**

8-35. A production process that fills 12-ounce cereal boxes is known to have a population standard deviation of 0.009 ounces. If a consumer protection agency would like to estimate the mean fill, in ounces, for 12-ounce cereal boxes with a confidence level of 92% and a margin of error of 0.001, what size sample must be used?

8-36. A public policy research group is conducting a study of health care plans and would like to estimate the average dollars contributed annually to health savings accounts by participating employees. A pilot study conducted a few months earlier indicated that the standard deviation of annual contributions to such plans was $1,225. The research group wants the study's findings to be within $100 of the true mean with a confidence level of 90%. What sample size is required?

8-37. With the high cost of fuel and intense competition, the major airline companies have had a very difficult time financially in recent years. Many carriers are now charging for checked bags. One carrier is considering charging a two-tiered rate based on the weight of checked bags. Before deciding at what rate to increase the charge, the airline wishes to estimate the mean weight per bag checked by passengers. It wants the estimate to be within ± 0.25 pounds of the true population mean. A pilot sample of bags checked gives the following results:

35	33	37	33	36	40	34	40	39	40
39	41	35	42	43	46	34	41	38	44

a. What size sample should the airline use if it wants to have 95% confidence?

b. Suppose the airline managers do not want to take as large a sample as the one you determined in part a. What general options do they have to lower the required sample size?

8-38. The Northwest Pacific Phone Company wishes to estimate the average number of minutes its customers spend on long-distance calls per month. The company wants the estimate made with 99% confidence and a margin of error of no more than 5 minutes.

a. A previous study indicated that the standard deviation for long-distance calls is 21 minutes per month. What should the sample size be?

b. Determine the required sample size if the confidence level were changed from 99% to 90%.

c. What would the required sample size be if the confidence level was 95% and the margin of error was 8 minutes?

8-39. An Associated Press article by Eileen Alt Powell discussed the changes that banks are making to the way they calculate the minimum payment due on credit card balances. The changes are being pushed by federal regulators. In the past, minimum payments were set at about 2% of the outstanding balance. Each credit card issuer is making its own changes. For example, Bank of America Corporation in Charlotte, North Carolina, went from a minimum of 2.2% of the balance to a flat amount of $10 plus all fees and interest due.

Suppose that a large California-based bank is in the process of considering what changes to make. It wishes to survey its customers to estimate the mean percent payment on their outstanding balance that customers would like to see. The bank wants to construct a 99% confidence interval estimate with a margin of error of ± 0.2 percent. A pilot sample of $n = 50$ customers showed a sample standard deviation of 1.4%.

How many more customers does the bank need to survey in order to construct the interval estimate?

8-40. The Longmont Computer Leasing Company leases computers and peripherals like laser printers. The printers have a counter that keeps track of the number of pages printed. The company wishes to estimate the mean number of pages that will be printed in a month on its leased printers. The plan is to select a random sample of printers and record the number on each printer's counter at the beginning of May. Then, at the end of May, the number on the counter will be recorded again and the difference will be the number of copies on that printer for the month. The company wants the estimate to be within ± 100 pages of the true mean with a 95% confidence level.

a. The standard deviation in pages printed is thought to be about 1,400 pages. How many printers should be sampled?

b. Suppose that the conjecture concerning the size of the standard deviation is off (plus or minus) by as much as 10%. What percentage change in the required sample size would this produce?

8-41. The Federal Communications Commission released a report (Leslie Cauley, *USA Today*, "Study: A la Carte Cable Would Be Cheaper," February 10, 2006) refuting an earlier report released in 2004 by the Federal Communications Commission (FCC) under the prior chairman, Michael Powell. The 2006 report indicates that cable subscribers would save as much as 13% on their cable television bills. The average monthly cable prices were estimated to be $41.04. Typically, such reports announce a margin of error of, say, $1.25 and a confidence level of 95%. Suppose the standard deviation of the monthly cost of cable television bills was $10.00.

a. Determine the sample size of the study released by the FCC in 2006.

b. Calculate the sample size required to decrease the margin of error by a dollar.

c. A typical sample size used in national surveys is 1,500 to 2,000. Determine a range for the margin of error corresponding to this range of sample sizes.

8-42. *Business Week* reports that film production companies are gravitating toward Eastern Europe. Studios there have a reputation of skilled technical work at a relatively low cost. But Bulgaria is even cheaper, with costs below those of Hollywood. As an example, weekly soundstage rental prices are quoted as $3.77 per square meter in Bulgaria and $16.50 for its U.S. counterparts. To verify these figures, a sample of 50 rentals was taken, producing the average quoted for Bulgaria.

a. Determine the standard deviation of the weekly rental prices if the margin of error associated with the estimate was $2 using a 95% confidence level.

b. How much would the sample size have to be increased to decrease the margin of error by $1?

c. Calculate the change in the standard deviation that would have to be realized to produce the same decrease in the margin of error as realized in part b.

8-43. A regional chain of fast-food restaurants would like to estimate the mean time required to serve its drive-thru customers. Because speed of service is a critical factor in the success of its restaurants, the chain wants to have as accurate an estimate of the mean service time as possible.

a. If the population standard deviation of service times is known to be 30 seconds, how large a sample must be used to estimate the mean service time for drive-thru customers if a margin of error of no more than ±10 seconds of the true mean with a 99% level of confidence is required?

b. Suppose the manager believes that a margin of error of ±10 seconds is too high and has decided it should be cut in half to a margin of error of ±5 seconds. He is of the opinion that by cutting the margin of error in half, the required sample size will double over what was required for a margin of error of ±10. Is the manager correct concerning the sample-size requirement for the reduced margin of error? (Provide supporting calculations.)

Computer Database **Exercises**

8-44. Bruce Leichtman is president of Leichtman Research Group, Inc. (LRG), which specializes in research and consulting on broadband, media, and entertainment industries. In a recent survey, the company determined the cost of extra high-definition (HD) gear needed to watch television in HD. The costs ranged from $5 a month for a set-top box to $200 for a new satellite receiver. The file titled **HDcosts** contains a sample of the costs of the extras whose purchase is required to watch television in HD.

a. Produce a 95% confidence interval for the population mean cost of the extras whose purchase would be required to watch television in HD.

b. Calculate the margin of error for this experiment.

c. If you were to view the sample used in part a to be a pilot sample, how many additional data values would be required to produce a margin of error of 5? Assume the population standard deviation is 50.353.

8-45. Suppose a random sample of 137 households in Detroit was selected to determine the average annual household spending on food at home for Detroit residents. The sample results are contained in the file **Detroit Eats**.

a. Using the sample standard deviation as an estimate for the population standard deviation, calculate the sample size required to estimate the true population mean to within ±$25 with 95% confidence. How many additional samples must be taken?

b. Using the sample standard deviation as an estimate for the population standard deviation, calculate the sample size required to estimate the true population mean to within ±$25 with 90% confidence. How many additional samples must be taken?

8-46. The Bureau of Labor Statistics, U.S. Office of Personnel Management, indicated that the average hourly compensation (salary plus benefits) for federal workers (not including military or postal service employees) was $44.82. The rates for private industry and state and local government workers are believed to be considerably less than that. The file titled **Paychecks** contains a random sample of the hourly amounts paid to state and local government workers.

a. Generate the margin of error for estimating the average hourly amounts paid to state and local government workers with a 98% confidence level.

b. Determine the sample size required to produce a margin of error equal to 1.40 with a confidence level of 98%. Assume the population standard deviation equals 6.22.

c. Does it appear that state and local government workers have a smaller average hourly compensation than federal workers? Support your opinion.

8-47. Phone Solutions, Inc., specializes in providing call center services for companies that wish to outsource their call center activities. There are two main ways that Phone Solutions has historically billed its clients: by the call or by the minute. Phone Solutions is currently negotiating with a new client who wants to be billed for the number of minutes that Phone Solutions is on the phone with customers. Before a contract is written, Phone Solutions plans to receive a random sample of calls and keep track of the minutes spent on the phone with the customer. From this, it plans to estimate the mean call time. It wishes to develop a 95% confidence interval estimate for the population mean call time and wants this estimate to be within ±0.15 minutes. The question is, how many calls should Phone Solutions use in its sample?

Since the population standard deviation is unknown, a pilot sample was taken by having three call centers operated by Phone Solutions each take 50 calls for a total pilot sample of 150 calls. The minutes for each of these calls are listed in the file called **PhoneSolutions**.

a. How many additional calls will be needed to compute the desired confidence interval estimate for the population mean?

b. In the event that the managers at Phone Solutions want a smaller sample size, what options do they have? Discuss in general terms.

8.3 Estimating a Population Proportion

The previous sections have illustrated the methods for developing confidence interval estimates when the population value of interest is the mean. However, you will encounter many situations in which the value of interest is the proportion of items in the population that possess a particular attribute. For example, you may wish to estimate the proportion of customers who are satisfied with the service provided by your company. The notation for the *population proportion* is p. The point estimate for p is the *sample proportion*, $\bar{p}$, which is computed using Equation 8.7.

Sample Proportion

$$\bar{p} = \frac{x}{n}$$

(8.7)

where:

$\bar{p}$ = Sample proportion
x = Number of items in the sample with the attribute of interest
n = Sample size

In Chapter 7, we introduced the sampling distribution for proportions. We indicated then that when the sample size is sufficiently large $[np \geq 5$ and $n(1 - p) \geq 5]$, the sampling distribution can be approximated by a normal distribution centered at p with a standard error for $\bar{p}$ computed using Equation 8.8.

Standard Error for $\bar{p}$

$$\sigma_{\bar{p}} = \sqrt{\frac{p(1-p)}{n}}$$

(8.8)

where:

p = Population proportion
n = Sample size

Notice that in Equation 8.8, the population proportion, p, is required. But if we already knew the value for p we would not need to determine its estimate. If p is unknown, we can estimate the value for the standard error by substituting $\bar{p}$ for p as shown in Equation 8.9, providing that $n\bar{p} \geq 5$ and $n(1 - \bar{p}) \geq 5$.

Estimate for the Standard Error of $\bar{p}$

$$\sigma_{\bar{p}} \approx \sqrt{\frac{\bar{p}(1-\bar{p})}{n}}$$

(8.9)

where:

$\bar{p}$ = Sample proportion
n = Sample size

Figure 8.7 illustrates the sampling distribution for $\bar{p}$.

Chapter Outcome 4. → ## Confidence Interval Estimate for a Population Proportion

The confidence interval estimate for a population proportion is formed using the same general format that we used to estimate a population mean. This was shown originally as Equation 8.1:

Point Estimate $\pm$ (Critical Value)(Standard Error)

FIGURE 8.7

Sample Distribution for $\bar{p}$

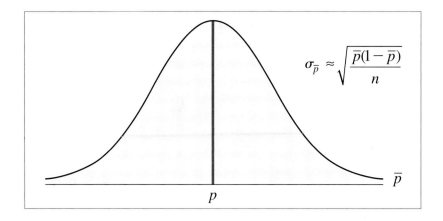

$$\sigma_{\bar{p}} \approx \sqrt{\frac{\bar{p}(1-\bar{p})}{n}}$$

Equation 8.10 shows the specific format for *confidence intervals involving population proportions*.

Confidence Interval Estimate for *p*

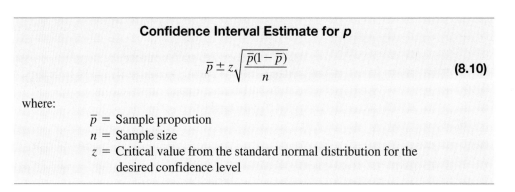

$$\bar{p} \pm z\sqrt{\frac{\bar{p}(1-\bar{p})}{n}} \qquad (8.10)$$

where:

$\bar{p}$ = Sample proportion
n = Sample size
z = Critical value from the standard normal distribution for the desired confidence level

---

The critical value for a confidence interval estimate of a population proportion will always be a *z*-value from the standard normal distribution. Recall from Table 8.1 the most commonly used critical values are

Critical Value	Confidence Level
$z = 1.28$	80%
$z = 1.645$	90%
$z = 1.96$	95%
$z = 2.575$	99%

For other confidence levels, you can find the critical *z*-value in the standard normal distribution table in Appendix D.

How to do it (Example 8-6)

Developing a Confidence Interval Estimate for a Population Proportion
Here are the steps necessary to develop a confidence interval estimate for a population proportion.

1. Define the population and variable of interest for which to estimate the population proportion.

2. Determine the sample size and select a random sample. Note, the sample must be large enough so that $np \geq 5$ and $n(1-p) \geq 5$.

3. Specify the level of confidence and obtain the critical value from the standard normal distribution table.

4. Calculate $\bar{p}$, the sample proportion.

5. Construct the interval estimate using Equation 8.10.

$$\bar{p} \pm z\sqrt{\frac{\bar{p}(1-\bar{p})}{n}}$$

EXAMPLE 8-6 | **CONFIDENCE INTERVAL FOR A POPULATION PROPORTION**

Iunamarina/Fotolia

Royal Haciendas Resort The Royal Haciendas Resort in Playa del Carmen, Mexico, is thinking of starting a new promotion. When a customer checks out of the resort after spending 5 or more days, the customer would be given a voucher that is good for 2 free nights on the next stay of 5 or more nights at the resort.

The marketing manager is interested in estimating the *proportion* of customers who return after getting a voucher. From a simple random sample of 100 customers, 62 returned within 1 year after receiving the voucher. A confidence interval estimate for the true population proportion is found using the following steps.

Step 1 **Define the population and the variable of interest.**
The population is all customers who received a voucher from Royal Haciendas, and the variable of interest is the number who use the voucher for two free nights.

Step 2 Determine the sample size.

A simple random sample of $n = 100$ customers who received vouchers. (Note, as long as $p \geq 0.05$ and $p \leq 0.95$, a sample size of 100 will meet the requirements that $np \geq 5$ and $n(1 - p) \geq 5$.

Step 3 Specify the desired level of confidence and determine the critical value.

Assuming that a 95% confidence level is desired, the critical value from the standard normal distribution table (Appendix D) will be $z = 1.96$.

Step 4 Compute the point estimate based on the sample data.

Equation 8.7 is used to compute the sample proportion.

$$\bar{p} = \frac{x}{n} = \frac{62}{100} = 0.62$$

Step 5 Compute the confidence interval using Equation 8.10.

The 95% confidence interval estimate is

$$\bar{p} \pm z\sqrt{\frac{\bar{p}(1 - \bar{p})}{n}}$$

$$0.62 \pm 1.96\sqrt{\frac{0.62(1 - 0.62)}{100}}$$

$$0.62 \pm 0.095$$

$$0.525 \text{ ———— } 0.715$$

Using the sample of 100 customers and a 95% confidence interval, the manager estimates that the true percentage of customers who will take advantage of the two-free night option will be between 52.5% and 71.5%.

>> **END EXAMPLE**

TRY PROBLEM 8-50 (pg. 325)

Chapter Outcome 5. → # Determining the Required Sample Size for Estimating a Population Proportion

Changing the confidence level affects the interval width. Likewise, changing the sample size will affect the interval width. An increase in sample size will reduce the standard error and reduce the interval width. A decrease in the sample size will have the opposite effect. For many applications, decision makers would like to determine a required sample size before doing the sampling. As was the case for estimating the population mean, the required sample size in a proportion application is based on the desired margin of error, the desired confidence level, and the variation in the population. The **margin of error**, e, is computed using Equation 8.11.

Margin of Error for Estimating p

$$e = z\sqrt{\frac{p(1 - p)}{n}} \tag{8.11}$$

where:

p = Population proportion
z = Critical value from standard normal distribution for the desired confidence level
n = Sample size

Equation 8.12 is used to determine the required sample size for a given confidence level and margin of error.

Sample Size for Estimating *p*

$$n = \frac{z^2 p (1 - p)}{e^2}$$ (8.12)

where:

p = Value used to represent the population proportion
e = Desired margin of error
z = Critical value from standard normal distribution for the desired confidence level

---

BUSINESS APPLICATION   **CALCULATING THE REQUIRED SAMPLE SIZE**

ROYAL HACIENDAS RESORT (*CONTINUED*)

Referring to Example 8-6, recall that the marketing manager developed a confidence interval estimate for the proportion of customers who would redeem the voucher for two free nights at the resort. This interval was

$$0.62 \pm 1.96 \sqrt{\frac{0.62(1 - 0.62)}{100}}$$

$$0.62 \pm 0.095$$

$$0.525 \text{ ———— } 0.715$$

The calculated margin of error in this situation is 0.095. Suppose the marketing manager wants the margin of error reduced to $e = \pm 0.04$ at a 95% confidence level. This will require an increase in sample size. To apply Equation 8.12, the margin of error and the confidence level are specified by the decision maker. However, the population proportion, p, is not something you can control. In fact, if you already knew the value for p, you wouldn't need to estimate it and the sample-size issue wouldn't come up.

Two methods overcome this problem. First, you can select a *pilot sample* and compute the sample proportion, $\bar{p}$, and substitute $\bar{p}$ for p. Then, once the sample size is computed, the pilot sample can be used as part of the overall required sample.

Second, you can select a conservative value for p. The closer p is to 0.50, the greater the variation because $p(1 - p)$ is greatest when $p = 0.50$. If the manager has reason to believe that the population proportion, p, will be about 0.60, he could use a value for p a little closer to 0.50—say, 0.55. If he doesn't have a good idea of what p is, he could conservatively use $p = 0.50$, which will give a sample size at least large enough to meet requirements.

Suppose the Royal Haciendas manager selects a pilot sample of $n = 100$ customers and provides them with the vouchers. Further, suppose $x = 62$ of these customers respond to the mailing. Then,

$$\bar{p} = \frac{62}{100} = 0.62$$

is substituted for p in Equation 8.12. For a 95% confidence level, the z-value is

$$z = 1.96$$

and the margin of error is equal to

$$e = 0.04$$

Substitute these values into Equation 8.12 and solve for the required sample size.

$$n = \frac{1.96^2 (0.62)(1 - 0.62)}{0.04^2} = 565.676 = 566$$

Because the pilot sample of 100 can be included, the Royal Haciendas Resort manager needs to give out an additional 466 vouchers to randomly selected customers. If this is more than the company can afford or wishes to include in the sample, the margin of error can be increased or the confidence level can be reduced.

EXAMPLE 8-7   SAMPLE SIZE DETERMINATION FOR ESTIMATING p

Naumann Research The customer account manager for Naumann Research, a marketing research company located in Cincinnati, Ohio, is interested in estimating the proportion of a client's customers who like a new television commercial. She wishes to develop a 90% confidence interval estimate and would like to have the estimate be within ±0.05 of the true population proportion. To determine the required sample size, she can use the following steps:

Step 1 **Define the population and variable of interest.**
The population is all potential customers in the market area. The variable of interest is the number of customers who like the new television commercial.

Step 2 **Determine the level of confidence and find the critical z-value using the standard normal distribution table.**
The desired confidence level is 90%. The z-value for 90% confidence is 1.645.

Step 3 **Determine the desired margin of error.**
The account manager wishes the margin of error to be 0.05.

Step 4 **Arrive at a value to use for p.**
Two options can be used to obtain a value for p:

1. Use a pilot sample and compute $\bar{p}$, the sample proportion. Use $\bar{p}$ to approximate p.
2. Select a value for p that is closer to 0.50 than you actually believe the value to be. If you have no idea what p might be, use $p = 0.50$, which will give the largest possible sample size for the stated confidence level and margin of error.

In this case, suppose the account manager has no idea what p is but wants to make sure that her sample is sufficiently large to meet her estimation requirements. Then she will use $p = 0.50$.

Step 5 **Use Equation 8.12 to determine the sample size.**

$$n = \frac{z^2 p(1-p)}{e^2} = \frac{1.645^2 (0.50)(1-0.50)}{0.05^2} = 270.0625 = 271$$

The account manager should randomly survey 271 customers. (Always round up.)

>> **END EXAMPLE**

TRY PROBLEM 8-49 (PG. 325)

MyStatLab

8-3: Exercises

Skill Development

8-48. Compute the 90% confidence interval estimate for the population proportion, p, based on a sample size of 100 when the sample proportion, $\bar{p}$, is equal to 0.40.

8-49. A pilot sample of 75 items was taken, and the number of items with the attribute of interest was found to be 15. How many more items must be sampled to construct a 99% confidence interval estimate for p with a 0.025 margin of error?

8-50. A decision maker is interested in estimating a population proportion. A sample of size $n = 150$ yields 115 successes. Based on these sample data, construct a 90% confidence interval estimate for the true population proportion.

8-51. At issue is the proportion of people in a particular county who do not have health care insurance coverage. A simple random sample of 240 people was asked if they have insurance coverage, and 66 replied that they did not have coverage. Based on these sample data, determine the 95% confidence interval estimate for the population proportion.

8-52. A magazine company is planning to survey customers to determine the proportion who will renew their subscription for the coming year. The magazine wants to estimate the population proportion with 95% confidence and a margin of error equal to ±0.02. What sample size is required?

8-53. A random sample of size 150 taken from a population yields a proportion equal to 0.35.
   a. Determine if the sample size is large enough so that the sampling distribution can be approximated by a normal distribution.
   b. Construct a 90% confidence interval for the population proportion.
   c. Interpret the confidence interval calculated in part b.
   d. Produce the margin of error associated with this confidence interval.

8-54. A random sample of 200 items reveals that 144 of the items have the attribute of interest.
   a. What is the point estimate for the population proportion for all items having this attribute?
   b. Use the information from the random sample to develop a 95% confidence interval estimate for the population proportion, p, of all items having this attribute of interest.

8-55. A random sample of 40 television viewers was asked if they had watched the current week's *American Idol* show. The following data represent their responses:

no	no	no	yes	no	no	no	yes	no	yes
no	no	no	yes	no	no	no	no	yes	no
yes	no	no	no	no	yes	no	no	no	no
no	no	no	no	no	no	no	no	no	no

   a. Calculate the proportion of viewers in the sample who indicated they watched the current week's episode of *American Idol*.
   b. Compute a 95% confidence interval for the proportion of viewers in the sample who indicated they watched the current week's episode of *American Idol*.
   c. Calculate the smallest sample size that would produce a margin of error of 0.025 if the population proportion is well represented by the sample proportion in part a.

Business Applications

8-56. As the automobile accident rate increases, insurers are forced to increase their premium rates. Companies such as Allstate have recently been running a campaign they hope will result in fewer accidents by their policyholders. For each six-month period that a customer goes without an accident, Allstate will reduce the customer's premium rate by a certain percentage. Companies like Allstate have reason to be concerned about driving habits, based on a survey conducted by Drive for Life, a safety group sponsored by Volvo of North America, in which 1,100 drivers were surveyed. Among those surveyed, 74% said that careless or aggressive driving was the biggest threat on the road. One-third of the respondents said that cell phone usage by other drivers was the driving behavior that annoyed them the most.

Based on these data, assuming that the sample was a simple random sample, construct and interpret a 95% confidence interval estimate for the true proportion in the population of all drivers who are annoyed by cell phone users.

8-57. A survey of 499 women for the American Orthopedic Foot and Ankle Society revealed that 38% wear flats to work.
   a. Use this sample information to develop a 99% confidence interval for the population proportion of women who wear flats to work.
   b. Suppose the society also wishes to estimate the proportion of women who wear athletic shoes to work with a margin of error of 0.01 with 95% confidence. Determine the sample size required.

8-58. The television landscape has certainly been changing in recent years as satellite and cable television providers compete for old-line television networks' viewers. In fact, prior to 2005, the networks had lost viewers in the 18–49 age group for more than 10 consecutive years, according to a May 2005 article in the *Wall Street Journal* by Brooks Barnes. However, according to the article, in 2005 the networks would post their first gain in viewers. Suppose that CBS plans to conduct interviews with television viewers in an attempt to estimate the proportion of viewers in the 18–49 age group who watch "most" of their television on network television as opposed to cable or satellite. CBS wishes to have 95% confidence and a margin of error in its estimate of ±0.03. A pilot sample of size 50 was selected, and the sample proportion was 0.61. To achieve these results with a simple random sample, how many additional viewers should be sampled?

8-59. Most major airlines allow passengers to carry two pieces of luggage (of a certain maximum size) onto the plane. However, their studies show that the more carry-on baggage passengers have, the longer it takes to unload and load passengers. One regional airline is considering changing its policy to allow only one carry-on per passenger. Before doing so, it decided to collect some data. Specifically, a random sample of 1,000 passengers was selected. The passengers were observed, and the number of bags carried on the plane was noted. Out of the 1,000 passengers, 345 had more than one bag.
   a. Based on this sample, develop and interpret a 95% confidence interval estimate for the proportion of the traveling population that would have been impacted had the one-bag limit been in effect. Discuss your result.
   b. The domestic version of Boeing's 747 has a capacity for 568 passengers. Determine an interval estimate of the number of passengers that you would expect to carry more than one piece of luggage on the plane. Assume the plane is at its passenger capacity.
   c. Suppose the airline also noted whether the passenger was male or female. Out of the 1,000 passengers observed, 690 were males. Of this group, 280 had more than one bag. Using this data, obtain and interpret a 95% confidence interval estimate for the proportion

of male passengers in the population who would have been affected by the one-bag limit. Discuss.

d. Suppose the airline decides to conduct a survey of its customers to determine their opinion of the proposed one-bag limit. The plan calls for a random sample of customers on different flights to be given a short written survey to complete during the flight. One key question on the survey will be: "Do you approve of limiting the number of carry-on bags to a maximum of one bag?" Airline managers expect that only about 15% will say "yes." Based on this assumption, what size sample should the airline take if it wants to develop a 95% confidence interval estimate for the population proportion who will say "yes" with a margin of error of ± 0.02?

8-60. Suppose the Akron Chamber of Commerce has decided to conduct a survey to estimate the proportion of adults between the ages of 25 and 35 living in the metropolitan area who have a college degree in a high-technology field. The chamber hopes to use the survey's results to attract more high-technology firms to the region. The chamber wants the survey to estimate the population proportion within a margin of error of 0.03 percentage points with a level of confidence of 95%.

a. If the chamber has no information concerning the proportion of adults between the ages of 25 and 35 who have a college degree in a high-technology field before the survey is taken, how large a sample size must be used?

b. Suppose the chamber conducted a pilot study of 200 adults between the ages of 25 and 35 that indicated 28 with the desired attribute. How large a sample would be needed for the survey to estimate the population proportion within a margin of error of ± 0.03 with a 95% level of confidence?

8-61. An Associated Press article written by Rukmini Callimachi pointed out that Nike, the world's largest maker of athletic shoes, has started to feature female models who are not the traditional rail-thin women who have graced billboards and magazine covers for the last 20 to 25 years. These new models, called "real people," may be larger than the former models, but they are still very athletic and represent what Nike spokeswoman Caren Ball calls "what is real" as opposed to "what is ideal." The article also reports on a survey of 1,000 women conducted by *Allure* magazine in which 91% of the respondents said they were satisfied with what they see in the mirror. Nike managers would like to use these data to develop a 90% confidence interval estimate for the true proportion of all women who are satisfied with their bodies. Develop and interpret the 90% confidence interval estimate.

8-62. A multinational corporation employing several thousand workers at its campus in a large city in the southwestern United States would like to estimate the proportion of its employees who commute to work by any means other than an automobile. The company hopes to use the information to develop a proposal to encourage more employees to forgo their automobiles

as a part of their commute. A pilot study of 100 randomly sampled employees found that 14 commute to work by means other than an automobile.

a. How many more employees must the company randomly sample to be able to estimate the true population of employees who commute to work by means other than an automobile with a margin of error of ± 0.03 and a level of confidence of 90%?

b. Suppose that after the full sample is taken, it was found that 50 employees commute to work by means other than an automobile. Construct a 90% confidence interval estimate for the true population of employees who commute to work using means other than an automobile. (*Hint*: Your sample size will be the total sample size required for part a.)

8-63. A survey of 777 teenagers between the ages of 13 and 18 conducted by JA Worldwide/Deloitte & Touche USA LLP found that 69% agree that people who practice good business ethics are more successful than those who do not.

a. Calculate the 90% confidence interval estimate for the true population proportion, p, given the survey information.

b. What is the largest possible sample size needed to estimate the true population proportion, p, within a margin of error of ± 0.02 with a confidence level of 95% if there was no prior knowledge concerning the proportion of respondents who would agree with the survey's question?

c. If the survey in part a had a margin of error of ± 0.04 percentage points, determine the level of confidence that was used in estimating the population proportion if there was no prior knowledge concerning the percentage of teenagers who would respond as they did.

8-64. The MainStay Investments of New York Life Investment Management survey of respondents between the ages of 26 to 82 indicated that 66% of seniors, 61% of baby boomers, and 58% of Generation X expect IRAs to be their primary source of income in retirement. The margin of error was given as ± 5 percentage points.

a. Calculate a 95% confidence interval for the proportion of seniors who expect IRAs to be their primary source of income in retirement.

b. Although the sample size for the entire survey was listed, the sample size for each of the three generations was not given. Assuming the confidence level was 95%, determine the sample size for each of the three generations.

8-65. A report released by the College Board asserted the percentage of students who took and passed Advanced Placement (AP) courses in all subjects has increased in every state and the District of Columbia since 2000. Among public school students, 14.1% earned a passing grade on at least one AP exam, the report indicated. In an attempt to determine if the proportion of those passing the math and science AP exams is equal to the 14.1% success rate, a random sample of 300 students enrolled in AP math and science classes has been selected.

a. If 35 of the students in the sample passed at least one AP math or science exam, calculate the proportion of those students who passed at least one AP math or science exam. Does this statistic indicate that the proportion of students who pass at least one AP math or science exam is less than that of those taking AP exams as a whole? Support your assertions.

b. Calculate the probability that a sample proportion equal to or less than that calculated in part a would occur if the population proportion was actually 0.141. Answer the question posed in part a using this probability.

c. Calculate a 98% confidence interval for the proportion of those students who passed at least one AP math or science exam. Answer the question posed in part a using this confidence interval. Does this answer correspond to that of part b? Support your assertions.

Computer Database Exercises

8-66. According to the Employee Benefit Research Institute (www.ebri.org), 34% of workers between the ages of 35 and 44 owned a 401(k)-type retirement plan. Suppose a recent survey was conducted by the Atlanta Chamber of Commerce to determine the participation rate of 35- to 44-year-old working adults in the Atlanta metropolitan area in 401(k)-type retirement plans. The Atlanta survey randomly sampled 144 working adults in Atlanta between the ages of 35 and 44. The results of the survey can be found in the file **Atlanta Retirement**.

a. Use the information in the file **Atlanta Retirement** to compute a 95% confidence interval estimate for the true population proportion of working adults in Atlanta between the ages of 35 and 44 in 401(k)-type retirement plans.

b. Based on the confidence interval calculated in part a, can the Atlanta Chamber of Commerce advertise that a greater percentage of working adults in Atlanta between the ages of 35 and 44 have 401(k) plans than in the nation as a whole for the same age group? Support your answer with the confidence level you calculated above.

8-67. A study by the Investment Company Institute (ICI), which randomly surveyed 3,500 households and drew on information from the Internal Revenue Service, found that 72% of households have funded at least one IRA rollover from an employer-sponsored retirement plan (www.financial-planning.com). Suppose a recent random sample of 90 households in the greater Miami area was taken and respondents were asked whether they had ever funded an IRA account with a rollover from an employer-sponsored retirement plan. The results are in the file **Miami Rollover**.

a. Based on the random sample of Miami households, what is the best point estimate for the proportion of all Miami households that have ever funded an IRA account with a rollover from an employer-sponsored retirement plan?

b. Construct a 99% confidence interval estimate for the true population proportion of Miami households that had ever funded an IRA account with a rollover from an employer-sponsored retirement plan.

c. If the sponsors of the Miami study found that the margin of error was too high, what could they do to reduce it if they were not willing to change the level of confidence?

8-68. Neverslip, Inc., produces belts for industrial use. As part of its continuous process-improvement program, Neverslip has decided to monitor on-time shipments of its products. Suppose a random sample of 140 shipments was taken from shipping records for the last quarter and the shipment was recorded as being either "on time" or "late." The results of the sample are contained in the file **Neverslip**.

a. Using the randomly sampled data, calculate a 90% confidence interval estimate for the true population proportion, p, for on-time shipments for Neverslip.

b. What is the margin of error for the confidence interval calculated in part a?

c. One of Neverslip's commitments to its customers is that 95% of all shipments will arrive on time. Based on the confidence interval calculated in part a, is Neverslip meeting its on-time commitment?

8-69. A survey by Frank N. Magid Associates Inc. concluded that men, of any age, are twice as likely as women to play console video games. The survey was based on a sample of men and women ages 12 and older. A file titled **Gameboys** contains responses that would result in the findings obtained by Magid Associates for the 18- to 34-year-old age group.

a. Calculate a 99% confidence interval for both the male and female responses.

b. Using the confidence intervals in part a, provide the minimum and maximum ratio of the population proportions.

c. Does your analysis in parts a and b substantiate the statement that men in this age group are twice as likely to play console video games? Support your assertions.

8-70. The Emerging Workforce Study conducted by Harris Interactive on behalf of Spherion, a leader in providing value-added staffing, recruiting, and workforce solutions, utilized a random sample of 502 senior human resources executives. The survey asked which methods the executives felt led them to find their best candidates. The file titled **Referrals** contains the responses indicating those that chose "referrals" as their best method.

a. Determine the margin of error that would accrue with a confidence level of 95%.

b. Calculate a 95% confidence interval for the proportion of executives who chose "referrals" as their best method.

c. Determine the sample size required to decrease the margin of error by 25%.

Visual Summary

Chapter 8: In many business situations decision makers need to know a population parameter. Unfortunately, if not impossible, gaining access to an entire population may be too time consuming and expensive to be feasible. In such situations decision makers will select a sample and use the sample data to compute a statistic that estimates the population parameter of interest. The decision maker needs to use procedures that ensure the sample will be large enough to provide valid estimates of the population parameter and needs to be confident that the estimate matches the population parameter of interest.

 8.1 Point and Confidence Interval Estimates for a Population Mean (pg. 296–314)

Summary

Whenever it is impossible to know the true population parameter, decision makers will rely on a point estimate. A point estimate is a single statistic, determined from a sample that is used to estimate the corresponding population parameter. Point estimates are subject to sampling error, which is the difference between a statistic and the corresponding population parameter. Sampling error cannot be eliminated, but it can be managed in the decision-making process by calculating a confidence interval. A confidence interval is an interval developed from sample values such that if all possible intervals of a given width are constructed, a percentage of these intervals, known as the confidence level, would include the true population parameter. A confidence interval can be calculated using the general format below:

Point estimate ± (Critical value) (Standard error)

The size of the sample and the confidence level chosen will have an impact on the interval estimate. The point estimate depends on the parameter being estimated. The critical value depends on the parameter being estimated and, for example, in the case where the population mean is being estimated, whether the population standard deviation is known or not. The standard error measures the spread of the sampling distribution. The amount that is added to and subtracted from the point estimate to determine the endpoints of the confidence interval is referred to as the margin of error. Lowering the confidence level is one way to reduce the margin of error. The margin of error can also be reduced by increasing the sample size.

When estimating a population mean it is necessary to distinguish between those cases where the population standard deviation is known and those cases where it is not known. When the population standard deviation is known the population mean is estimated using a critical value from the standard normal table for a specified confidence interval. When the population standard deviation is not known, the critical value is a *t*-value taken from a family of distributions called the Student's *t*-distributions. The specific *t*-distribution chosen depends on the number of independent data values available to estimate the population's standard deviation; a value known as the degrees of freedom.

Outcome 1. Distinguish between a point estimate and a confidence interval estimate.

Outcome 2. Construct and interpret a confidence interval estimate for a single population mean using both the standard normal and *t* distributions.

 8.2 Determining the Required Sample Size for Estimating a Population Mean (pg. 314–320)

Summary

A common question asked by decision makers who are conducting an estimation of a population parameter is "How large a sample size do I need?" The answer to this question depends on the resources available for sampling and the cost to select and measure each item sampled. The answers to these two questions will provide an upper limit on the sample size that can be selected. Before a definitive answer regarding the sample size can be given the decision maker must also specify the confidence level and the desired margin of error. If the population standard deviation is unknown one option may be to select a **pilot sample**—a sample taken from the population of interest of a size smaller than the anticipated sample size used to provide an estimate of the population standard deviation.

Outcome 3. Determine the required sample size for estimating a single population mean

 8.3 Estimating a Population Proportion (pg. 321–328)

Summary

In many situations the objective of sampling will be to estimate a population proportion. The confidence interval estimate for a **population proportion** is formed using the same general format to estimate a population mean:

Point Estimate ± (Critical Value) (Standard Error)

The critical value for a confidence interval estimate of a population proportion will always be a z-value from the standard normal distribution. Changing the confidence level affects the interval width. Likewise, changing the sample size will affect the interval width. An increase in the sample size will reduce the standard error and reduce the interval width. As was the case for estimating the population mean the required sample size for estimating a population proportion is based on the desired **margin of error**.

Outcome 4. Establish and interpret a confidence interval estimate for a single population proportion

Outcome 5. Determine the required sample size for estimating a single population proportion

● Conclusion

Many decision-making applications require that a decision be based on a sample which is used to estimate a population parameter. There are two types of estimates: point estimates and interval estimates. Point estimates are subject to potential sampling error. Point estimates are almost always different from the population value. A confidence interval estimate takes into account the potential for sampling error and provides a range within which we believe the true population value falls. The general format for all confidence interval estimates is:

Point Estimate ± (Critical Value) (Standard Error)

The point estimate falls in the center of the interval. The amount that is added and subtracted from the point estimate is called the margin of error. While the format stays the same, there are differences in the formulas used depending on what population value is being estimated and certain other conditions.

Figure 8-8 provides a useful flow diagram for the alternative confidence interval estimations discussed in the chapter.

FIGURE 8.8 |

Flow Diagram for Confidence
Interval Estimation Alternatives

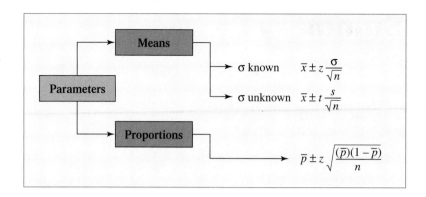

Equations

(8.1) Confidence Interval General Format pg. 299

Point estimate $\pm$ (Critical value)(Standard error)

(8.2) Confidence Interval Estimate for μ, σ Known pg. 299

$$\bar{x} \pm z \frac{\sigma}{\sqrt{n}}$$

(8.3) Margin of Error for Estimating μ, σ Known pg. 301

$$e = z \frac{\sigma}{\sqrt{n}}$$

(8.4) t-Value for $\bar{x}$ pg. 305

$$t = \frac{\bar{x} - \mu}{\dfrac{s}{\sqrt{n}}}$$

(8.5) Confidence Interval Estimate for μ, σ Unknown pg. 307

$$\bar{x} \pm t \frac{s}{\sqrt{n}}$$

(8.6) Sample Size Requirement for Estimating μ, σ Known pg. 315

$$n = \left(\frac{z\sigma}{e} \right)^2 = \frac{z^2 \sigma^2}{e^2}$$

(8.7) Sample Proportion pg. 321

$$\bar{p} = \frac{x}{n}$$

(8.8) Standard Error for $\bar{p}$ pg. 321

$$\sigma_{\bar{p}} = \sqrt{\frac{p(1-p)}{n}}$$

(8.9) Estimate for the Standard Error of $\bar{p}$ pg. 321

$$\sigma_{\bar{p}} \approx \sqrt{\frac{\bar{p}(1-\bar{p})}{n}}$$

(8.10) Confidence Interval Estimate for p pg. 322

$$\bar{p} \pm z \sqrt{\frac{\bar{p}(1-\bar{p})}{n}}$$

(8.11) Margin of Error for Estimating p pg. 323

$$e = z \sqrt{\frac{p(1-p)}{n}}$$

(8.12) Sample Size for Estimating p pg. 324

$$n = \frac{z^2 p(1-p)}{e^2}$$

Key Terms

Confidence interval pg. 296
Confidence level pg. 299
Degrees of freedom pg. 305

Margin of error pg. 301
Pilot sample pg. 316
Point estimate pg. 296

Sampling error pg. 296
Standard error pg. 297
Student's t-distributions pg. 304

Chapter Exercises _____ MyStatLab

Conceptual Questions

8-71. Explain why the critical value for a given confidence level when the population variance is not known is always greater than the critical value for the same confidence level when the population variance is known.

8-72. When we need to estimate the population mean, and the population standard deviation is unknown, we are hit with a "double whammy" when it comes to the margin of error. Explain what the "double whammy" is and why it occurs. (*Hint*: Consider the sources of variation in the margin of error.)

8-73. An insurance company in Iowa recently conducted a survey of its automobile policy customers to estimate the mean miles these customers commute to work each day. The result based on a random sample of 300 policyholders indicated the population mean was between 3.5 and 6.7 miles. This interval estimate was constructed using 95% confidence.

After receiving this result, one of the managers was overheard telling a colleague that 95% of all customers commute between 3.5 and 6.7 miles to work each day. How would you respond to this statement? Is it correct? Why or why not? Discuss.

8-74. Examine the equation for the margin of error when estimating a population mean

$$e = z \frac{\sigma}{\sqrt{n}}$$

Indicate the effect on the margin of error resulting from an increase in each of the following items:
a. confidence level
b. z-value
c. standard deviation
d. sample size
e. standard error

Business Applications

8-75. A random sample of 64 bicycle-riding adults in Portland indicated that 24 always wore a helmet while riding. Use the sample information to develop a 95% confidence interval estimate for the true population proportion of bicycle-riding adults in Portland who wear a helmet while riding.

8-76. Suppose a random sample of 197 accounts from a corporate credit card database revealed a sample average balance of $2,325 with a standard deviation of $144. Use the sample information to develop a 95% confidence interval for the true population of all credit card balances for this corporate credit card.

8-77. A random sample of 441 shoppers revealed that 76% made at least one purchase at a discount store last month.
a. Based on this sample information, what is the 90% confidence interval for the population proportion

of shoppers who made at least one discount store purchase last month?
b. The city of San Luis Obispo, California, has a population of 35,000 people. Referring to part a, determine a 90% confidence interval for the number of shoppers who made at least one discount store purchase last month.

8-78. According to an investigative reporter (Jim Drinkard, "Legislators Want to Ground 'Fact-Finding' Trips," *USA Today*, January 19, 2006), members of Congress are coming under scrutiny for "fact-finding" trips. Since 2000, members of Congress have made 6,666 trips paid for by private interests. The trips were worth about $19.6 million.
a. Calculate the average cost of these fact-finding trips.
b. If the cost of the trips could be considered to have a normal distribution, determine the standard deviation of the cost of the trips. (*Hint*: Recall the Empirical Rule.)
c. Choose a reasonable confidence level and calculate a confidence interval for the average cost of congressional fact-finding trips from the year 2000 until January 19, 2006.

8-79. Arco Manufacturing makes electronic pagers. As part of its quality efforts, the company wishes to estimate the mean number of days the pager is used before repair is needed. A pilot sample of 40 pagers indicates a sample standard deviation of 200 days. The company wishes its estimate to have a margin of error of no more than 50 days, and the confidence level must be 95%.
a. Given this information, how many additional pagers should be sampled?
b. The pilot study was initiated because of the costs involved in sampling. Each sampled observation costs approximately $10 to obtain. Originally, it was thought that the population's standard deviation might be as large as 300. Determine the amount of money saved by obtaining the pilot sample. (*Hint*: Determine the total cost of obtaining the required samples for both methods.)

8-80. A random sample of 25 sport utility vehicles (SUVs) of the same year and model revealed the following miles per gallon (mpg) values:

12.4	13.0	12.6	12.1	13.1
13.0	12.0	13.1	11.4	12.6
9.5	13.25	12.4	10.7	11.7
10.0	14.0	10.9	9.9	10.2
11.0	11.9	9.9	12.0	11.3

Assume that the population for mpg for this model year is normally distributed.

a. Use the sample results to develop a 95% confidence interval estimate for the population mean miles per gallon.

b. Determine the average number of gallons of gasoline the SUVs described here would use to travel between Los Angeles and San Francisco—a distance of approximately 400 miles.

c. Another sample of the same size is to be obtained. If you know that the average miles per gallon in the second sample will be larger than the one obtained in part a, determine the probability that the sample mean will be larger than the upper confidence limit of the confidence interval you calculated.

8-81. In an article titled "Airport Screeners' Strains, Sprains Highest among Workers," Thomas Frank reported that the injury rate for airport screeners was 29%, far exceeding the 4.5% injury rate for the rest of the federal workforce. The 48,000 full- and part-time screeners were reported to have missed nearly a quarter-million days because of injuries in the recent fiscal year.

a. Calculate the average number of days missed by airport screeners.

b. If one were to estimate the average number of days missed to within 1 hour in 2006 with a confidence level of 90%, determine the smallest sample size that would be required. Assume the standard deviation of the number of days missed is 1.5 days and that a work day consists of 8 hours.

c. How close could the estimate get if a sample of size 100 was used?

Computer Database Exercises

8-82. On its first day on the stock market, the Chinese Internet search engine, Baidu, increased its share price from $27.00 to $122.54, an increase of 454%. This was larger than any other Chinese initial public offering (IPO) and the second biggest for a foreign IPO. However, of the nine other biggest foreign IPOs with the largest first-day gains, all are trading below their IPO prices by an average of 88%. To determine the relationship between the IPOs with the largest first-day gains and the other IPOs, a sample might be taken to determine the average percentage decrease in the share prices of those IPOs not in the group of the nine IPOs with the largest first-day gains. A file titled **BigIPO$** contains such a sample. Note that an increase in share prices is represented as a negative decrease.

a. Calculate a 95% confidence interval for the average percentage decrease after the first-day offering in the share of those IPOs not in the 9 IPOs with the largest first-day gains.

b. Does it appear that there is a difference in the average percentage decrease in the share prices of the two groups? Support your assertions.

8-83. The Future-Vision Company is considering applying for a franchise to market satellite television dish systems in a Florida market area. As part of the company's research

into this opportunity, staff in the new acquisitions department conducted a survey of 548 homes selected at random in the market area. They asked a number of questions on the survey. The data for some of the variables are in a file called **Future-Vision**. One key question asked whether the household was currently connected to cable TV.

a. Using the sample information, what is the 95% confidence interval estimate for the true proportion of households in the market area that subscribe to cable television?

b. Based on the sample data, develop a 95% confidence interval estimate for the mean income and interpret this estimate.

8-84. The quality manager for a major automobile manufacturer is interested in estimating the mean number of paint defects in cars produced by the company. She wishes to have her estimate be within ± 0.10 of the true mean and wants 98% confidence in the estimate. The file called **CarPaint** contains data from a pilot sample that was conducted for the purpose of determining a value to use for the population standard deviation. How many additional cars need to be sampled to provide the estimate required by the quality manager?

8-85. The NPD Group recently released its annual U.S. Video Game Industry Retail Sales Report. The report contained the NPD Group's selection of the top 10 video games based on units sold. The top-selling video game was *Madden NFL 2012*, published by Electronic Arts. The average retail price for this video game last year was $56. The file titled **Madden** contains a sample of the current retail prices paid for *Madden NFL 2012*.

a. Calculate a 95% confidence interval for the current average retail price paid for *Madden NFL 2012*.

b. On the basis of the confidence interval constructed in part a, does it seem likely that the average retail price for *Madden NFL 2012* has decreased? Explain.

c. What sample size would be required to generate a margin of error of $1?

8-86. The Jordeen Bottling Company recently did an extensive sampling of its soft-drink inventory in which 5,000 cans were sampled. Employees weighed each can and used these weights to determine the fluid ounces in the cans. The data are in a file called **Jordeen**. Based on this sample data, should the company conclude that the mean volume is 12 ounces? Base your conclusion on a 95% confidence interval estimate and discuss.

8-87. Paper-R-Us is a national distributor of printer and copier paper for commercial use. The data file called **Sales** contains the annual, year-to-date sales values for each of the company's customers. Suppose the internal audit department has decided to audit a sample of these accounts. Specifically, they have decided to sample 36 accounts. However, before they actually conduct the in-depth audit (a process that involves tracking all transactions for each sampled account), they want to be sure that the sample they have selected is representative of the population.

a. Compute the population mean.

b. Use all the data in the population to develop a frequency distribution and histogram.

c. Calculate the proportion of accounts for customers in each region of the country.

d. Select a random sample of accounts. Develop a frequency distribution for these sample data. Compare this distribution to that of the population. (*Hint:* You might want to consider using relative frequencies for comparison purposes.)

e. Construct a 95% confidence interval estimate for the population mean sales per customer. Discuss how you would use this interval estimate to help determine whether the sample is a good representation of the population. (*Hint:* You may want to use the finite population correction factor since the sample is large relative to the size of the population.)

f. Use the information developed in parts a through e to draw a conclusion about whether the sample is a representative sample of the population. What other information would be desirable? Discuss.

Video Case 4

New Product Introductions @ McDonald's

New product ideas are a staple of our culture. Just take a look around you—how many billboards or television commercials can you count with new products or services? So, where do those ideas come from? If you're a company like McDonald's, the ideas don't come out of thin air. Instead, they're the result of careful monitoring of consumer preferences, trends, and tastes.

McDonald's menu is a good example of how consumer preferences have affected change in food offerings. What used to be a fairly limited lunch and dinner menu consisting of burgers, shakes, and fries has now become incredibly diverse. The Big Mac came along in 1968, and Happy Meals were introduced in 1979. Breakfast now accounts for nearly 30% of business in the United States, and chicken offerings comprise 30% of menu choices. Healthy offerings such as apple dippers, milk jugs, and fruit and yogurt parfaits are huge sellers. The company now rolls out at least three new products a year. Wade Thomas, VP U.S. Menu Management, leads the team behind most of today's menu options. He meets regularly with Chef Dan, the company's executive chef, to give the chef's team some idea anchor points with which to play.

When the chef's team is through playing with the concept, Wade's Menu Management team holds what they call a "rally." At a rally, numerous food concepts developed by Chef Dan's team are presented, tasted, discussed, and voted on. The winners move on to focus group testing. The focus groups are a huge source of the external data that helps the Menu Management team with its decision on whether to introduce a product. If a product scores 8 out of 10 on a variety of rankings, the idea moves forward.

The real test begins in the field. Wade and his team need to determine if the new product idea can actually be executed consistently in the restaurants. Data collected from the company's partnership with its owner/operators and suppliers is key. If a product takes five seconds too long to make or if the equipment doesn't fit into existing kitchen configurations, its chances of implementation are low, even though consumer focus groups indicated a high probability of success.

Throughout the idea-development process, various statistical methods are used to analyze the data collected. The data are handed over to the company's U.S. Consumer and Business Insights team for conversion into meaningful information the menu management team can use. At each step along the way, the statistical analyses are used to decide whether to move to the next step. The introduction of the new Asian chicken salad is a good example of a product offering that made it all the way to market. Analysis was performed on data collected in focus groups and eventually revealed the Asian salad met all the statistical hurdles for the salad to move forward.

Data collection and statistical analysis don't stop when the new products hit the market. Wade Thomas's team and the McDonald's U.S. Consumer and Business Insights group continue to forecast and monitor sales, the ingredient supply chain, customer preferences, competitive reactions, and more. As for the new Asian salad, time will tell just how successful it will become. But you can be sure techniques such as statistical estimation will be used to analyze it!

Discussion Questions:

1. During the past year, McDonald's introduced a new dessert product into its European market area. This product had already passed all the internal hurdles described in this case, including the focus group analysis and the operations analysis. The next step was to see how well the product would be received in the marketplace. In particular, McDonald's managers are interested in estimating the mean number of orders for this dessert per 1,000 customer transactions. A random sample of 142 stores throughout Europe was selected. Store managers tracked the number of dessert orders per 1,000 transactions during a two-week trial period. These sample data are in the data file called **McDonald's New Product Introduction**. Based on these sample data, construct and interpret a 95% confidence interval estimate for mean number of dessert orders per 1,000 orders.

2. Referring to question 1, suppose that Wade Thomas and his group are not happy with the margin of error associated with the confidence interval estimate and want the margin of error to be no greater than ± 3 dessert orders per 1,000 customer orders. To meet this objective, how many more stores should be included in the sample? Alternatively, if the managers don't wish to increase the sample size, what other option is available to reduce the margin of error? Discuss the pros and cons of both approaches.

Case 8.1

Management Solutions, Inc.

The round trip to the "site" was just under 360 miles, which gave Fred Kitchener and Mike Kyte plenty of time to discuss the next steps in the project. The site is a rural stretch of highway in Idaho where two visibility sensors are located. The project is part of a contract Fred's company, Management Solutions, Inc., has with the state of Idaho and the Federal Highway Administration. Under the contract, among other things, Management Solutions is charged with evaluating the performance of a new technology for measuring visibility. The larger study involves determining whether visibility sensors can be effectively tied to electronic message signs that would warn motorists of upcoming visibility problems in rural areas.

Mike Kyte, a transportation engineer and professor at the University of Idaho, has been involved with the project as a consultant to Fred's company since the initial proposal. Mike is very knowledgeable about visibility sensors and traffic systems. Fred's expertise is in managing projects like this one, in which it is important to get people from multiple organizations to work together effectively.

As the pair headed back toward Boise from the site, Mike was more excited than Fred had seen him in a long time. Fred reasoned that the source of excitement was that they had finally been successful in getting solid data to compare the two visibility sensors in a period of low visibility. The previous day at the site had been very foggy. The Scorpion Sensor is a tested technology that Mike has worked with for some time in urban applications. However, it has never before been installed in such a remote location as this stretch of Highway I-84, which connects Idaho and Utah. The other sensor produced by the Vanguard Company measures visibility in a totally new way using laser technology.

The data that had excited Mike so much were collected by the two sensors and fed back to a computer system at the port of entry near the test site. The measurements were collected every five minutes for the 24-hour day. As Fred took advantage of the 75-mph speed limit through southern Idaho, Mike kept glancing at the data on the printout he had made of the first few five-minute time periods. The Scorpion system had not only provided visibility readings, but it also had provided other weather-related data, such as temperature, wind speed, wind direction, and humidity.

Mike's eyes went directly to the two visibility columns. Ideally, the visibility readings for the two sensors would be the same at any five-minute period, but they weren't. After a few exclamations of surprise from Mike, Fred suggested that they come up with an outline for the report they would have to make from these data for the project team meeting next week. Both agreed that a full descriptive analysis of all the data, including graphs and numerical measures, was necessary. In addition, Fred wanted to use these early data to provide an estimate for the mean visibility provided by the two sensors. They agreed that estimates were needed for the day as a whole and also for only those periods when the Scorpion system showed visibility under 1.0 mile. They also felt that the analysis should look at the other weather factors, too, but they weren't sure just what was needed.

As the lights in the Boise Valley became visible, Mike agreed to work up a draft of the report, including a narrative based on the data in the file called **Visibility**. Fred said that he would set up the project team meeting agenda, and Mike could make the presentation. Both men agreed that the data were strictly a sample and that more low-visibility data would be collected when conditions occurred.

Case 8.2

Federal Aviation Administration

In January 2003, the FAA ordered that passengers be weighed before boarding 10- to 19-seat passenger planes. The order was instituted in response to a crash that occurred on January 8, 2003, in Charlotte, North Carolina, in which all 21 passengers, including the pilot and copilot, of a 19-seat Beech 1900 turboprop died. One possible cause of the crash was that the plane may have been carrying too much weight.

The airlines were asked to weigh adult passengers and carry-on bags randomly over a one-month period to estimate the mean weight per passenger (including luggage). A total of 426 people and their luggage were weighed, and the sample data are contained in a data file called **FAA**.

Required Tasks:

1. Prepare a descriptive analysis of the data using charts, graphs, and numerical measures.
2. Construct and interpret a 95% confidence interval estimate for the mean weight for male passengers.
3. Construct and interpret a 95% confidence interval estimate for the mean weight for female passengers.
4. Construct and interpret a 95% confidence interval estimate for the mean weight for all passengers.
5. Indicate what sample size would be required if the margin of error in the estimate for the mean of all passengers is to be reduced by half.

Case 8.3

Cell Phone Use

Helen Hutchins and Greg Haglund took the elevator together to the fourth-floor meeting room, where they were scheduled to meet the rest of the market research team at the Franklin

Company. On the way up, Helen mentioned that she had terminated her contract for the land-line telephone in her apartment and was going to be using her cell phone exclusively to save money. "I rarely use my house phone anymore and about the only calls I get are from organizations wanting donations or doing surveys," she said. Greg said that he and his wife were thinking about doing the same thing.

As Helen and Greg walked toward the meeting room, Helen suddenly stopped. "If everyone did what I am doing, wouldn't that affect our marketing research telephone surveys?" she asked. "I mean, when we make calls the numbers are all to land-line phones. Won't we be missing out on some people we should be talking to when we do our surveys?" Helen continued. Greg indicated that it could be a problem if very many people were using cell phones exclusively like Helen. "Maybe we need to discuss this at the meeting today," Greg said.

When Helen and Greg brought up the subject to the market research team, several others indicated that they had been having similar concerns. It was decided that a special study was needed among the Franklin customer base to estimate the proportion of customers who were now using only a cell phone for telephone service. It was decided to randomly sample customers using personal interviews at their business outlets, but no one had any idea of how many customers they needed to interview. One team member mentioned that he had read an Associated Press article recently that said about 8% of all households have only a cell phone. Greg mentioned that any estimate they came up with should have a margin of error of ± 0.03, and the others at the meeting agreed.

Required Tasks:

1. Assuming that the group wishes to develop a 95% confidence interval estimate, determine the required sample size if the population proportion of cell phone–only users is 8%.
2. Supposing the group is unwilling to use the 8% baseline proportion and wants to have the sample size be conservatively large enough to provide a margin of error of no greater than ± 0.03 with 95% confidence, determine the sample size that will be needed.

Chapter 9 Quick Prep Links

- **Review** the concepts associated with the Central Limit Theorem in Section 7.2.
- **Examine** Section 7.3 on the sampling distribution for proportions.

- **Familiarize** yourself with the Student's *t*-distributions in Section 8.1 and normal probability distributions in Section 6.1.

- **Review** the standard normal distribution and the Student's *t*-distribution tables, making sure you know how to find critical values in both tables.

Introduction to Hypothesis Testing

9.1 Hypothesis Tests for Means ←——— (pg. 337–358)

Outcome 1. Formulate null and alternative hypotheses for applications involving a single population mean or proportion.

9.2 Hypothesis Tests for a Proportion (pg. 358–365)

Outcome 2. Know what Type I and Type II errors are.

Outcome 3. Correctly formulate a decision rule for testing a hypothesis.

Outcome 4. Know how to use the test statistic, critical value, and *p*-value approaches to test a hypothesis.

9.3 Type II Errors (pg. 365–375) ←———

Outcome 5. Compute the probability of a Type II error.

Kitch Bain/Fotolia

Why you need to know

Estimating a population parameter based on a sample statistic is one area of business statistics called *statistical inference*. The basic tools for estimation were introduced in Chapter 8. Another important application of statistical inference is *hypothesis testing*. In hypothesis testing, a hypothesis (or statement) concerning a population parameter is made. We then use sample data to either deny or confirm the validity of the proposed hypothesis.

For example, suppose an orange juice plant in Orlando, Florida, produces approximately 120,000 bottles of orange juice daily. Each bottle is supposed to contain 32 fluid ounces. However, like all processes, the automated filling machine is subject to variation, and each bottle will contain either slightly more or less than the 32-ounce target. The important thing is that the mean fill is 32 fluid ounces. The manager might state the *hypothesis* that the mean fill is 32 ounces. Every two hours, the plant quality manager selects a random sample of bottles and computes the sample mean. If the sample mean is a "significant" distance from the desired 32 ounces, then the sample data will have provided sufficient evidence that the average fill is not 32 ounces and the manager's *hypothesis* would be rejected. The machine would then be stopped until repairs or adjustments had been made. However, if the sample mean is "close" to 32 ounces, the data would support the hypothesis and the machine would be allowed to continue filling bottles.

Hypothesis testing is performed regularly in many industries. Companies in the pharmaceutical industry must perform many hypothesis tests on new drug products before they are deemed to be safe and effective by the federal Food and Drug Administration (FDA). In these instances, the drug is hypothesized to be both unsafe and ineffective. Here, the FDA does not wish to certify that the drug is safe and effective unless sufficient evidence is obtained that this is the case. Then, if the sample results from the studies performed provide "significant" evidence that the drug is safe and effective, the FDA will allow the company to market the drug.

Hypothesis testing is the basis of the legal system in which judges and juries hear evidence in court cases. In a criminal case, the hypothesis in the American legal system is that the defendant is innocent. Based on the totality of the evidence presented in the trial, if the jury concludes that "beyond a reasonable doubt" the defendant committed the crime, the hypothesis of innocence will be rejected and the defendant will be found guilty. If the evidence is not strong enough, the defendant will be judged not guilty.

Hypothesis testing is a major part of business statistics. Chapter 9 introduces the fundamentals involved in conducting hypothesis tests. Many of the remaining chapters in this text will introduce additional hypothesis-testing techniques, so you need to gain a solid understanding of concepts presented in this chapter.

9.1 Hypothesis Tests for Means

By now you know that information contained in a sample is subject to sampling error. The sample mean will almost certainly not equal the population mean. Therefore, in situations in which you need to test a claim about a population mean by using the sample mean, you can't simply compare the sample mean to the claim and reject the claim if $\bar{x}$ and the claimed value of μ are different. Instead, you need a testing procedure that incorporates the potential for sampling error.

Statistical hypothesis testing provides managers with a structured analytical method for making decisions of this type. It lets them make decisions in such a way that the probability of decision errors can be controlled, or at least measured. Even though statistical hypothesis testing does not eliminate the uncertainty in the managerial environment, the techniques involved often allow managers to identify and control the level of uncertainty.

The techniques presented in this chapter assume the data are selected using an appropriate statistical sampling process and that the data are interval or ratio level. In short, we assume we are working with good data.

Formulating the Hypotheses

Null and Alternative Hypotheses In hypothesis testing, two hypotheses are formulated. One is the **null hypothesis**. The null hypothesis is represented by H_0 and contains an equality sign, such as "$=$," "$\leq$," or "$\geq$." The second hypothesis is the **alternative hypothesis** (represented by H_A). Based on the sample data, we either reject H_0 or we do not reject H_0.

Correctly specifying the null and alternative hypotheses is important. If done incorrectly, the results obtained from the hypothesis test may be misleading. Unfortunately, how you should formulate the null and alternative hypotheses is not always obvious. As you gain experience with hypothesis-testing applications, the process becomes easier. To help you get started, we have developed some general guidelines you should find helpful.

Testing the Status Quo In many cases, you will be interested in whether a situation has changed. We refer to this as testing the status quo, and this is a common application of hypothesis testing. For example, the Kellogg's Company makes many food products, including a variety of breakfast cereals. At the company's Battle Creek, Michigan, plant, Frosted Mini-Wheats are produced and packaged for distribution around the world. If the packaging process is working properly, the mean fill per box is 16 ounces. Every hour, quality analysts at the plant select a random sample of filled boxes and measure their contents. They do not wish to unnecessarily stop the packaging process since doing so can be quite costly. Thus, the packaging process will not be stopped unless there is sufficient evidence that the average fill is different from 16 ounces, i.e., H_A: $\mu \neq 16$. The analysts use the sample data to test the following null and alternative hypotheses:

$$H_0: \mu = 16 \text{ ounces (status quo)}$$
$$H_A: \mu \neq 16 \text{ ounces}$$

The null hypothesis is reasonable because the line supervisor would assume the process is operating correctly before starting production. As long as the sample mean is "reasonably" close to 16 ounces, the analysts will assume the filling process is working properly. Only when the sample mean is seen to be too large or too small will the analysts reject the null hypothesis (the status quo) and take action to identify and fix the problem.

Null Hypothesis

The statement about the population parameter that will be assumed to be true during the conduct of the hypothesis test. The null hypothesis will be rejected only if the sample data provide substantial contradictory evidence.

Alternative Hypothesis

The hypothesis that includes all population values not included in the null hypothesis. The alternative hypothesis will be selected only if there is strong enough sample evidence to support it. The alternative hypothesis is deemed to be true if the null hypothesis is rejected.

As another example, the Transportation Security Administration (TSA), which is responsible for screening passengers at U.S. airports, publishes on its Web site the average waiting times for customers to pass through security. For example, on Mondays between 9:00 A.M. and 10:00 A.M., the average waiting time at Atlanta's Hartsfield International Airport is supposed to be 15 minutes or less. Periodically, TSA staff will select a random sample of passengers during this time slot and will measure their actual wait times to determine if the average waiting time is longer than the guidelines require. The alternative hypothesis is, therefore, stated as: $H_A: \mu > 15$ minutes. The sample data will be used to test the following null and alternative hypotheses:

$$H_0: \mu \leq 15 \text{ minutes (status quo)}$$
$$H_A: \mu > 15 \text{ minutes}$$

Only if the sample mean wait time is "substantially" greater than 15 minutes will TSA employees reject the null hypothesis and conclude there is a problem with staffing levels. Otherwise, they will assume that the 15-minute standard (the status quo) is being met, and no action will be taken.

Testing a Research Hypothesis Many business and scientific applications involve research applications. For example, companies such as Intel, Procter & Gamble, Dell Computers, Pfizer, and 3M continually introduce new and hopefully improved products. However, before introducing a new product, the companies want to determine whether the new product is superior to the original. In the case of drug companies like Pfizer, the government requires them to show their products are both safe and effective. Because statistical evidence is needed to indicate that the new product is effective, the default position (or null hypothesis) is that it is no better than the original (or in the case of a drug, that it is unsafe and ineffective). The burden of proof is placed on the new product, and the alternative hypothesis is formulated as the **research hypothesis**.

Research Hypothesis

The hypothesis the decision maker attempts to demonstrate to be true. Because this is the hypothesis deemed to be the most important to the decision maker, it will be declared true only if the sample data strongly indicates that it is true.

For example, suppose the Goodyear Tire and Rubber Company has a new tread design that its engineers claim will outlast its competitor's leading tire. New technology is able to produce tires whose longevity is better than the competitors' tires but are less expensive. Thus, if Goodyear can be sure that the new tread design will last longer than the competition's, it will realize a profit that will justify the introduction of the tire with the new tread design. The competitor's tire has been demonstrated to provide an average of 60,000 miles of use. Therefore, the research hypothesis for Goodyear is that its tire will last longer than its competitor's, meaning that the tire will last an average of *more than* 60,000 miles. The research hypothesis becomes the alternative hypothesis:

$$H_0: \mu \leq 60,000$$
$$H_A: \mu > 60,000 \text{ (research hypothesis)}$$

The burden of proof is on Goodyear. Only if the sample data show a sample mean that is "substantially" larger than 60,000 miles will the null hypothesis be rejected and Goodyear's position be affirmed.

In another example, suppose the Nunhem Brothers Seed Company has developed a new variety of bean seed. Nunhem will introduce this seed variety on the market only if the seed provides yields superior to the current seed variety. Experience shows the current seed provides a mean yield of 60 bushels per acre. To test the new variety of beans, Nunhem Brothers researchers will set up the following null and alternative hypotheses:

$$H_0: \mu \leq 60 \text{ bushels}$$
$$H_A: \mu > 60 \text{ bushels (research hypothesis)}$$

The alternative hypothesis is the research hypothesis. If the null hypothesis is rejected, then Nunhem Brothers will have statistical evidence to show that the new variety of beans is superior to the existing product.

Testing a Claim about the Population Analyzing claims using hypothesis tests can be complicated. Sometimes you will want to give the benefit of the doubt to the claim, but in other instances you will be skeptical about the claim and will want to place the burden of proof on the claim. For consistency purposes, the rule adopted in this text is that if the claim contains the equality, the claim becomes the null hypothesis. If the claim does not contain the equality, the claim is the alternative hypothesis.

A recent radio commercial stated the average waiting time at a medical clinic is less than 15 minutes. A claim like this can be tested using hypothesis testing. The null and alternative hypotheses should be formulated such that one contains the claim and the other reflects the opposite position. Since in this example, the claim that the average wait time *is less* than 15 minutes does not contain the equality ($\mu < 15$), the claim should be the alternative hypothesis. The appropriate null and alternative hypotheses are, then, as follows:

$$H_0 : \mu \geq 15$$
$$H_A : \mu < 15 \text{ (claim)}$$

In cases like this where the claim corresponds to the alternative hypothesis, the *burden of proof* is on the claim. If the sample mean is "substantially" less than 15 minutes, the null hypothesis would be rejected and the alternative hypothesis (and the claim) would be accepted. Otherwise, the null hypothesis would not be rejected and the claim could not be accepted.

Chapter Outcome 1. →

How to do it (Example 9-1)

Formulating the Null and Alternative Hypotheses

1. The population parameter of interest (e.g., μ, p, or σ) must be identified.

2. The hypothesis of interest to the researcher or the analyst must be identified. This could encompass testing a status quo, a research hypothesis, or a claim.

3. The null hypothesis will contain the equal sign, the alternative hypothesis will not.

4. The range of possible values for the parameter must be divided between the null and alternative hypothesis. Therefore, if $H_0 : \mu \leq 15$, the alternative hypothesis must become $H_A : \mu > 15$.

EXAMPLE 9-1   **FORMULATING THE NULL AND ALTERNATIVE HYPOTHESES**

Student Work Hours In today's economy, university students often work many hours to help pay for the high costs of a college education. Suppose a university in the Midwest is considering changing its class schedule to accommodate students working long hours. The registrar has stated a change is needed because the mean number of hours worked by undergraduate students at the university is more than 20 per week. The following steps can be taken to establish the appropriate null and alternative hypotheses:

Step 1 Determine the population parameter of interest.
In this case, the population parameter of interest is the mean hours worked, μ. The null and alternative hypotheses must be stated in terms of the population parameter.

Step 2 Identify the hypothesis of interest.
In this case, the registrar has made a claim stating that the mean hours worked "is more than 20" per week. Because changing the class scheduling system would be expensive and time consuming, the claim should not be declared true unless the sample data strongly indicate that it is true. Thus, the burden of proof is placed on the registrar to justify her claim that the mean is greater than 20 hours.

Step 3 Formulate the null and alternative hypotheses.
Keep in mind that the equality goes in the null hypothesis.

$$H_0 : \mu \leq 20 \text{ hours}$$
$$H_A : \mu > 20 \text{ hours (claim)}$$

>> **END EXAMPLE**

TRY PROBLEM 9-13a (pg. 356)

Example 9-2 illustrates another example of how the null and alternative hypotheses are formulated.

EXAMPLE 9-2   **FORMULATING THE NULL AND ALTERNATIVE HYPOTHESES**

Nabisco Foods One of the leading products made by Nabisco foods is the snack cracker called Wheat Thins. Nabisco uses an automatic filling machine to fill the Wheat Thins boxes with the desired weight. For instance, when the company is running the product for Costco on the fill line, the machine is set to fill the oversized boxes with 20 ounces. If the machine is working properly, the mean fill will be 20 ounces. Each hour, a sample of boxes is collected and weighed, and the technicians determine whether the machine is still operating correctly or whether it needs adjustment. The following steps can be used to establish the null and alternative hypotheses to be tested:

Step 1 Determine the population parameter of interest.

In this case, the population parameter of interest is the mean weight per box, μ.

Step 2 Identify the hypothesis of interest.

The status quo is that the machine is filling the boxes with the proper amount, which is $\mu = 20$ ounces. We will believe this to be true unless we find evidence to suggest otherwise. If such evidence exists, then the filling process needs to be adjusted.

Step 3 Formulate the null and alternative hypotheses.

The null and alternative hypotheses are

$$H_0: \mu = 20 \text{ ounces (status quo)}$$
$$H_A: \mu \neq 20 \text{ ounces}$$

>> **END EXAMPLE**

TRY PROBLEM 9-14a (pg. 356)

Chapter Outcome 2. ⟶ **Types of Statistical Errors** Because of the potential for extreme sampling error, two possible errors can occur when a hypothesis is tested: **Type I** and **Type II errors**. These errors show the relationship between what actually exists (a state of nature) and the decision made based on the sample information.

Type I Error

Rejecting the null hypothesis when it is, in fact, true.

Type II Error

Failing to reject the null hypothesis when it is, in fact, false.

Figure 9.1 shows the possible actions and states of nature associated with any hypothesis-testing application. As you can see, there are three possible outcomes: no error (correct decision), Type I error, and Type II error. *Only one of these will be the outcome for a hypothesis test.* From Figure 9.1, if the null hypothesis is true and an error is made, it must be a Type I error. On the other hand, if the null hypothesis is false and an error is made, it must be a Type II error.

Many statisticians argue that you should never use the phrase "accept the null hypothesis." Instead, you should use "*do not reject* the null hypothesis." Thus, the only two hypothesis-testing decisions would be *reject H_0* or *do not reject H_0*. This is why in a jury verdict to acquit a defendant, the verdict is "not guilty" rather than innocent. Just because the evidence is insufficient to convict does not necessarily mean that the defendant is innocent. The same is true with hypothesis testing. Just because the sample data do not lead to rejecting the null hypothesis, we cannot be sure that the null hypothesis is true.

This thinking is appropriate when hypothesis testing is employed in situations in which some future action is not dependent on the results of the hypothesis test. However, in most business applications, the purpose of the hypothesis test is to direct the decision maker to take one action or another based on the test results. So, in this text, when hypothesis testing is applied to decision-making situations, *not rejecting* the null hypothesis is essentially the same as *accepting it*. The same action will be taken whether we conclude that the null hypothesis is not rejected or that it is accepted.[1]

FIGURE 9.1

The Relationship between Decisions and States of Nature

		State of Nature	
		Null Hypothesis True	Null Hypothesis False
Decision	Conclude Null True (Don't Reject H_0)	Correct Decision	Type II Error
	Conclude Null False (Reject H_0)	Type I Error	Correct Decision

[1]Whichever language you use, you should make an effort to understand both arguments and make an informed choice. If your instructor requests that you reference the action in a particular way, it would behoove you to follow the instructions. Having gone through this process ourselves, we prefer to state the choice as "don't reject the null hypothesis." This terminology will be used throughout this text.

BUSINESS APPLICATION **TYPE I AND TYPE II STATISTICAL ERRORS**

PRICE & ASSOCIATES CONSTRUCTION Price & Associates is a residential home developer in the Phoenix, Arizona, area. They build single-family homes in the $300,000 to $500,000 price range. Because of the volume of homes they build, they have refined their processes to be very efficient. For example, they have a company standard that a home should not require more than 25 days for framing and roofing. The managing partner at Price & Associates wishes to test whether the mean framing and roofing times have changed following the 2008 financial crisis, which reduced the number of homes the company has been building. Treating the average framing and roofing time of 25 days or less as the status quo, the null and alternative hypotheses to be tested are

$$H_0: \mu \le 25 \text{ days (status quo)}$$

$$H_A: \mu > 25 \text{ days}$$

The managing partner will select a random sample of homes built in 2012. In this application, a Type I error would occur if the sample data lead the manager to conclude that the mean framing and roofing time exceeds 25 days (H_0 is rejected) when in fact $\mu \le 25$ days. If a Type I error occurred, the manager would needlessly spend time and resources trying to speed up a process that already meets the original time frame.

Alternatively, a Type II error would occur if the sample evidence leads the manager to incorrectly conclude that $\mu \le 25$ days (H_0 is not rejected) when the mean framing and roofing time exceeds 25 days. Now the manager would take no action to improve framing and roofing times at Price & Associates when changes are needed to improve the building time.

Chapter Outcome 3. ➡ ## Significance Level and Critical Value

The objective of a hypothesis test is to use sample information to decide whether to reject the null hypothesis about a population parameter. How do decision makers determine whether the sample information supports or refutes the null hypothesis? The answer to this question is the key to understanding statistical hypothesis testing.

In hypothesis tests for a single population mean, the sample mean, $\bar{x}$, is used to test the hypotheses under consideration. Depending on how the null and alternative hypotheses are formulated, certain values of $\bar{x}$ will tend to support the null hypothesis, whereas other values will appear to support the alternative hypothesis. In the Price & Associates example, the null and alternative hypotheses were formulated as

$$H_0: \mu \le 25 \text{ days}$$

$$H_A: \mu > 25 \text{ days}$$

Values of $\bar{x}$ less than or equal to 25 days would tend to support the null hypothesis. By contrast, values of $\bar{x}$ greater than 25 days would tend to refute the null hypothesis. The larger the value of $\bar{x}$, the greater the evidence that the null hypothesis should be rejected. However, because we expect some sampling error, do we want to reject H_0 for any value of $\bar{x}$ that is greater than 25 days? Probably not. But should we reject H_0 if $\bar{x} = 26$ days, or $\bar{x} = 30$ days, or $\bar{x} = 35$ days? At what point do we stop attributing the result to sampling error?

To perform the hypothesis test, we need to select a *cutoff* point that is the demarcation between rejecting and not rejecting the null hypothesis. Our *decision rule* for the Price & Associates application is then

If $\bar{x} >$ Cutoff, reject H_0.

If $\bar{x} \le$ Cutoff, do not reject H_0.

If $\bar{x}$ is greater than the cutoff, we will reject H_0 and conclude that the average framing and roofing time *does* exceed 25 days. If $\bar{x}$ is less than or equal to the cutoff, we will not reject H_0; in this case our test does not give sufficient evidence that the faming and roofing time exceeds 25 days.

FIGURE 9.2

Sampling Distribution of $\bar{x}$ for Price & Associates

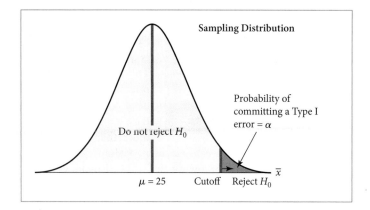

Recall from the Central Limit Theorem (see Chapter 7) that, for large samples, the distribution of the possible sample means is approximately normal, with a center at the population mean, μ. The null hypothesis in our example is $\mu \leq 25$ days. Figure 9.2 shows the sampling distribution for $\bar{x}$ assuming that $\mu = 25$. The shaded region on the right is called the *rejection region*. The area of the rejection region gives the probability of getting an $\bar{x}$ larger than the cutoff when μ is really 25, so it is the probability of making a Type I statistical error. This probability is called the **significance level** of the test and is given the symbol α (alpha).

The decision maker carrying out the test specifies the significance level, α. The value of α is determined based on the costs involved in committing a Type I error. If making a Type I error is costly, we will want the probability of a Type I error to be small. If a Type I error is less costly, then we can allow a higher probability of a Type I error.

However, in determining α, we must also take into account the probability of making a Type II error, which is given the symbol β (beta). The two error probabilities, α and β, are inversely related. That is, if we reduce α, then β will increase.[2] Thus, in setting α, you must consider both sides of the issue.[3]

Calculating the specific dollar costs associated with making Type I and Type II errors is often difficult and may require a subjective management decision. Therefore, any two managers might well arrive at different alpha levels. However, in the end, the choice for alpha must reflect the decision maker's best estimate of the costs of these two errors.

Having chosen a significance level, α, the decision maker then must calculate the corresponding cutoff point, which is called a **critical value**.

Significance Level

The maximum allowable probability of committing a Type I statistical error. The probability is denoted by the symbol α.

Critical Value

The value corresponding to a significance level that determines those test statistics that lead to rejecting the null hypothesis and those that lead to a decision not to reject the null hypothesis.

Chapter Outcome 4. ➜ # Hypothesis Test for μ, σ Known

Calculating Critical Values To calculate critical values corresponding to a chosen α, we need to know the sampling distribution of the sample mean $\bar{x}$. If our sampling conditions satisfy the Central Limit Theorem requirements or if the population is normally distributed and we know the population standard deviation σ, then the sampling distribution of $\bar{x}$ is a normal distribution with an average equal to the population mean μ and standard deviation $\sigma/\sqrt{n}$.[4] With this information, we can calculate a critical z-value, called z_α, or a critical $\bar{x}$-value, called $\bar{x}_\alpha$. We illustrate both calculations in the Price & Associates example.

---

[2]The sum of alpha and beta may coincidentally equal 1. However, in general, the sum of these two error probabilities does not equal 1 since they are not complements.

[3]We will discuss Type II errors more fully later in this chapter. Contrary to the Type I error situation in which we specify the desired alpha level, beta is computed based on certain assumptions. Methods for computing beta are shown in Section 9.3.

[4]For many population distributions, the Central Limit Theorem applies for sample sizes as small as 4 or 5. Sample sizes $n \geq 30$ assure us that the sampling distribution will be approximately normal regardless of population distribution.

PRICE & ASSOCIATES CONSTRUCTION (*CONTINUED*)

Suppose the managing partners decide they are willing to incur a 0.10 probability of committing a Type I error. Assume also that the population standard deviation, σ, for framing and roofing homes is three days and the sample size is 64 homes. Given that the sample size is large ($n \geq 30$) and that the population standard deviation is known ($\sigma = 3$ days), we can state the critical value in two ways. First, we can establish the critical value as a *z*-value.

Figure 9.3 shows that if the rejection region on the upper end of the sampling distribution has an area of 0.10, the critical *z*-value, z_α, from the standard normal table (or by using Excel's NORM.S.INV function) corresponding to the critical value is 1.28. Thus, $z_{0.10} = 1.28$. If the sample mean lies more than 1.28 standard deviations above $\mu = 25$ days, H_0 should be rejected; otherwise we will not reject H_0.

We can also express the critical value in the same units as the sample mean. In the Price & Associates example, we can calculate a critical $\bar{x}$ value, $\bar{x}_\alpha$, so that if $\bar{x}$ is greater than the critical value, we should reject H_0. If $\bar{x}$ is less than or equal to $\bar{x}_\alpha$, we should not reject H_0. Equation 9.1 shows how $\bar{x}_\alpha$ is computed. Figure 9.4 illustrates the use of Equation 9.1 for computing the critical value, $\bar{x}_\alpha$.

$\bar{x}_\alpha$ for Hypothesis Tests, σ Known

$$\bar{x}_\alpha = \mu + z_\alpha \frac{\sigma}{\sqrt{n}} \tag{9.1}$$

where:

μ = Hypothesized value for the population mean
z_α = Critical value from the standard normal distribution
σ = Population standard deviation
n = Sample size

Applying Equation 9.1, we determine the value for $\bar{x}_\alpha$ as follows:

$$\bar{x}_\alpha = \mu + z_\alpha \frac{\sigma}{\sqrt{n}}$$

$$\bar{x}_{0.10} = 25 + 1.28 \frac{3}{\sqrt{64}}$$

$$\bar{x}_{0.10} = 25.48 \text{ days}$$

If $\bar{x} > 25.48$ days, H_0 should be rejected and changes should be made in the construction process; otherwise, H_0 should not be rejected and the process should not be changed. Any sample mean between 25.48 and 25 days would be attributed to sampling error, and the null hypothesis would not be rejected. A sample mean of 25.48 or fewer days will support the null hypothesis.

FIGURE 9.3

Determining the Critical Value as a *z*-Value

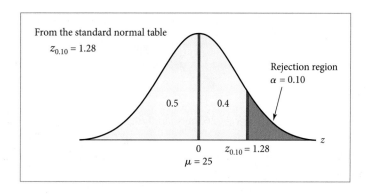

FIGURE 9.4

Determining the Critical Value as an $\bar{x}$-Value for the Price & Associates Example

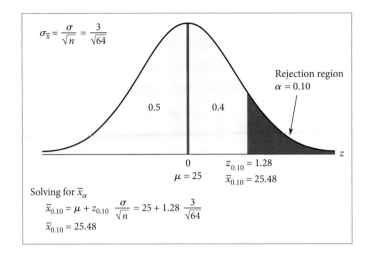

Decision Rules and Test Statistics To conduct a hypothesis test, you can use three equivalent approaches. You can calculate a z-value and compare it to the critical value, z_α. Alternatively, you can calculate the sample mean, $\bar{x}$, and compare it to the critical value, $\bar{x}_\alpha$. Finally, you can use a method called the p-value approach, to be discussed later in this section. It makes no difference which approach you use; each method yields the same conclusion.

Suppose $\bar{x} = 26$ days. How we test the null hypothesis depends on the procedure we used to establish the critical value. First, using the z-value method, we establish the following decision rule:

Hypotheses

$$H_0: \mu \leq 25 \text{ days}$$
$$H_A: \mu > 25 \text{ days}$$
$$\alpha = 0.10$$

Decision Rule

$$\text{If } z > z_{0.10}, \text{ reject } H_0.$$
$$\text{If } z \leq z_{0.10}, \text{ do not reject } H_0.$$

where:

$$z_{0.10} = 1.28$$

Recall that the number of homes sampled is 64 and the population standard deviation is assumed known at three days. The calculated z-value is called the **test statistic**.

The z-test statistic is computed using Equation 9.2.

Test Statistic

A function of the sampled observations that provides a basis for testing a statistical hypothesis.

---

z-Test Statistic for Hypothesis Tests for μ, σ Known

$$z = \frac{\bar{x} - \mu}{\dfrac{\sigma}{\sqrt{n}}} \tag{9.2}$$

where:

$\bar{x}$ = Sample mean
μ = Hypothesized value for the population mean
σ = Population standard deviation
n = Sample size

Given that $\bar{x} = 26$ days, applying Equation 9.2 we get

$$z = \frac{\bar{x} - \mu}{\dfrac{\sigma}{\sqrt{n}}} = \frac{26 - 25}{\dfrac{3}{\sqrt{64}}} = 2.67$$

Thus, $\bar{x} = 26$ is 2.67 standard deviations above the hypothesized mean. Because z is greater than the critical value,

$$z = 2.67 > z_{0.10} = 1.28, \text{ reject } H_0.$$

Now we use the second approach, which established (see Figure 9.4) a decision rule, as follows:

Decision Rule

$$\text{If } \bar{x} > \bar{x}_{0.10}, \text{ reject } H_0.$$
$$\text{Otherwise, do not reject } H_0.$$

Then,

$$\text{If } \bar{x} > 25.48 \text{ days, reject } H_0.$$
$$\text{Otherwise, do not reject } H_0.$$

Because

$$\bar{x} = 26 > \bar{x}_{0.10} = 25.48, \text{ reject } H_0.$$

Note that the two approaches yield the same conclusion, as they always will if you perform the calculations correctly. We have found that academic applications of hypothesis testing tend to use the z-value method, whereas business applications of hypothesis testing often use the $\bar{x}$ approach.

You will often come across a different language used to express the outcome of a hypothesis test. For instance, a statement for the hypothesis test just presented would be "The hypothesis test was significant at an α (or significance level) of 0.10." This simply means that the null hypothesis was rejected using a significance level of 0.10.

How to do it (Example 9-3)

One-Tailed Test for a Hypothesis about a Population Mean, σ Known
To test the hypothesis, perform the following steps:

1. Specify the population parameter of interest.

2. Formulate the null hypothesis and the alternative hypothesis in terms of the population mean, μ.

3. Specify the desired significance level (α).

4. Construct the rejection region. (We strongly suggest you draw a picture showing where in the distribution the rejection region is located.)

5. Compute the test statistic.

$$\bar{x} = \frac{\sum x}{n} \quad \text{or} \quad z = \frac{\bar{x} - \mu}{\frac{\sigma}{\sqrt{n}}}$$

6. Reach a decision. Compare the test statistic with $\bar{x}_\alpha$ or z_α.

7. Draw a conclusion regarding the null hypothesis.

EXAMPLE 9-3   ONE-TAILED HYPOTHESIS TEST FOR μ, σ KNOWN

Mountain States Surgery Center Mountain States Surgery Center in Denver, Colorado, performs many knee-replacement surgery procedures each year. Recently, research physicians at Mountain States have developed a surgery process they believe will reduce the average patient recovery time. The hospital board will not recommend the new procedure unless there is substantial evidence to suggest that it is better than the existing procedure. Records indicate that the current mean recovery rate for the standard procedure is 142 days, with a standard deviation of 15 days. To test whether the new procedure actually results in a lower mean recovery time, the procedure was performed on a random sample of 36 patients.

Step 1   Specify the population parameter of interest.
We are interested in the mean recovery time, μ.

Step 2   Formulate the null and alternative hypotheses.

$$H_0: \mu \geq 142 \text{ (status quo)}$$
$$H_A: \mu < 142$$

Step 3   Specify the desired significance level (α).
The researchers wish to test the hypothesis using a 0.05 level of significance.

Step 4   Construct the rejection region.
This will be a one-tailed test, with the rejection region in the lower (left-hand) tail of the sampling distribution. The critical value is $-z_{0.05} = -1.645$. Therefore, the decision rule becomes

$$\text{If } z < -1.645, \text{ reject } H_0; \text{ otherwise, do not reject } H_0.$$

Step 5   Compute the test statistic.
For this example, we will use z. Assume the sample mean, computed using $\bar{x} = \frac{\sum x}{n}$, is 140.2 days. Then,

$$z = \frac{\bar{x} - \mu}{\frac{\sigma}{\sqrt{n}}} = \frac{140.2 - 142}{\frac{15}{\sqrt{36}}} = -0.72$$

FIGURE 9.5

Mountain States Surgery
Hypothesis Test

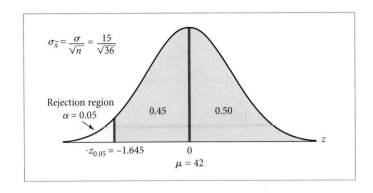

Step 6 Reach a decision. (See Figure 9.5.)
The decision rule is

$$\text{If } z < -1.645, \text{ reject } H_0.$$

Otherwise, do not reject.

Because $-0.72 > -1.645$, do not reject H_0.

Step 7 Draw a conclusion.
There is not sufficient evidence to conclude that the new knee replacement procedure results in a shorter average recovery period. Thus, Mountain States will not be able to recommend the new procedure on the grounds that it reduces recovery time.

>> **END EXAMPLE**

TRY PROBLEM 9-5 (pg. 355)

EXAMPLE 9-4   **HYPOTHESIS TEST FOR μ, α KNOWN**

Quality Car Care, Inc. Quality Car Care, Inc. performs vehicle maintenance services for car owners in Vancouver, B.C., Canada. The company has advertised that the mean time for a complete routine maintenance (lube, oil change, tire rotation, etc.) is 40 minutes or less. Recently the company has received complaints from several individuals saying the mean time required to complete the service exceeds the advertised mean of 40 minutes. Before responding, employees at Quality Car Care plan to test this claim using an alpha level equal to 0.05 and a random sample size of $n = 100$ past services. Based on previous studies, suppose that the population standard deviation is known to be $\sigma = 8$ minutes. The hypothesis test can be conducted using the following steps:

Step 1 Specify the population parameter of interest.
The population parameter of interest is the mean test time, μ.

Step 2 Formulate the null and alternative hypotheses.
The claim made by the company is $\mu \leq 40$. Thus, the null and alternative hypotheses are

$$H_0: \mu \leq 40 \text{ minutes (claim)}$$

$$H_A: \mu > 40 \text{ minutes}$$

Step 3 Specify the significance level.
The alpha level is specified to be 0.05.

Step 4 Construct the rejection region.
Alpha is the area under the standard normal distribution to the right of the critical value. The population standard deviation is known and the sample size is large, so the test statistic has a standard normal distribution. Therefore, the critical z-value, $z_{0.05}$, is found by locating the z-value that corresponds to an area equal to $0.50 - 0.05 = 0.45$. The critical z-value from the standard normal table is 1.645.

We can calculate $\bar{x}_\alpha = \bar{x}_{0.05}$ using Equation 9.1 as follows:

$$\bar{x}_\alpha = \mu + z_\alpha \frac{\sigma}{\sqrt{n}}$$

$$\bar{x}_{0.05} = 40 + 1.645\left(\frac{8}{\sqrt{100}}\right)$$

$$\bar{x}_{0.05} = 41.32$$

Step 5   Compute the test statistic.

Suppose that the sample of 100 service records produced a sample mean of 43.5 minutes.

Step 6   Reach a decision.

The decision rule is

If $\bar{x} > 41.32$, reject H_0.

Otherwise, do not reject.

Because $\bar{x} = 43.5 > 41.32$, we reject H_0.

Step 7   Draw a conclusion.

There is sufficient evidence to conclude that the mean time required to perform the maintenance service exceeds the advertised time of 40 minutes. Quality Car Care will likely want to modify its service process to shorten the average completion time or change its advertisement.

>> **END EXAMPLE**

TRY PROBLEM 9-7 (pg. 356)

p-Value Approach In addition to the two hypothesis-testing approaches discussed previously, a third approach for conducting hypothesis tests also exists. This third approach uses a **p-value** instead of a critical value.

If the calculated p-value is smaller than the probability in the rejection region (α), then the null hypothesis is rejected. If the calculated p-value is greater than or equal to α, then the hypothesis will not be rejected. The p-value approach is popular today because p-values are usually computed by statistical software packages, including Excel. The advantage to reporting test results using a p-value is that it provides more information than simply stating whether the null hypothesis is rejected. The decision maker is presented with a measure of the degree of significance of the result (i.e., the p-value). This allows the reader the opportunity to evaluate the *extent* to which the data disagree with the null hypothesis, not just whether they disagree.

p-Value

The probability (assuming the null hypothesis is true) of obtaining a test statistic at least as extreme as the test statistic we calculated from the sample. The p-value is also known as the *observed significance level*.

| **EXAMPLE 9-5** | **HYPOTHESIS TEST USING p-VALUES, σ KNOWN** |

Dodger Stadium Parking The parking manager for the Los Angeles Dodgers baseball team has studied the exit times for cars leaving the ballpark after a game and believes that recent changes to the traffic flow leaving the stadium have increased, rather than decreased, average exit times. Prior to the changes, the previous mean exit time per vehicle was 36 minutes, with a population standard deviation equal to 11 minutes. To test the parking manager's belief that the mean time exceeds 36 minutes, a simple random sample of $n = 200$ vehicles is selected, and a sample mean of 36.8 minutes is calculated. Using an alpha $= 0.05$ level, the following steps can be used to conduct the hypothesis test:

Step 1   Specify the population parameter of interest.

The Dodger Stadium parking manager is interested in the mean exit time per vehicle, μ.

Step 2   Formulate the null and alternative hypotheses.

Based on the manager's claim that the current mean exit time is longer than before the traffic flow changes, the null and alternative hypotheses are

$$H_0: \mu \leq 36 \text{ minutes}$$

$$H_A: \mu > 36 \text{ minutes (claim)}$$

Step 3 Specify the significance level.
The alpha level specified for this test is $\alpha = 0.05$.

Step 4 Construct the rejection region.
The decision rule is

If p-value $< \alpha = 0.05$, reject H_0.

Otherwise, do not reject H_0.

Step 5 Compute the test statistic (find the p-value.)
Because the sample size is large and the population standard deviation is assumed known, the test statistic will be a z-value, which is computed as follows:

$$z = \frac{\bar{x} - \mu}{\frac{\sigma}{\sqrt{n}}} = \frac{36.8 - 36}{\frac{11}{\sqrt{200}}} = 1.0285 = 1.03$$

In this example, the p-value is the probability of a z-value from the standard normal distribution being at least as large as 1.03. This is stated as

$$p\text{-value} = P(z \geq 1.03)$$

From the standard normal distribution table in Appendix D,

$$P(z \geq 1.03) = 0.5000 - 0.3485 = 0.1515$$

Step 6 Reach a decision.

Because the p-value $= 0.1515 > \alpha = 0.05$, do not reject the null hypothesis.

Step 7 Draw a conclusion.
The difference between the sample mean and the hypothesized population mean is not large enough to attribute the difference to anything but sampling error.

>> **END EXAMPLE**

TRY PROBLEM 9-6 (pg. 356)

Why do we need three methods to test the same hypothesis when they all give the same result? The answer is that we don't. However, you need to be aware of all three methods because you will encounter each in business situations. The p-value approach is especially important because many statistical software packages provide a p-value that you can use to test a hypothesis quite easily, and a p-value provides a measure of the degree of significance associated with the hypothesis test. This text will use both test-statistic approaches as well as the p-value approach to hypothesis testing.

Types of Hypothesis Tests

One-Tailed Test

A hypothesis test in which the entire rejection region is located in one tail of the sampling distribution. In a one-tailed test, the entire alpha level is located in one tail of the distribution.

Two-Tailed Test

A hypothesis test in which the entire rejection region is split into the two tails of the sampling distribution. In a two-tailed test, the alpha level is split evenly between the two tails.

Hypothesis tests are formulated as either **one-tailed tests** or **two-tailed tests** depending on how the null and alternative hypotheses are presented.

For instance, in the Price & Associates application, the null and alternative hypotheses are

Null hypothesis $H_0: \mu \leq 25 \text{ days}$

Alternative hypothesis $H_A: \mu > 25 \text{ days}$

This hypothesis test is one tailed because the entire rejection region is located in the upper tail and the null hypothesis will be rejected only when the sample mean falls in the extreme upper tail of the sampling distribution (see Figure 9.4). In this application, it will take a sample mean substantially larger than 25 days to reject the null hypothesis.

In Example 9-2 involving Nabisco Foods, the null and alternative hypotheses involving the mean fill of Wheat Thins boxes are

$$H_0: \mu = 20 \text{ ounces (status quo)}$$

$$H_A: \mu \neq 20 \text{ ounces}$$

In this two-tailed hypothesis test, the null hypothesis will be rejected if the sample mean is extremely large (upper tail) or extremely small (lower tail). The alpha level would be split evenly between the two tails.

p-Value for Two-Tailed Tests

In the previous *p*-value example about Dodger Stadium, the rejection region was located in one tail of the sampling distribution. In those cases, the null hypothesis was of the $\geq$ or $\leq$ format. However, sometimes the null hypothesis will be stated as a direct equality. The following application involving the Golden Peanut Company shows how to use the *p*-value approach for a two-tailed test.

BUSINESS APPLICATION   **USING *p*-VALUES TO TEST A NULL HYPOTHESIS**

GOLDEN PEANUT COMPANY Consider the Golden Peanut Company in Alpharetta, Georgia, which packages salted and unsalted unshelled peanuts in 16-ounce sacks. The company's filling process strives for an average fill amount equal to 16 ounces. Therefore, Golden would test the following null and alternative hypotheses:

$$H_0: \mu = 16 \text{ ounces (status quo)}$$
$$H_A: \mu \neq 16 \text{ ounces}$$

The null hypothesis will be rejected if the test statistic falls in either tail of the sampling distribution. The size of the rejection region is determined by α. Each tail has an area equal to $\alpha/2$.

The *p*-value for the two-tailed test is computed in a manner similar to that for a one-tailed test. First, determine the *z*-test statistic as follows:

$$z = (\bar{x} - \mu)/(\sigma/\sqrt{n})$$

Suppose for this situation, Golden managers calculated a $z = 3.32$. In a one-tailed test, the area that will be calculated to form the *p*-value is determined by the direction in which the inequality is pointing in the alternative hypotheses. However, in a two-tailed test, the tail area in which the test statistic is located is initially calculated. In this case, we find $P(z > 3.32)$ using either the standard normal table in Appendix D or Excel's **NORM.S.DIST** function. In this case, because $z = 3.32$ exceeds the table values, we will use Excel to obtain

$$P(z \leq 3.32) = 0.9995$$

Then

$$P(z > 3.32) = 1 - 0.9995 = 0.0005$$

However, because this is a two-tailed hypothesis test, the *p*-value is found by multiplying the 0.0005 value by 2 (to account for the chance that our sample result could have been on either side of the distribution). Thus

$$p\text{-value} = 2(0.0005) = 0.0010$$

Assuming an alpha $= 0.10$ level, then because the

$$p\text{-value} = 0.0010 < \alpha = 0.10, \text{ we reject } H_0.$$

Figure 9.6 illustrates the two-tailed test for the Golden Peanut Company example.

EXAMPLE 9-6   **TWO-TAILED HYPOTHESIS TEST FOR μ, σ KNOWN**

Hargrove Wood Products Hargrove Wood Products is a wood products company with lumber, plywood, and paper plants in several areas of the United States. At its La Grande, Oregon, plywood plant, the company makes plywood used in residential and commercial building. One product made at the La Grande plant is 3/8-inch plywood, which must have

---

How to do it (Example 9-6)

Two-Tailed Test for a Hypothesis about a Population Mean, σ Known
To conduct a two-tailed hypothesis test when the population standard deviation is known, you can perform the following steps:

1. Specify the population parameter of interest.

2. Formulate the null and alternative hypotheses in terms of the population mean, μ.

3. Specify the desired significance level, α.

4. Construct the rejection region. Determine the critical values for each tail, $z_{\alpha/2}$ and $-z_{\alpha/2}$ from the standard normal table. If needed, calculate $\bar{x}_{(\alpha/2)L}$ and $\bar{x}_{(\alpha/2)U}$.
Define the two-tailed decision rule using one of the following:
- If $z > z_{\alpha/2}$, or if $z < -z_{\alpha/2}$ reject H_0; otherwise, do not reject H_0.
- If $\bar{x} < \bar{x}_{(\alpha/2)L}$ or $\bar{x} > \bar{x}_{(\alpha/2)U}$ reject H_0; otherwise, do not reject H_0.
- If *p*-value $< \alpha$, reject H_0; otherwise, do not reject H_0.

5. Compute the test statistic, $z = (\bar{x} - \mu)/(\sigma/\sqrt{n})$, or $\bar{x}$, or find the *p*-value.

6. Reach a decision.

7. Draw a conclusion.

FIGURE 9.6

Two-Tailed Test for the
Golden Peanut Example

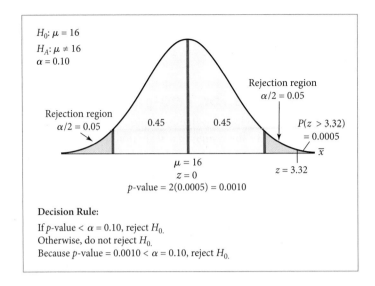

Decision Rule:

If p-value $< \alpha = 0.10$, reject H_0.
Otherwise, do not reject H_0.
Because p-value $= 0.0010 < \alpha = 0.10$, reject H_0.

a mean thickness of 0.375 inches. The standard deviation, σ, is known to be 0.05 inch. Before sending a shipment to customers, Hargrove managers test whether they are meeting the 0.375-inch requirements by selecting a random sample of $n = 100$ sheets of plywood and collecting thickness measurements.

Step 1 Specify the population parameter of interest.
The mean thickness of plywood is of interest.

Step 2 Formulate the null and the alternative hypotheses.
The null and alternative hypotheses are

$$H_0: \mu = 0.375 \text{ inch (status quo)}$$
$$H_A: \mu \neq 0.375 \text{ inch}$$

Note, the test is two tailed because the company is concerned that the plywood could be too thick or too thin.

Step 3 Specify the desired significance level (α).
The managers wish to test the hypothesis using an $\alpha = 0.05$.

Step 4 Construct the rejection region.
This is a two-tailed test. The critical z-values for the upper and lower tails are found in the standard normal table. These are

$$-z_{\alpha/2} = -z_{0.05/2} = -z_{0.025} = -1.96$$

and

$$z_{\alpha/2} = z_{0.05/2} = z_{0.025} = 1.96$$

Define the two-tailed decision rule:

If $z > 1.96$, or if $z < -1.96$, reject H_0; otherwise, do not reject H_0.

Step 5 Compute the test statistic.
Select the random sample and calculate the sample mean.
Suppose that the sample mean for the random sample of 100 measurements is

$$\bar{x} = \frac{\Sigma x}{n} = 0.378 \text{ inch}$$

The z-test statistic is

$$z = \frac{\bar{x} - \mu}{\dfrac{\sigma}{\sqrt{n}}} = \frac{0.378 - 0.375}{\dfrac{0.05}{\sqrt{100}}} = 0.60$$

Step 6 Reach a decision.
Because $-1.96 < z = 0.60 < 1.96$, do not reject the null hypothesis.

Step 7 Draw a conclusion.
The Hargrove Wood Products Company does not have sufficient evidence to reject the null hypothesis. Thus, it will ship the plywood.

>> **END EXAMPLE**

TRY PROBLEM 9-5 (pg. 355)

Hypothesis Test for μ, σ Unknown

In Chapter 8, we introduced situations in which the objective was to estimate a population mean when the population standard deviation was not known. In those cases, the critical value is a t-value from the t-distribution rather than a z-value from the standard normal distribution. The same logic is used in hypothesis testing when σ is unknown (which will usually be the case). Equation 9.3 is used to compute the test statistic for testing hypotheses about a population mean when the population standard deviation is unknown.

---

t-Test Statistic for Hypothesis Tests for μ, σ Unknown

$$t = \frac{\bar{x} - \mu}{\dfrac{s}{\sqrt{n}}} \tag{9.3}$$

where:

$\bar{x}$ = Sample mean

μ = Hypothesized value for the population mean

s = Sample standard deviation, $s = \sqrt{\dfrac{\Sigma(x - \bar{x})^2}{n-1}}$

n = Sample size

To employ the t-distribution, we must make the following assumption:

Assumption

The population is normally distributed.

If the population from which the simple random sample is selected is approximately normal, the t-test statistic computed using Equation 9.3 will be distributed according to a t-distribution with $n-1$ degrees of freedom.

EXAMPLE 9-7   **HYPOTHESIS TEST FOR μ, σ UNKNOWN**

Dairy Fresh Ice Cream The Dairy Fresh Ice Cream plant in Greensboro, Alabama, uses a filling machine for its 64-ounce cartons. There is some variation in the actual amount of ice cream that goes into the carton. The machine can go out of adjustment and put a mean amount either less or more than 64 ounces in the cartons. To monitor the filling process, the production manager selects a simple random sample of 16 filled ice cream cartons each day. He can test whether the machine is still in adjustment using the following steps:

Step 1 Specify the population parameter of interest.
The manager is interested in the mean amount of ice cream.

Step 2 Formulate the appropriate null and alternative hypotheses.
The status quo is that the machine continues to fill ice cream cartons with a mean equal to 64 ounces. Thus, the null and alternative hypotheses are

H_0: $\mu = 64$ ounces (Machine is in adjustment.)

H_A: $\mu \neq 64$ ounces (Machine is out of adjustment.)

How to do it (Example 9-7)

One- or Two-Tailed Tests for μ, σ Unknown

1. Specify the population parameter of interest, μ.

2. Formulate the null hypothesis and the alternative hypothesis.

3. Specify the desired significance level (α).

4. Construct the rejection region. If it is a two-tailed test, determine the critical values for each tail, $t_{\alpha/2}$ and $-t_{\alpha/2}$, from the t-distribution table. If the test is a one-tailed test, find either t_α or $-t_\alpha$, depending on the tail of the rejection region. Degrees of freedom are $n - 1$. If desired, the critical t-values can be used to find the appropriate $\bar{x}_\alpha$ or the $\bar{x}_{(\alpha/2)L}$ and $\bar{x}_{(\alpha/2)U}$ values.

   Define the decision rule.

   a. If the test statistic is in the rejection region, reject H_0; otherwise, do not reject H_0.

   b. If the p-value is less than α, reject H_0; otherwise, do not reject H_0.

5. Compute the test statistic or find the p-value.

   Select the random sample and calculate the sample mean, $\bar{x} = \Sigma x/n$, and the sample standard deviation,

   $$s = \sqrt{\frac{\Sigma(x - \bar{x})^2}{n-1}}.$$

   Then calculate

   $$t = \frac{\bar{x} - \mu}{\frac{s}{\sqrt{n}}}$$

   or the p-value.

6. Reach a decision.

7. Draw a conclusion.

Step 3 **Specify the desired level of significance.**

The test will be conducted using an alpha level equal to 0.05.

Step 4 **Construct the rejection region.**

We first produce a box and whisker plot for a rough check on the normality assumption.

The sample data are

62.7	64.7	64.0	64.5	64.6	65.0	64.4	64.2
64.6	65.5	63.6	64.7	64.0	64.2	63.0	63.6

The box and whisker plot is

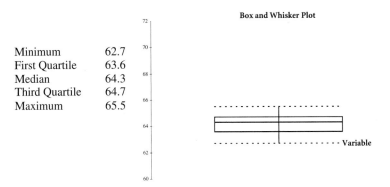

Minimum	62.7
First Quartile	63.6
Median	64.3
Third Quartile	64.7
Maximum	65.5

Box and Whisker Plot

The box and whisker diagram does not indicate that the population distribution is unduly skewed. The median line is close to the middle of the box, the whiskers extend approximately equal distances above and below the box, and there are no outliers. Thus, the normal distribution assumption is reasonable based on these sample data.

Now we determine the critical values from the t-distribution.

Based on the null and alternative hypotheses, this test is two tailed. Thus, we will split the alpha into two tails and determine the critical values from the t-distribution with $n - 1$ degrees of freedom. Using Appendix F, the critical t's for a two-tailed test with $\alpha = .05$ and $16 - 1 = 15$ degrees of freedom are $t = \pm 2.1315$.

The decision rule for this two-tailed test is

If $t < -2.1315$ or $t > 2.1315$, reject H_0.

Otherwise, do not reject H_0.

Step 5 **Compute the t-test statistic.**

The sample mean is

$$\bar{x} = \frac{\Sigma x}{n} = \frac{1{,}027.3}{16} = 64.2$$

The sample standard deviation is

$$s = \sqrt{\frac{\Sigma(x - \bar{x})^2}{n-1}} = 0.72$$

The t-test statistic, using Equation 9.3, is

$$t = \frac{\bar{x} - \mu}{\frac{s}{\sqrt{n}}} = \frac{64.2 - 64}{\frac{0.72}{\sqrt{16}}} = 1.11$$

Step 6 **Reach a decision.**

Because $t = 1.11$ is not less than -2.1315 and not greater than 2.1315, we do not reject the null hypothesis.

Step 7 Draw a conclusion.

Based on these sample data, the company does not have sufficient evidence to conclude that the filling machine is out of adjustment.

>> **END EXAMPLE**

TRY PROBLEM 9-12 (pg. 356)

EXAMPLE 9-8   **TESTING THE HYPOTHESIS FOR μ UNKNOWN**

United States Post Office The U.S. Post Office in Mobile, Alabama, has previously studied its service operations and has determined that the distribution of time required for a customer to be served is normally distributed, with a mean equal to 540 seconds. However, the manager overseeing all of Mobile's post offices has charged his staff with improving service times. Post Office officials have selected a random sample of 16 customers and wish to determine whether the mean service time is now fewer than 540 seconds.

Step 1 Specify the population parameter of interest.

The mean service time for all mobile post offices is the population parameter of interest.

Step 2 Formulate the null and alternative hypotheses.

The null and alternative hypotheses are

$$H_0: \mu \geq 540 \text{ seconds (status quo)}$$

$$H_A: \mu < 540 \text{ seconds}$$

Step 3 Specify the significance level.

The test will be conducted at the 0.01 level of significance. Thus, $\alpha = 0.01$.

Step 4 Construct the rejection region.

Because this is a one-tailed test and the rejection region is in the lower tail, as indicated in H_A, the critical value from the t-distribution with $16 - 1 = 15$ degrees of freedom is $-t_\alpha = -t_{0.01} = -2.6025$.

The decision rule for this one-tailed test is

If $t < -2.6025$, reject H_0.

Otherwise, do not reject H_0.

Step 5 Compute the test statistic.

The sample mean for the random sample of 16 customers is $\bar{x} = \Sigma x / n = 510$ seconds, and the sample standard deviation is $\sqrt{\dfrac{\Sigma(x - x)^2}{n - 1}} = 45$ seconds.

Assuming that the population distribution is approximately normal, the test statistic is

$$t = \frac{\bar{x} - \mu}{\dfrac{s}{\sqrt{n}}} = \frac{510 - 540}{\dfrac{45}{\sqrt{16}}} = -2.67$$

Step 6 Reach a decision.

Because $t = -2.67 < -2.6025$, the null hypothesis is rejected.

Step 7 Draw a conclusion.

There is sufficient evidence to conclude that the mean service time has been reduced below 540 seconds.

>> **END EXAMPLE**

TRY PROBLEM 9-15 (pg. 357)

Excel Tutorial

BUSINESS APPLICATION   **HYPOTHESIS TESTS USING SOFTWARE**

FRANKLIN TIRE AND RUBBER COMPANY The Franklin Tire and Rubber Company recently conducted a test on a new tire design to determine whether the company could make the claim that the mean tire mileage would exceed 60,000 miles. The test was conducted in

FIGURE 9.7

Excel 2010 (PHStat) Output for Franklin Tire Hypothesis Test Results

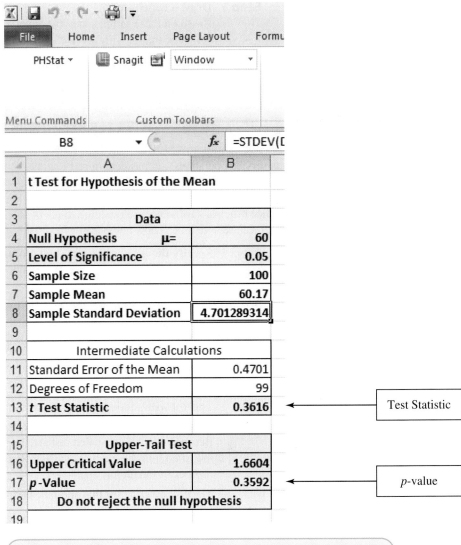

Excel 2010 Instructions:
1. Open **PHStat** and open File: **Franklin.xlsx**.
2. Click **Add-Ins** tab and then click the **PHStat** drop-down arrow.
3. Select **One-Sample Test**, *t*-test for **Mean, Sigma Unknown**.
4. Enter Null (hypothesized mean) and Level of Significance.
5. Check **Sample Statistics Unknown** and select data.
6. Check **Test Option > Upper Tail** test.

	A	B
1	t Test for Hypothesis of the Mean	
2		
3	**Data**	
4	Null Hypothesis μ=	60
5	Level of Significance	0.05
6	Sample Size	100
7	Sample Mean	60.17
8	Sample Standard Deviation	4.701289314
9		
10	Intermediate Calculations	
11	Standard Error of the Mean	0.4701
12	Degrees of Freedom	99
13	t Test Statistic	0.3616
14		
15	**Upper-Tail Test**	
16	Upper Critical Value	1.6604
17	p-Value	0.3592
18	Do not reject the null hypothesis	
19		

Test Statistic

p-value

Minitab Instructions (for similar results):
1. Open file: **Franklin.MTW**.
2. Choose **Stat > Basic Statistics > 1-sample *t***.
3. In **Samples in columns**, enter data column.
4. Select **Perform hypothesis test** and enter hypothesized mean.
5. Select **Options**, in **Confidence level** insert confidence level.
6. In **Alternative**, select hypothesis direction.
7. Click **OK**.

Alaska. A simple random sample of 100 tires was tested, and the number of miles each tire lasted until it no longer met the federal government minimum tread thickness was recorded. The data (shown in thousands of miles) are in the file called **Franklin**.

The null and alternative hypotheses to be tested are

$$H_0: \mu \leq 60$$
$$H_A: \mu > 60 \text{ (research hypothesis)}$$
$$\alpha = 0.05$$

Excel does not have a special procedure for testing hypotheses for single population means. However, the Excel add-ins software called PHStat has the necessary hypothesis-testing tools.[5] Figure 9.7 shows the Excel PHStat output.

---

[5]This test can be done in Excel without the benefit of the PHStat add-ins by using Excel equations. Please refer to the Excel tutorial for the specifics.

We denote the critical value of an upper- or lower-tail test with a significance level of α as t_α or $-t_\alpha$. The critical value for $\alpha = 0.05$ and 99 degrees of freedom is $t_{0.05} = 1.6604$. Using the critical value approach, the decision rule is:

If the t test statistic $> 1.6604 = t_{0.05}$, reject H_0; otherwise, do not reject H_0.

The sample mean, based on a sample of 100 tires, is $\bar{x} = 60.17$ (60,170 miles), and the sample standard deviation is $s = 4.701$ (4,701 miles). The t test statistic shown in Figure 9.7 is computed as follows:

$$t = \frac{\bar{x} - \mu}{\frac{s}{\sqrt{n}}} = \frac{60.17 - 60}{\frac{4.701}{\sqrt{100}}} = 0.3616$$

Because

$$t = 0.3616 < t_{0.05} = 1.6604, \text{ do not reject the null hypothesis.}$$

Thus, based on the sample data, the evidence is insufficient to conclude that the new tires have an average life exceeding 60,000 miles. Based on this test, the company would not be justified in making the claim.

Franklin managers could also use the p-value approach to test the null hypothesis because the output shown in Figures 9.7 provides the p-value. In this case, the p-value $= 0.3592$. The decision rule for a test is

If p-value $< \alpha$ reject H_0; otherwise, do not reject H_0.

Because

$$p\text{-value} = 0.3592 > \alpha = 0.05$$

we do not reject the null hypothesis. This is the same conclusion we reached using the t test statistic approach.

This section has introduced the basic concepts of hypothesis testing. There are several ways to test a null hypothesis. Each method will yield the same result; however, computer software such as Excel show the p-values automatically. Therefore, decision makers increasingly use the p-value approach.

MyStatLab

9-1: **Exercises**

Skill **Development**

9-1. Determine the appropriate critical value(s) for each of the following tests concerning the population mean:
   a. upper-tailed test: $\alpha = 0.025; n = 25; \sigma = 3.0$
   b. lower-tailed test: $\alpha = 0.05; n = 30; s = 9.0$
   c. two-tailed test: $\alpha = 0.02; n = 51; s = 6.5$
   d. two-tailed test: $\alpha = 0.10; n = 36; \sigma = 3.8$

9-2. For each of the following pairs of hypotheses, determine whether each pair represents valid hypotheses for a hypothesis test. Explain reasons for any pair that is indicated to be invalid.
   a. $H_0: \mu = 15, H_A: \mu > 15$
   b. $H_0: \mu = 20, H_A: \mu \neq 20$
   c. $H_0: \mu < 30, H_A: \mu > 30$
   d. $H_0: \mu \leq 40, H_A: \mu \geq 40$
   e. $H_0: \bar{x} \leq 45, H_A: \bar{x} > 45$
   f. $H_0: \mu \leq 50, H_A: \mu > 55$

9-3. Provide the relevant critical value(s) for each of the following circumstances:
   a. $H_A: \mu > 13, n = 15, \sigma = 10.3, \alpha = 0.05$
   b. $H_A: \mu \neq 21, n = 23, s = 35.40, \alpha = 0.02$

   c. $H_A: \mu \neq 35, n = 41, \sigma = 35.407, \alpha = 0.01$
   d. $H_A: \mu < 49$; data: 12.5, 15.8, 44.3, 22.6, 18.4; $\alpha = 0.10$
   e. $H_A: \bar{x} > 15, n = 27, \sigma = 12.4$

9-4. For each of the following z-test statistics, compute the p-value assuming that the hypothesis test is a one-tailed test:
   a. $z = 1.34$
   b. $z = 2.09$
   c. $z = -1.55$

9-5. For the following hypothesis test:

$$H_0: \mu = 200$$

$$H_A: \mu \neq 200$$

$$\alpha = 0.01$$

with $n = 64, \sigma = 9$, and $\bar{x} = 196.5$, state
   a. the decision rule in terms of the critical value of the test statistic
   b. the calculated value of the test statistic
   c. the conclusion

9-6. For the following hypothesis test:

$$H_0: \mu \leq 45$$
$$H_A: \mu > 45$$
$$\alpha = 0.02$$

with $n = 80$, $\sigma = 9$, and $\bar{x} = 47.1$, state
a. the decision rule in terms of the critical value of the test statistic
b. the calculated value of the test statistic
c. the appropriate p-value
d. the conclusion

9-7. For the following hypothesis, test:

$$H_0: \mu \geq 23$$
$$H_A: \mu < 23$$
$$\alpha = 0.025$$

with $n = 25$, $s = 8$, and $\bar{x} = 20$, state
a. the decision rule in terms of the critical value of the test statistic
b. the calculated value of the test statistic
c. the conclusion

9-8. For the following hypothesis, test:

$$H_0: \mu = 60.5$$
$$H_A: \mu \neq 60.5$$
$$\alpha = 0.05$$

with $n = 15$, $s = 7.5$, and $\bar{x} = 62.2$, state
a. the decision rule in terms of the critical value of the test statistic
b. the calculated value of the test statistic
c. the conclusion

9-9. For the following hypothesis:

$$H_0: \mu \leq 70$$
$$H_A: \mu > 70$$

with $n = 20$, $\bar{x} = 71.2$, $s = 6.9$, and $\alpha = 0.1$, state
a. the decision rule in terms of the critical value of the test statistic
b. the calculated value of the test statistic
c. the conclusion

9-10. A sample taken from a population yields a sample mean of 58.4. Calculate the p-value for each of the following circumstances:
a. $H_A: \mu > 58$, $n = 16$, $\sigma = 0.8$
b. $H_A: \mu \neq 45$, $n = 41$, $s = 35.407$
c. $H_A: \mu \neq 45$, $n = 41$, $\sigma = 35.407$
d. $H_A: \mu < 69$; data: 60.1, 54.3, 57.1, 53.1, 67.4

9-11. For each of the following scenarios, indicate which type of statistical error could have been committed or, alternatively, that no statistical error was made. When warranted, provide a definition for the indicated statistical error.
a. Unknown to the statistical analyst, the null hypothesis is actually true.
b. The statistical analyst fails to reject the null hypothesis.
c. The statistical analyst rejects the null hypothesis.
d. Unknown to the statistical analyst, the null hypothesis is actually true and the analyst fails to reject the null hypothesis.
e. Unknown to the statistical analyst, the null hypothesis is actually false.
f. Unknown to the statistical analyst, the null hypothesis is actually false and the analyst rejects the null hypothesis.

Business **Applications**

9-12. The National Club Association does periodic studies on issues important to its membership. The 2008 Executive Summary of the Club Managers Association of America reported that the average country club initiation fee was $31,912. Suppose a random sample taken in 2009 of 12 country clubs produced the following initiation fees:

$29,121	$31,472	$28,054	$31,005	$36,295	$32,771
$26,205	$33,299	$25,602	$33,726	$39,731	$27,816

Based on the sample information, can you conclude at the $\alpha = 0.05$ level of significance that the average 2009 country club initiation fees are lower than the 2008 average? Conduct your test at the $\alpha = 0.05$ level of significance.

9-13. The director of a state agency believes that the average starting salary for clerical employees in the state is less than $30,000 per year. To test her hypothesis, she has collected a simple random sample of 100 starting clerical salaries from across the state and found that the sample mean is $29,750.
a. State the appropriate null and alternative hypotheses.
b. Assuming the population standard deviation is known to be $2,500 and the significance level for the test is to be 0.05, what is the critical value (stated in dollars)?
c. Referring to your answer in part b, what conclusion should be reached with respect to the null hypothesis?
d. Referring to your answer in part c, which of the two statistical errors might have been made in this case? Explain.

9-14. A mail-order business prides itself in its ability to fill customers' orders in six calendar days or less on the average. Periodically, the operations manager selects a random sample of customer orders and determines the number of days required to fill the orders. Based on this sample information, he decides if the desired standard is not being met. He will assume that the average number of days to fill customers' orders is six or less unless the data suggest strongly otherwise.
a. Establish the appropriate null and alternative hypotheses.
b. On one occasion when a sample of 40 customers was selected, the average number of days was 6.65, with a sample standard deviation of 1.5 days. Can the operations manager conclude that his mail-order business is achieving its goal? Use a significance level of 0.025 to answer this question.

c. Calculate the *p*-value for this test. Conduct the test using this *p*-value.

d. The operations manager wishes to monitor the efficiency of his mail-order service often. Therefore, he does not wish to repeatedly calculate *t*-values to conduct the hypothesis tests. Obtain the critical value, $\bar{x}_\alpha$, so that the manager can simply compare the sample mean to this value to conduct the test.

9-15. A recent internal report issued by the marketing manager for a national oil-change franchise indicated that the mean number of miles between oil changes for franchise customers is at least 3,600 miles. One Texas franchise owner conducted a study to determine whether the marketing manager's statement was accurate for his franchise's customers. He selected a simple random sample of 10 customers and determined the number of miles each had driven the car between oil changes. The following sample data were obtained:

3,655	4,204	1,946	2,789	3,555
3,734	3,208	3,311	3,920	3,902

a. State the appropriate null and alternative hypotheses.

b. Use the test statistic approach with $\alpha = 0.05$ to test the null hypothesis.

9-16. The makers of Mini-Oats Cereal have an automated packaging machine that can be set at any targeted fill level between 12 and 32 ounces. Every box of cereal is not expected to contain exactly the targeted weight, but the average of all boxes filled should. At the end of every shift (eight hours), 16 boxes are selected at random and the mean and standard deviation of the sample are computed. Based on these sample results, the production control manager determines whether the filling machine needs to be readjusted or whether it remains all right to operate. Use $\alpha = 0.05$.

a. Establish the appropriate null and alternative hypotheses to be tested for boxes that are supposed to have an average of 24 ounces.

b. At the end of a particular shift during which the machine was filling 24-ounce boxes of Mini-Oats, the sample mean of 16 boxes was 24.32 ounces, with a standard deviation of 0.70 ounce. Assist the production control manager in determining if the machine is achieving its targeted average.

c. Why do you suppose the production control manager would prefer to make this hypothesis test a two-tailed test? Discuss.

d. Conduct the test using a *p*-value. (*Hint*: Use Excel's T.DIST.2T function.)

e. Considering the result of the test, which of the two types of errors in hypothesis testing could you have made?

9-17. Starting in 2008, an increasing number of people found themselves facing mortgages that were worth more than the value of their homes. A fund manager who had invested in debt obligations involving grouped

mortgages was interested in determining the group most likely to default on their mortgage. He speculates that older people are less likely to default on their mortgage and thinks the average age of those who do is 55 years. To test this, a random sample of 30 who had defaulted was selected; the following sample data reflect the ages of the sampled individuals:

40	55	78	27	55	33
51	76	54	67	40	31
60	61	50	42	78	80
25	38	74	46	48	57
30	65	80	26	46	49

a. State the appropriate null and alternative hypotheses.

b. Use the test statistic approach to test the null hypothesis with $\alpha = 0.01$.

Computer Database **Exercises**

9-18. At a recent meeting, the manager of a national call center for a major Internet bank made the statement that the average past-due amount for customers who have been called previously about their bills is now no larger than $20.00. Other bank managers at the meeting suggested that this statement may be in error and that it might be worthwhile to conduct a test to see if there is statistical support for the call center manager's statement. The file called **Bank Call Center** contains data for a random sample of 67 customers from the call center population. Assuming that the population standard deviation for past due amounts is known to be $60.00, what should be concluded based on the sample data? Test using $\alpha = 0.10$.

9-19. The *Consumer Expenditures* report released by the U.S. Bureau of Labor Statistics found the average annual household spending on food at home was $3,624. Suppose a random sample of 137 households in Detroit was taken to determine whether the average annual expenditure on food at home was less for consumer units in Detroit than in the nation as a whole. The sample results are in the file **Detroit Eats**. Based on the sample results, can it be concluded at the $\alpha = 0.02$ level of significance that average consumer-unit spending for food at home in Detroit is less than the national average?

9-20. The Center on Budget and Policy Priorities (www.cbpp.org) reported that average out-of-pocket medical expenses for prescription drugs for privately insured adults with incomes over 200% of the poverty level was $173 in 2002. Suppose an investigation was conducted in 2012 to determine whether the increased availability of generic drugs, Internet prescription drug purchases, and cost controls has reduced out-of-pocket drug expenses. The investigation randomly sampled 196 privately insured adults with incomes over 200% of the poverty level, and the respondents' 2012 out-of-pocket medical expenses for prescription drugs were recorded. These data are in the file **Drug Expenses**.

Based on the sample data, can it be concluded that 2012 out-of-pocket prescription drug expenses are lower than the 2002 average reported by the Center on Budget and Policy Priorities? Use a level of significance of 0.01 to conduct the hypothesis test.

9-21. A key factor in the world's economic condition is the population growth of the countries in the world. The file called **Country Growth** contains data for 231 countries. Consider these countries to be all the countries in the world.

   a. From this population, suppose a systematic random sample of every fifth country is selected starting with the fifth country on the list. From this sample, test the null hypothesis that the mean population growth percentage between the years 1990 and 2000 is equal to 1.5%. Test using $\alpha = 0.05$.

   b. Now compute the average population growth rate for all 231 countries. After examining the result of

the hypothesis test in part a, what type of statistical error, if any, was committed? Explain your answer.

9-22. Hono Golf is a manufacturer of golf products in Taiwan and China. One of the golf accessories it produces at its plant in Tainan Hsing, Taiwan, is plastic golf tees. The injector molder produces golf tees that are designed to have an average height of 66 mm. To determine if this specification is met, random samples are taken from the production floor. One sample is contained in the file labeled **THeight**.

   a. Determine if the process is not producing the tees to specification. Use a significance level of 0.01.

   b. If the hypothesis test determines the specification is not being met, the production process will be shut down while causes and remedies are determined. At times, this occurs even though the process is functioning to specification. What type of statistical error would this be?

END EXERCISES 9-1

9.2 Hypothesis Tests for a Proportion

So far, this chapter has focused on hypothesis tests about a single population mean. Although many decision problems involve a test of a population mean, there are also cases in which the parameter of interest is the population proportion. For example, a production manager might consider the proportion of defective items produced on an assembly line to determine whether the line should be restructured. Likewise, a life insurance salesperson's performance assessment might include the proportion of existing clients who renew their policies.

Chapter Outcome 1. → ## Testing a Hypothesis about a Single Population Proportion

The basic concepts of hypothesis testing for proportions are the same as for means.

1. The null and alternative hypotheses are stated in terms of a population parameter, now p instead of μ, and the sample statistic becomes $\bar{p}$ instead of $\bar{x}$.
2. The null hypothesis should be a statement concerning the parameter that includes the equality.
3. The significance level of the hypothesis determines the size of the rejection region.
4. The test can be one or two tailed, depending on how the alternative hypothesis is formulated.

BUSINESS APPLICATION **TESTING A HYPOTHESIS FOR A POPULATION PROPORTION**

SAMPSON AND KOENIG FINANCIAL CENTER The Sampson and Koenig Financial Center purchases installment loans that were originally made by independent appliance dealers and heating and air conditioning installers. Ideally, all loans purchased by Sampson and Koenig will be fully documented. However, the company's internal auditors periodically need to check to make sure the internal controls are being followed. Recently, the audit manager examined the documentation on the company's portfolio of 9,460 installment loans. The internal control procedures require that the file on each installment loan account contain certain specific documentation, such as a list of applicant assets, statement of monthly income, list of liabilities, and certificate of automobile insurance. If an account contains all the required documentation, then it complies with company procedures.

The audit manager has established a 1% noncompliance rate as the company's standard. If more than 1% of the 9,460 loans do not have appropriate documentation, then the internal

FIGURE 9.8

Decision Rule for Sampson
and Koenig Example

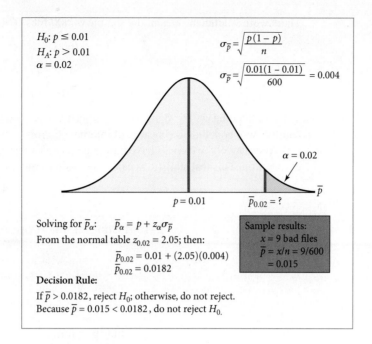

$H_0: p \leq 0.01$
$H_A: p > 0.01$
$\alpha = 0.02$

$\sigma_{\bar{p}} = \sqrt{\dfrac{p(1-p)}{n}}$

$\sigma_{\bar{p}} = \sqrt{\dfrac{0.01(1-0.01)}{600}} = 0.004$

$\alpha = 0.02$

$p = 0.01$ $\bar{p}_{0.02} = ?$

Solving for $\bar{p}_\alpha$: $\bar{p}_\alpha = p + z_\alpha \sigma_{\bar{p}}$
From the normal table $z_{0.02} = 2.05$; then:

$\bar{p}_{0.02} = 0.01 + (2.05)(0.004)$
$\bar{p}_{0.02} = 0.0182$

Sample results:
$x = 9$ bad files
$\bar{p} = x/n = 9/600$
$= 0.015$

Decision Rule:

If $\bar{p} > 0.0182$, reject H_0; otherwise, do not reject.
Because $\bar{p} = 0.015 < 0.0182$, do not reject H_0.

controls are not effective and the company needs to improve the situation. The audit staff does not have enough time to examine all 9,460 files to determine the true population noncompliance rate. As a result, the audit staff selects a random sample of 600 files, examines them, and determines the number of files not in compliance with bank documentation requirements. The sample findings will tell the manager if the bank is exceeding the 1% noncompliance rate for the population of all 9,460 loan files. The manager will not act unless the noncompliance rate exceeds 1%. The default position is that the internal controls are effective. Thus, the null and alternative hypotheses are

$$H_O: p \leq 0.01 \text{ (internal controls are effective)}$$

$$H_A: p > 0.01 \text{ (internal controls are effective)}$$

Suppose the sample of 600 accounts uncovered 9 files with inadequate loan documentation. The question is whether 9 out of 600 is sufficient to conclude that the company has a problem. To answer this question statistically, we need to recall a lesson from Chapter 7.

Requirement

The sample size, n, is large such that $np \geq 5$ and $n(1 - p) \geq 5$.[6]

If this requirement is satisfied, the sampling distribution is approximately normal with mean $= p$ and standard deviation $= \sqrt{p(1-p)/n}$.

The auditors have a general policy of performing these tests with a significance level of

$$\alpha = 0.02$$

They are willing to reject a true null hypothesis 2% of the time. In this case, if a Type I statistical error is committed, the internal controls will be considered ineffective when, in fact, they are working as intended.

Once the null and alternative hypotheses and the significance level have been specified, we can formulate the decision rule for this test. Figure 9.8 shows how the decision rule is developed. Notice the critical value, $\bar{p}_{0.02}$, is 2.05 standard deviations above $p = 0.01$. Thus, the decision rule is:

$$\text{If } \bar{p} > \bar{p}_{0.02} = 0.0182, \text{ reject } H_O$$

---

[6]A paper published in *Statistical Science* by L. Brown et al. titled "Interval Estimation for a Binomial Proportion" in 2001, pp. 101–133, suggests that the requirement should be $np \geq 15$ and $n(1 - p) > 15$. However, most sources still use the ≥ 5 limit.

There were 9 deficient files in the sample of 600 files. This means that

$$\bar{p} = 9/600 = 0.015$$

Because

$$\bar{p} = 0.015 < 0.0182 \text{ do not reject } H_0.$$

The null hypothesis, H_0, should not be rejected, based on these sample data. Therefore, the auditors will conclude the system of internal controls is working effectively.

Alternatively, we could have based the test on a test statistic (z) with a standard normal distribution. This test statistic is calculated using Equation 9.4.

---

z-Test Statistic for Proportions

$$z = \frac{\bar{p} - p}{\sqrt{\dfrac{p(1-p)}{n}}}$$ (9.4)

where:

$\bar{p}$ = Sample proportion
p = Hypothesized population proportion
n = Sample size

The z-value for this test statistic is

$$z = \frac{0.015 - 0.01}{0.004} = 1.25$$

As was established in Figure 9.8, the critical value is

$$z_{0.02} = 2.05$$

We reject the null hypothesis only if $z > z_{0.02}$. Because

$$z = 1.25 < 2.05$$

we don't reject the null hypothesis. This, of course, was the same conclusion we reached when we used $\bar{p}$ as the test statistic. Both test statistics must yield the same decision.

How to do it (Example 9-9)

Testing Hypotheses about a Single Population Proportion

1. Specify the population parameter of interest.

2. Formulate the null and alternative hypotheses.

3. Specify the significance level for testing the null hypothesis.

4. Construct the rejection region. For a one-tail test, determine the critical value, z_α, from the standard normal distribution table or

$$\bar{p}_\alpha = p + z_\alpha \sqrt{\frac{p(1-p)}{n}}$$

For a two-tail test, determine the critical values:

$z_{(\alpha/2)L}$ and $z_{(\alpha/2)U}$ from the standard normal table or
$\bar{p}_{(\alpha/2)L}$ and $\bar{p}_{(\alpha/2)U}$

5. Compute the test statistic,

$$\bar{p} = \frac{x}{n} \ \ or \ \ z = \frac{\bar{p} - p}{\sqrt{\dfrac{p(1-p)}{n}}}$$

or determine the p-value.

6. Reach a decision by comparing z to z_α or $\bar{p}$ to $\bar{p}_\alpha$ or by comparing the p-value to α.

7. Draw a conclusion.

EXAMPLE 9-9   **TESTING HYPOTHESES FOR A SINGLE POPULATION PROPORTION**

Mike Flippo/Shutterstock

The Developmental Basketball League Several years ago, when the Continental Basketball League folded, the NBA started a new professional basketball league called the Developmental League, or D-League for short, where players who were not on NBA rosters could fine-tune their skills in hopes of getting called up to the NBA. The teams in this league are privately owned but connected to NBA teams. One of the D-League's teams is considering increasing the season ticket prices for basketball games. The marketing manager is concerned that some people will terminate their ticket orders if this change occurs. If more than 10% of the season ticket orders would be terminated, the marketing manager does not want to implement the price increase. To test this, a random sample of ticket holders is surveyed and asked what they would do if the prices were increased.

Step 1   Specify the population parameter of interest.
The parameter of interest is the population proportion of season ticket holders who would terminate their orders.

Step 2 **Formulate the null and alternative hypotheses.**
The null and alternative hypotheses are

$$H_O: p \leq 0.10$$
$$H_A: p > 0.10$$

Step 3 **Specify the significance level.**
The alpha level for this test is $\alpha = 0.05$.

Step 4 **Construct the rejection region.**
1. Using the z critical value:
The critical value from the standard normal table for this upper-tailed test is $z_\alpha = z_{0.05} = 1.645$.
The decision rule is

If $z > 1.645$, reject H_0; otherwise, do not reject.

2. Using the $\bar{p}$ critical value:
As you learned in Section 9.1, there are alternative approaches to testing a hypothesis. In addition to the z-test statistic approach, you could compute the critical value, $\bar{p}_\alpha$, and compare $\bar{p}$ to $\bar{p}_\alpha$. The critical value is computed as follows:

$$\bar{p}_\alpha = p + z_\alpha \sqrt{\frac{p(1-p)}{n}}$$
$$\bar{p}_{0.05} = 0.10 + 1.645 \sqrt{\frac{0.10(1-0.10)}{100}} = 0.149$$

The decision rule is
If $\bar{p} > \bar{p}_{0.05} = 0.149$, reject H_0. Otherwise, do not reject.

3. Using the p-value:
The decision rule is
If p-value $< \alpha = 0.05$, reject H_0. Otherwise, do not reject.

Step 5 **Compute the test statistic or the p-value.**
The random sample of $n = 100$ season ticket holders showed that 14 would cancel their ticket orders if the price change were implemented.
1. The sample proportion and z-test statistic are

$$\bar{p} = \frac{x}{n} = \frac{14}{100} = 0.14$$
$$z = \frac{\bar{p} - p}{\sqrt{\frac{p(1-p)}{n}}} = \frac{0.14 - 0.10}{\sqrt{\frac{0.10(1-0.10)}{100}}} = 1.33$$

2. Using the $\bar{p}$-critical value:
The $\bar{p}$-critical value was previously calculated to be $p = 0.149$.
3. Using the p-value:
To find the p-value for a one-tailed test, we use the calculated z-value shown previously in step 5 to be $z = 1.33$. Then,

$$p\text{-value} = P(z > 1.33)$$

From the standard normal table, the probability associated with $z = 1.33$, i.e., $P(0 \leq z \leq 1.33)$, is 0.4082. Then,

$$p\text{-value} = 0.5 - 0.4082 = 0.0918$$

Step 6 **Reach a decision.**
1. Using the z-test statistic:
The decision rule is

If $z > z_{0.05}$, reject H_0.

Because $z = 1.33 < 1.645$, do not reject H_0.

2. Using the $\bar{p}$-critical value
The decision rule is

$$\text{If } \bar{p} > \bar{p}_{0.05}, \text{ reject } H_0.$$

Because $0.14 < 0.149$, do not reject H_0. This is the same decision we reached using the z-test statistic approach.
3. Using the p-value:
The decision rule is

$$\text{If } p\text{-value} < \alpha = 0.05, \text{ reject } H_0.$$

Because $p\text{-value} = 0.0918 > 0.05$, do not reject H_0.

All three hypothesis-testing approaches provide the same decision.

Step 7   Draw a conclusion.
Based on the sample data, the marketing manager does not have sufficient evidence to conclude that more than 10% of the season ticket holders will cancel their ticket orders.

>> **END EXAMPLE**

TRY PROBLEM 9-28 (pg. 362)

MyStatLab

9-2: **Exercises**

Skill Development

9-23. Determine the appropriate critical value(s) for each of the following tests concerning the population proportion:
   a. upper-tailed test: $\alpha = 0.025, n = 48$
   b. lower-tailed test: $\alpha = 0.05, n = 30$
   c. two-tailed test: $\alpha = 0.02, n = 129$
   d. two-tailed test: $\alpha = 0.10, n = 36$

9-24. Calculate the z-test statistic for a hypothesis test in which the null hypothesis states that the population proportion, p, equals 0.40 if the following sample information is present:

$$n = 150, x = 30$$

9-25. Given the following null and alternative hypotheses

$$H_O: p \geq 0.60$$
$$H_A: p < 0.60$$

test the hypothesis using $\alpha = 0.01$ assuming that a sample of $n = 200$ yielded $x = 105$ items with the desired attribute.

9-26. For the following hypothesis, test:

$$H_O: p = 0.40$$
$$H_A: p \neq 0.40$$
$$\alpha = 0.01$$

with $n = 64$ and $\bar{p} = 0.42$, state
   a. the decision rule in terms of the critical value of the test statistic
   b. the calculated value of the test statistic
   c. the conclusion

9-27. For the following hypothesis, test

$$H_O: p \geq 0.75$$
$$H_A: p < 0.75$$
$$\alpha = 0.025$$

with $n = 100$ and $\bar{p} = 0.66$, state
   a. the decision rule in terms of the critical value of the test statistic
   b. the calculated value of the test statistic
   c. the conclusion

9-28. A test of hypothesis has the following hypotheses:

$$H_O: p \leq 0.45$$
$$H_A: p > 0.45$$

For a sample size of 30, and a sample proportion of 0.55,
   a. For an $\alpha = 0.025$, determine the critical value.
   b. Calculate the numerical value of the test statistic.
   c. State the test's conclusion.
   d. Determine the p-value.

9-29. A sample of size 25 was obtained to test the hypotheses

$$H_O: p = 0.30$$
$$H_A: p \neq 0.30$$

Calculate the p-value for each of the following sample results:
   a. $\bar{p} = 0.12$
   b. $\bar{p} = 0.35$
   c. $\bar{p} = 0.42$
   d. $\bar{p} = 0.5$

Business Applications

9-30. Suppose a recent random sample of employees nationwide that have a 401(k) retirement plan found that 18% of them had borrowed against it in the last year. A random sample of 100 employees from a local company who have a 401(k) retirement plan found that 14 had borrowed from their plan. Based on the sample results, is it possible to conclude, at the $\alpha = 0.025$ level of significance, that the local company had a lower proportion of borrowers from its 401(k) retirement plan than the 18% reported nationwide?

9-31. An issue that faces individuals investing for retirement is allocating assets among different investment choices. Suppose a study conducted 10 years ago showed that 65% of investors preferred stocks to real estate as an investment. In a recent random sample of 900 investors, 360 preferred real estate to stocks. Is this new data sufficient to allow you to conclude that the proportion of investors preferring stocks to real estate has declined from 10 years ago? Conduct your analysis at the $\alpha = 0.02$ level of significance.

9-32. A major issue facing many states is whether to legalize casino gambling. Suppose the governor of one state believes that more than 55% of the state's registered voters would favor some form of legal casino gambling. However, before backing a proposal to allow such gambling, the governor has instructed his aides to conduct a statistical test on the issue. To do this, the aides have hired a consulting firm to survey a simple random sample of 300 voters in the state. Of these 300 voters, 175 actually favored legalized gambling.
a. State the appropriate null and alternative hypotheses.
b. Assuming that a significance level of 0.05 is used, what conclusion should the governor reach based on these sample data? Discuss.

9-33. A recent article in *The Wall Street Journal* titled "As Identity Theft Moves Online, Crime Rings Mimic Big Business" states that 39% of the consumer scam complaints by American consumers are about identity theft. Suppose a random sample of 90 complaints is obtained. Of these complaints, 40 were regarding identity theft. Based on these sample data, what conclusion should be reached about the statement made in *The Wall Street Journal*? (Test using $\alpha = 0.10$.)

9-34. Because of the complex nature of the U.S. income tax system, many people have questions for the Internal Revenue Service (IRS). Yet an article published by the *Detroit Free Press* titled "Assistance: IRS Help Centers Give the Wrong Information" discusses the propensity of IRS staff employees to give incorrect tax information to taxpayers who call with questions. Then IRS Inspector General Pamela Gardiner told a Senate subcommittee that "the IRS employees at 400 taxpayer assistance centers nationwide encountered 8.5 million taxpayers face-to-face last year. The problem: When inspector general auditors posing as taxpayers asked them to answer tax questions, the answers were right 69% of the time."

Suppose an independent commission was formed to test whether the 0.69 accuracy rate is correct or whether it is actually higher or lower. The commission has randomly selected $n = 180$ tax returns that were completed by IRS assistance employees and found that 105 of the returns were accurately completed.
a. State the appropriate null and alternative hypotheses.
b. Using an $\alpha = 0.05$ level, based on the sample data, what conclusion should be reached about the IRS rate of correct tax returns? Discuss your results.

9-35. A *Washington Post*–ABC News poll found that 72% of people are concerned about the possibility that their personal records could be stolen over the Internet. If a random sample of 300 college students at a Midwestern university were taken and 228 of them were concerned about the possibility that their personal records could be stolen over the Internet, could you conclude at the 0.025 level of significance that a higher proportion of the university's college students are concerned about Internet theft than the public at large? Report the *p*-value for this test.

9-36. Assume that the sports page of your local newspaper reported that 65% of males over the age of 17 in the United States would skip an important event such as a birthday party or an anniversary dinner to watch their favorite professional sports team play. A random sample of 676 adult males over the age of 17 in the Dallas-Fort Worth market reveals that 507 would be willing to skip an important event to watch their favorite team play. Given the results of the survey, can you conclude that the proportion of adult males who would skip an important event to watch their favorite team play is greater in the Dallas-Fort Worth area than in the nation as a whole? Conduct your test at the $\alpha = 0.01$ level of significance.

9-37. An Associated Press article written by Eileen Powell titled "Credit Card Payments Going Up" described a recent change in credit card policies. Under pressure from federal regulators, credit card issuers have started to raise the minimum payment that consumers are required to pay on outstanding credit card balances. Suppose a claim is made that more than 40% of all credit card holders pay the minimum payment. To test this claim, a random sample of payments made by credit card customers was collected. The sample contained data for 400 customers, of which 174 paid the minimum payment.
a. State the appropriate null and alternative hypotheses.
b. Based on the sample data, test the null hypothesis using an alpha level equal to 0.05. Discuss the results of the test.

9-38. CEO Chris Foreman of Pacific Theaters Exhibition Corp. is taking steps to reverse the decline in movie attendance. Moviegoers' comfort is one of the issues facing theaters. Pacific Theaters has begun offering assigned seating, no in-theater advertising, and a live announcer who introduces films and warns patrons to turn off cell phones. Despite such efforts, an Associated Press/America Online News poll of 1,000 adults discovered that 730 of those surveyed preferred seeing movies in their homes.

a. Using a significance level of 0.025, conduct a statistical procedure to determine if the Associated Press/America Online News poll indicates that more than 70% of adults prefer seeing movies in their homes. Use a *p*-value approach.

b. Express a Type II error in the context of this exercise's scenario.

9-39. The practice of "phishing," or using the Internet to pilfer personal information, has become an increasing concern, not only for individual computer users but also for online retailers and financial institutions. *The Wall Street Journal* reported 28% of people who bank online have cut back on their Internet use. The North Central Educators Credit Union instituted an extensive online security and educational program six months ago in an effort to combat phishing before the problem became extreme. The credit union's managers are certain that while Internet use may be down, the rate for their customers is much less than 28%. However, they believe that if more than 10% of their customers have cut back on their Internet banking transactions, they will be required to take more stringent action to lower this percentage.

The credit union's information technology department analyzed 200 randomly selected accounts and determined that 24 indicated they had cut back on their Internet banking transactions.

a. State the appropriate null and alternative hypotheses for this situation.

b. Using $\alpha = 0.05$ and the *p*-value approach, indicate whether the sample data support taking a more stringent action.

9-40. A large number of complaints has been received in the past six months regarding airlines losing fliers' baggage. The airlines claim the problem is nowhere near as great as the newspaper articles have indicated. In fact, one airline spokesman claimed that less than 1% of all bags fail to arrive at the destination with the passenger. To test this claim, 800 bags were randomly selected at various airports in the United States when they were checked with this airline. Of these, 6 failed to reach the destination when the passenger (owner) arrived.

a. Is this sufficient evidence to support the airline spokesman's claim? Test using a significance level of 0.05. Discuss.

b. Estimate the proportion of bags that fail to arrive at the proper destination using a technique for which 95% confidence applies.

9-41. Harris Interactive Inc., the 15th largest market research firm in the world, is a Rochester, New York–based

company. One of its surveys indicated that 56% of women have had experience with a global positioning system (GPS) device. The survey indicated that 66% of the men surveyed have used a GPS device.

a. If the survey was based on a sample size of 200 men, do these data indicate that the proportion of men is the same as the proportion of women who have had experience with a GPS device? Use a significance level of 0.05.

b. Obtain the *p*-value for the test indicated in part a.

Computer Database **Exercises**

9-42. A survey by the Pew Internet & American Life Project found that 21% of workers with an e-mail account at work say they are getting more spam than a year ago. Suppose a large multinational company, after implementing a policy to combat spam, asked 198 randomly selected employees with e-mail accounts at work whether they are receiving more spam today than they did a year ago. The results of the survey are in the file **Spam**. At the 0.025 level of significance, can the company conclude that the percentage of its employees receiving more spam than a year ago is smaller than that found by the Pew study?

9-43. A study by Fidelity Investment found that in a recent year, 40% of investors funded a Roth IRA rollover from an employer sponsored retirement account. A recent random sample of 90 households in the greater Miami area was taken, and respondents were asked whether they had ever funded a Roth IRA account with a rollover from an employer-sponsored retirement plan. The results are in the file **Miami Rollover**. Based on the sample data, can you conclude at the 0.10 level of significance that the proportion of households in the greater Miami area that have funded a Roth IRA with a rollover is different from the proportion for all households reported in the ICI study?

9-44. According to the Employee Benefit Research Institute (www.ebri.org), 34% of workers between the ages of 35 and 44 owned a 401(k)–type retirement plan in 2002. Suppose a recent survey was conducted by the Atlanta Chamber of Commerce to determine the rate of 35- to 44-year-old working adults in the Atlanta metropolitan area who owned 401(k)–type retirement plans. The results of the survey can be found in the file **Atlanta Retirement**. Based on the survey results, can the Atlanta Chamber of Commerce conclude that the participation rate for 35- to 44-year-old working adults in Atlanta is higher than the 2002 national rate? Conduct your analysis at the 0.025 level of significance.

9-45. The Electronic Controls Company (ECCO) is one of the largest makers of backup alarms in the world. Backup alarms are the safety devices that emit a high-pitched beeping sound when a truck, forklift, or other equipment is operated in reverse. ECCO is well known in the industry for its high quality and excellent customer service, but some products are returned under warranty due to quality problems. ECCO's operations manager recently stated that less than half of the warranty returns are wiring-related problems. To verify if she is correct, a company intern was asked to select a random sample of warranty returns and determine the proportion that were returned due to wiring problems. The data the intern collected are shown in the data file called **ECCO**.

a. State the appropriate null and alternative hypotheses.

b. Conduct the hypothesis test using $\alpha = 0.02$ and provide an interpretation of the result of the hypothesis test in terms of the operation manager's claim.

9-46. Cell phones are becoming an integral part of our daily lives. Commissioned by Motorola, a new behavioral study took researchers to nine cities worldwide from New York to London. Using a combination of personal interviews, field studies, and observation, the study identified a variety of behaviors that demonstrate the dramatic impact cell phones are having on the way people interact. The study found cell phones give people a newfound personal power, enabling unprecedented mobility and allowing them to conduct their business on the go. Interesting enough, gender differences can be found in phone use. Women see their cell phone as a means of expression and social communication, whereas males tend to use it as an interactive toy. A cell phone industry spokesman stated that half of all cell phones in use are registered to females.

a. State the appropriate null and alternative hypotheses for testing the industry claim.

b. Based on a random sample of cell phone owners shown in the data file called **Cell Phone Survey**, test the null hypothesis. (Use $\alpha = 0.05$.)

9-47. Joseph-Armand Bombardier in the 1930s founded the company that is now known as Seadoo in Canada. His initial invention of the snowmobile in 1937 led the way to what is now a 7,600-employee, worldwide company specializing in both snow and water sports vehicles. The company stresses high quality in both manufacturing and dealer service. Suppose that the company standard for customer satisfaction is 95% "highly satisfied." Company managers recently completed a customer survey of 700 customers from around the world. The responses to the question "What is your overall level of satisfaction with Seadoo?" are provided in the file called **Seadoo**.

a. State the appropriate null and alternative hypotheses to be tested.

b. Using an alpha level of 0.05, conduct the hypothesis test and discuss the conclusions.

END EXERCISES 9-2

9.3 Type II Errors

Sections 9.1 and 9.2 provided several examples that illustrated how hypotheses and decision rules for tests of the population mean or population proportion are formulated. In these examples, we determined the critical values by first specifying the significance level, alpha: the maximum allowable probability of committing a Type I error. As we indicated, if the cost of committing a Type I error is high, the decision maker will want to specify a small significance level.

This logic provides a basis for establishing the critical value for the hypothesis test. However, it ignores the possibility of committing a Type II error. Recall that a Type II error occurs if a false null hypothesis is "accepted." The probability of a Type II error is given by the symbol β, the Greek letter *beta*. We discussed in Section 9.1 that α and β are inversely related. That is, if we make α smaller, β will increase. However, the two are not proportional. A case in point: Cutting α in half will not necessarily double β.

Chapter Outcome 5. ⟶ **Calculating Beta**

Once α has been specified for a hypothesis test involving a particular sample size, β cannot also be specified. Rather, the β value is fixed for any specified value in that alternative hypothesis, and all the decision maker can do is calculate it. Therefore, β is not a single value; it depends on the selected value taken from the range of values in the alternative hypothesis. Because a Type II error occurs when a false null hypothesis is "accepted" (refer to Figure 9.1, "do not reject H_0" block), there is a β value for each possible population value for which the alternative hypothesis is true. To calculate beta, we must first specify a "what-if" value for a true population parameter taken from the alternative hypothesis. Then, β is computed conditional on that parameter being true. Keep in mind that β is computed before the sample is taken, so its value is not dependent on the sample outcome.

For instance, if the null hypothesis is that the mean income for a population is equal to or greater than $30,000, then β could be calculated for any value of μ less than $30,000. We would get a different β for each value of μ in that range. An application will help clarify this concept.

BUSINESS APPLICATION   **CALCULATING THE PROBABILITY OF A TYPE II ERROR**

WESTBERG PRODUCTS Westberg Products designs, manufactures, and distributes products for customers such as Lowe's and Home Depot. Westberg has developed a new, low-cost, energy-saving light bulb to last more than 700 hours on average. If a hypothesis test could confirm this, the company would use the "greater than 700 hours" statement in its advertising. The null and alternative hypotheses are

$$H_0: \mu \leq 700 \text{ hours}$$

$$H_A: \mu > 700 \text{ hours (research hypothesis)}$$

A type II error will occur if a false null hypothesis is "accepted." The null hypothesis is false for all possible values of $\mu > 700$ hours. Thus, for each of the infinite number of possibilities for $\mu > 700$, a value of β can be determined. (*Note:* σ is assumed to be a known value of 15 hours.)

Figure 9.9 shows how β is calculated if the true value of μ is 701 hours. By specifying the significance level to be 0.05 and a sample size of 100 bulbs, the chance of committing a Type II error is approximately 0.8365. This means that if the true population mean is 701 hours, there is nearly an 84% chance that the sampling plan Westberg Products is using will not reject the assumption that the mean is 700 hours or less.

Figure 9.10 shows that if the "what-if" mean value ($\mu = 704$) is farther from the hypothesized mean ($\mu = 700$), beta becomes smaller. The greater the difference between the mean specified in H_0 and the mean selected from H_A, the easier it is to tell the two apart, and the less likely we are to not reject the null hypothesis when it is actually false. Of course, the opposite is also true. As the mean selected from H_A moves increasingly closer to the mean specified in H_0, the harder it is for the hypothesis test to distinguish between the two.

FIGURE 9.9

Beta Calculation for "True"
$\mu = 701$

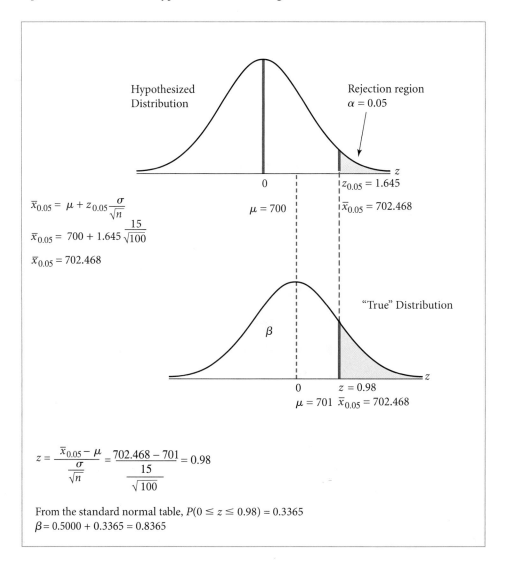

$$\bar{x}_{0.05} = \mu + z_{0.05}\frac{\sigma}{\sqrt{n}}$$

$$\bar{x}_{0.05} = 700 + 1.645\frac{15}{\sqrt{100}}$$

$$\bar{x}_{0.05} = 702.468$$

$$z = \frac{\bar{x}_{0.05} - \mu}{\frac{\sigma}{\sqrt{n}}} = \frac{702.468 - 701}{\frac{15}{\sqrt{100}}} = 0.98$$

From the standard normal table, $P(0 \leq z \leq 0.98) = 0.3365$
$\beta = 0.5000 + 0.3365 = 0.8365$

FIGURE 9.10 |

Beta Calculation for "True"
$\mu = 704$

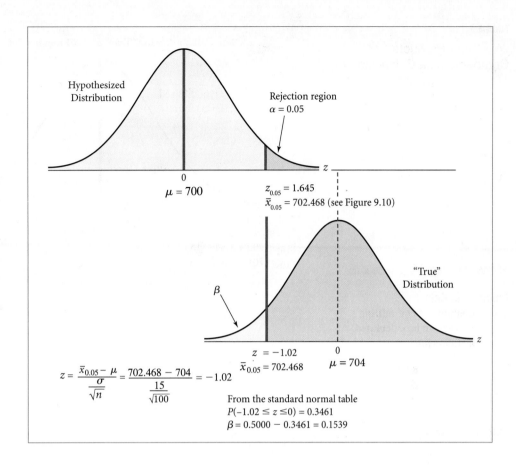

Controlling Alpha and Beta

Ideally, we want both alpha and beta to be as small as possible. Although we can set alpha at any desired level, for a specified sample size and standard deviation, the calculated value of beta depends on the population mean chosen from the alternative hypothesis and on the significance level. For a specified sample size, reducing alpha will increase beta. However, we can simultaneously control the size of both alpha and beta if we are willing to change the sample size.

Westberg Products planned to take a sample of 100 light bulbs. In Figure 9.9, we showed that beta = 0.8365 when the "true" population mean was 701 hours. This is a very large probability and would be unacceptable to the company. However, if the company is willing to incur the cost associated with a sample size of 500 bulbs, the probability of a Type II error could be reduced to 0.5596, as shown in Figure 9.11. This is a big improvement and is due to the fact that the standard error $(\sigma/\sqrt{n})$ is reduced because of the increased sample size.

EXAMPLE 9-10   **CALCULATING BETA**

Goldman Tax Software Goldman Tax Software develops software for use by individuals and small businesses to complete federal and state income tax forms. The company has claimed its customers save an average of more than $200 each by using the Goldman software. A consumer group plans to randomly sample 64 customers to test this claim. The standard deviation of the amount saved is assumed to be $100. Before testing, the consumer group is interested in knowing the probability that it will mistakenly conclude that the mean savings is less than or equal to $200 when, in fact, it does exceed $200, as the company claims. To find beta if the true population mean is $210, the company can use the following steps.

Step 1 Specify the population parameter of interest.
The consumer group is interested in the mean savings of Goldman Tax Software clients, μ.

FIGURE 9.11 |

Westberg Products Company, Beta Calculation for "True" $\mu = 701$ and $n = 500$

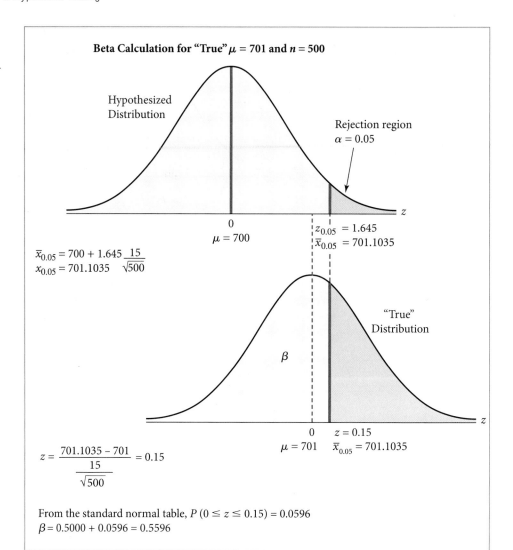

Beta Calculation for "True" $\mu = 701$ and $n = 500$

Hypothesized Distribution

Rejection region $\alpha = 0.05$

0
$\mu = 700$

$z_{0.05} = 1.645$
$\bar{x}_{0.05} = 701.1035$

$\bar{x}_{0.05} = 700 + 1.645 \dfrac{15}{\sqrt{500}}$
$x_{0.05} = 701.1035$

"True" Distribution

β

$0 \quad z = 0.15$
$\mu = 701 \quad \bar{x}_{0.05} = 701.1035$

$z = \dfrac{701.1035 - 701}{\dfrac{15}{\sqrt{500}}} = 0.15$

From the standard normal table, $P(0 \le z \le 0.15) = 0.0596$
$\beta = 0.5000 + 0.0596 = 0.5596$

How to do it (Example 9-10)

Calculating Beta

The probability of committing a Type II error can be calculated using the following steps.

1. Specify the population parameter of interest.

2. Formulate the null and alternative hypotheses.

3. Specify the significance level. (*Hint*: Draw a picture of the hypothesized sampling distribution showing the rejection region(s) and the "acceptance" region found by specifying the significance level.)

4. Determine the critical value, z_α, from the standard normal distribution.

5. Determine the critical value, $\bar{x}_\alpha = \mu + z_\alpha\sigma/\sqrt{n}$ for an upper-tail test, or $\bar{x}_\alpha = \mu - z_\alpha\sigma/\sqrt{n}$ for a lower-tail test.

6. Specify the stipulated value for μ, the "true" population mean for which you wish to compute β. (*Hint*: Draw the "true" distribution immediately below the hypothesized distribution.)

7. Compute the z-value based on the stipulated population mean as

$$z = \dfrac{\bar{x}_\alpha - \mu}{\dfrac{\sigma}{\sqrt{n}}}$$

8. Use the standard normal table to find β, the probability associated with "accepting" (not rejecting) the null hypothesis when it is false.

Step 2 Formulate the null and alternative hypotheses.
The null and alternative hypotheses are

$$H_0: \mu \le \$200$$
$$H_A: \mu > \$200 \text{ (claim)}$$

Step 3 Specify the significance level.
The one-tailed hypothesis test will be conducted using $\alpha = 0.05$.

Step 4 Determine the critical value, z_α, from the standard normal distribution.
The critical value from the standard normal is $z_\alpha = z_{0.05} = 1.645$.

Step 5 Calculate the $\bar{x}_\alpha$ critical value.

$$\bar{x}_{0.05} = \mu + z_{0.05}\dfrac{\sigma}{\sqrt{n}} = 200 + 1.645\dfrac{100}{\sqrt{64}} = 220.56$$

Thus, the null hypothesis will be rejected if $\bar{x} > 220.56$.

Step 6 Specify the stipulated value for μ.
The null hypothesis is false for all values greater than \$200. What is beta if the stipulated population mean is \$210?

Step 7   Compute the z-value based on the stipulated population mean.

The z-value based on stipulated population mean is

$$z = \frac{\overline{x}_{0.05} - \mu}{\frac{\sigma}{\sqrt{n}}} = \frac{220.56 - 210}{\frac{100}{\sqrt{64}}} = 0.84$$

Step 8   Determine beta.

From the standard normal table, the probability associated with $z = 0.84$ is 0.2995. Then $\beta = 0.5000 + 0.2995 = 0.7995$. There is a 0.7995 probability that the hypothesis test will lead the consumer agency to mistakenly believe that the mean tax savings is less than or equal to $200 when, in fact, the mean savings is $210.

>> **END EXAMPLE**

TRY PROBLEM 9-49 (pg. 373)

EXAMPLE 9-11   CALCULATING BETA FOR A TWO-TAILED TEST

Davidson Tree and Landscape Davidson Tree and Landscape provides trees to home and garden centers in the U.S. and Canada. One product is the Norway Maple. The ideal tree diameter for shipment to the nurseries is 2.25 inches. If the diameter is too large or small, it seems to affect the trees' ability to survive transport and planting. Before each large shipment is sent out, quality managers for Davidson randomly sample 20 Norway Maple trees and measure the diameter of each tree. The standard deviation is tightly controlled as well. Assume $\sigma = 0.005$ inches. Suppose that the quality manager is interested in how likely it is that if he conducts a hypothesis test, he will conclude that the mean diameter is equal to 2.25 inches when, in fact, the mean equals 2.255 inches. Thus, he wants to know the probability of a Type II error. To find beta for this test procedure under these conditions, the engineers can use the following steps:

Step 1   Specify the population parameter of interest.

The quality manager is interested in the mean diameter of Norway Maple trees, μ.

Step 2   Formulate the null and alternative hypotheses.

The null and alternative hypotheses are

$$H_0: \mu = 2.25 \text{ (status quo)}$$
$$H_A: \mu \neq 2.25$$

Step 3   Specify the significance level.

The two-tailed hypothesis test will be conducted using $\alpha = 0.05$.

Step 4   Determine the critical values, $z_{(\alpha/2)L}$ and $z_{(\alpha/2)U}$, from the standard normal distribution.

The critical value from the standard normal is $z_{(\alpha/2)L}$ and $z_{(\alpha/2)U} = \pm z_{0.025} = \pm 1.96$.

Step 5   Calculate the $\overline{x}_{(\alpha/2)L}$ and $\overline{x}_{(\alpha/2)U}$ critical values.

$$\overline{x}_{L,U} = \mu \pm z_{0.025} \frac{\sigma}{\sqrt{n}} = 2.25 \pm 1.96 \frac{0.005}{\sqrt{20}} \rightarrow \overline{x}_L = 2.2478; \overline{x}_U = 2.2522$$

Thus, the null hypothesis will be rejected if $\overline{x} < 2.2478$ or $\overline{x} > 2.2522$

Step 6   Specify the stipulated value of μ.

The stipulated value of μ is 2.255.

Step 7   Compute the z-values based on the stipulated population mean.

The z-values based on the stipulated population mean is

$$z = \frac{\overline{x}_L - \mu}{\frac{\sigma}{\sqrt{n}}} = \frac{2.2478 - 2.255}{\frac{0.005}{\sqrt{20}}} = -6.44 \quad \text{and} \quad z = \frac{\overline{x}_U - \mu}{\frac{\sigma}{\sqrt{n}}} = \frac{2.2522 - 2.255}{\frac{0.005}{\sqrt{20}}} = -2.50$$

Step 8   Determine beta and reach a conclusion.
Beta is the probability from the standard normal distribution between $z = -6.44$ and $z = -2.50$. From the standard normal table, we get

$$(0.5000 - 0.5000) + (0.5000 - 0.4938) = 0.0062$$

Thus, beta $= 0.0062$. There is a very small chance (only 0.0062) that this hypothesis test will fail to detect that the mean diameter has shifted to 2.255 inches from the desired mean of 2.25 inches. This low beta will give the quality manager confidence that his test can detect problems when they occur.

>> **END EXAMPLE**

TRY PROBLEM 9-59 (pg. 374)

As shown in Section 9.2, many business applications will involve hypotheses tests about population proportions rather than population means. Example 9-12 illustrates the steps needed to compute the beta for a hypothesis test involving proportions.

EXAMPLE 9-12   CALCULATING BETA FOR A TEST OF A POPULATION PROPORTION

The National Federation of Independent Business The National Federation of Independent Business (NFIB) has offices in Washington, D.C., and all 50 state capitals. NFIB is the nation's largest small-business lobbying group. Its research foundation provides policymakers, small-business owners, and other interested parties with empirically based information on small businesses. NFIB often initiates surveys to provide this information. A speech by a senior administration official claimed that at least 30% of all small businesses were owned or operated by women. NFIB internal analyses had the number at closer to 25%. As a result, the NFIB analysts planned to conduct a test to determine if the percentage of small businesses owned by women was less than 30%. Additionally, they were quite interested in determining the probability (beta) of "accepting" the claim ($\geq 30\%$) of the senior administration official if in fact the true percentage was 25%. A simple random sample of 500 small businesses will be selected.

Step 1   Specify the population parameter of interest.
NFIB is interested in the proportion of female-owned small businesses, p.

Step 2   Formulate the null and alternative hypotheses.

$$H_0: p \geq 0.30 \, (\text{claim})$$
$$H_A: p < 0.30$$

Step 3   Specify the significance level.
The one-tailed hypothesis test will be conducted using $\alpha = 0.025$.

Step 4   Determine the critical value, z_α, from the standard normal distribution.
The critical value from the standard normal is $z_\alpha = z_{0.025} = -1.96$.

Step 5   Calculate the $\bar{p}_\alpha$ critical value.

$$\bar{p}_{0.025} = p - z_{0.025}\sqrt{\frac{p(1-p)}{n}} = 0.30 - 1.96\sqrt{\frac{0.30(1-0.30)}{500}} = 0.2598$$

Therefore, the null hypothesis will be rejected if $\bar{p} < 0.2598$.

Step 6   Specify the stipulated value for the "true" p.
The stipulated value is 0.25.

Step 7   Compute the z-value based on the stipulated population proportion.
The z-value is

$$z = \frac{\bar{p}_\alpha - p}{\sqrt{\frac{p(1-p)}{n}}} = \frac{0.2598 - 0.25}{\sqrt{\frac{0.25(1-0.25)}{500}}} = 0.51$$

Step 8 Determine beta.

From the standard normal table, the probability associated with $z = 0.51$ is 0.1950. Then $\beta = 0.5000 - 0.1950 = 0.3050$. Thus, there is a 0.3050 chance that the hypothesis test will "accept" the null hypothesis that the percentage of women-owned or operated small businesses is $\geq 30\%$ if in fact the true percentage is only 25%. The NFIB may wish to increase the sample size to improve beta.

>> **END EXAMPLE**

TRY PROBLEM 9-57 (pg. 373)

As you now know, hypothesis tests are subject to error. The two potential statistical errors are

Type I (rejecting a true null hypothesis)

Type II (failing to reject or "accepting" a false null hypothesis)

In most business applications, there are adverse consequences associated with each type of error. In some cases, the errors can mean dollar costs to a company. For instance, suppose a health insurance company is planning to set its premium rates based on a hypothesized mean annual claims amount per participant as follows:

$$H_0: \mu \leq \$1,700$$
$$H_A: \mu > \$1,700$$

If the company tests the hypothesis and "accepts" the null, it will institute the planned premium rate structure. However, if a Type II error is committed, the actual average claim will exceed $1,700, and the company will incur unexpected payouts and suffer reduced profits. On the other hand, if the company rejects the null hypothesis, it will probably increase its premium rates. But if a Type I error is committed, there would be no justification for the rate increase, and the company may not be competitive in the marketplace and could lose customers.

In other cases, the costs associated with either a Type I or a Type II error may be even more serious. If a drug company's hypothesis tests for a new drug incorrectly conclude that the drug is safe when in fact it is not (Type I error), the company's customers may become ill or even die as a result. You might refer to recent reports dealing with pain medications such as Vicodin. On the other hand, a Type II error would mean that a potentially useful and safe drug would most likely not be made available to people who need it if the hypothesis tests incorrectly determined that the drug was not safe.

In the U.S. legal system where a defendant is hypothesized to be innocent, a Type I error by a jury would result in a conviction of an innocent person. DNA evidence has recently resulted in a number of convicted people being set free. A case in point is Hubert Geralds, who was convicted of killing Rhonda King in 1994 in the state of Illinois. On the other hand, Type II errors in our court system result in guilty people being set free to potentially commit other crimes.

The bottom line is that as a decision maker using hypothesis testing, you need to be aware of the potential costs associated with both Type I and Type II statistical errors and conduct your tests accordingly.

Power of the Test

In the previous examples, we have been concerned about the chance of making a Type II error. We would like beta to be as small as possible. If the null hypothesis is false, we want to reject it. Another way to look at this is that we would like the hypothesis test to have a high probability of rejecting a false null hypothesis. This concept is expressed by what is called the **power** of the test. When the alternative hypothesis is true, the power of the test is computed using Equation 9.5.

Power

The probability that the hypothesis test will correctly reject the null hypothesis when the null hypothesis is false.

Power

$$\text{Power} = 1 - \beta \qquad \textbf{(9.5)}$$

Refer again to the business application involving the Westberg Products Company. Beta calculations were presented in Figures 9.9, 9.10, and 9.11. For example, in Figure 9.9, the company was interested in the probability of a Type II error if the "true" population mean was 701 hours instead of the hypothesized mean of 700 hours. This probability, called beta, was shown to be 0.8365. Then for this same test,

$$\text{Power} = 1 - \beta$$

$$\text{Power} = 1 - 0.8365 = 0.1635$$

Thus, in this situation, there is only a 0.1635 chance that the hypothesis test will correctly reject the null hypothesis that the mean is 700 or fewer hours when in fact it really is 701 hours.

In Figure 9.10, when a "true" mean of 704 hours was considered, the value of beta dropped to 0.1539. Likewise, power is increased:

$$\text{Power} = 1 - 0.1539 = 0.8461$$

So the probability of correctly rejecting the null hypothesis increases to 0.8461 when the "true" mean is 704 hours.

We also saw in Figure 9.11 that an increase in sample size resulted in a decreased beta value. For a "true" mean of 701 but with a sample size increase from 100 to 500, the value of beta dropped from 0.8365 to 0.5596. That means that power is increased from 0.1635 to 0.4404 due to the increased size of the sample.

A graph called a **power curve** can be created to show the power of a hypothesis test for various levels of the "true" population parameter. Figure 9.12 shows the power curve for the Westberg Products Company application for a sample size of $n = 100$.

Power Curve

A graph showing the probability that the hypothesis test will correctly reject a false null hypothesis for a range of possible "true" values for the population parameter.

FIGURE 9.12

Westberg Products Company—Power Curve

$H_0: \mu \le 700$
$H_A: \mu > 700$
$\alpha = 0.05$
$\bar{x}_{0.05} = 702.468$

"True" μ	$z = \dfrac{702.468 - \mu}{\frac{15}{\sqrt{100}}}$	β	Power $(1-\beta)$
700.5	1.31	0.9049	0.0951
701	0.98	0.8365	0.1635
702	0.31	0.6217	0.3783
703	−0.36	0.3594	0.6406
704	−1.02	0.1539	0.8461
705	−1.69	0.0455	0.9545
706	−2.36	0.0091	0.9909

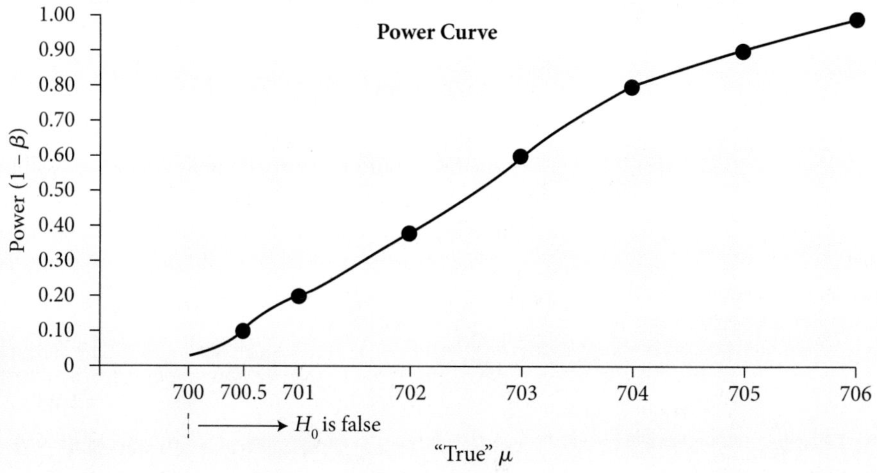

MyStatLab

9-3: Exercises

Skill Development

9-48. You are given the following null and alternative hypotheses:

$$H_0: \mu = 200$$
$$H_A: \mu \neq 200$$
$$\alpha = 0.10$$

Calculate the probability of committing a Type II error when the population mean is 197, the sample size is 36, and the population standard deviation is known to be 24.

9-49. You are given the following null and alternative hypotheses:

$$H_0: \mu = 1.20$$
$$H_A: \mu \neq 1.20$$
$$\alpha = 0.10$$

a. If the true population mean is 1.25, determine the value of beta. Assume the population standard deviation is known to be 0.50 and the sample size is 60.

b. Referring to part a, calculate the power of the test.

c. Referring to parts a and b, what could be done to increase power and reduce beta when the true population mean is 1.25? Discuss.

d. Indicate clearly the decision rule that would be used to test the null hypothesis, and determine what decision should be made if the sample mean were 1.23.

9-50. You are given the following null and alternative hypotheses:

$$H_0: \mu \geq 4,350$$
$$H_A: \mu < 4,350$$
$$\alpha = 0.05$$

a. If the true population mean is 4,345, determine the value of beta. Assume the population standard deviation is known to be 200 and the sample size is 100.

b. Referring to part a, calculate the power of the test.

c. Referring to parts a and b, what could be done to increase power and reduce beta when the true population mean is 4,345? Discuss.

d. Indicate clearly the decision rule that would be used to test the null hypothesis, and determine what decision should be made if the sample mean were 4,337.50.

9-51. You are given the following null and alternative hypotheses:

$$H_0: \mu \leq 500$$
$$H_A: \mu > 500$$
$$\alpha = 0.01$$

Calculate the probability of committing a Type II error when the population mean is 505, the sample size is 64, and the population standard deviation is known to be 36.

9-52. Consider the following hypotheses:

$$H_0: \mu \geq 103$$
$$H_A: \mu < 103$$

A sample of size 20 is to be taken from a population with a mean of 100 and a standard deviation of 4. Determine the probability of committing a Type II error for each of the following significance levels:

a. $\alpha = 0.01$

b. $\alpha = 0.025$

c. $\alpha = 0.05$

9-53. Solve for beta when the "true" population mean is 103 and the following information is given:

$$H_0: \mu \leq 100$$
$$H_A: \mu > 100$$
$$\alpha = 0.05$$
$$\sigma = 10$$
$$n = 49$$

9-54. For each of the following situations, indicate what the general impact on the Type II error probability will be:

a. The alpha level is increased.

b. The "true" population mean is moved farther from the hypothesized population mean.

c. The alpha level is decreased.

d. The sample size is increased.

9-55. Consider the following hypotheses:

$$H_0: \mu = 30$$
$$H_A: \mu \neq 30$$

A sample of size 50 is to be taken from a population with a standard deviation of 13. The hypothesis test is to be conducted using a significance level of 0.05. Determine the probability of committing a Type II error when

a. $\mu = 22$

b. $\mu = 25$

c. $\mu = 29$

9-56. Consider the following hypotheses:

$$H_0: \mu \leq 201$$
$$H_A: \mu > 201$$

A sample is to be taken from a population with a mean of 203 and a standard deviation of 3. The hypothesis test is to be conducted using a significance level of 0.05. Determine the probability of committing a Type II error when

a. $n = 10$

b. $n = 20$

c. $n = 50$

9-57. The following hypotheses are to be tested:

$$H_0: p \leq 0.65$$
$$H_A: p > 0.65$$

A random sample of 500 is taken. Using each set of information following, compute the power of the test.

a. $\alpha = 0.01$, true $p = 0.68$

b. $\alpha = 0.025$, true $p = 0.67$

c. $\alpha = 0.05$, true $p = 0.66$

9-58. The following hypotheses are to be tested:
$$H_O: p \geq 0.35$$
$$H_A: p < 0.35$$
A random sample of 400 is taken. Using each set of information following, compute the power of the test.
   a. $\alpha = 0.01$, true $p = 0.32$
   b. $\alpha = 0.025$, true $p = 0.33$
   c. $\alpha = 0.05$, true $p = 0.34$

Business Applications

9-59. According to data from the Environmental Protection Agency, the average daily water consumption for a household of four people in the United States is approximately at least 243 gallons. Suppose a state agency plans to test this claim using an alpha level equal to 0.05 and a random sample of 100 households with four people.
   a. State the appropriate null and alternative hypotheses.
   b. Calculate the probability of committing a Type II error if the true population mean is 230 gallons. Assume that the population standard deviation is known to be 40 gallons.

9-60. Swift is the holding company for Swift Transportation Co., Inc., a truckload carrier headquartered in Phoenix, Arizona. Swift operates the largest truckload fleet in the United States. Before Swift switched to its current computer-based billing system, the average payment time from customers was approximately 40 days. Suppose before purchasing the present billing system, it performed a test by examining a random sample of 24 invoices to see if the system would reduce the average billing time. The sample indicates that the average payment time is 38.7 days.
   a. The company that created the billing system indicates that the system would reduce the average billing time to less than 40 days. Conduct a hypothesis test to determine if the new computer-based billing system would reduce the average billing time to less than 40 days. Assume the standard deviation is known to be 6 days. Use a significance level of 0.025.
   b. If the billing system actually reduced the average billing time to 36 days, determine the probability that a wrong decision was made in part a.

9-61. Waiters at Finegold's Restaurant and Lounge earn most of their income from tips. Each waiter is required to "tip-out" a portion of tips to the table bussers and hostesses. The manager has based the "tip-out" rate on the assumption that the mean tip is at least 15% of the customer bill. To make sure that this is the correct assumption, he has decided to conduct a test by randomly sampling 60 bills and recording the actual tips.
   a. State the appropriate null and alternative hypotheses.
   b. Calculate the probability of a Type II error if the true mean is 14%. Assume that the population standard deviation is known to be 2% and that a significance level equal to 0.01 will be used to conduct the hypothesis test.

9-62. Nationwide Mutual Insurance, based in Columbus, Ohio, is one of the largest diversified insurance and financial services organizations in the world, with more than $140 billion in assets. Nationwide ranked 124th on the Fortune 500 list in 2010. The company provides a full range of insurance and financial services. In a recent news release, Nationwide reported the results of a new survey of 1,097 identity theft victims. The survey shows victims spend an average of 81 hours trying to resolve their cases. If the true average time spent was 81 hours, determine the probability that a test of hypothesis designed to test that the average was less than 85 hours would select the research hypothesis. Use $\alpha = 0.05$ and a standard deviation of 50.

9-63. According to CNN, the average starting salary for accounting graduates was $47,413. Suppose that the American Society for Certified Public Accountants planned to test this claim by randomly sampling 200 accountants who recently graduated.
   a. State the appropriate null and alternative hypotheses.
   b. Compute the power of the hypothesis test to reject the null hypothesis if the true average starting salary is only $47,000. Assume that the population standard deviation is known to be $4,600 and the test is to be conducted using an alpha level equal to 0.01.

9-64. According to the Internet source Smartbrief.com, per-capita U.S. beer consumption increased in 2008 after several years of decline. Current per-capita consumption is 22 gallons per year. A survey is designed to determine if the per-capita consumption has changed in the current year. A hypothesis test is to be conducted using a sample size of 1,500, a significance level of 0.01, and a standard deviation of 40. Determine the probability that the test will be able to correctly detect that the per-capita consumption has changed if it has declined by 10%.

9-65. Runzheimer International, a management consulting firm specializing in transportation reimbursement, released the results of a survey on July 28, 2005. It indicated that it costs more to own a car in Detroit, an amazing $11,844 a year for a mid-sized sedan, than in any other city in the country. The survey revealed that insurance, at $5,162 annually for liability, collision, and comprehensive coverage, is the biggest single reason that maintaining a car in the Motor City is so expensive. A sample size of 100 car owners in Los Angeles was used to determine if the cost of owning a car was more than 10% less than in Detroit. A hypothesis test with a significance level of 0.01 and a standard deviation of $750 is used. Determine the probability that the test will conclude the cost of owning a car in Los Angeles is not more than 10% less than in Detroit when in fact the average cost is $10,361.

9-66. The union negotiations between labor and management at the Stone Container paper mill in Minnesota hit a snag when management asked labor to take a cut in health insurance coverage. As part of its justification, management claimed that the average amount of insurance claims filed by union employees did not exceed $250 per employee. The union's chief negotiator requested that a sample of 100 employees' records be selected and that this claim be tested statistically. The claim would be accepted if the sample data did not strongly suggest otherwise. The significance level for the test was set at 0.10.

a. State the null and alternative hypotheses.

b. Before the sample was selected, the negotiator was interested in knowing the power of the test if the mean amount of insurance claims was $260. (Assume the standard deviation in claims is $70.00, as determined in a similar study at another plant location.) Calculate this probability for the negotiator.

c. Referring to part b, how would the power of the test change if $\alpha = 0.05$ is used?

d. Suppose alpha is left at 0.10, but the standard deviation of the population is $50.00 rather than $70.00. What will be the power of the test? State the generalization that explains the relationship between the answers to part b and d.

e. Referring to part d, based on the probability computed, if you were the negotiator, would you be satisfied with the sampling plan in this situation? Explain why or why not. What steps could be taken to improve the sampling plan?

Computer Database **Exercises**

9-67. *USA Today* reports (Gary Stoller, "Hotel Bill Mistakes Mean Many Pay Too Much") that George Hansen, CEO of Wichita-based Corporate Lodging

Consultants, conducted a recent review of hotel bills over a 12-month period. The review indicated that, on average, errors in hotel bills resulted in overpayment of $11.35 per night. To determine if such mistakes are being made at a major hotel chain, the CEO might direct a survey yielding the following data:

9.99	9.87	11.53	12.40	12.36	11.68	12.52	9.34	13.13	10.78
9.76	10.88	10.61	10.29	10.23	9.29	8.82	8.70	8.22	11.01
12.40	9.55	11.30	10.21	8.19	10.56	8.49	7.99	8.03	10.53

The file **OverPay** contains these data.

a. Conduct a hypothesis test with $\alpha = 0.05$ to determine if the average overpayment is smaller than that indicated by Corporate Lodging Consultants.

b. If the actual average overpayment at the hotel chain was $11 with an actual standard deviation of $1.50, determine the probability that the hypothesis test would correctly indicate that the actual average is less than $11.35.

9-68. In an article in *Business Week* ("Living on the Edge at American Apparel"), Dov Chaney, the CEO of American Apparel, indicated that the apparel store industry's average sales were $1,800/7 (= $257.14) a square foot. A hypothesis test was requested to determine if the data supported the statement made by the American Apparel CEO using an $\alpha = 0.05$ and a sample size of 41. Produce the probability that the data will indicate that American Apparel stores produce an average of seven times the apparel industry average when in fact they only produce an average six times the apparel industry average with a standard deviation of 100. The file called **Apparel** contains data for a random sample of several competitors' sales per square foot. Use $\alpha = 0.05$.

END EXERCISES 9-3

Visual Summary

Chapter 9: Hypothesis testing is a major part of business statistics. Statistical hypothesis testing provides managers with a structured analytical method for making decisions where a claim about a population parameter is tested using a sample statistic in a way that incorporates the potential for sampling error. By providing a structured approach, statistical hypothesis testing allows decision makers to identify and control the level of uncertainty associated with making decisions about a population based on a sample.

9.1 Hypothesis Tests for Means (pg. 337–358)

Summary

In hypothesis testing, two hypotheses are formulated: the **null hypothesis** and the **alternative hypothesis**. The **null hypothesis** is a statement about the population parameter which will be rejected only if the sample data provide substantial contradictory evidence. The null hypothesis always contains an equality sign. The **alternative hypothesis** is a statement that contains all population values not included in the null hypothesis. If the null hypothesis is rejected, then the alternative hypothesis is deemed to be true. It is important to specify the null and alternative hypotheses correctly so that the results obtained from the test are not misleading.

Because of sampling error, two possible errors can occur when a hypothesis is tested: **Type I** and **Type II errors**. A **Type I Error** occurs when the null hypothesis is rejected, when, in fact, it is true. The maximum allowable probability of committing a Type I statistical error is called the **significance level**. The significance level is specified by the decision maker conducting the test. **A Type II Error** occurs when the decision maker fails to reject the null hypothesis when it is, in fact, false. Controlling for this type of error is more difficult than controlling for the probability of committing a Type I error. Once the null and alternative hypotheses have been stated and the significance level specified, the decision maker must then determine the **critical value**. The **critical value** is the value corresponding to a significance level that determines those test statistics that lead to rejecting the null hypothesis and those that lead to not rejecting the null hypothesis. A **test statistic** is then calculated from the sample data and compared to the critical value. A decision regarding whether to reject or to not reject the null hypothesis is then made.

In many case, especially where hypothesis testing is conducted using a computer, a **p-value** is often used to test hypotheses. The **p-value** is the probability (assuming that the null hypothesis is true) of obtaining a test statistic at least as extreme as the test statistic calculated from the sample. If the p-value is smaller than the significance level, then the null hypothesis is rejected.

Hypothesis tests may be either **one-tailed** or **two-tailed**. A **one-tailed test** is a hypothesis test in which the entire rejection region is located in one tail of the sampling distribution. A **two-tailed test** is a hypothesis test in which the entire rejection region is divided evenly into the two tails of the sampling distribution.

Outcome 1. Formulate the null and alternative hypotheses for applications involving a single population mean or proportion.

Outcome 2. Know what Type I and Type II errors are.

Outcome 3. Correctly formulate a decision rule for testing a null hypothesis.

Outcome 4. Know how to use the test statistic, critical value, and p-value approaches to test the null hypothesis

9.2 Hypothesis Tests for Proportions (pg. 358–365)

Summary

Hypotheses tests for a single population proportion follow the same steps as hypotheses tests for a single population mean. Those steps are:

1. State the null and alternative hypotheses in terms of the population parameter, now **p** instead of μ.
2. The null hypothesis is a statement concerning the parameter that includes the equality sign.
3. The significance level specified by the decision maker determines the size of the rejection region.
4. The test can be a one- or two-tailed test, depending on how the alternative hypothesis is formulated.

9.3 Type II Errors (pg. 365–375)

Summary

A Type II error occurs when a false null hypothesis is "accepted." The probability of committing a Type II error is denoted by β. Unfortunately, once the significance level for a hypothesis test has been specified, β cannot also be specified. Rather, β is a fixed value and all the decision maker can do is calculate it. However, β is not a single value. Because a Type II error occurs when a false null hypothesis is "accepted," there is a β value for each possible population value for which the null hypothesis is false. To calculate β, the decision maker must first specify a "what-if" value for the true population parameter. Then, β is computed before the sample is taken, so its value is not dependent on the sample outcome. The size of both α and β can be simultaneously controlled if the decision maker is willing to increase the sample size.

The probability that the hypothesis test will correctly reject the null hypothesis when the null hypothesis is false is referred to as the **power** of the test. The power of the test is computed as 1-β. A **power curve** is a graph showing the probability that the hypothesis test will correctly reject a false null hypothesis for a range of possible "true" values for the population parameter.

Outcome 5. Compute the probability of a Type II error.

Conclusion

Many decision-making applications require that a hypothesis test of a single population parameter be conducted. This chapter discusses how to conduct hypothesis tests of a single population mean and a single population proportion. The chapter has emphasized the importance of recognizing that when a hypothesis is tested, an error might occur. Statistical hypothesis testing provides managers with a structured analytical method for making decisions where a claim about a population parameter is tested using a sample statistic in a way that incorporates the potential for sampling error. **Figure 9.13** provides a flowchart for deciding which hypothesis testing procedure to use.

FIGURE 9.13 |

Deciding Which Hypothesis
Testing Procedure to Use

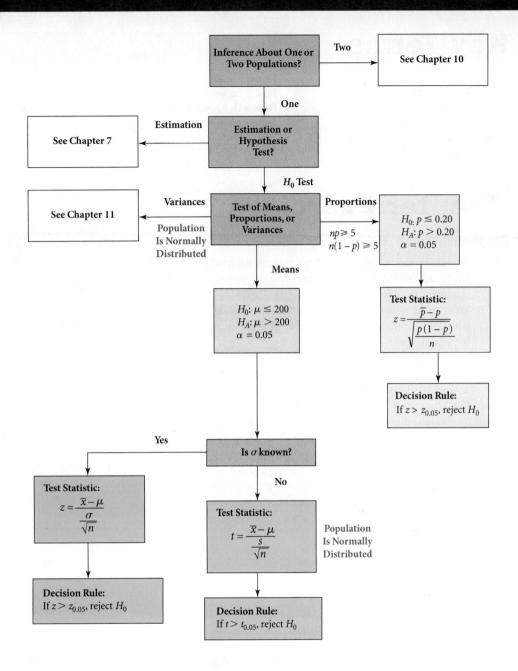

Equations

(9.1) $\bar{x}_\alpha$ for Hypothesis Tests, σ Known pg. 343

$$\bar{x}_\alpha = \mu + z_\alpha \frac{\sigma}{\sqrt{n}}$$

(9.2) z-Test Statistic for Hypothesis Tests for μ, σ Known pg. 344

$$z = \frac{\bar{x} - \mu}{\frac{\sigma}{\sqrt{n}}}$$

(9.3) t-Test Statistic for Hypothesis Tests for μ, σ Unknown pg. 351

$$t = \frac{\bar{x} - \mu}{\frac{s}{\sqrt{n}}}$$

(9.4) z-Test Statistic for Proportions pg. 360

$$z = \frac{\bar{p} - p}{\sqrt{\frac{p(1 - p)}{n}}}$$

(9.5) Power pg. 371

$$\text{Power} = 1 - \beta$$

Key Terms

Alternative hypothesis pg. 337
Critical value pg. 342
Null hypothesis pg. 337
One-tailed test pg. 348
p-value pg. 347

Power pg. 371
Power curve pg. 372
Research hypothesis pg. 338
Significance level pg. 342
Test statistic pg. 344

Two-tailed test pg. 348
Type I error pg. 340
Type II error pg. 340

Chapter Exercises   MyStatLab

Conceptual Questions

9-69. What is meant by the term *critical value* in a hypothesis-testing situation? Illustrate what you mean with a business example.

9-70. Discuss the issues a decision maker should consider when determining the significance level to use in a hypothesis test.

9-71. Discuss the two types of statistical errors that can occur when a hypothesis is tested. Illustrate what you mean by using a business example for each.

9-72. Discuss why it is necessary to use an estimate of the standard error for a confidence interval and not for a hypothesis test concerning a population proportion.

9-73. Examine the test statistic used in testing a population proportion. Why is it impossible to test the hypothesis that the population proportion equals zero using such a test statistic? Try to determine a way that such a test could be conducted.

9-74. Recall that the power of the test is the probability the null hypothesis is rejected when H_0 is false. Explain whether power is definable if the given parameter is the value specified in the null hypothesis.

9-75. What is the maximum probability of committing a Type I error called? How is this probability determined? Discuss.

9-76. In a hypothesis test, indicate the type of statistical error that can be made if
a. The null hypothesis is rejected.
b. The null hypothesis is not rejected.
c. The null hypothesis is true.
d. The null hypothesis is not true.

9-77. While conducting a hypothesis test, indicate the effect on
a. β when α is decreased while the sample size remains constant
b. β when α is held constant and the sample size is increased
c. the power when α is held constant and the sample size is increased
d. the power when α is decreased and the sample size is held constant

9-78. The Oasis Chemical Company develops and manufactures pharmaceutical drugs for distribution and sale in the United States. The pharmaceutical business can be very lucrative when useful and safe drugs are introduced into the market. Whenever the Oasis research lab considers putting a drug into production, the company must actually establish the following sets of null and alternative hypotheses:

Set 1	Set 2
H_0: The drug is not safe.	H_0: The drug is not effective.
H_A: The drug is safe.	H_A: The drug is effective.

Take each set of hypotheses separately.
a. Discuss the considerations that should be made in establishing alpha and beta.
b. For each set of hypotheses, describe what circumstances would suggest that a Type I error would be of more concern.
c. For each set of hypotheses, describe what circumstances would suggest that a Type II error would be of more concern.

9-79. For each of the following scenarios, indicate which test statistic would be used or which test could not be conducted using the materials from this chapter:
a. testing a mean when σ is known and the population sampled from has a normal distribution
b. testing a mean when σ is unknown and the population sampled from has a normal distribution
c. testing a proportion in which $np = 12$ and $n(1 - p) = 4$
d. Testing a mean when s is obtained from a small sample and the population sampled from has a skewed distribution

Business Applications

9-80. Fairfield Automotive is the local dealership selling Honda automobiles. It recently stated in an advertisement that Honda owners average more than 85,000 miles before trading in or selling their Hondas. To test this, an independent agency selected a simple random sample of 80 Honda owners who have either traded or sold their Hondas and determined the number of miles on the car when the owner parted with the car. It plans to test Fairfield's claim at the $\alpha = 0.05$ level.

a. State the appropriate null and alternative hypotheses.

b. If the sample mean is 86,200 miles and the sample standard deviation is 12,000 miles, what conclusion should be reached about the claim?

9-81. Sanchez Electronics sells electronic components for car stereos. It claims that the average life of a component exceeds 4,000 hours. To test this claim, it has selected a random sample of $n = 12$ of the components and traced the life between installation and failure. The following data were obtained:

| 1,973 | 4,838 | 3,805 | 4,494 | 4,738 | 5,249 |
| 4,459 | 4,098 | 4,722 | 5,894 | 3,322 | 4,800 |

a. State the appropriate null and alternative hypotheses.

b. Assuming that the test is to be conducted using a 0.05 level of significance, what conclusion should be reached based on these sample data? Be sure to examine the required normality assumption.

9-82. The Utah State Tax Commission attempts to set up payroll tax–withholding tables such that by the end of the year, an employee's income tax withholding is about $100 below his actual income tax owed to the state. The commission director claims that when all the Utah tax returns are in, the average additional payment will be less than $100.

A random sample of 50 accounts revealed an average additional payment of $114 with a sample standard deviation of $50.

a. Testing at a significance level of 0.10, do the sample data refute the director's claim?

b. Determine the largest sample mean (with the same sample size and standard deviation) that would fail to refute the director's claim.

9-83. Technological changes in golf equipment have meant people, in particular professional golfers, are able to hit golf balls much farther. *Golf Digest* reported on a survey conducted involving 300 golfers in which the respondents were asked their views about the impact of new technologies on the game of golf. Before the study, a group of United States Golf Association (USGA) officials believed that less than 50% of golfers thought professional golfers should have different equipment rules than amateurs. The survey conducted by *Golf Digest* found 67% did not favor different equipment rules.

a. If the claim made by the USGA is to be tested, what should the null and alternative hypotheses be?

b. Based on the sample data, and an alpha level equal to 0.05, use the *p*-value approach to conduct the hypothesis test.

9-84. *USA Today* reports (Darryl Haralson, "It's All about Overstock.com") on an ad for Overstock.com, which sells discounted merchandise on its Web site. To evaluate the effectiveness of the ads, Harris Interactive conducted a nationwide poll of 883 adults. Of the 883 adults, 168 thought the ads were very effective. This was compared to the Harris Ad Track average of 21%.

a. Determine if the sample size is large enough for the test to warrant approximating the sample proportion's distribution with a normal distribution.

b. Does the Harris poll provide evidence to contend that the proportion of adults who find Overstock.com's ads to be very effective is smaller than the Harris Ad Track average? Use a significance level of 0.05.

9-85. The college of business at a state university has a computer literacy requirement for all graduates. Students must show proficiency with a computer spreadsheet software package and with a word-processing software package. To assess whether students are computer literate, a test is given at the end of each semester. The test is designed so that at least 70% of all students who have taken a special microcomputer course will pass. The college does not wish to declare that fewer than 70% of the students pass the test unless there is strong sample evidence to indicate this. Suppose that, in a random sample of 100 students who have recently finished the microcomputer course, 63 pass the proficiency test.

a. Using a significance level of 0.05, what conclusions should the administrators make regarding the difficulty of the test?

b. Describe a Type II error in the context of this problem.

9-86. The makers of High Life Dog Food have an automated filling machine that can be set at any targeted fill level between 10 and 40 pounds. At the end of every shift (eight hours), 16 bags are selected at random and the mean and standard deviation of the sample are computed. Based on these sample results, the production control manager determines whether the filling machine needs to be readjusted or whether it remains all right to operate. Previous data suggest the fill level has a normal distribution with a standard deviation of 0.65 pounds. Use $\alpha = 0.05$. At the end of a run of 20-pound bags, a sample of 16 bags was taken and tested using a two-sided test to determine if the mean fill level was equal to 20 pounds.

a. Calculate the probability that the test procedure will detect that the average fill level is not equal to 20 pounds when in fact it equals 20.5 pounds.

b. On the basis of your calculation in part a, would you suggest a change in the test procedure? Explain what change you would make and the reasons you would make this change.

9-87. ACNielsen is a New York–based leading global provider of marketing research information services, analytical systems and tools, and professional client service. A recent issue of its magazine addressed, in part, consumers' attitudes to self-checkout lines. Of the

17,346 EDLP (everyday low price) shoppers, only 3,470 indicated an interest in this service. If Walmart's CEO had decided not to install self-checkout lines unless consumer interest was more than 17.5%, would he order the installation?

a. Determine if the sample size for the test indicated is large enough to warrant approximating the sample proportion's distribution with a normal distribution.

b. Use a significance level of 0.05 and the *p*-value approach to answer the question put forward above.

9-88. The Sledge Tire and Rubber Company plans to warranty its new mountain bike tire for 12 months. However, before it does this, the company wants to be sure that the mean lifetime of the tires is at least 18 months under normal operations. It will put the warranty in place unless the sample data strongly suggest that the mean lifetime of the tires is less than 18 months. The company plans to test this statistically using a random sample of tires. The test will be conducted using an alpha level of 0.03.

a. If the population mean is actually 16.5 months, determine the probability the hypothesis test will lead to incorrectly failing to reject the null hypothesis. Assume that the population standard deviation is known to be 2.4 months and the sample size is 60.

b. If the population mean is actually 17.3, calculate the chance of committing a Type II error. This is a specific example of a generalization relating the probability of committing a Type II error and the parameter being tested. State this generalization.

c. Without calculating the probability, state whether the probability of a Type II error would be larger or smaller than that calculated in part b if you were to calculate it for a hypothesized mean of 15 months. Justify your answer.

d. Suppose the company decides to increase the sample size from 60 to 100 tires. What can you expect to happen to the probabilities calculated in part a?

9-89. According to Freddie Mac, 74% of borrowers who refinanced their loans maintained the same loan value. If a sample size of 2,500 was used to obtain this information,

a. Determine if the sample size for the test is large enough to warrant approximating the sample proportion's distribution with a normal distribution.

b. Use this information to determine if less than 75% of new mortgages had a refinance loan amount equal to the same value as their original loan. Use a test statistic approach with $\alpha = 0.025$.

9-90. The personnel manager for a large airline has claimed that, on average, workers are asked to work no more than 3 hours overtime per week. Past studies show the standard deviation in overtime hours per worker to be 1.2 hours.

Suppose the union negotiators wish to test this claim by sampling payroll records for 250 employees. They believe that the personnel manager's claim is untrue but want to base their conclusion on the sample results.

a. State the research, null, and alternative hypotheses and discuss the meaning of Type I and Type II errors in the context of this case.

b. Establish the appropriate decision rule if the union wishes to have no more than a 0.01 chance of a Type I error.

c. The payroll records produced a sample mean of 3.15 hours. Do the union negotiators have a basis for a grievance against the airline? Support your answer with a relevant statistical procedure.

9-91. The Lazer Company has a contract to produce a part for Boeing Corporation that must have an average diameter of 6 inches and a standard deviation of 0.10 inch. The Lazer Company has developed the process that will meet the specifications with respect to the standard deviation, but it is still trying to meet the mean specifications. A test run (considered a random sample) of parts was produced, and the company wishes to determine whether this latest process that produced the sample will produce parts meeting the requirement of an average diameter equal to 6 inches.

a. Specify the appropriate research, null, and alternative hypotheses.

b. Develop the decision rule assuming that the sample size is 200 parts and the significance level is 0.01.

c. What should the Lazer Company conclude if the sample mean diameter for the 200 parts is 6.03 inches? Discuss.

9-92. Cisco Systems, Inc., is the leading maker of networking gear that connects computers to the Internet. Company managers are concerned with the productivity of their workers as well as their job satisfaction. Kate D'Camp is the senior vice president for human resources. She often initiates surveys concerning Cisco's personnel. A typical survey asked, "Do you feel it's OK for your company to monitor your Internet use?" Of the 405 respondents, 223 chose "Only after informing me." Cisco would consider monitoring if more than 50% of its workers wouldn't mind if informed beforehand that the company was going to monitor their Internet usage.

a. D'Camp may have read the *USA Today* issue that indicated 55% of American workers wouldn't object after being informed. So she might desire that the test indicate with a high probability that more than 50% of Cisco workers wouldn't object when in fact her workers reflect the opinion of all American workers. Calculate the probability that this would be the case. (*Hint*: Review the procedure concerning the sample mean and perform the analogous procedure for a proportion.)

b. Conduct the procedure to determine if the proportion of workers who wouldn't object to the company monitoring their Internet use after they were informed is more than 50%. Use a significance level of 0.05.

9-93. Many companies have moved employee retirement plans to ones based on 401(k) savings. In fact, most large mutual fund companies, like Vanguard, offer 401(k) options.

According to *US News and World Report,* the amount in an average plan depends not only on the age of the participant but also on the person's salary range. For someone in his or her 50s making between $60,000 and $80,000, the 401(k) plan would contain $226,266. A local investment advisor, seeing this figure, thinks those using her managed fund have more than the reported amount. She selects a random sample of 55 in that income range and finds a sample average of $241,387.

a. If the standard deviation for the amount in the investors' accounts is $1,734.23, determine if the investment advisor is correct in her assumption that those she is advising have more than the reported average amount. Use a significance level of 0.025 and discuss any assumptions you made to answer this question.

b. Determine the largest plausible average balance for the accounts of those using her managed fund in which you could have 90% confidence.

Computer Database Exercises

9-94. The Cell Tone Company sells cellular phones and airtime in several northwestern states. At a recent meeting, the marketing manager stated that the average age of its customers is under 40. This came up in conjunction with a proposed advertising plan that is to be directed toward a young audience. Before actually completing the advertising plan, Cell Tone decided to randomly sample customers. Among the questions asked in the survey of 50 customers in the Jacksonville, Florida, area was the customer's age. The data are available in a data file called **Cell Phone Survey**.

a. Based on the statement made by the marketing manager, formulate the appropriate null and alternative hypotheses.

b. The marketing manager must support his statement concerning average customer age in an upcoming board meeting. Using a significance level of 0.10, provide this support for the marketing manager.

c. Consider the result of the hypothesis test you conducted in part b. Which of the two types of hypothesis-test errors could you have committed? How could you discover if you had, indeed, made this error?

d. Calculate the critical value, $\bar{x}_\alpha$.

e. Determine the *p*-value and conduct the test using the *p*-value approach.

f. Note that the sample data list the customer's age to the nearest year. (1) If we denote a randomly

selected customer's age (to the nearest year) as x_i, is x_i a continuous or discrete random variable? (2) Is it possible that x_i has a normal distribution? Consider your answers to (1) and (2) and the fact that $\bar{x}$ must have a normal distribution to facilitate the calculation in part b. Does this mean that the calculation you have performed in part b is inappropriate? Explain your answer.

9-95. The AJ Fitness Center has surveyed 1,214 of its customers. Of particular interest is whether more than 60% of the customers who express overall service satisfaction with the club (represented by codes 4 or 5) are female. If this is not the case, the promotions director feels she must initiate new exercise programs that are designed specifically for women. Should the promotions director initiate the new exercise programs? Support your answer with the relevant hypothesis test utilizing a *p*-value to perform the test. The data are found in a data file called **AJ Fitness** ($\alpha = 0.05$).

9-96. The Wilson Company uses a great deal of water in the process of making industrial milling equipment. To comply with the federal clean water laws, it has a water purification system that all wastewater goes through before being discharged into a settling pond on the company's property. To determine whether the company is complying with the federal requirements, sample measures are taken every so often. One requirement is that the average pH levels not exceed 7.4. A sample of 95 pH measures has been taken. The data for these measures are shown in a file called **Wilson Water**.

a. Considering the requirement for pH level, state the appropriate null and alternative hypotheses. Discuss why it is appropriate to form the hypotheses with the federal standard as the alternative hypothesis.

b. Based on the sample data of pH level, what should the company conclude about its current status on meeting the federal requirement? Test the hypothesis at the 0.05 level. Discuss your results in a memo to the company's environmental relations manager.

9-97. The Haines Lumber Company makes plywood for the furniture industry. One product it makes is 3/4-inch oak veneer panels. It is very important that the panels conform to specifications. One specification calls for the panels to be made to an average thickness of 0.75 inches. Each hour, 5 panels are selected at random and measured. After 20 hours, a total of 100 panels have been measured. The thickness measures are in a file called **Haines**.

a. Formulate the appropriate null and alternative hypotheses relative to the thickness specification.

b. Based on the sample data, what should the company conclude about the status of its product meeting the thickness specification? Test at a significance level of 0.01. Discuss your results in a report to the production manager.

9-98. The Inland Empire Food Store Company has stated in its advertising that the average shopper will save more than $5.00 per week by shopping at Inland stores. A consumer group has decided to test this assertion by sampling 50 shoppers who currently shop at other stores. It selects the customers and then notes each item purchased at their regular stores. These same items are then priced at the Inland store, and the total bill is compared. The data in the file **Inland Foods** reflect savings at Inland for the 50 shoppers. Note that those cases where the bill was higher at Inland are marked with a minus sign.

a. Set up the appropriate null and alternative hypotheses to test Inland's claim.

b. Using a significance level of 0.05, develop the decision rule and test the hypothesis. Can Inland Empire support its advertising claim?

c. Which type of hypothesis error would the consumer group be most interested in controlling? Which type of hypothesis test error would the company be most interested in controlling? Explain your reasoning.

9-99. MBNA offers personal and business credit cards, loans, and savings products. It was bought by Bank of America in June 2005. One of the selling points for MBNA was its position relative to the rest of the credit card industry. MBNA's customers' average annual spending per active account before the purchase was $6,920. To demonstrate its relative position in the industry, MBNA's CFO, H. Vernon Wright, might authorize a survey producing the following data on the annual spending, to the nearest dollar, of accounts in the industry:

5,001	7,489	6,009	6,140
3,769	6,136	8,083	9,358
7,746	5,450	4,662	7,168
4,300	6,185	6,089	5,385
7,338	3,708	4,483	4,939
8,621	8,101	5,637	6,254
6,868	7,628	7,369	5,799
8,117	6,392	6,196	4,642
5,674	9,234	6,358	5,773
8,083	6,907	6,387	5,650

This sample is contained in the file labeled **ASpending**.

a. Conduct a hypothesis test to determine if MBNA has larger average annual spending per active account than the rest of the credit card industry. Use a p-value approach and a significance level of 0.025.

b. If the industry's annual spending per active account was normally distributed with a mean of $5,560 and a standard deviation of $1,140, determine the probability that a randomly chosen account would have an annual spending larger than MBNA's.

9-100. At the annual meeting of the Golf Equipment Manufacturer's Association, a speaker made the claim that at least 30% of all golf clubs being used by nonprofessional United States Golf Association (USGA) members are "knock-offs." These knock-offs are clubs that look very much like the more expensive originals, such as Big Bertha drivers, but are actually nonauthorized copies that are sold at a very reduced rate. This claim prompted the association to conduct a study to see if the problem was as big as the speaker said. A random sample of 400 golfers was selected from the USGA membership ranks. The players were called and asked to indicate the brand of clubs that they used and several other questions. Out of the 400 golfers, data were collected from 294 of them. Based on the response to club brand, a determination was made whether the club was "original" or a "copy." The data are in a file called **Golf Survey**.

a. Based on the sample data, what conclusion should be reached if the hypothesis is tested at a significance level of 0.05? Show the decision rule.

b. Determine whether a Type I or Type II error for this hypothesis test would be more severe. Given your determination, would you advocate raising or lowering the significance level for this test? Explain your reasoning.

c. Confirm that the sample proportion's distribution can be approximated by a normal distribution.

d. Based on the sample data, what should the USGA conclude about the use of knock-off clubs by the high-handicap golfers? Is the official's statement justified?

9-101. TOMRA Systems ASA is a Norwegian company that manufactures reverse vending machines (RVMs). In most cases, RVMs are used in markets that have deposits on beverage containers, offering an efficient and convenient method of identifying the deposit amount of each container returned and providing a refund to the customer. Prices for such machines range from about $9,000 for single-container machines to about $35,000 for higher-volume, multi-container (can, plastic, glass) machines. For a single-container machine to pay for itself in one year, it would need to generate an average monthly income of more than $750. The following sample of single-machine monthly incomes was obtained to determine if that goal could be reached:

765.37	748.21	813.77	633.21	714.74	802.96	696.06	880.65
701.80	696.16	905.01	688.51	922.43	753.97	728.60	690.06
839.48	1010.56	789.13	754.35	749.97	802.31	809.15	775.27

This sample is contained in the file labeled **RVMIncome**.

a. Conduct a hypothesis test to determine if the goal can be reached. Use a significance level of 0.05 and the p-value approach.

b. There are 10 sites in which an RVM could be placed. Unknown to the vendor, only four of the sites will allow the vendor to meet the goal of paying for the machine in one year. If he installs four of the RVMs, determine the probability that at least two of them will be paid off in a year.

Video Case 4

New Product Introductions @ McDonald's

New product ideas are a staple of our culture. Just take a look around you—how many billboards or television commercials can you count advertising new products or services? So, where do those ideas come from? If you're a company like McDonald's, the ideas don't come out of thin air. Instead, they're the result of careful monitoring of consumer preferences, trends, and tastes.

McDonald's menu is a good example of how consumer preferences have affected change in food offerings. What used to be a fairly limited lunch and dinner menu consisting of burgers, shakes, and fries has now become incredibly diverse. The Big Mac came along in 1968, and Happy Meals were introduced in 1979. Breakfast now accounts for nearly 30% of business in the United States, and chicken offerings comprise 30% of menu choices. Healthy offerings such as apple dippers, milk jugs, and fruit and yogurt parfaits are huge sellers. The company now rolls out at least three new products a year. Wade Thomas, VP U.S. Menu Management, leads the team behind most of today's menu options. He meets regularly with Chef Dan, the company's executive chef, to give the chef's team some idea anchor points to play with.

When the chef's team is through playing with the concept, Wade's Menu Management team holds what they call a "rally." At a rally, numerous food concepts developed by Chef Dan's team are presented, tasted, discussed, and voted on. The winners move on to focus group testing. The focus groups are a huge source of external data, which help the Menu Management team with its decision on whether to introduce a product. If a product scores 8 out of 10 on a variety of rankings, the idea moves forward.

The real test begins in the field. Wade and his team need to determine if the new product idea can be executed consistently in the restaurants. Data collected from the company's partnership with its owner/operators and suppliers are key. If a product takes five seconds too long to make or if the equipment doesn't fit into existing kitchen configurations, its chances of implementation are low, even though consumer focus groups indicated a high probability of success.

Throughout the idea development process, various statistical methods are used to analyze the data collected. The data are handed over to the company's U.S. Consumer and Business Insights team for conversion into meaningful information the menu management team can use. At each step along the way, the statistical analyses are used to decide whether to move to the next step. The introduction of the new Asian chicken salad is a good example of a new product offering that made it all the way to market. Analysis was performed on data collected in focus groups and eventually revealed that the Asian salad met all the statistical hurdles for the salad to move forward.

Data collection and statistical analysis don't stop when the new products hit the market. Wade Thomas's team and the McDonald's U.S. Consumer and Business Insights group continue to forecast and monitor sales, the ingredient supply chain, customer preferences, competitive reactions, and more. As for the new Asian salad, time will tell just how successful it will become. But you can be sure statistical techniques such as multiple regression will be used to analyze it!

Discussion Questions:

1. During the past year, McDonald's introduced a new dessert product into its European market area. This product had already passed all the internal hurdles described in this case, including the focus group analysis and the operations analysis. The next step was to see how well the product would be received in the marketplace. The hurdle rate that has been set for this product is a mean equal to 160 orders per 1,000 transactions. If the mean exceeds 160, the product will be introduced on a permanent basis. A random sample of 142 stores throughout Europe was selected. Store managers tracked the number of dessert orders per 1,000 transactions during a two-week trial period. These sample data are in the data file called **McDonald's New Product Introduction**. Using a significance level equal to 0.05, conduct the appropriate hypothesis test. Be sure to state the null and alternative hypotheses and show the results of the test. Write a short report that summarizes the hypothesis test and indicate what conclusion Wade Thomas and his group should reach about this new dessert product.

2. Referring to question 1, suppose a second hurdle is to be used in this case in determining whether the new dessert product should be introduced. This hurdle involves the proportion of every 1,000 transactions that the number of dessert orders exceeds 200. Wade Thomas has indicated that this proportion must exceed 0.15. Based on the sample data, using a significance level equal to 0.05, what conclusion should be reached? Write a short report that specifies the null and alternative hypotheses and shows the test results. Indicate what conclusion should be reached based on this hypothesis test.

Case 9.1

Campbell Brewery, Inc.—Part 1

Don Campbell and his younger brother, Edward, purchased Campbell Brewery from their father in 1983. The brewery makes and bottles beer under two labels and distributes it throughout the Southwest. Since purchasing the brewery, Don has been instrumental in modernizing operations.

One of the latest acquisitions is a filling machine that can be adjusted to fill at any average fill level desired. Because the bottles and cans filled by the brewery are exclusively the 12-ounce size, when they received the machine, Don set the fill level to 12 ounces and left it that way. According to the manufacturer's specifications, the machine will fill bottles or cans around the average, with a standard deviation of 0.15 ounce.

Don just returned from a brewery convention at which he attended a panel discussion related to problems with filling machines. One brewery representative discussed a problem her company had. It failed to learn that its machine's average fill went out of adjustment until several months later, when its cost accounting department reported some problems with beer production in bulk not matching output in bottles and cans. It turns out that the machine's average fill had increased from 12 ounces to 12.07 ounces. With large volumes of production, this deviation meant a substantial loss in profits.

Another brewery reported the same type of problem, but in the opposite direction. Its machine began filling bottles with slightly less than 12 ounces on the average. Although the consumers could not detect the shortage in a given bottle, the state and federal agencies responsible for checking the accuracy of packaged products discovered the problem in their testing and substantially fined the brewery for the underfill.

These problems were a surprise to Don Campbell. He had not considered the possibility that the machine might go out of adjustment and pose these types of problems. In fact, he became very concerned because the problems of losing profits and potentially being fined by the government were ones that he wished to avoid, if possible. After the convention, Don and Ed decided to hire a consulting firm with expertise in these matters to assist them in setting up a procedure for monitoring the performance of the filling machine.

The consultant suggested that they set up a sampling plan in which once a month, they would sample some number of bottles and measure their volumes precisely. If the average of the sample deviated too much from 12 ounces, they would shut the machine down and make the necessary adjustments. Otherwise, they would let the filling process continue. The consultant identified two types of problems that could occur from this sort of sampling plan:

1. They might incorrectly decide to adjust the machine when it was not really necessary to do so.
2. They might incorrectly decide to allow the filling process to continue when, in fact, the true average had deviated from 12 ounces.

After carefully considering what the consultant told them, Don indicated that he wanted no more than a 0.02 chance of the first problem occurring because of the costs involved. He also decided that if the true average fill had slipped to 11.99 ounces, he wanted no more than a 0.05 chance of not detecting this with his sampling plan. He wanted to avoid problems with state and federal agencies. Finally, if the true average fill had actually risen to 12.007 ounces, he wanted to be able to detect this 98% of the time with his sampling plan. Thus, he wanted to avoid the lost profits that would result from such a problem.

In addition, Don needs to determine how large a sample size is necessary to meet his requirements.

Case 9.2

Wings of Fire

Following his graduation from college, Tony Smith wanted to continue to live and work in Oxford. However, the community was small and there were not a lot of readily available opportunities for a new college graduate. Fortunately, Tony had some experience working in the food service industry gained in the summers and throughout high school at his uncle's restaurant in Buffalo. When Tony decided to leverage his experience into a small delivery and take-out restaurant located close to the university, he thought he had hit on a great idea. Tony would offer a limited fare consisting of the buffalo wings his uncle had perfected at his restaurant. Tony called his restaurant Wings of Fire. Although success came slowly, the uniqueness of Tony's offering coupled with the growth of the university community made Wings of Fire a success.

Tony's business was pretty simple. Tony purchased wings locally. The wings were then seasoned and prepared in Tony's restaurant. Once an order was received, Tony cooked the wings, which were then delivered or picked up by the customer. Tony's establishment was small, and there was no place for customers to dine in the restaurant. However, his wings proved so popular that over time, Tony hired several employees, including three delivery drivers. Business was steady and predictable during the week, with the biggest days being home-football Saturdays.

A little over a year ago, Oxford really began to grow and expand. Tony noticed that his business was beginning to suffer when other fast-food delivery restaurants opened around campus. Some of these restaurants were offering guarantees such as

"30 minutes or it's free." Tony's Wings of Fire now had to compete with fish tacos, specialty pizzas, and gourmet burgers. Most of these new restaurants, however, were dine-in establishments that provided carry-out and delivery as a customer convenience. However, Tony was certain that he would need to offer a delivery guarantee to remain competitive with the newer establishments.

Tony was certain that a delivery guarantee of "30 minutes or it's free" could easily be accomplished every day except on football Saturdays. Tony thought that if he could offer a 30-minute guarantee on his busiest day, he would be able to hold onto and perhaps even recover market share from the competition. However, before he was willing to commit to such a guarantee, Tony wanted to ensure that it was possible to meet the 30-minute promise.

Tony knew it would be no problem for customers to pick up orders within 30 minutes of phoning them in. However, he was less confident about delivering orders to customers in 30 minutes or less. Not only would the wings need to be cooked and packaged, but the delivery time might be affected by the availability of drivers. Tony decided that he needed to analyze the opportunity further.

As a part of his analysis, Tony decided to take a random sample of deliveries over five different football weekends. Cooking time and packaging time were not considered in his analysis because wings were not cooked for individual orders. Rather, large numbers of wings were cooked at a single time and then packaged in boxes of 12. Tony therefore decided to focus his analysis on the time required to deliver cooked and packaged wings. He collected information on the amount of time an order had to wait for a driver (the pick-up time) as well as the amount of time required to transport the wings to the customer (the drive time). The sampled information is in the file **Wings of Fire**. Tony is not willing to offer the guarantee on football Saturdays unless he can be reasonably sure that the total time to deliver a customer's order is less than 30 minutes, on average. Tony would also like to have an estimate of the actual time required to deliver a customer's order on football Saturdays. Finally, Tony would like to know how likely it is that the total time to make a delivery would take more than 30 minutes. Based on the sampled data, should Tony offer the guarantee? What percent of the Saturday deliveries would result in a customer receiving a free order? What recommendations might help Tony improve his Saturday delivery times?

Required Tasks:

1. Use the sample information to compute a measure of performance that Tony can use to analyze his delivery performance.
2. State a hypothesis test that would help Tony decide to offer the delivery guarantee or not.
3. Calculate sample statistics and formally test the hypothesis stated in (2).
4. Estimate the probability of an order taking longer than 30 minutes.
5. Summarize your findings and make a recommendation in a short report.

Chapter 10 Quick Prep Links

- **Review** material on calculating and interpreting sample means and standard deviations in Chapter 3.
- **Review** the normal distribution in Section 6.1.
- **Make sure** you understand the concepts associated with sampling distributions for $\bar{x}$ and $\bar{p}$ by reviewing Sections 7.1, 7.2, and 7.3.
- **Review** the steps for developing confidence interval estimates for a single population
- mean and a single population proportion in Sections 8.1 and 8.3.
- **Review** the methods for testing hypotheses about single population means and single population proportions in Chapter 9.

Estimation and Hypothesis Testing for Two Population Parameters

10.1 Estimation for Two Population Means Using Independent Samples (pg. 387–397)

10.2 Hypothesis Tests for Two Population Means Using Independent Samples (pg. 398–411)

10.3 Interval Estimation and Hypothesis Tests for Paired Samples (pg. 411–419)

10.4 Estimation and Hypothesis Tests for Two Population Proportions (pg. 419–426)

Outcome 1. Discuss the logic behind and demonstrate the techniques for using independent samples to test hypotheses and develop interval estimates for the difference between two population means.

Outcome 2. Develop confidence interval estimates and conduct hypothesis tests for the difference between two population means for paired samples.

Outcome 3. Carry out hypothesis tests and establish interval estimates, using sample data, for the difference between two population proportions.

Why you need to know

Chapter 9 introduced the concepts of hypothesis testing and illustrated its application through examples involving a single population parameter. However, in many business decision-making situations, managers must decide between two or more alternatives. For example, fleet managers in large companies must decide which model and make of car to purchase next year. Airlines must decide whether to purchase replacement planes from Boeing or Airbus. When deciding on a new advertising campaign, a company may need to evaluate proposals from competing advertising agencies. Hiring decisions may require a personnel director to select one employee from a list of applicants. Production managers are often confronted with decisions concerning whether to change a production process or leave it alone. Each day, consumers purchase a product from among several competing brands.

Fortunately, there are statistical procedures that can help decision makers use sample information to compare different populations. In this chapter, we introduce these procedures and techniques by discussing methods that can be used to make statistical comparisons between two populations. In a later chapter, we will discuss some methods to extend this comparison to more than two populations. Whether we are discussing cases involving two populations or those with more than two populations, the techniques we present are all extensions of the statistical tools involving a single population parameter introduced in Chapters 8 and 9.

Tatiana Popova/Shutterstock

10.1 Estimation for Two Population Means Using Independent Samples

In this section, we examine situations in which we are interested in the difference between two population means, looking first at the case in which the samples from the two populations are **independent**.

We will introduce techniques for estimating the difference between the means of two populations in the following situations:

1. The population standard deviations are known and the samples are independent.
2. The population standard deviations are unknown and the samples are independent.

Chapter Outcome 1. ➡ ## Estimating the Difference between Two Population Means When σ_1 and σ_2 Are Known, Using Independent Samples

Recall that in Chapter 8 the standard normal distribution z-values were used in establishing the critical value and developing the interval estimate when the population standard deviation was assumed known and the population distribution is assumed to be normally distributed.[1] The general format for a confidence interval estimate is shown in Equation 10.1.

Confidence Interval, General Format

$$\text{Point estimate} \pm (\text{Critical value})(\text{Standard error}) \qquad \textbf{(10.1)}$$

In business situations, you will often need to estimate the difference between two population means. For instance, you may wish to estimate the difference in mean starting salaries between males and females, the difference in mean production output in union and nonunion factories, or the difference in mean service times at two different fast-food businesses. In these situations, the best point estimate for $\mu_1 - \mu_2$ is

$$\text{Point estimate} = \bar{x}_1 - \bar{x}_2$$

In situations in which you know the population standard deviations, σ_1 and σ_2, and when the samples selected from the two populations are independent, an extension of the Central Limit Theorem tells us that the sampling distribution for all possible differences between $\bar{x}_1$ and $\bar{x}_2$ will be approximately normally distributed with a standard error computed as shown in Equation 10.2.

Standard Error of $\bar{x}_1 - \bar{x}_2$ When σ_1 and σ_2 Are Known

$$\sigma_{\bar{x}_1 - \bar{x}_2} = \sqrt{\frac{\sigma_1^2}{n_1} + \frac{\sigma_2^2}{n_2}} \qquad \textbf{(10.2)}$$

where:

$$\sigma_1^2 = \text{Variance of population 1}$$
$$\sigma_2^2 = \text{Variance of population 2}$$
$$n_1 \text{ and } n_2 = \text{Sample sizes from populations 1 and 2}$$

Further, the critical value for determining the confidence interval will be a z-value from the standard normal distribution. In these circumstances, the confidence interval estimate for $\mu_1 - \mu_2$ is found by using Equation 10.3.

---

[1] If the samples from the two populations are large $(n \geq 30)$ the normal distribution assumption is not required.

Confidence Interval Estimate for $\mu_1 - \mu_2$ When σ_1 and σ_2 Are Known, Independent Samples

$$(\bar{x}_1 - \bar{x}_2) \pm z\sqrt{\frac{\sigma_1^2}{n_1} + \frac{\sigma_2^2}{n_2}}$$

(10.3)

The z-values for several of the most commonly used confidence levels are

Confidence Level	Critical z-value
80%	$z = 1.28$
90%	$z = 1.645$
95%	$z = 1.96$
99%	$z = 2.575$

EXAMPLE 10-1   **CONFIDENCE INTERVAL ESTIMATE FOR $\mu_1 - \mu_2$ WHEN σ_1 AND σ_2 ARE KNOWN, USING INDEPENDENT SAMPLES**

Axiom Fitness Axiom Fitness is a small chain of fitness centers located primarily in the South but with some clubs scattered in other parts of the U.S. and Canada. Recently, the club in Winston-Salem, North Carolina, worked with a business class from a local university on a project in which a team of students observed Axiom customers with respect to their club usage. As part of the study, the students measured the time that customers spent in the club during a visit. The objective is to estimate the difference in mean time spent per visit for male and female customers. Previous studies indicate that the standard deviation is 11 minutes for males and 16 minutes for females. To develop a 95% confidence interval estimate for the difference in mean times, the following steps are taken:

Step 1   **Define the population parameter of interest and select independent samples from the two populations.**

In this case, the company is interested in estimating the difference in mean time spent in the club between males and females. The measure of interest is $\mu_1 - \mu_2$.

The student team has selected simple random samples of 100 males and 100 females at different times in the Winston-Salem club.

Step 2   **Specify the desired confidence level.**

The plan is develop a 95% confidence interval estimate.

Step 3   **Compute the point estimate.**

The resulting sample means are

Males: $\bar{x}_1 = 34.5$ minutes   Females: $\bar{x}_2 = 42.4$ minutes

The point estimate is

$$\bar{x}_1 - \bar{x}_2 = 34.5 - 42.4 = -7.9 \text{ minutes}$$

Women in the sample spent an average of 7.9 minutes longer in the club.

Step 4   **Determine the standard error of the sampling distribution.**

The standard error is calculated as

$$\sqrt{\frac{\sigma_1^2}{n_1} + \frac{\sigma_2^2}{n_2}} = \sqrt{\frac{11^2}{100} + \frac{16^2}{100}} = 1.9416$$

Step 5   **Determine the critical value, z, from the standard normal table.**

The interval estimate will be developed using a 95% confidence interval. Because the population standard deviations are known, the critical value is a z-value from the standard normal table. The critical value is

$$z = 1.96$$

Step 6 **Develop the confidence interval estimate using Equation 10.3.**

$$(\bar{x}_1 - \bar{x}_2) \pm z\sqrt{\frac{\sigma_1^2}{n_1} + \frac{\sigma_2^2}{n_2}}$$

$$-7.9 \pm 1.96\sqrt{\frac{11^2}{100} + \frac{16^2}{100}}$$

$$-7.9 \pm 3.8056$$

The 95% confidence interval estimate for the difference in mean time spent in the Winston-Salem Axiom Fitness center between men and women is

$$-11.7056 \le (\mu_1 - \mu_2) \le -4.0944$$

Thus, based on the sample data and the specified confidence level, women spend on average between 4.09 and 11.71 minutes longer at this Axiom Fitness Center.

>> **END EXAMPLE**

TRY PROBLEM 10-4 (pg. 395)

Chapter Outcome 1. → # Estimating the Difference between Two Means When σ_1 and σ_2 Are Unknown, Using Independent Samples

In Chapter 8, you learned that, when estimating a single population mean when the population standard deviation is unknown, the critical value is a t-value from the t-distribution. This is also the case when you are interested in estimating the difference between two population means, if the following assumptions hold:

Assumptions

- The populations are normally distributed.
- The populations have equal variances.
- The samples are independent.

The following application illustrates how a confidence interval estimate is developed using the t-distribution.

BUSINESS APPLICATION   **ESTIMATING THE DIFFERENCE BETWEEN TWO POPULATION MEANS**

Nick Barounis/Shutterstock

RETIREMENT INVESTING A major political issue for the past decade has focused on the long-term future of the U.S. Social Security system. Many people who have entered the workforce in the past 20 years believe the system will not be solvent when they retire, so they are actively investing in their own retirement accounts. One investment alternative is a tax-sheltered annuity (TSA) marketed by life insurance companies. Certain people, depending on occupation, qualify to invest part of their paychecks in a TSA and to pay no federal income tax on this money until it is withdrawn. While the money is invested, the insurance companies invest it in either stock or bond portfolios. A second alternative open to many people is a plan known as a 401(k), in which employees contribute a portion of their paychecks to purchase stocks, bonds, or mutual funds. In some cases, employers match all or part of the employee contributions. In many 401(k) systems, the employees can control how their funds are invested.

A recent study was conducted in North Dakota to estimate the difference in mean annual contributions for individuals covered by the two plans [TSA or 401(k)]. A simple random sample of 15 people from the population of adults who are eligible for a TSA investment was selected. A second sample of 15 people was selected from the population of adults in North Dakota who have 401(k) plans. The variable of interest is the dollar amount of money invested in the retirement plan during the previous year. Specifically, we are interested in estimating $\mu_1 - \mu_2$ using a 95% confidence interval estimate where:

μ_1 = Mean dollars invested by the TSA−eligible population during the past year
μ_2 = Mean dollars invested by the 401 (k)−eligible population during the past year

TSA–Eligible	401(k)–Eligible
$n_1 = 15$	$n_2 = 15$
$\bar{x}_1 = \$2,119.70$	$\bar{x}_2 = \$1,777.70$
$s_1 = \$709.70$	$s_2 = \$593.90$

Before applying the *t*-distribution, we need to determine whether the assumptions are likely to be satisfied. First, the samples are considered independent because the amount invested by one group should have no influence on the likelihood that any specific amount will be found for the second sample.

Next, Figure 10.1 shows the sample data and the box and whisker plots for the two samples. These plots exhibit characteristics that are reasonably consistent with those associated with normal distributions and approximately equal variances. Although using a box and whisker plot to check the *t*-distribution assumptions may seem to be imprecise, studies have shown the *t*-distribution to be applicable even when there are small violations of the assumptions. This is particularly the case when the sample sizes are approximately equal.[2]

Equation 10.4 can be used to develop the confidence interval estimate for the difference between two population means when you have small independent samples.

Confidence Interval Estimate for $\mu_1 - \mu_2$ When σ_1 and σ_2 Are Unknown, Independent Samples

$$(\bar{x}_1 - \bar{x}_2) \pm t s_p \sqrt{\frac{1}{n_1} + \frac{1}{n_2}}$$

(10.4)

where:

$$s_p = \sqrt{\frac{(n_1-1)s_1^2 + (n_2-1)s_2^2}{n_1 + n_2 - 2}} = \text{Pooled standard deviation}$$

$t = $ Critical *t*-value from the *t*-distribution, with degrees of freedom equal to $n_1 + n_2 - 2$

FIGURE 10.1

Sample Information for the Investment Study

Note: TSA, tax-sheltered annuity.

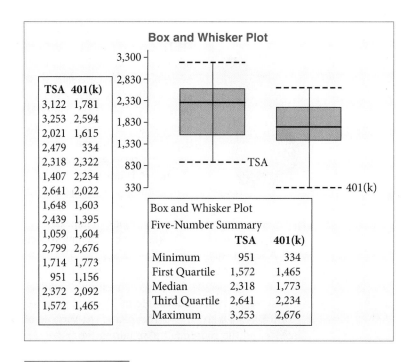

TSA	401(k)
3,122	1,781
3,253	2,594
2,021	1,615
2,479	334
2,318	2,322
1,407	2,234
2,641	2,022
1,648	1,603
2,439	1,395
1,059	1,604
2,799	2,676
1,714	1,773
951	1,156
2,372	2,092
1,572	1,465

Box and Whisker Plot
Five-Number Summary

	TSA	401(k)
Minimum	951	334
First Quartile	1,572	1,465
Median	2,318	1,773
Third Quartile	2,641	2,234
Maximum	3,253	2,676

---

[2] Chapter 11 introduces a statistical procedure for testing whether two populations have equal variances. Chapter 13 provides a statistical procedure for testing whether a population is normally distributed.

To use Equation 10.4, we must compute the pooled standard deviation, s_p. If the equal-variance assumption holds, then both s_1^2 and s_2^2 are estimators of the same population variance, σ^2. To use only one of these, say s_1^2, to estimate σ^2 would be disregarding the information obtained from the other sample. To use the average of s_1^2 and s_2^2, if the sample sizes were different, would ignore the fact that more information about σ^2 is obtained from the sample having the larger sample size. We therefore use a weighted average of s_1^2 and s_2^2, denoted as s_p^2, to estimate σ^2, where the weights are the degrees of freedom associated with each sample. The square root of s_p^2 is known as the *pooled standard deviation* and is computed using

$$s_p = \sqrt{\frac{(n_1-1)s_1^2 + (n_2-1)s_2^2}{n_1 + n_2 - 2}}$$

Notice that the sample size we have available to estimate σ^2 is $n_1 + n_2$. However, to produce s_p, we must first calculate s_1^2 and s_2^2. This requires that we estimate μ_1 and μ_2 using $\bar{x}_1$ and $\bar{x}_2$, respectively. The degrees of freedom are equal to the sample size minus the parameters estimated before the variance estimate is obtained. Therefore, our degrees of freedom must equal $n_1 + n_2 - 2$.

For the retirement investing example, the pooled standard deviation is

$$s_p = \sqrt{\frac{(n_1-1)s_1^2 + (n_2-1)s_2^2}{n_1 + n_2 - 2}} = \sqrt{\frac{(15-1)(709.7)^2 + (15-1)(593.9)^2}{15 + 15 - 2}} = 654.37$$

Using the *t*-distribution table, the critical *t*-value for

$$n_1 + n_2 - 2 = 15 + 15 - 2 = 28$$

degrees of freedom and 95% confidence is

$$t = 2.0484$$

Now we can develop the interval estimate using Equation 10.4:

$$(\bar{x}_1 - \bar{x}_2) \pm ts_p\sqrt{\frac{1}{n_1} + \frac{1}{n_2}}$$

$$(2{,}119.70 - 1{,}777.70) \pm 2.0484(654.37)\sqrt{\frac{1}{15} + \frac{1}{15}}$$

$$342 \pm 489.45$$

Thus, the 95% confidence interval estimate for the difference in mean dollars for people who invest in a TSA versus those who invest in a 401(k) is

$$-\$147.45 \le (\mu_1 - \mu_2) \le \$831.45$$

This confidence interval estimate crosses zero and therefore indicates there may be no difference between the mean contributions to TSA accounts and to 401(k) accounts by adults in North Dakota. The implication of this result is that the average amount invested by those individuals who invest in pretax TSA programs is no more or no less than that invested by those participating in after-tax 401(k) programs. Based on this result, there may be an opportunity to encourage the TSA investors to increase deposits.

> **EXAMPLE 10-2**   **CONFIDENCE INTERVAL ESTIMATE FOR $\mu_1 - \mu_2$ WHEN σ_1 AND σ_2 ARE UNKNOWN, USING INDEPENDENT SAMPLES**

Andreason Marketing, Inc. Andreason Marketing, Inc. has been hired by a major newspaper in the U.S. to estimate the difference in mean time that newspaper subscribers spend reading the Saturday newspaper when subscribers age 50 and under are compared with those more than 50 years old. A simple random sample of six people age 50 or younger and eight people over 50 participated in the study. The estimate can be developed using the following steps:

Step 1   **Define the population parameter of interest and select independent samples from the two populations.**

The objective here is to estimate the difference between the two age groups with respect to the mean time spent reading the Saturday edition of the newspaper. The parameter of interest is $\mu_1 - \mu_2$.

The marketing company has selected simple random samples of six "younger" and eight "older" people. Because the reading time by one person does not influence the reading time for any other person, the samples are independent.

Step 2   **Specify the confidence level.**

The marketing firm wishes to have a 95% confidence interval estimate.

Step 3   **Compute the point estimate.**

The resulting sample means and sample standard deviations for the two groups are

$$\text{age} \le 50: \quad \bar{x}_1 = 13.6 \text{ minutes} \qquad \text{age} > 50: \quad \bar{x}_2 = 11.2 \text{ minutes}$$
$$s_1 = 3.1 \text{ minutes} \qquad\qquad\qquad s_2 = 5.0 \text{ minutes}$$
$$n_1 = 6 \qquad\qquad\qquad\qquad n_2 = 8$$

The point estimate is

$$\bar{x}_1 - \bar{x}_2 = 13.6 - 11.2 = 2.4 \text{ minutes}$$

Step 4   **Determine the standard error of the sampling distribution.**

The pooled standard deviation is computed using

$$s_p = \sqrt{\frac{(n_1 - 1)s_1^2 + (n_2 - 1)s_2^2}{n_1 + n_2 - 2}} = \sqrt{\frac{(6-1)3.1^2 + (8-1)5^2}{6+8-2}} = 4.31$$

The standard error is then calculated as

$$s_p\sqrt{\frac{1}{n_1} + \frac{1}{n_1}} = 4.31\sqrt{\frac{1}{6} + \frac{1}{8}} = 2.3277$$

Step 5   **Determine the critical value, t, from the t-distribution table.**

Because the population standard deviations are unknown, the critical value will be a t-value from the t-distribution as long as the population variances are equal and the populations are assumed to be normally distributed.

The critical t for 95% confidence and $6 + 8 - 2 = 12$ degrees of freedom is

$$t = 2.1788$$

Step 6   **Develop a confidence interval using Equation 10.4.**

$$(\bar{x}_1 - \bar{x}_2) \pm ts_p\sqrt{\frac{1}{n_1} + \frac{1}{n_2}}$$

where:

$$s_p = \sqrt{\frac{(n_1 - 1)s_1^2 + (n_2 - 1)s_2^2}{n_1 + n_2 - 2}} = \sqrt{\frac{(6-1)3.1^2 + (8-1)5^2}{6+8-2}} = 4.31$$

Then the interval estimate is

$$2.4 \pm 2.1788(4.31)\sqrt{\frac{1}{6} + \frac{1}{8}}$$

$$2.4 \pm 5.0715$$

$$-2.6715 \le (\mu_1 - \mu_2) \le 7.4715$$

Because the interval crosses zero, we cannot conclude that a difference exists between the age groups with respect to the mean reading time for the Saturday edition. Thus, with respect to this factor, it does not seem to matter whether the person is 50 or younger or over 50.

>> **END EXAMPLE**

TRY PROBLEM 10-1 (pg. 395)

What If the Population Variances Are Not Equal? If you have reason to believe that the population variances are substantially different, Equation 10.4 is not appropriate for computing the confidence interval. Instead of computing the pooled standard deviation as part of the confidence interval formula, we use Equations 10.5 and 10.6.

Confidence Interval for $\mu_1 - \mu_2$ When σ_1 and σ_2 Are Unknown and Not Equal, Independent Samples

$$(\bar{x}_1 - \bar{x}_2) \pm t \sqrt{\frac{s_1^2}{n_1} + \frac{s_2^2}{n_2}} \tag{10.5}$$

where:

t is from the t-distribution with degrees of freedom computed using

Degrees of Freedom for Estimating Difference between Population Means When σ_1 and σ_2 Are Not Equal

$$df = \frac{(s_1^2/n_1 + s_2^2/n_2)^2}{\left(\dfrac{(s_1^2/n_1)^2}{n_1 - 1} + \dfrac{(s_2^2/n_2)^2}{n_2 - 1} \right)} \tag{10.6}$$

EXAMPLE 10-3   **ESTIMATING $\mu_1 - \mu_2$ WHEN THE POPULATION VARIANCES ARE NOT EQUAL**

Citibank The marketing managers at Citibank are planning to roll out a new marketing campaign addressed at increasing bank card use. As one part of the campaign, the company will be offering a low interest rate incentive to induce people to spend more money using its charge cards. However, the company is concerned whether this plan will have a different impact on married card holders than on unmarried card holders. So, prior to starting the marketing campaign nationwide, the company tests it on a random sample of 30 unmarried and 25 married customers. The managers wish to estimate the difference in mean credit card spending for unmarried versus married for a two-week period immediately after being exposed to the marketing campaign. Based on past data, the managers have reason to believe the spending distributions for unmarried and married will be approximately normally distributed, but they are unwilling to conclude the population variances for spending are equal for the two populations.

A 95% confidence interval estimate for the difference in population means can be developed using the following steps:

Step 1 Define the population parameter of interest.
The parameter of interest is the difference between the mean dollars spent on credit cards by unmarried versus married customers in the two-week period after being exposed to Citi's new marketing program.

Step 2 Specify the confidence level.
The research manager wishes to have a 95% confidence interval estimate.

Step 3 Compute the point estimate.
Independent samples of 30 unmarried and 25 married customers were taken, and the credit card spending for each sampled customer during

the two-week period was recorded. The following sample results were observed:

	Unmarried	Married
Mean	$455.10	$268.90
St. Dev.	$102.40	$ 77.25

The point estimate is the difference between the two sample means:

$$\text{Point estimate} = \bar{x}_1 - \bar{x}_2 = 455.10 - 268.90 = 186.20$$

Step 4 Determine the standard error of the sampling distribution.
The standard error is calculated as

$$\sqrt{\frac{s_1^2}{n_1} + \frac{s_2^2}{n_2}} = \sqrt{\frac{102.40^2}{30} + \frac{77.25^2}{25}} = 24.25$$

Step 5 Determine the critical value, t, from the t-distribution table.
Because we are unable to assume the population variances are equal, we must first use Equation 10.6 to calculate the degrees of freedom for the t-distribution. This is done as follows:

$$df = \frac{(s_1^2/n_1 + s_2^2/n_2)^2}{\left(\dfrac{(s_1^2/n_1)^2}{n_1 - 1} + \dfrac{(s_2^2/n_2)^2}{n_2 - 1}\right)}$$

$$= \frac{(102.40^2/30 + 77.25^2/25)^2}{\left(\dfrac{(102.40^2/30)^2}{29} + \dfrac{(77.25^2/25)^2}{24}\right)} = \frac{346,011.98}{6,586.81} = 52.53$$

Thus, the degrees of freedom (rounded down) will be 52. At the 95% confidence level, using the t-distribution table, the approximate t-value is 2.0086. Note, since there is no entry for 52 degrees of freedom in the table, we have selected the t-value associated with 95% confidence and 50 degrees of freedom, which provides a slightly larger t-value than would have been the case for 52 degrees of freedom. Thus, the interval estimate will be generously wide.

Step 6 Develop the confidence interval estimate using Equation 10.5.
The confidence interval estimate is computed using

$$(\bar{x}_1 - \bar{x}_2) \pm t\sqrt{\frac{s_1^2}{n_1} + \frac{s_2^2}{n_2}}$$

Then the interval estimate is

$$(\$455.10 - \$268.90) \pm 2.0086\sqrt{\frac{102.40^2}{30} + \frac{77.25^2}{25}}$$

$$\$186.20 \pm \$48.72$$

$$\$137.48 \leq (\mu_1 - \mu_2) \leq \$234.92$$

$$\$137.48 \text{———} \$234.92$$

The test provides evidence to conclude unmarried customers, after being introduced to the marketing program, spend more than married customers, on average, by anywhere from $137.48 to $234.92 in the two weeks following the marketing campaign. But before concluding that the campaign is more effective for unmarried than married customers, the managers would want to compare these results with data from customer accounts prior to the marketing campaign.

>> **END EXAMPLE**

TRY PROBLEM 10-6 (pg. 395)

MyStatLab

10-1: Exercises

Skill Development

10-1. The following information is based on independent random samples taken from two normally distributed populations having equal variances:

$n_1 = 15$	$n_2 = 13$
$\bar{x}_1 = 50$	$\bar{x}_2 = 53$
$s_1 = 5$	$s_2 = 6$

Based on the sample information, determine the 90% confidence interval estimate for the difference between the two population means.

10-2. The following information is based on independent random samples taken from two normally distributed populations having equal variances:

$n_1 = 24$	$n_2 = 28$
$\bar{x}_1 = 130$	$\bar{x}_2 = 125$
$s_1 = 19$	$s_2 = 17.5$

Based on the sample information, determine the 95% confidence interval estimate for the difference between the two population means.

10-3. Construct a 90% confidence interval estimate for the difference between two population means given the following sample data selected from two normally distributed populations with equal variances:

Sample 1			Sample 2		
29	25	31	42	39	38
35	35	37	42	40	43
21	29	34	46	39	35

10-4. Construct a 95% confidence interval estimate for the difference between two population means based on the following information:

Population 1	Population 2
$\bar{x}_1 = 355$	$\bar{x}_2 = 320$
$\sigma_1 = 34$	$\sigma_2 = 40$
$n_1 = 50$	$n_2 = 80$

10-5. Construct a 95% percent confidence interval for the difference between two population means using the following sample data that have been selected from normally distributed populations with different population variances:

Sample 1				Sample 2			
473	386	406	379	349	359	346	395
346	438	391	328	398	401	411	384
388	388	456	429	363	437	388	273

10-6. Two random samples were selected independently from populations having normal distributions. The following statistics were extracted from the samples:

$$\bar{x}_1 = 42.3 \quad \bar{x}_2 = 32.4$$

a. If $\sigma_1 = 3$ and $\sigma_2 = 2$ and the sample sizes are $n_1 = 50$ and $n_2 = 50$, construct a 95% confidence interval for the difference between the two population means.

b. If $\sigma_1 = \sigma_2$, $s_1 = 3$, and $s_2 = 2$, and the sample sizes are $n_1 = 10$ and $n_2 = 10$, construct a 95% confidence interval for the difference between the two population means.

c. If $\sigma_1 \neq \sigma_2$, $s_1 = 3$, and $s_2 = 2$, and the sample sizes are $n_1 = 10$ and $n_2 = 10$, construct a 95% confidence interval for the difference between the two population means.

Business Applications

10-7. Amax Industries operates two manufacturing facilities that specialize in doing custom manufacturing work for the semiconductor industry. The facility in Denton, Texas, is highly automated, whereas the facility in Lincoln, Nebraska, has more manual functions. For the past few months, both facilities have been working on a large order for a specialized product. The vice president of operations is interested in estimating the difference in mean time it takes to complete a part on the two lines. To do this, he has requested that a random sample of 15 parts at each facility be tracked from start to finish and the time required be recorded. The following sample data were recorded:

Denton, Texas	Lincoln, Nebraska
$\bar{x}_1 = 56.7$ hours	$\bar{x}_2 = 70.4$ hours
$s_1 = 7.1$ hours	$s_1 = 8.3$ hours

Assuming that the populations are normally distributed with equal population variances, construct and interpret a 95% confidence interval estimate.

10-8. A credit card company operates two customer service centers: one in Boise and one in Richmond. Callers to the service centers dial a single number, and a computer program routs callers to the center having the fewest calls waiting. As part of a customer service review program, the credit card center would like to determine whether the average length of a call (not including hold time) is different for the two centers. The managers of the customer service centers are willing to assume that the populations of interest are normally distributed with equal variances. Suppose a random sample of phone calls to the two centers is selected and the following results are reported:

	Boise	Richmond
Sample Size	120	135
Sample Mean (seconds)	195	216
Sample St. Dev. (seconds)	35.10	37.80

a. Using the sample results, develop a 90% confidence interval estimate for the difference between the two population means.

b. Based on the confidence interval constructed in part a, what can be said about the difference between the average call times at the two centers?

10-9. A pet food producer manufactures and then fills 25-pound bags of dog food on two different production lines located in separate cities. In an effort to determine whether differences exist between the average fill rates for the two lines, a random sample of 19 bags from line 1 and a random sample of 23 bags from line 2 were recently selected. Each bag's weight was measured and the following summary measures from the samples were reported:

	Production Line 1	Production Line 2
Sample Size, n	19	23
Sample Mean, $\bar{x}$	24.96	25.01
Sample Standard Deviation, s	0.07	0.08

Management believes that the fill rates of the two lines are normally distributed with equal variances.

a. Calculate the point estimate for the difference between the population means of the two lines.

b. Develop a 95% confidence interval estimate of the true mean difference between the two lines.

c. Based on the 95% confidence interval estimate calculated in part b, what can the managers of the production lines conclude about the differences between the average fill rates for the two lines?

10-10. Two companies that manufacture batteries for electronics products have submitted their products to an independent testing agency. The agency tested 200 of each company's batteries and recorded the length of time the batteries lasted before failure. The following results were determined:

Company A	Company B
$\bar{x} = 41.5$ hours	$\bar{x} = 39.0$ hours
$s = 3.6$	$s = 5.0$

a. Based on these data, determine the 95% confidence interval to estimate the difference in average life of the batteries for the two companies. Do these data indicate that one company's batteries will outlast the other company's batteries on average? Explain.

b. Suppose the manufacturers of each of these batteries wished to warranty their batteries. One small company to which they both ship batteries receives shipments of 200 batteries weekly. If the average length of time to failure of the batteries is less than a specified number, the manufacturer will refund the company's purchase price of that set of batteries. What value should each manufacturer set if they wish to refund money on at most 5% of the shipments?

10-11. Wilson Construction and Concrete Company is known as a very progressive company that is willing to try new ideas to improve its products and service. One of the key factors of importance in concrete work is the time it takes for the concrete to "set up." The company is considering a new additive that can be put in the concrete mix to help reduce the setup time. Before going ahead with the additive, the company plans to test it against the current additive. To do this, 14 batches of concrete are mixed using each of the additives. The following results were observed:

Old Additive	New Additive
$\bar{x} = 17.2$ hours	$\bar{x} = 15.9$ hours
$s = 2.5$ hours	$s = 1.8$ hours

a. Use these sample data to construct a 90% confidence interval estimate for the difference in mean setup time for the two concrete additives. On the basis of the confidence interval produced, do you agree that the new additive helps reduce the setup time for cement? (Assume the populations are normally distributed.) Explain your answer.

b. Assuming that the new additive is slightly more expensive than the old additive, do the data support switching to the new additive if the managers of the company are primarily interested in reducing average setup time?

10-12. A working paper (Mark Aguiar and Erik Hurst, "Measuring Trends in Leisure: The Allocation of Time over Five Decades," 2006) for the Federal Reserve Bank of Boston concluded that average leisure time spent per week by women in 2003 was 33.80 hours and 37.56 hours for men. The sample standard deviations were 40 and 70, respectively. These results were obtained from samples of women and men of size 8,492 and 6,752, respectively. In this study, *leisure* refers to the time individuals spent socializing, in passive leisure, in active leisure, volunteering, in pet care, gardening, and recreational child care. Assume that the amount of leisure time spent by men and women have normal distributions with equal population variances.

a. Determine the pooled estimate of the common populations' standard deviation.

b. Produce the margin of error to estimate the difference of the two population means with a confidence level of 95%.

c. Calculate a 95% confidence interval for the difference in the average leisure time between women and men.

d. Do your results in part c indicate that the average amount of men's leisure time was larger than that of women in 2003? Support your assertions.

e. Would your conclusion in part d change if you did not assume the population variances were equal?

10-13. The Graduate Management Admission Council reported a shift in the job-hunting strategies among second-year masters of business administration (MBA) candidates. Even though their prospective base salary has increased from $81,900 to $93,770 from 2002 to 2005, it appears that MBA candidates are submitting fewer job applications. Data obtained from online surveys of 1,442 MBA candidates at 30 business school programs indicate that in 2002 the average number of job applications per candidate was 38.9 and 2.0 in 2005. The sample variances were 64 and 0.32, respectively.

a. Examine the sample variances. Conjecture whether this sample evidence indicates that the two population variances are equal to each other. Support your assertion.

b. On the basis of your answer in part a, construct a 99% confidence interval for the difference in the average number of job applications submitted by MBA candidates between 2002 and 2005.

c. Using your result in part b, is it plausible that the difference in the average number of job applications submitted is 36.5? Is it plausible that the difference in the average number of job applications submitted is 37? Are your answers to these two questions contradictory? Explain.

Computer Database **Exercises**

10-14. Logston Enterprises operates a variety of businesses in and around the St. Paul, Minnesota, area. Recently, the company was notified by the law firm representing several female employees that a lawsuit was going to be filed claiming that males were given preferential treatment when it came to pay raises by the company. The Logston human resources manager has requested that an estimate be made of the difference between mean percentage raises granted to males versus females. Sample data are contained in the file **Logston Enterprises**. She wants you to develop and interpret a 95% confidence interval estimate. She further states that the distribution of percentage raises can be assumed approximately normal, and she expects the population variances to be about equal.

10-15. The owner of the A.J. Fitness Center is interested in estimating the difference in mean years that female members have been with the club compared with male members. He wishes to develop a 95% confidence interval estimate. Sample data are in the file called **AJ Fitness**. Assuming that the sample data are approximately normal and that the two populations have equal variances, develop and interpret the confidence interval estimate. Discuss the result.

10-16. Platinum Billiards, Inc., based in Jacksonville, Florida, is a retailer of billiard supplies. It stands out among billiard suppliers because of the research it does to assure its products are top notch. One experiment was conducted to measure the speed attained by a cue ball struck by various weighted pool cues. The conjecture is that a light cue generates faster speeds while breaking the balls at the beginning of a game of pool. Anecdotal experience has indicated that a billiard cue weighing less than 19 ounces generates faster speeds. Platinum used a robotic arm to investigate this claim. The research generated the data given in the file titled **Breakcue**.

a. Calculate the sample standard deviation and mean speed produced by cues in the two weight categories: (1) under 19 ounces and (2) at or above 19 ounces.

b. Calculate a 95% confidence interval for the difference in the average speed of a cue ball generated by each of the weight categories.

c. Is the anecdotal evidence correct? Support your assertion.

d. What assumptions are required so that your results in part b would be valid?

10-17. The Federal Reserve reported in its comprehensive Survey of Consumer Finances, released every three years, that the average income of families in the United States declined from 2001 to 2004. This was the first decline since 1989–1992. A sample of incomes was taken in 2001 and repeated in 2004. After adjusting for inflation, the data that arise from these samples are given in a file titled **Federal Reserve**.

a. Determine the percentage decline indicated by the two samples.

b. Using these samples, produce a 90% confidence interval for the difference in the average family income between 2001 and 2004.

c. Is it plausible that there has been no decline in the average income of U.S. families? Support your assertion.

d. How large an error could you have made by using the difference in the sample means to estimate the difference in the population means?

Chapter Outcome 1. → # 10.2 Hypothesis Tests for Two Population Means Using Independent Samples

You are going to encounter situations that will require you to test whether two populations have equal means or whether one population mean is larger (or smaller) than another. These hypothesis-testing applications are just an extension of the hypothesis-testing process introduced in Chapter 9 for a single population mean. They also build directly on the estimation process introduced in Section 10.1.

In this section, we will introduce hypothesis-testing techniques for the difference between the means of two populations in the following situations:

1. The population standard deviations are known and the samples are independent.
2. The population standard deviations are unknown and the samples are independent.

The remainder of this section presents examples of hypothesis tests for these different situations.

Testing for $\mu_1 - \mu_2$ When σ_1 and σ_2 Are Known, Using Independent Samples

Samples are considered to be *independent* when the samples from the two populations are taken in such a way that the occurrence of values in one sample has no influence on the probability of occurrence of the values in the second sample. In special cases in which the population standard deviations are known and the samples are independent, the test statistic is a z-value computed using Equation 10.7.

---

z-Test Statistic for $\mu_1 - \mu_2$ When σ_1 and σ_2 Are Known, Independent Samples

$$z = \frac{(\bar{x}_1 - \bar{x}_2) - (\mu_1 - \mu_2)}{\sqrt{\dfrac{\sigma_1^2}{n_1} + \dfrac{\sigma_2^2}{n_2}}}$$

(10.7)

where:

$(\mu_1 - \mu_2)$ = Hypothesized difference in population means

---

If the calculated z-value using Equation 10.7 exceeds the critical z-value from the standard normal distribution, the null hypothesis is rejected. Example 10-4 illustrates the use of this test statistic.

EXAMPLE 10-4   HYPOTHESIS TEST FOR $\mu_1 - \mu_2$ WHEN σ_1 AND σ_2 ARE KNOWN, INDEPENDENT SAMPLES

Brooklyn Brick, Inc. Brooklyn Brick, Inc. is a Pennsylvania-based company that makes bricks and concrete blocks for the building industry. One product is a brick facing material that looks like a real brick but is much thinner. The ideal thickness is 0.50 inches. The bricks that the company makes must be very uniform in their dimension so brickmasons can build straight walls. The company has two plants that produce brick facing products, and the technology used at the two plants is slightly different. At plant 1, the standard deviation in the thickness of brick facing products is known to be 0.025 inches, and the standard deviation at plant 2 is 0.034 inches. These are known values. However, the company is interested in determining whether there is a difference in the average thickness of brick facing products made at the two plants. Specifically, the company wishes to know whether plant 2 also provides brick facing products that have a greater mean thickness than the products produced at plant 1. If the test determines that plant 2 does provided thicker materials than plant 1, the managers will

The Hypothesis-Testing Process for Two Population Means
The hypothesis-testing process for tests involving two population means introduced in this section is essentially the same as for a single population mean. The process is composed of the following steps:

1. Specify the population parameter of interest.

2. Formulate the appropriate null and alternative hypotheses. The null hypothesis should contain the equality. Possible formats for hypotheses testing concerning two populations means are

$H_0: \mu_1 - \mu_2 = c$
$H_A: \mu_1 - \mu_2 \neq c$ two-tailed test
$H_0: \mu_1 - \mu_2 \leq c$
$H_A: \mu_1 - \mu_2 > c$ one-tailed test
$H_0: \mu_1 - \mu_2 \geq c$
$H_A: \mu_1 - \mu_2 < c$ one-tailed test

where c = any specified number.

3. Specify the significance level (α) for testing the hypothesis. Alpha is the maximum allowable probability of committing a Type I statistical error.

4. Determine the rejection region and develop the decision rule.

5. Compute the test statistic or the p-value. Of course, you must first select simple random samples from each population and compute the sample means.

6. Reach a decision. Apply the decision rule to determine whether to reject the null hypothesis.

7. Draw a conclusion.

have the maintenance department attempt to adjust the process to reduce the mean thickness. To test this, you can use the following steps:

Step 1 Specify the population parameter of interest.
This is $\mu_1 - \mu_2$, the difference in the two population means.

Step 2 Formulate the appropriate null and alternative hypotheses.
We are interested in determining whether the mean thickness for plant 2 exceeds that for plant 1. The following null and alternative hypotheses are specified:

$$H_0: \mu_1 - \mu_2 \geq 0.0 \qquad\qquad H_0: \mu_1 \geq \mu_2$$
$$\text{or}$$
$$H_A: \mu_1 - \mu_2 < 0.0 \qquad\qquad H_A: \mu_1 < \mu_2$$

Step 3 Specify the significance level for the test.
The test will be conducted using $\alpha = 0.05$.

Step 4 Determine the rejection region and state the decision rule.
Because the population standard deviations are assumed to be known, the critical value is a z-value from the standard normal distribution. This test is a one-tailed lower-tail test, with $\alpha = 0.05$. From the standard normal distribution, the critical z-value is

$$-z_{0.05} = -1.645$$

The decision rule compares the test statistic found in Step 5 to the critical z-value.

If $z < -1.645$, reject the null hypothesis;
Otherwise, do not reject the null hypothesis.

Alternatively, you can state the decision rule in terms of a p-value, as follows:

If p-value $< \alpha = 0.05$, reject the null hypothesis;
Otherwise, do not reject the null hypothesis.

Step 5 Compute the test statistic.
Select simple random samples of brick facing pieces from the two populations and compute the sample means. A simple random sample of 100 brick facing pieces is selected from plant 1's production, and another simple random sample of 100 brick facing pieces is selected from plant 2's production. The samples are independent because the thicknesses of the brick pieces made by one plant can in no way influence the thicknesses of the bricks made by the other plant. The means computed from the samples are

$$\bar{x}_1 = 0.501 \text{ inches} \quad \text{and} \quad \bar{x}_2 = 0.509 \text{ inches}$$

The test statistic is obtained using Equation 10.7.

$$z = \frac{(\bar{x}_1 - \bar{x}_2) - (\mu_1 - \mu_2)}{\sqrt{\dfrac{\sigma_1^2}{n_1} + \dfrac{\sigma_2^2}{n_2}}}$$

$$z = \frac{(0.501 - 0.509) - 0}{\sqrt{\dfrac{0.025^2}{100} + \dfrac{0.034^2}{100}}} = -1.90$$

Step 6 Reach a decision.
The critical $-z_{0.05} = -1.645$, and the test statistic value was computed to be $z = -1.90$. Applying the decision rule,

Because $z = -1.90 < -1.645$, reject the null hypothesis.

Figure 10.2 illustrates this hypothesis test.

FIGURE 10.2 |

Example 10-4 Hypothesis Test

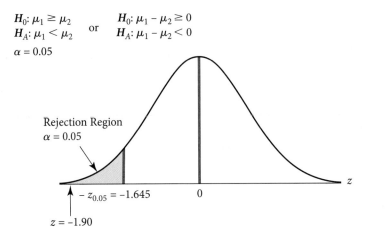

$H_0: \mu_1 \geq \mu_2$ or $H_0: \mu_1 - \mu_2 \geq 0$
$H_A: \mu_1 < \mu_2$ $H_A: \mu_1 - \mu_2 < 0$

$\alpha = 0.05$

Rejection Region
$\alpha = 0.05$

$-z_{0.05} = -1.645$ 0 z

$z = -1.90$

Test Statistic:

$$z = \frac{(\bar{x}_1 - \bar{x}_2) - (\mu_1 - \mu_2)}{\sqrt{\dfrac{\sigma_1^2}{n_1} + \dfrac{\sigma_2^2}{n_2}}} = \frac{(0.501 - 0.509) - 0}{\sqrt{\dfrac{0.025^2}{100} + \dfrac{0.034^2}{100}}} = -1.90$$

Decision Rule:
Since $z = -1.90 < z = -1.645$, reject H_0.
Conclude that the brick facings made by plant 2 have a larger mean thickness than those made by plant 1.

Step 7   Draw a conclusion.

There is statistical evidence to conclude that the brick facings made by plant 2 have a larger mean thickness than those made by plant 1. Thus, the managers of Brooklyn Brick, Inc. need to take action to reduce the mean thicknesses from plant 2.

>> **END EXAMPLE**

TRY PROBLEM 10-21 (pg. 408)

Using p-Values The z-test statistic computed in Example 10-4 indicates that the difference in sample means is 1.90 standard errors below the hypothesized difference of zero. Because this falls below the z critical level of -1.645, the null hypothesis is rejected. You could have also tested this hypothesis using the p-value approach introduced in Chapter 9. The p-value for this one-tailed test is the probability of a z-value in a standard normal distribution being less than -1.90. From the standard normal table, the probability associated with $z = -1.90$ is 0.4713. Then the p-value is

$$p\text{-value} = 0.5000 - 0.4713 = 0.0287$$

The decision rule to use with p-values is

If p-value $< \alpha$, reject the null hypothesis;
Otherwise, do not reject the null hypothesis.

Because

$$p\text{-value} = 0.0287 < \alpha = 0.05$$

reject the null hypothesis and conclude that the mean brick facing thickness for plant 2 is greater than the mean thickness for products produced by plant 1.

Testing $\mu_1 - \mu_2$ When σ_1 and σ_2 Are Unknown, Using Independent Samples

In Section 10.1 we showed that to develop a confidence interval estimate for the difference between two population means when the standard deviations are unknown, we used the t-distribution to obtain the critical value. As you might suspect, this same approach is taken for hypothesis-testing situations. Equation 10.8 shows the t-test statistic that will be used when σ_1 and σ_2 are unknown.

t-Test Statistic for $\mu_1 - \mu_2$ When σ_1 and σ_2 Are Unknown and Assumed Equal, Independent Samples

$$t = \frac{(\bar{x}_1 - \bar{x}_2) - (\mu_1 - \mu_2)}{s_p\sqrt{\dfrac{1}{n_1} + \dfrac{1}{n_2}}}, \quad df = n_1 + n_2 - 2 \tag{10.8}$$

where:

$\bar{x}_1$ and $\bar{x}_2$ = Sample means from populations 1 and 2

$\mu_1 - \mu_2$ = Hypothesized difference between population means

n_1 and n_2 = Sample sizes from the two populations

s_p = Pooled standard deviation (see Equation 10.4)

The test statistic in Equation 10.8 is based on three assumptions:

Assumptions

- Each population has a normal distribution.[3]
- The two population variances, σ_1^2 and σ_2^2, are equal.
- The samples are independent.

Notice that in Equation 10.8, we are using the pooled estimate for the common population standard deviation that we developed in Section 10.1.

BUSINESS APPLICATION | **HYPOTHESIS TEST FOR THE DIFFERENCE BETWEEN TWO POPULATION MEANS**

RETIREMENT INVESTING (CONTINUED) Recall the earlier example discussing a study in North Dakota involving retirement investing. The leaders of the study are interested in determining whether there is a difference in mean annual contributions for individuals covered by TSAs and those with 401(k) retirement programs. A simple random sample of 15 people from the population of adults who are eligible for a TSA investment was selected. A second sample of 15 people was selected from the population of adults in North Dakota who have 401(k) plans. The variables of interest are the dollars invested in the two retirement plans during the previous year.

Specifically, we are interested in testing the following null and alternative hypotheses:

$$H_0: \mu_1 - \mu_2 = 0.0 \qquad H_0: \mu_1 = \mu_2$$
$$\text{or}$$
$$H_A: \mu_1 - \mu_2 \neq 0.0 \qquad H_A: \mu_1 \neq \mu_2$$

μ_1 = Mean dollars invested by the TSA−eligible population during the past year
μ_2 = Mean dollars invested by the 401(k)−eligible population during the past year

The leaders of the study select a significance level of $\alpha = 0.05$. The sample results are

TSA–Eligible	401(k)–Eligible
$n_1 = 15$	$n_2 = 15$
$\bar{x}_1 = \$2{,}119.70$	$\bar{x}_2 = \$1{,}777.70$
$s_1 = \$709.70$	$s_2 = \$593.90$

Because the investments by individuals with TSA accounts are in no way influenced by investments by individuals with 401(k) accounts, the samples are considered independent. The box and whisker plots shown earlier in Figure 10.1 are consistent with what might be expected if the populations have equal variances and are approximately normally distributed.

---

[3]In Chapter 13, we will introduce a technique called the goodness-of-fit test, which we can use to test whether the sample data come from a population that is normally distributed.

We are now in a position to complete the hypothesis test to determine whether the mean dollar amount invested by TSA employees is different from the mean amount invested by 401(k) employees. We first determine the critical values from the t-distribution table in Appendix F with degrees of freedom equal to

$$n_1 + n_2 - 2 = 15 + 15 - 2 = 28$$

and $\alpha = 0.05$ for the two-tailed test.[4] The appropriate t-values are

$$t_{0.025} = \pm 2.0484 = \text{Critical values}$$

To continue the hypothesis test, we compute the pooled standard deviation.

$$s_p = \sqrt{\frac{(n_1-1)s_1^2 + (n_2-1)s_2^2}{n_1+n_2-2}} = \sqrt{\frac{(15-1)(709.7)^2 + (15-1)(593.9)^2}{15+15-2}} = 654.37$$

Note that the pooled standard deviation is partway between the two sample standard deviations. Now, keeping in mind that the hypothesized difference between μ_1 and μ_2 is zero, we compute the t-test statistic using Equation 10.8, as follows:

$$t = \frac{(\bar{x}_1 - \bar{x}_2) - (\mu_1 - \mu_2)}{s_p\sqrt{\frac{1}{n_1} + \frac{1}{n_2}}} = \frac{(2,119.70 - 1,777.70) - 0.0}{654.37\sqrt{\frac{1}{15} + \frac{1}{15}}} = 1.4313$$

This indicates that the difference in sample means is 1.4313 standard errors above the hypothesized difference of zero. Because

$$t = 1.4313 < t_{0.025} = 2.0484$$

the null hypothesis should not be rejected.

The difference in sample means is attributed to sampling error. Figure 10.3 summarizes this hypothesis test. Based on the sample data, there is no statistical justification to believe that the mean annual investment by individuals eligible for the TSA option is different from those individuals eligible for the 401(k) plan.

FIGURE 10.3

Hypothesis Test for the Equality of the Two Population Means for the North Dakota Investment Study

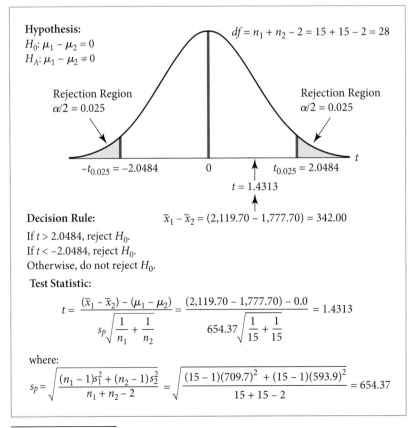

[4]You can also use Excel's T.INV.2T function (=T.INV.2T(0.05,28).

Excel Tutorial

USING EXCEL TO TEST FOR THE DIFFERENCE BETWEEN TWO POPULATION MEANS

SUV VEHICLE MILEAGE Excel has a procedure for performing the necessary calculations to test hypotheses involving two population means. Consider a national car rental company that is interested in testing to determine whether there is a difference in mean mileage for sport utility vehicles (SUVs) driven in town versus those driven on the highway. Based on its experience with regular automobiles, the company believes the mean highway mileage will exceed the mean city mileage.

To test this belief, the company has randomly selected 25 SUV rentals driven only on the highway and another random sample of 25 SUV rentals driven only in the city. The vehicles were filled with 14 gallons of gasoline. The company then asked each customer to drive the car until it ran out of gasoline. At that point, the elapsed miles were noted and the miles per gallon (mpg) were recorded. For their trouble, the customers received free use of the SUV and a coupon valid for one week's free rental. The results of the experiment are contained in the file **Mileage**.

Excel can be used to perform the calculations required to determine whether the manager's belief about SUV highway mileage is justified. We first formulate the null and alternative hypotheses to be tested:

$$H_0: \mu_1 - \mu_2 \leq 0.0 \qquad H_0: \mu_1 \leq \mu_2$$

or

$$H_A: \mu_1 - \mu_2 > 0.0 \qquad H_A: \mu_1 > \mu_2$$

Population 1 represents highway mileage, and population 2 represents city mileage. The test is conducted using a significance level of $0.05 = \alpha$.

Figure 10.4 shows the descriptive statistics for the two independent samples.

FIGURE 10.4

Excel 2010 Output—SUV Mileage Descriptive Statistics

Excel 2010 Instructions:
1. Open file: **Mileage.xlsx**.
2. Select **Data > Data Analysis**.
3. Select **Descriptive Statistics**.
4. Define the data range for all variables to be analyzed.
5. Select **Summary Statistics**.
6. Specify output location.
7. Click **OK**.

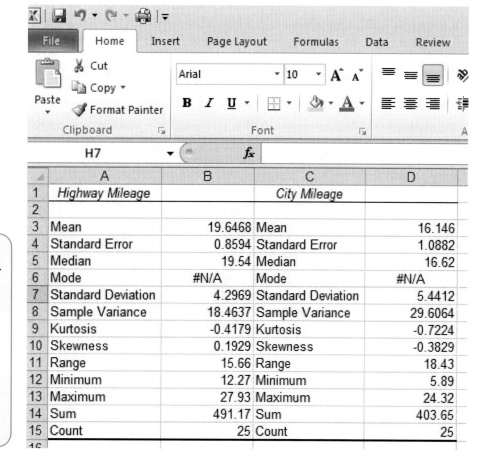

	A	B	C	D
1	*Highway Mileage*		*City Mileage*	
2				
3	Mean	19.6468	Mean	16.146
4	Standard Error	0.8594	Standard Error	1.0882
5	Median	19.54	Median	16.62
6	Mode	#N/A	Mode	#N/A
7	Standard Deviation	4.2969	Standard Deviation	5.4412
8	Sample Variance	18.4637	Sample Variance	29.6064
9	Kurtosis	-0.4179	Kurtosis	-0.7224
10	Skewness	0.1929	Skewness	-0.3829
11	Range	15.66	Range	18.43
12	Minimum	12.27	Minimum	5.89
13	Maximum	27.93	Maximum	24.32
14	Sum	491.17	Sum	403.65
15	Count	25	Count	25

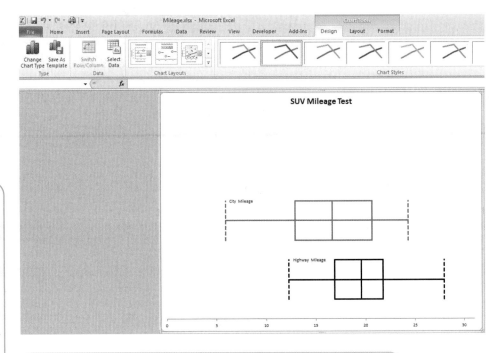

Excel 2010 Instructions:
1. Open **PHStat** and Enable Macros.
2. Open file: **Mileage.xlsx**.
3. Click **Add-Ins**.
4. Click **PHStat** down arrow.
5. Select **Descriptive Statistics**.
6. Select **Boxplot**.
7. Select data (both columns including headings).
8. Click **Multiple Groups–Unstacked**.
9. Click **OK**.
10. Add titles.

Minitab Instructions (for similar results):
1. Open file: **Mileage.MTW**.
2. Choose **Graph > Boxplot**.
3. Under **Multiple Ys**, select **Simple**.
4. Click **OK**.
5. In **Graph variables**, enter data columns.
6. Click **OK**.

Figure 10.5 displays the Excel box and whisker plots for the two samples. Based on these plots, the normal distribution and equal variance assumptions appear reasonable. We will proceed with the test of means assuming normal distributions and equal variances.

Figure 10.6 shows the Excel output for the hypothesis test. The mean highway mileage is 19.6468 mpg, whereas the mean for city driving is 16.146. At issue is whether this difference in sample means $(19.6468 - 16.146 = 3.5008 \text{ mpg})$ is sufficient to conclude the mean highway mileage exceeds the mean city mileage. The one-tail t critical value for $\alpha = 0.05$ is shown in Figure 10.6 to be

$$t_{0.05} = 1.6772$$

Figure 10.6 shows that the "t-Stat" value from Excel, which is the calculated test statistic (or t-value, based on Equation 10.8), is equal to

$$t = 2.52$$

The difference in sample means (3.5008 mpg) is 2.52 standard errors larger than the hypothesized difference of zero. Because the test statistic

$$t = 2.52 > t_{0.05} = 1.6772$$

we reject the null hypothesis. Thus, the sample data do provide sufficient evidence to conclude that mean SUV highway mileage exceeds mean SUV city mileage, and this study confirms the expectations of the rental company managers. This will factor into the company's fuel pricing.

The output shown in Figures 10.6 also provides the p-value for the one-tailed test, which can also be used to test the null hypothesis. Recall, if the calculated p-value is less than alpha, the null hypothesis should be rejected. The decision rule is

If p-value < 0.05, reject H_0.
Otherwise, do not reject H_0.

The p-value for the one-tailed test is 0.0075. Because $0.0075 < 0.05$, the null hypothesis is rejected. This is the same conclusion as the one we reached using the test statistic approach.

FIGURE 10.6 |

Excel 2010 Output for the SUV Mileage *t*-Test for Two Population Means

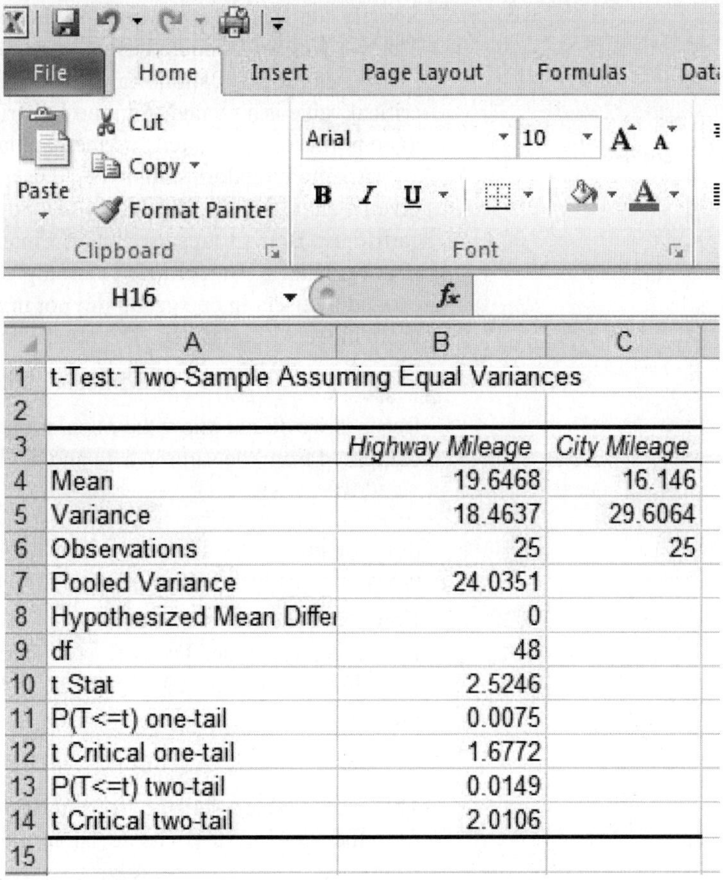

Excel 2010 Instructions:
1. Open file: **Mileage.xlsx**.
2. Select **Data > Data Analysis**.
3. Select **t-test: Two Sample Assuming Equal Variances**.
4. Define data ranges for the two variables of interest.
5. Set **Hypothesized Difference** to 0.0.
6. Set **Alpha** at 0.05.
7. Specify Output Location.
8. Click **OK**.
9. Click the **Home** tab and adjust decimal points in output.

	A	B	C
1	t-Test: Two-Sample Assuming Equal Variances		
2			
3		Highway Mileage	City Mileage
4	Mean	19.6468	16.146
5	Variance	18.4637	29.6064
6	Observations	25	25
7	Pooled Variance	24.0351	
8	Hypothesized Mean Differ	0	
9	df	48	
10	t Stat	2.5246	
11	P(T<=t) one-tail	0.0075	
12	t Critical one-tail	1.6772	
13	P(T<=t) two-tail	0.0149	
14	t Critical two-tail	2.0106	
15			

Minitab Instructions (for similar results):
1. Open file: **Mileage.MTW**.
2. Choose **Stat > Basic Statistics > 2-Sample *t***.
3. Choose **Samples in different columns**.
4. In **First**, enter the first data column.
5. In **Second**, enter the other data column.
6. Check **Assume equal variances**.
7. Click **Options** and enter $1 - \alpha$ in **Confidence level**.
8. In **Alternative** choose *greater than*.
9. Click **OK. OK**.

EXAMPLE 10-5   **HYPOTHESIS TEST FOR $\mu_1 - \mu_2$ WHEN σ_1 AND σ_2 ARE UNKNOWN, USING INDEPENDENT SAMPLES**

Color Printer Ink Cartridges A recent Associated Press news story out of Brussels, Belgium, indicated the European Union was considering a probe of computer makers after consumers complained that they were being overcharged for ink cartridges. Companies such as Canon, Hewlett-Packard, and Epson are the printer market leaders and make most of their printer-related profits by selling replacement ink cartridges. Suppose an independent test agency wishes to conduct a test to determine whether name-brand ink cartridges generate more color pages on average than competing generic ink cartridges. The test can be conducted using the following steps:

Step 1   Specify the population parameter of interest.
We are interested in determining whether the mean number of pages printed by name-brand cartridges (population 1) exceeds the mean pages printed by generic cartridges (population 2).

Step 2   Formulate the appropriate null and alternative hypotheses.
The following null and alternative hypotheses are specified:

$$H_0: \mu_1 - \mu_2 \leq 0.0 \qquad H_0: \mu_1 \leq \mu_2$$
$$\text{or}$$
$$H_A: \mu_1 - \mu_2 > 0.0 \qquad H_A: \mu_1 > \mu_2$$

Step 3 **Specify the significance level for the test.**

The test will be conducted using $\alpha = 0.05$.

When the populations have standard deviations that are unknown, the critical value is a t-value from the t-distribution if the populations are assumed to be normally distributed and the population variances are assumed to be equal.

A simple random sample of 10 users was selected, and the users were given a name-brand cartridge. A second sample of 8 users was given generic cartridges. Both groups used their printers until the ink ran out. The number of pages printed was recorded. The samples are independent because the pages printed by users in one group did not in any way influence the pages printed by users in the second group. The means computed from the samples are

$$\bar{x}_1 = 322.5 \text{ pages} \quad \text{and} \quad \bar{x}_2 = 298.3 \text{ pages}$$

Because we do not know the population standard deviations, these values are computed from the sample data and are

$$s_1 = 48.3 \text{ pages} \quad \text{and} \quad s_2 = 53.3 \text{ pages}$$

Suppose previous studies have shown that the number of pages printed by both types of cartridge tends to be approximately normal with equal variances.

Step 4 **Construct the rejection region.**

Based on a one-tailed test with $\alpha = 0.05$, the critical value is a t-value from the t-distribution with $10 + 8 - 2 = 16$ degrees of freedom. From the t-table, the critical t-value is

$$t_{0.05} = 1.7459 = \text{Critical value}$$

The calculated test statistic from step 5 is compared to the critical t-value to form the decision rule. The decision rule is

If $t > 1.7459$, reject the null hypothesis;
Otherwise, do not reject the null hypothesis.

Step 5 **Determine the test statistic using Equation 10.8.**

$$t = \frac{(\bar{x}_1 - \bar{x}_2) - (\mu_1 - \mu_2)}{s_p \sqrt{\dfrac{1}{n_1} + \dfrac{1}{n_2}}}$$

The pooled standard deviation is

$$s_p = \sqrt{\frac{(n_1 - 1)s_1^2 + (n_2 - 1)s_2^2}{n_1 + n_2 - 2}} = \sqrt{\frac{(10 - 1)48.3^2 + (8 - 1)53.3^2}{10 + 8 - 2}} = 50.55$$

Then the t-test statistic is

$$t = \frac{(322.5 - 298.3) - 0.0}{50.55 \sqrt{\dfrac{1}{10} + \dfrac{1}{8}}} = 1.0093$$

Step 6 **Reach a decision.**

Because

$$t = 1.0093 < t_{0.05} = 1.7459$$

do not reject the null hypothesis.

Figure 10.7 illustrates the hypothesis test.

Step 7 **Draw a conclusion.**

Based on these sample data, there is insufficient evidence to conclude that the mean number of pages produced by name-brand ink cartridges exceeds the mean for generic cartridges.

>> END EXAMPLE

TRY PROBLEM 10-20 (pg. 408)

FIGURE 10.7

Example 10-5 Hypothesis Test

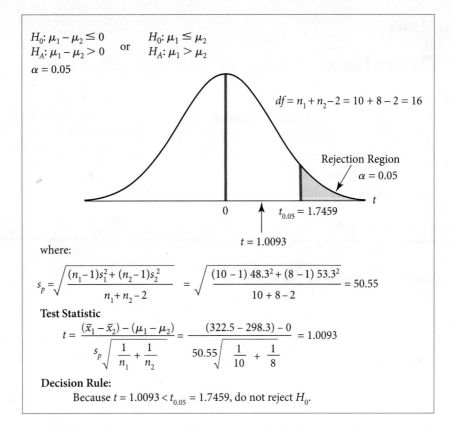

$H_0: \mu_1 - \mu_2 \leq 0$ $H_0: \mu_1 \leq \mu_2$
$H_A: \mu_1 - \mu_2 > 0$ or $H_A: \mu_1 > \mu_2$
$\alpha = 0.05$

$df = n_1 + n_2 - 2 = 10 + 8 - 2 = 16$

Rejection Region
$\alpha = 0.05$

0 $t_{0.05} = 1.7459$ t

$t = 1.0093$

where:

$$s_p = \sqrt{\frac{(n_1-1)s_1^2 + (n_2-1)s_2^2}{n_1 + n_2 - 2}} = \sqrt{\frac{(10-1)\,48.3^2 + (8-1)\,53.3^2}{10 + 8 - 2}} = 50.55$$

Test Statistic

$$t = \frac{(\bar{x}_1 - \bar{x}_2) - (\mu_1 - \mu_2)}{s_p\sqrt{\dfrac{1}{n_1} + \dfrac{1}{n_2}}} = \frac{(322.5 - 298.3) - 0}{50.55\sqrt{\dfrac{1}{10} + \dfrac{1}{8}}} = 1.0093$$

Decision Rule:
  Because $t = 1.0093 < t_{0.05} = 1.7459$, do not reject H_0.

What If the Population Variances Are Not Equal? In the previous examples, we assumed that the population variances were equal, and we carried out the hypothesis test for two population means using Equation 10.8. Even in cases in which the population variances are not equal, the t-test as specified in Equation 10.8 is generally considered to be appropriate as long as the sample sizes are equal.[5] However, if the sample sizes are not equal and if the sample data lead us to suspect that the variances are not equal, the t-test statistic must be approximated using Equation 10.9.[6] In cases in which the variances are not equal, the degrees of freedom are computed using Equation 10.10.

**t-Test Statistic for $\mu_1 - \mu_2$ When Population Variances Are
Unknown and Not Assumed Equal**

$$t = \frac{(\bar{x}_1 - \bar{x}_2) - (\mu_1 - \mu_2)}{\sqrt{\dfrac{s_1^2}{n_1} + \dfrac{s_2^2}{n_2}}}$$

(10.9)

**Degrees of Freedom for t-Test Statistic When Population
Variances Are Not Equal**

$$df = \frac{(s_1^2/n_1 + s_2^2/n_2)^2}{\left(\dfrac{(s_1^2/n_1)^2}{n_1 - 1} + \dfrac{(s_2^2/n_2)^2}{n_2 - 1}\right)}$$

(10.10)

---

[5]Studies show that when the sample sizes are equal or almost equal, the t distribution is appropriate even when one population variance is twice the size of the other.
[6]Chapter 11 introduces a statistical procedure for testing whether two populations have equal variances.

MyStatLab

10-2: Exercises

Skill Development

10-18. A decision maker wishes to test the following null and alternative hypotheses using an alpha level equal to 0.05:

$$H_0: \mu_1 - \mu_2 = 0$$
$$H_A: \mu_1 - \mu_2 \neq 0$$

The population standard deviations are assumed to be known. After collecting the sample data, the test statistic is computed to be

$$z = 1.78$$

a. Using the test statistic approach, what conclusion should be reached about the null hypothesis?
b. Using the p-value approach, what decision should be reached about the null hypothesis?
c. Will the two approaches (test statistic and p-value) ever provide different conclusions based on the same sample data? Explain.

10-19. The following null and alternative hypotheses have been stated:

$$H_0: \mu_1 - \mu_2 = 0$$
$$H_A: \mu_1 - \mu_2 \neq 0$$

To test the null hypothesis, random samples have been selected from the two normally distributed populations with equal variances. The following sample data were observed:

Sample from Population 1			Sample from Population 2		
33	29	35	46	43	42
39	39	41	46	44	47
25	33	38	50	43	39

Test the null hypothesis using an alpha level equal to 0.05.

10-20. Given the following null and alternative hypotheses

$$H_0: \mu_1 \geq \mu_2$$
$$H_A: \mu_1 < \mu_2$$

together with the following sample information

	Sample 1	Sample 2
	$n_1 = 14$	$n_2 = 18$
	$\bar{x}_1 = 565$	$\bar{x}_2 = 578$
	$s_1 = 28.9$	$s_2 = 26.3$

a. Assuming that the populations are normally distributed with equal variances, test at the 0.10 level of significance whether you would reject the null hypothesis based on the sample information. Use the test statistic approach.
b. Assuming that the populations are normally distributed with equal variances, test at the 0.05 level of significance whether you would reject the null hypothesis based on the sample information. Use the test statistic approach.

10-21. Given the following null and alternative hypotheses, conduct a hypothesis test using an alpha equal to 0.05. (*Note*: The population standard deviations are assumed to be known.)

$$H_0: \mu_1 \leq \mu_2$$
$$H_A: \mu_1 > \mu_2$$

The sample means for the two populations are shown as follows:

$\bar{x}_1 = 144$	$\bar{x}_2 = 129$
$\sigma_1 = 11$	$\sigma_2 = 16$
$n_1 = 40$	$n_2 = 50$

10-22. The following statistics were obtained from independent samples from populations that have normal distributions:

	1	2
n_i	41	51
$\bar{x}_i$	25.4	33.2
s_i	5.6	7.4

a. Use these statistics to conduct a test of hypothesis if the alternative hypothesis is $\mu_1 - \mu_2 < -4$. Use a significance level of 0.01.
b. Determine the p-value for the test described in part a.
c. Describe the type of statistical error that could have been made as a result of your hypothesis test.

10-23. Given the following null and alternative hypotheses

$$H_0: \mu_1 - \mu_2 = 0$$
$$H_A: \mu_1 - \mu_2 \neq 0$$

and the following sample information

	Sample 1	Sample 2
	$n_1 = 125$	$n_2 = 120$
	$s_1 = 31$	$s_2 = 38$
	$\bar{x}_1 = 130$	$\bar{x}_2 = 105$

a. Develop the appropriate decision rule, assuming a significance level of 0.05 is to be used.
b. Test the null hypothesis and indicate whether the sample information leads you to reject or fail to reject the null hypothesis. Use the test statistic approach.

10-24. Consider the following two independently chosen samples whose population variances are not equal to each other.

Sample 1	12.1	13.4	11.7	10.7	14.0
Sample 2	10.5	9.5	8.2	7.8	11.1

a. Using a significance level of 0.025, test the null hypothesis that $\mu_1 - \mu_2 \leq 0$.
b. Calculate the p-value.

Business Applications

10-25. Descent, Inc., produces a variety of climbing and mountaineering equipment. One of its products is a traditional three-strand climbing rope. An important characteristic of any climbing rope is its tensile strength. Descent produces the three-strand rope on two separate production lines: one in Bozeman and the other in Challis. The Bozeman line has recently installed new production equipment. Descent regularly tests the tensile strength of its ropes by randomly selecting ropes from production and subjecting them to various tests. The most recent random sample of ropes, taken after the new equipment was installed at the Bozeman plant, revealed the following:

Bozeman	Challis
$\bar{x}_1 = 7{,}200$ lb	$\bar{x}_2 = 7{,}087$ lb
$s_1 = 425$	$s_2 = 415$
$n_1 = 25$	$n_2 = 20$

Descent's production managers are willing to assume that the population of tensile strengths for each plant is approximately normally distributed with equal variances. Based on the sample results, can Descent's managers conclude that there is a difference between the mean tensile strengths of ropes produced in Bozeman and Challis? Conduct the appropriate hypothesis test at the 0.05 level of significance.

10-26. The management of the Seaside Golf Club regularly monitors the golfers on its course for speed of play. Suppose a random sample of golfers was taken in 2005 and another random sample of golfers was selected in 2006. The results of the two samples are as follows:

2005	2006
$\bar{x}_1 = 225$	$\bar{x}_2 = 219$
$s_1 = 20.25$	$s_2 = 21.70$
$n_1 = 36$	$n_2 = 31$

Based on the sample results, can the management of the Seaside Golf Club conclude that average speed of play was different in 2006 than in 2005? Conduct the appropriate hypothesis test at the 0.10 level of significance. Assume that the management of the club is willing to accept the assumption that the populations of playing times for each year are approximately normally distributed with equal variances.

10-27. The marketing manager for a major retail grocery chain is wondering about the location of the stores' dairy products. She believes that the mean amount spent by customers on dairy products per visit is higher in stores in which the dairy section is in the central part of the store compared with stores that have the dairy section at the rear of the store. To consider relocating the dairy products, the manager feels that the increase in the mean amount spent by customers must be at least 25 cents. To determine whether relocation is justified, her staff selected a random sample of 25 customers at stores in which the dairy section is central in the store. A second sample of 25 customers was selected in stores with the dairy section at the rear of the store. The following sample results were observed:

Central Dairy	Rear Dairy
$\bar{x}_1 = \$3.74$	$\bar{x}_2 = \$3.26$
$s_1 = \$0.87$	$s_2 = \$0.79$

a. Conduct a hypothesis test with a significance level of 0.05 to determine if the manager should relocate the dairy products in those stores displaying their dairy products in the rear of the store.
b. If a statistical error associated with hypothesis testing was made in this hypothesis test, what error could it have been? Explain.

10-28. Sherwin-Williams is a major paint manufacturer. Recently, the research and development (R&D) department came out with a new paint product designed to be used in areas that are particularly prone to periodic moisture and hot sun. They believe that this new paint will be superior to anything that Sherwin-Williams or its competitors currently offer. However, they are concerned about the coverage area that a gallon of the new paint will provide compared to their current products. The R&D department set up a test in which two random samples of paint were selected. The first sample consisted of 25 one-gallon containers of the company's best-selling paint, and the second sample consisted of 15 one-gallon containers of the new paint under consideration. The following statistics were computed from each sample and refer to the number of square feet that each gallon will cover:

Best-Selling Paint	New Paint Product
$\bar{x}_1 = 423$ sq.feet	$\bar{x}_2 = 406$ sq.feet
$s_1 = 22.4$ sq.feet	$s_2 = 16.8$ sq.feet
$n_1 = 25$	$n_2 = 15$

The R&D managers are concerned the average area covered per gallon will be less for the new paint than for the existing product. Based on the sample data, what should they conclude if they base their conclusion on a significance level equal to 0.01?

10-29. Albertsons was once one of the largest grocery chains in the United States, with more than 1,100 grocery stores, but in the early 2000s, the company began to feel the competitive pinch from companies like Wal-Mart and Costco. In January 2006, the company announced that it would be sold to SuperValu, Inc., headquartered in Minneapolis. Prior to the sale, Albertsons had attempted to lower prices to regain its competitive edge. In an effort to maintain its profit margins, Albertsons took several steps to lower costs. One was to replace some of the traditional checkout stands with automated self-checkout facilities. After making the change in some test stores, the company performed a study to determine whether the average purchase through a self-checkout facility was less than the average purchase at the traditional checkout stand.

To conduct the test, a random sample of 125 customer transactions at the self-checkout was obtained, and a second random sample of 125 transactions from customers using the traditional checkout process was obtained. The following statistics were computed from each sample:

Self-Checkout	Traditional Checkout
$\bar{x}_1 = \$45.68$	$\bar{x}_2 = \$78.49$
$s_1 = \$58.20$	$s_2 = \$62.45$
$n_1 = 125$	$n_2 = 125$

Based on these sample data, what should be concluded with respect to the average transaction amount for the two checkout processes? Test using an $\alpha = 0.05$ level.

10-30. The *Washington Post Weekly Edition* quoted an Urban Institute study that stated that about 80% of the estimated $200 billion of federal housing subsidies consisted of tax breaks (mainly deductions for mortgage interest payments). Samples indicated that the federal housing benefits average was $8,268 for those with incomes between $200,000 and $500,000 and only $365 for those with incomes of $40,000 to $50,000. The respective standard deviations were $2,100 and $150. They were obtained from sample sizes of 150.
   a. Examine the sample standard deviations. What do these suggest is the relationship between the two population standard deviations? Support your assertion.
   b. Conduct a hypothesis test to determine if the average federal housing benefits are at least $7,750 more for those in the $200,000 to $500,000 income range. Use a 0.05 significance level.
   c. Having reached your decision in part b, state the type of statistical error that you could have made.
   d. Is there any way to determine whether you were in error in the hypothesis selection you made in part b? Support your answer.

10-31. Although not all students have debt after graduating from college, more than half do. The College Board's *2008 Trends in Student Aid* addresses, among other topics, the difference in the average college debt accumulated by undergraduate bachelor of arts degree recipients by type of college for the 2006–2007 academic year. Samples might have been used to determine this difference in which the private, for-profit colleges' average was $38,300 and the public

college average was $11,800. Suppose the respective standard deviations were $2,050 and $2,084. The sample sizes were 75 and 205, respectively.
   a. Examine the sample standard deviations. What do these suggest is the relationship between the two population standard deviations? Support your assertion.
   b. Conduct a hypothesis test to determine if the average college debt for bachelor of arts degree recipients is at least $25,000 more for graduates from private colleges than from public colleges. Use a 0.01 significance level and a *p*-value approach for this hypothesis test.

Computer Database **Exercises**

10-32. Suppose a professional job-placement firm that monitors salaries in professional fields is interested in determining if the fluctuating price of oil and the outsourcing of computer-related jobs have had an effect on the starting salaries of chemical and electrical engineering graduates. Specifically, the job-placement firm would like to know if the 2007 average starting salary for chemical engineering majors is higher than the 2007 average starting salary for electrical engineering majors. To conduct its test, the job-placement firm has selected a random sample of 124 electrical engineering majors and 110 chemical engineering majors who graduated and received jobs in 2007. Each graduate was asked to report his or her starting salary. The results of the survey are contained in the file **Starting Salaries**.
   a. Conduct a hypothesis test to determine whether the mean starting salary for 2007 graduates in chemical engineering is higher than the mean starting salary for 2007 graduates in electrical engineering. Conduct the test at the 0.05 level of significance. Be sure to state a conclusion. (Assume that the firm believes the two populations from which the samples were taken are approximately normally distributed with equal variances.)
   b. Suppose the job-placement firm is unwilling to assume that the two populations are normally distributed with equal variances. Conduct the appropriate hypothesis test to determine whether a difference exists between the mean starting salaries for the two groups. Use a level of significance of 0.05. What conclusion should the job-placement firm reach based on the hypothesis test?

10-33. A *USA Today* editorial addressed the growth of compensation for corporate CEOs. Quoting a study made by *BusinessWeek*, *USA Today* indicated that the pay packages for CEOs have increased almost sevenfold on average from 1994 to 2004. The file titled **CEODough** contains the salaries of CEOs in 1994 and in 2004, adjusted for inflation.
   a. Determine the ratio of the average salary for 1994 and 2004. Does it appear that *BusinessWeek* was correct? Explain your answer.

b. Examine the sample standard deviations. What do these suggest is the relationship between the two population standard deviations? Support your assertion.

c. Based on your response to part b, conduct a test of hypothesis to determine if the difference in the average CEO salary between 1994 and 2004 is more than $9.8 million. Use a *p*-value approach with a significance level of 0.025.

10-34. The Marriott Corporation operates the largest chain of hotel and motel properties in the world. The Fairfield Inn and the Residence Inn are just two of the hotel brands that Marriott owns. At a recent managers' meeting, a question was posed regarding whether the average length of stay was different at these two properties in the United States. A summer intern was assigned the task of testing to see if there is a difference. She started by selecting a simple random sample of 100 hotel reservations from Fairfield Inn. Next, she selected a simple random sample of 100 hotel reservations from Residence Inn. In both cases, she recorded the number of nights' stay for each reservation. The resulting data are in the file called **Marriott**.

a. State the appropriate null and alternative hypotheses.

b. Based on these sample data and a 0.05 level of significance, what conclusion should be made about the average length of stay at these two hotel chains?

10-35. Airlines were severely affected by the oil price increases of 2008. Even Southwest lost money, the first time ever, during that time. Many airlines began charging for services that had previously been free, such as baggage and meals. One national airline had as an objective of getting an additional $5 to $10 per trip from its customers. Surveys could be used to determine the success of the company's actions. The file titled **AirRevenue** contains results of samples gathered before and after the company implemented its changes.

a. Produce a 95% confidence interval for the difference in the average fares paid by passengers before and after the change in policy. Based on the confidence interval, is it possible that revenue per passenger increased by at least $10? Explain your response.

b. Conduct a test of hypothesis to answer the question posed in part a. Use a significance level of 0.025.

c. Did you reach the same conclusion in both parts a and b? Is this a coincidence or will it always be so? Explain your response.

END EXERCISES 10-2

Chapter Outcome 2. → ## 10.3 Interval Estimation and Hypothesis Tests for Paired Samples

Sections 10.1 and 10.2 introduced the methods by which decision makers can estimate and test the hypotheses for the difference between the means for two populations when the two samples are independent. In each example, the samples were independent because the sample values from one population did not have the potential to influence the probability that values would be selected from the second population. However, there are instances in business in which you would want to use **paired samples** to control for sources of variation that might otherwise distort the conclusions of a study.

Paired Samples

Samples that are selected in such a way that values in one sample are matched with the values in the second sample for the purpose of controlling for extraneous factors. Another term for paired samples is *dependent samples*.

Why Use Paired Samples?

There are many situations in business in which using paired samples should be considered. For instance, a paint manufacturer might be interested in comparing the area that a new paint mix will cover per gallon with that of an existing paint mixture. One approach would be to have one random sample of painters apply a gallon of the new paint mixture. A second sample of painters would be given the existing mix. In both cases, the number of square feet that were covered by the gallon of paint would be recorded. In this case, the samples would be independent because the area covered by painters using the new mixture would not be in any way affected by the area covered by painters using the existing mixture.

This would be a fine way to do the study unless the painters themselves could influence the area that the paint will cover. For instance, suppose some painters, because of their technique or experience, are able to cover more area from a gallon of paint than other painters regardless of the type of paint used. Then, if by chance most of these "good" painters happened to get assigned to the new mix, the results might show that the new mix covers more area, not because it is a better paint, but because the painters that used it during the test were better.

To combat this potential problem, the company might want to use paired samples. To do this, one group of painters would be selected and each painter would use one gallon of each paint mix. We would measure the area covered by each painter for both paint mixes. Doing this controls for the effect of the painters' ability or technique. The following application involving gasoline supplemented with ethanol testing is one in which paired samples would most likely be warranted.

BUSINESS APPLICATION   ESTIMATION USING PAIRED SAMPLES

TESTING ETHANOL MIXED GASOLINE A major oil company wanted to estimate the difference in average mileage for cars using a regular gasoline compared with cars using a gasoline-and-ethanol mixture. The company used a paired-sample approach to control for any variation in mileage arising because of different cars and drivers. A random sample of 10 motorists (and their cars) was selected. Each car was filled with regular gasoline. The car was driven 200 miles on a specified route. The car then was filled again with gasoline and the miles per gallon were computed. After the 10 cars completed this process, the same steps were performed using the gasoline mixed with ethanol. Because the same cars and drivers tested both types of fuel, the miles-per-gallon measurements for the ethanol mixture and regular gasoline will most likely be related. The two samples are not independent but are instead considered paired samples. Thus, we will compute the *paired difference* between the values from each sample, using Equation 10.11.

Paired Difference

$$d = x_1 - x_2 \tag{10.11}$$

where:

d = Paired difference

x_1 and x_2 = Values from samples 1 and 2, respectively

Figure 10.8 shows the Excel spreadsheet for this mileage study with the paired differences computed. The data are in the file called **Ethanol-Gas**.

The first step to develop the interval estimate is to compute the *mean paired difference, $\bar{d}$,* using Equation 10.12. This value is the best point estimate for the population mean paired difference, μ_d.

Point Estimate for the Population Mean Paired Difference, μ_d

$$\bar{d} = \frac{\sum_{i=1}^{n} d_i}{n} \tag{10.12}$$

where:

d_i = ith paired difference value

n = Number of paired differrences

FIGURE 10.8

Excel 2010 Worksheet for Ethanol Mixed Gasoline Study

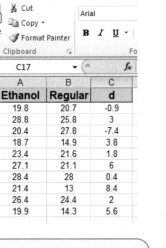

	A	B	C
1	Ethanol	Regular	d
2	19.8	20.7	-0.9
3	28.8	25.8	3
4	20.4	27.8	-7.4
5	18.7	14.9	3.8
6	23.4	21.6	1.8
7	27.1	21.1	6
8	28.4	28	0.4
9	21.4	13	8.4
10	26.4	24.4	2
11	19.9	14.3	5.6

Excel 2010 Instructions:
1. Open file: **Ethanol-Gas.xlsx**.

Using Equation 10.12, we determine $\bar{d}$ as follows:

$$\bar{d} = \frac{\sum d}{n} = \frac{22.7}{10} = 2.27$$

The next step is to compute the *sample standard deviation for the paired differences* using Equation 10.13.

Sample Standard Deviation for Paired Differences

$$s_d = \sqrt{\frac{\sum_{i=1}^{n}(d_i - \bar{d})^2}{n-1}} \tag{10.13}$$

where:

d_i = ith paired difference

$\bar{d}$ = Mean paired difference

The sample standard deviation for the paired differences is

$$s_d = \sqrt{\frac{\Sigma\left(d - \bar{d}\right)^2}{n-1}} = \sqrt{\frac{172.8}{10-1}} = 4.38$$

Assuming that the population of paired differences is normally distributed, the confidence interval estimate for the population mean paired difference is computed using Equation 10.14.

Confidence Interval Estimate for Population Mean Paired Difference, μ_d

$$\bar{d} \pm t\frac{s_d}{\sqrt{n}} \tag{10.14}$$

where:

t = Critical t value from t-distribution with $n - 1$ degrees of freedom

$\bar{d}$ = Sample mean paired difference

s_d = Sample standard deviation of paired differences

n = Number of paired differences (sample size)

For a 95% confidence interval with $10 - 1 = 9$ of freedom, we use a critical t from the t-distribution of

$$t = 2.2622$$

The interval estimate obtained from Equation 10.14 is

$$\bar{d} \pm t\frac{s_d}{\sqrt{n}}$$

$$2.27 \pm 2.2622\frac{4.38}{\sqrt{10}}$$

$$2.27 \pm 3.13$$

$$-0.86 \text{ mpg} \underline{\hspace{3cm}} 5.40 \text{ mpg}$$

Because the interval estimate contains zero, there may be no difference in the average mileage when either regular gasoline or the ethanol mixture is used.

EXAMPLE 10-6 **CONFIDENCE INTERVAL ESTIMATE FOR THE DIFFERENCE BETWEEN POPULATION MEANS, PAIRED SAMPLES**

sculpies/Shutterstock

PGA of America Testing Center Technology has done more to change golf than possibly any other group in recent years. Titanium woods, hybrid irons, and new golf ball designs have impacted professional and amateur golfers alike. PGA of America is the association that only professional golfers can belong to. The association provides many services for golf professionals, including operating an equipment training center in Florida. Recently, a maker of golf balls developed a new ball technology, and PGA of America is interested in estimating the mean difference in driving distance for this new ball versus the existing best-seller. To conduct the test, the PGA of America staff selected six professional golfers and had each golfer hit each ball one time. Here are the steps necessary to develop a confidence interval estimate for the difference in population means for paired samples:

Step 1 **Define the population parameter of interest.**
Because the same golfers hit each golf ball, the company is controlling for the variation in the golfers' ability to hit a golf ball. The samples are paired, and the population value of interest is μ_d, the mean paired difference in distance. We assume that the population of paired differences is normally distributed.

Step 2 **Specify the desired confidence level and determine the appropriate critical value.**
The research director wishes to have a 95% confidence interval estimate.

Step 3 **Collect the sample data and compute the point estimate, $\bar{d}$.**
The sample data, paired differences, are shown as follows.

Golfer	Existing Ball	New Ball	d
1	280	276	4
2	299	301	−2
3	278	285	−7
4	301	299	2
5	268	273	−5
6	295	300	−5

The point estimate is computed using Equation 10.12.

$$\bar{d} = \frac{\sum d}{n} = \frac{-13}{6} = -2.17 \text{ yards}$$

Step 4 **Calculate the standard deviation, s_d.**
The standard deviation for the paired differences is computed using Equation 10.13.

$$s_d = \sqrt{\frac{\sum (d - \bar{d})^2}{n-1}} = 4.36 \text{ yards}$$

Step 5 **Determine the critical value, t, from the t-distribution table.**
The critical t for 95% confidence and $6 - 1 = 5$ degrees of freedom is

$$t = 2.5706$$

Step 6 **Compute the confidence interval estimate using Equation 10.14.**

$$\bar{d} \pm t \frac{s_d}{\sqrt{n}}$$

$$-2.17 \pm 2.5706 \frac{4.36}{\sqrt{6}}$$

$$-2.17 \pm 4.58$$

$$-6.75 \text{ yards} \text{ ——————— } 2.41 \text{ yards}$$

Based on these sample data and the confidence interval estimate, which contains zero, the PGA of America must conclude that the new ball's average distance may not be any longer than that of the existing best-seller. This may affect whether the company that developed the new ball will continue to make it.

>> **END EXAMPLE**

TRY PROBLEM 10-38 (pg. 416)

The key in deciding whether to use paired samples is to determine whether a factor exists that might adversely influence the results of the estimation. In the ethanol mixed gasoline test example, we controlled for potential outside influence by using the same cars and drivers to test both gasolines. In Example 10-6, we controlled for golfer ability by having the same golfers hit both golf balls. If you determine there is no need to control for an outside source of variation, then independent samples should be used, as discussed earlier in this chapter.

Chapter Outcome 2. → ## Hypothesis Testing for Paired Samples

As we just illustrated, there will be instances in which paired samples can be used to control for an outside source of variation. For instance, in Example 10-5, involving the ink cartridges, the original test of whether name-brand cartridges yield a higher mean number of printed pages than generic cartridges involved different users for the two types of cartridges, so the samples were independent. However, different users may use more or less ink as a rule; therefore, we could control for that source of variation by having a sample of people use both types of cartridges in a paired test format.

If a paired-sample experiment is used, the test statistic is computed using Equation 10.15.

---

t-Test Statistic for Paired-Sample Test

$$t = \frac{\bar{d} - \mu_d}{\frac{s_d}{\sqrt{n}}}, \qquad df = (n-1)$$

(10.15)

where:

$$\bar{d} = \text{Mean paired difference} = \frac{\sum d}{n}$$

μ_d = Hypothesized population mean paired difference

$$s_d = \text{Sample standard deviation for paired differences} = \sqrt{\frac{\sum(d - \bar{d})^2}{n-1}}$$

n = Number of paired values in the sample

EXAMPLE 10-7   HYPOTHESIS TEST FOR μ_d, PAIRED SAMPLES

Color Printer Ink Cartridges Referring to Example 10-5, suppose the experiment regarding ink cartridges is conducted differently. Instead of having different samples of people use name-brand and generic cartridges, the test is done using paired samples. This means that the same people will use both types of cartridges, and the pages printed in each case will be recorded. The test under this paired-sample scenario can be conducted using the following steps. Six randomly selected people have agreed to participate.

Step 1 Specify the population value of interest.
In this case, we will form paired differences by subtracting the generic pages from the name-brand pages. We are interested in determining whether name-brand cartridges produce more printed pages, on average, than generic cartridges, so we would expect the paired difference to be positive. We assume that the paired differences are normally distributed.

Step 2 Formulate the null and alternative hypotheses.
The null and alternative hypotheses are

$$H_0: \mu_d \leq 0.0$$
$$H_A: \mu_d > 0.0$$

Step 3 Specify the significance level for the test.
The test will be conducted using $\alpha = 0.01$.

Step 4 Determine the rejection region.
The critical value is a *t*-value from the *t*-distribution, with $\alpha = 0.01$ and $6 - 1 = 5$ degrees of freedom. The critical value is

$$t_{0.01} = 3.3649$$

The decision rule is

If $t > 3.3649$, reject the null hypothesis;
otherwise, do not reject the null hypothesis.

Step 5 Compute the test statistic.
Select the random sample and compute the mean and standard deviation for the paired differences.

In this case, a random sample of six people tests each type of cartridge. The following data and paired differences were observed:

Printer User	Name-Brand	Generic	d
1	306	300	6
2	256	260	-4
3	402	357	45
4	299	286	13
5	306	290	16
6	257	260	-3

The mean paired difference is

$$\bar{d} = \frac{\Sigma d}{n} = \frac{73}{6} = 12.17$$

The standard deviation for the paired differences is

$$s_d = \sqrt{\frac{\Sigma(d - \bar{d})^2}{n-1}} = 18.02$$

The test statistic is calculated using Equation 10.15.

$$t = \frac{\bar{d} - \mu_d}{\frac{s_d}{\sqrt{n}}} = \frac{12.17 - 0.0}{\frac{18.02}{\sqrt{6}}} = 1.6543$$

Step 6 Reach a decision.
Because $t = 1.6543 < t_{0.01} = 3.3649$, do not reject the null hypothesis.

Step 7 Draw a conclusion.
Based on these sample data, there is insufficient evidence to conclude that name-brand ink cartridges produce more pages on average than generic brands.

>> **END EXAMPLE**

TRY PROBLEM 10-39 (pg. 417)

MyStatLab

10-3: **Exercises**

Skill **Development**

10-36. The following dependent samples were randomly selected. Use the sample data to construct a 95% confidence interval estimate for the population mean paired difference.

Sample 1	Sample 2	Sample 1	Sample 2
22	31	23	31
25	24	25	27
27	25	28	31
26	32	27	31
22	25	23	26
21	27		

10-37. The following paired sample data have been obtained from normally distributed populations. Construct a

90% confidence interval estimate for the mean paired difference between the two population means.

Sample #	Population 1	Population 2
1	3,693	4,635
2	3,679	4,262
3	3,921	4,293
4	4,106	4,197
5	3,808	4,536
6	4,394	4,494
7	3,878	4,094

10-38. You are given the following results of a paired-difference test:

$$\bar{d} = -4.6$$
$$s_d = 0.25$$
$$n = 16$$

a. Construct and interpret a 99% confidence interval estimate for the paired difference in mean values.

b. Construct and interpret a 90% confidence interval estimate for the paired difference in mean values.

10-39. The following sample data have been collected from a paired sample from two populations. The claim is that the first population mean will be at least as large as the mean of the second population. This claim will be assumed to be true unless the data strongly suggest otherwise.

Sample 1	Sample 2	Sample 1	Sample 2
4.4	3.7	2.6	4.2
2.7	3.5	2.4	5.2
1.0	4.0	2.0	4.4
3.5	4.9	2.8	4.3
2.8	3.1		

a. State the appropriate null and alternative hypotheses.

b. Based on the sample data, what should you conclude about the null hypothesis? Test using $\alpha = 0.10$.

c. Calculate a 90% confidence interval for the difference in the population means. Are the results from the confidence interval consistent with the outcome of your hypothesis test? Explain why or why not.

10-40. A paired sample study has been conducted to determine whether two populations have equal means. Twenty paired samples were obtained with the following sample results:

$$\bar{d} = 12.45 \qquad s_d = 11.0$$

Based on these sample data and a significance level of 0.05, what conclusion should be made about the population means?

10-41. The following samples are observations taken from the same elements at two different times:

Unit	Sample 1	Sample 2
1	15.1	4.8
2	12.3	5.7
3	14.9	6.2
4	17.5	9.4
5	18.1	2.3
6	18.4	4.7

a. Assume that the populations are normally distributed and construct a 90% confidence interval for the difference in the means of the distribution at the times in which the samples were taken.

b. Perform a test of hypothesis to determine if the difference in the means of the distribution at the first time period is 10 units larger than at the second time period. Use a level of significance equal to 0.10.

10-42. Consider the following set of samples obtained from two normally distributed populations whose variances are equal:

Sample 1:	11.2	11.2	7.4	8.7	8.5	13.5	4.5	11.9	
Sample 2:	11.7	9.5	15.6	16.5	11.3	17.6	17.0	8.5	

a. Suppose that the samples were independent. Perform a test of hypothesis to determine if there is a difference in the two population means. Use a significance level of 0.05.

b. Now suppose that the samples were paired samples. Perform a test of hypothesis to determine if there is a difference in the two population means.

c. How do you account for the difference in the outcomes of part a and part b? Support your assertions with a statistical rationale.

Business Applications

10-43. One of the advances that helped to diminish carpal tunnel syndrome is ergonomic keyboards. The ergonomic keyboards may also increase typing speed. Ten administrative assistants were chosen to type on both standard and ergonomic keyboards. The resulting word-per-minute typing speeds follow:

Ergonomic:	69	80	60	71	73	64	63	70	63	74
Standard:	70	68	54	56	58	64	62	51	64	53

a. Were the two samples obtained independently? Support your assertion.

b. Conduct a hypothesis test to determine if the ergonomic keyboards increase the average words per minute attained while typing. Use a *p*-value approach with a significance level of 0.01.

10-44. Production engineers at Sinotron believe that a modified layout on its assembly lines might increase average worker productivity (measured in the number of units produced per hour). However, before the engineers are ready to install the revised layout officially across the entire firm's production lines, they would like to study the modified line's effects on output. The following data represent the average hourly production output of 12 randomly sampled employees before and after the line was modified:

Employee	*1*	*2*	*3*	*4*	*5*	*6*	*7*	*8*	*9*	*10*	*11*	*12*
Before	49	45	43	44	48	42	46	46	49	42	46	44
After	49	46	48	50	46	50	45	46	47	51	51	49

At the 0.05 level of significance, can the production engineers conclude that the modified (after) layout has increased average worker productivity?

10-45. The United Way raises money for community charity activities. Recently, in one community, the fundraising committee was concerned about whether there is a difference in the proportion of employees who give to United Way depending on whether the employer is a private business or a government agency. A random sample of people who had been contacted about contributing last year was selected. Of those contacted, 70 worked for a private business and 50 worked for a government agency. For the 70 private-sector employees, the mean contribution was $230.25 with a standard deviation equal to $55.52. For the 50 government employees in the sample, the mean and standard deviation were $309.45 and $61.75, respectively.

a. Based on these sample data and $\alpha = 0.05$, what should be concluded? Be sure to show the decision rule.

b. Construct a 95% confidence interval for the difference between the mean contributions of private business and government agency employees who contribute to United Way. Do the hypothesis test and the confidence interval produce compatible results? Explain and give reasons for your answer.

10-46. An article on the PureEnergySystems.com website written by Louis LaPoint discusses a product called acetone. The article stated that "Acetone (CH_3COCH_3) is a product that can be purchased inexpensively in most locations around the world, such as in common hardware, auto parts, or drug stores. Added to the fuel tank in tiny amounts, acetone aids in the vaporization of the gasoline or diesel, increasing fuel efficiency, engine longevity, and performance—as well as reducing hydrocarbon emissions." To test whether this product actually does increase fuel efficiency in passenger cars, a consumer group has randomly selected 10 people to participate in the study. The following procedure is used:

1. People are to bring their cars into a specified gasoline station and have the car filled with regular, unleaded gasoline at a particular pump. Nothing extra is added to the gasoline at this fill-up. The car's odometer is recorded at the time of fill-up.

2. When the tank is nearly empty, the person is to bring the car to the same gasoline station and pump and have it refilled with gasoline. The odometer is read again and the miles per gallon are recorded. This time, a prescribed quantity of acetone is added to the fuel.

3. When the tank is nearly empty, the person is to bring the car back to the same station and pump to have it filled. The miles per gallon will be recorded.

Each person is provided with free tanks of gasoline and asked to drive his or her car normally.

The following miles per gallon (mpg) were recorded:

Driver	MPG: No Additive	MPG: Acetone Added
1	18.4	19.0
2	23.5	22.8
3	31.4	30.9
4	26.5	26.9
5	27.2	28.4
6	16.3	18.2
7	19.4	19.2
8	20.1	21.4
9	14.2	16.1
10	22.1	21.5

a. Discuss the appropriateness of the way this study was designed and conducted. Why didn't the consumer group select two samples with different drivers in each and have one group use the acetone and the other group not use it? Discuss.

b. Using a significance level of 0.05, what conclusion should be reached based on these sample data? Discuss.

10-47. An article in *The American Statistician* (M. L. R. Ernst, et al., "Scatterplots for Unordered Pairs," 50 (1996), pp. 260–265) reports on the difference in the measurements by two evaluators of the cardiac output of 23 patients using Doppler echocardiography. Both observers took measurements from the same patients. The measured outcomes were as follows:

Patient	1	2	3	4	5	6	7	8	9	10	11	12
Evaluator 1	4.8	5.6	6.0	6.4	6.5	6.6	6.8	7.0	7.0	7.2	7.4	7.6
Evaluator 2	5.8	6.1	7.7	7.8	7.6	8.1	8.0	8.21	6.6	8.1	9.5	9.6

Patient	13	14	15	16	17	18	19	20	21	22	23
Evaluator 1	7.7	7.7	8.2	8.2	8.3	8.5	9.3	10.2	10.4	10.6	11.4
Evaluator 2	8.5	9.5	9.1	10.0	9.1	10.8	11.5	11.5	11.2	11.5	12.0

a. Conduct a hypothesis test to determine if the average cardiac outputs measured by the two evaluators differ. Use a significance level of 0.02.

b. Calculate the standard error of the difference between the two average outputs assuming that the sampling was done independently. Compare this with the standard error obtained in part a.

Computer Database **Exercises**

10-48. A prime factor in the economic troubles that started in 2008 was the end of the "housing bubble." The file titled **House** contains data for a sample showing the average and median housing prices for selected areas in the country in November 2007 and November 2008. Assume the data can be viewed as samples of the relevant populations.

a. Discuss whether the two samples are independent or dependent.

b. Based on your answer to part a, calculate a 90% confidence interval for the difference between the means of the average and median selling prices for houses during November 2007.

c. Noting your answer to part b, would it be plausible to assert that the mean of the average selling prices for houses during the November 2007 is more than the average of the median selling prices during this period? Support your assertions.

d. Using a *p*-value approach and a significance level of 0.05, conduct a hypothesis test to determine if the mean of the average selling prices for houses during November 2007 is more than $30,000 larger than the mean of the median selling prices during this period.

10-49. A treadmill manufacturer has developed a new machine with softer tread and better fans than its current model. The manufacturer believes these new features will enable runners to run for longer times than they can on its current machines. To determine whether the desired result is achieved, the manufacturer randomly sampled 35 runners. Each runner was measured for one week on the current machine and for one week on the new machine. The weekly total number of minutes for each runner on the two types of machines was collected. The results are contained in the file **Treadmill**. At the 0.02 level of significance, can the treadmill manufacturer conclude that the new machine has the desired result?

10-50. As the number of air travelers with time on their hands increases, it would seem that spending on retail purchases in airports would increase as well. A study by *Airport Revenue News* addressed the per-person spending at selected airports for merchandise,

excluding food, gifts, and news items. A file titled **Revenues** contains sample data selected from airport retailers in 2005 and again in 2008.

a. Conduct a hypothesis test to determine if the average amount of retail spending by air travelers has increased as least as much as approximately $0.10 a year from 2005 to 2008. Use a significance level of 0.025.

b. Using the appropriate analysis (that of part a or other appropriate methodology), substantiate the statement that average retail purchases in airports increased over the time period between 2005 and 2008. Support your assertions.

c. Parts a and b give what seems to be a mixed message. Is there a way to determine what values are plausible for the difference between the average revenue in 2005 and 2008? If so, conduct the appropriate procedure.

END EXERCISES 10-3

10.4 Estimation and Hypothesis Tests for Two Population Proportions

The previous sections illustrated the methods for estimating and testing hypotheses involving two population means. There are many business situations in which these methods can be applied. However, there are other instances involving two populations in which the measures of interest are not the population means. For example, Chapter 9 introduced the methodology for testing hypotheses involving a single population proportion. This section extends that methodology to tests involving hypotheses about the difference between two population proportions. First, we will look at a confidence interval estimation involving two population proportions.

Chapter Outcome 3. → ## Estimating the Difference between Two Population Proportions

BUSINESS APPLICATION   **ESTIMATING THE DIFFERENCE BETWEEN TWO POPULATION PROPORTIONS**

BICYCLE DESIGN Recently, an outdoor magazine conducted an interesting study involving a prototype bicycle that was made by a Swiss manufacturer. The prototype had no identification on it to indicate the name of the manufacturer. Of interest was the difference in the proportion of men versus women who would rate the bicycle as high quality.

Obviously, there was no way to gauge the attitudes of the entire population of men and women who could eventually judge the quality of the bicycle. Instead, the reporter for the magazine asked a random sample of 425 men and 370 women to rate the bicycle's quality. In the results that follow, the variable x indicates the number in the sample who said the bicycle was high quality.

Men	Women
$n_1 = 425$	$n_2 = 370$
$x_1 = 240$	$x_2 = 196$

Based on these sample data, the sample proportions are

$$\bar{p}_1 = \frac{240}{425} = 0.565 \quad \text{and} \quad \bar{p}_2 = \frac{196}{370} = 0.530$$

The point estimate for the difference in population proportions is

$$\bar{p}_1 - \bar{p}_2 = 0.565 - 0.530 = 0.035$$

So, the single best estimate for the difference in the proportion of men versus women who rated the bicycle prototype as high quality is 0.035. However, all point estimates are subject to sampling error. A confidence interval estimate for the difference in population proportions can be developed using Equation 10.16, providing the sample sizes are sufficiently large. A rule of thumb for "sufficiently large" is that $n\bar{p}$ and $n(1-\bar{p})$ are greater than or equal to 5 for each sample.

Confidence Interval Estimate for $p_1 - p_2$

$$(\bar{p}_1 - \bar{p}_2) \pm z \sqrt{\frac{\bar{p}_1(1-\bar{p}_1)}{n_1} + \frac{\bar{p}_2(1-\bar{p}_2)}{n_2}} \tag{10.16}$$

where:

$\bar{p}_1$ = Sample proportion from population 1
$\bar{p}_2$ = Sample proportion from population 2
z = Critical value from the standard normal table

The analysts can substitute the sample results into Equation 10.16 to establish a 95% confidence interval estimate, as follows:

$$(0.565 - 0.530) \pm 1.96 \sqrt{\frac{0.565(1-0.565)}{425} + \frac{0.530(1-0.530)}{370}}$$

$$0.035 \pm 0.069$$

$$-0.034 \le (p_1 - p_2) \le 0.104$$

Thus, based on the sample data and using a 95% confidence interval, the analysts estimate that the true difference in proportion of males versus females who rate the prototype as high quality is between −0.034 and 0.104. At one extreme, 3.4% more females rate the bicycle as high in quality. At the other extreme, 10.4% more males rate the bicycle as high quality than females. Because zero is included in the interval, there may be no difference between the proportion of males and females who rate the prototype as high quality based on these data. Consequently, the reporter is not able to conclude that one group or the other would be more likely to rate the prototype bicycle high in quality.

Hypothesis Tests for the Difference between Two Population Proportions

BUSINESS APPLICATION **TESTING FOR THE DIFFERENCE BETWEEN TWO POPULATION PROPORTIONS**

POMONA FABRICATIONS Pomona Fabrications, Inc. produces handheld hair dryers that several major retailers sell as in-house brands. A critical component of a handheld hair dryer is the motor-heater unit, which accounts for most of the dryer's cost and for most of the product's reliability problems. Product reliability is important to Pomona because the company offers a one-year warranty. Of course, Pomona is also interested in reducing production costs.

Pomona's R&D department has recently created a new motor-heater unit with fewer parts than the current unit, which would lead to a 15% cost savings per hair dryer. However, the company's vice president of product development is unwilling to authorize the new component unless it is more reliable than the current motor-heater.

The R&D department has decided to test samples of both units to see which motor-heater is more reliable. Of each type, 250 will be tested under conditions that simulate one year's

Excel Tutorial

use, and the proportion of each type that fails within that time will be recorded. This leads to the formulation of the following null and alternative hypotheses:

$$H_0: p_1 - p_2 \geq 0.0 \qquad H_0: p_1 \geq p_2$$
$$\text{or}$$
$$H_A: p_1 - p_2 < 0.0 \qquad H_A: p_1 < p_2$$

where:

p_1 = Population proportion of new dryer type that fails in simulated one−year period
p_2 = Population proportion of existing dryer type that fails in simulated one−year period

The null hypothesis states that the new motor-heater is no better than the old, or current, motor-heater. The alternative states that the new unit has a smaller proportion of failures within one year than the current unit. In other words, the alternative states that the new unit is more reliable. The company wants clear evidence before changing units. If the null hypothesis is rejected, the company will conclude that the new motor-heater unit is more reliable than the old unit and should be used in producing the hair dryers. To test the null hypothesis, we can use the test statistic approach.

The test statistic is based on the sampling distribution of $\bar{p}_1 - \bar{p}_2$. In Chapter 7, we showed that when $np \geq 5$ and $n(1 - p) \geq 5$, the sampling distribution of the sample proportion is approximately normally distributed, with a mean equal to p and a variance equal to $p(1 - p)/n$.

Likewise, in the two-sample case, the sampling distribution of $\bar{p}_1 - \bar{p}_2$ will also be approximately normal if

Assumptions

$$n_1 p_1 \geq 5, \; n_1(1-p_1) \geq 5, \quad \text{and} \quad n_2 p_2 \geq 5, n_2(1-p_2) \geq 5$$

Because p_1 and p_2 are unknown, we substitute the sample proportions, $\bar{p}_1$ and $\bar{p}_2$, to determine whether the sample size requirements are satisfied.

The mean of the sampling distribution of $\bar{p}_1 - \bar{p}_2$ is the difference of the population proportions, $p_1 - p_2$. The variance is, however, the sum of the variances, $p_1(1 - p_1)/n_1 + p_2(1 - p_2)/n_2$. Because the test is conducted using the assumption that the null hypothesis is true, we assume that $p_1 = p_2 = p$ and estimate their common value, p, using a pooled estimate, as shown in Equation 10.17. The z-test statistic for the difference between two proportions is given as Equation 10.18.

Pooled Estimator for Overall Proportion

$$\bar{p} = \frac{n_1 \bar{p}_1 + n_2 \bar{p}_2}{n_1 + n_2} = \frac{x_1 + x_2}{n_1 + n_2} \qquad (10.17)$$

where:

x_1 and x_2 = Number from samples 1 and 2 with the characteristic of interest

---

z-Test Statistic for Difference between Population Proportions

$$z = \frac{(\bar{p}_1 - \bar{p}_2) - (p_1 - p_2)}{\sqrt{\bar{p}(1 - \bar{p})\left(\dfrac{1}{n_1} + \dfrac{1}{n_2}\right)}} \qquad (10.18)$$

where:

$(p_1 - p_2)$ = Hypothesized difference in proportions from populations 1 and 2, respectively
$\bar{p}_1$ and $\bar{p}_2$ = Sample proportions for samples selected from populations 1 and 2, respectively
$\bar{p}$ = Pooled estimator for the overall proportion for both populations combined

The reason for taking a weighted average in Equation 10.17 is to give more weight to the larger sample. Note that the numerator is the total number of items with the characteristic of interest in the two samples, and the denominator is the total sample size. Again, the pooled estimator, $\bar{p}$, is used when the null hypothesis is that there is no difference between the population proportions.

Assume that Pomona is willing to use a significance level of 0.05 and that 55 of the new motor-heaters and 75 of the originals failed the one-year test. Figure 10.9 illustrates the decision-rule development and the hypothesis test. As you can see, Pomona should reject the null hypothesis based on the sample data. Thus, the firm should conclude that the new motor-heater is more reliable than the old one. Because the new one is also less costly, the company should now use the new unit in the production of hair dryers.

The p-value approach to hypothesis testing could also have been used to test Pomona's hypothesis. In this case, the calculated value of the test statistic, $z = -2.04$, results in a p-value of $0.0207 (0.5 - 0.4793)$ from the standard normal table. Because this p-value is smaller than the significance level of 0.05, we would reject the null hypothesis. Remember, whenever your p-value is smaller than the alpha value, your sample contains evidence to reject the null hypothesis.

The PHStat add-in to Excel contains a procedure for performing hypothesis tests involving two population proportions. Figure 10.10 shows the PHStat output for the Pomona example. The output contains both the z-test statistic and the p-value. As we observed from our manual calculations, the difference in sample proportions is sufficient to reject the null hypothesis that there is no difference in population proportions.

FIGURE 10.9

Hypothesis Test of Two Population Proportions for Pomona Fabrications

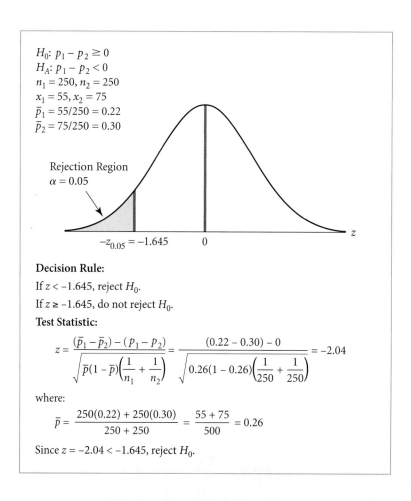

$H_0: p_1 - p_2 \geq 0$
$H_A: p_1 - p_2 < 0$
$n_1 = 250, n_2 = 250$
$x_1 = 55, x_2 = 75$
$\bar{p}_1 = 55/250 = 0.22$
$\bar{p}_2 = 75/250 = 0.30$

Rejection Region
$\alpha = 0.05$

$-z_{0.05} = -1.645$ 0 z

Decision Rule:

If $z < -1.645$, reject H_0.

If $z \geq -1.645$, do not reject H_0.

Test Statistic:

$$z = \frac{(\bar{p}_1 - \bar{p}_2) - (p_1 - p_2)}{\sqrt{\bar{p}(1-\bar{p})\left(\frac{1}{n_1} + \frac{1}{n_2}\right)}} = \frac{(0.22 - 0.30) - 0}{\sqrt{0.26(1-0.26)\left(\frac{1}{250} + \frac{1}{250}\right)}} = -2.04$$

where:

$$\bar{p} = \frac{250(0.22) + 250(0.30)}{250 + 250} = \frac{55 + 75}{500} = 0.26$$

Since $z = -2.04 < -1.645$, reject H_0.

FIGURE 10.10

Excel 2010 (PHStat) Output of the Two Proportions Test for Pomona Fabrications

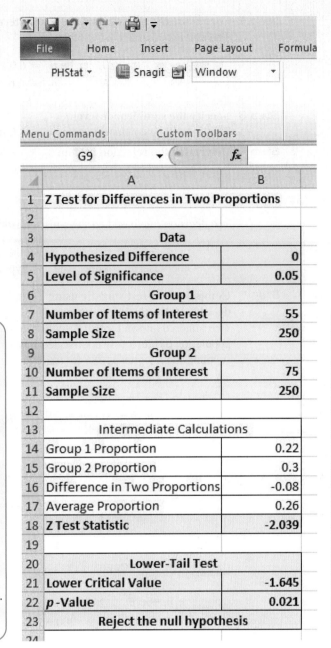

Excel 2010 Instructions:
1. Open **PHStat** and enable macros.
2. Click **Add-Ins**.
3. Click **PHStat** down arrow.
4. Select **Two Sample Tests (Summarized Data)**.
5. Select **Z test for Differences in Two Proportions**.
6. Specify **Hypothesized Difference** of 0 and **Alpha** equal to 0.05.
7. Enter **Number of Items of Interest** and **Sample Size** for both populations.
8. Indicate **Lower-tail test**.
9. Click **OK**.

Minitab Instructions (for similar results):
1. Choose **Stat > Basic Statistics > 2 Proportions**.
2. Choose **Summarized data**.
3. In **First** enter **Trials** and Events for sample 1 (e.g., 250 and 55).
4. In **Second** enter **Trials** and Events for sample 2 (e.g., 250 and 75).
5. Select **Options**, Insert $1 - \alpha$ in **Confidence level**.
6. In **Alternative** select *less than*.
7. Check **Use pooled estimate of p for test**.
8. Click **OK**. **OK**.

EXAMPLE 10-8 **HYPOTHESIS TEST FOR THE DIFFERENCE BETWEEN TWO POPULATION PROPORTIONS**

Transportation Security Administration Transportation Security Administration (TSA) is responsible for transportation security at all United States airports. The TSA is evaluating two suppliers of a scanning system it is considering purchasing. Both scanners are designed to detect forged IDs that might be used by passengers trying to board airlines. High-quality scanners and printers and home computers have made forging IDs an increasing security risk. The TSA is interested in determining whether there is a difference in the proportion of forged IDs detected by the two suppliers. To conduct this test, use the following steps:

Step 1 **Specify the population parameter of interest.**
In this case, the population parameter of interest is the population proportion of detected forged IDs. At issue is whether there is a difference between the two suppliers in terms of the proportion of forged IDs detected.

Step 2 **Formulate the appropriate null and alternative hypotheses.**
The null and alternative hypotheses are

$$H_0: p_1 - p_2 = 0.0$$
$$H_A: p_1 - p_2 \neq 0.0$$

Step 3 **Specify the significance level.**
The test will be conducted using an $\alpha = 0.02$.

Step 4 **Determine the rejection region.**
For a two-tailed test, the critical values for each side of the distribution are

$$-z_{0.01} = -2.33 \text{ and } z_{0.01} = 2.33$$

The decision rule based on the z-test statistic is

If $z < -2.33$ or $z > 2.33$, reject the null hypothesis;
Otherwise, do not reject the null hypothesis.

Step 5 **Compute the z-test statistic using Equation 10.18 and apply it to the decision rule.**
Two hundred known forged IDs will be randomly selected from a large population of previously confiscated IDs and scanned by systems from each supplier. For supplier 1, 186 forgeries are detected, and for supplier 2, 168 are detected. The sample proportions are

$$\bar{p}_1 = \frac{x_1}{n_1} = \frac{186}{200} = 0.93 \qquad \bar{p}_2 = \frac{x_2}{n_2} = \frac{168}{200} = 0.84$$

The test statistic is then calculated using Equation 10.18.

$$z = \frac{(\bar{p}_1 - \bar{p}_2) - (p_1 - p_2)}{\sqrt{\bar{p}(1-\bar{p})\left(\dfrac{1}{n_1} + \dfrac{1}{n_2}\right)}}$$

where:

$$\bar{p} = \frac{n_1\bar{p}_1 + n_2\bar{p}_2}{n_1 + n_2} = \frac{200(0.93) + 200(0.84)}{200 + 200} = 0.885 \qquad \text{(see Equation 10.17)}$$

then:

$$z = \frac{(0.93 - 0.84) - 0.0}{\sqrt{0.885(1-0.885)\left(\dfrac{1}{200} + \dfrac{1}{200}\right)}} = 2.8211$$

Step 6 **Reach a decision.**
Because $z = 2.8211 > z_{0.01} = 2.33$, reject the null hypothesis.

Step 7 **Draw a conclusion.**
The difference between the two sample proportions provides sufficient evidence to allow us to conclude a difference exists between the two suppliers. The TSA can infer that supplier 1 provides the better scanner for this purpose.

>> **END EXAMPLE**

TRY PROBLEM 10-54 (pg. 425)

MyStatLab

10-4: Exercises

Skill Development

10-51. In each of the following cases, determine if the sample sizes are large enough so that the sampling distribution of the differences in the sample proportions can be approximated with a normal distribution:
   a. $n_1 = 15$, $n_2 = 20$, $x_1 = 6$, and $x_2 = 16$
   b. $n_1 = 10$, $n_2 = 30$, $\bar{p}_1 = 0.6$, and $x_2 = 19$
   c. $n_1 = 25$, $n_2 = 16$, $x_1 = 6$, and $\bar{p}_2 = 0.40$
   d. $n_1 = 100$, $n_2 = 75$, $\bar{p}_1 = 0.05$, and $\bar{p}_2 = 0.05$

10-52. Given the following sample information randomly selected from two populations

Sample 1	Sample 2
$n_1 = 200$	$n_2 = 150$
$x_1 = 40$	$x_2 = 27$

   a. Determine if the sample sizes are large enough so that the sampling distribution for the difference between the sample proportions is approximately normally distributed.
   b. Calculate a 95% confidence interval for the difference between the two population proportions.

10-53. Given the following null and alternative hypotheses and level of significance

$$H_0: p_1 = p_2$$
$$H_A: p_1 \neq p_2$$
$$\alpha = 0.10$$

together with the sample information

Sample 1	Sample 2
$n_1 = 120$	$n_2 = 150$
$x_1 = 42$	$x_2 = 57$

conduct the appropriate hypothesis test using the p-value approach. What conclusion would be reached concerning the null hypothesis?

10-54. Given the following null and alternative hypotheses

$$H_0: p_1 - p_2 \leq 0.0$$
$$H_A: p_1 - p_2 > 0.0$$

and the following sample information

Sample 1	Sample 2
$n_1 = 60$	$n_2 = 80$
$x_1 = 30$	$x_2 = 24$

   a. Based on $\alpha = 0.02$ and the sample information, what should be concluded with respect to the null and alternative hypotheses? Be sure to clearly show the decision rule.

   b. Calculate the p-value for this hypothesis test. Based on the p-value, would the null hypothesis be rejected? Support your answer with calculations and/or reasons.

10-55. Independent random samples of size 50 and 75 are selected. The sampling results in 35 and 35 successes, respectively. Test the following hypotheses:
   a. $H_0: p_1 - p_2 = 0$ vs. $H_A: p_1 - p_2 \neq 0$.
      Use $\alpha = 0.05$.
   b. $H_0: p_1 - p_2 \geq 0$ vs. $H_A: p_1 - p_2 < 0$.
      Use $\alpha = 0.05$.
   c. $H_0: p_1 - p_2 \leq 0$ vs. $H_A: p_1 - p_2 > 0$.
      Use $\alpha = 0.025$.
   d. $H_0: p_1 - p_2 = 0.05$ vs. $H_A: p_1 - p_2 \neq 0.05$.
      Use $\alpha = 0.02$.

Business Applications

10-56. In an article titled "Childhood Pastimes Are Increasingly Moving Indoors," Dennis Cauchon asserts that there have been huge declines in spontaneous outdoor activities such as bike riding, swimming, and touch football. In the article, he cites separate studies by the national Sporting Goods Association and American Sports Data that indicate bike riding alone is down 31% from 1995 to 2004. According to the surveys, 68% of 7- to 11-year-olds rode a bike at least six times in 1995 and only 47% did in 2004. Assume the sample sizes were 1,500 and 2,000, respectively.
   a. Calculate a 95% confidence interval to estimate the proportion of 7- to 11-year-olds who rode their bike at least six times in 2004. Does this suggest that it is plausible to believe the proportion of 7- to 11-year-olds who rode their bike at least six times in 2004 is the same as in 1995?
   b. Conduct a test of hypothesis to answer the question posed in part a. Are the results of parts a and b contradictory? Explain.

10-57. Suppose, as part of a national study of economic competitiveness, a marketing research firm randomly sampled 200 adults between the ages of 27 and 35 living in metropolitan Seattle and 180 adults between the ages of 27 and 35 living in metropolitan Minneapolis. Each adult selected in the sample was asked, among other things, whether he or she had a college degree. From the Seattle sample, 66 adults answered yes, and from the Minneapolis sample, 63 adults answered yes when asked if they had a college degree. Based on the sample data, can we conclude that there is a difference between the population proportions of adults between the ages of 27 and 35 in the two cities with college degrees? Use a level of significance of 0.01 to conduct the appropriate hypothesis test.

10-58. Suppose a random sample of 100 U.S. companies taken in 2005 showed that 21 offered high-deductible health insurance plans to their workers. A separate random sample of 120 firms taken in 2006 showed that 30 offered high-deductible health insurance plans to their workers. Based on the sample results, can you conclude that there is a higher proportion of U.S. companies offering high-deductible health insurance plans to their workers in 2006 than in 2005? Conduct your hypothesis test at a level of significance $\alpha = 0.05$.

10-59. The American College Health Association produced the National College Health Assessment (Andy Gardiner, "Surfacing from Depression," February 6, 2006). The assessment indicates that the percentage of U.S. college students who report having been diagnosed with depression has risen from 2000. The assessment surveyed 47,202 students at 74 campuses. It discovered that 10.3% and 14.9% of students indicated that they had been diagnosed with depression in 2000 and 2004, respectively. Assume that half of the students surveyed were surveyed in 2004.

a. Conduct a hypothesis test to determine if there has been more than a 0.04 increase in the proportion of students who indicated they have been diagnosed with depression. Use a significance level of 0.05 and a p-value approach to this test.

b. Indicate the margin of error for estimating $p_1 - p_2$ with $\bar{p}_1 - \bar{p}_2$.

c. Determine the smallest difference between the two proportions of students who indicated that they had been diagnosed with depression in 2000 and 2004 that the test in part a would be able to detect.

Computer Database Exercises

10-60. As part of a nationwide study on home Internet use, researchers randomly sampled 150 urban households and 150 rural households. Among the questions asked of the sampled households was whether they used the Internet to download computer games. The survey results for this question are contained in the file **Internet Games**. Based on the sample results, can the researchers conclude that there is a difference between the proportion of urban households and rural households that use the Internet to download computer games? Conduct your test using a level of significance $\alpha = 0.01$.

10-61. The Boston Consulting Group released a survey of 940 executives representing 68 countries. One of the questions on the survey examined if the executives ranked innovation as the top priority for the coming year. The responses from 400 executives in the United

States and 300 in Asia are given in the file titled **Priority**.

a. Determine if the sample sizes are large enough to provide assurance that the sampling distribution of the difference in the sample proportion of executives who feel innovation is their top priority is normally distributed.

b. Determine if the same proportion of U.S. and Asian executives feel that innovation is their top priority for the coming year. Use a significance value of 0.05 and the p-value approach.

10-62. A marketing research firm is interested in determining whether there is a difference between the proportion of households in Chicago and the proportion of households in Milwaukee who purchase groceries online. The research firm decided to randomly sample households earning more than $50,000 a year in the two cities and ask them if they purchased any groceries online last year. The random sample involved 150 Chicago households and 135 Milwaukee households. The results of the sample can be found in the file **On-line Groceries**.

a. Construct a 95% confidence interval estimate for the difference between the two population proportions.

b. At the 0.10 level of significance, can the marketing research firm conclude that a greater proportion of households in Chicago earning more than $50,000 annually buys more groceries online than do similar households in Milwaukee? Support your answer with the appropriate hypothesis test.

10-63. *USA Today* notes (Mary Beth Marklein, "College Gender Gap Widens: 57% Are Women") that there are more men than women ages 18−24 in the United States—15 million versus 14.2 million. The male/female ratio in colleges today is 42.6/57.4. However, there is a discrepancy in the percentage of males dependent on their parents' income. The file titled **Diversity** contains the gender of undergrads (18−24) whose parents' income is in two categories: (1) low income—less than $30,000—and (2) upper income—$70,000 or more.

a. Determine if the sample sizes are large enough so that the sampling distribution of the difference between the sample proportions of male undergraduates in the two income categories can be approximated by a normal distribution.

b. Perform a test of hypothesis to determine that the proportion of male undergraduates in the upper-income category is more than 1% greater than that of the low-income category. Use a significance level of 0.01.

c. Calculate the difference between the two sample proportions. Given the magnitude of this difference, explain the results of part b.

Visual Summary

Chapter 10: Managers must often decide between two or more alternatives. Fortunately, there are statistical procedures that can help decision makers use sample information to compare alternative choices. This chapter introduces techniques that can be used to make statistical comparisons between two populations.

 10.1 Estimation for Two Population Means Using Independent Samples (pg. 387–397)

Summary

This section introduces estimation for those cases involving two population means where **independent samples** are selected. Techniques for estimating the difference between two population means are presented for each of the following situations:

- The population standard deviations are known and the samples are independent.
- The population standard deviations are unknown and the samples are independent.

Outcome 1. Discuss the logic behind, and demonstrate the techniques for, using independent samples to test hypotheses and develop interval estimates for the difference between two population means.

 10.2 Hypothesis Tests for Two Population Means Using Independent Samples (pg. 398–411)

Summary

This section introduces hypothesis-testing techniques for the difference between the means of two normally distributed populations in the following situations:

- The population standard deviations are known and the samples are independent.
- The population standard deviations are unknown and the samples are independent.

Just as was the case with hypothesis tests involving a single population parameter two possible errors can occur:

- Type I Error: Rejecting H_0 when it is true (alpha error).

- Type II Error: Not rejecting H_0 when it is false (beta error).

Outcome 1. Discuss the logic behind, and demonstrate the techniques for, using independent samples to test hypotheses and develop interval estimates for the difference between two population means.

 10.3 Interval Estimation and Hypothesis Tests for Paired Samples (pg. 411–419)

Summary

There are instances in business where **paired samples** are used to control for sources of variation that might otherwise distort the estimations or hypothesis tests. **Paired samples** are samples that are selected in such a way that values in one sample are matched with the values in the second sample for the purpose of controlling for extraneous factors. Paired samples are used in those cases where it is necessary to control for an outside source of variation. .

Outcome 2. Develop confidence interval estimates and conduct hypothesis tests for the difference between two population means for paired samples.

10.4 Estimation and Hypothesis Tests for Two Population Proportions (pg. 419–426)

Summary

Many business applications involve confidence intervals and hypothesis tests for two population proportions. The general format for confidence interval estimates for the difference between two population proportions is,

Point Estimate ± (Critical Value) (Standard Error)

Confidence intervals involving the difference between two population proportions always have a z-value as the critical value.

Hypothesis tests for the difference between two population proportions require the calculation of a pooled estimator for the overall proportion.

Outcome 3. Carry out hypothesis tests and establish interval estimates, using sample data, for the difference between two population proportions.

 Conclusion

Many decision-making applications require that a confidence interval for the difference between two population parameters be constructed and a hypothesis test for the difference between two population parameters be conducted. This chapter discussed the procedures and techniques for these situations. **Figure 10.11** provides a flowchart to assist you in selecting the appropriate procedures for establishing the confidence interval and conducting the hypothesis test when the decision-making situation involves two population parameters.

FIGURE 10.11

Estimation and Hypothesis
Testing Flow Diagram

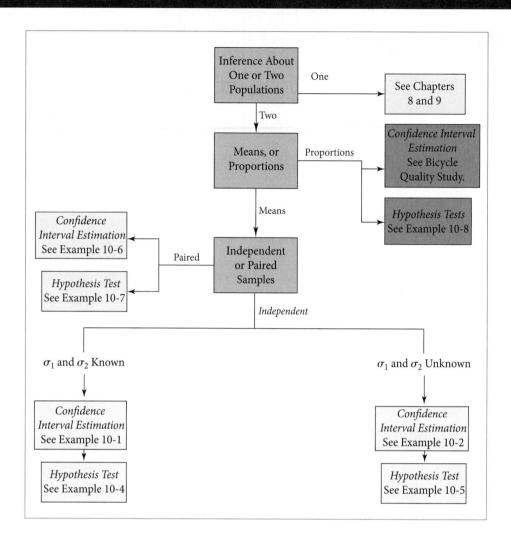

Equations

(10.1) Confidence Interval, General Format pg. 387

Point estimate $\pm$ (Critical value)(Standard error)

(10.2) Standard Error of $\bar{x}_1 - \bar{x}_{22}$ When σ_1 and σ_2 Are Known pg. 387

$$\sigma_{\bar{x}_1 - \bar{x}_2} = \sqrt{\frac{\sigma_1^2}{n_1} + \frac{\sigma_2^2}{n_2}}$$

(10.3) Confidence Interval Estimate for $\mu_1 - \mu_2$ When σ_1 and σ_2 Are Known, Independent Samples pg. 388

$$(\bar{x}_1 - \bar{x}_2) \pm z\sqrt{\frac{\sigma_1^2}{n_1} + \frac{\sigma_2^2}{n_2}}$$

(10.4) Confidence Interval Estimate for $\mu_1 - \mu_2$ When σ_1 and σ_2 Are Unknown, Independent Samples pg. 390

$$(\bar{x}_1 - \bar{x}_2) \pm t s_p \sqrt{\frac{1}{n_1} + \frac{1}{n_2}}$$

(10.5) Confidence Interval Estimate for $\mu_1 - \mu_2$ When σ_1 and σ_2 Are Unknown and Not Equal, Independent Samples pg. 393

$$(\bar{x}_1 - \bar{x}_2) \pm t\sqrt{\frac{s_1^2}{n_1} + \frac{s_2^2}{n_2}}$$

(10.6) Degrees of Freedom for Estimating Difference between Population Means When σ_1 and σ_2 Are Not Equal pg. 393

$$df = \frac{(s_1^2/n_1 + s_2^2/n_2)^2}{\left(\frac{(s_1^2/n_1)^2}{n_1 - 1} + \frac{(s_2^2/n_2)^2}{n_2 - 1}\right)}$$

(10.7) z-Test Statistic for $\mu_1 - \mu_2$ When σ_1 and σ_2 Are Known, Independent Samples pg. 398

$$z = \frac{(\bar{x}_1 - \bar{x}_2) - (\mu_1 - \mu_2)}{\sqrt{\frac{\sigma_1^2}{n_1} + \frac{\sigma_2^2}{n_2}}}$$

(10.8) t-Test Statistic for $\mu_1 - \mu_2$ When σ_1 and σ_2 Are Unknown and Assumed Equal, Independent Samples pg. 401

$$t = \frac{(\bar{x}_1 - \bar{x}_2) - (\mu_1 - \mu_2)}{s_p\sqrt{\frac{1}{n_1} + \frac{1}{n_2}}}, \quad df = n_1 + n_2 - 2$$

(10.9) *t*-Test Statistic for $\mu_1 - \mu_2$ When Population Variances Are Unknown and Not Assumed Equal pg. 407

$$t = \frac{(\bar{x}_1 - \bar{x}_2) - (\mu_1 - \mu_2)}{\sqrt{\dfrac{s_1^2}{n_1} + \dfrac{s_2^2}{n_2}}}$$

(10.10) Degrees of Freedom for *t*-Test Statistic When Population Variances Are Not Equal pg. 407

$$df = \frac{(s_1^2/n_1 + s_2^2/n_2)^2}{\left(\dfrac{(s_1^2/n_1)^2}{n_1 - 1} + \dfrac{(s_2^2/n_2)^2}{n_2 - 1}\right)}$$

(10.11) Paired Difference pg. 412

$$d = x_1 - x_2$$

(10.12) Point Estimate for the Population Mean Paired Difference, μ_d pg. 412

$$\bar{d} = \frac{\sum\limits_{i=1}^{n} d_i}{n}$$

(10.13) Sample Standard Deviation for Paired Differences pg. 412

$$s_d = \sqrt{\frac{\sum\limits_{i=1}^{n} (d_i - \bar{d})^2}{n - 1}}$$

(10.14) Confidence Interval Estimate for Population Mean Paired Difference, μ_d pg. 413

$$\bar{d} \pm t \frac{s_d}{\sqrt{n}}$$

(10.15) *t*-Test Statistic for Paired-Sample Test pg. 415

$$t = \frac{\bar{d} - \mu_d}{\dfrac{s_d}{\sqrt{n}}}, \qquad df = (n - 1)$$

(10.16) Confidence Interval Estimate for $p_1 - p_2$ pg. 420

$$(\bar{p}_1 - \bar{p}_2) \pm z \sqrt{\frac{\bar{p}_1(1 - \bar{p}_1)}{n_1} + \frac{\bar{p}_2(1 - \bar{p}_2)}{n_2}}$$

(10.17) Pooled Estimator for Overall Proportion pg. 421

$$\bar{p} = \frac{n_1 \bar{p}_1 + n_2 \bar{p}_2}{n_1 + n_2} = \frac{x_1 + x_2}{n_1 + n_2}$$

(10.18) *z*-Test Statistic for Difference Between Population Proportions pg. 421

$$z = \frac{(\bar{p}_1 - \bar{p}_2) - (p_1 - p_2)}{\sqrt{\bar{p}(1 - \bar{p})\left(\dfrac{1}{n_1} + \dfrac{1}{n_2}\right)}}$$

Key Terms

Independent samples pg. 387   **Paired samples** pg. 411

Chapter Exercises   MyStatLab

Conceptual Questions

10-64. Why, when dealing with two independent samples where you cannot assume the population variances are equal, should the degrees of freedom be adjusted?

10-65. Explain, in nontechnical terms, why pairing observations, if possible, is often a more effective tool than taking independent samples.

10-66. Consider the following set of samples obtained from two normally distributed populations whose variances are equal:

Sample 1:	11.2	11.2	7.4	8.7	8.5	13.5	4.5	11.9
Sample 2:	11.7	9.5	15.6	16.5	11.3	17.6	17.0	8.5

  a. Suppose that the samples were independent. Perform a test of hypothesis to determine if there is a difference in the two population means. Use a significance level of 0.05.

  b. Now suppose that the samples were paired samples. Perform a test of hypothesis to determine if there is a difference in the two population means.

  c. How do you account for the difference in the outcomes of part a and part b? Support your assertions with a statistical rationale.

10-67. Examine the following information:

	Sample 1	Sample 2
n_i	15	10
$\bar{x}_i$	12	7
s_i	3	4

  a. Construct a 95% confidence interval for $\mu_1 - \mu_2$.

  b. Calculate the test statistic that would be used to determine if $\mu_1 - \mu_2 =$ the upper confidence limit. Given this, what would the result of the test be if you wish to test $\mu_1 - \mu_2 =$ Any value larger than the upper confidence limit?

c. Calculate the test statistic that would be used to determine if $\mu_1 - \mu_2 =$ the lower confidence limit. Given this, what would the result of the test be if you wish to test $\mu_1 - \mu_2 =$ any value smaller than the lower confidence limit?

d. Given your answers to parts b and c, how could you use the confidence interval to conduct a two-tailed hypothesis test?

Business Applications

10-68. A student group at a university located in the Midwest is conducting a study to determine whether there is a difference between textbook prices for new textbooks sold by the on-campus bookstore and an Internet retailer. A random sample of 10 textbooks was taken, and the campus price and the Internet retailer's price for each textbook were collected. At the 0.01 level of significance, can the student group conclude that there is a difference in average textbook prices for new textbooks sold on campus and over the Internet?

Textbook	Physics	Chemistry	Spanish	Accounting	Calculus
Campus	108	114	114	110	118
Internet	124	120	107	112	122

Textbook	Economics	Art	Biology	History	English
Campus	108	119	115	119	114
Internet	123	125	108	117	119

10-69. Bach Photographs is a photography business with studios in two locations. The owner is interested in monitoring business activity closely at the two locations. Among the factors in which he is interested is whether the mean customer orders per day for the two locations are the same. A random sample of 11 days' orders for the two locations showed the following data:

Location A			Location B		
$444	$478	$501	$233	$127	$230
200	400	350	299	250	300
167	250	300	800	340	400
300	600		780	370	

The owner wishes to know the difference between the average amount in customer orders per day for the two locations. He has no idea what this difference might be. What procedure would you use under these circumstances? Explain your reasoning.

10-70. Allstate Insurance is one of the major automobile insurance companies in the country. Recently, the western region claims manager instructed an intern in her department to develop a confidence interval estimate of the difference between the mean years that male customers have been insured by Allstate versus female customers. The intern randomly selected 13 male and 13 female customers from the account records and recorded the number of years that the customer had been insured by Allstate. These data (rounded to the nearest year) are as follows:

Males				Females			
14	9	9	16	3	10	4	7
14	8	12	11	10	5	4	1
6	9	10	7	4	4	6	9
3				2			

Based on these data, construct and interpret a 90% confidence interval estimate for the difference between the mean years for male and female customers.

10-71. The Eaton Company sells breakable china through a mail-order system that has been very profitable. One of its major problems is freight damage. It insures the items at shipping, but the inconvenience to the customer when a piece gets broken can cause the customer not to place another order in the future. Thus, packaging is important to the Eaton Company.

In the past, the company has purchased two different packaging materials from two suppliers. The assumption was that there would be no difference in the proportion of damaged shipments resulting from use of either packaging material. The sales manager recently decided a study of this issue should be done. Therefore, a random sample of 300 orders using shipping material 1 and a random sample of 250 orders using material 2 were pulled from the files. The number of damaged parcels, x, was recorded for each material as follows:

Material 1	Material 2
$n_1 = 300$	$n_2 = 250$
$x_1 = 19$	$x_2 = 12$

a. Is the normal distribution a good approximation for the distribution of the difference between the sample proportions? Provide support for your answer.

b. Based on the sample information and $\alpha = 0.03$, what should the Eaton Company conclude?

10-72. Before the unprecedented decline in home sales that started in late 2008, the National Association of Realtors profile of home buyers and sellers indicated the percentage of home buyers who are single women has more than doubled since 1981, whereas the percentages of home buyers who are single men has declined. This occurred despite evidence indicating that women's salaries still lag behind those of men. The association's profile states that the median income for men and women home buyers was $58,939 and $47,315, respectively. Assume the respective standard deviations and sample sizes were $10,000 and $9,000 and 200 and 302.

a. Conduct a hypothesis test to determine if the median income for men buying homes is more than $10,000 larger than that of women. Use a significance level of 0.05.

b. Describe any additional assumptions required to validate the results of the hypothesis test in part a.

10-73. Turbo-Tax and Tax-Cut are two of the best-selling tax preparation software packages. Recently, a consumer group conducted a test to estimate the difference in the mean time it would take an individual to complete his or her federal income tax using these two products. To run the test, the group selected a random sample of 16 people. All 16 people used both software packages to complete their taxes. Half of the people were assigned Turbo-Tax first, followed by Tax-Cut. The other half used the products in the opposite order. The following values represent the time in minutes that it took to complete the returns:

Individual	Turbo-Tax	Tax-Cut
1	70	88
2	56	71
3	79	89
4	94	66
5	93	78
6	101	64
7	42	74
8	71	99
9	91	79
10	59	68
11	65	93
12	50	93
13	47	86
14	60	86
15	63	81
16	43	83

Based on these sample data, construct and interpret a 95% confidence interval estimate for the difference between the two population means.

10-74. Suppose a random sample taken in 2010 of 900 adults between the ages of 25 and 34 years of age indicated that 396 owned a home. In 1984, a random sample of 900 adults within the same age group showed that 432 owned a home. At the 0.02 level of significance, is there a difference between the proportion of homeowners in 2010 and 1984 for the 25 to 34 age group?

10-75. A random sample of 64 bicycle-riding adults in Portland indicated that 24 always wore a helmet while riding. A random sample of 80 bicycle-riding adults in Amsterdam indicated that 18 always rode a helmet while riding.

a. Use the sample information to develop a 95% confidence interval estimate for the difference between the proportions of bicycle-riding adults that wear a helmet in the two cities.

b. Based on the sample results, can you conclude that the population proportion of bicycle-riding adults in Portland who always wear a helmet is greater that the population proportion of bicycle-riding adults in Amsterdam who always wear a helmet? Use a 0.025 level of significance to conduct the test.

10-76. Surprisingly, injuries such as strains and sprains are higher among airport screeners than any other federal work group. A recent study found the injury rate for airport screeners was 29%, far exceeding the 4.5% injury rate for the rest of the federal workforce. Assume the sample sizes required to obtain these percentages were 75 and 125, respectively.

a. Determine if the sample sizes were large enough to allow the distribution of the difference of the sample proportions to be approximated with a normal distribution.

b. Conduct a hypothesis test to determine if the injury rate of airport screeners is more than 10% larger than that of the rest of the federal workforce. Use a significance level of 0.05.

Computer Database Exercises

10-77. Reviewers from the Oregon Evidence-Based Practice Center at the Oregon Health and Science University investigated the effectiveness of prescription drugs in assisting people to fall asleep and stay asleep. The Oregon reviewers, led by Susan Carson, M.P.H., concluded that Sonata was better than Ambien at putting people to sleep quickly, whereas patients on Ambien slept longer and reported having better-quality sleep than those taking Sonata. Samples taken by Carson and her associates are contained in a file titled **Shuteye**. The samples reflect an experiment in which individuals were randomly given the two brands of pills on separate evenings. Their time spent sleeping was recorded for each of the brands of sleeping pills.

a. Does the experiment seem to have dependent or independent samples? Explain your reasoning.

b. Do the data indicate that the researchers were correct? Conduct a statistical procedure to determine this.

c. Conduct a procedure to determine the plausible differences in the average number of hours slept by those taking Ambien and Sonata.

10-78. As part of a study on student loan debt, a national agency that underwrites student loans is examining the differences in student loan debt for undergraduate students. One question the agency would like to address specifically is whether the mean undergraduate debt of Hispanic students graduating in 2009 is less than the mean undergraduate debt of Asian-American students graduating in 2009. To conduct the study, a random sample of 92 Hispanic students and a random sample 110 Asian-American students who completed an undergraduate degree in 2009 were taken. The undergraduate debt incurred for financing college for each sampled student was collected. The sample results can be found in the file **Student Debt**.

a. Assume that the agency believes the two populations from which the samples were taken are approximately normally distributed with equal variances. Conduct a hypothesis test at the 0.01

level of significance to determine whether the mean undergraduate debt for Hispanic students is less than the mean undergraduate debt for Asian-American students.

b. For what values of alpha would your decision in part a change?

c. Suppose the agency is unwilling to assume the two populations from which the samples are taken are approximately normally distributed with equal variances. Conduct the appropriate test to determine whether the mean undergraduate debt for Hispanic students is less than the mean undergraduate debt for Asian-American students. Use the *p*-value approach to conduct the test. State a conclusion.

10-79. One of the statistics that the College Board monitors is the rising tuition at private and public four-year colleges. The tuition and fees for private and public four-year colleges for the 1980–1981 academic year in 2005 dollars were $8,180 and $1,818, respectively. The file titled **College$** contains data that yield the same average tuition and fees (adjusted for inflation) for private and public four-year colleges obtained by the College Board for 2005–2006.

a. Do the data indicate that the gap between tuition and fees at private and public colleges has more than doubled in the 2005–2006 academic year as compared to that of the 1980–1981 academic year? Use a significance level of 0.01. Assume the population variances are equal.

b. What statistical error could have been made based on the decision reached in part a? Provide an explanation.

10-80. Vintner Mortgage Company in Chicago, Illinois, markets residential and commercial loans to customers in the region. Although the company had generally tried to avoid the "sub-prime" loan market, recently the company's board of directors asked whether the company had experienced a difference in the proportion of loan defaults between residential and commercial customers. To prepare an answer to this question, company officials selected a random sample of 200 residential loans and 105 commercial loans that had been issued prior to 2005. The loans were analyzed to determine their status. A loan that is still being paid was labeled "Active" and a default loan was labeled "Default." The resulting data are in a file called **Vintner**.

a. Based on the sample data and a significance level equal to 0.05, does there appear to be a difference in the proportion of loan defaults between residential and commercial customers?

b. Prepare a short response to the Vintner board of directors. Include in your report a graph of the data that supports your statistical analysis.

c. Consider the outcome of the hypothesis test in part a. In the last five audits, 10 residential and 10 commercial customers were selected. In three of the audits, there were more residential than commercial loan defaults. Determine the probability of such an occurrence.

Case 10.1

Motive Power Company—Part 1

Cregg Hart is manufacturing manager for Motive Power Company, a locomotive engine and rail car manufacturer. The company has been very successful in recent years, and in July 2006 signed two major contracts totaling nearly $200 million. A key to the company's success has been its focus on quality. Customers from around the world have been very pleased with the attention to detail put forth by Motive Power.

One of the things Cregg has been adamant about is that Motive Power's suppliers also provide high quality. As a result, when the company finds good suppliers, it stays with them and tries to establish a long-term relationship. However, Cregg must also factor in the costs of parts and materials and has instructed his purchasing staff to be on the lookout for "better deals."

Recently, Sheryl Carleson, purchasing manager at Motive Power, identified a new rivet supplier in Europe that claims its rivets are as good or better quality than Motive Power's current supplier's but at a much lower cost. One key quality factor is the rivet diameter. When Sheryl approached Cregg about the possibility of going with the new supplier for rivets, he suggested they conduct a test to determine if there is any difference in the average diameter

of the rivets from the two companies. Sheryl requested that the new company send 100 rivets, and she pulled a random sample of 100 rivets from her inventory of rivets from the original supplier. She then asked an intern to measure the diameters to three decimal places using a micrometer. The resulting data from both suppliers are given in the file called **Motive Power**.

Required Tasks:

1. Develop histograms showing the distribution of rivet diameters from the two suppliers.
2. Compute the sample means and standard deviations for the two sets of data.
3. Comment on whether it appears the assumptions required for testing if the two populations have equal mean diameters are satisfied.
4. Select a level of significance for testing whether the two suppliers have rivets with equal mean diameters. Discuss the factors you used in arriving at the level of significance you have selected.
5. Perform the appropriate null and alternative hypothesis test. Discuss the results.
6. Prepare a short report outlining your recommendation.

Case 10.2

Hamilton Marketing Services

Alex Hamilton founded Hamilton Marketing Services in 1999 after leaving a major marketing consulting firm in Chicago. Hamilton Marketing Services focuses on small- to medium-sized retail firms and has been quite successful in providing a wide range of marketing and advertising services.

A few weeks ago, a relatively new customer that Alex himself has been working with for the past several months called with an idea. This customer, a pet-grooming company, is interested in changing the way it prices its full-service dog-grooming service. The customer is considering two options: (1) a flat $40.00 per-visit price and (2) a $30.00 per-visit price if the dog owner signs up for a series of four groomings. However, the pet-grooming service is unsure how these options would be received by its customers. The owner was hoping there was some type of study Alex could have his company do that would provide information on what the difference in response rate would be for the two pricing options. He was interested in determining if one option would bring in more revenue than the other.

At the time, Alex suggested that a flier with an attached coupon be sent to a random sample of potential customers. One sample of customers would receive the coupon listing the $40.00 price. A second sample of customers would receive the coupon listing the $30.00 price and the requirement for signing up for a series of four visits. Each coupon would have an expiration date of one month from the date of issue. Then the pet-grooming store owner could track the responses to these coupon offers and bring the data back to Alex for analysis.

Yesterday, the pet store owner e-mailed an Excel file called **Grooming Price Test** to Alex. Alex has now asked you to assist with the analysis. He has mentioned using a 95% confidence interval and wants a short report describing the data and summarizing which pricing strategy is preferred both from a proportion-response standpoint and from a revenue-producing standpoint.

Required Tasks:

1. Compute a sample proportion for the responses for the two coupon options under consideration.
2. Develop a 95% confidence interval for the difference between the proportions of responses between the two options.
3. Use the confidence interval developed in (2) to draw a conclusion regarding whether or not there is any statistical evidence that there is a difference in response rate between the two coupon options.
4. Determine whether or not there is a difference between the two coupon options in terms of revenue generated.
5. Identify any other issues or factors that should be considered in deciding which coupon option to use.
6. Develop a short report summarizing your analysis and conclusions.

Case 10.3

Green Valley Assembly Company

The Green Valley Assembly Company assembles consumer electronics products for manufacturers that need temporary extra production capacity. As such, it has periodic product changes. Because the products Green Valley assembles are marketed under the label of well-known manufacturers, high quality is a must.

Tom Bradley, of the Green Valley personnel department, has been very impressed by recent research concerning job-enrichment programs. In particular, he has been impressed with the increases in quality that seem to be associated with these programs. However, some studies have shown no significant increase in quality, and they imply that the money spent on such programs has not been worthwhile.

Tom has talked to Sandra Hansen, the production manager, about instituting a job-enrichment program in the assembly operation at Green Valley. Sandra was somewhat pessimistic about the potential, but she agreed to introduce the program. The plan was to implement the program in one wing of the plant and continue with the current method in the other wing. The procedure was to be in effect for six months. After that period, a test would be made to determine the effectiveness of the job-enrichment program.

After the six-month trial period, a random sample of employees from each wing produced the following output measures:

Old	Job-Enriched
$n_1 = 50$	$n_2 = 50$
$\bar{x}_1 = 11/\text{hr}$	$\bar{x}_2 = 9.7/\text{hr}$
$s_1 = 1.2/\text{hr}$	$s_2 = 0.9/\text{hr}$

Both Sandra and Tom wonder whether the job-enrichment program has affected production output. They would like to use these sample results to determine whether the average output has changed and to determine whether the employees' consistency has been affected by the new program.

A second sample from each wing was selected. The measure was the quality of the products assembled. In the "old" wing, 79 products were tested and 12% were found to be defectively assembled. In the "job-enriched" wing, 123 products were examined and 9% were judged defectively assembled.

With all these data, Sandra and Tom are beginning to get a little confused. However, they realize that there must be some way to use the information to make a judgment about the effectiveness of the job-enrichment program.

Case 10.4

U-Need-It Rental Agency

Richard Fundt has operated the U-Need-It rental agency in a northern Wisconsin city for the past five years. One of the biggest rental items has always been chainsaws; lately, the demand for these saws has increased dramatically. Richard buys chainsaws at a special industrial rate and then rents them for $10 per day. The chainsaws are used an average of 50 to 60 days per year. Although Richard makes money on any chainsaw, he obviously makes more on those saws that last the longest.

Richard worked for a time as a repairperson and can make most repairs on the equipment he rents, including chainsaws. However, he would also like to limit the time he spends making repairs. U-Need-It is currently stocking two types of saws: North Woods and Accu-Cut. Richard has an impression that one of the models, Accu-Cut, does not seem to break down as much as the other. Richard currently has 8 North Woods saws and 11 Accu-Cut

saws. He decides to keep track of the number of hours each is used between major repairs. He finds the following values, in hours:

Accu-Cut		North Woods	
48	46	48	78
39	88	44	94
84	29	72	59
76	52	19	52
41	57		
24			

The North Woods sales representative has stated that the company may be raising the price of its saws in the near future. This will make them slightly more expensive than the Accu-Cut models. However, the prices have tended to move with each other in the past.

Chapter 11 Quick Prep Links

- **Review** material on calculating and interpreting sample means and variances in Chapter 3.

- **Examine** Section 9.1 on formulating null and alternative hypotheses.

- **Make sure** you understand the concepts of Type I and Type II error discussed in Chapter 9.

Hypothesis Tests and Estimation for Population Variances

11.1 Hypothesis Tests and Estimation for a Single Population Variance (pg. 435–445)

Outcome 1. Formulate and carry out hypothesis tests for a single population variance.

Outcome 2. Develop and interpret confidence interval estimates for a population variance.

11.2 Hypothesis Tests for Two Population Variances (pg. 445–456)

Outcome 3. Formulate and carry out hypothesis tests for the difference between two population variances.

Why you need to know

In addition to hypothesis testing applications involving one and two population means and proportions like those presented in Chapters 9 and 10, there are also business situations in which decision makers must reach a conclusion about the value of a single population variance or about the relationship between two population variances. For example, knowing that a crate of strawberries weighs 4 pounds on average may not be enough. The produce manager for a supermarket chain may also be concerned about the variability in weight of the strawberries. If there is too much variability, then some crates may be underfilled, which will cause problems with consumers who believe they have been cheated. If the crate is overfilled, the store is giving away strawberries and unnecessary costs are incurred. The manager in this case must monitor both the average weight and the variation in weight of the strawberry crates.

A manager may also be required to decide if there is a difference in the variability of sales between two different sales territories or if the output of one production process is more or less variable than another. In this chapter, we discuss methods that can be used to make inferences concerning one and two population variances. The techniques presented in this chapter will also introduce new distributions that will be used in later chapters. When reading this chapter, keep in mind that the techniques discussed here are extensions of the estimation and hypothesis-testing concepts introduced in Chapters 8, 9, and 10.

olgaeolen/Fotolia

11.1 Hypothesis Tests and Estimation for a Single Population Variance

You can expect to encounter many cases in which you will be as interested in the spread or variation of a population as in its central location. For instance, military planes designed to penetrate enemy defenses have a ground-following radar system. The radar tells the pilot exactly how far the plane is above the ground. A radar unit that is correct *on the average* is useless if the readings are distributed widely around the average value. Many airport shuttle systems have stopping sensors to deposit passengers at the correct spot in a terminal. A sensor that, *on the average*, lets passengers off at the correct point could leave many irritated people long distances up and down the track. Therefore, many product specifications involve both an average value and some limit on the dispersion that the individual values can have. For example, the specification for a steel push pin may be an average length of 1.78 inches plus or minus 0.01 inch. A company using these pins would be interested in both the average length and how much these pins vary in length.

Business applications in which the population variance is important will use one of two statistical procedures: hypothesis tests or confidence interval estimates. In hypothesis-testing applications, a null hypothesis will be formulated in terms of the population variance, σ^2. For example, a bank manager might hypothesize that the population variance in customer service time, σ^2, is no greater than 36 minutes squared (remember, variance is in squared units). Then, based on sample data from the population of bank customers, the null hypothesis will either be rejected or not rejected.

In other cases, the application might require the population variance to be estimated. For instance, a regional transportation manager is planning to conduct a survey of residents in a suburb to determine the mean number of times per week they use their cars for purposes other than commuting to work. Before conducting the survey, she needs to determine the required sample size. One key factor in determining the sample size (see Chapter 9) is the value of the population variance. Thus, before she can determine the required sample size, she will need to estimate the population variance by taking a *pilot sample* and constructing a confidence interval estimate for σ^2.

This section introduces the methods for testing hypotheses and for constructing confidence interval estimates for a single population variance.

Chi-Square Test for One Population Variance

Usually when we think of measuring variation, the standard deviation is used as the measure because it is measured in the same units as the mean. Ideally, in the ground-following radar example, we would want to test to see whether the standard deviation exceeds a certain level, as determined by the product specifications. Unfortunately, there is no statistical test that directly tests the standard deviation. However, there is a procedure called the chi-square test that can be used to test the population variance. We can convert any standard deviation hypothesis test into one involving the variance, as shown in the following example.

Chapter Outcome 1. ➞ | BUSINESS APPLICATION | **HYPOTHESIS FOR A POPULATION VARIANCE**

CROSS TOWN MOVERS Cross Town Movers is a company started by four business majors at a local college. The company does small moving jobs for businesses and private residential customers. Looking at past records, the Cross Town operations manager has determined the mean job time for a properly trained moving crew is 2 hours, with a standard deviation not to exceed 0.5 hour. Recent data indicate that the 2-hour average is being achieved. However, the manager is worried that variability in move times may have increased. The company's job schedule is built around the assumptions of $\mu = 2$ hours and $\sigma = 0.5$ hour. If the move-time standard deviation exceeds 0.5 hour, the job schedule gets disrupted.

The operations manager has decided to select a random sample of recent jobs and to use the sample data to determine whether the move-time standard deviation exceeds 0.5 hour. Ideally, the manager would like to test the following null and alternative hypotheses:

$$H_0: \sigma \leq 0.5 \, (\text{service standard})$$
$$H_A: \sigma > 0.5$$

Because there is no statistical technique for directly testing hypotheses about a population standard deviation, he will use a test for a population variance. We first convert the standard deviation to a variance by squaring the standard deviation and then restate the null and alternative hypotheses as follows:

$$H_0: \sigma^2 \leq 0.25$$
$$H_A: \sigma^2 > 0.25$$

As with all hypothesis tests, the decision to reject or not reject the null hypothesis will be based on the statistic computed from the sample. In testing hypotheses about a single population variance, the appropriate sample statistic is s^2, the *sample variance*.

To test a null hypothesis about a population variance, we compare s^2 with the hypothesized population variance, σ^2. To do this, we need to standardize the distribution of the sample variance in much the same way as we did to use the z-distribution and the t-distribution when testing hypotheses about the population mean.

Assumption

> When the random sample is from a normally distributed population, the distribution for the standardized sample variance is a *chi-square distribution*.

The chi-square distribution is a continuous distribution of a standardized random variable, computed using Equation 11.1.

Chi-Square Test for a Single Population Variance

$$\chi^2 = \frac{(n-1)s^2}{\sigma^2} \qquad (11.1)$$

where:

$$\chi^2 = \text{Standardized chi-square variable}$$
$$n = \text{Sample size}$$
$$s^2 = \text{Sample variance}$$
$$\sigma^2 = \text{hypothesized variance}$$

The distribution of χ^2 is a chi-squared distribution with $n-1$ degrees of freedom.

The central location and shape of the chi-square distribution depends only on the degrees of freedom, $n-1$. Figure 11.1 illustrates chi-square distributions for various degrees of freedom. Note that as the degrees of freedom increase, the chi-square distribution comes closer to being symmetrical.

FIGURE 11.1

Chi-Square Distributions

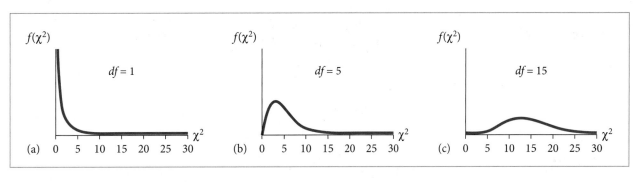

BUSINESS APPLICATION **TESTING A SINGLE POPULATION VARIANCE**

CROSS TOWN MOVERS (CONTINUED) Returning to the Cross Town Movers example, suppose the operations manager took a random sample of 20 service calls and found a variance of 0.33 hours squared. Figure 11.2 illustrates the hypothesis test at a significance level of 0.10.

Appendix G contains a table of upper-tail chi-square critical values for various probabilities and degrees of freedom. The use of the chi-square table is similar to the use of the *t*-distribution table. For example, to find the critical value, $\chi^2_{0.10}$, for the Cross Town Movers example, determine the degrees of freedom, $n - 1 = 20 - 1 = 19$, and the desired significance level, 0.10. Because this is an upper-tail, one-tail test, go to the chi-square table under the column headed 0.10 and find the χ^2 value in this column that intersects the row corresponding to the appropriate degrees of freedom. You should find the critical value of $\chi^2_{0.10} = 27.2036$.

As you can see in Figure 11.2, the chi-square test statistic, calculated using Equation 11.1, is

$$\chi^2 = \frac{(n - 1)s^2}{\sigma^2} = \frac{(19)(0.33)}{0.25} = 25.08$$

This falls to the left of the rejection region, meaning the manager should not reject the null hypothesis based on these sample data. Thus, based on these results, there is insufficient evidence to conclude that the moving teams are completing their moves with a standard deviation of more than 0.5 hour.

FIGURE 11.2

Chi-Square Test for One Population Variance for the Cross Town Movers Example

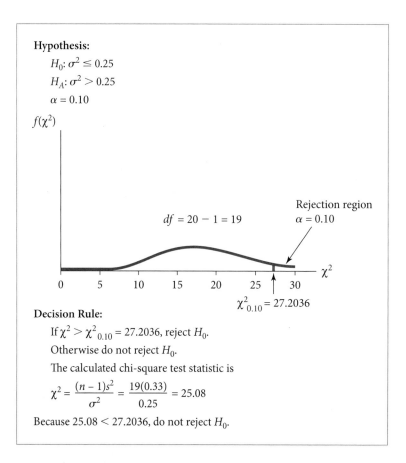

Hypothesis:

$H_0: \sigma^2 \le 0.25$

$H_A: \sigma^2 > 0.25$

$\alpha = 0.10$

$f(\chi^2)$

$df = 20 - 1 = 19$

Rejection region
$\alpha = 0.10$

χ^2

0   5   10   15   20   25   30

$\chi^2_{0.10} = 27.2036$

Decision Rule:

If $\chi^2 > \chi^2_{0.10} = 27.2036$, reject H_0.

Otherwise do not reject H_0.

The calculated chi-square test statistic is

$$\chi^2 = \frac{(n - 1)s^2}{\sigma^2} = \frac{19(0.33)}{0.25} = 25.08$$

Because $25.08 < 27.2036$, do not reject H_0.

How to do it (Example 11-1)

Hypotheses Tests for a Single Population Variance

To conduct a hypothesis test for a single population variance, you can use the following steps:

1. Specify the population parameter of interest.

2. Formulate the null and alternative hypotheses in terms of σ^2, the population variance.

3. Specify the level of significance for the hypothesis test.

4. Construct the rejection region and define the decision rule. Obtain the critical value, χ^2_α, from the chi-square distribution table.

5. Compute the test statistic.

   Select a random sample and compute the sample variance,

   $$s^2 = \frac{\Sigma(x - \bar{x})^2}{n - 1}$$

   Based on the sample variance, determine $\chi^2 = \frac{(n-1)s^2}{\sigma^2}$

6. Reach a decision.

7. Draw a conclusion.

EXAMPLE 11-1   **ONE-TAILED HYPOTHESES TESTS FOR A POPULATION VARIANCE**

Lockheed Martin Corporation The Lockheed Martin Corporation is a major defense contractor as well as the maker of commercial products such as space satellite systems. The quality specialist at the Sunnyvale, California, Space Systems facility has been informed that one specification listed in the contract between Lockheed Martin and the Department of Defense concerns the variability in the diameter of the part that will be installed on a satellite. Hundreds of these parts are used on each satellite made. Before installing these parts, Lockheed Martin quality specialists will take a random sample of 20 parts from the batch and test to see whether the standard deviation exceeds the 0.05-inch specification. This can be done using the following steps:

Step 1   Specify the population parameter of interest.
The standard deviation for the diameter of a part is the parameter of interest.

Step 2   Formulate the null and alternative hypotheses.
The null and alternative hypotheses must be stated in terms of the population variance, so we convert the specification, $\sigma = 0.05$, to the variance, $\sigma^2 = 0.0025$. The null and alternative hypotheses are

$$H_0: \sigma^2 \leq 0.0025$$
$$H_A: \sigma^2 > 0.0025$$

Step 3   Specify the significance level.
The hypothesis test will be conducted using $\alpha = 0.05$.

Step 4   Construct the rejection region and define the decision rule.
Note, this hypothesis test is a one-tailed, upper-tail test. Thus we obtain the critical value from the chi-square table where the area in the upper tail corresponds to $\alpha = 0.05$. The critical value from the chi-square distribution with $20 - 1 = 19$ degrees of freedom and 0.05 level of significance is

$$\chi^2_\alpha = \chi^2_{0.05} = 30.1435$$

The decision rule is stated as

If $\chi^2 > \chi^2_{0.05} = 30.1435$, reject H_0; otherwise, do not reject.

Step 5   Compute the test statistic.
The random sample of $n = 20$ parts gives a sample variance for part diameter of $s^2 = \frac{\Sigma(x - \bar{x})^2}{n - 1} = 0.0108$.

The test statistic is

$$\chi^2 = \frac{(n-1)s^2}{\sigma^2} = \frac{(20-1)0.0108}{0.0025} = 82.08$$

Step 6   Reach a decision.
Because $\chi^2 = 82.08 > 30.1435$, reject the null hypothesis.

Step 7   Draw a conclusion.
Conclude that the variance of the population does exceed the 0.0025 limit. The company appears to have a problem with the variation of this part. The quality specialist will likely contact the supplier to discuss the issue.

>> **END EXAMPLE**

TRY PROBLEM 11-3 (pg. 443)

EXAMPLE 11-2   **TWO-TAILED HYPOTHESES TESTS FOR A POPULATION VARIANCE**

Genesis Technology The research and development manager for Genesis Technology, a clean-tech start-up company headquartered in Pittsburgh, has spent the past several months overseeing a project in which the company has been experimenting with different designs of storage devices that can be used to store solar energy. One important attribute of a storage device for electricity is the variability in storage capacity. Consistent capacity is desirable so that consumers can more accurately predict the amount of time they can expect the "battery" system to last under normal conditions. Genesis Technology engineers have determined that one particular storage design will yield an average of 88 minutes per cell with a standard deviation of 6 minutes. During the past few weeks, the engineers have made some modifications to the design and are interested in determining whether this change has impacted the standard deviation either up or down. The test was conducted on a random sample of 12 individual storage cells containing the modified design. The following data show the minutes of use that were recorded:

89	85	91	95
95	97	81	89
94	86	87	83

This data can be analyzed using the following steps:

Step 1 Specify the population parameter of interest.
The engineers are interested in the standard deviation of the time (in minutes) that the storage cells last under normal use.

Step 2 Formulate the null and alternative hypotheses.
The null and alternative hypotheses are stated in terms of the population variance, since there is no test that deals specifically with the population standard deviation. Thus, we must convert the population standard deviation, $\sigma = 6$, to a variance, $\sigma^2 = 36$. Because the engineers are interested in whether there has been a change (up or down), the test will be a two-tailed test with the null and alternative hypotheses formulated as follows:

$$H_0: \sigma^2 = 36$$
$$H_A: \sigma^2 \neq 36$$

Step 3 Specify the significance level.
The hypothesis test will be conducted using an $\alpha = 0.10$.

Step 4 Construct the rejection region and define the decision rule.
Because this is a two-tail test, two critical values from the chi-square distribution in Appendix G are required, one for the upper (right) tail and one for the lower (left) tail. The alpha will be split evenly between the two tails with $\alpha/2 = 0.05$ in each tail. The degrees of freedom for the chi-square distribution are $n - 1 = 12 - 1 = 11$. The upper-tail critical value is found by locating the column headed 0.05 and going to the row for 11 degrees of freedom. This gives $\chi^2_{0.05} = 19.6752$. The lower critical value is found by going to the column headed 0.95 and to the row for 11 degrees of freedom. (Refer to Figure 11.3.) This gives $\chi^2_{0.95} = 4.5748$. Thus, the decision rule is

If $\chi^2 > \chi^2_{0.05} = 19.6752$, or if
$\chi^2 < \chi^2_{0.95} = 4.5748$, reject the null hypothesis

Otherwise, do not reject the null hypothesis.

Step 5 Compute the test statistic.
The random sample of $n = 12$ cells gives a sample standard variance computed as

$$s^2 = \frac{\sum(x - \bar{x})^2}{n - 1} = 26.6$$

FIGURE 11.3

Chi-Square Rejection Regions for Two-Tailed Test of One Population Variance

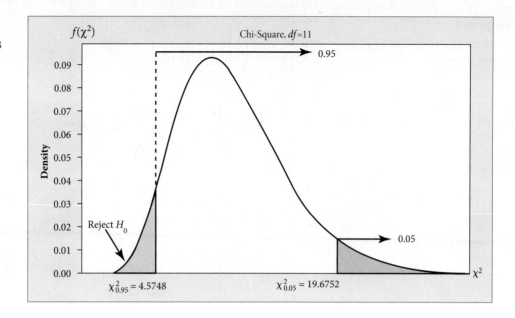

Then the test statistic is

$$\chi^2 = \frac{(n-1)s^2}{\sigma^2} = \frac{(12-1)26.6}{36} = 8.13$$

Step 6   Reach a decision.
Because $\chi^2 = 8.13 > \chi^2_{0.95} = 4.5748$ and $\chi^2 = 8.13 < \chi^2_{0.05} = 19.6752$, do not reject the null hypothesis based on these sample data.

Step 7   Draw a conclusion.
After conducting this test, the engineers at Genesis Technology can state there is insufficient evidence to conclude that the modified design has had any effect on the variability of storage life.

>> **END EXAMPLE**

TRY PROBLEM 11-2 (pg. 443)

Chapter Outcome 2. → # Interval Estimation for a Population Variance

Chapter 8 introduced confidence interval estimation for a single population mean and a single population proportion. We now extend those concepts to situations in which we are interested in estimating a population variance. Although the basic concepts are the same when we interpret a confidence interval estimate for a variance, the methodology for computing the interval estimate is slightly different. Equation 11.2 is used to construct the interval estimate.

Confidence Interval Estimate for a Population Variance

$$\frac{(n-1)s^2}{\chi^2_U} \le \sigma^2 \le \frac{(n-1)s^2}{\chi^2_L}$$ **(11.2)**

where:

$$s^2 = \text{Sample variance}$$
$$n = \text{Sample size}$$
$$\chi^2_L = \text{Lower critical value}$$
$$\chi^2_U = \text{Upper critical value}$$

FIGURE 11.4

Critical Values for
Estimating s^2

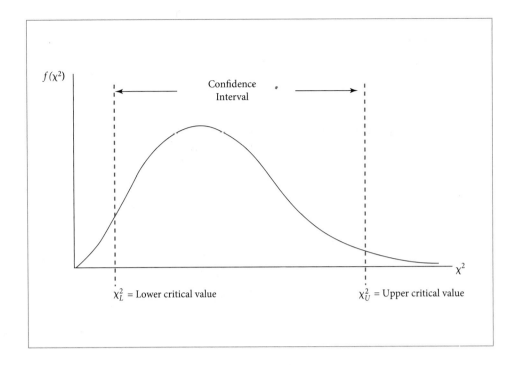

The logic of Equation 11.2 is best demonstrated using Figure 11.4. In a manner similar to the discussion associated with Figure 8.4 in Chapter 8 for estimating a population mean, when estimating a population variance, for a 95% confidence interval estimate, 95% of the area in the distribution will be between the lower and upper critical values. But since the chi-square distribution is not symmetrical and contains only positive numbers, two values must be found from the table in Appendix G.

In Equation 11.2, the denominators come from the chi-square distribution with $n - 1$ degrees of freedom. For example, in an application in which the sample size is $n = 10$ and the desired confidence level is 95%, there is 0.025 in both the lower and upper tails of the distribution. Then from the chi-square table in Appendix G, we get the critical value

$$\chi_U^2 = \chi_{0.025}^2 = 19.0228$$

Likewise, we get

$$\chi_L^2 = \chi_{0.975}^2 = 2.7004$$

Now suppose that the sample variance computed from the sample of $n = 10$ values is $s^2 = 44$. Then, using Equation 11.2, we construct the 95% confidence interval as follows:

$$\frac{(10-1)44}{19.0228} \leq \sigma^2 \leq \frac{(10-1)44}{2.7004}$$
$$20.82 \leq \sigma^2 \leq 146.64$$

Thus, at the 95% confidence level, we conclude that the population variance is in the range 20.82 to 146.64. By taking the square root, you can convert the interval estimate to one for the population standard deviation:

$$4.56 \leq \sigma \leq 12.11$$

MyStatLab

11-1: Exercises

Skill Development

11-1. A random sample of 20 values was selected from a population, and the sample standard deviation was computed to be 360. Based on this sample result, compute a 95% confidence interval estimate for the true population standard deviation.

11-2. Given the following null and alternative hypotheses

$$H_0: \sigma^2 = 100$$
$$H_A: \sigma^2 \neq 100$$

a. Test when $n = 27$, $s = 9$, and $\alpha = 0.10$. Be certain to state the decision rule.

b. Test when $n = 17$, $s = 6$, and $\alpha = 0.05$. Be certain to state the decision rule.

11-3. A manager is interested in determining if the population standard deviation has dropped below 130. Based on a sample of $n = 20$ items selected randomly from the population, conduct the appropriate hypothesis test at a 0.05 significance level. The sample standard deviation is 105.

11-4. The following sample data have been collected for the purpose of testing whether a population standard deviation is equal to 40. Conduct the appropriate hypothesis test using $\alpha = 0.05$.

318	255	323	325	334
354	266	308	321	297
316	272	346	266	309

11-5. Given the following null and alternative hypotheses

$$H_0: \sigma^2 = 50$$
$$H_A: \sigma^2 \neq 50$$

a. Test when $n = 12$, $s = 9$, and $\alpha = 0.10$. Be certain to state the decision rule.

b. Test when $n = 19$, $s = 6$, and $\alpha = 0.05$. Be certain to state the decision rule.

11-6. Suppose a random sample of 22 items produces a sample standard deviation of 16.

a. Use the sample results to develop a 90% confidence interval estimate for the population variance.

b. Use the sample results to develop a 95% confidence interval estimate for the population variance.

11-7. Historical data indicate that the standard deviation of a process is 6.3. A recent sample of size

a. 28 produced a variance of 66.2. Test to determine if the variance has increased using a significance level of 0.05.

b. 8 produced a variance of 9.02. Test to determine if the variance has decreased using a significance level of 0.025. Use the test statistic approach.

c. 18 produced a variance of 62.9. Test to determine if the variance has changed using a significance level of 0.10.

11-8. Examine the sample obtained from a normally distributed population:

5.2	10.4	5.1	2.1	4.8	15.5	10.2
8.7	2.8	4.9	4.7	13.4	15.6	14.5

a. Calculate the variance.

b. Calculate the probability that a randomly chosen sample would produce a sample variance at least as large as that produced in part a if the population variance was equal to 20.

c. What is the statistical term used to describe the probability calculated in part b?

d. Conduct a hypothesis test to determine if the population variance is larger than 15.3. Use a significance level equal to 0.05.

Business Applications

11-9. In an effort to increase public acceptance of a light rail system, the manager for City Transit Services in Seattle is interested in estimating the standard deviation for the time it takes a bus to travel between the University of Washington and the downtown bus terminal. To develop an estimate for the standard deviation, he has collected a random sample of the times required for 15 trips. The sample standard deviation is 6.2 minutes. Based on these data, what is the 90% confidence interval estimate for the true population standard deviation?

11-10. The consulting firm of Winston & Associates has been retained by an electronic component assembly company in Phoenix to design and program a computer simulation model of its operations. Winston & Associates plan to construct the model using ProModel software (see www.Promodel.com). This software allows the developer to program into the model probability distributions for things like machine downtime, defect rates, daily demand, and so forth. The closer the distributions specified in the computer model match those that actually occur in the assembly plant, the better the simulation model will perform. For one machine center, Winston consultants have assumed that when the center goes down for repairs, the time that it will be down will be normally distributed with an average of 30 minutes and a standard deviation equal to 10 minutes. Before finalizing the model, the consultants will collect a random sample of downtimes and test whether their downtime assumptions are valid. The following sample data reflect 10 randomly selected downtimes at this machine center from records over the past four weeks:

25	11	34	49	48
56	2	26	46	14

a. Using $\alpha = 0.05$, conduct the appropriate test for the mean downtime at this machine center.
b. Using $\alpha = 0.05$, conduct the appropriate test for the standard deviation in downtime.
c. Based on the hypothesis tests in parts a and b, what conclusions should the consulting company reach? Discuss.

11-11. The Flicks is a small, independent theater that shows foreign and limited-release films. One attraction of the Flicks is that it sells beer and wine as well as premium coffee and pastries at its snack bar. Friday and Saturday nights are the busiest nights at the Flicks, and the owners of the theater are interested in estimating the variance in sales at the snack bar on Friday nights. Suppose a random sample of 14 Friday evenings is selected and the snack bar sales for each evening are recorded. The results of the sample in dollars are as follows:

| 279.66 | 329.91 | 314.99 | 358.08 | 341.14 | 303.28 | 325.88 |
| 369.29 | 336.90 | 316.54 | 356.57 | 313.49 | 351.04 | 295.36 |

Use the random sample of sales to develop a 95% confidence interval estimate of the variance of Friday night snack bar sales at the Flicks.

11-12. Airlines face the challenging task of keeping their planes on schedule. One key measure is the number of minutes a plane deviates from the scheduled arrival time. Ideally, the measure for each arrival will be zero minutes, indicating that the plane arrived exactly on time. However, experience indicates that even under the best of circumstances, there will be inherent variability. Suppose one major airline has set standards that require the planes to arrive, on average, on time, with a standard deviation not to exceed two minutes. To determine whether these standards are being met, each month the airline selects a random sample of 12 airplane arrivals and determines the number of minutes early or late the flight is. For last month, the times, rounded to the nearest minute, are

| 3 | −7 | 4 | 2 | −2 | 5 | 11 | −3 | 4 | 6 | −4 | 1 |

a. State the appropriate null and alternative hypotheses for testing the standard regarding the mean value. Test the hypotheses using a significance level equal to 0.05. What assumption will be required?
b. State the appropriate null and alternative hypotheses regarding the standard deviation. Use the sample data to conduct the hypothesis test with $\alpha = 0.05$.
c. Discuss the results of both tests. What should the airline conclude regarding its arrival standards? What factors could influence the arrival times of flights?

11-13. A software design firm has recently developed a prototype educational computer game for children. One of the important factors in the success of a game like this is the time it takes the child to play the game. Two factors are important: the mean time it takes to

play and the variability in time required from child to child. Experience indicates that the mean time should be 10 minutes or less and the standard deviation should not exceed 4 minutes. The company has decided to test this prototype with 10 children selected at random from the local school district. The following values represent the time (rounded to the nearest minute) each child spent until completing the game:

| 9 | 14 | 11 | 8 | 13 | 15 | 11 | 10 | 7 | 12 |

a. The developers of the software will assume the mean time to completion of the game is 10 minutes or less unless the data strongly suggest otherwise. State the appropriate null and alternative hypotheses for testing the requirement regarding the mean value.
b. Referring to part a, test the hypotheses using a significance level equal to 0.10. What assumption will be required?
c. The developers of the software will assume the standard deviation of the time to completion of the game does not exceed 4 minutes unless the data strongly suggest otherwise. State the appropriate null and alternative hypotheses regarding the standard deviation. Use the sample data to conduct the hypothesis test with a significance level $= 0.10$.

11-14. A corporation makes CV joints for automobiles. An integral part of CV joints is the bearings that allow the joints to rotate differentially. One application utilizes six bearings in a CV joint that have an average diameter of 2.5 centimeters. The consistency of the diameters is vital to the operation of the joint. The specifications require that the variance of these diameters be no more than 0.0015 centimeters squared. The diameter is continually monitored by the quality-control team. Twenty subsamples of size 10 are obtained every day. One of these subsamples produced bearings that had a variance of 0.00317 centimeters squared.
a. Calculate the probability that a subsample of size 10 would produce a sample variance that would be at least 0.00317 centimeters squared if the population variance was 0.0015 centimeters squared.
b. On the basis of your calculation in part a, conduct a hypothesis test to determine if the quality control team should advise management to stop production and search for causes of the inconsistency of the bearing diameters. Use a significance level of 0.05.

11-15. The U.S. Bureau of Labor Statistics' most current figures indicate the average wage for construction workers was about $18.08 an hour. Its survey suggests that construction wages can vary widely. Hartford, Connecticut, wages are approximately 38% larger, and Brownsville, Texas, wages are about 30% lower than the national average. A sample of 25 construction workers in San Antonio, Texas, yielded an average wage of $13.27 and a standard deviation of $1.46.

a. Estimate the standard deviation of the nation's construction wages. (*Hint:* Recall the relationship between the standard deviation and the range of a normal distribution used in the sample-size calculations in the confidence interval for a population mean.)

b. Does it appear that both the average and the standard deviation of the construction workers' wages in San Antonio are smaller than those of the nation as a whole? Use hypotheses tests and a significance level of 0.05 to make your determination.

Computer Database **Exercises**

11-16. Due to the sharp rise in oil prices, the cost of heating a home has risen sharply. In a recent year, the average cost was $1,044, which was an increase of 33% above that in the previous year. In addition to concern over the increase in average heating costs was the possibility of a sharp increase in the variability in heating costs. This could signal that lower-income families were simply not heating their homes as much, whereas those in higher income brackets were heating their homes as required. The file titled **Homeheat** contains a sample of heating costs that accrued. Historical data indicate that heating costs have had a standard deviation of about $100.

a. Conduct a test of hypothesis to see if the variability in heating costs in the sample was larger than that indicated by historical data. Use both the test statistic and a significance level of 0.025.

b. Construct a box and whisker plot and determine whether it indicates that the hypothesis test of part a is valid.

11-17. Canidae Corporation, based in San Luis Obispo, California, is a producer of pet food. One of its products is Felidae cat food. The Chicken and Rice Cat and Kitten Formula is a dry cat food that comes in various sizes. Canidae guarantees that 32% of this cat food is crude protein. In the 6.6-pound (3-kilogram) size, this would indicate that 2.11 pounds would be

crude protein. Of course, these figures are averages. The amount of crude protein varies with each sack of cat food. The file titled **Catfood** contains the amounts of crude protein found in sacks randomly sampled from the production line. Assume the amount of crude protein in the 6.6-pound size is normally distributed.

a. If Canidae wishes to have the weight of crude protein sacks rounded off to 2.11 pounds, determine the standard deviation of the weight of crude protein. (*Hint:* Recall the relationship between the standard deviation and the range of a normal distribution used in the sample-size calculations in the confidence interval for a population mean.)

b. Using your result in part a, conduct a hypothesis test to determine if the standard deviation of the weight of crude protein in the 6.6-pound sack of Felidae cat food is too large to meet Canidae's wishes. Use a significance level of 0.01.

11-18. The Fillmore Institute has established a service designed to help charities increase the amount of money they collect from their direct-mail solicitations. Its consulting is aimed at increasing the mean dollar amount returned from each giver and also at reducing the variation in amount contributed from giver to giver. The Badke Foundation collects money for heart disease research. Over the last eight years, records show that the average contribution per returned envelope is $14.25 with a standard deviation of $6.44. The Badke Foundation directors decided to try the Fillmore services on a test basis. They used the recommended letters and other request materials and sent out 1,000 requests. From these, 166 were returned. The data showing the dollars returned per giver are in the file called **Badke**.

Based on the sample data, what conclusions should the Badke Foundation reach regarding the Fillmore consulting services? Use appropriate hypothesis tests with a significance level $= 0.05$ to reach your conclusions. (*Hint:* Use Excel's **CHISQ.INV** function to obtain the critical value for the chi-square distribution.)

END EXERCISES 11-1

11.2 Hypothesis Tests for Two Population Variances

Chapter Outcome 3. → **F-Test for Two Population Variances**

The previous section introduced a method for testing hypotheses involving a single population standard deviation. Recall that to conduct the test, we had to first convert the standard deviation to a variance. Then we used the chi-square distribution to determine whether the sample variance led us to reject the null hypothesis. However, decision makers are often faced with decision problems involving two population standard deviations. Although there is no hypothesis test that directly tests standard deviations, there is a procedure that can be used to test two population variances. We typically formulate null and alternative hypotheses using one of the following forms:

Two-Tailed Test	Upper One-Tailed Test	Lower One-Tailed Test
$H_0: \sigma_1^2 = \sigma_2^2$	$H_0: \sigma_1^2 \leq \sigma_2^2$	$H_0: \sigma_1^2 \geq \sigma_2^2$
$H_A: \sigma_1^2 \neq \sigma_2^2$	$H_A: \sigma_1^2 > \sigma_2^2$	$H_0: \sigma_1^2 < \sigma_2^2$

To test a hypothesis involving two population variances, we first compute the sample variances. We then compute the test statistic shown as Equation 11.3.

F-Test Statistic for Testing whether Two Populations Have Equal Variances

$$F = \frac{s_i^2}{s_j^2} \qquad (df: D_1 = n_i - 1 \quad \text{and} \quad D_2 = n_j - 1) \tag{11.3}$$

where:

n_i = Sample size from the ith population

n_j = Sample size from the jth population

s_i^2 = Sample variance from the ith population

s_j^2 = Sample variance from the jth population

Analyzing this test statistic requires that we introduce the *F*-distribution. Although it is beyond the scope of this book, statistical theory shows the *F*-distribution is formed by the ratio of two independent chi-square variables. Like the chi-square and the *t*-distributions, the appropriate *F*-distribution is determined by its degrees of freedom. However, the *F*-distribution has two degrees of freedom, D_1 and D_2, which depend on the sample sizes for the variances in the numerator and denominator, respectively, in Equation 11.3.

To apply the *F*-distribution to test two population variances, we must be able to assume the following are true:

Assumptions

- The populations are normally distributed.
- The samples are randomly and independently selected.

Independent Samples

Samples selected from two or more populations in such a way that the occurrence of values in one sample has no influence on the probability of the occurrence of values in the other sample(s).

Independent samples will occur when the sample data are obtained in such a way that the values in one sample do not influence the probability that the values in the second sample will be selected.

The test statistic shown in Equation 11.3 is formed as the ratio of two sample variances. There are two key points to remember when formulating this ratio.

1. To use the *F*-distribution table in this text, for a two-tailed test, always place the larger sample variance in the numerator. This will make the calculated *F*-value greater than 1.0 and push the *F*-value toward the upper tail of the *F*-distribution.
2. For the one-tailed test, examine the alternative hypothesis. For the population that is *predicted* (based on the alternative hypothesis) to have the larger variance, place that sample variance in the numerator.

The following applications and examples will illustrate the specific methods used for testing for a difference between two population variances.

E. COLI BACTERIA TESTING Recent years have seen several national scares involving meat contaminated with *E. coli* bacteria. The recommended preventative measure is to cook the meat at a required temperature. However, different meat patties cooked for the same amount of time will have different final internal temperatures because of variations in the patties and variations in burner temperatures. A regional hamburger chain will replace its current burners with one of two new digitally controlled models.

The chain's purchasing agents have arranged to randomly sample 11 patties of meat cooked by burner model 1 and 13 meat patties cooked by burner model 2 to learn if there is a difference in temperature variation between the two models. If a difference exists, the chain's managers have decided to select the model that provides the smaller variation in final internal meat temperature. Ideally, they would like a test that compares standard deviations, but no such test exists. Instead, they must convert the standard deviations to variances. The hypotheses are

$$H_0: \sigma_1^2 = \sigma_2^2$$

$$H_A: \sigma_1^2 \neq \sigma_2^2$$

The null and alternative hypotheses are formulated for a two-tailed test. Intuitively, you might reason that if the two population variances are actually equal, the sample variances should be approximately equal also. That would mean that the ratio of the two sample variances should be approximately 1. We will reject the null hypothesis if one sample variance is significantly larger than the other and if the ratio of sample variances is significantly greater than 1. The managers will use a significance level of $\alpha = 0.10$.

The next step is to collect the sample data. Figure 11.5 shows the sample data and the box and whisker plot. The assumption of independence is met because the two burners were used to cook different meat patties and the temperature measures are not related. The box and whisker plots provide no evidence to suggest that the distributions are highly skewed, so the assumption that the populations are normally distributed may hold.

FIGURE 11.5

E. coli Bacteria Testing Sample Data

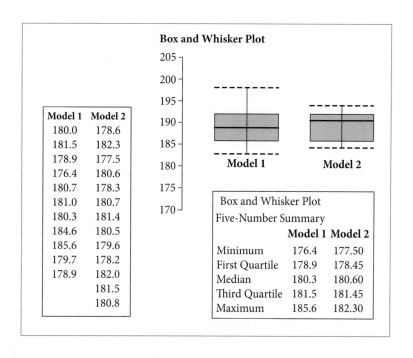

The sample variances are computed using Equation 11.4.

Sample Variance

$$s^2 = \frac{\Sigma(x - \bar{x})^2}{n - 1}$$

(11.4)

where:

$$\bar{x} = \frac{\Sigma x}{n} = \text{Sample mean}$$

$$n = \text{Sample size}$$

Based on the sample data shown in Figure 11.5, the sample variances are

$$s_1^2 = 6.7 \quad \text{and} \quad s_2^2 = 2.5$$

The null hypothesis is that the two population variances are equal, making this a two-tailed test. Thus, we form the test statistic using Equation 11.3 by placing the larger sample variance in the numerator. The calculated F-value is

$$F = \frac{s_1^2}{s_2^2} = \frac{6.7}{2.5} = 2.68$$

If the calculated F-value exceeds the critical value, then the null hypothesis is rejected. The critical F-value is determined by locating the appropriate F-distribution table for the desired alpha level and the correct degrees of freedom. This requires the following thought process:

1. If the test is two tailed, use the table corresponding to $\alpha/2$. For example, if $\alpha = 0.10$ for a two-tailed test, the appropriate F table is the one with the upper tail equal to 0.05.
2. If the test is one tailed, use the F table corresponding to the significance level. If $\alpha = 0.05$ for a one-tailed test, use the table with the upper-tail area equal to 0.05.

In this example, the test is two tailed and α is 0.10. Thus, we go to the F-distribution table in Appendix H for the upper-tail area equal to 0.05.

The next step is to determine the appropriate degrees of freedom. In Chapter 8, we stated that the degrees of freedom of any test statistic are equal to the number of independent data values available to estimate the population variance. We lose 1 degree of freedom for each parameter we are required to estimate. For both the numerator and denominator in Equation 11.3, we must estimate the population mean, $\bar{x}$, before we calculate s^2. In each case, we lose 1 degree of freedom. Therefore, we have two distinct degrees of freedom, D_1 and D_2, where D_1 is equal to $n_1 - 1$ for the variance in the numerator of the F-test statistic and D_2 is equal to $n_2 - 1$ for the variance in the denominator. Recall that for a two-tailed test, the larger sample variance is placed in the numerator. In this example, model 1 has the larger sample variance, so model 1 is placed in the numerator with a sample size of 11, so $D_1 = 11 - 1 = 10$ and $D_2 = 13 - 1 = 12$.

Locate the page of the F table corresponding to the desired upper-tail area. In this text, we have three options (0.05, 0.025, and 0.01). The F table is arranged in columns and rows. The columns correspond to the D_1 degrees of freedom and the rows correspond to the D_2 degrees of freedom. For this example, the critical F-value at the intersection of $D_1 = 10$ and $D_2 = 12$ degrees of freedom is 2.753.[1]

Figure 11.6 summarizes the hypothesis test. Note that the decision rule is

If calculated $F > 2.753$, reject H_0.

Otherwise, do not reject H_0.

Because $F = 2.68 < 2.753$, the conclusion is that the null hypothesis is not rejected based on these sample data; that is, there is not sufficient evidence to support a conclusion that there is a difference in the population variances of internal meat temperatures.

---

[1] If you prefer, you can use Excel's F.INV.RT function to determine the critical F-value. The F.INV.RT function is = F.INV.RT(.05,10,12) = 2.753.

FIGURE 11.6

F-Test for the *E. coli* Example

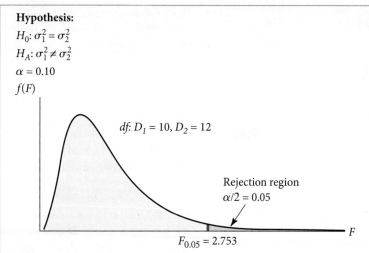

Hypothesis:

$H_0: \sigma_1^2 = \sigma_2^2$

$H_A: \sigma_1^2 \neq \sigma_2^2$

$\alpha = 0.10$

$f(F)$

df: $D_1 = 10, D_2 = 12$

Rejection region
$\alpha/2 = 0.05$

$F_{0.05} = 2.753$

F

Decision Rule:

If $F > 2.753$, reject H_0.

Otherwise, do not reject H_0.

The *F*-test is

$$F = \frac{s_1^2}{s_2^2} = \frac{6.7}{2.5} = 2.68$$

Because $F = 2.68 < F_{0.05} = 2.753$, do not reject H_0.

Note: The right-hand tail of the *F*-distribution always contains an area of $\alpha/2$ if the hypothesis is two-tailed.

EXAMPLE 11-3   **TWO-TAILED TEST FOR TWO POPULATION VARIANCES**

Phoenix Mass Transit Agency Phoenix, Arizona, has been one of the fastest-growing cities in the country. To accommodate the population growth, city leaders formed the Phoenix Mass Transit Agency, which has been responsible for expanding public transportation options, including bus service and light rail. However, mass transit will only work if the service is reliable. Suppose Agency leaders are concerned about the waiting times for passengers who use the downtown transit center between 4:00 P.M. and 6:00 P.M. Monday through Friday. Of particular interest is whether there is a difference in the standard deviations in waiting times at concourses A and B. The following steps can be used to test whether there is a difference in population standard deviations:

Step 1 Specify the population parameter of interest.
The population parameter of interest is the standard deviation in waiting times at the two concourses.

Step 2 Formulate the appropriate null and alternative hypotheses.
Because we are interested in determining if a difference exists in standard deviation and because neither concourse is predicted to have a higher variance, the test will be two-tailed, and the hypotheses are established as

$$H_0: \sigma_A^2 = \sigma_B^2$$

$$H_A: \sigma_A^2 \neq \sigma_B^2$$

Note: The hypotheses are stated in terms of the population variances.

Step 3 Specify the level of significance.
The test will be conducted using an $\alpha = 0.02$.

Step 4 Construct the rejection region.
To determine the critical value from the *F*-distribution, we can use either Excel's **F.INV.RT** function or the *F* table in Appendix H. The degrees of freedom are

D_1 = Numerator sample size − 1 and D_2 = Denominator sample size − 1. As shown in the statistics section of the stem and leaf display in Step 5, concourse B has the larger sample standard deviation, thus we get

$$D_1 = n_B - 1 = 31 - 1 = 30 \quad \text{and} \quad D_2 = n_A - 1 = 25 - 1 = 24$$

Then for $\alpha/2 = 0.01$, we get a critical $F_{0.01} = 2.577$. The null hypothesis is rejected if $F > F_{0.01} = 2.577$. Otherwise, do not reject the null hypothesis.

Step 5 Compute the test statistic.

The test statistic is formed by the ratio of the two sample variances. Because this is a two-tailed test, the larger sample variance is placed in the numerator.

Select random samples from each population of interest, determine whether the assumptions have been satisfied, and compute the test statistic.

Random samples of 25 passengers from concourse A and 31 passengers from concourse B were selected, and the waiting time for each passenger was recorded. There is no connection between the two samples, so the assumption of independence is satisfied. The stem and leaf diagrams do not dispute the assumption of normality.

		Stem and Leaf Display for Concourse A Stem unit: 1				**Stem and Leaf Display for Concourse B** Stem unit: 1	

Statistics				**Statistics**		
Sample Size	25	8 | 9		Sample Size	31	4 | 7
Mean	14.58	9 | 0		Mean	16.25	5 |
Median	14.16	10 | 2 3 7 9		Median	15.77	6 | 3
Std. Deviation	3.77	11 | 9		Std. Deviation	4.79	7 |
Minimum	8.89	12 | 2 4		Minimum	4.70	8 |
Maximum	22.16	13 | 2		Maximum	24.38	9 |
		14 | 0 0 2 2				10 | 8
		15 | 5 6 9				11 | 1 4 7
		16 | 2				12 | 2 4
		17 | 0 4				13 |
		18 | 2 4				14 | 2 2 2 8
		19 |				15 | 1 3 7 8
		20 | 8				16 |
		21 | 5				17 | 0 5
		22 | 2				18 | 3 6
						19 | 0 1 3 3
						20 | 4
						21 | 8 8
						22 | 1 4 9
						23 |
						24 | 4

$$F = \frac{4.79^2}{3.77^2} = 1.614$$

Step 6 Reach a decision.

Compare the test statistic to the critical value and reach a conclusion with respect to the null hypothesis.

Because $F = 1.641 < F_{0.01} = 2.577$, do not reject the null hypothesis.

Step 7 Draw a conclusion.

There is no reason to conclude that there is a difference in the variability of waiting time at concourses A and B.

>> END EXAMPLE

TRY PROBLEM 11-24 (pg. 454)

Excel Tutorial

BUSINESS APPLICATION **USING SOFTWARE TO TEST TWO POPULATION VARIANCES**

BANK ATMs One-tailed tests on two population variances are performed much like two-tailed tests. Consider the systems development group for a Midwestern bank, which has developed a new software algorithm for its automatic teller machines (ATMs). Although reducing average transaction time is an objective, the systems programmers also want to reduce the variability in transaction speed. They believe the standard deviation for transaction time will be less with the new software (population 2) than it was with the old algorithm (population 1). For their analysis, the programmers have performed 7 test runs using the original software and 11 test runs using the new system. Although the managers want to determine the standard deviation of transaction time, they must perform the test as a test of variances because no method exists for testing standard deviations directly. Thus, the null and alternative hypotheses are

$$H_0: \sigma_1^2 \leq \sigma_2^2 \quad \text{or} \quad \sigma_1^2 - \sigma_2^2 \leq 0$$
$$H_A: \sigma_1^2 > \sigma_2^2 \quad \text{or} \quad \sigma_1^2 - \sigma_2^2 > 0$$

The hypothesis is to be tested using a significance level of $\alpha = 0.01$.

In order to use the F-test to test whether these sample variances come from populations with equal variances, we need to make sure that the sample variances are independent and the populations are approximately normally distributed. Because the test runs using the two algorithms were unique, the variances are independent. The following box and whisker plots give no reason to indicate that, based on these small samples, the populations are not approximately normal.

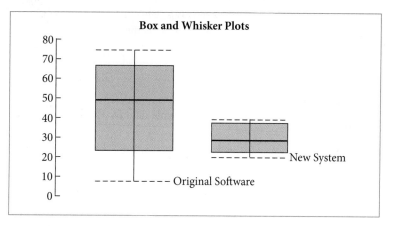

Figure 11.7 illustrates the one-tailed hypothesis test for this situation using a significance level of 0.01. Recall that in a two-tailed test, placing the larger sample variance in the numerator and the smaller variance in the denominator forms the F-ratio. In a one-tailed test, we look to the alternative hypothesis to determine which sample variance should go in the numerator. In this example, population 1 (the original software) is thought to have the larger variance. Then the sample variance from population 1 forms the numerator, regardless of the size of the sample variances. Excel correctly computes the calculated F-ratio.

If you are performing the test manually, the F-ratio needs to be formed correctly for two reasons. First, the correct F-ratio will be computed. Second, the correct degrees of freedom will be used to determine the critical value to test the null hypothesis. In this one-tailed example, the numerator represents population 1 and the denominator represents population 2. This means that the degrees of freedom are

$$D_1 = n_1 - 1 = 7 - 1 = 6 \quad \text{and} \quad D_2 = n_2 - 1 = 11 - 1 = 10$$

Using the F-distribution table in Appendix H or Excel's **F.INV.RT** function, you can determine

$$F_{0.01} = 5.386$$

for this one-tailed test with a $\alpha = 0.01$.

FIGURE 11.7

Excel 2010 Output—
F-Test Example of ATM
Transaction Time

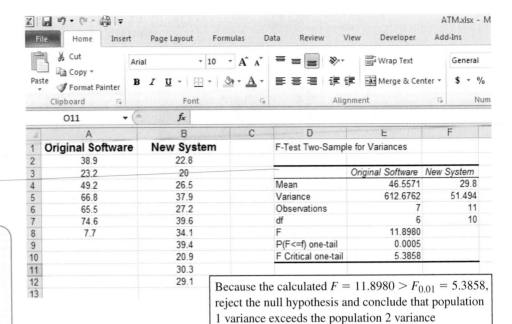

Because the calculated $F = 11.8980 > F_{0.01} = 5.3858$, reject the null hypothesis and conclude that population 1 variance exceeds the population 2 variance

Excel 2010 Instructions:
1. Open file: **ATM.xlsx**.
2. Select **Data > Data Analysis**.
3. Select **F-Test Two Sample Variances**.
4. Define the data range for the two variables.
5. Specify **Alpha** equal to 0.01.
6. Specify output location.
7. Click **OK**.
8. Click the **Home** tab and adjust decimal places in output.

Minitab Instructions (for similar results):
1. Open file: **ATM.MTW**.
2. Choose **Stat > Basic Statistics > 2 Variances**.
3. Select **Samples in different columns**, enter one data column in First and another in **Second**.
4. Click on **Options**.
5. In **Confidence Level**, enter $1 - \alpha$.
6. Click **OK. OK.**

The sample data for the test runs are in a file called **ATM**. The sample variances are

$$s_1^2 = 612.68$$
$$s_2^2 = 51.49$$

Thus, the calculated *F*-ratio is

$$F = \frac{612.68}{51.49} = 11.898$$

As shown in Figure 11.7, the calculated $F = 11.898 > F_{0.01} = 5.386$, so the null hypothesis, H_0, is rejected. Based on the sample data, the systems programmers have evidence to support their claim that the new ATM algorithm will result in reduced transaction-time variability.

There are many business decision-making applications in which you will need to test whether two populations have unequal variances.

EXAMPLE 11-4   **ONE-TAILED TEST FOR TWO POPULATION VARIANCES**

Goodyear Tire Company The Goodyear Tire Company has entered into a contract to supply tires for a leading Japanese automobile manufacturer. Goodyear executives were originally planning to make all the tires at their Ohio plant, but they also have an option to build some tires at their Michigan plant. A critical quality characteristic for the tires is tread thickness, and the automaker wants to know if the standard deviation in tread thickness of tires produced at the Ohio plant (population #1) exceeds the standard deviation for tires produced at the Michigan plant (population #2). If so, the automaker will specify that Goodyear use the

Michigan plant for all tires because a high standard deviation is not desirable. The following steps can be used to conduct a test for the two suppliers:

Step 1   Specify the population parameter of interest.
Goodyear is concerned with the standard deviation in tread thickness. Therefore, the population parameter of interest is the standard deviation, σ.

Step 2   Formulate the appropriate null and alternative hypotheses.
Because the Japanese automaker customers are concerned with whether the Ohio plant's tread standard deviation will exceed that for the Michigan plant, the test will be one tailed, and the null and alternative hypotheses are formed as follows:

$$H_0: \sigma_1^2 \leq \sigma_2^2$$
$$H_A: \sigma_1^2 > \sigma_2^2$$

Note: The hypotheses must be stated in terms of the population variances.

Step 3   Specify the significance level.
The test will be conducted using an alpha level equal to 0.05.

Step 4   Construct the rejection region.
Based on sample sizes of 11 tires from each Goodyear plant, the critical value for a one-tailed test with $\alpha = 0.05$ and $D_1 = 10$ and $D_2 = 10$ degrees of freedom is 2.978. The null hypothesis is rejected if $F > F_{0.05} = 2.978$. Otherwise, do not reject the null hypothesis.

Step 5   Compute the test statistic.
A simple random sample of 11 tires was selected from each Goodyear plant with the sample variances of

$$s_1^2 = 0.799 \quad \text{and} \quad s_2^2 = 0.547$$

The assumptions of independence and normal populations are believed to be satisfied in this case.

The test statistic is an F-ratio formed by placing the variance that is predicted to be larger (as shown in the alternative hypothesis) in the numerator. The Ohio plant is predicted to have the larger variance in the alternative hypothesis. Thus the test statistic is

$$F = \frac{0.799}{0.547} = 1.4607$$

Step 6   Reach a decision.
Because $F = 1.4607 < F_{0.05} = 2.978$, do not reject the null hypothesis.

Step 7   Draw a conclusion.
Based on the sample data, there is insufficient evidence to conclude that the variance of tread thickness from the Ohio plant (population #1) is greater than that for the Michigan plant (population #2). Therefore, Goodyear managers are free to produce tires at either manufacturing plant.

>> **END EXAMPLE**

TRY PROBLEM 11-19 (pg. 454)

Additional *F*-Test Considerations   Recall that in Chapter 10, the *t*-test for the difference between two population means with independent samples assumed that the two populations have equal variances. Oftentimes, decision makers use the *F*-test introduced in this section to test whether the assumption of equal variances is satisfied. However, studies have shown that the *F*-test may not be particularly effective in detecting certain differences in population variances that can adversely affect the *t*-test. Therefore, other tests for equality of variances, such as the Aspen-Welch test, may be preferred as preliminary tests to the *t*-test for two population means. (See the Markowski reference at the end of the book.)

MyStatLab

11-2: Exercises

Skill Development

11-19. Given the following null and alternative hypotheses

$$H_0: \sigma_1^2 \le \sigma_2^2$$
$$H_A: \sigma_1^2 > \sigma_2^2$$

and the following sample information

Sample 1	Sample 2
$n_1 = 13$	$n_2 = 21$
$s_1^2 = 1{,}450$	$s_2^2 = 1{,}320$

a. If $\alpha = 0.05$, state the decision rule for the hypothesis.

b. Test the hypothesis and indicate whether the null hypothesis should be rejected.

11-20. Given the following null and alternative hypotheses

$$H_0: \sigma_1^2 \le \sigma_2^2$$
$$H_A: \sigma_1^2 > \sigma_2^2$$

and the following sample information

Sample 1	Sample 2
$n_1 = 21$	$n_2 = 12$
$s_1^2 = 345.7$	$s_2^2 = 745.2$

a. If $\alpha = 0.01$, state the decision rule for the hypothesis. (Be careful to pay attention to the alternative hypothesis to construct this decision rule.)

b. Test the hypothesis and indicate whether the null hypothesis should be rejected.

11-21. Find the appropriate critical F-value, from the F-distribution table, for each of the following:

a. $D_1 = 16, D_2 = 14, \alpha = 0.01$

b. $D_1 = 5, D_2 = 12, \alpha = 0.05$

c. $D_1 = 16, D_2 = 20, \alpha = 0.01$

11-22. Given the following null and alternative hypotheses

$$H_0: \sigma_1^2 = \sigma_2^2$$
$$H_A: \sigma_1^2 \ne \sigma_2^2$$

and the following sample information

Sample 1	Sample 2
$n_1 = 11$	$n_2 = 21$
$s_1 = 15$	$s_2 = 33$

a. If $\alpha = 0.02$, state the decision rule for the hypothesis.

b. Test the hypothesis and indicate whether the null hypothesis should be rejected.

11-23. Consider the following two independently chosen samples:

Sample 1	Sample 2
12.1	10.5
13.4	9.5
11.7	8.2
10.7	7.8
14.0	11.1

Use a significance level of 0.05 for testing the null hypothesis that $\sigma_1^2 \le \sigma_2^2$.

11-24. You are given two random samples with the following information:

Item	Sample 1	Sample 2
1	19.6	21.3
2	22.1	17.4
3	19.5	19.0
4	20.0	21.2
5	21.5	20.1
6	20.2	23.5
7	17.9	18.9
8	23.0	22.4
9	12.5	14.3
10	19.0	17.8

Based on these samples, test at $\alpha = 0.10$ whether the true difference in population variances is equal to zero.

Business Applications

11-25. The manager of the Public Broadcasting System for Tennessee is considering changing from the traditional weeklong contribution campaign to an intensive one-day campaign. In an effort to better understand current donation patterns, she is studying past data. A staff member from a neighboring state has speculated that male viewers' donations have greater variability in amount than do those of females. To test this, random samples of 25 men and 25 women were selected from people who donated during last year's telethon. The following statistics were computed from the sample data:

Males	Females
$\bar{x} = \$12.40$	$\bar{x} = \$8.92$
$s = \$2.50$	$s = \$1.34$

Based on a significance level of 0.05, does it appear that male viewers' donations have greater variability in amount than do those of female viewers?

11-26. As purchasing agent for the Horner-Williams Company, you have primary responsibility for securing high-quality raw materials at the best possible price. One particular material that the Horner-Williams Company uses a great deal of is aluminum. After careful study, you have been able to reduce the prospective vendors to two. It is unclear whether these two vendors produce aluminum that is equally durable.

To compare durability, the recommended procedure is to put pressure on the aluminum until it cracks. The vendor whose aluminum requires the greatest average pressure will be judged to be the one that provides the most durable product.

To carry out this test, 14 pieces from vendor 1 and 14 pieces from vendor 2 are selected at random. The following results in pounds per square inch (psi) were noted:

Vendor 1	Vendor 2
$n_1 = 14$	$n_2 = 14$
$\bar{x}_1 = 2{,}345$ psi	$\bar{x}_2 = 2{,}411$ psi
$s_1 = 300$	$s_2 = 250$

Before testing the hypothesis about difference in population means, suppose the purchasing agent for the company was concerned about whether the assumption of equal population variances was satisfied.

a. Based on the sample data, what would you tell him if you tested at the significance level of 0.10?

b. Would your conclusion differ if you tested at the significance level of 0.02? Discuss.

c. What would be the largest significance level that would cause the null hypothesis to be rejected?

11-27. The production control manager at Ashmore Manufacturing is interested in determining whether there is a difference in standard deviation of product diameter for part #XC-343 for units made at the Trenton, New Jersey, plant versus those made at the Atlanta plant. The Trenton plant is highly automated and thought to provide better quality control. Thus, the parts produced in the Atlanta plant should be more variable than those made at the Trenton plant.

A random sample of 15 parts was selected from those produced last week at Trenton. The standard deviation for these parts was 0.14 inch. A sample of 13 parts was selected from those made in Atlanta. The sample standard deviation for these parts was 0.202 inch.

a. Based on these sample data, is there sufficient evidence to conclude that the Trenton plant produces parts that are less variable than those of the Atlanta plant? Test using $\alpha = 0.05$.

b. Consider the scenario that the Trenton plant is discovered to have a smaller variability than the Atlanta plant. Management, on this basis, decides that they must expend a large amount of money to upgrade the machinery in Atlanta. Suppose also that, in reality, the difference in the observed variability between the two plants is a result of sampling error. Specify the type of error associated with hypothesis testing that was made. How would

you modify the hypothesis procedure to guard against such an error?

11-28. Even before the "Ownership Society" programs of Presidents Clinton and Bush, the federal government was heavily involved in the housing market, primarily in the form of tax deductions for mortgage interest payments. In a study just prior to the foreclosure crisis starting in 2008, the Urban Institute stated about 80% of the estimated $200 billion of federal housing subsidies consisted of tax breaks (mainly deductions for mortgage interest payments). Samples indicated that federal housing benefits average $8,268 for those with incomes between $200,000 and $500,000 and only $365 for those with incomes of $40,000 to $50,000. The respective standard deviations were $2,100 and $150. They were obtained from sample sizes of 150.

To determine the appropriate hypothesis test concerning the average federal housing benefits of the two income groups, it is necessary to determine if the population variances are equal. Conduct a test of hypothesis to this effect using a significance level of 0.02.

11-29. A Midwest college admissions committee recently conducted a study to determine the relative debt incurred by students receiving their degrees in four years versus those taking more than four years. Some on the committee speculated a four-year student would likely be attending full time, whereas one taking more than four years could have a part-time job. However, average total debt provides only part of the information. Since the average, or mean, is affected by both large and small values, the committee also needed some way to determine the relative variances for the two groups. Samples of size 20 produced standard deviations of 2,636 for four-year graduates and 1,513 for those taking more than four years.

Conduct a test of hypothesis to determine if the standard deviation of the debt for four-year graduates is larger than those taking more than four years. Use a significance level of 0.05.

Computer Database **Exercises**

11-30. The Celltone company is in the business of providing cellular phone coverage. Recently, it conducted a study of its customers who have purchased either the Basic Plan or the Business Plan service. At issue is the number of minutes of use by the customers during the midnight-to-7:00 A.M. time period Monday through Friday over a four-week period. The belief of Celltone managers is that the standard deviation in minutes used by Basic Plan customers will be more than that for the Business Plan customers. Data for this study are in a file called **Celltone**. Assume that the managers wish to test this using a 0.05 level of significance. Determine if the standard deviation in minutes used by Basic Plan customers is more than that for the Business Plan customers using an alpha level equal to 0.05.

11-31. The First Night Stage Company operates a small, nonprofit theater group in Milwaukee. Each year, the company solicits donations to help fund its operations. This year, it obtained the help of a marketing research company in the city. This company's representatives proposed two different solicitation brochures. They are interested in determining whether there is a difference in the standard deviation of dollars returned between the two brochures. To test this, a random sample of 20 people was selected to receive brochure A and another random sample of 20 people was selected to receive brochure B. The data are contained in the file called **First-Night**. Based on these sample data, what should the First Night Company conclude about the two brochures with respect to their variability? Test using a significance level of 0.02.

11-32. The *Boston Globe* ("College Graduation Rates below National Average") examined the graduation rates at community colleges in Massachusetts. Overall, 16.4% of full-time community college students in Massachusetts earn a degree or certificate within three years. This appears to be well below the national average of 24.7%. To determine this, random samples were taken in both Massachusetts and in the nation as a whole. A file titled **Masspass** contains outcomes of this sampling. Assume the populations have normal distributions.

a. Determine if there is a difference in the variances of the percentage of community college students who earn a degree or certificate within three years in both Massachusetts and in the rest of the nation. Use a significance level of 0.05.

b. On the basis of the results of part a, select the appropriate procedure to determine if there is a significant difference between the average graduation rates for Massachusetts and for the remainder of the nation.

11-33. A *USA Today* editorial (Alejandro Gonzalez, "CEO Dough") addressed the growth of compensation for corporate CEOs. Part of the story quoted a study done for *BusinessWeek*, which indicated that the pay packages have increased almost sevenfold on average during a current 10-year period. The file titled **CEODough** contains the salaries of CEOs for this 10-year difference, adjusted for inflation. Assume the populations are normally distributed.

a. Determine if there is a difference in the standard deviations of the salaries of CEOs for the two years. Use a significance level of 0.02.

b. Calculate the proportion of CEO salaries for the later period that are larger than the average salaries for CEOs 10 years earlier. Assume the sample statistics are sufficiently good approximations to the populations' parameters.

END EXERCISES 11-2

Visual Summary

Chapter 11: Variability is the very heart of statistics. Knowing how spread out the data values of a population is essential to almost every procedure in business statistics. For instance in determining the number of airline tickets to issue for a given flight, the airline needs to know how variable the number of "no shows" will be. This chapter presents procedures to estimate and test values to provide knowledge of this kind. A large variance means that any estimates of the dispersion of the data will be imprecise making any prediction unreliable. It has also provided procedures to determine if the variances of two populations are equal so that tests that require this can be conducted as was the case for procedures in Chapter 10.

11.1 Hypothesis Tests and Estimation for a Single Population Variance (pg. 435–445)

Summary

A **Chi-Square test for one population variance** is used to determine if significant evidence exists in a randomly selected sample concerning a population variance to presume that the hypothesis of interest could be deemed to be true. If no hypothesis of interest concerning the population variance exists, the **Confidence Interval Estimate for** σ^2 is used to obtain a plausible range of values for the population variance. Often a standard deviation is the parameter of interest. In such cases, the standard deviation is converted into one involving the variance.

Outcome 1. Formulate and carry out hypothesis tests for a single population variance

Outcome 2. Develop and interpret confidence interval estimates for a population variance

11.2 Hypothesis Tests for Two Population Variances (pg. 445–456)

Summary

Chapter 10 presented a *t*-test for the difference between two population means. The test assumed that the two population variances equaled each other. The **F-Test for Two Population Variances** is one of the test procedures that tests such an assumption.

Outcome 3. Formulate and carry out hypothesis tests for the difference between two population variances.

Conclusion

The procedures developed in Chapter 11 introduced a hypothesis test and confidence interval for the variance of one population. Following these procedures, a hypothesis test to determine if two population variances equaled each other was introduced. Together with the procedures in Chapters 8, 9, and 10, the decision maker has the ability to deal with a wide range of circumstances. In Chapter 12, you will discover a procedure that utilizes a test statistic which is almost identical to that used in the test of hypothesis of two variances in this chapter. It, however, uses the test statistic to test whether three or more means (as opposed to two variances) are equal to each other.

Equations

(11.1) Chi-Square Test for a Single Population Variance pg. 437

$$\chi^2 = \frac{(n-1)s^2}{\sigma^2}$$

(11.2) Confidence Interval Estimate for a Population Variance pg. 441

$$\frac{(n-1)s^2}{\chi^2_U} \le \sigma^2 \le \frac{(n-1)s^2}{\chi^2_L}$$

(11.3) *F*-Test Statistic for Testing whether Two Populations Have Equal Variances pg. 446

$$F = \frac{s_i^2}{s_j^2} \qquad (df: D_1 = n_i - 1 \quad \text{and} \quad D_2 = n_j - 1)$$

(11.4) Sample Variance pg. 448

$$s^2 = \frac{\Sigma(x - \bar{x})^2}{n-1}$$

Key Term

Independent samples pg. 446

Chapter Exercises   MyStatLab

Conceptual Questions

11-34. Identify three situations in which the measured output of a process has a small variation and three situations in which the variation is larger (for instance, the time for a phone call to ring the other phone versus the time to speak to a person when making a service call).

11-35. In a journal related to your major, locate an article in which a hypothesis about one or two population variances is tested. Discuss why population variation was an important issue in the article, how the hypothesis was formulated, and the results of the test.

11-36. Much of the emphasis of modern quality-control efforts involves identifying sources of variation in the processes associated with service or manufacturing operations. Discuss why variation in a process may impact quality.

11-37. Identify three situations in which organizations would be interested in limiting the standard deviation of a process.

11-38. Consider testing the hypothesis $H_A: \sigma_1^2 > \sigma_2^2$ using samples of respective sizes 6 and 11. Note that we could represent this hypothesis as $H_A: \sigma_1^2/\sigma_2^2 > 1$. The samples yield $s_1^2 = 42.2$ and $s_2^2 = 1.1$. It hardly seems worth the time to conduct this test since the test statistic will obviously be very large, leading us to reject the null hypothesis. However, we might wish to test a hypothesis such as $H_A:\sigma_1^2/\sigma_2^2 > 10$. The test is conducted exactly the same way as the *F*-test of this chapter except that you use the test statistic $F = (s_1^2/s_2^2)(1/k)$, where $k = 10$ for this hypothesis. Conduct the indicated test using a significance level of 0.05.

Business Applications

11-39. In the production of its Nutty Toffee, Cordum Candies must carefully control the temperature of its cooking process. However, in response to customer surveys, the company has recently increased the size of the chopped nuts used in the process. The marketing manager is concerned that this change will affect the variability in the cooking temperature and compromise the taste and consistency of the toffee. The head cook finds this concern strange since the change was requested by the marketing department, but yesterday he took a random sample of 27 batches of toffee and found the standard deviation of the temperature to be 1.15°F. Realizing this is only a point estimate, the marketing manager has requested a 98% confidence interval estimate for the population variance in the cooking temperature.

11-40. Maher Saddles, Inc., produces bicycle seats. Among the many seats produced is one for the high-end mountain bicycle market. Maher's operation manager has recently made a change in the production process for this high-end seat and is scheduled to report on measures associated with the new process at the next staff meeting. After waiting for the process to become stable, he took a random sample of 25 assembly times and found a standard deviation of 47 seconds. He recognizes this is only a point estimate of the variation in completion times and so wants to report both a 90% and a 95% confidence interval estimate for the population variance.

11-41. A medical research group is investigating what differences might exist between two pain-killing drugs, Azerlieve and Zynumbic. The researchers have already established there is no difference between the two drugs in terms of the average amount of time required before they take effect. However, they are also interested in knowing if there is any difference between the variability of time until pain relief occurs. A random sample of 24 patients using Azerlieve and 32 patients using Zynumbic yielded the following results:

Azerlieve	Zynumbic
$n_A = 24$	$n_Z = 32$
$s_A = 37.5$ seconds	$s_Z = 41.3$ seconds

Based on these sample data, can the researchers conclude a difference exists between the two drugs?

11-42. Belden Inc. (NYSE: BWC) and Cable Design Technologies Corp. (NYSE: CDT) merged on Thursday, July 15, 2004. The new company, Belden CDT Inc., is one of the largest U.S.–based manufacturers of high-speed electronic cables and focuses on products for the specialty electronics and data networking markets, including connectivity. One of its products is a fiber-optic cable (TrayOptic). It is designed to have an overall diameter of 0.440 inch. A standard deviation greater than 0.05 inch would be unacceptable. A sample of size 20 was taken from the production line and yielded a standard deviation of 0.070.

   a. Determine if the standard deviation does not meet specifications using a significance level of 0.01.

   b. Describe a Type II error in the context of this exercise.

11-43. Coca-Cola Bottling Co. Consolidated (CCBCC), headquartered in Charlotte, North Carolina, uses quality-control techniques to assure that the average amount of Coke in the cans is 12 ounces. It maintains that a small standard deviation of 0.05 ounces is acceptable. Any significant deviation in this standard deviation would negate any of the quality-control measures concerning the average amount of Coke in the 12-ounce cans. A sample of size 20 indicated that the standard deviation was 0.070.

   a. Determine if the standard deviation of the amount of Coke in the cans differs from the standard deviation specified by the quality control division. Use a significance level of 0.10.

   b. The quality-control sampling occurs several times a day. In one day, seven samples were taken, and three indicated that the standard deviation was not 0.05. If the seven samples were taken at a time in which the standard deviation met specifications, determine the probability of having at least three out of seven samples indicate the specification was not being met.

11-44. While not all students who attend college graduate with debt, more than 50 percent do. The most recent College Board *Trends in Student Aid* addresses, among other topics, the difference in the average college debt accumulated by undergraduate students who complete their degrees. Samples were used to determine this value, in which the private, for-profit college average was $28,100 and the public college average was $22,000. Suppose the respective standard deviations were 2,050 and 2,084. The sample sizes were 75 and 205, respectively.

   a. To determine which hypothesis test procedure needs to be used to decide if a difference exists in the average undergraduate debt between private and public colleges, one of the verifications that must be performed is whether the population variances are equal. Perform this test using a significance level of 0.10.

   b. Indicate the appropriate test that should be used to determine if a difference exists in the average undergraduate debt between private and public colleges.

11-45. A Tillinghast-Towers-Perrin (TTP) study estimated the cost of the U.S. tort system to be $260 billion. This is approximately $886 per U.S. citizen. A response by the Economic Policy Institute (EPI) indicated that approximately half of the costs ($113 billion) were not costs in any real economic sense. It indicated they are transfer payments from wrongdoers to victims. To settle these points of contention, two samples of size 51 were obtained and produced sample standard deviations of $295 and $151.

   a. Determine if a two-sample t-distribution can be used to determine if at most half of the tort costs ($113 billion) were not costs in any real economic sense, i.e., the mean tort cost is $\leq \$886/2$.

   b. What other requirement must be met before the test indicated in part a can be utilized?

Computer Database Exercises

11-46. The California State Highway Patrol recently conducted a study on a stretch of interstate highway south of San Francisco to determine what differences, if any, existed in driving speeds of cars licensed in California and cars licensed in Nevada. One of the issues to be examined was whether there was a difference in the variability of driving speeds between cars licensed in the two states. The data file **Speed-Test** contains speeds of 140 randomly selected California cars and 75 randomly selected Nevada cars. Based on these sample results, can you conclude at the 0.05 level of significance there is a difference between the variations in driving speeds for cars licensed in the two states?

11-47. The operations manager for Cozine Corporation is concerned with variation in the number of pounds of garbage collected per truck. If this variation is too high, the manager will change the truck pickup routes to try to better balance the loads. The manager believes the current truck routing system provides for consistent garbage pickup per truck and is unwilling to reroute the trucks unless the variability, measured by the standard deviation in pounds per truck, is greater than 3,900 pounds. The data file **Cozine** contains 200 truck weights. Assuming the data represent a random sample of 200 trucks selected from Cozine's daily operations, is there evidence the manager needs to change the routes to better balance the loads? Conduct your analysis using a 0.10 level of significance. Be sure to state your conclusion in terms of the operations manager's decision.

11-48. The X-John Company makes batteries specifically designed for cellular telephones. Recently, the research and development (R&D) department developed a new battery it believes will be less expensive to produce. The R&D engineers are concerned, however, about the consistency in the lasting power of the battery. If there is too much variability in battery life, cellular phone users will be unwilling to buy X-John batteries even if they are less expensive. Engineers have specified the standard deviation of battery life must be less than 5 hours. Treat the measurements in the file **X-John** as a random sample of 100 of the new batteries. Based on this sample, is there evidence the standard deviation of battery life is less than 5 hours? Conduct the appropriate hypothesis test using a level of significance of 0.01. Report the p-value for this test and be sure to state a conclusion in business terms.

11-49. Freedom Hospital is in the midst of contract negotiations with its resident physicians. There has been a lot of discussion about the hospital's ability to pay and the way patients are charged. The doctors' negotiator recently mentioned the geriatric charge system does not make sense. The negotiator is concerned there is a greater variability in the total charges for men than in the total charges for women. To investigate this issue, the hospital collected a random sample of data for 138 patients. The data are contained in the file **Patients**. Using the data for total charges, conduct the appropriate test to respond to the negotiator's concern. Use a significance level of 0.05. State your conclusion in terms that address the issue raised by the negotiator.

11-50. The Transportation Security Administration (TSA) examined the possibility of a Registered Traveler program. This program is intended to be a way to shorten security lines for "trusted travelers." *USA Today* published an article on a study run at the Orlando International Airport. Thirteen thousand people paid an annual $80 fee to participate in the program. They spent an average of four seconds in security lines at Orlando, according to Verified Identity Pass, the company that ran the program. For comparison purposes, a sample of the time it took the

other passengers to pass through security at Orlando was obtained. The file titled **Passtime** contains these data.

a. Although the average time to pass through security is of importance, the standard deviation is also important. Conduct a hypothesis test to determine if the standard deviation is larger than $1\frac{1}{2}$ minutes (i.e., 90 seconds). Use a significance level of 0.01.

b. Considering the results of your hypothesis tests in part a, determine and define the type of statistical error that could have been made.

11-51. The U.S. Census Bureau reports family incomes on a yearly basis. Incomes increased between 2005 and 2010. The data that arise from samples from these years are given in a file titled **Incomes**.

a. Determine if the income of families in the United States in 2005 to 2010 had different standard deviations. Use a significance level of 0.05.

b. Would it be valid to use a two-sample t-test on these data to determine if the average of incomes of U.S. families was different between 2005 and 2010? Explain.

11-52. Phone Solutions provides assistance to users of a personal finance software package. Users of the software call with their questions, and trained consultants provide answers and information. One concern that Phone Solutions must deal with is the staffing of its call centers. As part of the staffing issue, it seeks to reduce the average variability in the time each consultant spends with each caller. A study of this issue is currently under way at the company's three call centers. Each call center manager has randomly sampled 50 days of calls, and the collected times, in minutes, are in the file **Phone Solutions**.

a. Call Center 1 has set the goal that the variation in phone calls, measured by the standard deviation of length of calls in minutes, should be less than 3.5 minutes. Using the data in the file, can the operations manager of Call Center 1 conclude her consultants are meeting the goal? Use a 0.10 level of significance.

b. Can the manager conclude there is greater variability in the average length of phone calls for Call Center 3 than for Call Center 2? Again, use a 0.10 level of significance to conduct the appropriate test.

Case 11.1

Motive Power Company—Part 2

Cregg Hart is manufacturing manager for Motive Power Company, a locomotive engine and rail car manufacturer (see Case 10.1). The company has been very successful in recent years, and in July 2006 signed two major contracts totaling nearly $200 million. A key to the company's success has been its focus on quality. Customers from around the world have been very pleased with the attention to detail put forth by Motive Power.

In Case 10.1, Sheryl Carleson came to Cregg with a new supplier of rivets that would provide a substantial price advantage for Motive Power over the current supplier. Cregg asked Sheryl to conduct a study in which samples of rivets were selected from both suppliers. (Data are in the file called **Motive Power**.) In Case 10.1, the focus was on the mean diameter and a test to determine whether the population means were the same for the two suppliers. However, Cregg reminds Sheryl that not only is the mean diameter important, so too is the variation in diameter. Too much variation in rivet diameter adversely affects quality. Cregg showed Sheryl the following table to emphasize what he meant:

Diameter		
Company A		**Company B**
0.375		0.375
0.376		0.400
0.374		0.350
0.375		0.325
0.375		0.425
0.376		0.340
0.374		0.410
0.375	Mean	0.375
0.00082	St. Dev.	0.03808

As Sheryl examined this example that Cregg had prepared, she was quickly convinced that looking at the mean diameters would not be enough to fully compare the rivet suppliers. She told Cregg that she would also ask her intern to perform the following tasks.

Required Tasks:

1. Review results from Case 10.1.
2. Conduct the appropriate hypothesis test to determine whether the two suppliers have equal standard deviations. (Test using a significance level equal to 0.05.)
3. Prepare a short report that ties together the results from Cases 10.1 and 11.1 to present to Cregg along with a conclusion as to whether the new supplier seems viable based on rivet diameters.

chapter 12

Chapter 12 Quick Prep Links

- **Review** the computational methods for the sample mean and the sample variance in Chapter 3.

- **Review** the basics of hypothesis testing discussed in Section 9.1.

- **Re-examine** the material on hypothesis testing for the difference between two population variances in Section 11.2.

Analysis of Variance

12.1 One-Way Analysis of Variance (pg. 463–482)

12.2 Randomized Complete Block Analysis of Variance (pg. 483–494)

12.3 Two-Factor Analysis of Variance with Replication (pg. 494–504)

Outcome 1. Understand the basic logic of analysis of variance.

Outcome 2. Perform a hypothesis test for a single-factor design using analysis of variance manually and with the aid of Excel software.

Outcome 3. Conduct and interpret post-analysis of variance pairwise comparisons procedures.

Outcome 4. Recognize when randomized block analysis of variance is useful and be able to perform analysis of variance on a randomized block design.

Outcome 5. Perform analysis of variance on a two-factor design of experiments with replications using Excel and interpret the output.

Why you need to know

After completing Chapters 9 through 11, you hopefully understand that regardless of the population parameter in question, hypothesis-testing steps are basically the same:

1. Specify the population parameter of interest.
2. Formulate the null and alternative hypotheses.
3. Specify the level of significance.
4. Determine a decision rule defining the rejection and "acceptance" regions.
5. Select a random sample of data from the population(s). Compute the appropriate sample statistic(s). Finally, calculate the test statistic.
6. Reach a decision. Reject the null hypothesis, H_0, if the sample statistic falls in the rejection region; otherwise, do not reject the null hypothesis. If the test is conducted using the p-value approach, H_0 is rejected whenever the p-value is smaller than the significance level; otherwise, H_0 is not rejected.
7. Draw a conclusion. State the result of your hypothesis test in the context of the exercise or analysis of interest.

Chapter 9 focused on hypothesis tests involving a single population. Chapters 10 and 11 expanded the hypothesis-testing process to include applications in which differences between two populations are involved. However, you will encounter many instances involving more than two populations. For example, the vice president of operations at Farber Rubber, Inc., oversees production at Farber's six different U.S. manufacturing plants. Because each plant uses slightly different manufacturing processes, the vice president needs to know if there are any differences in average strength of the products produced at the different plants.

maniacpixel/Shutterstock

Similarly, *Golf Digest*, a major publisher of articles about golf, might wish to determine which of five major brands of golf balls has the highest mean distance off the tee. The Environmental Protection Agency (EPA) might conduct a test to determine if there is a difference in the average miles-per-gallon performance of cars manufactured by the Big Three U.S. automobile producers. In each of these cases, testing a hypothesis involving more than two population means could be required.

This chapter introduces a tool called analysis of variance (ANOVA), which can be used to test whether there are differences among three or more population means. There are several ANOVA procedures, depending on the type of test being conducted. Our aim in this chapter is to introduce you to ANOVA and to illustrate how to use Microsoft Excel to perform the calculations involved in hypothesis tests involving three or more population means.

Chapter Outcome 1. → # 12.1 One-Way Analysis of Variance

In Chapter 10, we introduced the *t*-test for testing whether two populations have equal means when the samples from the two populations are independent. However, you will often encounter situations in which you are interested in determining whether three or more populations have equal means. To handle these situations, you will need a new tool called *analysis of variance (ANOVA)*. There are many different analysis of variance designs to fit different situations; the simplest is a **completely randomized design**. Completely randomized designs are handled through a procedure known as **one-way analysis of variance**.

Completely Randomized Design
An experiment is completely randomized if it consists of the independent random selection of observations representing each level of one factor.

Introduction to One-Way ANOVA

BUSINESS APPLICATION   APPLYING ONE-WAY ANALYSIS OF VARIANCE

One-Way Analysis of Variance
An analysis of variance design in which independent samples are obtained from two or more levels of a single factor for the purpose of testing whether the levels have equal means.

volff/Fotolia

CHICAGO CONNECTION SANDWICH COMPANY The Chicago Connection Sandwich Company is a privately held company that operates in several midwestern cities. For example, the company has four locations in Columbus, Ohio. The VP of sales for the company is interested in knowing whether the dollar value for orders made by individual customers differs, on average, between the four locations.

To answer this question, staff at the VP's office have selected a random sample of eight customers at each of the four locations and recorded the order amount. These are shown in Table 12.1.

In this example, we are interested in whether the different locations generate different mean order sizes. In other words, we are trying to determine if location is one of the possible causes of the variation in the dollar value of the order placed by customers (the response variable). In this case, location is called a **factor**.

Factor
A quantity under examination in an experiment as a possible cause of variation in the response variable.

The *single factor* of interest is location. This factor has four categories, measurements, or strata, called **levels**. These four levels are the four locations: 1, 2, 3, and 4. Because we are using only one factor, each dollar value of order is associated with only one level (that is, with location 1, 2, 3, or 4), as you can see in Table 12.1. Each level is a population of interest, and the values seen in Table 12.1 are sample values taken from those populations.

Levels
The categories, measurements, or strata of a factor of interest in the current experiment.

The null and alternative hypotheses to be tested are

$$H_0: \mu_1 = \mu_2 = \mu_3 = \mu_4 \text{ (mean order sizes are equal)}$$
$$H_A: \text{At least two of the population means are different}$$

The appropriate statistical tool for conducting the hypothesis test related to this experimental design is analysis of variance. Because this ANOVA addresses an experiment with only one factor, it is a one-way ANOVA, or a one-factor ANOVA. Because the sample size for each location (level) is the same, the experiment has a **balanced design**.

Balanced Design
An experiment has a balanced design if the factor levels have equal sample sizes.

ANOVA tests the null hypothesis that three or more populations have the same mean. The test is based on four assumptions:

Assumptions

1. All populations are normally distributed.
2. The population variances are equal.
3. The observations are independent—that is, the occurrence of any one individual value does not affect the probability that any other observation will occur.
4. The data are interval or ratio level.

TABLE 12.1 | **Chicago Connection Sandwich Company Order Data**

Customer	Store Locations 1	2	3	4	
1	$4.10	$6.90	$4.60	$12.50	
2	5.90	9.10	11.40	7.50	
3	10.45	13.00	6.15	6.25	
4	11.55	7.90	7.85	8.75	
5	5.25	9.10	4.30	11.15	
6	7.75	13.40	8.70	10.25	
7	4.78	7.60	10.20	6.40	
8	6.22	5.00	10.80	9.20	
					Grand Mean
Mean	$\bar{x}_1 = \$7.00$	$\bar{x}_2 = \$9.00$	$\bar{x}_3 = \$8.00$	$\bar{x}_4 = \$9.00$	$\bar{\bar{x}} = \$8.25$
Variance	$s_1^2 = 7.341$	$s_2^2 = 8.423$	$s_3^2 = 7.632$	$s_4^2 = 5.016$	

Note: Data are the dollar values of the orders by customers at the four locations.

If the null hypothesis is true, the populations have identical distributions. If so, the sample means for random samples from each population should be close in value. The basic logic of ANOVA is the same as the two-sample *t*-test introduced in Chapter 10. The null hypothesis should be rejected only if the sample means are substantially different.

Partitioning the Sum of Squares

To understand the logic of ANOVA, you should note several things about the data in Table 12.1. First, the dollar values of the orders are different throughout the data table. Some values are higher; others are lower. Thus, variation exists across all customer orders. This variation is called the **total variation** in the data.

Total Variation
The aggregate dispersion of the individual data values across the various factor levels is called the *total variation* in the data.

Next, within any particular location (i.e., factor level), not all customers had the same dollar order. For instance, within level 1, order amount ranged from $4.10 to $11.55. Similar differences occur within the other levels. The variation within the factor levels is called the **within-sample variation**.

Within-Sample Variation
The dispersion that exists among the data values within a particular factor level is called the *within-sample variation*.

Finally, the sample means for the four restaurant locations are not all equal. Thus, variation exists between the four averages. This variation between the factor levels is referred to as the **between-sample variation**.

Between-Sample Variation
Dispersion among the factor sample means is called the *between-sample variation*.

Recall that the sample variance is computed as

$$s^2 = \frac{\sum(x-\bar{x})^2}{n-1}$$

The sample variance is the sum of squared deviations from the sample mean divided by its degrees of freedom. When all the data from all the samples are included, s^2 is the estimator of the *total variation*. The numerator of this estimator is called the *total sum of squares (SST)* and can be partitioned into the sum of squares associated with the estimators of the between-sample variation and the within-sample variation, as shown in Equation 12.1.

Partitioned Sum of Squares

$$SST = SSB + SSW \qquad \text{(12.1)}$$

where:

SST = Total sum of squares
SSB = Sum of squares between
SSW = Sum of squares within

After separating the sum of squares, *SSB* and *SSW* are divided by their respective degrees of freedom to produce two estimates for the overall population variance. If the between-sample variance estimate is large relative to the within-sample estimate, the ANOVA procedure will lead us to reject the null hypothesis and conclude the population means are different. The question is, how can we determine at what point any difference is statistically significant?

The ANOVA Assumptions

Chapter Outcome 2. → | BUSINESS APPLICATION | **UNDERSTANDING THE ANOVA ASSUMPTIONS**

CHICAGO CONNECTION SANDWICH COMPANY (*CONTINUED*) Recall that the VP of sales for the Chicago Connection Sandwich Company in interested in testing whether the four locations generate orders of equal average dollar value. The null and alternative hypotheses are

$$H_0: \mu_1 = \mu_2 = \mu_3 = \mu_4$$
$$H_A: \text{At least two population means are different}$$

Before we jump into the ANOVA calculations, recall the four basic assumptions of ANOVA:

1. All populations are normally distributed.
2. The population variances are equal.
3. The sampled observations are independent.
4. The data's measurement level is interval or ratio.

Figure 12.1 illustrates the first two assumptions. The populations are normally distributed and the spread (variance) is the same for each population. However, this figure shows the populations have different means—and therefore the null hypothesis is false. Figure 12.2 illustrates the same assumptions but in a case in which the population means are equal; therefore, the null hypothesis is true.

You can do a rough check to determine whether the normality assumption is satisfied by developing graphs of the sample data from each population. Histograms are probably the best

FIGURE 12.1

Normal Populations with Equal Variances and Unequal Means

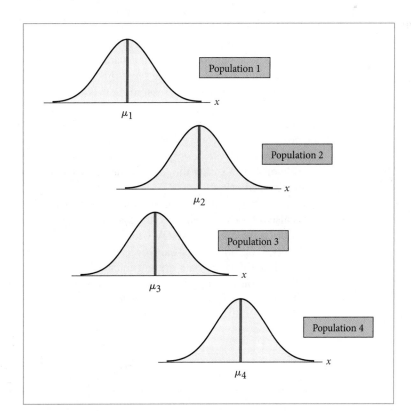

FIGURE 12.2

Normal Populations with Equal Variances and Equal Means

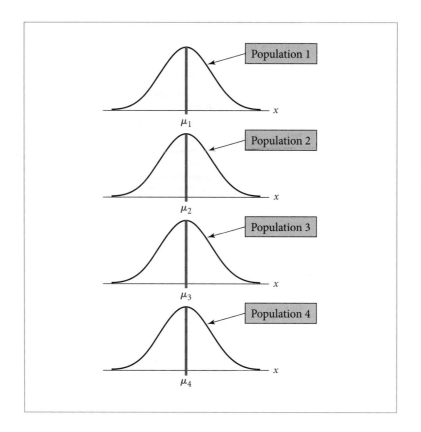

graphical tool for checking the normality assumption, but they require a fairly large sample size. The stem and leaf diagram and box and whisker plot are alternatives when sample sizes are smaller. If the graphical tools show plots consistent with a normal distribution, then that evidence suggests the normality assumption is satisfied.[1] Figure 12.3 illustrates the box and whisker plot for the Chicago Connection data. Note, when the sample sizes are very small, as they are here, the graphical techniques may not be very effective.[2]

Examining the sample data to see whether the basic assumptions are satisfied is always a good idea, but you should be aware that the analysis of variance procedures discussed in this chapter are *robust*, in the sense that the analysis of variance test is relatively unperturbed when the equal-variance assumption is not met. This is especially so when all samples are the same size, as in the Chicago Connection Company example. Hence, for one-way analysis of variance, or any other ANOVA design, try to have equal sample sizes when possible. Recall, we earlier referred to an analysis of variance design with equal sample sizes as a *balanced design*. If for some reason you are unable to use a balanced design, the rule of thumb is that the ratio of the largest sample size to the smallest sample size should not exceed 1.5.

When the samples are the same size (or meet the 1.5 ratio rule), the analysis of variance is also robust with respect to the assumption that the populations are normally distributed. So, in brief, the one-way ANOVA for independent samples can be applied to virtually any set of interval- or ratio-level data.

Finally, if the data are not interval or ratio level, or if they do not satisfy the normal distribution assumption, Chapter 17 introduces an ANOVA procedure called the Kruskal-Wallis One-Way ANOVA, which does not require these assumptions.

---

[1] Chapter 13 introduces a goodness-of-fit approach to testing whether sample data come from a normally distributed population.

[2] If we assume that the populations are approximately normally distributed, Hartley's F_{max} test can be used to test whether the populations have equal variances.

FIGURE 12.3

Box and Whisker Plot for Chicago Connection Sandwich Company

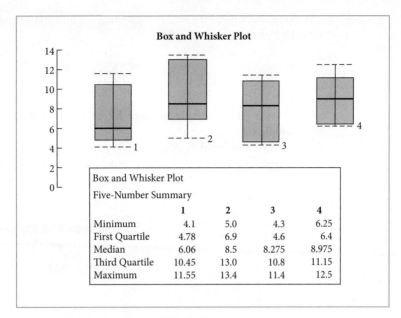

Applying One-Way ANOVA

Although the previous discussion covers the essence of ANOVA, to determine whether the null hypothesis should be rejected requires that we actually determine values of the estimators for the total variation, between-sample variation, and within-sample variation. Most ANOVA tests are done using a computer, but we will illustrate the manual computational approach one time to show you how it is done. Because software such as Excel can be used to perform all calculations, future examples will be done using the computer. The software packages will do all the computations while we focus on interpreting the results.

BUSINESS APPLICATION   **DEVELOPING THE ANOVA TABLE**

CHICAGO CONNECTION SANDWICH COMPANY (*CONTINUED*) Now we are ready to perform the necessary one-way ANOVA computations for the Chicago Connection Sandwich example. Recall from Equation 12.1 that we can partition the total sum of squares into two components:

$$SST = SSB + SSW$$

The *total sum of squares* is computed as shown in Equation 12.2.

Total Sum of Squares

$$SST = \sum_{i=1}^{k} \sum_{j=1}^{n_i} (x_{ij} - \bar{\bar{x}})^2 \qquad (12.2)$$

where:

SST = Total sum of squares
k = Number of populations (treatments)
n_i = Sample size from population i
x_{ij} = jth measurement from population i
$\bar{\bar{x}}$ = Grand mean (mean of all the data values)

Equation 12.2 is not as complicated as it appears. Manually applying Equation 12.2 to the data shown in Table 12.1 on page 464 (Grand mean = $\bar{\bar{x}}$ = 8.25), we can compute the *SST* as follows:

$$SST = (4.10 - 8.25)^2 + (5.90 - 8.25)^2 + (10.45 - 8.25)^2 + \cdots + (9.20 - 8.25)^2$$
$$SST = 220.88$$

Thus, the sum of the squared deviations of all values from the grand mean is 220.88. Equation 12.2 can also be restated as

$$SST = \sum_{i=1}^{k} \sum_{j=1}^{n_i} (x_{ij} - \bar{\bar{x}})^2 = (n_T - 1)s^2$$

where s^2 is the sample variance for all data combined, and n_T is the sum of the combined sample sizes.

We now need to determine how much of this total sum of squares is due to between-sample sum of squares and how much is due to within-sample sum of squares. The between-sample portion is called the *sum of squares between* and is found using Equation 12.3.

Sum of Squares Between

$$SSB = \sum_{i=1}^{k} n_i (\bar{x}_i - \bar{\bar{x}})^2 \tag{12.3}$$

where:

SSB = Sum of squares between samples
k = Number of populations
n_i = Sample size from population i
$\bar{x}_i$ = Sample mean from population i
$\bar{\bar{x}}$ = Grand mean

We can use Equation 12.3 to manually compute the sum of squares between for the Chicago Connection data, as follows:

$$SSB = 8(7 - 8.25)^2 + 8(9 - 8.25)^2 + 8(8 - 8.25)^2 + 8(9 - 8.25)^2$$
$$SSB = 22$$

Once both the SST and SSB have been computed, the *sum of squares within* (also called the sum of squares error, SSE) is easily computed using Equation 12.4. The sum of squares within can also be computed directly, using Equation 12.5.

Sum of Squares Within

$$SSW = SST - SSB \tag{12.4}$$

or

Sum of Squares Within

$$SSW = \sum_{i=1}^{k} \sum_{j=1}^{n_i} (x_{ij} - \bar{x}_i)^2 \tag{12.5}$$

where:

SSW = Sum of squares within samples
k = Number of populations
n_i = Sample size from population i
$\bar{x}_i$ = Sample mean from population i
x_{ij} = jth measurement from population i

For the Chicago Connection Sandwich example, the SSW is

$$SSW = 220.88 - 22.00$$
$$= 198.88$$

TABLE 12.2 | **One-Way ANOVA Table: The Basic Format**

Source of Variation	SS	df	MS	F-Ratio
Between samples	SSB	$k - 1$	MSB	$\dfrac{MSB}{MSW}$
Within samples	SSW	$n_T - k$	MSW	
Total	SST	$n_T - 1$		

where:

$$k = \text{Number of populations}$$
$$n_T = \text{Sum of the sample sizes from all populations}$$
$$df = \text{Degrees of freedom}$$
$$MSB = \text{Mean square between} = \frac{SSB}{k-1}$$
$$MSW = \text{Mean square within} = \frac{SSW}{n_T - k}$$

These computations are the essential first steps in performing the ANOVA test to determine whether the population means are equal. Table 12.2 illustrates the ANOVA table format used to conduct the test. The format shown in Table 12.2 is the standard ANOVA table layout. For the Chicago Connection example, we substitute the numerical values for SSB, SSW, and SST and complete the ANOVA table, as shown in Table 12.3. The mean square column contains the MSB (mean square between samples) and the MSW (mean square within samples).[3] These values are computed by dividing the sum of squares by their respective degrees of freedom, as shown in Table 12.3.

Restating the null and alternative hypotheses for the Chicago Connection example:

$$H_0: \mu_1 = \mu_2 = \mu_3 = \mu_4$$
$$H_A: \text{At least two population means are different}$$

Glance back at Figures 12.1 and 12.2. If the null hypothesis is true (that is, all the means are equal—Figure 12.2), the MSW and MSB will be equal, except for the presence of sampling error. However, the more the sample means differ (Figure 12.1), the larger the MSB becomes. As the MSB increases, it will tend to get larger than the MSW. When this difference gets too large, we will conclude that the population means must not be equal, and the null hypothesis

TABLE 12.3 | **One-Way ANOVA Table for the Chicago Connection Sandwich Company**

Source of Variation	SS	df	MS	F-Ratio
Between samples	22.00	3	7.33	$\dfrac{7.33}{7.10} = 1.03$
Within samples	198.88	28	7.10	
Total	220.88	31		

where:

$$MSB = \text{Mean square between} = \frac{SSB}{k-1} = \frac{22}{3} = 7.33$$
$$MSW = \text{Mean square between} = \frac{SSW}{n_T - k} = \frac{198.88}{28} = 7.10$$

---

[3]MSW is also known as the *mean square error (MSE)*.

FIGURE 12.4

Chicago Connection
Sandwich Company
Hypothesis Test

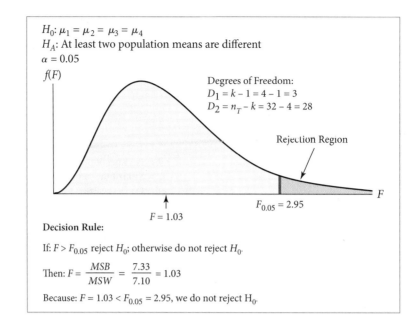

$H_0: \mu_1 = \mu_2 = \mu_3 = \mu_4$
H_A: At least two population means are different
$\alpha = 0.05$

$f(F)$

Degrees of Freedom:
$D_1 = k - 1 = 4 - 1 = 3$
$D_2 = n_T - k = 32 - 4 = 28$

Rejection Region

$F = 1.03$

$F_{0.05} = 2.95$

F

Decision Rule:

If: $F > F_{0.05}$ reject H_0; otherwise do not reject H_0.

Then: $F = \dfrac{MSB}{MSW} = \dfrac{7.33}{7.10} = 1.03$

Because: $F = 1.03 < F_{0.05} = 2.95$, we do not reject H_0.

will be rejected. But how do we determine what "too large" is? How do we know when the difference is due to more than just sampling error?

To answer these questions, recall from Chapter 11 the F-distribution is used to test whether two populations have the same variance. In the ANOVA test, if the null hypothesis is true, the ratio of MSB over MSW forms an F-distribution with $D_1 = k - 1$ and $D_2 = n_T - k$ degrees of freedom. If the calculated F-ratio in Table 12.3 gets too large, the null hypothesis is rejected.

Figure 12.4 illustrates the hypothesis test for a significance level of 0.05. Because the calculated F-ratio $= 1.03$ is less than the critical $F_{0.05} = 2.95$ (found using Excel's F.INV.RT function) with 3 and 28 degrees of freedom, the null hypothesis cannot be rejected. The F-ratio indicates that the between-levels estimate and the within-levels estimate are not different enough to conclude that the population means are different. This means there is insufficient statistical evidence to conclude that any one of the four locations will generate higher average-dollar lunch orders than any of the other locations. Therefore, the VP of sales has no reason to think that in Columbus, Ohio, location of his restaurants is influencing the size of customer orders.

Chapter Outcome 2. → | **EXAMPLE 12-1** **ONE-WAY ANALYSIS OF VARIANCE**

Roderick, Wilterding & Associates Roderick, Wilterding & Associates (RWA) operates automobile dealerships in three regions: the West, Southwest, and Northwest. Recently, RWA's general manager questioned whether the company's mean profit margin per vehicle sold differed by region. To determine this, the following steps can be performed:

Step 1 Specify the parameter(s) of interest.
The parameter of interest is the mean dollars of profit margin in each region.

Step 2 Formulate the null and alternative hypotheses.
The appropriate null and alternative hypotheses are

$$H_0: \mu_W = \mu_{SW} = \mu_{NW}$$
H_A: At least two populations have different means

Step 3 Specify the significance level (α) for testing the hypothesis.
The test will be conducted using an $\alpha = 0.05$.

Step 4 **Select independent simple random samples from each population, and compute the sample means and the grand mean.**

There are three regions. Simple random samples of vehicles sold in these regions have been selected: 10 in the West, 8 in the Southwest, and 12 in the Northwest. Note, even though the sample sizes are not equal, the largest sample is not more than 1.5 times as large as the smallest sample size. The following sample data were collected (in dollars):

West	Southwest	Northwest	West	Southwest	Northwest
3,700	3,300	2,900	5,300	2,700	3,300
2,900	2,100	4,300	2,200	4,500	3,700
4,100	2,600	5,200	3,700	2,400	2,400
4,900	2,100	3,300	4,800		4,400
4,900	3,600	3,600	3,000		3,300
					4,400
					3,200

The sample means are

$$\bar{x}_W = \frac{\Sigma x}{n} = \frac{\$39,500}{10} = \$3,950$$

$$\bar{x}_{SW} = \frac{\$23,300}{8} = \$2,912.50$$

$$\bar{x}_{NW} = \frac{\$44,000}{12} = \$3,666.67$$

and the grand mean, the mean of the data from all samples, is

$$\bar{\bar{x}} = \frac{\Sigma\Sigma x}{n_T} = \frac{\$3,700 + \$2,900 + \cdots + \$3,200}{30}$$

$$= \frac{\$106,800}{30}$$

$$= \$3,560$$

Step 5 **Determine the decision rule.**

The F-critical value from the F-distribution table in Appendix H for $D_1 = 2$ and $D_2 = 27$ degrees of freedom is a value between 3.316 and 3.403. The exact value $F_{0.05} = 3.354$ can be found using Excel's F.INV.RT function.

The decision rule is:

If $F > 3.354$, reject the null hypothesis;
otherwise, do not reject the null hypothesis.

Step 6 **Create the ANOVA table.**

Compute the total sum of squares, sum of squares between, and sum of squares within, and complete the ANOVA table.

Total Sum of Squares

$$SST = \sum_{i=1}^{k}\sum_{j=1}^{n_i}(x_{ij} - \bar{\bar{x}})^2$$

$$= (3,700 - 3,560)^2 + (2,900 - 3,560)^2 + \cdots + (3,200 - 3,560)^2$$

$$= 26,092,000$$

Sum of Squares Between

$$SSB = \sum_{i=1}^{k} n_i(\bar{x}_i - \bar{\bar{x}})^2$$

$$= 10(3,950 - 3,560)^2 + 8(2,912.50 - 3,560)^2 + 12(3,666.67 - 3,560)^2$$

$$= 5,011,583$$

Sum of Squares Within

$$SSW = SST - SSB = 26,092,000 - 5,011,583 = 21,080,417$$

The ANOVA table is

Source of Variation	SS	df	MS	F-Ratio
Between samples	5,011,583	2	2,505,792	$\dfrac{2,505,792}{780,756} = 3.209$
Within samples	21,080,417	27	780,756	
Total	26,092,000	29		

Step 7 Reach a decision.

Because the F-test statistic $= 3.209 < F_{0.05} = 3.354$, we do not reject the null hypothesis based on these sample data.

Step 8 Draw a conclusion.

We are not able to detect a difference in the mean profit margin per vehicle sold by region.

>> **END EXAMPLE**

TRY PROBLEM 12-2 (pg. 479)

Excel Tutorial

BUSINESS APPLICATION **USING SOFTWARE TO PERFORM ONE-WAY ANOVA**

HYDRONICS CORPORATION The Hydronics Corporation makes and distributes health products. Currently, the company's research department is experimenting with two new herb-based weight loss–enhancing products. To gauge their effectiveness, researchers at the company conducted a test using 300 human subjects over a six-week period. All the people in the study were between 30 and 40 pounds overweight.

One third of the subjects were randomly selected to receive a placebo—in this case, a pill containing only vitamin C. One third of the subjects were randomly selected and given product 1. The remaining 100 people received product 2. The subjects did not know which pill they had been assigned. Each person was asked to take the pill regularly for six weeks and otherwise observe his or her normal routine. At the end of six weeks, the subjects' weight loss was recorded. The company was hoping to find statistical evidence that at least one of the products is an effective weight-loss aid.

The file **Hydronics** shows the study data. Positive values indicate that the subject lost weight, whereas negative values indicate that the subject gained weight during the six-week study period. As often happens in studies involving human subjects, people drop out. Thus, at the end of six weeks, only 89 placebo subjects, 91 product 1 subjects, and 83 product 2 subjects with valid data remained. Consequently, this experiment resulted in an unbalanced design. Although the sample sizes are not equal, they are close to being the same size and do not violate the 1.5-ratio rule of thumb mentioned earlier.

The null and alternative hypotheses to be tested using a significance level of 0.05 are

$$H_0: \mu_1 = \mu_2 = \mu_3$$

$$H_A: \text{At least two population means are different}$$

The experimental design is completely randomized. The factor is diet supplement, which has three levels: placebo, product 1, and product 2. We will use a significance level of $\alpha = 0.05$.

FIGURE 12.5

Excel 2010 Output: Hydronics
Weight Loss ANOVA Results

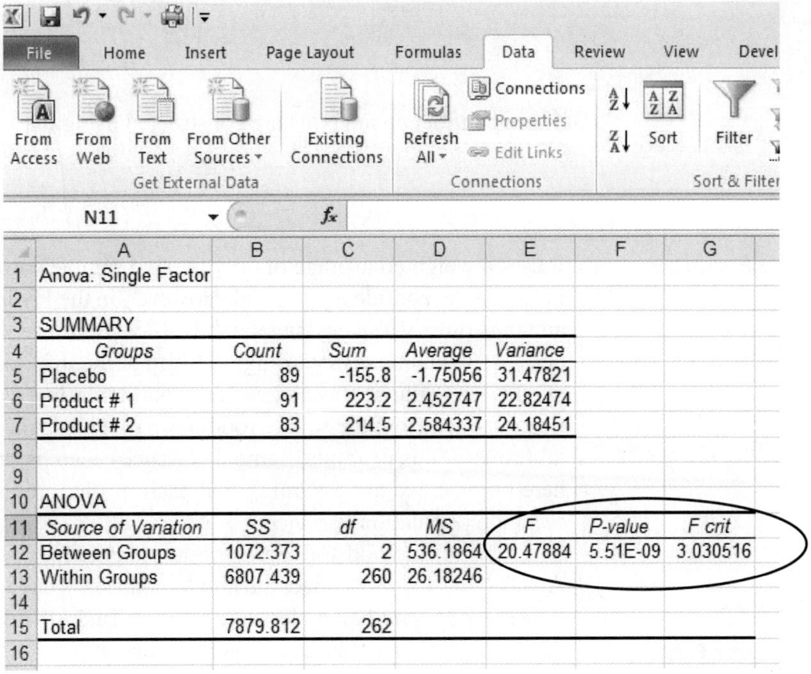

Excel 2010 Instructions:
1. Open File:
   Hydronics.xlsx.
2. Select **Data >
   Data Analysis.**
3. Select **ANOVA: Single
   Factor.**
4. Define data range
   (columns B, C, and D).
5. Specify **Alpha**
   equal 0.05.
6. Indicate output choice.
7. Click **OK.**

	A	B	C	D	E	F	G
1	Anova: Single Factor						
2							
3	SUMMARY						
4	*Groups*	*Count*	*Sum*	*Average*	*Variance*		
5	Placebo	89	-155.8	-1.75056	31.47821		
6	Product # 1	91	223.2	2.452747	22.82474		
7	Product # 2	83	214.5	2.584337	24.18451		
8							
9							
10	ANOVA						
11	*Source of Variation*	*SS*	*df*	*MS*	*F*	*P-value*	*F crit*
12	Between Groups	1072.373	2	536.1864	20.47884	5.51E-09	3.030516
13	Within Groups	6807.439	260	26.18246			
14							
15	Total	7879.812	262				
16							

Minitab Instructions (for similar results):
1. Open file: **Hydronics.MTW.**
2. Choose **Stat > ANOVA > One-way.**
3. In **Response**, enter data column, *Loss.*
4. In **Factor**, enter factor level
   column, *Program.*
5. Click **OK.**

Figure 12.5 shows the Excel analysis of variance results. The top section of the Excel ANOVA output provides descriptive information for the three levels. The ANOVA table is shown in the other section of the output. These tables look like the one we generated manually in the Chicago Connection Sandwich Company example. However, Excel also computes the p-value and displays the critical value, F-critical, from the F-distribution table. Thus, you can test the null hypothesis by comparing the calculated F to the F-critical or by comparing the p-value to the significance level.

The decision rule is

$$\text{If } F > F_{0.05} = 3.03, \text{ reject } H_0;$$
$$\text{otherwise, do not reject } H_0.$$

or

$$\text{If } p\text{-value} < \alpha = 0.05, \text{ reject } H_0;$$
$$\text{otherwise, do not reject } H_0.$$

Because

$$F = 20.48 > F_{0.05} = 3.03 \text{ (or } p\text{-value} = 0.0000 < \alpha = 0.05)$$

we reject the null hypothesis and conclude there is a difference in the mean weight loss for people on the three treatments. At least two of the populations have different means. The top portion of Figure 12.5 shows the descriptive measures for the sample data. For example, the subjects who took the placebo actually gained an average of 1.75 pounds. Subjects on product 1 lost an average of 2.45 pounds, and subjects on product 2 lost an average of 2.58 pounds.

Chapter Outcome 3. → **The Tukey-Kramer Procedure for Multiple Comparisons** What does this conclusion imply about which treatment results in greater weight loss? One approach to answering this question is to use confidence interval estimates for all possible pairs of population means, based on the pooling of the two relevant sample variances, as introduced in Chapter 10.

$$s_p = \sqrt{\frac{(n_1 - 1)s_1^2 + (n_2 - 1)s_2^2}{n_1 + n_2 - 2}}$$

These confidence intervals are constructed using the formula also given in Chapter 10:

$$(\bar{x}_1 - \bar{x}_2) \pm ts_p\sqrt{\frac{1}{n_1} + \frac{1}{n_2}}$$

It uses a weighted average of only the two sample variances corresponding to the two sample means in the confidence interval. However, in the Hydronics example, we have three samples, and thus three variances, involved. If we were to use the pooled standard deviation, s_p shown here, we would be disregarding one third of the information available to estimate the common population variance. Instead, we use confidence intervals based on the pooled standard deviation obtained from the square root of MSW. This is the square root of the weighted average of all (three in this example) sample variances. This is preferred to the interval estimate shown here because we are assuming that each of the three sample variances is an estimate of the common population variance.

A better method for testing which populations have different means after the one-way ANOVA has led us to reject the null hypothesis is called the *Tukey-Kramer procedure for multiple comparisons*.[4] To understand why the Tukey-Kramer procedure is superior, we introduce the concept of an **experiment-wide error rate**.

Experiment-Wide Error Rate

The proportion of experiments in which at least one of the set of confidence intervals constructed does not contain the true value of the population parameter being estimated.

The Tukey-Kramer procedure is based on the simultaneous construction of confidence intervals for all differences of pairs of treatment means. In this example, there are three different pairs of means $(\mu_1 - \mu_2, \mu_1 - \mu_3, \mu_2 - \mu_3)$. The Tukey-Kramer procedure simultaneously constructs three different confidence intervals for a specified confidence level, say 95%. Intervals that do not contain zero imply that a difference exists between the associated population means.

Suppose we repeat the study a large number of times. Each time, we construct the Tukey-Kramer 95% confidence intervals. The Tukey-Kramer method assures us that in 95% of these experiments, the three confidence intervals constructed will include the true difference between the population means, $\mu_i - \mu_j$. In 5% of the experiments, at least one of the confidence intervals will not contain the true difference between the population means. Thus, in 5% of the situations, we would make at least one mistake in our conclusions about which populations have different means. This proportion of errors (0.05) is known as the experiment-wide error rate.

For a 95% confidence interval, the Tukey-Kramer procedure controls the experiment-wide error to a 0.05 level. However, because we are concerned with only this one experiment (with one set of sample data), the error rate associated with any one of the three confidence intervals is actually less than 0.05.

The Tukey-Kramer procedure allows us to simultaneously examine all pairs of populations *after* the ANOVA test has been completed without increasing the true alpha level. Because these comparisons are made after the ANOVA F-test, the procedure is called a post-test (or post-hoc) procedure.

The first step in using the Tukey-Kramer procedure is to compute the absolute differences between each pair of sample means. Using the results shown in Figure 12.5, we get the following absolute differences:

$$|\bar{x}_1 - \bar{x}_2| = |-1.75 - 2.45| = 4.20$$
$$|\bar{x}_1 - \bar{x}_3| = |-1.75 - 2.58| = 4.33$$
$$|\bar{x}_2 - \bar{x}_3| = |2.45 - 2.58| = 0.13$$

The Tukey-Kramer procedure requires us to compare these absolute differences to the *critical range* that is computed using Equation 12.6.

---

[4]There are other methods for making these comparisons. Statisticians disagree over which method to use. Later, we introduce alternative methods.

Tukey-Kramer Critical Range

$$\text{Critical range} = q_{1-\alpha}\sqrt{\frac{MSW}{2}\left(\frac{1}{n_i}+\frac{1}{n_j}\right)} \tag{12.6}$$

where:

$q_{1-\alpha}$ = Value from studentized range table (Appendix J), with $D_1 = k$ and $D_2 = n_T - k$ degrees of freedom for the desired level of $1 - \alpha$ [k = Number of groups or factor levels, and n_T = Total number of data values from all populations (levels) combined]

MSW = Mean square within

n_i and n_j = Sample sizes from populations (levels) i and j, respectively

A critical range is computed for each pairwise comparison, but if the sample sizes are equal, only one critical-range calculation is necessary because the quantity under the radical in Equation 12.7 will be the same for all comparisons. If the calculated pairwise comparison value is greater than the critical range, we conclude the difference is significant.

To determine the q-value from the studentized range table in Appendix J for a significance level equal to

$$\alpha = 0.05$$

and

$$k = 3 \text{ and } n_T - k = 260 \text{ degrees of freedom}$$

For $D_2 = n_T - k = 260$ degrees of freedom, we use the row labeled ∞. The studentized range value for $1 - 0.05 = 0.95$ is approximately

$$q_{0.95} = 3.31$$

Then, for the placebo versus product 1 comparison,

$$n_1 = 89 \quad \text{and} \quad n_2 = 91$$

we use Equation 12.6 to compute the critical range, as follows:

$$\text{Critical range} = q_{1-\alpha}\sqrt{\frac{MSW}{2}\left(\frac{1}{n_i}+\frac{1}{n_j}\right)}$$

$$\text{Critical range} = 3.31\sqrt{\frac{26.18}{2}\left(\frac{1}{89}+\frac{1}{91}\right)} = 1.785$$

Because

$$|\bar{x}_1 - \bar{x}_2| = 4.20 > 1.785$$

we conclude that

$$\mu_1 \neq \mu_2$$

The mean weight loss for the placebo group is not equal to the mean weight loss for the product 1 group. Table 12.4 summarizes the results for the three pairwise comparisons. From

TABLE 12.4 | **Hydronics Pairwise Comparisons—Tukey-Kramer Test**

	$|\bar{x}_i - \bar{x}_j|$	Critical Range	Significant?
Placebo vs. product 1	4.20	1.785	Yes
Placebo vs. product 2	4.33	1.827	Yes
Product 1 vs. product 2	0.13	1.818	No

the table, we see that product 1 and product 2 both offer significantly higher average weight loss than the placebo. However, the sample data do not indicate a difference in the average weight loss between product 1 and product 2. Thus, the company can conclude that both product 1 and product 2 are superior to taking a placebo.

Chapter Outcome 3. →

Excel Tutorial

EXAMPLE 12-2 **THE TUKEY-KRAMER PROCEDURE FOR MULTIPLE COMPARISON**

Digitron, Inc. Digitron, Inc., makes disc brakes for automobiles. Digitron's research and development (R&D) department recently tested four brake systems to determine if there is a difference in the average stopping distance among them. Forty identical mid-sized cars were driven on a test track. Ten cars were fitted with brake A, 10 with brake B, and so forth. An electronic, remote switch was used to apply the brakes at exactly the same point on the road. The number of feet required to bring the car to a full stop was recorded. The data are in the file **Digitron**. Because we care to determine only whether the four brake systems have the same or different mean stopping distances, the test is a one-way (single-factor) test with four levels and can be completed using the following steps:

Step 1 **Specify the parameter(s) of interest.**

The parameter of interest is the mean stopping distance for each brake type. The company is interested in knowing whether a difference exists in mean stopping distance for the four brake types.

Step 2 **Formulate the appropriate null and alternative hypotheses.**

The appropriate null and alternative hypotheses are

$$H_0: \mu_1 = \mu_2 = \mu_3 = \mu_4$$
$$H_A: \text{At least two population means are different}$$

Step 3 **Specify the significance level for the test.**

The test will be conducted using $\alpha = 0.05$.

Step 4 **Select independent simple random samples from each population.**

Step 5 **Check to see that the normality and equal-variance assumptions have been satisfied.**

Because of the small sample size, the box and whisker plot is used.

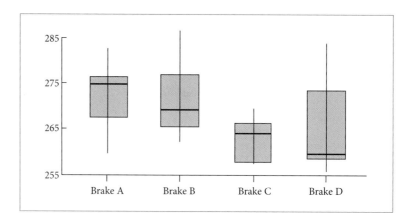

The box plots indicate some skewness in the samples and question the assumption of equality of variances.[5]

---

[5]If we assume that the populations are approximately normally distributed, Hartley's F_{max} test can be used to test whether the four populations have equal variances.

FIGURE 12.6

Excel 2010 One-Way ANOVA Output for the Digitron Example

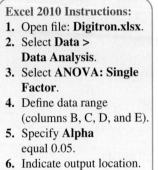

Excel 2010 Instructions:
1. Open file: **Digitron.xlsx**.
2. Select **Data > Data Analysis**.
3. Select **ANOVA: Single Factor**.
4. Define data range (columns B, C, D, and E).
5. Specify **Alpha** equal 0.05.
6. Indicate output location.
7. Click **OK**.

	A	B	C	D	E	F	G
1	Anova: Single Factor						
2							
3	SUMMARY						
4	*Groups*	*Count*	*Sum*	*Average*	*Variance*		
5	Brake A	10	2723.590	272.359	49.900		
6	Brake B	10	2713.299	271.330	61.856		
7	Brake C	10	2623.140	262.314	21.736		
8	Brake D	10	2652.357	265.236	106.439		
9							
10							
11	ANOVA						
12	*Source of Variation*	*SS*	*df*	*MS*	*F*	*P-value*	*F crit*
13	Between Groups	699.164	3	233.055	3.885	0.017	2.866
14	Within Groups	2159.369	36	59.982			
15							
16	Total	2858.532					
17							

Because calculated F = 3.885 > F critical = 2.866, reject the null hypothesis and conclude that the population means are not equal.

Minitab Instructions (for similar results):
1. Open file: **Digitron.MTW**.
2. Choose **Stat > ANOVA > One-way**.
3. In **Response**, enter data column, *Distance*.
4. In **Factor**, enter factor level column, *Brake*.
5. Click **OK**.

Recall our earlier discussion stating that when the sample sizes are equal, as they are in this example, the ANOVA test is robust in regard to both the equal variance and normality assumptions.

Step 6 Determine the decision rule.
Because $k - 1 = 3$ and $n_T - k = 36$, from Excel $F_{0.05} = 2.8663$. The decision rule is

If the calculated $F > F_{0.05} = 2.8663$, reject H_0, or
if the p-value $< \alpha = 0.05$, reject H_0; otherwise, do not reject H_0.

Step 7 Use Excel to construct the ANOVA table.
Figure 12.6 shows the Excel output for the ANOVA.

Step 8 Reach a decision.
From Figure 12.6, we see that

$$F = 3.89 > F_{0.05} = 2.8663, \text{ and } p\text{-value} = 0.017 < 0.05$$

We reject the null hypothesis.

Step 9 Draw a conclusion.
We conclude that not all population means are equal. But which systems are different? Is one system superior to all the others?

Step 10 Use the Tukey-Kramer test to determine which populations have different means.
Because we have rejected the null hypothesis of equal means, we need to perform a post–ANOVA multiple comparisons test. Using Equation 12.6

to construct the critical range to compare to the absolute differences in all possible pairs of sample means, the critical range is[6]

$$\text{Critical range} = q_{1-\alpha}\sqrt{\frac{MSW}{2}\left(\frac{1}{n_i}+\frac{1}{n_j}\right)} = 3.85\sqrt{\frac{59.98}{2}\left(\frac{1}{10}+\frac{1}{10}\right)}$$

$$\text{Critical range} = 9.43$$

Only one critical range is necessary because the sample sizes are equal. If any pair of sample means has an absolute difference $|\bar{x}_i - \bar{x}_j|$, greater than the critical range, we can infer that a difference exists in those population means. The possible pairwise comparisons (part of a family of comparisons called *contrasts*) are

Contrast	Significant Difference
$|\bar{x}_1 - \bar{x}_2| = |272.3590 - 271.3299| = 1.0291 < 9.43$	No
$|\bar{x}_1 - \bar{x}_3| = |272.3590 - 262.3140| = 10.0450 > 9.43$	Yes
$|\bar{x}_1 - \bar{x}_4| = |272.3590 - 265.2357| = 7.1233 < 9.43$	No
$|\bar{x}_2 - \bar{x}_3| = |271.3299 - 262.3140| = 9.0159 < 9.43$	No
$|\bar{x}_2 - \bar{x}_4| = |271.3299 - 265.2357| = 6.0942 < 9.43$	No
$|\bar{x}_3 - \bar{x}_4| = |262.3140 - 265.2357| = 2.9217 < 9.43$	No

Therefore, based on the Tukey-Kramer procedure, we can infer that population 1 (brake system A) and population 3 (brake system C) have different mean stopping distances. Because short stopping distances are preferred, system C would be preferred over system A, but no other differences are supported by these sample data. For the other contrasts, the difference between the two sample means is insufficient to conclude that a difference in population means exists.

>> **END EXAMPLE**

TRY PROBLEM 12-6 (pg. 480)

Fixed Effects Versus Random Effects in Analysis of Variance

In the Digitron brake example, the company was testing four brake systems. These were the only brake systems under consideration. The ANOVA was intended to determine whether there was a difference in these four brake systems only. In the Hydronics weight-loss example, the company was interested in determining whether there was a difference in mean weight loss for two supplements and the placebo. In the Chicago Connection Sandwich example involving locations, the company analyzed orders at four selected locations, and the ANOVA test was used to determine whether there was a difference in means for these four locations only. Thus, in each of these examples, the inferences extend only to the factor levels being analyzed, and the levels are assumed to be the only levels of interest. This type of test is called a *fixed effects analysis of variance test*.

Suppose in the Chicago Connection example that instead of reducing the list of possible restaurant locations to the four in Columbus, Ohio, the company had simply selected a random sample of four of its restaurants from all its Midwest locations. In that case, the

---

[6]The q-value from the studentized range table with $\alpha = 0.05$ and degrees of freedom equal to $k = 4$ and $n_T - k = 36$ must be approximated using degrees of freedom 4 and 30 because the table does not show degrees of freedom of 4 and 36. This value is 3.85. Rounding down to 30 will give a larger q value and a conservatively large critical range.

factor levels included in the test would be a random sample of the possible levels. Then, if the ANOVA leads to rejecting the null hypothesis, the conclusion applies to all possible Chicago Connections Sandwich locations rather than just the four in Columbus. The assumption is the possible levels have a normal distribution and the tested levels are a random sample from this distribution. When the factor levels are selected through random sampling, the analysis of variance test is called a *random effects test*.

MyStatLab

12-1: Exercises

Skill Development

12-1. A start-up cell phone applications company is interested in determining whether household incomes are different for subscribers to three different service providers. A random sample of 25 subscribers to each of the three service providers was taken, and the annual household income for each subscriber was recorded. The partially completed ANOVA table for the analysis is shown here:

ANOVA				
Source of Variation	**SS**	**df**	**MS**	**F**
Between Groups	2,949,085,157			
Within Groups				
Total	9,271,678,090			

a. Complete the ANOVA table by filling in the missing sums of squares, the degrees of freedom for each source, the mean square, and the calculated F-test statistic.
b. Based on the sample results, can the start-up firm conclude that there is a difference in household incomes for subscribers to the three service providers? You may assume normal distributions and equal variances. Conduct your test at the $\alpha = 0.10$ level of significance. Be sure to state a critical F-statistic, a decision rule, and a conclusion.

12-2. An analyst is interested in testing whether four populations have equal means. The following sample data have been collected from populations that are assumed to be normally distributed with equal variances:

Sample 1	Sample 2	Sample 3	Sample 4
9	12	8	17
6	16	8	15
11	16	12	17
14	12	7	16
14	9	10	13

Conduct the appropriate hypothesis test using a significance level equal to 0.05.

12-3. A manager is interested in testing whether three populations of interest have equal population means. Simple random samples of size 10 were selected from each population. The following ANOVA table and related statistics were computed:

ANOVA: Single Factor				
Summary				
Groups	**Count**	**Sum**	**Average**	**Variance**
Sample 1	10	507.18	50.72	35.06
Sample 2	10	405.79	40.58	30.08
Sample 3	10	487.64	48.76	23.13

ANOVA						
Source	**SS**	**df**	**MS**	**F**	**p-value**	**F-crit**
Between Groups	578.78	2	289.39	9.84	0.0006	3.354
Within Groups	794.36	27	29.42			
Total	1,373.14	29				

a. State the appropriate null and alternative hypotheses.
b. Based on your answer to part a, what conclusions can be reached about the null and alternative hypotheses. Use a 0.05 level of significance.
c. If warranted, use the Tukey-Kramer procedure for multiple comparisons to determine which populations have different means. (Assume $\alpha = 0.05$.)

12-4. Respond to each of the following questions using this partially completed one-way ANOVA table:

Source of Variation	SS	df	MS	F-ratio
Between Samples	1,745			
Within Samples		240		
Total	6,504	246		

a. How many different populations are being considered in this analysis?
b. Fill in the ANOVA table with the missing values.
c. State the appropriate null and alternative hypotheses.

d. Based on the analysis of variance *F*-test, what conclusion should be reached regarding the null hypothesis? Test using a significance level of 0.01.

12-5. Respond to each of the following questions using this partially completed one-way ANOVA table:

Source of Variation	SS	df	MS	F-ratio
Between Samples	483	3	161	11.13
Within Samples	405	28	14.46	
Total	888	31		

a. How many different populations are being considered in this analysis?
b. Fill in the ANOVA table with the missing values.
c. State the appropriate null and alternative hypotheses.
d. Based on the analysis of variance *F*-test, what conclusion should be reached regarding the null hypothesis? Test using $\alpha = 0.05$.

12-6. Given the following sample data

Item	Group 1	Group 2	Group 3	Group 4
1	20.9	28.2	17.8	21.2
2	27.2	26.2	15.9	23.9
3	26.6	21.6	18.4	19.5
4	22.1	29.7	20.2	17.4
5	25.3	30.3	14.1	
6	30.1	25.9		
7	23.8			

a. Based on the computations for the within- and between-sample variation, develop the ANOVA table and test the appropriate null hypothesis using $\alpha = 0.05$. Use the *p*-value approach.
b. If warranted, use the Tukey-Kramer procedure to determine which populations have different means. Use $\alpha = 0.05$.

12-7. Examine the three samples obtained independently from three populations:

Item	Group 1	Group 2	Group 3
1	14	17	17
2	13	16	14
3	12	16	15
4	15	18	16
5	16		14
6			16

a. Conduct a one-way analysis of variance on the data. Use alpha = 0.05.
b. If warranted, use the Tukey-Kramer procedure to determine which populations have different means. Use an experiment-wide error rate of 0.05.

Business **Applications**

12-8. In conjunction with the housing foreclosure crisis of 2009, many economists expressed increasing concern about the level of credit card debt and efforts of banks to raise interest rates on these cards. The banks claimed the increases were justified. A Senate subcommittee decided to determine if the average credit card balance depends on the type of credit card used. Under consideration are Visa, MasterCard, Discover, and American Express. The sample sizes to be used for each level are 25, 25, 26, and 23, respectively.

a. Describe the parameter of interest for this analysis.
b. Determine the factor associated with this experiment.
c. Describe the levels of the factor associated with this analysis.
d. State the number of degrees of freedom available for determining the between-samples variation.
e. State the number of degrees of freedom available for determining the within-samples variation.
f. State the number of degrees of freedom available for determining the total variation.

12-9. EverRun Incorporated produces treadmills for use in exercise clubs and recreation centers. EverRun assembles, sells, and services its treadmills, but it does not manufacture the treadmill motors. Rather, treadmill motors are purchased from an outside vendor. Currently, EverRun is considering which motor to include in its new ER1500 series. Three potential suppliers have been identified: Venetti, Madison, and Edison; however, only one supplier will be used. The motors produced by these three suppliers are identical in terms of noise and cost. Consequently, EverRun has decided to make its decision based on how long a motor operates at a high level of speed and incline before it fails. A random sample of 10 motors of each type is selected, and each motor is tested to determine how many minutes (rounded to the nearest minute) it operates before it needs to be repaired. The sample information for each motor is as follows:

Venetti	Madison	Edison
14,722	13,649	13,296
14,699	13,592	13,262
12,627	11,788	11,552
13,010	12,623	11,036
13,570	14,552	12,978
14,217	13,441	12,170
13,687	13,404	12,674
13,465	13,427	11,851
14,786	12,049	12,342
12,494	11,672	11,557

a. At the $\alpha = 0.01$ level of significance, is there a difference in the average time before failure for the three different suppliers' motors?
b. Is it possible for EverRun to decide on a single motor supplier based on the analysis of the sample results? Support your answer by conducting the appropriate post-test analysis.

12-10. Lanhu Cement Corporation is a leading North American cement producer, with more than 6.5 million metric tons of annual capacity. With headquarters in Nazareth, Pennsylvania, Lanhu operates production facilities strategically located throughout the United States, Canada, and Puerto Rico. One of its products is Portland cement. Portland cement's properties and performance standards are defined by its type designation. Each type is designated by a Roman numeral. Ninety-two percent of the Portland cement produced in North America is Type I, II, or I/II. One characteristic of the type of cement is its compressive strength. Sample data for the compressive strength (psi) are shown as follows:

Type	Compressive Strength			
I	4,972	4,983	4,889	5,063
II	3,216	3,399	3,267	3,357
I/II	4,073	3,949	3,936	3,925

a. Develop the appropriate ANOVA table to determine if there is a difference in the average compressive strength among the three types of Portland cement. Use a significance level of 0.01.
b. If warranted, use the Tukey-Kramer procedure to determine which populations have different mean compressive strengths. Use an experiment-wide error rate of 0.01.

12-11. The Weidmann Group Companies, with headquarters in Rapperswil, Switzerland, are worldwide leaders in insulation systems technology for power and distribution transformers. One facet of its expertise is the development of dielectric fluids in electrical equipment. Mineral oil–based dielectric fluids have been used more extensively than other dielectric fluids. Their only shortcomings are their relatively low flash and fire points. One study examined the fire point of mineral oil, high-molecular-weight hydrocarbon (HMWH), and silicone. The fire points for each of these fluids were as follows:

Fluid	Fire Points (°C)				
Mineral Oil	162	151	168	165	169
HMWH	312	310	300	311	308
Silicone	343	337	345	345	337

a. Develop the appropriate ANOVA table to determine if there is a difference in the average fire points among the types of dielectric fluids. Use a significance level of 0.05.
b. If warranted, use the Tukey-Kramer procedure to determine which populations have different mean fire points. Use an experiment-wide error rate of 0.05.

12-12. The manager at the Lawrence National Bank is interested in determining whether there is a difference in the mean time that customers spend completing their transactions depending on which of four tellers they use. To conduct the test, the manager has selected simple random samples of 15 customers for each

of the tellers and has timed them (in seconds) from the moment they start their transaction to the time the transaction is completed and they leave the teller station. The manager then asked one of her assistants to perform the appropriate statistical test. The assistant returned with the following partially completed ANOVA table.

Summary				
Groups	Count	Sum	Average	Variance
Teller 1	15	3,043.9		827.4
Teller 2	15	3,615.5		472.2
Teller 3	15	3,427.7		445.6
Teller 4	15	4,072.4		619.4

ANOVA						
Source of Variation	SS	df	MS	F-ratio	p-value	F-crit
Between Groups	36,530.6				0.0000	2.7694
Within Groups						
Total	69,633.7	59				

a. State the appropriate null and alternative hypotheses.
b. Fill in the missing parts of the ANOVA table and perform the statistical hypothesis test using $\alpha = 0.05$.
c. Based on the result of the test in part c, if warranted, use the Tukey-Kramer method with $\alpha = 0.05$ to determine which teller require the most time on average to complete a customer's transaction.

12-13. Suppose as part of your job you are responsible for installing emergency lighting in a series of state office buildings. Bids have been received from four manufacturers of battery-operated emergency lights. The costs are about equal, so the decision will be based on the length of time the lights last before failing. A sample of four lights from each manufacturer has been tested with the following values (time in hours) recorded for each manufacturer:

Type A	Type B	Type C	Type D
1,024	1,270	1,121	923
1,121	1,325	1,201	983
1,250	1,426	1,190	1,087
1,022	1,322	1,122	1,121

a. Using a significance level equal to 0.01, what conclusion should you reach about the four manufacturers' battery-operated emergency lights? Explain.
b. If the test conducted in part a reveals that the null hypothesis should be rejected, what manufacturer should be used to supply the lights? Can you eliminate one or more manufacturers based on these

data? Use the appropriate test and $\alpha = 0.01$ for multiple comparisons. Discuss.

Computer Database **Exercises**

12-14. Damage to homes caused by burst piping can be expensive to repair. By the time the leak is discovered, hundreds of gallons of water may have already flooded the home. Automatic shutoff valves can prevent extensive water damage from plumbing failures. The valves contain sensors that cut off water flow in the event of a leak, thereby preventing flooding. One important characteristic is the time (in milliseconds) required for the sensor to detect the water leak. Sample data obtained for four different shutoff valves are contained in the file titled **Waterflow**.

   a. Produce the relevant ANOVA table and conduct a hypothesis test to determine if the mean detection time differs among the four shutoff valve models. Use a significance level of 0.05.

   b. Use the Tukey-Kramer multiple comparison technique to discover any differences in the average detection time. Use a significance level of 0.05.

   c. Which of the four shutoff valves would you recommend? State your criterion for your selection.

12-15. A regional package delivery company is considering changing from full-size vans to minivans. The company sampled minivans from each of three manufacturers. The number sampled represents the number the manufacturer was able to provide for the test. Each minivan was driven for 5,000 miles, and the operating cost per mile was computed. The operating costs, in cents per mile, for the 12 are provided in the data file called **Delivery**:

Mini 1	Mini 2	Mini 3
13.3	12.4	13.9
14.3	13.4	15.5
13.6	13.1	15.2
12.8		14.5
14.0		

   a. Perform an analysis of variance on these data. Assume a significance level of 0.05. Do the experimental data provide evidence that the average operating costs per mile for the three types of minivans are different? Use a *p*-value approach.

   b. Referring to part a, based on the sample data and the appropriate test for multiple comparisons, what conclusions should be reached concerning which type of car the delivery company should adopt? Discuss and prepare a report to the company CEO. Use $\alpha = 0.05$.

   c. Provide an estimate of the maximum and minimum difference in average savings per year if the CEO chooses the "best" versus the "worst" minivan using operating costs as a criterion. Assume that minivans are driven 30,000 miles a year. Use a 90% confidence interval.

12-16. The Lottaburger restaurant chain in central New Mexico is conducting an analysis of its restaurants, which take pride in serving burgers and fries to go faster than the competition. As a part of its analysis, Lottaburger wants to determine if its speed of service is different across its four outlets. Orders at Lottaburger restaurants are tracked electronically, and the chain is able to determine the speed with which every order is filled. The chain decided to randomly sample 20 orders from each of the four restaurants it operates. The speed of service for each randomly sampled order was noted and is contained in the file **Lottaburger**.

   a. At the $\alpha = 0.05$ level of service, can Lottaburger conclude that the speed of service is different across the four restaurants in the chain?

   b. If the chain concludes that there is a difference in speed of service, is there a particular restaurant the chain should focus its attention on? Use the appropriate test for multiple comparisons to support your decision. Use $\alpha = 0.05$.

12-17. Most auto batteries are made by just three manufacturers—Delphi, Exide, and Johnson Controls Industries. Each makes batteries sold under several different brand names. Delphi makes ACDelco and some EverStart (Walmart) models. Exide makes Champion, Exide, Napa, and some EverStart batteries. Johnson Controls makes Diehard (Sears), Duralast (AutoZone), Interstate, Kirkland (Costco), Motorcraft (Ford), and some EverStarts. To determine if who makes the auto batteries affects the average length of life of the battery, the samples in the file titled **Start** were obtained. The data represent the length of life (months) for batteries of the same specifications for each of the three manufacturers.

   a. Determine if the average length of battery life is different among the batteries produced by the three manufacturers. Use a significance level of 0.05.

   b. Which manufacturer produces the battery with the longest average length of life? If warranted, conduct the Tukey-Kramer procedure to determine this. Use a significance level of 0.05. (*Note:* You will need to manipulate the data columns to obtain the appropriate factor levels).

END EXERCISES 12-1

Chapter Outcome 4. → # 12.2 Randomized Complete Block Analysis of Variance

Section 12.1 introduced one-way ANOVA for testing hypotheses involving three or more population means. This ANOVA method is appropriate as long as we are interested in analyzing one factor at a time and we select independent random samples from the populations. For instance, Example 12-2 involving brake assembly systems at the Digitron Corporation (Figure 12.6) illustrated a situation in which we were interested in only one factor: type of brake assembly system. The measurement of interest was the stopping distance with each brake system. To test the hypothesis that the four brake systems were equal with respect to average stopping distance, four groups of the same make and model cars were assigned to each brake system independently. Thus, the one-way ANOVA design was appropriate.

There are, however, situations in which another factor may affect the observed response in a one-way design. Often, this additional factor is unknown. This is the reason for randomization within the experiment. However, there are also situations in which we know the factor that is impinging on the response variable of interest. Chapter 10 introduced the concept of paired samples and indicated that there are instances when you will want to test for differences in two population means by controlling for sources of variation that might adversely affect the analysis. For instance, in the Digitron example, we might be concerned that, even though we used the same make and model of car in the study, the cars themselves may interject a source of variability that could affect the result. To control for this, we could use the concept of *paired samples* by using the same 10 cars for each of the four brake systems. When an additional factor with two or more levels is involved, a design technique called *blocking* can be used to eliminate the additional factor's effect on the statistical analysis of the main factor of interest.

Randomized Complete Block ANOVA

BUSINESS APPLICATION **A RANDOMIZED BLOCK DESIGN**

Excel Tutorial

CITIZEN'S STATE BANK At Citizen's State Bank, homeowners can borrow money against the equity they have in their homes. To determine equity, the bank determines the home's value and subtracts the mortgage balance. The maximum loan is 90% of the equity.

The bank outsources the home appraisals to three companies: Allen & Associates, Heist Appraisal, and Appraisal International. The bank managers know that appraisals are not exact. Some appraisal companies may overvalue homes on average, whereas others might undervalue homes.

Bank managers wish to test the hypothesis that there is no difference in the average house appraisal among the three different companies. The managers could select a random sample of homes for Allen & Associates to appraise, a second sample of homes for Heist Appraisal to work on, and a third sample of homes for Appraisal International. One-way ANOVA would be used to compare the sample means. Obviously a problem could occur if, by chance, one company received larger, higher-quality homes located in better neighborhoods than the other companies. This company's appraisals would naturally be higher on average, not because it tended to appraise higher, but because the homes were simply more expensive.

Citizen's State Bank officers need to control for the variation in size, quality, and location of homes to fairly test that the three companies' appraisals are equal on the average. To do this, they select a random sample of properties and have each company appraise the same properties. In this case, the properties are called *blocks*, and the test design is called a *randomized complete block design*.

The data in Table 12.5 were obtained when each appraisal company was asked to appraise the same five properties. The bank managers wish to test the following hypothesis:

$$H_0: \mu_1 = \mu_2 = \mu_3$$

H_A: At least two populations have different means

The randomized block design requires the following assumptions:

Assumptions

1. The populations are normally distributed.
2. The populations have equal variances.
3. The observations within samples are independent.
4. The data measurement must be interval or ratio level.

TABLE 12.5 | **Citizen's State Bank Property Appraisals (in thousands of dollars)**

Property (Block)	Appraisal Company			
	Allen & Associates	Heist Appraisal	Appraisal International	Block Mean
1	78	82	79	79.67
2	102	102	99	101.00
3	68	74	70	70.67
4	83	88	86	85.67
5	95	99	92	95.33
Factor-Level Mean	$\bar{x}_1 = 85.2$	$\bar{x}_2 = 89$	$\bar{x}_3 = 85.2$	$\bar{\bar{x}} = 86.47 =$ Grand mean

Because the managers have chosen to have the same properties appraised by each company (block on property), the samples are not independent, and a method known as *randomized complete block ANOVA* must be employed to test the hypothesis. This method is similar to the one-way ANOVA in Section 12.1. However, there is one more source of variation to be accounted for: the block variation. As was the case in Section 12.1, we must find estimators for each source of variation. Identifying the appropriate sums of squares and then dividing each by its degrees of freedom does this. As was the case in the one-way ANOVA, the sums of squares are obtained by partitioning the total sum of squares (*SST*). However, in this case the *SST* is divided into three components instead of two, as shown in Equation 12.7.

Sum of Squares Partitioning for Randomized Complete Block Design

$$SST = SSB + SSBL + SSW \qquad (12.7)$$

where:

$$SST = \text{Total sum of squares}$$
$$SSB = \text{Sum of squares between factor levels}$$
$$SSBL = \text{Sum of squares between blocks}$$
$$SSW = \text{Sum of squares within levels}$$

Both *SST* and *SSB* are computed just as we did with one-way ANOVA, using Equations 12.2 and 12.3. The *sum of squares for blocking (SSBL)* is computed using Equation 12.8.

Sum of Squares for Blocking

$$SSBL = \sum_{j=1}^{b} k(\bar{x}_j - \bar{\bar{x}})^2 \qquad (12.8)$$

where:

$$k = \text{Number of levels for the factor}$$
$$b = \text{Number of blocks}$$
$$\bar{x}_j = \text{The mean of the } j\text{th block}$$
$$\bar{\bar{x}} = \text{Grand mean}$$

Finally, the *sum of squares within (SSW)* is computed using Equation 12.9. This sum of squares is what remains (the residual) after the variation for all known factors has been removed. This residual sum of squares may be due to the inherent variability of the data, measurement error, or other unidentified sources of variation. Therefore, the sum of squares within is also known as the sum of squares error, *SSE*.

Sum of Squares Within	
$$SSW = SST - (SSB + SSBL)$$	**(12.9)**

The effect of computing $SSBL$ and subtracting it from SST in Equation 12.9 is that SSW is reduced. Also, if the corresponding variation in the blocks is significant, the variation within the factor levels will be significantly reduced. This can make it easier to detect a difference in the population means if such a difference actually exists. If it does, the estimator for the within variability will in all likelihood be reduced, and thus, the denominator for the F-test statistic will be smaller. This will produce a larger F-test statistic, which will more likely lead to rejecting the null hypothesis. This will depend, of course, on the relative size of $SSBL$ and the respective changes in the degrees of freedom.

Table 12.6 shows the completely randomized block ANOVA table format and equations for degrees of freedom, mean squares, and F-ratios. As you can see, we now have two F-ratios. The reason for this is that we test not only to determine whether the population means are equal but also to obtain an indication of whether the blocking was necessary by examining the ratio of the mean square for blocks to the mean square within.

Although you could manually compute the necessary values for the randomized block design, Excel has a procedure that will do all the computations and build the ANOVA table. The Citizen's State Bank appraisal data are included in the file **Citizens**. (Note that the first column contains labels for each block.)

Figures 12.7 shows the ANOVA output. Using Excel to perform the computations frees the decision maker to focus on interpreting the results. Note that Excel refers to the randomized block ANOVA as Two-Factor ANOVA without replication.

The main issue is to determine whether the three appraisal companies differ in average appraisal values. The primary test is

$$H_0: \mu_1 = \mu_2 = \mu_3$$
H_A: At least two populations have different means
$$\alpha = 0.05$$

Using the output presented in Figure 12.7, you can test this hypothesis two ways. First, we can use the F-distribution approach. Figure 12.8 shows the results of this test. Based on the

TABLE 12.6 | **Basic Format for the Randomized Block ANOVA Table**

Source of Variation	SS	df	MS	F-ratio
Between blocks	$SSBL$	$b-1$	$MSBL$	$\dfrac{MSBL}{MSW}$
Between samples	SSB	$k-1$	MSB	$\dfrac{MSB}{MSW}$
Within samples	SSW	$(k-1)(b-1)$	MSW	
Total	SST	n_T-1		

where:
$$k = \text{Number of levels}$$
$$b = \text{Number of blocks}$$
$$df = \text{Degrees of freedom}$$
$$n_T = \text{Combined sample size}$$
$$MSBL = \text{Mean square blocking} = \frac{SSBL}{b-1}$$
$$MSB = \text{Mean square between} = \frac{SSB}{k-1}$$
$$MSW = \text{Mean square within} = \frac{SSW}{(k-1)(b-1)}$$

Note: Some randomized block ANOVA tables put SSB first, followed by $SSBL$.

FIGURE 12.7

Excel 2010 Output: Citizen's State Bank Analysis of Variance

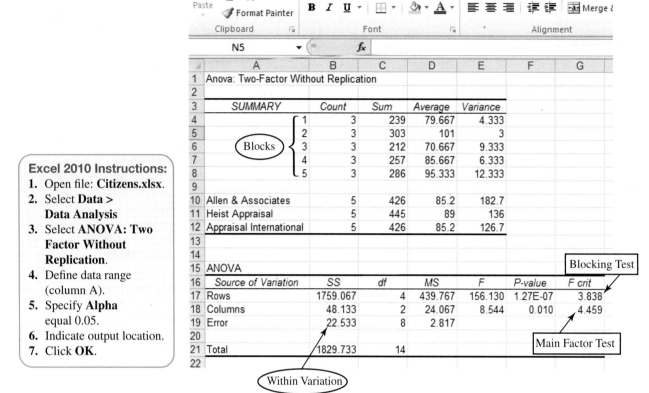

Excel 2010 Instructions:
1. Open file: **Citizens.xlsx**.
2. Select **Data > Data Analysis**
3. Select **ANOVA: Two Factor Without Replication**.
4. Define data range (column A).
5. Specify **Alpha** equal 0.05.
6. Indicate output location.
7. Click **OK**.

Minitab Instructions (for similar results):
1. Open file: **Citizens.MTW**.
2. Choose **Stat > ANOVA > Two-way**.
3. In Response, enter the data column (*Appraisal*).
4. In **Row Factor**, enter main factor indicator column (*Company*) and select **Display Means**.
5. In **Column Factor**, enter the block indicator column (*Property*) and select **Display Means**.
6. Choose **Fit additive model**.
7. Click **OK**.

FIGURE 12.8

Appraisal Company Hypothesis Test for Citizen's State Bank

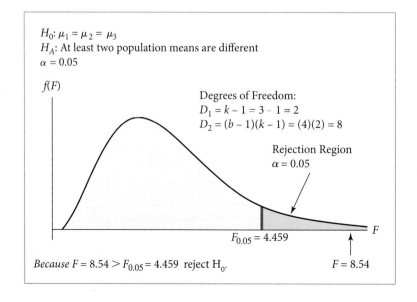

$H_0: \mu_1 = \mu_2 = \mu_3$
H_A: At least two population means are different
$\alpha = 0.05$

$f(F)$

Degrees of Freedom:
$D_1 = k - 1 = 3 - 1 = 2$
$D_2 = (b - 1)(k - 1) = (4)(2) = 8$

Rejection Region
$\alpha = 0.05$

$F_{0.05} = 4.459$

$F = 8.54$

Because $F = 8.54 > F_{0.05} = 4.459$ reject H_0.

sample data, we reject the null hypothesis and conclude that the three appraisal companies do not provide equal average values for properties.

The second approach to testing the null hypothesis is the p-value approach. The decision rule in an ANOVA application for p-values is

$$\text{If } p\text{-value } < \alpha \text{ reject } H_0; \text{ otherwise, do not reject } H_0.$$

In this case, $\alpha = 0.05$ and the p-value in Figure 12.7 is 0.010. Because p-value $= 0.010 < \alpha = 0.05$ we reject the null hypothesis.

Both the F-distribution approach and the p-value approach give the same result, as they must.

Was Blocking Necessary? Before we take up the issue of determining which company provides the highest mean property values, we need to discuss one other issue. Recall that the bank managers chose to control for variation between properties by having each appraisal company evaluate the same five properties. This restriction is called blocking, and the properties are the blocks. The ANOVA output in Figure 12.7 contains information that allows us to test whether blocking was necessary.

If blocking was necessary, it would mean that appraisal values are in fact influenced by the particular property being appraised. The blocks then form a second factor of interest, and we formulate a secondary hypothesis test for this factor, as follows:

$$H_0: \mu_{b1} = \mu_{b2} = \mu_{b3} = \mu_{b4} = \mu_{b5}$$
$$H_A: \text{Not all block means are equal}$$

Note that we are using μ_{bj} to represent the mean of the jth block.

It seems only natural to use a test statistic that consists of the ratio of the mean square for blocks to the mean square within. However, certain (randomization) restrictions placed on the complete block design make this proposed test statistic invalid from a theoretical statistics point of view. As an approximate procedure, however, the examination of the ratio $MSBL/MSW$ is certainly reasonable. If it is large, it implies that the blocks had a large effect on the response variable and that they were probably helpful in improving the precision of the F-test for the primary factor's means.[7] In performing the analysis of variance, we may also conduct a pseudo test to see whether the average appraisals for each property are equal. If the null hypothesis is rejected, we have an indication that the blocking is necessary and that the randomized block design is justified. However, we should be careful to present this only as an indication and not as a precise test of hypothesis for the blocks. The output in Figure 12.7 provides the F-value and p-value for this pseudo test to determine if the blocking was a necessity. Because $F = 156.13 > F_{0.05} = 3.838$, we definitely have an indication that the blocking design was necessary.

If a hypothesis test indicates blocking is not necessary, the chance of a Type II error for the primary hypothesis has been unnecessarily increased by the use of blocking. The reason is that by blocking, we not only partition the sum of squares, we also partition the degrees of freedom. Therefore, the denominator of MSW is decreased, and MSW will most likely increase. If blocking isn't needed, the MSW will tend to be relatively larger than if we had run a one-way design with independent samples. This can lead to failing to reject the null hypothesis for the primary test when it actually should have been rejected.

Therefore, if blocking is indicated to be unnecessary, follow these rules:

1. If the primary H_0 is rejected, proceed with your analysis and decision making. There is no concern.
2. If the primary H_0 is not rejected, redo the study without using blocking. Run a one-way ANOVA with independent samples.

---

[7]Many authors argue that the randomization restriction imposed by using blocks means that the F-ratio really is a test for the equality of the block means plus the randomization restriction. For a summary of this argument and references, see D. C. Montgomery, *Design and Analysis of Experiments*, 4th ed. (New York City: John Wiley & Sons, 1997), pp. 175–176.

Chapter Outcome 4. ⟶ | **EXAMPLE 12-3**   **PERFORMING A RANDOMIZED BLOCK ANALYSIS OF VARIANCE** |

Online Course Exams A business statistics professor at a Philadelphia, Pennsylvania, university has developed an online course for business statistics that is available through the school's Division of Extended Studies. To reduce the possibility of students sharing exam questions with one another, the professor has developed three different midterm exams that are to be graded on a 1,000 point scale. However, before she uses the exams in a live class, she wants to determine if the tests will yield the same mean scores. To test this, a random sample of fourteen people who have been through the course material covered in the course prior to midterms is selected. Each student will take each test. The order in which the tests are taken is randomized and the scores are recorded. A randomized block analysis of variance test can be performed using the following steps:

Step 1 **Specify the parameter of interest and formulate the appropriate null and alternative hypotheses.**

The parameter of interest is the mean test score for the three different exams, and the question is whether there is a difference among the mean scores for the three. The appropriate null and alternative hypotheses are

$$H_0: \mu_1 = \mu_2 = \mu_3$$
$$H_A: \text{At least two populations have different means}$$

In this case, the professor wants to control for variation in student ability by having the same students take all three tests. The test scores will be independent because the scores achieved by one student do not influence the scores achieved by other students. Here, the students are the blocks.

Step 2 **Specify the level of significance for conducting the tests.**

The tests will be conducted using $\alpha = 0.05$.

Step 3 **Select simple random samples from each population, and compute treatment means, block means, and the grand mean.**

The following sample data were observed:

Student	Exam 1	Exam 2	Exam 3	Block Means
1	830	647	630	702.33
2	743	840	786	789.67
3	652	747	730	709.67
4	885	639	617	713.67
5	814	943	632	796.33
6	733	916	410	686.33
7	770	923	727	806.67
8	829	903	726	819.33
9	847	760	648	751.67
10	878	856	668	800.67
11	728	878	670	758.67
12	693	990	825	836.00
13	807	871	564	747.33
14	901	980	719	866.67
Treatment means	793.57	849.50	668.00	770.36 = Grand mean

Step 4 **Compute the sums of squares and complete the ANOVA table.**

Four sums of squares are required:

Total Sum of Squares (Equation 12.2)

$$SST = \sum_{i=1}^{k}\sum_{j=1}^{n_i}(x_{ij} - \bar{\bar{x}})^2 = 614{,}641.6$$

Sum of Squares Between (Equation 12.3)

$$SSB = \sum_{i=1}^{k} n_i(\bar{x}_i - \bar{\bar{x}})^2 = 241{,}912.7$$

Sum of Squares Blocking (Equation 12.8)

$$SSBL = \sum_{j=1}^{b} k(\bar{x}_j - \bar{\bar{x}})^2 = 116{,}605.0$$

Sum of Squares Within (Equation 12.9)

$$SSW = SST - (SSB + SSBL) = 256{,}123.9$$

The ANOVA table is (see Table 12.6 format)

Source	SS	df	MS	F-Ratio
Between blocks	116,605.0	13	8,969.6	0.9105
Between samples	241,912.7	2	120,956.4	12.2787
Within samples	256,123.9	26	9,850.9	
Total	614,641.6	41		

Step 5 **Test to determine whether blocking is effective.**
Fourteen people were used to evaluate the three tests. These people constitute the blocks, so if blocking is effective, the mean test scores across the three tests will not be the same for all 14 students. The null and alternative hypotheses are

$$H_0: \mu_{b1} = \mu_{b2} = \mu_{b3} = \cdots = \mu_{b14}$$
$$H_A: \text{Not all means are equal (blocking is effective)}$$

As shown in Step 3, the F-test statistic to test this null hypothesis is formed by

$$F = \frac{MSBL}{MSW} = \frac{8{,}969.6}{9{,}850.9} = 0.9105$$

The F-critical from the F-distribution, with $\alpha = 0.05$ and $D_1 = 13$ and $D_2 = 26$ degrees of freedom, can be approximated using the F-distribution table in Appendix H as

$$F_{\alpha=0.05} \approx 2.15$$

The exact F-critical can be found using the F.INV.RT function in Excel as $F_{0.05} = 2.119$. Then, because

$$F = 0.9105 < F_{\alpha=0.05} = 2.119, \text{ do not reject the null hypothesis.}$$

This means that based on these sample data we cannot conclude that blocking was effective.

Step 6 **Conduct the main hypothesis test to determine whether the populations have equal means.**
We have three different statistics exams being considered. At issue is whether the mean score is equal for the three exams. The appropriate null and alternative hypotheses are

$$H_0: \mu_1 = \mu_2 = \mu_3$$
$$H_A: \text{At least two populations have different means}$$

As shown in the ANOVA table in Step 3, the F-test statistic for this null hypothesis is formed by

$$F = \frac{MSB}{MSW} = \frac{120{,}956.4}{9{,}850.9} = 12.2787$$

The F-critical from the F-distribution, with $\alpha = 0.05$ and $D_1 = 2$ and $D_2 = 26$ degrees of freedom, can be approximated using the F-distribution table in Appendix H as

$$F_{\alpha=0.05} \approx 3.40$$

The exact F-critical can be found using the F.INV.RT function in Excel as $F = 3.369$. Then, because

$$F = 12.2787 > F_{\alpha=0.05} = 3.369,\ \text{reject the null hypothesis.}$$

Even though in Step 5 we concluded that blocking was not effective, the sample data still lead us to reject the primary null hypothesis and conclude that the three tests do not all have the same mean score. The professor will now be interested in looking into the issue in more detail to determine which tests yield higher or lower average scores.

>> **END EXAMPLE**

TRY PROBLEM 12-21 (pg. 492)

Chapter Outcome 3. → # Fisher's Least Significant Difference Test

An analysis of variance test can be used to test whether the populations of interest have different means. However, even if the null hypothesis of equal population means is rejected, the ANOVA does not specify which population means are different. In Section 12.1, we showed how the Tukey-Kramer multiple comparisons procedure is used to determine where the population differences occur for a one-way ANOVA design. Likewise, *Fisher's least significant difference test* is one test for multiple comparisons that we can use for a randomized block ANOVA design.

If the primary null hypothesis has been rejected, then we can compare the absolute differences in sample means from any two populations to the *least significant difference (LSD)*, as computed using Equation 12.10.

Fisher's Least Significant Difference

$$LSD = t_{\alpha/2}\sqrt{MSW}\sqrt{\frac{2}{b}} \tag{12.10}$$

where:

$$t_{\alpha/2} = \text{One-tailed value from Student's } t\text{-distribution for } \alpha/2$$
$$\text{and } (k-1)(b-1) \text{ degrees of freedom}$$
$$MSW = \text{Mean square within from ANOVA table}$$
$$b = \text{Number of blocks}$$
$$k = \text{Number of levels of the main factor}$$

EXAMPLE 12-4   **APPLYING FISHER'S LEAST SIGNIFICANT DIFFERENCE TEST**

Online Course Exams (*Continued*) Recall that in Example 12-3, the business statistics professor used a randomized block ANOVA design to conclude that the midterm exams do not all have the same mean test score. To determine which populations (tests) have different means, you can use the following steps:

Step 1 **Compute the *LSD* statistic using Equation 12.10.**

$$LSD = t_{\alpha/2}\sqrt{MSW}\sqrt{\frac{2}{b}}$$

Using a significance level equal to 0.05, the t-critical value for $(3 - 1)(14 - 1) = 26$ degrees of freedom is

$$t_{0.05/2} = 2.0555$$

The mean square within from the ANOVA table (see Example 12-3, Step 3) is

$$MSW = 9,850.9$$

The LSD is

$$LSD = t_{\alpha/2}\sqrt{MSW}\sqrt{\frac{2}{b}} = 2.0555\sqrt{9,850.9}\sqrt{\frac{2}{14}} = 77.11$$

Step 2 Compute the sample means from each population.

$$\bar{x}_1 = \frac{\sum x}{n} = 793.57 \qquad \bar{x}_2 = \frac{\sum x}{n} = 849.50 \qquad \bar{x}_3 = \frac{\sum x}{n} = 668$$

Step 3 Form all possible contrasts by finding the absolute differences between all pairs of sample means. Compare these to the LSD value.

Absolute Difference	Comparison	Significant Difference
$\|\bar{x}_1 - \bar{x}_2\| = \|793.57 - 849.50\| = 55.93$	$55.93 < 77.11$	No
$\|\bar{x}_1 - \bar{x}_3\| = \|793.57 - 668\| = 125.57$	$125.57 > 77.11$	Yes
$\|\bar{x}_2 - \bar{x}_3\| = \|849.50 - 668\| = 181.50$	$181.50 > 77.11$	Yes

We infer, based on the sample data, that the mean score for test 1 exceeds the mean for test 3, and the mean for test 2 exceeds the mean for test 3. Now the professor may wish to evaluate test 3 to see why the scores are lower than for the other two tests. No difference is detected between tests 1 and 2.

>> **END EXAMPLE**

TRY PROBLEM 12-22 (pg. 492)

MyStatLab

12-2: **Exercises**

Skill **Development**

12-18. A study was conducted to determine if differences in new textbook prices exist between on-campus bookstores, off-campus bookstores, and Internet bookstores. To control for differences in textbook prices that might exist across disciplines, the study randomly selected 12 textbooks and recorded the price of each of the 12 books at each of the three retailers. You may assume normality and equal-variance assumptions have been met. The partially completed ANOVA table based on the study's findings is shown here:

ANOVA				
Source of Variation	**SS**	**df**	**MS**	**F**
Textbooks	16,624			
Retailer	2.4			
Error				
Total	17,477.6			

a. Complete the ANOVA table by filling in the missing sums of squares, the degrees of freedom for each source, the mean square, and the calculated F-test statistic for each possible hypothesis test.

b. Based on the study's findings, was it correct to block for differences in textbooks? Conduct the appropriate test at the $\alpha = 0.10$ level of significance.

c. Based on the study's findings, can it be concluded that there is a difference in the average price of textbooks across the three retail outlets? Conduct the appropriate hypothesis test at the $\alpha = 0.10$ level of significance.

12-19. The following data were collected for a randomized block analysis of variance design with four populations and eight blocks:

	Group 1	Group 2	Group 3	Group 4
Block 1	56	44	57	84
Block 2	34	30	38	50
Block 3	50	41	48	52

	Group 1	Group 2	Group 3	Group 4
Block 4	19	17	21	30
Block 5	33	30	35	38
Block 6	74	72	78	79
Block 7	33	24	27	33
Block 8	56	44	56	71

a. State the appropriate null and alternative hypotheses for the treatments and determine whether blocking is necessary.
b. Construct the appropriate ANOVA table.
c. Using a significance level equal to 0.05, can you conclude that blocking was necessary in this case? Use a test-statistic approach.
d. Based on the data and a significance level equal to 0.05, is there a difference in population means for the four groups? Use a p-value approach.
e. If you found that a difference exists in part d, use the *LSD* approach to determine which populations have different means.

12-20. The following ANOVA table and accompanying information are the result of a randomized block ANOVA test.

Summary	Count	Sum	Average	Variance
1	4	443	110.8	468.9
2	4	275	68.8	72.9
3	4	1,030	257.5	1891.7
4	4	300	75.0	433.3
5	4	603	150.8	468.9
6	4	435	108.8	72.9
7	4	1,190	297.5	1891.7
8	4	460	115.0	433.3
Sample 1	8	1,120	140.0	7142.9
Sample 2	8	1,236	154.5	8866.6
Sample 3	8	1,400	175.0	9000.0
Sample 4	8	980	122.5	4307.1

ANOVA

Source of Variation	SS	df	MS	F	p-value	F-crit
Rows	199,899	7	28557.0	112.8	0.0000	2.488
Columns	11,884	3	3961.3	15.7	0.0000	3.073
Error	5,317	21	253.2			
Total	217,100	31				

a. How many blocks were used in this study?
b. How many populations are involved in this test?
c. Test to determine whether blocking is effective using an alpha level equal to 0.05.
d. Test the main hypothesis of interest using $\alpha = 0.05$.
e. If warranted, conduct an *LSD* test with $\alpha = 0.05$ to determine which population means are different.

12-21. The following sample data were recently collected in the course of conducting a randomized block analysis of variance. Based on these sample data,

what conclusions should be reached about blocking effectiveness and about the means of the three populations involved? Test using a significance level equal to 0.05.

Block	Sample 1	Sample 2	Sample 3
1	30	40	40
2	50	70	50
3	60	40	70
4	40	40	30
5	80	70	90
6	20	10	10

12-22. A randomized complete block design is carried out, resulting in the following statistics:

Source	$\bar{x}_1$	$\bar{x}_2$	$\bar{x}_3$	$\bar{x}_4$
Primary Factor	237.15	315.15	414.01	612.52
Block	363.57	382.22	438.33	
$SST = 364{,}428$				

a. Determine if blocking was effective for this design.
b. Using a significance level of 0.05, produce the relevant ANOVA and determine if the average responses of the factor levels are equal to each other.
c. If you discovered that there were differences among the average responses of the factor levels, use the *LSD* approach to determine which populations have different means.

Business **Applications**

12-23. The Goodson Company manufactures four different products that it ships to customers throughout Canada. Delivery times are not a driving factor in the decision as to which type of carrier to use (rail, plane, or truck) to deliver the product. However, breakage cost is very expensive, and Goodson would like to select a mode of delivery that reduces the amount of product breakage. To help it reach a decision, the managers have decided to examine the dollar amount of breakage incurred by the three alternative modes of transportation under consideration. Because each product's fragility is different, the executives conducting the study wish to control for differences due to type of product. The company randomly assigns each product to each carrier and monitors the dollar breakage that occurs over the course of 100 shipments. The dollar breakage per shipment (to the nearest dollar) is as follows:

	Rail	Plane	Truck
Product 1	$7,960	$8,053	$8,818
Product 2	$8,399	$7,764	$9,432
Product 3	$9,429	$9,196	$9,260
Product 4	$6,022	$5,821	$5,676

a. Was the Goodson Company correct in its decision to block for type of product? Conduct the appropriate hypothesis test using a level of significance of 0.01.

b. Is there a difference due to carrier type? Conduct the appropriate hypothesis test using a level of significance of 0.01.

12-24. The California Lettuce Research Board was originally formed as the Iceberg Lettuce Advisory Board in 1973. The primary function of the board is to fund research on iceberg and leaf lettuce. The California Lettuce Research Board published research (M. Cahn and H. Ajwa, "Salinity Effects on Quality and Yield of Drip Irrigated Lettuce") concerning the effect of varying levels of sodium absorption ratios (SAR) on the yield of head lettuce. The trials followed a randomized complete block design where variety of lettuce (Salinas and Sniper) was the main factor and salinity levels were the blocks. The measurements (the number of lettuce heads from each plot) of the kind observed were

SAR	Salinas	Sniper
3	104	109
5	160	163
7	142	146
10	133	156

a. Determine if blocking was effective for this design.
b. Using a significance level of 0.05, produce the relevant ANOVA and determine if the average number of lettuce heads among the SARs are equal to each other.
c. If you discovered that there were differences among the average number of lettuce heads among the SARs, use the *LSD* approach to determine which populations have different means.

12-25. D&G Industries operates three shifts every day of the week. Each shift includes full-time hourly workers, nonsupervisory salaried employees, and supervisors/ managers. D&G Industries would like to know if there is a difference among the shifts in terms of the number of hours of work missed due to employee illness. To control for differences that might exist across employee groups, D&G Industries randomly selects one employee from each employee group and shift and records the number of hours missed for one year. The results of the study are shown here:

	Shift 1	Shift 2	Shift 3
Hourly	48	54	60
Nonsupervisory	31	36	55
Supervisors/Managers	25	33	40

a. Develop the appropriate test to determine whether blocking is effective or not. Conduct the test at the $\alpha = 0.05$ level of significance.
b. Develop the appropriate test to determine whether there are differences in the average number of hours missed due to illness across the three shifts. Conduct the test at the $\alpha = 0.05$ level of significance.

c. If it is determined that a difference in the average hours of work missed due to illness is not the same for the three shifts, use the *LSD* approach to determine which shifts have different means.

12-26. Grant Thornton LLP is the U.S. member firm of Grant Thornton International, one of the six global accounting, tax, and business advisory organizations. It provides firm-wide auditing training for its employees in three different auditing methods. Auditors were grouped into four blocks according to the education they had received: (1) high school, (2) bachelor's, (3) master's, and (4) doctorate. Three auditors at each education level were used—one assigned to each method. They were given a post training examination consisting of complicated auditing scenarios. The scores for the 12 auditors were as follows:

	Method 1	Method 2	Method 3
Doctorate	83	81	82
Master's	77	75	79
Bachelor's	74	73	75
High School	72	70	69

a. Indicate why blocking was employed in this design.
b. Determine if blocking was effective for this design by producing the relevant ANOVA.
c. Using a significance level of 0.05, determine if the average post training examination scores among the auditing methods are equal to each other.
d. If you discovered that there were differences among the average post training examination scores among the auditing methods, use the *LSD* approach to determine which populations have different means.

Computer Database **Exercises**

12-27. Applebee's International, Inc., is a U.S. company that develops, franchises, and operates the Applebee's Neighborhood Grill and Bar restaurant chain. It is the largest chain of casual dining restaurants in the country, with more than 1,500 restaurants across the United States. The headquarters is located in Overland Park, Kansas. The company is interested in determining if mean weekly revenue differs among three restaurants in a particular city. The file titled **Applebees** contains revenue data for a sample of weeks for each of the three locations.
a. Test to determine if blocking the week on which the testing was done was necessary. Use a significance level of 0.05.
b. Based on the data gathered by Applebee's, can it be concluded that there is a difference in the average revenue among the three restaurants?
c. If you did conclude that there was a difference in the average revenue, use Fisher's *LSD* approach to determine which restaurant has the lowest mean sales.

12-28. In a local community, there are three grocery chain stores. The three have been carrying out a spirited advertising campaign in which each claims to have the lowest prices. A local news station recently sent a reporter to the three stores to check prices on several items. She found that for certain, items each store had the lowest price. This survey didn't really answer the question for consumers. Thus, the station set up a test in which 20 shoppers were given a list of grocery items and were sent to each of the three chain stores. The sales receipts from each of the three stores are recorded in the data file **Groceries**.

a. Why should this price test be conducted using the design that the television station used? What was it attempting to achieve by having the same shopping lists used at each of the three grocery stores?

b. Based on a significance level of 0.05 and these sample data, test to determine whether blocking was necessary in this example. State the null and alternative hypotheses. Use a test-statistic approach.

c. Based on these sample data, can you conclude the three grocery stores have different sample means? Test using a significance level of 0.05. State the appropriate null and alternative hypotheses. Use a *p*-value approach.

d. Based on the sample data, which store has the highest average prices? Use Fisher's *LSD* test if appropriate.

12-29. The Cordage Institute, based in Wayne, Pennsylvania, is an international association of manufacturers, producers, and resellers of cordage, rope, and twine. It is a not-for-profit corporation that reports on research concerning these products. Although natural fibers like manila, sisal, and cotton were once the predominant rope materials, industrial synthetic fibers dominate the marketplace today, with most ropes made of nylon, polyester, or polypropylene. One of the principal traits of rope material is its breaking strength. A research project generated data given in the file titled **Knots**. The data listed were gathered on 10 different days from $\frac{1}{2}''$-diameter ropes.

a. Test to determine if inserting the day on which the testing was done was necessary. Use a significance level of 0.05.

b. Based on the data gathered by the Cordage Institute, can it be concluded that there is a difference in the average breaking strength of nylon, polyester, and polypropylene?

c. If you concluded that there was a difference in the average breaking strength of the rope material, use Fisher's *LSD* approach to determine which material has the highest breaking strength.

12-30. When the world's largest retailer, Walmart, decided to enter the grocery marketplace in a big way with its Super Stores, it changed the retail grocery landscape significantly. The other major chains such as Albertsons have struggled to stay competitive. In addition, regional discounters such as WinCo in the western United States have made it difficult for the traditional grocery chains. Recently, a study was conducted in which a "market basket" of products was selected at random from those items offered in three stores in Boise, Idaho: Walmart, WinCo, and Albertsons. At issue was whether the mean prices at the three stores are equal or whether there is a difference in prices. The sample data are in the data file called **Food Price Comparisons**. Using an alpha level equal to 0.05, test to determine whether the three stores have equal population mean prices. If you conclude that there are differences in the mean prices, perform the appropriate posttest to determine which stores have different means.

END EXERCISES 12-2

Chapter Outcome 5. → **12.3** **Two-Factor Analysis of Variance with Replication**

Section 12.2 introduced an ANOVA procedure called the randomized complete block ANOVA. This method is used when we are interested in testing whether the means for the populations (levels) for a factor of interest are equal and we want to control for potential variation due to a second factor. The second factor is called the blocking factor. Consider again the Citizen's State Bank property appraisal application, in which the bank was interested in determining whether the mean property valuation was the same for three different appraisal companies. The company used the same five properties to test each appraisal company in an attempt to reduce any variability that might exist due to the properties involved in the test. The properties were the blocks in that example, but we were not really interested in knowing whether the mean appraisal was the same for all properties. The single factor of interest was the appraisal companies.

However, you will encounter many situations in which there are actually two or more factors of interest in the same study. In this section, we limit our discussion to situations involving only two factors. The technique that is used when we wish to analyze two factors is called *two-factor ANOVA with replications*.

Two-Factor ANOVA with Replications

Excel Tutorial

FLY HIGH AIRLINES Like other major U.S. airlines, Fly High Airlines is concerned because many of its frequent flier program members have accumulated large quantities of free miles.[8] The airline worries that at some point in the future, there will be a big influx of customers wanting to use their miles and the airline will have difficulty satisfying all the requests at once. Thus, Fly High recently conducted an experiment in which each of three methods for redeeming frequent flier miles was offered to a sample of 16 customers. Each customer had accumulated more than 100,000 frequent flier miles. The customers were equally divided into four age groups. The variable of interest was the number of miles redeemed by the customers during the six-week trial. Table 12.7 shows the number of miles redeemed for each person in the study. These data are also contained in the **Fly High** file.

Method 1 offered cash inducements to use miles. Method 2 offered discount vacation options, and method 3 offered access to a discount-shopping program through the Internet. The airline wants to know if the mean number of miles redeemed under the three redemption methods is equal and whether the mean miles redeemed is the same across the four age groups.

A *two-factor ANOVA* design is the appropriate method in this case because the airline has two factors of interest. Factor A is the redemption offer type with three levels. Factor B is the age group of each customer with four levels. As shown in Table 12.7, there are $3 \times 4 = 12$ cells in the study and four customers in each cell. The measurements are called *replications* because we get four measurements (miles redeemed) at each combination of redemption offer level (factor A) and age level (factor B).

Two-factor ANOVA follows the same logic as all other ANOVA designs. Each factor of interest introduces variability into the experiment. As was the case in Sections 12.1 and 12.2, we must find estimators for each source of variation. Identifying the appropriate sums of squares and then dividing each by its degrees of freedom does this. As in the one-way ANOVA, the total sum of squares (*SST*) in two-factor ANOVA can be partitioned. The *SST* is partitioned into four parts as follows:

1. One part is due to differences in the levels of factor A (SS_A).
2. Another part is due to the levels of factor B (SS_B).
3. Another part is due to the *interaction* between factor A and factor B (SS_{AB}). (We will discuss the concept of interaction between factors later.)
4. The final component making up the total sum of squares is the sum of squares due to the inherent random variation in the data (SSE).

TABLE 12.7 | **Fly High Airlines Frequent Flier Miles Data**

	Cash Option	Vacation	Shopping
Under 25 years	30,000	40,000	25,000
	0	25,000	25,000
	25,000	0	75,000
	0	0	5,000
25 to 40 years	60,000	40,000	30,000
	0	25,000	25,000
	0	5,000	50,000
	25,000	25,000	0
41 to 60 years	40,000	25,000	25,000
	25,000	50,000	50,000
	25,000	0	0
	0	25,000	0
Over 60 years	0	45,000	30,000
	5,000	25,000	25,000
	25,000	0	25,000
	50,000	50,000	50,000

---

[8]Name changed at request of the airline.

FIGURE 12.9 |

Two-Factor ANOVA—
Partitioning of Total Sums of
Squares

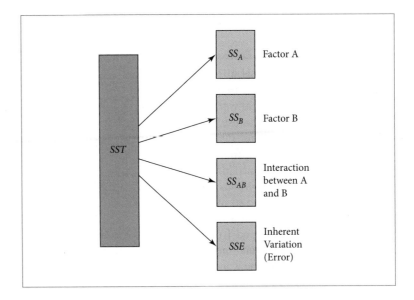

Figure 12.9 illustrates this partitioning concept. The variations due to each of these components will be estimated using the respective *mean squares* obtained by dividing the sums of squares by their degrees of freedom. If the variation accounted for by factor A and factor B is large relative to the error variation, we will tend to conclude that the factor levels have different means.

Table 12.8 illustrates the format of the two-factor ANOVA. Three different hypotheses can be tested from the information in this ANOVA table. First, for factor A (redemption options), we have

$$H_0: \mu_{A1} = \mu_{A2} = \mu_{A3}$$
$$H_A: \text{Not all factor A means are equal}$$

For factor B (age levels):

$$H_0: \mu_{B1} = \mu_{B2} = \mu_{B3} = \mu_{B4}$$
$$H_A: \text{Not all factor B means are equal}$$

TABLE 12.8 | **Basic Format of the Two-Factor ANOVA Table**

Source of Variation	SS	df	MS	F-Ratio
Factor A	SS_A	$a - 1$	MS_A	$\dfrac{MS_A}{MSE}$
Factor B	SS_B	$b - 1$	MS_B	$\dfrac{MS_B}{MSE}$
AB interaction	SS_{AB}	$(a - 1)(b - 1)$	MS_{AB}	$\dfrac{MS_{AB}}{MSE}$
Error	$\underline{SSE}$	$n_T - ab$	MSE	
Total	SST	$n_T - 1$		

where:

$$a = \text{Number of levels of factor A}$$
$$b = \text{Number of levels of factor B}$$
$$n_T = \text{Total number of observation in all cells}$$
$$MS_A = \text{Mean square factor A} = \frac{SS_A}{a-1}$$
$$MS_B = \text{Mean square factor B} = \frac{SS_B}{b-1}$$
$$MS_{AB} = \text{Mean square interaction} = \frac{SS_{AB}}{(a-1)(b-1)}$$
$$MSE = \text{Mean square error} = \frac{SSE}{n_T - ab}$$

Test to determine whether interaction exists between the two factors:

H_0: Factors A and B do not interact to affect the mean response

H_A: Factors A and B do interact

Here is what we must assume to be true to use two-factor ANOVA:

Assumptions

1. The population values for each combination of pairwise factor levels are normally distributed.
2. The variances for each population are equal.
3. The samples are independent.
4. The data measurement is interval or ratio level.

Although all the necessary values to complete Table 12.8 could be computed manually using the equations shown in Table 12.9, this would be a time-consuming task for even a small example because the equations for the various sum-of-squares values are quite complicated. Instead, you will want to use software such as Excel to perform the two-factor ANOVA.

TABLE 12.9 | **Two-Factor ANOVA Equations**

Total Sum of Squares

$$SST = \sum_{i=1}^{a}\sum_{j=1}^{b}\sum_{k=1}^{n}(x_{ijk} - \bar{\bar{x}})^2 \qquad \textbf{(12.11)}$$

Sum of Squares Factor A

$$SS_A = bn\sum_{i=1}^{a}(\bar{x}_{i..} - \bar{\bar{x}})^2 \qquad \textbf{(12.12)}$$

Sum of Squares Factor B

$$SS_B = an\sum_{j=1}^{b}(\bar{x}_{.j.} - \bar{\bar{x}})^2 \qquad \textbf{(12.13)}$$

Sum of Squares Interaction between Factors A and B

$$SS_{AB} = n\sum_{i=1}^{a}\sum_{j=1}^{b}(\bar{x}_{ij.} - \bar{x}_{i..} - \bar{x}_{.j.} + \bar{\bar{x}})^2 \qquad \textbf{(12.14)}$$

Sum of Squares Error

$$SSE = \sum_{i=1}^{a}\sum_{j=1}^{b}\sum_{k=1}^{n}(x_{ijk} - \bar{x}_{ij.})^2 \qquad \textbf{(12.15)}$$

where:

$$\bar{\bar{x}} = \frac{\sum_{i=1}^{a}\sum_{j=1}^{b}\sum_{k=1}^{n}}{abn} = \text{Grand mean}$$

$$\bar{x}_{i..} = \frac{\sum_{j=1}^{b}\sum_{k=1}^{n}x_{ijk}}{bn} = \text{Mean of each level of factor A}$$

$$\bar{x}_{.j.} = \frac{\sum_{i=1}^{a}\sum_{k=1}^{n}x_{ijk}}{an} = \text{Mean of each level of factor B}$$

$$\bar{x}_{ij.} = \sum_{k=1}^{n}\frac{x_{ijk}}{n} = \text{Mean of each cell}$$

a = Number of levels of factor A

b = Number of levels of factor B

n = Number of replications in each cell

FIGURE 12.10

Differences between Factor-Level Mean Values: No Interaction

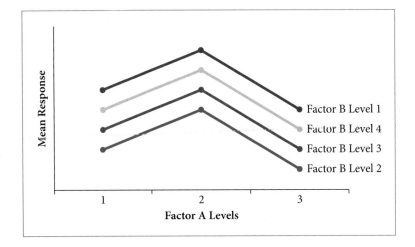

Interaction Explained Before we share the ANOVA results for the Fly High Airlines example, a few comments regarding the concept of *factor interaction* are needed. Consider our example involving the two factors: miles-redemption-offer type and age category of customer. The response variable is the number of miles redeemed in the six weeks after the offer. Suppose one redemption-offer type is really better and results in a higher average miles being redeemed. If there is no interaction between age and offer type, then customers of all ages will have uniformly higher average miles redeemed for this offer type compared with the other offer types. If another offer type yields lower average miles, and if there is no interaction, all age groups receiving this offer type will redeem uniformly lower miles on average than the other offer types. Figure 12.10 illustrates a situation with no interaction between the two factors.

However, if interaction exists between the factors, we would see a graph similar to the one shown in Figure 12.11. Interaction would be indicated if one age group redeemed higher average miles than the other age groups with one program but lower average miles than the other age groups on the other mileage-redemption programs. In general, interaction occurs if the differences in the averages of the response variable for the various levels of one factor—say, factor A—are not the same for each level of the other factor—say, factor B. The general idea is that interaction between two factors means that the effect due to one of them is not uniform across all levels of the other factor.

Another example in which potential interaction might exist occurs in plywood manufacturing, where thin layers of wood called veneer are glued together to form plywood. One of the important quality attributes of plywood is its strength. However, plywood is made from different species of wood (pine, fir, hemlock, etc.), and different types of glue are available. If some species of wood work better (stronger plywood) with certain glues, whereas other species work better with different glues, we say that the wood species and the glue type interact.

FIGURE 12.11

Differences between Factor-Level Mean Values when Interaction is Present

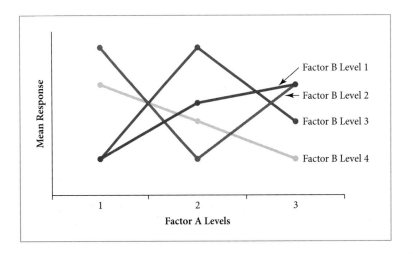

FIGURE 12.12

Excel 2010 Data Format for Two-Factor ANOVA for Fly High Airlines

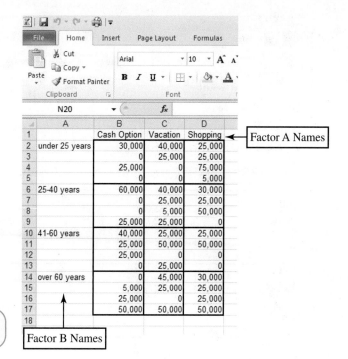

Excel 2010 Instructions:
1. Open file: **Fly High.xlsx**.

If interaction is suspected, it should be accounted for by subtracting the interaction term (SS_{AB}) from the total sum-of-squares term in the ANOVA. From a strictly arithmetic point of view, the effect of computing SS_{AB} and subtracting it from SST is that SSE is reduced. Also, if the corresponding variation due to interaction is significant, the variation within the factor levels (error) will be significantly reduced. This can make it easier to detect a difference in the population means if such a difference actually exists. If so, MSE will most likely be reduced. This will produce a larger F-test statistic, which will more likely lead to correctly rejecting the null hypothesis. Thus, by considering potential interaction, your chances of finding a difference in the factor A and factor B mean values, if such a difference exists, is improved. This will depend, of course, on the relative size of SS_{AB} and the respective changes in the degrees of freedom. We will comment later on the appropriateness of testing the factor hypotheses if interaction is present. *Note that to measure the interaction effect, the sample size for each combination of factor A and factor B must be 2 or greater.*

Excel contains a data analysis tool for performing two-factor ANOVA with replications. It can be used to compute the different sums of squares and complete the ANOVA table. However, Excel requires that the data be organized in a special way, as shown in Figure 12.12. (Note, Excel's first row must contain the names for each level of factor A. Also, Excel's column A contains the factor B level names. These must be in the row corresponding to the first sample item value for each factor B level.)

The Excel two-factor ANOVA output for this example is actually too big to fit on one screen. The top portion of the printout shows summary information for each cell, including means and variances (see Figure 12.13). At the bottom of the output (scroll down) is the ANOVA table shown in Figure 12.14. Excel changes a few labels. For example, factor A (the miles redemption options) is now referred to as *Columns*. Factor B (age groups) is referred to as *Sample*. In Figure 12.14, we see all the information necessary to test whether the three redemption offers (factor A) result in different mean miles redeemed.

$$H_0: \mu_{A1} = \mu_{A2} = \mu_{A3}$$
$$H_A: \text{Not all factor A means are equal}$$
$$\alpha = 0.05$$

Both the p-value and F-distribution approaches can be used. Because

$$p\text{-value (columns)} = 0.561 > \alpha = 0.05$$

FIGURE 12.13

Excel 2010 Output (Part 1) for Two-Factor ANOVA for Fly High Airlines

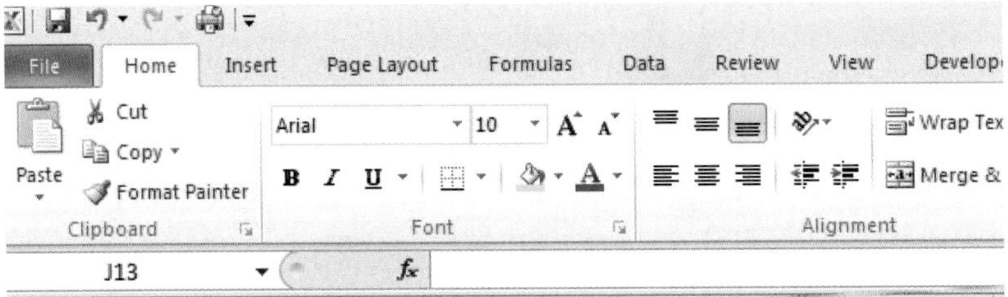

	A	B	C	D	E
1	Anova: Two-Factor With Replication				
2					
3	SUMMARY	Cash Option	Vacation	Shopping	Total
4	*under 25 years*				
5	Count	4	4	4	12
6	Sum	55,000	65,000	130,000	250,000
7	Average	13,750	16,250	32,500	20,833
8	Variance	256,250,000	389,583,333	891,666,667	494,696,970
9					
10	*25-40 years*				
11	Count	4	4	4	12
12	Sum	85,000	95,000	105,000	285,000
13	Average	21,250	23,750	26,250	23,750
14	Variance	806,250,000	206,250,000	422,916,667	396,022,727
15					
16	*41-60 years*				
17	Count	4	4	4	12
18	Sum	90,000	100,000	75,000	265,000
19	Average	22,500	25,000	18,750	22,083
20	Variance	275,000,000	416,666,667	572,916,667	352,083,333
21					
22	*over 60 years*				
23	Count	4	4	4	12
24	Sum	80,000	120,000	130,000	330,000
25	Average	20,000	30,000	32,500	27,500
26	Variance	516,666,667	516,666,667	141,666,667	352,272,727

Excel 2010 Instructions:
1. Open file: **Fly High.xlsx**.
2. Select **Data > Data Analysis**.
3. Select **ANOVA: Two Factor With Replication**.
4. Define data range (include factor A and B labels).
5. Specify the number of **rows per sample: 4**.
6. Specify **Alpha** equal 0.05.
7. Indicate output range.

Minitab Instructions (for similar results):
1. Open file: **Fly High.MTW**.
2. Choose **Stat > ANOVA > Two-way**.
3. In **Response**, enter the data column, (*Value*).
4. In **Row Factor**, enter main factor indicator column (*Redemption Option*).
5. In **Column Factor**, enter the block indicator column (*Age*).
6. Click **OK**.

the null hypothesis H_0 is not rejected. (Also, $F = 0.59 < F_{0.05} = 3.259$; the null hypothesis is not rejected.) This means the test data do not indicate that a difference exists between the average amounts of mileage redeemed for the three types of offers. None seems superior to the others.

We can also test to determine if age level makes a difference in frequent flier miles redeemed.

$$H_0: \mu_{B1} = \mu_{B2} = \mu_{B3} = \mu_{B4}$$
$$H_A: \text{Not all factor B means are equal}$$
$$\alpha = 0.05$$

In Figure 12.14, we see that the

$$p\text{-value} = 0.880 > \alpha = 0.05$$
$$(\text{Also, } F = 0.22 < F_{0.05} = 2.866)$$

Thus, the null hypothesis is not rejected. The test data do not indicate that customer age significantly influences the average number of frequent flier miles that will be redeemed.

FIGURE 12.14

Excel 2010 Output (Part 2) for Two-Factor ANOVA for Fly High Airlines

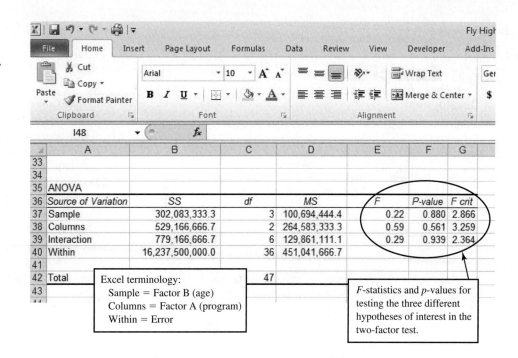

Finally, we can also test for interaction. The null hypothesis is that no interaction exists. The alternative is that interaction does exist between the two factors. The ANOVA table in Figure 12.14 shows a p-value of 0.939, which is greater than $\alpha = 0.05$. Based on these data, interaction between the two factors does not appear to exist. This would indicate that the differences in the average mileage redeemed between the various age categories are the same for each redemption-offer type.

A Caution about Interaction

In this example, the sample data indicate that no interaction between factors A and B is present. Based on the sample data, we were unable to conclude that the three redemption offers resulted in different average frequent flier miles redeemed. Finally, we were unable to conclude that a difference in average miles redeemed occurred over the four different age groups.

The appropriate approach is to begin by testing for interaction. If the interaction null hypothesis is not rejected, proceed to test the factor A and factor B hypotheses. However, if we conclude that interaction is present between the two factors, hypothesis tests for factors A and B generally *should not* be performed. The reason is that findings of significance for either factor might be due only to interactive effects when the two factors are combined and not to the fact that the levels of the factor differ significantly. It is also possible that interactive effects might mask differences between means of one of the factors for at least some of the levels of the other factor. If significant interaction is present, the experimenter may conduct a one-way ANOVA to test the levels of one of the factors, for example, factor A, using only one level of the other factor, factor B.

Thus, when conducting hypothesis tests for a two-factor ANOVA:

1. Test for interaction.
2. If interaction is present, conduct a one-way ANOVA to test the levels of one of the factors using only one level of the other factor.[9]
3. If no interaction is found, test factor A and factor B.

---

[9]There are, however, some instances in which the effects of the factors provide important and meaningful information even though interaction is present. See D. R. Cox, *Planning of Experiments* (New York City: John Wiley and Sons, 1992), pp. 107–108.

MyStatLab

12-3: Exercises

Skill Development

12-31. Consider the following data from a two-factor experiment:

		Factor A	
Factor B	Level 1	Level 2	Level 3
Level 1	43	25	37
	49	26	45
Level 2	50	27	46
	53	31	48

a. Determine if there is interaction between factor A and factor B. Use the p-value approach and a significance level of 0.05.
b. Does the average response vary among the levels of factor A? Use the test-statistic approach and a significance level of 0.05.
c. Determine if there are differences in the average response between the levels of factor B. Use the p-value approach and a significance level of 0.05.

12-32. Examine the following two-factor analysis of variance table:

Source	SS	df	MS	F-Ratio
Factor A	162.79	4		
Factor B			28.12	
AB Interaction	262.31	12		
Error	_____	__		
Total	1,298.74	84		

a. Complete the analysis of variance table.
b. Determine if interaction exists between factor A and factor B. Use $\alpha = 0.05$.
c. Determine if the levels of factor A have equal means. Use a significance level of 0.05.
d. Does the ANOVA table indicate that the levels of factor B have equal means? Use a significance level of 0.05.

12-33. Consider the following data for a two-factor experiment:

		Factor A	
Factor B	Level 1	Level 2	Level 3
Level 1	33	30	21
	31	42	30
	35	36	30
Level 2	23	30	21
	32	27	33
	27	25	18

a. Based on the sample data, do factors A and B have significant interaction? State the appropriate

null and alternative hypotheses and test using a significance level of 0.05.
b. Based on these sample data, can you conclude that the levels of factor A have equal means? Test using a significance level of 0.05.
c. Do the data indicate that the levels of factor B have different means? Test using a significance level equal to 0.05.

12-34. Consider the following partially completed two-factor analysis of variance table, which is an outgrowth of a study in which factor A has four levels and factor B has three levels. The number of replications was 11 in each cell.

Source of Variation	SS	df	MS	F-Ratio
Factor A	345.1	4		
Factor B			28.12	
AB Interaction	1,123.2	12		
Error	256.7			
Total	1,987.3	84		

a. Complete the analysis of variance table.
b. Based on the sample data, can you conclude that the two factors have significant interaction? Test using a significance level equal to 0.05.
c. Based on the sample data, should you conclude that the means for factor A differ across the four levels or the means for factor B differ across the three levels? Discuss.
d. Considering the outcome of part b, determine what can be said concerning the differences of the levels of factors A and B. Use a significance level of 0.10 for any hypothesis tests required. Provide a rationale for your response to this question.

12-35. A two-factor experiment yielded the following data:

		Factor A	
Factor B	Level 1	Level 2	Level 3
Level 1	375	402	395
	390	396	390
Level 2	335	336	320
	342	338	331
Level 3	302	485	351
	324	455	346

a. Determine if there is interaction between factor A and factor B. Use the p-value approach and a significance level of 0.05.
b. Given your findings in part a, determine any significant differences among the response means of the levels of factor A for level 1 of factor B.
c. Repeat part b at levels 2 and 3 of factor B, respectively.

Business Applications

12-36. A PEW Research Center survey concentrated on the issue of weight loss. It investigated how many pounds heavier the respondents were than their perceived ideal weight. It investigated whether these perceptions differed among different regions of the country and gender of the respondents. The following data (pounds) reflect the survey results:

| | | Region | | |
Gender	West	Midwest	South	Northeast
Men	14	18	15	16
	13	16	15	14
Women	16	20	17	17
	13	18	17	13

a. Determine if there is interaction between Region and Gender. Use the *p*-value approach and a significance level of 0.05.
b. Given your findings in part a, determine any significant differences among the discrepancy between the average existing and desired weights in the regions.
c. Repeat part b for the Gender factor.

12-37. The Lanier Company produces a single product on three production lines. Because the lines were developed at different points in Lanier's history, they use different equipment. The production manager is considering changing the layouts of the lines and would like to know what effects different layouts would have on production output. A study was conducted to determine the average output for each line over four randomly selected weeks using each of the three layouts under consideration. The output (in hundreds of units produced) was measured for each line for each of the four weeks for each layout being evaluated. The results of the study are as follows:

	Line 1	Line 2	Line 3
Layout 1	12	12	11
	10	14	10
	12	10	14
	12	11	12
Layout 2	17	16	18
	18	15	18
	15	16	17
	17	17	18
Layout 3	12	10	11
	12	11	11
	11	11	10
	11	11	12

a. Based on the sample data, can the production manager conclude that there is an interaction effect between the type of layout and the production line? Conduct the appropriate test at the 0.05 level of significance.

b. At the 0.05 level of significance, can the production manager conclude that there is a difference in mean output across the three production lines?
c. At the 0.05 level of significance, can the production manager conclude that there is a difference in mean output due to the type of layout used?

12-38. A popular consumer staple was displayed in different locations in the same aisle of a grocery store to determine what, if any, effect different placement might have on its sales. The product was placed at one of three heights on the aisle—low, medium, and high—and at one of three locations in the store—at the front of the store, at the middle of the store, or at the rear of the store. The number of units sold of the product at the various height and distance combinations was recorded each week for five weeks. The following results were obtained:

	Front	Middle	Rear
Low	125	195	126
	143	150	136
	150	160	129
	138	195	136
	149	162	147
Medium	141	186	128
	137	161	133
	145	157	148
	150	165	145
	130	194	141
High	129	157	149
	141	152	137
	148	186	138
	130	164	126
	137	176	138

a. At the 0.10 level of significance, is there an interaction effect?
b. At the 0.10 level of significance, does the height of the product's placement have an effect on the product's mean sales?
c. At the 0.10 level of significance, does the location in the store have an effect on the product's mean sales?

Computer Database Exercises

12-39. Mt. Jumbo Plywood Company makes plywood for use in furniture production. The first major step in the plywood process is the peeling of the logs into thin layers of veneer. A lathe that rotates the logs through a knife that peels the log into layers 3/8-inch thick conducts the peeling process. Ideally, when a log is reduced to a 4-inch core diameter, the lathe releases the core and a new log is loaded onto the lathe. However, a problem called "spinouts" occurs if the lathe kicks out a core that has more than 4 inches left. This wastes wood and costs the company money.

Before going to the lathe, the logs are conditioned in a heated water-filled vat to warm them. The company is concerned that improper log conditioning may lead to excessive spinouts. Two factors are believed to affect the core diameter: the vat temperature and the time the logs spend in the vat prior to peeling. The lathe supervisor has recently conducted a test during which logs were peeled at each combination of temperature and time. The sample data for this experiment are in the data file called **Mt Jumbo**. The data are the core diameters in inches.

a. Based on the sample data, is there an interaction between water temperature and vat hours? Test using a significance level of 0.01. Discuss what interaction would mean in this situation. Use a p-value approach.

b. Based on the sample data, is there a difference in mean core diameter at the three water temperatures? Test using a significance level of 0.01.

c. Do the sample data indicate a difference in mean core diameter across the three vat times analyzed in this study? Use a significance level of 0.10 and a p-value approach.

12-40. A psychologist is conducting a study to determine whether there are differences between the ability of history majors and mathematics majors to solve various types of puzzles. Five mathematics majors and five history majors were randomly selected from the students at a liberal arts college in Maine. Each student was given the same five different puzzles to complete: a crossword puzzle, a cryptogram, a logic problem, a maze, and a cross sums. The time in minutes (rounded to the nearest minute) was recorded for each student in the study. If a student could not complete a puzzle in the maximum time allowed, or completed a puzzle incorrectly, then a penalty of 10 minutes was added to his or her time. The results are shown in the file **Puzzle**.

a. Plot the mean time to complete a puzzle for each puzzle type by major. What conclusion would you reach about the interaction between major and puzzle type?

b. At the 0.05 level of significance, is there an interaction effect?

c. If interaction is present, conduct a one-way ANOVA to test whether the mean time to complete a puzzle for history majors depends on the type of puzzle. Does the mean time to complete a puzzle for mathematics majors depend on the type of puzzle?

Conduct the one-way ANOVA tests at a level of significance of 0.05.

12-41. The Iams Company sells Eukanuba and Iams premium dog and cat foods (dry and canned) in 70 countries. Iams makes dry dog and cat food at plants in Lewisburg, Ohio; Aurora, Nebraska; Henderson, North Carolina; Leipsic, Ohio; and Coevorden, the Netherlands. Its Eukanuba brand dry dog foods come in five formulas. One of the ingredients is of particular importance: crude fat. To discover if there is a difference in the average percentage of crude fat among the five formulas and among the production sites, the sample data found in the file titled **Eukanuba** were obtained.

a. Determine if there is interaction between the Eukanuba formulas and the plant sites where they are produced. Use the p-value approach and a significance level of 0.025.

b. Given your findings in part a, determine if there is a difference in the average percentage of crude fat in the Eukanuba formulas. Use a test-statistic approach with a significance level of 0.025.

c. Repeat part b for the plant sites in which the formulas are produced.

d. One important finding will be whether the average percent of crude fat for the "Reduced Fat" formula is equal to the advertised 9%. Conduct a relevant hypothesis test to determine this using a significance level of 0.05.

12-42. The amount of sodium in food has been of increasing concern due to its health implications. Beers from various producers have been analyzed for their sodium content. The file titled **Sodium** contains the amount of sodium (mg) discovered in 12 fluid ounces of beer produced by the four major producers: Anheuser-Busch Inc., Miller Brewing Co., Coors Brewing Co., and Pabst Brewing Co. The types of beer (ales, lager, and specialty beers) were also scrutinized in the analysis.

a. Determine if there is interaction between the producer and the type of beer. Use a significance level of 0.05.

b. Given your findings in part a, determine if there is a difference in the average amount of sodium in 12 ounces of beer among the producers of the beer. Use a significance level of 0.05.

c. Repeat part b for the types of beer. Use a significance level of 0.05.

END EXERCISES 12-3

Visual Summary

Chapter 12: A group of procedures known as analysis of variance, ANOVA, was introduced in this chapter. The procedures presented here represent a wide range of techniques used to determine whether three or more populations have equal means. Depending upon the experimental design employed, there are different hypothesis tests that must be performed. The one-way design is used to test whether three or more populations have equal mean values when the samples from the populations are considered to be independent. If an outside source of variation is present, the randomized complete block design is used. If there are two factors of interest and we wish to test to see whether the levels of each separate factor have equal means, then a two-factor design with replications is used. Regardless of which method is used, if the null hypothesis of equal means is rejected, methods presented in this chapter enable you to determine which pairs of populations have different means.

Analysis of variance is actually an array of statistical techniques used to test hypotheses related to these (and many other) experimental designs. By completing this chapter, you have been introduced to some of the most popular ANOVA techniques.

12.1 One-Way Analysis of Variance (pg. 463–482)

Summary

There are often circumstances in which independent samples are obtained from two or more levels of a single **factor** to determine if the **levels** have equal means. The experimental design which produces the data for this experiment is referred to as a **completely randomized design**. The appropriate statistical tool for conducting the hypothesis test related to this experimental design is analysis of variance. Because this procedure addresses an experiment with only one factor, it is called a **one-way analysis of variance**. The concept acknowledges that the data produced by the completely randomized design will not all be the same value. This indicates that there is variation in the data. This is referred to as the **total variation**. Each level's data exhibits dispersion as well and is called the **within-sample variation**. The dispersion between the factor levels is designated as the **between-sample variation**. The ratio between estimators of these two variances forms the test statistic used to detect differences in the levels' means. If the null hypothesis of equal means is rejected, the Tukey-Kramer procedure was presented to determine which pairs of populations have different means.

> **Outcome 1.** Understand the basic logic of analysis of variance.
> **Outcome 2.** Perform a hypothesis test for a single-factor design using analysis of variance manually and with the aid of Excel software.
> **Outcome 3.** Conduct and interpret post-analysis of variance pairwise comparisons procedures.

12.2 Randomized Complete Block Analysis of Variance (pg. 483–494)

Summary

Section 12.1 addressed procedures for determining the equality of three or more population means of the levels of a single factor. In this case all other unknown sources of variation are addressed by the use of randomization. However, there are situations in which an additional known factor with at least two levels is impinging on the response variable of interest. A technique called blocking is used in such cases to eliminate the effects of the levels of the additional known factor on the analysis of variance.

As was the case in Section 12.1, a multiple comparisons procedure known as *Fisher's least significant difference* can be used to determine any difference among the population means of a randomized block ANOVA design.

> **Outcome 3.** Conduct and interpret post-analysis of variance pairwise comparisons procedures.
> **Outcome 4.** Recognize when randomized block analysis of variance is useful and be able to perform analysis of variance on a randomized block design.

12.3 Two-Factor Analysis of Variance with Replication (pg. 494–504)

Summary

Two-factor ANOVA follows the same logic as was the case in the one-way and complete block ANOVA designs. In the latter two procedures, there is only one factor of interest. In the two-factor ANOVA, there are two factors of interest. Each factor of interest introduces variability into the experiment. There are circumstances in which the presence of a level of one factor affects the relationship between the response variable and the levels of the other factor. This effect is called interaction and, if present, is another source of variation. As was the case in Sections 12.1 and 12.2, we must find estimators for each source of variation. Identifying the appropriate sums of squares and then dividing each by its degrees of freedom does this. If the variation accounted for by factor A, factor B, and interaction is large relative to the error variation, we will tend to conclude that the factor levels have different means. The technique that is used when we wish to analyze two factors as described above is called *two-factor ANOVA with replications*.

> **Outcome 5.** Perform analysis of variance on a two-factor design of experiments with replications using Excel and interpret the output.

Conclusion

Chapter 12 has illustrated there are many instances in business in which we are interested in testing to determine whether three or more populations have equal means. The technique for performing such tests is called analysis of variance. If the sample means tend to be substantially different, then the hypothesis of equal means is rejected. The most elementary ANOVA experimental design is the one-way design, which is used to test whether three or more populations have equal mean values when the samples from the populations are considered to be independent. If we need to control for an outside source of variation (analogous to forming paired samples in Chapter 10), we can use the randomized complete block design. If there are two factors of interest and we wish to test to see whether the levels of each separate factor have equal means, then a two-factor design with replications is used.

Equations

(12.1) Partitioned Sum of Squares pg. 464

$$SST = SSB + SSW$$

(12.2) Total Sum of Squares pg. 467

$$SST = \sum_{i=1}^{k} \sum_{j=1}^{n_i} (x_{ij} - \bar{\bar{x}})^2$$

(12.3) Sum of Squares Between pg. 468

$$SSB = \sum_{i=1}^{k} n_i (\bar{x}_i - \bar{\bar{x}})^2$$

(12.4) Sum of Squares Within pg. 468

$$SSW = SST - SSB$$

(12.5) Sum of Squares Within pg. 468

$$SSW = \sum_{i=1}^{k} \sum_{j=1}^{n_i} (x_{ij} - \bar{x}_i)^2$$

(12.6) Tukey-Kramer Critical Range pg. 475

$$\text{Critical range} = q_{1-\alpha} \sqrt{\frac{MSW}{2} \left(\frac{1}{n_i} + \frac{1}{n_j} \right)}$$

(12.7) Sum of Squares Partitioning for Randomized Complete Block Design pg. 484

$$SST = SSB + SSBL + SSW$$

(12.8) Sum of Squares for Blocking pg. 484

$$SSBL = \sum_{j=1}^{b} k(\bar{x}_j - \bar{\bar{x}})^2$$

(12.9) Sum of Squares Within pg. 485

$$SSW = SST - (SSB + SSBL)$$

(12.10) Fisher's Least Significant Difference pg. 490

$$LSD = t_{\alpha/2} \sqrt{MSW} \sqrt{\frac{2}{b}}$$

(12.11) Total Sum of Squares pg. 497

$$SST = \sum_{i=1}^{a} \sum_{j=1}^{b} \sum_{k=1}^{n} (x_{ijk} - \bar{\bar{x}})^2$$

(12.12) Sum of Squares Factor A pg. 497

$$SS_A = bn \sum_{i=1}^{a} (\bar{x}_{i..} - \bar{\bar{x}})^2$$

(12.13) Sum of Squares Factor B pg. 497

$$SS_B = an \sum_{j=1}^{b} (\bar{x}_{.j.} - \bar{\bar{x}})^2$$

(12.14) Sum of Squares Interaction between Factors A and B pg. 497

$$SS_{AB} = n \sum_{i=1}^{a} \sum_{j=1}^{b} (\bar{x}_{ij.} - \bar{x}_{i..} - \bar{x}_{.j.} + \bar{\bar{x}})^2$$

(12.15) Sum of Squares Error pg. 497

$$SSE = \sum_{i=1}^{a} \sum_{j=1}^{b} \sum_{k=1}^{n} (x_{ijk} - \bar{x}_{ij.})^2$$

Key Terms

Balanced design pg. 463
Between-sample variation pg. 464
Completely randomized design pg. 463

Experiment-wide error rate pg. 474
Factor pg. 463
Levels pg. 463

One-way analysis of variance pg. 463
Total variation pg. 464
Within-sample variation pg. 464

Chapter Exercises
MyStatLab

Conceptual Questions

12-43. A one-way analysis of variance has just been performed. The conclusion reached is that the null hypothesis stating the population means are equal has not been rejected. What would you expect the Tukey-Kramer procedure for multiple comparisons to show if it were performed for all pairwise comparisons? Discuss.

12-44. In journals related to your major, locate two articles in which tests of three or more population means were important. Discuss the issue being addressed, how the data were collected, the results of the statistical test, and any conclusions drawn based on the analysis.

12-45. Discuss why in some circumstances it is appropriate to use the randomized complete block design. Give an example other than those discussed in the text in which this design could be used.

12-46. A two-way analysis of variance experiment is to be conducted to examine CEO salaries ($K) as a function of the number of years the CEO has been with the company and the size of the company's sales. The years spent with the company are categorized into $0 - 3, 4 - 6, 7 - 9$, and > 9 years. The size of the company is categorized using sales ($million) per year into three categories: $0 - 50, 51 - 100$, and > 100.
   a. Describe the factors associated with this experiment.
   b. List the levels of each of the factors identified in part a.
   c. List the treatment combinations of the experiment.
   d. Indicate the components of the ANOVA table that will be used to explain the variation in the CEOs' salaries.
   e. Determine the degrees of freedom for each of the components in the ANOVA if two replications are used.

12-47. In any of the multiple comparison techniques (Tukey-Kramer, *LSD*), the estimate of the within-sample variance uses data from the entire experiment. However, if one were to do a two-sample *t*-test to determine if there were a difference between any two means, the estimate of the population variances would only include data from the two specific samples under consideration. Explain this seeming discrepancy.

Business Applications

12-48. The development of the Internet has made many things possible, in addition to downloading music. In particular, it allows an increasing number of people to telecommute, or work from home. Although this has many advantages, it has required some companies to provide employees with the necessary equipment, which has made your job as office manager more difficult. Your company provides computers, printers, and Internet service to a number of engineers and programmers, and although the cost of hardware has decreased, the cost of supplies, in this case printer cartridges, has not. Because of the cost of name-brand printer replacement cartridges, several companies have entered the secondary market. You are currently considering offers from four companies. The prices are equivalent, so you will make your decision based on length of service, specifically number of pages printed. You have given samples of four cartridges to 16 programmers and engineers and have received the following values:

Supplier A	Supplier B	Supplier C	Supplier D
424	650	521	323
521	725	601	383
650	826	590	487
422	722	522	521

a. Using a significance level equal to 0.01, what conclusion should you reach about the four manufacturers' printer cartridges? Explain.
b. If the test conducted in part a reveals that the null hypothesis should be rejected, which supplier should be used? Is there one or more you can eliminate based on these data? Use the appropriate test for multiple comparisons. Discuss.

12-49. The Promise Seed Co. was founded in Baltimore in 1876 by a 19-year-old with a passion for plants and animals and a father willing to lend him $1,000 of "seed money" to get started in business. Today, it is owned by Tim Carlton Jr. One of Promise's most demanded seeds is corn. Promise continues to increase production to meet the growing demand. To this end, an experiment such as the one presented here is used to determine the combination of fertilizer and seed type that produces the largest number of kernels per ear.

	Fert. 1	Fert. 2	Fert. 3	Fert. 4
Seed A	807	995	894	903
	800	909	907	904
Seed B	1,010	1,098	1,000	1,008
	912	987	801	912
Seed C	1,294	1,286	1,298	1,199
	1,097	1,099	1,099	1,201

a. Determine if there is interaction between the type of seed and the type of fertilizer. Use a significance level of 0.05.
b. Given your findings in part a, determine if there is a difference in the average number of kernels per ear among the seeds.
c. Repeat part b for the types of fertilizer. Use a significance level of 0.05.

12-50. Recent news stories have highlighted errors national companies such as H&R Block have made in preparing taxes. However, many people rely on local accountants to handle their tax work. A local television station, which prides itself on doing investigative reporting, decided to determine whether similar preparation problems occur in its market area.

The station selected eight people to have their taxes figured at each of three accounting offices in its market area. The following data shows the tax bills (in dollars) as figured by each of the three accounting offices:

Return	Office 1	Office 2	Office 3
1	4,376.20	5,100.10	4,988.03
2	5,678.45	6,234.23	5,489.23
3	2,341.78	2,242.60	2,121.90
4	9,875.33	10,300.30	9,845.60
5	7,650.20	8,002.90	7,590.88
6	1,324.80	1,450.90	1,356.89
7	2,345.90	2,356.90	2,345.90
8	15,468.75	16,080.70	15,376.70

a. Discuss why this test was conducted as a randomized block design. Why did the station think it important to have all three offices do the returns for each of the eight people?

b. Test to determine whether blocking was necessary in this situation. Use a significance level of 0.01. State the null and alternative hypotheses.

c. Based on the sample data, can the station report statistical evidence that there is a difference in the mean taxes due on tax returns? Test using a significance level of 0.01. State the appropriate null and alternative hypotheses.

d. Referring to part c, if you did conclude that a difference exists, use the appropriate test to determine which office has the highest mean tax due.

12-51. A senior analyst working for Ameritrade has reviewed purchases his customers have made over the last six months. He has categorized the mutual funds purchased into eight categories: (1) Aggressive Growth (AG), (2) Growth (G), (3) Growth-Income (G-I), (4) Income Funds (IF), (5) International (I), (6) Asset Allocation (AA), (7) Precious Metal (PM), and (8) Bond (B). The percentage gains accrued by 3 randomly selected customers in each group are as follows:

Mutual Fund	AG	G	G-I	IF	I	AA	PM	B
	6	7	5	1	14	−3	5	−1
	7	−2	6	0	13	7	7	3
	12	0	2	6	10	7	5	2

a. Develop the appropriate ANOVA table to determine if there is a difference in the average percentage gains accrued by his customers among the mutual fund types. Use a significance level of 0.05.

b. Use the Tukey-Kramer procedure to determine which mutual fund type has the highest average percentage gain. Use an experiment-wide error rate of 0.05.

12-52. Anyone who has gone into a supermarket or discount store has walked by displays at the end of aisles. These are referred to as endcaps and are often prized because they increase the visibility of products. A manufacturer of tortilla chips has recently developed a new product, a blue corn tortilla chip. The manufacturer has arranged with a regional supermarket chain to display the chips on endcaps at four different locations in stores that have had similar weekly sales in snack foods. The dollar volumes of sales for the last six weeks in the four stores are as follows:

	Store			
Week	1	2	3	4
1	$1,430	$ 980	$1,780	$2,300
2	$2,200	$1,400	$2,890	$2,680
3	$1,140	$1,200	$1,500	$2,000
4	$ 880	$1,300	$1,470	$1,900
5	$1,670	$1,300	$2,400	$2,540
6	$ 990	$ 550	$1,600	$1,900

a. If the assumptions of a one-way ANOVA design are satisfied in this case, what should be concluded about the average sales at the four stores? Use a significance level of 0.05.

b. Discuss whether you think the assumptions of a one-way ANOVA are satisfied in this case and indicate why or why not. If they are not, what design is appropriate? Discuss.

c. Perform a randomized block analysis of variance test using a significance level of 0.05 to determine whether the mean sales for the four stores are different.

d. Comment on any differences between the means in parts b and c.

e. Suppose blocking was necessary and the researcher chooses not to use blocks. Discuss what impact this could have on the results of the analysis of variance.

f. Use Fisher's least significant difference procedure to determine which, if any, stores have different true average weekly sales.

Computer Database Exercises

12-53. A *USA Today* editorial addressed the growth of compensation for corporate CEOs. As an example, quoting a study made by *BusinessWeek*, *USA Today* indicated that the pay packages for CEOs have increased almost sevenfold on average from 1994 to 2004. The file titled **CEODough** contains the salaries of CEOs in 1994 and in 2004, adjusted for inflation.

a. Use analysis of variance to determine if there is a difference in the CEOs' average salaries between 1994 and 2004, adjusted for inflation.

b. Determine if there is a difference in the CEOs' average salaries between 1994 and 2004 using the two-sample *t*-test procedure.

c. What is the relationship between the two test statistics and the critical values, respectively, that were used in parts a and b?

12-54. The use of high-technology materials and design has dramatically impacted the game of golf. Not only are the professionals hitting the balls farther but so too are the average players. This has led to a rush to design new and better equipment.

Gordon Manufacturing produces golf balls. Recently, Gordon developed a golf ball made from a space-age material. This new golf ball promises greater distance off the tee. To test Gordon Manufacturing's claim, a test was set up to measure the average distance of four different golf balls (the New Gordon, Competitor 1, Competitor 2, Competitor 3) hit by a driving machine using three different types of drivers (Driver 1, Driver 2, Driver 3). The results (rounded to the nearest yard) are listed in the data file called **Gordon**. Conduct a test to determine if there are significant differences due to type of golf ball.

a. Does there appear to be interaction between type of golf ball and type of driver?

b. Conduct a test to determine if there is a significant effect due to the type of driver used.

c. How could the results of the tests be used by Gordon Manufacturing?

12-55. Maynards, a regional home improvement store chain located in the Intermountain West, is considering upgrading to a new series of scanning systems for its automatic checkout lanes. Although scanners can save customers a great deal of time, scanners will sometimes misread an item's price code. Before investing in one of three new systems, Maynards would like to determine if there is a difference in scanner accuracy. To investigate possible differences in scanner accuracy, 30 shopping carts were randomly selected from customers at the Golden, Colorado, store. The 30 carts differed from each other in both the number and types of items each contained. The items in each cart were then scanned by the three new scanning systems under consideration as well as by the current scanner used in all stores at a specially designed test facility for the purposes of the analysis. Each item was also checked manually, and a count was kept of the number of scanning errors made by each scanner for each basket. Each of the scannings was repeated 30 times, and the average number of scanning errors was determined. The sample data are in the data file called **Maynards**.

a. What type of experimental design did Maynards use to test for differences among scanning systems? Why was this type of design selected?

b. State the primary hypotheses of interest for this test.

c. At the 0.01 level of significance, is there a difference in the average number of errors among the four different scanners?

d. (1) Is there a difference in the average number of errors by cart? (2) Was Maynards correct in blocking by cart?

e. If you determined that there is a difference in the average number of errors among the four different scanners, identify where those differences exist.

f. Do you think that Maynards should upgrade from its existing scanner to Scanner A, Scanner B, or Scanner C? What other factors may it want to consider before making a decision?

12-56. PhoneEx provides call center services for many different companies. A large increase in its business has made it necessary to establish a new call center. Four cities are being considered—Little Rock, Wichita, Tulsa, and Memphis. The new center will employ approximately 1,500 workers, and PhoneEx will transfer 75 people from its Omaha center to the new location. One concern in the choice of where to locate the new center is the cost of housing for the employees who will be moving there. To help determine whether significant housing cost differences exist across the competing sites, PhoneEx has asked a real estate broker in each city to randomly select a list of 33 homes between 5 and 15 years old and ranging in size between 1,975 and 2,235 square feet. The prices (in dollars) that were recorded for each city are contained in the file called **PhoneEx**.

a. At the 0.05 level of significance, is there evidence to conclude that the average price of houses between 5 and 15 years old and ranging in size between 1,975 and 2,235 square feet is not the same in the four cities? Use the *p*-value approach.

b. At the 0.05 level of significance, is there a difference in average housing price between Wichita and Little Rock? Between Little Rock and Tulsa? Between Tulsa and Memphis?

c. Determine the sample size required to estimate the average housing price in Wichita to within $500 with a 95% confidence level. Assume the required parameters' estimates are sufficient for this calculation.

12-57. An investigation into the effects of various levels of nitrogen (M. L. Vitosh, *Tri-State Fertilizer Recommendations for Corn, Soybeans, Wheat and Alfalfa*, Bulletin E-2567) at Ohio State University addressed the pounds per acre of nitrogen required to produce certain yield levels of corn on fields that had previously been planted with other crops. The file titled **Nitrogen** indicates the amount of nitrogen required to produce given quantities of corn planted.

a. Determine if there is interaction between the yield levels of corn and the crop that had been previously planted in the field. Use a significance level of 0.05.

b. Given your findings in part a, determine any significant differences among the average pounds per acre of nitrogen required to produce yield levels of corn on fields that had been planted with corn as the previous crop.

c. Repeat part b for soybeans and grass sod, respectively.

Video Case 3

Drive-Thru Service Times @ McDonald's

When you're on the go and looking for a quick meal, where do you go? If you're like millions of people every day, you make a stop at McDonald's. Known as "quick service restaurants" in the industry (not "fast food"), companies such as McDonald's invest heavily to determine the most efficient and effective ways to provide fast, high-quality service in all phases of their business.

Drive-thru operations play a vital role. It's not surprising that attention is focused on the drive-thru process. After all, more than 60% of individual restaurant revenues in the United States come from the drive-thru experience. Yet understanding the process is more complex than just counting cars. Marla King, professor at the company's international training center, Hamburger University, got her start 25 years ago working at a McDonald's drive-thru. She now coaches new restaurant owners and managers. "Our stated drive-thru service time is 90 seconds or less. We train every manager and team member to understand that a quality customer experience at the drive-thru depends on them," says Marla. Some of the factors that affect a customer's ability to complete a purchase within 90 seconds include restaurant staffing, equipment layout in the restaurant, training, efficiency of the grill team, and frequency of customer arrivals, to name a few. Customer-order patterns also play a role. Some customers will just order drinks, whereas others seem to need enough food to feed an entire soccer team. And then there are the special orders. Obviously, there is plenty of room for variability here.

Yet that doesn't stop the company from using statistical techniques to better understand the drive-thru action. In particular, McDonald's utilizes statistical techniques to display data and to help transform the data into useful information. For restaurant managers to achieve the goal in their own restaurants, they need training in proper restaurant and drive-thru operations. Hamburger University, McDonald's training center located near Chicago, satisfies that need. In the mock-up restaurant service lab, managers go thru a "before and after" training scenario. In the "before" scenario, they run the restaurant for 30 minutes as if they were back in their home restaurants. Managers in the training class are assigned to be crew, customers, drive-thru cars, special-needs guests (such as hearing impaired, indecisive, or clumsy), or observers. Statistical data about the operations, revenues, and service times are collected and analyzed. Without the right training, the restaurant's operations usually start breaking down after 10–15 minutes. After debriefing and analyzing the data collected, the managers make

suggestions for adjustments and head back to the service lab to try again. This time, the results usually come in well within standards. "When presented with the quantitative results, managers are pretty quick to make the connections between better operations, higher revenues, and happier customers," Marla states.

When managers return to their respective restaurants, the training results and techniques are shared with staff charged with implementing the ideas locally. The results of the training eventually are measured when McDonald's conducts a restaurant operations improvement process study, or ROIP. The goal is simple: improved operations. When the ROIP review is completed, statistical analyses are performed and managers are given their results. Depending on the results, decisions might be made that require additional financial resources, building construction, staff training, or reconfiguring layouts. Yet one thing is clear: Statistics drive the decisions behind McDonald's drive-thru service operations.

Discussion Questions:

1. After returning from the training session at Hamburger University, a McDonald's store owner selected a random sample of 362 drive-thru customers and carefully measured the time it took from when a customer entered the McDonald's property until the customer had received the order at the drive-thru window. These data are in the file called **McDonald's Drive-Thru Waiting Times**. Note, the owner selected some customers during the breakfast period, others during lunch, and others during dinner. Test, using an alpha level equal to 0.05, to determine whether the mean drive-thru time is equal during the three dining periods (breakfast, lunch, and dinner.)

2. Referring to question 1, write a short report discussing the results of the test conducted. Make sure to include a discussion of any ramifications the results of this test might have regarding the efforts the manager will need to take to reduce drive-thru times.

Case 12.1

Agency for New Americans

Denise Walker collapsed at home after her first outing as a volunteer for the Agency for New Americans in Raleigh, North Carolina. Denise had a fairly good career going with various federal agencies after graduating with a degree in accounting. She decided to stay at home after she and her husband started a family. Now that their youngest was in high school, Denise decided she needed something more to do than manage the household. She decided on volunteer work and joined the Agency for New Americans.

The purpose of the Agency for New Americans is to help new arrivals become comfortable with the basic activities necessary to function in American society. One of the major activities, of course, is shopping for food and other necessities. Denise had just returned from her first outing to a supermarket with a recently arrived Somali Bantu family. It was their first time also, and they were astonished by both the variety and selection. Since the family was on a very limited budget, Denise spent much time talking

about comparison shopping, and for someone working with a new currency, this was hard. She didn't even want to tell them the store they were in was only one of four possible chains within a mile of their apartment. Denise realized the store she started with would be the one they would automatically return to when on their own.

Next week, Denise and the family were scheduled to go to a discount store. Denise typically goes to a national chain close to her house but hasn't felt the need to be primarily a value shopper for some time. Since she feels the Somali family will automatically return to the store she picks, and she has her choice of two national chains and one regional chain, she decides to not automatically take them to "her" store. Because each store advertises low prices and meeting all competitors' prices, she also doesn't want to base her decision on what she hears on commercials. Instead, she picks a random selection of items and finds the prices in each store. The items and prices are shown in the file **New Americans**. In looking at the data, Denise sees there are differences in some prices but wonders if there is any way to determine which store to take the family to.

Required Tasks:

1. Identify the major issue in the case.
2. Identify the appropriate statistical test that could be conducted to address the case's major issue.
3. Explain why you selected the test you choose in (2).
4. State the appropriate null and alternative hypotheses for the statistical test you identified.
5. Perform the statistical test(s). Be sure to state your conclusion(s).
6. If possible, identify the stores that Denise should recommend to the family.
7. Summarize your analysis and findings in a short report.

Case 12.2

McLaughlin Salmon Works

John McLaughlin's father correctly predicted that a combination of declining wild populations of salmon and an increase in demand for fish in general would create a growing market for salmon grown in "fish farms." Over recent years, an increasing percentage of salmon, trout, and catfish, for example, come from commercial operations. At first, operating a fish farm consisted of finding an appropriate location, installing the pens, putting in smelt, and feeding the fish until they grew to the appropriate size. However, as the number of competitors increased, successful operation required taking a more scientific approach to raising fish.

Over the past year, John has been looking at the relationship between food intake and weight gain. Since food is a major cost of the operation, the higher the weight gain for a given amount of food, the more cost-effective the food. John's most recent effort involved trying to determine the relationship between four component mixes and three size progressions for the food pellets. Since smaller fish require smaller food pellets but larger pellets contain more food, one question John was addressing was at what rate to move from smaller to larger pellets. Also, since fish are harder to individually identify than livestock, the study involved constructing small individual pens and giving fish in each pen a different combination of pellet mix and size progression. This involved a reasonable cost but a major commitment of time, and John's father wasn't sure the cost and time were justified. John had just gathered his first set of data and has started to analyze it. The data are shown in the file called **McLaughlin Salmon Works**. John is not only interested in whether one component mix, or one pellet size progression, seemed to lead to maximum weight gain but would really like to find one combination of mix and size progression that proved to be superior.

Required Tasks:

1. Identify the major issues in the case.
2. Identify an appropriate statistical analysis to perform.
3. Explain why you selected the test you choose in (2).
4. State the appropriate null and alternative hypotheses for the statistical test you identified.
5. Perform the statistical test(s). Be sure to state your conclusion(s).
6. Is there one combination of mix and size progression that is superior to the others?
7. Summarize your analysis and findings in a short report.

Case 12.3

NW Pulp and Paper

Cassie Coughlin had less than a week to finish her presentation to the CEO of NW Pulp and Paper. Cassie had inherited a project started by her predecessor as head of the new-product development section of the company, and by the nature of the business, dealing with wood products, projects tended to have long lifetimes. Her predecessor had successfully predicted the consequences of a series of events that, in fact, had occurred:

1. The western United States, where NW Pulp and Paper had its operations, was running out of water, caused by a combination of population growth and increased irrigation. The situation had currently been made worse by several years of drought. This meant many farming operations were becoming unprofitable.
2. The amount of timber harvesting from national forests continued to be limited.
3. At least some of the land that had been irrigated would become less productive due to alkaline deposits caused by taking water from rivers.

Based on these three factors, Cassie's predecessor had convinced the company to purchase a 2,000-acre farm that had four types of soil commonly found in the West and also had senior water rights. Water rights in the West are given by the state, and senior rights are those that will continue to be able to get irrigation water after those with junior rights are cut off. His idea had been to plant three types of genetically modified poplar trees (these are generally fast-growing trees) on the four types of soil and assess growth rates. His contention was it might be economically feasible for the company to purchase more farms that were becoming less productive and to become self-sufficient in its supply of raw material for making paper.

The project had been started 15 years ago, and since her predecessor had since retired, Cassie was now in charge of the project. The primary focus of the 15-year review was tree growth. Growth in this case did not refer to height but wood volume. Volume is assessed by measuring the girth of the tree three feet above the ground. She had just received data from the foresters who had been managing the experiment. They had taken a random sample of measurements from each of the tree types. The data are shown in the file **NW Pulp and Paper**. Cassie knew the CEO would at least be interested in whether one type of tree was generally superior and whether there was some unique combination of soil type and tree type that stood out.

Case 12.4

Quinn Restoration

Last week John Quinn sat back in a chair with his feet on his deck and nodded at his wife, Kate. They had just finished a conversation that would likely influence the direction of their lives for the next several years or longer.

John retired a little less than a year ago after 25 years in the Lake Oswego police department. He had steadily moved up the ranks and retired as a captain. Although his career had, in his mind, gone excellently, he had been working much more than he had been home. Initially upon retiring, he had reveled in the ability to spend time doing things he was never able to do while working: complete repairs around the house, travel with his wife, spend time with the children still at home, and visit those who had moved out. He was even able to knock five strokes off his golf handicap. However, he had become increasingly restless, and both he and Kate agreed he needed something to do, but that something did not involve a full-time job.

John had, over the years, bought, restored, and sold a series of older Corvettes. Although this had been entirely a hobby, it also had been a profitable one. The discussion John and Kate just concluded involved expanding this hobby, not into a full-time job, but into a part-time business. John would handle the actual restoration, which he enjoyed, and Kate would cover the paperwork, ordering parts, keeping track of expenses, and billing clients, which John did not like. The last part of their conversation involved ordering parts.

In the past, John had ordered parts for old Corvettes from one of three possible sources: Weckler's, American Auto Parts, or Corvette Central. Kate, however, didn't want to call all three any time John needed a part but instead wanted to set up an account with one of the three and be able to order parts over the Internet. The question was which company, if any, would be the appropriate choice. John agreed to develop a list of common parts. Kate would then call each of the companies asking for their prices, and, based on this information, determine with which company to establish the account. Kate spent time over the last week on the phone developing the data located in the data file called **Quinn Restoration**. The question John now faced is whether the prices he found could lead him to conclude one company will be less expensive, on average, than the other two.

Business Statistics Capstone Project

Theme: Analysis of Variance

Project Objective:

The objective of this business statistics capstone project is to provide you with an opportunity to integrate the statistical tools and concepts you have learned in your business statistics course. As in all real-world applications, it is not expected through the completion of this project that you will have utilized every statistical technique you have been taught in this course. Rather, an objective of the assignment will be for you to determine which of the statistical tools and techniques are appropriate to employ for the situation you have selected.

Project Description:

You are to identify a business or organizational issue that is appropriately addressed using analysis of variance or experimental design. You will need to specify one or more sets of null and alternative hypotheses to be tested in order to reach conclusions pertaining to the business or organizational issue you have selected. You are responsible for designing and carrying out an "experiment" or otherwise collecting appropriate data required to test the hypotheses using one or more of the analysis of variance designs introduced in your text and statistics course.

There is no minimum sample size. The sample size should depend on the design you choose and the cost and difficulty in obtaining the data. You are responsible for making sure that the data are accurate. All methods (or sources) for data collection should be fully documented.

Project Deliverables:

To successfully complete this capstone project, you are required to deliver, at a minimum, the following items in the context of a management report:

- A complete description of the central issue of your project and of the background of the company or organization you have selected as the basis for the project

- A clear and concise explanation of the data-collection method used. Included should be a discussion of your rationale for selecting the analysis of variance technique(s) used in your analysis.
- A complete descriptive analysis of all variables in the data set, including both numerical and graphical analysis. You should demonstrate the extent to which the basic assumptions of the analysis of variance designs have been satisfied.
- Provide a clear and concise review of the hypotheses tests that formed the objective of your project. Show any post–ANOVA multiple comparison tests where appropriate.
- Offer a summary and conclusion section that relates back to the central issue(s) of your project and discusses the results of the hypothesis tests.
- All pertinent appendix materials.

The final report should be presented in a professional format using the style or format suggested by your instructor.

Special Review Section

Chapter 8   Estimating Single Population Parameters

Chapter 9   Introduction to Hypothesis Testing

Chapter 10   Estimation and Hypothesis Testing for Two Population
             Parameters

Chapter 11   Hypothesis Tests and Estimation for Population
             Variances

Chapter 12   Analysis of Variance

This review section, which is presented using block diagrams and flowcharts, is intended to help you tie together the material from several key chapters. This section is not a substitute for reading and studying the chapters covered by the review. However, you can use this review material to add to your understanding of the individual topics in the chapters.

Chapters 8–12

Statistical inference is the process of reaching conclusions about a population based on a random sample selected from the population. Chapters 8 to 12 introduced the fundamental concepts of statistical inference involving two major categories of inference, *estimation* and *hypothesis testing*. These chapters have covered a fairly wide range of different situations that, for beginning students, can sometimes seem overwhelming. The following diagrams will, we hope, help you better identify which specific estimation or hypothesis-testing technique to use in a given situation. These diagrams form something resembling a decision support system that you should be able to use as a guide through the estimation and hypothesis-testing processes.

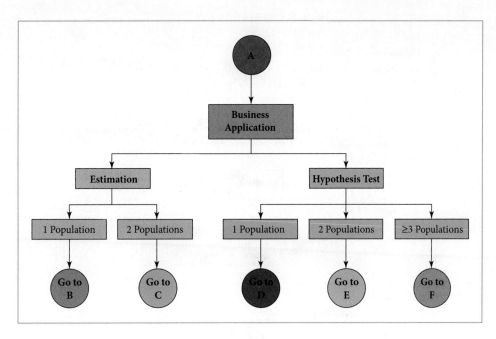

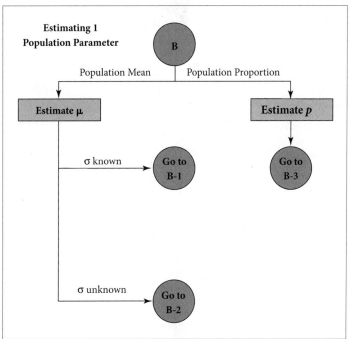

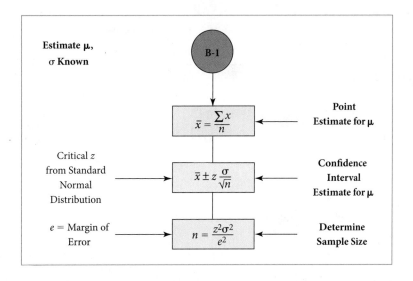

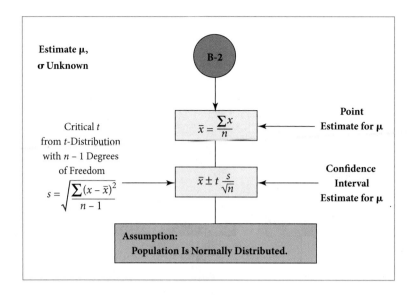

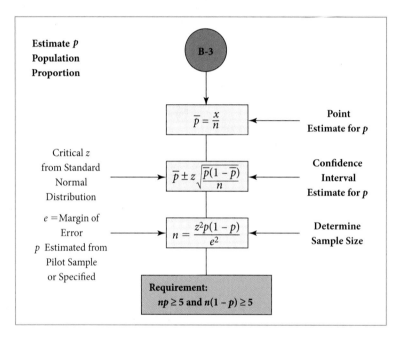

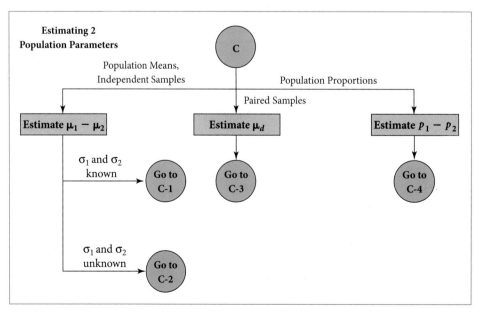

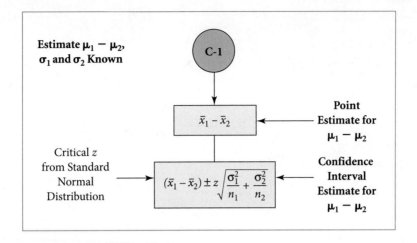

Estimate $\mu_1 - \mu_2$, σ_1 and σ_2 Known

C-1

$\bar{x}_1 - \bar{x}_2$

Point Estimate for $\mu_1 - \mu_2$

Critical z from Standard Normal Distribution

$(\bar{x}_1 - \bar{x}_2) \pm z \sqrt{\dfrac{\sigma_1^2}{n_1} + \dfrac{\sigma_2^2}{n_2}}$

Confidence Interval Estimate for $\mu_1 - \mu_2$

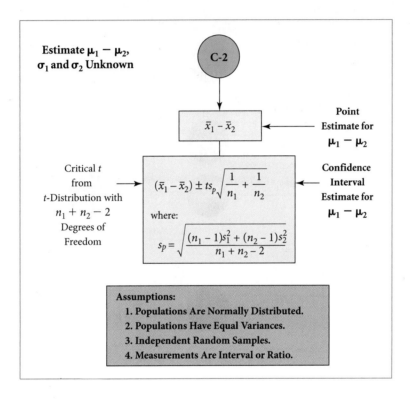

Estimate $\mu_1 - \mu_2$, σ_1 and σ_2 Unknown

C-2

$\bar{x}_1 - \bar{x}_2$

Point Estimate for $\mu_1 - \mu_2$

Critical t from t-Distribution with $n_1 + n_2 - 2$ Degrees of Freedom

$(\bar{x}_1 - \bar{x}_2) \pm t s_p \sqrt{\dfrac{1}{n_1} + \dfrac{1}{n_2}}$

where:

$s_p = \sqrt{\dfrac{(n_1 - 1)s_1^2 + (n_2 - 1)s_2^2}{n_1 + n_2 - 2}}$

Confidence Interval Estimate for $\mu_1 - \mu_2$

Assumptions:
1. **Populations Are Normally Distributed.**
2. **Populations Have Equal Variances.**
3. **Independent Random Samples.**
4. **Measurements Are Interval or Ratio.**

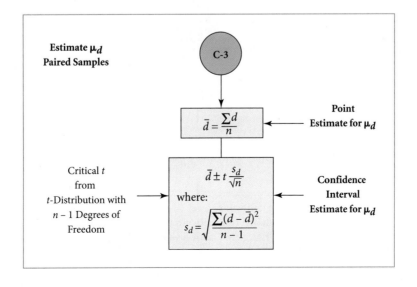

Estimate μ_d Paired Samples

C-3

$\bar{d} = \dfrac{\sum d}{n}$

Point Estimate for μ_d

Critical t from t-Distribution with $n - 1$ Degrees of Freedom

$\bar{d} \pm t \dfrac{s_d}{\sqrt{n}}$

where:

$s_d = \sqrt{\dfrac{\sum(d - \bar{d})^2}{n - 1}}$

Confidence Interval Estimate for μ_d

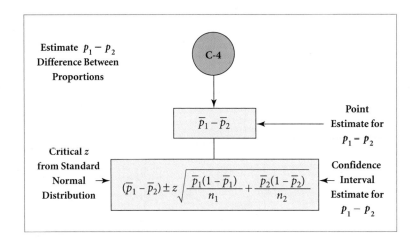

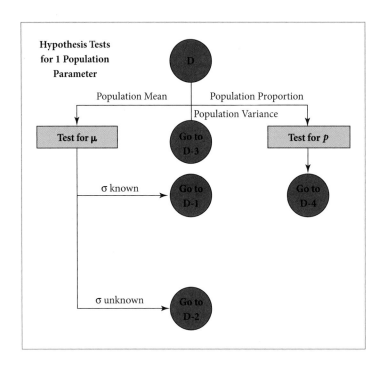

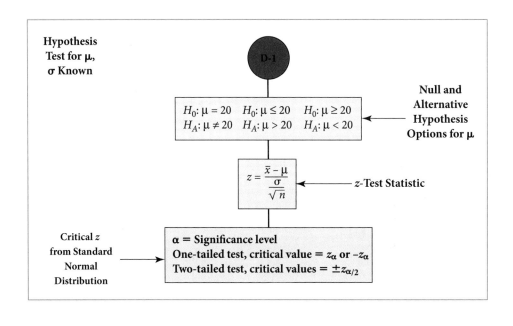

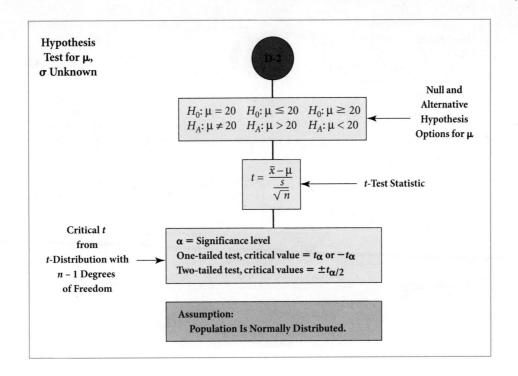

Hypothesis Test for μ, σ Unknown

D-2

$H_0: \mu = 20$ $H_0: \mu \leq 20$ $H_0: \mu \geq 20$
$H_A: \mu \neq 20$ $H_A: \mu > 20$ $H_A: \mu < 20$

Null and Alternative Hypothesis Options for μ

$t = \dfrac{\bar{x} - \mu}{\dfrac{s}{\sqrt{n}}}$

t-Test Statistic

Critical t from t-Distribution with $n - 1$ Degrees of Freedom

α = Significance level
One-tailed test, critical value = t_α or $-t_\alpha$
Two-tailed test, critical values = $\pm t_{\alpha/2}$

Assumption:
  Population Is Normally Distributed.

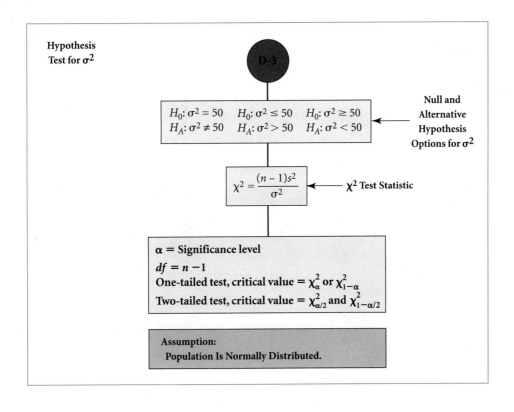

Hypothesis Test for σ^2

D-3

$H_0: \sigma^2 = 50$ $H_0: \sigma^2 \leq 50$ $H_0: \sigma^2 \geq 50$
$H_A: \sigma^2 \neq 50$ $H_A: \sigma^2 > 50$ $H_A: \sigma^2 < 50$

Null and Alternative Hypothesis Options for σ^2

$\chi^2 = \dfrac{(n-1)s^2}{\sigma^2}$

χ^2 Test Statistic

α = Significance level
$df = n - 1$
One-tailed test, critical value = χ^2_α or $\chi^2_{1-\alpha}$
Two-tailed test, critical value = $\chi^2_{\alpha/2}$ and $\chi^2_{1-\alpha/2}$

Assumption:
  Population Is Normally Distributed.

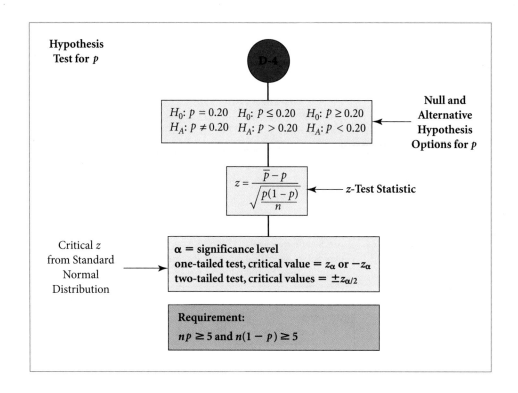

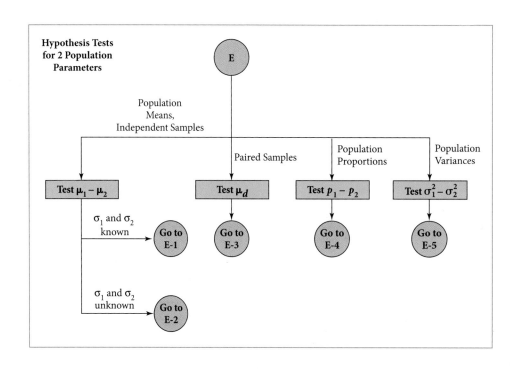

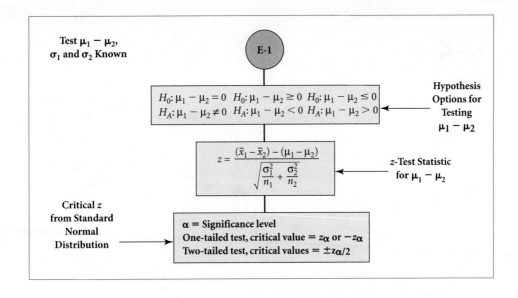

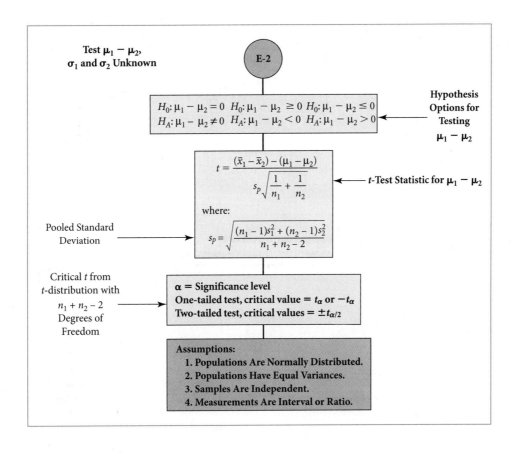

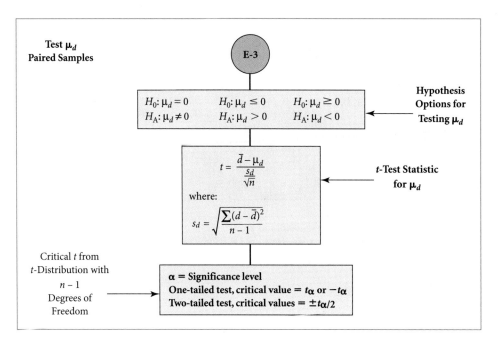

Test μ_d
Paired Samples

E-3

$H_0: \mu_d = 0$ $H_0: \mu_d \leq 0$ $H_0: \mu_d \geq 0$
$H_A: \mu_d \neq 0$ $H_A: \mu_d > 0$ $H_A: \mu_d < 0$

Hypothesis
Options for
Testing μ_d

$$t = \frac{\bar{d} - \mu_d}{\frac{s_d}{\sqrt{n}}}$$

where:

$$s_d = \sqrt{\frac{\sum(d - \bar{d})^2}{n-1}}$$

t-Test Statistic
for μ_d

Critical t from
t-Distribution with
$n - 1$
Degrees of
Freedom

α = Significance level
One-tailed test, critical value = t_α or $-t_\alpha$
Two-tailed test, critical values = $\pm t_{\alpha/2}$

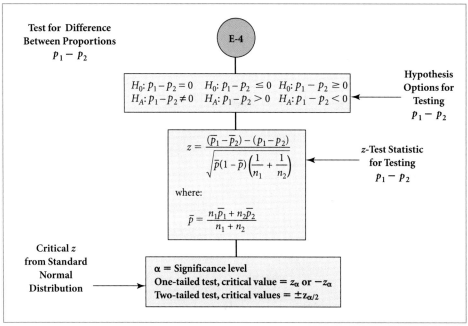

Test for Difference
Between Proportions
$p_1 - p_2$

E-4

$H_0: p_1 - p_2 = 0$ $H_0: p_1 - p_2 \leq 0$ $H_0: p_1 - p_2 \geq 0$
$H_A: p_1 - p_2 \neq 0$ $H_A: p_1 - p_2 > 0$ $H_A: p_1 - p_2 < 0$

Hypothesis
Options for
Testing
$p_1 - p_2$

$$z = \frac{(\bar{p}_1 - \bar{p}_2) - (p_1 - p_2)}{\sqrt{\bar{p}(1 - \bar{p})\left(\frac{1}{n_1} + \frac{1}{n_2}\right)}}$$

where:

$$\bar{p} = \frac{n_1\bar{p}_1 + n_2\bar{p}_2}{n_1 + n_2}$$

z-Test Statistic
for Testing
$p_1 - p_2$

Critical z
from Standard
Normal
Distribution

α = Significance level
One-tailed test, critical value = z_α or $-z_\alpha$
Two-tailed test, critical values = $\pm z_{\alpha/2}$

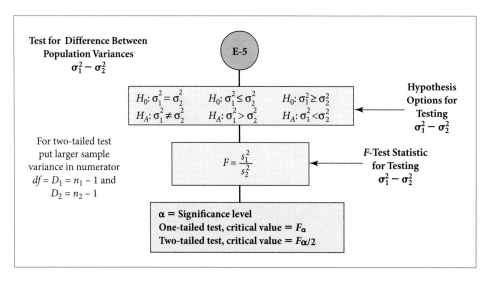

Test for Difference Between
Population Variances
$\sigma_1^2 - \sigma_2^2$

E-5

$H_0: \sigma_1^2 = \sigma_2^2$ $H_0: \sigma_1^2 \leq \sigma_2^2$ $H_0: \sigma_1^2 \geq \sigma_2^2$
$H_A: \sigma_1^2 \neq \sigma_2^2$ $H_A: \sigma_1^2 > \sigma_2^2$ $H_A: \sigma_1^2 < \sigma_2^2$

Hypothesis
Options for
Testing
$\sigma_1^2 - \sigma_2^2$

For two-tailed test
put larger sample
variance in numerator
$df = D_1 = n_1 - 1$ and
$D_2 = n_2 - 1$

$$F = \frac{s_1^2}{s_2^2}$$

F-Test Statistic
for Testing
$\sigma_1^2 - \sigma_2^2$

α = Significance level
One-tailed test, critical value = F_α
Two-tailed test, critical value = $F_{\alpha/2}$

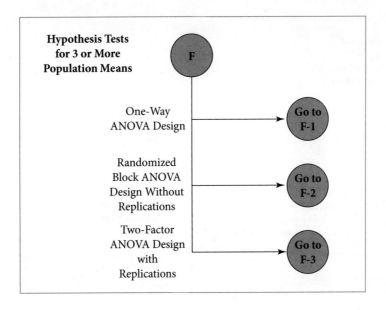

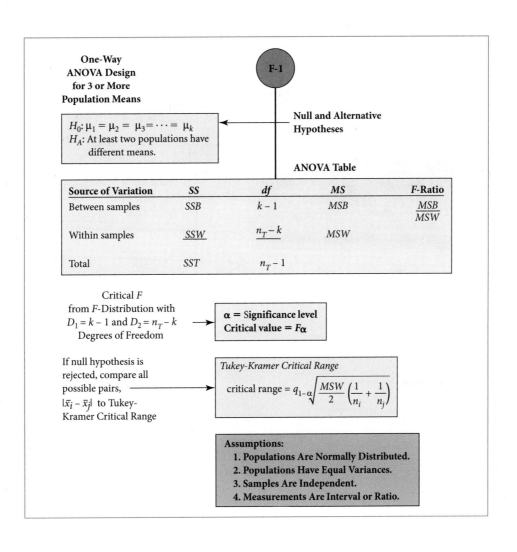

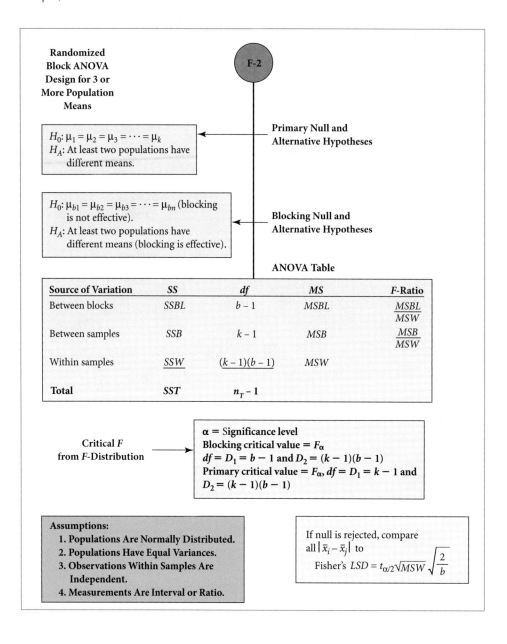

Randomized Block ANOVA Design for 3 or More Population Means

F-2

$H_0: \mu_1 = \mu_2 = \mu_3 = \cdots = \mu_k$
$H_A:$ At least two populations have different means.

Primary Null and Alternative Hypotheses

$H_0: \mu_{b1} = \mu_{b2} = \mu_{b3} = \cdots = \mu_{bn}$ (blocking is not effective).
$H_A:$ At least two populations have different means (blocking is effective).

Blocking Null and Alternative Hypotheses

ANOVA Table

Source of Variation	SS	df	MS	F-Ratio
Between blocks	SSBL	$b - 1$	MSBL	$\dfrac{MSBL}{MSW}$
Between samples	SSB	$k - 1$	MSB	$\dfrac{MSB}{MSW}$
Within samples	SSW	$(k - 1)(b - 1)$	MSW	
Total	SST	$n_T - 1$		

Critical F from F-Distribution

α = Significance level
Blocking critical value = F_α
$df = D_1 = b - 1$ and $D_2 = (k - 1)(b - 1)$
Primary critical value = F_α, $df = D_1 = k - 1$ and $D_2 = (k - 1)(b - 1)$

Assumptions:
1. Populations Are Normally Distributed.
2. Populations Have Equal Variances.
3. Observations Within Samples Are Independent.
4. Measurements Are Interval or Ratio.

If null is rejected, compare all $|\bar{x}_i - \bar{x}_j|$ to
Fisher's $LSD = t_{\alpha/2}\sqrt{MSW}\sqrt{\dfrac{2}{b}}$

**Two-Factor
ANOVA Design
with Replications**

F-3

**Factor A Null and
Alternative Hypotheses**

$H_0: \mu_{A1} = \mu_{A1} = \mu_{A3} = \cdots = \mu_{Ak}$
H_A: Not all Factor A means are equal.

**Factor B Null and
Alternative Hypotheses**

$H_0: \mu_{B1} = \mu_{B2} = \mu_{B3} = \cdots = \mu_{Bn}$
H_A: Not all Factor B means are equal.

H_0: Factors A and B do not interact
to affect the mean response.
H_A: Factors A and B do interact.

**Null and alternative hypotheses
for testing whether the two
factors interact**

ANOVA Table

Source of Variation	SS	df	MS	F-Ratio
Factor A	SS_A	$a - 1$	MS_A	$\dfrac{MS_A}{MSE}$
Factor B	SS_B	$b - 1$	MS_B	$\dfrac{MS_B}{MSE}$
AB Interaction	SS_{AB}	$(a - 1)(b - 1)$	MS_{AB}	$\dfrac{MS_{AB}}{MSE}$
Error	$\underline{SSE}$	$\underline{n_T - ab}$	MSE	
Total	**SST**	$\mathbf{n_T - 1}$		

α = Significance level
Factor A critical value = $F_\alpha, df = D_1 = a - 1$ and $D_2 = n_T - ab$
Factor B critical value = $F_\alpha, df = D_1 = b - 1$ and $D_2 = n_T - ab$
Interaction critical value = $F_\alpha, df = D_1 = (a-1)(b-1)$ and $D_2 = n_T - ab$

Assumptions:
1. The Population Values for Each Combination of Pairwise Factor Levels
   Are Normally Distributed.
2. The Variances for Each Population Are Equal.
3. The Samples Are Independent.
4. Measurements Are Interval or Ratio.

Using the Flow Diagrams

Example Problem: A travel agent in Florida is interested in determining whether there is a difference in the mean out-of-pocket costs incurred by customers on two major cruise lines. To test this, she has selected a simple random sample of 20 customers who have taken cruise line I and has asked these people to track their costs over and above the fixed price of the cruise. She did the same for a second simple random sample of 15 people who took cruise line II.

You can use the flow diagrams to direct you to the appropriate statistical tool.

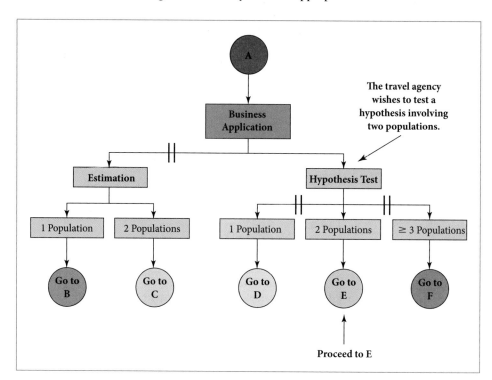

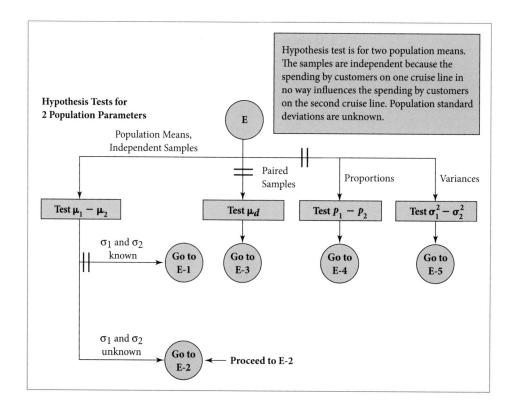

At E-2, we determine the null hypothesis to be

$$H_0: \mu_1 - \mu_2 = 0$$
$$H_A: \mu_1 - \mu_2 \neq 0$$

Next, we establish the test statistic as

$$t = \frac{(\bar{x}_1 - \bar{x}_2) - (\mu_1 - \mu_2)}{s_p \sqrt{\dfrac{1}{n_1} + \dfrac{1}{n_2}}}$$

where:

$$s_p = \sqrt{\frac{(n_1 - 1)s_1^2 + (n_2 - 1)s_2^2}{n_1 + n_2 - 2}}$$

Finally, the critical value is a t-value from the t-distribution with $20 + 15 - 2 = 33$ degrees of freedom. Note, if the degrees of freedom are not shown in the t table, use Excel's **TINV** to determine the t-value.

Thus, by using the flow diagrams and answering a series of basic questions, you should be successful in identifying the statistical tools required to address any problem or application covered in Chapters 8 to 12. You are encouraged to apply this process to the application problems and projects listed here.

MyStatLab

Exercises

Integrative **Application Problems**

SR.1. Brandon Outdoor Advertising supplies neon signs to retail stores. A major complaint from its clients is that letters in the signs can burn out and leave the signs looking silly, depending on which letters stop working. The primary cause of neon letters not working is the failure of the starter unit attached to each letter. Starter units fail primarily based on turn-on/turn-off cycles. The present unit bought by Brandon averages 1,000 cycles before failure. A new manufacturer has approached Brandon claiming to have a model that is superior to the current unit. Brandon is skeptical but agrees to sample 50 starter units. It says it will buy from the new supplier if the sample results indicate the new unit is better. The sample of 50 gives the following values:

Sample mean $= 1,010$ cycles

Sample standard deviation $= 48$ cycles

Would you recommend changing suppliers?

SR.2. PestFree Chemicals has developed a new fungus preventative that may have a significant market among potato growers. Unfortunately, the actual extent of the fungus problem in any year depends on rainfall, temperature, and many other factors. To test the new chemical, PestFree has used it on 500 acres of potatoes and has used the leading competitor on an additional 500 acres. At the end of the season, 120 acres treated

by the new chemical show significant levels of fungus infestation, whereas 160 of the acres treated by the leading chemical show significant infestation.

Do these data provide statistical proof that the new product is superior to the leading competitor?

SR.3. Last year, Tucker Electronics decided to try to do something about turnover among assembly-line workers at its plants. It implemented two trial personnel policies, one based on an improved hiring policy and the other based on increasing worker responsibility. These policies were put into effect at two different plants, with the following results:

	Plant 1	Plant 2
	Improved Hiring	Increased Responsibility
Workers in trial group	800	900
Turnover proportion	0.05	0.09

Do these data provide evidence that there is a difference between the turnover rates for the two trial policies?

SR.4. A Big 10 University has been approached by Wilson Sporting Goods. Wilson has developed a football designed specifically for practice sessions. Wilson would like to claim the ball will last for 500 practice hours before it needs to be replaced. Wilson has supplied six balls for use during spring and fall practice. The following data have been gathered on the time used before the ball must be replaced.

Hours	
551	511
479	435
440	466

Do you see anything wrong with Wilson claiming the ball will last 500 hours?

SR.5. The management of a chain of movie theaters believes the average weekend attendance at its downtown theater is greater than at its suburban theater. The following sample results were found from their accounting data.

	Downtown	Suburban
Number of weekends	11	10
Average attendance	855	750
Sample variance	1,684	1,439

Do these data provide sufficient evidence to indicate there is a difference in average attendance? The company is also interested in whether there is a significant difference in the variability of attendance.

SR.6. A large mail-order company has placed an order for 5,000 thermal-powered fans to sit on wood-burning stoves from a supplier in Canada, with the stipulation that no more than 2% of the units will be defective. To check the shipment, the company tests a random sample of 400 fans and finds 11 defective. Should this sample evidence lead the company to conclude the supplier has violated the terms of the contract?

SR.7. A manufacturer of automobile shock absorbers is interested in comparing the durability of its shocks with that of its two biggest competitors. To make the comparison, a set of one each of the manufacturer's and of the competitor's shocks were randomly selected and installed on the rear wheels of each of six randomly selected cars of the same type. After the cars had been driven 20,000 miles, the strength of each test shock was measured, coded, and recorded.

Car number	Manufacturer's	Competitor 1	Competitor 2
1	8.8	9.3	8.6
2	10.5	9.0	13.7
3	12.5	8.4	11.2
4	9.7	13.0	9.7
5	9.6	12.0	12.2
6	13.2	10.1	8.9

Do these data present sufficient evidence to conclude there is a difference in the mean strength of the three types of shocks after 20,000 miles?

SR.8. AstraZeneca is the maker of the stomach medicine Prilosec, which is the second-best-selling drug in the world. Recently, the company has come under close scrutiny concerning the cost of its medicines. The company's internal audit department selected a random sample of 300 purchases for Prilosec. They wished to characterize how much is being spent on this medicine. In the sample, the mean price per 20-milligram tablet of Prilosec was $2.70. The sample had a standard deviation of $0.30. Determine an estimate that will characterize the average range of values charged for a tablet of Prilosec.

SR.9. A manufacturer of PC monitors is interested in the effects that the type of glass and the type of phosphor used in the manufacturing process have on the brightness of the monitors. The director of research and development has received anecdotal evidence that the type of glass does not affect the brightness of the monitor as long as phosphor type 2 is used. However, the evidence seems to indicate that the type of glass does make a difference if two other phosphor types are used. Here are data to validate this anecdotal evidence.

	Phosphor Type		
Glass Type	1	2	3
1	279	307	287
	254	313	290
	297	294	285
2	243	253	252
	245	232	236
	267	223	278

Conduct a procedure to verify or repudiate the anecdotal evidence.

SR.10. The Vilmore Corporation is considering two word-processing programs for its PCs. One factor that will influence its decision is the ease of use in preparing a business report. Consequently, Jody Vilmore selected a random sample of nine typists from the clerical pool and asked them to type a typical report using both word processors. The typists then were timed (in seconds) to determine how quickly they could type one of the frequently used forms. The results were as follows.

Typist	Processor 1	Processor 2
1	82	75
2	76	80
3	90	70
4	55	58
5	49	53
6	82	75
7	90	80
8	45	45
9	70	80

Jody wishes to have an estimate of the smallest and biggest differences that might exist in the average time required for typing the business form using the two programs. Provide this information.

SR.11. The research department of an appliance manufacturing firm has developed a solid-state switch for its blender that the department claims will reduce the percentage of appliances being returned under the one-year full warranty by a range of 3% to 6%. To determine if the claim can be supported, the testing department selects a group of the blenders manufactured with the new switch and the old switch and subjects them to a normal year's worth of wear. Out of 250 blenders tested with the new switch, 9 would have been returned. Sixteen would have been returned out of the 250 blenders with the old switch. Use a statistical procedure to verify or refute the department's claim.

SR.12. The Ecco Company makes electronics products for distribution throughout the world. As a member of the quality department, you are interested in the warranty claims that are made by customers who have experienced problems with Ecco products. The file called **Ecco** contains data for a random sample of warranty claims. Large warranty claims not only cost the company money but also provide adverse publicity. The quality manager has asked you to provide her with a range of values that would represent the percentage of warranty claims filed for more than $300. Provide this information for your quality manager.

END EXERCISES

Term Project Assignments

Investigate whether there are differences in grocery prices for three or more stores in your city.

a. Specify the type of testing procedure you will use.
b. What type of experimental design will be used? Why?
c. Develop a "typical" market basket of at least 10 items that you will price-check. Collect price data on these items at three or more different stores that sell groceries.
d. Analyze your price data using the testing procedure and experimental design you specified in parts a and b.
e. Present your findings in a report. Did you find differences in average prices of the "market basket" across the different grocery stores?

Business Statistics Capstone Project

Theme: Financial Data Analysis

Project Objective

The objective of this business statistics capstone project is to provide you with an opportunity to integrate the statistical tools and concepts that you have learned in your business statistics course. Like all real-world applications, it is not expected that through the completion of this project you will have utilized every statistical technique you have been taught in this course. Rather, an objective of the assignment will be for you to determine which of the statistical tools and techniques are appropriate to apply for the situation you have selected.

Project Description

Assume that you are working as an intern for a financial management company. Your employer has a large number of clients who trust the company managers to invest their funds. In your position, you have the responsibility for producing reports for clients when they request information. Your company has two large data files with financial information for a large number of U.S. companies. The first is called **US Companies 2003**, which contains financial information for the companies' 2001 or 2002 fiscal-year end. The

second file is called **US Companies 2005**, which has data for the fiscal 2003 or 2004 year-end. The 2003 file has data for 7,441 companies. The 2005 file has data for 6,992 companies. Thus, many companies are listed in both files, but some are just in one or the other.

The two files have many of the same variables, but the 2003 file has a larger range of financial variables than the 2005 file. For some companies, the data for certain variables are not available and a code of NA is used to so indicate. The 2003 file has a special worksheet containing the description of each variable. These descriptions apply to the 2005 data file as well.

You have been given access to these two data files for use in preparing your reports. Your role will be to perform certain statistical analyses that can be used to help convert these data into useful information in order to respond to the clients' questions.

This morning, one of the partners of your company received a call from a client who asked for a report that would compare companies in the financial services industry (SIC codes in the 6000s) to companies in production-oriented industries (SIC codes in the 2000s and 3000s). There are no firm guidelines on what the report should entail, but the partner has suggested the following:

- Start with the 2005 data file. Pull the data for all companies with the desired SIC codes into a new worksheet.
- Prepare a complete descriptive analysis of key financial variables using appropriate charts and graphs to help compare the two types of businesses.
- Determine whether there are statistical differences between the two classes of companies in terms of key financial measures.
- Using data from the 2003 file for companies that have these SIC codes and that are also in the 2005 file, develop a comparison that shows the changes over the time span both within SIC code grouping and between SIC code grouping.

Project Deliverables

To successfully complete this capstone project, you are required to deliver a management report that addresses the partner's requests (listed above) and also contains at least one other substantial type of analysis not mentioned by the partner. This latter work should be set off in a special section of the report.

The final report should be presented in a professional format using the style or format suggested by your instructor.

Chapter 13 Quick Prep Links

- **Review** the logic involved in testing a hypothesis discussed in Chapter 9.
- **Review** the characteristics of probability distributions such as the binomial, Poisson, uniform, and normal distributions in Chapters 5 and 6.
- **Review** the definitions of Type I and Type II errors in Chapter 9.

Goodness-of-Fit Tests and Contingency Analysis

13.1 Introduction to Goodness-of-Fit Tests (pg. 530–543) ← **Outcome 1.** Utilize the chi-square goodness-of-fit test to determine whether data from a process fit a specified distribution.

13.2 Introduction to Contingency Analysis (pg. 544–553) ← **Outcome 2.** Set up a contingency analysis table and perform a chi-square test of independence.

3d brained/Shutterstock

Why you need to know

So far, we have discussed numerous descriptive tools and techniques, as well as estimation and hypothesis tests for one and two populations, hypothesis tests using the *t*-distribution, and analysis of variance. However, as we have often mentioned, these statistical tools are limited to use under those conditions for which they were originally developed. For example, the tests that employ the *t*-distribution assume that the sampled populations are normally distributed. In other situations, we assumed that the binomial or Poisson distribution applied. How do we know which distribution applies to our situation? Fortunately, a statistical technique called *goodness of fit* exists that can help us answer this question. Using goodness-of-fit tests, we can decide whether a set of data comes from a specific hypothesized distribution.

You will also encounter many business situations in which the level of data measurement for the variable of interest is either nominal or ordinal, not interval or ratio. For example, a bank may use a code to indicate whether a customer is a good or poor credit risk. The bank may also have data for these customers that indicate, by a code, whether each person is buying or renting a home. The loan officer may be interested in determining whether credit-risk status is independent of home ownership. Because both credit risk and home ownership are qualitative, or categorical, variables, their measurement level is nominal and the statistical techniques introduced in Chapters 8 through 12 cannot be used to analyze this problem. We therefore need a new statistical tool to assist the manager in reaching an inference about the customer population. This statistical tool is contingency analysis. Contingency analysis is a widely used tool for analyzing the relationship between qualitative variables, one that decision makers in all business areas find helpful for data analysis.

Chapter Outcome 1. → **13.1 Introduction to Goodness-of-Fit Tests**

Many of the statistical procedures introduced in earlier chapters require that the sample data come from populations that are normally distributed. For example, when we use the *t*-distribution in confidence interval estimation or hypothesis testing about one or two population means, the population(s) of interest is (are) assumed to be normally distributed. The *F*-test introduced in Chapters 11 and 12 is based on the assumption that the populations are normally distributed. But how can you determine whether these assumptions are satisfied? In other instances, you may wish to employ a particular probability distribution to help solve a problem related to an actual business process. To solve the problem, you may find it necessary to know whether the actual data from the process fit the probability distribution being considered. In such instances, a statistical technique known as a *goodness-of-fit test* can be used.

The term *goodness of fit* aptly describes the technique. Suppose Nordstrom's, a major retail department store, believes the proportions of customers who use each of the four entrances to its Seattle, Washington, store are the same. This would mean that customer arrivals are *uniformly* distributed across the four entrances. Suppose a sample of 1,000 customers is observed entering the store, and the entrance (East, West, North, South) selected by each customer is recorded. Table 13.1 shows the results of the sample. If the manager's assumption about the entrances being used uniformly holds and if there was no sampling error involved, we would expect one fourth of the customers, or 250, to enter through each door. When we allow for the potential of sampling error, we would still expect close to 250 customers to enter through each entrance. The question is, how "good is the fit" between the sample data in Table 13.1 and the expected number of 250 people at each entrance? At what point do we no longer believe that the differences between what is actually observed at each entrance and what we expected can be attributed to sampling error? If these differences get too big, we will reject the uniformity assumption and conclude that customers prefer some entrances to others.

TABLE 13.1 | Customer Door Entrance Data

Entrance	Number of Customers
East	260
West	290
North	230
South	220

Chi-Square Goodness-of-Fit Test

The *chi-square goodness-of-fit test* is one of the statistical tests that can be used to determine whether the sample data come from any hypothesized distribution. Consider the following application.

BUSINESS APPLICATION   **CONDUCTING A GOODNESS-OF-FIT TEST**

corepics/Fotolia

CHECKER CAB COMPANY The Checker Cab Company in Boston operates taxi service in the city seven days a week. The operations manager for Checker Cab is interested in matching the number of cabs in service with customer demand throughout the week.

Currently, the company runs the same number of taxis Monday through Friday, with reduced staffing on Saturday and Sunday. This is because the operations manager believes that demand for taxicabs is fairly level throughout the week and about 25% less on weekends. The manager has decided to study demand to see whether the assumed demand pattern still applies.

The operations manager requested a random sample of 20 days for each day of the week that showed the number of customers using Checker Cabs on each of the sample days. A portion of those data follows:

TABLE 13.2 | Customer Count Data for the Checker Cab Company Example

Day	Total Customer Count
Sunday	4,502
Monday	6,623
Tuesday	8,308
Wednesday	10,420
Thursday	11,032
Friday	10,754
Saturday	4,361
Total	56,000

Day	Customer Count	Day	Customer Count
Monday, May 6	325	Monday, July 15	323
Monday, October 7	379	Wednesday, April 3	467
Tuesday, July 2	456	etc.	etc.

For the 140 days observed, the total count was 56,000 Checker customers. The total customer counts for each day of the week are shown in Table 13.2 and are graphed in Figure 13.1.

Recall that the previous operations manager at Checker Cab Company bases his cab supply on the premise that from Monday to Friday the customer demand is essentially the same, and on Saturdays and Sundays, it is down 25%. If this is so, how many of the 56,000 taxi customers would we expect on Monday? How many on Tuesday, and so forth? To figure out this demand, we determine weighting factors by allocating four units each

FIGURE 13.1

Graph of Actual Frequencies
for Checker Cab Company

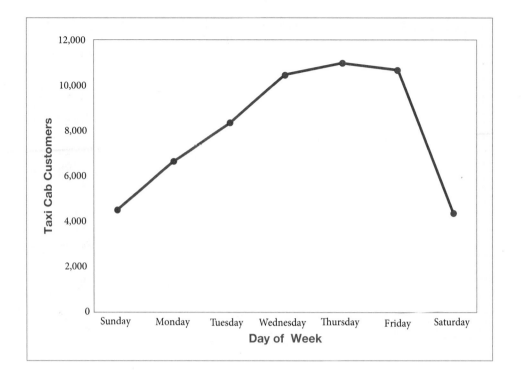

to days Monday through Friday and three units each (representing the 25% reduction) to Saturday and Sunday. The total number of units is then $(5 \times 4) + (2 \times 3) = 26$. The proportion of total customers expected on each weekday is $4/26$ and the proportion expected on each weekend day is $3/26$. The expected number of customers on a weekday is $(4/26) \times 56,000 = 8,615.38$, and the expected number on each weekend day is $(3/26) \times 56,000 = 6,461.54$.

Figure 13.2 shows a graph with the actual sample data and the expected values. With the exception of what might be attributed to sampling error, if the taxi demand distribution assumed by the operations manager is correct, the actual frequencies for each day of the week should fit quite closely with the expected frequencies. As you can see in Figure 13.2, the actual data and the expected data do not match perfectly. However, is the difference enough to warrant changing how the company's taxis are scheduled? The situation facing Checker Cab Company is one for which a number of statistical tests have been developed. One of the most frequently used is the *chi-square goodness-of-fit test*. What we need to examine is how well the sample data fit the hypothesized distribution. The following null and alternative hypotheses can represent this:

H_0: The customer demand distribution is evenly spread through the weekdays and is 25% lower on the weekend.

H_A: The customer demand follows some other distribution.

Equation 13.1 is the equation for the chi-square goodness-of-fit test statistic. The logic behind this test is based on determining how far the actual *observed frequency* is from the *expected frequency*. Because we are interested in whether a difference exists, positive or negative, we remove the effect of negative values by squaring the differences. In addition, how important this difference is really depends on the magnitude of the expected frequency (e.g., a difference of 5 is more important if the expected frequency is 10 than if the expected frequency is 1,000), so we divide the squared difference by the expected frequency. Finally, we sum these difference ratios for all days. This sum is a statistic that has an approximate chi-square distribution.

FIGURE 13.2

Actual and Expected Frequencies for Checker Cab Company

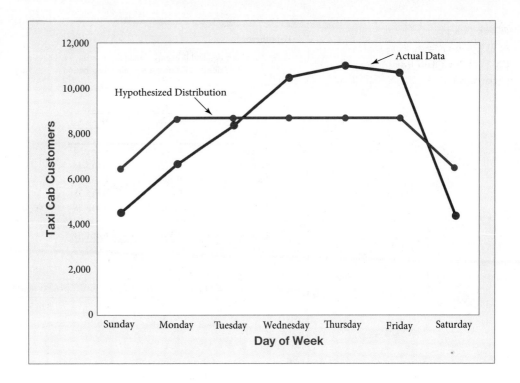

Chi-Square Goodness-of-Fit Test Statistic

$$\chi^2 = \sum_{i=1}^{k} \frac{(o_i - e_i)^2}{e_i}$$

(13.1)

where:

o_i = Observed frequency for category i
e_i = Expected frequency for category i
k = Number of categories

The χ^2 statistic is distributed approximately as a chi-square only if the sample size is large.

Special Note

A sample size of at least 30 is sufficient in most cases provided that none of the expected frequencies is too small.

This issue of expected cell frequencies will be discussed later. If the calculated chi-square statistic gets large, this is evidence to suggest that the fit of the actual data to the hypothesized distribution is not good and that the null hypothesis should be rejected.

Figure 13.3 shows the hypothesis-test process and results for this chi-square goodness-of-fit test. Note that the degrees of freedom for the chi-square test are equal to $k - 1$, where k is the number of categories or observed cell frequencies. In this example, we have 7 categories corresponding to the days of the week, so the degrees of freedom are $7 - 1 = 6$. The critical value of 12.5916 is found in Appendix G for an upper-tail test with 6 degrees of freedom and a significance level of 0.05.

As Figure 13.3 indicates, $\chi^2 = 3{,}335.6 > 12.5916$, so the null hypothesis is rejected and the manager should conclude that the demand pattern does not match the previously defined distribution. The data in Figure 13.3 indicate that demand is heavier than expected Wednesday through Friday and less than expected on the other days. The operations manager may now wish to increase the number of taxicabs in service on Wednesday, Thursday, and Friday to more closely approximate current demand patterns.

FIGURE 13.3

Chi-Square Goodness-of-Fit Test for Checker Cab Company

Hypotheses:

H_0: Customer demand is evenly spread through the weekdays and is 25% lower on weekends.
H_A: Customer demand follows some other distribution.

$\alpha = 0.05$

	Total Customer Count	
	Observed	Expected
Day	o_i	e_i
Sunday	4,502	6,461.54
Monday	6,623	8,615.38
Tuesday	8,308	8,615.38
Wednesday	10,420	8,615.38
Thursday	11,032	8,615.38
Friday	10,754	8,615.38
Saturday	4,361	6,461.54
Total	56,000	56,000

Test Statistic:

$$\chi^2 = \sum_{i=1}^{k} \frac{(o_i - e_i)^2}{e_i} = \frac{(4{,}502 - 6{,}461.54)^2}{6{,}461.54} + \frac{(6{,}623 - 8{,}615.38)^2}{8{,}615.38} + \cdots + \frac{(4{,}361 - 6{,}461.54)^2}{6{,}461.54}$$

$$\chi^2 = 594.2 + 460.8 + \cdots + 682.9$$

$$\chi^2 = 3{,}335.6$$

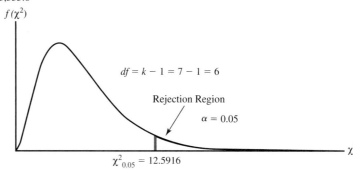

$df = k - 1 = 7 - 1 = 6$

Rejection Region

$\alpha = 0.05$

$\chi^2_{0.05} = 12.5916$

Decision Rule:

If $\chi^2 > 12.5916$, reject H_0.

Otherwise, do not reject H_0.

Because $3{,}335.6 > 12.5916$, reject H_0.

Based on the sample data, we can conclude that the customer distribution is not the same as previously indicated.

EXAMPLE 13-1   **CHI-SQUARE GOODNESS-OF-FIT TEST**

M.studio/Fotolia

Central University Food Service One of the challenges in managing a food service on a college campus is predicting how many students will show up for meals. Central University operates three different food service facilities on campus. All three are the "all-you-can-eat" style where students pay a fixed fee to enter the dining hall and then can eat as much as they want from the various food stations in the hall. One of these is the River View Café on campus, which is open five days a week—Monday through Friday—for breakfast, lunch, and dinner. The manager has been ordering food products for the three meals under the assumption that there is no difference in demand for various food products by day of the week. For example, at dinner, she provides pie as one of the dessert choices. She orders the same number of pies from a local bakery each day. Recently, the manager has received complaints that the café frequently runs out of pie. As a first step in analyzing this issue, the manager decides to conduct a test to determine if student demand for pie is *uniformly distributed* across the five days of the week or whether some other demand distribution applies. She starts by ordering enough pie every day so that there is no possible chance of running out and counts the number of pieces that are selected each day. A chi-square goodness-of-fit test can then be conducted to test this using the following steps:

Step 1 **Formulate the appropriate null and alternative hypotheses.**
Because the number of pieces of pie demanded is supposed to be the same across the five days of the week, the following null and alternative hypotheses are formed:

H_0: Distribution of pie demand is uniform across the five days.
H_A: Distribution of pie demand is not uniform.

Step 2 **Specify the significance level.**
The test will be conducted using $\alpha = 0.05$.

Step 3 **Determine the critical value.**
The critical value for the goodness-of-fit test is a chi-square value from the chi-square distribution, with $k - 1 = 5 - 1 = 4$ degrees of freedom, and $\alpha = 0.05$ is 9.4877.

Step 4 **Collect the sample data and compute the chi-square test statistic.**
The manager collects the data over the course of a representative four-week period. The following data represent the number of pieces of pie used on each day of the week:

Day	Mon	Tue	Wed	Thu	Fri
Pieces of Pie	358	402	577	403	380

A total of 2,120 pieces of pie were taken by students over the test period. Under the hypothesis of a uniform distribution, 20% of this total (424) should be selected on each day of the week. Thus, the expected number of pieces needed each day, if the null hypothesis of a uniform distribution is true, is 424. This number is the expected cell frequency.

Equation 13.1 is used to form the test statistic based on these sample data.

$$\chi^2 = \sum_{i=1}^{k} \frac{(o_i - e_i)^2}{e_i} = \frac{(358 - 424)^2}{424} + \frac{(402 - 424)^2}{424}$$
$$+ \frac{(577 - 424)^2}{424} + \frac{(403 - 424)^2}{424} + \frac{(380 - 424)^2}{424}$$
$$= 72.231$$

Step 5 **Reach a decision.**
The decision rule is

If $\chi^2 > 9.4877$, reject H_0.
Otherwise, do not reject H_0.

Because $\chi^2 = 72.231 > 9.4877$, reject the null hypothesis.

Step 6 **Draw a conclusion.**
The manager of the River View Café should conclude that the demand for pie is not occurring equally across the five days of the week. As a result, she will need to alter the ordering process to account for a nonuniform demand distribution for this food item.

>> **END EXAMPLE**

TRY PROBLEM 13-2 (pg. 541)

BUSINESS APPLICATION   **USING SOFTWARE TO CONDUCT A GOODNESS-OF-FIT TEST**

WOODTRIM PRODUCTS, INC. Woodtrim Products, Inc., makes wood moldings, doorframes, and window frames. It purchases lumber from mills throughout New England and eastern Canada. The first step in the production process is to rip the lumber into narrower strips. Different widths are used for different products. For example, wider pieces with no

Excel Tutorial

imperfections are used to make door and window frames. Once an operator decides on the appropriate width, that information is locked into a computer and a ripsaw automatically cuts the board to the desired size. The manufacturer of the saw claims that the ripsaw cuts an average deviation of zero from target and that the differences from target will be normally distributed, with a standard deviation of 0.01 inch.

Woodtrim has recently become concerned that the ripsaw may not be cutting to the manufacturer's specifications because operators at other machines downstream in the production process are finding excessive numbers of ripped pieces that are too wide or too narrow.

A quality improvement team (QIT) has started to investigate the problem. Team members selected a random sample of 300 boards just as they came off the ripsaw. To provide a measure of control, the only pieces sampled in the initial study had stated widths of $2\frac{7}{8}$ (2.875) inches. Each piece's width was measured halfway from its end. A portion of the data and the differences between the target 2.875 inches and the actual measured width are shown in Figure 13.4. The full data set is contained in the file **Woodtrim**. The team can use these data and the chi-square goodness-of-fit testing procedure to test the following null and alternative hypotheses:

H_0: The differences are normally distributed, with $\mu = 0$ and $\sigma = 0.01$.
H_A: The differences are not normally distributed, with $\mu = 0$ and $\sigma = 0.01$.

This example differs slightly from the previous examples because the hypothesized distribution is continuous rather than discrete. Thus, we must organize the data into a grouped-data frequency distribution (see Chapter 2), as shown in the Excel output in Figure 13.5. Our choice of classes requires careful consideration. The chi-square goodness-of-fit test compares the actual cell frequencies with the expected cell frequencies. The test statistic from Equation 13.1,

$$\chi^2 = \sum_{i=1}^{k} \frac{(o_i - e_i)^2}{e_i}$$

is approximately chi-square distributed if the expected cell frequencies are large. Because the expected cell frequencies are used in computing the test statistic, the general recommendation is that the goodness-of-fit test be performed only when all expected cell frequencies are at least 5. If any of the cells have expected frequencies less than 5, the cells should be combined in a meaningful way such that the expected frequencies are at least 5. We have chosen to use $k = 6$ classes. The number of classes is your choice. You can perform the chi-square goodness-of-fit test using Excel. (The tutorial that accompany this text take you through the specific steps required to complete this example.) Figure 13.5 shows the normal distribution probabilities, expected cell frequencies, and the chi-square calculation. The calculated chi-square statistic is $\chi^2 = 26.432$. The p-value associated with $\chi^2 = 26.432$ and $6 - 1 = 5$

FIGURE 13.4

Excel 2010 Woodtrim Products Test Data

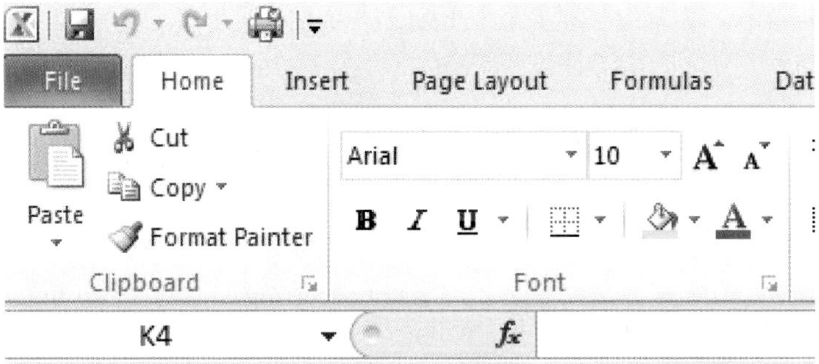

Excel 2010 Instructions:
1. Open file: **Woodtrim.xlsx**.

	A	B	C	D
1	Sample	Actual Width	Target Width	Difference
2	1	2.870	2.875	-0.005
3	2	2.863	2.875	-0.012
4	3	2.885	2.875	0.010
5	4	2.872	2.875	-0.003
6	5	2.891	2.875	0.016
7	6	2.893	2.875	0.018
8	7	2.868	2.875	-0.007
9	8	2.861	2.875	-0.014

FIGURE 13.5

Excel 2010 Results—
Goodness-of-Fit Test for the
Woodtrim Example

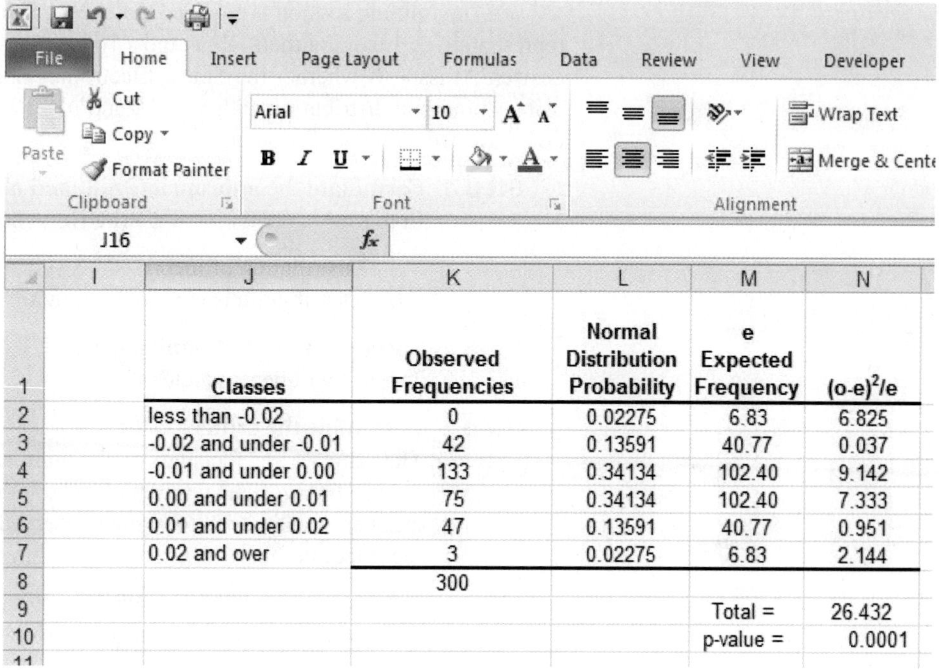

**Minitab Instructions
(for similar results):**
1. Open file:
   Woodtrim.MTW.
2. Choose **Stat > Basic
   Statistics > Normality
   Test**.
3. In **Variable**, enter
   column *Difference*.
4. Under Normality select
   Kolmogorov-Smirnov.
5. Click **OK**.

Classes	Observed Frequencies	Normal Distribution Probability	e Expected Frequency	(o-e)²/e
less than -0.02	0	0.02275	6.83	6.825
-0.02 and under -0.01	42	0.13591	40.77	0.037
-0.01 and under 0.00	133	0.34134	102.40	9.142
0.00 and under 0.01	75	0.34134	102.40	7.333
0.01 and under 0.02	47	0.13591	40.77	0.951
0.02 and over	3	0.02275	6.83	2.144
	300			
			Total =	26.432
			p-value =	0.0001

Excel 2010 Instructions:
1. Open file: **Woodtrim.xlsx**.
2. Define classes (column J).
3. Determine observed frequencies [i.e. cell K4 is **=COUNTIF($D$2: $D$301,"0.0")-SUM($K$2:K3)**].
4. Determine normal distribution probabilities, assuming mean = 0.0, and st. deviation = 0.01—i.e., cell L4 formula is **=NORM.DIST (0,0,.01,TRUE)-SUM($L$2:L3)**.
5. Determine expected frequencies by multiplying the normal probabilities by the sample size ($n = 300$).
6. Compute values for the chi-square in column N—i.e., for cell N5, the formula is **=(K5-M5)^2/M5**.
7. Sum column N to get chi-square statistic.
8. Find *p*-value using **CHISQ.TEST** function—i.e., for cell N10 the formula is **CHISQ.TEST(K2:K7,M2:M7)**.

degrees of freedom is 0.0001. Therefore, because *p*-value = 0.0001 is less than any reasonable level of alpha, we reject the null hypothesis and conclude the ripsaw is not currently meeting the manufacturer's specification. The saw errors are not normally distributed with mean equal to 0 and a standard deviation equal to 0.01.

Special Note

Note that in this case, because the null hypothesis specified both the mean and the standard deviation, the normal distribution probabilities were computed using these values. However, if the mean and/or the standard deviation had not been specified, the sample mean and standard deviation would be used in the probability computation. You would lose 1 additional degree of freedom for each parameter that was estimated from the sample data. This is true any time sample statistics are specified in place of population parameters in the hypothesis.

EXAMPLE 13-2　**GOODNESS-OF-FIT TEST**

Call Center Support, Specialty Electronics Specialty Electronics sells a wide variety of electronics products over the Internet. One of the features that differentiates Specialty Electronics from other online electronics retailers is the 24-7 call center support it provides to customers. A key component is that the answers provided by the call center representatives are accurate. Because of the high volume of calls received each week, the call center quality-assurance manager can't analyze every call for accuracy of assistance provided. Instead, every day, 10 calls are randomly recorded for quality purposes. The manager has a policy that if two or more of the 10 calls result in incorrect answers, all call center representatives are required to come in after hours for a special training session. If the review finds one or fewer incorrect answers, no training session is required that week. The manager believes that if the call center representatives are doing their job, at most 10% of the customers who call in will get a wrong answer. At issue is whether the Select Electronics manager can evaluate this sampling plan using a binomial distribution with $n = 10$ and $p = .10$. To test this, a goodness-of-fit test can be performed using the following steps:

Step 1 Formulate the appropriate null and alternative hypotheses.
In this case, the null and alternative hypotheses are

H_0: Distribution of incorrect answers is binomial, with $n = 10$ and $p = .10$
H_A: Distribution is not binomial, with $n = 10$ and $p = .10$

Step 2 Specify the level of significance.
The test will be conducted using $\alpha = 0.025$.

Step 3 Determine the critical value.
The critical value depends on the number of degrees of freedom and the level of significance. The degrees of freedom will be equal to $k - 1$, where k is the number of categories for which observed and expected frequencies will be recorded. In this case, the managers have set up the following four groups:

Incorrect Answers: 0, 1, 2, 3 and over

Therefore, $k = 4$, and the degrees of freedom are $4 - 1 = 3$. The critical chi-square value for $\alpha = 0.025$ found in Appendix G is 9.3484.

Step 4 Collect the sample data and compute the chi-square test statistic using Equation 13.1.
The company selected a simple random sample of 100 days' test results from past recorded calls and counted the number of incorrect answers in each sample of 10 calls. The following table shows the computations for the chi-square statistic.

Incorrect Answers	o Observed Defects	Binomial Probability $n = 10, p = 0.10$	e Expected Frequency	$\dfrac{(o_i - e_i)^2}{e_i}$
0	30	0.3487	34.87	0.6802
1	40	0.3874	38.74	0.0410
2	20	0.1937	19.37	0.0205
3 and over	10	0.0702	7.02	1.2650
Total	100			2.0067

The calculated chi-square test statistic is $\chi^2 = 2.0067$.

Step 5 Reach a decision.
Because $\chi^2 = 2.0067$ is less than the critical value of 9.3484, we do not reject the null hypothesis.

Step 6 Draw a conclusion.
The binomial distribution may be the appropriate distribution to describe the company's sampling plan.

>> **END EXAMPLE**

TRY PROBLEM 13-1 (pg. 541)

EXAMPLE 13-3   **GOODNESS-OF-FIT TEST**

University Internet Service Students in a computer information systems class at a major university have established an Internet service provider (ISP) company for the university's students, faculty, and staff. Customers of this ISP connect via a wireless signal available throughout the campus and surrounding business area. Capacity is always an issue for an ISP, and the students had to estimate the capacity demands for their service. Before opening for business, the students conducted a survey of likely customers. Based on this survey, they estimated that demand during the late afternoon and evening hours is Poisson distributed (refer to Chapter 5) with a mean equal to 10 users per hour. Based on this assumption, the students developed the ISP with the capacity to handle 20 users simultaneously. However, they have lately been receiving complaints from customers saying they have been denied access to the system because 20 users are already online. The students are now interested in determining whether the demand distribution is still Poisson distributed with a mean equal to 10 per hour. To test this, they have collected data on the number of user requests for ISP access for 225 randomly selected time periods during the heavy-use hours. The following steps can be used to conduct the statistical test:

Step 1 State the appropriate null and alternative hypotheses.
The null and alternative hypotheses are

H_0: Demand distribution is Poisson distributed with mean equal to 10 users per time period.

H_A: The demand distribution is not distributed as a Poisson distribution with mean equal to 10 per period.

Step 2 Specify the level of significance.
The hypothesis test will be conducted using $\alpha = 0.05$.

Step 3 Determine the critical value.
The critical value depends on the level of significance and the number of degrees of freedom. The degrees of freedom is equal to $k - 1$, where k is the number of categories. In this case, after collapsing the categories to get the expected frequencies to be at least 5, we have 13 categories (see Step 4). Thus, the degrees of freedom for the chi-square critical value is $13 - 1 = 12$. For 12 degrees of freedom and a level of significance equal to 0.05, from Appendix G we find a critical value of $\chi^2 = 21.0261$. Thus the decision rule is

If $\chi^2 > 21.0261$, reject the null hypothesis

Otherwise, do not reject.

Step 4 Collect the sample data and compute the chi-square test statistic using Equation 13.1.
A random sample of 225 time periods was selected, and the number of users requesting access to the ISP at each time period was recorded. The observed frequencies based on the sample data are as follows:

Number of Requests	Observed Frequency	Number of Requests	Observed Frequency
0	0	10	18
1	2	11	14
2	1	12	17
3	3	13	18
4	4	14	25
5	3	15	28
6	8	16	23
7	6	17	17
8	11	18	9
9	7	19 and over	11
		Total	225

To compute the chi-square test statistic, you must determine the expected frequencies. Start by determining the probability for each number of user requests based on the hypothesized distribution. (Poisson with $\lambda t = 10$.)

The expected frequencies are calculated by multiplying the probability by the total observed frequency of 225. These results are as follows:

Number of Requests	Observed Frequency	Poisson Probability $\lambda t = 10$	Expected Frequency
0	0	0.0000	0.00
1	2	0.0005	0.11
2	1	0.0023	0.52
3	3	0.0076	1.71
4	4	0.0189	4.25
5	3	0.0378	8.51
6	8	0.0631	14.20
7	6	0.0901	20.27
8	11	0.1126	25.34
9	7	0.1251	28.15
10	18	0.1251	28.15
11	14	0.1137	25.58
12	17	0.0948	21.33
13	18	0.0729	16.40
14	25	0.0521	11.72
15	28	0.0347	7.81
16	23	0.0217	4.88
17	17	0.0128	2.88
18	9	0.0071	1.60
19 and over	11	0.0072	1.62
Total	225	1.0000	225.00

Now you need to check if any of the expected cell frequencies are less than 5. In this case, we see there are several instances where this is so. To deal with this, collapse categories so that all expected frequencies are at least 5. Doing this gives the following:

Number of Requests	Observed Frequency	Poisson Probability $\lambda t = 10$	Expected Frequency
4 or fewer	10	0.0293	6.59
5	3	0.0378	8.51
6	8	0.0631	14.20
7	6	0.0901	20.27
8	11	0.1126	25.34
9	7	0.1251	28.15
10	18	0.1251	28.15
11	14	0.1137	25.58
12	17	0.0948	21.33
13	18	0.0729	16.40
14	25	0.0521	11.72
15	28	0.0347	7.81
16 or more	60	0.0488	10.98
Total	225	1.0000	225.00

Now we can compute the chi-square test statistic using Equation 13.1 as follows:

$$\chi^2 = \sum_{i=1}^{k} \frac{(o_i - e_i)^2}{e_i}$$

$$= \frac{(10 - 6.59)^2}{6.59} + \frac{(3 - 8.51)^2}{8.51} + \cdots + \frac{(60 - 10.98)^2}{10.98}$$

$$= 338.1$$

Step 5 Reach a decision.

Because $\chi^2 = 338.1 > 21.0261$, reject the null hypothesis.

Step 6 Draw a conclusion.

The demand distribution is not Poisson distributed with a mean of 10. The students should conclude that either the mean demand per period has increased from 10 or the distribution is not Poisson or both. They may need to add more capacity to the ISP business.

>> **END EXAMPLE**

TRY PROBLEM 13-3 (pg. 541)

MyStatLab

13-1: Exercises

Skill Development

13-1. A large retailer receives shipments of batteries for consumer electronic products in packages of 50 batteries. The packages are held at a distribution center and are shipped to retail stores as requested. Because some packages may contain defective batteries, the retailer randomly samples 400 packages from its distribution center and tests to determine whether the batteries are defective or not. The most recent sample of 400 packages revealed the following observed frequencies for defective batteries per package:

# of Defective Batteries per Package	Frequency of Occurrence
0	165
1	133
2	65
3	28
4 or more	9

The retailer's managers would like to know if they can evaluate this sampling plan using a binomial distribution with $n = 50$ and $p = 0.02$. Test at the $\alpha = 0.01$ level of significance.

13-2. The following frequency distribution shows the number of times an outcome was observed from the toss of a die. Based on the frequencies that were observed from 2,400 tosses of the die, can it be concluded at the 0.05 level of significance that the die is fair?

Outcome	Frequency
1	352
2	418
3	434
4	480
5	341
6	375

13-3. Based on the sample data in the following frequency distribution, conduct a test to determine whether the population from which the sample data were selected is Poisson distributed with mean equal to 6. Test using $\alpha = 0.05$.

x	Frequency	x	Frequency
2 or less	7	9	53
3	29	10	35
4	26	11	28
5	52	12	18
6	77	13	13
7	77	14 or more	13
8	72	Total	500

13-4. A chi-square goodness-of-fit test is to be conducted to test whether a population is normally distributed. No statement has been made regarding the value of the population mean and standard deviation. A frequency distribution has been formed based on a random sample of 1,000 values. The frequency distribution has $k = 8$ classes. Assuming that the test is to be conducted at the $\alpha = 0.10$ level, determine the correct decision rule to be used.

13-5. An experiment is run that is claimed to have a binomial distribution with $p = 0.15$ and $n = 18$ and the number of successes is recorded. The experiment is conducted 200 times with the following results:

Number of Successes	0	1	2	3	4	5
Observed Frequency	80	75	39	6	0	0

Using a significance level of 0.01, is there sufficient evidence to conclude that the distribution is binomially distributed with $p = 0.15$ and $n = 18$?

13-6. Data collected from a hospital emergency room reflect the number of patients per day that visited the emergency room due to cardiac-related symptoms. It is believed that the distribution of the number of cardiac patients entering the emergency room per day over a two-month period has a Poisson distribution with a mean of 8 patients per day.

6	7	9	7	5	6	7	7	5	10
9	9	7	2	8	5	7	10	6	7
12	12	10	8	8	14	7	9	10	**7**
4	9	6	4	11	9	10	7	5	10
8	8	10	7	9	2	10	12	10	9
8	11	7	9	11	7	16	7	9	10

Use a chi-square goodness-of-fit test to determine if the data come from a Poisson distribution with mean of 8. Test using a significance level of 0.01.

Business Applications

13-7. HSBC Bank is a large, London-based international banking company. One of its most important sources of income is home loans. A component of its effort to maintain and increase its customer base is excellent service. The loan manager at one of its branches in New York keeps track of the number of loan applicants who visit his branch's loan department per week. Having enough loan officers available is one of the ways of providing excellent service. Over the last year, the loan manager accumulated the following data:

Number of Customers	0	1	2	3	4	5	≥6
Frequencies	1	2	9	11	14	6	9

From previous years, the manager believes that the distribution of the number of customer arrivals has a Poisson distribution with an average of 3.5 loan applicants per week. Determine if the loan officer's belief is correct using a significance level of 0.025.

13-8. Managers of a major book publisher believe that the occurrence of typographical errors in the books the company publishes is Poisson distributed with a mean of 0.2 per page. Because of some customer quality complaints, the managers have arranged for a test to be conducted to determine if the error distribution still holds. A total of 400 pages were randomly selected and the number of errors per page was counted. These data are summarized in the following frequency distribution:

Errors	Frequency
0	335
1	56
2	7
3	2
Total	400

Conduct the appropriate hypothesis test using a significance level equal to 0.01. Discuss the results.

13-9. The Baltimore Steel and Pipe Company recently developed a new pipe product for a customer. According to specifications, the pipe is supposed to have an average outside diameter of 2.00 inches with a standard deviation equal to 0.10 inch, and the distribution of outside diameters is to be normally distributed. Before going into full-scale production, the company selected a random sample of 30 sections of pipe from the initial test run. The following data were recorded:

Pipe Section	Diameter (inches)	Pipe Section	Diameter (inches)
1	2.04	16	1.96
2	2.13	17	1.89
3	2.07	18	1.99
4	1.99	19	2.13
5	1.90	20	1.90
6	2.06	21	1.91
7	2.19	22	1.95
8	2.01	23	2.18
9	2.05	24	1.94
10	1.98	25	1.93
11	1.95	26	2.08
12	1.90	27	1.82
13	2.10	28	1.94
14	2.02	29	1.96
15	2.11	30	1.81

a. Using a significance level of 0.01, perform the appropriate test.
b. Based on these data, should the company conclude that it is meeting the product specifications? Explain your reasoning.

13-10. Quality-control managers work in every type of production environment possible, from producing dictionaries to dowel cutting for boat plugs. The Cincinnati Dowel & Wood Products Co., located in Mount Orab, Ohio, manufactures wood dowels and wood turnings. Four-inch-diameter boat plugs are one of its products. The quality control procedures aimed at maintaining the 4-inch diameter are only valid if the diameters have a normal distribution. The quality-control manager recently obtained the following summary diameters taken from randomly selected boat plugs on the production line:

Interval	Frequency	Interval	Frequency
<3.872	4	4.001–4.025	8
3.872–3.916	6	4.026–4.052	2
3.917–3.948	11	4.053–4.084	4
3.949–3.975	9	4.085–4.128	0
3.976–4.000	5	> 4.128	1

The boat plug diameters are specified to have a normal distribution with a mean of 4 inches and a standard deviation of 0.10. Determine if the distribution of the 4-inch boat plugs is currently adhering to specification. Use a chi-square goodness-of-fit test and a significance level of 0.05.

Computer Database Exercises

13-11. The owners of Big Boy Burgers are considering remodeling their facility to include a drive-thru window. There will be room for three cars in the drive-thru line if they build it. However, they are concerned that the capacity may be too low during their busy lunchtime hours between 11:00 A.M. and 1:30 P.M. One of the factors they need to know is the distribution of the length of time it takes to fill an order for cars coming to the drive-thru. To collect information on this, the owners have received permission from a similar operation owned by a relative in a nearby town to collect some data at that drive-thru. The data in the file called **Clair's Deli** reflect the service time per car.

Based on these sample data, is there sufficient evidence to conclude that the distribution of service time is not normally distributed? Test using the chi-square distribution and $\alpha = 0.05$.

13-12. Executives at the Walt Disney Company are interested in estimating the mean spending per capita for people who visit Disney World in Orlando, Florida. Since they do not know the population standard deviation, they plan to use the t-distribution (see Chapter 9) to conduct the test. However, they realize that the t-distribution requires that the population be normally distributed. Six hundred customers were randomly surveyed, and the amount spent during their stay at Disney World was recorded. These data are in the file called **Disney**. Before using these sample data to estimate the population mean, the managers wish to test to determine whether the population is normally distributed.
  a. State the appropriate null and alternative hypotheses.
  b. Organize the data into six classes and form the grouped data frequency distribution (refer to Chapter 2).
  c. Using the sample mean and sample standard deviation, calculate the expected frequencies, assuming that the null hypothesis is true.
  d. Conduct the test statistic and compare it to the appropriate critical value for a significance level equal to 0.05. What conclusion should be reached? Discuss.

13-13. Again, working with the data in Problem 13-11, the number of cars that arrive in each 10-minute period is another factor that will determine whether there will be the capacity to handle the drive-thru business. In addition to studying the service times, the owners also counted the number of cars that arrived at the deli in the nearby town in a sample of 10-minute time periods. These data are as follows:

3	2	0
2	3	3
3	3	3
0	2	3
0	3	3
1	1	0
2	4	9
1	2	4
2	1	1
4	1	3

Based on these data, is there evidence to conclude that the arrivals are not Poisson distributed? State the appropriate null and alternative hypotheses and test using a significance level of 0.025.

13-14. Damage to homes caused by burst piping can be expensive to repair. By the time the leak is discovered, hundreds of gallons of water may have already flooded the home. Automatic shutoff valves can prevent extensive water damage from plumbing failures. The valves contain sensors that cut off water flow in the event of a leak, thereby preventing flooding. One important characteristic is the time (in milliseconds) required for the sensor to detect the water flow. The data obtained for four different shutoff valves are contained in the file titled **Waterflow**. The differences between the observed time for the sensor to detect the water flow and the predicted time (termed *residuals*) are listed and are assumed to be normally distributed. Using the four sets of residuals given in the data file, determine if the residuals have a normal distribution. Use a chi-square goodness-of-fit test and a significance level of 0.05. Use five groups of equal width to conduct the test.

13-15. An article in the *San Francisco Chronicle* indicated that just 38% of drivers crossing the San Francisco Bay Area's seven state-owned bridges pay their tolls electronically, compared with rates nearing 80% at systems elsewhere in the nation. Albert Yee, director of highway and arterial operations for the regional Metropolitan Transportation Commission, indicated that the commission is eager to drive up the percentage of tolls paid electronically. In an attempt to see if its efforts are producing the required results, 15 vehicles each day are tracked through the toll lanes of the Bay Area bridges. The number of drivers using electronic payment to pay their toll for a period of three months appears in the file titled **Fastrak**.
  a. Determine if the distribution of the number of FasTrak users could be described as a binomial distribution with a population proportion equal to 0.50. Use a chi-square goodness-of-fit test and a significance level of 0.05.
  b. Conduct a test of hypothesis to determine if the percent of tolls paid electronically has increased to more than 70% since Yee's efforts.

Chapter Outcome 2.→ # 13.2 Introduction to Contingency Analysis

In Chapters 9 and 10, you were introduced to hypothesis tests involving one and two population proportions. Although these techniques are useful in many cases, you will also encounter many situations involving multiple population proportions. For example, a mutual fund company offers six different mutual funds. The president of the company may wish to determine if the proportion of customers selecting each mutual fund is related to the four sales regions in which the customers reside. A hospital administrator who collects service-satisfaction data from patients might be interested in determining whether there is a significant difference in patient rating by hospital department. A personnel manager for a large corporation might be interested in determining whether there is a relationship between level of employee job satisfaction and job classification. In each of these cases, the proportions relate to characteristic categories of the variable of interest. The six mutual funds, four sales regions, hospital departments, and job classifications are all specific categories.

These situations involving categorical data call for a new statistical tool known as *contingency analysis* to help make decisions when multiple proportions are involved. Contingency analysis can be used when a level of data measurement is either nominal or ordinal and the values are determined by counting the number of occurrences in each category.

2 × 2 Contingency Tables

BUSINESS APPLICATION **APPLYING CONTINGENCY ANALYSIS**

DALGARNO PHOTO, INC. Dalgarno Photo, Inc., gets much of its business from taking photographs for college yearbooks. Dalgarno hired a first-year masters of business administration (MBA) student to develop the survey it mailed to 850 yearbook editors at the colleges and universities in its market area. The representatives were unaware that Dalgarno Photo had developed the survey.

The survey asked about the photography and publishing activities associated with yearbook development. For instance, what photographer and publisher services did the schools use, and what factors were most important in selecting services? The survey instrument contained 30 questions, which were coded into 137 separate variables.

Among his many interests in this study, Dalgarno's marketing manager questioned whether college funding source and gender of the yearbook editor were related in some manner. To analyze this issue, we examine these two variables more closely. Source of university funding is a categorical variable, coded as follows:

$$1 = \text{Private funding}$$
$$2 = \text{State funding}$$

Of the 221 respondents who provided data for this variable, 155 came from privately funded colleges or universities and 66 were from state-funded institutions.

The second variable, gender of the yearbook editor, is also a categorical variable, with two response categories, coded as follows:

$$1 = \text{Male}$$
$$2 = \text{Female}$$

Of the 221 responses to the survey, 164 were from females and 57 were from males.

In cases in which the variables of interest are both categorical and the decision maker is interested in determining whether a relationship exists between the two, a statistical technique known as contingency analysis is useful. We first set up a two-dimensional table called a **contingency table**. The contingency table for these two variables is shown in Table 13.3.

Table 13.3 shows that 14 of the respondents were males from schools that are privately funded. The numbers at the extreme right and along the bottom are called the *marginal frequencies*. For example, 57 respondents were males, and 155 respondents were from privately funded institutions.

The issue of whether there is a relationship between responses to these two variables is formally addressed through a hypothesis test, in which the null and alternative hypotheses are stated as follows:

H_0: Gender of yearbook editor is independent of the college's funding source.
H_A: Gender of yearbook editor *is not* independent of the college's funding source.

Contingency Table

A table used to classify sample observations according to two or more identifiable characteristics. It is also called a *crosstabulation table*.

TABLE 13.3 | **Contingency Table for Dalgarno Photo**

	Source of Funding		
Gender	Private	State	
Male	14	43	57
Female	141	23	164
	155	66	221

If the null hypothesis is true, the population proportion of yearbook editors from private institutions who are males should be equal to the proportion of male editors from state-funded institutions. These two proportions should also equal the population proportion of male editors without regard to a school's funding source. To illustrate, we can use the sample data to determine the sample proportion of male editors as follows:

$$p_M = \frac{\text{Number of male editors}}{\text{Number of respondents}} = \frac{57}{221} = 0.2579$$

Then, if the null hypothesis is true, we would expect 25.79% of the 155 privately funded schools, or 39.98 schools, to have a male yearbook editor. We would also expect 25.79% of the 66 state-funded schools, or 17.02, to have male yearbook editors. (Note that the expected numbers need not be integer values. Note also that the sum of expected frequencies in any column or row add up to the marginal frequency.) We can use this reasoning to determine the expected number of respondents in each cell of the contingency table, as shown in Table 13.4.

You can simplify the calculations needed to produce the expected values for each cell. Note that the first cell's expected value, 39.98, was obtained by the following calculation:

$$e_{11} = 0.2579\,(155) = 39.98$$

However, because the probability, 0.2579, is calculated by dividing the row total, 57, by the grand total, 221, the calculation can also be represented as

$$e_{11} = \frac{(\text{Row total})(\text{Column total})}{\text{Grand total}} = \frac{(57)(155)}{221} = 39.98$$

As a further example, we can calculate the expected value for the next cell in the same row. The expected number of male yearbook editors in state-funded schools is

$$e_{12} = \frac{(\text{Row total})(\text{Column total})}{\text{Grand total}} = \frac{(57)(66)}{221} = 17.02$$

Keep in mind that the row and column totals (the marginal frequencies) must be the same for the expected values as for the observed values. Therefore, when there is only one cell left in a row or a column for which you must calculate an expected value, you can obtain it by subtraction. So, as an example, the expected value e_{12} could have been calculated as

$$e_{12} = 57 - 39.98 = 17.02$$

Allowing for sampling error, we would expect the actual frequencies in each cell to approximately match the corresponding expected cell frequencies when the null hypothesis is true. The greater the difference between the actual and the expected frequencies, the more likely the null hypothesis of independence is false and should be rejected. The statistical test to determine whether the sample data support or refute the null hypothesis is given by Equation 13.2. Do not be confused by the double summation in Equation 13.2; it merely indicates that all rows and columns must be used in calculating χ^2. As was the case in the goodness-of-fit tests, the degrees of freedom are the number of independent data values obtained from the experiment. In any given row, once you know $c - 1$ of the data values, the remaining data

TABLE 13.4 | **Contingency Table for Dalgarno Photo**

	Source of Funding		
Gender	Private	State	Total
Male	$o_{11} = 14$ $e_{11} = 39.98$	$o_{12} = 43$ $e_{12} = 17.02$	57
Female	$o_{21} = 141$ $e_{21} = 115.02$	$o_{22} = 23$ $e_{22} = 48.98$	164
Total	155	66	221

value is determined. For instance, once you know that 14 of the 57 male editors were from privately funded institutions, you know that 43 were from state-funded institutions.

Chi-Square Contingency Test Statistic

$$\chi^2 = \sum_{i=1}^{r} \sum_{j=1}^{c} \frac{(o_{ij} - e_{ij})^2}{e_{ij}} \qquad \text{with } df = (r-1)(c-1)$$ **(13.2)**

where:

o_{ij} = Observed frequency in cell (i, j)
e_{ij} = Expected frequency in cell (i, j)
r = Number of rows
c = Number of columns

FIGURE 13.6

Chi-Square Contingency
Analysis Test for
Dalgarno Photo

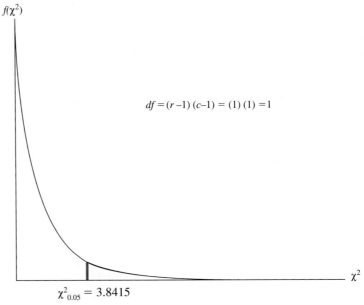

Hypotheses:

H_0: Gender of yearbook editor is independent of college's funding source.
H_A: Gender of yearbook editor is not independent of college's funding source.
$\alpha = 0.05$

	Private	State
Male	$o_{11} = 14$ $e_{11} = 39.98$	$o_{12} = 43$ $e_{12} = 17.02$
Female	$o_{21} = 141$ $e_{21} = 115.02$	$o_{22} = 23$ $e_{22} = 48.98$

Test Statistic:

$$\chi^2 = \sum_{i=1}^{r} \sum_{j=1}^{c} \frac{(o_{ij} - e_{ij})^2}{e_{ij}} = \frac{(14 - 39.98)^2}{39.98} + \frac{(43 - 17.02)^2}{17.02}$$
$$+ \frac{(141 - 115.02)^2}{115.02} + \frac{(23 - 48.98)^2}{48.98} = 76.19$$

$f(\chi^2)$

$df = (r-1)(c-1) = (1)(1) = 1$

$\chi^2_{0.05} = 3.8415$

χ^2

Decision Rule:

If $\chi^2 > 3.8415$, reject H_0;
Otherwise, do not reject H_0.
Because $76.19 > 3.8415$, reject H_0. Thus, the gender of the yearbook editor and the school's source of funding are not independent.

Similarly, once $r - 1$ data values in a column are known, the remaining data value is determined. Therefore, the degrees of freedom are obtained by the expression $(r - 1)(c - 1)$.

Figure 13.6 presents the hypotheses and test results for this example. As was the case in the goodness-of-fit tests, the test statistic has a distribution that can be approximated by the chi-square distribution if the expected values are larger than 5. Note that the calculated chi-square statistic is compared to the tabled value of chi-square for an $\alpha = 0.05$ and degrees of freedom $= (2 - 1)(2 - 1) = 1$. Because $\chi^2 = 76.19 > 3.8415$, the null hypothesis of independence should be rejected. Dalgarno Photo representatives should conclude that the gender of the yearbook editor and each school's source of funding are not independent. By examining the data in Figure 13.6, you can see that private schools are more likely to have female editors, whereas state schools are more likely to have male yearbook editors.

EXAMPLE 13-4   **2 × 2 CONTINGENCY ANALYSIS**

Jury Selection In major cases, trial attorneys often spend significant time and resources trying to better understand how potential jurors may respond to particular testimony. For example, in a civil case involving a high-profile client in Pittsburg, Pennsylvania, the lawyers were interested in understanding whether potential jurors might recall a DUI arrest of their client a year ago. They are specifically concerned about whether there is a relationship between gender and the ability to recall the DUI incident. They conducted a test in which they randomly called 100 people (potential jurors) and asked them to indicate whether they recalled a DUI conviction by the client. The law firm is interested in determining whether there is a relationship between gender and a person's ability to recall the DUI arrest. To test this, the following steps can be used:

Step 1 Specify the null and alternative hypotheses.
The law firm is interested in testing whether a relationship exists between gender and recall ability. Here are the appropriate null and alternative hypotheses.

H_0: Ability to correctly recall the client's arrest is independent of gender.
H_A: Recall ability and gender are not independent.

Step 2 Determine the significance level.
The test will be conducted using a 0.01 level of significance.

Step 3 Determine the critical value.
The critical value for this test will be the chi-square value, with $(r - 1)(c - 1) = (2 - 1)(2 - 1) = 1$ degree of freedom with an $\alpha = 0.01$. From Appendix G, the critical value is 6.6349.

Step 4 Collect the sample data and compute the chi-square test statistic using Equation 13.2.
The following contingency table shows the results of the sampling:

	Female	Male	Total
Correct Recall	33	25	58
Incorrect Recall	22	20	42
Total	55	45	100

Note that 58% of the entire data values result in a correct recall. If the ability to correctly recall the client's DUI arrest is independent of gender, you would expect the same percentage (58%) would occur for each gender. Thus, 58% of the males $[.58(45) = 26.10]$ would be expected to have a correct recall. In general, the expected cell frequencies are determined by multiplying the row total by the column total and dividing by the overall sample size. For example, for the cell corresponding to female and correct recall, we get

$$\text{Expected} = \frac{58 \times 55}{100} = 31.90$$

The expected cell values for all cells are

	Female	Male	Total
Correct Recall	$o = 33$ $e = 31.90$	$o = 25$ $e = 26.10$	58
Incorrect Recall	$o = 22$ $e = 23.10$	$o = 20$ $e = 18.90$	42
Total	55	45	100

After checking to make sure all the expected cell frequencies ≥ 5, the test statistic is computed using Equation 13.2.

$$\chi^2 = \sum_{i=1}^{r}\sum_{j=1}^{c}\frac{(o_{ij}-e_{ij})^2}{e_{ij}}$$

$$= \frac{(33-31.90)^2}{31.90}+\frac{(25-26.10)^2}{26.10}+\frac{(22-23.10)^2}{23.10}+\frac{(20-18.90)^2}{18.90} = 0.20$$

Step 5   Reach a decision.
Because $\chi^2 = 0.20 < 6.6349$, do not reject the null hypothesis.

Step 6   Draw a conclusion.
Based on the sample data, there is no reason to believe that being able to recall that the client was previously arrested for DUI is related to gender. Thus, based on this issue, the lawyers would have no reason to prefer male or female jurors.

>> **END EXAMPLE**

TRY PROBLEM 13-17 (pg. 551)

$r \times c$ Contingency Tables

BUSINESS APPLICATION   **LARGER CONTINGENCY TABLES**

Excel Tutorial

BENTON STONE & TILE Benton Stone & Tile makes a wide variety of products for the building industry. It pays market wages, provides competitive benefits, and offers attractive options for employees in an effort to create a satisfied workforce and reduce turnover. Recently, however, several supervisors have complained that employee absenteeism is becoming a problem. In response to these complaints, the human resources manager studied a random sample of 500 employees. One aim of this study was to determine whether there is a relationship between absenteeism and marital status. Absenteeism during the past year was broken down into three levels:

  1. 0 absences
  2. 1 to 5 absences
  3. Over 5 absences

Marital status was divided into four categories:

  1. Single 2. Married
  3. Divorced 4. Widowed

Table 13.5 shows the contingency table for the sample of 500 employees. The table is also shown in the file **Benton**. The null and alternative hypotheses to be tested are

  H_0: Absentee behavior is independent of marital status.
  H_A: Absentee behavior is not independent of marital status.

As with 2×2 contingency analysis, the test for independence can be made using the chi-square test, where the expected cell frequencies are compared to the actual cell frequencies

TABLE 13.5 | **Contingency Table for Benton Stone & Tile**

Marital Status	Absentee Rate			Row Totals
	0	1–5	Over 5	
Single	84	82	34	200
Married	50	64	36	150
Divorced	50	34	16	100
Widowed	16	20	14	50
Column Totals	200	200	100	500

and the test statistic shown as Equation 13.2 is used. The logic of the test says that if the actual and expected frequencies closely match, then the null hypothesis of independence is not rejected. However, if the actual and expected cell frequencies are substantially different overall, the null hypothesis of independence is rejected. The calculated chi-square statistic is compared to an Appendix G critical value for the desired significance and degrees of freedom equal to $(r - 1)(c - 1)$.

The expected cell frequencies are determined assuming that the row and column variables are independent. This means, for example, that the probability of a married person being absent more than 5 days during the year is the same as the probability of any employee being absent more than 5 days. An easy way to compute the expected cell frequencies, e_{ij}, is given by Equation 13.3.

Expected Cell Frequencies

$$e_{ij} = \frac{(i\text{th row total})(j\text{th column total})}{\text{total sample size}} \tag{13.3}$$

For example, the expected cell frequency for row 1, column 1 is

$$e_{11} = \frac{(200)(200)}{500} = 80$$

and the expected cell frequency for row 2, column 3 is

$$e_{23} = \frac{(150)(100)}{500} = 30$$

Figure 13.7 shows the completed contingency table with the actual and expected cell frequencies that were developed using Excel. The calculated chi-square test value is computed as follows:

$$\chi^2 = \sum_{i=1}^{r}\sum_{j=1}^{c} \frac{(o_{ij} - e_{ij})^2}{e_{ij}}$$

$$= \frac{(84 - 80)^2}{80} + \frac{(82 - 80)^2}{80} + \cdots + \frac{(20 - 20)^2}{20} + \frac{(14 - 10)^2}{10}$$

$$= 10.88$$

The degrees of freedom are $(r - 1)(c - 1) = (4 - 1)(3 - 1) = 6$. You can use the chi-square table in Appendix G to get the chi-square critical value for $\alpha = 0.05$ and 6 degrees of freedom, or you can use Excel's CHISQ.INV.RT function (CHISQ.INV.RT(.05,6) = 12.5916). Because the calculated chi-square value (10.883) shown in Figure 13.7 is less than 12.5916, we cannot reject the null hypothesis. Based on these sample data, there is *insufficient evidence* to conclude that absenteeism and marital status are not independent.

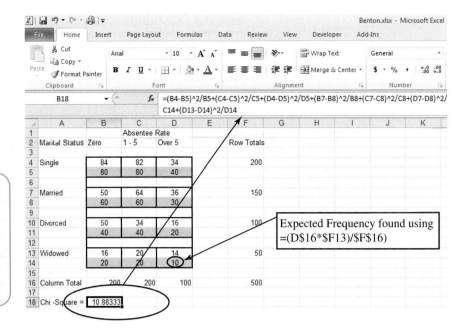

Excel 2010 Instructions:
1. Open file: **Benton.xlsx**.
2. Compute expected cell frequencies using Excel formula.
3. Compute chi-square statistic using Excel formula.

Minitab Instructions (for similar results):
1. Open file: **Benton.MTW**.
2. Choose **Stat > Tables > Chi-Square Test**.
3. In Columns containing the table, enter data columns.
4. Click **OK**.

Chi-Square Test Limitations

The chi-square distribution is only an approximation for the true distribution for contingency analysis. We use the chi-square approximation because the true distribution is impractical to compute in most instances. However, the approximation (and, therefore, the conclusion reached) is quite good when all expected cell frequencies are at least 5.0. When expected cell frequencies drop below 5.0, the calculated chi-square value tends to be inflated and may inflate the true probability of a Type I error beyond the stated significance level. As a rule, if the null hypothesis is not rejected, you do not need to worry when the expected cell frequencies drop below 5.0.

There are two alternatives that can be used to overcome the small expected-cell-frequency problem. The first is to increase the sample size. This may increase the marginal frequencies in each row and column enough to increase the expected cell frequencies. The second option is to combine the categories of the row and/or column variables. If you do decide to group categories together, there should be some logic behind the resulting categories. You don't want to lose the meaning of the results through poor groupings. You will need to examine each situation individually to determine whether the option of grouping classes to increase expected cell frequencies makes sense.

MyStatLab

13-2: Exercises

Skill Development

13-16. A university recently completed a study to determine whether the number of classes students dropped during their college course work was related to whether the student lived on campus or commuted. The following data were collected.

Courses dropped	Where Lived	
	Commuted	On Campus
0	70	90
1	60	50

Courses dropped	Where Lived	
	Commuted	On Campus
2	45	28
3	42	47
Over 3	36	48

Using an $\alpha = 0.05$ level, determine whether the number of courses dropped is independent of where a student lives.

13-17. The billing department of a national cable service company is conducting a study of how customers pay their monthly cable bills. The cable company accepts payment in one of four ways: in person at a local office, by mail, by credit card, or by electronic funds transfer from a bank account. The cable company randomly sampled 400 customers to determine if there is a relationship between the customer's age and the payment method used. The following sample results were obtained:

Payment Method	Age of Customer			
	20–30	31–40	41–50	Over 50
In Person	8	12	11	13
By Mail	29	67	72	50
By Credit Card	26	19	5	7
By Funds Transfer	23	35	17	6

Based on the sample data, can the cable company conclude that there is a relationship between the age of the customer and the payment method used? Conduct the appropriate test at the $\alpha = 0.01$ level of significance.

13-18. A contingency analysis table has been constructed from data obtained in a phone survey of customers in a market area in which respondents were asked to indicate whether they owned a domestic or foreign car and whether they were a member of a union or not. The following contingency table is provided.

Car	Union	
	Yes	No
Domestic	155	470
Foreign	40	325

a. Use the chi-square approach to test whether type of car owned (domestic or foreign) is independent of union membership. Test using an $\alpha = 0.05$ level.
b. Calculate the p-value for this hypothesis test.

13-19. Utilize the following contingency table to answer the questions listed below.

	C_1	C_2
R_1	51	207
R_2	146	185
R_3	240	157

a. State the relevant null and alternative hypotheses.
b. Calculate the expected values for each of the cells.

c. Compute the chi-square test statistic for the hypothesis test.
d. Determine the appropriate critical value and reach a decision for the hypothesis test. Use a significance level of 0.05.
e. Obtain the p-value for this hypothesis test.

13-20. A manufacturer of sports drinks has randomly sampled 198 men and 202 women. Each sampled participant was asked to taste an unflavored version and a flavored version of a new sports drink currently in development. The participants' preferences are shown below:

	Flavored	Unflavored
Men	101	97
Women	68	134

a. State the relevant null and alternative hypotheses.
b. Conduct the appropriate test and state a conclusion. Use a level of significance of 0.05.

13-21. A marketing research firm is conducting a study to determine if there is a relationship between an individual's age and the individual's preferred source of news. The research firm asked 1,000 individuals to list their preferred source for news: newspaper, radio and television, or the Internet. The following results were obtained:

Preferred News Source	Age of Respondent			
	20–30	31–40	41–50	Over 50
Newspaper	19	62	95	147
Radio/TV	27	125	168	88
Internet	104	113	37	15

At the 0.01 level of significance, can the marketing research firm conclude that there is a relationship between the age of the individual and the individual's preferred source for news?

13-22. A loan officer wished to determine if the marital status of loan applicants was independent of the approval of loans. The following table presents the result of her survey:

	Approved	Rejected
Single	213	189
Married	374	231
Divorced	358	252

a. Conduct the appropriate hypothesis test that will provide an answer to the loan officer. Use a significance level of 0.01.
b. Calculate the p-value for the hypothesis test in part a.

13-23. An instructor in a large accounting class is interested in determining whether the grades that students get are related to how close to the front of the room the students sit. He has categorized the room seating as "Front," "Middle," and "Back." The following data were collected over two sections with 400 total students. Based on the sample data, can you conclude that there is a dependency relationship between seating location and grade using a significance level equal to 0.05?

	A	B	C	D	F	Total
Front	18	55	30	3	0	106
Middle	7	42	95	11	1	156
Back	3	15	104	14	2	138
Total	28	112	229	28	3	400

Business Applications

13-24. A study was conducted to determine if there is a difference between the investing preferences of mid-level managers working in the public and private sectors in New York City. A random sample of 320 public-sector employees and 380 private-sector employees was taken. The sampled participants were then asked about their retirement investment decisions and classified as being either "aggressive," if they invested only in stocks or stock mutual funds, or "balanced," if they invested in some combination of stocks, bonds, cash, and other. The following results were found:

	Aggressive	Balanced
Public	164	156
Private	236	144

a. State the hypothesis of interest and conduct the appropriate hypothesis test to determine whether there is a relationship between employment sector and investing preference. Use a level of significance of 0.01.
b. State the conclusion of the test conducted in part a.
c. Calculate the p-value for the hypothesis test conducted in part a.

13-25. The following table classifies a stock's price change as up, down, or no change for both today's and yesterday's prices. Price changes were examined for 100 days. A financial theory states that stock prices follow what is called a "random walk." This means, in part, that the price change today for a stock must be independent of yesterday's price change. Test the hypothesis that daily stock price changes for this stock are independent. Let $\alpha = 0.05$.

Price Change Today	Price Change Previous Day		
	Up	No Change	Down
Up	14	16	12
No Change	6	8	6
Down	16	14	8

13-26. A local appliance retailer handles four washing machine models for a major manufacturer: standard, deluxe, superior, and XLT. The marketing manager has recently conducted a study on the purchasers of the washing machines. The study recorded the model of appliance purchased and the credit account balance of the customer at the time of purchase. The sample data are in the following table. Based on these data, is there evidence of a relationship between the account balance and the model of washer purchased? Use a significance level of 0.025. Conduct the test using a p-value approach.

Credit Balance	Washer Model Purchased			
	Standard	Deluxe	Superior	XLT
Under $200	10	16	40	5
$200–$800	8	12	24	15
Over $800	16	12	16	30

13-27. A random sample of 980 heads of households was taken from the customer list for State Bank and Trust. Those sampled were asked to classify their own attitudes and their parents' attitudes toward borrowing money as follows:
A: Borrow only for real estate and car purchases
B: Borrow for short-term purchases such as appliances and furniture
C: Never borrow money
The following table indicates the responses from those in the study.

Parent	Respondent		
	A	B	C
A	240	80	20
B	180	120	40
C	180	80	40

Test the hypothesis that the respondents' borrowing habits are independent from what they believe their parents' attitudes to be. Let $\alpha = 0.01$.

13-28. The California Lettuce Research board was originally formed as the Iceberg Lettuce Advisory Board in 1973. The primary function of the board is to fund research on iceberg and leaf lettuce. A recent project involved studying the effect of varying levels of sodium absorption ratios (SAR) on the yield of head lettuce. The measurements (the number of lettuce heads from each plot) of the kind observed were as follows:

SAR	Lettuce Type	
	Salinas	Sniper
3	104	109
5	160	163
7	142	146
10	133	156

a. Determine if the number of lettuce heads harvested for the two lettuce types is independent of the levels of sodium absorption ratios (SAR). Use a significance level of 0.025 and a p-value approach.
b. Which type of lettuce would you recommend?

13-29. In its ninth year, the Barclaycard Business Travel Survey has become an information source for business travelers not only in the United Kingdom but internationally as well. Each year, as a result of the research, Barclaycard Business has been able to predict and comment on trends within the business travel industry. One question asked in two consecutive years was, "Have you considered reducing hours spent away from home to increase quality of life?" The following table represents the responses:

	Year 1	Year 2	Total
Yes—have reduced	400	384	784
Yes—not been able to	400	300	700
No—not certain	400	516	916
Total	1200	1200	2400

a. Determine if the response to the survey question was independent of the year in which the question was asked. Use a significance level of 0.05.

b. Determine if there is a significant difference between the proportion of travelers who say they have reduced hours spent away from home between the two years.

Computer Database Exercises

13-30. Daniel Vinson of the University of Missouri–Columbia led a team of researchers investigating the increased risk when people are angry of serious injuries in the workplace requiring emergency medical care. The file titled **Angry** contains the data collected by the team of researchers. It displays the emotions reported by patients just before they were injured.

a. Use the data in the file titled **Angry** to construct a contingency table.

b. Determine if the type of emotion felt by patients just before they were injured is independent of the severity of that emotion. Use a contingency analysis and a significance level of 0.05.

13-31. *Gift of the Gauche*, a left-handedness information Web site (www.left-handedness.info), provides information concerning left-handed activities, products, and demography. It indicates that about 10% to 11% of the population of Europe and North America is left-handed. It also reports on demographic surveys. It cites an American study in which more than one million magazine respondents found that 12.6% of the male respondents were left-handed, as were 9.9% of the female respondents, although this was not a random sample. The data obtained by a British survey of more than 8,000 randomly selected men and women,

published in *The Graphologist*, is furnished in a file titled **Lefties**. Based on this data, determine if the "handedness" of an individual is independent of gender. Use a significance level of 0.01 and a *p*-value approach.

13-32. The Marriott Company owns and operates a number of different hotel chains, including the Courtyard chain. Recently, a survey was mailed to a random sample of 400 Courtyard customers. A total of 62 customers responded to the survey. The customers were asked a number of questions related to their satisfaction with the chain as well as several demographic questions. Among the issues of interest was whether there is a relationship between the likelihood that customers will stay at the chain again and whether this was the customer's first stay at the Courtyard. The following contingency table has been developed from the data set contained in the file called **CourtyardSurvey**:

Stay Again?	First Stay		
	Yes	No	Total
Definitely Will	9	12	21
Probably Will	18	2	20
Maybe	15	3	18
Probably Not	2	1	3
Total	44	18	62

Using a significance level equal to 0.05, test to see whether these sample data imply a relationship between the two variables. Discuss the results.

13-33. ECCO (Electronic Controls Company) makes backup alarms that are used on such equipment as forklifts and delivery trucks. The quality manager recently performed a study involving a random sample of 110 warranty claims. One of the questions the manager wanted to answer was whether there is a relationship between the type of warranty complaint and the plant at which the alarm was made. The data are in the file called **ECCO**.

a. Calculate the expected values for the cells in this analysis. Suggest a way in which cells can be combined to assure that the expected value of each cell is at least 5 so that as many level combinations of the two variables as possible are retained.

b. Using a significance level of 0.01, conduct a relevant hypothesis test and provide an answer to the manager's question.

13-34. Referring to Problem 13-32, can the quality control manager conclude that the type of warranty problem is independent of the shift on which the alarm was manufactured? Test using a significance level of 0.05. Discuss your results.

Visual Summary

Chapter 13: Many of the statistical procedures introduced in earlier chapters require that the sample data come from populations that are normally distributed and that the data be measured at least at the interval level. However, you will encounter many situations in which these specifications are not met. This chapter introduces two sets of procedures that are used to address each of these issues in turn. Goodness-of–fit procedures are used to determine if sample data has been drawn from a specific hypothesized distribution. Contingency analysis is an often used technique to determine the relationship between qualitative variables. Though these procedures are not used as much as those requiring normal populations, you will discover that far too few of the procedures presented in this chapter are used when they should be. It is, therefore, important that you learn when and how to use the procedures presented in this chapter.

13.1 Introduction to Goodness-of-Fit Tests (pg. 530–543)

Summary

The chi-square goodness-of-fit test can be used to determine if a set of data comes from a specific hypothesized distribution. Recall that several of the procedures presented in Chapters 8-12 require that the sampled populations are normally distributed. For example, tests involving the *t*-distribution are based on such a requirement. In order to verify this requirement, the goodness-of-fit test determines if the observed set of values agree with a set of data obtained from a specified probability distribution. Perhaps the goodness-of-fit test is most often used to verify a normal distribution. However, it can be used to detect many other probability distributions.

> **Outcome 1.** Utilize the chi-square goodness-of-fit test to determine whether data from a process fit a specified distribution

13.2 Introduction to Contingency Analysis (pg. 544–553)

Summary
You will encounter many business situations in which the level of data measurement for the variable of interest is either nominal or ordinal, not interval or ratio. In Chapters 9 and 10 you were introduced to hypothesis tests involving one and two population proportions. However, you will also encounter many situations involving multiple population proportions for which two-population procedures are not applicable. In each of these cases, the proportions relate to characteristic categories of the variable of interest. These situations involving categorical data call for a new statistical tool known as *contingency analysis* to help make decisions when multiple proportions are involved. Contingency analysis can be used when a level of data measurement is either nominal or ordinal and the values are determined by counting the number of occurrences in each category.

> **Outcome 2.** Set up a contingency analysis table and perform a chi-square test of independence

Conclusion

This chapter has introduced two very useful statistical tools: goodness-of-fit tests and contingency analysis. Goodness-of-fit testing is used when a decision maker wishes to determine whether sample data come from a population having specific characteristics. The chi-square goodness-of-fit procedure that was introduced in this chapter addresses this issue. This test relies on the idea that if the distribution of the sample data is substantially different from the hypothesized population distribution, then the population distribution from which these sample data came must not be what was hypothesized.

Contingency analysis is a frequently used statistical tool that allows the decision maker to test whether responses to two variables are independent. Market researchers, for example, use contingency analysis to determine whether attitude about the quality of their company's product is independent of the gender of a customer. By using contingency analysis and the chi-square contingency test, they can make this determination based on a sample of customers.

Equations

(13.1) Chi-Square Goodness-of-Fit Test Statistic pg. 533

$$\chi^2 = \sum_{i=1}^{k} \frac{(o_i - e_i)^2}{e_i}$$

(13.2) Chi-Square Contingency Test Statistic pg. 546

$$\chi^2 = \sum_{i=1}^{r}\sum_{j=1}^{c} \frac{(o_{ij} - e_{ij})^2}{e_{ij}} \quad \text{with } df = (r-1)(c-1)$$

(13.3) Expected Cell Frequencies pg. 549

$$e_{ij} = \frac{(i\text{th row total})(j\text{th column total})}{\text{total sample size}}$$

Key Term

Contingency table pg. 544

Chapter Exercises _____ MyStatLab

Conceptual Questions

13-35. Locate a journal article that uses either contingency analysis or a goodness-of-fit test. Discuss the article, paying particular attention to the reasoning behind using the particular statistical test.

13-36. Find a marketing research book (or borrow one from a friend). Does it discuss either of the tests considered in this chapter? If yes, outline the discussion. If no, determine where in the text such a discussion would be appropriate.

13-37. One of the topics in Chapter 10 was hypothesis testing for the difference between two population proportions. For the test to have validity, there were conditions set on the sample sizes with respect to the sample proportions. A 2×2 contingency table may also be utilized to test the difference between proportions of two independent populations. This procedure has conditions placed on the expected value of each cell. Discuss the relationship between these two conditions.

13-38. A 2×2 contingency table and a hypothesis test of the difference between two population proportions can be used to analyze the same data set. However, besides all the similarities of the two methods, the hypothesis test of the difference between two proportions has two advantages. Identify these advantages.

Business Applications

13-39. The College Bookstore has just hired a new manager, one with a business background. Claudia Markman has been charged with increasing the profitability of the bookstore, with the profits going to the general scholarship fund. Claudia started her job just before the beginning of the semester and was analyzing the sales during the days when students are buying their textbooks. The store has four checkout stands, and Claudia noticed registers three and four served fewer students than registers one and two. She is not sure whether the layout of the store channels customers into these registers, whether the checkout clerks in these lines are simply slower than the other two, or whether she was just seeing random differences.

Claudia kept a record of which stands the next 1,000 students chose for checkout. The students checked out of the four stands according to the following pattern:

Stand 1	Stand 2	Stand 3	Stand 4
338	275	201	186

a. Based on these data, can Claudia conclude the proportion of students using the four checkout stands is equal? (Use an $\alpha = 0.05$.)

b. A friend suggested that you could just as well conduct four hypothesis tests that the proportion of customers visiting each stand is equal to $p = 0.25$. Discuss the merits of this suggestion.

13-40. A regional cancer treatment center has had success treating localized cancers with a linear accelerator. Whereas admissions for further treatment nationally average 2.1 per patient per year, the center's director thinks that readmissions with the new treatment are Poisson distributed, with a mean of 1.2 patients per year. He has collected the following data on a random sample of 300 patients:

Re-admissions Last Year	Patients
0	139
1	87
2	48

Re-admissions Last Year	Patients
3	14
4	8
5	1
6	1
7	0
8	2
	300

a. Adjust the data so that you can test the director's claim using a test statistic whose sampling distribution can be approximated by a chi-square distribution.
b. Assume the Type I error rate is to be controlled at 0.05. Do you agree with the director's claim? Why? Conduct a statistical procedure to support your opinion.

13-41. Cooper Manufacturing, Inc., of Dallas, Texas, has a contract with the U.S. Air Force to produce a part for a new fighter plane being manufactured. The part is a bolt that has specifications requiring that the length be normally distributed with a mean of 3.05 inches and a standard deviation of 0.015 inch. As part of the company's quality-control efforts, each day Cooper's engineers select a random sample of 100 bolts produced that day and carefully measure the bolts to determine whether the production is within specifications. The following data were collected yesterday:

Length (inches)	Frequency
Under 3.030	5
3.030 and under 3.035	16
3.035 and under 3.040	7
3.040 and under 3.050	20
3.050 and under 3.060	36
3.060 and under 3.065	8
3.065 and over	8

Based on these sample data, what should Cooper's engineers conclude about the production output if they test using an $\alpha = 0.01$? Discuss.

13-42. The Cooper Company discussed in Problem 13-40 has a second contract with a private firm for which it makes fuses for an electronic instrument. The quality-control department at Cooper periodically selects a random sample of five fuses and tests each fuse to determine whether it is defective. Based on these findings, the production process is either shut down (if too many defectives are observed) or allowed to run. The quality-control department believes that the sampling process follows a binomial distribution, and it has been using the binomial distribution to compute the probabilities associated with the sampling outcomes.

The contract allows for at most 5% defectives. The head of quality control recently compiled a list of the sampling results for the past 300 days in which five randomly selected fuses were tested, with the following

frequency distribution for the number of defectives observed. She is concerned that the binomial distribution with a sample size of 5 and a probability of defectives of 0.05 may not be appropriate.

Number of Defectives	Frequency
0	209
1	33
2	43
3	10
4	5
5	0

a. Calculate the expected values for the cells in this analysis. Suggest a way in which cells can be combined to assure that the expected value of each cell is at least 5.
b. Using a significance level of 0.10, what should the quality control manager conclude based on these sample data? Discuss.

13-43. A survey performed by Simmons Market Research investigated the percentage of individuals in various age groups who indicated they were willing to pay more for environmentally friendly products. The results were presented in *USA Today* "Snapshots." The survey had approximately 3,240 respondents in each age group. Results of the survey follow:

Age Group	18–24	25–34	35–44	45–54	55–64	65 and over
Percentage	11	17	19	20	14	19

Conduct a goodness-of-fit test analysis to determine if the proportions of individuals willing to pay more for environmentally friendly products in the various age groups are equal. Use a significance level of 0.01.

13-44. An article published in *USA Today* asserts that many children are abandoning outdoor for indoor activities. The National Sporting Goods Association annual survey compared activity levels to the levels found nine years earlier. A random selection of children (7- to 11-year-olds) indicating their favorite outdoor activity is given in the following table:

	Bicycling	Swimming	Baseball	Fishing	Touch Football
Earlier	68	60	29	25	16
Present	47	42	22	18	10

Construct a contingency analysis to determine if the type of preferred outdoor activity is dependent on the year in this survey. Use a significance level of 0.05 and the *p*-value approach.

Computer Database Exercises

13-45. With the economic downturn that started in late 2007, many people started worrying about retirement and whether they even would be able to retire. A study recently done by the Employee Benefit Research

Institute (EBRI) found about 69% of workers said they and/or their spouses have saved for retirement. The file titled **Retirement** contains the total savings and investments indicated. Use a contingency analysis to determine if the amount of total savings and investments is dependent on the age of the worker.

13-46. The airport manager at the Sacramento, California, airport recently conducted a study of passengers departing from the airport. A random sample of 100 passengers was selected. The data are in the file called **Airline Passengers**. An earlier study showed the following usage by airline:

Delta	20%	7
Horizon	10%	29
Northwest	10%	10
Skywest	3%	8
Southwest	25%	20
United	32%	18

a. If the manager wishes to determine whether the airline usage pattern has changed from that reported in the earlier study, state the appropriate null and alternative hypotheses.

b. Based on the sample data, what should be concluded? Test using a significance level of 0.01.

13-47. A pharmaceutical company is planning to market a drug that is supposed to help reduce blood pressure. The company claims that if the drug is taken properly, the amount of blood pressure decrease will be normally distributed with a mean equal to 10 points on the diastolic reading and a standard deviation equal to 4.0. One hundred patients were administered the drug, and data were collected showing the reduction in blood pressure at the end of the test period. The data are located in the file labeled **Blood Pressure**.

a. Using a goodness-of-fit test and a significance level equal to 0.05, what conclusion should be reached with respect to the distribution of diastolic blood pressure reduction? Discuss.

b. Conduct a hypothesis test to determine if the standard deviation for this population could be considered to be 4.0. Use a significance level of 0.10.

c. Given the results of the two tests in parts a and b, is it appropriate to construct a confidence interval based on a normal distribution with a population standard deviation of 4.0? Explain your answer.

d. If appropriate, construct a 99% confidence interval for the mean reduction in blood pressure. Based on this confidence interval, does an average diastolic loss of 10 seem reasonable for this procedure? Explain your reasoning.

13-48. An Ariel Capital Management and Charles Schwab survey addressed the proportion of African Americans and White Americans who have money invested in the stock market. Suppose the file titled **Stockrace** contains data obtained in the surveys. The survey asked 500 African American and 500 White respondents if they personally had money invested in the stock market.

a. Create a contingency table using the data in the file **Stockrace**.

b. Conduct a contingency analysis to determine if the proportion of African Americans differs from the proportion of White Americans who invest in stocks. Use a significance level of 0.05.

13-49. The state transportation department recently conducted a study of motorists in Idaho. Two main factors of interest were whether the vehicle was insured with liability insurance and whether the driver was wearing a seat belt. A random sample of 100 cars was stopped at various locations throughout the state. The data are in the file called **Liabins**. The investigators were interested in determining whether seat belt status is independent of insurance status.

Conduct the appropriate hypothesis test using a 0.05 level of significance and discuss your results.

Case 13.1

American Oil Company

Chad Williams sat back in his airline seat to enjoy the hour-long flight between Los Angeles and Oakland, California. The hour would give him time to reflect on his upcoming trip to Australia and the work he had been doing the past week in Los Angeles.

Chad is one man on a six-man crew employed by the American Oil Company to literally walk the earth searching for oil. His college degrees in geology and petroleum engineering landed him the job with American, but he never dreamed he would be doing the exciting work he now does. Chad and his crew spend several months in special locations around the world using highly sensitive electronic equipment for oil exploration.

The upcoming trip to Australia is one that Chad has been looking forward to since it was announced that his crew would be going there to search the Outback for oil. In preparation for the trip, the crew has been in Los Angeles at American's engineering research facility working on some new equipment that will be used in Australia.

Chad's thoughts centered on the problem he was having with a particular component part on the new equipment. The specifications called for 200 of the components, with each having a diameter of between 0.15 and 0.18 inch. The only available supplier of the component manufactures the components in New Jersey to specifications calling for normally distributed output, with a mean of 0.16 inches and a standard deviation of 0.02 inches.

Chad faces two problems. First, he is unsure that the supplier actually does produce parts with means of 0.16 inches and standard deviations of 0.02 inches according to a normal distribution. Second, if the parts are made to specifications, he needs to determine how many components to purchase if enough acceptable components are to be received to make two oil exploration devices.

The supplier has sent Chad the following data for 330 randomly selected components. Chad believes that the supplier is honest and that he can rely on the data.

Chad needs to have a report ready for Monday indicating whether he believes the supplier delivers at its stated specifications and, if so, how many of the components American should order to have enough acceptable components to outfit two oil exploration devices.

Diameter (Inch)	Frequency
Under 0.14	5
0.14 and under 0.15	70
0.15 and under 0.16	90
0.16 and under 0.17	105
0.17 and under 0.18	50
Over 0.18	10
Total	330

Required Tasks:

1. State the problems faced by Chad Williams.
2. Identify the statistical test Chad Williams can use to determine whether the supplier's claim is true.
3. State the null and alternative hypotheses for the test to determine whether the supplier's claim is true.
4. Assuming that the supplier produces output whose diameter is normally distributed with a mean of 0.16 inches and a standard deviation of 0.02 inches, determine the expected frequencies that Chad would expect to see in a sample of 330 components.
5. Based on the observed and expected frequencies, calculate the appropriate test statistic.
6. Calculate the critical value of the test statistic. Select an alpha value.
7. State a conclusion. Is the supplier's claim with respect to specifications of the component parts supported by the sample data?
8. Provide a short report that summarizes your analysis and conclusion.

Case 13.2

Bentford Electronics—Part 1

On Saturday morning, Jennifer Bentford received a call at her home from the production supervisor at Bentford Electronics Plant 1. The supervisor indicated that she and the supervisors from Plants 2, 3, and 4 had agreed that something must be done to improve company morale and thereby increase the production output of their plants. Jennifer Bentford, president of Bentford Electronics, agreed to set up a Monday morning meeting with the supervisors to see if they could arrive at a plan for accomplishing these objectives.

By Monday, each supervisor had compiled a list of several ideas, including a four-day work week and interplant competitions of various kinds. A second meeting was set for Wednesday to discuss the issue further.

Following the Wednesday afternoon meeting, Jennifer Bentford and her plant supervisors agreed to implement a weekly contest called the NBE Game of the Week. The plant producing the most each week would be considered the NBE Game of the Week winner and would receive 10 points. The second-place plant would receive 7 points, and the third- and fourth-place plants would receive 3 points and 1 point, respectively. The contest would last 26 weeks. At the end of that period, a $200,000 bonus would be divided among the employees in the four plants proportional to the total points accumulated by each plant.

The announcement of the contest created a lot of excitement and enthusiasm at the four plants. No one complained about the rules because the four plants were designed and staffed to produce equally.

At the close of the contest, Jennifer Bentford called the supervisors into a meeting, at which time she asked for data to determine whether the contest had significantly improved productivity. She indicated that she had to know this before she could authorize a second contest. The supervisors, expecting this request, had put together the following data:

Units Produced (4 Plants Combined)	Before-Contest Frequency	During-Contest Frequency
0–2,500	11	0
2,501–8,000	23	20
8,001–15,000	56	83
15,001–20,000	15	52
	105 days	155 days

Jennifer examined the data and indicated that the contest looked to be a success, but she wanted to base her decision to continue the contest on more than just an observation of the data. "Surely there must be some way to statistically test the worthiness of this contest," Jennifer stated. "I have to see the results before I will authorize the second contest."

- **Review** the methods for testing a null hypothesis using the *t*-distribution in Chapter 9.
- **Review** confidence intervals discussed in Chapter 8.

- **Make sure** you review the discussion about scatter plots in Chapter 2.
- **Review** the concepts associated with selecting a simple random sample in Chapter 1.

- **Review** the *F*-distribution and the approach for finding critical values from the *F*-table as discussed in Chapters 11 and 12.

chapter 14

Introduction to Linear Regression and Correlation Analysis

14.1   Scatter Plots and ⟵——————— **Outcome 1.** Calculate and interpret the correlation between
Correlation (pg. 560–569)   two variables.

Outcome 2. Determine whether the correlation is significant.

14.2   Simple Linear Regression ⟵——————— **Outcome 3.** Calculate the simple linear regression equation
Analysis (pg. 570–592)   for a set of data and know the basic assumptions behind
                                         regression analysis.

Outcome 4. Determine whether a regression model is significant.

14.3   Uses for Regression ⟵——————— **Outcome 5.** Recognize regression analysis applications for
Analysis (pg. 592–603)   purposes of description and prediction.

Outcome 6. Calculate and interpret confidence intervals for
the regression analysis.

Outcome 7. Recognize some potential problems if regression
analysis is used incorrectly.

Why you need to know

Many business situations will require you to consider the relationship between two or more variables. For example, a stock analyst might be interested in the relationship between stock prices and the dividends issued by a publicly traded company. A company might be interested in examining the relationship between product sales and the amount of money spent on advertising. In another case, consider a loan manager at a bank who is interested in determining the market value of a home before granting a real estate loan to a customer. She would begin by collecting data on a sample of comparable properties that have sold recently. In addition to the selling price, she would collect data on other factors, such as the size and age of the property. She might then analyze the relationship between the price and the other variables and use this relationship to determine an appraised price for the property in question.

Simple linear regression and correlation analysis are introduced in this chapter. These techniques are two of the most often applied statistical procedures used by business decision makers for analyzing the relationship between two variables. In Chapter 15, we will extend the discussion to include three or more variables.

robybret/Shutterstock

14.1 Scatter Plots and Correlation

Scatter Plot

A two-dimensional plot showing the values for the joint occurrence of two quantitative variables. The scatter plot may be used to graphically represent the relationship between two variables. It is also known as a scatter diagram.

Decision-making situations that call for understanding the relationship between two quantitative variables are aided by the use of **scatter plots**, or *scatter diagrams*. Figure 14.1 shows scatter plots that depict several potential relationships between values of a dependent variable, *y*, and an independent variable, *x*. A *dependent* (or *response*) *variable* is the variable whose variation we wish to explain. An *independent* (or *explanatory*) *variable* is a variable used to explain variation in the dependent variable. In Figure 14.1, (a) and (b) are examples of strong *linear* (or straight line) relationships between *x* and *y*. Note that the linear relationship can be either positive (as the *x* variable increases, the *y* variable also increases) or negative (as the *x* variable increases, the *y* variable decreases).

Figures 14.1 (c) and (d) illustrate situations in which the relationship between the *x* and *y* variable is nonlinear. There are many possible nonlinear relationships that can occur. The scatter plot is very useful for visually identifying the nature of the relationship.

Figures 14.1 (e) and (f) show examples in which there is no identifiable relationship between the two variables. This means that as *x* increases, *y* sometimes increases and sometimes decreases but with no particular pattern.

The Correlation Coefficient

In addition to analyzing the relationship between two variables graphically, we can also measure the strength of the linear relationship between two variables using a measure called the **correlation coefficient**.

Correlation Coefficient

A quantitative measure of the strength of the linear relationship between two variables. The correlation ranges from −1.0 to +1.0. A correlation of ±1.0 indicates a perfect linear relationship, whereas a correlation of 0 indicates no linear relationship.

The correlation coefficient of two variables can be estimated from sample data using Equation 14.1 or the algebraic equivalent, Equation 14.2.

Chapter Outcome 1. ⟶

Sample Correlation Coefficient

$$r = \frac{\sum(x - \bar{x})(y - \bar{y})}{\sqrt{[\sum(x - \bar{x})^2][\sum(y - \bar{y})^2]}}$$

(14.1)

FIGURE 14.1

Two-Variable Relationships

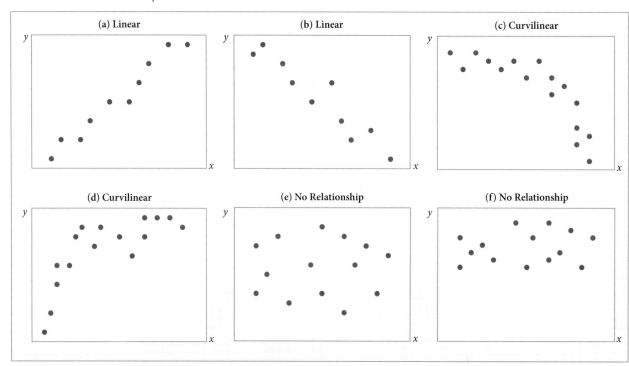

or the algebraic equivalent:

$$r = \frac{n\sum xy - \sum x \sum y}{\sqrt{[n(\sum x^2) - (\sum x)^2][n(\sum y^2) - (\sum y)^2]}}$$ (14.2)

where:

r = Sample correlation coefficient
n = Sample size
x = Value of the independent variable
y = Value of the dependent variable

The sample correlation coefficient computed using Equations 14.1 and 14.2 is called the *Pearson Product Moment Correlation*. The sample correlation coefficient, r, can range from a perfect positive correlation, $+1.0$, to a perfect negative correlation, -1.0. A perfect correlation occurs if all points on the scatter plot fall on a straight line. If two variables have no linear relationship, the correlation between them is 0 and there is no linear relationship between the change in x and y. Consequently, the more the correlation differs from 0.0, the stronger the linear relationship between the two variables. The sign of the correlation coefficient indicates the direction of the relationship.

Figure 14.2 illustrates some examples of correlation between two variables. Once again, for the correlation coefficient to equal plus or minus 1.0, all the (x, y) points form a perfectly straight line. The more the points depart from a straight line, the weaker (closer to 0.0) the correlation is between the two variables.

BUSINESS APPLICATION   **TESTING FOR SIGNIFICANT CORRELATIONS**

Excel Tutorial

MIDWEST DISTRIBUTION COMPANY Consider the Midwest Distribution Company, which supplies soft drinks and snack foods to convenience stores in Michigan, Illinois, and Iowa. Although Midwest Distribution has been profitable, the director of marketing has been concerned about the rapid turnover in her sales force. In the course of exit interviews, she discovered a major concern with the compensation structure.

FIGURE 14.2

Correlation between Two Variables

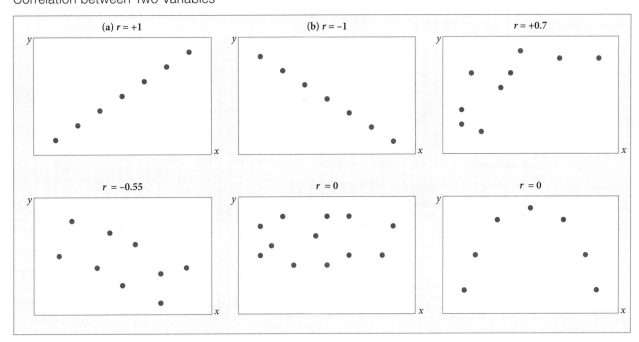

Midwest Distribution has a two-part wage structure: a base salary and a commission computed on monthly sales. Typically, about half of the total wages paid come from the base salary, which increases with longevity with the company. This portion of the wage structure is not an issue. The concern expressed by departing employees is that new employees tend to be given parts of the sales territory previously covered by existing employees and are assigned prime customers as a recruiting inducement.

At issue, then, is the relationship between sales (on which commissions are paid) and number of years with the company. The data for a random sample of 12 sales representatives are in the file called **Midwest**. The first step is to develop a scatter plot of the data. Excel can be used to construct a scatter plot and compute the correlation coefficient.

The scatter plot for the Midwest data is shown in Figure 14.3. Based on this plot, total sales and years with the company appear to be linearly related. However, the strength of this relationship is uncertain. That is, how close do the points come to being on a straight line? To answer this question, we need a quantitative measure of the strength of the linear relationship between the two variables. That measure is the correlation coefficient.

Equation 14.1 is used to determine the correlation between sales and years with the company. Table 14.1 shows the manual calculations that were used to determine this correlation coefficient of 0.8325. However, because the calculations are rather tedious and long, we almost always use computer software such as Excel to perform the computation, as shown in Figure 14.4. The $r = 0.8325$ indicates that there is a fairly strong, positive correlation between these two variables for the sample data.

Significance Test for the Correlation Although a correlation coefficient of 0.8325 seems quite large (relative to 0), you should remember that this value is based on a sample of 12 data points and is subject to sampling error. Therefore, a formal hypothesis-testing procedure is needed to determine whether the linear relationship between sales and years with the company is significant.

FIGURE 14.3

Excel 2010 Scatter Plot of Sales vs. Years with Midwest Distribution

Excel 2010 Instructions:
1. Open file: **Midwest.xlsx**.
2. Move the *Sales* column to the right of *Years* column.
3. Select data to be used in the chart.
4. On **Insert** tab, click **Scatter**, and then click the **Scatter with only Markers** option.
5. Use the **Layout** tab of the **Chart Tools** to add titles and remove the grid lines.
6. Use the **Design** tab of **Chart Tools** to move the chart to a new worksheet.

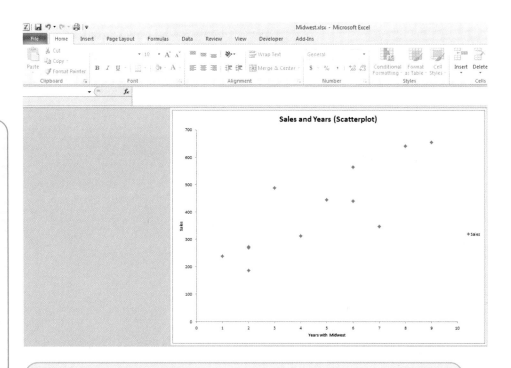

Minitab Instructions (for similar results):
1. Open file: **Midwest.MTW**.
2. Choose **Graph > Scatterplot**.
3. Under **Scatterplot**, choose **Simple OK**.
4. Under **Y variable**, enter y column.
5. In **X variable**, enter x column.
6. Click **OK**.

TABLE 14.1 | **Correlation Coefficient Calculations for the Midwest Distribution Example**

Sales	Years					
y	x	$x - \bar{x}$	$y - \bar{y}$	$(x - \bar{x})(y - \bar{y})$	$(x - \bar{x})^2$	$(y - \bar{y})^2$
487	3	−1.58	82.42	−130.22	2.50	6,793.06
445	5	0.42	40.42	16.98	0.18	1,633.78
272	2	−2.58	−132.58	342.06	6.66	17,577.46
641	8	3.42	236.42	808.56	11.70	55,894.42
187	2	−2.58	−217.58	561.36	6.66	47,341.06
440	6	1.42	35.42	50.30	2.02	1,254.58
346	7	2.42	−58.58	−141.76	5.86	3,431.62
238	1	−3.58	−166.58	596.36	12.82	27,748.90
312	4	−0.58	−92.58	53.70	0.34	8,571.06
269	2	−2.58	−135.58	349.80	6.66	18,381.94
655	9	4.42	250.42	1,106.86	19.54	62,710.18
563	6	1.42	158.42	224.96	2.02	25,096.90
$\Sigma = 4{,}855$	$\Sigma = 55$			$\Sigma = 3{,}838.92$	$\Sigma = 76.92$	$\Sigma = 276{,}434.92$

$$\bar{y} = \frac{\Sigma y}{n} = \frac{4{,}855}{12} = 404.58 \qquad \bar{x} = \frac{\Sigma x}{n} = \frac{55}{12} = 4.58$$

Using Equation 14.1,

$$r = \frac{\Sigma(x - \bar{x})(y - \bar{y})}{\sqrt{\Sigma(x - \bar{x})^2 \, \Sigma(y - \bar{y})^2}} = \frac{3{,}838.92}{\sqrt{(76.92)(276{,}434.92)}} = 0.8325$$

FIGURE 14.4

Excel 2010 Correlation Output for Midwest Distribution

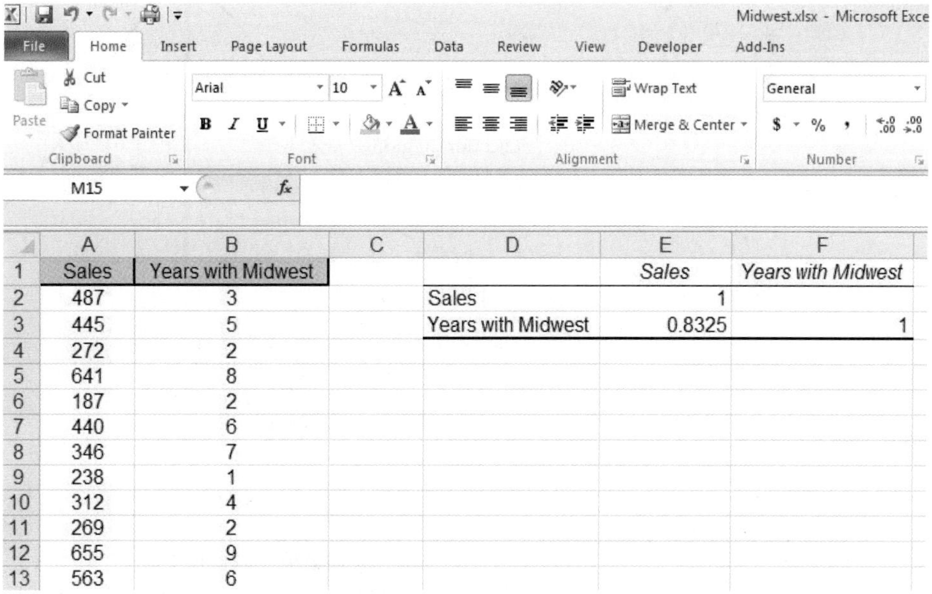

Excel 2010 Instructions:
1. Open File: **Midwest.xlsx**.
2. Select **Data > Data Analysis**.
3. Select **Correlation**.
4. Define the data range.
5. Click on **Labels in First Row**.
6. Specify Output Location.
7. Click **OK**.

	A	B	C	D	E	F
1	Sales	Years with Midwest			Sales	Years with Midwest
2	487	3		Sales	1	
3	445	5		Years with Midwest	0.8325	1
4	272	2				
5	641	8				
6	187	2				
7	440	6				
8	346	7				
9	238	1				
10	312	4				
11	269	2				
12	655	9				
13	563	6				

Minitab Instructions (for similar results):
1. Open file: **Midwest.MTW**.
2. Choose **Stat > Basic Statistics > Correlation**.
3. In **Variables**, enter Y and X columns.
4. Click **OK**.

The null and alternative hypotheses to be tested are

$$H_0: \rho = 0 \quad \text{(no correlation)}$$
$$H_A: \rho \neq 0 \quad \text{(correlation exists)}$$

where the Greek symbol ρ (rho) represents the population correlation coefficient.

We must test whether the sample data support or refute the null hypothesis. The test procedure utilizes the t-test statistic in Equation 14.3.

Chapter Outcome 2. ⟶

Test Statistic for Correlation

$$t = \frac{r}{\sqrt{\dfrac{1-r^2}{n-2}}} \qquad df = n - 2$$

(14.3)

where:

$$t = \text{Number of standard errors } r \text{ is from 0}$$
$$r = \text{Sample correlation coefficient}$$
$$n = \text{Sample size}$$

The degrees of freedom for this test are $n - 2$, because we lose 1 degree of freedom for each of the two sample means ($\bar{x}$ and $\bar{y}$) that are used to estimate the population means for the two variables.

Figure 14.5 shows the hypothesis test for the Midwest Distribution example using an alpha level of 0.05. Recall that the sample correlation coefficient was $r = 0.8325$.

FIGURE 14.5

Correlation Significance Test for the Midwest Distribution Example

Hypothesis:

$H_0: \rho = 0$ (no correlation)
$H_A: \rho \neq 0$
$\alpha = 0.05$

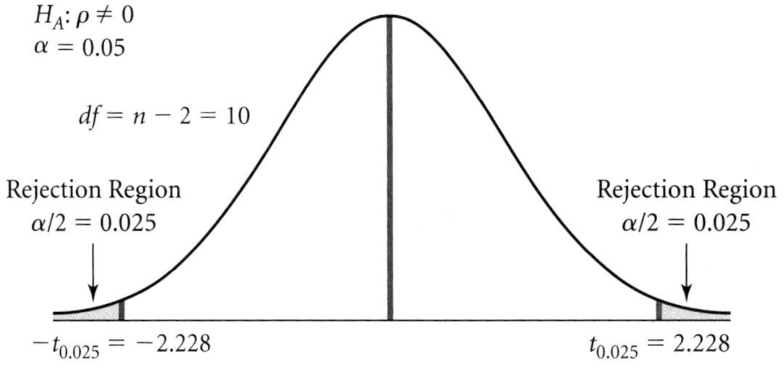

$df = n - 2 = 10$

Rejection Region
$\alpha/2 = 0.025$

Rejection Region
$\alpha/2 = 0.025$

$-t_{0.025} = -2.228$

$t_{0.025} = 2.228$

The calculated t-value is

$$t = \frac{r}{\sqrt{\dfrac{1-r^2}{n-2}}} = \frac{0.8325}{\sqrt{\dfrac{1-0.6931}{10}}} = 4.752$$

Decision Rule:

If $t > t_{0.025} = 2.228$, reject H_0.
If $t < -t_{0.025} = -2.228$, reject H_0.
Otherwise, do not reject H_0.
Because $4.752 > 2.228$, reject H_0.

Based on the sample evidence, we conclude there is a significant positive linear relationship between years with the company and sales volume.

Based on these sample data, we should conclude there is a significant, positive linear relationship in the population between years of experience and total sales for Midwest Distribution sales representatives. The implication is that the more years an employee has been with the company, the more sales that employee generates. This runs counter to the claims made by some of the departing employees. The manager will probably want to look further into the situation to see whether a problem might exist in certain regions.

The *t*-test for determining whether the population correlation is significantly different from 0 requires the following assumptions:

Assumptions

1. The data are interval or ratio-level.
2. The two variables (*y* and *x*) are distributed as a *bivariate normal* distribution.

Although the formal mathematical representation is beyond the scope of this text, *two variables are bivariate normal if their joint distribution is normally distributed*. Although the *t*-test assumes a bivariate normal distribution, it is robust—that is, correct inferences can be reached even with slight departures from the normal-distribution assumption. (See Kutner et al., *Applied Linear Statistical Models*, for further discussion of bivariate normal distributions.)

| **EXAMPLE 14-1** | **CORRELATION ANALYSIS** |

mdd/Shutterstock

Stock Portfolio Analysis A student intern at the investment firm of McMillan & Associates was given the assignment of determining whether there is a positive correlation between the number of individual stocks in a client's portfolio (*x*) and the annual rate of return (*y*) for the portfolio. The intern selected a simple random sample of 10 client portfolios and determined the number of individual company stocks and the annual rate of return earned by the client on his or her portfolio. To determine whether there is a statistically significant positive correlation between the two variables, the following steps can be employed:

Step 1 Specify the population parameter of interest.
The intern wishes to determine whether the number of stocks is positively correlated with the rate of return earned by the client. The parameter of interest is, therefore, the population correlation, ρ.

Step 2 Formulate the appropriate null and alternative hypotheses.
Because the intern was asked to determine whether a positive correlation exists between the variables of interest, the hypothesis test will be one tailed, as follows:

$$H_0: \rho \leq 0$$
$$H_A: \rho > 0$$

Step 3 Specify the level of significance.
A significance level of 0.05 is chosen.

Step 4 Compute the correlation coefficient and the test statistic.
Compute the sample correlation coefficient using Equation 14.1 or 14.2, or by using software such as Excel.

The following sample data were obtained:

Number of Stocks	Rate of Return
9	0.13
16	0.16
25	0.21
16	0.18
20	0.18
16	0.19
20	0.15
20	0.17
16	0.13
9	0.11

Using Equation 14.1, we get

$$r = \frac{\Sigma(x - \bar{x})(y - \bar{y})}{\sqrt{[\Sigma(x - \bar{x})^2][\Sigma(y - \bar{y})^2]}} = 0.7796$$

Compute the *t*-test statistic using Equation 14.3:

$$t = \frac{r}{\sqrt{\dfrac{1 - r^2}{n - 2}}} = \frac{0.7796}{\sqrt{\dfrac{1 - 0.7796^2}{10 - 2}}} = 3.52$$

Step 5 Construct the rejection region and decision rule.
For an alpha level equal to 0.05, the one-tailed, upper-tail, critical value for $n - 2 = 10 - 2 = 8$ degrees of freedom is $t_{0.05} = 1.8595$. The decision rule is

If $t > 1.8595$, reject the null hypothesis.

Otherwise, do not reject the null hypothesis.

Step 6 Reach a decision.
Because

$t = 3.52 > 1.8595$, reject the null hypothesis.

Step 7 Draw a conclusion.
Because the null hypothesis is rejected, the sample data do support the contention that there is a positive linear relationship between the number of individual stocks in a client's portfolio and the portfolio's rate of return.

>> **END EXAMPLE**

TRY PROBLEM 14-3 (pg. 567)

Cause-and-Effect Interpretations Care must be used when interpreting the correlation results. For example, even though we found a significant linear relationship between years of experience and sales for the Midwest Distribution sales force, the correlation does not imply cause and effect. Although an increase in experience may, in fact, cause sales to change, simply because the two variables are correlated does not guarantee a cause-and-effect situation. Two seemingly unconnected variables may be highly correlated. For example, over a period of time, teachers' salaries in North Dakota might be highly correlated with the price of grapes in Spain. Yet we doubt that a change in grape prices will *cause* a corresponding change in salaries for teachers in North Dakota, or vice versa. When a correlation exists between two seemingly unrelated variables, the correlation is said to be a *spurious correlation*. You should take great care to avoid basing conclusions on spurious correlations.

The Midwest Distribution marketing director has a logical reason to believe that years of experience with the company and total sales are related. That is, sales theory and customer feedback hold that product knowledge is a major component in successfully marketing a product. However, a statistically significant correlation alone does not prove that this cause-and-effect relationship exists. When two seemingly unrelated variables are correlated, they may both be responding to changes in some third variable. For example, the observed correlation could be the effect of a company policy of giving better sales territories to more senior salespeople.

MyStatLab

14-1: Exercises

Skill Development

14-1. An industry study was recently conducted in which the sample correlation between units sold and marketing expenses was 0.57. The sample size for the study included 15 companies. Based on the sample results, test to determine whether there is a significant positive correlation between these two variables. Use an $\alpha = 0.05$.

14-2. The following data for the dependent variable, y, and the independent variable, x, have been collected using simple random sampling:

x	y
10	120
14	130
16	170
12	150
20	200
18	180
16	190
14	150
16	160
18	200

   a. Construct a scatter plot for these data. Based on the scatter plot, how would you describe the relationship between the two variables?

   b. Compute the correlation coefficient.

14-3. A random sample of the following two variables was obtained:

x	29	48	28	22	28	42	33	26	48	44
y	16	46	34	26	49	11	41	13	47	16

   a. Calculate the correlation between these two variables.

   b. Conduct a test of hypothesis to determine if there exists a correlation between the two variables in the population. Use a significance level of 0.10.

14-4. A random sample of two variables, x and y, produced the following observations:

x	y
19	7
13	9
17	8
9	11
12	9
25	6
20	7
17	8

   a. Develop a scatter plot for the two variables and describe what relationship, if any, exists.

   b. Compute the correlation coefficient for these sample data.

   c. Test to determine whether the population correlation coefficient is negative. Use a significance level of 0.05 for the hypothesis test.

14-5. You are given the following data for variables x and y:

x	y
3.0	1.5
2.0	0.5
2.5	1.0
3.0	1.8
2.5	1.2
4.0	2.2
1.5	0.4
1.0	0.3
2.0	1.3
2.5	1.0

   a. Plot these variables in scatter plot format. Based on this plot, what type of relationship appears to exist between the two variables?

   b. Compute the correlation coefficient for these sample data. Indicate what the correlation coefficient measures.

   c. Test to determine whether the population correlation coefficient is positive. Use the $\alpha = 0.01$ level to conduct the test. Be sure to state the null and alternative hypotheses and show the test and decision rule clearly.

14-6. For each of the following circumstances, perform the indicated hypothesis tests:

   a. $H_A: \rho > 0, r = 0.53$, and $n = 30$ with $\alpha = 0.01$, using a test-statistic approach.

   b. $H_A: \rho \neq 0, r = -0.48$, and $n = 20$ with $\alpha = 0.05$, using a p-value approach.

   c. $H_A: \rho \neq 0, r = 0.39$, and $n = 45$ with $\alpha = 0.02$, using a test-statistic approach.

   d. $H_A: \rho < 0, r = 0.34$, and $n = 25$ with $\alpha = 0.05$, using a test-statistic approach.

Business Applications

14-7. The Federal No Child Left Behind Act requires periodic testing in standard subjects. A random sample of 50 junior high school students from Atlanta was selected, and each student's scores on a standardized mathematics examination and a standardized English examination were recorded. School administrators were interested in the relationship between the two scores. Suppose the correlation coefficient for the two examination scores is 0.75.

   a. Provide an explanation of the sample correlation coefficient in this context.

b. Using a level of significance of $\alpha = 0.01$, test to determine whether there is a positive linear relationship between mathematics scores and English scores for junior high school students in Atlanta.

14-8. Because of the current concern over credit card balances, a bank's chief financial officer is interested in whether there is a relationship between account balances and the number of times a card is used each month. A random sample of 50 accounts was selected. The account balance and the number of charges during the past month were the two variables recorded. The correlation coefficient for the two variables was -0.23.

a. Discuss what the $r = -0.23$ measures. Make sure to frame your discussion in terms of the two variables mentioned here.

b. Using an $\alpha = 0.10$ level, test to determine whether there is a significant linear relationship between account balance and the number of card uses during the past month. State the null and alternative hypotheses and show the decision rule.

c. Consider the decision you reached in part b. Describe the type of error you could have made in the context of this problem.

14-9. Farmers National Bank issues MasterCard credit cards to its customers. A main factor in determining whether a credit card will be profitable to the bank is the average monthly balance that the customer will maintain on the card that will be subject to finance charges. Bank analysts wish to determine whether there is a relationship between the average monthly credit card balance and the income stated on the original credit card application form. The following sample data have been collected from existing credit card customers:

Income	Credit Balance
$43,000	$345
$35,000	$1,370
$47,000	$1,140
$55,000	$201
$55,000	$56
$59,000	$908
$28,000	$2,345
$43,000	$104
$54,000	$0
$36,000	$1,290
$39,000	$130
$31,000	$459
$30,000	$0
$37,000	$1,950
$39,000	$240

a. Indicate which variable is to be the independent variable and which is to be the dependent variable in the bank's analysis and indicate why.

b. Construct a scatter plot for these data and describe what, if any, relationship appears to exist between these two variables.

c. Calculate the correlation coefficient for these two variables and test to determine whether there is a significant correlation at the $\alpha = 0.05$ level.

14-10. Amazon.com has become one of the most successful online merchants. Two measures of its success are sales and net income/loss figures (all figures in $million). These values for the years 1995–2007 are shown as follows.

Year	Net Income/Loss	Sales
1995	−0.3	0.5
1996	−5.7	15.7
1997	−27.5	147.7
1998	−124.5	609.8
1999	−719.9	1,639.8
2000	−1,411.2	2,761.9
2001	−567.3	3,122.9
2002	−149.1	3,933
2003	35.3	5,263.7
2004	588.5	6,921
2005	359	8,490
2006	190	10,711
2007	476	14,835

a. Produce a scatter plot for Amazon's net income/loss and sales figures for the period 1995 to 2007. Does there appear to be a linear relationship between these two variables? Explain your response.

b. Calculate the correlation coefficient between Amazon's net income/loss and sales figures for the period 1995 to 2007.

c. Conduct a hypothesis test to determine if a positive correlation exists between Amazon's net income/loss and sales figures. Use a significance level of 0.05 and assume that these figures form a random sample.

14-11. Complaints concerning excessive commercials seem to grow as the amount of "clutter," including commercials and advertisements for other television shows, steadily increases on network and cable television. A recent analysis by Nielsen Monitor-Plus compares the average nonprogram minutes in an hour of prime time for both network and cable television. Data for selected years are shown as follows.

Year	1996	1999	2001	2004
Network	9.88	14.00	14.65	15.80
Cable	12.77	13.88	14.50	14.92

a. Calculate the correlation coefficient for the average nonprogram minutes in an hour of prime time between network and cable television.

b. Conduct a hypothesis test to determine if a positive correlation exists between the average nonprogram minutes in an hour of prime time between network and cable television. Use a significance level of 0.05 and assume that these figures form a random sample.

14-12. A regional retailer would like to determine if the variation in average monthly store sales can, in part, be explained by the size of the store measured in square feet. A random sample of 21 stores was selected and the store size and average monthly sales were computed. The following results are shown

Store Size (Sq. Ft)	Average Monthly Sales
17400	$581,241.00
15920	$538,275.00
17440	$636,059.00
17320	$574,477.00
15760	$558,043.00
20200	$689,256.00
15280	$552,569.00
17000	$584,737.00
11920	$470,551.00
12400	$520,798.00
15640	$619,703.00
12560	$465,416.00
21680	$730,863.00
14120	$501,501.00
16680	$624,255.00
14920	$567,043.00
18360	$612,974.00
18440	$618,122.00
16720	$691,403.00
19880	$719,275.00
17880	$536,592.00

a. Construct a scatter plot using this data. What, if any relationship, appears to exist between the two variables?
b. Calculate the sample correlation coefficient between store size and average monthly sales.
c. Conduct a hypothesis test to determine if a positive correlation exists between store size and average monthly sales. Use a level of significance of 0.025.

Computer Database **Exercises**

14-13. Platinum Billiards, Inc., is a retailer of billiard supplies based in Jacksonville, Florida. It stands out among billiard suppliers because of the research it does to assure its products are top notch. One experiment was conducted to measure the speed attained by a cue ball struck by various weighted pool cues. The conjecture is that a light cue generates faster speeds while breaking the balls at the beginning of a game of pool. Anecdotal experience has indicated that a billiard cue weighing less than 19 ounces generates faster speeds. Platinum used a robotic arm to investigate this claim. Its research generated the data given in the file titled **Breakcue**.
a. To determine if there is a negative relationship between the weight of the pool cue and the speed attained by the cue ball, calculate a correlation coefficient.
b. Conduct a test of hypothesis to determine if there is a negative relationship between the weight of the

pool cue and the speed attained by the cue ball. Use a significance level of 0.025 and a p-value approach.

14-14. Customers who made online purchases last quarter from an Internet retailer were randomly sampled from the retailer's database. The dollar value of each customer's quarterly purchases along with the time the customer spent shopping the company's online catalog that quarter were recorded. The sample results are contained in the file **Online**.
a. Create a scatter plot of the variables Time (x) and Purchases (y). What relationship, if any, appears to exist between the two variables?
b. Compute the correlation coefficient for these sample data. What does the correlation coefficient measure?
c. Conduct a hypothesis test to determine if there is a positive relationship between time viewing the retailer's catalog and dollar amount purchased. Use a level of significance equal to 0.025. Provide a managerial explanation of your results.

14-15. A regional accreditation board for colleges and universities is interested in determining whether a relationship exists between student applicant verbal SAT scores and the in-state tuition costs at the university. Data have been collected on a sample of colleges and universities and are in the data file called **Colleges and Universities**.
a. Develop a scatter plot for these two variables and discuss what, if any, relationship you see between the two variables based on the scatter plot.
b. Compute the sample correlation coefficient.
c. Based on the correlation coefficient computed in part b, test to determine whether the population correlation coefficient is positive for these two variables. That is, can we expect schools that charge higher in-state tuition will attract students with higher average verbal SAT scores? Test using a 0.05 significance level.

14-16. As the number of air travelers with time on their hands increases, logic would indicate spending on retail purchases in airports would increase as well. A study by *Airport Revenue News* addressed the per-person spending at select airports for merchandise, excluding food, gifts, and news items. A file titled **Revenues** contains sample data selected from airport retailers in 2001 and again in 2004.
a. Produce a scatter plot for the per-person spending at selected airports for merchandise, excluding food, gifts, and news items, for the years 2001 and 2004. Does there appear to be a linear relationship between spending in 2001 and spending in 2004? Explain your response.
b. Calculate the correlation coefficient between the per-person spending in 2001 and the per-person spending in 2004. Does it appear that an increase in per-person spending in 2001 would be associated with an increase in spending in 2004? Support your assertion.
c. Conduct a hypothesis test to determine if a positive correlation exists between the per-person spending in 2001 and that in 2004. Use a significance level of 0.05 and assume that these figures form a random sample.

14.2 Simple Linear Regression Analysis

In the Midwest Distribution application in Section 14.1, we determined that the relationship between years of experience and total sales is linear and statistically significant, based on the correlation analysis performed in the previous section. Because hiring and training costs have been increasing, we would like to use this relationship to help formulate a more acceptable wage package for the sales force.

The statistical method we will use to analyze the relationship between years of experience and total sales is *regression analysis*. When we have only two variables—a dependent variable, such as sales, and an independent variable, such as years with the company—the technique is referred to as *simple regression analysis*. When the relationship between the dependent variable and the independent variable is linear, the technique is **simple linear regression**.

Simple Linear Regression
The method of regression analysis in which a single independent variable is used to predict the dependent variable.

The Regression Model and Assumptions

The objective of simple linear regression (which we shall call *regression analysis*) is to represent the relationship between values of x and y with a model of the form shown in Equation 14.4.

Simple Linear Regression Model (Population Model)

$$y = \beta_0 + \beta_1 x + \varepsilon \qquad (14.4)$$

where:

y = Value of the dependent variable
x = Value of the independent variable
β_0 = Population's y intercept
β_1 = Slope of the population regression line
ε = Random error term

The simple linear regression population model described in Equation 14.4 has four assumptions:

Assumptions

---

1. Individual values of the error terms, ε, are statistically independent of one another, and these values represent a random sample from the population of possible ε-values at each level of x.
2. For a given value of x, there can exist many values of y and therefore many values of ε. Further, the distribution of possible ε-values for any x-value is normal.
3. The distributions of possible ε-values have equal variances for all values of x.
4. The means of the dependent variable, y, for all specified values of the independent variable, $(\mu_{y|x})$, can be connected by a straight line called the population regression model.

Figure 14.6 illustrates assumptions 2, 3, and 4. The regression model (straight line) connects the average of the y-values for each level of the independent variable, x. The actual y-values for each level of x are normally distributed around the mean of y. Finally, observe that the spread of possible y-values is the same regardless of the level of x. The population regression line is determined by two values, β_0 and β_1. These values are known as the population *regression coefficients*. Value β_0 identifies the y intercept and β_1 the slope of the regression line. Under the regression assumptions, the coefficients define the true population model.

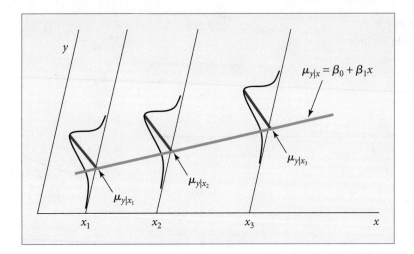

For each observation, the actual value of the dependent variable, y, for any x is the sum of two components:

$$y = \underbrace{\beta_0 + \beta_1 x}_{\text{Linear component}} + \underbrace{\varepsilon}_{\text{Random error component}}$$

The random error component, ε, may be positive, zero, or negative, depending on whether a single value of y for a given x falls above, on, or below the population regression line. Section 15.5 in Chapter 15 discusses how to check whether assumptions have been violated and the possible courses of action if the violations occur.

Meaning of the Regression Coefficients

Coefficient β_1, the **regression slope coefficient** of the population regression line, measures the average change in the value of the dependent variable, y, for each unit change in x. The regression slope can be either positive, zero, or negative, depending on the relationship between x and y. For example, a positive population slope of 12 ($\beta_1 = 12$) means that for a 1-unit increase in x, we can expect an average 12-unit increase in y. Correspondingly, if the population slope is negative 12 ($\beta_1 = -12$), we can expect an average decrease of 12 units in y for a 1-unit increase in x.

The population's y intercept, β_0, indicates the mean value of y when x is 0. However, this interpretation holds only if the population could have x values equal to 0. When this cannot occur, β_0 does not have a meaningful interpretation in the regression model.

BUSINESS APPLICATION **SIMPLE LINEAR REGRESSION ANALYSIS**

MIDWEST DISTRIBUTION (*CONTINUED*) The Midwest Distribution marketing manager has data for a sample of 12 sales representatives. In Section 14.1, she has established that a significant linear relationship exists between years of experience and total sales using correlation analysis. (Recall that the sample correlation between the two variables was $r = 0.8325$.) Now she would like to estimate the regression equation that defines the *true* linear relationship (that is, the population's linear relationship) between years of experience and sales. Figure 14.3 showed the scatter plot for two variables: years with the company and sales. We need to use the sample data to estimate β_0 and β_1, the true intercept and slope of the line representing the relationship between two variables. The *regression line* through the sample data is the best estimate of the population regression line. However, there are an infinite number of possible regression lines for a set of points. For example, Figure 14.7 shows three of the possible different lines that pass through the Midwest Distribution data. Which line should be used to estimate the true regression model?

FIGURE 14.7

Possible Regression Lines

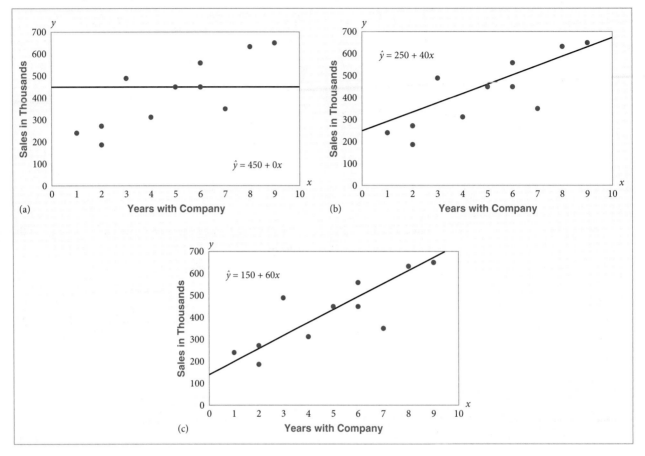

Least Squares Criterion

The criterion for determining a regression line that minimizes the sum of squared prediction errors.

Residual

The difference between the actual value of the dependent variable and the value predicted by the regression model.

We must establish a criterion for selecting the best line. The criterion used is the **least squares criterion**. To understand the least squares criterion, you need to know about prediction error, or **residual**, which is the distance between the actual y coordinate of an (x, y) point and the predicted value of that y coordinate produced by the regression line. Figure 14.8 shows how the prediction error is calculated for the employee who was with Midwest for four years $(x = 4)$ using one possible regression line: (where $\hat{y}$ is the predicted sales value). The predicted sales value is

$$\hat{y} = 150 + 60(4) = 390$$

However, the actual sales (y) for this employee is 312 (see Table 14.2). Thus, when $x = 4$, the difference between the observed value, $y = 312$, and the predicted value, $\hat{y} = 390$, is $312 - 390 = -78$. The residual (or prediction error) for this case when $x = 4$ is -78. Table 14.2 shows the calculated prediction errors and sum of squared errors for each of the three regression lines shown in Figure 14.7.[1] Of these three potential regression models, the line with the equation $\hat{y} = 150 + 60x$ has the smallest sum of squared errors. However, is there a better line than this? That is, would $\sum_{i=1}^{n}(y_i - \hat{y}_i)^2$ be smaller for some other line? One way to determine this is to calculate the sum of squared errors for all other regression lines. However, because there are an infinite number of these lines, this approach is not feasible. Fortunately, through the use of calculus, equations can be derived to directly determine the

---

[1]The reason we are using the sum of the squared residuals is that the sum of the residuals will be zero for the best regression line (the positive values of the residuals will balance the negative values).

FIGURE 14.8

Computation of Regression
Error for the Midwest
Distribution Example

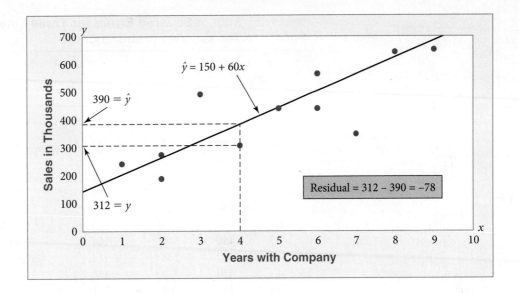

slope and intercept estimates such that $\sum_{i=1}^{n} (y_i - \hat{y}_i)^2$ is minimized.[2] This is accomplished by letting the estimated regression model be of the form shown in Equation 14.5.

Chapter Outcome 3. →

Estimated Regression Model (Sample Model)

$$\hat{y} = b_0 + b_1 x \qquad (14.5)$$

where:

$\hat{y}$ = Estimated, or predicted, y–value
b_0 = Unbiased estimate of the regression intercept, found using Equation 14.8
b_1 = Unbiased estimate of the regression slope, found using Equation 14.6 or 14.7
x = Value of the independent variable

Equations 14.6 and 14.8 are referred to as the solutions to the *least squares equations* because they provide the slope and intercept that minimize the sum of squared errors. Equation 14.7 is the algebraic equivalent of Equation 14.6 and may be easier to use when the computation is performed using a calculator.

Least Squares Equations

$$b_1 = \frac{\sum (x_i - \bar{x})(y_i - \bar{y})}{\sum (x_i - \bar{x})^2} \qquad (14.6)$$

algebraic equivalent:

$$b_1 = \frac{\sum xy - \dfrac{\sum x \sum y}{n}}{\sum x^2 - \dfrac{(\sum x)^2}{n}} \qquad (14.7)$$

and

$$b_0 = \bar{y} - b_1 \bar{x} \qquad (14.8)$$

---

[2]The calculus derivation of the least squares equations is contained in the Kutner et al. reference shown at the end of the book.

TABLE 14.2 | **Sum of Squared Errors for Three Linear Equations for Midwest Distribution**

From Figure 14.7(a):

$\hat{y} = 450 + 0x$

			Residual	
x	$\hat{y}$	y	$y - \hat{y}$	$(y - \hat{y})^2$
3	450	487	37	1,369
5	450	445	−5	25
2	450	272	−178	31,684
8	450	641	191	36,481
2	450	187	−263	69,169
6	450	440	−10	100
7	450	346	−104	10,816
1	450	238	−212	44,944
4	450	312	−138	19,044
2	450	269	−181	32,761
9	450	655	205	42,025
6	450	563	113	12,769
				$\Sigma = 301{,}187$

From Figure 14.7(b):

$\hat{y} = 250 + 40x$

			Residual	
x	$\hat{y}$	y	$y - \hat{y}$	$(y - \hat{y})^2$
3	370	487	117	13,689
5	450	445	−5	25
2	330	272	−58	3,364
8	570	641	71	5,041
2	330	187	−143	20,449
6	490	440	−50	2,500
7	530	346	−184	33,856
1	290	238	−52	2,704
4	410	312	−98	9,604
2	330	269	−61	3,721
9	610	655	45	2,025
6	490	563	73	5,329
				$\Sigma = 102{,}307$

From Figure 14.7(c):

$\hat{y} = 150 + 60x$

			Residual	
x	$\hat{y}$	y	$y - \hat{y}$	$(y - \hat{y})^2$
3	330	487	157	24,649
5	450	445	−5	25
2	270	272	2	4
8	630	641	11	121
2	270	187	−83	6,889
6	510	440	−70	4,900
7	570	346	−224	50,176
1	210	238	28	784
4	390	312	−78	6,084
2	270	269	−1	1
9	690	655	−35	1,225
6	510	563	53	2,809
				$\Sigma = 97{,}667$

TABLE 14.3 | **Manual Calculations for Least Squares Regression Coefficients for the Midwest Distribution Example**

y	x	xy	x^2	y^2
487	3	1,461	9	237,169
445	5	2,225	25	198,025
272	2	544	4	73,984
641	8	5,128	64	410,881
187	2	374	4	34,969
440	6	2,640	36	193,600
346	7	2,422	49	119,716
238	1	238	1	56,644
312	4	1,248	16	97,344
269	2	538	4	72,361
655	9	5,895	81	429,025
563	6	3,378	36	316,969
$\Sigma y = 4{,}855$	$\Sigma x = 55$	$\Sigma xy = 26{,}091$	$\Sigma x^2 = 329$	$\Sigma y^2 = 2{,}240{,}687$

$$\bar{y} = \frac{\Sigma y}{n} = \frac{4{,}855}{12} = 404.58 \qquad \bar{x} = \frac{\Sigma x}{n} = \frac{55}{12} = 4.58$$

$$b_1 = \frac{\Sigma xy - \dfrac{\Sigma x \, \Sigma y}{n}}{\Sigma x^2 - \dfrac{(\Sigma x)^2}{n}} = \frac{26{,}091 - \dfrac{55(4{,}855)}{12}}{329 - \dfrac{(55)^2}{12}}$$

$$= 49.91$$

Then,

$$b_0 = \bar{y} - b_1 \bar{x} = 404.58 - 49.91(4.58) = 175.99$$

The least squares regression line is, therefore,

$$\hat{y} = 175.99 + 49.91x$$

There is a slight difference between the manual calculation and the computer result due to rounding.

Table 14.3 shows the manual calculations, which are subject to rounding, for the least squares estimates for the Midwest Distribution example. However, you will almost always use a software package to perform these computations. (Figure 14.9 shows the Excel output.) In this case, the "best" regression line, given the least squares criterion, is $\hat{y} = 175.8288 + 49.9101(x)$. Figure 14.10 shows the predicted sales values along with the prediction errors and squared errors associated with this best simple linear regression line. Keep in mind that the prediction errors are also referred to as residuals. From Figure 14.10, the sum of the squared errors is 84,834.29. This is the smallest sum of squared residuals possible for this set of sample data. No other simple linear regression line through these 12 (x, y) points will produce a smaller sum of squared errors. Equation 14.9 presents a formula that can be used to calculate the sum of squared errors manually.

Sum of Squared Errors

$$SSE = \sum y^2 - b_0 \sum y - b_1 \sum xy \tag{14.9}$$

Figure 14.11 shows the scatter plot of sales and years of experience and the least squares regression line for Midwest Distribution. This line is the *best fit* for these sample data. The regression line passes through the point corresponding to $(\bar{x}, \bar{y})$. This will always be the case.

FIGURE 14.9

Excel 2010 Midwest
Distribution Regression
Results

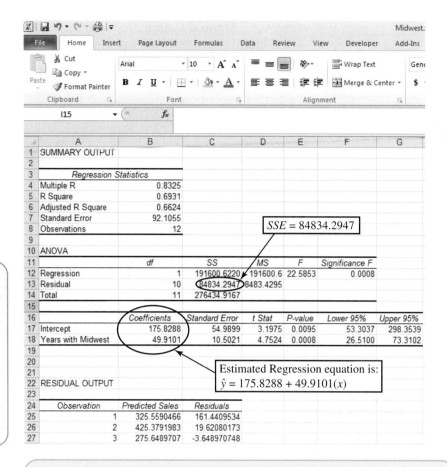

Excel 2010 Instructions:
1. Open File: **Midwest.xlsx**.
2. Select **Data > Data Analysis**.
3. Select **Regression**.
4. Define *y* (*Sales*) and *x* (*Years* with *Midwest*) variable data range.
5. Select **Labels**.
6. Select **Residuals**.
7. Select output location.

Minitab Instructions (for similar results):
1. Open file: **Midwest.MTW**.
2. Choose **Stat > Regression > Regression**.
3. In **Response**, enter the *y* variable column.
4. In **Predictors**, enter the *x* variable column.

5. Click **Storage; under Diagnostic Measures** select **Residuals**.
6. Click **OK**.

Least Squares Regression Properties

There are several important properties of least squares regression. These are as follows:

1. The sum of the residuals from the least squares regression line is 0 (Equation 14.10). The total underprediction by the regression model is exactly offset by the total overprediction (see Figure 14.10).

Sum of Residuals

$$\sum_{i=1}^{n}(y_i - \hat{y}_i) = 0$$

(14.10)

---

2. The sum of the squared residuals is the minimum (Equation 14.11).

Sum of Squared Residuals (Errors)

$$SSE = \sum_{i=1}^{n}(y_i - \hat{y}_i)^2$$

(14.11)

FIGURE 14.10

Excel 2010 Residuals and Squared Residuals for the Midwest Distribution Example

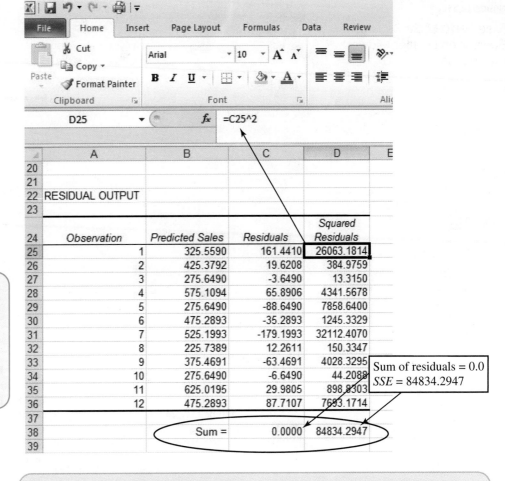

Excel 2010 Instructions:
1. Using output from Excel's Regression (See Figure 14.9), create Squared Residuals.
2. Sum the residuals and squared residuals columns.

D25 f_x =C25^2

	A	B	C	D	E
20					
21					
22	RESIDUAL OUTPUT				
23					
24	Observation	Predicted Sales	Residuals	Squared Residuals	
25	1	325.5590	161.4410	26063.1814	
26	2	425.3792	19.6208	384.9759	
27	3	275.6490	-3.6490	13.3150	
28	4	575.1094	65.8906	4341.5678	
29	5	275.6490	-88.6490	7858.6400	
30	6	475.2893	-35.2893	1245.3329	
31	7	525.1993	-179.1993	32112.4070	
32	8	225.7389	12.2611	150.3347	
33	9	375.4691	-63.4691	4028.3295	
34	10	275.6490	-6.6490	44.2088	
35	11	625.0195	29.9805	898.8303	
36	12	475.2893	87.7107	7693.1714	
37					
38		Sum =	0.0000	84834.2947	
39					

Sum of residuals = 0.0
$SSE = 84834.2947$

Minitab Instructions (for similar results):
1. Choose **Calc > Column Statistics**.
2. Under **Statistics**, Choose **Sum**.
3. In **Input variable**, enter residual column.
4. Click **OK**.
5. Choose **Calc > Column Statistics**.
6. Under **Statistic**, choose **Sum of Squares**.
7. In **Input variable**, enter residual column.
8. Click **OK**.

This property provided the basis for developing the equations for b_0 and b_1.

3. The simple regression line always passes through the mean of the y variable, $\bar{y}$, and the mean of the x variable, $\bar{x}$. So, to manually draw any simple linear regression line, all you need to do is to draw a line connecting the least squares y intercept with the $(\bar{x}, \bar{y})$ point.
4. The least squares coefficients are unbiased estimates of β_0 and β_1. Thus, the expected values of b_0 and b_1 equal β_0 and β_1, respectively.

EXAMPLE 14-2   **SIMPLE LINEAR REGRESSION AND CORRELATION**

NAN/Shutterstock

Harmonic Investments The investment firm Harmonic Investments wants to manage the pension fund of a major Chicago retailer. For their presentation to the retailer, the Harmonic analysts want to use simple linear regression to model the relationship between profits and numbers of employees for 50 Fortune 500 companies in the firm's portfolio. The data for the analysis are contained in the file **Fortune 50**. This analysis can be done using the following steps:

Step 1   Specify the independent and dependent variables.
The object in this example is to model the linear relationship between number of employees (the independent variable) and each company's profits in millions (the dependent variable).

FIGURE 14.11 |

Excel 2010 Least Squares
Regression Line for Midwest
Distribution

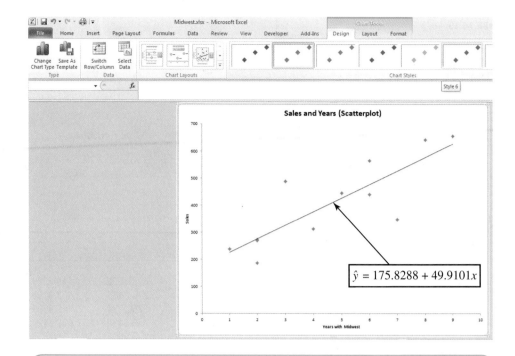

Excel 2010 Instructions:
1. Open file: **Midwest.xlsx**.
2. Move the *Sales* column to the right of the *Years* column.
3. Select data to be used in the chart.
4. On **Insert** tab, click **Scatter**, and then click the **Scatter with only Markers** option.
5. Use the **Layout** tab of the **Chart Tools** to add titles and remove the grid lines.
6. Use the **Design** tab of **Chart Tools** to move the chart to a new worksheet.
7. Click on one of the chart points.
8. Right click and select **Add Trendline**.
9. Select **Linear**.

Excel Tutorial

Step 2 **Develop a scatter plot to graphically display the relationship between the independent and dependent variables.**
Figure 14.12 shows the scatter plot, where the dependent variable, y, is company profits and the independent variable, x, is number of employees. There appears to be a slight positive linear relationship between the two variables.

Step 3 **Calculate the correlation coefficient and the linear regression equation.**
Do either manually using Equations 14.1, 14.6 (or 14.7), and 14.8, respectively, or by using Excel. Figure 14.13 shows the regression results. The sample correlation coefficient (called "Multiple R" in Excel) is

$$r = 0.3638$$

The regression equation is

$$\hat{y} = 2,556.88 + 0.0048x$$

The regression slope is estimated to be 0.0048, which means that for each additional employee, the average increase in company profit is 0.0048 million dollars, or $4,800. The intercept can only be interpreted when a value equal to zero for the x variable (employees) is plausible. Clearly, no company has zero employees, so the intercept in this case has no meaning other than it locates the height of the regression line for $x = 0$.

FIGURE 14.12

Excel 2010 Scatter Plot for
Harmonic Investments

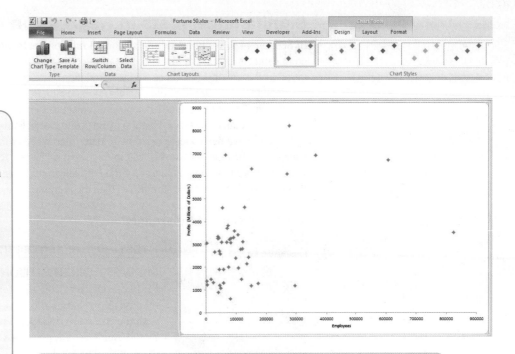

Excel 2010 Instructions:

1. Open file:
   Fortune 50.xlsx.
2. Move the *Profits* column
   to the right *Employees*
   column.
3. Select data to be used in
   the chart (Employees
   and Profits).
4. On **Insert** tab, click
   Scatter, and then click
   the **Scatter with only
   Markers** option.
5. Use the **Layout** tab of
   the **Chart Tools** to add
   titles and remove the
   grid lines.
6. Use the **Design** tab of
   Chart Tools to move the
   chart to a new worksheet.

Minitab Instructions (for similar results):

1. Open file: **Fortune 50.MTW**.
2. Choose **Graph > Character Graphs >
   Scatterplot**.
3. In **Y variable**, enter *y* column.
4. In **X variable**, enter *x* column.
5. Click **OK**.

FIGURE 14.13

Excel 2010 Regression
Results for Harmonic
Investments

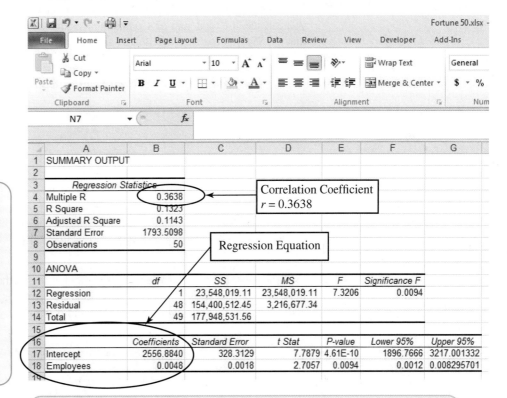

Excel 2010 Instructions:

1. Open File:
   Fortune 50.xlsx.
2. Select **Data > Data
   Analysis**.
3. Select **Regression**.
4. Define *y* (*Profits*) and *x*
   (*Employees*) variable
   data range.
5. Select **Labels**.
6. Select **Residuals**.
7. Select output location.

Minitab Instructions (for similar results):

1. Open file: **Fortune 50.MTW**.
2. Choose **Stat > Regression > Regression**.
3. In **Response**, enter the *y* variable column.
4. In **Predictors**, enter the *x* variable
   column.
5. Click **OK**.

>> **END EXAMPLE**

TRY PROBLEM 14-17 a,b,c (pg. 589)

Chapter Outcome 4. → # Significance Tests in Regression Analysis

In Section 14.1, we pointed out that the correlation coefficient computed from sample data is a point estimate of the population correlation coefficient and is subject to sampling error. We also introduced a test of significance for the correlation coefficient. Likewise, the regression coefficients developed from a sample of data are also point estimates of the true regression coefficients for the population. The regression coefficients are subject to sampling error. For example, due to sampling error, the estimated slope coefficient may be positive or negative while the population slope is really 0. Therefore, we need a test procedure to determine whether the regression slope coefficient is statistically significant. As you will see in this section, the test for the simple linear regression slope coefficient is equivalent to the test for the correlation coefficient. That is, if the correlation between two variables is found to be significant, then the regression slope coefficient will also be significant.

The Coefficient of Determination, R^2

BUSINESS APPLICATION   **TESTING THE REGRESSION MODEL**

MIDWEST DISTRIBUTION (*CONTINUED*) Recall that the Midwest Distribution marketing manager was analyzing the relationship between the number of years an employee had been with the company (independent variable) and the sales generated by the employee (dependent variable). We note when looking at the sample data for 12 employees (see Table 14.3) that sales vary among employees. Regression analysis aims to determine the extent to which an independent variable can explain this variation. In this case, does number of years with the company help explain the variation in sales from employee to employee?

The *SST* (total sum of squares) can be used in measuring the variation in the dependent variable. *SST* is computed using Equation 14.12. For Midwest Distribution, the total sum of squares for sales is provided in the output generated by Excel, as shown in Figure 14.14. As you can see, the total sum of squares in sales that needs to be explained is 276,434.92. Note that the *SST* value is in squared units and has no particular meaning.

Total Sum of Squares

$$SST = \sum_{i=1}^{n} (y_i - \overline{y})^2 \qquad \text{(14.12)}$$

where:

$$SST = \text{Total sum of squares}$$
$$n = \text{Sample size}$$
$$y_i = i\text{th value of the dependent variable}$$
$$\overline{y} = \text{Average value of the dependent variable}$$

The least squares regression line is computed so that the sum of squared residuals is minimized (recall the discussion of the least squares equations). The sum of squared residuals is also called the *sum of squares error (SSE)* and is defined by Equation 14.13.

Sum of Squares Error

$$SSE = \sum_{i=1}^{n} (y_i - \hat{y}_i)^2 \qquad \text{(14.13)}$$

where:

$$n = \text{Sample size}$$
$$y_i = i\text{th value of the dependent variable}$$
$$\hat{y}_i = i\text{th predicted value of } y \text{ given the } i\text{th value of } x$$

FIGURE 14.14 |

Excel 2010 Regression
Results for Midwest
Distribution

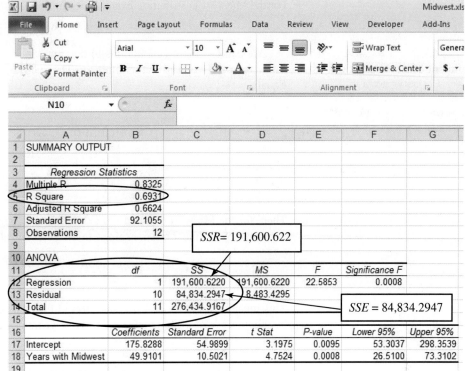

Excel 2010 Instructions:
1. Open File: **Midwest.xlsx**.
2. Select **Data > Data Analysis**.
3. Select **Regression**.
4. Define *y* (*Sales*) and *x* (*Years* with *Midwest*) variable data range.
5. Select **Labels**.
6. Select **Residuals**.
7. Select output location.

Minitab Instructions (for similar results):
1. Open file: **Midwest.MTW**.
2. Choose **Stat > Regression > Regression**.
3. In **Response**, enter the *y* variable column.
4. In **Predictors**, enter the *x* variable column.
5. Click **OK**.

SSE represents the amount of the total sum of squares in the dependent variable that *is not explained* by the least squares regression line. Excel refers to *SSE* as *sum of squares residual.* This value is contained in the regression output shown in Figure 14.14.

$$SSE = \sum (y - \hat{y})^2 = 84{,}834.29$$

Thus, of the total sum of squares (*SST* = 276,434.92), the regression model leaves *SSE* = 84,834.2947 unexplained. Then, the portion of the total sum of squares that *is explained* by the regression line is called the *sum of squares regression* (*SSR*) and is calculated by Equation 14.14.

Sum of Squares Regression

$$SSR = \sum_{i=1}^{n} (\hat{y}_i - \overline{y})^2$$ **(14.14)**

where:

$\hat{y}_i$ = Estimated value of *y* for each value of *x*

$\overline{y}$ = Average value of the *y* variable

The sum of squares regression (*SSR* = 191,600.62) is also provided in the regression output shown in Figure 14.14. You should also note that the following holds:

$$SST = SSR + SSE$$

For the Midwest Distribution example, in the Excel output (rounded) we get

$$276,435 = 191,601 + 84,834$$

Coefficient of Determination

The portion of the total variation in the dependent variable that is explained by its relationship with the independent variable. The coefficient of determination is also called R-squared and is denoted as R^2.

We can use these calculations to compute an important measure in regression analysis called the **coefficient of determination**. The coefficient of determination is calculated using Equation 14.15.

Coefficient of Determination, R^2

$$R^2 = \frac{SSR}{SST} \qquad \textbf{(14.15)}$$

Then, for the Midwest Distribution example, the proportion of variation in sales that can be explained by its linear relationship with the years of sales force experience is

$$R^2 = \frac{SSR}{SST} = \frac{191,600.62}{276,434.92} = 0.6931$$

This means that 69.31% of the variation in the sales data for this sample can be explained by the linear relationship between sales and years of experience. Notice that R^2 is part of the regression output in Figure 14.14.

R^2 can be a value between 0 and 1.0. If there is a perfect linear relationship between two variables, then the coefficient of determination, R^2, will be 1.0. This would correspond to a situation in which the least squares regression line would pass through each of the points in the scatter plot. R^2 is the measure used by many decision makers to indicate how well the linear regression line fits the (x, y) data points. The better the fit, the closer R^2 will be to 1.0. R^2 will be close to 0 when there is a weak linear relationship.

Finally, when you are employing *simple linear regression* (a linear relationship between a single independent variable and the dependent variable), there is an alternative way of computing R^2, as shown in Equation 14.16.

Coefficient of Determination for the Single Independent Variable Case

$$R^2 = r^2 \qquad \textbf{(14.16)}$$

where:

$$R^2 = \text{Coefficient of determination}$$
$$r = \text{Sample correlation coefficient}$$

Therefore, by squaring the correlation coefficient, we can get R^2 for the simple regression model. Figure 14.14 shows the correlation, $r = 0.8325$, which is referred to as *Multiple R* in Excel. Then, using Equation 14.16, we get R^2.

$$R^2 = r^2$$
$$= 0.8325^2$$
$$= 0.6931$$

Keep in mind that $R^2 = 0.6931$ is based on the random sample of size 12 and is subject to sampling error. Thus, just because $R^2 = 0.6931$ for the sample data does not mean that knowing the number of years an employee has worked for the company will explain 69.31% of the variation in sales for the population of all employees with the company. Likewise, just because $R^2 > 0.0$ for the sample data does not mean that the population coefficient of determination, noted as ρ^2 (rho-squared), is greater than zero.

However, a statistical test exists for testing the following null and alternative hypotheses:

$$H_0: \rho^2 = 0$$
$$H_A: \rho^2 > 0$$

The test statistic is an F-test with the test statistic defined as shown in Equation 14.17.

Test Statistic for Significance of the Coefficient of Determination

$$F = \frac{\dfrac{SSR}{1}}{\dfrac{SSE}{(n-2)}} \quad df = (D_1 = 1,\ D_2 = n - 2) \qquad (14.17)$$

where:

$$SSR = \text{Sum of squares regression}$$
$$SSE = \text{Sum of squares error}$$

For the Midwest Distribution example, the test statistic is computed using Equation 14.17 as follows:

$$F = \frac{\dfrac{191,600.62}{1}}{\dfrac{84,834.29}{(12 - 2)}} = 22.58$$

The critical value from the F-distribution table in Appendix for $\alpha = 0.05$ and for 1 and 10 degrees of freedom is 4.965. This gives the following decision rule:

> If $F > 4.965$, reject the null hypothesis.
> Otherwise, do not reject the null hypothesis.

Because $F = 22.58 > 4.965$, we reject the null hypothesis and conclude the population coefficient of determination (ρ^2) is greater than zero. This means the independent variable explains a significant proportion of the variation in the dependent variable.

For a simple regression model (a regression model with a single independent variable), the test for ρ^2 is equivalent to the test shown earlier for the population correlation coefficient, ρ. Refer to Figure 14.5 to see that the t-test statistic for the correlation coefficient was $t = 4.752$. If we square this t-value we get

$$t^2 = 4.752^2 = F = 22.58$$

Thus, the tests are equivalent. They will provide the same conclusions about the relationship between the x and y variables.

Significance of the Slope Coefficient For a simple linear regression model (one independent variable), there are three equivalent statistical tests:

1. Test for significance of the correlation between x and y.
2. Test for significance of the coefficient of determination.
3. Test for significance of the regression slope coefficient.

We have already introduced the first two of these tests. The third one deals specifically with the significance of the regression slope coefficient. The null and alternative hypotheses to be tested are

$$H_0: \beta_1 = 0$$
$$H_A: \beta_1 \neq 0$$

To test the significance of the simple linear regression slope coefficient, we are interested in determining whether the population regression slope coefficient is 0. A slope of 0 would imply that there is no linear relationship between x and y variables and that the x variable, in its linear form, is of no use in explaining the variation in y. If the linear relationship is useful, then we should reject the hypothesis that the regression slope is 0. However, because the estimated regression slope coefficient, b_1, is calculated from sample data, it is subject to sampling error. Therefore, even though b_1 is not 0, we must determine whether its difference from 0 is greater than would generally be attributed to sampling error.

If we selected several samples from the same population and for each sample determined the least squares regression line, we would likely get regression lines with different slopes and different y intercepts. This is analogous to getting different sample means from different samples when attempting to estimate a population mean. Just as the distribution of possible sample means has a standard error, the possible regression slopes also have a standard error, which is given in Equation 14.18.

Simple Regression Standard Error of the Slope Coefficient (Population)

$$\sigma_{b_1} = \frac{\sigma_\varepsilon}{\sqrt{\sum(x - \overline{x})^2}} \qquad \textbf{(14.18)}$$

where:

σ_{b_1} = Standard deviation of the regression slope (called the *standard error of the slope*)

σ_ε = Population standard error of the estimate

Equation 14.18 requires that we know the *standard error of the estimate*. It measures the dispersion of the dependent variable about its mean value at each value of the dependent variable in the original units of the dependent variable. However, because we are sampling from the population, we can estimate σ_ε as shown in Equation 14.19.

Simple Regression Estimator for the Standard Error of the Estimate

$$s_\varepsilon = \sqrt{\frac{SSE}{n - 2}} \qquad \textbf{(14.19)}$$

where:

SSE = Sum of squares error

n = Sample size

Equation 14.18, the standard error of the regression slope, applies when we are dealing with a population. However, in most cases, such as the Midwest Distribution example, we are dealing with a sample from the population. Thus, we need to estimate the regression slope's standard error using Equation 14.20.

Simple Regression Estimator for the Standard Error of the Slope

$$s_{b_1} = \frac{s_\varepsilon}{\sqrt{\sum(x - \overline{x})^2}} \qquad \textbf{(14.20)}$$

where:

s_{b_1} = Estimate of the standard error of the least squares slope

$s_\varepsilon = \sqrt{\dfrac{SSE}{n - 2}}$ = Sample standard error of the estimate (the measure of deviation of the actual y-values around the regression line)

BUSINESS APPLICATION | **REGRESSION ANALYSIS USING COMPUTER SOFTWARE**

MIDWEST DISTRIBUTION (*CONTINUED*) For Midwest Distribution, the regression outputs in Figure 14.15 shows $b_1 = 49.91$. The question is whether this value is different enough from 0 to have not been caused by sampling error. We find the answer by looking at the value of the estimate of the standard error of the slope, calculated using Equation 14.20, which is also shown in Figure 14.15. The standard error of the slope coefficient is 10.50.

If the standard error of the slope σ_{b_1} is large, then the value of b_1 will be quite variable from sample to sample. Conversely, if σ_{b_1} is small, the possible slope values will be less variable. However, regardless of the standard error of the slope, the average value of b_1 will equal β_1, the true regression slope, if the assumptions of the regression analysis are satisfied. Figure 14.16 illustrates what this means. Notice that when the standard error of the slope is large, the sample slope can take on values *much* different from the true population slope. As Figure 14.16(a) shows, a sample slope and the true population slope can even have different signs. However, when σ_{b_1} is small, the sample regression lines will cluster closely around the true population line as shown in Figure 14.16(b).

Because the sample regression slope will most likely not equal the true population slope, we must test to determine whether the true slope could possibly be 0. A slope of 0 in the linear model means that the independent variable will not explain any variation in the dependent

FIGURE 14.15

Excel 2010 Regression Results for Midwest Distribution

Excel 2010 Instructions:
1. Open File: **Midwest.xlsx**.
2. Select **Data > Data Analysis**.
3. Select **Regression**.
4. Define *y* (*Sales*) and *x* (*Years* with *Midwest*) variable data range.
5. Select **Labels**.
6. Select **Residuals**.
7. Select output location.

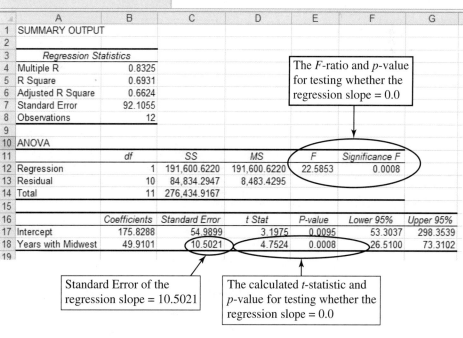

Minitab Instructions (for similar results):
1. Open file: Midwest.MTW.
2. Choose **Stat > Regression > Regression**.
3. In **Response**, enter the *y* variable column.
4. In **Predictors** enter the *x* variable column.
5. Click **OK**.

FIGURE 14.16

Standard Error of the Slope

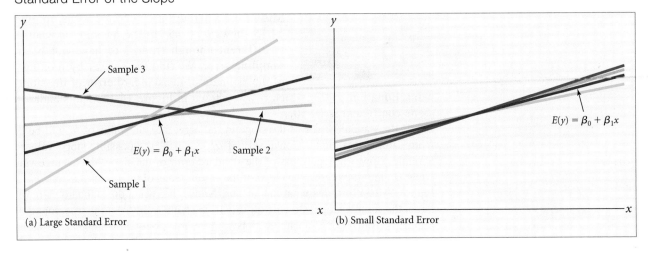

(a) Large Standard Error (b) Small Standard Error

variable, nor will it be useful in predicting the dependent variable. Assuming a 0.05 level of significance, the null and alternative hypotheses to be tested are

$$H_0: \beta_1 = 0$$
$$H_A: \beta_1 \neq 0$$

To test the significance of a slope coefficient, we use the *t*-test value in Equation 14.21.

FIGURE 14.17

Significance Test of the Regression Slope for Midwest Distribution

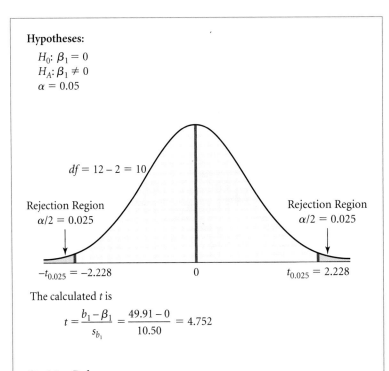

Hypotheses:

$H_0: \beta_1 = 0$
$H_A: \beta_1 \neq 0$
$\alpha = 0.05$

$df = 12 - 2 = 10$

Rejection Region
$\alpha/2 = 0.025$

Rejection Region
$\alpha/2 = 0.025$

$-t_{0.025} = -2.228$ 0 $t_{0.025} = 2.228$

The calculated *t* is

$$t = \frac{b_1 - \beta_1}{s_{b_1}} = \frac{49.91 - 0}{10.50} = 4.752$$

Decision Rule:

If $t > t_{0.025} = 2.228$, reject H_0.
If $t < -t_{0.025} = -2.228$, reject H_0.
Otherwise, do not reject H_0.
Because 4.752 > 2.228, we should reject the null hypothesis and conclude that the true slope is not 0. Thus, the simple linear relationship that utilizes the independent variable, years with the company, is useful in explaining the variation in the dependent variable, sales volume.

Simple Linear Regression Test Statistic for Test of the Significance of the Slope

$$t = \frac{b_1 - \beta_1}{s_{b_1}} \qquad df = n - 2 \qquad \text{(14.21)}$$

where:

b_1 = Sample regression slope coefficient

β_1 = Hypothesized slope $(\text{usually } \beta_1 = 0)$

s_{b_1} = Estimator of the standard error of the slope

How to do it (Example 14-3)

Simple Linear Regression Analysis
The following steps outline the process that can be used in developing a simple linear regression model and the various hypotheses tests used to determine the significance of a simple linear regression model.

1. Define the independent (x) and dependent (y) variables and select a simple random sample of pairs of (x, y) values.

2. Develop a scatter plot of y and x. You are looking for a linear relationship between the two variables.

3. Compute the correlation coefficient for the sample data.

4. Calculate the least squares regression line for the sample data and the coefficient of determination, R^2. The coefficient of determination measures the proportion of variation in the dependent variable explained by the independent variable.

5. Conduct any of the following tests for determining whether the regression model is statistically significant.

  a. Test to determine whether the true regression slope is 0. The test statistic with $df = n - 2$ is

$$t = \frac{b_1 - \beta_1}{s_{b_1}} = \frac{b_1 - 0}{s_{b_1}}$$

  b. Test to see whether ρ is significantly different from 0. The test statistic is

$$t = \frac{r}{\sqrt{\dfrac{1 - r^2}{n - 2}}}$$

  c. Test to see whether ρ^2 is significantly greater than 0. The test statistic is

$$F = \frac{\dfrac{SSR}{1}}{\dfrac{SSE}{(n - 2)}}$$

6. Reach a decision.

7. Draw a conclusion.

Figure 14.17 illustrates this test for the Midwest Distribution example. The calculated t-value of 4.752 exceeds the critical value, $t = 2.228$, from the t-distribution with 10 degrees of freedom and $\alpha/2 = 0.025$. This indicates that we should reject the hypothesis that the true regression slope is 0. Thus, years of experience can be used to help explain the variation in an individual representative's sales. This is not a coincidence. This test is always equivalent to the tests for ρ and ρ^2 presented earlier.

The output shown in Figure 14.15 also contains the calculated t statistic. The p-value for the calculated t statistic is also provided. As with other situations involving two-tailed hypothesis tests, if the p-value is less than α, the null hypothesis is rejected. In this case, because p-value $= 0.0008 < 0.05$, we reject the null hypothesis.

EXAMPLE 14-3 | SIMPLE LINEAR REGRESSION ANALYSIS

Denis Dryashkin/Shutterstock

Vantage Electronic Systems Consider the example involving Vantage Electronic Systems in Deerfield, Michigan, which started out supplying electronic equipment for the automobile industry but in recent years has ventured into other areas. One area is visibility sensors used by airports to provide takeoff and landing information and by transportation departments to detect low visibility on roadways during fog and snow. The recognized leader in the visibility sensor business is the SCR Company, which makes a sensor called the Scorpion. The research and development (R&D) department at Vantage has recently performed a test on its new unit by locating a Vantage sensor and a Scorpion sensor side by side. Various data, including visibility measurements, were collected at randomly selected points in time over a two-week period. These data are contained in a file called **Vantage**.

Step 1 Define the independent (x) and dependent (y) variables.
The analysis included a simple linear regression using the Scorpion visibility measurement as the dependent variable, y, and the Vantage visibility measurement as the independent variable, x.

Step 2 Develop a scatter plot of y and x.
The scatter plot is shown in Figure 14.18. There does not appear to be a strong linear relationship.

Step 3 Compute the correlation coefficient for the sample data.
Equation 14.1 or 14.2 can be used for manual computation, or we can use Excel. The sample correlation coefficient is

$$r = 0.5778$$

Step 4 Calculate the least squares regression line for the sample data and the coefficient of determination, R^2.
Equations 14.7 and 14.8 can be used to manually compute the regression slope coefficient and intercept, respectively, and Equation 14.15 or 14.16 can be used to manually compute R^2. Excel can also be used to eliminate the computational burden. The coefficient of determination is

$$R^2 = r^2 = 0.5778^2 = 0.3339$$

FIGURE 14.18

Scatter Plot—Example 14-3

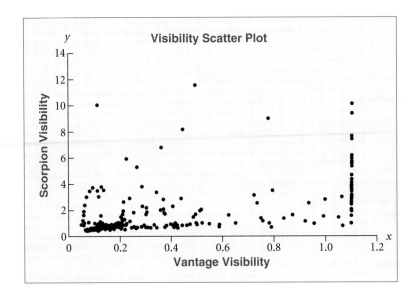

Thus, approximately 33% of the variation in the Scorpion visibility measures is explained by knowing the corresponding Vantage system visibility measure. The least squares regression equation is

$$\hat{y} = 0.586 + 3.017x$$

tutorials

Excel Tutorial

Step 5   **Conduct a test to determine whether the regression model is statistically significant (or whether the population correlation is equal to 0).**

The null and alternative hypotheses to test the correlation coefficient are

$$H_0: \rho = 0$$
$$H_A: \rho \neq 0$$

The t-test statistic using Equation 14.3 is

$$t = \frac{r}{\sqrt{\dfrac{1-r^2}{n-2}}} = \frac{0.5778}{\sqrt{\dfrac{1-0.5778^2}{280-2}}} = 11.8$$

The $t = 11.8$ exceeds the critical t for any reasonable level of α for 278 degrees of freedom, so the null hypothesis is rejected and we conclude that there is a statistically significant linear relationship between visibility measures for the two visibility sensors.

Alternatively, the null and alternative hypotheses to test the regression slope coefficient are

$$H_0: \beta_1 = 0$$
$$H_A: \beta_1 \neq 0$$

The t-test statistic is

$$t = \frac{b_1 - \beta_1}{s_{b_1}} = \frac{3.017 - 0}{0.2557} = 11.8$$

Step 6   **Reach a decision.**

The t-test statistic of 11.8 exceeds the t-critical for any reasonable level of α for 278 degrees of freedom.

Step 7   **Draw a conclusion.**

The population regression slope coefficient is not equal to 0. This means that knowing the Vantage visibility reading provides useful help in knowing what the Scorpion visibility reading will be.

>> **END EXAMPLE**

TRY PROBLEM 14-17 (pg. 589)

MyStatLab

14-2: Exercises

Skill Development

14-17. You are given the following sample data for variables y and x:

y	140	120	80	100	130	90	110	120	130	130	100
x	5	3	2	4	5	4	4	5	6	5	4

a. Develop a scatter plot for these data and describe what, if any, relationship exists.

b. (1) Compute the correlation coefficient. (2) Test to determine whether the correlation is significant at the significance level of 0.05. Conduct this hypothesis test using the p-value approach. (3) Compute the regression equation based on these sample data and interpret the regression coefficients.

c. Test the significance of the overall regression model using a significance level equal to 0.05.

14-18. You are given the following sample data for variables x and y:

x (independent)	y (dependent)
1	16
7	50
3	22
8	59
11	63
5	46
4	43

a. Construct a scatter plot for these data and describe what, if any, relationship appears to exist.

b. Compute the regression equation based on these sample data and interpret the regression coefficients.

c. Based on the sample data, what percentage of the total variation in the dependent variable can be explained by the independent variable?

d. Test the significance of the overall regression model using a significance level of 0.01.

e. Test to determine whether the true regression slope coefficient is equal to 0. Use a significance level of 0.01.

14-19. The following data for the dependent variable, y, and the independent variable, x, have been collected using simple random sampling:

x	y
10	120
14	130
16	170
12	150
20	200
18	180
16	190

x	y
14	150
16	160
18	200

a. Develop a simple linear regression equation for these data.

b. Calculate the sum of squared residuals, the total sum of squares, and the coefficient of determination.

c. Calculate the standard error of the estimate.

d. Calculate the standard error for the regression slope.

e. Conduct the hypothesis test to determine whether the regression slope coefficient is equal to 0. Test using $\alpha = 0.02$.

14-20. Consider the following sample data for the variables y and x:

x	30.3	4.8	15.2	24.9	8.6	20.1	9.3	11.2
y	14.6	27.9	17.6	15.3	19.8	13.2	25.6	19.4

a. Calculate the linear regression equation for these data.

b. Determine the predicted y-value when $x = 10$.

c. Estimate the change in the y variable resulting from the increase in the x variable of 10 units.

d. Conduct a hypothesis test to determine if an increase of 1 unit in the x variable will result in the decrease of the average value of the y variable. Use a significance of 0.025.

14-21. Examine the following sample data for the variables y and x:

x	1	2	3	4	5
y	4	2	5	8	9

a. Construct a scatter plot of these data. Describe the relationship between x and y.

b. Calculate the sum of squares error for the following equations: (1) $\hat{y} = 0.8 + 1.60x$, (2) $\hat{y} = 1 + 1.50x$, and (3) $\hat{y} = 0.7 + 1.60x$.

c. Which of these equations provides the "best" fit of these data? Describe the criterion you used to determine "best" fit.

d. Determine the regression line that minimizes the sum of squares error.

Business Applications

14-22. The Skelton Manufacturing Company recently did a study of its customers. A random sample of 50 customer accounts was pulled from the computer records. Two variables were observed:

y = Total doll volume of business this year
x = Miles customer is from corporate headquarters

The following statistics were computed:

$$\hat{y} = 2,140.23 - 10.12x$$
$$s_{b_1} = 3.12$$

a. Interpret the regression slope coefficient.
b. Using a significance level of 0.01, test to determine whether it is true that the farther a customer is from the corporate headquarters, the smaller the total dollar volume of business.

14-23. A shipping company believes that the variation in the cost of a customer's shipment can be explained by differences in the weight of the package being shipped. To investigate whether this relationship is useful, a random sample of 20 customer shipments was selected, and the weight (in lb) and the cost (in dollars, rounded to the nearest dollar) for each shipment were recorded. The following results were obtained:

Weight (x)	Cost (y)
8	11
6	8
5	11
7	11
12	17
9	11
17	27
13	16
8	9
18	25
17	21
17	24
10	16
20	24
9	21
5	10
13	21
6	16
6	11
12	20

a. Construct a scatter plot for these data. What, if any, relationship appears to exist between the two variables?
b. Compute the linear regression model based on the sample data. Interpret the slope and intercept coefficients.
c. Test the significance of the overall regression model using a significance level equal to 0.05.
d. What percentage of the total variation in shipping cost can be explained by the regression model you developed in part b?

14-24. College tuition has risen at a pace faster than inflation for more than two decades, according to an article in *USA Today*. The following data indicate the average college tuition (in 2003 dollars) for private and public colleges:

Period	1983–1984	1988–1989	1993–1994	1998–1999	2003–2004	2008–2009
Private	9,202	12,146	13,844	16,454	19,710	21,582
Public	2,074	2,395	3,188	3,632	4,694	5,652

a. Conduct a simple linear regression analysis of these data in which the average tuition for private colleges is predicted by the average public college tuition. Test the significance of the model using an $\alpha = 0.10$.
b. How much does the average private college tuition increase when the average public college tuition increases by $100?
c. When the average public college tuition reaches $7,500, how much would you expect the average private college tuition to be?

14-25. A regional retailer would like to determine if the variation in average monthly store sales can, in part, be explained by the size of the store measured in square feet. A random sample of 21 stores was selected and the store size and average monthly sales were computed. The following results are shown

Store Size (Sq. Ft)	Average Monthly Sales
17400	$581,241.00
15920	$538,275.00
17440	$636,059.00
17320	$574,477.00
15760	$558,043.00
20200	$689,256.00
15280	$552,569.00
17000	$584,737.00
11920	$470,551.00
12400	$520,798.00
15640	$619,703.00
12560	$465,416.00
21680	$730,863.00
14120	$501,501.00
16680	$624,255.00
14920	$567,043.00
18360	$612,974.00
18440	$618,122.00
16720	$691,403.00
19880	$719,275.00
17880	$536,592.00

a. Compute the simple linear regression model using the sample data to determine whether variation in average monthly sales can be explained by store size. Interpret the slope and intercept coefficients.
b. Test for the significance of the slope coefficient of the regression model. Use a level of significance of 0.05.
c. Based on the estimated regression model, what percentage of the total variation in average monthly sales can be explained by store size?

14-26. An engineering firm is interested in investigating whether the variability in the cost of small projects (defined as projects under $10 million) can be accounted for, in part, by differences in the number of direct engineering consulting hours billed. A random sample of 24 small projects was randomly selected from small projects performed over the past two years. The number of engineering consulting hours billed for each project, along with the project's cost, was recorded. The results are shown below:

Project	Billed Consulting Hours	Total Project Cost
1	3932	$4,323,826
2	3097	$3,750,964
3	2972	$3,579,570
4	3994	$5,053,149
5	4906	$5,528,308
6	5147	$5,631,967
7	4003	$5,257,756
8	4279	$5,681,909
9	3158	$4,133,012
10	4123	$4,596,329
11	2566	$3,344,851
12	3253	$3,868,200
13	3888	$4,865,998
14	3177	$4,042,509
15	3938	$5,067,679
16	3135	$4,111,731
17	5142	$6,554,583
18	5091	$6,042,445
19	4301	$5,192,769
20	2914	$3,581,835
21	3890	$4,745,269
22	2869	$3,353,559
23	3683	$5,169,469
24	4217	$5,147,689

a. Develop a scatter plot based on the sample data. What type of relationship, if any, appears to exist between the two variables?

b. Calculate the sample correlation coefficient between billed consulting hours and total project costs.

c. Conduct a hypothesis test to determine if there is a significant positive correlation between billed consulting hours and total project costs. Use a level of significance of 0.01.

Computer Database Exercises

14-27. The file **Online** contains a random sample of 48 customers who made purchases last quarter from an online retailer. The file contains information related to the time each customer spent viewing the online catalog and the dollar amount of purchases made. The retailer would like to analyze the sample data to determine whether a relationship exists between the time spent viewing the online catalog and the dollar amount of purchases.

a. Compute the regression equation based on these sample data and interpret the regression coefficients.

b. Compute the coefficient of determination and interpret its meaning.

c. Test the significance of the overall regression model using a significance level of 0.01.

d. Test to determine whether the true regression slope coefficient is equal to 0. Use a significance level of 0.01 to conduct the hypothesis test.

14-28. The National Football League (NFL) is arguably the most successful professional sports league in the United States. Following the recent season, the commissioner's office staff performed an analysis in which a simple linear regression model was developed with average home attendance used as the dependent variable and the total number of games won during the season as the independent variable. The staff was interested in determining whether games won could be used as a predictor for average attendance. Develop the simple linear regression model. The data are in the file called **NFL**.

a. What percentage of total variation in average home attendance is explained by knowing the number of games the team won?

b. What is the standard error of the estimate for this regression model?

c. Using $\alpha = 0.05$, test to determine whether the regression slope coefficient is significantly different from 0.

d. After examining the regression analysis results, what should the NFL staff conclude about how the average attendance is related to the number of games the team won?

14-29. The consumer price index (CPI) is a measure of the average change in prices over time in a fixed market basket of goods and services typically purchased by consumers. The CPI for all urban consumers covers about 80% of the total population. It is prepared and published by the Bureau of Labor Statistics of the Department of Labor, which measures average changes in prices of goods and services. The CPI is one way the government measures the general level of inflation— the annual percentage change in the value of this index is one way of measuring the annual inflation rate. The file titled **CPI** contains the monthly CPI and inflation rate for the period 2000–2005.

a. Construct a scatter plot of the CPI versus inflation for the period 2000 through 2005. Describe the relationship that appears to exist between these two variables.

b. Conduct a hypothesis test to confirm your preconception of the relationship between the CPI and the inflation rate. Use $\alpha = 0.05$.

c. Does it appear that the CPI and the inflation rate are measuring the same component of our economy? Support your assertion with statistical reasoning.

14-30. The College Board, administrator of the SAT test for college entrants, has made several changes to the test in recent years. One recent change occurred between years 2005 and 2006. In a press release, the College Board announced SAT scores for students in the class of 2005, the last class to take the former version of the SAT featuring math and verbal sections. The board indicated that for the class of 2005, the average SAT math scores continued their strong upward trend, increasing from 518 in 2004 to 520 in 2005, 14 points above 10 years previous and an all-time high. The file titled **MathSAT** contains the math SAT scores for the interval 1967 to 2005.

a. Produce a scatter plot of the average SAT math scores versus the year the test was taken for all students (male and female) during the last 10 years (1996–2005).

b. Construct a regression equation to predict the average math scores with the year as the predictor.

c. Use regression to determine if the College Board's assertion concerning the improvement in SAT average math test scores over the last 10 years is overly optimistic.

14-31. One of the editors of a major automobile publication has collected data on 30 of the best-selling cars in the United States. The data are in a file called **Automobiles**. The editor is particularly interested in the relationship between highway mileage and curb weight of the vehicles.

a. Develop a scatter plot for these data. Discuss what the plot implies about the relationship between the two variables. Assume that you wish to predict highway mileage by using vehicle curb weight.

b. Compute the correlation coefficient for the two variables and test to determine whether there is a linear relationship between the curb weight and the highway mileage of automobiles.

c. (1) Compute the linear regression equation based on the sample data. (2) A CTS Sedan weighs approximately 4,012 pounds. Provide an estimate of the average highway mileage you would expect to obtain from this model.

14-32. *The Insider View of Las Vegas* Web site (www. insidervlv.com) furnishes information and facts concerning Las Vegas. A set of data published by them provides the amount of gaming revenue for various portions of Clark County, Nevada. The file titled **Vegas** provides the gaming revenue for the year 2005.

a. Compute the linear regression equation to predict the gaming revenue for Clark County based on the gaming revenue of the Las Vegas Strip.

b. Conduct a hypothesis test to determine if the gaming revenue from the Las Vegas Strip can be used to predict the gaming revenue for all of Clark County.

c. Estimate the increased gaming revenue that would accrue to all of Clark County if the gaming revenue on the Las Vegas Strip were to increase by a million dollars.

END EXERCISES 14-2

Chapter Outcome 5. ➞ **14.3 Uses for Regression Analysis**

Regression analysis is a statistical tool that is used for two main purposes: description and prediction. This section discusses these two applications.

Regression Analysis for Description

BUSINESS APPLICATION USING REGRESSION ANALYSIS FOR DECISION-MAKING

VEHICLE MILEAGE In the summer of 2012, gasoline prices reached near-record-high levels in the United States, heightening motor vehicle customers' concern for fuel economy. Analysts at a major automobile company collected data on a variety of variables for a sample of 30 different cars and small trucks. Included among those data were the Environmental Protection Agency (EPA)'s highway mileage rating and the horsepower of each vehicle. The analysts were interested in the relationship between horsepower (x) and highway mileage (y). The data are contained in the file **Automobiles**.

A simple linear regression model can be developed using Excel. The Excel output is shown in Figure 14.19. For these sample data, the coefficient of determination $R^2 = 0.3016$, indicates that knowing the horsepower of the vehicle explains 30.16% of the variation in the highway mileage. The estimated regression equation is

$$\hat{y} = 31.1658 - 0.0286x$$

Excel Tutorial

Before the analysts attempt to describe the relationship between horsepower and highway mileage, they first need to test whether there is a statistically significant linear relationship

FIGURE 14.19 |

Excel 2010 Regression
Results for the Automobile
Mileage Study

Excel 2010 Instructions
1. Open File:
   Automobiles.xlsx.
2. Select **Data > Data
   Analysis**.
3. Select **Regression**.
4. Define *y* (*Mileage,
   highway*) and *x*
   (*Horsepower*) variable
   data range.
5. Select **Labels**.
6. Select **Residuals**.
7. Select output location.

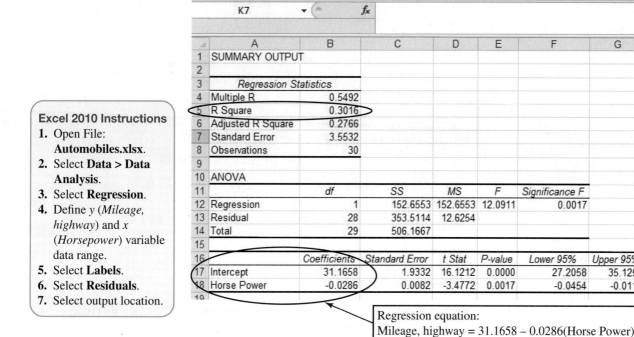

Regression equation:
Mileage, highway = 31.1658 − 0.0286(Horse Power)

Minitab Instructions (for similar results):
1. Open file: **Automobiles.MTW**.
2. Choose **Stat > Regression > Regression**.
3. In **Response**, enter the *y* variable column.
4. In **Predictors**, enter the *x* variable column.
5. Click **OK**.

between the two variables. To do this, they can apply the *t*-test described in Section 14.2 to test the following null and alternative hypotheses:

$$H_0: \beta_1 = 0$$
$$H_A: \beta_1 \neq 0$$

at the significance level

$$\alpha = 0.05$$

The calculated *t* statistic and the corresponding *p*-value are shown in Figure 14.19. Because the

$$p\text{-}value = 0.0017 < 0.05$$

the null hypothesis, H_0, is rejected and the analysts can conclude that the population regression slope is not equal to 0.

The sample slope, b_1, equals -0.0286. This means that for each 1-unit increase in horsepower, the highway mileage is estimated to decrease by an average of 0.0286 miles per gallon. However, b_1 is subject to sampling error and is considered a *point estimate* for the true regression slope coefficient. From earlier discussions about point estimates in Chapters 8 and 10, we expect that $b_1 \neq \beta_1$. Therefore, to help describe the relationship between the independent variable, horsepower, and the dependent variable, highway miles per gallon, we need to develop a *confidence interval estimate* for β_1. Equation 14.22 is used to do this.

Chapter Outcome 6. →

Confidence Interval Estimate for the Regression Slope, Simple Linear Regression

$$b_1 \pm ts_{b_1}$$ (14.22)

or equivalently,

$$b_1 \pm t \frac{s_\varepsilon}{\sqrt{\sum(x-\bar{x})^2}} \qquad df = n-2$$

where:

s_{b_1} = Standard error of the regression slope coefficient
s_ε = Standard error of the estimate

The regression output shown in Figure 14.19 contains the 95% confidence interval estimate for the slope coefficient, which is

$$-0.0454 \text{———} -0.0117$$

Thus, at the 95% confidence level, based on the sample data, the analysts for the car company can conclude that a 1-unit increase in horsepower will result in a drop in mileage by an average amount between approximately 0.012 and 0.045 miles per gallon.

There are many other situations in which the prime purpose of regression analysis is description. Economists use regression analysis for descriptive purposes as they search for a way of explaining the economy. Market researchers also use regression analysis, among other techniques, in an effort to describe the factors that influence the demand for products.

| **EXAMPLE 14-4** | **DEVELOPING A CONFIDENCE INTERVAL ESTIMATE FOR THE REGRESSION SLOPE** |

Home Prices Home values are determined by a variety of factors. One factor is the size of the house (square feet). Recently, a study was conducted by First City Real Estate aimed at estimating the average value of each additional square foot of space in a house. A simple random sample of 319 homes sold within the past year was collected. Here are the steps required to compute a confidence interval estimate for the regression slope coefficient:

Step 1 Define the y (dependent) and x (independent) variables.
The dependent variable is sales price, and the independent variable is square feet.

Step 2 Obtain the sample data.
The study consists of sales prices and corresponding square feet for a random sample of 319 homes. The data are in a file called **First-City**.

Step 3 Compute the regression equation and the standard error of the slope coefficient.
These computations can be performed manually using Equations 14.7 and 14.8 for the regression model and Equation 14.20 for the standard error of the slope. Alternatively, we can use Excel to obtain these values.

	Coefficients	Standard Error
Intercept (b_0)	39,838.48	7,304.95
Square Feet (b_1)	75.70	3.78

The point estimate for the regression slope coefficient is $75.70. Thus, for a 1-square-foot increase in the size of a house, house prices increase by an average of $75.70. This is a point estimate and is subject to sampling error.

Step 4 Construct and interpret the confidence interval estimate for the regression slope using Equation 14.22.
The confidence interval estimate is

$$b_1 \pm ts_{b_1}$$

where the degrees of freedom for the critical t is $319 - 2 = 317$. The critical t for a 95% confidence interval estimate is approximately 1.97, and the interval estimate is

$$\$75.70 \pm 1.97(\$3.78)$$
$$\$75.70 \pm \$7.45$$
$$\$68.25 \text{————} \$83.15$$

So, for a 1-square-foot increase in house size, at the 95% confidence level, we estimate that homes increase in price by an average of between $68.25 and $83.15.

>> **END EXAMPLE**

TRY PROBLEM 14-34 (pg. 599)

Chapter Outcome 5. → # Regression Analysis for Prediction

| BUSINESS APPLICATION | **PREDICTING HOSPITAL COSTS USING REGRESSION ANALYSIS** |

Excel Tutorial

FREEDOM HOSPITAL One of the main uses of regression analysis is *prediction*. You may need to predict the value of the dependent variable based on the value of the independent variable. Consider the administrator for Freedom Hospital, who has been asked by the hospital's board of directors to develop a model to predict the total charges for a geriatric patient. The file **Patients** contains the data that the administrator has collected.

Although the Regression tool in Excel works well for generating the simple linear regression equation and other useful information, it does not provide predicted values for the dependent variable. However, the PHStat add-ins do provide predictions.

The administrator is attempting to construct a simple linear regression model, with total charges as the dependent (y) variable and length of stay as the independent (x) variable. Figure 14.20 shows the Excel (and PHStat) regression output. The administrator is interested in predicting total charges for a patient whose length of stay is 5 days. To do this using PHStat, as Step 5 of the Excel instructions shows, $x = 5$ is used. The point estimate for the predicted total charges is shown in Figure 14.20 as $7,291.59. The true charges will be either higher or lower than this amount. To account for this uncertainty, the administrator can develop a prediction interval, which is similar to the confidence interval estimates developed in Chapter 8.

Chapter Outcome 6. → **Confidence Interval for the Average y, Given x** The administrator might like a 95% confidence interval for *average*, or expected value, for charges of patients who stay in the hospital five days. The confidence interval for the expected value of a dependent variable, given a specific level of the independent variable, is determined by Equation 14.23. Observe that the specific value of x used to provide the prediction is denoted as x_p.

Confidence Interval for $E(y)|x_p$

$$\hat{y} \pm t s_\varepsilon \sqrt{\frac{1}{n} + \frac{(x_p - \bar{x})^2}{\sum(x - \bar{x})^2}}$$

(14.23)

where:

$\hat{y} = $ Point estimate of the dependent variable
$t = $ Critical value with $n-2$ degrees of freedom
$n = $ Sample size
$x_p = $ Specific value of the independent variable
$\bar{x} = $ Mean of the independent variable observations in the sample
$s_\varepsilon = $ Estimate of the standard error of the estimate

---

FIGURE 14.20

Excel 2010 (PHStat) Prediction Interval for Freedom Hospital

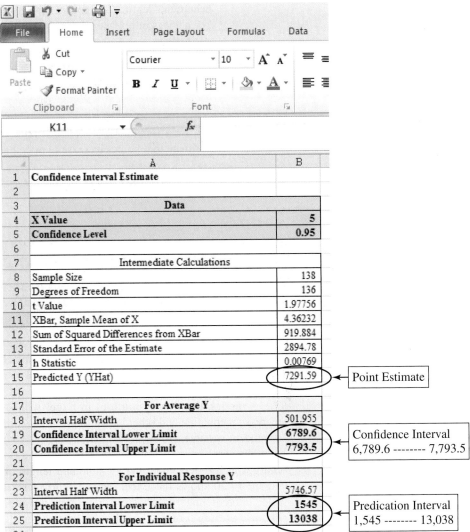

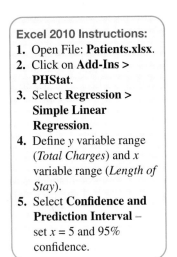

Excel 2010 Instructions:
1. Open File: **Patients.xlsx**.
2. Click on **Add-Ins > PHStat**.
3. Select **Regression > Simple Linear Regression**.
4. Define *y* variable range (*Total Charges*) and *x* variable range (*Length of Stay*).
5. Select **Confidence and Prediction Interval** – set *x* = 5 and 95% confidence.

Although the confidence interval estimate can be manually computed using Equation 14.23, using your computer is much easier. Excel using PHStat generates the confidence interval estimate for the average value of the dependent variable for a given value of the *x* variable as shown in Figure 14.20 near the bottom of the printout. Given a five-day length of stay, the point estimate for the mean total charges is $7,291.59, and at the 95% confidence level, the administrators believe the mean total charges will be in the interval $6,789.60 to $7,793.50.

Prediction Interval for a Particular *y*, Given *x*   The confidence interval just discussed is for the average value of *y* given x_p. The administrator might also be interested in predicting the total charges for a *particular* patient with a five-day stay, rather than the average of the charges for all patients staying five days. Developing this 95% prediction interval requires only a slight modification to Equation 14.23. This prediction interval is given by Equation 14.24.

Prediction Interval for $y\,|\,x_p$

$$\hat{y} \pm t s_\varepsilon \sqrt{1 + \frac{1}{n} + \frac{(x_p - \bar{x})^2}{\sum(x - \bar{x})^2}}$$ **(14.24)**

As was the case with the confidence interval application discussed previously, the manual computations required to use Equation 14.24 can be onerous. We recommend using software such

FIGURE 14.21

Regression Lines Illustrating the Increase in Potential Variation in y as x_p Moves Farther from $\bar{x}$

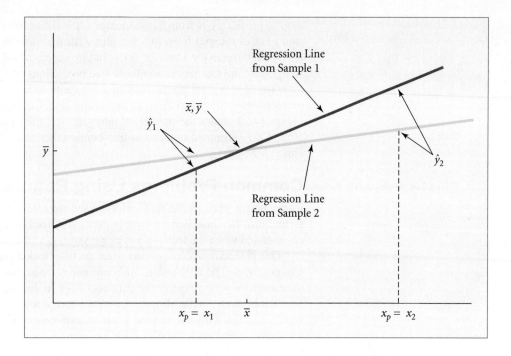

as Excel with PHStat to find the prediction interval. Figure 14.20 also shows the prediction interval for an individual value of the dependent variable (total charges) for a five-day length of stay.

Based on this regression model, at the 95% confidence level, the hospital administrators can predict total charges for any specific patient with length of stay of five days to be between \$1,545 and \$13,038. As you can see, this prediction has extremely poor precision. We doubt any hospital administrator will use a prediction interval that is so wide. Although the regression model explains a significant proportion of variation in the dependent variable, it is relatively imprecise for predictive purposes. To improve the precision, we might decrease the confidence level or increase the sample size and redevelop the model.

The prediction interval for a specific value of the dependent variable is wider (less precise) than the confidence interval for predicting the average value of the dependent variable. This will always be the case, as seen in Equations 14.23 and 14.24. From an intuitive viewpoint, we should expect to come closer to predicting an average value than a single value.

Note, the term $(x_p - \bar{x})^2$ has a particular effect on the confidence interval determined by both Equations 14.23 and 14.24. The farther x_p (the value of the independent variable

FIGURE 14.22

Confidence Intervals for $y|x_p$ and $E(y)|x_p$

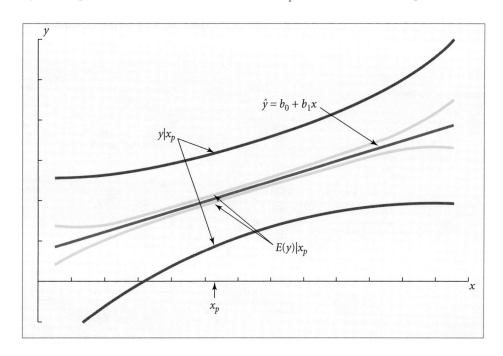

used to predict y), is from $\bar{x}$, the greater $(x_p - \bar{x})^2$ becomes. Figure 14.21 shows two regression lines developed from two samples with the same set of x-values. We have made both lines pass through the same $(\bar{x}, \bar{y})$ point; however, they have different slopes and intercepts. At $x_p = x_1$, the two regression lines give predictions of y that are close to each other. However, for $x_p = x_2$, the predictions of y are quite different. Thus, when x_p is close to $\bar{x}$, the problems caused by variations in regression slopes are not as great as when x_p is far from $\bar{x}$. Figure 14.22 shows the prediction intervals over the range of possible x_p values. The band around the estimated regression line bends away from the regression line as x_p moves in either direction from $\bar{x}$.

Chapter Outcome 7. →

Common Problems Using Regression Analysis

Regression is perhaps the most widely used statistical tool other than descriptive statistical techniques. Because it is so widely used, you need to be aware of the common problems encountered when the technique is employed.

One potential problem occurs when decision makers apply regression analysis for predictive purposes. The conclusions and inferences made from a regression line are statistically valid only over the range of the data contained in the sample used to develop the regression line. For instance, in the Midwest Distribution example, we analyzed the performance of sales representatives with one to nine years of experience. Therefore, predicting sales levels for employees with one to nine years of experience would be justified. However, if we were to try to predict the sales performance of someone with more than nine years of experience, the relationship between sales and experience might be different. Because no observations were taken for experience levels beyond the one- to nine-year range, we have no information about what might happen outside that range. Figure 14.23 shows a case in which the true relationship between sales and experience reaches a peak value at about 20 years and then starts to decline. If a linear regression equation were used to predict sales based on experience levels beyond the relevant range of data, large prediction errors could occur.

A second important consideration, one that was discussed previously, involves correlation and causation. The fact that a significant linear relationship exists between two variables does not imply that one variable causes the other. Although there may be a cause-and-effect relationship, you should not infer that such a relationship is present based only on regression and/or correlation analysis. You should also recognize that a cause-and-effect relationship between two variables is not necessary for regression analysis to be an effective tool. What matters is that the regression model accurately reflects the relationship between the two variables and that the relationship remains stable.

Many users of regression analysis mistakenly believe that a high coefficient of determination (R^2) guarantees that the regression model will be a good predictor. You should remember that R^2 is a measure of the variation in the dependent variable explained by the

FIGURE 14.23

Graph for a Sales Peak at 20 Years

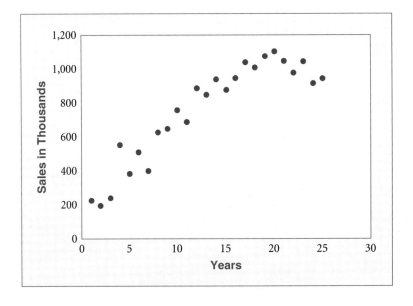

independent variable. Although the least squares criterion assures us that R^2 will be maximized (because the sum of squares error is a minimum) for the given set of sample data, the value applies only to those data used to develop the model. Thus, R^2 measures the fit of the regression line to the sample data. There is no guarantee that there will be an equally good fit with new data. The only true test of a regression model's predictive ability is how well the model actually predicts.

Finally, we should mention that you might find a large R^2 with a large standard error. This can happen if total sum of squares is large in comparison to the *SSE*. Then, even though R^2 is relatively large, so too is the estimate of the model's standard error. Thus, confidence and prediction errors may simply be too wide for the model to be used in many situations. This is discussed more fully in Chapter 15.

MyStatLab

14-3: Exercises

Skill Development

14-33. The following data have been collected by an accountant who is performing an audit of paper products at a large office supply company. The dependent variable, y, is the time taken (in minutes) by the accountant to count the units. The independent variable, x, is the number of units on the computer inventory record.

| y | 23.1 | 100.5 | 242.9 | 56.4 | 178.7 | 10.5 | 94.2 | 200.4 | 44.2 | 128.7 | 180.5 |
| x | 24 | 120 | 228 | 56 | 190 | 13 | 85 | 190 | 32 | 120 | 230 |

a. Develop a scatter plot for these data.
b. Determine the regression equation representing the data. Is the model significant? Test using a significance level of 0.10 and the p-value approach.
c. Develop a 90% confidence interval estimate for the true regression slope and interpret this interval estimate. Based on this interval, could you conclude the accountant takes an additional minute to count each additional unit?

14-34. You are given the following sample data:

x	y
10	3
6	7
9	3
3	8
2	9
8	5
3	7

a. Develop a scatter plot for these data.
b. Determine the regression equation for the data.
c. Develop a 95% confidence interval estimate for the true regression slope and interpret this interval estimate.

d. Provide a 95% prediction interval estimate for a particular y, given $x_p = 7$.

Problems 14-35 and **14-36** refer to the following output for a simple linear regression model:

Summary Output

Regression Statistics	
Multiple R	0.1027
R-Square	0.0105
Adjusted R-Square	−0.0030
Standard Error	9.8909
Observations	75

Anova

	df	SS	MS	F	Significance F
Regression	1	76.124	76.12	0.778	0.3806
Residual	73	7141.582	97.83		
Total	74	7217.706			

	Coefficients	Standard Error	t-Statistic
Intercept	4.0133	3.878	1.035
x	0.0943	0.107	0.882

	p-value	Lower 95%	Upper 95%
Intercept	0.3041	−3.715	11.742
x	0.3806	−0.119	0.307

14-35. Referring to the displayed regression model, what percent of variation in the y variable is explained by the x variable in the model?

14-36. Construct and interpret a 90% confidence interval estimate for the regression slope coefficient.

14-37. You are given the following summary statistics from a regression analysis:

$$\hat{y} = 200 + 150x$$
$$SSE = 25.25$$
$$SSX = \text{Sum of squares } X = \sum(x - \bar{x})^2 = 99,645$$
$$n = 18$$
$$\bar{x} = 52.0$$

a. Determine the point estimate for y if $x_p = 48$ is used.
b. Provide a 95% confidence interval estimate for the average y, given $x_p = 48$. Interpret this interval.
c. Provide a 95% prediction interval estimate for a particular y, given $x_p = 48$. Interpret.
d. Discuss the difference between the estimates provided in parts b and c.

14-38. The sales manager at Sun City Real Estate Company in Tempe, Arizona, is interested in describing the relationship between condo sales prices and the number of weeks the condo is on the market before it sells. He has collected a random sample of 17 low-end condos that have sold within the past three months in the Tempe area. These data are shown as follows:

Weeks on the Market	Selling Price
23	$76,500
48	$102,000
9	$53,000
26	$84,200
20	$73,000
40	$125,000
51	$109,000
18	$60,000
25	$87,000
62	$94,000
33	$76,000
11	$90,000
15	$61,000
26	$86,000
27	$70,000
56	$133,000
12	$93,000

a. Develop a simple linear regression model to explain the variation in selling price based on the number of weeks the condo is on the market.
b. Test to determine whether the regression slope coefficient is significantly different from 0 using a significance level equal to 0.05.
c. Construct and interpret a 95% confidence interval estimate for the regression slope coefficient.

14-39. A sample of 10 yields the following data:

x	10	8	11	7	10	11	6	7	15	9
y	103	85	115	73	97	102	65	75	155	95

a. Provide a 95% confidence interval for the average y when $x_p = 9.4$.

b. Provide a 95% confidence interval for the average y when $x_p = 10$.
c. Obtain the margin of errors for both part a and part b. Explain why the margin of error obtained in part b is larger than that in part a.

14-40. A regression analysis from a sample of 15 produced the following:

$$\sum(x_i - \bar{x})(y_i - \bar{y}) = 156.4$$
$$\sum(x_i - \bar{x})^2 = 173.5$$
$$\sum(y_i - \bar{y})^2 = 181.6$$
$$\sum(y_i - \hat{y})^2 = 40.621$$
$$\bar{x} = 13.4 \text{ and } \bar{y} = 56.4$$

a. Produce the regression line.
b. Determine if there is a linear relationship between the dependent and independent variables. Use a significance level of 0.05 and a p-value approach.
c. Calculate a 90% confidence interval for the amount the dependent variable changes when the independent variable increases by 1 unit.

Business **Applications**

14-41. During the recession that began in 2008, not only did some people stop making house payments, they also stopped making payments for local government services such as trash collection and water and sewer services. The following data have been collected by an accountant who is performing an audit of account balances for a major city billing department. The population from which the data were collected represent those accounts for which the customer had indicated the balance was incorrect. The dependent variable, y, is the actual account balance as verified by the accountant. The independent variable, x, is the computer account balance.

y	233	10	24	56	78	102	90	200	344	120	18
x	245	12	22	56	90	103	85	190	320	120	23

a. Compute the least squares regression equation.
b. If the computer account balance was 100, what would you expect to be the actual account balance as verified by the accountant?
c. The computer balance for Timothy Jones is listed as 100 in the computer account record. Provide a 90% interval estimate for Mr. Jones's actual account balance.
d. Provide a 90% interval estimate for the average of all customers' actual account balances in which a computer account balance is the same as that of Mr. Jones (part c). Interpret.

14-42. Gym Outfitters sells and services exercise equipment such as treadmills, ellipticals, and stair climbers to gymnasiums and recreational centers. The company's management would like to determine if there is a relationship between the number of minutes required to complete a routine service call and the number of machines serviced. A random sample of 12 records revealed the following information concerning the number of machines serviced and the time (in minutes) to complete the routine service call:

Number of Machines	Service Time (minutes)
11	115
8	60
9	80
10	90
7	55
6	65
8	70
4	33
10	95
5	50
5	40
12	110

a. Estimate the least squares regression equation.
b. If a gymnasium had six machines, how many minutes should Gym Outfitters expect a routine service call to require?
c. Provide a 90% confidence interval for the average amount of time required to complete a routine service call when the number of machines being serviced is nine.
d. Provide a 90% prediction interval for the time required to complete a particular routine service call for a gymnasium that has seven machines.

14-43. The National Association of Realtors (NAR) Existing-Home Sales Series provides a measurement of the residential real estate market. On or about the 25th of each month, NAR releases statistics on sales and prices of condos and co-ops, in addition to existing single-family homes, for the nation and the four regions. The data presented here indicate the number of (in thousands) existing-home sales as well as condo/co-op sales:

Year	Month	Single-Family Sales	Condo/Co-op Sales
2009	Apr	6,270	895
	May	6,230	912
	Jun	6,330	943
	Jul	6,220	914
	Aug	6,280	928
	Sept	6,290	908
	Oct	6,180	867
	Nov	6,150	876
	Dec	5,860	885
2010	Jan	5,790	781
	Feb	6,050	852
	Mar	6,040	862
	Apr	5,920	839

a. Construct the regression equation that would predict the number of condo/co-op sales using the number of single-family sales.

b. One might conjecture that these two markets (single-family sales and condo/co-op sales) would be competing for the same audience. Therefore, we would expect that as the number of single-family sales increases, the number of condo/co-op sales would decrease. Conduct a hypothesis test to determine this using a significance level of 0.05.
c. Provide a prediction interval for the number of condo/co-op sales when the number of single-family sales is 6,000 (thousands). Use a confidence level of 95%.

14-44. J.D. Power and Associates conducts an initial quality study (IQS) each year to determine the quality of newly manufactured automobiles. IQS measures 135 attributes across nine categories, including ride/handling/braking, engine and transmission, and a broad range of quality problem symptoms reported by vehicle owners. The 2008 IQS was based on responses from more than 62,000 purchasers and lessees of new 2008 model-year cars and trucks, who were surveyed after 90 days of ownership. The data given here portray the industry average of the number of reported problems per 100 vehicles for 1998–2008.

Year	1998	1999	2000	2001	2002	2003	2004	2005	2006	2007	2008
Problems	176	167	154	147	133	133	125	121	119	118	118

a. Construct a scatter plot of the number of reported problems per 100 vehicles as a function of the year.
b. Determine if the average number of reported problems per 100 vehicles declines from year to year. Use a significance level of 0.01 and a p-value approach.
c. Assume the relationship between the number of reported problems per 100 vehicles and the year continues into the future. Provide a 95% prediction interval for the initial quality industry average of the number of reported problems per 100 vehicles for 2010.

14.45. An engineering firm is interested in investigating whether the variability in the cost of small projects (defined as projects under $10 million) can be accounted for, in part, by differences in the number of direct engineering consulting hours billed. A random sample of 24 small projects was randomly selected from small projects performed over the past two years. The number of engineering consulting hours billed for each project, along with the project's cost, was recorded. The results are shown below:

Project	Billed Consulting Hours	Total Project Cost
1	3932	$4,323,826
2	3097	$3,750,964
3	2972	$3,579,570
4	3994	$5,053,149
5	4906	$5,528,308

Project	Billed Consulting Hours	Total Project Cost
6	5147	$5,631,967
7	4003	$5,257,756
8	4279	$5,681,909
9	3158	$4,133,012
10	4123	$4,596,329
11	2566	$3,344,851
12	3253	$3,868,200
13	3888	$4,865,998
14	3177	$4,042,509
15	3938	$5,067,679
16	3135	$4,111,731
17	5142	$6,554,583
18	5091	$6,042,445
19	4301	$5,192,769
20	2914	$3,581,835
21	3890	$4,745,269
22	2869	$3,353,559
23	3683	$5,169,469
24	4217	$5,147,689

a. Develop a simple linear regression model to explain the variation in total project cost based on the number of billed consulting hours.
b. Construct and interpret a 95% confidence interval estimate for the regression slope coefficient.
c. Provide a 95% confidence interval for the average value of y when $x_p = 3,500$.
d. Provide a 95% prediction interval for total project cost for a particular project with 3,500 billed consulting hours.

14.46. A regional retailer would like to determine if the variation in average monthly store sales can, in part, be explained by the size of the store measured in square feet. A random sample of 21 stores was selected and the store size and average monthly sales were computed. The following results are shown

Store Size (Sq. Ft)	Average Monthly Sales
17400	$581,241.00
15920	$538,275.00
17440	$636,059.00
17320	$574,477.00
15760	$558,043.00
20200	$689,256.00
15280	$552,569.00
17000	$584,737.00
11920	$470,551.00
12400	$520,798.00
15640	$619,703.00
12560	$465,416.00
21680	$730,863.00
14120	$501,501.00
16680	$624,255.00
14920	$567,043.00

Store Size (Sq. Ft)	Average Monthly Sales
18360	$612,974.00
18440	$618,122.00
16720	$691,403.00
19880	$719,275.00
17880	$536,592.00

a. Develop a simple linear regression model to explain the variation in average monthly sales based on the size of the store.
b. Construct and interpret a 95% confidence interval estimate for the regression slope coefficient.
c. Provide a 90% confidence interval for the average value of monthly sales when $x_p = 15,000$.
d. Provide a 90% prediction interval for a particular month's average sales when the store size is 15,000 square feet.

Computer Database **Exercises**

14-47. A manufacturer produces a wash-down motor for the food service industry. The company manufactures the motors to order by modifying a base model to meet the specifications requested by the customer. The motors are produced in a batch environment with the batch size equal to the number ordered. The manufacturer has recently sampled 50 customer orders. The motor manufacturer would like to determine if there is a relationship between the cost of producing the order and the order size so that it could estimate the cost of producing a particular size order. The sampled data are contained in the file **Washdown Motors**.
a. Use the sample data to estimate the least squares regression model.
b. Provide an interpretation of the regression coefficients.
c. Test the significance of the overall regression model using a significance level of 0.01.
d. The company has just received an order for 30 motors. Use the regression model developed in part a to estimate the cost of producing this particular order.
e. Referring to part d, what is the 90% confidence interval for an average cost of an order of 30 motors?

14-48. Each month, the Bureau of Labor Statistics (BLS) of the U.S. Department of Labor announces the total number of employed and unemployed persons in the United States for the previous month. At the same time, it also publishes the inflation rate, which is the rate of change in the price of goods and services from one month to the next. It seems quite plausible that there should be some relationship between these two indicators. The file titled **CPI** provides the monthly unemployment and inflation rates for the period 2000 through 2005.

a. Construct a scatter plot of the unemployment rate versus inflation rate for the period 2000 through 2005. Describe the relationship that appears to exist between these two variables.

b. Produce a 95% prediction interval for the unemployment rate for the maximum inflation rate in the period 2000 through 2005. Interpret the interval.

c. Produce a 95% prediction interval for the unemployment rate when the inflation rate -is 0.00.

d. Which of the prediction intervals in parts b and c has the larger margin of error? Explain why this is the case.

14-49. The National Highway Transportation Safety Administration's National Center for Statistics and Analysis released its Vehicle Survivability Travel Mileage Schedules in January 2006. One item investigated was the relationship between the annual vehicle miles traveled (VMT) as a function of vehicle age for passenger cars up to 25 years old. The VMT data were collected by asking consumers to estimate the number of miles driven in a given year. The data were collected over a 14-month period. The file titled **Miles** contains this data.

a. Produce a regression equation modeling the relationship between VMT and the age of the vehicle. Estimate how many more annual vehicle miles would be traveled for a vehicle that is 10 years older than another vehicle.

b. Provide a 90% confidence interval estimate for the average annual vehicle miles traveled when the age of the vehicle is 15 years.

c. Determine if it is plausible for a vehicle that is 10 years old to travel 12,000 miles in a year. Support your answer with statistical reasoning.

END EXERCISES 14-3

Visual Summary

Chapter 14: Although some business situations involve only one variable, others require decision makers to consider the relationship between two or more variables. In analyzing the relationship between two variables, there are two basic models that we can use. The regression model covered in this chapter is referred to as **simple linear regression**. This relationship between x and y assumes that the x variable takes on known values specifically selected from all the possible values for x. The y variable is a random variable observed at the different levels of x. Testing that a linear relationship exists between the dependent and independent variables is performed using the standard statistical procedures of hypothesis testing and confidence intervals. A second model is referred to as the correlation model and is used in applications in which both the x and y variables are considered to be random variables. These two models arise in practice by the way in which the data are obtained. Regression analysis and correlation analysis are two of the most often applied statistical tools for business decision making.

14.1 Scatter Plots and Correlation (pg. 560–569)

Summary

Decision-making situations that call for understanding the relationship between two quantitative variables are aided by the use of **scatter plots**, or *scatter diagrams*. A scatter plot is a two-dimensional plot showing the values for the joint occurrence of two quantitative variables. The scatter plot may be used to graphically represent the relationship between two variables. A numerical quantity that measures the strength of the linear relationship between two variables is labeled the **correlation coefficient**. The sample correlation coefficient, r, can range from a perfect positive correlation, $+1.0$, to a perfect negative correlation, -1.0. A test based upon the t-distribution can determine whether the population correlation coefficient is significantly different from 0 and, therefore, whether a linear relationship exists between the dependent and independent variables.

Outcome 1. Calculate and interpret the correlation between two variables.
Outcome 2. Determine whether the correlation is significant.

14.2 Simple Linear Regression Analysis (pg. 570–592)

Summary

The statistical technique we use to analyze the relationship between the dependent variable and the independent variable is known as regression analysis. When the relationship between the dependent variable and the independent variable is linear, the technique is referred as **simple linear regression**. The population regression model is determined by three values known as the population regression coefficients: (1) the y-intercept, (2) the slope of the regression line, and (3) the random error term. The criterion used to determine the best estimate of the population regression line is known as the **least squares criterion**. It chooses values for the y-intercept and slope that will produce the smallest possible sum of squared prediction errors. Testing that the population's slope coefficient is equal to zero provides a method to determine if there is no linear relationship between the dependent and independent variables. The test for the simple linear regression is equivalent to the test that the correlation coefficient is significant. A less involved procedure that indicates the goodness of fit of the regression equation to the data is known as the **coefficient of determination**. Simple linear regression, which is introduced in this chapter, is one of the most often applied statistical tools by business decision makers for analyzing the relationship between two variables.

Outcome 3. Calculate the simple linear regression equation for a set of data and know the basic assumptions behind regression analysis.
Outcome 4. Determine whether a regression model is significant.

 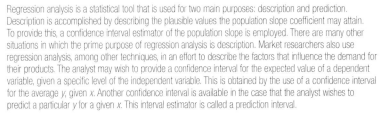

14.3 Uses for Regression Analysis (pg. 592–603)

Summary

Regression analysis is a statistical tool that is used for two main purposes: description and prediction. Description is accomplished by describing the plausible values the population slope coefficient may attain. To provide this, a confidence interval estimator of the population slope is employed. There are many other situations in which the prime purpose of regression analysis is description. Market researchers also use regression analysis, among other techniques, in an effort to describe the factors that influence the demand for their products. The analyst may wish to provide a confidence interval for the expected value of a dependent variable, given a specific level of the independent variable. This is obtained by the use of a confidence interval for the average y, given x. Another confidence interval is available in the case that the analyst wishes to predict a particular y for a given x. This interval estimator is called a prediction interval.

Any procedure in statistics is valid only if the assumptions it is built upon are valid. This is particularly true in regression analysis. Therefore, before using a regression model for description or prediction, you should check to see if the assumptions associated with linear regression analysis are valid. Residual analysis is the procedure that is used for that purpose

Outcome 5. Recognize regression analysis applications for purposes of description and prediction.
Outcome 6. Calculate and interpret confidence intervals for the regression analysis.
Outcome 7. Recognize some potential problems if regression analysis is used incorrectly.

Conclusion

Correlation and regression analysis are two of the most frequently used statistical techniques by business decision makers. This chapter has introduced the basics of these two topics. The discussion of regression analysis has been limited to situations in which you have one dependent variable and one independent variable. Chapter 15 will extend the discussion of regression analysis by showing how two or more independent variables are included in the analysis. The focus of that chapter will be on building a model for explaining the variation in the dependent variable. However, the basic concepts presented in this chapter will be carried forward.

Equations

(14.1) Sample Correlation Coefficient pg. 560

$$r = \frac{\Sigma(x - \bar{x})(y - \bar{y})}{\sqrt{[\Sigma(x - \bar{x})^2][\Sigma(y - \bar{y})^2]}}$$

(14.2) or the algebraic equivalent: pg. 561

$$r = \frac{n\Sigma xy - \Sigma x \Sigma y}{\sqrt{[n(\Sigma x^2) - (\Sigma x)^2][n(\Sigma y^2) - (\Sigma y)^2]}}$$

(14.3) Test Statistic for Correlation pg. 564

$$t = \frac{r}{\sqrt{\frac{1 - r^2}{n - 2}}} \qquad df = n - 2$$

(14.4) Simple Linear Regression Model (Population Model) pg. 570

$$y = \beta_0 + \beta_1 x + \varepsilon$$

(14.5) Estimated Regression Model (Sample Model) pg. 573

$$\hat{y} = b_0 + b_1 x$$

(14.6) Least Squares Equation pg. 573

$$b_1 = \frac{\Sigma(x_i - \bar{x})(y_i - \bar{y})}{\Sigma(x_i - \bar{x})^2}$$

(14.7) or the algebraic equivalent: pg. 573

$$b_1 = \frac{\Sigma xy - \frac{\Sigma x \Sigma y}{n}}{\Sigma x^2 - \frac{(\Sigma x)^2}{n}}$$

(14.8) and pg. 573

$$b_0 = \bar{y} - b_1 \bar{x}$$

(14.9) Sum of Squared Errors pg. 575

$$SSE = \Sigma y^2 - b_0 \Sigma y - b_1 \Sigma xy$$

(14.10) Sum of Residuals pg. 576

$$\sum_{i=1}^{n}(y_i - \hat{y}_i) = 0$$

(14.11) Sum of Squared Residuals (Errors) pg. 576

$$SSE = \sum_{i=1}^{n}(y_i - \hat{y}_i)^2$$

(14.12) Total Sum of Squares pg. 580

$$SST = \sum_{i=1}^{n}(y_i - \bar{y})^2$$

(14.13) Sum of Squares Error pg. 580

$$SSE = \sum_{i=1}^{n}(y_i - \hat{y}_i)^2$$

(14.14) Sum of Squares Regression pg. 581

$$SSR = \sum_{i=1}^{n}(\hat{y}_i - \bar{y})^2$$

(14.15) Coefficient of Determination, R^2 pg. 582

$$R^2 = \frac{SSR}{SST}$$

(14.16) Coefficient of Determination for the Single Independent Variable Case pg. 582

$$R^2 = r^2$$

(14.17) Test Statistic for Significance of the Coefficient of Determination pg. 583

$$F = \frac{\frac{SSR}{1}}{\frac{SSE}{(n - 2)}} \qquad df = (D_1 = 1, D_2 = n - 2)$$

(14.18) Simple Regression Standard Error of the Slope Coefficient (Population) pg. 584

$$\sigma_{b_1} = \frac{\sigma_\varepsilon}{\sqrt{\Sigma(x - \bar{x})^2}}$$

(14.19) Simple Regression Estimator for the Standard Error of the Estimate pg. 584

$$s_\varepsilon = \sqrt{\frac{SSE}{n - 2}}$$

(14.20) Simple Regression Estimator for the Standard Error of the Slope pg. 584

$$s_{b_1} = \frac{s_\varepsilon}{\sqrt{\Sigma(x - \bar{x})^2}}$$

(14.21) Simple Linear Regression Test Statistic for Test of the Significance of the Slope pg. 587

$$t = \frac{b_1 - \beta_1}{s_{b_1}} \qquad df = n - 2$$

(14.22) Confidence Interval Estimate for the Regression Slope, Simple Linear Regression pg. 594

$$b_1 \pm t s_{b_1}$$

or equivalently,

$$b_1 \pm t \frac{s_\varepsilon}{\sqrt{\Sigma(x - \bar{x})^2}} \qquad df = n - 2$$

(14.23) Confidence Interval for $E(y)\,|x_p$ pg. 595

$$\hat{y} \pm t s_\varepsilon \sqrt{\frac{1}{n} + \frac{(x_p - \bar{x})^2}{\Sigma(x - \bar{x})^2}}$$

(14.24) Prediction Interval for $y\,|x_p$ pg. 596

$$\hat{y} \pm t s_\varepsilon \sqrt{1 + \frac{1}{n} + \frac{(x_p - \bar{x})^2}{\Sigma(x - \bar{x})^2}}$$

Key Terms

Coefficient of determination pg. 582
Correlation coefficient pg. 560
Least squares criterion pg. 572

Regression slope coefficient pg. 571
Residual pg. 572
Scatter plot pg. 560

Simple linear regression pg. 570

Chapter Exercises _____ MyStatLab

Conceptual Questions

14-50. A statistics student was recently working on a class project that required him to compute a correlation coefficient for two variables. After careful work, he arrived at a correlation coefficient of 0.45. Interpret this correlation coefficient for the student who did the calculations.

14-51. Referring to the previous problem, another student in the same class computed a regression equation relating the same two variables. The slope of the equation was found to be −0.735. After trying several times and always coming up with the same result, she felt that she must have been doing something wrong since the value was negative and she knew that this could not be right. Comment on this student's conclusion.

14-52. If we select a random sample of data for two variables and, after computing the correlation coefficient, conclude that the two variables may have zero correlation, can we say that there is no relationship between the two variables? Discuss.

14-53. Discuss why prediction intervals that attempt to predict a particular y-value are less precise than confidence intervals for predicting an average y.

14-54. Consider the two following scenarios:

a. The number of new workers hired per week in your county has a high positive correlation with the average weekly temperature. Can you conclude that an increase in temperature causes an increase in the number of new hires? Discuss.

b. Suppose the stock price and the common dividends declared for a certain company have a high positive correlation. Are you safe in concluding on the basis of the correlation coefficient that an increase in the common dividends declared causes an increase in the stock price? Present other reasons than the correlation coefficient that might lead you to conclude that an increase in common dividends declared causes an increase in the stock price.

14-55. Consider the following set of data:

x	48	27	34	24	49	29	39	38	46	32
y	47	23	31	20	50	48	47	47	42	47

a. Calculate the correlation coefficient of these two variables.

b. Multiply each value of the variable x by 5 and add 10 to the resulting products. Now multiply each value of the variable y by 3 and subtract 7 from the resulting products. Finally, calculate the correlation coefficient of the new x and y variables.

c. Describe the principle that the example developed in parts a and b demonstrates.

14-56. Go to the library and locate an article in a journal related to your major (*Journal of Marketing*, *Journal of Finance*, etc.) that uses linear regression. Discuss the following:

a. How the author chose the dependent and independent variables

b. How the data were gathered

c. What statistical tests the author used

d. What conclusions the analysis allowed the author to draw

Business Applications

14-57. The Smithfield Organic Milk Company recently studied a random sample of 30 of its distributors and found the correlation between sales and advertising dollars to be 0.67.

a. Is there a significant linear relationship between sales and advertising? If so, is it fair to conclude that advertising causes sales to increase?

b. If a regression model were developed using sales as the dependent variable and advertising as the independent variable, determine the proportion of the variation in sales that would be explained by its relationship to advertising. Discuss what this says about the usefulness of using advertising to predict sales.

14-58. A previous exercise discussed the relationship between the average college tuition (in 2003 dollars) for private and public colleges. The data indicated in the article follow:

Period	1983–1984	1988–1989	1993–1994
Private	9,202	12,146	13,844
Public	2,074	2,395	3,188
Period	1998–1999	2003–2004	2008–2009
Private	16,454	19,710	21,582
Public	3,632	4,694	5,652

a. Construct the regression equation that would predict the average college tuition for private colleges using that of the public colleges.

b. Determine if there is a linear tendency for the average college tuition for private colleges to increase when the average college tuition for public colleges increases. Use a significance level of 0.05 and a p-value approach.

c. Provide a 95% confidence interval for the average college tuition for private colleges when the average college tuition for public colleges reaches $7,000.

d. Is it plausible that the average college tuition for private colleges would be larger than $35,000 when the average college tuition for public colleges reaches $7,000? Support your assertion with statistical reasoning.

14-59. The Farmington City Council recently commissioned a study of park users in their community. Data were collected on the age of the person surveyed and the amount of hours he or she spent in the park in the past month. The data collected were as follows:

Time in Park	Age	Time in Park	Age
7.2	16	4.4	48
3.5	15	8.8	18
6.6	28	4.9	24
5.4	16	5.1	33
1.5	29	1.0	56
2.3	38		

a. Draw a scatter plot for these data and discuss what, if any, relationship appears to be present between the two variables.

b. Compute the correlation coefficient between age and the amount of time spent in the park. Provide an explanation to the Farmington City Council of what the correlation measures.

c. Test to determine whether the amount of time spent in the park decreases with increases in the age of the park user. Use a significance level of 0.10. Use a p-value approach to conduct this hypothesis test.

14-60. At State University, a study was done to establish whether a relationship exists between students' graduating grade point average (GPA) and the SAT verbal score when the student originally entered the university. The sample data are reported as follows:

GPA	2.5	3.2	3.5	2.8	3.0	2.4	3.4	2.9	2.7	3.8
SAT	640	700	550	540	620	490	710	600	505	710

a. Develop a scatter plot for these data and describe what, if any, relationship exists between the two variables, GPA and SAT score.

b. (1) Compute the correlation coefficient. (2) Does it appear that the success of students at State University is related to the SAT verbal scores of those students? Conduct a statistical procedure to answer this question. Use a significance level of 0.01.

c. (1) Compute the regression equation based on these sample data if you wish to predict the university GPA using the student SAT score. (2) Interpret the regression coefficients.

14-61. An American airline company recently performed a customer survey in which it asked a random sample of 100 passengers to indicate their income and the total cost of the airfares they purchased for pleasure trips during the past year. A regression model was developed for the purpose of determining whether income could be used as a variable to explain the variation in the total cost of airfare on airlines in a year. The following regression results were obtained:

$$\hat{y} = 0.25 + 0.0150x$$
$$s_\varepsilon = 721.44$$
$$R^2 = 0.65$$
$$s_{b_1} = 0.0000122$$

a. Determine whether income is a significant variable in explaining the variation in the total cost of airfare on airlines in a year by using a 90% confidence interval.

b. Can the intercept of the regression equation be interpreted in this case, assuming that no one who was surveyed had an income of 0 dollars? Explain.

14-62. One of the advances that have helped to diminish carpal tunnel syndrome is ergonomic keyboards. The ergonomic keyboards may also increase typing speed. Ten administrative assistants were chosen to type on both standard and ergonomic keyboards. The resulting typing speeds follow:

Ergonomic:	69	80	60	71	73	64	63	70	63	74
Standard:	70	68	54	56	58	64	62	51	64	53

a. Produce a scatter plot of the typing speed of administrative assistants using ergonomic and standard keyboards. Does there appear to be a linear relationship between these two variables? Explain your response.

b. Calculate the correlation coefficient of the typing speed of administrative assistants using ergonomic and standard keyboards.

c. Conduct a hypothesis test to determine if a positive correlation exists between administrative assistants using ergonomic and standard keyboards. Use a significance level of 0.05.

14-63. A company is considering recruiting new employees from a particular college and plans to place a great deal of emphasis on the student's college GPA. However, the company is aware that not all schools have the same grading standards, so it is possible that a student at this school might have a lower (or higher) GPA than a student from another school, yet really be on par with the other student. To make this comparison between schools, the company has devised a test that it has administered utilizing a sample size of 400 students. With the results of the test, it has developed a regression model that it uses to predict student GPA. The following equation represents the model:

$$\hat{y} = 1.0 + 0.028x$$

The R^2 for this model is 0.88 and the standard error of the estimate is 0.20, based on the sample data used to develop the model. Note that the dependent variable is the GPA and the independent variable is test score, where this score can range from 0 to 100. For the sample data used to develop the model, the following values are known:

$$\bar{y} = 2.76$$
$$\bar{x} = 68$$
$$\Sigma (x - \bar{x})^2 = 148,885.73$$

a. Based on the information contained in this problem, can you conclude that as the test score increases, the GPA will also increase, using a significance level of 0.05?

b. Suppose a student interviews with this company, takes the company test, and scores 80 correct. What is the 90% prediction interval estimate for this student's GPA? Interpret the interval.

c. Suppose the student in part b actually has a 2.90 GPA at this school. Based on this evidence, what might be concluded about this person's actual GPA compared with other students with the same GPA at other schools? Discuss the limitations you might place on this conclusion.

d. Suppose a second student with a 2.45 GPA took the test and scored 65 correct. What is the 90% prediction interval for this student's "real" GPA? Interpret.

Computer Database Exercises

14-64. Although the Jordan Banking System, a smaller regional bank, generally avoided the subprime mortgage market and consequently did not take money from the Federal Troubled Asset Relief Program (TARP), its board of directors has decided to look into all aspects of revenues and costs. One service the bank offers is free checking, and the board is interested in whether the costs of this service are offset by revenues from interest earned on the deposits. One aspect in studying checking accounts is to determine whether changes in average checking account balance can be explained by knowing the number of checks written per month. The sample data selected are contained in the data file named **Jordan**.

a. Draw a scatter plot for these data.

b. Develop the least squares regression equation for these data.

c. Develop the 90% confidence interval estimate for the change in the average checking account balance when a person who formerly wrote 25 checks a month doubles the number of checks used.

d. Test to determine if an increase in the number of checks written by an individual can be used

to predict the checking account balance of that individual. Use $\alpha = 0.05$. Comment on this result and the result of part c.

14-65. An economist for the state government of Mississippi recently collected the data contained in the file called **Mississippi** on the percentage of people unemployed in the state at randomly selected points in time over the past 25 years and the interest rate of Treasury bills offered by the federal government at that point in time.

a. (1) Develop a plot showing the relationship between the two variables. (2) Describe the relationship as being either linear or curvilinear.

b. (1) Develop a simple linear regression model with unemployment rate as the dependent variable. (2) Write a short report describing the model and indicating the important measures.

14-66. Terry Downes lost his job as an operations analyst last year in a company downsizing effort. In looking for job opportunities, Terry remembered reading an article in *Fortune* stating companies were looking to outsource activities they were currently doing that were not part of their core competence. Terry decided no company's core competence involved cleaning its facilities, and so using his savings, he started a cleaning company. In a surprise to his friends, Terry's company proved to be successful. Recently, Terry decided to survey customers to determine how satisfied they are with the work performed. He devised a rating scale between 0 and 100, with 0 being poor and 100 being excellent service. He selected a random sample of 14 customers and asked them to rate the service. He also recorded the number of worker hours spent in the customer's facility. These data are in the data file named **Downes**.

a. (1) Draw a scatter plot showing these two variables, with the y variable on the vertical axis and the x variable on the horizontal axis. (2) Describe the relationship between these two variables.

b. (1) Develop a linear regression model to explain the variation in the service rating. (2) Write a short report describing the model and showing the results of pertinent hypothesis tests, using a significance level of 0.10.

14-67. A previous problem discussed the College Board changing the SAT test between 2005 and 2006. The class of 2005 was the last to take the former version of the SAT featuring math and verbal sections. The file titled **MathSAT** contains the math SAT scores for the interval 1967 to 2005. One point of interest concerning the data is the relationship between the average scores of male and female students.

a. Produce a scatter plot depicting the relationship between the average math SAT score of males (the dependent variable) and females (independent variable) over the period 1967 to 2005. Describe the relationship between these two variables.

b. Is there a linear relationship between the average score for males and females over the period 1967 to 2005? Use a significance level of 0.05 and the *p*-value approach to determine this.

14-68. The housing market in the United States saw a major decrease in value between 2007 and 2008. The file titled **House** contains the data on average and median housing prices between November 2007 and November 2008. Assume the data can be viewed as samples of the relevant populations.

    a. Determine the linear relationship that could be used to predict the average selling prices for November 2007 using the median selling prices for that period.

    b. Conduct a hypothesis test to determine if the median selling prices for November 2007 could be used to determine the average selling prices in that period. Use a significance level of 0.05 and the *p*-value approach to conduct the test.

    c. Provide an interval estimate of the average selling price of homes in November 2007 if the median selling price was $195,000. Use a 90% confidence interval.

14-69. The Grinfield Service Company's marketing director is interested in analyzing the relationship between her company's sales and the advertising dollars spent. In the course of her analysis, she selected a random sample of 20 weeks and recorded the sales for each week and the amount spent on advertising. These data are contained in the data file called **Grinfield**.

    a. Identify the independent and dependent variables.

    b. Draw a scatter plot with the dependent variable on the vertical axis and the independent variable on the horizontal axis.

    c. The marketing director wishes to know if increasing the amount spent on advertising increases sales. As a first attempt, use a statistical test that will provide the required information. Use a significance level of 0.025. On careful consideration, the marketing manager realizes that it takes a certain amount of time for the effect of advertising to register in terms of increased sales. She therefore asks you to calculate a correlation coefficient for sales of the current week against amount of advertising spent in the previous week and to conduct a hypothesis test to determine if, under this model, increasing the amount spent on advertising increases sales. Again, use a significance level of 0.025.

14-70. Refer to the Grinfield Service Company discussed in Problem 14-69.

    a. Develop the least squares regression equation for these variables. Plot the regression line on the scatter plot.

    b. Develop a 95% confidence interval estimate for the increase in sales resulting from increasing the advertising budget by $50. Interpret the interval.

    c. Discuss whether it is appropriate to interpret the intercept value in this model. Under what conditions is it appropriate? Discuss.

    d. Develop a 90% confidence interval for the mean sales amount achieved during all weeks in which advertising is $200 for the week.

    e. Suppose you are asked to use this regression model to predict the weekly sales when advertising is to be set at $100. What would you reply to the request? Discuss.

Case 14.1

A & A Industrial Products

Alex Court, the cost accountant for A & A Industrial Products, was puzzled by the repair cost analysis report he had just reviewed. This was the third consecutive report in which unscheduled plant repair costs were out of line with the repair cost budget allocated to each plant. A & A budgets for both scheduled maintenance and unscheduled repair costs for its plants' equipment, mostly large industrial machines. Budgets for scheduled maintenance activities are easy to estimate and are based on the equipment manufacturer's recommendations. The unscheduled repair costs, however, are harder to determine. Historically, A & A Industrial Products has estimated unscheduled maintenance using a formula based on the average number of hours of operation between major equipment failures at a plant. Specifically, plants were given a budget of $65.00 per hour of operation between major failures. Alex had arrived at this amount by dividing aggregate historical repair costs by the total number of hours between failures. Then plant averages would be used to estimate unscheduled repair cost. For example, if a plant averaged 450 hours of run time before a major repair occurred, the plant would be allocated a repair budget of 450 × $65 = $29,250 per repair. If the plant was expected to be in operation 3,150 hours per year, the company would anticipate seven unscheduled repairs (3,150/450) annually and budget $204,750 for annual unscheduled repair costs.

Alex was becoming more and more convinced that this approach was not working. Not only was upper management upset about the variance between predicted and actual costs of repair, but plant managers believed that the model did not account for potential differences among the company's three plants when allocating dollars for unscheduled repairs. At the weekly management meeting, Alex was informed that he needed to analyze his cost projections further and produce a report that provided a more reliable method for predicting repair costs. On leaving the meeting, Alex had his assistant randomly pull 64 unscheduled repair reports. The data are in the file **A & A Costs**. The management team is anxiously waiting for Alex's analysis.

Required Tasks:

1. Identify the major issue(s) of the case.
2. Analyze the overall cost allocation issues by developing a scatterplot of Cost v. Hours of Operation. Which variable, cost or hours of operation, should be the dependent variable? Explain why.
3. Fit a linear regression equation to the data.
4. Explain how the results of the linear regression equation could be used to develop a cost allocation formula. State any adjustments or modifications you have made to the regression output to develop a cost allocation formula that can be used to predict repair costs.
5. Sort the data by plant.
6. Fit a linear regression equation to each plant's data.
7. Explain how the results of the individual plant regression equations can help the manager determine whether a different linear regression equation could be used to develop a cost allocation formula for each plant. State any adjustments or modifications you have made to the regression output to develop a cost allocation formula.
8. Based on the individual plant regression equations determine whether there is reason to believe there are differences among the repair costs of the company's three plants.
9. Summarize your analysis and findings in a report to the company's manager.

Case 14.2

Sapphire Coffee—Part 1

Jennie Garcia could not believe that her career had moved so far so fast. When she left graduate school with a master's degree in anthropology, she intended to work at a local coffee shop until something else came along that was more related to her academic background. But after a few months, she came to enjoy the business, and in a little more than a year, she was promoted to store manager. When the company for which she worked continued to grow, Jennie was given oversight of a few stores.

Now, eight years after she started as a barista, Jennie was in charge of operations and planning for the company's southern region. As a part of her responsibilities, Jennie tracks store revenues and forecasts coffee demand. Historically, Sapphire Coffee would base its demand forecast on the number of stores, believing that each store sold approximately the same amount of coffee. This approach seemed to work well when the company had shops of similar size and layout, but as the company grew, stores became more varied. Now, some stores had drive-thru windows, a feature that top management added to some stores believing that it would increase coffee sales for customers who wanted a cup of coffee on their way to work but who were too rushed to park and enter the store to place an order.

Jennie noticed that weekly sales seemed to be more variable across stores in her region and was wondering what, if anything, might explain the differences. The company's financial vice

president had also noticed the increased differences in sales across stores and was wondering what might be happening. In an e-mail to Jennie, he stated that weekly store sales are expected to average $5.00 per square foot. Thus, a 1,000-square-foot store would have average weekly sales of $5,000. He asked that Jennie analyze the stores in her region to see if this rule of thumb was a reliable measure of a store's performance.

The vice president of finance was expecting the analysis to be completed by the weekend. Jennie decided to randomly select weekly sales records for 53 stores. The data are in the file **Sapphire Coffee-1**. A full analysis needs to be sent to the corporate office by Friday.

Required Tasks:

1. Identify the major issue(s) of the case.
2. Develop a scatter plot of the variables Store Size and Weekly Sales. Identify the dependent variable. Briefly describe the relationship between the two variables.
3. Fit a linear regression equation to the data. Does the variable Store Size explain a significant amount of the variation in Weekly Sales?
4. Based on the estimated regression equation does it appear the $5.00 per square foot weekly sales expectation the company currently uses is a valid one?
5. Summarize your analysis and findings in a report to the company's vice president of finance.

Case 14.3

Alamar Industries

While driving home in northern Kentucky at 8:00 P.M., Juan Alamar wondered whether his father had done him any favor by retiring early and letting him take control of the family machine tool–restoration business. When his father started the business

of overhauling machine tools (both for resale and on a contract basis), American companies dominated the tool manufacturing market. During the past 30 years, however, the original equipment industry had been devastated, first by competition from Germany and then from Japan. Although foreign competition had not yet invaded the overhaul segment of the business, Juan had heard about foreign companies establishing operations on the West Coast.

The foreign competitors were apparently stressing the high-quality service and operations that had been responsible for their great inroads into the original equipment market. Last week, Juan attended a daylong conference on total quality management that had discussed the advantages of competing for the Baldrige Award, the national quality award established in 1987. Presenters from past Baldrige winners, including Xerox, Federal Express, Cadillac, and Motorola, stressed the positive effects on their companies of winning and said similar effects would be possible for any company. This assertion of only positive effects was what Juan questioned. He was certain that the effect on his remaining free time would not be positive.

The Baldrige Award considers seven corporate dimensions of quality. Although the award is not based on a numerical score, an overall score is calculated. The maximum score is 1,000, with most recent winners scoring about 800. Juan did not doubt the award was good for the winners, but he wondered about the nonwinners. In particular, he wondered about any relationship between attempting to improve quality according to the Baldrige dimensions and company profitability. Individual company scores are not released,

but Juan was able to talk to one of the conference presenters, who shared some anonymous data, such as companies' scores in the year they applied, their returns on investment (ROIs) in the year applied, and returns on investment in the year after application. Juan decided to commit the company to a total quality management process if the data provided evidence that the process would lead to increased profitability.

Baldrige Score	ROI Application Year	ROI Next Year
470	11%	13%
520	10	11
660	14	15
540	12	12
600	15	16
710	16	16
580	11	12
600	12	13
740	16	16
610	11	14
570	12	13
660	17	19

Case 14.4

Continental Trucking

Norm Painter is the newly hired cost analyst for Continental Trucking. Continental is a nationwide trucking firm, and until recently, most of its routes were driven under regulated rates. These rates were set to allow small trucking firms to earn an adequate profit, leaving little incentive to work to reduce costs by efficient management techniques. In fact, the greatest effort was made to try to influence regulatory agencies to grant rate increases.

A recent rash of deregulation has made the long-distance trucking industry more competitive. Norm has been hired to analyze Continental's whole expense structure. As part of this study, Norm is looking at truck repair costs. Because the trucks are involved in long hauls, they inevitably break down. In the past, little preventive maintenance was done, and if a truck broke down in the middle of a haul, either a replacement tractor was sent or an independent contractor finished the haul. The truck was then repaired at the nearest local shop. Norm is sure this procedure has led to more expense than if major repairs had been made before the trucks failed.

Norm thinks that some method should be found for determining when preventive maintenance is needed. He believes that fuel consumption is a good indicator of possible breakdowns; as trucks begin to run badly, they will consume more fuel. Unfortunately, the major determinants of fuel consumption are the weight of a

truck and headwinds. Norm picks a sample of a single truck model and gathers data relating fuel consumption to truck weight. All trucks in the sample are in good condition. He separates the data by direction of the haul, realizing that winds tend to blow predominantly out of the west.

Although he can rapidly gather future data on fuel consumption and haul weight, now that Norm has these data, he is not quite sure what to do with them.

East-West Haul		West-East Haul	
Miles/Gallon	**Haul Weight**	**Miles/Gallon**	**Haul Weight**
4.1	41,000 lb	4.3	40,000 lb
4.7	36,000	4.5	37,000
3.9	37,000	4.8	36,000
4.3	38,000	5.2	38,000
4.8	32,000	5.0	35,000
5.1	37,000	4.7	42,000
4.3	46,000	4.9	37,000
4.6	35,000	4.5	36,000
5.0	37,000	5.2	42,000
		4.8	41,000

Chapter 15 Quick Prep Links

- **Review** the methods for testing a null hypothesis using the *t*-distribution in Chapter 9.
- **Review** confidence intervals discussed in Chapter 8.
- **Make sure** you review the discussion about scatter plots in Chapters 2 and 14.
- **Review** the concepts associated with simple linear regression and correlation analysis presented in Chapter 14.
- **In Chapter 14**, review the steps involved in using the *t*-distribution for testing the significance of a correlation coefficient and a regression coefficient.

Multiple Regression Analysis and Model Building

15.1 Introduction to Multiple Regression Analysis (pg. 613–631)

Outcome 1. Understand the general concepts behind model building using multiple regression analysis.

Outcome 2. Apply multiple regression analysis to business decision-making situations.

Outcome 3. Analyze the computer output for a multiple regression model and interpret the regression results.

Outcome 4. Test hypotheses about the significance of a multiple regression model and test the significance of the independent variables in the model.

Outcome 5. Recognize potential problems when using multiple regression analysis and take steps to correct the problems.

15.2 Using Qualitative Independent Variables (pg. 631–638)

Outcome 6. Incorporate qualitative variables into a regression model by using dummy variables.

15.3 Working with Nonlinear Relationships (pg. 639–654)

Outcome 7. Apply regression analysis to situations in which the relationship between the independent variable(s) and the dependent variable is nonlinear.

15.4 Stepwise Regression (pg. 654–663)

Outcome 8. Understand the uses of stepwise regression.

15.5 Determining the Aptness of the Model (pg. 664–674)

Outcome 9. Analyze the extent to which a regression model satisfies the regression assumptions.

Why you need to know

Chapter 14 introduced linear regression and correlation analyses for analyzing the relationship between two variables. As you might expect, business problems are not limited to linear relationships involving only two variables. Many practical situations involve analyzing the relationships among three or more variables. For example, a vice president of planning for an automobile manufacturer would be interested in the relationship between her company's automobile sales and the variables that influence those sales. Included in her analysis might be such independent or explanatory variables as automobile price, competitors' sales, and advertising, as well as economic variables such as disposable personal income, the inflation rate, and the unemployment rate.

When multiple independent variables are to be included in an analysis simultaneously, the technique introduced in this chapter—multiple linear regression—is very useful. When a relationship between variables is nonlinear, we may be able to transform the independent variables in ways that allow us to use multiple linear

egd / Shutterstock

regression analysis to model the nonlinear relationships. This chapter examines the general topic of model building by extending the concepts of simple linear regression analysis provided in Chapter 14.

15.1 Introduction to Multiple Regression Analysis

Chapter 14 introduced the concept of simple linear regression analysis. The simple regression model is characterized by two variables: y, the *dependent variable*, and x, the *independent variable*. The single independent variable explains some variation in the dependent variable, but unless x and y are perfectly correlated, the proportion explained will be less than 100%. In multiple regression analysis, additional independent variables are added to the regression model to clear up some of the as yet unexplained variation in the dependent variable. Multiple regression is merely an extension of simple regression analysis; however, as we expand the model for the population from one independent variable to two or more, there are some new considerations.

The general format of a *multiple regression model for the population* is given by Equation 15.1.

Population Multiple Regression Model

$$y = \beta_0 + \beta_1 x_1 + \beta_2 x_2 + \cdots + \beta_k x_k + \varepsilon \tag{15.1}$$

where:

β_0 = Population's regression constant
β_j = Population's regression coefficient for each variable, $x_j = 1, 2, \cdots k$
k = Number of independent variables
ε = Model error

Four assumptions similar to those that apply to the simple linear regression model must also apply to the multiple regression model.

Assumptions

1. Individual model errors, ε, are statistically independent of one another, and these values represent a random sample from the population of possible errors at each level of x.
2. For a given value of x, there can exist many values of y, and therefore many possible values for ε. Further, the distribution of possible model errors for any level of x is normally distributed.
3. The distributions of possible ε-values have equal variances at each level of x.
4. The means of the dependent variable, y, for all specified values of x can be connected with a line called the population regression model.

Equation 15.1 represents the multiple regression model for the population. However, in most instances, you will be working with a random sample from the population. Given the preceding assumptions, the estimated multiple regression model, based on the sample data, is of the form shown in Equation 15.2.

Estimated Multiple Regression Model

$$\hat{y} = b_0 + b_1 x_1 + b_2 x_2 + \cdots + b_k x_k \tag{15.2}$$

This estimated model is an extension of an estimated simple regression model. The principal difference is that whereas the estimated simple regression model is the equation for a straight

TABLE 15.1 | **Sample Data to Illustrate the Difference between Simple and Multiple Regression Models**

(A) One Independent Variable		(B) Two Independent Variables		
y	x_1	y	x_1	x_2
564.99	50	564.99	50	10
601.06	60	601.06	60	13
560.11	40	560.11	40	14
616.41	50	616.41	50	12
674.96	60	674.96	60	15
630.58	45	630.58	45	16
554.66	53	554.66	53	14

Regression Hyperplane

The multiple regression equivalent of the simple regression line. The plane typically has a different slope for each independent variable.

line in a two-dimensional space, the estimated multiple regression model forms a hyperplane (or response surface) through multidimensional space. Each regression coefficient represents a different slope. Therefore, using Equation 15.2, a value of the dependent variable can be estimated using values of two or more independent variables. The **regression hyperplane** represents the relationship between the dependent variable and the k independent variables.

For example, Table 15.1A shows sample data for a dependent variable, y, and one independent variable, x_1. Figure 15.1 shows a scatter plot and the regression line for the simple regression analysis for y and x_1. The points are plotted in two-dimensional space, and the regression model is represented by a line through the points such that the sum of squared errors $[SSE = \Sigma (y - \hat{y})^2]$ is minimized.

If we add variable x_2 to the model, as shown in Table 15.1B, the resulting multiple regression equation becomes

$$\hat{y} = 307.71 + 2.85x_1 + 10.94x_2$$

For the time being, don't worry about how this equation was computed. That will be discussed shortly. Note, however, that the (y, x_1, x_2) points form a three-dimensional space, as shown in Figure 15.2. The regression equation forms a slice (hyperplane) through the data such that $\Sigma(y - \hat{y})^2$ is minimized. This is the same *least squares criterion* that is used with simple linear regression.

FIGURE 15.1 |

Simple Regression Line

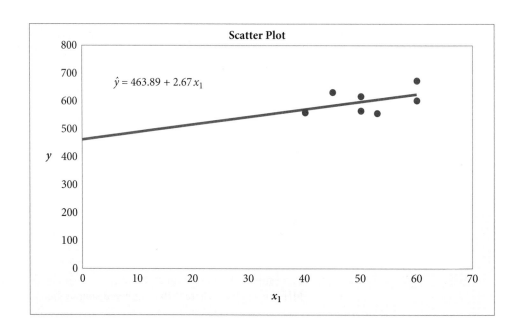

FIGURE 15.2 |

Multiple Regression
Hyperplane for Population

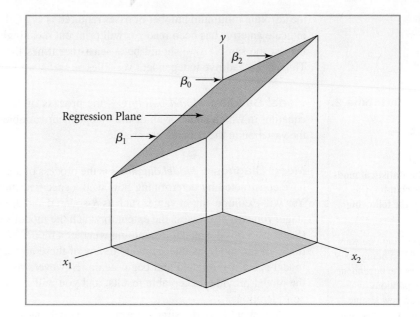

The mathematics for developing the least squares regression equation for simple linear regression involves differential calculus. The same is true for the multiple regression equation, but the mathematical derivation is beyond the scope of this text.[1]

Multiple regression analysis is usually performed with the aid of a computer and appropriate software. Excel contains a procedure for performing multiple regression, and the PHStat Excel add-in expands Excel's capabilities. However, other statistical software such as Minitab, SPSS and SAS offer more extensive regression options. Each software package presents the output in a slightly different format; however, the same basic information will appear in all regression output.

Chapter Outcome 1. → # Basic Model-Building Concepts

Model

A representation of an actual system using either a physical or a mathematical portrayal.

An important activity in business decision making is referred to as **model** building. Models are often used to test changes in a system without actually having to change the real system. Models are also used to help describe a system or to predict the output of a system based on certain specified inputs. You are probably quite aware of physical models. Airlines use flight simulators to train pilots. Wind tunnels are used to determine the aerodynamics of automobile designs. Golf ball makers use a physical model of a golfer called Iron Mike that can be set to swing golf clubs in a very controlled manner to determine how far a golf ball will fly. Although physical models are very useful in business decision making, our emphasis in this chapter is on statistical models that are developed using multiple regression analysis.

Modeling is both an art and a science. Determining an appropriate model is a challenging task, but it can be made manageable by employing a model-building process consisting of the following three components: model specification, model building, and model diagnosis.

Model Specification *Model specification*, or model identification, is the process of determining the dependent variable, deciding which independent variables should be included in the model, and obtaining the sample data for all variables. As with any statistical procedure, the larger the sample size the better, because the potential for extreme sampling error is reduced when the sample size is large. However, at a minimum, the sample size required to compute a regression model must be at least one greater than the number of independent variables.[2] If we are thinking of developing a regression model with five independent variables,

---

[1]For a complete treatment of the matrix algebra approach for estimating multiple regression coefficients, consult *Applied Linear Statistical Models* by Kutner et al. listed at the end of the book in References.
[2]There are mathematical reasons for this sample-size requirement that are beyond the scope of this text. In essence, there is no unique solution to the regression coefficient in Equation 15.2 if the sample size is not at least one larger than the number of independent variables.

the absolute minimum number of cases required is six. Otherwise, the computer software will indicate an error has been made or will print out meaningless values. However, as a practical matter, the sample size should be at least four times the number of independent variables. Thus, if we had five independent variables ($k = 5$), we would want a sample of at least 20.

Chapter Outcome 2.

How to do it

Model Specification
In the context of the statistical models discussed in this chapter, this component involves the following three steps:

1. Decide what question you want to ask. The question being asked usually indicates the dependent variable. In the previous chapter, we discussed how simple linear regression analysis could be used to describe the relationship between a dependent and an independent variable.

2. List the potential independent variables for your model. Here, your knowledge of the situation you are modeling guides you in identifying potential independent variables.

3. Gather the sample data (observations) for all variables.

How to do it

Developing a Multiple Regression Model
The following steps are employed in developing a multiple regression model:

1. Specify the model by determining the dependent variable and potential independent variables, and select the sample data.

2. Formulate the model. This is done by computing the correlation coefficients for the dependent variable and each independent variable, and for each independent variable with all other independent variables. The multiple regression equation is also computed. The computations are performed using Excel.

3. Perform diagnostic checks on the model to determine how well the specified model fits the data and how well the model appears to meet the multiple regression assumptions.

Model Building *Model building* is the process of actually constructing a mathematical equation in which some or all of the independent variables are used in an attempt to explain the variation in the dependent variable.

Model Diagnosis *Model diagnosis* is the process of analyzing the quality of the model you have constructed by determining how well a specified model fits the data you just gathered. You will examine output values such as R-squared and the standard error of the model. At this stage, you will also assess the extent to which the model's assumptions appear to be satisfied. (Section 15.5 is devoted to examining whether a model meets the regression analysis assumptions.) If the model is unacceptable in any of these areas, you will be forced to revert to the model-specification step and begin again. However, you will be the final judge of whether the model provides acceptable results, and you will always be constrained by time and cost considerations.

You should use the simplest available model that will meet your needs. The objective of model building is to help you make better decisions. You do not need to feel that a sophisticated model is better if a simpler one will provide acceptable results.

> **EXAMPLE 15-1** **DEVELOPING A MULTIPLE REGRESSION MODEL**

Sai Yeung Chan/Shutterstock

First City Real Estate First City Real Estate executives wish to build a model to predict sales prices for residential property. Such a model will be valuable when working with potential sellers who might list their homes with First City. This can be done using the following steps:

Step 1 **Model Specification.**
The question being asked is how can the real estate firm determine the selling price for a house? Thus, the dependent variable is the sales price. This is what the managers want to be able to predict. The managers met in a brainstorming session to determine a list of possible independent (explanatory) variables. Some variables, such as "condition of the house," were eliminated because of lack of data. Others, such as "curb appeal" (the appeal of the house to people as they drive by), were eliminated because the values for these variables would be too subjective and difficult to quantify. From a wide list of possibilities, the managers selected the following variables as good candidates:

$$x_1 = \text{Home size (in square feet)}$$
$$x_2 = \text{Age of house}$$
$$x_3 = \text{Number of bedrooms}$$
$$x_4 = \text{Number of bathrooms}$$
$$x_5 = \text{Garage size (number of cars)}$$

Data were obtained for a sample of 319 residential properties that had sold within the previous two months in an area served by two of First City's offices. For each house in the sample, the sales price and values for each potential independent variable were collected. The data are in the file **First City**.

Step 2 **Model Building.**
The regression model is developed by including independent variables from among those for which you have complete data. There is no way to determine whether an independent variable will be a good predictor variable by analyzing the individual

variable's descriptive statistics, such as the mean and standard deviation. Instead, we need to look at the correlation between the independent variables and the dependent variable, which is measured by the **correlation coefficient**.

>> **END EXAMPLE**

Correlation Coefficient

A quantitative measure of the strength of the linear relationship between two variables. The correlation coefficient, r, ranges from -1.0 to $+1.0$.

Correlation Matrix

A table showing the pairwise correlations between all variables (dependent and independent).

When we have multiple independent variables and one dependent variable, we can look at the correlation between all pairs of variables by developing a **correlation matrix**. Each correlation is computed using one of the equations in Equation 15.3. The appropriate formula is determined by whether the correlation is being calculated for an independent variable and the dependent variable or for two independent variables.

Correlation Coefficient

$$r = \frac{\Sigma(x - \bar{x})(y - \bar{y})}{\sqrt{\Sigma(x - \bar{x})^2 \, \Sigma(y - \bar{y})^2}} \quad \text{or} \quad r = \frac{\Sigma(x_i - \bar{x}_i)(x_j - \bar{x}_j)}{\sqrt{\Sigma(x_i - \bar{x}_i)^2 \, \Sigma(x_j - \bar{x}_j)^2}} \qquad (15.3)$$

$$\text{One } x \text{ variable with } y \qquad\qquad \text{One } x \text{ variable with another } x$$

The actual calculations are done using Excel's correlation tool, and the result is shown in Figure 15.3. The output provides the correlation between y and each x variable and between each pair of independent variables. Recall that in Chapter 14, a t-test (see Equation 14-3) was used to test whether the correlation coefficient is statistically significant.

$$H_0: \rho = 0 \quad H_A: \rho \neq 0$$

We will conduct the test with a significance level of

$$\alpha = 0.05$$

FIGURE 15.3

Excel 2010 Results Showing First City Real Estate Correlation Matrix

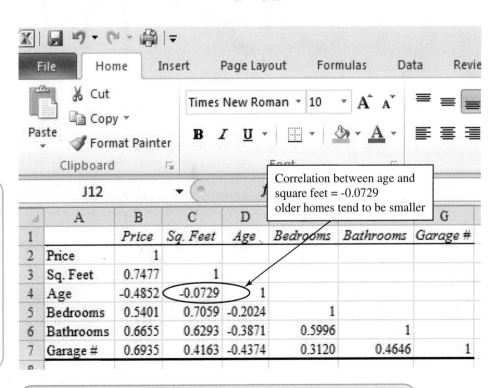

Correlation between age and square feet = -0.0729 older homes tend to be smaller

	Price	Sq. Feet	Age	Bedrooms	Bathrooms	Garage #
Price	1					
Sq. Feet	0.7477	1				
Age	-0.4852	-0.0729	1			
Bedrooms	0.5401	0.7059	-0.2024	1		
Bathrooms	0.6655	0.6293	-0.3871	0.5996	1	
Garage #	0.6935	0.4163	-0.4374	0.3120	0.4646	1

Excel 2010 Instructions:
1. Open file: **First City.xlsx**.
2. Use the Homes-Sample 1 Worksheet.
3. Select **Data > Data Analysis**.
4. Select **Correlation**.
5. Define **Input Range**— all rows and columns.
6. Click **Labels**.
7. Specify output location.
8. Click **OK**.

Minitab Instructions (for similar results):
1. Open file: **First City.MTW**.
2. Choose **Stat > Basic Statistics > Correlation**.
3. In **Variables**, enter variable columns.
4. Click **OK**.

FIGURE 15.4

First City Real Estate Scatter Plots

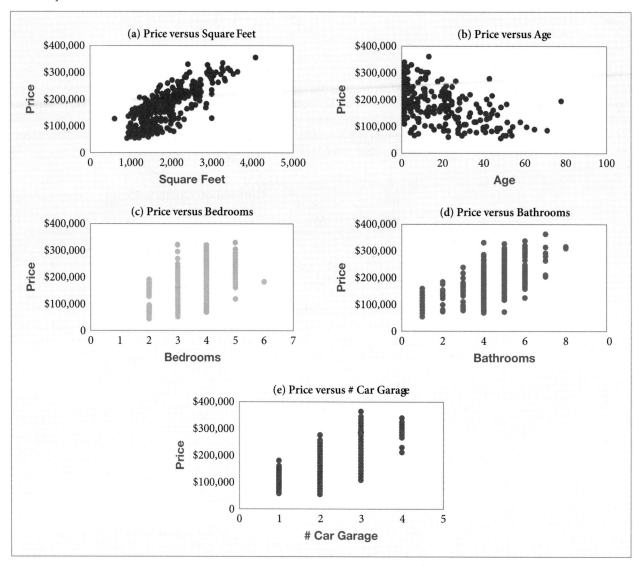

Given degrees of freedom equal to

$$n - 2 = 319 - 2 = 317$$

the critical t (see Appendix E) for a two-tailed test is approximately ± 1.96.[3]

Any correlation coefficient generating a t-value greater than 1.96 or less than -1.96 is determined to be significant.

For now, we will focus on the correlations in the first column in Figure 15.3, which measures the strength of the linear relationship between each independent variable and the dependent variable, sales price. For example, the t statistic for price and square feet is

$$t = \frac{r}{\sqrt{\dfrac{1-r^2}{n-2}}} = \frac{0.7477}{\sqrt{\dfrac{1-0.7477^2}{319-2}}} = 20.048$$

Because

$$t = 20.048 > 1.96$$

we reject H_0 and conclude that the correlation between sales price and square feet is statistically significant.

---

[3]You can use the Excel **T.INV.2T** function to get the precise t-value, which is ± 1.967.

Similar calculations for the other independent variables with price show that all variables are statistically correlated with price. This indicates that a significant linear relationship exists between each independent variable and sales price. Variable x_1, square feet, has the highest correlation at 0.748. Variable x_2, age of the house, has the lowest correlation at -0.485. The negative correlation implies that older homes tend to have lower sales prices.

As we discussed in Chapter 14, it is always a good idea to develop scatter plots to visualize the relationship between two variables. Figure 15.4 shows the scatter plots for each independent variable and the dependent variable, sales price. In each case, the plots indicate a linear relationship between the independent variable and the dependent variable. Note that several of the independent variables (bedrooms, bathrooms, garage size) are quantitative but discrete. The scatter plots for these variables show points at each level of the independent variable rather than over a continuum of values.

Chapter Outcome 3. → **Computing the Regression Equation** First City's goal is to develop a regression model to predict the appropriate selling price for a home, using certain measurable characteristics. The first attempt at developing the model will be to run a multiple regression computer program using all available independent variables. The regression outputs from Excel are shown in Figure 15.5.

The estimate of the multiple regression model given in Figure 15.5 is

$$\hat{y} = 31{,}127.6 + 63.1\,(\text{sq.ft.}) - 1{,}144.4\,(\text{age}) - 8{,}410.4\,(\text{bedrooms})$$
$$+ 3{,}522.0\,(\text{bathrooms}) + 28{,}203.5\,(\text{garage})$$

FIGURE 15.5 |

Excel 2010 Multiple Regression Model Results for First City Real Estate

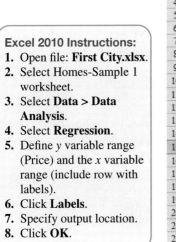

Excel 2010 Instructions:
1. Open file: **First City.xlsx**.
2. Select Homes-Sample 1 worksheet.
3. Select **Data > Data Analysis**.
4. Select **Regression**.
5. Define y variable range (Price) and the x variable range (include row with labels).
6. Click **Labels**.
7. Specify output location.
8. Click **OK**.

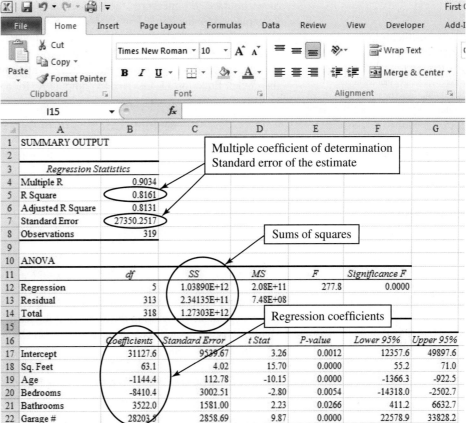

Minitab Instructions (for similar results):
1. Open file: **First City.MTW**.
2. Choose **Stat > Regression**.
3. In **Response**, enter dependent (y) variable.
4. In **Predictors**, enter independent (x) variables.
5. Click **OK**.

The coefficients for each independent variable represent an estimate of the average change in the dependent variable for a 1-unit change in the independent variable, holding all other independent variables constant. For example, for houses of the same age, with the same number of bedrooms, baths, and garage size, a 1-square-foot increase in the size of the house is estimated to increase its price by an average of $63.10. Likewise, for houses with the same square footage, bedrooms, bathrooms, and garages, a 1-year increase in the age of the house is estimated to result in an average drop in sales price of $1,144.40. The other coefficients are interpreted in the same way. Note, in each case, we are interpreting the regression coefficient for one independent variable while holding the other variables constant.

To estimate the value of a residential property, First City Real Estate brokers would substitute values for the independent variables into the regression equation. For example, suppose a house with the following characteristics is considered:

$$x_1 = \text{Square feet} = 2{,}100$$
$$x_2 = \text{Age} = 15$$
$$x_3 = \text{Number of bedrooms} = 4$$
$$x_4 = \text{Number of bathrooms} = 3$$
$$x_5 = \text{Size of garage} = 2$$

The point estimate for the sales price is

$$\hat{y} = 31{,}127.6 + 63.1\,(2{,}100) - 1{,}144.4\,(15) - 8{,}410.4\,(4) + 3{,}522.0\,(3)$$
$$+\ 28{,}203.5\,(2)$$
$$\hat{y} = \$179{,}802.70$$

The Coefficient of Determination You learned in Chapter 14 that the *coefficient of determination*, R^2, measures the proportion of variation in the dependent variable that can be explained by the dependent variable's relationship to a single independent variable. When there are multiple independent variables in a model, R^2 is called the **multiple coefficient of determination** and is used to determine the proportion of variation in the dependent variable that is explained by the dependent variable's relationship to all the independent variables in the model. Equation 15.4 is used to compute R^2 for a multiple regression model.

Multiple coefficient of determination (R^2)

The proportion of the total variation of the dependent variable in a multiple regression model that is explained by its relationship to the independent variables. It is, as is the case in the simple linear model, called *R*-squared and is denoted as R^2.

Multiple Coefficient of Determination (R^2)

$$R^2 = \frac{\text{Sum of squares regression}}{\text{Total sum of squares}} = \frac{SSR}{SST} \qquad \text{(15.4)}$$

As shown in Figure 15.5, $R^2 = 0.8161$. Both *SSR* and *SST* are also included in the output. Therefore, you can also use Equation 15.4 to get R^2, as follows:

$$\frac{SSR}{SST} = \frac{1.0389E+12}{1.27303E+12} = 0.8161$$

More than 81% of the variation in sales price can be explained by the linear relationship of the five independent variables in the regression model to the dependent variable. However, as we shall shortly see, not all independent variables are equally important to the model's ability to explain this variation.

Model Diagnosis Before First City actually uses this regression model to estimate the sales price of a house, there are several questions that should be answered.

1. Is the overall model significant?
2. Are the individual variables significant?
3. Is the standard deviation of the model error too large to provide meaningful results?
4. Is multicollinearity a problem?
5. Have the regression analysis assumptions been satisfied?

We shall answer the first four questions in order. We will have to wait until Section 15.5 before we have the procedures to answer the fifth important question.

Chapter Outcome 4. → **Is the Model Significant?** Because the regression model we constructed is based on a sample of data from the population and is subject to sampling error, we need to test the statistical significance of the overall regression model. The specific null and alternative hypotheses tested for First City Real Estate are

$$H_0: \beta_1 = \beta_2 = \beta_3 = \beta_4 = \beta_5 = 0$$
$$H_A: \text{At least one } \beta_i \neq 0$$

If the null hypothesis is true and all the slope coefficients are simultaneously equal to zero, the overall regression model is not useful for predictive or descriptive purposes.

The F-test is a method for testing whether the regression model explains a significant proportion of the variation in the dependent variable (and whether the overall model is significant). The F-test statistic for a multiple regression model is shown in Equation 15.5.

F-Test Statistic

$$F = \frac{\dfrac{SSR}{k}}{\dfrac{SSE}{n-k-1}}$$ **(15.5)**

where:

$$SSR = \text{Sum of squares regression} = \Sigma(\hat{y} - \bar{y})^2$$
$$SSE = \text{Sum of squares error} = \Sigma(y - \hat{y})^2$$
$$n = \text{Sample size}$$
$$k = \text{Number of independent variables}$$
$$\text{Degrees of freedom} = D_1 = k \quad \text{and} \quad D_2 = (n - k - 1)$$

The ANOVA portion of the output shown in Figure 15.5 contains values for SSR, SSE, and the F-value. The general format of the ANOVA table in a regression analysis is as follows:

ANOVA

Source	df	SS	MS	F	Significance F
Regression	k	SSR	$MSR = SSR/k$	MSR/MSE	computed p-value
Residual	$n - k - 1$	SSE	$MSE = SSE/(n - k - 1)$		
Total	$n - 1$	SST			

The ANOVA portion of the output from Figure 15.5 is as follows:

ANOVA

Source	df	SS	MS	F	Significance F
Regression	5	$1.04E + 12$	$2.08E + 11$	277.8	0.0000
Residual	313	$2.34E + 11$	$7.48E + 08$		
Total	318	$1.27303E + 12$			

We can test the model's significance

$$H_0: \beta_1 = \beta_2 = \beta_3 = \beta_4 = \beta_5 = 0$$
$$H_A: \text{At least one } \beta_i \neq 0$$

by either comparing the calculated F-value, 277.8, with a critical value for a given alpha level

$$\alpha = 0.01$$

and $k = 5$ and $n - k - 1 = 313$ degrees of freedom using Excel's F.INV.RT function ($F_{0.01} = 3.076$) or comparing the p-value in the output with a specified alpha level. Because

$$F = 277.8 > 3.076, \text{ reject } H_0$$

or because

$$p\text{-value} \approx 0.0 < 0.01, \text{reject } H_0$$

we should therefore conclude that the regression model *does* explain a significant proportion of the variation in sales price. Thus, the overall model is statistically significant. This means we can conclude that at least one of the regression slope coefficients is not equal to zero.

Excel provides a measure called the R-sq(adj), which is the **adjusted R-squared** value (see Figure 15.5). It is calculated by Equation 15.6.

Adjusted R-squared

A measure of the percentage of explained variation in the dependent variable in a multiple regression model that takes into account the relationship between the sample size and the number of independent variables in the regression model.

Adjusted R-Squared

A measure of the percentage of explained variation in the dependent variable that takes into account the relationship between the sample size and the number of independent variables in the regression model.

$$R\text{-sq(adj)} = R_A^2 = 1 - (1 - R^2)\left(\frac{n-1}{n-k-1}\right) \tag{15.6}$$

where:

$$n = \text{Sample size}$$
$$k = \text{Number of independent variables}$$
$$R^2 = \text{Coefficient of determination}$$

Adding independent variables to the regression model will always increase R^2, even if these variables have no relationship to the dependent variable. Therefore, as the number of independent variables is increased (regardless of the quality of the variables), R^2 will increase. However, each additional variable results in the loss of one degree of freedom. This is viewed as part of the cost of adding the specified variable. The addition to R^2 may not justify the reduction in degrees of freedom. The R_A^2 value takes into account this cost and adjusts the R_A^2 value accordingly. R_A^2 will always be less than R^2. When a variable is added that does not contribute its fair share to the explanation of the variation in the dependent variable, the R_A^2 value may actually decline, even though R^2 will always increase. The adjusted R-squared is a particularly important measure when the number of independent variables is large relative to the sample size. It takes into account the relationship between sample size and number of variables. R^2 may appear artificially high if the number of variables is large compared with the sample size.

In this example, in which the sample size is quite large relative to the number of independent variables, the adjusted R-squared is 81.3%, only slightly less than $R^2 = 81.6\%$.

Chapter Outcome 4. → **Are the Individual Variables Significant?** We have concluded that the overall model is significant. This means *at least* one independent variable explains a significant proportion of the variation in sales price. This does not mean that *all* the variables are significant, however. To determine which variables are significant, we test the following hypotheses:

$$H_0: \beta_j = 0$$
$$H_A: \beta_j \neq 0 \quad \text{for all } j$$

We can test the significance of each independent variable using significance level

$$\alpha = 0.05$$

and a t-test, as discussed in Chapter 14. The calculated t-values should be compared to the critical t-value with

$$n - k - 1 = 319 - 5 - 1 = 313$$

degrees of freedom, which is approximately

$$t_{0.025} \approx 1.97$$

for $\alpha = 0.05$. The calculated t-value for each variable is provided on the computer print-out in Figure 15.5. Recall that the t statistic is determined by dividing the regression coefficient by the estimator of the standard deviation of the regression coefficient, as shown in Equation 15.7.

---

t-Test for Significance of Each Regression Coefficient

$$t = \frac{b_j - 0}{s_{b_j}} \qquad df = n - k - 1 \qquad \textbf{(15.7)}$$

where:

b_j = Sample slope coefficient for the jth independent variable

s_{b_j} = Estimate of the standard error for the jth sample slope coefficient

---

For example, the t-value for square feet shown in Figure 15.5 is 15.70. This was computed using Equation 15.7, as follows:

$$t = \frac{b_j - 0}{s_{b_j}} = \frac{63.1 - 0}{4.02} = 15.70$$

Because

$$t = 15.70 > 1.97, \text{ we reject } H_0,$$

and conclude that, given the other independent variables in the model, the regression slope for square feet is not zero.

We can also look at the Excel output and compare the p-value for each regression slope coefficient with alpha. If the p-value is less than alpha, we reject the null hypothesis and conclude that the independent variable is statistically significant in the model. Both the t-test and the p-value techniques will give the same results.

You should consider that these t-tests are *conditional* tests. This means that the null hypothesis is *the value of each slope coefficient is 0, given that the other independent variables are already in the model.*[4] Figure 15.6 shows the hypothesis tests for each independent variable using a 0.05 significance level. We conclude that all five independent variables in the model are significant. When a regression model is to be used for prediction, the model should contain no insignificant variables. If insignificant variables are present, they should be dropped and a new regression equation obtained before the model is used for prediction purposes. We will have more to say about this later.

Is the Standard Deviation of the Regression Model Too Large?

The purpose of developing the First City regression model is to be able to determine values of the dependent variable when corresponding values of the independent variables are known. An indication of how good the regression model is can be found by looking at the relationship between the measured values of the dependent variable and those values that would be predicted by the regression model. The standard deviation of the regression model (also called the *standard error of the estimate*) measures the dispersion of observed home sale values, y, around values predicted by the regression model. The standard error of the estimate is shown in Figure 15.5 and can be computed using Equation 15.8.

---

[4]Note that the t-tests may be affected if the independent variables in the model are themselves correlated. A procedure known as the *sum of squares drop F-test*, discussed by Kutner et al. in *Applied Linear Statistical Models*, should be used in this situation. Each t-test considers only the marginal contribution of the independent variables and may indicate that none of the variables in the model are significant, even though the ANOVA procedure indicates otherwise.

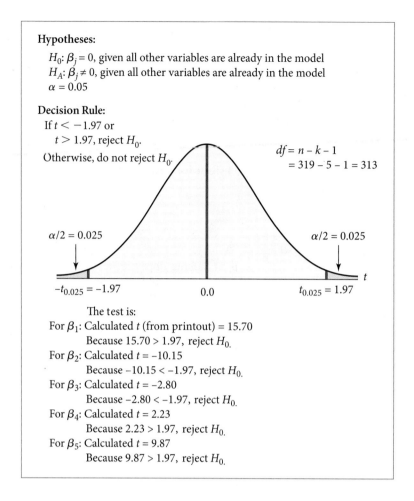

Hypotheses:

H_0: $\beta_j = 0$, given all other variables are already in the model
H_A: $\beta_j \neq 0$, given all other variables are already in the model
$\alpha = 0.05$

Decision Rule:

If $t < -1.97$ or
$t > 1.97$, reject H_0.
Otherwise, do not reject H_0.

$df = n - k - 1$
$= 319 - 5 - 1 = 313$

$\alpha/2 = 0.025$ $\alpha/2 = 0.025$

$-t_{0.025} = -1.97$ 0.0 $t_{0.025} = 1.97$

The test is:

For β_1: Calculated t (from printout) = 15.70
 Because $15.70 > 1.97$, reject H_0.
For β_2: Calculated $t = -10.15$
 Because $-10.15 < -1.97$, reject H_0.
For β_3: Calculated $t = -2.80$
 Because $-2.80 < -1.97$, reject H_0.
For β_4: Calculated $t = 2.23$
 Because $2.23 > 1.97$, reject H_0.
For β_5: Calculated $t = 9.87$
 Because $9.87 > 1.97$, reject H_0.

Standard Error of the Estimate

$$s_\varepsilon = \sqrt{\frac{SSE}{n-k-1}} = \sqrt{MSE} \qquad (15.8)$$

where:

SSE = Sum of squares error (residual)
n = Sample size
k = Number of independent variables

Examining Equation 15.8 closely, we see that this standard error of the estimate is the square root of the mean square error of the residuals found in the analysis of variance table.

Sometimes, even though a model has a high R^2, the standard error of the estimate will be too large to provide adequate precision for confidence and prediction intervals. A rule of thumb that we have found useful is to examine the range $\pm 2s_\varepsilon$. Taking into account the mean value of the dependent variable, if this range is acceptable from a practical viewpoint, the standard error of the estimate might be considered acceptable.[5]

In this First City Real Estate Company example, the standard error, shown in Figure 15.5, is $27,350. Thus, the rough prediction range for the price of an individual home is

$$\pm 2(\$27,350) = \pm \$54,700$$

---

[5]The actual confidence interval for prediction of a new observation requires the use of matrix algebra. However, when the sample size is large and dependent variable values near the means of the dependent variables are used, the rule of thumb given here is a close approximation. Refer to *Applied Linear Statistical Models* by Kutner et al. for further discussion.

Considering that the mean price of homes in this study is in the low $200,000s, a potential error of $54,700 high or low is probably not acceptable. Not many homeowners would be willing to have their appraisal value set by a model with a possible error this large. Even though the model is statistically significant, the company needs to take steps to reduce the standard deviation of the estimate. Subsequent sections of this chapter discuss some ways we can attempt to reduce it.

Chapter Outcome 5. → Is Multicollinearity a Problem? Even if the overall regression model is significant and each independent variable is significant, decision makers should still examine the regression model to determine whether it appears reasonable. This is referred to as checking for *face validity*. Specifically, you should check to see that signs on the regression coefficients are consistent with the signs on the correlation coefficients between the independent variables and the dependent variable. Does any regression coefficient have an unexpected sign?

Before answering this question for the First City Real Estate example, we should review what the regression coefficients mean. First, the constant term, b_0, is the estimate of the model's y intercept. If the data used to develop the regression model contain values of $x_1, x_2, x_3, x_4,$ and x_5 that are simultaneously 0 (such as would be the case for vacant land), b_0 is the mean value of y, given that $x_1, x_2, x_3, x_4,$ and x_5 all equal 0. Under these conditions b_0 would estimate the average value of a vacant lot. However, in the First City example, no vacant land was in the sample, so b_0 has no particular meaning.

The coefficient for square feet, b_1, estimates the average change in sales price corresponding to a change in house size of 1 square foot, holding the other independent variables constant. The value shown in Figure 15.5 for b_1 is 63.1. The coefficient is positive, indicating that an increase in square footage is associated with an increase in sales price. This relationship is expected. All other things being equal, bigger houses should sell for more money.

Likewise, the coefficient for x_5, the size of the garage, is positive, indicating that an increase in size is also associated with an increase in price. This is expected. The coefficient for x_2, the age of the house, is negative, indicating that an older house is worth less than a similar younger house. This also seems reasonable. Finally, variable x_4 for bathrooms has the expected positive sign. However, the coefficient for variable x_3, the number of bedrooms, is −$8,410.4, meaning that if we hold the other variables constant but increase the number of bedrooms by one, the average price will *drop* by $8,410.40. Does this seem reasonable?

Referring to the correlation matrix that was shown earlier in Figure 15.3, the correlation between variable x_3, bedrooms, and y, the sales price, is +0.540. This indicates that without considering the other independent variables, the linear relationship between number of bedrooms and sales price is positive. But why does the regression coefficient for variable x_3 turn out to be negative in the model? The answer lies in what is called **multicollinearity**.

Multicollinearity

A high correlation between two independent variables such that the two variables contribute redundant information to the model. When highly correlated independent variables are included in the regression model, they can adversely affect the regression results.

Multicollinearity occurs when independent variables are correlated with each other and therefore overlap with respect to the information they provide in explaining the variation in the dependent variable. For example, x_3 and the other independent variables have the following correlations (see Figure 15.3):

$$r_{x_3, x_1} = 0.706$$
$$r_{x_3, x_2} = -0.202$$
$$r_{x_3, x_4} = 0.600$$
$$r_{x_3, x_5} = 0.312$$

All four correlations have t-values indicating a significant linear relationship. Refer to the correlation matrix in Figure 15.3 to see that other independent variables are also correlated with each other.

The problems caused by multicollinearity, and how to deal with them, continue to be of prime concern to statisticians. From a decision maker's viewpoint, you should be aware that multicollinearity can (and often does) exist and recognize the basic problems it can cause. The following are some of the most obvious problems and indications of severe multicollinearity:

1. Unexpected, therefore potentially incorrect, signs on the coefficients
2. A sizable change in the values of the previously estimated coefficients when a new variable is added to the model

3. A variable that was previously significant in the regression model becomes insignificant when a new independent variable is added.
4. The estimate of the standard deviation of the model error increases when a variable is added to the model.

Mathematical approaches exist for dealing with multicollinearity and reducing its impact. Although these procedures are beyond the scope of this text, one suggestion is to eliminate the variables that are the chief cause of the multicollinearity problems.

If the independent variables in a regression model are correlated and multicollinearity is present, another potential problem is that the *t*-tests for the significance of the individual independent variables may be misleading. That is, a *t*-test may indicate that the variable is not statistically significant when in fact it is.

One method of measuring multicollinearity is known as the **variance inflation factor** (**VIF**). Equation 15.9 is used to compute the *VIF* for each independent variable.

Variance Inflation Factor

A measure of how much the variance of an estimated regression coefficient increases if the independent variables are correlated. A *VIF* equal to 1.0 for a given independent variable indicates that this independent variable is not correlated with the remaining independent variables in the model. The greater the multicollinearity, the larger the *VIF*.

Variance Inflation Factor

$$VIF = \frac{1}{(1 - R_j^2)} \qquad (15.9)$$

where:

R_j^2 = Coefficient of determination when the *j*th independent variable is regressed against the remaining $k - 1$ independent variables

---

The PHStat add-in to Excel contains an option that provides *VIF* values.[6]

Figure 15.7 shows the Excel (PHStat) output of the *VIF*s for the First City Real Estate example. The effect of multicollinearity is to decrease the test statistic, thus reducing the probability that the variable will be declared significant. A related impact is to increase the width of the confidence interval estimate of the slope coefficient in the regression model. Generally, if the *VIF* < 5 for a particular independent variable, multicollinearity is not considered a problem for that variable. *VIF* values ≥ 5 imply that the correlation between the independent variables is too extreme and should be dealt with by dropping variables from the model. As Figure 15.7 illustrates, the *VIF* values for each independent variable are less than 5, so based on variance inflation factors, even though the sign on the variable, bedrooms, has switched from positive to negative, the other multicollinearity issues do not exist among these independent variables.

Confidence Interval Estimation for Regression Coefficients Previously, we showed how to determine whether the regression coefficients are statistically significant. This was necessary because the estimates of the regression coefficients are developed from sample data and are subject to sampling error. The issue of sampling error also comes into play when interpreting the slope coefficients.

Consider again the regression model for First City Real Estate shown in Figure 15.8. The regression coefficients shown are *point estimates* for the true regression coefficients. For example, the coefficient for the variable square feet is $b_1 = 63.1$. We interpret this to mean that, holding the other variables constant, for each increase in the size of a home by 1 square foot, the average price of a house is estimated to increase by $63.1. But like all point estimates, this is subject to sampling error. In Chapter 14, you were introduced to the concept of confidence interval estimates for the regression coefficients. That same concept applies in multiple regression models. Equation 15.10 is used to develop the confidence interval estimate for the regression coefficients.

---

[6]Excel's Regression procedure in the Data Analysis Tools area does not provide *VIF* values directly. Without PHStat, you would need to compute each regression analysis individually and record the *R*-squared value to compute the *VIF*.

FIGURE 15.7

Excel 2010 (PHStat) Multiple Regression Model Results for First City Real Estate with Variance Inflation Factors

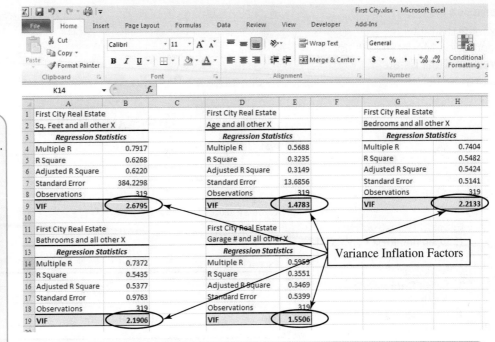

Excel 2010 Instructions:
1. Open file: **First City.xlsx**.
2. Select Homes-Sample 1 worksheet.
3. Select **Add-Ins PHStat**.
4. Select **Regression > Multiple Regression**.
5. Define *y* variable range (Price) and the *x* variable range (include row with labels).
6. Select **Regression Statistics Table** and **ANOVA** and **Coefficients Table**.
7. Select **Variance Inflation Factor (VIF)**.
8. Click **OK** (note: VIFs consolidated to one page for display in Figure 15.7).

Minitab Instructions (for similar results):
1. Open file: **First City.MTW**.
2. Choose **Stat > Regression > Regression**.
3. In **Response** enter dependent (*y*) variable.
4. In **Predictors,** enter independent (*x*) variables.
5. Click **Options**.
6. In **Display**, select Variance Inflation factors.
7. Click **OK. OK**.

Confidence Interval Estimate for the Regression Slope

$$b_j \pm ts_{b_j} \qquad\qquad (15.10)$$

where:

b_j = Point estimate for the regression coefficient for x_j

t = Critical *t*-value for the specified confidence level

s_{b_j} = The standard error of the *j*th regression coefficient

---

The Excel output in Figure 15.8 provides the confidence interval estimates for each regression coefficient. For example, the 95% interval estimate for square feet is

$$\$55.2 \text{———} \$71.0$$

To manually calculate the confidence interval associated with the square feet variable, use Equation 15.10 as[7]

$$b_1 \pm ts_{b_1}$$
$$63.1 \pm 1.967\,(4.017)$$
$$63.1 \pm 7.90$$
$$\$55.2 \text{———} \$71.0$$

---

[7]Note, we used Excel's **T.INV.2T** function to get the precise *t*-value of ± 1.967.

FIGURE 15.8

Excel 2010 Multiple Regression Model Results for First City Real Estate

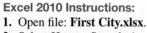

Excel 2010 Instructions:
1. Open file: **First City.xlsx**.
2. Select Homes-Sample 1 worksheet.
3. Select **Data > Data Analysis**.
4. Select **Regression**.
5. Define *y* variable range (Price) and the *x* variable range (include row with labels).
6. Click **Labels**.
7. Specify output location.
8. Click **OK**.

	A	B	C	D	E	F	G
1	SUMMARY OUTPUT						
2							
3	*Regression Statistics*						
4	Multiple R	0.9034					
5	R Square	0.8161					
6	Adjusted R Square	0.8131					
7	Standard Error	27350.2517					
8	Observations	319					
9							
10	ANOVA						
11		*df*	*SS*	*MS*	*F*	*Significance F*	
12	Regression	5	1.03890E+12	2.08E+11	277.8	0.0000	
13	Residual	313	2.34135E+11	7.48E+08			
14	Total	318	1.27303E+12				
15							
16		*Coefficients*	*Standard Error*	*t Stat*	*P-value*	*Lower 95%*	*Upper 95%*
17	Intercept	31127.6	9539.67	3.26	0.0012	12357.6	49897.6
18	Sq. Feet	63.1	4.02	15.70	0.0000	55.2	71.0
19	Age	-1144.4	112.78	-10.15	0.0000	-1366.3	-922.5
20	Bedrooms	-8410.4	3002.51	-2.80	0.0054	-14318.0	-2502.7
21	Bathrooms	3522.0	1581.00	2.23	0.0266	411.2	6632.7
22	Garage #	28203.5	2858.69	9.87	0.0000	22578.9	33828.2

95% confidence interval estimates for the regression coefficients

Minitab Instructions (for similar results):
1. Open file: **First City.MTW**.
2. Choose **Stat > Regression > Regression**.
3. In **Response** enter dependent (*y*) variable.
4. In **Predictors**, enter independent (*x*) variables.
5. Click **OK**.

We interpret this interval as follows: Holding the other variables constant, using a 95% confidence level, a change in square feet by 1 foot is estimated to generate an average change in home price of between $55.20 and $71.00. Each of the other regression coefficients can be interpreted in the same manner.

MyStatLab

15-1: **Exercises**

Skill **Development**

15-1. The following output is associated with a multiple regression model with three independent variables:

	df	SS	MS	F	Significance F
Regression	3	16,646.091	5,548.697	5.328	0.007
Residual	21	21,871.669	1,041.508		
Total	24	38,517.760			

	Coefficients	Standard Error	t Stat	p-value
Intercept	87.790	25.468	3.447	0.002
x_1	-0.970	0.586	-1.656	0.113
x_2	0.002	0.001	3.133	0.005
x_3	-8.723	7.495	-1.164	0.258

	Lower 95%	Upper 95%	Lower 90%	Upper 90%
Intercept	34.827	140.753	43.966	131.613
x_1	−2.189	0.248	−1.979	0.038
x_2	0.001	0.004	0.001	0.004
x_3	−24.311	6.864	−21.621	4.174

a. What is the regression model associated with these data?
b. Is the model statistically significant?
c. How much of the variation in the dependent variable can be explained by the model?
d. Are all of the independent variables in the model significant? If not, which are not and how can you tell?
e. How much of a change in the dependent variable will be associated with a one-unit change in x_2? In x_3?
f. Do any of the 95% confidence interval estimates of the slope coefficients contain zero? If so, what does this indicate?

15-2. You are given the following estimated regression equation involving a dependent and two independent variables:

$$\hat{y} = 12.67 + 4.14x_1 + 8.72x_2$$

a. Interpret the values of the slope coefficients in the equation.
b. Estimate the value of the dependent variable when $x_1 = 4$ and $x_2 = 9$.

15-3. In working for a local retail store, you have developed the following estimated regression equation:

$$\hat{y} = 22,167 - 412x_1 + 818x_2 - 93x_3 - 71x_4$$

where:

y = Weekly sales
x_1 = Local unemployment rate
x_2 = Weekly average high temperature
x_3 = Number of activities in the local community
x_4 = Average gasoline price

a. Interpret the values of b_1, b_2, b_3, and b_4 in this estimated regression equation.
b. What is the estimated sales if the unemployment rate is 5.7%, the average high temperature is 61°, there are 14 activities, and gasoline average price is $3.39?

15-4. The following correlation matrix is associated with the same data used to build the regression model in Problem 15-1:

	y	x_1	x_2	x_3
y	1			
x_1	−0.406	1		
x_2	0.459	0.051	1	
x_3	−0.244	0.504	0.272	1

Does this output indicate any potential multicollinearity problems with the analysis?

15-5. Consider the following set of data:

x_1	29	48	28	22	28	42	33	26	48	44
x_2	15	37	24	32	47	13	43	12	58	19
y	16	46	34	26	49	11	41	13	47	16

a. Obtain the estimated regression equation.
b. Develop the correlation matrix for this set of data. Select the independent variable whose correlation magnitude is the smallest with the dependent variable. Determine if its correlation with the dependent variable is significant.
c. Determine if the overall model is significant. Use a significance level of 0.05.
d. Calculate the variance inflation factor for each of the independent variables. Indicate if multicollinearity exists between the two independent variables.

15-6. Consider the following set of data:

x_2	10	8	11	7	10	11	6
x_1	50	45	37	32	44	51	42
y	103	85	115	73	97	102	65

a. Obtain the estimated regression equation.
b. Examine the coefficient of determination and the adjusted coefficient of determination. Does it seem that either of the independent variables' addition to R^2 does not justify the reduction in degrees of freedom that results from its addition to the regression model? Support your assertions.
c. Conduct a hypothesis test to determine if the dependent variable increases when x_2 increases. Use a significance level of 0.025 and the p-value approach.
d. Construct a 95% confidence interval for the coefficient of x_1.

Computer Database **Exercises**

15-7. An investment analyst collected data about 20 randomly chosen companies. The data consisted of the 52-week-high stock prices, price-to-earnings (PE) ratio, and the market value of the company. These data are in the file titled **Investment**.
a. Produce a regression equation to predict the market value using the 52-week-high stock price and the PE ratio of the company.
b. Determine if the overall model is significant. Use a significance level of 0.05.
c. OmniVision Technologies (Sunnyvale, CA) in April 2006 had a 52-week-high stock price of 31 and a PE ratio of 19. Estimate its market value for that time period. (*Note*: Its actual market value for that time period was $1,536.)

15-8. An article in *BusinessWeek* presents a list of the 100 companies perceived as having "hot growth" characteristics. A company's rank on the list is the sum of 0.5 times its rank in return on total capital and 0.25 times its sales and profit-growth ranks. The file titled **Growth** contains sales ($million), sales increase (%), return on capital, market value ($million), and recent stock price of the top 20 ranked companies.

a. Produce a correlation matrix for the variables contained in the file titled **Growth**.

b. Select the two variables that are most highly correlated with the recent stock price and produce the regression equation to predict the recent stock price as a function of the two variables you chose.

c. Determine if the overall model is significant. Use a significance level of 0.10.

d. Examine the coefficient of determination and the adjusted coefficient of determination. Does it seem that either of the independent variables' addition to R^2 does not justify the reduction in degrees of freedom that results from its addition to the regression model? Support your assertions.

e. Select the variable that is most correlated with the stock price and test to see if it is a significant predictor of the stock price. Use a significance level of 0.10 and the *p*-value approach.

15-9. Refer to Problem 15-8, which referenced a list of the 100 companies perceived as having "hot growth" characteristics. The file titled **Logrowth** contains sales ($million), sales increase (%), return on capital, market value ($million), and recent stock price of the companies ranked from 81 to 100. In Problem 15-8, stock prices were the focus. Examine the sales of the companies.

a. Produce a regression equation that will predict the sales as a function of the other variables.

b. Determine if the overall model is significant. Use a significance level of 0.05.

c. Conduct a test of hypothesis to discover if market value should be removed from this model.

d. To see that a variable can be insignificant in one model but very significant in another, construct a regression equation in which sales is the dependent variable and market value is the independent variable. Test the hypothesis that market value is a significant predictor of sales for those companies ranked from 81 to 100. Use a significance level of 0.05 and the *p*-value approach.

15-10. The National Association of Theatre Owners is the largest exhibition trade organization in the world, representing more than 26,000 movie screens in all 50 states and in more than 20 countries worldwide. Its membership includes the largest cinema chains and hundreds of independent theatre owners. It publishes statistics concerning the movie sector of the economy. The file titled **Flicks** contains data on total U.S. box office grosses ($billion), total number of admissions (billion), average U.S. ticket price ($), and number of movie screens.

a. Construct a regression equation in which total U.S. box office grosses are predicted using the other variables.

b. Determine if the overall model is significant. Use a significance level of 0.05.

c. Determine the range of plausible values for the change in box office grosses if the average ticket price were to be increased by $1. Use a confidence level of 95%.

d. Calculate the variance inflation factor for each of the independent variables. Indicate if multicollinearity exists between any two independent variables.

e. Produce the regression equation suggested by your answer to part d.

15-11. The athletic director of State University is interested in developing a multiple regression model that might be used to explain the variation in attendance at football games at his school. A sample of 16 games was selected from home games played during the past 10 seasons. Data for the following factors were determined:

$$y = \textit{Game attendance}$$
$$x_1 = \text{Team win/loss percentage to date}$$
$$x_2 = \text{Opponent win/loss percentage to date}$$
$$x_3 = \text{Games played this season}$$
$$x_4 = \text{Temperature at game time}$$

The data collected are in the file called **Football**.

a. Produce scatter plots for each independent variable versus the dependent variable. Based on the scatter plots, produce a model that you believe represents the relationship between the dependent variable and the group of predictor variables represented in the scatter plots.

b. Based on the correlation matrix developed from these data, comment on whether you think a multiple regression model will be effectively developed from these data.

c. Use the sample data to estimate the multiple regression model that contains all four independent variables.

d. What percentage of the total variation in the dependent variable is explained by the four independent variables in the model?

e. Test to determine whether the overall model is statistically significant. Use $\alpha = 0.05$.

f. Which, if any, of the independent variables is statistically significant? Use a significance level of $\alpha = 0.08$ and the *p*-value approach to conduct these tests.

g. Estimate the standard deviation of the model error and discuss whether this regression model is acceptable as a means of predicting the football attendance at State University at any given game.

h. Define the term *multicollinearity* and indicate the potential problems that multicollinearity can cause for this model. Indicate what, if any, evidence there is of multicollinearity problems with this regression model. Use the variance inflation factor to assist you in this analysis.

i. Develop a 95% confidence interval estimate for each of the regression coefficients and interpret each estimate. Comment on whether the interpretation of the intercept is relevant in this situation.

END EXERCISES 15-1

Chapter Outcome 6. → ## 15.2 Using Qualitative Independent Variables

In Example 15-1 involving the First City Real Estate Company, the independent variables were quantitative and ratio level. However, you will encounter many situations in which you may wish to use a qualitative, lower-level variable as an explanatory variable.

If a variable is nominal and numerical codes are assigned to the categories, you already know not to perform mathematical calculations using those data. The results would be meaningless. Yet we may wish to use a variable such as marital status, gender, or geographical location as an independent variable in a regression model. If the variable of interest is coded as an ordinal variable, such as education level or job performance ranking, computing means and variances is also inappropriate. Then how are these variables incorporated into a multiple regression analysis? The answer lies in using what are called **dummy (or indicator) variables**.

For instance, consider the variable gender, which can take on two possible values: male or female. Gender can be converted to a dummy variable as follows:

Dummy Variable

A variable that is assigned a value equal to either 0 or 1, depending on whether the observation possesses a given characteristic.

$$x_1 = 1 \text{ if female}$$
$$x_1 = 0 \text{ if male}$$

Thus, a data set consisting of males and females will have corresponding values for x_1 equal to 0s and 1s, respectively. Note that it makes no difference which gender is coded 1 and which is coded 0.

If a categorical variable has more than two mutually exclusive outcome possibilities, multiple dummy variables must be created. Consider the variable marital status, with the following possible outcomes:

never married   married   divorced   widowed

In this case, marital status has four values. To account for all the possibilities, you would create three dummy variables, one less than the number of possible outcomes for the original variable. They could be coded as follows:

$$x_1 = 1 \text{ if never married, 0 if not}$$
$$x_2 = 1 \text{ if married, 0 if not}$$
$$x_3 = 1 \text{ if divorced, 0 if not}$$

Note that we don't need the fourth variable because we would know that a person is widowed if $x_1 = 0$, $x_2 = 0$, and $x_3 = 0$. If the person isn't single, married, or divorced, he or she must be widowed. *Always use one fewer dummy variables than categories.* The mathematical reason that the number of dummy variables must be one less than the number of possible responses is called the *dummy variable trap.* Perfect multicollinearity is introduced, and the least squares regression estimates cannot be obtained if the number of dummy variables equals the number of possible categories.

| **EXAMPLE 15-2** | **INCORPORATING DUMMY VARIABLES** |

Losevsky/Shutterstock

Executive Salary Analysis To illustrate the effect of incorporating dummy variables into a regression model, consider the sample data displayed in the scatter plot in Figure 15.9. The population from which the sample was selected consists of executives between the ages of 24 and 60 who are working in the U.S. high-tech industry. Data for annual salary (y) and age (x_1) are

FIGURE 15.9

Executive Salary Data—
Scatter Plot

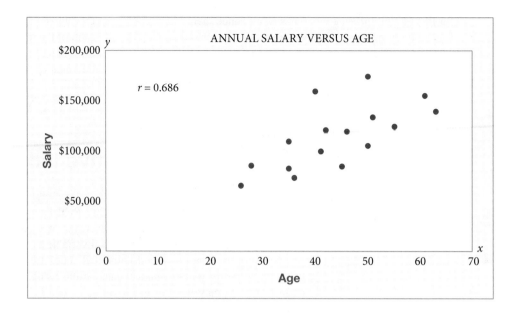

available. The objective is to determine whether a model can be generated to explain the variation in annual salary for business executives. Even though age and annual salary are significantly correlated $(r = 0.686)$ at the $\alpha = 0.05$ level, the coefficient of determination is only 47%. Therefore, we would likely search for other independent variables that could help us to further explain the variation in annual salary.

Suppose we can determine which of the 16 people in the sample had a master of business administration (MBA) degree. Figure 15.10 shows the scatter plot for these same data, with the MBA data represented by triangles. To incorporate a qualitative variable into the analysis, use the following steps:

Step 1 **Code the qualitative variable as a dummy variable.**
Create a new variable, x_2, which is a dummy variable coded as

$$x_2 = 1 \text{ if MBA, 0 if not}$$

The data with the new variable are shown in Table 15.2.

FIGURE 15.10

Impact of a Dummy Variable

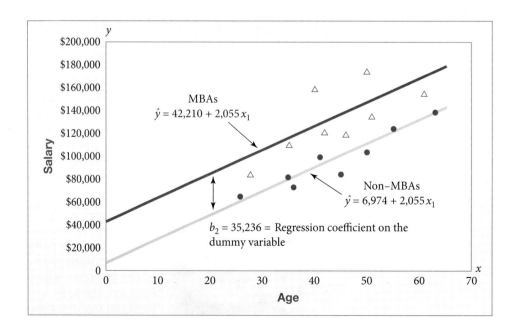

TABLE 15.2 | Executive Salary Data Including MBA Variable

Salary($)	Age	MBA
65,000	26	0
85,000	28	1
74,000	36	0
83,000	35	0
110,000	35	1
160,000	40	1
100,000	41	0
122,000	42	1
85,000	45	0
120,000	46	1
105,000	50	0
135,000	51	1
125,000	55	0
175,000	50	1
156,000	61	1
140,000	63	0

Step 2 **Develop a multiple regression model with the dummy variables incorporated as independent variables.**

The two-variable population multiple regression model has the following form:

$$y = \beta_0 + \beta_1 x_1 + \beta_2 x_2 + \varepsilon$$

Using Excel, we get the following regression equation as an estimate of the population model:

$$\hat{y} = 6,974 + 2,055x_1 + 35,236x_2$$

Because the dummy variable, x_2, has been coded 0 or 1 depending on MBA status, incorporating it into the regression model is like having two simple linear regression lines with the same slopes, but different intercepts. For instance, when $x_2 = 0$, the regression equation is

$$\hat{y} = 6,974 + 2,055x_1 + 35,236(0)$$
$$= 6,974 + 2,055x_1$$

This line is shown in Figure 15.10. However, when $x_2 = 1$ (the executive has an MBA), the regression equation is

$$\hat{y} = 6,974 + 2,055x_1 + 35,236(1)$$
$$= 42,210 + 2,055x_1$$

This regression line is also shown in Figure 15.10. As you can see, incorporating the dummy variable affects the regression intercept. In this case, the intercept for executives with an MBA degree is $35,236 higher than for those without an MBA. We interpret the regression coefficient on this dummy variable as follows: Based on these data, and holding age (x_1) constant, we estimate that executives with an MBA degree make an average of $35,236 per year more in salary than their non–MBA counterparts.

>> **END EXAMPLE**

TRY PROBLEM 15-17 (pg. 637)

Excel Tutorial

BUSINESS APPLICATION **REGRESSION MODELS USING DUMMY VARIABLES**

FIRST CITY REAL ESTATE (*CONTINUED*) The regression model developed in Example 15-1 for First City Real Estate showed potential because the overall model was statistically significant. Looking back at Figure 15.8, we see that the model explained nearly 82% of the variation in sales prices for the homes in the sample. All of the independent variables were significant, given that the other independent variables were in the model. However, the standard error of the estimate is quite high at $27,350.

The managers have decided to try to improve the model. First, they have decided to add a new variable: area. However, at this point, the only area variable they have access to defines whether the home is in the foothills. Because this is a categorical variable with two possible outcomes (foothills or not foothills), a dummy variable can be created as follows:

$$x_6\,(\text{area}) = 1 \text{ if foothills, 0 if not}$$

Of the 319 homes in the sample, 249 were homes in the foothills and 70 were not. Figure 15.11a shows the revised Excel multiple regression with the variable, area, added. This model is an improvement over the original model because the adjusted R-squared has increased from 0.813 to 0.902 and the standard error of the estimate has decreased from $27,350 to $19,828. The conditional t-tests show that all of the

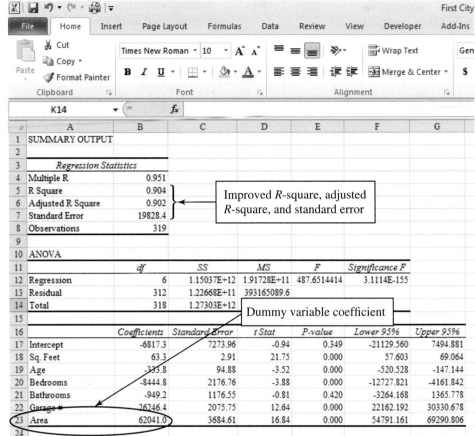

Excel 2010 Instructions:
1. Open file: **First City.xlsx**.
2. Select Homes-Sample 2 worksheet.
3. Select **Data > Data Analysis**.
4. Select **Regression**.
5. Define y variable range (Price) and the x variable range (include row with labels).
6. Click **Labels**.
7. Specify output location.
8. Click **OK**.

Minitab Instructions (for similar results):
1. Open file: **First City.MTW**.
2. Choose **Stat > Regression > Regression**.
3. In **Response** enter dependent (y) variable.
4. In **Predictors**, enter independent (x) variables.
5. Click **Options**.
6. In **Display**, select **Variance inflation Factors**.
7. Click **OK. OK**.

regression models' slope coefficients, except that for the variable bathrooms, differ significantly from 0.

The resulting regression model is

$$\hat{y} = -6{,}817.3 + 63.3\,(\text{sq. ft.}) - 333.8\,(\text{age}) - 8{,}444.8\,(\text{bedrooms}) - 949.2\,(\text{bathrooms})$$
$$+ 26{,}246\,(\text{garage}) + 62{,}041\,(\text{area})$$

Because the variable *bathrooms* is not significant in the presence of the other variables, we can remove the variable and rerun the multiple regression. The resulting model shown in Figure 15.11b is

$$\text{Price} = -7{,}050.2 + 62.5\,(\text{sq. ft.}) - 322\,(\text{age}) - 8{,}830\,(\text{bedrooms})$$
$$+ 26{,}053.9\,(\text{garage}) + 61{,}370.1\,(\text{area})$$

Based on the sample data and this regression model, we estimate that a house with the same characteristics (square footage, age, bedrooms, and garage size) is worth an average of $61,370 more if it is located in the foothills (based on how the dummy variable was coded).

There are still signals of multicollinearity problems. The coefficient on the independent variable bedrooms is negative, when we might expect homes with more bedrooms to sell for more. Also, the standard error of the estimate is still very large ($19,817) and does not provide the precision the managers need to set prices for homes. More work needs to be done before the model is complete.

FIGURE 15.11b

Excel 2010 Output—First City Real Estate Revised Regression Model (Bathrooms Removed)

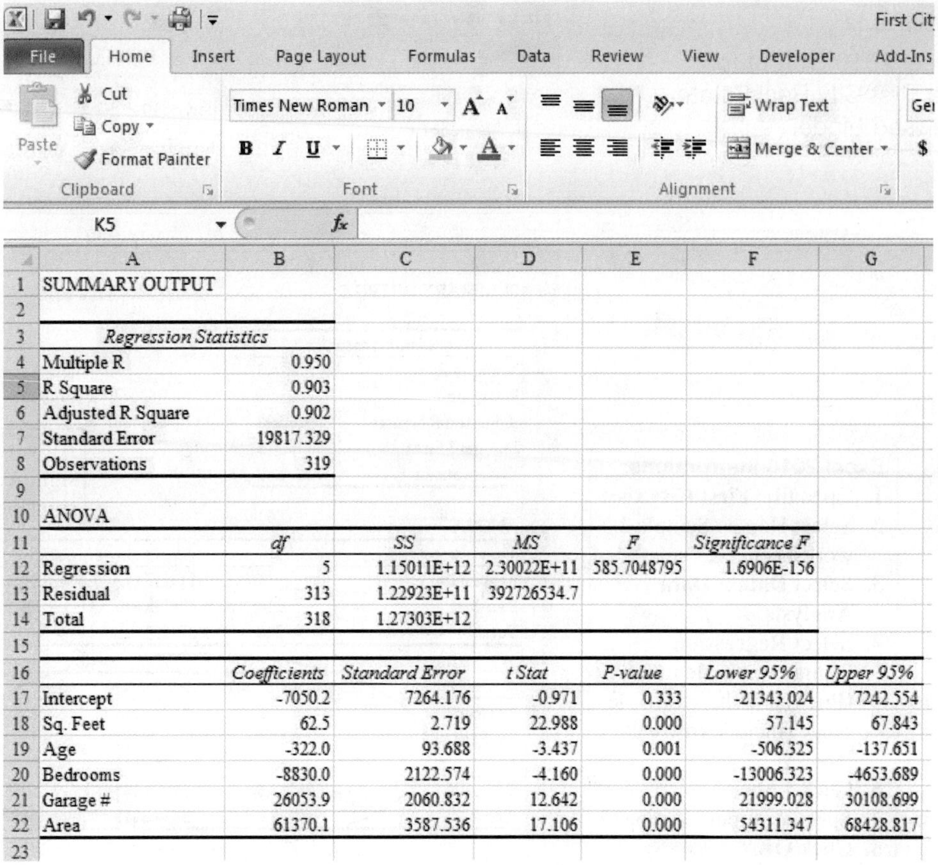

Excel 2010 Instructions:
1. Open file: **First City.xlsx**.
2. Select Homes-Sample 2 worksheet.
3. Select **Data > Data Analysis**.
4. Select **Regression**.
5. Define y variable range (Price) and the x variable range (include row with labels).
6. Click **Labels**.
7. Specify output location.
8. Click **OK**.

	A	B	C	D	E	F	G
1	SUMMARY OUTPUT						
2							
3	*Regression Statistics*						
4	Multiple R	0.950					
5	R Square	0.903					
6	Adjusted R Square	0.902					
7	Standard Error	19817.329					
8	Observations	319					
9							
10	ANOVA						
11		*df*	*SS*	*MS*	*F*	*Significance F*	
12	Regression	5	1.15011E+12	2.30022E+11	585.7048795	1.6906E-156	
13	Residual	313	1.22923E+11	392726534.7			
14	Total	318	1.27303E+12				
15							
16		*Coefficients*	*Standard Error*	*t Stat*	*P-value*	*Lower 95%*	*Upper 95%*
17	Intercept	-7050.2	7264.176	-0.971	0.333	-21343.024	7242.554
18	Sq. Feet	62.5	2.719	22.988	0.000	57.145	67.843
19	Age	-322.0	93.688	-3.437	0.001	-506.325	-137.651
20	Bedrooms	-8830.0	2122.574	-4.160	0.000	-13006.323	-4653.689
21	Garage #	26053.9	2060.832	12.642	0.000	21999.028	30108.699
22	Area	61370.1	3587.536	17.106	0.000	54311.347	68428.817
23							

Possible Improvements to the First City Appraisal Model Because the standard error of the estimate is still too high, we look to improve the model. We could start by identifying possible problems:

1. We may be missing useful independent variables.
2. Independent variables may have been included that should not have been included.

There is no sure way of determining the correct model specification. However, a recommended approach is for the decision maker to try adding variables or removing variables from the model.

We begin by removing the bedrooms variable, which has an unexpected sign on the regression slope coefficient. (*Note*: If the regression model's sole purpose is for prediction, independent variables with unexpected signs do not automatically pose a problem and do not necessarily need to be deleted. However, insignificant variables should be deleted.) The resulting model is shown in Figure 15.12. Now, all the variables in the model have the expected signs. However, the standard error of the estimate has increased slightly.

Adding other explanatory variables might help. For instance, consider whether the house has central air conditioning, which might affect sales. If we can identify whether a house has air conditioning, we could add a dummy variable coded as follows:

$$\text{If air conditioning, } x_7 = 1$$

$$\text{If no air conditioning, } x_7 = 0$$

Other potential independent variables might include a more detailed location variable, a measure of the physical condition, or whether the house has one or two stories. Can you think of others?

The First City example illustrates that even though a regression model may pass the statistical tests of significance, it may not be functional. Good appraisal models can be developed using multiple regression analysis, provided more detail is available about such characteristics as finish quality, landscaping, location, neighborhood characteristics, and so forth. The cost and effort required to obtain these data can be relatively high.

Developing a multiple regression model is more of an art than a science. The real decisions revolve around how to select the best set of independent variables for the model.

FIGURE 15.12

Excel 2010 Output for the First City Real Estate Revised Model

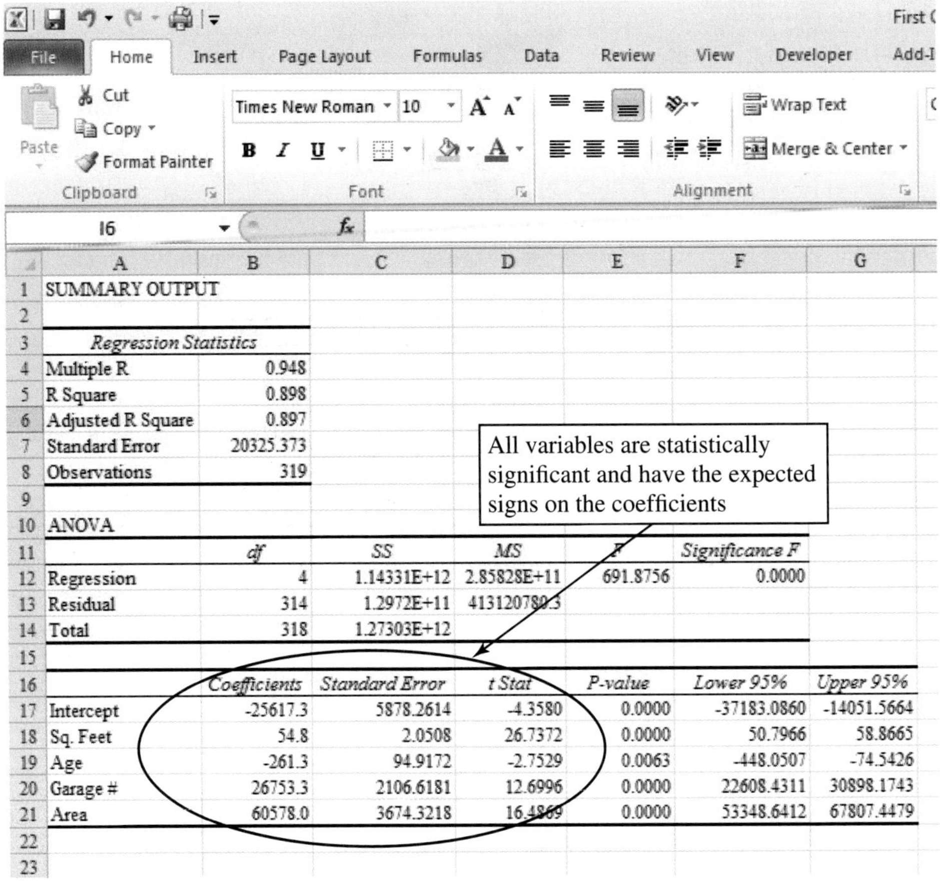
All variables are statistically significant and have the expected signs on the coefficients

SUMMARY OUTPUT

Regression Statistics	
Multiple R	0.948
R Square	0.898
Adjusted R Square	0.897
Standard Error	20325.373
Observations	319

ANOVA

	df	*SS*	*MS*	*F*	*Significance F*
Regression	4	1.14331E+12	2.85828E+11	691.8756	0.0000
Residual	314	1.2972E+11	413120780.3		
Total	318	1.27303E+12			

	Coefficients	*Standard Error*	*t Stat*	*P-value*	*Lower 95%*	*Upper 95%*
Intercept	-25617.3	5878.2614	-4.3580	0.0000	-37183.0860	-14051.5664
Sq. Feet	54.8	2.0508	26.7372	0.0000	50.7966	58.8665
Age	-261.3	94.9172	-2.7529	0.0063	-448.0507	-74.5426
Garage #	26753.3	2106.6181	12.6996	0.0000	22608.4311	30898.1743
Area	60578.0	3674.3218	16.4869	0.0000	53348.6412	67807.4479

Excel 2010 Instructions:

1. Open file: **First City.xlsx**.
2. Select Homes-Sample 2 worksheet.
3. Select **Data > Data Analysis**.
4. Select **Regression**.
5. Define *y* variable range (Price) and the *x* variable range (include row with labels).
6. Click **Labels**.
7. Specify output location.
8. Click **OK**.

Minitab Instructions (for similar results):

1. Open file: **First City.MTW**.
2. Choose **Stat > Regression > Regression**.
3. In **Response** enter dependent (*y*) variable.
4. In **Predictors**, enter independent (*x*) variables.
5. Click **OK**.

MyStatLab

15-2: Exercises

Skill Development

15-12. Consider the following regression model:

$$y = \beta_0 + \beta_1 x_1 + \beta_2 x_2 + \varepsilon$$

where:

$$x_1 = \text{A quantitative variable}$$

$$x_2 = \begin{cases} 1 \text{ if } x_1 < 20 \\ 0 \text{ if } x_1 \geq 20 \end{cases}$$

The following estimated regression equation was obtained from a sample of 30 observations:

$$\hat{y} = 24.1 + 5.8x_1 + 7.9x_2$$

a. Provide the estimated regression equation for instances in which $x_1 < 20$.
b. Determine the value of $\hat{y}$ when $x_1 = 10$.
c. Provide the estimated regression equation for instances in which $x_1 > 20$.
d. Determine the value of $\hat{y}$ when $x_1 = 30$.

15-13. You are considering developing a regression equation relating a dependent variable to two independent variables. One of the variables can be measured on a ratio scale, but the other is a categorical variable with two possible levels.

a. Write a multiple regression equation relating the dependent variable to the independent variables.

b. Interpret the meaning of the coefficients in the regression equation.

15-14. You are considering developing a regression equation relating a dependent variable to two independent variables. One of the variables can be measured on a ratio scale, but the other is a categorical variable with four possible levels.

a. How many dummy variables are needed to represent the categorical variable?

b. Write a multiple regression equation relating the dependent variable to the independent variables.

c. Interpret the meaning of the coefficients in the regression equation.

15-15. A real estate agent wishes to estimate the monthly rental for apartments based on the size (square feet) and the location of the apartments. She chose the following model:

$$y = \beta_0 + \beta_1 x_1 + \beta_2 x_2 + \varepsilon$$

where:

$x_1 =$ Square footage of the apartment

$x_2 = \begin{cases} 1 \text{ if located in town center} \\ 0 \text{ if not located in town center} \end{cases}$

This linear regression model was fitted to a sample of size 50 to produce the following regression equation:

$$\hat{y} = 145 + 1.2x_1 + 300x_2$$

a. Predict the average monthly rent for an apartment located in the town center that has 1,500 square feet.

b. Predict the average monthly rent for an apartment located in the suburbs that has 1,500 square feet.

c. Interpret b_2 in the context of this exercise.

Business Applications

15-16. The Polk Utility Corporation is developing a multiple regression model that it plans to use to predict customers' utility usage. The analyst currently has three quantitative variables (x_1, x_2, and x_3) in the model, but she is dissatisfied with the R-squared and the estimate of the standard deviation of the model's error. Two variables she thinks might be useful are whether the house has a gas water heater or an electric water heater and whether the house was constructed after the 1974 energy crisis or before.

Provide the model she should use to predict customers' utility usage. Specify the dummy variables to be used, the values these variables could assume, and what each value will represent.

15-17. A study was recently performed by the American Automobile Association in which it attempted to develop a regression model to explain variation in Environmental Protection Agency (EPA) mileage ratings of new cars. At one stage of the analysis, the estimate of the model took the following form:

$$\hat{y} = 34.20 - 0.003x_1 + 4.56x_2$$

where:

$x_1 =$ Vehicle weight

$x_2 = \begin{cases} 1, \text{ if standard transmission} \\ 0, \text{ if automatic transmission} \end{cases}$

a. Interpret the regression coefficient for variable x_1.

b. Interpret the regression coefficient for variable x_2.

c. Present an estimate of a model that would predict the average EPA mileage rating for an automobile with standard transmission as a function of the vehicle's weight.

d. Cadillac's STS-V with automatic transmission weighs approximately 3,973 pounds. Provide an estimate of the average highway mileage you would expect to obtain from this model.

e. Discuss the effect of a dummy variable being incorporated in a regression equation like this one. Use a graph if it is helpful.

15-18. A real estate agent wishes to determine the selling price of residences using the size (square feet) and whether the residence is a condominium or a single-family home. A sample of 20 residences was obtained with the following results:

Price($)	Type	Square Feet	Price($)	Type	Square Feet
199,700	Family	1,500	200,600	Condo	1,375
211,800	Condo	2,085	208,000	Condo	1,825
197,100	Family	1,450	210,500	Family	1,650
228,400	Family	1,836	233,300	Family	1,960
215,800	Family	1,730	187,200	Condo	1,360
190,900	Condo	1,726	185,200	Condo	1,200
312,200	Family	2,300	284,100	Family	2,000
313,600	Condo	1,650	207,200	Family	1,755
239,000	Family	1,950	258,200	Family	1,850
184,400	Condo	1,545	203,100	Family	1,630

a. Produce a regression equation to predict the selling price for residences using a model of the following form:

$$y_i = \beta_0 + \beta_1 x_1 + \beta_2 x_2 + \varepsilon$$

where:

$x_1 =$ Square footage   and $x_2 = \begin{cases} 1 \text{ if a condo} \\ 0 \text{ if single-family home} \end{cases}$

b. Interpret the parameters β_1 and β_2 in the model given in part a.

c. Produce an equation that describes the relationship between the selling price and the square footage of (1) condominiums and (2) single-family homes.

d. Conduct a test of hypothesis to determine if the relationship between the selling price and the square footage is different between condominiums and single-family homes.

Computer Database **Exercises**

15-19. For years, import cars have held an advantage over domestic automobiles according to data collected by J.D. Power and Associates, which generates a widely respected report on initial quality. The 2011 data showed a general decrease in quality due primarily to voice-activated electronic systems that didn't work as well as advertised. The data are contained in the file **PP100**. Initial quality is measured by the number of problems per 100 vehicles (PP100).

  a. Produce a regression equation to predict the PP100 for vehicles in the model

$$y_i = \beta_0 + \beta_1 x_1 + \beta_2 x_2 + \varepsilon$$

  where $x_1 = 1$ if considered an Asian brand and 0 if not and $x_2 = 1$ if considered a European car and 0 if not.

  b. Interpret the parameters β_0, β_1, and β_2 in the model given in part a.

  c. Conduct a test of hypothesis using the model in part a to determine if the average PP100 is the same for the three groups of companies.

15-20. The Energy Information Administration (EIA), created by Congress in 1977, is a statistical agency of the U.S. Department of Energy. It provides data, forecasts, and analyses to promote sound policymaking and public understanding regarding energy and its interaction with the economy and the environment. One of the most important areas of analysis is petroleum. The file titled **Crude** contains data for the period 1995 through 2010 concerning the price, supply, and demand for fuel. It has been conjectured that the pricing structure of gasoline changed at the turn of the century.

  a. Produce a regression equation to predict the selling price of gasoline:

$$y_i = \beta_0 + \beta_1 x_1 + \varepsilon$$

  where:

$$x_1 = \begin{cases} 1 \text{ if in twenty-first century} \\ 0 \text{ if in twentieth century} \end{cases}$$

  b. Conduct a hypothesis test to address the conjecture. Use a significance level of 0.05 and the test statistic approach.

  c. Produce a 95% confidence interval to estimate the change of the average selling price of gasoline between the twentieth and the twenty-first centuries.

15-21. The Gilmore Accounting firm, in an effort to explain variation in client profitability, collected the data found in the file called **Gilmore**, where:

  y = Net profit earned from the client
  x_1 = Number of hours spent working with the client
  x_2 = Type of client:
      1, if manufacturing
      2, if service
      3, if governmental

  a. Develop a scatter plot of each independent variable against the client income variable. Comment on what, if any, relationship appears to exist in each case.

  b. Run a simple linear regression analysis using only variable x_1 as the independent variable. Describe the resulting estimate fully.

  c. Test to determine if the number of hours spent working with the client is useful in predicting client profitability.

15-22. Using the data from the Gilmore Accounting firm found in the data file **Gilmore** (see Problem 15-21),

  a. Incorporate the client type into the regression analysis using dummy variables. Describe the resulting multiple regression estimate.

  b. Test to determine if this model is useful in predicting the net profit earned from the client.

  c. Test to determine if the number of hours spent working with the client is useful in this model in predicting the net profit earned from a client.

  d. Considering the tests you have performed, construct a model and its estimate for predicting the net profit earned from the client.

  e. Predict the average difference in profit if the client is governmental versus one in manufacturing. Also state this in terms of a 95% confidence interval estimate.

15-23. Several previous problems have dealt with the College Board changing the format of the SAT test taken by many entering college freshmen. Many reasons were given for changing the format. The class of 2005 was the last to take the former version of the SAT, featuring math and verbal sections. There had been conjecture about whether a relationship between the average math SAT score and the average verbal SAT score and the gender of the student taking the SAT examination existed. Consider the following relationship:

$$y_i = \beta_0 + \beta_1 x_1 + \beta_2 x_2 + \varepsilon$$

  where:

  $x_1 = $ Average verbal SAT score and $x_2 = \begin{cases} 1 \text{ if female} \\ 0 \text{ if male} \end{cases}$

  a. Use the file **MathSAT** to compute the linear regression equation to predict the average math SAT score using the gender and the average verbal SAT score of the students taking the SAT examination.

  b. Interpret the parameters in the model.

  c. Conduct a hypothesis test to determine if the gender of the student taking the SAT examination is a significant predictor of the student's average math SAT score for a given average verbal SAT score.

  d. Predict the average math SAT score of female students with an average verbal SAT score of 500.

Chapter Outcome 7. ➔ ## 15.3 Working with Nonlinear Relationships

Section 14.1 in Chapter 14 showed there are a variety of ways in which two variables can be related. Correlation and regression analysis techniques are tools for measuring and modeling linear relationships between variables. Many situations in business have a linear relationship between two variables, and regression equations that model that relationship will be appropriate to use in these situations. However, there are also many instances in which the relationship between two variables will be curvilinear rather than linear. For instance, demand for electricity has grown at an almost exponential rate relative to the population growth in some areas. Advertisers believe that a diminishing returns relationship will occur between sales and advertising if advertising is allowed to grow too large. These two situations are shown in Figures 15.13 and 15.14, respectively. They represent just two of the great many possible curvilinear relationships that could exist between two variables.

As you will soon see, models with nonlinear relationships become more complicated than models showing only linear relationships. Although complicated models are sometimes necessary, decision makers should use them with caution for several reasons. First, management researchers and authors have written that people use decision aids they understand and don't use those they don't understand. So, the more complicated a model is, the less likely it is to be used. Second, the scientific principle of parsimony suggests using the simplest model possible that provides a reasonable fit of the data, because complex models typically do not reflect the underlying phenomena that produce the data in the first place.

This section provides a brief introduction to how linear regression analysis can be used in dealing with curvilinear relationships. To model such curvilinear relationships, we must incorporate terms into the multiple regression model that will create "curves" in the model we are building. Including terms whose independent variable has an exponent larger than 1 generates these curves. When a model possesses such terms we refer to it as a *polynomial model*. The general equation for a polynomial with one independent variable is given in Equation 15.11.

FIGURE 15.13

Exponential Relationship of Increased Demand for Electricity versus Population Growth

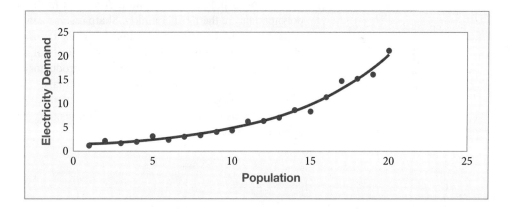

FIGURE 15.14

Diminishing Returns Relationship of Advertising versus Sales

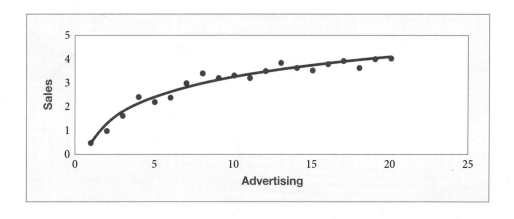

Polynomial Population Regression Model

$$y = \beta_0 + \beta_1 x + \beta_2 x^2 + \cdots + \beta_p x^p + \varepsilon \qquad \textbf{(15.11)}$$

where:

β_0 = Population regression's constant
β_j = Population's regression coefficient for variable $x^j; j = 1, 2, \ldots, p$
p = Order (or degree) of the polynomial
ε = Model error

The order, or degree, of the model is determined by the largest exponent of the independent variable in the model. For instance, the model

$$y = \beta_0 + \beta_1 x + \beta_2 x^2 + \varepsilon$$

is a second-order polynomial because the largest exponent in any term of the polynomial is 2. You will note that this model contains terms of all orders less than or equal to 2. A polynomial with this property is said to be a *complete* polynomial. Therefore, the previous model would be referred to as a complete *second-order regression model*. A second-order model produces a parabola. The parabola either opens upward $(\beta_2 > 0)$ or downward $(\beta_2 < 0)$, shown in Figure 15.15. You will notice that the models in Figures 15.13, 15.14, and 15.15 possess a single curve.

As more curves appear in the data, the order of the polynomial must be increased. A general (complete) third-order polynomial is given by the equation

$$y = \beta_0 + \beta_1 x + \beta_2 x^2 + \beta_3 x^3 + \varepsilon$$

This model produces a curvilinear model that reverses the direction of the initial curve to produce a second curve, as shown in Figure 15.16. Note that there are two curves in the third-order model. In general, a pth-order polynomial will exhibit $p - 1$ curves.

Although polynomials of all orders exist in the business sector, perhaps second-order polynomials are the most common. Sharp reversals in the curvature of a relationship between variables in the business environment usually point to some unexpected or perhaps severe changes that were not foreseen. The vast majority of organizations try to avoid such reverses. For this reason, and the fact that this is an introductory business statistics book, we will direct most of our attention to second-order polynomials.

The following examples illustrate two of the most common instances in which curvilinear relationships can be used in decision making. They should give you an idea of how to approach similar situations.

FIGURE 15.15

Second-Order Regression Models

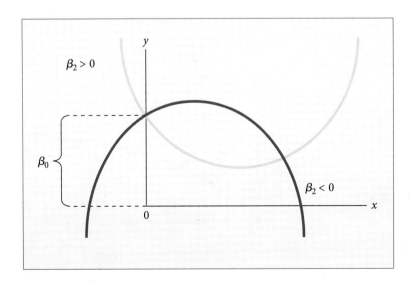

FIGURE 15.16 |

Third-Order Regression
Models

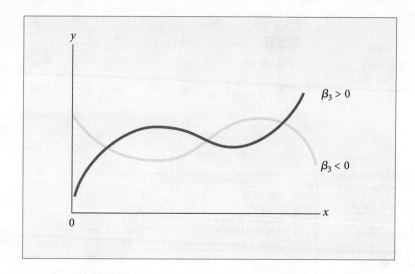

Chapter Outcome 7. ➡ | **EXAMPLE 15-3**   **MODELING CURVILINEAR RELATIONSHIPS**

Ashley Investment Services Ashley Investment Services was severely shaken by the downturn in the stock market during the summer and fall of 2008. To maintain profitability and save as many jobs as possible, since then everyone has been extra busy analyzing new investment opportunities. The director of personnel has noticed an increased number of people suffering from "burnout," in which physical and emotional fatigue hurt job performance. Although he cannot change the job's pressures, he has read that the more time a person spends socializing with coworkers away from the job, the more likely there is to be a higher degree of burnout. With the help of the human resources lab at the local university, the personnel director has administered a questionnaire to company employees. A burnout index has been computed from the responses to the survey. Likewise, the survey responses are used to determine quantitative measures of socialization. Sample data from questionnaires are contained in the file **Ashley**. The following steps can be used to model the relationship between the socialization index and the burnout index for Ashley employees:

Step 1   Specify the model by determining the dependent and potential independent variables.
The dependent variable is the burnout index. The company wishes to explain the variation in burnout level. One potential independent variable is the socialization index.

Step 2   Formulate the model.
We begin by proposing that a linear relationship exists between the two variables. Figure 15.17 shows the linear regression analysis results using Excel. The correlation between the two variables is $r = 0.818$, which is statistically different from zero at any reasonable significance level. The estimate of the population linear regression model shown in Figure 15.17 is

$$\hat{y} = -66.164 + 9.589x$$

Step 3   Perform diagnostic checks on the model.
The sample data and the regression line are plotted in Figure 15.18. The line appears to fit the data. However, a closer inspection reveals instances in which several consecutive points lie above or below the line. The points are not randomly dispersed around the regression line, as should be the case given the regression analysis assumptions.
As you will recall from earlier discussions, we can use an F-test to test whether a regression model explains a significant amount of variation in the dependent variable.

$$H_0: \rho^2 = 0$$
$$H_A: \rho^2 > 0$$

FIGURE 15.17

Excel 2010 Output of a Simple Linear Regression for Ashley Investment Services

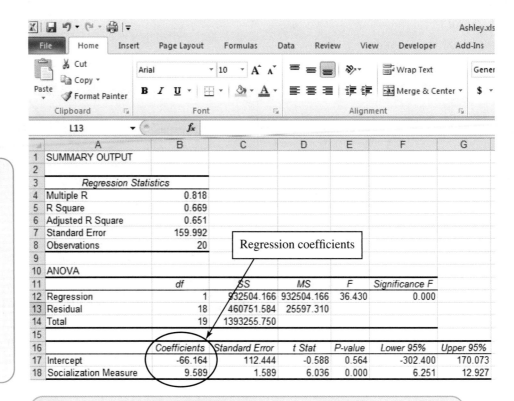

Excel 2010 Instructions:
1. Open file: **Ashley.xlsx**.
2. Select **Data > Data Analysis**.
3. Select **Regression**.
4. Define *y* variable range (Burnout) and the *x* variable range (Socialization Measure—include row with labels).
5. Click **Labels**.
6. Specify output location.
7. Click **OK**.

Minitab Instructions (for similar results):
1. Open file: **Ashley.MTW**.
2. Choose **Stat > Regression > Regression**.
3. In **Response**, enter the *y* variable column.
4. In **Predictors**, enter the *x* variable column.
5. Click **OK**.

From the output in Figure 15.17,

$$F = 36.43$$

which has a *p*-value ≈ 0.000.

Thus, we conclude that the simple linear model is statistically significant. However, we should also examine the data to determine if any curvilinear relationships may be present.

Step 4   Model the curvilinear relationship.

Finding instances of nonrandom patterns in the residuals for a regression model indicates the possibility of using a curvilinear relationship rather than

FIGURE 15.18

Plot of Regression Line for the Ashley Investment Services Example

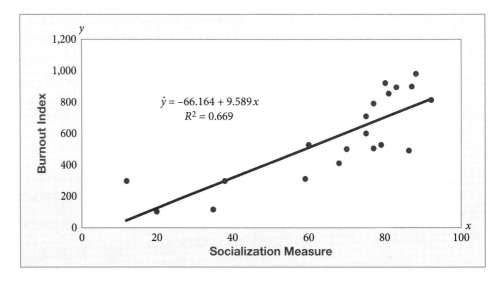

FIGURE 15.19

Excel 2010 Output of a
Second-Order Polynomial Fit
for Ashley Investment

Excel 2010 Instructions:
1. Open file: **Ashley.xlsx**.
2. Use Excel equation to create a new variable in column C (i.e., for the first data value in row 2, use =A2^2. Then copy down to the last row.).
3. Rearrange columns so both independent variables are together.
4. Select **Data > Data Analysis**.
5. Select **Regression**.
6. Define *y* variable range (Burnout) and the *x* variable range (include Socialization Measure and the new variable—include row with labels).
7. Click **Labels**.
8. Specify output location.
9. Click **OK**.

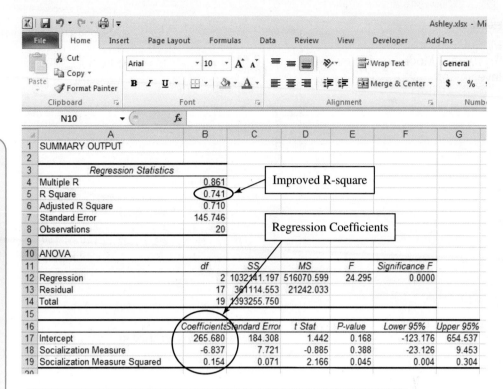

Minitab Instructions (for similar results):
1. Open file: **Ashley.MTW**.
2. Use **Calc > Calculator** to create socialization column.
3. Choose **Stat > Regression > Fitted Line Plot**.
4. In **Response**, enter *y* variable.
5. In **Predictor**, enter *x* variables.
6. Under **Type of Regression Model**, choose **Quadratic**.
7. Click **OK**.

a linear one. One possible approach to modeling the curvilinear nature of the data in the Ashley Investments example is with the use of polynomials. From Figure 15.18, we can see that there appears to be one curve in the data. This suggests fitting the second-order polynomial

$$y = \beta_0 + \beta_1 x + \beta_2 x^2 + \varepsilon$$

Before fitting the estimate for this population model, you will need to create the new independent variable by squaring the socialization measure variable. In Excel, use the formula option to create the new variable. Figure 15.19 shows the output after fitting this second-order polynomial model.

Step 5   Perform diagnostics on the revised curvilinear model.
Notice the second-order polynomial provides a model whose estimated regression equation has an R^2 of 0.741. This is higher than the R^2 of 0.669 for the linear model. Figure 15.20 shows the plot of the second-order polynomial model. Comparing Figure 15.20 with Figure 15.18, we can see that the polynomial model does appear to fit the sample data better than the linear model.

>> **END EXAMPLE**

TRY PROBLEM 15-24 (pg. 651)

Analyzing Interaction Effects

BUSINESS APPLICATION   **DEALING WITH INTERACTION**

ASHLEY INVESTMENT SERVICES (*CONTINUED*) Referring to Example 15-3 involving Ashley Investment Services, the director of personnel wondered if the effects of burnout differ among male and female workers. He therefore identified the gender of the

Excel Tutorial

FIGURE 15.20

Plot of Second-Order
Polynomial Model for Ashley
Investment

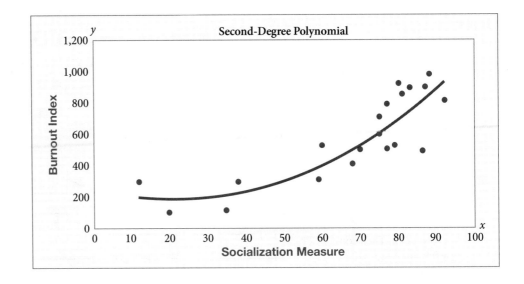

previously surveyed employees (see file **Ashley-2**). A multiple scatter plot of the data appears as Figure 15.21.

The personnel director tried to determine the relationship between the burnout index and socialization measure for men and women. The graphical result is presented in Figure 15.21.

FIGURE 15.21

Excel 2010 Multiple Scatter
Plot for Ashley Investment
Services

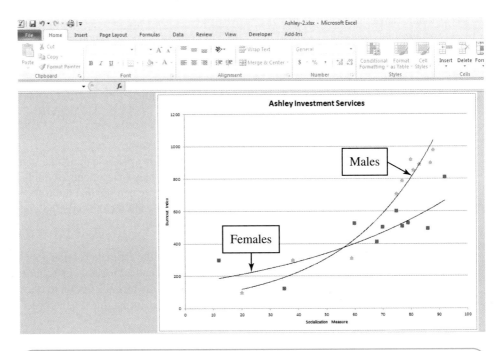

Excel 2010 Instructions:

1. Open file: **Ashley-2.xlsx**.
2. Select Socialization Measure and Burnout Index columns.
3. Select **Insert** tab.
4. Select **Scatter > Scatter with only Markers**.
5. Select **Chart** and click the right mouse button—choose **Select Data**.
6. Click on **Add** on the **Legend Entry (Series)** section.
7. Enter **Series Name**—(Females)—for **Series X Values**, select data from Socialization column for row corresponding

to females (rows 2–11). **For Series Y Values**, select data from the Burnout column corresponding to females (rows 2–11).
8. Repeat step 7 for males.
9. Select **Layout** tab to remove legend and to add chart and axis titles.
10. Select data points for males—right click and select **Add Trendline > Exponential**.
11. Repeat step 10 for females.
12. Click **Design** tab and click **Move Chart**.

Note that both relationships appear to be curvilinear, with a similarly shaped curve. As we showed earlier, curvilinear shapes often can be modeled by the second-order polynomial

$$\hat{y} = b_0 + b_1 x_1 + b_2 x_1^2$$

However, the regression equations that estimate this second-order polynomial for men and women are not the same. The two equations seem to have different locations and different rates of curvature. Whether an employee is a man or woman seems to change the basic relationship between burnout index (y) and socialization measure (x_1). To represent this difference, the equation's coefficients b_0, b_1, and b_2 must be different for male and female employees. Thus, we could use two models, one for each gender. Alternatively, we could use one model for both male and female employees by incorporating a dummy independent variable with two levels, which is shown as

$$x_2 = 1 \text{ if male, } 0 \text{ if female}$$

As x_2 changes values from 0 to 1, it affects the values of the coefficients b_0, b_1, and b_2. Suppose the director fitted the second-order model for the female employees only. He obtained the following regression equation:

$$\hat{y} = 291.70 - 4.62x_1 + 0.102x_1^2$$

The equation for only male employees was

$$\hat{y} = 149.59 - 4.40x_1 + 0.160x_1^2$$

Interaction

The case in which one independent variable (such as x_2) affects the relationship between another independent variable (x_1) and the dependent variable (y).

To explain how a change in gender can cause this kind of change, we must introduce **interaction**. In our example, gender (x_2) interacts with the relationship between socialization measure (x_1) and burnout index (y). The question is how do we obtain the interaction terms to model such a relationship? To answer this question, we first obtain the model for the basic relationship between the x_1 and the y variables. The population model is

$$y = \beta_0 + \beta_1 x_1 + \beta_2 x_1^2 + \varepsilon$$

To obtain the interaction terms, multiply the terms on the right-hand side of this model by the variable that is interacting with this relationship between y and x_1. In this case, that interacting variable is x_2. Then the interaction terms would be

$$\beta_3 x_2 + \beta_4 x_1 x_2 + \beta_5 x_1^2 x_2$$

Notice that we have changed the coefficient subscripts so we do not duplicate those in the original model. Then the interaction terms are added to the original model to produce the **composite model**.

Composite Model

The model that contains both the basic terms and the interaction terms.

$$y = \beta_0 + \beta_1 x_1 + \beta_2 x_1^2 + \beta_3 x_2 + \beta_4 x_1 x_2 + \beta_5 x_1^2 x_2 + \varepsilon$$

Note, the model for women is obtained by substituting $x_2 = 0$ into the composite model. This gives

$$y = \beta_0 + \beta_1 x_1 + \beta_2 x_1^2 + \beta_3(0) + \beta_4 x_1(0) + \beta_5 x_1^2(0) + \varepsilon$$
$$= \beta_0 + \beta_1 x_1 + \beta_2 x_1^2 + \varepsilon$$

Similarly, for men we substitute the value of $x_2 = 1$. The model then becomes

$$y = \beta_0 + \beta_1 x_1 + \beta_2 x_1^2 + \beta_3(1) + \beta_4 x_1(1) + \beta_5 x_1^2(1) + \varepsilon$$
$$= (\beta_0 + \beta_3) + (\beta_1 + \beta_4)x_1 + (\beta_2 + \beta_5)x_1^2 + \varepsilon$$

This illustrates how the coefficients are changed for different values of x_2 and, therefore, how x_2 is interacting with the relationship between x_1 and y. Once we know β_3, β_4, and β_5, we know the effect of the interaction of gender on the original relationship between the burnout index (y) and the socialization measure (x_1). To estimate the composite model, we need to create the required variables, as shown in Figure 15.22. Figure 15.23 shows the regression for the composite model. The estimate for the composite model is

$$\hat{y} = 291.706 - 4.615x_1 + 0.102x_1^2 - 142.113x_2 + 0.215x_1 x_2 + 0.058x_1^2 x_2$$

FIGURE 15.22

Excel 2010 Data Preparation for Estimating Interactive Effects for Second-Order Model for Ashley Investment

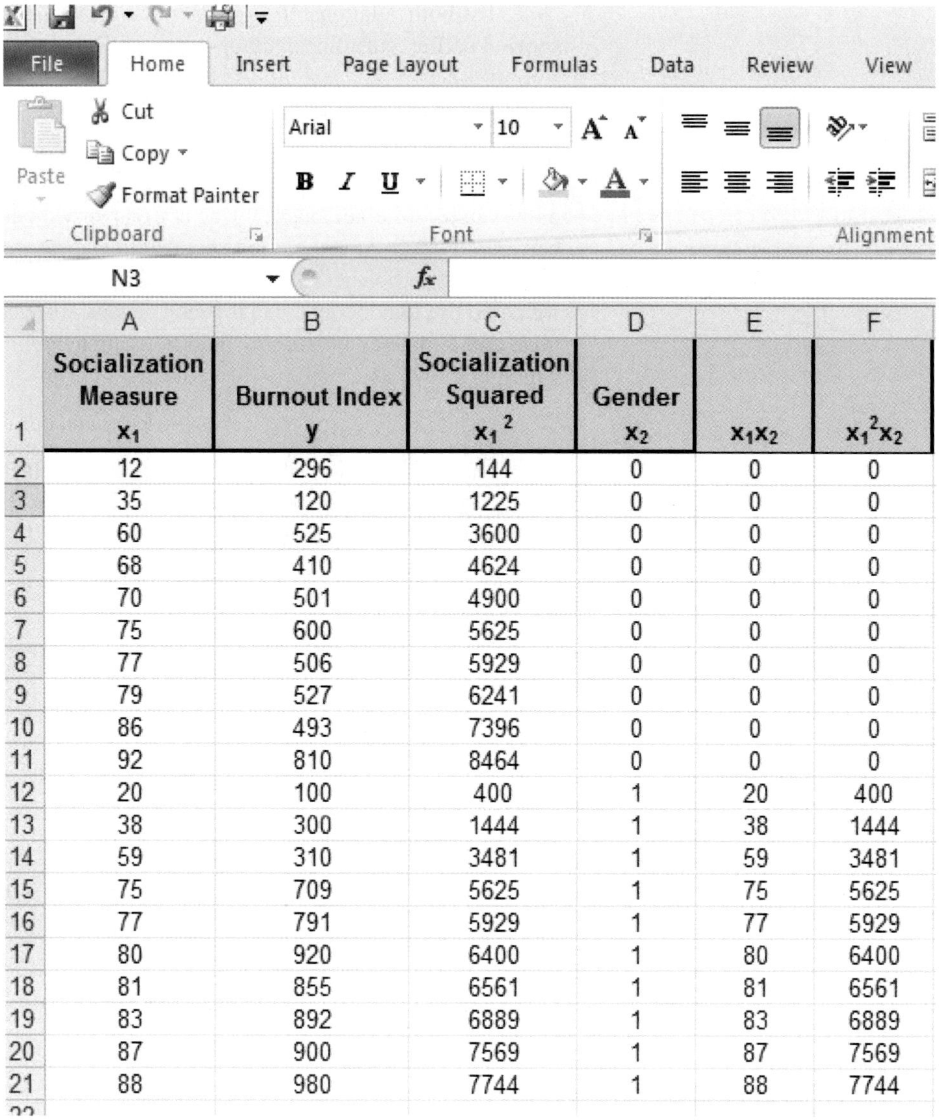

	A	B	C	D	E	F
1	Socialization Measure x_1	Burnout Index y	Socialization Squared x_1^2	Gender x_2	x_1x_2	$x_1^2x_2$
2	12	296	144	0	0	0
3	35	120	1225	0	0	0
4	60	525	3600	0	0	0
5	68	410	4624	0	0	0
6	70	501	4900	0	0	0
7	75	600	5625	0	0	0
8	77	506	5929	0	0	0
9	79	527	6241	0	0	0
10	86	493	7396	0	0	0
11	92	810	8464	0	0	0
12	20	100	400	1	20	400
13	38	300	1444	1	38	1444
14	59	310	3481	1	59	3481
15	75	709	5625	1	75	5625
16	77	791	5929	1	77	5929
17	80	920	6400	1	80	6400
18	81	855	6561	1	81	6561
19	83	892	6889	1	83	6889
20	87	900	7569	1	87	7569
21	88	980	7744	1	88	7744

Excel 2010 Instructions:

1. Open file: **Ashley-2.xlsx**.
2. Use Excel formulas to create new variables in columns C, E, and F.

We obtain the model for females by substituting $x_2 = 0$, giving

$$\hat{y} = 291.706 - 4.615x_1 + 0.102x_1^2 - 142.113(0) + 0.215x_1(0) + 0.058x_1^2(0)$$
$$\hat{y} = 291.706 - 4.615x_1 + 0.102x_1^2$$

For males, we substitute $x_2 = 1$, giving

$$\hat{y} = 291.706 - 4.615x_1 + 0.102x_1^2 - 142.113(1) + 0.215x_1(1) + 0.058x_1^2(1)$$
$$\hat{y} = 149.593 - 4.40x_1 + 0.160x_1^2$$

Note that these equations for male and female employees are the same as those we found earlier when we generated two separate regression models, one for each gender.

In this example, we have looked at a case in which a dummy variable interacts with the relationship between another independent variable and the dependent variable. However, the interacting variable need not be a dummy variable. It can be any independent variable. Also, strictly speaking, interaction is not said to exist if the only effect of the interaction variable is to change the y intercept of the equation, relating another independent variable to the dependent variable. Therefore, when you examine a scatter plot to detect interaction, you are trying to determine if the relationships produced, when the interaction variable changes values, are parallel or not. If the relationships are parallel, that indicates that only the y intercept is being affected by the change of the interacting variable and that interaction does not exist. Figure 15.24 demonstrates this concept graphically.

FIGURE 15.23 | Excel 2010 Composite Model for Ashley Investment Services

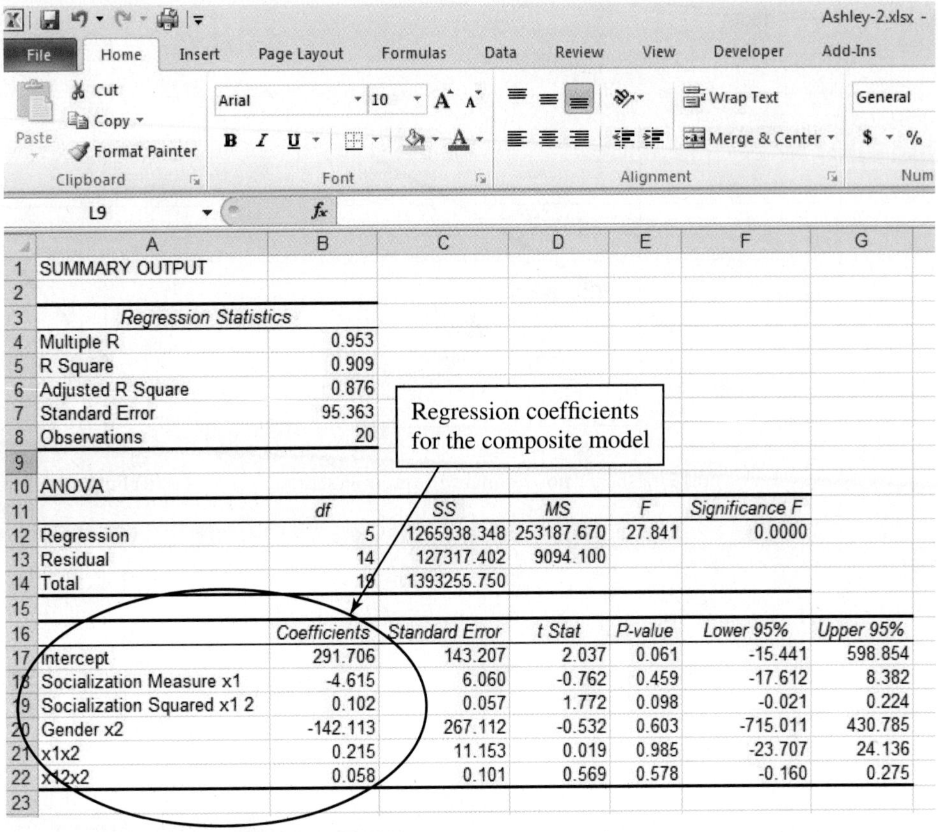

	A	B	C	D	E	F	G
1	SUMMARY OUTPUT						
2							
3	*Regression Statistics*						
4	Multiple R	0.953					
5	R Square	0.909					
6	Adjusted R Square	0.876					
7	Standard Error	95.363					
8	Observations	20					
9							
10	ANOVA						
11		*df*	*SS*	*MS*	*F*	*Significance F*	
12	Regression	5	1265938.348	253187.670	27.841	0.0000	
13	Residual	14	127317.402	9094.100			
14	Total	19	1393255.750				
15							
16		*Coefficients*	*Standard Error*	*t Stat*	*P-value*	*Lower 95%*	*Upper 95%*
17	Intercept	291.706	143.207	2.037	0.061	-15.441	598.854
18	Socialization Measure x1	-4.615	6.060	-0.762	0.459	-17.612	8.382
19	Socialization Squared x1 2	0.102	0.057	1.772	0.098	-0.021	0.224
20	Gender x2	-142.113	267.112	-0.532	0.603	-715.011	430.785
21	x1x2	0.215	11.153	0.019	0.985	-23.707	24.136
22	x12x2	0.058	0.101	0.569	0.578	-0.160	0.275
23							

Excel 2010 Instructions:

1. Open file: **Ashley-2.xlsx**.
2. Use Excel equation to create new variables (see Figure 15.22 Excel 2010 Instructions).
3. Rearrange columns so all independent variables are together.
4. Select **Data > Data Analysis**.
5. Select **Regression**.
6. Define *y* variable range (Burnout) and the *x* variable range (include Socialization Measure and the new variables—include row with labels).
7. Click **Labels**.
8. Specify output location.
9. Click **OK**.

Minitab Instructions (for similar results):

1. Continue from Step 2.
2. Choose **Stat > Regression > Regression**.
3. In **Response**, enter dependent (*y*) variable.
4. In **Predictors**, enter independent (*x*) variables.
5. Click **OK**.

The Partial-*F* Test

So far you have been given the procedures required to test the significance of either one or all of the coefficients in a regression model. For instance, in Example 15-3, a hypothesis test was used to determine that a second-order model involving the socialization measure fit the sample data better than the linear model. Comparing the *R*-squared values was the mechanism used to establish this. We could have determined whether both the linear and quadratic components were useful in predicting the burnout index level by testing the hypothesis H_0: $\beta_1 = \beta_2 = 0$. However, more complex models occur. The interaction model involving Ashley Investment Services containing five predictor variables was

$$y_i = \beta_0 + \beta_1 x_{1i} + \beta_2 x_{1i}^2 + \beta_3 x_{2i} + \beta_4 x_{1i} x_{2i} + \beta_5 x_{1i}^2 x_{2i} + \varepsilon$$

Two of these predictor variables (*i.e.*, $x_{1i}x_{2i}$ and $x_{1i}^2 x_{2i}$) existing in the model would indicate interaction is evident in this regression model. If the two interaction variables were absent, the model would be

$$y_i = \beta_0 + \beta_1 x_{1i} + \beta_2 x_{1i}^2 + \beta_3 x_{2i} + \varepsilon$$

To determine whether there is statistical evidence of interaction, we must determine if the coefficients of the interaction terms are all equal to 0. If they are, there is no interaction. Otherwise, at least some interaction exists. For the Ashley Investment example, we test the hypotheses

$$H_0: \beta_4 = \beta_5 = 0$$
$$H_A: \text{Either } B_4 \text{ or } B_5 \neq 0$$

FIGURE 15.24

Graphical Evidence of Interaction

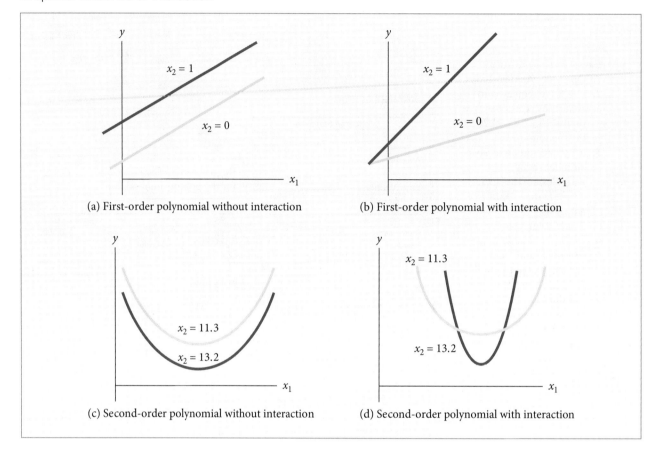

(a) First-order polynomial without interaction

(b) First-order polynomial with interaction

(c) Second-order polynomial without interaction

(d) Second-order polynomial with interaction

Earlier in this chapter, we introduced procedures for testing whether all of the coefficients of a model equaled 0. In that case, you use the analysis of variance F-test found on Excel output. However, to test whether there is significant interaction, we must test more than one but fewer than all the regression coefficients. The method for doing this is the *partial-F test*. This test relies on the fact that if given a choice between two models, one model is a better fit if its sum of squares of error (SSE) is significantly smaller than for the other model. Therefore, to determine if interaction exists in our model, we must obtain the SSE for the model with the interaction terms and for the model without the interaction terms. The model without the interaction terms is called the *reduced model*. The model containing the interaction terms is called the *complete model*. We will denote the respective sum of squares as SSE_R and SSE_C.

This procedure is appropriate to test any subset greater than one but less than all of the model's coefficients. We use the interaction terms in this example just as one such procedure. There are many models not containing interaction terms in which the partial-F test is applicable.

The test is based on the concept that the SSE will be significantly reduced if not all of the regression coefficients being tested equal zero. Of course, if the SSE is significantly reduced, then $SSE_R - SSE_C$ must be significantly different from zero. To determine if this difference is significantly different from zero, we use the partial-F test statistic given by Equation 15.12.

Partial-F Test Statistic

$$F = \frac{(SSE_R - SSE_C)/(c-r)}{MSE_C}$$

(15.12)

where:

$$MSE_C = \text{Mean square error for the complete model}$$
$$= SSE_C/(n - c - 1)$$
$$r = \text{The number of coefficients in the reduced model}$$
$$c = \text{The number of coefficients in the complete model}$$
$$n = \text{Sample size}$$

The numerator of this test statistic is basically the average SSE per degree of freedom reduced by including the coefficients being tested in the model. This is compared to the average SSE per degree of freedom for the complete model. If these averages are significantly different, then the null hypothesis is rejected. This test statistic has an F-distribution whose numerator degrees of freedom equals the number of parameters being tested $(c - r)$ and whose denominator degrees of freedom equals the degrees of freedom for the complete model $(n - c - 1)$.

We are now prepared to determine if the director's data indicate a significant interaction between gender and the relationship between the Socialization Measure and the Burnout Index. In order to conduct the test of hypothesis, the director produced regression equations for both models (Figures 15.25a and 15.25b). He obtained the SSE_C, MSE_C from Figure 15.25a, and SSE_R from Figure 15.25b. He was then able to conduct the hypothesis test to determine if there was any interaction. Figure 15.25c displays this test.

Since the null hypothesis was rejected, we can conclude that interaction does exist in this model. Apparently, gender of the employee does affect the relationship between the Burnout Index and the Socialization Measure. The relationship between the Burnout Index and the Socialization Measure is different within men and women.

You must be very careful with interpretations of regression coefficients when interaction exists. Notice that the equation that contains interaction terms is given by

$$\hat{y}_i = 292 - 4.61x_{1i} + 0.102x_{1i}^2 - 142x_{2i} + 0.2x_{1i}x_{2i} + 0.058x_{1i}^2x_{2i}$$

When interpreting the coefficient b_1, you may be tempted to say that the Burnout Index will decrease by an average of 4.61 units for every unit the Socialization Measure (x_{1i}) increases,

FIGURE 15.25a

Sum of Squares for the Complete Model

Excel 2010 Instructions:
1. Open file: **Ashley-2.xlsx**.
2. Use Excel equation to create new variables (see Figure 15.22 Excel 2010 Instructions).
3. Rearrange columns so all independent variables are together.
4. Select **Data > Data Analysis**.
5. Select **Regression**.
6. Define y variable range (Burnout) and the x variable range (include Socialization Measure and the new variables—include row with labels).
7. Click **Labels**.
8. Specify output location.
9. Click **OK**.

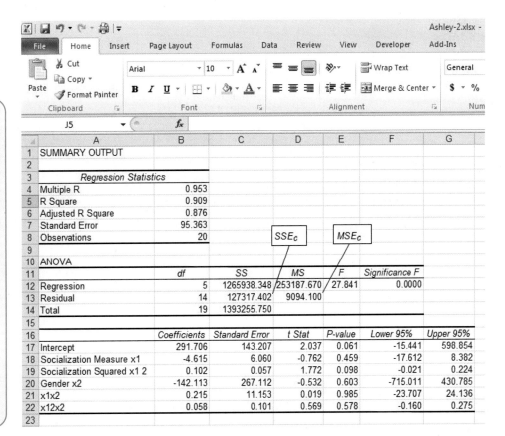

	A	B	C	D	E	F	G
1	SUMMARY OUTPUT						
2							
3		*Regression Statistics*					
4	Multiple R	0.953					
5	R Square	0.909					
6	Adjusted R Square	0.876					
7	Standard Error	95.363					
8	Observations	20		SSE_C		MSE_C	
9							
10	ANOVA						
11			*df*	*SS*	*MS*	*F*	*Significance F*
12	Regression		5	1265938.348	253187.670	27.841	0.0000
13	Residual		14	127317.402	9094.100		
14	Total		19	1393255.750			
15							
16			*Coefficients*	*Standard Error*	*t Stat*	*P-value*	*Lower 95%*	*Upper 95%*
17	Intercept		291.706	143.207	2.037	0.061	-15.441	598.854
18	Socialization Measure x1		-4.615	6.060	-0.762	0.459	-17.612	8.382
19	Socialization Squared x1 2		0.102	0.057	1.772	0.098	-0.021	0.224
20	Gender x2		-142.113	267.112	-0.532	0.603	-715.011	430.785
21	x1x2		0.215	11.153	0.019	0.985	-23.707	24.136
22	x12x2		0.058	0.101	0.569	0.578	-0.160	0.275
23							

FIGURE 15.25b

Sum of Squares for the
Reduced Model

Excel 2010 Instructions:
1. Open file: **Ashley-2.xlsx**.
2. Use Excel equation to create new variable in column C (i.e., for first data value use = A2^2, then copy down to end last row of data).
3. Rearrange columns so all independent variables are together.
4. Select **Data > Data Analysis**.
5. Select **Regression**.
6. Define y variable range (Burnout) and the x variable range (include Socialization Measure and the new variable— include row with labels).
7. Click **Labels**.
8. Specify output location.
9. Click **OK**.

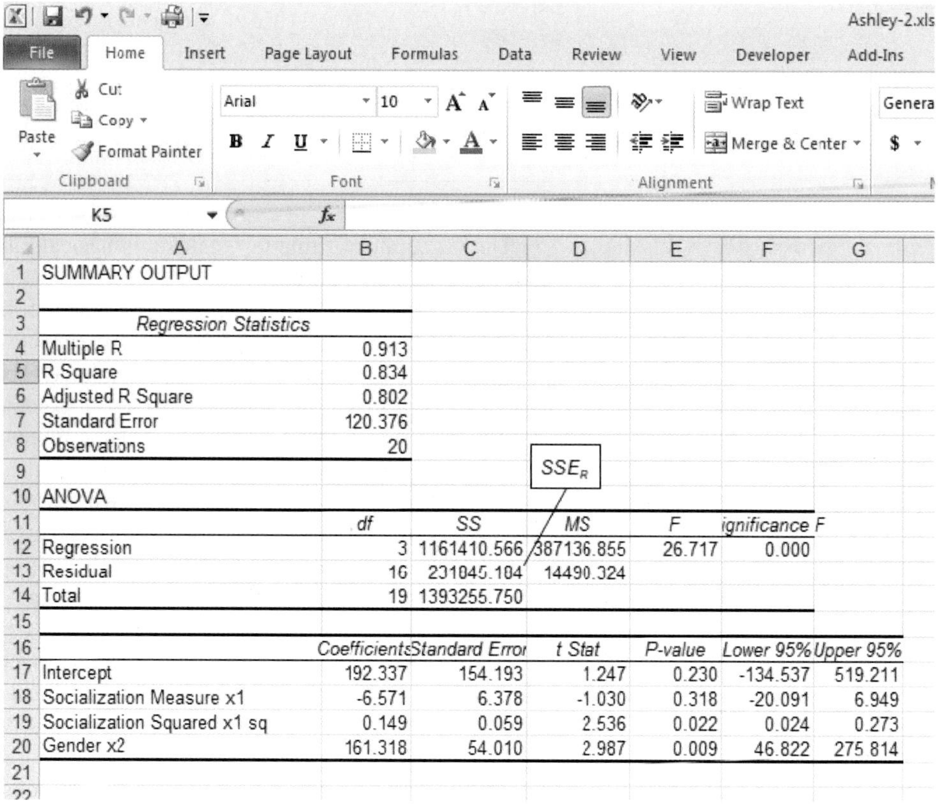

	A	B	C	D	E	F	G
1	SUMMARY OUTPUT						
2							
3	*Regression Statistics*						
4	Multiple R	0.913					
5	R Square	0.834					
6	Adjusted R Square	0.802					
7	Standard Error	120.376					
8	Observations	20					
9				SSE_R			
10	ANOVA						
11		*df*	*SS*	*MS*	*F*	*ignificance F*	
12	Regression	3	1161410.566	387136.855	26.717	0.000	
13	Residual	16	231845.184	14490.324			
14	Total	19	1393255.750				
15							
16		*Coefficients*	*Standard Error*	*t Stat*	*P-value*	*Lower 95%*	*Upper 95%*
17	Intercept	192.337	154.193	1.247	0.230	-134.537	519.211
18	Socialization Measure x1	-6.571	6.378	-1.030	0.318	-20.091	6.949
19	Socialization Squared x1 sq	0.149	0.059	2.536	0.022	0.024	0.273
20	Gender x2	161.318	54.010	2.987	0.009	46.822	275.814
21							

FIGURE 15.25c

Partial-F Hypothesis Test for
Interaction

$H_0: \beta_4 = \beta_5 = 0$
$H_A:$ At least one of the β_is $\neq 0$

$\alpha = 0.05$

Test Statistic:

$$F = \frac{(SSE_R - SSE_C)/(c - r)}{MSE_C} = \frac{(231,845.184 - 127,317.402)/(5 - 3)}{9,094.1} = 5.747$$

Rejection Region:

df: $D_1 = c - r = 5 - 3 = 2$
$D_2 = (n - c - 1) = 20 - 5 - 1 = 14$

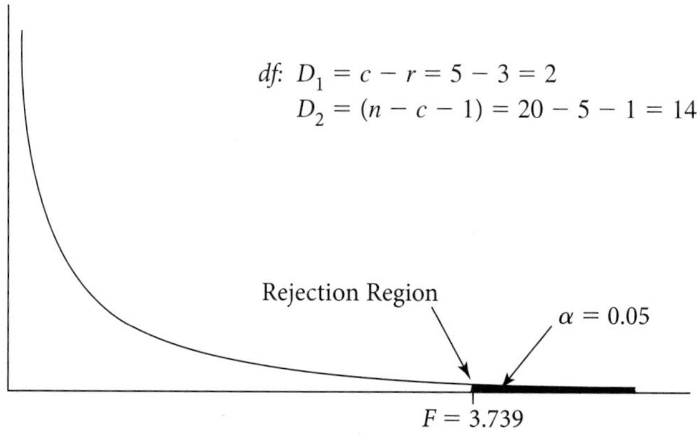

Rejection Region

$\alpha = 0.05$

$F = 3.739$

Because Partial-$F = 5.747 > 3.739$, we reject H_0.

holding all other predictor variables constant. However, this is not true; there are three other components of this regression equation that contain x_{1i}. When x_{1i} increases by one unit x_{1i}^2 will also increase. In addition, the interaction terms also contain x_{1i}, and therefore, those terms will change as well. This being the case, every time the variable x_2 changes, the rate of change of the interaction terms are also affected. Perhaps you will see this more clearly if we rewrite the equation as

$$\hat{y}_i = (292 - 142x_{2i}) + (0.2x_{2i} - 4.61)x_{1i} + (0.102 + 0.058x_{2i})x_{1i}^2$$

In this form, you can see that the coefficients of x_{1i} and x_{1i}^2 change whenever x_2 changes. Thus, the interpretation of any of these components depends on the value x_2, as well as x_{1i}. Whenever interaction or higher-order components are present, you should be very careful in your attempts to interpret the results of your regression analysis.

MyStatLab

15-3: Exercises

Skill Development

15-24. Consider the following values for the dependent and independent variables:

x	y
5	10
15	15
40	25
50	44
60	79
80	112

a. Develop a scatter plot of the data. Does the plot suggest a linear or nonlinear relationship between the dependent and independent variables?
b. Develop an estimated linear regression equation for the data. Is the relationship significant? Test at an $\alpha = 0.05$ level.
c. Develop a regression equation of the form $\hat{y} = b_0 + b_1x + b_2x^2$. Does this equation provide a better fit to the data than that found in part b?

15-25. Consider the following values for the dependent and independent variables:

x	y
6	5
9	20
14	28
18	30
22	33
27	35

a. Develop a scatter plot of the data. Does the plot suggest a linear or nonlinear relationship between the dependent and independent variables?
b. Develop an estimated linear regression equation for the data. Is the relationship significant? Test at an $\alpha = 0.05$ level.

c. Develop a regression equation of the form $\hat{y} = b_0 + b_1 \ln(x)$. Does this equation provide a better fit to the data than that found in part b?

15-26. Examine the following data:

x	2	8	9	12	15	22	21	25	37	39
y	4	75	175	415	620	7,830	7,551	7,850	11,112	11,617

a. Construct a scatter plot of the data. Determine the order of the polynomial that is represented by the data.
b. Obtain an estimate of the model identified in part a.
c. Conduct a test of hypothesis to determine if a third-order, as opposed to a second-order, polynomial is a better representation of the relationship between y and x. Use a significance level of 0.05 and the p-value approach.

15-27. Examine the following two sets of data:

When $x_2 = 1$		When $x_2 = 2$	
x_1	y	x_1	y
1	2	2	3
4	15	3	9
5	23	6	5
7	52	7	10
8	60	9	48
12	154	10	50
11	122	14	87
14	200	13	51
19	381	16	63
20	392	21	202

a. Produce a distinguishable scatter plot for each of the data sets on the same graph. Does it appear that there is interaction between x_2 and the relationship between y and x_1? Support your assertions.
b. Consider the following model to represent the relationship among y, x_1, and x_2:

$$y_i = \beta_0 + \beta_1 x_1 + \beta_2 x_1^2 + \beta_3 x_1 x_2 + \beta_4 x_1^2 x_2 + \varepsilon$$

Produce the estimated regression equation for this model.

c. Conduct a test of hypothesis for each interaction term. Use a significance level of 0.05 and the p-value approach.

d. Based on the two hypothesis tests in part c, does it appear that there is interaction between x_2 and the relationship between y and x_1? Support your assertions.

15-28. Consider the following data:

x	1	4	5	7	8	12	11	14	19	20
y	1	54	125	324	512	5,530	5,331	5,740	7,058	7,945

a. Construct a scatter plot of the data. Determine the order of the polynomial that is represented by this data.

b. Obtain an estimate of the model identified in part a.

c. Conduct a test of hypothesis to determine if a third-order, as opposed to a first-order, polynomial is a better representation of the relationship between y and x. Use a significance level of 0.05 and the p-value approach.

15-29. A regression equation to be used to predict a dependent variable with four independent variables is developed from a sample of size 10. The resulting equation is

$$\hat{y} = 32.8 + 0.470x_1 + 0.554x_2 - 4.77x_3 + 0.929x_4$$

Two other equations are developed from the sample:

$$\hat{y} = 12.4 + 0.60x_1 + 1.60x_2$$

and

$$\hat{y} = 49.7 - 5.38x_3 + 1.35x_4$$

The respective sum of squares errors for the three equations are 201.72, 1,343, and 494.6.

a. Use the summary information to determine if the independent variables x_3 and x_4 belong in the complete regression model. Use a significance level of 0.05.

b. Repeat part a for the independent variables x_1 and x_2. Use the p-value approach and a significance level of 0.05.

Computer Database **Exercises**

15-30. In a bit of good news for male students, American men have closed the gap with women on life span, according to a *USA Today* article. Male life expectancy attained a record 75.2 years, and women's reached 80.4. The National Center for Health Statistics provided the data given in the file titled **Life**.

a. Produce a scatter plot depicting the relationship between the life expectancy of women and men.

b. Determine the order of the polynomial that is represented on the scatter plot obtained in part a. Produce the estimated regression equation that represents this relationship.

c. Determine if women's average life expectancy can be used in a second-order polynomial to predict the average life expectancy of men. Use a significance level of 0.05.

d. Use the estimated regression equation computed in part b to predict the average length of life of men when women's length of life equals 100. What does this tell you about the wisdom (or lack thereof) of extrapolation in regression models?

15-31. The Gilmore Accounting firm previously mentioned, in an effort to explain variation in client profitability, collected the data found in the file called **Gilmore**, where:

y = Net profit earned from the client
x_1 = Number of hours spent working with the client
x_2 = Type of client:
   1, if manufacturing
   2, if service
   3, if governmental

Gilmore has asked if it needs the client type in addition to the number of hours spent working with the client to predict the net profit earned from the client. You are asked to provide this information.

a. Fit a model to the data that incorporates the number of hours spent working with the client and the type of client as independent variables. (*Hint*: Client type has three levels.)

b. Fit a second-order model to the data, again using dummy variables for client type. Does this model provide a better fit than that found in part a? Which model would you recommend be used?

15-32. McCullom's International Grains is constantly searching out areas in which to expand its market. Such markets present different challenges since tastes in the international market are often different from domestic tastes. India is one country on which McCullom's has recently focused. Paddy is a grain used widely in India, but its characteristics are unknown to McCullom's. Charles Walters has been assigned to take charge of the handling of this grain. He has researched its various characteristics. During his research he came across an article, "Determination of Biological Maturity and Effect of Harvesting and Drying Conditions on Milling Quality of Paddy" [*Journal of Agricultural Engineering Research* (1975), pp. 353–361], which examines the relationship between y, the yield (kg/ha) of paddy, as a function of x, and the number of days after flowering at which harvesting took place. The accompanying data appeared in the article and are in a file called **Paddy**.

y	x
2,508	16
2,518	18
3,304	20

y	x
3,423	22
3,057	24
3,190	26
3,500	28
3,883	30
3,823	32
3,646	34
3,708	36
3,333	38
3,517	40
3,241	42
3,103	44
2,776	46

a. Construct a scatter plot of the yield (kg/ha) of paddy as a function of the number of days after flowering at which harvesting took place. Display at least two models that would explain the relationship you see in the scatter plot.

b. Conduct tests of hypotheses to determine if the models you selected are useful in predicting the yield of paddy.

c. Consider the model that includes the second-order term x^2. Would a simple linear regression model be preferable to the model containing the second-order term? Conduct a hypothesis test using the p-value approach to arrive at your answer.

d. Which model should Charles use to predict the yield of paddy? Explain your answer.

15-33. The National Association of Realtors Existing-Home Sales Series provides a measurement of the residential real estate market. One of the measurements it produces is the Housing Affordability Index (HAI). It is a measure of the financial ability of U.S. families to buy a house: 100 means that families earning the national median income have just the amount of money needed to qualify for a mortgage on a median-priced home; higher than 100 means they have more than enough, and lower than 100 means they have less than enough. The file titled **Index** contains the HAI and associated variables.

a. Construct a scatter plot relating the HAI to the median family income.

b. Determine the order of the polynomial that is suggested by the scatter plot produced in part a. Obtain the estimated regression equation of the polynomial selected.

c. Determine if monthly principal and interest interact with the relationship between the HAI and the median family income indicated in part b. (*Hint*: You may need to conduct more than one hypothesis test.) Use a significance level of 0.05 and the p-value approach.

15-34. Badeaux Brothers Louisiana Treats ships packages of Louisiana coffee, cakes, and Cajun spices to individual customers around the United States. The cost to ship

these products depends primarily on the weight of the package being shipped. Badeaux charges the customers for shipping and then ships the product itself. As a part of a study of whether it is economically feasible to continue to ship products itself, Badeaux sampled 20 recent shipments to determine what, if any, relationship exists between shipping costs and package weight. These data are in the file called **Badeaux**.

a. Develop a scatter plot of the data with the dependent variable, cost, on the vertical axis and the independent variable, weight, on the horizontal axis. Does there appear to be a relationship between the two variables? Is the relationship linear?

b. Compute the sample correlation coefficient between the two variables. Conduct a test, using a significance level of 0.05, to determine whether the population correlation coefficient is significantly different from zero.

c. Badeaux Brothers has been using a simple linear regression equation to predict the cost of shipping various items. Would you recommend it use a second-order polynomial model instead? Is the second-order polynomial model a significant improvement on the simple linear regression equation?

d. Badeaux Brothers has made a decision to stop shipping products if the shipping charges exceed $100. The company has asked you to determine the maximum weight for future shipments. Do this for both the first- and second-order models you have developed.

15-35. The National Association of Theatre Owners is the largest exhibition trade organization in the world, representing more than 26,000 movie screens in all 50 states and in more than 20 countries worldwide. Its membership includes the largest cinema chains and hundreds of independent theater owners. It publishes statistics concerning the movie sector of the economy. The file titled **Flicks** contains data on total U.S. box office grosses ($billion), total number of admissions (billion), average U.S. ticket price ($), and number of movie screens. One concern is the effect the increasing ticket prices have on the number of individuals who go to the theaters to view movies.

a. Construct a scatter plot depicting the relationship between the total number of admissions and the U.S. ticket price.

b. Determine the order of the polynomial that is suggested by the scatter plot produced in part a. Obtain the estimated regression equation of the polynomial selected.

c. Examine the p-value associated with the F-test for the polynomial you have selected in part a. Relate these results to those of the t-tests for the individual parameters and the adjusted coefficient of determination. To what is this attributed?

d. Conduct t-tests to remove higher order components until no components can be removed.

15-36. The Energy Information Administration (EIA), created by Congress in 1977, is a statistical agency of the U.S. Department of Energy. It provides data, forecasts, and analyses to promote sound policymaking and public understanding regarding energy and its interaction with the economy and the environment. One of the most important areas of analysis is petroleum. The file titled **Crude** contains data for the period 1995 through 2010 concerning the price, supply, and demand for fuel. One concern has been the increase in imported oil into the United States.

a. Examine the relationship between price of gasoline and the annual amount of imported crude oil. Construct a scatter plot depicting this relationship.

b. Determine the order of the polynomial that would fit the data displayed in part a. Express "Imports" in millions of gallons, i.e., $3,146,454/1,000,000 = 3.146454$. Produce an estimate of this polynomial.

c. Is a linear or quadratic model more appropriate for predicting the price of gasoline using the annual quantity of imported oil? Conduct the appropriate hypothesis test to substantiate your answer.

15-37. The National Association of Realtors Existing-Home Sales Series provides a measurement of the residential real estate market. One of the measurements it produces is the Housing Affordability Index (HAI). It is a measure of the financial ability of U.S. families to buy a house. A value of 100 means that families earning the national median income have just the amount of money needed to qualify for a mortgage on a median-priced home; higher than 100 means they have more than enough and lower than 100 means they have less than enough. The file titled **Index** contains the HAI and associated variables.

a. Construct a second order of the polynomial relating the HAI to the median family income.

b. Conduct a test of hypothesis to determine if this polynomial is useful in predicting the HAI. Use a p-value approach and a significance level of 0.01.

c. Determine if monthly principal and interest interact with the relationship between the HAI and the median family income indicated in part b. Use a significance level of 0.01. *Hint:* You must produce another regression equation with the interaction terms inserted. You must then use the appropriate test to determine if the interaction terms belong in this latter model.

15-38. An investment analyst collected data on 20 randomly chosen companies. The data consisted of the 52-week-high stock prices, PE ratio, and the market value of the company. These data are in the file titled **Investment**. The analyst wishes to produce a regression equation to predict the market value using the 52-week-high stock price and the PE ratio of the company. He creates a complete second-degree polynomial.

a. Construct an estimate of the regression equation using the indicated variables.

b. Determine if any of the quadratic terms are useful in predicting the average market value. Use a p-value approach with a significance level of 0.10.

c. Determine if any of the PE ratio terms are useful in predicting the average market value. Use a test statistic approach with a significance level of 0.05.

END EXERCISES 15-3

Chapter Outcome 8. → # 15.4 Stepwise Regression

One option in regression analysis is to bring all possible independent variables into the model in one step. This is what we have done in the previous sections. We use the term *full regression* to describe this approach. Another method for developing a regression model is called *stepwise regression*. Stepwise regression, as the name implies, develops the least squares regression equation in steps, either through *forward selection, backward elimination,* or *standard stepwise* regression.

Forward Selection

The forward selection procedure begins (Step 1) by selecting a single independent variable from all those available. The independent variable selected at Step 1 is the variable that is most highly correlated with the dependent variable. A *t*-test is used to determine if this variable explains a significant amount of the variation in the dependent variable. At Step 1, if the variable does explain a significant amount of the dependent variable's variation, it is selected to be part of the final model used to predict the dependent variable. If it does not, the process is terminated. If no variables are found to be significant, the researcher will have to search for different independent variables than the ones already tested.

In the next step (Step 2), a second independent variable is selected based on its ability to explain the remaining unexplained variation in the dependent variable. The independent

Coefficient of Partial Determination

The measure of the marginal contribution of each independent variable, given that other independent variables are in the model.

variable selected in the second and each subsequent step is the variable with the highest **coefficient of partial determination**.

Recall that the coefficient of determination (R^2) measures the proportion of variation explained by all of the independent variables in the model. Thus, after the first variable (say, x_1) is selected, R^2 will indicate the percentage of variation explained by this variable. The forward selection routine will then compute all possible two-variable regression models, with x_1 included, and determine the R^2 for each model. The coefficient of partial determination at Step 2 is the proportion of the as yet unexplained variation (after x_1 is in the model) that is explained by the additional variable. The independent variable that adds the most to R^2, given the variable(s) already in the model, is the one selected. Then, a t-test is conducted to determine if the newly added variable is significant. This process continues until either all independent variables have been entered or the remaining independent variables do not add appreciably to R^2. For the forward selection procedure, the model begins with no variables. Variables are entered one at a time, and after a variable is entered, it cannot be removed.

Backward Elimination

Backward elimination is just the reverse of the forward selection procedure. In the backward elimination procedure, all variables are forced into the model to begin the process. Variables are removed one at a time until no more insignificant variables are found. Once a variable has been removed from the model, it cannot be re-entered.

EXAMPLE 15-4   **APPLYING FORWARD SELECTION STEPWISE REGRESSION ANALYSIS**

B. T. Longmont Company The B. T. Longmont Company operates a large retail department store in Macon, Georgia. Like other department stores, Longmont has incurred heavy losses due to shoplifting and employee pilferage. The store's security manager wants to develop a regression model to explain the monthly dollar loss. The following steps can be used when developing a multiple regression model using stepwise regression:

Step 1 **Specify the model by determining the dependent variable and potential independent variables.**

The dependent variable (y) is the monthly dollar losses due to shoplifting and pilferage. The security manager has identified the following potential independent variables:

x_1 = Average monthly temperature (degrees Fahrenheit)
x_2 = Number of sales transactions
x_3 = Dummy variable for holiday month (1 if holiday during month, 0 if not)
x_4 = Number of persons on the store's monthly payroll

The data are contained in the file **Longmont**.

Step 2 **Formulate the regression model.**

The correlation matrix for the data is presented in Figure 15.26. The forward selection procedure will select the independent variable most highly correlated with the dependent variable. By examining the bottom row in the correlation matrix in Figure 15.26, you can see the variable x_2, number of sales transactions, is most highly correlated ($r = 0.6307$) with dollars lost. Once this variable is entered into the model, the remaining independent variables will be entered based on their ability to explain the remaining variation in the dependent variable.

Figure 15.27 shows the PHStat stepwise regression output. At Step 1 of the process, variable x_2, Number of Sales Transactions enters the model.

Step 3 **Perform diagnostic checks on the model.**

Although PHStat does not provide R^2 or the standard error of the estimate directly, they can be computed from the output in the ANOVA section of the printout. Recall from Chapter 14 that R^2 is computed as

FIGURE 15.26

Excel 2010 Correlation Matrix Output for the B.T. Longmont Company

Excel 2010 Instructions:
1. Open file: **Longmont.xlsx**.
2. Select **Data**.
3. Select **Data Analysis >**
   Correlation.
4. Specify data range
   (include labels).
5. Click **Labels**.
6. Specify output location.
7. Click **OK**.

	A	B	C	D	E	F
1		Average Temperature	Number of Sales Transactions	Holiday	Employees	Shoplifting Loss
2	Average Temperature	1				
3	Number of Sales Transactions	-0.0241	1			
4	Holiday	-0.1432	0.0626	1		
5	Employees	-0.0821	0.9185	-0.1966	1	
6	Shoplifting Loss	0.2858	0.6307	0.1361	0.4132	1
7						

$$R^2 = \frac{SSR}{SST} = \frac{1,270,172.193}{3,192,631.529} = 0.398$$

This single independent variable explains 39.8% ($R^2 = 0.398$) of the variation in the dependent variable. The standard error of the estimate is the square root of the mean square residual:

$$s_\varepsilon = \sqrt{MSE} = \sqrt{MS \text{ residual}} = \sqrt{128,163.96} = 358$$

Now at Step 1, we test the following:

$$H_0: \beta_2 = 0 \text{ (slope for variable } x_2 = 0)$$
$$H_A: \beta_2 \neq 0$$
$$\alpha = 0.05$$

FIGURE 15.27

Excel 2010 (PHStat) Forward Selection Results for the B.T. Longmont Company—Step 1

Excel 2010 Instructions:
1. Select **Add-Ins**.
2. Select **PHStat**.
3. Open file:
   Longmont.xlsx.
4. Select **Regression >**
   Stepwise Regression.
5. Define data range for *y*
   variable (dollar losses)
   and data range for *x*
   variable.
6. Check *p*-**value** criteria.
7. Select **Forward**
   Selection.
8. Click **OK**.

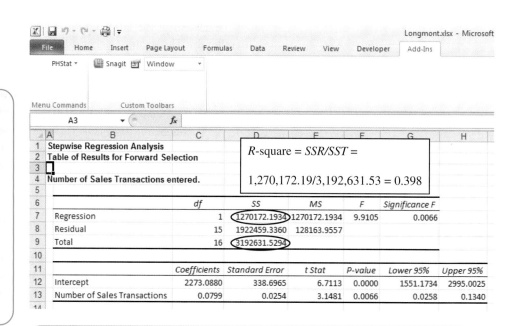

	A	B	C	D	E	F	G	H
1	Stepwise Regression Analysis							
2	Table of Results for Forward Selection			*R*-square = SSR/SST =				
3								
4	Number of Sales Transactions entered.			1,270,172.19/3,192,631.53 = 0.398				
5								
6			df	SS	MS	F	Significance F	
7	Regression		1	1270172.1934	1270172.1934	9.9105	0.0066	
8	Residual		15	1922459.3360	128163.9557			
9	Total		16	3192631.5294				
10								
11			Coefficients	Standard Error	t Stat	P-value	Lower 95%	Upper 95%
12	Intercept		2273.0880	338.6965	6.7113	0.0000	1551.1734	2995.0025
13	Number of Sales Transactions		0.0799	0.0254	3.1481	0.0066	0.0258	0.1340

Minitab Instructions (for similar results):
1. Open file: **Longmont.MTW**.
2. Choose **Stat > Regression >**
   Stepwise.
3. In **Response**, enter dependent
   variable (*y*).
4. In **Predictors**, enter independent variable (*x*).
5. Select **Methods**.
6. Select **Forward selection**, enter > in **Alpha to**
   enter and *F* in **F to enter**.
7. Click **OK**.

As shown in Figure 15.27, the calculated t-value is 3.1481. We compare this to the critical value from the t-distribution for $\alpha/2 = (0.05/2) = 0.025$ and degrees of freedom equal to

$$n - k - 1 = 17 - 1 - 1 = 15$$

This critical value is

$$t_{0.025} = 2.1315$$

Because

$$t = 3.1481 > 2.1315$$

we reject the null hypothesis and conclude that the regression slope coefficient for the variable, Number of Sales Transactions, is not zero. Note also, because the

$$p\text{-value} = 0.0066 < \alpha = 0.05$$

we would reject the null hypothesis.[8]

Step 4 **Continue to formulate and diagnose the model by adding other independent variables.**

The next variable to be selected will be the one that can do the most to increase R^2. If you were doing this manually, you would try each variable to see which one yields the highest R^2, given that the transactions variable is already in the model. The PHStat add-in for Excel does this automatically. As shown in Figure 15.28, the variable selected in Step 2 of the process is x_4, Employees. Using the ANOVA section, we can determine R^2 and s_ε as before.

$$R^2 = \frac{SSR}{SST} = \frac{1,833,270.524}{3,192,631.529} = 0.5742 \quad \text{and}$$

$$s_\varepsilon = \sqrt{MS \text{ residual}} = \sqrt{97,097.22} = 311.6$$

The model now explains 57.42% of the variation in the dependent variable. The t-values for both slope coefficients exceed $t = 2.145$ (the critical value from the t-distribution table with a one-tailed area equal to 0.025 and $17 - 2 - 1 = 14$ degrees of freedom), so we conclude that both variables are significant in explaining the variation in the dependent variable, shoplifting loss.

The forward selection routine continues to enter variables as long as each additional variable explains a significant amount of the remaining variation in the dependent variable. Note that PHStat allows you to set the significance level in terms of a p-value or in terms of the t statistic. Then, as long as the calculated p-value for an incoming variable is less than your limit, the variable is allowed to enter the model. Likewise, if the calculated t-statistic exceeds your t limit, the variable is allowed to enter.

In this example, with the p-value limit set at 0.05, neither of the two remaining independent variables would explain a significant amount of the remaining variation in the dependent variable. The procedure is, therefore, terminated. The resulting regression equation provided by forward selection is

$$\hat{y} = 4600.8 + 0.203x_2 - 21.57x_4$$

---

[8]Some authors use an F-distribution to perform these tests. This is possible, since squaring a random variable that has a t-distribution produces a random variable that has an F-distribution with one degree of freedom in the numerator and the same number of degrees as the t-distribution in the denominator.

FIGURE 15.28

Excel 2010 (PHStat) Forward Selection Results for the B.T. Longmont Company—Step 2

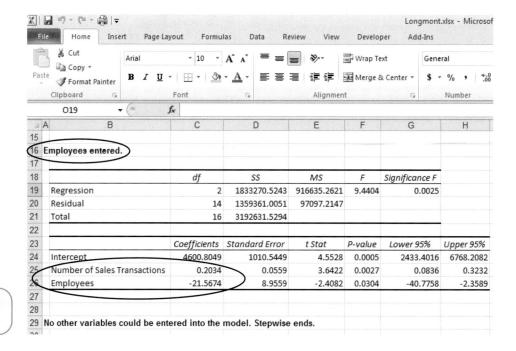

Excel 2010 Instructions:
1. See Figure 15.27.

Note that Average Temperature and the dummy variables for Holiday did not enter the model. This implies that, given the other variables are already included, knowing whether the month in question has a holiday or knowing its average temperature does not add significantly to the model's ability to explain the variation in the dependent variable.

The B.T. Longmont Company can now use this regression model to explain variation in shoplifting and pilferage losses based on knowing the number of sales transactions and the number of employees.

>> **END EXAMPLE**

TRY PROBLEM 15-40 (pg. 662)

Standard Stepwise Regression

The standard stepwise procedure (sometimes referred to as *forward stepwise regression*—not to be confused with forward selection) combines attributes of both backward elimination and forward selection. The standard stepwise method serves one more important function. If two or more independent variables are correlated, a variable selected in an early step may become insignificant when other variables are added at later steps. The standard stepwise procedure will drop this insignificant variable from the model. Standard stepwise regression also offers a means of observing multicollinearity problems, because we can see how the regression model changes as each new variable is added to it.

The standard stepwise procedure is widely used in decision-making applications and is generally recognized as a useful regression method. However, care should be exercised when using this procedure because it is easy to rely too heavily on the automatic selection process. Remember, the order of variable selection is conditional, based on the variables already in the model. There is no guarantee that stepwise regression will lead you to the best set of independent variables from those available. Decision makers still must use common sense in applying regression analysis to make sure they have usable regression models.

Best Subsets Regression

Another method for developing multiple regression models is called the *best subsets* method. As the name implies, the best subsets method works by selecting subsets from the chosen possible independent variables to form models. The user can then select the "best" model based on such measures as *R*-squared or the standard error of the estimate. The PHStat add-in for Excel contains a procedure for performing best subsets regression.

EXAMPLE 15-5	**APPLYING BEST SUBSETS REGRESSION**

Suzanne Tucker/Shutterstock

Winston Investment Advisors Charles L. Winston, founder and CEO at Winston Investment Advisors in Burbank, California, is interested in developing a regression model to explain the variation in dividends paid per share by U.S. companies. Such a model would be useful in advising his clients. The following steps show how to develop such a model using the best subsets regression approach:

Step 1 **Specify the model.**

Some publicly traded companies pay higher dividends than others. The CEO is interested in developing a multiple regression model to explain the variation in dividends per share paid to shareholders. The dependent variable will be dividends per share. The CEO met with other analysts in his firm to identify potential independent variables for which data would be readily available. The following list of potential independent variables was selected:

x_1 = Return on equity (net income/equity)
x_2 = Earnings per share
x_3 = Current assets in millions of dollars
x_4 = Year-ending stock price
x_5 = Current ratio (current assets/current liabilities)

A random sample of 35 publicly traded U.S. companies was selected. For each company in the sample, the analysis obtained data on the dividend per share paid last year and the year-ending data on the five independent variables. These data are contained in the data file **Company Financials**.

Step 2 **Formulate the regression model.**

The CEO is interested in developing the "best" regression model for explaining the variation in the dependent variable, dividends per share. The approach taken is to use best subsets, which requires that multiple regression models be developed, each containing a different mix of variables. The models tried will contain from one to five independent variables. The resulting models will be evaluated by comparing values for *R*-squared and the standard error of the estimate. High *R*-squares and low standard errors are desirable. Another statistic often provided by statistical software is, identified as C_p, and is sometimes used to evaluate regression models. Values of C_p close to $p = k + 1$ (k is the number of independent variables in the model) are preferred.

The PHStat Excel add-in can be used to perform best subsets regression analysis. Figure 15.29 shows output. Notice that all possible combinations of models with $k = 1$ to $k = 5$ independent variables are included. Several models appear to be good candidates based on

FIGURE 15.29

Excel 2010 (PHStat) Best Subsets Regression Output for Winston Investment Advisors

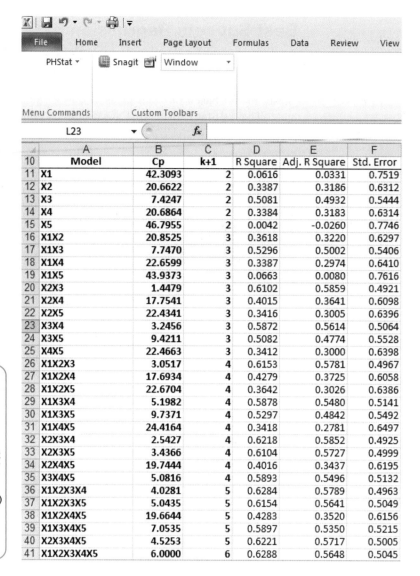

Excel 2010 Instructions:
1. Select **Add-Ins**.
2. Select **PHStat**.
3. Open file: **Company Financials.xlsx**.
4. Select **Regression > Best Subsets Regression**.
5. Define data range for y variable (dividends/share) and data range for x variables.
6. Click **OK**.

R-squared, adjusted R-squared, standard error of the estimate, and C_p values. These are as follows:

Model	C_p	$k + 1$	R-square	Adj. R-square	Std. Error
$x_1 x_2 x_3 x_4$	4.0	5	0.628	0.579	0.496
$x_1 x_2 x_3 x_4 x_5$	6.0	6	0.629	0.565	0.505
$x_1 x_2 x_3 x_5$	5.0	5	0.615	0.564	0.505
$x_2 x_3$	1.4	3	0.610	0.586	0.492
$x_2 x_3 x_4$	2.5	4	0.622	0.585	0.493
$x_2 x_3 x_4 x_5$	4.5	5	0.622	0.572	0.500
$x_2 x_3 x_5$	3.4	4	0.610	0.573	0.500

There is little difference in these seven models in terms of the statistics shown. We can examine any of them in more detail by looking at further PHStat output. For instance, the model containing variables x_1, x_2, x_3, and x_5 is shown in Figure 15.30. Note that although this model is among the best with respect to R-squared, adjusted R-squared, standard error of the estimate, and C_p value, two of the four variables ($x_1 =$ ROE and $x_5 =$ Current ratio) have statistically insignificant regression coefficients. Figure 15.31 shows the regression model with the two statistically significant variables remaining. The R-squared value is 0.61, the adjusted R^2 has increased, and the overall model is statistically significant.

FIGURE 15.30 |

Excel 2010 (PHStat) One
Potential Model for Winston
Investment Advisors

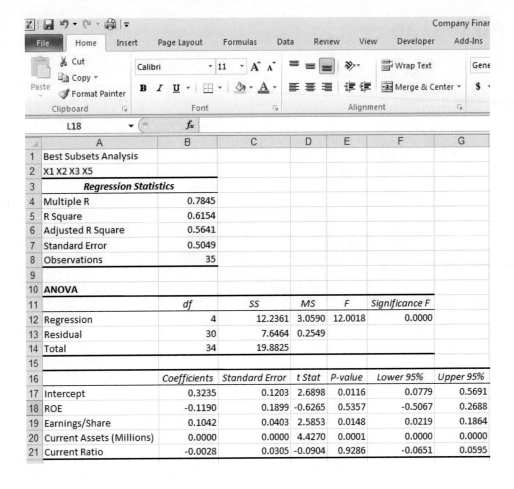

	A	B	C	D	E	F	G
1	Best Subsets Analysis						
2	X1 X2 X3 X5						
3	*Regression Statistics*						
4	Multiple R	0.7845					
5	R Square	0.6154					
6	Adjusted R Square	0.5641					
7	Standard Error	0.5049					
8	Observations	35					
9							
10	**ANOVA**						
11		*df*	*SS*	*MS*	*F*	*Significance F*	
12	Regression	4	12.2361	3.0590	12.0018	0.0000	
13	Residual	30	7.6464	0.2549			
14	Total	34	19.8825				
15							
16		*Coefficients*	*Standard Error*	*t Stat*	*P-value*	*Lower 95%*	*Upper 95%*
17	Intercept	0.3235	0.1203	2.6898	0.0116	0.0779	0.5691
18	ROE	-0.1190	0.1899	-0.6265	0.5357	-0.5067	0.2688
19	Earnings/Share	0.1042	0.0403	2.5853	0.0148	0.0219	0.1864
20	Current Assets (Millions)	0.0000	0.0000	4.4270	0.0001	0.0000	0.0000
21	Current Ratio	-0.0028	0.0305	-0.0904	0.9286	-0.0651	0.0595

FIGURE 15.31 |

Excel 2010 (PHStat) A Final
Model for Winston Investment
Advisors

	A	B	C	D	E	F	G
1	Best Subsets Analysis						
2	X2 X3						
3	*Regression Statistics*						
4	Multiple R	0.7812					
5	R Square	0.6102					
6	Adjusted R Square	0.5859					
7	Standard Error	0.4921					
8	Observations	35					
9							
10	**ANOVA**						
11		*df*	*SS*	*MS*	*F*	*Significance F*	
12	Regression	2	12.1332	6.0666	25.0512	0.0000	
13	Residual	32	7.7493	0.2422			
14	Total	34	19.8825				
15							
16		*Coefficients*	*Standard Error*	*t Stat*	*P-value*	*Lower 95%*	*Upper 95%*
17	Intercept	0.3385	0.0941	3.5960	0.0011	0.1468	0.5302
18	Earnings/Share	0.0882	0.0305	2.8954	0.0068	0.0261	0.1502
19	Current Assets (Millions)	0.000003	0.000001	4.7218	0.0000	0.0000	0.0000

>> **END EXAMPLE**

TRY PROBLEM 15-43 (pg. 662)

MyStatLab

15-4: Exercises

Skill Development

15-39. Suppose you have four potential independent variables, x_1, x_2, x_3, and x_4, from which you want to develop a multiple regression model. Using stepwise regression, x_2 and x_4 entered the model.
   a. Why did only two variables enter the model? Discuss.
   b. Suppose a full regression with only variables x_2 and x_4 had been run. Would the resulting model be different from the stepwise model that included only these two variables? Discuss.
   c. Now, suppose a full regression model had been developed, with all four independent variables in the model. Which would have the higher R^2 value, the full regression model or the stepwise model? Discuss.

15-40. You are given the following set of data:

y	x_1	x_2	x_3	y	x_1	x_2	x_3
33	9	192	40	45	12	296	52
44	11	397	47	25	9	235	27
34	10	235	37	53	10	295	57
60	13	345	61	45	13	335	50
20	11	245	23	37	11	243	41
30	7	235	35	44	13	413	51

   a. Determine the appropriate correlation matrix and use it to predict which variable will enter in the first step of a stepwise regression model.
   b. Use standard stepwise regression to construct a model, entering all significant variables.
   c. Construct a full regression model. What are the differences in the model? Which model explains the most variation in the dependent variable?

15-41. You are given the following set of data:

y	x_1	x_2	x_3	y	x_1	x_2	x_3
45	40	41	39	45	42	39	37
41	31	41	35	43	37	52	41
43	45	49	39	34	40	47	40
38	43	41	41	49	35	44	44
50	42	42	51	45	39	40	45
39	48	40	42	40	43	30	42
50	44	44	41	43	53	34	34

   a. Determine the appropriate correlation matrix and use it to predict which variable will enter in the first step of a stepwise regression model.
   b. Use standard stepwise regression to construct a model, entering all significant variables.
   c. Construct a full regression model. What are the differences in the model? Which model explains the most variation in the dependent variable?

15-42. The following data represent a dependent variable and four independent variables:

y	x_1	x_2	x_3	x_4	y	x_1	x_2	x_3	x_4
61	37	13	10	21	68	35	17	3	33
69	35	19	9	23	48	12	8	8	30
37	25	7	11	32	65	37	11	17	19
24	23	14	7	31	66	34	15	2	33
22	23	6	7	18	45	30	9	24	31

   a. Use the standard stepwise regression to produce an estimate of a multiple regression model to predict y. Use 0.15 as the alpha to enter and to remove.
   b. Change the alpha to enter to 0.01. Repeat the standard stepwise procedure.
   c. Change the alpha to remove to 0.35, leaving alpha to enter to be 0.15. Repeat the standard stepwise procedure.
   d. Change the alpha to remove to 0.15, leaving alpha to enter to be 0.05. Repeat the standard stepwise procedure.
   e. Change the alpha to remove and to enter to 0.35. Repeat the standard stepwise procedure.
   f. Compare the estimated regression equations developed in parts a–e.

15-43. Consider the following set of data:

y	x_1	x_2	x_3	x_4	y	x_1	x_2	x_3	x_4
61	37	18	2	13	69	35	21	2	20
37	25	5	4	10	24	23	7	6	9
22	23	12	7	4	68	35	15	3	14
48	12	6	2	15	65	37	19	2	19
66	34	14	3	25	45	30	12	3	12

   a. Use standard stepwise regression to produce an estimate of a multiple regression model to predict y.
   b. Use forward selection stepwise regression to produce an estimate of a multiple regression model to predict y.
   c. Use backwards elimination stepwise regression to produce an estimate of a multiple regression model to predict y.
   d. Use best subsets regression to produce an estimate of a multiple regression model to predict y.

Computer Database Exercises

15-44. The U.S. Energy Information Administration publishes summary statistics concerning the energy sector of the U.S. economy. The electric power industry continues to grow. Electricity generation and sales rose to record levels. The file titled **Energy** presents the revenue from retail sales ($million) and the net generation by energy source for a recent 12-year period.

   a. Produce the correlation matrix of all the variables. Predict the variables that will remain in the estimated regression equation if standard stepwise regression is used to predict the revenues from retail sales of energy.

   b. Use standard stepwise regression to develop an estimate of a model that is to predict the revenue from retail sales of energy ($million).

   c. Compare the results of parts a and b. Explain any difference between the two models.

15-45. The Western State Tourist Association gives out pamphlets, maps, and other tourist-related information to people who call a toll-free number and request the information. The association orders the packets of information from a document-printing company and likes to have enough available to meet the immediate need without having too many sitting around taking up space. The marketing manager decided to develop a multiple regression model to be used in predicting the number of calls that will be received in the coming week. A random sample of 12 weeks is selected, with the following variables:

y = Number of calls
x_1 = Number of advertisements placed the previous week
x_2 = Number of calls received the previous week
x_3 = Number of airline tour bookings into Western cities for the current week

These data are in the data file called **Western States**.

   a. Develop the multiple regression model for predicting the number of calls received, using backward elimination stepwise regression.

   b. At the final step of the analysis, how many variables are in the model?

   c. Discuss why the variables were removed from the model in the order shown by the stepwise regression.

15-46. Refer to Problem 15-45.

   a. Develop the correlation matrix that includes all independent variables and the dependent variable. Predict the order that the variables will be selected into the model if forward selection stepwise regression is used.

   b. Use forward selection stepwise regression to develop a model for predicting the number of calls that the company will receive. Write a report that describes what has taken place at each step of the regression process.

   c. Compare the forward selection stepwise regression results in part b with the backward elimination results determined in Problem 15-45. Which model would you choose? Explain your answer.

15-47. An investment analyst collected data of 20 randomly chosen companies. The data consisted of the 52-week-high stock prices, PE ratios, and the market values of the companies. These data are in the file titled **Investment**. The analyst wishes to produce a regression equation to predict the market value using the 52-week-high stock price and the PE ratio of the company. He creates a complete second-degree polynomial.

   a. Produce two scatter plots: (1) market value versus stock price and (2) market value versus PE ratio. Do the scatter plots support the analyst's decision to produce a second-order polynomial? Support your assertion with statistical reasoning.

   b. Use forward selection stepwise regression to eliminate any unneeded components from the analyst's model.

   c. Does forward selection stepwise regression support the analyst's decision to produce a second-order polynomial? Support your assertion with statistical reasoning.

15-48. A variety of sources suggest that individuals assess their health, at least in part, by estimating their percentage of body fat. A widely accepted measure of body fat uses an underwater weighing technique. There are, however, more convenient methods using only a scale and a measuring tape. An article in the *Journal of Statistics Education* by Roger W. Johnson explored regression models to predict body fat. The file titled **Bodyfat** lists a portion of the data presented in the cited article.

   a. Use best subsets stepwise regression to establish the relationship between body fat and the variables in the specified file.

   b. Predict the body fat of an individual whose age is 21, weight is 170 pounds, height is 70 inches, chest circumference is 100 centimeters, abdomen is 90 centimeters, hip is 105 centimeters, and thigh is 60 centimeters around.

15-49. The consumer price index (CPI) is a measure of the average change in prices over time in a fixed market basket of goods and services typically purchased by consumers. One of the items in this market basket that affects the CPI is the price of oil and its derivatives. Of course, prices are affected by inflation, and so the file titled **Consumer** contains the price of the derivatives of oil and the CPI adjusted to 2005 levels for a recent 15-month period.

   a. Use backward elimination stepwise regression to determine which combination of the oil derivative prices drive the CPI. If you encounter difficulties in completing this task, explain what caused the difficulties.

   b. Eliminate the source of the difficulties in part a by producing a correlation matrix to determine where the difficulty lies.

   c. Delete one of the variables indicated in part b and complete the instructions in part a.

Chapter Outcome 9. → # 15.5 Determining the Aptness of the Model

In Section 15.1, we discussed the basic steps involved in building a multiple regression model. These are as follows:

1. Specify the model.
2. Build the model.
3. Perform diagnostic checks on the model.

The final step is the diagnostic step in which you examine the model to determine how well it performs. In Section 15.2, we discussed several statistics that you need to consider when performing the diagnostic step, including analyzing R^2, adjusted R^2, and the standard error of the estimate. In addition, we discussed the concept of multicollinearity and the impacts that can occur when multicollinearity is present. Section 15.3 introduced another diagnostic step that involves looking for potential curvilinear relationships between the independent variables and the dependent variable. We presented some basic data transformation techniques for dealing with curvilinear situations. However, a major part of the diagnostic process involves an analysis of how well the model fits the regression analysis assumptions.

The assumptions required to use multiple regression include the following:

Assumptions

1. Individual model errors, ε, are statistically independent of one another, and these values represent a random sample from the population of possible residuals at each level of x.
2. For a given value of x, there can exist many values of y, and therefore many possible values for ε. Further, the distribution of possible ε-values for any level of x is normally distributed.
3. The distributions of possible ε-values have equal variances at each level of x.
4. The means of the dependent variable, y, for all specified values of x can be connected with a line called the population regression model.

The degree to which a regression model satisfies these assumptions is called *aptness*.

Analysis of Residuals

Residual

The difference between the actual value of the dependent variable and the value predicted by the regression model.

The **residual** is computed using Equation 15.13.

Residual

$$e_i = y_i - \hat{y}_i \tag{15.13}$$

A residual value can be computed for each observation in the data set. A great deal can be learned about the aptness of the regression model by analyzing the residuals. The principal means of residual analysis is a study of residual plots. The following problems can be inferred through graphical analysis of residuals:

1. The regression function is not linear.
2. The residuals do not have a constant variance.
3. The residuals are not independent.
4. The residual terms are not normally distributed.

We will address each of these in order. The regression options in Excel provide extensive residual analysis.

Checking for Linearity A plot of the residuals (on the vertical axis) against the independent variable (on the horizontal axis) is useful for detecting whether a linear function is the appropriate regression function. Figure 15.32 illustrates two different residual plots. Figure 15.32a shows residuals that systematically depart from 0. When x is small, the residuals are negative.

FIGURE 15.32

Residual Plots Showing Linear and Nonlinear Patterns

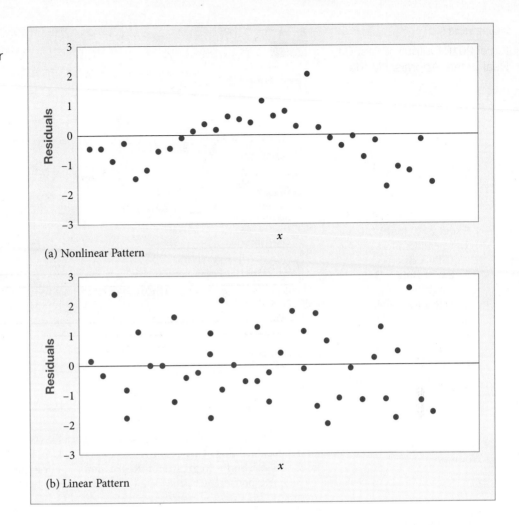

(a) Nonlinear Pattern

(b) Linear Pattern

When x is in the midrange, the residuals are positive, and for large x-values, the residuals are negative again. This type of plot suggests that the relationship between y and x is nonlinear. Figure 15.32b shows a plot in which residuals do not show a systematic variation around 0, implying that the relationship between x and y is linear.

If a linear model is appropriate, we expect the residuals to band around 0 with no systematic pattern displayed. If the residual plot shows a systematic pattern, it may be possible to transform the independent variable (refer to Section 15.3) so that the revised model will produce residual plots that will not systematically vary from 0.

BUSINESS APPLICATION   **RESIDUAL ANALYSIS**

Excel Tutorial

Sai Yeung Chan/Shutterstock

FIRST CITY REAL ESTATE (CONTINUED) We have been using First City Real Estate to introduce multiple regression tools throughout this chapter. Remember, the managers wish to develop a multiple regression model for predicting the sales prices of homes in their market. Suppose that the most current model (**First City-3**) incorporates a transformation of the lot size variable as log of lot size. The output for this model is shown in Figure 15.33. Notice the model now has a R^2 value of 96.9%.

There are currently four independent variables in the model: square feet, bedrooms, garage size, and the log of lot size. Excel provides procedures for automatically producing residual plots. Figure 15.34 shows the plots of the residuals against each of the independent variables. The transformed variable, log lot size, has a residual pattern that shows a systematic pattern (Figure 15.34d). The residuals are positive for small values of log lot size, negative for intermediate values of log lot size, and positive again for large values of log lot size. This pattern suggests that the curvature of the relationship between sales prices of homes and lot size is even more pronounced than the logarithm implies. Potentially, a second- or third-degree polynomial in the lot size should be pursued.

FIGURE 15.33

Excel 2010 Output of First City Real Estate Appraisal Model

Excel 2010 Instructions:
1. Open file: **First City-3.xlsx**.
2. Select **Data > Data Analysis**.
3. Select **Regression**.
4. Define *y* variable range (Price) and the *x* variable range.
5. Click **Labels**.
6. Specify output location.
7. Click **OK**.

	A	B	C	D	E	F	G
1	SUMMARY OUTPUT						
2							
3	*Regression Statistics*						
4	Multiple R	0.984					
5	R Square	0.969					
6	Adjusted R Square	0.968					
7	Standard Error	11249.939					
8	Observations	319					
9							
10	ANOVA						
11		*df*	*SS*	*MS*	*F*	*Significance F*	
12	Regression	4	1,233,292,449,609.030	308,323,112,402.257	2436.160	0.000	
13	Residual	314	39,740,194,152.727	126,561,127.875			
14	Total	318	1,273,032,643,761.750				
15							
16		*Coefficients*	*Standard Error*	*t Stat*	*P-value*	*Lower 95%*	*Upper 95%*
17	Intercept	-521919.558	10797.808	-48.336	0.000	-543164.759	-500674.357
18	Sq. Feet	17.858	1.682	10.617	0.000	14.548	21.167
19	Bedrooms	-2319.027	1173.993	-1.975	0.049	-4628.915	-9.140
20	Garage #	6012.740	1299.306	4.628	0.000	3456.294	8569.187
21	log Lot Size	159050.177	3286.101	48.401	0.000	152584.618	165515.737

Minitab Instructions (for similar results):
1. Open file: **First City-3.MTW**.
2. Choose **Stat > Regression > Regression**.
3. In **Response**, enter dependent (*y*) variable.
4. In **Predictors**, enter independent (*x*) variables.
5. Click **OK**.

FIGURE 15.34

First City Real Estate Residual Plots versus the Independent Variables

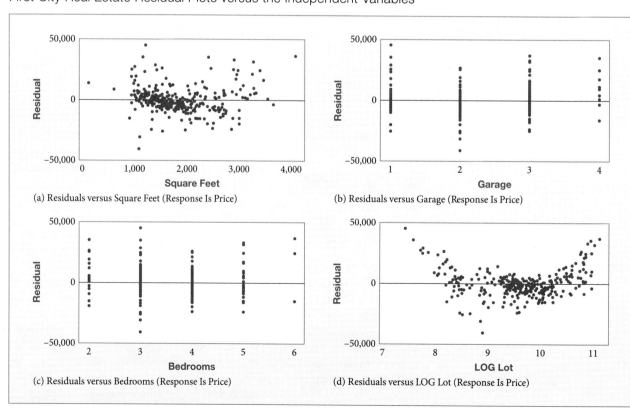

(a) Residuals versus Square Feet (Response Is Price)

(b) Residuals versus Garage (Response Is Price)

(c) Residuals versus Bedrooms (Response Is Price)

(d) Residuals versus LOG Lot (Response Is Price)

FIGURE 15.35

Residual Plots Showing
Constant and Nonconstant
Variances

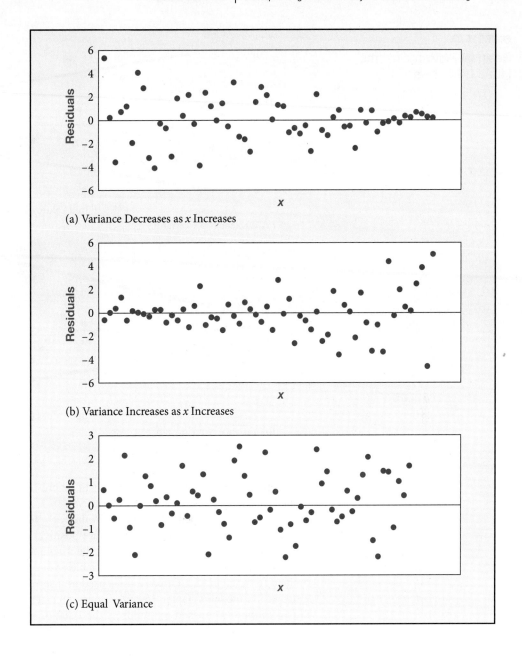

(a) Variance Decreases as x Increases

(b) Variance Increases as x Increases

(c) Equal Variance

Do the Residuals Have Equal Variances at all Levels of Each x Variable? Residual plots also can be used to determine whether the residuals have a constant variance. Consider Figure 15.35, in which the residuals are plotted against an independent variable. The plot in Figure 15.35a shows an example in which as x increases, the residuals become less variable. Figure 15.35b shows the opposite situation. When x is small, the residuals are tightly packed around 0, but as x increases, the residuals become more variable. Figure 15.35c shows an example in which the residuals exhibit a constant variance around the zero mean.

When a multiple regression model has been developed, we can analyze the equal variance assumption by plotting the residuals against the fitted $(\hat{y})$ values. When the residual plot is cone-shaped, as in Figure 15.36, it suggests that the assumption of equal variance has been violated. This is evident because the residuals are wider on one end than the other. That indicates that the standard error of the estimate is larger on one end than the other—that is, it is not constant.

Figure 15.37 shows the residuals plotted against the $\hat{y}$-values for First City Real Estate's appraisal model. We have drawn a band around the residuals that shows that the variance of the residuals stays quite constant over the range of the fitted values.

Are the Residuals Independent? If the data used to develop the regression model are measured over time, a plot of the residuals against time is used to determine whether the residuals are correlated. Figure 15.38a shows an example in which the residual plot against

FIGURE 15.36

Residual Plots against the Fitted ($\hat{y}$) Values

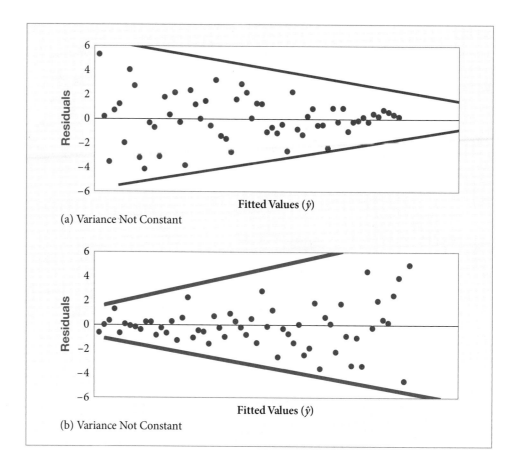

(a) Variance Not Constant

(b) Variance Not Constant

time suggests independence. The residuals in Figure 15.38a appear to be randomly distributed around the mean of zero over time. However, in Figure 15.38b, the plot suggests that the residuals are not independent, because in the early time periods, the residuals are negative, and in later time periods, the residuals are positive. This, or any other nonrandom pattern in the residuals over time, indicates that the assumption of independent residuals has been violated. Generally, this means some variable associated with the passage of time has been omitted from the model. Often, time is used as a surrogate for other time-related variables in a regression model. Chapter 16 will discuss time-series data analysis and forecasting techniques in more detail and will address the issue of incorporating the time variable into the model. In Chapter 16, we introduce a procedure called the Durbin-Watson test to determine whether residuals are correlated over time.

Checking for Normally Distributed Error Terms The need for normally distributed model errors occurs when we want to test a hypothesis about the regression model. Small departures from normality do not cause serious problems. However, if the model errors depart dramatically from a normal distribution, there is cause for concern. Examining the sample residuals will allow us to detect such dramatic departures. One method for graphically analyzing the residuals is to form a frequency histogram of the residuals to determine whether the general shape is normal. The chi-square goodness-of-fit test presented in Chapter 13 can be used to test whether the residuals fit a normal distribution.

Another method for determining normality is to calculate and plot the *standardized residuals*. In Chapter 3, you learned that a random variable is standardized by subtracting its mean and dividing the result by its standard deviation. The mean of the residuals is zero. Therefore, dividing each residual by an estimate of its standard deviation gives the standardized residual.[9] Although the proof is beyond the scope of this text, it can be shown that the standardized residual for any particular observation for a simple linear regression model is found using Equation 15.14.

---

[9]The standardized residual is also referred to as the *studentized residual*.

FIGURE 15.37

Excel 2010 Plot of Residuals versus Fitted Values for First City Real Estate

Excel 2010 Instructions:
1. Open file: **First City-3.xlsx**.
2. Follow the instructions from Steps 3–5 on Figure 15.33.
3. Check **Residuals** option.
4. Specify output location.
5. Click **OK**.
6. Insert a Scatter Plot of Predicted Price and Residuals columns.
7. Insert Title, x-axis title, and y-axis title.
8. Click on the vertical axis, right mouse click, and select **Format Axis…**
9. Under **Horizontal axis crosses**, set **Axis Value** to −50000.
10. Click **Close**.

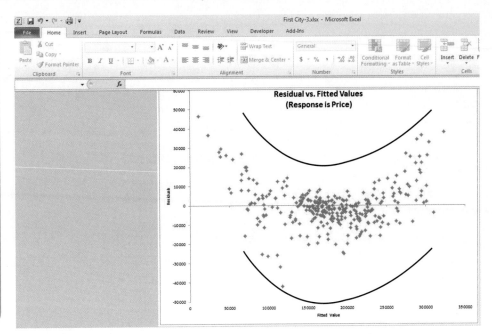

Minitab Instructions (for similar results):
1. Open file: **First City-3.MTW**.
2. Choose **Stat > Regression > Regression**.
3. In **Response**, enter dependent (*y*) variable.
4. In **Predictors**, enter independent (*x*) variables.
5. Choose **Graphs**.
6. Under **Residual Plots**, select **Residuals versus fits**.
7. Click **OK. OK**.

Standardized Residual for Linear Regression

$$s_{e_i} = \frac{e_i}{s_\varepsilon \sqrt{1 + \dfrac{1}{n} + \dfrac{(x_i - \bar{x})^2}{\sum x^2 - \dfrac{(\sum x)^2}{n}}}} \qquad \text{(15.14)}$$

where:

e_i = *i*th residual value

s_ε = Standard error of the estimate

x_i = Value of *x* used to generate the predicted *y*-value for the *i*th observation

---

Computing the standardized residual for an observation in a multiple regression model is too complicated to be done by hand. However, the standardized residuals are generated from most statistical software, including Excel. The Excel tutorial illustrate the methods required to generate the standardized residuals and residual plots. Because other problems such as nonconstant variance and nonindependent residuals can result in residuals that seem to be abnormal, you should check these other factors before addressing the normality assumption.

Recall that for a normal distribution, approximately 68% of the values will fall within ±1 standard deviation of the mean, 95% will fall within ±2 standard deviations of the mean, and virtually all values will fall within ±3 standard deviations of the mean.

Figure 15.39 illustrates the histogram of the residuals for the First City Real Estate example. The distribution of residuals looks to be close to a normal distribution. Figure 15.40 shows the histogram for the standardized residuals, which will have the same basic shape as the residual distribution in Figure 15.39.

FIGURE 15.38

Plot of Residuals against Time

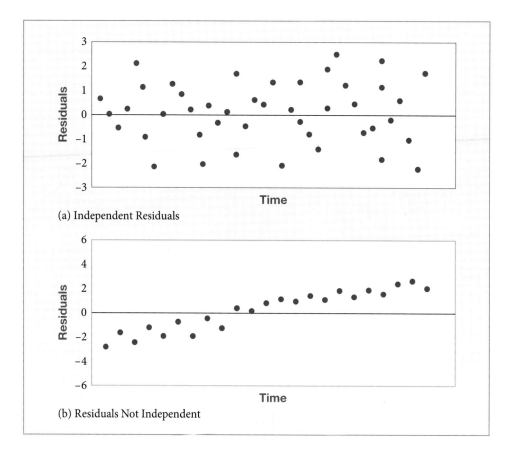

(a) Independent Residuals

(b) Residuals Not Independent

FIGURE 15.39

Excel 2010 Histogram of
Residuals for First City
Real Estate

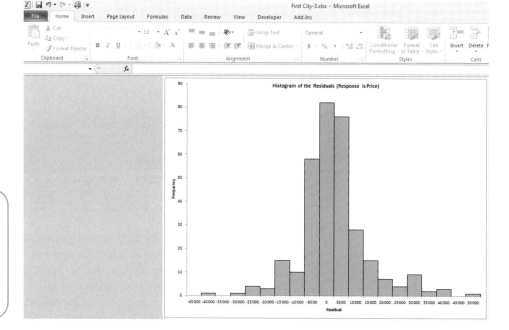

Excel 2010 Instructions:
1. Open file: **First City-3.xlsx**.
2. Follow the instructions from Steps 2–5 on Figure 15.37.
3. Create a Histogram using the Residuals column.
4. Add appropriate titles.

Minitab Instructions (for similar results):
1. Open file: **First City-3.MTW**.
2. Choose **Stat > Regression > Regression**.
3. In **Response**, enter dependent (y) variable.
4. In **Predictors**, enter independent (x) variables.
5. Choose **Graphs**.
6. Under **Residual Plots**, select **Histogram of residuals**.
7. Click **OK. OK.**

FIGURE 15.40

Excel 2010 Histogram of Standardized Residuals for First City Real Estate

Excel 2010 Instructions:
1. Open file: **First City-3.xlsx**.
2. Follow the instructions from Steps 3–5 on Figure 15.33.
3. Check **Residuals** option.
4. Check **Standardized Residuals** option.
5. Specify output location.
6. Click **OK**.
7. Create a Histogram using the Standardized Residuals column.
8. Add appropriate titles.

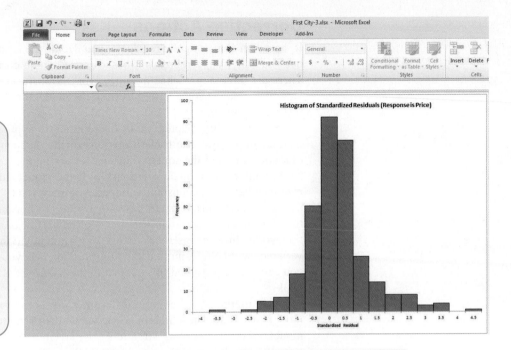

Minitab Instructions (for similar results):
1. Open file: **First City-3.MTW**.
2. Choose **Stat > Regression > Regression**.
3. In **Response**, enter dependent (*y*) variable.
4. In **Predictors**, enter independent (*x*) variables.
5. Choose **Graphs**.
6. Under **Residual for Plots**, select **Standardized**.
7. Under **Residual Plots**, select **Histogram of residuals**.
8. Click **OK. OK**.

Another approach for checking for normality of the residuals is to form a *probability plot*. We start by arranging the residuals in numerical order from smallest to largest. The standardized residuals are plotted on the horizontal axis, and the corresponding expected value for the standardized residual is plotted on the vertical axis. Although we won't delve into how the expected value is computed, you can examine the normal probability plot to see whether the plot forms a straight line. The closer the line is to linear, the closer the residuals are to being normally distributed. Figure 15.41 shows the normal probability plot for the First City Real Estate example.

FIGURE 15.41

Excel 2010 Normal Probability Plot of Residuals for First City Real Estate

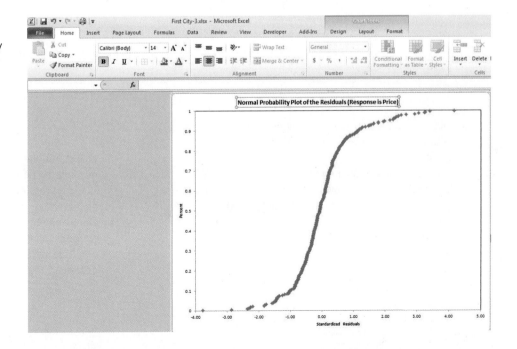

Corrective Actions

If, based on analyzing the residuals, you decide the model constructed is not appropriate, but you still want a regression-based model, some corrective action may be warranted. There are three approaches that may work: Transform some of the existing independent variables, remove some variables from the model, or start over in the development of the regression model.

Earlier in this chapter, we discussed a basic approach involved in variable transformation. In general, the transformations of the independent variables (such as raising x to a power, taking the square root of x, or taking the log of x) are used to make the data better conform to a linear relationship. If the model suffers from nonlinearity and if the residuals have a nonconstant variance, you may want to transform both the independent and dependent variables. In cases in which the normality assumption is not satisfied, transforming the dependent variable is often useful. In many instances, a log transformation works. In some instances, a transformation involving the product of two independent variables will help. A more detailed discussion is beyond the scope of this text. However, you can read more about this subject in the Kutner et al. reference listed at the end of the book.

The alternative of using a different regression model means that we respecify the model to include new independent variables or remove existing variables from the model. In most modeling situations, we are in a continual state of model respecification. We are always seeking to improve the regression model by finding new independent variables.

MyStatLab

15-5: Exercises

Skill Development

15-50. Consider the following values for an independent and dependent variable:

x	y
6	5
9	20
14	28
18	30
22	33
27	35
33	45

a. Determine the estimated linear regression equation relating the dependent and independent variables.
b. Is the regression equation you found significant? Test at the $\alpha = 0.05$ level.
c. Determine both the residuals and standardized residuals. Is there anything about the residuals that would lead you to question whether the assumptions necessary to use regression analysis are satisfied? Discuss.

15-51. Consider the following values for an independent and dependent variable:

x	y
6	5
9	20
14	28
18	15
22	27
27	31
33	32
50	60
61	132
75	160

a. Determine the estimated linear regression equation relating the dependent and independent variables.
b. Is the regression equation you found significant? Test at the $\alpha = 0.05$ level.
c. Determine both the residuals and standardized residuals. Is there anything about the residuals that would lead you to question whether the assumptions necessary to use regression analysis are satisfied?

15-52. Examine the following data set:

y	x
25	10
35	10
14	10
45	20
52	20
41	20
65	30
63	30
68	30

a. Determine the estimated regression equation for this data set.
b. Calculate the residuals for this regression equation.
c. Produce the appropriate residual plot to determine if the linear function is the appropriate regression function for this data set.
d. Use a residual plot to determine if the residuals have a constant variance.
e. Produce a residual plot to determine if the residuals are independent. Assume the order of appearance is the time order of the data.
f. Use a probability plot to determine if the error terms are normally distributed.

15-53. Examine the following data set:

y	x_1	x_2
25	5	25
35	5	5
14	5	5
45	25	40
52	25	5
41	25	25
65	30	30
63	30	30
68	30	25
75	40	30

a. Determine the estimated regression equation for this data set.
b. Calculate the residuals and the standardized residuals for this regression equation.
c. Produce the appropriate residual plot to determine if the linear function is the appropriate regression function for this data set.
d. Use a residual plot to determine if the residuals have a constant variance.
e. Produce the appropriate residual plot to determine if the residuals are independent.
f. Construct a probability plot to determine if the error terms are normally distributed.

Computer Database Exercises

15-54. Refer to Problem 15-9, which referenced an article in *BusinessWeek* that presented a list of the 100 companies perceived as having "hot growth" characteristics. The file titled **Logrowth** contains sales ($million), sales increase (%), return on capital, market value ($million), and recent stock price of the companies ranked from 81 to 100. In Problem 15-9, a regression equation was constructed in which the sales of the companies was predicted using their market value.

a. Determine the estimated regression equation for this data set.
b. Calculate the residuals and the standardized residuals for this regression equation.
c. Produce the appropriate residual plot to determine if the linear function is the appropriate regression function for this data set.
d. Use a residual plot to determine if the residuals have a constant variance.
e. Produce the appropriate residual plot to determine if the residuals are independent. Assume the data were extracted in the order listed.
f. Construct a probability plot to determine if the error terms are normally distributed.

15-55. The White Cover Snowmobile Association promotes snowmobiling in both the Upper Midwest and the Rocky Mountain region. The industry has been affected in the West because of uncertainty associated with conflicting court rulings about the number of snowmobiles allowed in national parks. The Association advertises in outdoor- and tourist-related publications and then sends out pamphlets, maps, and other regional related information to people who call a toll-free number and request the information. The association orders the packets from a document-printing company and likes to have enough available to meet the immediate need without having too many sitting around taking up space. The marketing manager decided to develop a multiple regression model to be used in predicting the number of calls that will be received in the coming week. A random sample of 12 weeks is selected, with the following variables:

y = Number of calls
x_1 = Number of advertisements placed the previous week
x_2 = Number of calls received the previous week
x_3 = Number of airline tour bookings into Western cities for the current week

The data are in the file called **Winter Adventures**.

a. Construct a multiple regression model using all three independent variables. Write a short report discussing the model.
b. Based on the appropriate residual plots, what can you conclude about the constant variance assumption? Discuss.

c. Based on the appropriate residual analysis, does it appear that the residuals are independent? Discuss.

d. Use an appropriate analysis of the residuals to determine whether the regression model meets the assumption of normally distributed error terms. Discuss.

15-56. The athletic director of State University is interested in developing a multiple regression model that might be used to explain the variation in attendance at football games at his school. A sample of 16 games was selected from home games played during the past 10 seasons. Data for the following factors were determined:

y = Game attendance
x_1 = Team win/loss percentage to date
x_2 = Opponent win/loss percentage to date
x_3 = Games played this season
x_4 = Temperature at game time

The sample data are in the file called **Football**.

a. Build a multiple regression model using all four independent variables. Write a short report that outlines the characteristics of this model.

b. Develop a table of residuals for this model. What is the average residual value? Why do you suppose it came out to this value? Discuss.

c. Based on the appropriate residual plot, what can you conclude about the constant variance assumption? Discuss.

d. Based on the appropriate residual analysis, does it appear that the model errors are independent? Discuss.

e. Can you conclude, based on the appropriate method of analysis, that the model error terms are approximately normally distributed?

15-57. The consumer price index (CPI) is a measure of the average change in prices over time in a fixed market basket of goods and services typically purchased by consumers. One of the items in this market basket that affects the CPI is the price of oil and its derivatives. The file titled **Consumer** contains the price of the derivatives of oil and the CPI adjusted to 2005 levels. In Problem 15-49, backward elimination stepwise regression was used to determine the relationship between CPI and two independent variables: the price of heating oil and of diesel fuel.

a. Construct an estimate of the regression equation using the same variables.

b. Produce the appropriate residual plots to determine if the linear function is the appropriate regression function for this data set.

c. Use a residual plot to determine if the residuals have a constant variance.

d. Produce the appropriate residual plot to determine if the residuals are independent. Assume the data were extracted in the order listed.

e. Construct a probability plot to determine if the error terms are normally distributed.

15-58. In Problem 15-48, you were asked to use best subsets stepwise regression to establish the relationship between body fat and the independent variables weight, abdomen circumference, and thigh circumference based on data in the file **Bodyfat**. This is an extension of that exercise.

a. Construct an estimate of the regression equation using the same variables.

b. Produce the appropriate residual plots to determine if the linear function is the appropriate regression function for this data set.

c. Use a residual plot to determine if the residuals have a constant variance.

d. Produce the appropriate residual plot to determine if the residuals are independent. Assume the data were extracted in the order listed.

e. Construct a probability plot to determine if the error terms are normally distributed.

15-59. The National Association of Theatre Owners is the largest exhibition trade organization in the world, representing more than 26,000 movie screens in all 50 states and in more than 20 countries worldwide. Its membership includes the largest cinema chains and hundreds of independent theater owners. It publishes statistics concerning the movie sector of the economy. The file titled **Flicks** contains data on total U.S. box office grosses ($billion), total number of admissions (billion), average U.S. ticket price ($), and number of movie screens.

a. Construct a regression equation in which total U.S. box office grosses are predicted using the other variables.

b. Produce the appropriate residual plots to determine if the linear function is the appropriate regression function for this data set.

c. Square each of the independent variables and add them to the model on which the regression equation in part a was built. Produce the new regression equation.

d. Use a residual plot to determine if the quadratic model in part c alleviates the problem identified in part b.

e. Construct a probability plot to determine if the error terms are normally distributed for the updated model.

Visual Summary

Chapter 15: Chapter 14 introduced linear regression, concentrating on analyzing a linear relationship between two variables. However, business problems are not limited to linear relationships involving only two variables, many situations involve linear and nonlinear relationships among three or more variables. This chapter introduces several extensions of the techniques covered in the last chapter including: multiple linear regression, incorporating qualitative variables in the regression model, working with nonlinear relationships, techniques for determining how "good" the model fits the data, and stepwise regression.

15.1 Introduction to Multiple Regression Analysis (pg. 613–631)

Summary
Multiple linear regression analysis examines the relationship between a dependent and more than one independent variable. Determining the appropriate relationship starts with **model specification**, where the appropriate variables are determined, then moves to **model building**, followed by **model diagnosis**, where the quality of the model built is determined. The purpose of the model is to explain variation in the dependent variable. Useful independent variables are those **highly correlated** with the dependent variable. The percentage of variation in the dependent variable explained by the model is determined by the **coefficient of determination**, R^2. The overall model can be tested for significance as can the individual terms in the model. A common problem in multiple regressions models occurs when the independent variables are highly correlated, this is called **multicollinearity**.

Outcome 1. Understand the general concepts behind model building using multiple regression analysis.
Outcome 2. Apply multiple regression analysis to business decision-making situations.
Outcome 3. Analyze the computer output for a multiple regression model and interpret the regression results.
Outcome 4. Test hypotheses about the significance of a multiple regression model and test the significance of the independent variables in the model.
Outcome 5. Recognize potential problems when using multiple regression analysis and take steps to correct the problems.

15.2 Using Qualitative Independent Variables (pg. 631–638)

Summary
Independent variables are not always quantitative and ratio level. Important independent variables might include determining if someone is married, or not, owns her home, or not, is recently employed and type of car owned. All of these are qualitative, not quantitative, variables and are incorporated into multiple regression analysis using dummy variables. Dummy variables are numerical codes, 0 or 1, depending on whether the observation has the indicated characteristic. Be careful to insure you use one fewer dummy variables than categories to avoid the dummy variable trap.

Outcome 6. Incorporate qualitative variables into a regression model by using dummy variables.

15.3 Working with Nonlinear Relationships (pg. 639–654)

Summary
Sometimes business situations involve a nonlinear relationship between the dependent and independent variables. Regression models with nonlinear relationships become more complicated to build and analyze. Start by plotting the data to see the relationships between the dependent variable and independent variable. Exponential, or second or third-order polynomial relationships are commonly found. Once the appropriate relationship is determined, the independent variable is modified and used in the model.

Outcome 7. Apply regression analysis to situations where the relationship between the independent variable(s) and the dependent variable is nonlinear.

15.4 Stepwise Regression (pg. 654–663)

Summary
Stepwise regression develops the regression equation either through **forward selection**, **backward elimination**, or **standard stepwise regression**. **Forward selection** begins by selecting a single independent variable which is most highly correlated with the dependent variable. Additional variables will be added to the model as long as they reduce a significant amount of the remaining variation in the dependent variable. **Backward elimination** starts with all variables in the model to begin the process. Variables are removed one at a time until no more insignificant variables are found. **Standard stepwise** is similar to forward selection. However, if two or more variables are correlated, a variable selected in an early step may become insignificant when other variables are added at later steps. The standard stepwise procedure will drop this insignificant variable from the model.

Outcome 8. Understand the uses of stepwise regression.

15.5 Determining the Aptness of the Model (pg. 664–674)

Summary
Determining the aptness of a model relies on an analysis of **residuals**, the difference between the observed value of the dependent variable and the value predicted by the model. The residuals should be randomly scattered about the regression line with a normal distribution and constant variance. If a plot of the residuals indicates any of the preceding does not occur, corrective action should be taken which might involve transforming some independent variables, dropping some variables or adding new ones, or even starting over with the model-building process.

Outcome 9. Analyze the extent to which a regression model satisfies the regression assumptions.

Conclusion
Multiple regression uses two or more independent variables to explain the variation in the dependent variable. As a decision maker, you will generally not be required to manually develop the regression model, but you will have to judge its applicability based on a computer printout. Consequently, this chapter has largely involved an analysis of computer printouts. You no doubt will encounter printouts that look somewhat different from those shown in this text and some of the terms used may differ slightly, but Excel is representative of the many software packages that are available.

Equations

(15.1) Population Multiple Regression Model pg. 613

$$y = \beta_0 + \beta_1 x_1 + \beta_2 x_2 + \cdots + \beta_k x_k + \varepsilon$$

(15.2) Estimated Multiple Regression Model pg. 613

$$\hat{y} = b_0 + b_1 x_1 + b_2 x_2 + \cdots + b_k x_k$$

(15.3) Correlation Coefficient pg. 617

$$r = \frac{\Sigma(x - \bar{x})(y - \bar{y})}{\sqrt{\Sigma(x - \bar{x})^2 \Sigma(y - \bar{y})^2}} \quad \text{or} \quad r = \frac{\Sigma(x_i - \bar{x}_i)(x_j - \bar{x}_j)}{\sqrt{\Sigma(x_i - \bar{x}_i)^2 \Sigma(x_j - \bar{x}_j)^2}}$$

One x variable with y One x variable with another x

(15.4) Multiple Coefficient of Determination (R^2) pg. 620

$$R^2 = \frac{\text{Sum of squares regression}}{\text{Total sum of squares}} = \frac{SSR}{SST}$$

(15.5) F-Test Statistic pg. 621

$$F = \frac{\dfrac{SSR}{k}}{\dfrac{SSE}{n-k-1}}$$

(15.6) Adjusted R-Squared pg. 622

$$R\text{-sq(adj)} = R_A^2 = 1 - (1 - R^2)\left(\frac{n-1}{n-k-1}\right)$$

(15.7) t-Test for Significance of Each Regression Coefficient pg. 623

$$t = \frac{b_j - 0}{s_{b_j}} \qquad df = n - k - 1$$

(15.8) Standard Error of the Estimate pg. 624

$$s_\varepsilon = \sqrt{\frac{SSE}{n-k-1}} = \sqrt{MSE}$$

(15.9) Variance Inflation Factor pg. 626

$$VIF = \frac{1}{(1 - R_j^2)}$$

(15.10) Confidence Interval Estimate for the Regression Slope pg. 627

$$b_j \pm t s_{b_j}$$

(15.11) Polynomial Population Regression Model pg. 640

$$y = \beta_0 + \beta_1 x + \beta_2 x^2 + \cdots + \beta_p x^p + \varepsilon$$

(15.12) Partial-F Test Statistic pg. 648

$$F = \frac{(SSE_R - SSE_C)/(c - r)}{MSE_C}$$

(15.13) Residual pg. 664

$$e_i = y_i - \hat{y}_i$$

(15.14) Standardized Residual for Linear Regression pg. 669

$$s_{e_i} = \frac{e_i}{s_\varepsilon \sqrt{1 + \dfrac{1}{n} + \dfrac{(x_i - \bar{x})^2}{\Sigma x^2 - \dfrac{(\Sigma x)^2}{n}}}}$$

Key Terms

Adjusted R-squared pg. 622
Coefficient of partial determination pg. 655
Composite model pg. 645
Correlation coefficient pg. 617
Correlation matrix pg. 617
Dummy variable pg. 631

Interaction pg. 645
Model pg. 615
Multicollinearity pg. 625
Multiple coefficient of determination (R²) pg. 620

Regression hyperplane pg. 614
Residual pg. 664
Variance inflation factor (**VIF**) pg. 626

Chapter Exercises

MyStatLab

Conceptual Questions

15-60. Go to the library or use the Internet to locate three articles using a regression model with more than one independent variable. For each article, write a short summary covering the following points:

Purpose for using the model
How the variables in the model were selected
How the data in the model were selected

Any possible violations of the needed assumptions
The conclusions drawn from using the model

15-61. Discuss in your own terms the similarities and differences between simple linear regression analysis and multiple regression analysis.

15-62. Discuss what is meant by the least squares criterion as it pertains to multiple regression analysis. Is the least squares criterion any different for simple regression analysis? Discuss.

15-63. List the basic assumptions of regression analysis and discuss in your own terms what each means.

15-64. What does it mean if we have developed a multiple regression model and have concluded that the model is apt?

15-65. Consider the following model:

$$\hat{y} = 5 + 3x_1 + 5x_2$$

a. Provide an interpretation of the coefficient of x_1.

b. Is the interpretation provided in part a true regardless of the value of x_2? Explain.

c. Now consider the model $\hat{y} = 5 + 3x_1 + 5x_2 + 4x_1x_2$. Let $x_2 = 1$.
Give an interpretation of the coefficient of x_1 when $x_2 = 1$.

d. Repeat part c when $x_2 = 2$. Is the interpretation provided in part a true regardless of the value of x_2? Explain.

e. Considering your answers to parts c and d, what type of regression components has conditional interpretations?

Computer Database Exercises

15-66. Amazon.com has become one of the most successful online merchants. Two measures of its success are sales and net income/loss figures. The data can be found in the file **Amazon.**

a. Produce a scatter plot for Amazon's net income/ loss and sales figures for the period 1995 to 2011. Determine the order (or degree) of the polynomial that could be used to predict Amazon's net income/ loss using sales figures for the period 1995 to 2011.

b. To simplify the analysis, consider only the values from 1995–2004. Produce the polynomial indicated by this data.

c. Test to determine whether the overall model from part b is statistically significant. Use a significance level of 0.10.

d. Conduct a hypothesis test to determine if curvature exists in the model that predicts Amazon's net income/ loss using sales figures from part b. Use a significance level of 0.02 and the test statistic approach.

The following information applies to Problems 15-67, 15-68, and 15-69.
A publishing company in New York is attempting to develop a model that it can use to help predict textbook sales for books it is considering for future publication. The marketing department has collected data on several variables from a random sample of 15 books. These data are given in the file **Textbooks.**

15-67. Develop the correlation matrix showing the correlation between all possible pairs of variables. Test statistically to determine which independent variables are significantly correlated with the dependent variable, book sales. Use a significance level of 0.05.

15-68. Develop a multiple regression model containing all four independent variables. Show clearly the regression

coefficients. Write a short report discussing the model. In your report make sure you cover the following issues:

a. How much of the total variation in book sales can be explained by these four independent variables? Would you conclude that the model is significant at the 0.05 level?

b. Develop a 95% confidence interval for each regression coefficient and interpret these confidence intervals.

c. Which of the independent variables can you conclude to be significant in explaining the variation in book sales? Test using $\alpha = 0.05$.

d. How much of the variation in the dependent variable is explained by the independent variables? Is the model statistically significant at the $\alpha = 0.01$ level? Discuss.

e. How much, if at all, does adding one more page to the book impact the sales volume of the book? Develop and interpret a 95% confidence interval estimate to answer this question.

f. Perform the appropriate analysis to determine the aptness of this regression model. Discuss your results and conclusions.

15-69. The publishing company recently came up with some additional data for the 15 books in the original sample. Two new variables, production expenditures (x_5) and number of prepublication reviewers (x_6), have been added. These additional data are as follows:

Book	$x_5(\$)$	x_6
1	38,000	5
2	86,000	8
3	59,000	3
4	80,000	9
5	29,500	3
6	31,000	3
7	40,000	5
8	69,000	4
9	51,000	4
10	34,000	6
11	20,000	2
12	80,000	5
13	60,000	5
14	87,000	8
15	29,000	3

Incorporating these additional data, calculate the correlation between each of these additional variables and the dependent variable, book sales.

a. Test the significance of the correlation coefficients, using $\alpha = 0.05$. Comment on your results.

b. Develop a multiple regression model that includes all six independent variables. Which, if any, variables would you recommend be retained if this model is going to be used to predict book sales for the publishing company? For any statistical tests you might perform, use a significance level of 0.05. Discuss your results.

c. Use the F-test approach to test the null hypothesis that all slope coefficients are 0. Test with a significance level of 0.05. What do these results mean? Discuss.

d. Do multicollinearity problems appear to be present in the model? Discuss the potential consequences of multicollinearity with respect to the regression model.

e. Discuss whether the standard error of the estimate is small enough to make this model useful for predicting the sales of textbooks.

f. Plot the residuals against the predicted value of y and comment on what this plot means relative to the aptness of the model.

g. Compute the standardized residuals and form these into a frequency histogram. What does this indicate about the normality assumption?

h. Comment on the overall aptness of this model and indicate what might be done to improve the model.

The following information applies to Problems 15-70 through 15-79.

The J. J. McCracken Company has authorized its marketing research department to make a study of customers who have been issued a McCracken charge card. The marketing research department hopes to identify the significant variables that explain the variation in purchases. Once these variables are determined, the department intends to try to attract new customers who would be predicted to make a high volume of purchases.

Twenty-five customers were selected at random, and values for the following variables were recorded in the file called **McCracken**:

y = Average monthly purchases (in dollars) at McCracken

x_1 = Customer age

x_2 = Customer family income

x_3 = Family size

15-70. A first step in regression analysis often involves developing a scatter plot of the data. Develop the scatter plots of all the possible pairs of variables, and with a brief statement indicate what each plot says about the relationship between the two variables.

15-71. Compute the correlation matrix for these data. Develop the decision rule for testing the significance of each coefficient. Which, if any, correlations are not significant? Use $\alpha = 0.05$.

15-72. Use forward selection stepwise regression to develop the multiple regression model. The variable x_2, family income, was brought into the model. Discuss why this happened.

15-73. Test the significance of the regression model at Step 1 of the process. Justify the significance level you have selected.

15-74. Develop a 95% confidence level for the slope coefficient for the family income variable at Step 1 of the model. Be sure to interpret this confidence interval.

15-75. Describe the regression model at Step 2 of the analysis. In your discussion, be sure to discuss the effect of adding a new variable on the standard error of the estimate and on R^2.

15-76. Referring to Problem 15-75, suppose the manager of McCracken's marketing department questions the appropriateness of adding a second variable. How would you respond to her question?

15-77. Looking carefully at the stepwise regression model, you can see that the value of the slope coefficient for variable x_2, family income, changes as a new variable is added to the regression model. Discuss why this change takes place.

15-78. Analyze the stepwise regression model. Write a report to the marketing manager pointing out the strengths and weaknesses of the model. Be sure to comment on the department's goal of being able to use the model to predict which customers will purchase high volumes from McCracken.

15-79. Plot the residuals against the predicted value of y and comment on what this plot means relative to the aptness of the model.

a. Compute the standardized residuals and form these in a frequency histogram. What does this indicate about the normality assumption?

b. Comment on the overall aptness of this model and indicate what might be done to improve the model.

15-80. The National Association of Realtors Existing-Home Sales Series provides a measurement of the residential real estate market. One of the measurements it produces is the Housing Affordability Index (HAI), which is a measure of the financial ability of U.S. families to buy a house. A value of 100 means that families earning the national median income have just the amount of money needed to qualify for a mortgage on a median-priced home; higher than 100 means they have more than enough, and lower than 100 means they have less than enough. The file titled **Index** contains the HAI and associated variables.

a. Produce the correlation matrix of all the variables. Predict the variables that will remain in the estimated regression equation if standard stepwise regression is used.

b. Use standard stepwise regression to develop an estimate of a model that is to predict the HAI from the associated variables found in the file titled **Index**.

c. Compare the results of parts a and b. Explain any difference between the two models.

15-81. An investment analyst collected data from 20 randomly chosen companies. The data consisted of the 52-week-high stock prices, PE ratios, and the market values of the companies. This data are in the file titled **Investment**.

The analyst wishes to produce a regression equation to predict the market value using the 52-week-high stock price and the PE ratio of the company. He creates a complete second-degree polynomial.

a. Construct an estimate of the regression equation using the indicated variables.

b. Produce the appropriate residual plots to determine if the polynomial function is the appropriate regression function for this data set.

c. Use a residual plot to determine if the residuals have a constant variance.

d. Produce the appropriate residual plot to determine if the residuals are independent. Assume the data were extracted in the order listed.

e. Construct a probability plot to determine if the error terms are normally distributed.

15-82. The consumer price index (CPI) is a measure of the average change in prices over time in a fixed market basket of goods and services typically purchased by consumers. One of the items in this market basket that affects the CPI is the price of oil and its derivatives. The file titled **Consumer** contains the price of the derivatives of oil and the CPI adjusted to 2005 levels.

a. Produce a multiple regression equation depicting the relationship between the CPI and the price of the derivatives of oil.

b. Conduct a t-test on the coefficient that has the highest p-value. Use a significance level of 0.02 and the p-value approach.

c. Produce a multiple regression equation depicting the relationship between the CPI and the price of the derivatives of oil leaving out the variable tested in part b.

d. Referring to the regression results in part c, repeat the tests indicated in part b.

e. Perform a test of hypothesis to determine if the resulting overall model is statistically significant. Use a significance level of 0.02 and the p-value approach.

15-83. Badeaux Brothers Louisiana Treats ships packages of Louisiana coffee, cakes, and Cajun spices to individual customers around the United States. The cost to ship these products depends primarily on the weight of the package being shipped. Badeaux charges the customers for shipping and then ships the product itself. As a part of a study of whether it is economically feasible to continue to ship products themselves, Badeaux sampled 20 recent shipments to determine what if any relationship exists between shipping costs and package weight. The data are contained in the file **Badeaux**.

a. Develop a scatter plot of the data with the dependent variable, cost, on the vertical axis and the independent variable, weight, on the horizontal axis. Does there appear to be a relationship between the two variables? Is the relationship linear?

b. Compute the sample correlation coefficient between the two variables. Conduct a test, using an alpha value of 0.05, to determine whether the population correlation coefficient is significantly different from zero.

c. Determine the simple linear regression model for this data. Plot the simple linear regression model together with the data. Would a nonlinear model better fit the sample data?

d. Now develop a nonlinear model and plot the model against the data. Does the nonlinear model provide a better fit than the linear model developed in part c?

15-84. The State Tax Commission must download information files each morning. The time to download the files primarily depends on the size of the file. The Tax Commission has asked your computer consulting firm to determine what, if any, relationship exists between download time and size of files. The Tax Commission randomly selected a sample of days and provided the information contained in the file **Tax Commission.**

a. Develop a scatter plot of the data with the dependent variable, download time, on the vertical axis and the independent variable, size, on the horizontal axis. Does there appear to be a relationship between the two variables? Is the relationship linear?

b. Compute the sample correlation coefficient between the two variables. Conduct a test, using an alpha value of 0.05, to determine whether the population correlation coefficient is significantly different from zero.

c. Determine the simple linear regression model for these data. Plot the simple linear regression model together with the data. Would a nonlinear model better fit the sample data?

d. Now determine a nonlinear model and plot the model against the data. Does the nonlinear model provide a better fit than the linear model developed in part c?

15-85. Refer to the State Department of Transportation data set called **Liabins**. The department was interested in determining the rate of compliance with the state's mandatory liability insurance law, as well as other things. *Assume the data were collected using a simple random sampling process.* Develop the best possible linear regression model using vehicle year as the dependent variable and any or all of the other variables as potential independent variables. Assume that your objective is to develop a predictive model. Write a report that discusses the steps you took to develop the final model. Include a correlation matrix and all appropriate statistical tests. Use an $\alpha = 0.05$. If you are using a nominal or ordinal variable, remember that you must make sure it is in the form of one or more dummy variables.

Case 15.1

Dynamic Scales, Inc.

In 2005, Stanley Ahlon and three financial partners formed Dynamic Scales, Inc. The company was based on an idea Stanley had for developing a scale to weigh trucks in motion and thus eliminate the need for every truck to stop at weigh stations along highways. This dynamic scale would be placed in the highway approximately one-quarter mile from the regular weigh station. The scale would have a minicomputer that would automatically record truck speed, axle weights, and climate variables, including temperature, wind, and moisture. Stanley Ahlon and his partners believed that state transportation departments in the United States would be the primary market for such a scale.

As with many technological advances, developing the dynamic scale has been difficult. When the scale finally proved accurate for trucks traveling 40 miles per hour, it would not perform for trucks traveling at higher speeds. However, eight months ago, Stanley announced that the dynamic scale was ready to be field-tested by the Nebraska State Department of Transportation under a grant from the federal government. Stanley explained to his financial partners, and to Nebraska transportation officials, that the dynamic weight would not exactly equal the static weight (truck weight on a static scale). However, he was sure a statistical relationship between dynamic weight and static weight could be determined, which would make the dynamic scale useful.

Nebraska officials, along with people from Dynamic Scales, installed a dynamic scale on a major highway in Nebraska. Each month for six months, data were collected for a random sample of trucks weighed on both the dynamic scale and a static scale. Table 15.3 presents these data.

Once the data were collected, the next step was to determine whether, based on this test, the dynamic scale measurements could be used to predict static weights. A complete report will be submitted to the U.S. government and to Dynamic Scales.

TABLE 15.3 | **Test Data for the Dynamic Scales Example**

Month	Front-Axle Static Weight (lb.)	Front-Axle Dynamic Weight (lb.)	Truck Speed (mph)	Temperature (°F)	Moisture (%)
January	1,800	1,625	52	21	0.00
	1,311	1,904	71	17	0.15
	1,504	1,390	48	13	0.40
	1,388	1,402	50	19	0.10
	1,250	1,100	61	24	0.00
February	2,102	1,950	55	26	0.10
	1,410	1,475	58	32	0.20
	1,000	1,103	59	38	0.15
	1,430	1,387	43	24	0.00
	1,073	948	59	18	0.40
March	1,502	1,493	62	34	0.00
	1,721	1,902	67	36	0.00
	1,113	1,415	48	42	0.21
	978	983	59	29	0.32
	1,254	1,149	60	48	0.00
April	994	1,052	58	37	0.00
	1,127	999	52	34	0.21
	1,406	1,404	59	40	0.40
	875	900	47	48	0.00
	1,350	1,275	68	51	0.00
May	1,102	1,120	55	52	0.00
	1,240	1,253	57	57	0.00
	1,087	1,040	62	63	0.00
	993	1,102	59	62	0.10
	1,408	1,400	67	68	0.00
June	1,420	1,404	58	70	0.00
	1,808	1,790	54	71	0.00
	1,401	1,396	49	83	0.00
	933	1,004	62	88	0.40
	1,150	1,127	64	81	0.00

Case 15.2

Glaser Machine Works

Glaser Machine Works has experienced a significant change in its business operations over the past 50 years. Glaser started business as a machine shop that produced specialty tools and products for the timber and lumber industry. This was a logical fit, given its location in the southern part of the United States. However, over the years, Glaser looked to expand its offerings beyond the lumber and timber industry. Initially, its small size coupled with its rural location made it difficult to attract the attention of large companies that could use its products. All of that began to change as Glaser developed the ability not only to fabricate parts and tools but also to assemble products for customers who needed special components in large quantities. Glaser's business really took off when first foreign and then domestic automakers began to build automobile plants in the southern United States. Glaser was able to provide quality parts quickly for firms that expected high quality and responsive delivery. Many of Glaser's customers operated with little inventory and required that suppliers be able to provide shipments with short lead times.

As part of its relationship with the automobile industry, Glaser was expected to buy into the lean-manufacturing and quality-improvement initiatives of its customers. Glaser had always prided itself on its quality, but as the number and variety of its products increased, along with ever higher expectations by its customers, Glaser knew that it would have to respond by ensuring its quality and operations were continually improving. Of recent concern was the performance of its manufacturing line 107B. This line produced a component part for a Japanese automobile company. The Japanese firm had initially been pleased with Glaser's performance, but lately the number of defects was approaching an unacceptable level. Managers of the 107B line knew the line and its workers had been asked to ramp up production to meet increased demand and that some workers were concerned with the amount of

overtime being required. There was also concern about the second shift now being run at 107B. Glaser had initially run only one shift, but when demand for its product became so high that there was not sufficient capacity with one shift, additional workers were hired to operate a night shift.

Management was wondering if the new shift had been stretched beyond its capabilities. Glaser plant management asked Kristi Johnson, the assistant production supervisor for line 107B, to conduct an analysis of product defects for the line. Kristi randomly selected several days of output and counted the number of defective parts produced on the 107B line. This information, along with other data, is contained in the file **Glaser Machine Works**. Kristi promised to have a full report for the management team by the end of the month.

Required Tasks:

1. Identify the primary issue of the case.
2. Identify a statistical model you might use to help analyze the case.
3. Develop a multiple regression model that can be used to help Kristi Johnson analyze the product defects for line 107B. Be sure to carefully specify the dependent variable and the independent variables.
4. Discuss how the variables overtime hours, supervisor training, and shift will be modeled.
5. Run the regression model you developed and interpret the results.
6. Which variables are significant?
7. Provide a short report that describes your analysis and explains in managerial terms the findings of your model. Be sure to explain which variables, if any, are significant explanatory variables. Provide a recommendation to management.

Case 15.3

Hawlins Manufacturing

Ross Hawlins had done it all at Hawlins Manufacturing, a company founded by his grandfather 63 years ago. Among his many duties, Ross oversaw all the plant's operations, a task that had grown in responsibility given the company's rapid growth over the past three decades. When Ross's grandfather founded the company, there were only two manufacturing sites. Expansion and acquisition of competitors over the years had caused that number to grow to more than 50 manufacturing plants in 18 states.

Hawlins had a simple process that produced only two products, but the demand for these products was strong, and Ross had spent millions of dollars upgrading his facilities over the past decade. Consequently, most of the company's equipment was less than 10 years old on average. Hawlins's two products were produced for local markets, as prohibitive shipping costs prevented shipping the product long distances. Product demand was sufficiently strong to support two manufacturing shifts (day

and night) at every plant, and every plant had the capability to produce both products sold by Hawlins. Recently, the management team at Hawlins noticed that there were differences in output levels across the various plants. They were uncertain what, if anything, might explain these differences. Clearly, if some plants were more productive than others, there might be some meaningful insights that could be standardized across plants to boost overall productivity.

Ross Hawlins asked Lisa Chandler, an industrial engineer at the company's headquarters, to conduct a study of the plant's productivity. Lisa randomly sampled 159 weeks of output from various plants together with the number of plant employees working that week, the plants' average age in years, the product mix produced that week (either product A or B), and whether the output was from the day or night shift. The sampled data are contained in the file **Hawlins Manufacturing**. The Hawlins management team is expecting a written report and a presentation by Lisa when it meets again next Tuesday.

Required Tasks:

1. Identify the primary issue of the case.
2. Identify a statistical model you might use to help analyze the case.
3. Develop a multiple regression model for Lisa Chandler. Be sure to carefully specify the dependent variable and the independent variables.
4. Discuss how the type of product (A or B) and the shift (day or night) can be included in the regression model.
5. Run the regression model you developed and interpret the results.
6. Which variables are significant?
7. Provide a short report that describes your analysis and explains in management terms the findings of your model. Be sure to explain which variables, if any, are significant explanatory variables. Provide a recommendation to management.

Case 15.4

Sapphire Coffee—Part 2

Jennie Garcia could not believe that her career had moved so far so fast. When she left graduate school with a master's degree in anthropology, she intended to work at a local coffee shop until something else came along that was more related to her academic background. But after a few months, she came to enjoy the business, and in a little over a year, she was promoted to store manager. When the company for whom she worked continued to grow, Jennie was given oversight of a few stores.

Now, eight years after she started as a barista, Jennie is in charge of operations and planning for the company's southern region. As a part of her responsibilities, Jennie tracks store revenues and forecasts coffee demand. Historically, Sapphire Coffee would base its demand forecast on the number of stores, believing that each store sold approximately the same amount of coffee. This approach seemed to work well when the company had shops of similar size and layout, but as the company grew, stores became more varied. Now, some stores have drive-thru windows, a feature that top management added to some stores believing that it would increase coffee sales for customers who wanted a cup of coffee on their way to work but who were too rushed to park and enter the store.

Jennie noticed that weekly sales seemed to be more variable across stores in her region and was wondering what, if anything, might explain the differences. The company's financial vice president had also noticed the increased differences in sales across stores and was wondering what might be happening. In an e-mail to Jennie, he stated that weekly store sales are expected to average $5.00 per square foot. Thus, a 1,000-square-foot store would have average weekly sales of $5,000. He asked that Jennie analyze the stores in her region to see if this rule of thumb was a reliable measure of a store's performance.

Jennie had been in the business long enough to know that a store's size, although an important factor, was not the only thing that might influence sales. She had never been convinced of the efficacy of the drive-thru window, believing that it detracted from the coffee house experience that so many of Sapphire Coffee's customers had come to expect. The VP of finance was expecting the analysis to be completed by the weekend. Jennie decided to randomly select weekly sales records for 53 stores, along with each store's size, whether it was located close to a college, and whether it had a drive-thru window. The data are in the file **Sapphire Coffee-2**. A full analysis would need to be sent to the corporate office by Friday.

Case 15.5

Wendell Motors

Wendell Motors manufactures and ships small electric motors and drives to a variety of industrial and commercial customers in and around St. Louis. Wendell is a small operation with a single manufacturing plant. Wendell's products are different from other motor and drive manufacturers because Wendell only produces small motors (25 horsepower or less) and because its products are used in a variety of industries and businesses that appreciate Wendell's quality and speed of delivery. Because it has only one plant, Wendell ships motors directly from the plant to its customers. Wendell's reputation for quality and speed of delivery allows it to maintain low inventories of motors and to ship make-to-order products directly.

As part of its ongoing commitment to lean manufacturing and continuous process improvement, Wendell carefully monitors the cost associated with both production and shipping. The manager of shipping for Wendell, Tyler Jenkins, regularly reports the shipping costs to Wendell's management team. Because few finished goods inventories are maintained, competitive delivery times often require that Wendell expedite shipments. This is almost always the case for those customers who operate their business around the clock every day of the week. Such customers might

maintain their own backup safety stock of a particular motor or drive, but circumstances often result in cases where replacement products have to be rushed through production and then expedited to the customer.

Wendell's management team wondered if these special orders were too expensive to handle in this way and if it might be less expensive to produce and hold certain motors as finished goods inventory, enabling off-the-shelf delivery using less expensive modes of shipping. This might especially be true for orders that must be filled on a holiday, incurring an additional shipping charge. At the last meeting of the management team, Tyler Jenkins was asked to analyze expedited shipping costs and to develop a model that could be used to estimate the cost of expediting a customer's order.

Donna Layton, an industrial engineer in the plant, was asked to prepare an inventory cost analysis to determine the expenses of holding additional finished goods inventory. Tyler began his analysis by randomly selecting 45 expedited shipping records. The sampled data can be found in the file **Wendell Motors**. The management team expects a full report in five days. Tyler knew he would need a model for explaining shipping costs for expedited orders and that he would also need to answer the questions as to what effect, if any, shipping on a holiday had on costs.

- **Review** the steps used to develop a line chart discussed in Chapter 2.

- **Make sure** you understand the steps necessary to construct and interpret linear and nonlinear regression models in Chapters 14 and 15.

- **Review** the concepts and properties associated with means discussed in Chapter 3.

Analyzing and Forecasting Time-Series Data

16.1 Introduction to Forecasting, Time-Series Data, and Index Numbers (pg. 683–697)

Outcome 1. Identify the components present in a time series.

Outcome 2. Understand and compute basic index numbers.

16.2 Trend-Based Forecasting Techniques (pg. 697–723)

Outcome 3. Apply the fundamental steps in developing and implementing forecasting models.

Outcome 4. Apply trend-based forecasting models, including linear trend, nonlinear trend, and seasonally adjusted trend.

16.3 Forecasting Using Smoothing Methods (pg. 723–733)

Outcome 5. Use smoothing-based forecasting models, including single and double exponential smoothing.

Why you need to know

Every organization has a need to forecast the demand for the goods or services it provides. A retail clothing store must forecast the demand for the shirts it sells by shirt size. A concert promoter must forecast how many tickets will be sold before signing a contract with a performer and the concert venue. Apple relies on forecasts of the units of a new iPhone that will be demanded in order to determine how many of the product to produce. Your state's elected officials must forecast tax revenues in order to establish a budget each year. For many organizations, the success of the forecasting effort will play a major role in determining the general success of the organization.

Forecasters won't have access to a crystal ball on which to rely for an accurate prediction of the future. Instead, they need tools to assist in preparing the forecast. This chapter provides an introduction to several basic forecasting techniques and illustrates how and when to apply them. We urge you to focus on the material and take with you the tools that will give you a competitive advantage over those who are not familiar with forecasting techniques.

16.1 Introduction to Forecasting, Time-Series Data, and Index Numbers

The concepts of forecasting and planning are often confused. Planning is the process of determining how to deal with the future. On the other hand, *forecasting* is the process of predicting what the future will be like. Forecasts are used as inputs for the planning process.

Liveshot/Shutterstock

There are two broad categories of forecasting techniques: qualitative and quantitative. *Qualitative forecasting* techniques are based on expert opinion and judgment. *Quantitative forecasting* techniques are based on statistical methods for analyzing quantitative historical data. This chapter focuses on quantitative forecasting techniques.

In general, quantitative forecasting techniques are used whenever the following conditions are true: Historical data relating to the variable to be forecast exist, the historical data can be quantified, and you are willing to assume that the historical pattern will continue into the future.

General Forecasting Issues

Forecasting is both an art and a science. The role of a forecaster is to model a real-world system. Determining the appropriate forecasting model is a challenging task, but it can be made manageable by employing the model-building process discussed in Chapter 15 consisting of **model specification**, **model building**, and **model diagnosis**. As we will point out in later sections, guidelines exist for determining which forecasting techniques may be more appropriate than others in certain situations. However, you may have to specify (and try) several model forms for a given situation before deciding on one that is most acceptable. For example, if Walmart expects future sales patterns at a given store to look like the past sales patterns, then any model it develops should adequately fit the past data to have a reasonable chance of forecasting the future. As a forecaster, you will spend much time selecting a model's specification and estimating its parameters to reach an acceptable fit of the past data. You will need to determine how well a model fits past data, how well it performs in mock forecasting trials, and how well its assumptions appear to be satisfied. If the model is unacceptable in any of these areas, you will be forced to revert to the model specification step and begin again.

An important consideration when you are developing a forecasting model is to use the simplest available model that will meet your forecasting needs. The objective of forecasting is to provide good forecasts. You do not need to feel that a sophisticated approach is better if a simpler one will work just as well. As in football, in which some players specialize in defense and others in offense, forecasting techniques have been developed for special situations, which are generally dependent on the **forecasting horizon**. For the purpose of categorizing forecasting techniques in most business situations, the forecast horizon, or lead time, is typically divided into four categories:

1. Immediate term—less than one month
2. Short term—one to three months
3. Medium term—three months to two years
4. Long term—two years or more

As we introduce various forecasting techniques, we will indicate the forecasting horizon(s) for which each is typically best suited.

In addition to determining the desired forecasting horizon, the forecaster must determine the **forecasting period**. For instance, the forecasting period might be a day, a week, a month, a quarter, or a year. Thus, the forecasting horizon consists of one or more forecasting periods. If quantitative forecasting techniques are to be employed, historical quantitative data must be available for a similar period. If we want weekly forecasts, weekly historical data must be available. The **forecasting interval** is generally the same length as the forecast period. That is, if the forecast period is one week, then we will provide a new forecast each week.

Components of a Time Series

Quantitative forecasting models have one factor in common: They use past measurements of the variable of interest to generate a forecast of the future. The past data, measured over time, are called *time-series data*. The decision maker who plans to develop a quantitative forecasting model must analyze the relevant time-series data.

Model Specification

The process of selecting the forecasting technique to be used in a particular situation.

Model Building

The process of estimating the specified model's parameters to achieve an adequate fit of the historical data.

Model Diagnosis

The process of determining how well a model fits past data and how well the model's assumptions appear to be satisfied.

Forecasting Horizon

The number of future periods covered by a forecast. It is sometimes referred to as *forecast lead time*.

Forecasting Period

The unit of time for which forecasts are to be made.

Forecasting Interval

The frequency with which new forecasts are prepared.

INTERMOUNTAIN OFFICE SUPPLY The owner of Intermountain Office Supply needs to forecast revenues for the copier service portion of the company in order to make sure he has ample cash flows to operate the business. When forecasting this portion of the company's revenue for next year, he plans to consider the historical pattern over the prior four years. The issue is whether demand for copier services has generally increased or decreased and whether there have been times during the year when demand was typically higher than at other times. The forecasters can perform a time-series analysis of the historical sales.

Table 16.1 presents the time-series data for the revenue generated by this portion of the company for the four-year period. An effective means for analyzing these data is to develop a *time-series plot*, or line chart, as shown in Figure 16.1. By graphing the data, much can be observed about the firm's revenue over the past four years. The time-series plot is an important tool in identifying the time-series components. All time-series data exhibit one or more of the following:

1. Trend component
2. Seasonal component
3. Cyclical component
4. Random component

Trend Component A *trend* is the long-term increase or decrease in a variable being measured over time. Figure 16.1 shows that Intermountain's revenues exhibited an upward trend over the four-year period. In other situations, the time series may exhibit a downward trend.

Linear Trend

A long-term increase or decrease in a time series in which the rate of change is relatively constant.

Trends can be classified as **linear** or nonlinear. A trend can be observed when a time series is measured in any time increment, such as years, quarters, months, or days. Figure 16.1 shows a good example of a positive linear trend. Time-series data that exhibit a linear trend will tend to increase or decrease at a fairly constant rate. However, not all trends are linear. Many time series will show a *nonlinear trend*. For instance, in the 11 years between 2001 and 2011, total annual game attendance for the New York Yankees Major League Baseball team is shown in Figure 16.2. Attendance was fairly flat between 2001 and 2003, increased dramatically between 2003 and 2006, slowed down again through 2008, and then declined sharply during 2009 through 2011.

Seasonal Component

A wavelike pattern that is repeated throughout a time series and has a recurrence period of at most one year.

Seasonal Component Another component that may be present in time-series data is the **seasonal component**. Many time series show a repeating pattern over time. For instance, Figure 16.1 showed a time series that exhibits a wavelike pattern. This pattern repeats itself

TABLE 16.1 | **Time-Series Data for Sales Revenues (Thousands of Dollars)**

Month	Billing Total			
	2009	2010	2011	2012
January	170	390	500	750
February	200	350	470	700
March	190	300	510	680
April	220	320	480	710
May	180	310	530	710
June	230	350	500	660
July	220	380	540	630
August	260	420	580	670
September	300	460	630	700
October	330	500	690	720
November	370	540	770	850
December	390	560	760	880

FIGURE 16.1

Time-Series Plot for
Intermountain Office Supply
Copier Services Revenue

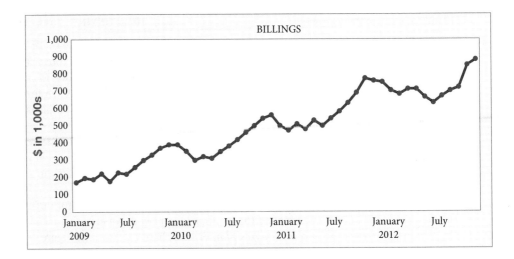

throughout the time series. Copier services revenues reach an annual maximum around January and then decline to an annual minimum around April. This pattern repeats itself every 12 months. The shortest period of repetition for a pattern is known as its *recurrence period*. A seasonal component's recurrence period is at most one year. If the time series exhibits a repetitious pattern with a recurrence period longer than a year, the time series is said to exhibit a cyclical effect—a concept to be explored shortly.

In analyzing past sales data for a retail toy store, we would expect to see sales increase in the months leading into Christmas and then substantially decrease after Christmas. Automobile gasoline sales might show a seasonal increase during the summer months, when people drive more, and a decrease during the cold winter months. These predictable highs and lows at specific times during the year indicate seasonality in data.

To view seasonality in a time series, the data must be measured quarterly, monthly, weekly, or daily. Annual data will not show seasonal patterns of highs and lows. Figure 16.3 shows quarterly sales data for a major hotel chain from June 2004 through December 2009. Notice that the data exhibit a definite seasonal pattern. The local maximums occur in the spring. The recurrence period of the component in the time series is, therefore, one year. The winter quarter tends to be low, whereas the following quarter (spring) is the high quarter each year.

FIGURE 16.2

New York Yankees Annual
Attendance Showing a
Nonlinear Trend

Excel 2010 Instructions:
1. Open Blank worksheet.
2. Enter *Year* and *Attendance* data.
3. Select the *Attendance* data to be graphed.
4. On the **Insert** tab, click the **Line** chart.
5. Click the **Line with Markers** option.
6. Use the **Layout** tab in the **Chart Tools** to remove the Legend, change the Chart Title, add the Axis Titles.

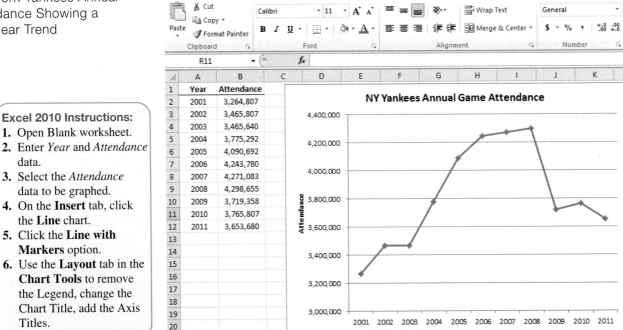

FIGURE 16.3 |

Hotel Sales by Quarter

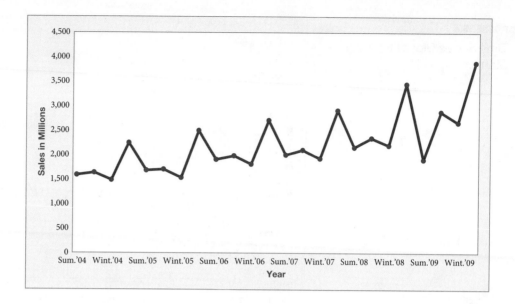

Seasonality can be observed in time-series data measured over time periods shorter than a year. For example, the number of checks processed daily by a bank may show predictable highs and lows at certain times during a month. The pattern of customers arriving at the bank during any hour may be "seasonal" within a day, with more customers arriving near opening time, around the lunch hour, and near closing time.

Cyclical Component

A wavelike pattern within the time series that repeats itself throughout the time series and has a recurrence period of more than one year.

Cyclical Component If you observe time-series data over a long enough time span, you may see sustained periods of high values followed by periods of lower values. If the recurrence period of these fluctuations is larger than a year, the data are said to contain a **cyclical component**.

National economic measures such as the unemployment rate, gross national product, stock market indexes, and personal saving rates tend to cycle. The cycles vary in length and magnitude. That is, some cyclical time series may have longer runs of high and low values than others. Also, some time series may exhibit deeper troughs and higher crests than others. Figure 16.4 shows quarterly housing starts in the United States between 1995 and 2006. Note the definite cyclical pattern, with low periods in 1995, 1997, and 2000. Although the pattern resembles the shape of a seasonal component, the length of the recurrence period identifies this pattern as being the result of a cyclical component.

Random Component

Changes in time-series data that are unpredictable and cannot be associated with a trend, seasonal, or cyclical component.

Random Component Although not all time series possess a trend, seasonal, or cyclical component, virtually all time series will have a **random component**. The random component is often referred to as "noise" in the data. A time series with no identifiable pattern is completely random and contains only noise. In addition to other components, each of the time series in Figures 16.1 through 16.4 contains random fluctuations.

In the following sections of this chapter, you will see how various forecasting techniques deal with the time-series components. An important first step in forecasting is to identify which components are present in the time series to be analyzed. As we have shown, constructing a time-series plot is the first step in this process.

Chapter Outcome 2. → # Introduction to Index Numbers

When analyzing time-series data, decision makers must often compare one value measured at one point in time with other values measured at different points in time. For example, a real estate broker may wish to compare house prices in 2012 with house prices in previous years. A common procedure for making relative comparisons is to begin by determining a **base period index** to which all other data values can be fairly compared.

Base Period Index

The time-series value to which all other values in the time series are compared. The index number for the base period is defined as 100.

Equation 16.1 is used to make relative comparisons for data found in different periods by calculating a *simple index number*.

FIGURE 16.4

Time-Series Plot of Housing
Starts

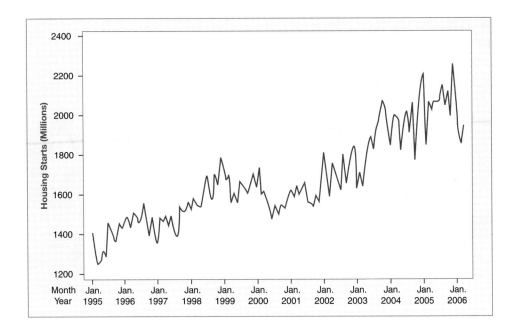

Simple Index Number

$$I_t = \frac{y_t}{y_0} 100$$ (16.1)

where:

I_t = Index number at time period t

y_t = Value of the time series at time t

y_0 = Value of the time series at the index base period

EXAMPLE 16-1   **COMPUTING SIMPLE INDEX NUMBERS**

Computrol, Inc. The managers at Computrol, Inc., a company that makes electronic control equipment for electric utilities, are considering the purchase of another controls manufacturer in North Carolina. The agents representing the company's current owners have touted their company's rapid sales growth over the past 10 years as a reason for their asking price. To gain a better understanding of the sales history, Computrol executives wish to convert the company's sales data to index numbers. The following steps can be used to do this:

Step 1   **Obtain the time-series data.**
The company has sales data for each of the 10 years since 2003.

Step 2   **Select a base period.**
Computrol managers have selected 2003 as the index base period. Sales in 2003 were $14.0 million.

Step 3   **Compute the simple index numbers for each year using Equation 16.1.**
For instance, sales in 2004 were $15.2 million. Using Equation 16.1, the index for 2004 is

$$I_t = \frac{y_t}{y_0} 100$$

$$I_{2001} = \frac{15.2}{14.0} 100 = 108.6$$

For the 10 years, we get:

Year	Sales ($ millions)	Index
2003	14.0	100.0
2004	15.2	108.6
2005	17.8	127.1
2006	21.4	152.9
2007	24.6	175.7
2008	30.5	217.9
2009	29.8	212.9
2010	32.4	231.4
2011	37.2	265.7
2012	39.1	279.3

>> **END EXAMPLE**

TRY PROBLEM 16-8 (pg. 696)

Referring to Example 16-1, we can use the index numbers to determine the percentage change any year is from the base year. For instance, sales in 2010 have an index of 231.4. This means that sales in 2010 are 131.4% above sales in the base year of 2003. Sales in 2012 are 179.3% higher than they were in 2003.

Note that although you can use the index number to compare values between any one time period and the base period and can express the difference in percentage-change terms, you cannot compare period-to-period changes by subtracting the index numbers. For instance, in Example 16-1, when comparing sales for 2011 and 2012, we cannot say that the growth has been

$$279.3 - 265.7 = 13.6\%$$

To determine the actual percentage growth, we do the following:

$$\frac{279.3 - 265.7}{265.7}100 = 5.1\%$$

Thus, the sales growth rate between 2011 and 2012 has been 5.1%, not 13.6%.

Aggregate Price Indexes

"The dollar's not worth what it once was" is a saying that everyone has heard. The problem is that nothing is worth what it used to be; sometimes it is worth more, and other times it is worth less. The simple index shown in Equation 16.1 works well for comparing prices when we wish to analyze the price of a single item over time. For instance, we could use the simple index to analyze how apartment rents have changed over time or how college tuition has increased over time. However, if we wish to compare prices of a group of items, we might construct an **aggregate price index**.

Aggregate Price Index
An index that is used to measure the rate of change from a base period for a group of two or more items.

Equation 16.2 is used to compute an unweighted aggregate price index.

Unweighted Aggregate Price Index

$$I_t = \frac{\sum p_t}{\sum p_0}(100)$$

(16.2)

where:

I_t = Unweighted aggregate index at time period t
p_t = Sum of the prices for the group of items at time period t
p_0 = Sum of the prices for the group of items at base time period

EXAMPLE 16-2   **COMPUTING AN UNWEIGHTED AGGREGATE PRICE INDEX**

College Costs There have been many news stories recently discussing the rate of growth of college and university costs. One university is interested in analyzing the growth in the total costs for students over the past five years. The university wishes to consider three main costs: tuition and fees, room and board, and books and supplies. Rather than analyzing these factors individually using three simple indexes, an unweighted aggregate price index can be developed using the following steps:

Step 1 Define the variables to be included in the index and gather the time-series data.
The university has identified three main categories of costs: tuition fees, room and board, and books and supplies. Data for the past five years have been collected. Full-time tuition and fees for two semesters are used. The full dorm-and-meal package offered by the university is priced for the room-and-board variable, and the books-and-supplies cost for a "typical" student are used for that component of the total costs.

Step 2 Select a base period.
The base period for this study will be the 2007–2008 academic year.

Step 3 Use Equation 16.2 to compute the unweighted aggregate price index.
The equation is

$$I_t = \frac{\sum p_t}{\sum p_0}(100)$$

The sum of the prices for the three components during the base academic year of 2007–2008 is $13,814. The sum of the prices in the 2011–2012 academic year is $19,492. Applying Equation 16.2, the unweighted aggregate price index is

$$I_{2008-2009} = \frac{\$19,492}{\$13,814}(100) = 141.1$$

This means, as a group, the components making up the cost of attending this university have increased by 41.1% since the 2007–2008 academic year. The indexes for the other years are shown as follows:

Academic Year	Tuition & Fees ($)	Room & Board ($)	Books & Supplies ($)	$\sum p_t$ ($)	Index
2007–2008	7,300	5,650	864	13,814	100.0
2008–2009	7,720	5,980	945	14,645	106.0
2009–2010	8,560	6,350	1,067	15,977	115.7
2010–2011	9,430	6,590	1,234	17,254	124.9
2011–2012	10,780	7,245	1,467	19,492	141.1

>> **END EXAMPLE**

TRY PROBLEM 16-9 (pg. 696)

Weighted Aggregate Price Indexes

Example 16-2 utilized an unweighted aggregate price index to determine the change in university costs. This was appropriate because each student would incur the same set of three costs. However, in some situations, the items composing a total cost are not equally weighted. For instance, in a consumer price study of a "market basket" of 10 food items, a typical household will not use the same number (or volume) of each item. During a week, a typical household might use three gallons of milk but only two loaves of bread. In these types of situations, we need to compute a weighted aggregate price index to account for the different levels of use. Two common weighted indexes are the Paasche Index and the Laspeyres Index.

The Paasche Index Equation 16.3 is used to compute a Paasche Index. Note that the weighting percentage in Equation 16.3 for the Paasche Index is always the percentage for the time period for which the index is being computed. The idea is that the prices in the base period should be weighted relative to their current use, not to what that use level was in other periods.

Paasche Index

$$I_t = \frac{\sum q_t p_t}{\sum q_t p_0}(100)$$

(16.3)

where:

q_t = Weighting percentage at time t
p_t = Price in time period t
p_0 = Price in the base period

EXAMPLE 16-3   **COMPUTING THE PAASCHE INDEX**

Sergey Ilin/Shutterstock

Wage Rates Before a company makes a decision to locate a new manufacturing plant in a community, the managers will be interested in knowing how the wage rates have changed. Two categories of wages are to be analyzed as a package: production hourly wages and administrative/clerical hourly wages. Annual data showing the average hourly wage rates since 2003 are available. Each year, the makeup of the labor market differs in terms of the percentage of employees in the two categories. To compute a Paasche Index, use the following steps:

Step 1   Define the variables to be included in the index and gather the time-series data.
The variables are the mean hourly price for production workers and the mean average price for administrative/clerical workers. Data are collected for the 10-year period through 2012.

Step 2   Select the base period.
Because similar data for another community are available only back to 2006, the company will use 2006 as the base period to make comparisons between the two communities easier.

Step 3   Use Equation 16.3 to compute the Paasche Index.
The equation is

$$I_t = \frac{\sum q_t p_t}{\sum q_t p_0}(100)$$

The hourly wage rate for production workers in the base year 2006 was $10.80, whereas the average hourly administrative/clerical rate was $10.25.

In 2012, the production hourly rate had increased to $15.45, and the administrative/clerical rate was $13.45. In 2012, 60% of the employees in the community were designated as working in production and 40% were administrative/clerical. Equation 16.3 is used to compute the Paasche Index for 2012, as follows:

$$I_{2012} = \frac{(0.60)(\$15.45) + (0.40)(\$13.45)}{(0.60)(\$10.80) + (0.40)(\$10.25)}(100) = 138.5$$

This means that, overall, the wage rates in this community have increased by 38.5% since the base year of 2006. The following table shows the Paasche Indexes for all years.

Year	Production Wage Rate ($)	Percent Production	Administrative/Clerical Wage Rate ($)	Percent Admin./ Clerical	Paasche Index
2003	8.50	0.78	9.10	0.22	80.8
2004	9.10	0.73	9.45	0.27	86.3
2005	10.00	0.69	9.80	0.31	93.5
2006	10.80	0.71	10.25	0.29	100.0
2007	11.55	0.68	10.60	0.32	105.9
2008	12.15	0.67	10.95	0.33	110.7
2009	12.85	0.65	11.45	0.35	116.5
2010	13.70	0.65	11.90	0.35	123.2
2011	14.75	0.62	12.55	0.38	131.4
2012	15.45	0.60	13.45	0.40	138.5

>> **END EXAMPLE**

TRY PROBLEM 16-12 (pg. 696)

The Laspeyres Index The Paasche Index is computed using the logic that the index for the current period should be compared to a base period with the current period weightings. An alternate index, called the Laspeyres Index, uses the base-period weighting in its computation, as shown in Equation 16.4.

Laspeyres Index

$$I_t = \frac{\sum q_0 p_t}{\sum q_0 p_0}(100)$$

(16.4)

where:

q_0 = Weighting percentage at base period
p_t = Price in time period t
p_0 = Price in base period

EXAMPLE 16-4   **COMPUTING THE LASPEYRES INDEX**

Sergey Ilin/Shutterstock

Wage Rates Refer to Example 16-3, in which the managers of a company are interested in knowing how the wage rates have changed in the community in which they are considering building a plant. Two categories of wages are to be analyzed as a package: production hourly wages and administrative/clerical hourly wages. Annual data showing the average hourly wage rate since 2003 are available. Each year, the makeup of the labor market differs in terms of the percentage of employees in the two categories. To compute a Laspeyres Index, use the following steps:

Step 1 **Define the variables to be included in the index and gather the time-series data.**

The variables are the mean hourly price for production workers and the mean average price for administrative/clerical workers. Data are collected for the 10-year period through 2012.

Step 2 **Select the base period.**

Because similar data for another community are available only back to 2006, the company will use 2006 as the base period to make comparisons between the two communities easier.

Step 3 Use Equation 16.4 to compute the Laspeyres Index.
The equation is

$$I_t = \frac{\Sigma q_0 p_t}{\Sigma q_0 p_0}(100)$$

The hourly wage rate for production workers in the base year of 2006 was $10.80, whereas the average hourly administrative/clerical rate was $10.25.

In that year, 71% of the workers were classified as production. In 2012, the production hourly rate had increased to $15.45, and the administrative/clerical rate was at $13.45. Equation 16.4 is used to compute the Laspeyres Index for 2012, as follows:

$$I_{2012} = \frac{(0.71)(\$15.45)+(0.29)(\$13.45)}{(0.71)(\$10.80)+(0.29)(\$10.25)}(100) = 139.7$$

This means that, overall, the wage rates in this community have increased by 39.7% since the base year of 2006. The following table shows the Laspeyres Indexes for all years.

Year	Production Wage Rate ($)	Percent Production	Administrative/Clerical Wage Rate ($)	Percent Admin./ Clerical	Laspeyres Index
2003	8.50	0.78	9.10	0.22	81.5
2004	9.10	0.73	9.45	0.27	86.5
2005	10.00	0.69	9.80	0.31	93.4
2006	10.80	0.71	10.25	0.29	100.0
2007	11.55	0.68	10.60	0.32	106.0
2008	12.15	0.67	10.95	0.33	110.9
2009	12.85	0.65	11.45	0.35	116.9
2010	13.70	0.65	11.90	0.35	123.8
2011	14.75	0.62	12.55	0.38	132.6
2012	15.45	0.60	13.45	0.40	139.7

>> **END EXAMPLE**

TRY PROBLEM 16-13 (pg. 696)

Commonly Used Index Numbers

In addition to converting time-series data to index numbers, you will encounter a variety of indexes in your professional and personal life.

Consumer Price Index To most of us, inflation has come to mean increased prices and less purchasing power for our dollar. The Consumer Price Index (CPI) attempts to measure the overall changes in retail prices for goods and services. The CPI, originally published in 1913 by the U.S. Department of Labor, uses a "market basket" of goods and services purchased by a typical wage earner living in a city. The CPI, a weighted aggregate index similar to a Laspeyres Index, is based on items grouped into seven categories, including food, housing, clothing, transportation, medical care, entertainment, and miscellaneous items. The items

TABLE 16.2 | **CPI Index (1999 to 2011)**

Year	1999	2000	2001	2002	2003	2004	2005	2006	2007	2008	2009	2010	2011
CPI	166.6	172.2	177.1	179.9	184.0	188.9	195.3	201.6	207.3	215.3	214.5	218.0	224.9

Base = 1982 to 1984 (Index = 100)
Source: Bureau of Labor Statistics: http://www.bls.gov/cpi/home.htm#data

TABLE 16.3 | **PPI Index (1996 to 2005)**

Year	1996	1997	1998	1999	2000	2001	2002	2003	2004	2005
PPI	127.7	127.6	124.4	125.5	132.7	134.2	131.1	138.1	142.7	157.4

Base = 1984 (Index = 100)
Source: Bureau of Labor Statistics: http://www.bls.gov/ppi/home.htm#data

in the market basket have changed over time to keep pace with the buying habits of our society and as new products and services have become available.

Since 1945, the base period used to construct the CPI has been updated. Currently, the base period, 1982 to 1984, has an index of 100. Table 16.2 shows the CPI index values for 1999 to 2011. For instance, the index for 2008 is 215.3, which means that the price of the market basket of goods increased 115.3% between 1984 and 2008. Remember also that you cannot determine the inflation rate by subtracting index values for successive years. Instead, you must divide the difference by the earlier year's index. For instance, the rate of inflation between 2007 and 2008 was

$$\text{Inflation rate} = \frac{215.3 - 207.3}{207.3}(100) = 3.86\%$$

Thus, in general terms, if your income did not increase by at least 3.86% between 2007 and 2008, you failed to keep pace with inflation and your purchasing power was reduced.

Producer Price Index The U.S. Bureau of Labor Statistics publishes the *Producer Price Index* (PPI) on a monthly basis to measure the rate of change in nonretail prices. Like the CPI, the PPI is a Laspeyres weighted aggregate index. This index is used as a leading indicator of upcoming changes in the CPI. Table 16.3 shows the PPI between 1996 and 2005.

Stock Market Indexes

Every night on the national and local TV news, reporters tell us what happened on the stock market that day by reporting on the *Dow Jones Industrial Average* (DJIA). The Dow, as this index is commonly referred to, is not the same type of index as the CPI or PPI, in that it is not a percentage of a base year. Rather, the DJIA is the sum of the stock prices for 30 large industrial companies whose stocks trade on the New York Stock Exchange divided by a factor that is adjusted for stock splits. Many analysts use the DJIA, which is computed daily, as a measure of the health of the stock market. Other analysts prefer other indexes, such as the *Standard and Poor's 500* (S&P 500). The S&P 500 includes stock prices for 500 companies and is thought by some to be more representative of the broader market.

The *NASDAQ* is an index made up of stocks on the NASDAQ exchange and is heavily influenced by technology-based companies that are traded on this exchange. Publications such as *The Wall Street Journal* and *Barrons* publish all these indexes and others every day for investors to use in their investing decisions.

Using Index Numbers to Deflate a Time Series

A common use of index numbers is to convert values measured at different times into more directly comparable values. For instance, if your wages increase, but at a rate less than inflation, you will in fact be earning less in "real terms." A company experiencing increasing sales at a rate of increase less than inflation is actually not increasing in "real terms."

BUSINESS APPLICATION   **DEFLATING TIME-SERIES VALUES USING INDEX VALUES**

WYMAN-GORMAN COMPANY The Wyman-Gorman Company, located in Massachusetts, designs and produces forgings, primarily for internal combustion engines. In 2005, the company experienced financial difficulty and discontinued its agricultural and earthmoving divisions.

TABLE 16.4 | **Deflated Sales Data—Using Producer Price Index (PPI)**

Year	Sales ($ millions)	PPI (Base = 1984)	Sales ($ millions, adjusted to 1984 dollars)
1996	610.3	127.7	477.9
1997	473.1	127.6	370.8
1998	383.5	124.4	308.3
1999	425.5	125.5	339.0
2000	384.1	132.7	289.4
2001	341.1	134.2	254.2
2002	310.3	131.1	236.7
2003	271.6	138.1	196.7
2004	371.6	142.7	260.4
2005	390.2	157.4	247.9

Table 16.4 shows sales in millions of dollars for the company for 1996 to 2005. Also shown is the PPI (Producer Price Index) for the same years. Finally, sales, adjusted to 1984 dollars, are also shown.

Equation 16.5 is used to determine the adjusted time-series values.

Deflation Formula

$$y_{adj_t} = \frac{y_t}{I_t}(100) \tag{16.5}$$

where:

$$y_{adj_t} = \text{Deflated time-series value at time } t$$
$$y_t = \text{Actual value of the time series at time } t$$
$$I_t = \text{Index (such as CPI or PPI) at time } t$$

For instance, in 1996 sales were $610.3 million. The PPI for that year was 127.7. The sales, adjusted to 1984 dollars, is

$$y_{adj_{1996}} = \frac{610.3}{127.7}(100) = \$477.9$$

MyStatLab

16-1: **Exercises**

Skill Development

16-1. What is meant by time-series data? Give an example.

16-2. Explain the difference between time-series data and cross-sectional data. Are these two types of data sets mutually exclusive? What do they have in common? How do they differ?

16-3. What are the differences between quantitative and qualitative forecasting techniques? Under what conditions is it appropriate to use a quantitative technique?

16-4. Provide an example of a business decision that requires (1) a short-term forecast, (2) a medium-term forecast, and (3) a long-term forecast.

16-5. What is meant by the trend component of a time series? How is a linear trend different from a nonlinear trend?

16-6. Must a seasonal component be associated with the seasons (fall, spring, summer, winter) of the year? Provide an example of a seasonal effect that is not associated with the seasons of the year.

16-7. A Greek entrepreneur followed the olive harvests. He noted that olives ripen in September. Each March he would try to determine if the upcoming olive harvest would be especially bountiful. If his analysis indicated it would, he would enter into agreements with the owners of all the olive oil presses in the region. In exchange for a small deposit months ahead of the harvest, he would obtain the right to lease the presses at market prices during the harvest. If he was correct about the harvest and demand for olive oil presses boomed, he could make a great deal of money. Identify the following quantities in the context of this scenario:
  a. forecasting horizon
  b. category that applies to the forecasting horizon identified in part a
  c. forecasting period
  d. forecasting interval

16-8. Consider the following median selling prices ($thousands) for homes in a community:

Year	Price
1	320
2	334
3	329
4	344
5	358
6	347
7	383
8	404
9	397
10	411

  a. Use year 1 as a base year and construct a simple index number to show how the median selling price has increased.
  b. Determine the actual percentage growth in the median selling price between the base year and year 10.
  c. Determine the actual percentage growth in the median selling price between the base year and year 5.
  d. Determine the actual percentage growth in the median selling price between year 5 and year 10.

16-9. The following values represent advertising rates paid by a regional catalog retailer that advertises either on radio or in newspapers:

Year	Radio Rates ($)	Newspaper Rates ($)
1	300	400
2	310	420
3	330	460
4	346	520
5	362	580
6	380	640
7	496	660

  a. Determine a relative index for each type of advertisement using year 1 as the base year.

  b. Determine an unweighted aggregate index for the two types of advertisement.
  c. In year 1, the retailer spent 30% of the advertisement budget on radio advertising. Construct a Laspeyres index for the data.
  d. Using year 1 as the base, construct a Paasche index for the same data.

Business Applications

Problems **16-10 through 16-13** refer to Gallup Construction and Paving, a company whose primary business has been constructing homes in planned communities in the upper Midwest. The company has kept a record of the relative cost of labor and materials in its market areas for the last 11 years. These data are as follows:

Year	Hourly Wages ($)	Average Material Cost ($)
1999	30.10	66,500
2000	30.50	68,900
2001	31.70	70,600
2002	32.50	70,900
2003	34.00	71,200
2004	35.50	71,700
2005	35.10	72,500
2006	35.05	73,700
2007	34.90	73,400
2008	33.80	74,100
2009	34.20	74,000

16-10. Using 1999 as the base year, construct a separate index for each component in the construction of a house.

16-11. Plot both series of data and comment on the trend you see in both plots.

16-12. Construct a Paasche index for 2004 using the data. Use 1999 as the base year and assume that in 2004, 60% of the cost of a townhouse was in materials.

16-13. Construct a Laspeyres index using the data, assuming that in 1999, 40% of the cost of a townhouse was labor.

16-14. Retail Forward, Inc., is a global management consulting and market research firm specializing in retail intelligence and strategies. One of its press releases (*June Consumer Outlook: Spending Plans Show Resilience*, June 1, 2006) divulged the result of the Retail Forward ShopperScape™ survey conducted each month from a sample of 4,000 U.S. primary household shoppers. A measure of consumer spending is represented by the figure at the top of the next page:
  a. Describe the type of index used by Retail Forward to explore consumer spending.
  b. Determine the actual percentage change in the Future Spending Index between December 2005 and June 2006.
  c. Determine the actual percentage change in the Future Spending Index between June 2005 and June 2006.

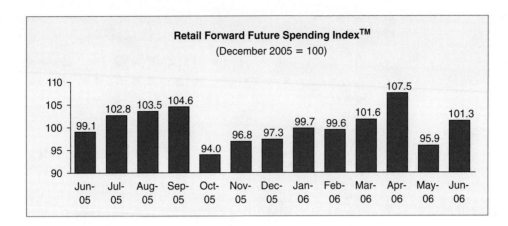

Retail Forward Future Spending Index™
(December 2005 = 100)

Computer Database Exercises

16-15. The Energy Information Administration (EIA), created by Congress in 1977, is a statistical agency of the U.S. Department of Energy. It provides data, forecasts, and analyses to promote sound policymaking and public understanding regarding energy and its interaction with the economy and the environment. The price of the sources of energy is becoming more and more important as our natural resources are consumed. The file titled **Prices** contains data for the period 1993–2008 concerning the price of gasoline ($/gal.), natural gas ($/cu. ft.), and electricity (cents/kilowatt hr.).
   a. Using 1993 as the base, calculate an aggregate energy price index for these three energy costs.
   b. Determine the actual percentage change in the aggregate energy prices between 1993 and 2008.
   c. Determine the actual percentage change in the aggregate energy prices between 1998 and 2008.

16-16. The federal funds rate is the interest rate charged by banks when banks borrow "overnight" from each other. The funds rate fluctuates according to supply and demand and is not under the direct control of the Federal Reserve Board but is strongly influenced by the Fed's actions. The file titled **The Fed** contains the federal funds rates for the period 1955–2008.
   a. Construct a time-series plot for the federal funds rate for the period 1955–2008.
   b. Describe the time-series components that are present in the data set.
   c. Indicate the recurrence periods for any seasonal or cyclical components.

16-17. The Census Bureau of the Department of Commerce released the U.S. retail e-commerce sales for the period Fourth Quarter 1999–Fourth Quarter 2008. The file titled **E-Commerce** contains that data.
   a. Using the fourth quarter of 1999 as the base, calculate a Laspeyres Index for the retail sales for the period of Fourth Quarter 1999–Fourth Quarter 2008.
   b. Determine the actual percentage change in the retail sales for the period Fourth Quarter 1999–First Quarter 2004.
   c. Determine the actual percentage change in the retail sales for the period First Quarter 2004–First Quarter 2006.

END EXERCISES 16-1

16.2 Trend-Based Forecasting Techniques

As we discussed in Section 16.1, some time series exhibit an increasing or decreasing trend. Further, the trend may be linear or nonlinear. A plot of the data will be very helpful in identifying which, if any, of these trends exist.

Developing a Trend-Based Forecasting Model

In this section, we introduce *trend-based forecasting techniques*. As the name implies, these techniques are used to identify the presence of a trend and to model that trend. Once the trend model has been defined, it is used to provide forecasts for future time periods.

Chapter Outcomes 3 and 4. ➝ **BUSINESS APPLICATION** LINEAR TREND FORECASTING

THE TAFT ICE CREAM COMPANY The Taft Ice Cream Company is a family-operated company selling gourmet ice cream to resort areas, primarily on the North Carolina coast. Figure 16.5 displays the annual sales data for the 10-year period 2003–2012 and shows the time-series plot illustrating that sales have trended up in the 10-year period. These data are in a file called **Taft**.

FIGURE 16.5 |

Excel 2010 Output Showing
Taft Ice Cream Sales
Trend Line

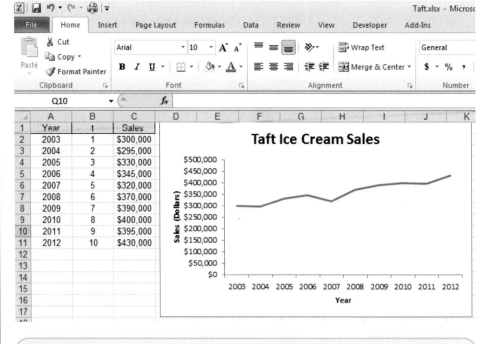

Excel 2010 Instructions:
1. Open file: **Taft.xlsx**.
2. Select the data in the
   Sales column.
3. Select **Insert > Line
   Chart**.
4. Click **Select Data**.
5. Under **Horizontal
   (categories) Axis Labels**
   select data in *Year* column.
6. Click **Layout > Chart
   Title** and enter desired
   title.
7. Click **Layout > Axis
   Titles** and enter horizontal
   and vertical axes labels.
8. Click on grid line, right
   click and click **Delete** to
   remove gridlines.

Minitab Instructions (for similar results):
1. Open file: **Taft.MTW**.
2. Choose **Graph > Time Series Plot**.
3. Select **Simple**.
4. Under **Series**, enter time series' column.
5. Click **Time/Scale**.
6. Under **Time Scale** select **Calendar** and
   Year.
7. Under **Start Values**, insert the starting
   year.
8. Click **OK. OK**.

Excel Tutorial

Taft's owners are considering expanding their ice cream manufacturing facilities. As part of the bank's financing requirements, the managers are asked to supply a forecast of future sales. Recall from our earlier discussions that the forecasting process has three steps: (1) model specification, (2) model fitting, and (3) model diagnosis.

Step 1   Model Specification

The time-series plot in Figure 16.5 indicates that sales have exhibited a linear growth pattern. A possible forecasting tool is a linear trend (straight-line) model.

Step 2   Model-Fitting

Because we have specified a linear trend model, the process of fitting can be accomplished using least squares regression analysis of a form described by Equation 16.6.

Linear Trend Model

$$y_t = \beta_0 + \beta_1 t + \varepsilon_t \tag{16.6}$$

where:

y_t = Value of the trend at time t
β_0 = y intercept of the trend line
β_1 = Slope of the trend line
t = Time period ($t = 1, 2, \ldots$).
ε_t = Model error at time t

We let the first period in the time series be $t = 1$, the second period be $t = 2$, and so forth. The values for time form the independent variable, with sales being the dependent variable. Referring to Chapter 14, the least squares regression equations for the slope and intercept are estimated by Equations 16.7 and 16.8. Here the sums are taken over the values of t ($t = 1, 2 \ldots$).

Least Squares Equations Estimates

$$b_1 = \frac{\sum ty_t - \dfrac{\sum t \sum y_t}{n}}{\sum t^2 - \dfrac{(\sum t)^2}{n}}$$

(16.7)

$$b_0 = \frac{\sum y_t}{n} - b_1 \frac{\sum t}{n}$$

(16.8)

where:

n = Number of periods in the time series
t = Time period (independent variable)
y_t = Dependent variable at time t

The linear regression procedure in Excel can be used to compute the least squares trend model. Figure 16.6 shows the Excel output for the Taft Ice Cream Company example. The least squares trend model for the Taft Company is

$$\hat{y}_t = b_0 + b_1 t$$
$$\hat{y}_t = 277{,}333.33 + 14{,}575.76(t)$$

FIGURE 16.6

Excel 2010 Output for Taft Ice Cream Trend Model

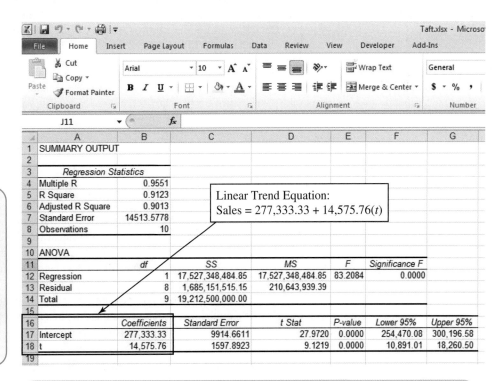

Excel 2010 Instructions:
1. Open file: **Taft.xlsx**.
2. Select **Data > Data Analysis**.
3. Select **Regression**.
4. Enter range for y variable (*Sales*).
5. Enter range for x variable ($t = 1,2,3,\ldots$).
6. Click **Labels**.
7. Specify output location.

Minitab Instructions (for similar results):
1. Open file: **Taft.MTW**.
2. Choose **Stat > Regression > Regression**.
3. In **Response**, enter the time series column, *Sales*.
4. In **Predictors**, enter the time variable column, *t*.
5. Click **OK**.

FIGURE 16.7 |

Excel 2010 Output for Taft Ice
Cream Trend Line

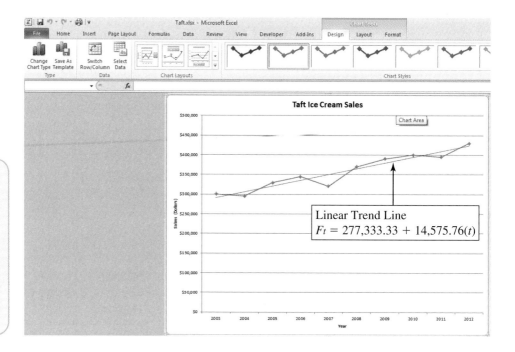

**Minitab Instructions
(for similar results):**
1. Open file: **Taft.MTW**.
2. Choose **Stat > Time
   Series > Trend
   Analysis**.
3. In **Variable**, enter the
   time series column.
4. Under **Model Type**
   choose **Linear**.
5. Click **OK**.

Excel 2010 Instructions:
1. Open file: **Taft.xlsx**.
2. Select the data in *Sales* column.
3. Click **Insert > Line Chart > Line
   with Markers**.
4. Click **Select Data**.
5. Under **Horizontal (categories) Axis
   Labels, click Edit**, select data in
   Year column.
6. Click **Layout > Chart Title > Above
   Chart** and enter desired title.
7. Click **Layout > Axis Titles, position
   desired** and enter horizontal and vertical
   axes titles.
8. Select the data in the chart.
9. Right-click and select **Add Trendline >
   Linear**.
10. To set color, select **Line Color**, choose
    Solid Line, select desired color.
11. Delete Legend.
12. Move Chart to new sheet.

For a forecast, we use F_t as the forecast value or predicted value at time
period t. Thus,

$$F_t = 277,333.33 + 14,575.76\,(t)$$

Step 3 Model Diagnosis

The linear trend regression output in Figure 16.6 offers some conclusions
about the potential capabilities of our model. R-squared $= 0.9123$ shows that
for these 10 years of data, the linear trend model explains more than 91% of
the variation in sales. The p-value for the regression slope coefficient to four
decimal places is 0.0000. This means that time (t) can be used to explain a
significant portion of the variation in sales. Figure 16.7 shows the plot of the
trend line through the data. You can see the trend model fits the historical data
quite closely. Although these results are a good sign, the model diagnosis step
requires further analysis.

Comparing the Forecast Values to the Actual Data

The slope of the trend line indicates the Taft Ice Cream Company has experienced an average increase in sales of $14,575.76 per year over the 10-year period. The linear trend model's
fitted sales values for periods $t = 1$ through $t = 10$ can be found by substituting for t in the
following forecast equation:

$$F_t = 277,333.33 + 14,575.76\,(t)$$

FIGURE 16.8

Excel 2010 Residual Output
for Taft Ice Cream

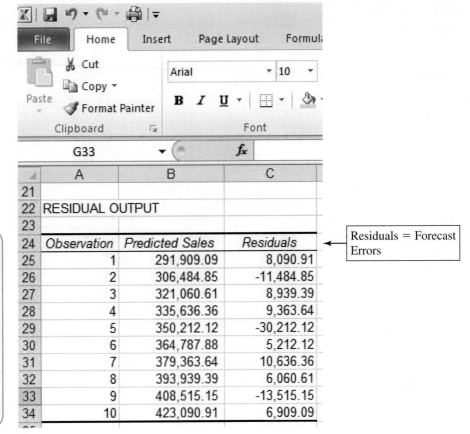

Excel 2010 Instructions:
1. Open File: **Taft.xlsx**.
2. Select **Data > Data Analysis**.
3. Select **Regression**.
4. Click **Residuals**.
5. Enter range for *y* variable (*Sales*).
6. Enter range for *x* variable (*t* = 1,2,3,…).
7. Click **Labels**.
8. Specify output location.

For example, for $t = 1$, we get

$$F_t = 277{,}333.33 + 14{,}575.76\,(1)$$
$$= \$291{,}909.09$$

Note that the actual sales figure, y_1, for period 1 was $300,000. The difference between the actual sales in time t and the forecast values in time t, found using the trend model, is called the *forecast error* or the *residual*. Figure 16.8 shows the forecasts for periods 1 through 10 and the forecast errors at each period.

Computing the forecast error by comparing the trend-line values with actual past data is an important part of the model diagnosis step. The errors measure how closely the model fits the actual data at each point. A perfect fit would lead to residuals of 0 each time. We would like to see small residuals and an overall good fit. Two commonly used measures of fit are mean squared residual, or *mean squared error* (*MSE*), and *mean absolute deviation* (*MAD*). These measures are computed using Equations 16.9 and 16.10, respectively. *MAD* measures the average magnitude of the forecast errors. *MSE* is a measure of the variability in the forecast errors. The forecast error is the observed value, y_t, minus the predicted value, F_t.

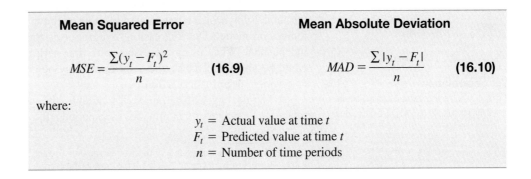

Mean Squared Error		Mean Absolute Deviation	
$MSE = \dfrac{\Sigma(y_t - F_t)^2}{n}$	**(16.9)**	$MAD = \dfrac{\Sigma \lvert y_t - F_t \rvert}{n}$	**(16.10)**

where:

y_t = Actual value at time t
F_t = Predicted value at time t
n = Number of time periods

FIGURE 16.9

Excel 2010 *MSE* and *MAD* Computations for Taft Ice Cream

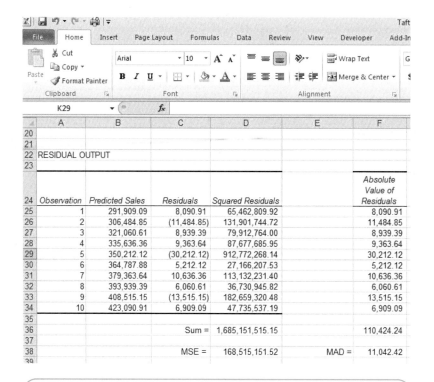

Excel 2010 Instructions:
1. Open file: **Taft.xlsx**.
2. Select **Data > Data Analysis**.
3. Select **Regression**.
4. Click **Residuals**.
5. Enter range for *y* variable (*Sales*).
6. Enter range for *x* variable ($t = 1,2,3,\dots$).
7. Click **Labels**.
8. Specify output location.
9. Create a new column of squared residuals (i.e.,

   cell D25 use equation =C25^2).
10. Create a column of absolute values of the residuals (i.e., cell F25 use equation = ABS(C25).
11. Use Equations 16.9 and 16.10 to calculate *MSE* and *MAD*.

Figure 16.9 shows the *MSE* and *MAD* calculations using Excel for the Taft Ice Cream example. The *MAD* value of $11,042.42 indicates the linear trend model has an average absolute error of $11,042.42 per period. The *MSE* (in squared units) equals 168,515,151.52. The square root of the *MSE* (often referred to as *RMSE*, root mean square error) is $12,981.34, and although it is not equal to the *MAD* value, it does provide similar information about the relationship between the forecast values and the actual values of the time series.[1]

These error measures are particularly helpful when comparing two or more forecasting techniques. We can compute the *MSE* and/or the *MAD* for each forecasting technique. The forecasting technique that gives the smallest *MSE* or *MAD* is generally considered to provide the best fit.

Autocorrelation In addition to examining the fit of the forecasts to the actual time series, the model-diagnosis step also should examine how a model meets the assumptions of the regression model. One regression assumption is that the error terms are uncorrelated, or independent. When using regression with time-series data, the assumption of independence could be violated. That is, the error terms may be correlated over time. We call this *serial correlation*, or **autocorrelation**.

When dealing with a time-series variable, the value of *y* at time period *t* is commonly related to the value of *y* at previous time periods. If a relationship between y_t and y_{t-1} exists,

Autocorrelation

Correlation of the error terms (residuals) occurs when the residuals at points in time are related.

---
[1]Technically this is the square root of the average squared distance between the forecasts and the observed data values. Algebraically, of course, this is not the same as the average forecast error, but it is comparable.

we conclude that first-order autocorrelation exists. If y_t is related to y_{t-2}, second-order autocorrelation exists, and so forth. If the time-series values are autocorrelated, the assumption that the error terms are independent is violated.

The autocorrelation can be positive or negative. For instance, when the values are first-order positively autocorrelated, we expect a positive residual to be followed by a positive residual in the next period, and we expect a negative residual to be followed by another negative residual. With negative first-order autocorrelation, we expect a positive residual to be followed by a negative residual, followed by a positive residual, and so on. The presence of autocorrelation can have adverse consequences on tests of statistical significance in a regression model. Thus, you need to be able to detect the presence of autocorrelation and take action to remove the problem. The *Durbin-Watson statistic*, which is shown in Equation 16.11, is used to test whether residuals are autocorrelated.

Durbin-Watson Statistic

$$d = \frac{\sum_{t=2}^{n}(e_t - e_{t-1})^2}{\sum_{t=1}^{n}e_t^2}$$

(16.11)

where:

d = Durbin-Watson test statistic
$e_t = (y_t - \hat{y}_t)$ = Residual at time t
n = Number of time periods in the time series

Figure 16.10 shows the PHStat add-in for Excel output providing the Durbin-Watson statistic for the Taft Ice Cream data, as follows:

$$d = \frac{\sum_{t=2}^{n}(e_t - e_{t-1})^2}{\sum_{t=1}^{n}e_t^2} = 2.65$$

Examining Equation 16.11, we see that if successive values of the residual are close in value, the Durbin-Watson d statistic will be small. This would describe residuals that are positively correlated.

FIGURE 16.10 |

Excel 2010—Durbin-Watson Statistic: Taft Ice Cream Company Example

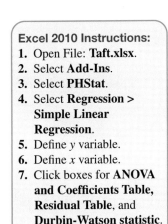

Excel 2010 Instructions:
1. Open File: **Taft.xlsx**.
2. Select **Add-Ins**.
3. Select **PHStat**.
4. Select **Regression > Simple Linear Regression**.
5. Define *y* variable.
6. Define *x* variable.
7. Click boxes for **ANOVA and Coefficients Table, Residual Table**, and **Durbin-Watson statistic**.
8. Click **OK**.

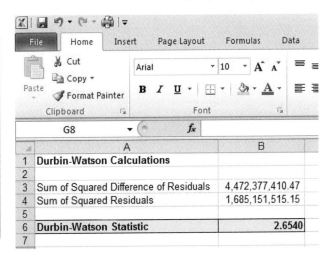

Minitab Instructions (for similar results):
1. Open File: **Taft.xlsx**.
2. Choose **Stat > Regression > Regression**.
3. In **Response**, enter the time series column, *Sales*.
4. In **Predictors**, enter the time variable column, *t*.
5. Select **Options**.
6. Under **Display**, select **Durbin-Watson statistic**.
7. Click **OK. OK**.

The Durbin-Watson statistic can have a value ranging from 0 to 4. A value of 2 indicates no autocorrelation. However, like any other statistics computed from a sample, the Durbin-Watson d is subject to sampling error. We may wish to test formally to determine whether positive autocorrelation exists.

$$H_0: \rho = 0$$
$$H_A: \rho > 0$$

If the d statistic is too small, we will reject the null hypothesis and conclude that positive autocorrelation exists. If the d statistic is too large, we will not reject and will not be able to conclude that positive autocorrelation exists. Appendix N contains a table of one-tailed Durbin-Watson critical values for $\alpha = 0.05$ and $\alpha = 0.01$ levels. (*Note*: The critical values in Appendix N are for one-tailed tests with $\alpha = 0.05$ or 0.01. For a two-tailed test, the alpha is doubled.) The Durbin-Watson table provides two critical values: d_L and d_U. In this test for positive autocorrelation, the decision rule is

If $d < d_L$, *reject H_0* and conclude that positive autocorrelation exists.

If $d > d_U$, do not reject H_0 and conclude that no positive autocorrelation exists.

If $d_L < d < d_U$, the test is inconclusive.

The Durbin-Watson test is not reliable for sample sizes smaller than 15. Therefore, for the Taft Ice Cream Company application, we are unable to conduct the hypothesis test for autocorrelation. However, Example 16-5 shows a Durbin-Watson test carried out.

EXAMPLE 16-5   **TESTING FOR AUTOCORRELATION**

SSI Foods, Inc. SSI Foods supplied hamburger patties to fast-food companies such as Burger-King and Jack-In-The-Box and operated between 1992 and 2009, when it was sold to another meat supplier. During this time, revenues grew steadily. Figure 16.11 displays the data in a time-series plot. The data are in a file called **SSI Foods**.

Recently the managers of the current company developed a linear trend regression model they hope to use to forecast revenue for the next two years to determine whether they can support adding another processing line to their Ohio factory. They are now interested in determining whether the linear model is subject to positive autocorrelation. To test for this, the following steps can be used:

Step 1 Specify the model.
Based on a study of the line chart, the forecasting model is to be a simple linear trend regression model, with revenue as the dependent variable and time (t) as the independent variable.

FIGURE 16.11

Time-Series Plot of SSI
Foods, Inc. Revenue Data

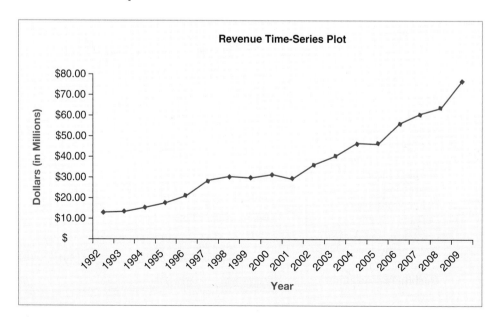

Step 2 Fit the model.

Because we have specified a linear trend model, the process of fitting can be accomplished using least squares regression analysis and Excel to estimate the slope and intercept for the model. Fitting the 18 data points with a least squares line, we find the following:

$$F_t = 5.0175 + 3.3014\,(t)$$

Step 3 Diagnose the model.

The following values were also found:

$$R^2 = 0.935$$
$$F\text{-statistic} = 230.756$$
$$\text{Standard error} = 4.78$$

The large F-statistic indicates that the model explains a significant amount of variation in revenue over time. However, looking at a plot of the trend line shown in Figure 16.12, we see a pattern of actual revenue values first above, and then below, the trend line. This pattern indicates possible autocorrelation among the error terms. We will test for autocorrelation by calculating the Durbin-Watson d statistic or by using the PHStat add-in for Excel have the option to generate the Durbin-Watson statistic. The output is shown in Figure 16.13.

Figure 16.13 shows the Durbin-Watson d statistic as

$$d = 0.661$$

The null and alternative hypotheses for testing for positive autocorrelation are

$$H_0\text{: } \rho = 0$$
$$H_A\text{: } \rho > 0$$

We next go to the Durbin-Watson table (Appendix N) for $\alpha = 0.05$, sample size 18, and number of independent variables, $P = 1$. The values from the table for d_L and d_U are

$$d_L = 1.16 \quad \text{and} \quad d_U = 1.39$$

The decision rule for testing whether we have positive autocorrelation is

If $d < 1.16$, reject H_0 and conclude that positive autocorrelation exists.
If $d > 1.39$, conclude that no positive autocorrelation exists.
If $1.16 < d < 1.39$, the test is inconclusive.

FIGURE 16.12

SSI Foods, Inc. Trend Line

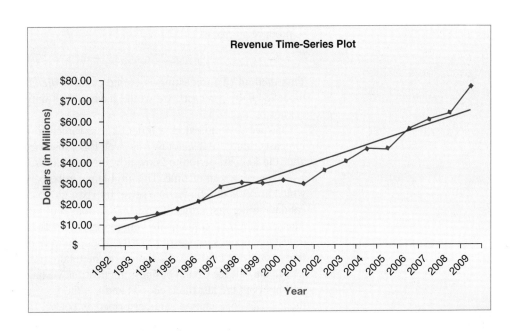

FIGURE 16.13

Excel 2010 (PHStat) Output—Durbin-Watson Statistic for SSI Foods, Inc.

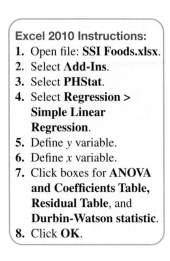

Excel 2010 Instructions:
1. Open file: **SSI Foods.xlsx**.
2. Select **Add-Ins**.
3. Select **PHStat**.
4. Select **Regression >**
   Simple Linear
   Regression.
5. Define *y* variable.
6. Define *x* variable.
7. Click boxes for **ANOVA**
   and Coefficients Table,
   Residual Table, and
   Durbin-Watson statistic.
8. Click **OK**.

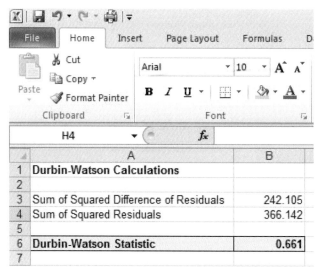

Minitab Instructions (for
similar results):
1. Open file:
   SSI Foods.MTW.
2. Choose **Stat >**
   Regression > Regression.
3. In **Response**, enter the
   time series column,
   Revenue.
4. In **Predictors**, enter the
   time variable column, *t*.
5. Select **Options**.
6. Under **Display**, select
   Durbin-Watson statistic.
7. Click **OK. OK**.

Because $d = 0.661 < d_L = 1.16$, we must reject the null hypothesis and conclude that significant positive autocorrelation exists in the regression model. This means that the assumption of uncorrelated error terms has been violated in this case. Thus, the linear trend model is not the appropriate model to provide the annual revenue forecasts for the next two years.

>> **END EXAMPLE**

TRY PROBLEM 16-18 (pg. 720)

There are several techniques for dealing with the problem of autocorrelation. Some of these are beyond the scope of this text. (Refer to books by Nelson and Wonnacott.) However, one option is to attempt to fit a nonlinear trend to the data, which is discussed starting on page 708.

True Forecasts Although a decision maker is interested in how well a forecasting technique can fit historical data, the real test comes with how well it forecasts future values. Recall in the Taft example, we had 10 years of historical data. If we wish to forecast ice cream sales for year 11 using the linear trend model, we substitute $t = 11$ into the forecast equation to produce a forecast as follows:

$$F_{11} = 277,333.33 + 14,575.76(11) = \$437,666.69$$

This method of forecasting is called *trend projection*. To determine how well our trend model actually forecasts, we would have to wait until the actual sales amount for period 11 is known.

As we just indicated, a model's true forecasting ability is determined by how well it forecasts future values, not by how well it fits historical values. However, having to wait until after the forecast period to know how effective a forecast is doesn't help us assess a model's effectiveness ahead of time. This problem can be partially overcome by using *split samples*, which involves dividing a time series into two groups. You put the first (n_1) periods of historical data in the first group. These (n_1) periods will be used to develop the forecasting model. The second group contains the remaining (n_2) periods of historical data, which will be used to test the model's forecasting ability. These data are called the *holdout data*. Usually, three to five periods are held out, depending on the total number of periods in the time series.

In the Taft Ice Cream business application, we have only 10 years of historical data, so we will hold out the last three periods and use the first seven periods to develop the linear trend model. The computations are performed as before, using Excel or Equations 16.7 and 16.8.

Because we are using a different data set to develop the linear equation, we get a slightly different trend line than when all 10 periods were used. The new trend line is

$$F_t = 277,142.85 + 14,642.85\,(t)$$

This model is now used to provide forecasts for periods 8 through 10 by using trend projection. These forecasts are

Year	Actual	Forecast	Error
t	y_t	F_t	$(y_t - F_t)$
8	400,000	394,285.65	5,714.35
9	395,000	408,928.50	−13,928.50
10	430,000	423,571.35	6,428.65

Then we can compute the *MSE* and the *MAD* values for periods 8 through 10.

$$MSE = \frac{[(5,714.35)^2 + (-13,928.50)^2 + (6,428.65)^2]}{3} = 89,328,149.67$$

and

$$MAD = \frac{(|5,714.35| + |-13,928.50| + |6,428.65|)}{3} = 8,690.50$$

These values could be compared with those produced using other forecasting techniques or evaluated against the forecaster's own standards. Smaller values are preferred. Other factors should also be considered. For instance, in some cases, the forecast values might tend to be higher (or lower) than the actual values. This may imply the linear trend model isn't the best model to use. Forecasting models that tend to over- or underforecast are said to contain *forecast bias*. Equation 16.12 is used as an estimator of the bias.

Forecast Bias

$$\text{Forecast bias} = \frac{\Sigma(y_t - F_t)}{n} \tag{16.12}$$

The forecast bias can be either positive or negative. A positive value indicates a tendency to underforecast. A negative value indicates a tendency to overforecast. The estimated bias taken from the forecasts for periods 8 through 10 in our example is

$$\text{Forecast bias} = \frac{[(5,714.35) + (-13,928.50) + (6,428.65)]}{3} = -595.17$$

This means that, on average, the model overforecasts sales by $595.17.

Suppose that on the basis of our bias estimate, we judge that the linear trend model does an acceptable job in forecasting. Then all available data (periods 1 through 10) would be used to develop a linear trend model (see Figure 16.6), and a trend projection would be used to forecast for future time periods by substituting appropriate values for t into the trend model.

$$F_t = 277,333.33 + 14,575.76\,(t)$$

However, if the linear model is judged to be unacceptable, the forecaster will need to try a different technique. For the purpose of the bank loan application, the Taft Ice Cream Company needs to forecast sales for the next three years (periods 11 through 13). Assuming the linear trend model is acceptable, these forecasts are

$$F_{11} = 277,333.33 + 14,575.76\,(11) = \$437,666.69$$
$$F_{12} = 277,333.33 + 14,575.76\,(12) = \$452,242.45$$
$$F_{13} = 277,333.33 + 14,575.76\,(13) = \$466,818.21$$

Nonlinear Trend Forecasting

As we indicated earlier, you may encounter a time series that exhibits a nonlinear trend. Figure 16.2 showed an example of a nonlinear trend. When the historical data show a nonlinear trend, you should consider using a nonlinear trend forecasting model. A common method for dealing with nonlinear trends is to use an extension of the linear trend method. This extension calls for making a data transformation before applying the least squares regression analysis.

Excel Tutorial

Chapter Outcome 4. ➞

BUSINESS APPLICATION   **FORECASTING NONLINEAR TRENDS**

HARRISON EQUIPMENT COMPANY Consider Harrison Equipment Company, which leases large construction equipment to contractors in the Southwest. The lease arrangements call for Harrison to perform all repairs and maintenance on this equipment. Figure 16.14 shows a line chart for the repair costs for a crawler tractor leased to a contractor in Phoenix for the past 20 quarters. The data are contained in the file **Harrison**.

Model Specification

Harrison Equipment is interested in forecasting future repair costs for the crawler tractor. Recall that the first step in forecasting is model specification. Even though the plot in Figure 16.14 indicates a sharp upward nonlinear trend, the forecaster may start by specifying a linear trend model.

Model Fitting

As a part of the model-fitting step, the forecaster could use Excel's regression procedure to obtain the linear forecasting model shown in Figure 16.15. As shown the linear trend model is

$$F_t = -1,022.7 + 570.9 \, (t)$$

FIGURE 16.14

Excel 2010 Time-Series Plot for Harrison Equipment Repair Costs

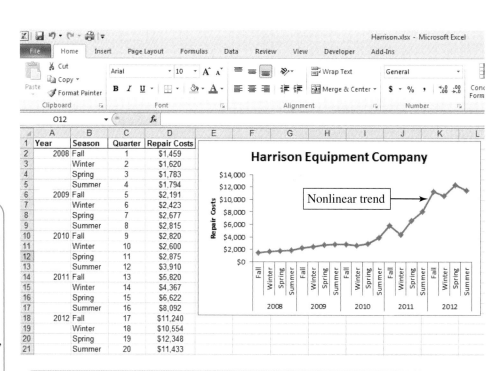

Excel 2010 Instructions:
1. Open file: **Harrison.xlsx**.
2. Select data in the *Repair Costs* data column.
3. Click **Insert > Line Chart**.
4. Click **Select Data**.
5. Under **Horizontal (categories) Axis Labels**, select data in *Year* and *Quarter* columns.
6. Click **Layout > Chart Title**, desired location and enter desired title.
7. Click **Layout > Axis Titles**, desired location and enter vertical title.
8. Remove Gridlines.

Minitab Instructions (for similar results):
1. Open file: **Harrison.MTW**.
2. Select **Graph > Time Series Plot**.
3. Select Simple.
4. Under **Series**, enter time series column.
5. Click **Time/Scale**.
6. Under **Time Scale** select **Calendar** and **Quarter Year**.
7. Under **Start Values**, insert the starting quarter and year.
8. Click **OK. OK**.

FIGURE 16.15

Excel 2010 (PHStat) Output for the Harrison Equipment Company Linear Trend Model

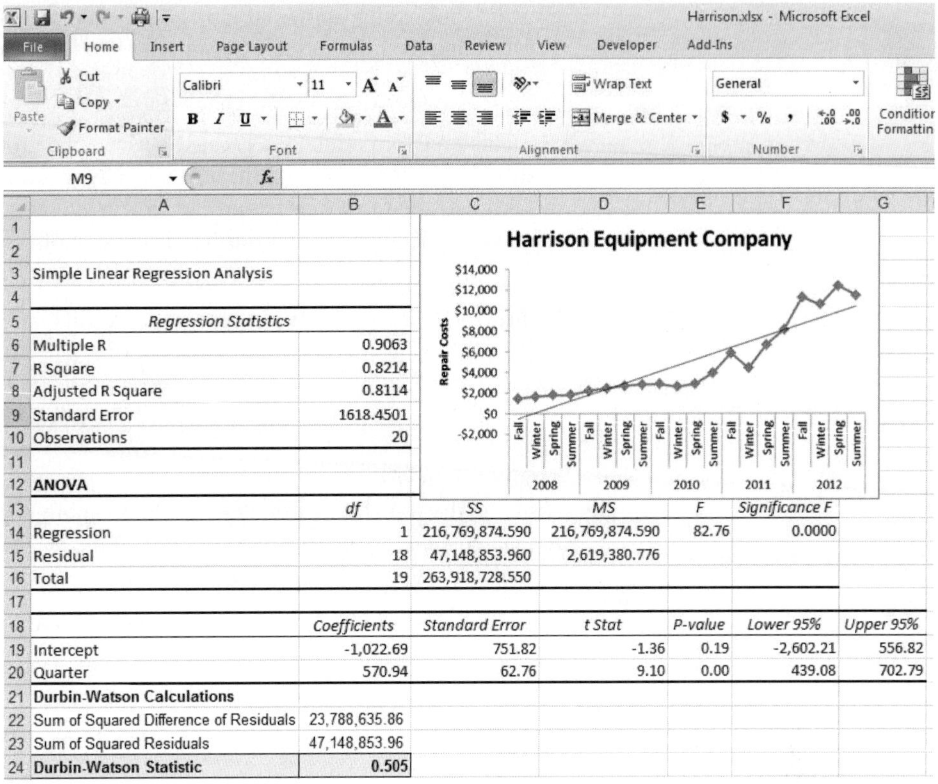

Excel 2010 Instructions:
1. Open file: **Harrison.xlsx**.
2. Select **Add-Ins**.
3. Select **PHStat**.
4. Select **Regression > Simple Linear Regression**.
5. Specify the *y* variable data range.
6. Specify *x* variable data range (Time = *t* values).
7. Check Boxes for **ANOVA and Coefficients Table, Residuals Table** and **Durbin-Watson Statistic**.
8. Paste chart output from Figure 16.14.
9. Right click on the line and select **Add Trendline**, select **Linear**, click **Close**.

	A	B	C	D	E	F	G
3	Simple Linear Regression Analysis						
5	*Regression Statistics*						
6	Multiple R	0.9063					
7	R Square	0.8214					
8	Adjusted R Square	0.8114					
9	Standard Error	1618.4501					
10	Observations	20					
12	ANOVA						
13		*df*	*SS*	*MS*	*F*	*Significance F*	
14	Regression	1	216,769,874.590	216,769,874.590	82.76	0.0000	
15	Residual	18	47,148,853.960	2,619,380.776			
16	Total	19	263,918,728.550				
18		*Coefficients*	*Standard Error*	*t Stat*	*P-value*	*Lower 95%*	*Upper 95%*
19	Intercept	-1,022.69	751.82	-1.36	0.19	-2,602.21	556.82
20	Quarter	570.94	62.76	9.10	0.00	439.08	702.79
21	**Durbin-Watson Calculations**						
22	Sum of Squared Difference of Residuals	23,788,635.86					
23	Sum of Squared Residuals	47,148,853.96					
24	**Durbin-Watson Statistic**	0.505					

Minitab Instructions (for similar results):
1. Open file: **Harrison.MTW**.
2. Follow Minitab instructions in Figure 16.13.
3. Choose **Stat > Time Series > Trend Analysis**.
4. In **Variable**, enter time-series column.
5. Under **Model Type**, Choose **Linear**.
6. Click **OK**.

Model Diagnosis

The fit is pretty good with an *R*-squared = 0.8214 and a standard error of 1,618.5. But we need to look closer. Figure 16.15 shows a plot of the trend line compared with the actual data. A close inspection indicates the linear trend model may not be best for this case. Notice that the linear model underforecasts, then overforecasts, then underforecasts again. From this we might suspect positive autocorrelation.

We can establish the following null and alternative hypotheses:

$$H_0: \rho = 0$$
$$H_A: \rho > 0$$

Equation 16.11 could be used to manually compute the Durbin-Watson *d* statistic, or more likely, we would use the PHStat. The calculated Durbin-Watson is

$$d = 0.505$$

The d_L critical value from the Durbin-Watson table in Appendix N for $\alpha = 0.05$ and a sample size of $n = 20$ and $p = 1$ independent variable is 1.20.

Because $d = 0.505 < d_L = 1.20$, we reject the null hypothesis.

We conclude that the error terms are significantly positively autocorrelated. The model-building process needs to be repeated.

Model Specification

After examining Figure 16.15 and determining the results of the test for positive autocorrelation, a nonlinear trend will likely provide a better fit for these data. To account for the nonlinear growth trend, which starts out slowly and then builds rapidly, the forecaster might consider transforming the time variable by squaring t to form a model of the form

$$y = \beta_0 + \beta_1 t + \beta_2 t^2 + \varepsilon$$

This transformation is suggested because the growth in costs appears to be increasing at an increasing rate. Other nonlinear trends may require different types of transformations, such as taking a square root or natural log. Each situation must be analyzed separately. (See the reference by Kutner et al. for further discussion of transformations.)

Model Fitting

Figure 16.16 shows the Excel regression results, and Figure 16.17 shows the revised time-series plot using the polynomial transformation. The resulting nonlinear trend regression model is

$$F_t = 2{,}318.7 - 340.4\,(t) + 43.4\,(t^2)$$

Model Diagnosis

Visually, the transformed model now looks more appropriate. The fit is much better as the R-squared value is increased to 0.9466 and the standard error is reduced to 910.35. The null and alternative hypotheses for testing whether positive autocorrelation exists are

$$H_0: \rho = 0$$
$$H_A: \rho > 0$$

FIGURE 16.16

Excel 2010 (PHStat)
Transformed Regression
Model for Harrison Equipment

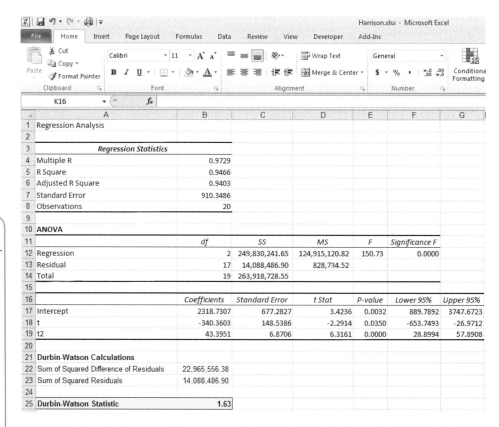

Excel 2010 Instructions:
1. Open file: **Harrison.xlsx**.
2. Select **Add-Ins**.
3. Select **PHStat**.
4. Insert a new column between columns C and D.
5. Create a new variable, t^2 in the newly added column.
6. Select **Regression > Multiple Regression**.
7. Specify the y variable data range.
8. Specify x variables data range (*Quarter* = t and t^2).
9. Check Boxes for **ANOVA and Coefficients Table, Residuals Table** and **Durbin-Watson Statistic**.
10. **Click OK.**

Minitab Instructions (for similar results):
1. Open file: **Harrison.MTW**.
2. Choose **Calc > Calculator**.
3. In **Store result in variable**, enter destination column *Qrt square*.
4. With cursor in **Expressions**, enter *Quarter* column then **2.
5. Click **OK**.
6. Choose **Stat > Regression > Regression**.
7. In **Response**, enter *Repair Costs*. In **Predictors**, enter *Qrt square*.
8. Click **Storage**.
9. Under **Diagnostic Measures**, select **Residuals**. Under **Characteristics of Estimated Equation**, select **Fits**.
10. Click **OK. OK.**

FIGURE 16.17 |

Excel 2010 Transformed
Model for Harrison Equipment
Company

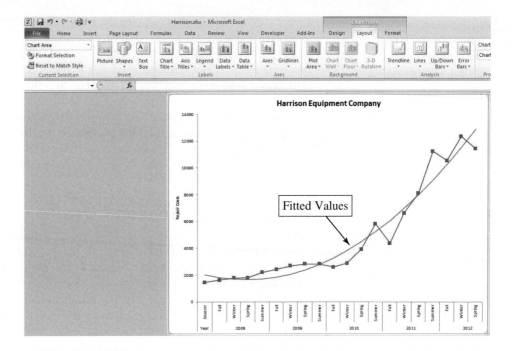

Excel 2010 Instructions:

1. Open file: **Harrison.xlsx**.
2. Insert a new column between columns C and D.
3. Create a new variable, t^2 in the newly added column
4. Select **Add-Ins**.
5. Select **PHStat**.
6. Select **Regression > Multiple Regression**.
7. Specify the *y* variable data range.
8. Specify *x* variables data range (*Quarter* = *t* and t^2).
9. Check Boxes for **ANOVA and Coefficients Table, Residuals Table** and **Durbin-Watson Statistic**.
10. Click **Insert > Line Chart > Line with Markers**.
11. Click **Select Data**.
12. Specify the data range (*Repair Costs*).
13. Under **Horizontal (categories) Axis Labels**, select **Edit**, select data in *Year* and *Quarter* columns.
14. Click OK twice.
15. Click on **Layout > Chart Title**, desired location and enter desired title.
16. Click on **Layout > Axis Titles**, desired location and enter vertical title.
17. Click on **Residuals Table**.
18. Copy and Paste **Predicted Values** on the line chart.
19. Remove markers from predicted values line.

As seen in Figure 16.16, the calculated Durbin-Watson statistic is

$$d = 1.63$$

The d_L and d_U critical values from the Durbin-Watson table in Appendix N for $\alpha = 0.05$ and a sample size of $n = 20$ and $p = 2$ independent variables are 1.10 and 1.54, respectively.

Because $d = 1.63 > 1.54$, the Durbin-Watson test indicates that there is no positive autocorrelation. Given this result and the improvements to *R*-squared and the standard error of the estimate, the nonlinear model is judged superior to the original linear model.

Forecasts for periods 21 and 22, using this latest model, are obtained using the trend projection method.

For period $t = 21$:

$$F_{21} = 2{,}318.7 - 340.4\,(21) + 43.4\,(21^2) = \$14{,}310$$

For period $t = 22$:

$$F_{22} = 2{,}318.7 - 340.4\,(22) + 43.4\,(22^2) = \$15{,}836$$

Using transformations often provides a very effective way of improving the fit of a time series. However, a forecaster should be careful not to get caught up in an exercise of "curve-fitting." One suggestion is that only explainable terms—terms that can be justified—be used for transforming data. For instance, in our example, we might well expect repair costs to increase at a faster rate as a tractor gets older and begins wearing out. Thus, the t^2 transformation seems to make sense.

Some Words of Caution The trend projection method relies on the future behaving in a manner similar to the past. In the previous example, if equipment repair costs continue to follow the pattern displayed over the past 20 quarters, these forecasts may prove acceptable. However, if the future pattern changes, there is no reason to believe these forecasts will be close to actual costs.

Adjusting for Seasonality

In Section 16.1, we discussed seasonality in a time series. The seasonal component represents those changes (highs and lows) in the time series that occur at approximately the same time every period. If the forecasting model you are using does not already explicitly account for seasonality, you should adjust your forecast to take into account the seasonal component. The linear and non-linear trend models discussed thus far do not automatically incorporate the seasonal component. Forecasts using these models should be adjusted as illustrated in the following application.

BUSINESS APPLICATION   **FORECASTING WITH SEASONAL DATA**

BIG MOUNTAIN SKI RESORT Most businesses in the tourist industry know that sales are seasonal. For example, at the Big Mountain Ski Resort, business peaks at two times during the year: winter for skiing and summer for golf and tennis. These peaks can be identified in a time series if the sales data are measured on at least a quarterly basis. Figure 16.18 shows the quarterly sales data for the past four years in spreadsheet form. The line chart for these data is also shown. The data are in the file **Big Mountain**. The time-series plot clearly shows that

Excel Tutorial

FIGURE 16.18

Excel 2010 Big Mountain Resort Quarterly Sales Data

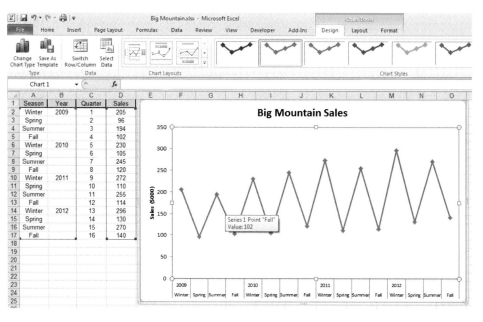

Excel 2010 Instructions:
1. Open file: **Big Mountain.xlsx**.
2. Select data in the *Sales* column.
3. Click **Insert > Line Chart**.
4. Click **Select Data**.
5. Under **Horizontal (categories) Axis Labels**, select data in *Year* and *Season* columns.
6. Click **Layout > Chart Title** and enter desired title.
7. Click **Layout > Axis Titles** and enter vertical title.
8. Click on one of the gridlines, right click, and select **Delete**.

the summer and winter quarters are the busy times. There has also been a slightly increasing linear trend in sales over the four years.

Big Mountain Resort wants to forecast sales for each quarter of the coming year, and it hopes to use a linear trend model. When the historical data show a trend and seasonality, the trend-based forecasting model needs to be adjusted to incorporate the seasonality. One method for doing this involves computing **seasonal indexes**.

For instance, when we have quarterly data, we can develop four seasonal indexes, one each for winter, spring, summer, and fall. A seasonal index below 1.00 indicates that the quarter has a value that is typically below the average value for the year. On the other hand, an index greater than 1.00 indicates that the quarter's value is typically higher than the yearly average.

Computing Seasonal Indexes Although there are several methods for computing the seasonal indexes, the procedure introduced here is the *ratio-to-moving-average method*. This method assumes that the actual time-series data can be represented as a product of the four time-series components—trend, seasonal, cyclical, and random—which produces the multiplicative model shown in Equation 16.13.

> ### Multiplicative Time-Series Model
>
> $$y_t = T_t \times S_t \times C_t \times I_t \tag{16.13}$$
>
> where:
>
> y_t = Value of the time series at time t
> T_t = Trend value at time t
> S_t = Seasonal value at time t
> C_t = Cyclical value at time t
> I_t = Irregular or random value at time t

The ratio-to-moving-average method begins by removing the seasonal and irregular components, S_t and I_t, from the data, leaving the combined trend and cyclical components, T_t and C_t. This is done by first computing successive four-period moving averages for the time series. A moving average is the average of n consecutive values of a time series. Using the Big Mountain sales data in Figure 16.19, we find that the **moving average** using the first four quarters is

$$\frac{205 + 96 + 194 + 102}{4} = 149.25$$

This moving average is associated with the middle time period of the data values in the moving average. The middle period of the first four quarters is 2.5 (between quarter 2 and quarter 3).

The second moving average is found by dropping the value from period 1 and adding the value from period 5, as follows:

$$\frac{96 + 194 + 102 + 230}{4} = 155.50$$

This moving average is associated with time period 3.5, the middle period between quarters 3 and 4.

Figure 16.19 shows the moving averages for the Big Mountain sales data in Excel spreadsheet form. We selected 4 data values for the moving average because we have quarterly data; with monthly data, 12 data values would have been used.

The next step is to compute the *centered moving averages* by averaging each successive pair of moving averages. Centering the moving averages is necessary so that the resulting moving average will be associated with one of the data set's original time periods. In this example, Big Mountain is interested in quarterly sales data—that is, time periods 1, 2, 3, and so on. Therefore, the moving averages we have representing time periods 2.5, 3.5, and so forth are not of interest to Big Mountain. Centering these averaged time series values, however,

Seasonal Index

A number used to quantify the effect of seasonality in time-series data.

Moving Average

The successive averages of n consecutive values in a time series.

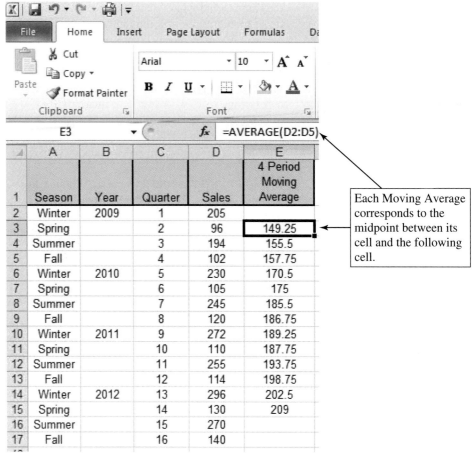

Each Moving Average
corresponds to the
midpoint between its
cell and the following
cell.

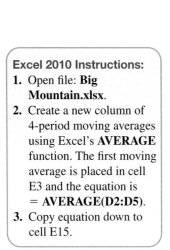

Excel 2010 Instructions:
1. Open file: **Big Mountain.xlsx**.
2. Create a new column of 4-period moving averages using Excel's **AVERAGE** function. The first moving average is placed in cell E3 and the equation is = **AVERAGE(D2:D5)**.
3. Copy equation down to cell E15.

produces moving averages for the (quarterly) time periods of interest. For example, the first two moving averages are averaged to produce the first centered moving average. We get

$$\frac{149.25 + 155.5}{2} = 152.38$$

This centered moving average is associated with quarter 3.[2] The centered moving averages are shown in Figure 16.20. These values estimate the $T_t \times C_t$ value.

If the number of data values used for a moving average is odd, the moving average will be associated with the time period of the middle observation. In such cases, we would not have to center the moving average, as we did in Figure 16.20, because the moving averages would already be associated with one of the time periods from the original time series.

Next, we estimate the $S_t \times I_t$ value. Dividing the actual sales value for each quarter by the corresponding centered moving average, as in Equation 16.14, does this. As an example, we examine the third time period: summer of 2009. The sales value of 194 is divided by the centered moving average of 152.38 to produce 1.273. This value is called the *ratio-to-moving-average*. Figure 16.21 shows these values for the Big Mountain data.

Ratio-to-Moving-Average

$$S_t \times I_t = \frac{y_t}{T_t \times C_t} \tag{16.14}$$

---

[2]Excel's tabular format does not allow the uncentered moving averages to be displayed with their "interquarter" time periods. That is, 149.25 is associated with time period 2.5, 155.50 with time period 3.5, and so forth.

FIGURE 16.20

Excel 2010 Seasonal Index—
Step 2: Big Mountain Resort
Centered Moving Averages

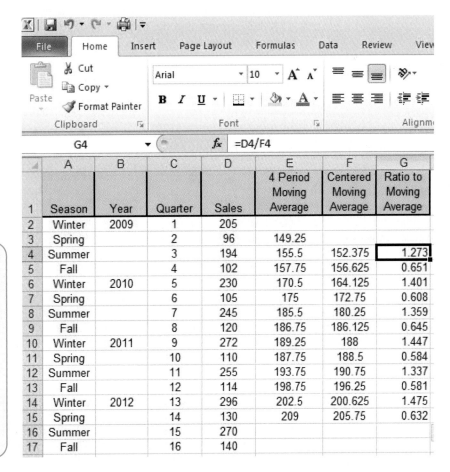

Excel 2010 Instructions:
1. Follow Figure 16.19
   Instructions 1–3.
2. Create a new column of
   centered moving averages
   using Excel's **AVERAGE**
   function. The first moving
   average is placed in cell
   F4 using the equation
   = **AVERAGE(E3:E4)**.
3. Copy the equation down
   to cell F15.

F4 f_x =AVERAGE(E3:E4)

	A	B	C	D	E	F
1	Season	Year	Quarter	Sales	4 Period Moving Average	Centered Moving Average
2	Winter	2009	1	205		
3	Spring		2	96	149.25	
4	Summer		3	194	155.5	152.375
5	Fall		4	102	157.75	156.625
6	Winter	2010	5	230	170.5	164.125
7	Spring		6	105	175	172.75
8	Summer		7	245	185.5	180.25
9	Fall		8	120	186.75	186.125
10	Winter	2011	9	272	189.25	188
11	Spring		10	110	187.75	188.5
12	Summer		11	255	193.75	190.75
13	Fall		12	114	198.75	196.25
14	Winter	2012	13	296	202.5	200.625
15	Spring		14	130	209	205.75
16	Summer		15	270		
17	Fall		16	140		

FIGURE 16.21

Excel 2010 Seasonal Index—
Step 3: Big Mountain Resort
Ratio-to-Moving-Averages

Excel 2010 Instructions:
1. Open File: **Big
   Mountain.xlsx**.
2. Follow Instructions 2 and
   3 in Figures 16.19 and
   16.20.
3. Create a new column of
   ratio-to-moving-averages
   using equation = **D4/F4**
   in column G beginning in
   cell G4.
4. Copy equation down to
   cell G15.

G4 f_x =D4/F4

	A	B	C	D	E	F	G
1	Season	Year	Quarter	Sales	4 Period Moving Average	Centered Moving Average	Ratio to Moving Average
2	Winter	2009	1	205			
3	Spring		2	96	149.25		
4	Summer		3	194	155.5	152.375	1.273
5	Fall		4	102	157.75	156.625	0.651
6	Winter	2010	5	230	170.5	164.125	1.401
7	Spring		6	105	175	172.75	0.608
8	Summer		7	245	185.5	180.25	1.359
9	Fall		8	120	186.75	186.125	0.645
10	Winter	2011	9	272	189.25	188	1.447
11	Spring		10	110	187.75	188.5	0.584
12	Summer		11	255	193.75	190.75	1.337
13	Fall		12	114	198.75	196.25	0.581
14	Winter	2012	13	296	202.5	200.625	1.475
15	Spring		14	130	209	205.75	0.632
16	Summer		15	270			
17	Fall		16	140			

The final step in determining the seasonal indexes is to compute the mean ratio-to-moving-average value for each season. Each quarter's ratio-to-moving-average is averaged over the years to produce the *seasonal index* for that quarter. Figure 16.22 shows the seasonal indexes. The seasonal index for the winter quarter is 1.441. This indicates that sales for Big Mountain during the winter are 44.1% above the average for the year. Also, sales in the spring quarter are only 60.8% of the average for the year.

One important point about the seasonal indexes is that the sum of the indexes is equal to the number of seasonal indexes. That is, the average of all seasonal indexes equals 1.0. In the Big Mountain Resort example, we find

Summer		Fall		Winter		Spring	
1.323	+	0.626	+	1.441	+	0.608 = 3.998 (difference from 4 due to rounding)	

Likewise, in an example with monthly data instead of quarterly data, we would generate 12 seasonal indexes, one for each month. The sum of these indexes should be 12.

The Need to Normalize the Indexes If the sum of the seasonal indexes does not equal the number of time periods in the recurrence period of the time series, an adjustment is necessary. In the Big Mountain Resort example, the sum of the four seasonal indexes may have been something other than 4 (the recurrence period). In such cases, we must adjust the seasonal indexes by multiplying each by the number of time periods in the recurrence period over the sum of the unadjusted seasonal indexes. For quarterly data such as the Big Mountain Resort example, we would multiply each seasonal index by 4/(Sum of the unadjusted seasonal indexes). Performing this multiplication will *normalize* the seasonal indexes. This adjustment is necessary if the seasonal adjustments are going to even out over the recurrence period.

Deseasonalizing A strong seasonal component may partially mask a trend in the time-series data. Consequently, to identify the trend, you should first remove the effect of the seasonal component. This is called *deseasonalizing* the time series.

Again, assume that the multiplicative model shown previously in Equation 16.13 is appropriate:

$$y_t = T_t \times S_t \times C_t \times I_t$$

FIGURE 16.22

Excel 2010 Seasonal Index—Step 4: Big Mountain Resort Mean Ratios

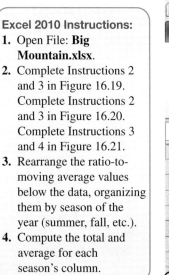

Excel 2010 Instructions:
1. Open File: **Big Mountain.xlsx**.
2. Complete Instructions 2 and 3 in Figure 16.19. Complete Instructions 2 and 3 in Figure 16.20. Complete Instructions 3 and 4 in Figure 16.21.
3. Rearrange the ratio-to-moving average values below the data, organizing them by season of the year (summer, fall, etc.).
4. Compute the total and average for each season's column.

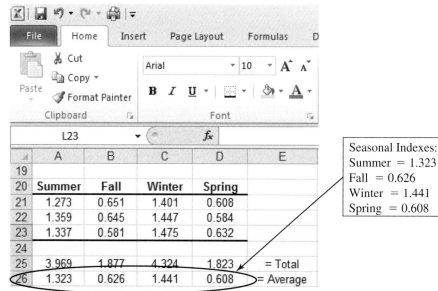

Deseasonalizing is accomplished by dividing y_t by the appropriate seasonal index, S_t, as shown in Equation 16.15.

Deseasonalization

$$T_t \times C_t \times I_t = \frac{y_t}{S_t} \qquad \qquad \textbf{(16.15)}$$

For time period 1, which is the winter quarter, the seasonal index is 1.441. The deseasonalized value for y_1 is

$$205/1.441 = 142.26$$

Figure 16.23 presents the deseasonalized values and the graph of these deseasonalized sales data for the Big Mountain example. This shows that there has been a gentle upward trend over the four years.

Once the data have been deseasonalized, the next step is to determine the trend based on the deseasonalized data. As in the previous examples of trend estimation, you can use Excel to develop the linear model for the deseasonalized data. The results are shown in Figure 16.24. The linear regression trend line equation is

$$F_t = 142.096 + 4.683\,(t)$$

You can use this trend line and the trend projection method to forecast sales for period $t = 17$:

$$F_{17} = 142.096 + 4.683\,(17) = 221.707 = \$221{,}707$$

Seasonally Unadjusted Forecast

A forecast made for seasonal data that does not include an adjustment for the seasonal component in the time series.

This is a **seasonally unadjusted forecast**, because the time-series data used in developing the trend line were deseasonalized.

Now we need to adjust the forecast for period 17 to reflect the quarterly fluctuations. We do this by multiplying the unadjusted forecast values by the appropriate seasonal index. In this case, period 17 corresponds to the winter quarter. The winter quarter has a seasonal index of 1.441, indicating a high sales period. The adjusted forecast is

$$F_{17} = (221.707)(1.441) = 319.480, \text{ or } \$319{,}480$$

FIGURE 16.23 |

Excel 2010 Deseasonalized Time Series for Big Mountain Sales Data

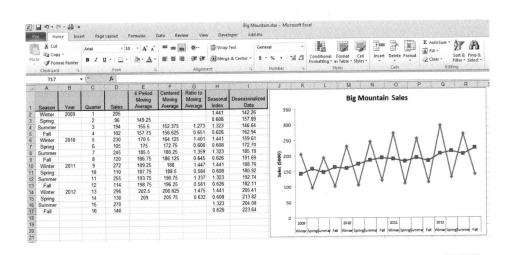

Excel 2010 Instructions:
1. Open file: **Big Mountain.xlsx**.
2. Follow instructions for Figures 16.18 through 16.22.
3. Create a new column to contain the deseasonalized values. Use Excel

equation to form text equation 16.15. For example, in cell I2, use = **D2/1.441**. In cell I2 use, = **D3/0.608**, etc.

4. Select new deseasonalized data from column I and paste onto the line graph.

FIGURE 16.24

Excel 2010 Regression Trend Line of Big Mountain Deseasonalized Data

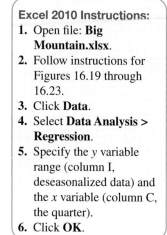

Excel 2010 Instructions:
1. Open file: **Big Mountain.xlsx**.
2. Follow instructions for Figures 16.19 through 16.23.
3. Click **Data**.
4. Select **Data Analysis > Regression**.
5. Specify the y variable range (column I, deseasonalized data) and the x variable (column C, the quarter).
6. Click **OK**.

	A	B	C	D	E	F	G
1	SUMMARY OUTPUT						
2							
3	*Regression Statistics*						
4	Multiple R	0.9416					
5	R Square	0.8865					
6	Adjusted R Square	0.8784					
7	Standard Error	8.2557					
8	Observations	16					
9							
10	ANOVA						
11		*df*	*SS*	*MS*	*F*	*Significance F*	
12	Regression	1	7455.934	7455.934	109.394	0.0000	
13	Residual	14	954.191	68.156			
14	Total	15	8410.125				
15							
16		*Coefficients*	*Standard Error*	*t Stat*	*P-value*	*Lower 95%*	*Upper 95%*
17	Intercept	142.096	4.329	32.822	0.000	132.810	151.381
18	Quarter	4.683	0.448	10.459	0.000	3.723	5.643

Linear Trend Equation:
$F_t = 142.096 + 4.683(t)$

How to do it

The Seasonal Adjustment Process: The Multiplicative Model

We can summarize the steps for performing a seasonal adjustment to a trend-based forecast as follows:

1. Compute each moving average from the k appropriate consecutive data values, where k is the number of values in one period of the time series.

2. Compute the centered moving averages.

3. Isolate the seasonal component by computing the ratio-to-moving-average values.

4. Compute the seasonal indexes by averaging the ratio-to-moving-average values for comparable periods.

5. Normalize the seasonal indexes (if necessary).

6. Deseasonalize the time series by dividing the actual data by the appropriate seasonal index.

7. Use least squares regression to develop the trend line using the deseasonalized data.

8. Develop the unadjusted forecasts using trend projection.

9. Seasonally adjust the forecasts by multiplying the unadjusted forecasts by the appropriate seasonal index.

The seasonally adjusted forecasts for each quarter in 2013 are as follows:

Quarter (2013)	t	Unadjusted Forecast	Index	Adjusted Forecast
Winter	17	221.707	1.441	319.480 = $319,480
Spring	18	226.390	0.608	137.645 = $137,645
Summer	19	231.073	1.323	305.710 = $305,710
Fall	20	235.756	0.626	147.583 = $147,583

You can use the seasonally adjusted trend model when a time series exhibits both a trend and seasonality. This process allows for a better identification of the trend and produces forecasts that are more sensitive to seasonality in the data.

Using Dummy Variables to Represent Seasonality The multiplicative model approach for dealing with seasonal data in a time-series forecasting application is one method that is commonly used by forecasters. Another method used to incorporate the seasonal component into a linear trend forecast involves the use of dummy variables. To illustrate, we again use the Big Mountain example, which had four years of quarterly data. Because of quarterly data, start by constructing 3 dummy variables (one less than the number of data values in the year; if you have monthly data, construct 11 dummy variables). Form dummy variables as follows:

$$x_1 = 1 \text{ if season is winter} \qquad x_1 = 0 \text{ if not winter}$$
$$x_2 = 1 \text{ if season is spring} \qquad x_2 = 0 \text{ if not spring}$$
$$x_3 = 1 \text{ if season is summer} \qquad x_3 = 0 \text{ if not summer}$$

Table 16.5 shows the revised data set for the Big Mountain Company.

Next form a multiple regression model:

$$F_t = \beta_0 + \beta_1 t + \beta_2 x_1 + \beta_3 x_2 + \beta_4 x_3 + \varepsilon$$

Note, this model formulation is an extension of the linear trend model where the seasonality is accounted for by adding the regression coefficient for the season to the linear trend fitted value.

TABLE 16.5 | **Big Mountain Sales Output Using Dummy Variables**

Season	Year	y Sales	Quarter = t	x_1 Winter Dummy	x_2 Spring Dummy	x_3 Summer Dummy
Winter	2009	205	1	1	0	0
Spring		96	2	0	1	0
Summer		194	3	0	0	1
Fall		102	4	0	0	0
Winter	2010	230	5	1	0	0
Spring		105	6	0	1	0
Summer		245	7	0	0	1
Fall		120	8	0	0	0
Winter	2011	272	9	1	0	0
Spring		110	10	0	1	0
Summer		255	11	0	0	1
Fall		114	12	0	0	0
Winter	2012	296	13	1	0	0
Spring		130	14	0	1	0
Summer		270	15	0	0	1
Fall		140	16	0	0	0

Figure 16.25 shows the Excel multiple regression output. The regression equation is

$$F_t = 71.0 + 4.8t + 146.2(x_1) + 0.9(x_2) + 126.8(x_3)$$

The R-square value is very high at 0.9710, indicating the regression model fits the historical data quite well. The F-ratio of 92.07 is significant at any reasonable level of significance, indicating the overall regression model is statistically significant. However, the p-value for x_2,

FIGURE 16.25

Excel 2010 Regression Output with Dummy Variables Included—Big Mountain Example

Excel 2010 Instructions:
1. Open file: **Big Mountain.xlsx**.
2. Between columns C and D, insert 3 dummy variable columns for winter, spring, summer (i.e., Winter variable = 1 if Winter, 0 if not Winter).
3. Click **Data**.
4. Select **Data Analysis > Regression**.
5. Specify y variable, Sales (column D) and x variables (Quarter and three new dummy variables).
6. Click **OK**.

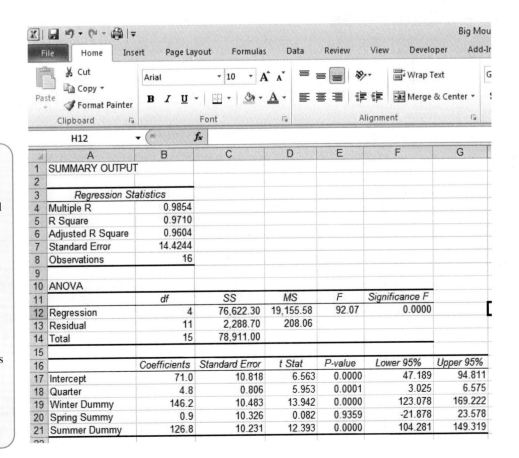

	A	B	C	D	E	F	G
1	SUMMARY OUTPUT						
2							
3	Regression Statistics						
4	Multiple R	0.9854					
5	R Square	0.9710					
6	Adjusted R Square	0.9604					
7	Standard Error	14.4244					
8	Observations	16					
9							
10	ANOVA						
11		df	SS	MS	F	Significance F	
12	Regression	4	76,622.30	19,155.58	92.07	0.0000	
13	Residual	11	2,288.70	208.06			
14	Total	15	78,911.00				
15							
16		Coefficients	Standard Error	t Stat	P-value	Lower 95%	Upper 95%
17	Intercept	71.0	10.818	6.563	0.0000	47.189	94.811
18	Quarter	4.8	0.806	5.953	0.0001	3.025	6.575
19	Winter Dummy	146.2	10.483	13.942	0.0000	123.078	169.222
20	Spring Summy	0.9	10.326	0.082	0.9359	-21.878	23.578
21	Summer Dummy	126.8	10.231	12.393	0.0000	104.281	149.319

the spring dummy variable, is 0.9359, indicating that variable is insignificant. Consequently, we will drop this variable and rerun the regression analysis with only three independent variables. The resulting model is

$$F_t = 71.5 + 4.8t + 145.7x_1 + 126.4x_3$$

This overall model is significant, and all three variables are statistically significant at any reasonable level of alpha. The coefficients on the two dummy variables can be interpreted as the seasonal indexes for winter and summer. The indexes for spring and fall are incorporated into the intercept value. We can now use this model to develop forecasts for year 5 (periods 17–20) as follows:

$$\text{Winter} (t = 17): F_t = 71.5 + 4.8\,(17) + 145.7\,(1) + 126.4\,(0) = 298.80 = \$298{,}800$$
$$\text{Spring} (t = 18): F_t = 71.5 + 4.8\,(18) + 145.7\,(0) + 126.4\,(0) = 157.90 = \$157{,}900$$
$$\text{Summer} (t = 19): F_t = 71.5 + 4.8\,(19) + 145.7\,(0) + 126.4\,(1) = 289.10 = \$289{,}100$$
$$\text{Fall} (t = 20): F_t = 71.5 + 4.8\,(20) + 145.7\,(0) + 126.4\,(0) = 167.50 = \$167{,}500$$

If you compare these forecasts to the ones we previously obtained using the multiplicative model approach, the forecasts for winter and summer are lower with the dummy variable model but higher for spring and fall. You could use the split-sample approach to test the two alternative approaches to see which, in this case, seems to provide more accurate forecasts based on *MAD* and *MSE* calculations.

Both the multiplicative and the dummy variable approach have their advantages and both methods are commonly used by business forecasters.

MyStatLab

16-2: Exercises

Skill Development

Problems **16-18 to 16-22** refer to Tran's Furniture Store, which has maintained monthly sales records for the past 48 months, with the following results:

Month	Sales ($)	Month	Sales ($)
1 (Jan.)	23,500	19	31,100
2	21,700	20	32,400
3	18,750	21	34,500
4	22,000	22	35,700
5	23,000	23	42,000
6	26,200	24	42,600
7	27,300	25 (Jan.)	31,000
8	29,300	26	30,400
9	31,200	27	29,800
10	34,200	28	32,500
11	39,500	29	34,500
12	43,400	30	33,800
13 (Jan.)	23,500	31	34,200
14	23,400	32	36,700
15	21,400	33	39,700
16	24,200	34	42,400
17	26,900	35	43,600
18	29,700	36	47,400

Month	Sales ($)	Month	Sales ($)
37 (Jan)	32,400	43	37,500
38	35,600	44	40,000
39	31,200	45	43,200
40	34,600	46	46,700
41	36,800	47	50,100
42	35,700	48	52,100

16-18. Based on the Durbin-Watson statistic, is there evidence of autocorrelation in these data? Use a linear trend model.

16-19. Using the multiplicative model, estimate the $T \times C$ portion by computing a 12-month moving average and then the centered 12-month moving average.

16-20. Estimate the $S \times I$ portion of the multiplicative model by finding the ratio-to-moving-averages for the time-series data. Determine whether these ratio-to-moving-averages are stable from year to year.

16-21. Extract the irregular component by taking the normalized average of the ratio-to-moving-averages.

Make a table that shows the normalized seasonal indexes. Interpret what the index for January means relative to the index for July.

16-22. Based on your work in the previous three problems,
  a. Determine a seasonally adjusted linear trend forecasting model. Compare this model with an unadjusted linear trend model. Use both models to forecast Tran's sales for period 49.
  b. Which of the two models developed has the lower *MAD* and lower *MSE*?

16-23. Consider the following set of sales data, given in millions of dollars:

2006	2008
1st quarter 152	1st quarter 217
2nd quarter 162	2nd quarter 209
3rd quarter 157	3rd quarter 202
4th quarter 167	4th quarter 221

2007	2009
1st quarter 182	1st quarter 236
2nd quarter 192	2nd quarter 242
3rd quarter 191	3rd quarter 231
4th quarter 197	4th quarter 224

  a. Plot these data. Based on your visual observations, what time-series components are present in the data?
  b. Determine the seasonal index for each quarter.
  c. Fit a linear trend model to the data and determine the *MAD* and *MSE* values. Comment on the adequacy of the linear trend model based on these measures of forecast error.
  d. Provide a seasonally unadjusted forecast using the linear trend model for each quarter of the year 2010.
  e. Use the seasonal index values computed in part b to provide seasonal adjusted forecasts for each quarter of 2010.

16-24. Examine the following time series:

t	1	2	3	4	5	6	7	8	9	10
y_t	52	72	58	66	68	60	46	43	17	3

  a. Produce a scatter plot of this time series. Indicate the appropriate forecasting model for this time series.
  b. Construct the equation for the forecasting model identified in part a.
  c. Produce forecasts for time periods 11, 12, 13, and 14.
  d. Obtain the forecast bias for the forecasts produced in part c if the actual time series values are -35, -41, -79, and -100 for periods 11 through 14, respectively.

16-25. Examine the following quarterly data:

t	1	2	3	4	5	6	7	8	9	10	11	12
y_t	2	12	23	20	18	32	48	41	35	52	79	63

  a. Compute the four-period moving averages for this set of data.
  b. Compute the centered moving averages from the moving averages of part a.
  c. Compute the ratio-to-moving-averages values.
  d. Calculate the seasonal indexes. Normalize them if necessary.
  e. Deseasonalize the time series.
  f. Produce the trend line using the deseasonalized data.
  g. Produce seasonally adjusted forecasts for each of the time periods 13, 14, 15, and 16.

Business Applications

16-26. "The average college senior graduated this year with more than $19,000 in debt" was the beginning sentence of a recent article in *USA Today*. The majority of students have loans that are not due until the student leaves school. This can result in the student ignoring the size of debt that piles up. Federal loans obtained to finance college education are steadily mounting. The data given here show the amount of loans ($million) for the last 13 academic years, with year 20 being the most recent.

Year	Amount	Year	Amount	Year	Amount
1	9,914	8	16,221	15	37,228
2	10,182	9	22,557	16	39,101
3	12,493	10	26,011	17	42,761
4	13,195	11	28,737	18	49,360
5	13,414	12	31,906	19	57,463
6	13,890	13	33,930	20	62,614
7	15,232	14	34,376		

  a. Produce a time-series plot of these data. Indicate the time-series components that exist in the data.
  b. Conduct a test of hypothesis to determine if there exists a linear trend in these data. Use a significance level of 0.10 and the *p*-value approach.
  c. Provide a 90% prediction interval for the amount of federal loans for the 26th academic year.

16-27. The average monthly price of regular gasoline in Southern California is monitored by the Automobile Club of Southern California's monthly Fuel Gauge Report. The prices of the time period July 2004 to June 2006 are given here.

Month	Price ($)	Month	Price ($)	Month	Price ($)
7/04	2.247	3/05	2.344	11/05	2.637
8/04	2.108	4/05	2.642	12/05	2.289
9/04	2.111	5/05	2.532	1/06	2.357
10/04	2.352	6/05	2.375	2/06	2.628
11/04	2.374	7/05	2.592	3/06	2.626
12/04	2.192	8/05	2.774	4/06	2.903
1/05	1.989	9/05	3.031	5/06	3.417
2/05	2.130	10/05	2.943	6/06	3.301

  a. Produce a time-series plot of the average price of regular gas in Southern California. Identify any time-series components that exist in the data.

b. Identify the recurrence period of the time series. Determine the seasonal index for each month within the recurrence period.

c. Fit a linear trend model to the deseasonalized data.

d. Provide a seasonally adjusted forecast using the linear trend model for July 2006 and July 2010.

16-28. Manuel Gutierrez correctly predicted the increasing need for home health care services due to the country's aging population. Five years ago, he started a company offering meal delivery, physical therapy, and minor housekeeping services in the Galveston area. Since that time, he has opened offices in seven additional Gulf State cities. Manuel is currently analyzing the revenue data from his first location for the first five years of operation.

	Revenue ($10,000s)				
	2005	2006	2007	2008	2009
January	23	67	72	76	81
February	34	63	64	75	72
March	45	65	64	77	71
April	48	71	77	81	83
May	46	75	79	86	85
June	49	70	72	75	77
July	60	72	71	80	79
August	65	75	77	82	84
September	67	80	79	86	91
October	60	78	78	87	86
November	71	89	87	91	94
December	76	94	92	96	99

a. Plot these data. Based on your visual observations, what time-series components are present in the data?

b. Determine the seasonal index for each month.

c. (1) Fit a linear trend model to the deseasonalized data for the years 2005–2009 and determine the *MAD* and *MSE* for forecasts for each of the months in 2010. (2) Conduct a test of hypothesis to determine if the linear trend model fits the existing data. (3) Comment on the adequacy of the linear trend model based on the measures of forecast error and the hypothesis test you conducted.

d. Manuel had hoped to reach $2,000,000 in revenue by the time he had been in business for 10 years. From the results in part c, is this a feasible goal based on the historical data provided? Consider and comment on the size of the standard error for this prediction. What makes this value so large? How does it affect your conclusion?

e. Use the seasonal index values computed in part b to provide seasonal adjusted forecasts for each month of the year 2010.

16-29. A major brokerage company has an office in Miami, Florida. The manager of the office is evaluated based on the number of new clients generated each quarter. The following data reflect the number of new customers added during each quarter between 2006 and 2009.

2006	2007
1st quarter 218	1st quarter 250
2nd quarter 190	2nd quarter 220
3rd quarter 236	3rd quarter 265
4th quarter 218	4th quarter 241

2008	2009
1st quarter 244	1st quarter 229
2nd quarter 228	2nd quarter 221
3rd quarter 263	3rd quarter 248
4th quarter 240	4th quarter 231

a. Plot the time series and discuss the components that are present in the data.

b. Referring to part a, fit the linear trend model to the data for the years 2006 through 2008. Then use the resulting model to forecast the number of new brokerage customers for each quarter in the year 2009. Compute the *MAD* and *MSE* for these forecasts and discuss the results.

c. Using the data for the years 2006 through 2008, determine the seasonal indexes for each quarter.

d. Develop a seasonally unadjusted forecast for the four quarters of year 2009.

e. Using the seasonal indexes computed in part d, determine the seasonally adjusted forecast for each quarter for the year 2009. Compute the *MAD* and *MSE* for these forecasts.

f. Examine the values for the *MAD* and *MSE* in parts b and e. Which of the two forecasting techniques would you recommend the manager use to forecast the number of new clients generated each quarter? Support your choice by giving your rationale.

Computer Database **Exercises**

16-30. Logan Pickens is a plan/build construction company specializing in resort area construction projects. Plan/build companies typically have a cash flow problem since they tend to be paid in lump sums when projects are completed or hit milestones. However, their expenses, such as payroll, must be paid regularly. Consequently, such companies need bank lines of credit to finance their initial costs, but in 2009, lines of credit were difficult to negotiate. The data file **Logan-Pickens** contains month-end cash balances for the past 16 months.

a. Plot the data as a time-series graph. Discuss what the graph implies concerning the relationship between cash balance and the time variable, month.

b. Fit a linear trend model to the data. Compute the coefficient of determination for this model and show the trend line on the time-series graph. Discuss the appropriateness of the linear trend model. What are the strengths and weaknesses of the model?

c. Referring to part b, compute the *MAD* and *MSE* for the 16 data points.

d. Use the t^2 transformation approach and recompute the linear model using the transformed time variable. Plot the new trend line against the transformed data. Discuss whether this model appears to provide a better fit than did the model without the transformation. Compare the coefficients of determination for the two models. Which model seems to be superior, using the coefficient of determination as the criterion?

e. Refer to part d. Compute the *MAD* and *MSE* for the 16 data values. Discuss how these compare to those that were computed in part c, prior to transformation. Do the measures of fit (R^2, *MSE*, or *MAD*) agree on the best model to use for forecasting purposes?

16-31. Refer to Problem 16-30.

a. Use the linear trend model (without transformation) for the first 15 months and provide a cash balance forecast for month 16. Then make the t^2 transformation and develop a new linear trend forecasting model based on months 1 through 15. Forecast the cash balance for month 16. Now compare the accuracy of the forecasts with and without the transformation. Which of the two forecast models would you prefer? Explain your answer.

b. Provide a 95% prediction interval for the cash balance forecast for month 16 using the linear trend model both with and without the transformation. Which interval has the widest width? On this basis, which procedure would you choose?

16-32. The federal funds rate is the interest rate charged by banks when banks borrow "overnight" from each other. The funds rate fluctuates according to supply and demand and is not under the direct control of the Federal Reserve Board but is strongly influenced by the Fed's actions. The file titled **The Fed** contains the federal funds rates for the period 1955 through 2008.

a. Produce a scatter plot of the federal funds rate for the period 1955 through 2008. Identify any time-series components that exist in the data.

b. Identify the recurrence period of the time series. Determine the seasonal index for each month within the recurrence period.

c. Fit a nonlinear trend model that uses coded years and coded years squared as predictors for the deseasonalized data.

d. Provide a seasonally adjusted forecast using the nonlinear trend model for 2010 and 2012.

e. Diagnose the model.

16-33. The Census Bureau of the Department of Commerce released the U.S. retail e-commerce sales ("Quarterly Retail E-Commerce Sales 1st Quarter 2006," May 18, 2006) for the period of Fourth Quarter 1999 through Fourth Quarter 2008. The file titled **E-Commerce** contains those data.

a. Produce a time-series plot of this data. Indicate the time-series components that exist in the data.

b. Conduct a test of hypothesis to determine if there exists a linear trend in these data. Use a significance level of 0.10 and the *p*-value approach.

c. Provide forecasts for the e-commerce retail sales for the next four quarters.

d. Presume the next four quarters exhibit e-commerce retail sales of $35,916, $36,432, $35,096, and $36,807, respectively. Produce the forecast bias. Interpret this number in the context of this exercise.

END EXERCISES 16-2

16.3 Forecasting Using Smoothing Methods

The trend-based forecasting technique introduced in the previous section is widely used and can be very effective in many situations. However, it has a disadvantage in that it gives as much weight to the earliest data in the time series as it does to the data that are close to the period for which the forecast is required. Also, this trend approach does not provide an opportunity for the model to "learn" or "adjust" to changes in the time series.

A class of forecasting techniques called *smoothing models* is widely used to overcome these problems and to provide forecasts in situations in which there is no pronounced trend in the data. These models attempt to "smooth out" the random or irregular component in the time series by an averaging process. In this section we introduce two frequently used smoothing-based forecasting techniques: single exponential smoothing and double exponential smoothing. Double exponential smoothing offers a modification to the single exponential smoothing model that specifically deals with trends.

Chapter Outcome 5. → # Exponential Smoothing

The trend-based forecasting methods discussed in Section 16.2 are used in many forecasting situations. As we showed, the least squares trend line is computed using all available historical data. Each observation is given equal input in establishing the trend line, thus allowing the trend line to reflect all the past data. If the future pattern looks like the past, the forecast should be reasonably accurate.

However, in many situations involving time-series data, the more recent the observation, the more indicative it is of possible future values. For example, this month's sales are probably a better indicator of next month's sales than would be sales from 20 months ago. However, the regression analysis approach to trend-based forecasting does not take this fact into account. The data from 20 periods ago will be given the same weight as data from the most current period in developing a forecasting model. This equal valuation can be a drawback to the trend-based forecasting approach.

Exponential Smoothing
A time-series and forecasting technique that produces an exponentially weighted moving average in which each smoothing calculation or forecast is dependent on all previous observed values.

With **exponential smoothing**, current observations can be weighted more heavily than older observations in determining the forecast. Therefore, if in recent periods the time-series values are much higher (or lower) than those in earlier periods, the forecast can be made to reflect this difference. The extent to which the forecast reflects the current data depends on the weights assigned by the decision maker.

We will introduce two classes of exponential smoothing models: single exponential smoothing and double exponential smoothing. Double smoothing is used when a time series exhibits a linear trend. Single smoothing is used when no linear trend is present in the time series. Both single and double exponential smoothing are appropriate for short-term forecasting and for time series that are not seasonal.

Single Exponential Smoothing   Just as its name implies, single exponential smoothing uses a single smoothing constant. Equations 16.16 and 16.17 represent two equivalent methods for forecasting using single exponential smoothing.

Exponential Smoothing Model

$$F_{t+1} = F_t + \alpha(y_t - F_t) \tag{16.16}$$

or

$$F_{t+1} = \alpha y_t + (1 - \alpha)F_t \tag{16.17}$$

where:

F_{t+1} = Forecast value for period $t + 1$
y_t = Actual value of the time series at time t
F_t = Forecast value for period t
α = Alpha (smoothing constant $0 \leq \alpha \leq 1$)

The logic of the exponential smoothing model is that the forecast made for the next period will equal the forecast made for the current period, plus or minus some adjustment factor. The adjustment factor is determined by the difference between this period's forecast and the actual value $(y_t - F_t)$, multiplied by the smoothing constant, α. The idea is that if we forecast low, we will adjust next period's forecast upward, by an amount determined by the smoothing constant.

Excel Tutorial

EXAMPLE 16-6   **DEVELOPING A SINGLE EXPONENTIAL SMOOTHING MODEL**

Dawson Graphic Design Consider the past 10 weeks of potential incoming customer sales calls for Dawson Graphic Design located in Orlando, Florida. These data and their line graph are shown in Figure 16.26. The data showing the number of incoming calls from potential customers are in the file **Dawson**. Suppose the current time period is the end of week 10 and we wish to forecast the number of incoming calls for week 11 using a single exponential smoothing model.

FIGURE 16.26

Incoming Sales Calls Data and Line Graph for Dawson Graphic Design

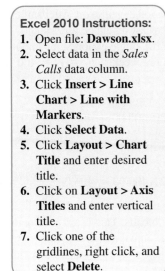

Excel 2010 Instructions:
1. Open file: **Dawson.xlsx**.
2. Select data in the *Sales Calls* data column.
3. Click **Insert > Line Chart > Line with Markers**.
4. Click **Select Data**.
5. Click **Layout > Chart Title** and enter desired title.
6. Click on **Layout > Axis Titles** and enter vertical title.
7. Click one of the gridlines, right click, and select **Delete**.

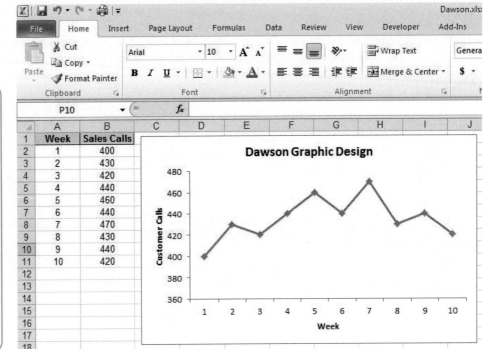

The following steps can be used:

Step 1 Specify the model.

Because the data do not exhibit a pronounced trend and because we are interested in a short-term forecast (one period ahead), the single exponential smoothing model with a single smoothing constant can be used.

Step 2 Fit the model.

We start by selecting a value for α, the smoothing constant, between 0.0 and 1.0. The closer α is to 0.0, the less influence the current observations have in determining the forecast. Small α values will result in greater smoothing of the time series. Likewise, when α is near 1.0, the current observations have greater impact in determining the forecast and less smoothing will occur. There is no firm rule for selecting the value for the smoothing constant. However, in general, if the time series is quite stable, a small α should be used to lessen the impact of random or irregular fluctuations. Because the time series shown in Figure 16.26 appears to be relatively stable, we will use $\alpha = 0.20$ in this example.

The forecast value for period $t = 11$ is found using Equation 16.17, as follows:

$$F_{11} = 0.20y_{10} + (1 - 0.20)F_{10}$$

This demonstrates that the forecast for period 11 is a weighted average of the actual number of calls in period 10 and the forecast for period 10. Although we know the number of calls for period 10, we don't know the forecast for period 10. However, we can determine it by

$$F_{10} = 0.20y_9 + (1 - 0.20)F_9$$

Again, this forecast is a weighted average of the actual number of calls in period 9 and the forecast calls for period 9. We would continue in this manner until we get to

$$F_2 = 0.20y_1 + (1 - 0.20)F_1$$

This requires a forecast for period 1. Because we have no data before period 1 from which to develop a forecast, a rule often used is to assume that $F_1 = y_1$.[3]

Forecast for period 1 = Actual value in period 1

---

[3]Another approach for establishing the starting value, F_1, is to use the mean value for some portion of the available data. Regardless of the method used, the quantity of available data should be large enough to dampen out the impact of the starting value.

Because setting the starting value is somewhat arbitrary, you should obtain as much historical data as possible to "warm" the model and dampen out the effect of the starting value. In our example, we have 10 periods of data to warm the model before the forecast for period 11 is made. Note that when using an exponential smoothing model, the effect of the initial forecast is reduced by $(1 - \alpha)$ in the forecast for period 2, then reduced again for period 3, and so on. After sufficient periods, any error due to the arbitrary initial forecast should be very small.

Figure 16.27 shows the results of using the single exponential smoothing equation and Excel for weeks 1 through 10. For week 1, $F_1 = y_1 = 400$. Then, for week 2, we get

$$F_2 = 0.20y_1 + (1 - 0.20)F_1$$
$$F_2 = (0.20)400 + (1 - 0.20)400.00 = 400.00$$

For week 3,

$$F_3 = 0.20y_2 + (1 - 0.20)F_2$$
$$F_3 = (0.20)430 + (1 - 0.20)400.00 = 406.00$$

At the end of week 2, after seeing what actually happened to the number of calls in week 2, our forecast for week 3 is 406 calls. This is a 6-unit increase over the forecast for week 2 of 400 calls. The actual number of calls in week 2 was 430, rather than 400. The number of calls for week 2 was 30 units higher than the forecast for that time period. Because the actual calls were larger than the forecast, an adjustment must be made. The 6-unit adjustment is determined by multiplying the smoothing constant by the forecast error $[0.20(30) = 6]$, as specified in Equation 16.16. The adjustment compensates for the forecast error in week 2.

FIGURE 16.27

Dawson Graphic Design
Single Exponential
Smoothing—Excel
Spreadsheet

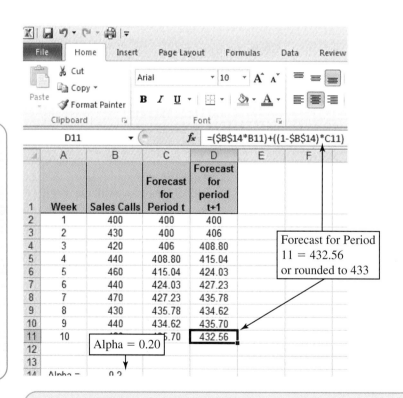

Excel 2010 Instructions:
1. Open file: **Dawson.xlsx**.
2. Create and label two new columns.
3. Enter the smoothing constant (alpha) in an empty cell. (e.g., B14 = 0.20).
4. Enter initial starting value forecast for period 1 in cell C3 = 400.
5. Use text equation 16.17 to create forecast of period t + 1 in cell D2.
6. Copy equation down to cell D12.

Minitab Instructions (for similar results):
1. Open file: **Dawson.MTW**.
2. Choose **Stat > Time Series > Single Exp Smoothing**.
3. In **Variable**, enter time series column.
4. Under **Weight to use in smoothing**, select Use and insert α.
5. Click on **Storage** and select **Fits (one-period-ahead forecasts)**.
6. Click **OK. OK.**

Continuing for week 4 again using Equation 16.17,

$$F_4 = 0.20y_3 + (1 - 0.20)F_3$$
$$F_4 = (0.20)420 + (1 - 0.20)406.00 = 408.80$$

Recall that our forecast for week 3 was 406. However, actual calls were higher than forecast at 420, and we underforecast by 14 calls. The adjustment for week 4 is then $0.20(14) = 2.80$, and the forecast for week 4 is $406 + 2.80 = 408.80$.

This process continues through the data until we are ready to forecast week 11, as shown in Figure 16.27.

$$F_{11} = 0.20y_{10} + (1 - 0.20)F_{10}$$
$$F_{11} = (0.20)420 + (1 - 0.20)435.70 = 432.56$$

Dawson Graphic Design managers would forecast incoming customer calls for week 11 of 433. If we wished to forecast week 12 calls, we would either use the week 11 forecast or wait until the actual week 11 calls are known and then update the smoothing equations to get a new forecast for week 12.

Step 3 Diagnose the model.

However, before we actually use the exponential smoothing forecast for decision-making purposes, we need to determine how successfully the model fits the historical data. Unlike the trend-based forecast, which uses least squares regression, there is no need to use split samples to test the forecasting ability of an exponential smoothing model, because the forecasts are "true forecasts." The forecast for a given period is made before considering the actual value for that period.

Figure 16.28 shows the *MAD* for the forecast model with $\alpha = 0.20$ and a plot of the forecast values versus the actual call values. This plot shows

FIGURE 16.28

Excel 2010 Output for Dawson Graphic Design *MAD* Computation for Single Exponential Smoothing, $\alpha = 0.20$

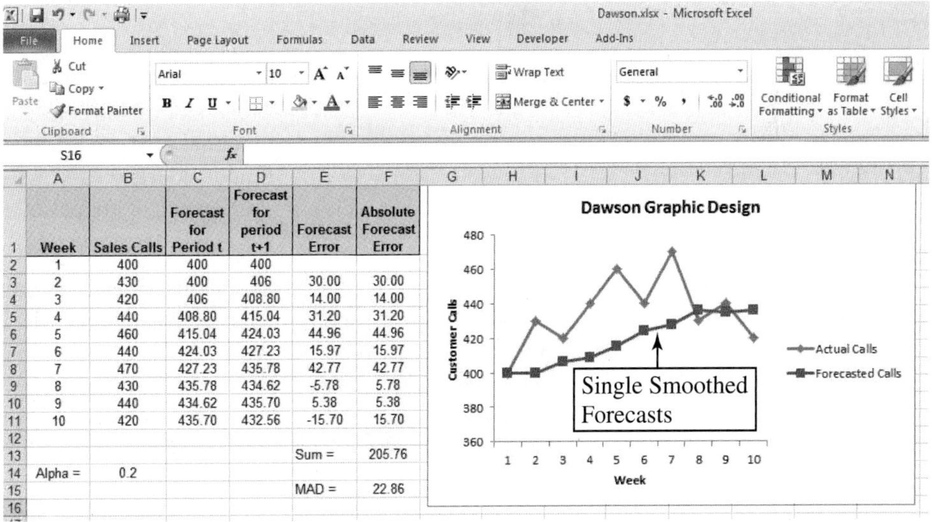

Week	Sales Calls	Forecast for Period t	Forecast for period t+1	Forecast Error	Absolute Forecast Error
1	400	400	400		
2	430	400	406	30.00	30.00
3	420	406	408.80	14.00	14.00
4	440	408.80	415.04	31.20	31.20
5	460	415.04	424.03	44.96	44.96
6	440	424.03	427.23	15.97	15.97
7	470	427.23	435.78	42.77	42.77
8	430	435.78	434.62	-5.78	5.78
9	440	434.62	435.70	5.38	5.38
10	420	435.70	432.56	-15.70	15.70
				Sum =	205.76
Alpha =	0.2				
				MAD =	22.86

Minitab Instructions (for similar results):

1. Open file: **Dawson.MTW**.
2. Choose **Stat > Time Series > Single Exp Smoothing**.
3. In **Variable**, enter time series column.
4. Under **Weight to Use in Smoothing**, select **Optimal ARIMA**.
5. Click **OK**.

Excel 2010 Instructions:

1. Open File: **Dawson.xlsx**.
2. Follow Figure 16.27 instructions.
3. Create a column of forecast errors using an Excel equation starting in E3.
4. Starting in cell F3, create a column of absolute forecast errors using Excel's **ABS** function.
5. Compute the *MAD* starting in F3 using the **AVERAGE** function for the column on absolute errors.
6. Select *Sales Calls* and *Forecast* data.
7. Click **Insert > Line Chart**.
8. Click **Layout > Chart Title** and enter desired title.
9. Click **Layout > Axis Titles** and enter vertical title.
10. Click one of the gridlines, right click, and select **Delete**.

the smoothing that has occurred. Note, we don't include period 1 in the *MAD* calculation since the forecast is set equal to the actual value.

Our next step would be to try different smoothing constants and find the *MAD* for each new α. The forecast for period 11 would be made using the smoothing constant that generates the smallest *MAD*.

>> **END EXAMPLE**

TRY PROBLEM 16-34 (pg. 731)

A major advantage of the single exponential smoothing model is that it is easy to update. In Example 16-6, the forecast for week 12 using this model is found by simply plugging the actual data value for week 11, once it is known, into the smoothing formula.

$$F_{12} = \alpha y_{11} + (1 - \alpha)F_{11}$$

We do not need to go back and recompute the entire model, as would have been necessary with a trend-based regression model.

Chapter Outcome 5. →   **Double Exponential Smoothing**   When the time series has an increasing or decreasing trend, a modification to the single exponential smoothing model is used to explicitly account for the trend. The resulting technique is called *double exponential smoothing*. The double exponential smoothing model is often referred to as *exponential smoothing with trend*. In double exponential smoothing, a second smoothing constant, beta (β), is included to account for the trend. Equations 16.18, 16.19, and 16.20 are needed to provide the forecasts.

Double Exponential Smoothing Model

$$C_t = \alpha y_t + (1 - \alpha)(C_{t-1} + T_{t-1}) \qquad (16.18)$$

$$T_t = \beta(C_t - C_{t-1}) + (1 - \beta)T_{t-1} \qquad (16.19)$$

$$F_{t+1} = C_t + T_t \qquad (16.20)$$

where:

y_t = Value of the time series at time t
α = Constant-process smoothing constant
β = Trend-smoothing constant
C_t = Smoothed constant-process value for period t
T_t = Smoothed trend value for period t
F_{t+1} = Forecast value for period $t + 1$
t = Current time period

Equation 16.18 is used to smooth the time-series data; Equation 16.19 is used to smooth the trend; and Equation 16.20 combines the two smoothed values to form the forecast for period $t + 1$.

EXAMPLE 16-7   **DOUBLE EXPONENTIAL SMOOTHING**

Excel Tutorial

Pakhnyushchyy/Fotolia

Billingsley Insurance Company   The Billingsley Insurance Company has maintained data on the number of automobile claims filed at its Denver office over the past 12 months. These data, which are in the file **Billingsley**, are listed and graphed in Figure 16.29. The claims manager wants to forecast claims for month 13. A double exponential smoothing model can be developed using the following steps:

Step 1   **Specify the model.**
The time series contains a strong upward trend, so a double exponential smoothing model might be selected.

As was the case with single exponential smoothing, we must select starting values. In the case of the double exponential smoothing model, we must select

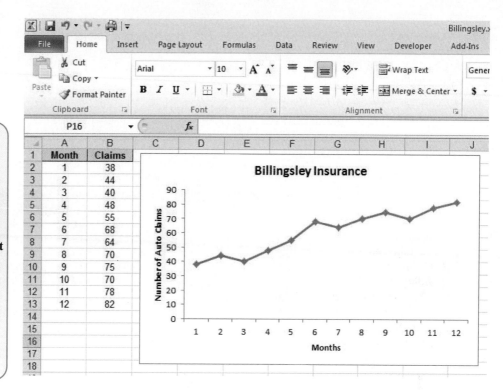

Excel 2010 Instructions:
1. Open file:
   Billingsley.xlsx.
2. Select data in the *Claims*
   data column.
3. Click on **Insert > Line
   Chart**.
4. Click on **Layout > Chart
   Title** and enter desired
   title.
5. Click on **Layout > Axis
   Titles** and enter vertical
   title.
6. Click on one of the
   gridlines, right click, and
   select **Delete**.

initial values for C_0, T_0, and the smoothing constants α and β. The choice of
smoothing constant values (α and β) depends on the same issues as those discussed
earlier for single exponential smoothing. That is, use larger smoothing constants
when less smoothing is desired and values closer to 0 when more smoothing is
desired. The larger the smoothing constant value, the more impact that current data
will have on the forecast. Suppose we use $\alpha = 0.20$ and $\beta = 0.30$ in this example. There are several approaches for selecting starting values for C_0 and T_0. The
method we use here is to fit the least squares trend to the historical data,

$$\hat{y}_t = b_0 + b_1 t$$

where the y intercept, b_0, is used as the starting value, C_0, and the slope, b_1, is
used as the starting value for the trend, T_0. We can use the regression procedure
in Excel to perform these calculations, giving

$$\hat{y}_t = 34.273 + 4.1119\,(t)$$

So,

$$C_0 = 34.273 \quad \text{and} \quad T_0 = 4.1119$$

Keep in mind that these are arbitrary starting values, and as with single exponential smoothing, their effect will be dampened out as you proceed through
the sample data to the current period. The more historical data you have, the
less impact the starting values will have in the forecast.

Step 2 Fit the model.

The forecast for period 1 made at the beginning of period 1 is

$$F_1 = C_0 + T_0$$
$$F_1 = 34.273 + 4.1119 = 38.385$$

At the close of period 1, in which actual claims were 38, the smoothing equations are updated as follows.

$$C_1 = 0.20\,(38) + (1 - 0.20)(34.273 + 4.1119) = 38.308$$
$$T_1 = 0.30\,(38.308 - 34.273) + (1 - 0.30)(4.1119) = 4.089$$

FIGURE 16.30

Excel 2010 Double Exponential Smoothing Spreadsheet for Billingsley Insurance

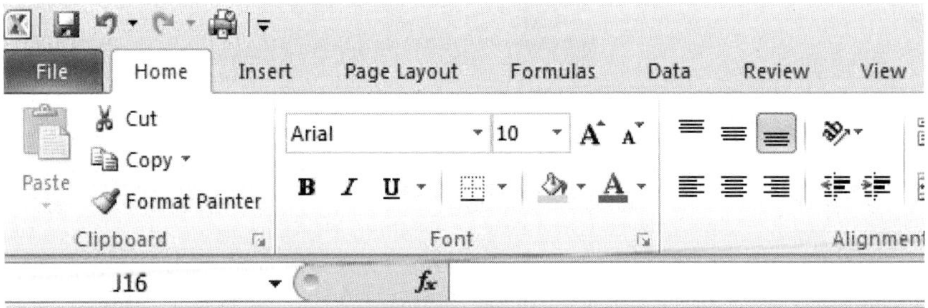

	A	B	C	D	E	F	G
1	Month	Claims	Constant	Trend	Forecast	Forecast Error	Absolute Error
2	t	y_t	C_t	T_t	$F_t = C_{t-1} + T_{t-1}$	$y_t - F_t$	$\lvert y_t - f_t \rvert$
3	1	38	38.308	4.089	38.385	-0.385	0.385
4	2	44	42.717	4.185	42.397	1.603	1.603
5	3	40	45.522	3.771	46.902	-6.902	6.902
6	4	48	49.034	3.693	49.293	-1.293	1.293
7	5	55	53.182	3.830	52.728	2.272	2.272
8	6	68	59.209	4.489	57.012	10.988	10.988
9	7	64	63.759	4.507	63.698	0.302	0.302
10	8	70	68.613	4.611	68.266	1.734	1.734
11	9	75	73.579	4.718	73.224	1.776	1.776
12	10	70	76.637	4.220	78.297	-8.297	8.297
13	11	78	80.286	4.048	80.857	-2.857	2.857
14	12	82	83.867	3.908	84.334	-2.334	2.334
15				Month 13 forecast →	87.776		
16						Sum =	40.745
17	Alpha =	0.2	C_o =	34.273		MAD =	3.395
18	Beta =	0.3	T_o =	4.1119			

Minitab Instructions (for similar results):
1. Open file: **Billingsley.MTW**.
2. Choose **Stat > Time Series > Double Exp Smoothing**.
3. In **Variable**, enter time series column.
4. Check **Generate forecasts** and enter 1 in **Number of forecasts** and 12 in **Starting from origin**.
5. Click **OK**.

Excel 2010 Instructions:
1. Open file: **Billingsley.xlsx**.
2. Create 5 new columns as shown in Figure 16.30 above.
3. Place smoothing constants (alpha and beta) in empty cells (B17 and B18).
4. Place starting values for the constant process and the trend in empty cells (D17 and D18).
5. Use text equations 16.18 and 16.19 to create values for C_t and T_t in columns C and D.
6. Use text equation 16.20 to create forecasts in column E.
7. Calculate forecast errors in column F by subtracting column E value from column B value.
8. Calculate a column of absolute errors using Excel's **ABS** function.
9. Calculate the *MAD* by using Excel's **AVERAGE** function (= **AVERAGE (G3:G14)**).

Next, the forecast for period 2 is

$$F_2 = 38.308 + 4.089 = 42.397$$

We then repeat the process through period 12 to find the forecast for period 13.

Step 3   Diagnose the model.

Figure 16.30 show the results of the computations and the *MAD* value. The forecast for period 13 is

$$F_{13} = C_{12} + T_{12}$$
$$F_{13} = 83.867 + 3.908 = 87.776$$

Based on this double exponential smoothing model, the number of claims for period 13 is forecast to be about 88. However, before settling on this forecast, we should try different smoothing constants to determine whether a smaller *MAD* can be found.

>> **END EXAMPLE**

TRY PROBLEM 16-39 (pg. 732)

As you can see, the computations required for double exponential smoothing are somewhat tedious and are ideally suited for your computer. Although Excel does not have a double exponential smoothing procedure, in Figure 16.30 we have used Excel formulas to develop our model in conjunction with the regression tool for determining the starting values.

MyStatLab

16-3: **Exercises**

Skill **Development**

16-34. The following table represents two years of data:

Year 1		Year 2	
1st quarter	242	1st quarter	272
2nd quarter	252	2nd quarter	267
3rd quarter	257	3rd quarter	276
4th quarter	267	4th quarter	281

a. Prepare a single exponential smoothing forecast for the first quarter of year 3 using an alpha value of 0.10. Let the initial forecast value for quarter 1 of year 1 be 250.
b. Prepare a single exponential smoothing forecast for the first quarter of year 3 using an alpha value of 0.25. Let the initial forecast value for quarter 1 of year 1 be 250.
c. Calculate the *MAD* value for the forecasts you generated in parts a and b. Which alpha value provides the smaller *MAD* value at the end of the 4th quarter in year 2?

16-35. The following data represent enrollment in a major at your university for the past six semesters (*Note*: semester 1 is the oldest data; semester 6 is the most recent data):

Semester	Enrollment
1	87
2	110
3	123
4	127
5	145
6	160

a. Prepare a graph of enrollment for the six semesters.
b. Based on the graph you prepared in part a, does it appear that a trend is present in the enrollment figures?
c. Prepare a single exponential smoothing forecast for semester 7 using an alpha value of 0.35. Assume that the initial forecast for semester 1 is 90.
d. Prepare a double exponential smoothing forecast for semester 7 using an alpha value of 0.20 and a beta value of 0.25. Assume that the initial smoothed constant value for semester 1 is 80 and the initial smoothed trend value for semester 1 is 10.
e. Calculate the *MAD* values for the simple exponential smoothing model and the double exponential smoothing model at the end of semester 6. Which model appears to be doing the better job of

forecasting course enrollment? Don't include period 1 in the calculation.

16-36. The following data represent the average number of employees in outlets of a large consumer electronics retailer:

Year	2001	2002	2003	2004	2005	2006	2007	2008	2009	2010
Number	20.6	17.3	18.6	21.5	23.2	19.9	18.7	15.6	19.7	20.4

a. Construct a time-series plot of this time series. Does it appear that a linear trend exists in the time series?
b. Calculate forecasts for each of the years in the time series. Use a smoothing constant of 0.25 and single exponential smoothing.
c. Calculate the *MAD* value for the forecasts you generated in part b.
d. Construct a single exponential smoothing forecast for 2011. Use a smoothing constant of 0.25.

16-37. A brokerage company is interested in forecasting the number of new accounts the office will obtain next month. It has collected the following data for the past 12 months:

Month	Accounts
1	19
2	20
3	21
4	25
5	26
6	24
7	24
8	21
9	27
10	30
11	24
12	30

a. Produce a time-series plot for these data. Specify the exponential forecasting model that should be used to obtain next month's forecast.
b. Assuming a double exponential smoothing model, fit the least squares trend to the historical data, to determine the smoothed constant-process value and the smoothed trend value for period 0.
c. Produce the forecasts for periods 1 through 12 using $\alpha = 0.15, \beta = 0.25$. Indicate the number of new accounts the company may expect to receive next month based on the forecast model.
d. Calculate the *MAD* for this model.

Business Applications

16-38. With tax revenues declining in many states, school districts have been searching for methods of cutting costs without affecting classroom academics. One district has been looking at the cost of extracurricular activities ranging from band trips to athletics. The district business manager has gathered the past six months' costs for these activities as shown here.

Month	Expenditures ($)
September	23,586.41
October	23,539.22
November	23,442.06
December	23,988.71
January	23,727.13
February	23,799.69

Using this past history, prepare a single exponential smoothing forecast for March using an α value of 0.25.

16-39. "The average college senior graduated this year with more than $19,000 in debt" was the beginning sentence of a recent article in *USA Today*. The majority of students have loans that are not due until the student leaves school. This can result in the student ignoring the size of debt that piles up. Federal loans obtained to finance college education are steadily mounting. The data given here show the amount of loans ($million) for the last 20 academic years, with year 20 being the most recent.

Year	Amount	Year	Amount	Year	Amount
1	9,914	8	16,221	15	37,228
2	10,182	9	22,557	16	39,101
3	12,493	10	26,011	17	42,761
4	13,195	11	28,737	18	49,360
5	13,414	12	31,906	19	57,463
6	13,890	13	33,930	20	62,614
7	15,232	14	34,376		

a. Produce a time-series plot for these data. Specify the exponential forecasting model that should be used to obtain next year's forecast.
b. Assuming a double exponential smoothing model, fit the least squares trend to the historical data to determine the smoothed constant-process value and the smoothed trend value for period 0.
c. Using data for periods 1 through 20 and using $\alpha = 0.20$ and $\beta = 0.30$, forecast the total student loan volume for the year 21.
d. Calculate the *MAD* for this model.

16-40. The human resources manager for a medium-sized business is interested in predicting the dollar value of medical expenditures filed by employees of her company for the year 2011. From her company's database, she has collected the following information showing the dollar value of medical expenditures made by employees for the previous seven years:

Year	Medical Claims
2004	$405,642.43
2005	$407,180.60
2006	$408,203.30
2007	$410,088.03
2008	$411,085.64
2009	$412,200.39
2010	$414,043.90

a. Prepare a graph of medical expenditures for the years 2004 through 2010. Which forecasting technique do you think is most appropriate for this time series, single exponential smoothing or double exponential smoothing? Why?
b. Use an α value of 0.25 and a β value of 0.15 to produce a double exponential forecast for the medical claims data. Use linear trend analysis to obtain the starting values for C_0 and T_0.
c. Compute the *MAD* value for your model for the years 2004 to 2010. Also produce a graph of your forecast values.

16-41. Retail Forward, Inc., is a global management consulting and market research firm specializing in retail intelligence and strategies. One of its press releases (*June Consumer Outlook: Spending Plans Show Resilience*, June 1, 2006) divulged the result of the Retail Forward ShopperScape™ survey conducted each month from a sample of 4,000 U.S. primary household shoppers. A measure of consumer spending is represented by the following figure:

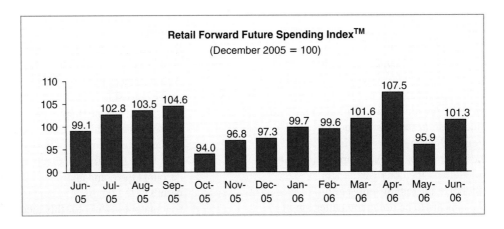

a. Construct a time-series plot of these data. Does it appear that a linear trend exists in the time series?

b. Calculate forecasts for each of the months in the time series. Use a smoothing constant of 0.25.

c. Calculate the *MAD* value for the forecasts you generated in part b.

d. Construct a single exponential smoothing forecast for July 2006. Use a smoothing constant of 0.25.

Computer Database **Exercises**

16-42. The National Association of Theatre Owners is the largest exhibition trade organization in the world, representing more than 26,000 movie screens in all 50 states and in more than 20 countries worldwide. Its membership includes the largest cinema chains and hundreds of independent theater owners. It publishes statistics concerning the movie sector of the economy. The file titled **Flicks** contains data on average U.S. ticket prices ($). One concern is the rapidly increasing price of tickets.

a. Produce a time-series plot for these data. Specify the exponential forecasting model that should be used to obtain next year's forecast.

b. Assuming a double exponential smoothing model, fit the least squares trend to the historical data to determine the smoothed constant-process value and the smoothed trend value for period 0.

c. Use $\alpha = 0.20$ and $\beta = 0.30$ to forecast the average yearly ticket price for the year 2010.

d. Calculate the *MAD* for this model.

16-43. Inflation is a fall in the market value or purchasing power of money. Measurements of inflation are prepared and published by the Bureau of Labor Statistics of the Department of Labor, which measures average changes in prices of goods and services. The file titled **CPI** contains the monthly CPI and inflation rate for the period January 2000 through December 2005.

a. Construct a plot of this time series. Does it appear that a linear trend exists in the time series? Specify the exponential forecasting model that should be used to obtain next month's forecast.

b. Assuming a single exponential smoothing model, calculate forecasts for each of the months in the time series. Use a smoothing constant of 0.15.

c. Calculate the *MAD* value for the forecasts you generated in part b.

d. Construct a single exponential smoothing forecast for January 2006. Use a smoothing constant of 0.15.

16-44. The sales manager at Grossmieller Importers in New York City needs to determine a monthly forecast for the number of men's golf sweaters that will be sold so that he can order an appropriate amount of packing boxes. Grossmieller ships sweaters to retail stores throughout the United States and Canada. Shirts are packed six to a box. Data for the past 12 months are contained in the data file called **Grossmieller**.

a. Plot the sales data using a time-series plot. Based on the graph, what time series components are present? Discuss.

b. (1) Use a single exponential smoothing model with $\alpha = 0.30$ to forecast sales for month 17. Assume that the initial forecast for period 1 is 36,000. (2) Compute the *MAD* for this model. (3) Graph the smoothing-model-fitted values on the time-series plot.

c. (1) Referring to part b, try different alpha levels to determine which smoothing constant value you would recommend. (2) Indicate why you have selected this value and then develop the forecast for month 17. (3) Compare this to the forecast you got using $\alpha = 0.30$ in part b.

16-45. Referring to Problem 16-44, in which the sales manager for Grossmieller Imports of New York City needs to forecast monthly sales,

a. Discuss why a double exponential smoothing model might be preferred over a single exponential smoothing model.

b. (1) Develop a double exponential smoothing model using $\alpha = 0.20$ and $\beta = 0.30$ as smoothing constants. To obtain the starting values, use the regression trend line approach discussed in this section. (2) Determine the forecast for month 17. (3) Also compute the *MAD* for this model. (4) Graph the fitted values on the time-series graph.

c. Compare the results for this double exponential smoothing model with the "best" single exponential smoothing model developed in part c of Problem 16-44. Discuss which model is preferred.

d. Referring to part b, try different alpha and beta values in an attempt to determine an improved forecast model for monthly sales. For each model, show the forecast for period 17 and the *MAD*. Write a short report that compares the different models.

e. Referring to part d and to part c for Problem 16-44, write a report to the Grossmieller sales manager that indicates your choice for the forecasting model, complete with your justification for the selection.

Visual Summary

Chapter 16: Organizations must operate effectively in the environment they face today, but also plan to continue to effectively operate in the future. To plan for the future organizations must **forecast**. This chapter introduces the two basic types of forecasting: qualitative forecasting and quantitative forecasting. Qualitative forecasting techniques are based on expert opinion and judgment. **Quantitative forecasting** techniques are based on statistical methods for analyzing quantitative historical data. The chapter focuses on **quantitative forecasting** techniques. Numerous techniques exist, often determined by the **forecasting horizon**. Forecasts are often divided into four phases, **immediate forecasts** of one month or less, **short term** of one to three months, **medium term** of three months to two years and **long term** of two years of more. The forecasting technique used is often determined by the length of the forecast, called the forecasting horizon. The model building issues discussed in Chapter 15 involving **model specification**, **model fitting**, and **model diagnosis** also apply to forecasting models.

16.1 Introduction to Forecasting, Time-Series Data, and Index Numbers (pg. 683–697)

Summary

Quantitative forecasting techniques rely on data gathered in the past to forecast what will happen in the future. **Time-series** analysis is a commonly used quantitative forecasting technique. Time-series analysis involves looking for patterns in the past data that will hopefully continue into the future. It involves looking for four components, trend, seasonal, cyclical and random. A **trend** is the long-term increase or decrease in a variable being measured over time and can be linear or nonlinear. **A seasonal component** is present if the data shows a repeating pattern over time. If when observing time-series data you see sustained periods of high values followed by periods of lower values and the recurrence period of these fluctuations is larger than a year, the data are said to contain a **cyclical component**. Although not all time series possess a trend, seasonal, or cyclical component, virtually all time series will have a random component. The **random component** is often referred to as "noise" in the data. When analyzing time-series data, you will often compare one value measured at one point in time with other values measured at different points in time. A common procedure for making relative comparisons is to begin by determining a **base period index** to which all other data values can be fairly compared. The simplest index is an **unweighted aggregate index**. More complicated weighted indexes include the **Paasche** and **Lespeyres** indexes.

Outcome 1. Identify the components present in a time series.
Outcome 2. Understand and compute basic index numbers.

16.2 Trend-Based Forecasting Techniques (pg. 697–723)

Summary

Trend-based forecasting techniques begin by identifying and modeling that trend. Once the trend model has been defined, it is used to provide forecasts for future time periods. Regression analysis is often used to identify the trend component. How well the trend fits the actual data can be determined by the **Mean Squared Error (MSE)** or **Mean Absolute Deviation (MAD)**. In general the smaller the MSE and MAD the better the model fits the actual data. Using regression analysis to determine the trend carries some risk, one of which is that the error terms in the analysis are not independent. Related error terms indicate autocorrelation in the data and is tested for using the **Durbin-Watson Statistic**. Seasonality is often found in trend based forecasting models and, if found, is dealt with by computing seasonal indexes. While alternate methods are used to compute **seasonal indexes** this section concentrates on the **ratio-to-moving-average method**. Once the seasonal indexes are determined, they are used to deseasonalize the data to allow for a better trend forecast. The indexes are then used to determine a **seasonally adjusted forecast**. Determining the trend and seasonal components to a time series model allows the cyclical and random components to be better determined.

Outcome 3. Apply the fundamental steps in developing and implementing forecasting models.

Outcome 4. Apply trend-based forecasting models, including linear trend, nonlinear trend, and seasonally adjusted trend.

16.3 Forecasting Using Smoothing Methods (pg. 723–733)

Summary

A disadvantage of trend-based forecasting is that it gives as much weight to the earliest data in the time series as it does to the data that are close to the period for which the forecast is required. It does not, therefore, allow model to "learn" or "adjust" to changes in the time series. This section introduces exponential smoothing models. With **exponential smoothing**, current observations can be weighted more heavily than older observations in determining the forecast. Therefore, if in recent periods the time-series values are much higher (or lower) than those in earlier periods, the forecast can be made to reflect this difference. The section discusses **single exponential smoothing** models and double exponential smoothing models. **Single exponential smoothing** models are used when only random fluctuations are seen in the data while **double exponential smoothing** models are used if the data seems to combine both random variations with a trend. Both models weigh recent data more heavily than past data. As with all forecast models the basic steps of model building: specification, fitting and diagnosing the model are followed.

Outcome 5. Use smoothing-based forecasting models, including single and double exponential smoothing

Conclusion

While both qualitative and quantitative forecasting techniques are used, this chapter has emphasized quantitative techniques. Quantitative forecasting techniques require historical data for the variable to be forecasted. The success of a quantitative model is determined by how well the model fits the historical time-series data and how closely the future resembles the past. Forecasting is as much an art as it is a science. The more experience you have in a given situation, the more effective you likely will be at identifying and applying the appropriate forecasting tool. You will find that the techniques introduced in this chapter are used frequently as an initial basis for a forecast. However, in most cases, the decision maker will modify the forecast based on personal judgment and other qualitative inputs that are not considered by the quantitative model.

Equations

(16.1) Simple Index Number pg. 688

$$I_t = \frac{y_t}{y_0} 100$$

(16.2) Unweighted Aggregate Price Index pg. 689

$$I_t = \frac{\sum p_t}{\sum p_0}(100)$$

(16.3) The Paasche Index pg. 691

$$I_t = \frac{\sum q_t p_t}{\sum q_t p_0}(100)$$

(16.4) Laspeyres Index pg. 692

$$I_t = \frac{\sum q_0 p_t}{\sum q_0 p_0}(100)$$

(16.5) Deflation Formula pg. 695

$$y_{adj_t} = \frac{y_t}{I_t}(100)$$

(16.6) Linear Trend Model pg. 698

$$y_t = \beta_0 + \beta_1 t + \varepsilon_t$$

(16.7) Least Squares Equations Estimates pg. 699

$$b_1 = \frac{\sum t y_t - \dfrac{\sum t \sum y_t}{n}}{\sum t^2 - \dfrac{(\sum t)^2}{n}}$$

(16.8)

$$b_0 = \frac{\sum y_t}{n} - b_1 \frac{\sum t}{n}$$

(16.9) Mean Squared Error pg. 701

$$MSE = \frac{\sum(y_t - F_t)^2}{n}$$

(16.10) Mean Absolute Deviation pg. 701

$$MAD = \frac{\sum |y_t - F_t|}{n}$$

(16.11) Durbin-Watson Statistic pg. 703

$$d = \frac{\displaystyle\sum_{t=2}^{n}(e_t - e_{t-1})^2}{\displaystyle\sum_{t=1}^{n} e_t^2}$$

(16.12) Forecast Bias pg. 707

$$\text{Forecast bias} = \frac{\sum(y_t - F_t)}{n}$$

(16.13) Multiplicative Time-Series Model pg. 713

$$y_t = T_t \times S_t \times C_t \times I_t$$

(16.14) Ratio-to-Moving-Average pg. 714

$$S_t \times I_t = \frac{y_t}{T_t \times C_t}$$

(16.15) Deseasonalization pg. 717

$$T_t \times C_t \times I_t = \frac{y_t}{S_t}$$

(16.16) Exponential Smoothing Model pg. 724

$$F_{t+1} = F_t + \alpha(y_t - F_t)$$

or

(16.17)

$$F_{t+1} = \alpha y_t + (1 - \alpha)F_t$$

(16.18) Double Exponential Smoothing Model pg. 728

$$C_t = \alpha y_t + (1 - \alpha)(C_{t-1} + T_{t-1})$$

(16.19)

$$T_t = \beta(C_t - C_{t-1}) + (1 - \beta)T_{t-1}$$

(16.20)

$$F_{t+1} = C_t + T_t$$

Key Terms

Aggregate price index pg. 689
Autocorrelation pg. 702
Base period index pg. 687
Cyclical component pg. 687
Exponential smoothing pg. 724
Forecasting horizon pg. 684

Forecasting interval pg. 684
Forecasting period pg. 684
Linear trend pg. 685
Model diagnosis pg. 684
Model building pg. 684
Model specification pg. 684

Moving average pg. 713
Random component pg. 687
Seasonal component pg. 685
Seasonal index pg. 713
Seasonally unadjusted forecast pg. 717

Chapter Exercises

Conceptual Questions

16-46. Go to the library or use the Internet to find data showing your state's population for the past 20 years. Plot these data and indicate which of the time-series components are present.

16-47. A time series exhibits the pattern stated below. Indicate the type of time-series component described.
  a. The pattern is "wavelike" with a recurrence period of nine months.
  b. The time series is steadily increasing.
  c. The pattern is "wavelike" with a recurrence period of two years.
  d. The pattern is unpredictable.
  e. The pattern steadily decreases, with a "wavelike" shape that reoccurs every 10 years.

16-48. Identify the businesses in your community that might be expected to have sales that exhibit a seasonal component. Discuss.

16-49. Discuss the difference between a cyclical component and a seasonal component. Which component is more predictable, seasonal or cyclical? Discuss and illustrate with examples.

16-50. In the simple linear regression model, confidence and prediction intervals are utilized to provide interval estimates for an average and a particular value, respectively, of the dependent variable. The linear trend model in time series is an application of simple linear regression. This being said, discuss whether a confidence or a prediction interval is the relevant interval estimate for a linear trend model's forecast.

Business Applications

Problems **16-51 through 16-54** refer to Malcar Autoparts Company, which has started producing replacement control microcomputers for automobiles. This has been a growth industry since the first control units were introduced in 1985. Sales data since 1994 are as follows:

Year	Sales ($)
1994	240,000
1995	218,000
1996	405,000
1997	587,000
1998	795,000
1999	762,000
2000	998,000
2001	1,217,000
2002	1,570,000
2003	1,947,000
2004	2,711,000
2005	3,104,000
2006	2,918,000
2007	4,606,000
2008	5,216,000
2009	5,010,000

16-51. As a start in analyzing these data,
  a. Graph these data and indicate whether they appear to have a linear trend.
  b. Develop a simple linear regression model with time as the independent variable. Using this regression model, describe the trend and the strength of the linear trend over the 16 years. Is the trend line statistically significant? Plot the trend line against the actual data.
  c. Compute the *MAD* value for this model.
  d. Provide the Malcar Autoparts Company an estimate of its expected sales for the next 5 years.
  e. Provide the maximum and minimum sales Malcar can expect with 90% confidence for the year 2014.

16-52. Develop a single exponential smoothing model using $\alpha = 0.20$. Use as a starting value the average of the first 6 years' data. Determine the forecasted value for year 2010.
  a. Compute the *MAD* for this model.
  b. Plot the forecast values against the actual data.
  c. Use the same starting value but try different smoothing constants (say, 0.05, 0.10, 0.25, and 0.30) in an effort to reduce the *MAD* value.
  d. Is it possible to answer part d of Problem 16-51 using this forecasting technique? Explain your answer.

16-53. Develop a double exponential smoothing model using smoothing constants $\alpha = 0.20$ and $\beta = 0.40$. As starting values, use the least squares trend line slope and intercept values.
  a. Compute the *MAD* for this model.
  b. Plot the forecast values against the actual data.
  c. Use the same starting values but try different smoothing constants, [say, $(\alpha, \beta) = (0.10, 0.50)$, $(0.30, 0.30)$, and $(0.40, 0.20)$] in an effort to reduce the *MAD* value.

16-54. Using whatever diagnostic tools you are familiar with, determine which of the three forecasting methods utilized to forecast sales for Malcar Autoparts Company in the previous three problems provides superior forecasts. Explain the reasons for your choice.

16-55. Amazon.com has become one of the most successful online merchants. Two measures of its success are sales and net income/loss figures. They are given here.

Year	Net Income/Loss	Sales
1995	−0.3	0.5
1996	−5.7	15.7
1997	−27.5	147.7
1998	−124.5	609.8
1999	−719.9	1,639.8
2000	−1,411.2	2,761.9
2001	−567.3	3,122.9
2002	−149.1	3,933
2003	35.3	5,263.7

Year	Net Income/Loss	Sales
2004	588.5	6,921
2005	359	8,490
2006	190	10,711
2007	476	14,835

a. Produce a time-series plot for these data. Specify the exponential forecasting model that should be used to obtain the following years' forecasts.
b. Assuming a double exponential smoothing model, fit the least squares trend to the historical data to determine the smoothed constant-process value and the smoothed trend value for period 0.
c. Produce the forecasts for periods 1 through 13 using $\alpha = 0.10$ and $\beta = 0.20$. Indicate the sales Amazon should expect for 2008 based on the forecast model.
d. Calculate the *MAD* for this model.

16-56. College tuition has risen at a pace faster than inflation for more than two decades, according to an article in *USA Today*. The following data indicate the average college tuition (in 2003 dollars) for public colleges:

Period	1983–1984	1988–1989	1993–1994	1998–1999	2003–2004	2008–2009
Public	2,074	2,395	3,188	3,632	4,694	5,652

a. Produce a time-series plot of these data. Indicate the time-series components that exist in the data.
b. Provide a forecast for the average tuition for public colleges in the academic year 2013 through 2014. (*Hint*: One time-series time period represents five academic years.)
c. Provide an interval of plausible values for the average tuition change after five academic periods have gone by. Use a confidence level of 0.90.

16-57. Loans and leases data for the years 2000 through 2010 for the Bank of the Ozarks are shown below:

Year	Loans & Leases ($ millions)
2000	511
2001	616
2002	718
2003	909
2004	1,135
2005	1,371
2006	1,677
2007	1,871
2008	2,021
2009	1,904
2010	2,354

Source: 2010 Annual Report—Bank of the Ozarks

a. Produce a time-series plot of these data.
b. Fit a linear trend line to these data.
c. Conduct a hypothesis test of the significance of the linear trend model developed in part b. Use a level of significance of 0.05.
d. For the years 2000 through 2010, what is the predicted value each year for loans and leases using the linear trend model estimated in part b.
e. Calculate the *MAD* for the linear trend forecasts developed in part d.
f. Use the linear trend model to forecast loans and leases for the Bank of the Ozarks for 2011 and 2012.

16-58. Tom and Hank's is a regional convenience store with locations in several small towns along the Mississippi River. The quarterly revenue for the store beginning with the first quarter of 2005 and ending with the second quarter of 2011 is shown below:

Period	Sales	Period	Sales
1Q05	$ 304,072	2Q08	$ 414,776
2Q05	$ 241,146	3Q08	$ 409,164
3Q05	$ 251,719	4Q08	$ 397,537
4Q05	$ 247,792	1Q09	$ 548,111
1Q06	$ 370,434	2Q09	$ 412,788
2Q06	$ 291,448	3Q09	$ 417,408
3Q06	$ 297,308	4Q09	$ 406,495
4Q06	$ 286,892	1Q10	$ 586,479
1Q07	$ 415,718	2Q10	$ 468,013
2Q07	$ 325,157	3Q10	$ 480,706
3Q07	$ 336,537	4Q10	$ 466,087
4Q07	$ 387,424	1Q11	$ 667,478
1Q08	$ 546,057	2Q11	$ 522,337

a. Produce a time-series plot of the store's revenues by quarter. What time-series components appear to be present in the data?
b. Determine a seasonal index for each quarter.
c. Use the seasonal indexes from part b to deseasonalize the data.
d. Graph and fit a linear trend line to the deseasonalized data.
e. Use the linear trend line and the seasonal indexes to produce a seasonally adjusted forecast for each quarter beginning with quarter 1 of 2005 and ending with quarter 2 of 2011.
f. Calculate a forecast error for each period.
g. Calculate the *MAD* and the *MSE* for the forecasts you developed in part e.
h. Using the seasonal indexes and the estimated trend line, produce a forecast for quarters 3 and 4 for 2011.

16-59. Suppose the median weekly earnings for recent college graduates in a large city by quarter for the years 2004 to 2011 are as follows:

Quarter	Median Weekly Earnings	Quarter	Median Weekly Earnings
Qtr 1 2004	816	Qtr 1 2008	947.2
Qtr 2 2004	816	Qtr 2 2008	961.6
Qtr 3 2004	835.2	Qtr 3 2008	963.2
Qtr 4 2004	836.8	Qtr 4 2008	964.8
Qtr 1 2005	852.8	Qtr 1 2009	976
Qtr 2 2005	865.6	Qtr 2 2009	972.8
Qtr 3 2005	864	Qtr 3 2009	984
Qtr 4 2005	889.6	Qtr 4 2009	982.4
Qtr 1 2006	908.8	Qtr 1 2010	998.4
Qtr 2 2006	894.4	Qtr 2 2010	990.4
Qtr 3 2006	912	Qtr 3 2010	1006.4
Qtr 4 2006	921.6	Qtr 4 2010	1020.8
Qtr 1 2007	929.6	Qtr 1 2011	1033.6
Qtr 2 2007	931.2	Qtr 2 2011	1016
Qtr 3 2007	936	Qtr 3 2011	1046.4
Qtr 4 2007	940.8	Qtr 4 2011	1038.4

a. Prepare a line chart of the median earnings by quarter.

b. Estimate a linear trend line for this set of data.

c. Produce a forecast for each quarter using the linear trend line you estimated in part b.

d. Calculate the error for each period.

e. Calculate the Durbin-Watson statistic and test for positive autocorrelation. Use a level of significance of 0.05.

Computer Database Exercises

16-60. HSH® Associates, financial publishers, is the nation's largest publisher of mortgage and consumer loan information. Every week it collects current data from 2,000 mortgage lenders across the nation. It tracks a variety of adjustable rate mortgage (ARM) indexes and makes them available on its Web site. The file **ARM** contains the national monthly average one-year ARM for the time period January 2004 to December 2008.

a. Produce a scatter plot of the federal ARM for the time period January 2004 to December 2008. Identify any time-series components that exist in the data.

b. Identify the recurrence period of the time series. Determine the seasonal index for each month within the recurrence period.

c. Fit a nonlinear trend model containing coded years and coded years squared as predictors for the deseasonalized data.

d. Provide a seasonally adjusted forecast using the nonlinear trend model for January 2009.

e. Diagnose the model.

16-61. DataNet is an Internet service through which clients can find information and purchase various items such as airline tickets, stereo equipment, and listed stocks. DataNet has been in operation for four years. Data on monthly calls for service for the time that the company has been in business are in the data file called **DataNet**.

a. Plot these data in a time-series graph. Based on the graph, what time-series components are present in the data?

b. Develop the seasonal indexes for each month. Describe what the seasonal index for August means.

c. Fit a linear trend model to the deseasonalized data for months 1 through 48 and determine the *MAD* value. Comment on the adequacy of the linear trend model based on these measures of forecast error.

d. Provide a seasonally unadjusted forecast using the linear trend model for each month of the year.

e. Use the seasonal index values computed in part b to provide seasonal adjusted forecasts for months 49 through 52.

16-62. Referring to Problem 16-61, the managers of DataNet, the Internet company through which users can purchase products like airline tickets, need to forecast monthly call volumes in order to have sufficient capacity. Develop a single exponential smoothing model using $\alpha = 0.30$. Use as a starting value the average of the first six months' data.

a. Compute the *MAD* for this model.

b. Plot the forecast values against the actual data.

c. Use the same starting value but try different smoothing constants (say, 0.10, 0.20, 0.40, and 0.50) in an effort to reduce the *MAD* value.

d. Reflect on the type of time series for which the single exponential smoothing model is designed to provide forecasts. Does it surprise you that the *MAD* for this method is relatively large for these data? Explain your reasoning.

16-63. Continuing with the DataNet forecasting problems, develop a double exponential smoothing model using smoothing constants $\alpha = 0.20$ and $\beta = 0.20$. As starting values, use the least squares trend line slope and intercept values.

a. Compute the *MAD* for this model.

b. Plot the forecast values against the actual data.

c. Compare this with a linear trend model. Which forecast method would you use? Explain your rationale.

d. Use the same starting values but try different smoothing constants [say, $(\alpha, \beta) = (0.10, 0.30)$, $(0.15, 0.25)$, and $(0.30, 0.10)$] in an effort to reduce the *MAD* value. Prepare a short report that summarizes your efforts.

16-64. The College Board, administrator of the SAT test for college entrants, has made several changes to the test in recent years. One recent change occurred between years 2005 and 2006. In a press release, the College Board announced SAT scores for students in the class of 2005, the last to take the former version of the SAT featuring math and verbal sections. The board indicated that for the class of 2005, the average SAT math scores continued their strong upward trend, increasing from 518 in 2004 to 520 in 2005, 14 points higher than 10 years ago and an all-time high. The file titled

MathSAT contains the math SAT scores for the interval 1967 to 2005.

   a. Produce a time-series plot for the combined gender math SAT scores for the period 1980 to 2005. Indicate the time-series components that exist in the data.

   b. Conduct a test of hypothesis to determine if the average SAT math scores of students continued to increase in the period indicated in part a. Use a significance level of 0.10 and the test statistic approach.

   c. Produce a forecast for the average SAT math scores for 2010.

   d. Beginning with the March 12, 2005, administration of the exam, the SAT Reasoning Test, was modified and lengthened. How does this affect the forecast produced in part c? What statistical concept is exhibited by producing the forecast in part c?

Video Case 2

Restaurant Location and Re-imaging Decisions @ McDonald's

In the early days of his restaurant company's growth, McDonald's founder Ray Kroc knew that finding the right location was key. He had a keen eye for prime real estate locations. Today, the company is more than 30,000 restaurants strong. When it comes to picking prime real estate locations for its restaurants and making the most of them, McDonald's is way ahead of the competition. In fact, when it comes to global real estate holdings, no corporate entity has more.

From urban office and airport locations to Walmart stores and the busiest street corner in your town, McDonald's has grown to become one of the world's most recognized brands. Getting there hasn't been just a matter of buying all available real estate on the market. Instead, the company has used the basic principles and process Ray Kroc believed in to investigate and secure the best possible sites for its restaurants. Factors such as neighborhood demographics, traffic patterns, competitor proximity, workforce, and retail shopping center locations all play a role.

Many of the company's restaurant locations have been in operation for decades. And although the restaurants have adapted to changing times—including diet fads and reporting nutrition information, staff uniform updates, and menu innovations such as Happy Meals, Chicken McNuggets, and premium salads—there's more to bringing customers back time and again than an updated menu and a good location. Those same factors that played a role in the original location decision need to be periodically examined to learn what's changed and, as a result, what changes the local McDonald's needs to consider.

Beginning in 2003, McDonald's started work on "re-imaging" its existing restaurants while continuing to expand the brand globally. More than 6,000 restaurants have been re-imaged to date. Sophia Galassi, vice president of U.S. Restaurant Development, is responsible for the new look nationwide. According to Sophia, re-imaging is more than new landscaping and paint. In some cases, the entire store is torn down and rebuilt with redesigned drive-thru lanes to speed customers through faster, interiors with contemporary colors and coffee-house seating, entertainment zones with televisions, and free wi-fi.

"We work very closely with our owner/operators to collect solid data about their locations, and then help analyze them so we can present the business case to them," says Sophia. Charts and graphs, along with the detailed statistical results, are vital to the decision process.

One recent project provides a good example of how statistics supported the re-imaging decision. Dave Traub, owner/operator, had been successfully operating a restaurant in Midlothian, Virginia, for more than 30 years. The location was still prime, but the architecture and décor hadn't kept up with changing times. After receiving the statistical analysis on the location from McDonald's, Dave had the information he needed to make the decision to invest in re-imaging the restaurant. With revenues and customer traffic up, he has no regrets. "We've become the community's gathering place. The local senior citizens group now meets here regularly in the mornings," he says.

The re-imaging effort doesn't mean the end to new restaurant development for the company. "As long as new communities are developed and growth continues in neighborhoods across the country, we'll be analyzing data about them to be sure our restaurants are positioned in the best possible locations," states Sophia. Ray Kroc would be proud.

Discussion Questions:

1. Sophia Galassi, vice president of U.S. Restaurant Development for McDonald's, indicated that she and her staff work very closely with owner/operators to collect data about McDonald's restaurant locations. Describe some of the kinds of data that Sophia's staff would collect and the respective types of charts that could be used to present their findings to the owner/operators.

2. At the end of 2001, Sophia Galassi and her team led a remodel and re-imaging effort for the McDonald's franchises in a major U.S. city. This entailed a total change in store layout and design and a renewed emphasis on customer service. Once this work had been completed, the company put in place a comprehensive customer satisfaction data collection and tracking system. The data in the file called **McDonald's Customer Satisfaction** consist of the overall percentage of customers at the franchise McDonald's in this city who have rated the customer service as Excellent or Very Good during each quarter since the re-imaging and remodeling was completed. Develop a line chart and discuss what time-series components appear to be contained in these data.

3. Referring to question 2, based on the available historical data, develop a seasonally adjusted forecast for the percentage of customers who will rate the stores as Excellent or Very Good for Quarter 3 and Quarter 4 of 2006. Discuss the process you used to arrive at these forecasts.

4. Referring to questions 2 and 3, use any other forecasting method discussed in this chapter to arrive at a forecast for Quarters 3 and 4 of 2006. Compare your chosen model with the seasonally adjusted forecast model specified in question 3. Use appropriate measures of forecast error. Prepare a short report outlining your forecasting attempts along with your recommendation of which method McDonald's should use in this case.

5. Prior to remodeling or re-imaging a McDonald's store, extensive research is conducted. This includes the use of "mystery shoppers," who are people hired by McDonald's to go to stores as customers to observe various attributes

of the store and the service being provided. The file called **McDonald's Mystery Shopper** contains data pertaining to the "cleanliness" rating provided by the mystery shoppers who visited a particular McDonald's location each month between January 2004 and June 2006. The values represent the average rating on a 0-to-100 percent scale provided by five shoppers. A score of 100% is considered perfect. Using these time-series data, develop a line chart and discuss what time-series components are present in these data.

6. Referring to question 5, develop a double exponential smoothing model to forecast the rating for July 2006 (use alpha = 0.20 and beta = 0.30 smoothing constants). Compare the results of this forecasting approach with a simple linear trend forecasting approach. Write a short report describing the methods you have used and the results. Use linear trend analysis to obtain the starting values for C_0 and T_0.

Case 16.1

Park Falls Chamber of Commerce

Masao Sugiyama is the recently elected president of the Chamber of Commerce in Park Falls, Wisconsin. He is the long-time owner of the only full-service hardware store in this small farming town. Being president of the Chamber of Commerce has been considered largely a ceremonial post because business conditions have not changed in Park Falls for as long as anyone can remember. However, Masao has just read an article in *The Wall Street Journal* that has made him think he needs to take a more active interest in the business conditions of his town.

The article concerned Walmart, the largest retailer in the United States. Walmart has expanded primarily by locating in small towns and avoiding large suburban areas. The Park Falls merchants have not had to deal with either Lowes or Home Depot because these companies have located primarily in large urban centers. In addition, a supplier has recently told Masao that both Lowes and Home Depot are considering locating stores in smaller towns. Sugiyama knows that Walmart has moved into the outskirts of metropolitan areas and now is considering stores for smaller, untapped markets. He also has heard that Lowes and Home Depot have recently had difficulty.

Masao decided he needs to know more about all three retailers. He asked the son of a friend to locate the following sales data, which are also in a file called **Park Falls**.

Quarterly Sales Values in Millions of Dollars

		Lowes	Home Depot	Walmart
Fiscal 1999	Q1	$ 3,772	$ 8,952	$29,819
	Q2	$ 4,435	$10,431	$33,521
	Q3	$ 3,909	$ 9,877	$33,509
	Q4	$ 3,789	$ 9,174	$40,785
Fiscal 2000	Q1	$ 4,467	$11,112	$34,717

Quarterly Sales Values in Millions of Dollars

		Lowes	Home Depot	Walmart
	Q2	$ 5,264	$12,618	$38,470
	Q3	$ 4,504	$11,545	$40,432
	Q4	$ 4,543	$10,463	$51,394
Fiscal 2001	Q1	$ 5,276	$12,200	$42,985
	Q2	$ 6,127	$14,576	$46,112
	Q3	$ 5,455	$13,289	$45,676
	Q4	$ 5,253	$13,488	$56,556
Fiscal 2002	Q1	$ 6,470	$14,282	$48,052
	Q2	$ 7,488	$16,277	$52,799
	Q3	$ 6,415	$14,475	$52,738
	Q4	$ 6,118	$13,213	$64,210
Fiscal 2003	Q1	$ 7,118	$15,104	$51,705
	Q2	$ 8,666	$17,989	$56,271
	Q3	$ 7,802	$16,598	$55,241
	Q4	$ 7,252	$15,125	$66,400
Fiscal 2004	Q1	$ 8,681	$17,550	$56,718
	Q2	$10,169	$19,960	$62,637
	Q3	$ 9,064	$18,772	$62,480
	Q4	$ 8,550	$16,812	$74,494
Fiscal 2005	Q1	$ 9,913	$18,973	$64,763
	Q2	$11,929	$22,305	$69,722
	Q3	$10,592	$30,744	$68,520
	Q4	$10,808	$19,489	$82,216

Masao is interested in what all these data tell him. How much faster has Walmart grown than the other two firms? Is there any evidence Walmart's growth has leveled off? Does Lowes seem to be rebounding, based on sales? Are seasonal fluctuations an issue in these sales figures? Is there any evidence that one firm is more affected by the cyclical component than the others? He needs some help in analyzing these data.

Case 16.2

The St. Louis Companies

An irritated Roger Hatton finds himself sitting in the St. Louis airport after hearing that his flight to Chicago has been delayed—and, if the storm in Chicago continues, possibly cancelled. Because he must get to Chicago if at all possible, Roger is stuck at the airport. He decides he might as well try to get some work done, so he opens his laptop computer and calls up the **Claimnum** file.

Roger was recently assigned as an analyst in the worker's compensation section of the St. Louis Companies, one of the biggest issuers of worker's compensation insurance in the country. Until this year, the revenues and claim costs for all parts of the company were grouped together to determine any yearly profit or loss. Therefore, no one really knew if an individual department was profitable. Now, however, the new president is looking at each part of the company as a profit center. The clear implication is that money-losing departments may not have a future unless they develop a clear plan to become profitable.

When Roger asked the accounting department for a listing, by client, of all policy payments and claims filed and paid, he was told that the information is available but he may have to wait two or three months to get it. He was able to determine, however, that the department has been keeping track of the clients who file frequent

(at least one a month) claims and the total number of firms that purchase workers' compensation insurance. Using the data from this report, Roger divides the number of clients filing frequent claims by the corresponding number of clients. These ratios, in the file **Claimnum**, are as follows:

Year	Ratio (%)	Year	Ratio (%)
1	3.8	12	6.1
2	3.6	13	7.8
3	3.5	14	7.1
4	4.9	15	7.6
5	5.9	16	9.7
6	5.6	17	9.6
7	4.9	18	7.5
8	5.6	19	7.9
9	8.5	20	8.3
10	7.7	21	8.4
11	7.1		

Staring at these figures, Roger feels there should be some way to use them to project what the next several years may hold if the company doesn't change its underwriting policies.

Case 16.3

Wagner Machine Works

Mary Lindsey has recently agreed to leave her upper-level management job at a major paper manufacturing firm and return to her hometown to take over the family machine-products business. The U.S. machine-products industry had a strong position of world dominance until recently, when it was devastated by foreign competition, particularly from Germany and Japan. Among the many problems facing the American industry is that it is made up of many small firms that must compete with foreign industrial giants.

Wagner Machine Works, the company Mary is taking over, is one of the few survivors in its part of the state, but it, too, faces increasing competitive pressure. Mary's father let the business slide as he approached retirement, and Mary sees the need for an immediate modernization of their plant. She has arranged for a loan from the local bank, but now she must forecast sales for the next three years to ensure that the company has enough cash flow to repay the debt. Surprisingly, Mary finds that her father has no forecasting system in place, and she cannot afford the time or money to install a system like that used at her previous company.

Wagner Machine Works' quarterly sales (in millions of dollars) for the past 15 years are as follows:

Year	Quarter 1	2	3	4
1995	10,490	11,130	10,005	11,058
1996	11,424	12,550	10,900	12,335
1997	12,835	13,100	11,660	13,767
1998	13,877	14,100	12,780	14,738
1999	14,798	15,210	13,785	16,218
2000	16,720	17,167	14,785	17,725
2001	18,348	18,951	16,554	19,889
2002	20,317	21,395	19,445	22,816
2003	23,335	24,179	22,548	25,029
2004	25,729	27,778	23,391	27,360
2005	28,886	30,125	26,049	30,300
2006	30,212	33,702	27,907	31,096
2007	31,715	35,720	28,554	34,326
2008	35,533	39,447	30,046	37,587
2009	39,093	44,650	30,046	37,587

While looking at these data, Mary wonders whether they can be used to forecast sales for the next three years. She wonders how much, if any, confidence she can have in a forecast made with these data. She also wonders if the recent increase in sales is due to growing business or just to inflationary price increases in the national economy.

Required Tasks:

1. Identify the central issue in the case.
2. Plot the quarterly sales for the past 15 years for Wagner Machine Works.
3. Identify any patterns that are evident in the quarterly sales data.
4. If a seasonal pattern is identified, estimate quarterly seasonal factors.
5. Deseasonalize the data using the quarterly seasonal factors developed.
6. Run a regression model on the deseasonalized data using the time period as the independent variable.
7. Develop a seasonally adjusted forecast for the next three years.
8. Prepare a report that includes graphs and analysis.

Chapter 17 Quick Prep Links

- **Review** the concepts associated with hypothesis testing for a single population mean using the *t*-distribution in Chapter 9.

- **Make sure** you are familiar with the steps involved in testing hypotheses for the difference between two population means discussed in Chapter 10.

- **Review** the concepts and assumptions associated with analysis of variance in Chapter 12.

Introduction to Nonparametric Statistics

17.1 The Wilcoxon Signed Rank Test for One Population Median (pg. 743–749) ← **Outcome 1.** Recognize when and how to use the Wilcoxon signed rank test for a population median.

17.2 Nonparametric Tests for Two Population Medians (pg. 749–761) ← **Outcome 2.** Recognize the situations for which the Mann–Whitney *U*-test for the difference between two population medians applies and be able to use it in a decision-making context.

Outcome 3. Know when to apply the Wilcoxon matched-pairs signed rank test for related samples.

17.3 Kruskal–Wallis One-Way Analysis of Variance (pg. 761–767) ← **Outcome 4.** Perform nonparametric analysis of variance using the Kruskal–Wallis one-way ANOVA.

Why you need to know

In previous chapters, you were introduced to a wide variety of statistical techniques that are used extensively to analyze data and aid in the decision-making process. However, some of the estimation and hypothesis testing techniques discussed earlier may not be appropriate in certain situations if the assumptions of those procedures are not satisfied. For instance, housing prices are particularly important when a company considers potential locations for a new manufacturing plant because the company would like affordable housing to be available for employees who transfer to the new location. A company that is in the midst of relocation has taken a sample of real estate listings from the four cities in contention for the new plant and would like to make a statistically valid comparison of home prices based on this sample information. The analysis of variance (ANOVA) *F*-test introduced in Chapter 12 would seem appropriate. However, this test is based on the assumptions that all populations are normally distributed and have equal variances. Unfortunately, housing prices are generally not normally distributed because most cities have home prices that are highly right skewed with most home prices clustered around the median price with a few very expensive houses that pull the mean value up. A class of statistical techniques known as nonparametric statistics is available for situations such as the housing price case.

17.1 The Wilcoxon Signed Rank Test for One Population Median

Up to this point, the text has presented a wide array of statistical tools for describing data and for drawing inferences about a population based on sample information from that population. These tools are widely used in decision-making situations. However, you will

mmaxer/Shutterstock

also encounter decision situations in which major departures from the required assumptions exist. For example, many populations, such as family income levels and house prices, are highly skewed. In other instances, the level of data measurement will be too low (ordinal or nominal) to warrant use of the techniques presented earlier. In such cases, the alternative is to employ a *nonparametric statistical procedure* that has been developed to meet specific inferential needs. Such procedures have fewer restrictive assumptions concerning data level and underlying probability distributions. There are a great many nonparametric procedures that cover a wide range of applications. The purpose of this chapter is to introduce you to the concept of nonparametric statistics and illustrate some of the more frequently used methods.

Chapter Outcome 1. → # The Wilcoxon Signed Rank Test—Single Population

Chapter 9 introduced examples that involved testing hypotheses about a single population mean. Recall that if the data were interval or ratio level and the population was normally distributed, a *t*-test was used to test whether a population mean had a specified value. However the *t*-test is not appropriate in cases in which the data level is ordinal or when populations are not believed to be approximately normally distributed. To overcome data limitation issues, a nonparametric statistical technique known as the *Wilcoxon signed rank test* can be used. This test makes no highly restrictive assumption about the shape of the population distribution.

The Wilcoxon test is used to test hypotheses about a population median rather than a population mean. The basic logic of the Wilcoxon test is straightforward. Because the median is the midpoint in a population, allowing for sampling error, we would expect approximately half the data values in a random sample to be below the hypothesized median and about half to be above it. The hypothesized median will be rejected if the actual data distribution shows too large a departure from this expectation.

BUSINESS APPLICATION **APPLYING THE WILCOXON SIGNED RANK TEST**

Jorge Salcedo/Shutterstock

STUDENT LOANS March, 2012, news stories indicate that the total outstanding debt for student loans in the United States has reached $1 trillion. In an address to the State Legislature, one university President in the southwest has stated that the median student loan balance for graduates of her university exceeds $35,000. She also stated that the distribution of student loan balances is highly skewed to the right with some students amassing very high loans, which are why she used the median in her speech rather than the mean.

The student body Vice President is interested in testing whether the President's assertion is right and wants to apply an appropriate statistical test to do so. The *t*-test from Chapter 9, which requires that the population be normally distributed, is not appropriate. Besides, that test is used for testing hypotheses about population means, not medians. Thus, the VP will need to use a test that can accommodate a non-normal distribution and that can be used in a test of the median of a population. The Wilcoxon signed rank test can be used to test whether the population median exceeds $35,000. The student body leader has selected a simple random sample of $n = 10$ graduates and collected data on the loan balance for each student.

As with all tests, we start by stating the appropriate null and alternative hypotheses. The null and alternative hypotheses for the one-tailed test are

$$H_0: \widetilde{\mu} \leq \$35,000$$
$$H_A: \widetilde{\mu} > \$35,000$$

The test will be conducted using

$$\alpha = 0.05$$

For small samples, the hypothesis is tested using a *W*-test statistic determined by the following steps:

Step 1 Collect the sample data.

Step 2 Compute d_i, the deviation between each value and the hypothesized median.

Step 3 Convert the d_i values to absolute differences.

Step 4 Determine the ranks for each d_i value, eliminating any zero d_i values.

The lowest d_i value receives a rank of 1. If observations are tied, assign the average rank of the tied observations to each of the tied values.

Step 5 For any data value greater than the hypothesized median, place the rank in an $R+$ column. For data values less than the hypothesized median, place the rank in an $R-$ column.

Step 6 The test statistic W is the sum of the ranks in the $R+$ column.

For a lower tail test use the sum in the $R-$ column. For an equal to hypothesis use either.

Table 17.1 shows the results for a random sample of 10 loan balances. The hypothesis is tested comparing the calculated W-value with the critical values for the Wilcoxon signed rank test that are shown in Appendix O. Both upper and lower critical values are shown, corresponding to $n = 5$ to $n = 20$ for various levels of alpha. Note that n equals the number of nonzero d_i values. In this example, we have $n = 9$ nonzero d_i values. The lower critical value for $n = 9$ and a one-tailed $\alpha = 0.05$ is 8. The corresponding upper-tailed critical value is 37.

Because this is an upper-tail test, we are interested only in the upper critical value $W_{0.05}$. Therefore, the decision rule is

$$\text{If } W > 37, \text{ reject } H_0.$$

Because $W = 29.5 < 37$, we do not reject the null hypothesis and are unable to conclude that the median loan balance for graduates from this university does exceed \$35,000 as the President suggested in her speech.

The loan balance example illustrates how the Wilcoxon signed rank test is used when the sample sizes are small. The W-test statistic approaches a normal distribution as n increases. Therefore, for sample sizes >20, the Wilcoxon test can be approximated using the normal distribution where the test statistic is a z-value, as shown in Equation 17.1.

Large-Sample Wilcoxon Signed Rank Test Statistic

$$z = \frac{W - \dfrac{n(n+1)}{4}}{\sqrt{\dfrac{n(n+1)(2n+1)}{24}}} \qquad \textbf{(17.1)}$$

where:

$$W = \text{Sum of the } R+ \text{ ranks}$$
$$n = \text{Number of nonzero } d_i \text{ values}$$

TABLE 17.1 | **Wilcoxon Ranking Table for the Student Loans Example**

Loan Balance	$d_i = x_i - \$35,000$	$|d_i|$	Rank	$R+$	$R-$
36,400	1,400	1,400	2	2	
38,500	3,500	3,500	3	3	
27,000	−8,000	8,000	8		8
35,000	0	0			
29,000	−6,000	6,000	6.5		6.5
40,000	5,000	5,000	5	5	
52,000	17,000	17,000	9	9	
34,000	−1,000	1,000	1		1
38,900	3,900	3,900	4	4	
41,000	6,000	6,000	6.5	6.5	
			Total = W =	29.5	15.5

EXAMPLE 17-1   **WILCOXON SIGNED RANK TEST, ONE SAMPLE, *n* > 20**

Executive Salaries A recent article in the business section of a regional newspaper indicated that the median salary for C-level executives (CEO, CFO, CIO, etc.) in the United States is less than $276,200. A shareholder advocate group has decided to test this assertion. A random sample of 25 C-level executives was selected. Since we would expect that executive salaries are highly right-skewed, a *t*-test is not appropriate. Instead a large-sample Wilcoxon signed rank test can be conducted using the following steps:

Step 1   Specify the null and alternative hypotheses.
In this case, the null and alternative hypotheses are

$$H_0: \widetilde{\mu} \geq \$276,200$$
$$H_A: \widetilde{\mu} < \$276,200 \text{ (claim)}$$

Step 2   Determine the significance level for the test.
The test will be conducted using

$$\alpha = 0.01$$

Step 3   Collect the sample data and compute the *W*-test statistic.
Using the steps outlined on pages 744–745, we manually compute the *W*-test statistic as shown in Table 17.2.

TABLE 17.2 │ **Wilcoxon Ranking Table for Executive Salaries Example**

Salary = x_i ($)	d_i	$\|d_i\|$	Rank	R+	R−
273,000	−3,200	3,200	1		1
269,900	−6,300	6,300	2		2
263,500	−12,700	12,700	3		3
260,600	−15,600	15,600	4		4
259,200	−17,000	17,000	5		5
257,200	−19,000	19,000	6		6
256,500	−19,700	19,700	7		7
255,400	−20,800	20,800	8		8
255,200	−21,000	21,000	9		9
297,750	21,550	21,550	10	10	
254,200	−22,000	22,000	11		11
300,750	24,550	24,550	12	12	
249,500	−26,700	26,700	13		13
303,000	26,800	26,800	14	14	
304,900	28,700	28,700	15	15	
245,900	−30,300	30,300	16		16
243,500	−32,700	32,700	17		17
237,650	−38,550	38,550	18		18
316,250	40,050	40,050	19	19	
234,500	−41,700	41,700	20		20
228,900	−47,300	47,300	21		21
217,000	−59,200	59,200	22		22
212,400	−63,800	63,800	23		23
204,500	−71,700	71,700	24		24
202,600	−73,600	73,600	25		25
				70	255

Step 4 **Compute the z-test statistic.**
The z-test statistic using the sum of the positive ranks is

$$z = \frac{W - \dfrac{n(n+1)}{4}}{\sqrt{\dfrac{n(n+1)(2n+1)}{24}}} = \frac{70 - \dfrac{25(25+1)}{4}}{\sqrt{\dfrac{25(25+1)(2(25)+1)}{24}}} = -2.49$$

Step 5 **Reach a decision.**
The critical value for a one-tailed test for alpha $= 0.01$ from the standard normal distribution is -2.33.
Because $z = -2.49 < -2.33$, we reject the null hypothesis.

Step 6 **Draw a conclusion.**
Thus, based on the sample data, the shareholder group should conclude the median executive salary is less than $276,200.

>> **END EXAMPLE**

TRY PROBLEM 17-1 (pg. 747)

MyStatLab

17-1: **Exercises**

Skill **Development**

17-1. Consider the following set of observations:

9.0 15.6 21.1 11.1 13.5 9.2 13.6 15.8 12.5 18.7 18.9

You should not assume these data come from a normal distribution. Test the hypothesis that the median of these data is greater than or equal to 14.

17-2. Consider the following set of observations:

10.21 13.65 12.30 9.51 11.32 12.77 6.16 8.55 11.78 12.32

You should not assume these data come from a normal distribution. Test the hypothesis that these data come from a distribution with a median less than or equal to 10.

17-3. Consider the following set of observations:

3.1   4.8   2.3   5.6   2.8   2.9   4.4

You should not assume these data come from a normal distribution. Test the hypothesis that these data come from a distribution with a median equal to 4. Use $\alpha = 0.10$.

Business **Applications**

17-4. Sigman Corporation makes batteries that are used in highway signals in rural areas. The company managers claim that the median life of a battery exceeds 4,000 hours. To test this claim, they have selected a random sample of $n = 12$ batteries and have traced their life spans between installation and failure. The following data were obtained:

1,973	4,838	3,805	4,494	4,738	5,249
4,459	4,098	4,722	5,894	3,322	4,800

a. State the appropriate null and alternative hypotheses.
b. Assuming that the test is to be conducted using a 0.05 level of significance, what conclusion should be reached based on these sample data? Be sure to examine the required normality assumption.

17-5. A cable television customer call center has a goal that states that the median time for each completed call should not exceed four minutes. If calls take too long, productivity is reduced and other customers have to wait too long on hold. The operations manager does not want to incorrectly conclude that the goal isn't being satisfied unless sample data justify that conclusion. A sample of 12 calls was selected, and the following times (in seconds) were recorded:

| 194 | 278 | 302 | 140 | 245 | 234 | 268 | 208 | 102 | 190 | 220 | 255 |

    a. Construct the appropriate null and alternative hypotheses.

    b. Based on the sample data, what should the operations manager conclude? Test at the 0.05 significance level.

17-6. A recent trade newsletter reported that during the initial 6-month period of employment, new sales personnel in an insurance company spent a median of 119 hours per month in the field. A random sample of 20 new salespersons was selected. The numbers of hours spent in the field by members in a randomly chosen month are listed here:

163	103	112	96	134
147	102	95	134	126
189	126	135	114	129
142	111	103	89	115

Do the data support the trade newsletter's claim? Conduct the appropriate hypothesis test with a significance level of 0.05.

17-7. At Hershey's, the chocolate maker, a particular candy bar is supposed to weigh 11 ounces. However, the company has received complaints that the bars are under weight. To assess this situation, the company has conducted a statistical study that concluded that the average weight of the candy is indeed 11 ounces. However, a consumer organization, while acknowledging the finding that the mean weight is 11 ounces, claims that more than 50% of the candy bars weigh less than 11 ounces and that a few heavy bars pull the mean up, thereby cheating a majority of customers. A sample of 20 candy bars was selected. The data obtained follow:

10.9	11.7	10.5	11.8	10.2
11.5	10.8	11.2	11.8	10.7
10.6	10.9	11.6	11.2	11.0
10.7	10.8	10.5	11.3	10.1

Test the consumer organization's claim at a significance level of 0.05.

17-8. Sylvania's quality control division is constantly monitoring various parameters related to its products. One investigation addressed the life of incandescent light bulbs (in hours). Initially, they were satisfied with examining the average length of life. However, a recent sample taken from the production floor gave them pause for thought. The data follow:

1,100	1,140	1,550	1,210	1,280	840	1,620	1,500
1,460	1,940	2,080	1,350	1,150	730	2,410	1,060
1,150	1,260	1,760	1,250	1,500	1,560	1,210	1,440
1,770	1,270	1,210	1,230	1,230	2,100	1,630	500

Their initial efforts indicated that the average length of life of the light bulbs was 1,440 hours.

    a. Construct a box and whisker plot of these data. On this basis, draw a conclusion concerning the distribution of the population from which this sample was drawn.

    b. Conduct a hypothesis test to determine if the median length of life of the light bulbs is longer than the average length of life. Use $\alpha = 0.05$.

17-9. The Penn Oil Company wished to verify the viscosity of its premium 30-weight oil. A simple random sample of specimens taken from automobiles running at normal temperatures was obtained. The viscosities observed were as follows:

25	24	21	35	25
25	35	38	32	36
35	29	30	27	28
27	31	32	30	30

Determine if the median viscosity at normal running temperatures is equal to 30 as advertised for Penn's premium 30-weight oil. (Use $\alpha = 0.05$.)

Computer Database **Exercises**

17-10. The Cell Tone Company sells cellular phones and airtime in several states. At a recent meeting, the marketing manager stated that the median age of its customers is less than 40. This came up in conjunction with a proposed advertising plan that is to be directed toward a young audience. Before actually completing the advertising plan, Cell Tone decided to randomly sample customers. Among the questions asked in a survey of 50 customers in the Jacksonville, Florida, area was the customers' ages. The data are in the file **Cell Phone Survey**.

    a. Examine the sample data. Is the variable being measured a discrete or a continuous variable? Does it seem feasible that these data could have come from a normal distribution?

    b. The marketing manager must support his statement concerning customer age in an upcoming board meeting. Using a significance level of 0.10, provide this support for the marketing manager.

17-11. The Wilson Company uses a great deal of water in the process of making industrial milling equipment. To comply with federal clean-water laws, it has a water purification system that all wastewater goes through before being discharged into a settling pond on the company's property. To determine whether the company is complying with federal requirements, sample measures are taken every so often. One requirement is that the median pH level must be less than 7.4. A sample of 95 pH measures has been taken. The data for these measures are shown in the file **Wilson Water**.

a. Carefully examine the data. Use an appropriate procedure to determine if the data could have been sampled from a normal distribution. (*Hint:* Review the goodness-of-fit test in Chapter 13.)

b. Based on the sample data of pH level, what should the company conclude about its current status on meeting federal requirements? Test the hypothesis at the 0.05 level.

END EXERCISES 17-1

17.2 Nonparametric Tests for Two Population Medians

You should recall that one of the assumptions for the *t*-test involving two population means is that the two populations are normally distributed. Another assumption is the data are interval or ratio level. In this section we introduce two nonparametric techniques that do not require such stringent assumptions and data requirements: the *Mann–Whitney U-test*[1] and the *Wilcoxon matched-pairs signed rank test*. Both tests can be used with ordinal (ranked) data, and neither requires that the populations be normally distributed. The Mann–Whitney *U*-test is used when the samples are independent, whereas the Wilcoxon matched-pairs signed rank test is used when the design has paired samples.

The Mann–Whitney *U*-Test

Chapter Outcome 2. → **BUSINESS APPLICATION**   **TESTING TWO POPULATION MEDIANS**

BLAINE COUNTY HIGHWAY DISTRICT The workforce of the Blaine County Highway District (BCHD) is made up of the rural and urban divisions. A few months ago, several rural division supervisors began claiming that the urban division employees waste gravel from the county gravel pit. The supervisors claimed the urban division uses more gravel per mile of road maintenance than the rural division. In response to these claims, the BCHD materials manager performed a test. He selected a random sample from the district's job-cost records of jobs performed by the urban (U) division and another sample of jobs performed by the rural (R) division. The yards of gravel per mile for each job are recorded.

Even though the data are ratio-level, the manager is not willing to make the normality assumptions necessary to employ the two-sample *t*-test (discussed in Chapter 10). However, the Mann–Whitney *U*-test will allow him to compare the gravel use of the two divisions.

The Mann–Whitney *U*-test is one of the most commonly used nonparametric tests to compare samples from two populations in those cases when the following assumptions are satisfied:

Assumptions

> 1. The two samples are independent and random.
> 2. The value measured is a continuous variable.
> 3. The measurement scale used is at least ordinal.
> 4. If they differ, the distributions of the two populations will differ only with respect to central location.

The fourth point is instrumental in setting your null and alternative hypotheses. We are interested in determining whether two populations have the same or different medians. The test can be performed using the following steps:

Step 1 State the appropriate null and alternative hypotheses.
In this situation, the variable of interest is cubic yards of gravel used. This is a ratio-level variable: However, the populations are suspected to be skewed, so

---
[1] An equivalent test to the Mann–Whitney *U*-test is the Wilcoxon rank-sum test.

the materials manager has decided to test the following hypotheses, stated in terms of the population medians:

$$H_0: \widetilde{\mu}_U \leq \widetilde{\mu}_R \text{ (Median urban gravel use is less than or}$$
$$\text{equal to median rural use.)}$$
$$H_A: \widetilde{\mu}_U > \widetilde{\mu}_R \text{ (Urban median exceeds rural median.)}$$

Step 2   Specify the desired level of significance.

The decision makers have determined that the test will be conducted using

$$\alpha = 0.05$$

Step 3   Select the sample data and compute the appropriate test statistic.

Computing the test statistic manually requires several steps:

1. Combine the raw data from the two samples into one set of numbers, keeping track of the sample from which each value came.
2. Rank the numbers in this combined set from low to high. Note that we expect no ties to occur because the values are considered to have come from continuous distributions. However, in actual situations ties will sometimes occur. When they do, we give tied observations the average of the rank positions for which they are tied. For instance, if the lowest four data points were each 460, each of the four 460s would receive a rank of $(1 + 2 + 3 + 4)/4 = 10/4 = 2.5$.[2]
3. Separate the two samples; listing each observation with the rank it has been assigned. This leads to the rankings shown in Table 17.3.

   The logic of the Mann–Whitney U-test is based on the idea that if the sum of the rankings of one sample differs greatly from the sum of the rankings of the second sample, we should conclude that there is a difference in the population medians.

4. Calculate a U-value for each sample, as shown in Equations 17.2 and 17.3.

U Statistics

$$U_1 = n_1 n_2 + \frac{n_1(n_1 + 1)}{2} - \Sigma R_1 \qquad \textbf{(17.2)}$$

$$U_2 = n_1 n_2 + \frac{n_2(n_2 + 1)}{2} - \Sigma R_2 \qquad \textbf{(17.3)}$$

where:

$$n_1 \text{ and } n_2 = \text{Sample sizes from populations 1 and 2}$$
$$\Sigma R_1 \text{ and } \Sigma R_2 = \text{Sum of ranks for samples 1 and 2}$$

For our example using the ranks in Table 17.3,

$$U_1 = 12(12) + \frac{12(13)}{2} - 142$$
$$= 80$$
$$U_2 = 12(12) + \frac{12(13)}{2} - 158$$
$$= 64$$

Note that $U_1 + U_2 = n_1 n_2$. This is always the case, and it provides a good check on the correctness of the rankings in Table 17.3.

---

[2]Noether provides an adjustment when ties occur. He, however, points out that using the adjustment has little effect unless a large proportion of the observations are tied or there are ties of considerable extent. See the References at the end of the book.

TABLE 17.3 | **Ranking of Yards of Gravel per Mile for the Blaine County Highway District Example**

Urban ($n_1 = 12$)		Rural ($n_2 = 12$)	
Yards of Gravel	**Rank**	**Yards of Gravel**	**Rank**
460	2	600	6
830	16	652	9
720	12	603	7
930	20	594	5
500	4	1,402	23
620	8	1,111	21
703	11	902	18
407	1	700	10
1,521	24	827	15
900	17	490	3
750	13	904	19
800	14	1,400	22
	$\Sigma R_1 = 142$		$\Sigma R_2 = 158$

5. Select the U-value to be the test statistic.

The Mann–Whitney U tables in Appendices K and L give the lower tail of the U-distribution. For one-tailed tests such as our Blaine County example, you need to look at the alternative hypothesis to determine whether U_1 or U_2 should be selected as the test statistic. Recall that

$$H_A: \tilde{\mu}_U > \tilde{\mu}_R$$

If the alternative hypothesis indicates that population 1 has a higher median, as in this case, then U_1 is selected as the test statistic. If population 2 is expected to have a higher median, then U_2 should be selected as the test statistic. The reason is that the population with the larger median should have the larger sum of ranked values, thus producing the smaller U-value. It is very important to note that this logic must be made in terms of the alternative hypothesis and not on the basis of the U-values obtained from the samples.

Now, we select the U-value that the alternative hypothesis indicates should be the smaller and call this U. Because population 1 (Urban) should have the smaller U-value (larger median) if the alternative hypothesis is true, the sample data give a

$$U = 80$$

This is actually larger than the U-value for the rural population, but we still use it as the test statistic because the alternative hypothesis indicates that $\tilde{\mu}_U > \tilde{\mu}_R$.[3]

Step 4 **Determine the critical value for the Mann–Whitney U-test.**

For sample sizes less than 9, use the Mann–Whitney U table in Appendix K for the appropriate sample size. For sample sizes from 9 to 20, as in this example, the null hypothesis can be tested by comparing U with the appropriate critical value given in the Mann–Whitney U table in Appendix L. We begin by locating the part of the table associated with the desired significance level. In this case, we have a one-tailed test with

$$\alpha = 0.05$$

---

[3]For a two-tailed test, you should select the smaller U-value as your test statistic. This will force you toward the lower tail. If the U-value is smaller than the critical value in the Mann–Whitney U table, you will reject the null hypothesis.

Go across the top of the Mann–Whitney U table to locate the value corresponding to the sample size from population 2 (Rural) and down the left side of the table to the sample size from population 1 (Urban).

In the Blaine County example, both sample sizes are 12, so we will use the Mann–Whitney table in Appendix L for a one-tailed test at $\alpha = 0.05$. Go across the top of the table to

$$n_2 = 12$$

and down the left-hand side to

$$n_1 = 12$$

The intersection of these column and row values gives a critical value of

$$U_{0.05} = 42$$

We can now form the decision rule as follows:

If $U < 42$, reject H_0.
Otherwise, do not reject H_0.

Step 5 **Reach a decision.**
Now because

$$U = 80 > 42$$

we do not reject the null hypothesis.

Step 6 **Draw a conclusion.**
Therefore, based on the sample data, there is not sufficient evidence to conclude that the median yards of gravel per mile used by the urban division is greater than that for the rural division.

Mann–Whitney *U*-Test—Large Samples

When you encounter a situation with sample sizes in excess of 20, the previous approaches to the Mann–Whitney U-test cannot be used because of table limitations. However, the U statistic approaches a normal distribution as the sample sizes increase, and the Mann–Whitney U-test can be conducted using a normal approximation approach, where the mean and standard deviation for the U statistic are as given in Equations 17.4 and 17.5, respectively.

Mean and Standard Deviation for *U* Statistic

$$\mu = \frac{n_1 n_2}{2} \tag{17.4}$$

$$\sigma = \sqrt{\frac{(n_1)(n_2)(n_1 + n_2 + 1)}{12}} \tag{17.5}$$

where:

n_1 and n_2 = Sample sizes from populations 1 and 2

Equations 17.4 and 17.5 are used to form the U-test statistic in Equation 17.6.

Mann–Whitney *U*-Test Statistic

$$z = \frac{U - \dfrac{n_1 n_2}{2}}{\sqrt{\dfrac{(n_1)(n_2)(n_1 + n_2 + 1)}{12}}} \tag{17.6}$$

BUSINESS APPLICATION   **LARGE SAMPLE TEST OF TWO POPULATION MEDIANS**

TAX PREPARATION SOFTWARE Over the past few years, two tax preparation software products have emerged as the leaders—TurboTax and TaxCut. These software options have pulled a lot of business away from accounting firms and tax services businesses. A recent article in a business periodical suggested that median household income for families that use software to do their own taxes is actually less than the median income for those who use a professional tax service.

The authors used the median (as opposed to the mean) income in their story because data such as household income are notorious for having large outliers and skewed distributions. In such cases, the median, which is not sensitive to outliers, is a preferable measure of the center of the data. The skewed distribution is another reason to use a nonparametric procedure such as the Mann–Whitney test.

The Mann–Whitney U-test can be used to test the authors' assertion about median incomes for families using software versus professional tax preparation services. The correct procedure is:

Step 1   Specify the null and alternative hypotheses.
Given that the author stated that that median household income for software customers (C) is less than the median for those customers who don't use software (NC) the null and alternative hypotheses to be tested are

$$H_0: \widetilde{\mu}_C \geq \widetilde{\mu}_{NC}$$
$$H_A: \widetilde{\mu}_C < \widetilde{\mu}_{NC} \text{ (claim)}$$

Step 2   Specify the desired level of significance.
The test is to be conducted using

$$\alpha = 0.05$$

Step 3   Select the random sample and compute the test statistic.
To test this hypothesis, take a survey in the market area for a total of 548 households in this case (144 who use professional services and 404 who use tax software). The results of the survey are contained in the file **Tax Software**. Because of the sample size, we can use the large-sample approach to the Mann–Whitney U-test. To compute the test statistic shown in Equation 17.6, use the following steps:

1. The income data must be converted to ranks. The sample data and ranks are in a file called **Tax Software-Ranks**. Note that when data are tied in value, they share the same average rank. For example, if four values are tied for the fifth position, each one is assigned the average of rankings 5, 6, 7, and 8, or $(5 + 6 + 7 + 8)/4 = 6.5$.

2. Next, we compute the U-value. The sum of the ranks for the families using a professional service is

$$\Sigma R_1 = 41,204$$

and the sum of the ranks for the families using software is

$$\Sigma R_2 = 109,222$$

3. Based on sample sizes of

$$n_1 = 144$$

tax professional users and

$$n_2 = 404$$

software users, we compute the U-values using Equations 17.2 and 17.3.

$$U_1 = 144(404) + \frac{144(145)}{2} - 41,204 = 27,412$$

$$U_2 = 144(404) + \frac{404(405)}{2} - 109,222 = 30,764$$

Because the alternative hypothesis predicts that families that use a tax professional will have a higher median, U_1 is selected to be U. Thus,

$$U = 27,412$$

4.　We now substitute appropriate values into Equations 17.4 and 17.5.

$$\mu = \frac{n_1 n_2}{2} = \frac{(144)(404)}{2} = 29,088$$

and

$$\sigma = \sqrt{\frac{(n_1)(n_2)(n_1 + n_2 + 1)}{12}} = \sqrt{\frac{(144)(404)(144 + 404 + 1)}{12}} = 1,631.43$$

5.　The test statistic is computed using Equation 17.6.

$$z = \frac{U - \frac{n_1 n_2}{2}}{\sqrt{\frac{(n_1)(n_2)(n_1 + n_2 + 1)}{12}}} = \frac{27,412 - 29,088}{\sqrt{\frac{(144)(404)(144 + 404 + 1)}{12}}}$$

$$= \frac{-1,676}{1,631.43} = -1.027$$

Step 4　Determine the critical value for the test.
Based on a one-tailed test with $\alpha = 0.05$, the critical value from the standard normal distribution table is

$$z_{0.05} = -1.645$$

Step 5　Reach a decision.
Since $z = -1.027 > -1.645$, the null hypothesis cannot be rejected.

Step 6　Draw a conclusion.
This means that the claim that families that use a tax professional to prepare their income taxes have higher median incomes than families who use a tax software package is not supported by the sample data.

Chapter Outcome 3. ➔ **The Wilcoxon Matched-Pairs Signed Rank Test** The Mann–Whitney U-test is a very useful nonparametric technique. However, as discussed in the Blaine County Highway District example, its use is limited to those situations in which the samples from the two populations are independent. As we discussed in Chapter 10, you will encounter decision situations in which the samples will be paired and, therefore, are not independent.

The *Wilcoxon matched-pairs signed rank test* has been developed for situations in which you have related samples and are unwilling or unable (due to data-level limitations) to use the paired-sample t-test. It is useful when the two related samples have a measurement scale that allows us to determine not only whether the pairs of observations differ but also the magnitude of any difference. The Wilcoxon matched-pairs test can be used in those cases in which the following assumptions are satisfied:

Assumptions

1. The differences are measured on a continuous variable.
2. The measurement scale used is at least interval.
3. The distribution of the population differences is symmetric about their median.

EXAMPLE 17-2 **SMALL-SAMPLE WILCOXON TEST**

Financial Systems Associates Financial Systems Associates develops and markets financial planning software. To differentiate its products from the other packages on the market, Financial Systems has built many macros into its software. According to Financial Systems, once a user learns the macro keystrokes, complicated financial computations become much easier to perform.

As part of its product-development testing program, software engineers at Financial Systems have selected a focus group of seven people who frequently use spreadsheet packages. Each person is given complicated financial and accounting data and is asked to prepare a detailed analysis. The software tracks the amount of time each person takes to complete the task. Once the analysis is complete, these same seven individuals are given a training course in Financial Systems add-ons. After the training course, they are given a similar set of data and are asked to do the same analysis. Again, the systems software determines the time needed to complete the analysis.

You should recognize that the samples in this application are not independent because the same subjects are used in both cases. If the software engineers performing the analysis are unwilling to make the normal distribution assumption required of the paired-sample t-test, they can use the Wilcoxon matched-pairs signed rank test. This test can be conducted using the following steps:

Step 1 **Specify the appropriate null and alternative hypotheses.**
The null and alternative hypotheses being tested are

$$H_0: \widetilde{\mu}_b \leq \widetilde{\mu}_a$$
$$H_A: \widetilde{\mu}_b > \widetilde{\mu}_a \text{ (Median time will be less } after \text{ the training.)}$$

Step 2 **Specify the desired level of significance.**
The test will be conducted using

$$\alpha = 0.025$$

Step 3 **Collect the sample data and compute the test statistic.**
The data are shown in Table 17.4.

First, we convert the data in Table 17.4 to differences. The column of differences, d, gives the "before minus after" differences. The next column is the rank of the d-values from low to high. Note that the ranks are determined without considering the sign on the d-value. However, once the rank is determined, the original sign on the d-value is attached to the rank. For example, $d = 13$ is given a rank of 7, whereas $d = -4$ has a rank of -3.

The final column is titled "Ranks with Smallest Expected Sum." To determine the values in this column, we take the absolute values of either the positive or the negative ranks, depending on which group has the smallest expected sum of absolute-valued ranks. We look to the alternative hypothesis, which is

$$H_A: \widetilde{\mu}_b > \widetilde{\mu}_a$$

TABLE 17.4 | **Financial Systems Associates Ranked Data**

Subject	Before Training	After Training	d	Rank of d	Ranks with Smallest Expected Sum
1	24	11	13	7	
2	20	18	2	1	
3	19	23	−4	−3	3
4	20	15	5	4	
5	13	16	−3	−2	2
6	28	22	6	5	
7	15	8	7	6	
					$T = \overline{5}$

Because the before median is predicted to exceed the after median, we would expect the positive differences to exceed the negative differences. Therefore, the negative ranks should have the smaller sum, and therefore should be used in the final column, as shown in Table 17.4. The test statistic, T, is equal to the sum of absolute values of these negative ranks. Thus, $T = 5$.

Step 4 **Determine the critical value.**

To determine whether T is small enough to reject the null hypothesis, we consult the Wilcoxon table of critical T-values in Appendix M. If the calculated T is less than or equal to the critical T from the table, the null hypothesis is rejected. For instance, with $\alpha = 0.025$ for our one-tailed test and $n = 7$, we get a critical value of

$$T_{0.025} = 2$$

Step 5 **Reach a decision.**

Because

$$T = 5 > 2, \text{do not reject } H_0.$$

Step 6 **Draw a conclusion.**

Based on these sample data, Financial Systems Associates does not have a statistical basis for stating that its product will reduce the median time required to perform complicated financial analyses.

>> **END EXAMPLE**

TRY PROBLEM 17-20 (pg. 758)

Ties in the Data If the two measurements of an observed data pair have the same values and, therefore, a d-value of 0, that case is dropped from the analysis and the sample size is reduced accordingly. You should note that this procedure favors rejecting the null hypothesis because we are eliminating cases in which the two sample points have exactly the same values.

If two or more d-values have the same absolute values, we assign the same average rank to each one using the same approach as with the Mann–Whitney U-test. For example, if we have two d-values that tie for ranks 4 and 5, we average them as $(4 + 5)/2 = 4.5$ and assign both a rank of 4.5. Studies have shown that this method of assigning ranks to ties has little effect on the Wilcoxon test results. For a more complete discussion of the effect of ties on the Wilcoxon matched-pairs signed rank test, please see the text by Marascuilo and McSweeney referenced at the end of this book.

Large-Sample Wilcoxon Test If the sample size (number of matched pairs) exceeds 25, the Wilcoxon table of critical T-values in Appendix M cannot be used. However, it can be shown that for large samples, the distribution of T-values is approximately normal, with a mean and standard deviation given by Equations 17.7 and 17.8, respectively.

Wilcoxon Mean and Standard Deviation

$$\mu = \frac{n(n+1)}{4} \qquad \textbf{(17.7)}$$

$$\sigma = \sqrt{\frac{n(n+1)(2n+1)}{24}} \qquad \textbf{(17.8)}$$

where:

$$n = \text{Number of paired values}$$

The *Wilcoxon test statistic* is given by Equation 17.9.

Wilcoxon Test Statistic

$$z = \frac{T - \dfrac{n(n+1)}{4}}{\sqrt{\dfrac{n(n+1)(2n+1)}{24}}} \qquad (17.9)$$

Then, the z-value is compared to the critical value from the standard normal table in the usual manner.

MyStatLab

17-2: Exercises

Skill Development

17-12. For each of the following tests, determine which of the two U statistics (U_1 or U_2) you would choose, the appropriate test statistic, and the rejection region for the Mann–Whitney test:

a. H_A: $\tilde{\mu}_1 < \tilde{\mu}_2$, $\alpha = 0.05$, $n_1 = 5$, and $n_2 = 10$
b. H_A: $\tilde{\mu}_1 > \tilde{\mu}_2$, $\alpha = 0.05$, $n_1 = 15$, and $n_2 = 12$
c. H_A: $\tilde{\mu}_1 \neq \tilde{\mu}_2$, $\alpha = 0.10$, $n_1 = 12$, and $n_2 = 17$
d. H_A: $\tilde{\mu}_1 < \tilde{\mu}_2$, $\alpha = 0.05$, $n_1 = 22$, and $n_2 = 25$
e. H_A: $\tilde{\mu}_1 \neq \tilde{\mu}_2$, $\alpha = 0.10$, $n_1 = 44$, and $n_2 = 15$

17-13. The following sample data have been collected from two independent samples from two populations. Test the claim that the second population median will exceed the median of the first population.

Sample 1		Sample 2	
12	11	9	20
21	14	18	7
15	12	16	12
10	8	17	19

a. State the appropriate null and alternative hypotheses.
b. If you are unwilling to assume that the two populations are normally distributed, based on the sample data, what should you conclude about the null hypothesis? Test using $\alpha = 0.05$.

17-14. The following sample data have been collected from independent samples from two populations. The claim is that the first population median will be larger than the median of the second population.

Sample 1		Sample 2	
4.4	2.6	3.7	4.2
2.7	2.4	3.5	5.2
1.0	2.0	4.0	4.4
3.5	2.8	4.9	4.3
2.8		3.1	

a. State the appropriate null and alternative hypotheses.
b. Using the Mann–Whitney U-test, based on the sample data, what should you conclude about the null hypothesis? Test using $\alpha = 0.05$.

17-15. The following sample data have been collected from two independent random samples from two populations. Test the claim that the first population median will exceed the median of the second population.

Sample 1		Sample 2	
50	43	38	31
47	46	44	38
44	72	38	39
48	40	37	54
40	55	43	41
36	38	44	40

a. State the appropriate null and alternative hypotheses.
b. Using the Mann–Whitney U-test, based on the sample data, what should you conclude about the null hypothesis? Test using a significance level of 0.01.

17-16. Determine the rejection region for the Mann–Whitney U-test in each of the following cases:

a. H_A: $\tilde{\mu}_1 < \tilde{\mu}_2$, $\alpha = 0.05$, $n_1 = 3$, and $n_2 = 15$
b. H_A: $\tilde{\mu}_1 \neq \tilde{\mu}_2$, $\alpha = 0.10$, $n_1 = 5$, and $n_2 = 20$
c. H_A: $\tilde{\mu}_1 < \tilde{\mu}_2$, $\alpha = 0.025$, $n_1 = 9$, and $n_2 = 12$
d. H_A: $\tilde{\mu}_1 \neq \tilde{\mu}_2$, $\alpha = 0.10$, $n_1 = 124$, and $n_2 = 25$

17-17. The following sample data have been collected from independent samples from two populations. Do the populations have different medians? Test at a significance level of 0.05. Use the Mann–Whitney U-test.

Sample 1		Sample 2	
550	489	594	538
483	480	542	505
379	433	447	486
438	436	466	425
398	540	560	497
582	415	447	511
528	532	526	576
502	412	446	558
352	572	573	500
488	579	542	467
400	556	473	556
451	383	418	383
571	515	511	515
382	501	510	501
588	353	577	353
465	369	585	
492	475	436	
384	470	461	
563	595	545	
506	361	441	

17-18. For each of the following tests, determine which of the two sums of absolute ranks (negative or positive) you would choose, the appropriate test statistic, and the rejection region for the Wilcoxon matched-pairs signed rank test:

a. $H_A: \tilde{\mu}_1 < \tilde{\mu}_2, \alpha = 0.025, n = 15$
b. $H_A: \tilde{\mu}_1 > \tilde{\mu}_2, \alpha = 0.01, n = 12$
c. $H_A: \tilde{\mu}_1 \neq \tilde{\mu}_2, \alpha = 0.05, n = 9$
d. $H_A: \tilde{\mu}_1 < \tilde{\mu}_2, \alpha = 0.05, n = 26$
e. $H_A: \tilde{\mu}_1 \neq \tilde{\mu}_2, \alpha = 0.10, n = 44$

17-19. You are given two paired samples with the following information:

Item	Sample 1	Sample 2
1	3.4	2.8
2	2.5	3.0
3	7.0	5.5
4	5.9	6.7
5	4.0	3.5
6	5.0	5.0
7	6.2	7.5
8	5.3	4.2

a. Based on these paired samples, test at the $\alpha = 0.05$ level whether the true median paired difference is 0.
b. Answer part a assuming data given here were sampled from normal distributions with equal variances.

17-20. You are given two paired samples with the following information:

Item	Sample 1	Sample 2
1	19.6	21.3
2	22.1	17.4
3	19.5	19.0
4	20.0	21.2
5	21.5	20.1
6	20.2	23.5
7	17.9	18.9
8	23.0	22.4
9	12.5	14.3
10	19.0	17.8

Based on these paired samples, test at the $\alpha = 0.05$ level whether the true median paired difference is 0.

17-21. You are given two paired samples with the following information:

Item	Sample 1	Sample 2
1	1,004	1,045
2	1,245	1,145
3	1,360	1,400
4	1,150	1,000
5	1,300	1,350
6	1,450	1,350
7	900	1,140

Based on these paired samples, test at the $\alpha = 0.05$ level whether the true median paired difference is 0.

17-22. From a recent study we have collected the following data from two independent random samples:

Sample 1	Sample 2
405	300
450	340
290	400
370	250
345	270
460	410
425	435
275	390
380	225
330	210
500	395
215	315

Suppose we do not wish to assume normal distributions. Use the appropriate nonparametric test to determine whether the populations have equal medians. Test at $\alpha = 0.05$.

17-23. You are given two paired samples with the following information:

Item	Sample 1	Sample 2
1	234	245
2	221	224
3	196	194
4	245	267
5	234	230
6	204	198

Based on these paired samples, test at the $\alpha = 0.05$ level whether the true median paired difference is 0.

17-24. Consider the following data for two paired samples:

Case #	Sample 1	Sample 2
1	258	304
2	197	190
3	400	500
4	350	340
5	237	250
6	400	358
7	370	390
8	130	100

a. Test the following null and alternative hypotheses at an $\alpha = 0.05$ level:

H_0: There is no difference between the two population distributions.

H_A: There is a difference between the two populations.

b. Answer part a as if the samples were independent samples from normal distributions with equal variances.

Business Applications

17-25. National Reading Academy claims that graduates of its program have a higher median reading speed per minute than people who do not take the course. An independent agency conducted a study to determine whether this claim was justified. Researchers from the agency selected a random sample of people who had taken the speed reading course and another random sample of people who had not taken the course. The agency was unwilling to make the assumption that the populations were normally distributed. Therefore, a nonparametric test was needed. The following summary data were observed:

With Course	Without Course
$n = 7$	$n = 5$
Sum of ranks = 42	Sum of ranks = 36

Assuming that higher ranks imply more words per minute being read, what should the testing agency conclude based on the sample data? Test at an $\alpha = 0.05$ level.

17-26. The makers of the Plus 20 Hardcard, a plug-in hard disk unit on a PC board, have recently done a marketing research study in which they asked two independently selected groups to rate the Hardcard on a scale of 1 to 100, with 100 being perfect satisfaction. The first group consisted of professional computer programmers. The second group consisted of home computer users. The company hoped to be able to say that the product would receive the same median ranking from each group. The following summary data were recorded:

Professionals	Home Users
$n = 10$	$n = 8$
Sum of ranks = 92	Sum of ranks = 79

Based on these data, what should the company conclude? Test at the $\alpha = 0.02$ level.

17-27. Property taxes are based on assessed values of property. In most states, the law requires that assessed values be "at or near" market value of the property. In one Washington county, a tax protest group has claimed that assessed values are higher than market values. To address this claim, the county tax assessor, together with representatives from the protest group, has selected 15 properties at random that have sold within the past six months. Both parties agree that the sales price was the market value at the time of the sale.

The assessor then listed the assessed values and the sales values side by side, as shown.

House	Assessed Value ($)	Market Value ($)
1	302,000	198,000
2	176,000	182,400
3	149,000	154,300
4	198,500	198,500
5	214,000	218,000
6	235,000	230,000
7	305,000	298,900
8	187,500	190,000
9	150,000	149,800
10	223,000	222,000
11	178,500	180,000
12	245,000	250,900
13	167,000	165,200
14	219,000	220,700
15	334,000	320,000

a. Assuming that the population of assessed values and the population of market values have the same distribution shape and that they may differ only with respect to medians, state the appropriate null and alternative hypotheses.

b. Test the hypotheses using an $\alpha = 0.01$ level.

c. Discuss why one would not assume that the samples were obtained from normal distributions for this problem. What characteristic about the market values of houses would lead you to conclude that these data were not normally distributed?

17-28. The Kansas Tax Commission recently conducted a study to determine whether there is a difference in median deductions taken for charitable contributions depending on whether a tax return is filed as a single or a joint return. A random sample from each category was selected, with the following results:

Single	Joint
$n = 6$	$n = 8$
Sum of ranks = 43	Sum of ranks = 62

Based on these data, what should the tax commission conclude? Use an $\alpha = 0.05$ level.

17-29. A cattle feedlot operator has collected data for 40 matched pairs of cattle showing weight gain on two different feed supplements. His purpose in collecting the data is to determine whether there is a difference in the median weight gain for the two supplements. He has no preconceived idea about which supplement might produce higher weight gain. He wishes to test using an $\alpha = 0.05$ level.

Assuming that the T-value for these data is 480, what should be concluded concerning which supplement might produce higher weight gain? Use the large-sample Wilcoxon matched-pairs signed rank test normal approximation. Conduct the test using a p-value approach.

17-30. Radio advertisements have been stressing the virtues of an audiotape program to help children learn to read. To test whether this tape program can cause a quick improvement in reading ability, 10 children were given a nationally recognized reading test that measures reading ability. The same 10 children were then given the tapes to listen to for 4 hours spaced over a 2-day period. The children then were tested again. The test scores were as follows:

Child	Before	After
1	60	63
2	40	38
3	78	77
4	53	50
5	67	74
6	88	96
7	77	80
8	60	70
9	64	65
10	75	75

If higher scores are better, use the Wilcoxon matched-pairs signed rank test to test whether this tape program produces quick improvement in reading ability. Use an $\alpha = 0.025$.

17-31. The Montgomery Athletic Shoe Company has developed a new shoe-sole material it thinks provides superior wear compared with the old material the company has been using for its running shoes. The company selected 10 cross-country runners and supplied each runner with a pair of shoes. Each pair had one sole made of the old material and the other made of the new material. The shoes were monitored until the soles wore out. The following lifetimes (in hours) were recorded for each material:

Runner	Old Material	New Material
1	45.5	47.0
2	50.0	51.0
3	43.0	42.0

Runner	Old Material	New Material
4	45.5	46.0
5	58.5	58.0
6	49.0	50.5
7	29.5	39.0
8	52.0	53.0
9	48.0	48.0
10	57.5	61.0

a. If the populations from which these samples were taken could be considered to have normal distributions, determine if the soles made of the new material have a longer mean lifetime than those made from the old material. Use a significance level of 0.025.

b. Suppose you were not willing to consider that the populations have normal distributions. Make the determination requested in part a.

c. Given only the information in this problem, which of the two procedures indicated in parts a and b would you choose to use? Give reasons for your answer.

Computer Database **Exercises**

17-32. For at least the past 20 years, there has been a debate over whether children who are placed in child-care facilities while their parents work suffer as a result. A recent study of 6,000 children discussed in *Developmental Psychology* found "no permanent negative effects caused by their mothers' absence." In fact, the study indicated that there might be some positive benefits from the day-care experience. To investigate this premise, a nonprofit organization called Child Care Connections conducted a small study in which children were observed playing in neutral settings (not at home or at a day-care center). Over a period of 20 hours of observation, 15 children who did not go to day care and 21 children who had spent much time in day care were observed. The variable of interest was the total minutes of play in which each child was actively interacting with other students. Child Care Connections leaders hoped to show that the children who had been in day care would have a higher median time in interactive situations than the stay-at-home children. The file **Children** contains the results of the study.

a. Conduct a hypothesis test to determine if the hopes of the Child Care Connections leaders can be substantiated. Use a significance level of 0.05, and write a short statement that describes the results of the test.

b. Based on the outcome of the hypothesis test, which statistical error might have been committed?

17-33. The California State Highway Patrol recently conducted a study on a stretch of interstate highway south of San Francisco to determine whether the mean speed for California vehicles exceeded the mean speed for Nevada vehicles. A total of 140 California cars were included in the study, and 75 Nevada cars were included. Radar was used to measure the speed. The file **Speed-Test** contains the data collected by the California Highway Patrol.

a. Past studies have indicated that the speeds at which both Nevada and California drivers drive have normal distributions. Using a significance level equal to 0.10, obtain the results desired by the California Highway Patrol. Use a *p*-value approach to conduct the relevant hypothesis test. Discuss the results of this test in a short written statement.

b. Describe, in the context of this problem, what a Type I error would be.

17-34. The Sunbeam Corporation makes a wide variety of appliances for the home. One product is a digital blood pressure gauge. For obvious reasons, the blood pressure readings made by the monitor need to be accurate. When a new model is being designed, one of the steps is to test it. To do this, a sample of people is selected. Each person has his or her systolic blood pressure taken by a highly respected physician. They then immediately have their systolic blood pressure taken using the Sunbeam monitor. If the mean blood pressure is the same for the monitor as it is as determined by the physician, the monitor is determined to pass the test.

In a recent test, 15 people were randomly selected to be in the sample. The blood pressure readings for these people using both methods are contained in the file **Sunbeam**.

a. Based on the sample data and a significance level equal to 0.05, what conclusion should the Sunbeam engineers reach regarding the latest blood pressure monitor? Discuss your answer in a short written statement.

b. Conduct the test as a paired *t*-test.

c. Discuss which of the two procedures in parts a and b is more appropriate to analyze the data presented in this problem.

17-35. The Hersh Corporation is considering two word-processing systems for its computers. One factor that will influence its decision is the ease of use in preparing a business report. Consequently, nine typists were selected from the clerical pool and asked to type a typical report using both word-processing systems. The typists then rated the systems on a scale of 0 to 100. The resulting ratings are in the file **Hersh**.

a. Which measurement level describes the data collected for this analysis?

b. (1) Could a normal distribution describe the population distribution from which these data were sampled? (2) Which measure of central tendency would be appropriate to describe the center of the populations from which these data were sampled?

c. Choose the appropriate hypothesis procedure to determine if there is a difference in the measures of central tendency you selected in part b between these two word-processing systems. Use a significance level of 0.01.

d. Which word-processing system would you recommend the Hersh Corporation adopt? Support your answer with statistical reasoning.

END EXERCISES 17-2

Chapter Outcome 4. → # 17.3 Kruskal–Wallis One-Way Analysis of Variance

Section 17.2 showed that the Mann–Whitney *U*-test is a useful nonparametric procedure for determining whether two independent samples are from populations with the same median. However, as discussed in Chapter 12, many decisions involve comparing more than two populations. Chapter 12 introduced one-way analysis of variance and showed how, if the assumptions of normally distributed populations with equal variances are satisfied, the *F*-distribution can be used to test the hypothesis of equal population means. However, what if decision makers are not willing to assume normally distributed populations? In that case, they can turn to a nonparametric procedure to compare the populations. *Kruskal–Wallis One-Way Analysis of Variance* is the nonparametric counterpart to the one-way ANOVA procedure. It is applicable any time the variables in question satisfy the following conditions:

Assumptions

> 1. They have a continuous distribution.
> 2. The data are at least ordinal.
> 3. The samples are independent.
> 4. The samples come from populations whose only possible difference is that at least one may have a different central location than the others.

USING THE KRUSKAL-WALLIS ONE-WAY ANOVA TEST

WESTERN STATES OIL AND GAS Western States Oil and Gas is considering outsourcing its information systems activities, including demand-supply analysis, general accounting, and billing. On the basis of cost and performance standards, the company's information systems manager has reduced the possible suppliers to three, each using different computer systems. One critical factor in the decision is downtime (the time when the system is not operational). When the system goes down, the online applications stop and normal activities are interrupted. The information systems manager received from each supplier a list of firms using its service. From these lists, the manager selected random samples of nine users of each service. In a telephone interview, she found the number of hours of downtime in the previous month for each service. At issue is whether the three computer downtime populations have the same or different medians. If the manager is unwilling to make the assumptions of normality and equal variances required for the one-way ANOVA technique, introduced in Chapter 12, she can implement the Kruskal–Wallis nonparametric test using the following steps.

Step 1 **Specify the appropriate null and alternative hypotheses to be tested.**
In this application the information systems manager is interested in determining whether a difference exists between median downtime for the three systems. Thus, the null and alternative hypotheses are

$$H_0: \widetilde{\mu}_A = \widetilde{\mu}_B = \widetilde{\mu}_C$$
$$H_A: \text{Not all population medians are equal}$$

Step 2 **Specify the desired level of significance for the test.**
The test will be conducted using a significance level equal to

$$\alpha = 0.10$$

Step 3 **Collect the sample data and compute the test statistic.**
The data represent a random sample of downtimes from each service. The samples are independent. To use the Kruskal–Wallis ANOVA, first replace each downtime measurement by its *relative ranking* within all groups combined. The smallest downtime is given a rank of 1, the next smallest a rank of 2, and so forth, until all downtimes for the three services have been replaced by their relative rankings. Table 17.5 shows the sample data and the rankings for the 27 observations. Notice that the rankings are summed for each service. The Kruskal–Wallis test will determine whether these sums are so different that it is not likely that they came from populations with equal medians.
   If the samples actually do come from populations with equal medians (that is, the three services have the same per-month median downtime), then the

TABLE 17.5 | **Sample Data and Rankings of System Downtimes for the Western States Gas and Oil Example**

Service A		Service B		Service C	
Data	Ranking	Data	Ranking	Data	Ranking
4.0	11	6.9	19	0.5	1
3.7	10	11.3	23	1.4	4
5.1	15	21.7	27	1.0	2
2.0	6	9.2	20	1.7	5
4.6	12	6.5	17	3.6	9
9.3	21	4.9	14	5.2	16
2.7	8	12.2	25	1.3	3
2.5	7	11.7	24	6.8	18
4.8	13	10.5	22	14.1	26
Sum of ranks = 103		Sum of ranks = 191		Sum of ranks = 84	

H statistic, calculated by Equation 17.10, will be approximately distributed as a chi-square variable with $k - 1$ degrees of freedom, where k equals the number of populations (systems in this application) under study.

H Statistic

$$H = \frac{12}{N(N+1)} \sum_{i=1}^{k} \frac{R_i^2}{n_i} - 3(N+1) \qquad \text{(17.10)}$$

where:

N = Sum of the sample sizes from all populations
k = Number of populations
R_i = Sum of ranks in the sample from the ith population
n_i = Size of the sample from the ith population

Using Equation 17.10, the H statistic is

$$H = \frac{12}{N(N+1)} \sum_{i=1}^{k} \frac{R_i^2}{n_i} - 3(N+1)$$

$$= \frac{12}{27(27+1)} \left[\frac{103^2}{9} + \frac{191^2}{9} + \frac{84^2}{9} \right] - 3(27+1) = 11.50$$

Step 4 Determine the critical value from the chi-square distribution.
If H is larger than χ^2 from the chi-square distribution with $k - 1$ degrees of freedom in Appendix G, the hypothesis of equal medians should be rejected. The critical value for $\alpha = 0.10$ and

$$k - 1 = 3 - 1 = 2$$

degrees of freedom is

$$\chi^2_{0.10} = 4.6052$$

Step 5 Reach a decision.
Since $H = 11.50 > 4.6052$, reject the null hypothesis based on these sample data.

Step 6 Draw a conclusion.
The Kruskal–Wallis one-way ANOVA shows the information systems manager should conclude, based on the sample data, that the three services *do not* have equal median downtimes. From this analysis, the supplier with system B would most likely be eliminated from consideration unless other factors such as price or service support offset the apparent longer downtimes.

EXAMPLE 17-3   USING KRUSKAL–WALLIS ONE-WAY ANOVA

Amalgamated Sugar Amalgamated Sugar has recently begun a new effort called total productive maintenance (TPM). The TPM concept is to increase the overall operating effectiveness of the company's equipment. One component of the TPM process attempts to reduce unplanned machine downtime. The first step is to gain an understanding of the current downtime situation. To do this, a sample of 20 days has been collected for each of the three shifts (day, swing, and graveyard). The variable of interest is the minutes of unplanned downtime per shift per day. The minutes are tabulated by summing the downtime minutes

Excel

tutorials

Excel Tutorial

for all equipment in the plant. The Kruskal–Wallis test can be performed using the following steps:

Step 1 **State the appropriate null and alternative hypotheses.**

The Kruskal–Wallis one-way ANOVA procedure can test whether the medians are equal, as follows:

$$H_0: \tilde{\mu}_1 = \tilde{\mu}_2 = \tilde{\mu}_3$$
$$H_A: \text{Not all population medians are equal}$$

Step 2 **Specify the desired significance level for the test.**

The test will be conducted using an

$$\alpha = 0.05$$

Step 3 **Collect the sample data and compute the test statistic.**

The sample data are in the **Amalgamated** file.

Excel (using the PHStat add-in) can be used to perform the Kruskal–Wallis nonparametric ANOVA test. Figures 17.1 illustrates the Excel output for these sample data. The calculated H statistic is

$$H = 0.1859$$

Step 4 **Determine the critical value from the chi-square distribution.**

The critical value for $\alpha = 0.05$ and $k - 1 = 2$ degrees of freedom is

$$\chi^2_{0.05} = 5.9915$$

FIGURE 17.1

Excel 2010 (PHStat) Kruskal–Wallis ANOVA Output for Amalgamated Sugar

Excel 2010 Instructions:
1. Open File: **Amalgamated.xlsx**.
2. Select **Add-Ins**.
3. Select **PHStat**.
4. Select **Multiple Sample Test > Kruskal-Wallis Rank Test**.
5. Specify significance level (0.05).
6. Define data range (Columns B through D) including labels.
7. Click **OK**.

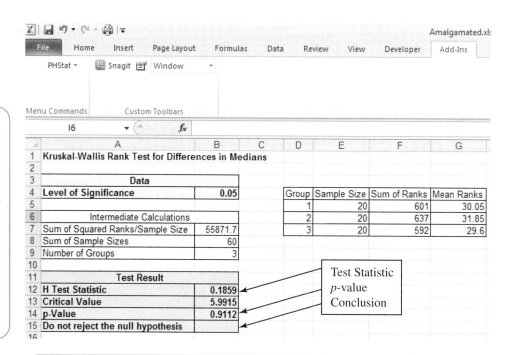

Minitab Instructions (for similar results):
1. Open file: **Amalgamated.MTW**.
2. Choose **Data > Stack > Columns**.
3. In **Stack the following columns**, enter data columns.
4. In **Store the stacked data in** select **Column of current worksheet**, and enter column name: *Downtime*.
5. In **Store subscripts in**, enter column name: *Shifts*. Click **OK**.
6. Choose **Stat > Nonparametrics > Kruskal–Wallis**.
7. In **Response**, enter data column: *Downtime*.
8. In **Factor**, enter factor levels column: *Shifts*.
9. Click **OK**.

Step 5   Reach a decision.
Because

$$H = 0.1859 < 5.9915$$

we do not reject the null hypothesis.

The PHStat output provides the p-value associated with the H statistic. The p-value of 0.9112 far exceeds an alpha of 0.05.

Step 6   Draw a conclusion.
Based on the sample data, the three shifts do not appear to differ with respect to median equipment downtime. The company can now begin to work on steps that will reduce the downtime across the three shifts.

>> **END EXAMPLE**

TRY PROBLEM 17-37 (pg. 766)

Limitations and Other Considerations

The Kruskal–Wallis one-way ANOVA does *not* require the assumption of normality and is, therefore, often used instead of the ANOVA technique discussed in Chapter 12. However, the Kruskal–Wallis test as discussed here applies only if the sample size from each population is at least 5, the samples are independently selected, and each population has the same distribution except for a possible difference in central location.

When ranking observations, you will sometimes encounter ties. When ties occur, each observation is given the average rank for which it is tied. The H statistic is influenced by ties and should be corrected by dividing Equation 17.10 by Equation 17.11.

Correction for Tied Rankings—Kruskal–Wallis Test

$$1 - \frac{\sum_{i=1}^{g}(t_i^3 - t_i)}{N^3 - N}$$

(17.11)

where:

g = Number of different groups of ties
t_i = Number of tied observations in the ith tied group of scores
N = Total number of observations

The correct formula for calculating the Kruskal–Wallis H statistic when ties are present is Equation 17.12.

Correcting for ties increases H. This makes rejecting the null hypothesis more likely than if the correction is not used. A rule of thumb is that if no more than 25% of the observations are involved in ties, the correction factor is not required. The PHStat add-in to Excel for performing the Kruskal–Wallis test does not provide the adjusted H statistic. However, the adjustment is only necessary when the null hypothesis is not rejected and the H statistic is "close" to the rejection region. In that case, making the proper adjustment could lead to rejecting the null hypothesis.

H Statistic Corrected for Tied Rankings

$$H = \frac{\dfrac{12}{N(N+1)}\sum_{i=1}^{k}\dfrac{R_i^2}{n_i} - 3(N+1)}{1 - \dfrac{\sum_{i=1}^{g}(t_i^3 - t_i)}{N^3 - N}}$$

(17.12)

MyStatLab

17-3: **Exercises**

Skill **Development**

17-36. Given the following sample data:

Group 1	Group 2	Group 3
21	17	29
25	15	38
36	34	28
35	22	27
33	16	14
23	19	26
31	30	39
32	20	36

a. State the appropriate null and alternative hypotheses to test whether there is a difference in the medians of the three populations.

b. Based on the sample data and a significance level of 0.05, what conclusion should be reached about the medians of the three populations if you are not willing to make the assumption that the populations are normally distributed?

c. Test the hypothesis stated in part a, assuming that the populations are normally distributed with equal variances.

d. Which of the procedures described in parts b and c would you select to analyze the data? Explain your reasoning.

17-37. Given the following sample data:

Group 1	Group 2	Group 3
10	8	13
9	6	12
11	8	12
12	9	11
13	10	13
12	10	15

a. State the appropriate null and alternative hypotheses for determining whether a difference exists in the median value for the three populations.

b. Based on the sample data, use the Kruskal–Wallis ANOVA procedure to test the null hypothesis using $\alpha = 0.05$. What conclusion should be reached?

17-38. Given the following data:

Group 1	Group 2	Group 3	Group 4
20	28	17	21
27	26	15	23
26	21	18	19
22	29	20	17
25	30	14	20
30	25		
23			

a. State the appropriate null and alternative hypotheses for determining whether a difference exists in the median value for the four populations.

b. Based on the sample data, use the Kruskal–Wallis one-way ANOVA procedure to test the null hypothesis. What conclusion should be reached using a significance level of 0.10? Discuss.

c. Determine the H-value adjusted for ties.

d. Given the results in part b, is it necessary to use the H-value adjusted for ties? If it is, conduct the hypothesis test using this adjusted value of H. If not, explain why not.

17-39. A study was conducted in which samples were selected independently from four populations. The sample size from each population was 20. The data were converted to ranks. The sum of the ranks for the data from each sample is as follows:

	Sample 1	Sample 2	Sample 3	Sample 4
Sum of ranks	640	780	460	1,360

a. State the appropriate null and alternative hypotheses if we wish to determine whether the populations have equal medians.

b. Use the information in this exercise to perform a Kruskal–Wallis one-way ANOVA.

Business **Applications**

17-40. The American Beef Growers Association is trying to promote the consumption of beef products. The organization performs numerous studies, the results of which are often used in advertising campaigns. One such study involved a quality perception test. Three grades of beef were involved: choice, standard, and economy. A random sample of people was provided pieces of choice-grade beefsteak and was asked to rate its quality on a scale of 1 to 100. A second sample of people was given pieces of standard-grade beefsteak, and a third sample was given pieces of economy-grade beefsteak, with instructions to rate the beef on the 100-point scale. The following data were obtained:

Choice	Standard	Economy
78	67	65
87	80	62
90	78	70
87	80	66
89	67	70
90	70	73

a. What measurement level do these data possess? Would it be appropriate to assume that such data

could be obtained from a normal distribution?
Explain your answers.

b. Based on the sample data, what conclusions should be reached concerning the median quality perception scores for the three grades of beef? Test using an $\alpha = 0.01$.

17-41. A study was conducted by the sports department of a national network television station in which the objective was to determine whether a difference exists between median annual salaries of National Basketball Association (NBA) players, National Football League (NFL) players, and Major League Baseball (MLB) players. The analyst in charge of the study believes that the normal distribution assumption is violated in this study. Thus, she thinks that a nonparametric test is in order.

The following summary data have been collected:

NBA	NFL	MLB
$n = 20$	$n = 30$	$n = 40$
$\Sigma R_i = 1,655$	$\Sigma R_i = 1,100$	$\Sigma R_i = 1,340$

a. Why would the sports department address the median as the parameter of interest in this analysis, as opposed to the mean? Explain your answer.

b. What characteristics of the salaries of professional athletes suggest that such data are not normally distributed? Explain.

c. Based on these data, what can be concluded about the median salaries for the three sports? Test at an $\alpha = 0.05$. Assume no ties.

17-42. Referring to Problem 17-41, suppose that there were 40 ties at eight different salary levels. The following shows how many scores were ties at each salary level:

Level	t
1	2
2	3
3	2
4	4
5	8
6	10
7	6
	5

a. Given the results in the previous exercise, is it necessary to use the H-value adjusted for ties?

b. If your answer to part a is yes, conduct the test of hypothesis using this adjusted value of H. If it is not, explain why not.

17-43. Suppose as part of your job you are responsible for installing emergency lighting in a series of state office buildings. Bids have been received from four manufacturers of battery-operated emergency lights. The costs are about equal, so the decision will be based on the length of time the lights last before failing.

A sample of four lights from each manufacturer has been tested, with the following values (time in hours) recorded for each manufacturer:

Type A	Type B	Type C	Type D
1,024	1,270	1,121	923
1,121	1,325	1,201	983
1,250	1,426	1,190	1,087
1,022	1,322	1,122	1,121

Using $\alpha = 0.01$, what conclusion for the four manufacturers should you reach about the median length of time the lights last before failing? Explain.

Computer Database **Exercises**

17-44. As purchasing agent for the Horner-Williams Company, you have primary responsibility for securing high-quality raw materials at the best possible prices. One particular material the Horner-Williams Company uses a great deal of is aluminum. After careful study, you have been able to reduce the prospective vendors to three. It is unclear whether these three vendors produce aluminum that is equally durable.

To compare durability, the recommended procedure is to put pressure on aluminum until it cracks. The vendor whose aluminum requires the highest median pressure will be judged to provide the most durable product. To carry out this test, 14 pieces from each vendor have been selected. These data are in the file **Horner-Williams**. (The data are pounds per square inch pressure.) Using $\alpha = 0.05$, what should the company conclude about whether there is a difference in the median strength of the three vendors' aluminum?

17-45. A large metropolitan police force is considering changing from full-size to mid-size cars. The police force sampled cars from each of three manufacturers. The number sampled represents the number that the manufacturer was able to provide for the test. Each car was driven for 5,000 miles, and the operating cost per mile was computed. The operating costs, in cents per mile, for the 12 cars are provided in the file **Police**. Perform the appropriate ANOVA test on these data. Assume a significance level of 0.05. State the appropriate null and alternative hypotheses. Do the experimental data provide evidence that the median operating costs per mile for the three types of police cars are different?

17-46. A nationwide moving company is considering five different types of nylon tie-down straps. The purchasing department randomly selected straps from each company and determined their breaking strengths in pounds. The sample data are contained in the file **Nylon**. Based on your analysis, with a Type I error rate of 0.05, can you conclude that a difference exists among the median breaking strengths of the types of nylon ropes?

Visual Summary

Chapter 17: Previous chapters introduced a wide variety of commonly used statistical techniques all of which rely on underlying assumptions about the data used. The *t*-distribution assumes the population from which the sample is selected is normally distributed. Analysis of Variance is based on the assumptions that all populations are normally distributed and have equal variances. In addition, each of these techniques requires the data measurement level for the variables of interest to be either interval or ratio level.

In decision-making situations, you will encounter situations in which either the level of data measurement is too low or the distribution assumptions are clearly violated. To handle such cases as these, a class of statistical tools called nonparametric statistics has been developed. While many different nonparametric statistics tests exist, this chapter introduces some of the more commonly used: **The Wilcoxon Signed Rank Test** for one population median, two nonparametric tests for two population medians, **The Mann-Whitney *U* Test** and the **Wilcoxon Matched Pairs Signed Rank Test** and finally the **Kruskal-Wallis One Way Analysis of Variance** test.

 17.1 The Wilcoxon Signed Rank Test for One Population Median (pg. 743–749)

 Summary

In chapter 9 we introduced the *t*-test which is used to test whether a population mean has a specified value. However the *t*-test is not appropriate if the data is ordinal or when populations are not believed to be approximately normally distributed. In these cases, the **Wilcoxon signed rank test** can be used. This test makes no highly restrictive assumption about the shape of the population distribution.

The Wilcoxon test is used to test hypotheses about a population median rather than a population mean. The logic of the Wilcoxon test is because the median is the midpoint in a population, we would expect approximately half the data values in a random sample to lie below the hypothesized median and about half to lie above it. The hypothesized median will be rejected if the actual data distribution shows too large a departure from a 50-50 split.

> **Outcome 1.** Recognize when and how to use the Wilcoxon signed rank test for a population median.

 17.2 Nonparametric Tests for Two Population Medians (pg. 749–761)

 Summary

Chapter 10 discussed testing the difference between two population means using the Student's *t*-distribution. Again, the *t*-distribution assumes the two populations are normally distributed and the data are restricted to being interval or ratio level. Although in many situations these assumptions and the data requirements will be satisfied, you will often encounter situations where they are not.

This section introduces two nonparametric techniques that do not require the distribution and data level assumptions of the *t*-test: the **Mann–Whitney *U*-test** and the **Wilcoxon matched-pairs signed rank test**. Both tests can be used with ordinal (ranked) data, and neither requires that the populations be normally distributed. The Mann–Whitney *U*-test is used when the samples are independent, whereas the Wilcoxon matched-pairs signed rank test is used when the design has paired samples.

> **Outcome 2.** Recognize the situations for which the Mann–Whitney *U*-test for the difference between two population medians applies and be able to use it in a decision-making context.
>
> **Outcome 3.** Know when to apply the Wilcoxon matched-pairs signed rank test for related samples.

  Conclusion

 17.3 Kruskal-Wallis One-Way Analysis of Variance (pg. 761–767)

 Summary

Decision makers are often faced with deciding between three or more alternatives. Chapter 12 introduced one-way analysis of variance and showed how, if the assumptions of normally distributed populations with equal variances are satisfied, the *F*-distribution can be used to test the hypothesis of equal population means. If the assumption of normally distributed populations can not be made, the **Kruskal–Wallis One-Way Analysis of Variance** is the nonparametric counterpart to the one-way ANOVA procedure presented in Chapter 12. However, it has its own set of assumptions:

1. The distributions are continuous.
2. The data are at least ordinal.
3. The samples are independent.
4. The samples come from populations whose only possible difference is that at least one may have a different central location than the others.

> **Outcome 4.** Perform nonparametric analysis of variance using the Kruskal–Wallis one-way ANOVA

Conclusion

Many statistical techniques discussed in this book are based on the assumptions the data being analyzed are interval or ratio and the underlying populations are normal. If these assumptions come close to being satisfied, many of the tools discussed before this chapter apply and are useful. However, in many practical situations these assumptions just do not apply. In such cases nonparametric statistical tests may be appropriate. While this chapter introduced some common nonparametric tests, many other nonparametric statistical techniques have been developed for specific applications. Many are aimed at situations involving small samples. **Figure 17.2** may help you determine which nonparametric test to use in different situations.

FIGURE 17.2

Nonparametric Tests
Introduced in Chapter 17

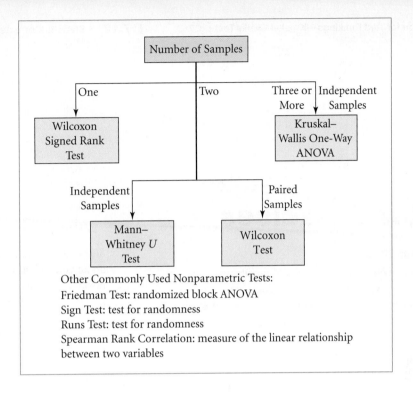

Other Commonly Used Nonparametric Tests:
Friedman Test: randomized block ANOVA
Sign Test: test for randomness
Runs Test: test for randomness
Spearman Rank Correlation: measure of the linear relationship
between two variables

Equations

(17.1) Large-Sample Wilcoxon Signed Rank Test Statistic pg. 745

$$z = \frac{W - \dfrac{n(n+1)}{4}}{\sqrt{\dfrac{n(n+1)(2n+1)}{24}}}$$

(17.2) U Statistics pg. 750

$$U_1 = n_1 n_2 + \frac{n_1(n_1+1)}{2} - \sum R_1$$

(17.3)
$$U_2 = n_1 n_2 + \frac{n_2(n_2+1)}{2} - \sum R_2$$

(17.4) Mean and Standard Deviation for U Statistic pg. 752

$$\mu = \frac{n_1 n_2}{2}$$

(17.5)
$$\sigma = \sqrt{\frac{(n_1)(n_2)(n_1 + n_2 + 1)}{12}}$$

(17.6) Mann–Whitney U-Test Statistic pg. 752

$$z = \frac{U - \dfrac{n_1 n_2}{2}}{\sqrt{\dfrac{(n_1)(n_2)(n_1 + n_2 + 1)}{12}}}$$

(17.7) Wilcoxon Mean and Standard Deviation pg. 756

$$\mu = \frac{n(n+1)}{4}$$

(17.8)
$$\sigma = \sqrt{\frac{n(n+1)(2n+1)}{24}}$$

(17.9) Wilcoxon Test Statistic pg. 757

$$z = \frac{T - \dfrac{n(n+1)}{4}}{\sqrt{\dfrac{n(n+1)(2n+1)}{24}}}$$

(17.10) H Statistic pg. 763

$$H = \frac{12}{N(N+1)} \sum_{i=1}^{k} \frac{R_i^2}{n_i} - 3(N+1)$$

(17.11) Correction for Tied Rankings—Kruskal–Wallis Test pg. 765

$$1 - \frac{\sum_{i=1}^{g}(t_i^3 - t_i)}{N^3 - N}$$

(17.12) *H* Statistic Corrected for Tied Rankings pg. 765

$$H = \frac{\frac{12}{N(N+1)}\sum_{t=1}^{k}\frac{R_i^2}{n_i} - 3(N+1)}{1 - \frac{\sum_{i=1}^{g}(t_i^3 - t_i)}{N^3 - N}}$$

Chapter Exercises   MyStatLab

Conceptual Questions

17-47. Find an organization you think would be interested in data that would violate the measurement scale or known distribution assumptions necessary to use the statistical tools found in Chapters 10–12 (retail stores are a good candidate). Determine to what extent this organization considers these problems and whether it uses any of the techniques discussed in this chapter.

17-48. Discuss the data conditions that would lead you to use the Kruskal–Wallis test as opposed to the ANOVA procedure introduced in Chapter 12. Present an example illustrating these conditions.

17-49. In the library, locate two journal articles that use one of the nonparametric tests discussed in this chapter. Prepare a brief outline of the articles, paying particular attention to the reasons given for using the particular test.

17-50. As an example of how the sampling distribution for the Mann–Whitney Test is derived, consider two samples with sample sizes $n_1 = 2$ and $n_2 = 3$. The distribution is obtained under the assumption that the two variables, say x and y, are identically distributed. Under this assumption, each measurement is equally likely to obtain one of the ranks between 1 and $n_1 + n_2$.
   a. List all the possible sets of two ranks that could be obtained from five ranks. Calculate the Mann–Whitney U-value for each of these sets of two ranks.
   b. The number of ways in which we may choose n_1 ranks from $n_1 + n_2$ is given by $(n_1 + n_2)!/n_1!n_2!$. Calculate this value for $n_1 = 2$ and $n_2 = 3$. Now calculate the probability of any one of the possible Mann–Whitney U-values.
   c. List all the possible Mann–Whitney U-values you obtained in part a. Then using part b, calculate the probability that each of these U-values occurs, thereby producing the sampling distribution for the Mann–Whitney U statistic when $n_1 = 2$ and $n_2 = 3$.

17-51. Let us examine how the sampling distribution of the Wilcoxon test statistic is obtained. Consider the sampling distributions of the positive ranks from a sample size of 4. The ranks to be considered are, therefore, 1, 2, 3, and 4. Under the null hypothesis, the

differences to be ranked are distributed symmetrically about zero. Thus, each difference is just as likely to be positively as negatively ranked.
   a. For a sample size of four, there are $2^4 = 16$ possible sets of signs associated with the four ranks. List the 16 possible sets of ranks that could be positive—that is, (none), (1), (2)...(1, 2, 3, 4). Each of these sets of positive ranks (under the null hypothesis) has the same probability of occurring.
   b. Calculate the sum of the ranks of each set specified in part a.
   c. Using parts a and b, produce the sampling distribution for the Wilcoxon test statistic when $n = 4$.

Business Applications

17-52. Students attending West Valley Community College buy their textbooks online from one of two different book sellers because the college does not have a bookstore. The following data represent sample amounts that students spend on books per term:

Company 1 ($)	Company 2 ($)
246	300
211	305
235	308
270	325
411	340
310	295
450	320
502	330
311	240
200	360

   a. Do these data indicate a difference in mean textbook prices for the two companies? Apply the Mann–Whitney U test with a significance level of 0.10.
   b. Apply the t-test to determine whether the data indicate a difference between the mean amount spent on books at the two companies. Use a significance level of 0.10. Indicate what assumptions must be made to apply the t-test.

17-53. The Hunter Family Corporation owns roadside diners in numerous locations across the country. For the past few months, the company has undertaken a new advertising study. Initially, company executives selected 22 of its retail outlets that were similar with respect to sales volume, profitability, location, climate, economic status of customers, and experience of store management. Each of the outlets was randomly assigned one of two advertising plans promoting a new sandwich product. The accompanying data represent the number of new sandwiches sold during the specific test period at each retail outlet.

Hunter executives want you to determine which of the two advertising plans leads to the largest average sales levels for the new product. They are not willing to make the assumptions necessary for you to use the t-test. They do not wish to have an error rate of more than 0.05.

Advertising Plan 1 ($)	Advertising Plan 2 ($)
1,711	2,100
1,915	2,210
1,905	1,950
2,153	3,004
1,504	2,725
1,195	2,619
2,103	2,483
1,601	2,520
1,580	1,904
1,475	1,875
1,588	1,943

17-54. The Miltmore Corporation performs consulting services for companies that think they have image problems. Recently, the Bluedot Beer Company approached Miltmore. Bluedot executives were concerned that the company's image, relative to its two closest competitors, had diminished. Miltmore conducted an image study in which a random sample of 8 people was asked to rate Bluedot's image. Five people were asked to rate competitor A's image, and 10 people were asked to rate competitor B's image. The image ratings were made on a 100-point scale, with 100 being the best possible rating. Here are the results of the sampling.

Bluedot	Competitor A	Competitor B
40	95	50
60	53	80
70	55	82
40	92	87
55	90	93
90		51
20		63
20		72
		96
		88

a. Based on these sample results, should Bluedot conclude there is an image difference among the three companies? Use a significance level equal to 0.05.

b. Should Bluedot infer that its image has been damaged by last year's federal government recall of its product? Discuss why or why not.

c. Why might the decision maker wish to use parametric ANOVA rather than the corresponding nonparametric test? Discuss.

17-55. The Style-Rite Company of Atlanta makes windbreaker jackets for people who play golf and who are active outdoors during the spring and fall months. The company recently developed a new material and is in the process of test-marketing jackets made from the material. As part of this test-marketing effort, 10 people were each supplied with a jacket made from the original material and were asked to wear it for two months, washing it at least twice during that time. A second group of 10 people was each given a jacket made from the new material and asked to wear it for two months with the same washing requirements.

Following the two-month trial period, the individuals were asked to rate the jackets on a scale of 0 to 100, with 0 being the worst performance rating and 100 being the best. The ratings for each material are shown as follows:

Original Material	New Material
76	55
34	90
70	72
23	17
45	56
80	69
10	91
46	95
67	86
75	74

The company expects that, on the average, the performance ratings will be superior for the new material.

a. Examine the data given. What characteristics of these data sets would lead you to reject the assumption that the data came from populations that had normal distributions and equal variances?

b. Do the sample data support this belief at a significance level of 0.05? Discuss.

17-56. A study was recently conducted by the Bonneville Power Association (BPA) to determine attitudes regarding the association's policies in western U.S. states. One part of the study asked respondents to rate the performance of the BPA on its responsiveness to environmental issues. The following responses were obtained for a sample of 12 urban residents and 10 rural residents. The ratings are on a 1 to 100 scale, with 100 being perfect.

Urban	Rural
76	55
90	80
86	94
60	40
43	85
96	92
50	77
20	68
30	35
82	59
75	
84	

a. Based on the sample data, should the BPA conclude that there is no difference between the urban and rural residents with respect to median environmental rating? Test using a significance level of 0.02.

b. Perform the appropriate parametric statistical test and indicate the assumptions necessary to use this test that were not required by the Mann–Whitney tests. Use a significance level of 0.02. (Refer to Chapter 10 if needed.)

17-57. The manager of credit card operations for a small regional bank has determined that last year's median credit card balance was $1,989.32. A sample of 18 customer balances this year revealed the following figures, in dollars:

Sample 1	Sample 2	Sample 3	Sample 4	Sample 5	Sample 6
1,827.85	1,992.75	2,012.35	1,955.64	2,023.19	1,998.52

Sample 7	Sample 8	Sample 9	Sample 10	Sample 11	Sample 12
2,003.75	1,752.55	1,865.32	2,013.13	2,225.35	2,100.35

Sample 13	Sample 14	Sample 15	Sample 16	Sample 17	Sample 18
2,002.02	1,850.37	1,995.35	2,001.18	2,252.54	2,035.75

Based on the 18 customer balances sampled, is there enough evidence to allow you to conclude the median balance has changed? Test at the 0.05 level of significance.

17-58. During the production of a textbook, there are many steps between when the author begins preparing the manuscript and when the book is finally printed and bound. Tremendous effort is made to minimize the number of errors of any type in the text. One type of error that is especially difficult to eliminate is the typographical error that can creep in when the book is typeset. The Prolythic Type Company does contract work for many publishers. As part of its quality control efforts, it charts the number of corrected errors per page in its manuscripts. In one particularly difficult to typeset

book, the following data were observed for a sample of 15 pages (in sequence):

Page	1	2	3	4	5	6	7	8	9	10	11	12	13	14	15
Errors	2	4	1	0	6	7	4	2	9	4	3	6	2	4	2

Is there sufficient evidence to conclude the median number of errors per page is greater than 6?

17-59. A Vermont company is monitoring a process that fills maple syrup bottles. When the process is filling correctly, the median average fill in an 8-ounce bottle of syrup is 8.03 ounces. The last 15 bottles sampled revealed the following levels of fill:

7.95	8.02	8.07	8.06	8.05	8.04	7.97	8.01
8.04	8.05	8.08	8.11	7.99	8.00	8.02	

a. Formulate the null and alternative hypotheses needed in this situation.

b. Do the sample values support the null or alternative hypothesis?

Computer Database Exercises

17-60. A major car manufacturer is experimenting with three new methods of pollution control. The testing lab must determine whether the three methods produce equal pollution reductions. Readings from a calibrated carbon monoxide meter are taken from groups of engines randomly equipped with one of the three control units. The data are in the file **Pollution**. Determine whether the three pollution-control methods will produce equal results.

17-61. A business statistics instructor at State University has been experimenting with her testing procedure. This term, she has taken the approach of giving two tests over each section of material. The first test is a problem-oriented exam, in which students have to set up and solve applications problems. The exam is worth 50 points. The second test, given a day later, is a multiple-choice test, covering the concepts introduced in the section of the text covered by the exam. This exam is also worth 50 points.

In one class of 15 students, the observed test scores over the first section of material in the course are contained in the file **State University**.

a. If the instructor is unwilling to make the assumptions for the paired-sample *t*-test, what should she conclude based on these data about the distribution of scores for the two tests if she tests at a significance level of 0.05?

b. In the context of this problem, define a Type II error.

17-62. Two brands of tires are being tested for tread wear. To control for vehicle and driver variation, one tire of each brand is put on the front wheels of 10 cars. The cars are driven under normal driving conditions for a total of 15,000 miles. The tread wear is then measured using a very sophisticated instrument. The data that were observed are in the file **Tread Wear**. (Note that the larger the number, the less wear in the tread.)

a. What would be the possible objection in this case for employing the paired-sample *t*-test? Discuss.

b. Assuming that the decision makers in this situation are not willing to make the assumptions required to perform the paired-sample *t*-test, what decision should be reached using the appropriate nonparametric test if a significance level of 0.05 is used? Discuss.

17-63. High Fuel Company markets a gasoline additive for automobiles that it claims will increase a car's miles per gallon (mpg) performance. In an effort to determine whether High Fuel's claim is valid, a consumer testing agency randomly selected eight makes of automobiles. Each car's tank was filled with gasoline and driven around a track until empty. Then the car's tank was refilled with gasoline and the additive, and the car was driven until the gas tank was empty again. The miles per gallon were measured for each car with and without the additive. The results are reported in the file **High Fuel**.

The testing agency is unwilling to accept the assumption that the underlying probability distribution is normally distributed, but it would still like to perform a statistical test to determine the validity of High Fuel's claim.

a. What statistical test would you recommend the testing agency use in this case? Why?

b. Conduct the test that you believe to be appropriate. Use a significance level of 0.025.

c. State your conclusions based on the test you have just conducted. Is High Fuel's claim supported by the test's findings?

17-64. A company assembles remote controls for television sets. The company's design engineers have developed a revised design that they think will make it faster to assemble the controls. To test whether the new design leads to faster assembly, 14 assembly workers were randomly selected and each worker was asked to assemble a control using the current design and then asked to assemble a control using the revised design. The times in seconds to assemble the controls are shown in the file **Remote Control**. The company's engineers are unable to assume that the assembly times are normally distributed, but they would like to test whether assembly times are lower using the revised design.

a. What statistical test do you recommend the company use? Why?

b. State the null and alternative hypotheses of interest to the company.

c. At the 0.025 level of significance, is there any evidence to support the engineers' belief that the revised design reduces assembly time?

d. How might the results of the statistical test be used by the company's management?

Case 17.1

Bentford Electronics—Part 2

On Saturday morning, Jennifer Bentford received a call at her home from the production supervisor at Bentford Electronics Plant 1. The supervisor indicated that she and the supervisors from Plants 2, 3, and 4 had agreed that something must be done to improve company morale and, thereby, increase the production output of their plants. Jennifer Bentford, president of Bentford Electronics, agreed to set up a Monday morning meeting with the supervisors to see if they could arrive at a plan for accomplishing these objectives.

By Monday each supervisor had compiled a list of several ideas, including a 4-day work week and interplant competition of various kinds.

After listening to the discussion for some time, Jennifer Bentford asked if anyone knew if there was a difference in average daily output for the four plants. When she heard no positive response, she told the supervisors to select a random sample of daily production reports from each plant and test whether there was a difference. They were to meet again on Wednesday afternoon with test results.

By Wednesday morning, the supervisors had collected the following data on units produced:

Plant 1	Plant 2	Plant 3	Plant 4
4,306	1,853	2,700	1,704
2,852	1,948	2,705	2,320
1,900	2,702	2,721	4,150
4,711	4,110	2,900	3,300
2,933	3,950	2,650	3,200
3,627	2,300	2,480	2,975

The supervisors had little trouble collecting the data, but they were at a loss about how to determine whether there was a difference in the output of the four plants. Jerry Gibson, the company's research analyst, told the supervisors that there were statistical procedures that could be used to test hypotheses regarding multiple samples if the daily output was distributed in a bell shape (normal distribution) at each plant. The supervisors expressed dismay because no one thought his or her output was normally distributed. Jerry Gibson indicated that there were techniques that did not require the normality assumption, but he did not know what they were.

The meeting with Jennifer Bentford was scheduled to begin in 3 hours, so he needed some statistical-analysis help immediately.

chapter 18

Chapter 18 Quick Prep Links

Modern quality control is based on many of the statistical concepts you have covered up to now, so to adequately understand the material, you need to review many previous topics.

- **Review** how to construct and interpret line charts, covered in Chapter 2.
- **Make sure** you are familiar with the steps involved in determining the mean and standard deviation of the binomial and Poisson distributions, covered in Chapter 5.

- **Review** how to determine the mean and standard deviation of samples and the meaning of the Central Limit Theorem from Chapter 7.
- **Finally,** become familiar again with how to determine a confidence interval estimate and test a hypothesis of a single population parameter as covered in Chapters 8 and 9.

Introduction to Quality and Statistical Process Control

18.1 Introduction to Statistical Process Control Charts
(pg. 774–795)

Outcome 1. Construct and interpret $\bar{x}$-charts and R-charts.

Outcome 2. Construct and interpret p-charts.

Outcome 3. Construct and interpret c-charts.

Why you need to know

Keeping existing customers and gaining new customers are important criteria for any business to succeed. One key to making this happen is to deliver high-quality products and services. Do you think the Apple iPad would have been such a great success if it suffered from quality issues? What if Coca-Cola products had unreliable quality? Think about your favorite restaurant. What is it about that place that makes it your favorite? Chances are it is the quality of the food or the service.

Successful organizations know that having high quality requires hard work and a continual focus on improving the processes that produce the products and services. Over the past several decades, a number of techniques and methods for process improvement have been developed and used by organizations. As a group, these are referred to as the *Tools of Quality*. Many of these tools are based on statistical procedures and data analysis.

One set of quality tools known as *statistical process control charts* is so prevalent in business today and is so closely linked to the material in Chapters 5 through 9 that its coverage merits a separate chapter. This chapter is designed to introduce you to the fundamental tools and techniques of quality management and to show you how to construct and interpret statistical process control charts.

18.1 Introduction to Statistical Process Control Charts

In this section, we provide an overview of statistical process control (SPC) charts. As you will see, SPC is actually an application of hypothesis testing.

Zoom Team/Shutterstock

The Existence of Variation

After studying the material in Chapters 1 through 17, you should be well aware of the importance of variation in business decision making. Variation exists naturally in the world around us. In any process or activity, the day-to-day outcomes are rarely the same. As a practical example, think about the time it takes you to travel to the university each morning. You know it's about a 15-minute trip, and even though you travel the same route, your actual time will vary somewhat from day to day. You will notice this variation in many other daily occurrences. The next time you are in a drive-thru restaurant, notice that some cars get through faster than others. The same is true at a bank, where the time customers spend competing their transactions varies considerably.

Even in instances when variation is hard to detect, it is present. For example, when you measure a stack of 4-foot-by-8-foot sheets of plywood using a tape measure, they will all appear to be 4 feet wide. However, when the stack is measured using an engineer's scale, you may be able to detect slight variations among sheets, and using a caliper, you can detect even more (see Figure 18.1).

Therefore, three concepts to remember about variation are

1. Variation is natural; it is inherent in the world around us.
2. No two products or service experiences are exactly the same.
3. With a fine-enough gauge, all things can be seen to differ.

Sources of Variation What causes variation? Variation in the output of a process comes from variation in the inputs to the process. Let's go back to your travel time to school. Why isn't it always the same? Your travel time depends on many factors, such as what route you take, how much traffic you encounter, whether you are in a hurry, how your car is running, and so on.

The six most common sources of variation are

1. People
2. Machines
3. Materials
4. Methods
5. Measurement
6. Environment

FIGURE 18.1

Plywood Variation

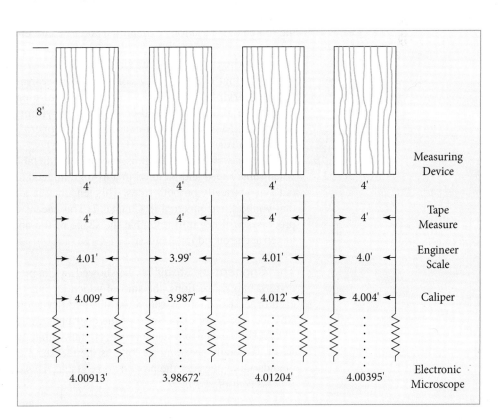

Types of Variation Although variation is always present, we can define two major types that occur. The first is called *common cause variation*, which means it is naturally occurring or expected in the system. Other terms people use for common cause variation include *normal*, *random*, *chance occurrence*, *inherent*, and *stable variation*.

The other type of variation is called *special cause variation*. This type of variation is abnormal, indicating that something out of the ordinary has happened. This type of variation is also called *nonrandom*, *unstable*, and *assignable cause variation*.

In our example of travel time to school, there are common causes of variation such as traffic lights, traffic patterns, weather, and departure time. On the days when it takes you significantly more or less time to arrive at work, there are also special causes of variation occurring. These may be factors such as accidents, road construction detours, or needing to stop for gas. Examples of the two types of variation and some sources are as follows:

Sources of Common Cause Variation	Sources of Special Cause Variation
Weather conditions	Equipment not maintained and cleaned
Inconsistent work methods	Poor training
Machine wear	Worker fatigue
Temperature	Procedures not followed
Employee skill levels	Misuse of tools
Computer response times	Incorrect data entry

In any process or system, the total process variation is a combination of common cause and special cause factors. This can be expressed by Equation 18.1.

Variation Components

$$\text{Total process variation} = \text{Common cause variation} + \text{Special cause variation} \qquad \textbf{(18.1)}$$

In process improvement efforts, the goal is first to remove the special cause variation and then to reduce the common cause variation in a system. Removing special cause variation requires the source of a variation be identified and its cause eliminated.

The Predictability of Variation: Understanding the Normal Distribution

A system that contains only common cause variations is very predictable. Though the outputs vary, they exhibit an important feature called *stability*. This means that some percentage of the output will continue to lie within given limits hour after hour, day after day, so long as the common-cause system is operating. When a process exhibits stability, it is in control.

The reason that the outputs vary in a predictable manner is because measurable data, when subgrouped and pictured in a histogram, tend to cluster around the average and spread out symmetrically on both sides. This tendency is a function of the Central Limit Theorem that you first encountered in Chapter 7. This means that the frequency distribution of many processes will begin to resemble the shape of the normal distribution as the values are collected and grouped into classes.

The Concept of Stability We showed in Chapter 6 that the normal distribution can be divided into six sections, the sum of which includes 99.7% of the data values. The width of each of these sections is called the standard deviation. The standard deviation is the primary way the spread (or dispersion) of the distribution is measured. Thus, we expect virtually all (99.7%) of the data in a stable process to fall within plus or minus 3 standard deviations of the mean. Generally speaking, as long as the measurements fall within the 3-standard-deviation boundary, we consider the process to be stable. This concept provides the basis for *statistical process control charts*.

Introducing Statistical Process Control Charts

Cars are equipped with a temperature gauge that measures engine temperature. We come to rely on the gauge to let us know if "everything is all right." As long as the gauge points to the *normal* range, we conclude that there is no problem. However, if the gauge moves outside the *normal* range toward the *hot* mark, it's a signal that the engine is overheating and something is wrong. If the gauge moves out of the *normal* range toward the *cold* mark, it's also a signal of potential problems.

Under typical driving conditions, engine temperature will fluctuate. The normal range on the car's gauge defines the expected temperature variation when the car is operating properly. Over time driving our own car, we come to know what to expect. If something changes, the gauge is designed to give us a signal. The engine temperature gauge is analogous to a process control chart. Like the engine gauge, process control charts are used in business to define the boundaries that represent the amount of variation that can be considered normal.

Figure 18.2 illustrates the general format of a process control chart. The upper and lower *control limits* define the normal operating region for the process. The horizontal axis reflects the passage of time, or order of production. The vertical axis corresponds to the variable of interest.

There are a number of different types of process control charts. In this section, we introduce four of the most commonly used process control charts:

1. $\bar{x}$-chart
2. R-chart (range chart)
3. p-chart
4. c-chart

Each of these charts is designed for a special purpose. However, as you will see, the underlying logic is the same for each. The $\bar{x}$-chart and R-chart are always used in tandem. The $\bar{x}$-charts are used to monitor a process average. R-charts are used to monitor the variation of individual process values. They require the variable of interest to be quantitative. The following Business Application shows how these two charts are developed and used.

FIGURE 18.2

Process Control Chart Format

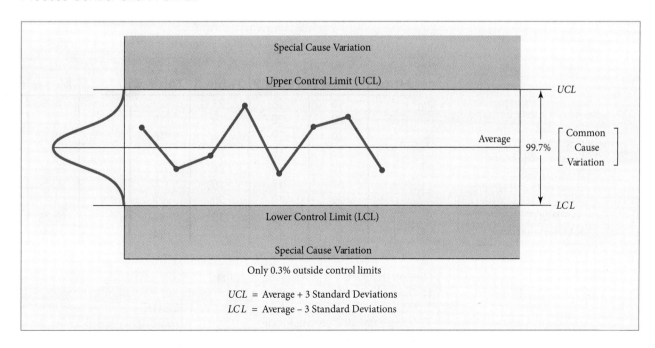

Chapter Outcome 1. → **x̄ Chart and R-Chart**

Excel Tutorial

Dallas Events Inc./Shutterstock

BUSINESS APPLICATION   **MONITORING A PROCESS USING x̄ AND R CHARTS**

CATTLEMEN'S BAR AND GRILL The Cattlemen's Bar and Grill in Kansas City, Missouri, has developed a name for its excellent food and service. To maintain this reputation, the owners have established key measures of product and service quality, and they monitor these regularly. One measure is the amount of time customers wait from the time they are seated until they are served.

Every day, each hour that the business is open, four tables are randomly selected. The elapsed time from when customers are seated at these tables until their orders arrive is recorded. The owners wish to use these data to construct an x̄-chart and an R-chart. These control charts can be developed using the following steps:

Step 1   Collect the initial sample data from which the control charts will be developed.
Four measurements during each hour for 30 hours are contained in the file **Cattlemen**. The four values recorded each hour make up a *subgroup*. The x̄-chart and R-charts are typically generated from small subgroups (three to six observations), and the general recommendation is that data from a minimum of 20 subgroups be gathered before a chart is constructed. Once the subgroup size is determined, all subgroups must be the same size. In this case, the subgroup size is four tables.

Step 2   Calculate subgroup means and ranges.
Figure 18.3 shows the Excel worksheet with a partial listing of the data after the means and ranges have been computed for each subgroup.

Step 3   Compute the average of the subgroup means and the average range value.
The average of the subgroup means and the average range value are computed using Equations 18.2 and 18.3.

FIGURE 18.3

Excel 2010 Worksheet of Cattlemen's Service-Time Data, Including Subgroup Means and Ranges

Excel 2010 Instructions:
1. Open file: **Cattlemen.xlsx**.
2. Subgroup Mean and Range values in columns G and H were computed using Excel's **AVERAGE** and **RANGE** functions.

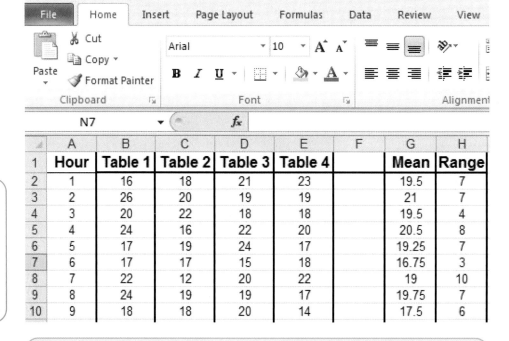

	A	B	C	D	E	F	G	H
1	Hour	Table 1	Table 2	Table 3	Table 4		Mean	Range
2	1	16	18	21	23		19.5	7
3	2	26	20	19	19		21	7
4	3	20	22	18	18		19.5	4
5	4	24	16	22	20		20.5	8
6	5	17	19	24	17		19.25	7
7	6	17	17	15	18		16.75	3
8	7	22	12	20	22		19	10
9	8	24	19	19	17		19.75	7
10	9	18	18	20	14		17.5	6

Minitab Instructions (for similar results):
1. Open file: **Cattlemen.MTW**.
2. Choose **Calc > Row Statistics**.
3. Under **Statistics**, choose **Mean**.
4. In **Input variables**, enter data columns.
5. In **Store result in**, enter storage column.
6. Click **OK**.
7. Repeat 3 through 6 choosing **Range** under **Statistics**.

Average Subgroup Mean

$$\bar{\bar{x}} = \frac{\sum_{i=1}^{k} \bar{x}_i}{k}$$

(18.2)

where:

$\bar{x}_i = i$th subgroup average
$k =$ Number of subgroups

Average Subgroup Range

$$\bar{R} = \frac{\sum_{i=1}^{k} R_i}{k}$$

(18.3)

where:

$R_i = i$th subgroup range
$k =$ Number of subgroups

Using Equations 18.2 and 18.3, we get:

$$\bar{\bar{x}} = \frac{\sum \bar{x}}{k} = \frac{19.5 + 21 + \cdots + 20.75}{30} = 19.24$$

$$\bar{R} = \frac{\sum R}{k} = \frac{7 + 7 + \cdots + 3}{30} = 5.73$$

Step 4 Prepare graphs of the subgroup means and ranges as a line chart.
On one graph, plot the $\bar{x}$-values in time order across the graph and draw a line across the graph at the value corresponding to $\bar{\bar{x}}$. This is shown in Figure 18.4. Likewise, graph the R-values and $\bar{R}$ as a line chart, as shown in Figure 18.5.

FIGURE 18.4

Line Chart for $\bar{x}$-Values for Cattlemen's Data

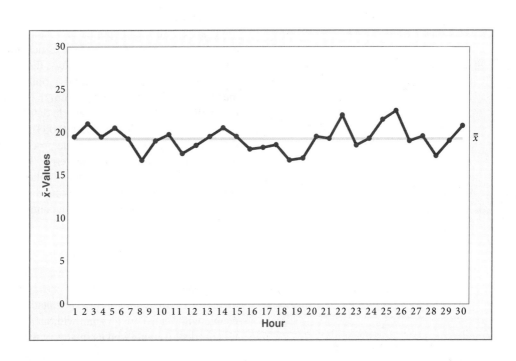

FIGURE 18.5

Line Chart for *R*-Values for Cattlemen's Data

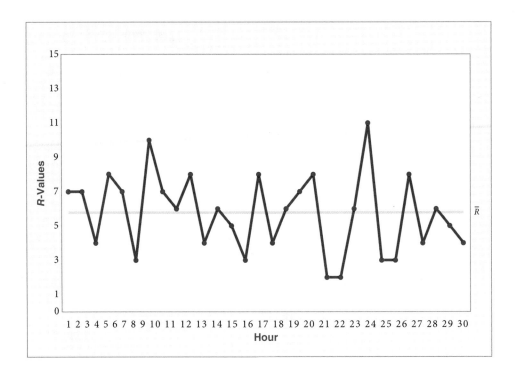

The $\bar{\bar{x}}$ and $\bar{R}$ values in Figures 18.4 and 18.5 are called the "process control centerlines." The *centerline* is a graph of the mean value of the sample data. We use $\bar{\bar{x}}$ as the notation for centerline, which represents the current process average. For these sample data, the average time people in the subgroups wait between being seated and being served is 19.24 minutes. However, as seen in Figure 18.4, there is variation around the centerline. The next step is to establish the boundaries that define the limits for what is considered *normal* variation in the process.

Step 5 **Compute the upper and lower control limits for the $\bar{x}$-chart.**
For a normal distribution with mean μ and standard deviation σ, approximately 99.7% of the values will fall within $\mu \pm 3\sigma$. Most process control charts are developed as 3-sigma control charts, meaning that the range of inherent variation is ± 3 standard deviations from the mean.

Because the $\bar{x}$-chart is a graph of subgroup (sample) means, the control limits are established at points ± 3 standard errors from the centerline, $\bar{\bar{x}}$. The control limits are analogous to the critical values we establish in hypothesis-testing problems. Using this analogy, the null hypothesis is that the process is in control. We will reject this null hypothesis whenever we obtain a subgroup mean beyond 3 standard errors from the centerline in either direction. Because the control chart is based on sample data, our conclusions are subject to error. Approximately 3 times in 1,000 (0.003), a subgroup mean should be outside the control limits when, in fact, the process is still in control. If this happens, we will have committed a Type I error. The 0.003 value is the significance level for the test. This small alpha level implies that 3-sigma control charts are very conservative when it comes to saying that a process is out of control. We might also conclude that the process is in control when in fact it isn't. If this happens, we have committed a Type II error.

To construct the control limits, we must determine the standard error of the sample means, $\sigma / \sqrt{n}$. Based on what you have learned in previous chapters, you might suspect that we would use $s / \sqrt{n}$. However, in most applications this is not done. In the 1930s, when process control charts were first introduced, there was no such thing as pocket calculators. To make control charts usable by people without calculators and without statistical training, a simpler approach was needed. An unbiased estimator of the standard error of the sample means, $\sigma / \sqrt{n}$, that was relatively easy to calculate was developed by Walter Shewhart.[1] The unbiased estimator is

$$\frac{A_2}{3} \bar{R}$$

where:

$\bar{R}$ = The mean of the subgroups' ranges

A_2 = A Shewhart factor that makes $(A_2/3)\bar{R}$ an unbiased estimator of the standard error of the sample means, $\sigma / \sqrt{n}$

Thus, 3 standard errors of the sample means can be estimated by

$$3\left(\frac{A_2}{3} \bar{R}\right) = A_2 \bar{R}$$

Appendix P displays the Shewhart factors for various subgroup sizes. Equations 18.4 and 18.5 are used to compute the upper and lower control limits for the $\bar{x}$-chart.[2]

Upper Control Limit, $\bar{x}$-Chart

$$UCL = \bar{\bar{x}} + A_2(\bar{R}) \qquad\qquad \textbf{(18.4)}$$

Lower Control Limit, $\bar{x}$-Chart

$$LCL = \bar{\bar{x}} - A_2(\bar{R}) \qquad\qquad \textbf{(18.5)}$$

where:

A_2 = Shewhart factor for subgroup size = n

For the Cattlemen's Bar and Grill example, the subgroup size is 4. Thus, the A_2 factor from the Shewhart table (Appendix P) is 0.729. We can compute the upper and lower control limits as follows:

$$UCL = \bar{\bar{x}} + A_2(\bar{R})$$
$$UCL = 19.24 + 0.729(5.73)$$
$$UCL = 23.42$$

$$LCL = \bar{\bar{x}} - A_2(\bar{R})$$
$$LCL = 19.24 - 0.729(5.73)$$
$$LCL = 15.06$$

Step 6 Compute the upper and lower control limits for the *R*-chart.

The D_3 and D_4 factors in the Shewhart table presented in Appendix P are used to compute the 3-sigma control limits for the R-chart. The control limits are established at points ± 3 standard errors from the centerline, $\bar{R}$. However, unlike the case for the $\bar{x}$-chart, the unbiased estimator of the standard error of the sample ranges is a constant multiplied by $\bar{R}$. The constant for the lower control limit is the D_3 value from the Shewhart table. The D_4 value from the Shewhart table is the constant for the upper control limit.

---

[1]The leader of a group at the Bell Telephone Laboratories that did much of the original work in SPC, Shewhart is credited with developing the idea of control charts.

[2]When $A_2/3$ is multiplied by $\bar{R}$, this product becomes an unbiased estimator of the standard error, which is the reason for A_2's use here.

Equations 18.6 and 18.7 are used to find the *UCL* and *LCL* values. Because the subgroup size is 4 in our example, $D_3 = 0.0$ and $D_4 = 2.282$.[3]

Upper Control Limit, *R*-chart

$$UCL = D_4(\overline{R})\tag{18.6}$$

Lower Control Limit, *R*-chart

$$LCL = D_3(\overline{R})\tag{18.7}$$

where:

D_3 and D_4 are taken from Appendix P, the Shewhart table, for subgroup size $= n$

Using Equations 18.6 and 18.7, we get:

$$UCL = D_4(\overline{R})$$
$$UCL = 2.282(5.73)$$
$$UCL = 13.08$$

$$LCL = D_3(\overline{R})$$
$$LCL = 0.0(5.73)$$
$$LCL = 0.0$$

Step 7　Finish constructing the control chart by locating the control limits on the $\overline{x}$- and *R*-charts.

Graph the *UCL* and *LCL* values on the $\overline{x}$-chart and *R*-chart, as shown in Figure 18.6 and Figure 18.7, which were constructed using the PHStat add-in to Excel.[4]

Both students and people in industry sometimes confuse control limits and specification limits. Specification limits are arbitrary and are defined by a customer, by an industry standard, or by engineers who designed the item. The specification limits are defined as values above and below the "target" value for the item. The specification limits pertain to individual items—an item either meets specifications or it does not. Process control limits are computed from actual data from the process. These limits define the range of inherent variation that is actually occurring in the process. The control limits are values above and below the current process average (which may be higher or lower than the "target").

Therefore, a process may be operating in a state of control, but it may be producing individual items that do not meet the specifications. Companies interested in improving quality must first bring the process under control before attempting to make changes in the process to reduce the defect level.

Using the Control Charts Once control charts for Cattlemen's service time have been developed, they can be used to determine whether the time it takes to serve customers remains *in control*. The concept involved is essentially a hypothesis test in which the null and alternative hypotheses can be stated as

H_0: The process is in control; the variation around the centerline is a result of common causes inherent in the process.

H_A: The process is out of control; the variation around the centerline is due to some special cause and is beyond what is normal for the process.

In the Cattlemen's Bar and Grill example, the hypothesis is tested every hour, when four tables are selected and the service time is recorded for each table. The $\overline{x}$- and *R*-values for the new subgroup are computed and plotted on their respective control charts.

---

[3]Because a range cannot be negative, the constant is adjusted to indicate that the lower boundary for the range must equal 0.

[4]See the Excel Tutorial for the specific steps required to obtain the $\overline{x}$- and *R*-charts.

FIGURE 18.6

Excel 2010 (PHStat)
Cattlemen's $\bar{x}$-Chart Output

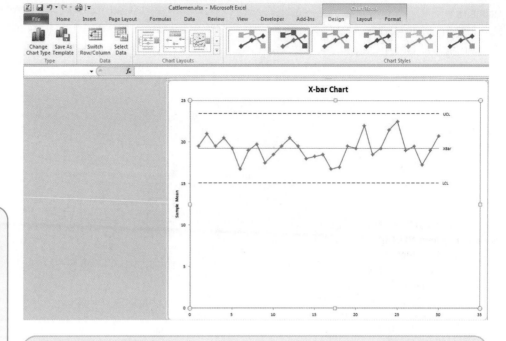

Excel 2010 Instructions:
1. Open File:
   Cattlemen.xlsx.
2. Select **Add-Ins**.
3. Select **PHStat**.
4. Select **Control Charts >
   R and X-Bar Charts**.
5. Specify
   SubgroupSize (4).
6. Define cell range for
   the subgroup ranges
   (H1:H31).
7. Check **R** and **X-Bar
   Chart** options.
8. Define cell range for
   subgroup means
   (G1:G31).
9. Click **OK**.

Minitab Instructions (for similar results):
1. Open file: **Cattlemen.MTW**.
2. Choose **Stat > Control Charts > Variables
   Charts for Subgroups > X-bar**.
3. Select *Observations for a subgroup are in
   one row of columns*.
4. Enter data columns in box.
5. Because file contains additional data select
   Data Options, **Specify which rows to**
   exclude. Select **Row Numbers** and
   enter **31, 32, 33, 34, 35, 36**. Click **OK**.
6. Click on **Xbar Options** and select
   Tests tab.
7. Select *Perform the following tests for
   special courses* and select the first
   four tests.
8. Click **OK**. **OK**.

There are three main process changes that can be detected with a process control chart:

1. The process average has shifted up or down from normal.
2. The process average is trending up or down from normal.
3. The process is behaving in such a manner that the existing variation is not random in nature.

If any of these has happened, the null hypothesis is considered false and the process is considered to be *out of control*.

The control charts are used to provide signals that something has changed. There are four primary signals that indicate a change and that, if observed, will cause us to reject the null hypothesis.[5] These are

Signals

1. One or more points outside the upper or lower control limits
2. Nine or more points in a row above (or below) the centerline
3. Six or more consecutive points moving in the same direction (increasing or decreasing)
4. Fourteen points in a row, alternating up and down

These signals were derived such that the probability of a Type I error is less than 0.01. Thus, there is a very small chance that we will conclude the process has changed when, in fact, it has not. If we examine the control charts in Figures 18.6 and 18.7, we find that none of these signals occur. Thus, the process is deemed in control during the period in which the initial sample data were collected.

---

[5]There is some minor disagreement on the signals, depending on which process control source you refer to.

FIGURE 18.7

Excel 2010 (PHStat)
Cattlemen's *R*-Chart Output

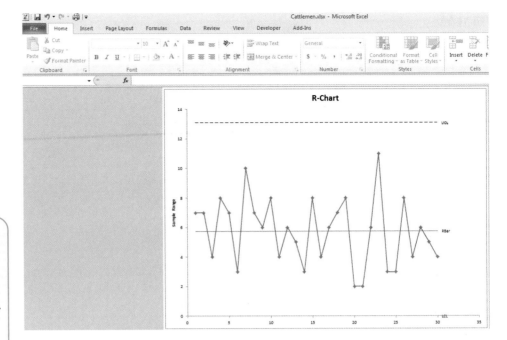

Excel 2010 Instructions:
1. Open **PHStat**.
2. Open file: **Cattlemen.xlsx**.
3. Select **Add-Ins**.
4. Select **Control Charts > R and X-Bar Charts**.
5. Specify **Subgroup Size** (4).
6. Define cell range for the subgroup ranges (H1:H31).
7. Check **R** and **X-Bar Chart** options.
8. Define cell range for subgroup means (G1:G31).
9. Click **OK**.

Minitab Instructions (for similar results):
1. Open file: **Cattlemen. MTW**.
2. Choose **Stat > Control Charts > Variables Charts for Subgroups > R-bar**.
3. Select *Observations for a subgroup are in one row of columns*.
4. Enter data columns in box.
5. Because file contains additional
data select **Data Options, Specify which rows to exclude**. Select **Row Numbers** and enter **31, 32, 33, 34, 35, 36**. Click **OK**.
6. Click on **R-bar Options** and select **Tests** tab.
7. Select *Perform the following tests for special courses* and select the first four tests.
8. Click **OK. OK.**

Suppose that the Cattlemen's owners monitor the process for the next 5 hours. Table 18.1 shows these new values, along with the mean and range for each hour. The means are plotted on the $\bar{x}$-chart, and the *R*-values are plotted on the *R*-chart, as shown in Figures 18.8 and 18.9.

When $\bar{x}$- and *R*-charts are used, we first look at the *R*-chart. Figure 18.9 shows the range (*R*) has been below the centerline ($\bar{R} = 5.733$) for seven consecutive hours. Although this doesn't quite come up to the nine points of signal 2, the owners should begin to suspect something unusual might be happening to cause a downward shift in the variation in service time between tables. Although the *R*-chart does not indicate the reason for the shift, the owners should be pleased, because this might indicate greater consistency in service times. This change may represent a quality improvement. If this trend continues, the owners will want to study the situation so they will be able to retain these improvements in service-time variability.

The $\bar{x}$-chart in Figure 18.8 indicates that the average service time is out of control because in hour 35, the mean service time exceeded the upper control limit of 23.42 minutes. The mean wait time for the four tables during this hour was 25.5 minutes. The chance of this

TABLE 18.1 | **Data for Hours 31 to 35 for Cattlemen's Bar and Grill**

Hour	Table 1	Table 2	Table 3	Table 4	Mean	Range
31	20	21	24	22	21.75	4
32	17	22	18	20	19.25	5
33	23	20	22	22	21.75	3
34	24	23	19	20	21.50	5
35	24	25	26	27	25.50	3

FIGURE 18.8

Cattlemen's $\bar{x}$-Chart

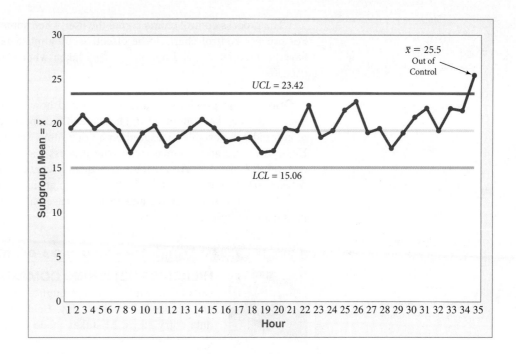

happening is extremely low unless something has changed in the process. This should be a signal to the owners that a special cause exists. They should immediately investigate possible problems to determine if there has been a system change (e.g., training issue) or if this is truly a one-time event (e.g., fire in the kitchen). An important point is that analysis of each of the control charts should not be done in isolation. A moment's consideration will lead you to see that if the variation of the process has gotten out of control (above the upper control limit), then trying to interpret the $\bar{x}$-chart can be very misleading. Widely fluctuating variation could make it much more probable that an $\bar{x}$-value would exceed the control limits even though the process mean had not changed.

Adding (or subtracting) a given number from all of the numbers in a data set does not change the variance of that data set, so a shift in the mean of a process can occur without that shift affecting the variation of the process. However, a change in the variation almost always affects the $\bar{x}$ control chart. For this reason, the general advice is to control the variation of a process before the mean of the process is subjected to control chart analysis.

FIGURE 18.9

Cattlemen's R-Chart

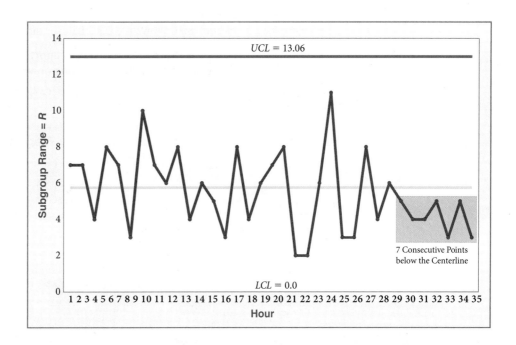

The process control charts signal the user when something in the process has changed. For process control charts to be effective, they must be updated immediately after data have been collected, and action must be taken when the charts signal that a change has occurred.

Chapter Outcome 2. ⟶ **p-Charts** The previous example illustrated how $\bar{x}$-charts and R-charts can be developed and used. They are used in tandem and are applicable when the characteristic being monitored is a variable measured on a continuous scale (e.g., time, weight, length, etc.). However, there are instances when the process issue involves an *attribute* rather than a quantitative variable. An attribute is a quality characteristic that is either present or not present. In many quality control situations, an attribute is whether an item is good (meets specifications) or defective, and in those cases a *p-chart* can be used to monitor the proportion of defects.

BUSINESS APPLICATION CONSTRUCTING *p*-CHARTS

HILDER'S PUBLISHING COMPANY Hilder's Publishing Company sells books and records through a catalog, processing hundreds of mail and phone orders each day. Each customer order requires numerous data-entry steps. Mistakes made in data entry can be costly, resulting in shipping delays, incorrect prices, or the wrong items being shipped. As part of its ongoing efforts to improve quality, Hilder's managers and employees want to reduce errors.

The manager of the order-entry department has developed a process control chart to monitor order-entry errors. For each of the past 30 days, she has selected a random sample of 100 orders. These orders were examined, with the attribute being

- Order entry is correct.
- Order entry is incorrect.

In developing a *p*-chart, the sample size should be large enough such that $np \geq 5$ and $n(1 - p) \geq 5$. Unlike the $\bar{x}$- and R-chart cases, the sample size may differ from sample to sample. However, this complicates the development of the *p*-chart.

The *p*-chart can be developed using the following steps:

Step 1 Collect the sample data.
The sample size is 100 orders. This size sample was selected for each of 30 days. The subgroup proportion of incorrect orders, called *nonconformances*, is displayed in the file **Hilders**. The proportions are given the notation *p*.

Step 2 Plot the subgroup proportions as a line chart.
Figure 18.10 shows the line chart for the 30 days.

Step 3 Compute the mean subgroup proportion for all samples using Equation 18.8 or 18.9, depending on whether the sample sizes are equal.

Mean Subgroup Proportion

For equal-size samples

$$\bar{p} = \frac{\sum_{i=1}^{k} p_i}{k}$$

(18.8)

where:

p_i = Sample proportion for subgroup i
k = Number of samples of size n

FIGURE 18.10

Excel 2010 (PHStat) *p*-Chart for Hilder's Publishing

Excel 2010 Instructions:
1. Open file: **Hilders.xlsx**.
2. Select **Add-Ins**.
3. Select **PHStat**.
4. Select **Control Charts > p Chart**.
5. Define cell range for the number of nonconformances (C1:C31).
6. Check **Sample/Subgroup Size** does not vary.
7. Enter sample/subgroup size (100).
8. Click **OK**.

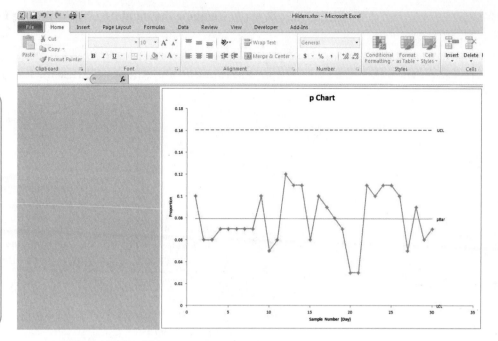

Minitab Instructions (for similar results):
1. Open file: **Hilders.MTW**.
2. Choose **Stat > Control Charts > Attribute Charts > P**.
3. In **Variable**, enter *number of orders with errors* column.
4. In **Subgroup Sizes** enter size of subgroup: 100.
5. Click on **P Chart Options** and select **Tests** tab.
6. Select *Perform all tests for special causes*.
7. Click **OK. OK**.

Mean Subgroup Proportion

For unequal sample sizes:

$$\bar{p} = \frac{\sum\limits_{i=1}^{k} n_i p_i}{\sum\limits_{i=1}^{k} n_i} \tag{18.9}$$

where:

n_i = The number of items in sample i

p_i = Sample proportion for subgroup i

$\sum\limits_{i=1}^{k} n_i$ = Total number of items sampled in k samples

k = Number of samples of size n

Because we have equal sample sizes, we use Equation 18.8, as follows:

$$\bar{p} = \frac{\sum p_i}{k} = \frac{0.10 + 0.06 + 0.06 + 0.07 + \cdots}{30} = \frac{2.38}{30} = 0.0793$$

Thus, the average proportion of orders with errors is 0.0793.

Step 4 Compute the standard error of p using Equation 18.10.

Estimate for the Standard Error for the Subgroup Proportions

For equal sample sizes:

$$s_{\bar{p}} = \sqrt{\frac{(\bar{p})(1-\bar{p})}{n}} \qquad (18.10)$$

where:

$$\bar{p} = \text{Mean subgroup proportion}$$
$$n = \text{Common sample size}$$

For unequal sample sizes:

Option 1   *Compute $s_{\bar{p}}$ using largest sample size and $s_{\bar{p}}$ using the smallest sample size. Construct control limits using each value.*

Option 2 $s_{\bar{p}} = \sqrt{\dfrac{\bar{p}(1-\bar{p})}{n_i}}$ *Compute a unique value of $s_{\bar{p}}$ for each different sample size, n_i. Construct control limits for each $s_{\bar{p}}$ value producing "wavy" control limits.*

We compute $s_{\bar{p}}$ using Equation 18.10, as follows:

$$s_{\bar{p}} = \sqrt{\frac{(\bar{p})(1-\bar{p})}{n}} = \sqrt{\frac{(0.0793)(1-0.0793)}{100}} = 0.027$$

Step 5 Compute the 3-sigma control limits using Equations 18.11 and 18.12.

Control Limits for p-Chart

$$UCL = \bar{p} + 3s_{\bar{p}} \qquad (18.11)$$

$$LCL = \bar{p} - 3s_{\bar{p}} \qquad (18.12)$$

where:

$$\bar{p} = \text{Mean subgroup proportion}$$

$$s_{\bar{p}} = \text{Estimated standard error of } \bar{p} = \sqrt{\frac{(\bar{p})(1-\bar{p})}{n}}$$

Using Equations 18.11 and 18.12, we get the following control limits:

$$UCL = \bar{p} + 3s_{\bar{p}} = 0.079 + 3(0.027) = 0.160$$
$$LCL = \bar{p} - 3s_{\bar{p}} = 0.079 - 3(0.027) = -0.002 \rightarrow 0.0$$

Because a proportion of nonconforming items cannot be negative, the lower control limit is set to 0.0.

Step 6 Plot the centerline and control limits on the control chart.
Both upper and lower control limits are plotted on the control charts in Figure 18.10.

Using the *p*-Chart Once the control chart is developed, the same rules are used as for the $\bar{x}$- and *R*-charts:

Signals

1. One or more points outside the upper or lower control limits
2. Nine or more points in a row above (or below) the centerline
3. Six or more consecutive points moving in the same direction (increasing or decreasing)
4. Fourteen points in a row, alternating up and down

The *p*-chart shown in Figure 18.10 indicates the process is in control. None of the signals are present in these data. The variation in the nonconformance rates is assumed to be due to the common cause issues.

For future days, the managers would select random samples of 100 orders, count the number with errors, and compute the proportion. This value would be plotted on the *p*-chart. For each day, the managers would use the control chart to test the hypotheses:

H_0: The process is in control. The variation around the centerline is a result of common causes and is inherent in the process.

H_A: The process is out of control. The variation around the centerline is due to some special cause and is beyond what is normal for the process.

The signals mentioned previously would be used to test the null hypothesis. Remember, control charts are most useful when the charts are updated as soon as the new sample data become available. When a signal of special cause variation is present, you should take action to determine the source of the problem and address it as quickly as possible.

Chapter Outcome 3. → ***c*-Charts** The *p*-chart just discussed is used when you select a sample of items and you determine the number of the sampled items that possess a specific attribute of interest. Each item either has or does not have that attribute. You will encounter other situations that involve attribute data but differ from the *p*-chart applications. In these situations, you have what is defined as a sampling unit (or experimental unit), which could be a sheet of plywood, a door panel on a car, a textbook page, an hour of service, or any other defined unit of space, volume, time, and so on. Each sampling unit could have one or more of the attributes of interest, and you would be able to count the number of attributes present in each sampling unit. In cases in which the sampling units are the same size, the appropriate control chart is a *c*-chart.

BUSINESS APPLICATION **CONSTRUCTING *c*-CHARTS**

Vladimir Mucibabic/Fotolia

CHANDLER TILE COMPANY The Chandler Tile Company makes ceramic tile. In recent years, there has been a big demand for tile products in private residences for kitchens and bathrooms and in commercial establishments for decorative counter and wall covering. Although the demand has increased, so has the competition. The senior management at Chandler knows that three factors are key to winning business from contractors: price, quality, and service.

One quality issue is scratches on a tile. The production managers wish to set up a control chart to monitor the level of scratches per tile to determine whether the production process remains in control.

Special Note

Control charts monitor a process as it currently operates, not necessarily how you would like it to operate. Thus, a process that is in control might still yield a higher number of scratches per tile than the managers would like.

The managers believe that the numbers of scratches per tile are independent of each other and that the prevailing operating conditions are consistent from tile to tile. In this case, the proper control chart is a *c*-chart. Here the tiles being sampled are the same size, and the managers will tally the number of scratches per tile. However, if we asked, "How many opportunities were there to scratch each tile?" we probably would not be able to answer the question. There are more opportunities than we could count. For this reason, the *c*-chart is based on the Poisson probability distribution introduced in Chapter 5 rather than the binomial distribution. You might recall that the Poisson distribution is defined by the mean number of *successes* per interval, or sampling unit, as shown in Equation 18.13. A success can be regarded as a defect, a nonconformance, or any other characteristic of interest. In the Chandler example, a success is a scratch on a tile.

Mean for *c*-Chart

$$\bar{c} = \frac{\displaystyle\sum_{i=1}^{k} c_i}{k}$$

(18.13)

where:

c_i = Number of successes per sampling unit
k = Number of sampling units

Because the Poisson distribution is skewed when the mean of the sampling unit is small, we must define the sampling unit so that it is large enough to provide an average of at least 5 successes per sampling unit ($\bar{c} \geq 5$). This may require that you combine smaller sampling units into a larger unit size. In this case we combine six tiles to form a sampling unit.

The mean and the variance of the Poisson distribution are identical. Therefore, the standard deviation of the Poisson distribution is the square root of its mean. For this reason, the estimator of the standard deviation for the Poisson distribution is computed as the square root of the sample mean, as shown in Equation 18.14.

Standard Deviation for *c*-Chart

$$s_c = \sqrt{\bar{c}}$$

(18.14)

Then Equations 18.15 and 18.16 are used to compute the 3-sigma (3 standard deviation) control limits for the *c*-chart.

_c_-Chart Control Limits

$$UCL = \bar{c} + 3\sqrt{\bar{c}}$$

(18.15)

and

$$LCL = \bar{c} - 3\sqrt{\bar{c}}$$

(18.16)

You can use the following steps to construct a *c*-chart:

Step 1   Collect the sample data.

The original plan called for the Chandler Tile Company to select six tiles each hour from the production line and to perform a thorough inspection to count the number of scratches per tile. Like all control charts, at least 20 samples are desired in developing the initial control chart. After collecting 40 sampling

FIGURE 18.11 |

Excel 2010 PhStat *c*-Chart for
Chandler Tile Company

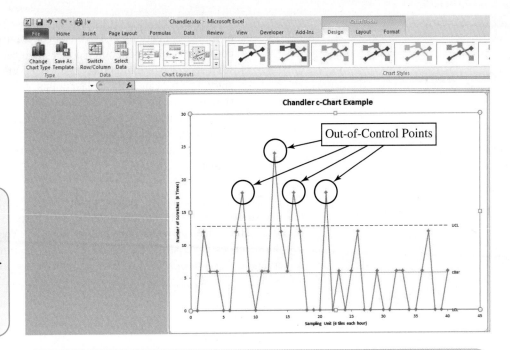

Excel 2010 Instructions:
1. Open file: **Candler.xlsx**.
2. Select **Add-Ins**
3. Select **PHStat**.
4. Select **Control Charts > c Chart**.
5. Select Nonconformance Cell Range (B1:B41).
6. Click **OK**.

Minitab Instructions (for similar results):
1. Open file: **Chandler.MTW**.
2. Choose **Stat > Control Chart > Attributes Charts > C**.
3. In **Variable**, enter number of defectives column.
4. Click on **C Chart Options** and select **Tests** tab.
5. Select *Perform all tests for special causes.*
6. Click **OK. OK.**

How to do it

Constructing SPC charts
The following steps are employed when constructing statistical quality control charts:

1. Collect the sample data.

2. Plot the subgroup statistics as a line chart.

3. Compute the average subgroup statistic, i.e., the centerline value. The centerline on the control chart is the average value for the sample data. This is the current process average.

4. Compute the appropriate standard error.

5. Compute the upper and lower control limits.

6. Plot the appropriate data on the control chart, along with the centerline and control limits.

units of six tiles each, the total number of scratches found was 228. The data set is contained in the file **Chandler**.

Step 2 Plot the subgroup number of occurrences as a line chart.
Figure 18.11 shows the line chart for the 40 sampling units.

Step 3 Compute the average number of occurrences per sampling unit using Equation 18.13.
The mean is

$$\bar{c} = \frac{\sum x}{k} = \frac{228}{40} = 5.70$$

Step 4 Compute the standard error of s_c using Equation 18.14.
The standard error is

$$s_c = \sqrt{\bar{c}} = \sqrt{5.70} = 2.387$$

Step 5 Construct the 3-sigma control limits, using Equations 18.15 and 18.16.
The upper and lower 3-sigma control limits are

$$UCL = \bar{c} + 3\sqrt{\bar{c}} = 5.7 + 3(2.387) = 12.86$$
$$LCL = \bar{c} - 3\sqrt{\bar{c}} = 5.7 - 3(2.387) = -1.46 \rightarrow 0.0$$

Step 6 Plot the centerline and control limits on the control chart.
Both upper and lower control limits are plotted on the control chart in Figure 18.11.
As with the *p*-chart, the lower control limit can't be negative. We change it to zero, which is the fewest possible scratches on a tile. The completed *c*-chart is shown in Figure 18.11.

Note in Figure 18.11 that four samples of six tiles each had a total number of scratches that fell outside the upper control limit of 12.86. The managers need to consult production records and other information to determine what special cause might have generated this level of scratches. If they can determine the cause, these data points should be removed and the control limits should be recomputed from the remaining 36 values. You might also note that the graph changes beginning with about sample 22. The process seems more stable from sample 22 onward. Managers might consider inspecting for another 13 to 15 hours and recomputing the control limits using data from hours 22 and higher.

Other Control Charts Our purpose in this chapter has been to introduce SPC charts. We have illustrated a few of the most frequently used charts. However, there are many other types of control charts that can be used in special situations. You are encouraged to consult several of the references listed at the end of the textbook for information about these other charts. Regardless of the type of statistical quality control chart you are using, the same general steps are used.

MyStatLab

18-1: Exercises

Skill Development

18-1. Fifty sampling units of equal size were inspected, and the number of nonconforming situations was recorded. The total number of instances was 449.
  a. Determine the appropriate control chart to use for this process.
  b. Compute the mean value for the control chart.
  c. Compute the upper and lower control limits.

18-2. Data were collected on a quantitative measure with a subgroup size of five observations. Thirty subgroups were collected, with the following results:

$$\bar{\bar{x}} = 44.52 \qquad \bar{R} = 5.6$$

  a. Determine the Shewhart factors that will be needed if $\bar{x}$- and R-charts are to be developed.
  b. Compute the upper and lower control limits for the R-chart.
  c. Compute the upper and lower control limits for the $\bar{x}$-chart.

18-3. Data were collected from a process in which the factor of interest was whether the finished item contained a particular attribute. The fraction of items that did not contain the attribute was recorded. A total of 30 samples were selected. The common sample size was 100 items. The total number of nonconforming items was 270. Based on these data, compute the upper and lower control limits for the p-chart.

18-4. Explain why it is important to update the control charts as soon as new data become available.

Computer Database Exercises

18-5. Grandfoods, Inc., makes energy supplement bars for use by athletes and others who need an energy boost. One of the critical quality characteristics is the weight of the bars. Too much weight implies that too many liquids have been added to the mix and the bar will be too chewy. If the bars are light, the implication is that the bars are too dry. To monitor the weights, the production manager wishes to use process control charts. Data for 30 subgroups of size 4 bars are contained in the file **Grandfoods**. Note that a subgroup is selected every 15 minutes as bars come off the manufacturing line.
  a. Use these data to construct the appropriate process control chart(s).
  b. Discuss what each chart is used for. Why do we need both charts?
  c. Examine the control charts and indicate which, if any, of the signals are present. Is the process currently in control?
  d. Develop a histogram for the energy bar weights. Discuss the shape of the distribution and the implications of this toward the validity of the control chart procedures you have used.

18-6. The Haines Lumber Company makes plywood for residential and commercial construction. One of the key quality measures is plywood thickness. Every hour, five pieces of plywood are selected and the thicknesses are measured. The data (in inches) for the first 20 subgroups are in the file **Haines**.

a. Construct an $\bar{x}$-chart based on these data. Make sure you plot the centerline and both 3-sigma upper and lower control limits.

b. Construct an R-chart based on these data.

c. Examine both control charts and determine if there are any special causes of variation that require attention in this process.

18-7. Referring to Problem 18-6, suppose the process remained in control for the next 40 hours. The thickness measurements for hours 41 through 43 are as follows:

Hour 41	0.764	0.737	0.724	0.716	0.752
Hour 42	0.766	0.785	0.777	0.790	0.799
Hour 43	0.812	0.774	0.767	0.799	0.821

a. Based on these data and the two control charts, what should you conclude about the process? Has the process gone out of control? Discuss.

b. Was it necessary to obtain your answer to Problem 18-15 before part a could be answered? Explain your reasoning.

18-8. Referring to the process control charts developed in Problem 18-5, data for periods 31 to 40 are contained in the file **Grandfoods-Extra**.

a. Based on these data, what would you conclude about the energy bar process?

b. Write a report discussing the results, and show the control charts along with the new data.

18-9. Wilson, Ryan, and Reed is a large certified public accounting (CPA) firm in Charleston, South Carolina. It has been monitoring the accuracy of its employees and wishes to get the number of accounts with errors under statistical control. It has sampled 100 accounts for each of the last 30 days and has examined them for errors. The data are presented in the file **Accounts**.

a. Construct the relevant control chart for the account process.

b. What does the chart indicate about the statistical stability of the process? Give reasons for your answers.

c. Suppose that for the next 3 days, sample sizes of 100 accounts are examined with the following results:

| Number of Errors | 6 | 7 | 9 |

Plot the appropriate data on the control chart and indicate whether any of the control chart signals are present. Discuss your results.

18-10. Trinkle & Sons performs subcontract body paint work for one of the "Big Three" automakers. One of its recent contracts called for the company to paint 12,500 door panels. Several quality characteristics are very important to the manufacturer, one of which is blemishes in the paint. The manufacturer has required Trinkle & Sons to have control charts to monitor the number of paint blemishes per door panel. The panels

are all for the same model car and are the same size. To initially develop the control chart, data for 88 door panels were collected and are provided in the file **CarPaint**.

a. Determine the appropriate type of process control chart to develop.

b. Develop a 3-sigma control chart.

c. Based on the control chart and the standard signals discussed in this chapter, what conclusions can you reach about whether the paint process is in control? Discuss.

18-11. Tony Perez is the manager of one of the largest chains of service stores that specialize in oil and lubrication of automobiles, Fastlube, Inc. One of the company's stated goals is to provide a lube and oil change for anyone's automobile in 15 minutes. Tony has thought for some time now that there is a growing disparity among his workers in the time it takes to lube and change the oil of an automobile. To monitor this aspect of Fastlube, Tony has selected a sample of 20 days and has recorded the time it took five randomly selected employees to service an automobile. The data are located in the file **Fastlube**.

a. Tony glanced through the data and noticed that the longest time it took to service a car was 25.33 minutes. Suppose the distribution of times to service a car was normal, with a mean of 15. Use your knowledge of a normal distribution to let Tony know what the standard deviation is for the time it takes to service a car.

b. Use the **Fastlube** data to construct an $\bar{x}$ and an R-chart.

c. Based on these data, what would you conclude about the service process?

d. Based on your findings on the R-chart, would it be advisable to draw conclusions based on the $\bar{x}$-chart?

18-12. The Ajax Taxi company in Manhattan, New York, wishes to set up an $\bar{x}$-chart and an R-chart to monitor the number of miles driven per day by its taxi drivers. Each week, the scheduler selects four taxis and (without the drivers' knowledge) monitors the number of miles driven. He has done this for the past 40 weeks. The data are in the file **Ajax**.

a. Construct the R-chart for these 40 subgroups.

b. Construct the $\bar{x}$-chart for these 40 subgroups. Be sure to label the chart correctly.

c. Look at both control charts and determine if any of the control chart signals are present to indicate that the process is not in control. Explain the implications of what you have found for the Ajax Taxi Company.

18-13. Referring to Problem 18-12, assume the Ajax managers determine any issues identified by the control charts were caused by one time events. The data for weeks 41 through 45 are in the **Ajax-Extra** file.

a. Using the control limits developed from the first 40 weeks, do these data indicate that the process is now out of control? Explain.

b. If a change has occurred, brainstorm some of the possible reasons.

c. What will be the impact on the control charts when the new data are included?

d. Use the data in the files **Ajax** and **Ajax-Extra** to develop the new control charts.

e. Are any of the typical control chart signals present? Discuss.

18-14. The Kaiser Corporation makes aluminum at various locations around the country. One of the key factors in being profitable is keeping the machinery running. One particularly troublesome machine is a roller that flattens the sheets to the appropriate thickness. This machine tends to break down for various reasons. Consequently, the maintenance manager has decided to develop a process control chart. Over a period of 10 weeks, 20 subgroups consisting of 5 downtime measures (in minutes) were collected (one measurement at the end of each of the two shifts). The subgroup means and ranges are shown as follows and are contained in the file called **Kaiser**.

Subgroup Mean	104.8	85.9	78.6	72.8	102.6	84.8	67.0
Subgroup Range	9.6	14.3	8.6	10.6	11.2	13.5	10.8
Subgroup Mean	91.1	79.5	71.9	47.6	106.7	80.7	81.0
Subgroup Range	5.2	14.2	14.1	14.9	12.7	13.3	15.4
Subgroup Mean	57.0	98.9	87.9	64.9	101.6	83.9	
Subgroup Range	15.5	13.8	16.6	11.2	9.6	11.5	

a. Explain why the $\bar{x}$- and R-charts would be appropriate in this case.

b. Find the centerline value for the $\bar{x}$-chart.

c. Calculate the centerline value for the R-chart.

d. Compute the upper and lower control limits for the R-chart, and construct the chart with appropriate labels.

e. Compute the upper and lower control limits for the $\bar{x}$-chart, and construct the chart with appropriate labels.

f. Examine the charts constructed in parts d and e and determine whether the process was in control during the period for which the control charts were developed. Explain.

18-15. Referring to Problem 18-14, if necessary delete any out-of-control points and construct the appropriate $\bar{x}$- and R-charts. Now, suppose the process stays in control for the next six weeks (subgroups 18 through 23). The subgroup means and ranges for subgroups 33 to 38 are as follows:

Subgroup	33	34	35	36	37	38
Subgroup Mean	89.0	88.4	85.2	89.3	97.2	105.3
Subgroup Range	11.4	5.4	14.2	11.7	9.5	10.2

a. Plot the ranges on the R-chart. Is there evidence based on the range chart that the process has gone out of control? Discuss.

b. Plot the subgroup means on the $\bar{x}$-chart. Is there evidence to suggest that the process has gone out of control with respect to the process mean? Discuss.

18-16. Regis Printing Company performs printing services for individuals and business customers. Many of the jobs require that brochures be folded for mailing. The company has a machine that does the folding. It generally does a good job, but it can have problems that cause it to do improper folds. To monitor this process, the company selects a sample of 50 brochures from every order and counts the number of incorrectly folded items in each sample. Until now, nothing has been done with the 300 samples that have been collected. The data are located in the file **Regis**.

a. What is the appropriate control chart to use to monitor this process?

b. Using the data in this file, construct the appropriate control chart and label it properly.

c. Suppose that for the next three orders, sample sizes of 50 brochures are examined with the following results:

Sample Number	301	302	303
Number of Bad Folds	6	9	7

Plot the appropriate data to the control chart and indicate whether any of the control chart signals are present. Discuss your results.

d. Suppose that the next sample of 50 has 14 improperly folded brochures. What conclusion should be reached based on the control chart? Discuss.

18-17. Recall from Problem 18-11 that Tony Perez is the manager of one of the largest chains of service stores that specialize in oil and lubrication of automobiles, Fastlube, Inc. One of the company's stated goals is to provide a lube and oil change for anyone's automobile in 15 minutes. Tony has thought for some time now that there is a growing disparity among his workers in the time it takes to lube and change the oil of an automobile. To monitor this aspect of Fastlube, Tony has selected a sample of 24 days and has recorded the time it took to service 100 automobiles each day. The number of times the service was performed in 15 minutes or less (≤ 15) is given in the file **Lubeoil**.

a. (1) Convert the sample data to proportions and plot the data as a line graph. (2) Compute $\bar{p}$ and plot this value on the line graph. (3) Compute s_p and interpret what it measures.

b. Construct a p-chart and determine if the process of the time required for oil and lube jobs is in control.

c. Specify the signals that are used to indicate an out-of-control situation on a p-chart.

18-18. Susan Booth is the director of operations for National Skyways, a small commuter airline with headquarters in Cedar Rapids, Iowa. Since airlines have started charging for checked baggage, National Skyways has seen in increase in carry-on luggage. She collected data concerning the number of pieces of baggage that were taken on board over a one-month period. The data collected are provided in the file **Carryon**. *Hint:* Consider a *U*-chart from the optional topics.

a. Set up a control chart for the number of carry-on bags per day.

b. Is the process in a state of statistical control? Explain your answer.

c. Suppose that National Skyways' aircraft were full for each of the 30 days. Each Skyways aircraft holds 40 passengers. Describe the control chart you would use. Is it necessary that you use this latter alternative or is it just a preference? Explain your answer.

18-19. Sid Luka is the service manager for Brakes Unlimited, a franchise corporation that specializes in servicing automobile brakes. He wants to study the length of time required to replace the rear drum brakes of automobiles. A subgroup of 10 automobiles needing their brakes replaced was selected on each day for a period of 20 days. The subgroup times required (in hours) for this service were recorded and are presented in the file **Brakes**.

a. Sid has been trying to get the average time required to replace the rear drum brakes of an automobile to be under 1.65 hours. Use the data Sid has collected to determine if he has reached his goal.

b. Set up the appropriate control charts to determine if this process is under control.

c. Determine whether the process is under control. If the process is not under control, brainstorm suggestions that might help Sid bring it under control. What tools of quality might Sid find useful?

END EXERCISES 18-1

Visual Summary

Chapter 18: Organizations across the United States and around the world have turned to quality management in an effort to meet the competitive challenges of the international marketplace. Their efforts have generally followed two distinctive, but complementary, tracks. The first track involves a change in managerial philosophy following principles set out by **W. Edwards Deming** and **Joseph Juran,** two pioneers in the quality movement. It generally involves employees at all levels to be brought into the effort as members of process improvement teams. These teams are assisted by training in the **Tools of Quality.** The second track involves a process of continual improvement using a set of statistically based tools involving **process control charts**. This chapter discusses four of the most commonly used statistical process control charts.

18.1 Introduction to Statistical Process Control Charts (pg. 774–795)

Summary

Process control charts are based on the idea that all processes exhibit variation. Although variation is always present, two major types occur. The first is **common cause variation**, which means it is naturally occurring or expected in the system. Other terms people use for common cause variation include *normal, random, chance occurrence, inherent,* and *stable variation.* The other type of variation is **special cause variation**, it indicates that something out of the ordinary has happened. This type of variation is also called *nonrandom, unstable,* and *assignable cause variation.* Process control charts are used to separate special cause variation from common cause variation. Process control charts are constructed by determining a centerline (a process average) and construction upper and lower control limits around the centerline (three standard deviation lines above and below the average). The charts considered in this chapter are the most commonly used: the $\bar{x}$ and R-charts (used in tandem), p-charts and c-charts. Data is gathered continually from the process being monitored and plotted on the chart. Data points between the upper and lower control limits generally indicate the process is stable, but not always. Process control charts are continually monitored to indicate signs of going "out of control". Common signals include: one or more points outside the upper or lower control limits, nine or more points in a row above (or below) the centerline, six or more consecutive points moving in the same direction (increasing or decreasing), fourteen points in a row, alternating up and down. Generally, continual process improvement procedures involve identifying and addressing the reason for special cause variation and then working to reduce the common cause variation.

Outcome 1. Construct and interpret $\bar{x}$ charts and R-charts.
Outcome 2. Construct and interpret p-charts.
Outcome 3. Construct and interpret c-charts.

Conclusion

The quality movement throughout the United States and much of the rest of the world has created great expectations among consumers. Ideas such as continuous process improvement and customer focus have become a central part in raising these expectations. Statistics has played a key role in increasing expectations of quality products. The enemy of quality is variation, which exists in everything. Through the use of appropriate statistical tools and the concept of statistical reasoning, managers and employees have developed better understandings of their processes. Although they haven't yet figured out how to eliminate variation, statistics has helped reduce it and understand how to operate more effectively when it exists.

Statistical process control (SPC) has played a big part in the understanding of variation. SPC is quite likely the most frequently used quality tool. This chapter has introduced SPC. Hopefully, you realize that these tools are merely extensions of the hypothesis-testing and estimation concepts presented in Chapters 8–10. You will very likely have the opportunity to use SPC in one form or another after you leave this course and enter the workforce. **Figure 18.12** summarizes some of the key SPC charts and the conditions under which each is developed.

FIGURE 18.12

Statistical Process Control
Chart Option

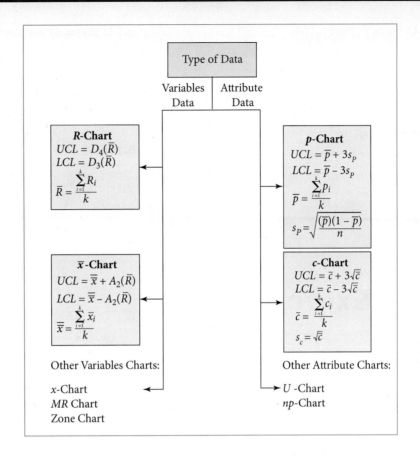

Equations

(18.1) **Variation Components** pg. 776

Total process variation = Common cause variation
+ Special cause variation

(18.2) **Average Subgroup Means** pg. 779

$$\bar{\bar{x}} = \frac{\sum\limits_{i=1}^{k} \bar{x}_i}{k}$$

(18.3) **Average Subgroup Range** pg. 779

$$\bar{R} = \frac{\sum\limits_{i=1}^{k} R_i}{k}$$

(18.4) **Upper Control Limit, $\bar{x}$-Chart** pg. 781

$$UCL = \bar{\bar{x}} + A_2(\bar{R})$$

(18.5) **Lower Control Limit, $\bar{x}$-Chart** pg. 781

$$LCL = \bar{\bar{x}} - A_2(\bar{R})$$

(18.6) **Upper Control Limit, R-Chart** pg. 782

$$UCL = D_4(\bar{R})$$

(18.7) **Lower Control Limit, R-Chart** pg. 782

$$LCL = D_3(\bar{R})$$

(18.8) **Mean Subgroup Proportion** pg. 786
For equal-size samples:

$$\bar{p} = \frac{\sum\limits_{i=1}^{k} p_i}{k}$$

(18.9) **For unequal sample sizes:** pg. 787

$$\bar{p} = \frac{\sum\limits_{i=1}^{k} n_i p_i}{\sum\limits_{i=1}^{k} n_i}$$

(18.10) **Estimate for the Standard Error for the Subgroup Proportions** pg. 788
For equal sample sizes:

$$s_{\bar{p}} = \sqrt{\frac{(\bar{p})(1-\bar{p})}{n}}$$

(18.11) Standard Deviation for c-Chart pg. 788

$$UCL = \bar{p} + 3s_{\bar{p}}$$

(18.12)

$$LCL = \bar{p} - 3s_{\bar{p}}$$

(18.13) Mean for c-Chart pg. 790

$$\bar{c} = \frac{\sum\limits_{i=1}^{k} c_i}{k}$$

(18.14) Standard Deviation for c-Chart pg. 790

$$s_c = \sqrt{\bar{c}}$$

(18.15) c-Chart Control Limits pg. 790

$$UCL = \bar{c} + 3\sqrt{\bar{c}}$$

(18.16)

$$LCL = \bar{c} - 3\sqrt{\bar{c}}$$

Chapter Exercises _____ MyStatLab

Conceptual Questions

18-20. Data were collected on a quantitative measure with a subgroup size of three observations. Thirty subgroups were collected, with the following results:

$$\bar{\bar{x}} = 1{,}345.4 \qquad \bar{R} = 209.3$$

a. Determine the Shewhart factors that will be needed if $\bar{x}$- and R-charts are to be developed.
b. Compute the upper and lower control limits for the R-chart.
c. Compute the upper and lower control limits for the $\bar{x}$-chart.

18-21. Data were collected on a quantitative measure with subgroups of four observations. Twenty-five subgroups were collected, with the following results:

$$\bar{\bar{x}} = 2.33 \qquad \bar{R} = 0.80$$

a. Determine the Shewhart factors that will be needed if $\bar{x}$- and R-charts are to be developed.
b. Compute the upper and lower control limits for the R-chart.
c. Compute the upper and lower control limits for the $\bar{x}$-chart.

18-22. Data were collected from a process in which the factor of interest was whether a finished item contained a particular attribute. The fraction of items that did not contain the attribute was recorded. A total of 20 samples were selected. The common sample size was 150 items. The total number of nonconforming items was 720. Based on these data, compute the upper and lower control limits for the p-chart.

18-23. Data were collected from a process in which the factor of interest was whether a finished item contained a particular attribute. The fraction of items that did not contain the attribute was recorded. A total of 30 samples were selected. The common sample size was 100 items. The average number of nonconforming items per sample was 14. Based on these data, construct the upper and lower control limits for the p-chart.

Computer Database Exercises

18-24. CC, Inc., provides billing services for the health care industry. To ensure that its processes are operating as intended, CC selects 100 billing records at random every day and inspects each record to determine if it is free of errors. A billing record is classified as defective whenever there is an error that requires that the bill be reprocessed and mailed again. Such errors can occur for a variety of reasons. For example, a defective bill could have an incorrect mailing address, a wrong insurance identification number, or an improper doctor or hospital reference. The sample data taken from the most recent five weeks of billing records are contained in the file **CC Inc**.

Use the sample information to construct the appropriate 3-sigma control chart. Does CC's billing process appear to be in control? What, if any, comments can you make regarding the performance of its billing process?

18-25. A & A Enterprises ships integrated circuits to companies that assemble computers. Because computer manufacturing operations run on little inventory, parts must be available when promised. Thus, a critical element of A & A's customer satisfaction is on-time delivery performance. To ensure that the delivery process is performing as intended, a quality improvement team decided to monitor the firm's distribution and delivery process. From the A & A corporate database, 100 monthly shipping records were randomly selected for the previous 21 months, and the number of on-time shipments was counted. This information is contained in the file **A & A On Time Shipments**. Develop the appropriate 3-sigma control chart(s) for monitoring this process. Does it appear that the delivery process is in control? If not, can you suggest some possible assignable causes?

18-26. Fifi Carpets, Inc., produces carpet for homes and offices. Fifi has recently opened a new production process dedicated to the manufacture of a special type of carpet used by firms who want a floor covering for high-traffic spaces. As a part of their ongoing quality improvement activities, the managers of Fifi regularly monitor their production processes using statistical process control. For their new production process, Fifi managers would like to develop control charts to help them in their monitoring activities. Thirty samples of carpet sections, with each section having an area of 50 square meters, were randomly selected, and the numbers of stains, cuts, snags, and tears were counted on each section. The sample data are contained in the file **Fifi Carpets**.

Use the sample data to construct the appropriate 3-sigma control chart(s) for monitoring the production process. Does the process appear to be in statistical control?

18-27. The order-entry, order-processing call center for PS Industries is concerned about the amounts of time that customers must wait before their calls are handled. A quality improvement consultant suggests that it monitor call-wait times using control charts. Using call center statistics maintained by the company's database system, the consultant randomly selects four calls every hour for 30 different hours and examines the wait time, in seconds, for each call. This information is contained in the file **PS Industries**.

Use the sample data to construct the appropriate control chart(s). Does the process appear to be in statistical control? What other information concerning

the call center's process should the consultant be aware of?

18-28. Varians Controls manufactures a variety of different electric motors and drives. One step in the manufacturing process involves cutting copper wire from large reels into smaller lengths. For a particular motor, there is a dedicated machine for cutting wire to the required length. As a part of its regular quality improvement activities, the continuous process improvement team at Varians took a sample size of 5 cuttings every hour for 30 consecutive hours of operation. At the time the samples were taken, Varians had every reason to believe that its process was working as intended. The automatic cutting machine records the length of each cut, and the results are reported in the file **Varians Controls**.

a. Develop the appropriate 3-sigma control chart(s) for this process. Does the process appear to be working as intended (in control)?

b. A few weeks after the previous data were sampled, a new operator was hired to calibrate the company's cutting machines. The first 5 samples taken from the machine after the calibration adjustments (samples 225 to 229) are shown as follows:

	Cutting 1	Cutting 2	Cutting 3	Cutting 4	Cutting 5
Sample 225	0.7818	0.7760	0.7814	0.7824	0.7702
Sample 226	0.7694	0.7838	0.7675	0.7834	0.7730
Sample 227	0.7875	0.7738	0.7737	0.7594	0.7837
Sample 228	0.7762	0.7711	0.7700	0.7823	0.7673
Sample 229	0.7805	0.7724	0.7748	0.7823	0.7924

Based on these sample values, what can you say about the cutting process? Does it appear to be in control?

Case 18.1

Izbar Precision Casters, Inc.

Izbar Precision Casters, Inc., manufactures a variety of structural steel products for the construction trade. Currently, there is a strong demand for its I-beam product produced at a mill outside Memphis. Beams at this facility are shipped throughout the Midwest and mid-South, and demand for the product is high due to the strong economy in the regions served by the plant. Angie Schneider, the mill's manager, wants to ensure that the plant's operations are in control, and she has selected several characteristics to monitor. Specifically, she collects data on the number of weekly accidents at the plant, the number of orders shipped on time, and the thickness of the steel I-beams produced.

For the number of reported accidents, Angie selected 30 days at random from the company's safety records. Angie and all the plant employees are very concerned about workplace safety, and management, labor, and government officials have worked together to help create a safe work environment. As a part of the safety program, the company requires employees to report every accident regardless of how minor it may be. In fact, most accidents are very minor, but Izbar still records them and works to prevent them from recurring. Because of Izbar's strong reporting requirement, Angie was able to get a count of the number of reported accidents for each of the 30 sampled days. These data are shown in Table 18.2.

TABLE 18.2 | **Accident Data**

Day	Number of Reported Accidents	Day	Number of Reported Accidents
1	9	16	4
2	11	17	11
3	9	18	7
4	9	19	7
5	11	20	10
6	10	21	11
7	10	22	6
8	10	23	6
9	4	24	7
10	7	25	4
11	7	26	9
12	8	27	11
13	11	28	9
14	10	29	6
15	7	30	5

TABLE 18.3 | **Late Shipments**

Day	Number of Late Shipments	Day	Number of Late Shipments
1	5	11	8
2	3	12	2
3	1	13	5
4	6	14	6
5	5	15	2
6	8	16	7
7	5	17	7
8	6	18	3
9	4	19	2
10	4	20	7

To monitor the percentage of on-time shipments, Angie randomly selected 50 records from the firm's shipping and billing system every day for 20 different days over the past six months. These records contain the actual and promised shipping dates for each order. Angie used a spreadsheet to determine the number of shipments that were made after the promised shipment dates. The number of late shipments from the 50 sampled records was then reported. These data are shown in Table 18.3.

Finally, to monitor the thickness of the I-beam produced at the plant, Angie randomly selected six I-beams every day for 30 days and had each sampled beam measured. The thickness of each beam, in inches, was recorded. All of the data collected by Angie are contained in the file **Izbar**. She wants to use the information she has collected to construct and analyze the appropriate control charts for the plant's production processes. She intends to present this information at the next manager's meeting on Monday morning.

Required Tasks:

a. Use the data that Angie has collected to develop and analyze the appropriate control charts for this process. Be sure to label each control chart carefully and also to identify the type of control chart used.
b. Do the processes analyzed appear to be in control? Why or why not? What would you suggest that Angie do?
c. Does Angie need to continue to monitor her processes on a regular basis? How should she do this? Also, are there other variables that might be of interest to her in monitoring the plant's performance? If so, what do you think they might be?

List of **Appendix Tables**

APPENDIX A   Random Numbers Table   802

APPENDIX B   Cumulative Binomial Distribution Table   803

APPENDIX C   Cumulative Poisson Probability Distribution Table   816

APPENDIX D   Standard Normal Distribution Table   821

APPENDIX E   Exponential Distribution Table   822

APPENDIX F   Values of t for Selected Probabilities   823

APPENDIX G   Values of χ^2 for Selected Probabilities   824

APPENDIX H F-Distribution Table   825

APPENDIX I   Distribution of the Studentized Range (q-values)   831

APPENDIX J   Critical Values of r in the Runs Test   833

APPENDIX K   Mann-Whitney U Test Probabilities ($n < 9$)   834

APPENDIX L   Mann-Whitney U Test Critical Values ($9 \leq n \leq 20$)   836

APPENDIX M   Critical Values of T in the Wilcoxon Matched-Pairs Signed-Ranks Test ($n \leq 25$)   838

APPENDIX N   Critical Values d_L and d_U of the Durbin-Watson Statistic D   839

APPENDIX O   Lower and Upper Critical Values W of Wilcoxon Signed-Ranks Test   841

APPENDIX P   Control Chart Factors   842

Random Numbers Table

1511	4745	8716	2793	9142	4958	5245	8312	8925
6249	7073	0460	0819	0729	6806	2713	6595	5149
2587	4800	3455	7565	1196	7768	6137	4941	0488
0168	1379	7838	7487	7420	5285	8045	6679	1361
9664	9021	4990	5570	4697	7939	5842	5353	7503
1384	4981	2708	6437	2298	6230	7443	9425	5384
6390	8953	4292	7372	7197	2121	6538	2093	7629
6944	8134	0704	8500	6996	3492	4397	8802	3253
3610	3119	7442	6218	7623	0546	8394	3286	4463
9865	0028	1783	9029	2858	8737	7023	0444	8575
7044	6712	7530	0018	0945	8803	4467	0979	1342
9304	4857	5476	8386	1540	5760	9815	7191	3291
1717	8278	0072	2636	3217	1693	6081	1330	3458
2461	3598	5173	9666	6165	7438	6805	2357	6994
8240	9856	0075	7599	8468	7653	6272	0573	4344
1697	6805	1386	2340	6694	9786	0536	6423	1083
4695	2251	8962	5638	9459	5578	0676	2276	4724
3056	8558	3020	7509	5105	4283	5390	5715	8405
6887	9035	8520	6571	3233	7175	2859	1615	3349
1267	8824	5588	2821	1247	0967	4355	1385	0727
4369	9267	9377	8205	6479	7002	0649	4731	7086
2888	0333	5347	4849	5526	2975	5295	5071	6011
9893	7251	6243	4617	9256	4039	4800	9393	3263
8927	3977	6054	5979	8566	8120	2566	4449	2414
2676	7064	2198	3234	3796	5506	4462	5121	9052
0775	7316	2249	5606	9411	3818	5268	7652	6098
3828	9178	3726	0743	4075	3560	9542	3922	7688
3281	3419	6660	7968	1238	2246	2164	4567	1801
0328	7471	5352	2019	5842	1665	5939	6337	9102
8406	1826	8437	3078	9068	1425	1232	0573	7751
7076	8418	6778	1292	2019	3506	7474	0141	6544
0446	8641	3249	5431	4068	6045	1939	5626	1867
3719	9712	7472	1517	8850	6862	6990	5475	6227
5648	0563	6346	1981	9512	0659	5694	6668	2563
3694	8582	3434	4052	8392	3883	5126	0477	4034
3554	9876	4249	9473	9085	6594	2434	9453	8883
4934	8446	4646	2054	1136	1023	6295	6483	9915
7835	1506	0019	5011	0563	4450	1466	6334	2606
1098	2113	8287	3487	8250	2269	1876	3684	8856
1186	2685	7225	8311	3835	8059	9163	2539	6487
4618	1522	0627	0448	0669	4086	4083	0881	4270
5529	4173	5711	7419	2535	5876	8435	2564	3031
0754	5808	8458	2218	9180	6213	5280	4753	0696
5865	0806	2070	7986	4800	3076	2866	0515	7417
6168	8963	0235	1514	7875	2176	3095	1171	7892
7479	4144	6697	2255	5465	7233	4981	3553	8144
4608	6576	9422	4198	2578	1701	4764	7460	3509
0654	2483	6001	4486	4941	1500	3502	9693	1956
3000	9694	6616	5599	7759	1581	9896	2312	8140
2686	3675	5760	2918	0185	7364	9985	5930	9869
4713	4121	5144	5164	8104	0403	4984	3877	8772
9281	6522	7916	8941	6710	1670	1399	5961	4714
5736	9419	5022	6955	3356	5732	1042	0527	7441
2383	0408	2821	7313	5781	6951	7181	0608	2864
8740	8038	7284	6054	2246	1674	9984	0355	0775

APPENDIX B

Cumulative Binomial Distribution Table

$$P(x \leq X) = \sum_{i=0}^{X} \frac{n!}{i!(n-i)!} p^i (1-p)^{n-i}$$

n = 1

x	p = 0.01	p = 0.02	p = 0.03	p = 0.04	p = 0.05	p = 0.06	p = 0.07	p = 0.08	p = 0.09
0	0.9900	0.9800	0.9700	0.9600	0.9500	0.9400	0.9300	0.9200	0.9100
1	1.0000	1.0000	1.0000	1.0000	1.0000	1.0000	1.0000	1.0000	1.0000

x	p = 0.10	p = 0.15	p = 0.20	p = 0.25	p = 0.30	p = 0.35	p = 0.40	p = 0.45	p = 0.50
0	0.9000	0.8500	0.8000	0.7500	0.7000	0.6500	0.6000	0.5500	0.5000
1	1.0000	1.0000	1.0000	1.0000	1.0000	1.0000	1.0000	1.0000	1.0000

x	p = 0.55	p = 0.60	p = 0.65	p = 0.70	p = 0.75	p = 0.80	p = 0.85	p = 0.90	p = 0.91
0	0.4500	0.4000	0.3500	0.3000	0.2500	0.2000	0.1500	0.1000	0.0900
1	1.0000	1.0000	1.0000	1.0000	1.0000	1.0000	1.0000	1.0000	1.0000

x	p = 0.92	p = 0.93	p = 0.94	p = 0.95	p = 0.96	p = 0.97	p = 0.98	p = 0.99	p = 1.00
0	0.0800	0.0700	0.0600	0.0500	0.0400	0.0300	0.0200	0.0100	0.0000
1	1.0000	1.0000	1.0000	1.0000	1.0000	1.0000	1.0000	1.0000	1.0000

n = 2

x	p = 0.01	p = 0.02	p = 0.03	p = 0.04	p = 0.05	p = 0.06	p = 0.07	p = 0.08	p = 0.09
0	0.9801	0.9604	0.9409	0.9216	0.9025	0.8836	0.8649	0.8464	0.8281
1	0.9999	0.9996	0.9991	0.9984	0.9975	0.9964	0.9951	0.9936	0.9919
2	1.0000	1.0000	1.0000	1.0000	1.0000	1.0000	1.0000	1.0000	1.0000

x	p = 0.10	p = 0.15	p = 0.20	p = 0.25	p = 0.30	p = 0.35	p = 0.40	p = 0.45	p = 0.50
0	0.8100	0.7225	0.6400	0.5625	0.4900	0.4225	0.3600	0.3025	0.2500
1	0.9900	0.9775	0.9600	0.9375	0.9100	0.8775	0.8400	0.7975	0.7500
2	1.0000	1.0000	1.0000	1.0000	1.0000	1.0000	1.0000	1.0000	1.0000

x	p = 0.55	p = 0.60	p = 0.65	p = 0.70	p = 0.75	p = 0.80	p = 0.85	p = 0.90	p = 0.91
0	0.2025	0.1600	0.1225	0.0900	0.0625	0.0400	0.0225	0.0100	0.0081
1	0.6975	0.6400	0.5775	0.5100	0.4375	0.3600	0.2775	0.1900	0.1719
2	1.0000	1.0000	1.0000	1.0000	1.0000	1.0000	1.0000	1.0000	1.0000

x	p = 0.92	p = 0.93	p = 0.94	p = 0.95	p = 0.96	p = 0.97	p = 0.98	p = 0.99	p = 1.00
0	0.0064	0.0049	0.0036	0.0025	0.0016	0.0009	0.0004	0.0001	0.0000
1	0.1536	0.1351	0.1164	0.0975	0.0784	0.0591	0.0396	0.0199	0.0000
2	1.0000	1.0000	1.0000	1.0000	1.0000	1.0000	1.0000	1.0000	1.0000

n = 3

x	p = 0.01	p = 0.02	p = 0.03	p = 0.04	p = 0.05	p = 0.06	p = 0.07	p = 0.08	p = 0.09
0	0.9703	0.9412	0.9127	0.8847	0.8574	0.8306	0.8044	0.7787	0.7536
1	0.9997	0.9988	0.9974	0.9953	0.9928	0.9896	0.9860	0.9818	0.9772
2	1.0000	1.0000	1.0000	0.9999	0.9999	0.9998	0.9997	0.9995	0.9993
3	1.0000	1.0000	1.0000	1.0000	1.0000	1.0000	1.0000	1.0000	1.0000

x	p = 0.10	p = 0.15	p = 0.20	p = 0.25	p = 0.30	p = 0.35	p = 0.40	p = 0.45	p = 0.50
0	0.7290	0.6141	0.5120	0.4219	0.3430	0.2746	0.2160	0.1664	0.1250
1	0.9720	0.9393	0.8960	0.8438	0.7840	0.7183	0.6480	0.5748	0.5000
2	0.9990	0.9966	0.9920	0.9844	0.9730	0.9571	0.9360	0.9089	0.8750
3	1.0000	1.0000	1.0000	1.0000	1.0000	1.0000	1.0000	1.0000	1.0000

x	p = 0.55	p = 0.60	p = 0.65	p = 0.70	p = 0.75	p = 0.80	p = 0.85	p = 0.90	p = 0.91
0	0.0911	0.0640	0.0429	0.0270	0.0156	0.0080	0.0034	0.0010	0.0007
1	0.4253	0.3520	0.2818	0.2160	0.1563	0.1040	0.0608	0.0280	0.0228
2	0.8336	0.7840	0.7254	0.6570	0.5781	0.4880	0.3859	0.2710	0.2464
3	1.0000	1.0000	1.0000	1.0000	1.0000	1.0000	1.0000	1.0000	1.0000

x	p = 0.92	p = 0.93	p = 0.94	p = 0.95	p = 0.96	p = 0.97	p = 0.98	p = 0.99	p = 1.00
0	0.0005	0.0003	0.0002	0.0001	0.0001	0.0000	0.0000	0.0000	0.0000
1	0.0182	0.0140	0.0104	0.0073	0.0047	0.0026	0.0012	0.0003	0.0000
2	0.2213	0.1956	0.1694	0.1426	0.1153	0.0873	0.0588	0.0297	0.0000
3	1.0000	1.0000	1.0000	1.0000	1.0000	1.0000	1.0000	1.0000	1.0000

(continued)

n = 4

x	p = 0.01	p = 0.02	p = 0.03	p = 0.04	p = 0.05	p = 0.06	p = 0.07	p = 0.08	p = 0.09
0	0.9606	0.9224	0.8853	0.8493	0.8145	0.7807	0.7481	0.7164	0.6857
1	0.9994	0.9977	0.9948	0.9909	0.9860	0.9801	0.9733	0.9656	0.9570
2	1.0000	1.0000	0.9999	0.9998	0.9995	0.9992	0.9987	0.9981	0.9973
3	1.0000	1.0000	1.0000	1.0000	1.0000	1.0000	1.0000	1.0000	0.9999
4	1.0000	1.0000	1.0000	1.0000	1.0000	1.0000	1.0000	1.0000	1.0000

x	p = 0.10	p = 0.15	p = 0.20	p = 0.25	p = 0.30	p — 0.35	p = 0.40	p = 0.45	p = 0.50
0	0.6561	0.5220	0.4096	0.3164	0.2401	0.1785	0.1296	0.0915	0.0625
1	0.9477	0.8905	0.8192	0.7383	0.6517	0.5630	0.4752	0.3910	0.3125
2	0.9963	0.9880	0.9728	0.9492	0.9163	0.8735	0.8208	0.7585	0.6875
3	0.9999	0.9995	0.9984	0.9961	0.9919	0.9850	0.9744	0.9590	0.9375
4	1.0000	1.0000	1.0000	1.0000	1.0000	1.0000	1.0000	1.0000	1.0000

x	p = 0.55	p = 0.60	p = 0.65	p = 0.70	p = 0.75	p = 0.80	p = 0.85	p = 0.90	p = 0.91
0	0.0410	0.0256	0.0150	0.0081	0.0039	0.0016	0.0005	0.0001	0.0001
1	0.2415	0.1792	0.1265	0.0837	0.0508	0.0272	0.0120	0.0037	0.0027
2	0.6090	0.5248	0.4370	0.3483	0.2617	0.1808	0.1095	0.0523	0.0430
3	0.9085	0.8704	0.8215	0.7599	0.6836	0.5904	0.4780	0.3439	0.3143
4	1.0000	1.0000	1.0000	1.0000	1.0000	1.0000	1.0000	1.0000	1.0000

x	p = 0.92	p = 0.93	p = 0.94	p = 0.95	p = 0.96	p = 0.97	p = 0.98	p = 0.99	p = 1.00
0	0.0000	0.0000	0.0000	0.0000	0.0000	0.0000	0.0000	0.0000	0.0000
1	0.0019	0.0013	0.0008	0.0005	0.0002	0.0001	0.0000	0.0000	0.0000
2	0.0344	0.0267	0.0199	0.0140	0.0091	0.0052	0.0023	0.0006	0.0000
3	0.2836	0.2519	0.2193	0.1855	0.1507	0.1147	0.0776	0.0394	0.0000
4	1.0000	1.0000	1.0000	1.0000	1.0000	1.0000	1.0000	1.0000	1.0000

n = 5

x	p = 0.01	p = 0.02	p = 0.03	p = 0.04	p = 0.05	p = 0.06	p = 0.07	p = 0.08	p = 0.09
0	0.9510	0.9039	0.8587	0.8154	0.7738	0.7339	0.6957	0.6591	0.6240
1	0.9990	0.9962	0.9915	0.9852	0.9774	0.9681	0.9575	0.9456	0.9326
2	1.0000	0.9999	0.9997	0.9994	0.9988	0.9980	0.9969	0.9955	0.9937
3	1.0000	1.0000	1.0000	1.0000	1.0000	0.9999	0.9999	0.9998	0.9997
4	1.0000	1.0000	1.0000	1.0000	1.0000	1.0000	1.0000	1.0000	1.0000
5	1.0000	1.0000	1.0000	1.0000	1.0000	1.0000	1.0000	1.0000	1.0000

x	p = 0.10	p = 0.15	p = 0.20	p = 0.25	p = 0.30	p = 0.35	p = 0.40	p = 0.45	p = 0.50
0	0.5905	0.4437	0.3277	0.2373	0.1681	0.1160	0.0778	0.0503	0.0313
1	0.9185	0.8352	0.7373	0.6328	0.5282	0.4284	0.3370	0.2562	0.1875
2	0.9914	0.9734	0.9421	0.8965	0.8369	0.7648	0.6826	0.5931	0.5000
3	0.9995	0.9978	0.9933	0.9844	0.9692	0.9460	0.9130	0.8688	0.8125
4	1.0000	0.9999	0.9997	0.9990	0.9976	0.9947	0.9898	0.9815	0.9688
5	1.0000	1.0000	1.0000	1.0000	1.0000	1.0000	1.0000	1.0000	1.0000

x	p = 0.55	p = 0.60	p = 0.65	p = 0.70	p = 0.75	p = 0.80	p = 0.85	p = 0.90	p = 0.91
0	0.0185	0.0102	0.0053	0.0024	0.0010	0.0003	0.0001	0.0000	0.0000
1	0.1312	0.0870	0.0540	0.0308	0.0156	0.0067	0.0022	0.0005	0.0003
2	0.4069	0.3174	0.2352	0.1631	0.1035	0.0579	0.0266	0.0086	0.0063
3	0.7438	0.6630	0.5716	0.4718	0.3672	0.2627	0.1648	0.0815	0.0674
4	0.9497	0.9222	0.8840	0.8319	0.7627	0.6723	0.5563	0.4095	0.3760
5	1.0000	1.0000	1.0000	1.0000	1.0000	1.0000	1.0000	1.0000	1.0000

x	p = 0.92	p = 0.93	p — 0.94	p = 0.95	p = 0.96	p = 0.97	p = 0.98	p = 0.99	p = 1.00
0	0.0000	0.0000	0.0000	0.0000	0.0000	0.0000	0.0000	0.0000	0.0000
1	0.0002	0.0001	0.0001	0.0000	0.0000	0.0000	0.0000	0.0000	0.0000
2	0.0045	0.0031	0.0020	0.0012	0.0006	0.0003	0.0001	0.0000	0.0000
3	0.0544	0.0425	0.0319	0.0226	0.0148	0.0085	0.0038	0.0010	0.0000
4	0.3409	0.3043	0.2661	0.2262	0.1846	0.1413	0.0961	0.0490	0.0000
5	1.0000	1.0000	1.0000	1.0000	1.0000	1.0000	1.0000	1.0000	1.0000

n = 6

x	p = 0.01	p = 0.02	p = 0.03	p = 0.04	p = 0.05	p = 0.06	p = 0.07	p = 0.08	p = 0.09
0	0.9415	0.8858	0.8330	0.7828	0.7351	0.6899	0.6470	0.6064	0.5679
1	0.9985	0.9943	0.9875	0.9784	0.9672	0.9541	0.9392	0.9227	0.9048
2	1.0000	0.9998	0.9995	0.9988	0.9978	0.9962	0.9942	0.9915	0.9882
3	1.0000	1.0000	1.0000	1.0000	0.9999	0.9998	0.9997	0.9995	0.9992

4	1.0000	1.0000	1.0000	1.0000	1.0000	1.0000	1.0000	1.0000	
5	1.0000	1.0000	1.0000	1.0000	1.0000	1.0000	1.0000	1.0000	
6	1.0000	1.0000	1.0000	1.0000	1.0000	1.0000	1.0000	1.0000	

x	p = 0.10	p = 0.15	p = 0.20	p = 0.25	p = 0.30	p = 0.35	p = 0.40	p = 0.45	p = 0.50
0	0.5314	0.3771	0.2621	0.1780	0.1176	0.0754	0.0467	0.0277	0.0156
1	0.8857	0.7765	0.6554	0.5339	0.4202	0.3191	0.2333	0.1636	0.1094
2	0.9842	0.9527	0.9011	0.8306	0.7443	0.6471	0.5443	0.4415	0.3438
3	0.9987	0.9941	0.9830	0.9624	0.9295	0.8826	0.8208	0.7447	0.6563
4	0.9999	0.9996	0.9984	0.9954	0.9891	0.9777	0.9590	0.9308	0.8906
5	1.0000	1.0000	0.9999	0.9998	0.9993	0.9982	0.9959	0.9917	0.9844
6	1.0000	1.0000	1.0000	1.0000	1.0000	1.0000	1.0000	1.0000	1.0000

x	p = 0.55	p = 0.60	p = 0.65	p = 0.70	p = 0.75	p = 0.80	p = 0.85	p = 0.90	p = 0.91
0	0.0083	0.0041	0.0018	0.0007	0.0002	0.0001	0.0000	0.0000	0.0000
1	0.0692	0.0410	0.0223	0.0109	0.0046	0.0016	0.0004	0.0001	0.0000
2	0.2553	0.1792	0.1174	0.0705	0.0376	0.0170	0.0059	0.0013	0.0008
3	0.5585	0.4557	0.3529	0.2557	0.1694	0.0989	0.0473	0.0159	0.0118
4	0.8364	0.7667	0.6809	0.5798	0.4661	0.3446	0.2235	0.1143	0.0952
5	0.9723	0.9533	0.9246	0.8824	0.8220	0.7379	0.6229	0.4686	0.4321
6	1.0000	1.0000	1.0000	1.0000	1.0000	1.0000	1.0000	1.0000	1.0000

x	p = 0.92	p = 0.93	p = 0.94	p = 0.95	p = 0.96	p = 0.97	p = 0.98	p = 0.99	p = 1.00
0	0.0000	0.0000	0.0000	0.0000	0.0000	0.0000	0.0000	0.0000	0.0000
1	0.0000	0.0000	0.0000	0.0000	0.0000	0.0000	0.0000	0.0000	0.0000
2	0.0005	0.0003	0.0002	0.0001	0.0000	0.0000	0.0000	0.0000	0.0000
3	0.0085	0.0058	0.0038	0.0022	0.0012	0.0005	0.0002	0.0000	0.0000
4	0.0773	0.0608	0.0459	0.0328	0.0216	0.0125	0.0057	0.0015	0.0000
5	0.3936	0.3530	0.3101	0.2649	0.2172	0.1670	0.1142	0.0585	0.0000
6	1.0000	1.0000	1.0000	1.0000	1.0000	1.0000	1.0000	1.0000	1.0000

n = 7

x	p = 0.01	p = 0.02	p = 0.03	p = 0.04	p = 0.05	p = 0.06	p = 0.07	p = 0.08	p = 0.09
0	0.9321	0.8681	0.8080	0.7514	0.6983	0.6485	0.6017	0.5578	0.5168
1	0.9980	0.9921	0.9829	0.9706	0.9556	0.9382	0.9187	0.8974	0.8745
2	1.0000	0.9997	0.9991	0.9980	0.9962	0.9937	0.9903	0.9860	0.9807
3	1.0000	1.0000	1.0000	0.9999	0.9998	0.9996	0.9993	0.9988	0.9982
4	1.0000	1.0000	1.0000	1.0000	1.0000	1.0000	1.0000	0.9999	0.9999
5	1.0000	1.0000	1.0000	1.0000	1.0000	1.0000	1.0000	1.0000	1.0000
6	1.0000	1.0000	1.0000	1.0000	1.0000	1.0000	1.0000	1.0000	1.0000
7	1.0000	1.0000	1.0000	1.0000	1.0000	1.0000	1.0000	1.0000	1.0000

x	p = 0.10	p = 0.15	p = 0.20	p = 0.25	p = 0.30	p = 0.35	p = 0.40	p = 0.45	p = 0.50
0	0.4783	0.3206	0.2097	0.1335	0.0824	0.0490	0.0280	0.0152	0.0078
1	0.8503	0.7166	0.5767	0.4449	0.3294	0.2338	0.1586	0.1024	0.0625
2	0.9743	0.9262	0.8520	0.7564	0.6471	0.5323	0.4199	0.3164	0.2266
3	0.9973	0.9879	0.9667	0.9294	0.8740	0.8002	0.7102	0.6083	0.5000
4	0.9998	0.9988	0.9953	0.9871	0.9712	0.9444	0.9037	0.8471	0.7734
5	1.0000	0.9999	0.9996	0.9987	0.9962	0.9910	0.9812	0.9643	0.9375
6	1.0000	1.0000	1.0000	0.9999	0.9998	0.9994	0.9984	0.9963	0.9922
7	1.0000	1.0000	1.0000	1.0000	1.0000	1.0000	1.0000	1.0000	1.0000

x	p = 0.55	p = 0.60	p = 0.65	p = 0.70	p = 0.75	p = 0.80	p = 0.85	p = 0.90	p = 0.91
0	0.0037	0.0016	0.0006	0.0002	0.0001	0.0000	0.0000	0.0000	0.0000
1	0.0357	0.0188	0.0090	0.0038	0.0013	0.0004	0.0001	0.0000	0.0000
2	0.1529	0.0963	0.0556	0.0288	0.0129	0.0047	0.0012	0.0002	0.0001
3	0.3917	0.2898	0.1998	0.1260	0.0706	0.0333	0.0121	0.0027	0.0018
4	0.6836	0.5801	0.4677	0.3529	0.2436	0.1480	0.0738	0.0257	0.0193
5	0.8976	0.8414	0.7662	0.6706	0.5551	0.4233	0.2834	0.1497	0.1255
6	0.9848	0.9720	0.9510	0.9176	0.8665	0.7903	0.6794	0.5217	0.4832
7	1.0000	1.0000	1.0000	1.0000	1.0000	1.0000	1.0000	1.0000	1.0000

x	p = 0.92	p = 0.93	p = 0.94	p = 0.95	p = 0.96	p = 0.97	p = 0.98	p = 0.99	p = 1.00
0	0.0000	0.0000	0.0000	0.0000	0.0000	0.0000	0.0000	0.0000	0.0000
1	0.0000	0.0000	0.0000	0.0000	0.0000	0.0000	0.0000	0.0000	0.0000
2	0.0001	0.0000	0.0000	0.0000	0.0000	0.0000	0.0000	0.0000	0.0000
3	0.0012	0.0007	0.0004	0.0002	0.0001	0.0000	0.0000	0.0000	0.0000
4	0.0140	0.0097	0.0063	0.0038	0.0020	0.0009	0.0003	0.0000	0.0000
5	0.1026	0.0813	0.0618	0.0444	0.0294	0.0171	0.0079	0.0020	0.0000
6	0.4422	0.3983	0.3515	0.3017	0.2486	0.1920	0.1319	0.0679	0.0000
7	1.0000	1.0000	1.0000	1.0000	1.0000	1.0000	1.0000	1.0000	1.0000

(continued)

$n = 8$

x	p = 0.01	p = 0.02	p = 0.03	p = 0.04	p = 0.05	p = 0.06	p = 0.07	p = 0.08	p = 0.09
0	0.9227	0.8508	0.7837	0.7214	0.6634	0.6096	0.5596	0.5132	0.4703
1	0.9973	0.9897	0.9777	0.9619	0.9428	0.9208	0.8965	0.8702	0.8423
2	0.9999	0.9996	0.9987	0.9969	0.9942	0.9904	0.9853	0.9789	0.9711
3	1.0000	1.0000	0.9999	0.9998	0.9996	0.9993	0.9987	0.9978	0.9966
4	1.0000	1.0000	1.0000	1.0000	1.0000	1.0000	0.9999	0.9999	0.9997
5	1.0000	1.0000	1.0000	1.0000	1.0000	1.0000	1.0000	1.0000	1.0000
6	1.0000	1.0000	1.0000	1.0000	1.0000	1.0000	1.0000	1.0000	1.0000
7	1.0000	1.0000	1.0000	1.0000	1.0000	1.0000	1.0000	1.0000	1.0000
8	1.0000	1.0000	1.0000	1.0000	1.0000	1.0000	1.0000	1.0000	1.0000

x	p = 0.10	p = 0.15	p = 0.20	p = 0.25	p = 0.30	p = 0.35	p = 0.40	p = 0.45	p = 0.50
0	0.4305	0.2725	0.1678	0.1001	0.0576	0.0319	0.0168	0.0084	0.0039
1	0.8131	0.6572	0.5033	0.3671	0.2553	0.1691	0.1064	0.0632	0.0352
2	0.9619	0.8948	0.7969	0.6785	0.5518	0.4278	0.3154	0.2201	0.1445
3	0.9950	0.9786	0.9437	0.8862	0.8059	0.7064	0.5941	0.4770	0.3633
4	0.9996	0.9971	0.9896	0.9727	0.9420	0.8939	0.8263	0.7396	0.6367
5	1.0000	0.9998	0.9988	0.9958	0.9887	0.9747	0.9502	0.9115	0.8555
6	1.0000	1.0000	0.9999	0.9996	0.9987	0.9964	0.9915	0.9819	0.9648
7	1.0000	1.0000	1.0000	1.0000	0.9999	0.9998	0.9993	0.9983	0.9961
8	1.0000	1.0000	1.0000	1.0000	1.0000	1.0000	1.0000	1.0000	1.0000

x	p = 0.55	p = 0.60	p = 0.65	p = 0.70	p = 0.75	p = 0.80	p = 0.85	p = 0.90	p = 0.91
0	0.0017	0.0007	0.0002	0.0001	0.0000	0.0000	0.0000	0.0000	0.0000
1	0.0181	0.0085	0.0036	0.0013	0.0004	0.0001	0.0000	0.0000	0.0000
2	0.0885	0.0498	0.0253	0.0113	0.0042	0.0012	0.0002	0.0000	0.0000
3	0.2604	0.1737	0.1061	0.0580	0.0273	0.0104	0.0029	0.0004	0.0003
4	0.5230	0.4059	0.2936	0.1941	0.1138	0.0563	0.0214	0.0050	0.0034
5	0.7799	0.6846	0.5722	0.4482	0.3215	0.2031	0.1052	0.0381	0.0289
6	0.9368	0.8936	0.8309	0.7447	0.6329	0.4967	0.3428	0.1869	0.1577
7	0.9916	0.9832	0.9681	0.9424	0.8999	0.8322	0.7275	0.5695	0.5297
8	1.0000	1.0000	1.0000	1.0000	1.0000	1.0000	1.0000	1.0000	1.0000

x	p = 0.92	p = 0.93	p = 0.94	p = 0.95	p = 0.96	p = 0.97	p = 0.98	p = 0.99	p = 1.00
0	0.0000	0.0000	0.0000	0.0000	0.0000	0.0000	0.0000	0.0000	0.0000
1	0.0000	0.0000	0.0000	0.0000	0.0000	0.0000	0.0000	0.0000	0.0000
2	0.0000	0.0000	0.0000	0.0000	0.0000	0.0000	0.0000	0.0000	0.0000
3	0.0001	0.0001	0.0000	0.0000	0.0000	0.0000	0.0000	0.0000	0.0000
4	0.0022	0.0013	0.0007	0.0004	0.0002	0.0001	0.0000	0.0000	0.0000
5	0.0211	0.0147	0.0096	0.0058	0.0031	0.0013	0.0004	0.0001	0.0000
6	0.1298	0.1035	0.0792	0.0572	0.0381	0.0223	0.0103	0.0027	0.0000
7	0.4868	0.4404	0.3904	0.3366	0.2786	0.2163	0.1492	0.0773	0.0000
8	1.0000	1.0000	1.0000	1.0000	1.0000	1.0000	1.0000	1.0000	1.0000

$n = 9$

x	p = 0.01	p = 0.02	p = 0.03	p = 0.04	p = 0.05	p = 0.06	p = 0.07	p = 0.08	p = 0.09
0	0.9135	0.8337	0.7602	0.6925	0.6302	0.5730	0.5204	0.4722	0.4279
1	0.9966	0.9869	0.9718	0.9522	0.9288	0.9022	0.8729	0.8417	0.8088
2	0.9999	0.9994	0.9980	0.9955	0.9916	0.9862	0.9791	0.9702	0.9595
3	1.0000	1.0000	0.9999	0.9997	0.9994	0.9987	0.9977	0.9963	0.9943
4	1.0000	1.0000	1.0000	1.0000	1.0000	0.9999	0.9998	0.9997	0.9995
5	1.0000	1.0000	1.0000	1.0000	1.0000	1.0000	1.0000	1.0000	1.0000
6	1.0000	1.0000	1.0000	1.0000	1.0000	1.0000	1.0000	1.0000	1.0000
7	1.0000	1.0000	1.0000	1.0000	1.0000	1.0000	1.0000	1.0000	1.0000
8	1.0000	1.0000	1.0000	1.0000	1.0000	1.0000	1.0000	1.0000	1.0000
9	1.0000	1.0000	1.0000	1.0000	1.0000	1.0000	1.0000	1.0000	1.0000

x	p = 0.10	p = 0.15	p = 0.20	p = 0.25	p = 0.30	p = 0.35	p = 0.40	p = 0.45	p = 0.50
0	0.3874	0.2316	0.1342	0.0751	0.0404	0.0207	0.0101	0.0046	0.0020
1	0.7748	0.5995	0.4362	0.3003	0.1960	0.1211	0.0705	0.0385	0.0195
2	0.9470	0.8591	0.7382	0.6007	0.4628	0.3373	0.2318	0.1495	0.0898
3	0.9917	0.9661	0.9144	0.8343	0.7297	0.6089	0.4826	0.3614	0.2539
4	0.9991	0.9944	0.9804	0.9511	0.9012	0.8283	0.7334	0.6214	0.5000
5	0.9999	0.9994	0.9969	0.9900	0.9747	0.9464	0.9006	0.8342	0.7461
6	1.0000	1.0000	0.9997	0.9987	0.9957	0.9888	0.9750	0.9502	0.9102
7	1.0000	1.0000	1.0000	0.9999	0.9996	0.9986	0.9962	0.9909	0.9805
8	1.0000	1.0000	1.0000	1.0000	1.0000	0.9999	0.9997	0.9992	0.9980
9	1.0000	1.0000	1.0000	1.0000	1.0000	1.0000	1.0000	1.0000	1.0000

x	p = 0.55	p = 0.60	p = 0.65	p = 0.70	p = 0.75	p = 0.80	p = 0.85	p = 0.90	p = 0.91
0	0.0008	0.0003	0.0001	0.0000	0.0000	0.0000	0.0000	0.0000	0.0000
1	0.0091	0.0038	0.0014	0.0004	0.0001	0.0000	0.0000	0.0000	0.0000
2	0.0498	0.0250	0.0112	0.0043	0.0013	0.0003	0.0000	0.0000	0.0000
3	0.1658	0.0994	0.0536	0.0253	0.0100	0.0031	0.0006	0.0001	0.0000
4	0.3786	0.2666	0.1717	0.0988	0.0489	0.0196	0.0056	0.0009	0.0005
5	0.6386	0.5174	0.3911	0.2703	0.1657	0.0856	0.0339	0.0083	0.0057
6	0.8505	0.7682	0.6627	0.5372	0.3993	0.2618	0.1409	0.0530	0.0405
7	0.9615	0.9295	0.8789	0.8040	0.6997	0.5638	0.4005	0.2252	0.1912
8	0.9954	0.9899	0.9793	0.9596	0.9249	0.8658	0.7684	0.6126	0.5721
9	1.0000	1.0000	1.0000	1.0000	1.0000	1.0000	1.0000	1.0000	1.0000

x	p = 0.92	p = 0.93	p = 0.94	p = 0.95	p = 0.96	p = 0.97	p = 0.98	p = 0.99	p = 1.00
0	0.0000	0.0000	0.0000	0.0000	0.0000	0.0000	0.0000	0.0000	0.0000
1	0.0000	0.0000	0.0000	0.0000	0.0000	0.0000	0.0000	0.0000	0.0000
2	0.0000	0.0000	0.0000	0.0000	0.0000	0.0000	0.0000	0.0000	0.0000
3	0.0000	0.0000	0.0000	0.0000	0.0000	0.0000	0.0000	0.0000	0.0000
4	0.0003	0.0002	0.0001	0.0000	0.0000	0.0000	0.0000	0.0000	0.0000
5	0.0037	0.0023	0.0013	0.0006	0.0003	0.0001	0.0000	0.0000	0.0000
6	0.0298	0.0209	0.0138	0.0084	0.0045	0.0020	0.0006	0.0001	0.0000
7	0.1583	0.1271	0.0978	0.0712	0.0478	0.0282	0.0131	0.0034	0.0000
8	0.5278	0.4796	0.4270	0.3698	0.3075	0.2398	0.1663	0.0865	0.0000
9	1.0000	1.0000	1.0000	1.0000	1.0000	1.0000	1.0000	1.0000	1.0000

$$n = 10$$

x	p = 0.01	p = 0.02	p = 0.03	p = 0.04	p = 0.05	p = 0.06	p = 0.07	p = 0.08	p = 0.09
0	0.9044	0.8171	0.7374	0.6648	0.5987	0.5386	0.4840	0.4344	0.3894
1	0.9957	0.9838	0.9655	0.9418	0.9139	0.8824	0.8483	0.8121	0.7746
2	0.9999	0.9991	0.9972	0.9938	0.9885	0.9812	0.9717	0.9599	0.9460
3	1.0000	1.0000	0.9999	0.9996	0.9990	0.9980	0.9964	0.9942	0.9912
4	1.0000	1.0000	1.0000	1.0000	0.9999	0.9998	0.9997	0.9994	0.9990
5	1.0000	1.0000	1.0000	1.0000	1.0000	1.0000	1.0000	1.0000	0.9999
6	1.0000	1.0000	1.0000	1.0000	1.0000	1.0000	1.0000	1.0000	1.0000
7	1.0000	1.0000	1.0000	1.0000	1.0000	1.0000	1.0000	1.0000	1.0000
8	1.0000	1.0000	1.0000	1.0000	1.0000	1.0000	1.0000	1.0000	1.0000
9	1.0000	1.0000	1.0000	1.0000	1.0000	1.0000	1.0000	1.0000	1.0000
10	1.0000	1.0000	1.0000	1.0000	1.0000	1.0000	1.0000	1.0000	1.0000

x	p = 0.10	p = 0.15	p = 0.20	p = 0.25	p = 0.30	p = 0.35	p = 0.40	p = 0.45	p = 0.50
0	0.3487	0.1969	0.1074	0.0563	0.0282	0.0135	0.0060	0.0025	0.0010
1	0.7361	0.5443	0.3758	0.2440	0.1493	0.0860	0.0464	0.0233	0.0107
2	0.9298	0.8202	0.6778	0.5256	0.3828	0.2616	0.1673	0.0996	0.0547
3	0.9872	0.9500	0.8791	0.7759	0.6496	0.5138	0.3823	0.2660	0.1719
4	0.9984	0.9901	0.9672	0.9219	0.8497	0.7515	0.6331	0.5044	0.3770
5	0.9999	0.9986	0.9936	0.9803	0.9527	0.9051	0.8338	0.7384	0.6230
6	1.0000	0.9999	0.9991	0.9965	0.9894	0.9740	0.9452	0.8980	0.8281
7	1.0000	1.0000	0.9999	0.9996	0.9984	0.9952	0.9877	0.9726	0.9453
8	1.0000	1.0000	1.0000	1.0000	0.9999	0.9995	0.9983	0.9955	0.9893
9	1.0000	1.0000	1.0000	1.0000	1.0000	1.0000	0.9999	0.9997	0.9990
10	1.0000	1.0000	1.0000	1.0000	1.0000	1.0000	1.0000	1.0000	1.0000

x	p = 0.55	p = 0.60	p = 0.65	p = 0.70	p = 0.75	p = 0.80	p = 0.85	p = 0.90	p = 0.91
0	0.0003	0.0001	0.0000	0.0000	0.0000	0.0000	0.0000	0.0000	0.0000
1	0.0045	0.0017	0.0005	0.0001	0.0000	0.0000	0.0000	0.0000	0.0000
2	0.0274	0.0123	0.0048	0.0016	0.0004	0.0001	0.0000	0.0000	0.0000
3	0.1020	0.0548	0.0260	0.0106	0.0035	0.0009	0.0001	0.0000	0.0000
4	0.2616	0.1662	0.0949	0.0473	0.0197	0.0064	0.0014	0.0001	0.0001
5	0.4956	0.3669	0.2485	0.1503	0.0781	0.0328	0.0099	0.0016	0.0010
6	0.7340	0.6177	0.4862	0.3504	0.2241	0.1209	0.0500	0.0128	0.0088
7	0.9004	0.8327	0.7384	0.6172	0.4744	0.3222	0.1798	0.0702	0.0540
8	0.9767	0.9536	0.9140	0.8507	0.7560	0.6242	0.4557	0.2639	0.2254
9	0.9975	0.9940	0.9865	0.9718	0.9437	0.8926	0.8031	0.6513	0.6106
10	1.0000	1.0000	1.0000	1.0000	1.0000	1.0000	1.0000	1.0000	1.0000

x	p = 0.92	p = 0.93	p = 0.94	p = 0.95	p = 0.96	p = 0.97	p = 0.98	p = 0.99	p = 1.00
0	0.0000	0.0000	0.0000	0.0000	0.0000	0.0000	0.0000	0.0000	0.0000
1	0.0000	0.0000	0.0000	0.0000	0.0000	0.0000	0.0000	0.0000	0.0000
2	0.0000	0.0000	0.0000	0.0000	0.0000	0.0000	0.0000	0.0000	0.0000

(continued)

x									
3	0.0000	0.0000	0.0000	0.0000	0.0000	0.0000	0.0000	0.0000	0.0000
4	0.0000	0.0000	0.0000	0.0000	0.0000	0.0000	0.0000	0.0000	0.0000
5	0.0006	0.0003	0.0002	0.0001	0.0000	0.0000	0.0000	0.0000	0.0000
6	0.0058	0.0036	0.0020	0.0010	0.0004	0.0001	0.0000	0.0000	0.0000
7	0.0401	0.0283	0.0188	0.0115	0.0062	0.0028	0.0009	0.0001	0.0000
8	0.1879	0.1517	0.1176	0.0861	0.0582	0.0345	0.0162	0.0043	0.0000
9	0.5656	0.5160	0.4614	0.4013	0.3352	0.2626	0.1829	0.0956	0.0000
10	1.0000	1.0000	1.0000	1.0000	1.0000	1.0000	1.0000	1.0000	1.0000

$n = 11$

x	$p = 0.01$	$p = 0.02$	$p = 0.03$	$p = 0.04$	$p = 0.05$	$p = 0.06$	$p = 0.07$	$p = 0.08$	$p = 0.09$
0	0.8953	0.8007	0.7153	0.6382	0.5688	0.5063	0.4501	0.3996	0.3544
1	0.9948	0.9805	0.9587	0.9308	0.8981	0.8618	0.8228	0.7819	0.7399
2	0.9998	0.9988	0.9963	0.9917	0.9848	0.9752	0.9630	0.9481	0.9305
3	1.0000	1.0000	0.9998	0.9993	0.9984	0.9970	0.9947	0.9915	0.9871
4	1.0000	1.0000	1.0000	1.0000	0.9999	0.9997	0.9995	0.9990	0.9983
5	1.0000	1.0000	1.0000	1.0000	1.0000	1.0000	1.0000	0.9999	0.9998
6	1.0000	1.0000	1.0000	1.0000	1.0000	1.0000	1.0000	1.0000	1.0000
7	1.0000	1.0000	1.0000	1.0000	1.0000	1.0000	1.0000	1.0000	1.0000
8	1.0000	1.0000	1.0000	1.0000	1.0000	1.0000	1.0000	1.0000	1.0000
9	1.0000	1.0000	1.0000	1.0000	1.0000	1.0000	1.0000	1.0000	1.0000
10	1.0000	1.0000	1.0000	1.0000	1.0000	1.0000	1.0000	1.0000	1.0000
11	1.0000	1.0000	1.0000	1.0000	1.0000	1.0000	1.0000	1.0000	1.0000

x	$p = 0.10$	$p = 0.15$	$p = 0.20$	$p = 0.25$	$p = 0.30$	$p = 0.35$	$p = 0.40$	$p = 0.45$	$p = 0.50$
0	0.3138	0.1673	0.0859	0.0422	0.0198	0.0088	0.0036	0.0014	0.0005
1	0.6974	0.4922	0.3221	0.1971	0.1130	0.0606	0.0302	0.0139	0.0059
2	0.9104	0.7788	0.6174	0.4552	0.3127	0.2001	0.1189	0.0652	0.0327
3	0.9815	0.9306	0.8389	0.7133	0.5696	0.4256	0.2963	0.1911	0.1133
4	0.9972	0.9841	0.9496	0.8854	0.7897	0.6683	0.5328	0.3971	0.2744
5	0.9997	0.9973	0.9883	0.9657	0.9218	0.8513	0.7535	0.6331	0.5000
6	1.0000	0.9997	0.9980	0.9924	0.9784	0.9499	0.9006	0.8262	0.7256
7	1.0000	1.0000	0.9998	0.9988	0.9957	0.9878	0.9707	0.9390	0.8867
8	1.0000	1.0000	1.0000	0.9999	0.9994	0.9980	0.9941	0.9852	0.9673
9	1.0000	1.0000	1.0000	1.0000	1.0000	0.9998	0.9993	0.9978	0.9941
10	1.0000	1.0000	1.0000	1.0000	1.0000	1.0000	1.0000	0.9998	0.9995
11	1.0000	1.0000	1.0000	1.0000	1.0000	1.0000	1.0000	1.0000	1.0000

x	$p = 0.55$	$p = 0.60$	$p = 0.65$	$p = 0.70$	$p = 0.75$	$p = 0.80$	$p = 0.85$	$p = 0.90$	$p = 0.91$
0	0.0002	0.0000	0.0000	0.0000	0.0000	0.0000	0.0000	0.0000	0.0000
1	0.0022	0.0007	0.0002	0.0000	0.0000	0.0000	0.0000	0.0000	0.0000
2	0.0148	0.0059	0.0020	0.0006	0.0001	0.0000	0.0000	0.0000	0.0000
3	0.0610	0.0293	0.0122	0.0043	0.0012	0.0002	0.0000	0.0000	0.0000
4	0.1738	0.0994	0.0501	0.0216	0.0076	0.0020	0.0003	0.0000	0.0000
5	0.3669	0.2465	0.1487	0.0782	0.0343	0.0117	0.0027	0.0003	0.0002
6	0.6029	0.4672	0.3317	0.2103	0.1146	0.0504	0.0159	0.0028	0.0017
7	0.8089	0.7037	0.5744	0.4304	0.2867	0.1611	0.0694	0.0185	0.0129
8	0.9348	0.8811	0.7999	0.6873	0.5448	0.3826	0.2212	0.0896	0.0695
9	0.9861	0.9698	0.9394	0.8870	0.8029	0.6779	0.5078	0.3026	0.2601
10	0.9986	0.9964	0.9912	0.9802	0.9578	0.9141	0.8327	0.6862	0.6456
11	1.0000	1.0000	1.0000	1.0000	1.0000	1.0000	1.0000	1.0000	1.0000

x	$p = 0.92$	$p = 0.93$	$p = 0.94$	$p = 0.95$	$p = 0.96$	$p = 0.97$	$p = 0.98$	$p = 0.99$	$p = 1.00$
0	0.0000	0.0000	0.0000	0.0000	0.0000	0.0000	0.0000	0.0000	0.0000
1	0.0000	0.0000	0.0000	0.0000	0.0000	0.0000	0.0000	0.0000	0.0000
2	0.0000	0.0000	0.0000	0.0000	0.0000	0.0000	0.0000	0.0000	0.0000
3	0.0000	0.0000	0.0000	0.0000	0.0000	0.0000	0.0000	0.0000	0.0000
4	0.0000	0.0000	0.0000	0.0000	0.0000	0.0000	0.0000	0.0000	0.0000
5	0.0001	0.0000	0.0000	0.0000	0.0000	0.0000	0.0000	0.0000	0.0000
6	0.0010	0.0005	0.0003	0.0001	0.0000	0.0000	0.0000	0.0000	0.0000
7	0.0085	0.0053	0.0030	0.0016	0.0007	0.0002	0.0000	0.0000	0.0000
8	0.0519	0.0370	0.0248	0.0152	0.0083	0.0037	0.0012	0.0002	0.0000
9	0.2181	0.1772	0.1382	0.1019	0.0692	0.0413	0.0195	0.0052	0.0000
10	0.6004	0.5499	0.4937	0.4312	0.3618	0.2847	0.1993	0.1047	0.0000
11	1.0000	1.0000	1.0000	1.0000	1.0000	1.0000	1.0000	1.0000	1.0000

$n = 12$

x	p = 0.01	p = 0.02	p = 0.03	p = 0.04	p = 0.05	p = 0.06	p = 0.07	p = 0.08	p = 0.09
0	0.8864	0.7847	0.6938	0.6127	0.5404	0.4759	0.4186	0.3677	0.3225
1	0.9938	0.9769	0.9514	0.9191	0.8816	0.8405	0.7967	0.7513	0.7052
2	0.9998	0.9985	0.9952	0.9893	0.9804	0.9684	0.9532	0.9348	0.9134
3	1.0000	0.9999	0.9997	0.9990	0.9978	0.9957	0.9925	0.9880	0.9820
4	1.0000	1.0000	1.0000	0.9999	0.9998	0.9996	0.9991	0.9984	0.9973
5	1.0000	1.0000	1.0000	1.0000	1.0000	1.0000	0.9999	0.9998	0.9997
6	1.0000	1.0000	1.0000	1.0000	1.0000	1.0000	1.0000	1.0000	1.0000
7	1.0000	1.0000	1.0000	1.0000	1.0000	1.0000	1.0000	1.0000	1.0000
8	1.0000	1.0000	1.0000	1.0000	1.0000	1.0000	1.0000	1.0000	1.0000
9	1.0000	1.0000	1.0000	1.0000	1.0000	1.0000	1.0000	1.0000	1.0000
10	1.0000	1.0000	1.0000	1.0000	1.0000	1.0000	1.0000	1.0000	1.0000
11	1.0000	1.0000	1.0000	1.0000	1.0000	1.0000	1.0000	1.0000	1.0000
12	1.0000	1.0000	1.0000	1.0000	1.0000	1.0000	1.0000	1.0000	1.0000

x	p = 0.10	p = 0.15	p = 0.20	p = 0.25	p = 0.30	p = 0.35	p = 0.40	p = 0.45	p = 0.50
0	0.2824	0.1422	0.0687	0.0317	0.0138	0.0057	0.0022	0.0008	0.0002
1	0.6590	0.4435	0.2749	0.1584	0.0850	0.0424	0.0196	0.0083	0.0032
2	0.8891	0.7358	0.5583	0.3907	0.2528	0.1513	0.0834	0.0421	0.0193
3	0.9744	0.9078	0.7946	0.6488	0.4925	0.3467	0.2253	0.1345	0.0730
4	0.9957	0.9761	0.9274	0.8424	0.7237	0.5833	0.4382	0.3044	0.1938
5	0.9995	0.9954	0.9806	0.9456	0.8822	0.7873	0.6652	0.5269	0.3872
6	0.9999	0.9993	0.9961	0.9857	0.9614	0.9154	0.8418	0.7393	0.6128
7	1.0000	0.9999	0.9994	0.9972	0.9905	0.9745	0.9427	0.8883	0.8062
8	1.0000	1.0000	0.9999	0.9996	0.9983	0.9944	0.9847	0.9644	0.9270
9	1.0000	1.0000	1.0000	1.0000	0.9998	0.9992	0.9972	0.9921	0.9807
10	1.0000	1.0000	1.0000	1.0000	1.0000	0.9999	0.9997	0.9989	0.9968
11	1.0000	1.0000	1.0000	1.0000	1.0000	1.0000	1.0000	0.9999	0.9998
12	1.0000	1.0000	1.0000	1.0000	1.0000	1.0000	1.0000	1.0000	1.0000

x	p = 0.55	p = 0.60	p = 0.65	p = 0.70	p = 0.75	p = 0.80	p = 0.85	p = 0.90	p = 0.91
0	0.0001	0.0000	0.0000	0.0000	0.0000	0.0000	0.0000	0.0000	0.0000
1	0.0011	0.0003	0.0001	0.0000	0.0000	0.0000	0.0000	0.0000	0.0000
2	0.0079	0.0028	0.0008	0.0002	0.0000	0.0000	0.0000	0.0000	0.0000
3	0.0356	0.0153	0.0056	0.0017	0.0004	0.0001	0.0000	0.0000	0.0000
4	0.1117	0.0573	0.0255	0.0095	0.0028	0.0006	0.0001	0.0000	0.0000
5	0.2607	0.1582	0.0846	0.0386	0.0143	0.0039	0.0007	0.0001	0.0000
6	0.4731	0.3348	0.2127	0.1178	0.0544	0.0194	0.0046	0.0005	0.0003
7	0.6956	0.5618	0.4167	0.2763	0.1576	0.0726	0.0239	0.0043	0.0027
8	0.8655	0.7747	0.6533	0.5075	0.3512	0.2054	0.0922	0.0256	0.0180
9	0.9579	0.9166	0.8487	0.7472	0.6093	0.4417	0.2642	0.1109	0.0866
10	0.9917	0.9804	0.9576	0.9150	0.8416	0.7251	0.5565	0.3410	0.2948
11	0.9992	0.9978	0.9943	0.9862	0.9683	0.9313	0.8578	0.7176	0.6775
12	1.0000	1.0000	1.0000	1.0000	1.0000	1.0000	1.0000	1.0000	1.0000

x	p = 0.92	p = 0.93	p = 0.94	p = 0.95	p = 0.96	p = 0.97	p = 0.98	p = 0.99	p = 1.00
0	0.0000	0.0000	0.0000	0.0000	0.0000	0.0000	0.0000	0.0000	0.0000
1	0.0000	0.0000	0.0000	0.0000	0.0000	0.0000	0.0000	0.0000	0.0000
2	0.0000	0.0000	0.0000	0.0000	0.0000	0.0000	0.0000	0.0000	0.0000
3	0.0000	0.0000	0.0000	0.0000	0.0000	0.0000	0.0000	0.0000	0.0000
4	0.0000	0.0000	0.0000	0.0000	0.0000	0.0000	0.0000	0.0000	0.0000
5	0.0000	0.0000	0.0000	0.0000	0.0000	0.0000	0.0000	0.0000	0.0000
6	0.0002	0.0001	0.0000	0.0000	0.0000	0.0000	0.0000	0.0000	0.0000
7	0.0016	0.0009	0.0004	0.0002	0.0001	0.0000	0.0000	0.0000	0.0000
8	0.0120	0.0075	0.0043	0.0022	0.0010	0.0003	0.0001	0.0000	0.0000
9	0.0652	0.0468	0.0316	0.0196	0.0107	0.0048	0.0015	0.0002	0.0000
10	0.2487	0.2033	0.1595	0.1184	0.0809	0.0486	0.0231	0.0062	0.0000
11	0.6323	0.5814	0.5241	0.4596	0.3873	0.3062	0.2153	0.1136	0.0000
12	1.0000	1.0000	1.0000	1.0000	1.0000	1.0000	1.0000	1.0000	1.0000

$n = 13$

x	p = 0.01	p = 0.02	p = 0.03	p = 0.04	p = 0.05	p = 0.06	p = 0.07	p = 0.08	p = 0.09
0	0.8775	0.7690	0.6730	0.5882	0.5133	0.4474	0.3893	0.3383	0.2935
1	0.9928	0.9730	0.9436	0.9068	0.8646	0.8186	0.7702	0.7206	0.6707
2	0.9997	0.9980	0.9938	0.9865	0.9755	0.9608	0.9422	0.9201	0.8946

3	1.0000	0.9999	0.9995	0.9986	0.9969	0.9940	0.9897	0.9837	0.9758
4	1.0000	1.0000	1.0000	0.9999	0.9997	0.9993	0.9987	0.9976	0.9959
5	1.0000	1.0000	1.0000	1.0000	1.0000	0.9999	0.9999	0.9997	0.9995
6	1.0000	1.0000	1.0000	1.0000	1.0000	1.0000	1.0000	1.0000	0.9999
7	1.0000	1.0000	1.0000	1.0000	1.0000	1.0000	1.0000	1.0000	1.0000
8	1.0000	1.0000	1.0000	1.0000	1.0000	1.0000	1.0000	1.0000	1.0000
9	1.0000	1.0000	1.0000	1.0000	1.0000	1.0000	1.0000	1.0000	1.0000
10	1.0000	1.0000	1.0000	1.0000	1.0000	1.0000	1.0000	1.0000	1.0000
11	1.0000	1.0000	1.0000	1.0000	1.0000	1.0000	1.0000	1.0000	1.0000
12	1.0000	1.0000	1.0000	1.0000	1.0000	1.0000	1.0000	1.0000	1.0000
13	1.0000	1.0000	1.0000	1.0000	1.0000	1.0000	1.0000	1.0000	1.0000

x	$p = 0.10$	$p = 0.15$	$p = 0.20$	$p = 0.25$	$p = 0.30$	$p = 0.35$	$p = 0.40$	$p = 0.45$	$p = 0.50$
0	0.2542	0.1209	0.0550	0.0238	0.0097	0.0037	0.0013	0.0004	0.0001
1	0.6213	0.3983	0.2336	0.1267	0.0637	0.0296	0.0126	0.0049	0.0017
2	0.8661	0.6920	0.5017	0.3326	0.2025	0.1132	0.0579	0.0269	0.0112
3	0.9658	0.8820	0.7473	0.5843	0.4206	0.2783	0.1686	0.0929	0.0461
4	0.9935	0.9658	0.9009	0.7940	0.6543	0.5005	0.3530	0.2279	0.1334
5	0.9991	0.9925	0.9700	0.9198	0.8346	0.7159	0.5744	0.4268	0.2905
6	0.9999	0.9987	0.9930	0.9757	0.9376	0.8705	0.7712	0.6437	0.5000
7	1.0000	0.9998	0.9988	0.9944	0.9818	0.9538	0.9023	0.8212	0.7095
8	1.0000	1.0000	0.9998	0.9990	0.9960	0.9874	0.9679	0.9302	0.8666
9	1.0000	1.0000	1.0000	0.9999	0.9993	0.9975	0.9922	0.9797	0.9539
10	1.0000	1.0000	1.0000	1.0000	0.9999	0.9997	0.9987	0.9959	0.9888
11	1.0000	1.0000	1.0000	1.0000	1.0000	1.0000	0.9999	0.9995	0.9983
12	1.0000	1.0000	1.0000	1.0000	1.0000	1.0000	1.0000	1.0000	0.9999
13	1.0000	1.0000	1.0000	1.0000	1.0000	1.0000	1.0000	1.0000	1.0000

x	$p = 0.55$	$p = 0.60$	$p = 0.65$	$p = 0.70$	$p = 0.75$	$p = 0.80$	$p = 0.85$	$p = 0.90$	$p = 0.91$
0	0.0000	0.0000	0.0000	0.0000	0.0000	0.0000	0.0000	0.0000	0.0000
1	0.0005	0.0001	0.0000	0.0000	0.0000	0.0000	0.0000	0.0000	0.0000
2	0.0041	0.0013	0.0003	0.0001	0.0000	0.0000	0.0000	0.0000	0.0000
3	0.0203	0.0078	0.0025	0.0007	0.0001	0.0000	0.0000	0.0000	0.0000
4	0.0698	0.0321	0.0126	0.0040	0.0010	0.0002	0.0000	0.0000	0.0000
5	0.1788	0.0977	0.0462	0.0182	0.0056	0.0012	0.0002	0.0000	0.0000
6	0.3563	0.2288	0.1295	0.0624	0.0243	0.0070	0.0013	0.0001	0.0001
7	0.5732	0.4256	0.2841	0.1654	0.0802	0.0300	0.0075	0.0009	0.0005
8	0.7721	0.6470	0.4995	0.3457	0.2060	0.0991	0.0342	0.0065	0.0041
9	0.9071	0.8314	0.7217	0.5794	0.4157	0.2527	0.1180	0.0342	0.0242
10	0.9731	0.9421	0.8868	0.7975	0.6674	0.4983	0.3080	0.1339	0.1054
11	0.9951	0.9874	0.9704	0.9363	0.8733	0.7664	0.6017	0.3787	0.3293
12	0.9996	0.9987	0.9963	0.9903	0.9762	0.9450	0.8791	0.7458	0.7065
13	1.0000	1.0000	1.0000	1.0000	1.0000	1.0000	1.0000	1.0000	1.0000

x	$p = 0.92$	$p = 0.93$	$p = 0.94$	$p = 0.95$	$p = 0.96$	$p = 0.97$	$p = 0.98$	$p = 0.99$	$p = 1.00$
0	0.0000	0.0000	0.0000	0.0000	0.0000	0.0000	0.0000	0.0000	0.0000
1	0.0000	0.0000	0.0000	0.0000	0.0000	0.0000	0.0000	0.0000	0.0000
2	0.0000	0.0000	0.0000	0.0000	0.0000	0.0000	0.0000	0.0000	0.0000
3	0.0000	0.0000	0.0000	0.0000	0.0000	0.0000	0.0000	0.0000	0.0000
4	0.0000	0.0000	0.0000	0.0000	0.0000	0.0000	0.0000	0.0000	0.0000
5	0.0000	0.0000	0.0000	0.0000	0.0000	0.0000	0.0000	0.0000	0.0000
6	0.0000	0.0000	0.0000	0.0000	0.0000	0.0000	0.0000	0.0000	0.0000
7	0.0003	0.0001	0.0001	0.0000	0.0000	0.0000	0.0000	0.0000	0.0000
8	0.0024	0.0013	0.0007	0.0003	0.0001	0.0000	0.0000	0.0000	0.0000
9	0.0163	0.0103	0.0060	0.0031	0.0014	0.0005	0.0001	0.0000	0.0000
10	0.0799	0.0578	0.0392	0.0245	0.0135	0.0062	0.0020	0.0003	0.0000
11	0.2794	0.2298	0.1814	0.1354	0.0932	0.0564	0.0270	0.0072	0.0000
12	0.6617	0.6107	0.5526	0.4867	0.4118	0.3270	0.2310	0.1225	0.0000
13	1.0000	1.0000	1.0000	1.0000	1.0000	1.0000	1.0000	1.0000	1.0000

$n = 14$

x	$p = 0.01$	$p = 0.02$	$p = 0.03$	$p = 0.04$	$p = 0.05$	$p = 0.06$	$p = 0.07$	$p = 0.08$	$p = 0.09$
0	0.8687	0.7536	0.6528	0.5647	0.4877	0.4205	0.3620	0.3112	0.2670
1	0.9916	0.9690	0.9355	0.8941	0.8470	0.7963	0.7436	0.6900	0.6368
2	0.9997	0.9975	0.9923	0.9833	0.9699	0.9522	0.9302	0.9042	0.8745
3	1.0000	0.9999	0.9994	0.9981	0.9958	0.9920	0.9864	0.9786	0.9685
4	1.0000	1.0000	1.0000	0.9998	0.9996	0.9990	0.9980	0.9965	0.9941
5	1.0000	1.0000	1.0000	1.0000	1.0000	0.9999	0.9998	0.9996	0.9992

6	1.0000	1.0000	1.0000	1.0000	1.0000	1.0000	1.0000	1.0000	0.9999
7	1.0000	1.0000	1.0000	1.0000	1.0000	1.0000	1.0000	1.0000	1.0000
8	1.0000	1.0000	1.0000	1.0000	1.0000	1.0000	1.0000	1.0000	1.0000
9	1.0000	1.0000	1.0000	1.0000	1.0000	1.0000	1.0000	1.0000	1.0000
10	1.0000	1.0000	1.0000	1.0000	1.0000	1.0000	1.0000	1.0000	1.0000
11	1.0000	1.0000	1.0000	1.0000	1.0000	1.0000	1.0000	1.0000	1.0000
12	1.0000	1.0000	1.0000	1.0000	1.0000	1.0000	1.0000	1.0000	1.0000
13	1.0000	1.0000	1.0000	1.0000	1.0000	1.0000	1.0000	1.0000	1.0000
14	1.0000	1.0000	1.0000	1.0000	1.0000	1.0000	1.0000	1.0000	1.0000

x	$p = 0.10$	$p = 0.15$	$p = 0.20$	$p = 0.25$	$p = 0.30$	$p = 0.35$	$p = 0.40$	$p = 0.45$	$p = 0.50$
0	0.2288	0.1028	0.0440	0.0178	0.0068	0.0024	0.0008	0.0002	0.0001
1	0.5846	0.3567	0.1979	0.1010	0.0475	0.0205	0.0081	0.0029	0.0009
2	0.8416	0.6479	0.4481	0.2811	0.1608	0.0839	0.0398	0.0170	0.0065
3	0.9559	0.8535	0.6982	0.5213	0.3552	0.2205	0.1243	0.0632	0.0287
4	0.9908	0.9533	0.8702	0.7415	0.5842	0.4227	0.2793	0.1672	0.0898
5	0.9985	0.9885	0.9561	0.8883	0.7805	0.6405	0.4859	0.3373	0.2120
6	0.9998	0.9978	0.9884	0.9617	0.9067	0.8164	0.6925	0.5461	0.3953
7	1.0000	0.9997	0.9976	0.9897	0.9685	0.9247	0.8499	0.7414	0.6047
8	1.0000	1.0000	0.9996	0.9978	0.9917	0.9757	0.9417	0.8811	0.7880
9	1.0000	1.0000	1.0000	0.9997	0.9983	0.9940	0.9825	0.9574	0.9102
10	1.0000	1.0000	1.0000	1.0000	0.9998	0.9989	0.9961	0.9886	0.9713
11	1.0000	1.0000	1.0000	1.0000	1.0000	0.9999	0.9994	0.9978	0.9935
12	1.0000	1.0000	1.0000	1.0000	1.0000	1.0000	0.9999	0.9997	0.9991
13	1.0000	1.0000	1.0000	1.0000	1.0000	1.0000	1.0000	1.0000	0.9999
14	1.0000	1.0000	1.0000	1.0000	1.0000	1.0000	1.0000	1.0000	1.0000

x	$p = 0.55$	$p = 0.60$	$p = 0.65$	$p = 0.70$	$p = 0.75$	$p = 0.80$	$p = 0.85$	$p = 0.90$	$p = 0.91$
0	0.0000	0.0000	0.0000	0.0000	0.0000	0.0000	0.0000	0.0000	0.0000
1	0.0003	0.0001	0.0000	0.0000	0.0000	0.0000	0.0000	0.0000	0.0000
2	0.0022	0.0006	0.0001	0.0000	0.0000	0.0000	0.0000	0.0000	0.0000
3	0.0114	0.0039	0.0011	0.0002	0.0000	0.0000	0.0000	0.0000	0.0000
4	0.0426	0.0175	0.0060	0.0017	0.0003	0.0000	0.0000	0.0000	0.0000
5	0.1189	0.0583	0.0243	0.0083	0.0022	0.0004	0.0000	0.0000	0.0000
6	0.2586	0.1501	0.0753	0.0315	0.0103	0.0024	0.0003	0.0000	0.0000
7	0.4539	0.3075	0.1836	0.0933	0.0383	0.0116	0.0022	0.0015	0.0008
8	0.6627	0.5141	0.3595	0.2195	0.1117	0.0439	0.0115	0.0092	0.0059
9	0.8328	0.7207	0.5773	0.4158	0.2585	0.1298	0.0467	0.0441	0.0315
10	0.9368	0.8757	0.7795	0.6448	0.4787	0.3018	0.1465	0.1584	0.1255
11	0.9830	0.9602	0.9161	0.8392	0.7189	0.5519	0.3521	0.4154	0.3632
12	0.9971	0.9919	0.9795	0.9525	0.8990	0.8021	0.6433	0.7712	0.7330
13	0.9998	0.9992	0.9976	0.9932	0.9822	0.9560	0.8972		
14	1.0000	1.0000	1.0000	1.0000	1.0000	1.0000	1.0000	1.0000	1.0000

x	$p = 0.92$	$p = 0.93$	$p = 0.94$	$p = 0.95$	$p = 0.96$	$p = 0.97$	$p = 0.98$	$p = 0.99$	$p = 1.00$
0	0.0000	0.0000	0.0000	0.0000	0.0000	0.0000	0.0000	0.0000	0.0000
1	0.0000	0.0000	0.0000	0.0000	0.0000	0.0000	0.0000	0.0000	0.0000
2	0.0000	0.0000	0.0000	0.0000	0.0000	0.0000	0.0000	0.0000	0.0000
3	0.0000	0.0000	0.0000	0.0000	0.0000	0.0000	0.0000	0.0000	0.0000
4	0.0000	0.0000	0.0000	0.0000	0.0000	0.0000	0.0000	0.0000	0.0000
5	0.0000	0.0000	0.0000	0.0000	0.0000	0.0000	0.0000	0.0000	0.0000
6	0.0000	0.0000	0.0000	0.0000	0.0000	0.0000	0.0000	0.0000	0.0000
7	0.0000	0.0000	0.0000	0.0000	0.0000	0.0000	0.0000	0.0000	0.0000
8	0.0004	0.0002	0.0001	0.0000	0.0000	0.0000	0.0000	0.0000	0.0000
9	0.0035	0.0020	0.0010	0.0004	0.0002	0.0000	0.0000	0.0000	0.0000
10	0.0214	0.0136	0.0080	0.0042	0.0019	0.0006	0.0001	0.0000	0.0000
11	0.0958	0.0698	0.0478	0.0301	0.0167	0.0077	0.0025	0.0003	0.0000
12	0.3100	0.2564	0.2037	0.1530	0.1059	0.0645	0.0310	0.0084	0.0000
13	0.6888	0.6380	0.5795	0.5123	0.4353	0.3472	0.2464	0.1313	0.0000
14	1.0000	1.0000	1.0000	1.0000	1.0000	1.0000	1.0000	1.0000	1.0000

$$n = 15$$

x	$p = 0.01$	$p = 0.02$	$p = 0.03$	$p = 0.04$	$p = 0.05$	$p = 0.06$	$p = 0.07$	$p = 0.08$	$p = 0.09$
0	0.8601	0.7386	0.6333	0.5421	0.4633	0.3953	0.3367	0.2863	0.2430
1	0.9904	0.9647	0.9270	0.8809	0.8290	0.7738	0.7168	0.6597	0.6035
2	0.9996	0.9970	0.9906	0.9797	0.9638	0.9429	0.9171	0.8870	0.8531
3	1.0000	0.9998	0.9992	0.9976	0.9945	0.9896	0.9825	0.9727	0.9601
4	1.0000	1.0000	0.9999	0.9998	0.9994	0.9986	0.9972	0.9950	0.9918

(continued)

5	1.0000	1.0000	1.0000	1.0000	0.9999	0.9999	0.9997	0.9993	0.9987
6	1.0000	1.0000	1.0000	1.0000	1.0000	1.0000	1.0000	0.9999	0.9998
7	1.0000	1.0000	1.0000	1.0000	1.0000	1.0000	1.0000	1.0000	1.0000
8	1.0000	1.0000	1.0000	1.0000	1.0000	1.0000	1.0000	1.0000	1.0000
9	1.0000	1.0000	1.0000	1.0000	1.0000	1.0000	1.0000	1.0000	1.0000
10	1.0000	1.0000	1.0000	1.0000	1.0000	1.0000	1.0000	1.0000	1.0000
11	1.0000	1.0000	1.0000	1.0000	1.0000	1.0000	1.0000	1.0000	1.0000
12	1.0000	1.0000	1.0000	1.0000	1.0000	1.0000	1.0000	1.0000	1.0000
13	1.0000	1.0000	1.0000	1.0000	1.0000	1.0000	1.0000	1.0000	1.0000
14	1.0000	1.0000	1.0000	1.0000	1.0000	1.0000	1.0000	1.0000	1.0000
15	1.0000	1.0000	1.0000	1.0000	1.0000	1.0000	1.0000	1.0000	1.0000

x	$p = 0.10$	$p = 0.15$	$p = 0.20$	$p = 0.25$	$p = 0.30$	$p = 0.35$	$p = 0.40$	$p = 0.45$	$p = 0.50$
0	0.2059	0.0874	0.0352	0.0134	0.0047	0.0016	0.0005	0.0001	0.0000
1	0.5490	0.3186	0.1671	0.0802	0.0353	0.0142	0.0052	0.0017	0.0005
2	0.8159	0.6042	0.3980	0.2361	0.1268	0.0617	0.0271	0.0107	0.0037
3	0.9444	0.8227	0.6482	0.4613	0.2969	0.1727	0.0905	0.0424	0.0176
4	0.9873	0.9383	0.8358	0.6865	0.5155	0.3519	0.2173	0.1204	0.0592
5	0.9978	0.9832	0.9389	0.8516	0.7216	0.5643	0.4032	0.2608	0.1509
6	0.9997	0.9964	0.9819	0.9434	0.8689	0.7548	0.6098	0.4522	0.3036
7	1.0000	0.9994	0.9958	0.9827	0.9500	0.8868	0.7869	0.6535	0.5000
8	1.0000	0.9999	0.9992	0.9958	0.9848	0.9578	0.9050	0.8182	0.6964
9	1.0000	1.0000	0.9999	0.9992	0.9963	0.9876	0.9662	0.9231	0.8491
10	1.0000	1.0000	1.0000	0.9999	0.9993	0.9972	0.9907	0.9745	0.9408
11	1.0000	1.0000	1.0000	1.0000	0.9999	0.9995	0.9981	0.9937	0.9824
12	1.0000	1.0000	1.0000	1.0000	1.0000	0.9999	0.9997	0.9989	0.9963
13	1.0000	1.0000	1.0000	1.0000	1.0000	1.0000	1.0000	0.9999	0.9995
14	1.0000	1.0000	1.0000	1.0000	1.0000	1.0000	1.0000	1.0000	1.0000
15	1.0000	1.0000	1.0000	1.0000	1.0000	1.0000	1.0000	1.0000	1.0000

x	$p = 0.55$	$p = 0.60$	$p = 0.65$	$p = 0.70$	$p = 0.75$	$p = 0.80$	$p = 0.85$	$p = 0.90$	$p = 0.91$
0	0.0000	0.0000	0.0000	0.0000	0.0000	0.0000	0.0000	0.0000	0.0000
1	0.0001	0.0000	0.0000	0.0000	0.0000	0.0000	0.0000	0.0000	0.0000
2	0.0011	0.0003	0.0001	0.0000	0.0000	0.0000	0.0000	0.0000	0.0000
3	0.0063	0.0019	0.0005	0.0001	0.0000	0.0000	0.0000	0.0000	0.0000
4	0.0255	0.0093	0.0028	0.0007	0.0001	0.0000	0.0000	0.0000	0.0000
5	0.0769	0.0338	0.0124	0.0037	0.0008	0.0001	0.0000	0.0000	0.0000
6	0.1818	0.0950	0.0422	0.0152	0.0042	0.0008	0.0001	0.0000	0.0000
7	0.3465	0.2131	0.1132	0.0500	0.0173	0.0042	0.0006	0.0000	0.0000
8	0.5478	0.3902	0.2452	0.1311	0.0566	0.0181	0.0036	0.0003	0.0002
9	0.7392	0.5968	0.4357	0.2784	0.1484	0.0611	0.0168	0.0022	0.0013
10	0.8796	0.7827	0.6481	0.4845	0.3135	0.1642	0.0617	0.0127	0.0082
11	0.9576	0.9095	0.8273	0.7031	0.5387	0.3518	0.1773	0.0556	0.0399
12	0.9893	0.9729	0.9383	0.8732	0.7639	0.6020	0.3958	0.1841	0.1469
13	0.9983	0.9948	0.9858	0.9647	0.9198	0.8329	0.6814	0.4510	0.3965
14	0.9999	0.9995	0.9984	0.9953	0.9866	0.9648	0.9126	0.7941	0.7570
15	1.0000	1.0000	1.0000	1.0000	1.0000	1.0000	1.0000	1.0000	1.0000

x	$p = 0.92$	$p = 0.93$	$p = 0.94$	$p = 0.95$	$p = 0.96$	$p = 0.97$	$p = 0.98$	$p = 0.99$	$p = 1.00$
0	0.0000	0.0000	0.0000	0.0000	0.0000	0.0000	0.0000	0.0000	0.0000
1	0.0000	0.0000	0.0000	0.0000	0.0000	0.0000	0.0000	0.0000	0.0000
2	0.0000	0.0000	0.0000	0.0000	0.0000	0.0000	0.0000	0.0000	0.0000
3	0.0000	0.0000	0.0000	0.0000	0.0000	0.0000	0.0000	0.0000	0.0000
4	0.0000	0.0000	0.0000	0.0000	0.0000	0.0000	0.0000	0.0000	0.0000
5	0.0000	0.0000	0.0000	0.0000	0.0000	0.0000	0.0000	0.0000	0.0000
6	0.0000	0.0000	0.0000	0.0000	0.0000	0.0000	0.0000	0.0000	0.0000
7	0.0000	0.0000	0.0000	0.0000	0.0000	0.0000	0.0000	0.0000	0.0000
8	0.0001	0.0000	0.0000	0.0000	0.0000	0.0000	0.0000	0.0000	0.0000
9	0.0007	0.0003	0.0001	0.0001	0.0000	0.0000	0.0000	0.0000	0.0000
10	0.0050	0.0028	0.0014	0.0006	0.0002	0.0001	0.0000	0.0000	0.0000
11	0.0273	0.0175	0.0104	0.0055	0.0024	0.0008	0.0002	0.0000	0.0000
12	0.1130	0.0829	0.0571	0.0362	0.0203	0.0094	0.0032	0.0004	0.0000
13	0.3403	0.2832	0.2262	0.1710	0.1191	0.0730	0.0353	0.0096	0.0000
14	0.7137	0.6633	0.6047	0.5367	0.4579	0.3667	0.2614	0.1399	0.0000
15	1.0000	1.0000	1.0000	1.0000	1.0000	1.0000	1.0000	1.0000	1.0000

$n = 20$

x	p = 0.01	p = 0.02	p = 0.03	p = 0.04	p = 0.05	p = 0.06	p = 0.07	p = 0.08	p = 0.09
0	0.8179	0.6676	0.5438	0.4420	0.3585	0.2901	0.2342	0.1887	0.1516
1	0.9831	0.9401	0.8802	0.8103	0.7358	0.6605	0.5869	0.5169	0.4516
2	0.9990	0.9929	0.9790	0.9561	0.9245	0.8850	0.8390	0.7879	0.7334
3	1.0000	0.9994	0.9973	0.9926	0.9841	0.9710	0.9529	0.9294	0.9007
4	1.0000	1.0000	0.9997	0.9990	0.9974	0.9944	0.9893	0.9817	0.9710
5	1.0000	1.0000	1.0000	0.9999	0.9997	0.9991	0.9981	0.9962	0.9932
6	1.0000	1.0000	1.0000	1.0000	1.0000	0.9999	0.9997	0.9994	0.9987
7	1.0000	1.0000	1.0000	1.0000	1.0000	1.0000	1.0000	0.9999	0.9998
8	1.0000	1.0000	1.0000	1.0000	1.0000	1.0000	1.0000	1.0000	1.0000
9	1.0000	1.0000	1.0000	1.0000	1.0000	1.0000	1.0000	1.0000	1.0000
10	1.0000	1.0000	1.0000	1.0000	1.0000	1.0000	1.0000	1.0000	1.0000
11	1.0000	1.0000	1.0000	1.0000	1.0000	1.0000	1.0000	1.0000	1.0000
12	1.0000	1.0000	1.0000	1.0000	1.0000	1.0000	1.0000	1.0000	1.0000
13	1.0000	1.0000	1.0000	1.0000	1.0000	1.0000	1.0000	1.0000	1.0000
14	1.0000	1.0000	1.0000	1.0000	1.0000	1.0000	1.0000	1.0000	1.0000
15	1.0000	1.0000	1.0000	1.0000	1.0000	1.0000	1.0000	1.0000	1.0000
16	1.0000	1.0000	1.0000	1.0000	1.0000	1.0000	1.0000	1.0000	1.0000
17	1.0000	1.0000	1.0000	1.0000	1.0000	1.0000	1.0000	1.0000	1.0000
18	1.0000	1.0000	1.0000	1.0000	1.0000	1.0000	1.0000	1.0000	1.0000
19	1.0000	1.0000	1.0000	1.0000	1.0000	1.0000	1.0000	1.0000	1.0000
20	1.0000	1.0000	1.0000	1.0000	1.0000	1.0000	1.0000	1.0000	1.0000

x	p = 0.10	p = 0.15	p = 0.20	p = 0.25	p = 0.30	p = 0.35	p = 0.40	p = 0.45	p = 0.50
0	0.1216	0.0388	0.0115	0.0032	0.0008	0.0002	0.0000	0.0000	0.0000
1	0.3917	0.1756	0.0692	0.0243	0.0076	0.0021	0.0005	0.0001	0.0000
2	0.6769	0.4049	0.2061	0.0913	0.0355	0.0121	0.0036	0.0009	0.0002
3	0.8670	0.6477	0.4114	0.2252	0.1071	0.0444	0.0160	0.0049	0.0013
4	0.9568	0.8298	0.6296	0.4148	0.2375	0.1182	0.0510	0.0189	0.0059
5	0.9887	0.9327	0.8042	0.6172	0.4164	0.2454	0.1256	0.0553	0.0207
6	0.9976	0.9781	0.9133	0.7858	0.6080	0.4166	0.2500	0.1299	0.0577
7	0.9996	0.9941	0.9679	0.8982	0.7723	0.6010	0.4159	0.2520	0.1316
8	0.9999	0.9987	0.9900	0.9591	0.8867	0.7624	0.5956	0.4143	0.2517
9	1.0000	0.9998	0.9974	0.9861	0.9520	0.8782	0.7553	0.5914	0.4119
10	1.0000	1.0000	0.9994	0.9961	0.9829	0.9468	0.8725	0.7507	0.5881
11	1.0000	1.0000	0.9999	0.9991	0.9949	0.9804	0.9435	0.8692	0.7483
12	1.0000	1.0000	1.0000	0.9998	0.9987	0.9940	0.9790	0.9420	0.8684
13	1.0000	1.0000	1.0000	1.0000	0.9997	0.9985	0.9935	0.9786	0.9423
14	1.0000	1.0000	1.0000	1.0000	1.0000	0.9997	0.9984	0.9936	0.9793
15	1.0000	1.0000	1.0000	1.0000	1.0000	1.0000	0.9997	0.9985	0.9941
16	1.0000	1.0000	1.0000	1.0000	1.0000	1.0000	1.0000	0.9997	0.9987
17	1.0000	1.0000	1.0000	1.0000	1.0000	1.0000	1.0000	1.0000	0.9998
18	1.0000	1.0000	1.0000	1.0000	1.0000	1.0000	1.0000	1.0000	1.0000
19	1.0000	1.0000	1.0000	1.0000	1.0000	1.0000	1.0000	1.0000	1.0000
20	1.0000	1.0000	1.0000	1.0000	1.0000	1.0000	1.0000	1.0000	1.0000

x	p = 0.55	p = 0.60	p = 0.65	p = 0.70	p = 0.75	p = 0.80	p = 0.85	p = 0.90	p = 0.91
0	0.0000	0.0000	0.0000	0.0000	0.0000	0.0000	0.0000	0.0000	0.0000
1	0.0000	0.0000	0.0000	0.0000	0.0000	0.0000	0.0000	0.0000	0.0000
2	0.0000	0.0000	0.0000	0.0000	0.0000	0.0000	0.0000	0.0000	0.0000
3	0.0003	0.0000	0.0000	0.0000	0.0000	0.0000	0.0000	0.0000	0.0000
4	0.0015	0.0003	0.0000	0.0000	0.0000	0.0000	0.0000	0.0000	0.0000
5	0.0064	0.0016	0.0003	0.0000	0.0000	0.0000	0.0000	0.0000	0.0000
6	0.0214	0.0065	0.0015	0.0003	0.0000	0.0000	0.0000	0.0000	0.0000
7	0.0580	0.0210	0.0060	0.0013	0.0002	0.0000	0.0000	0.0000	0.0000
8	0.1308	0.0565	0.0196	0.0051	0.0009	0.0001	0.0000	0.0000	0.0000
9	0.2493	0.1275	0.0532	0.0171	0.0039	0.0006	0.0000	0.0000	0.0000
10	0.4086	0.2447	0.1218	0.0480	0.0139	0.0026	0.0002	0.0000	0.0000
11	0.5857	0.4044	0.2376	0.1133	0.0409	0.0100	0.0013	0.0001	0.0000
12	0.7480	0.5841	0.3990	0.2277	0.1018	0.0321	0.0059	0.0004	0.0002
13	0.8701	0.7500	0.5834	0.3920	0.2142	0.0867	0.0219	0.0024	0.0013
14	0.9447	0.8744	0.7546	0.5836	0.3828	0.1958	0.0673	0.0113	0.0068
15	0.9811	0.9490	0.8818	0.7625	0.5852	0.3704	0.1702	0.0432	0.0290
16	0.9951	0.9840	0.9556	0.8929	0.7748	0.5886	0.3523	0.1330	0.0993
17	0.9991	0.9964	0.9879	0.9645	0.9087	0.7939	0.5951	0.3231	0.2666
18	0.9999	0.9995	0.9979	0.9924	0.9757	0.9308	0.8244	0.6083	0.5484
19	1.0000	1.0000	0.9998	0.9992	0.9968	0.9885	0.9612	0.8784	0.8484
20	1.0000	1.0000	1.0000	1.0000	1.0000	1.0000	1.0000	1.0000	1.0000

(continued)

x	p = 0.92	p = 0.93	p = 0.94	p = 0.95	p = 0.96	p = 0.97	p = 0.98	p = 0.99	p = 1.00
0	0.0000	0.0000	0.0000	0.0000	0.0000	0.0000	0.0000	0.0000	0.0000
1	0.0000	0.0000	0.0000	0.0000	0.0000	0.0000	0.0000	0.0000	0.0000
2	0.0000	0.0000	0.0000	0.0000	0.0000	0.0000	0.0000	0.0000	0.0000
3	0.0000	0.0000	0.0000	0.0000	0.0000	0.0000	0.0000	0.0000	0.0000
4	0.0000	0.0000	0.0000	0.0000	0.0000	0.0000	0.0000	0.0000	0.0000
5	0.0000	0.0000	0.0000	0.0000	0.0000	0.0000	0.0000	0.0000	0.0000
6	0.0000	0.0000	0.0000	0.0000	0.0000	0.0000	0.0000	0.0000	0.0000
7	0.0000	0.0000	0.0000	0.0000	0.0000	0.0000	0.0000	0.0000	0.0000
8	0.0000	0.0000	0.0000	0.0000	0.0000	0.0000	0.0000	0.0000	0.0000
9	0.0000	0.0000	0.0000	0.0000	0.0000	0.0000	0.0000	0.0000	0.0000
10	0.0000	0.0000	0.0000	0.0000	0.0000	0.0000	0.0000	0.0000	0.0000
11	0.0000	0.0000	0.0000	0.0000	0.0000	0.0000	0.0000	0.0000	0.0000
12	0.0001	0.0000	0.0000	0.0000	0.0000	0.0000	0.0000	0.0000	0.0000
13	0.0006	0.0003	0.0001	0.0000	0.0000	0.0000	0.0000	0.0000	0.0000
14	0.0038	0.0019	0.0009	0.0003	0.0001	0.0000	0.0000	0.0000	0.0000
15	0.0183	0.0107	0.0056	0.0026	0.0010	0.0003	0.0000	0.0000	0.0000
16	0.0706	0.0471	0.0290	0.0159	0.0074	0.0027	0.0006	0.0000	0.0000
17	0.2121	0.1610	0.1150	0.0755	0.0439	0.0210	0.0071	0.0010	0.0000
18	0.4831	0.4131	0.3395	0.2642	0.1897	0.1198	0.0599	0.0169	0.0000
19	0.8113	0.7658	0.7099	0.6415	0.5580	0.4562	0.3324	0.1821	0.0000
20	1.0000	1.0000	1.0000	1.0000	1.0000	1.0000	1.0000	1.0000	1.0000

$n = 25$

x	p = 0.01	p = 0.02	p = 0.03	p = 0.04	p = 0.05	p = 0.06	p = 0.07	p = 0.08	p = 0.09
0	0.7778	0.6035	0.4670	0.3604	0.2774	0.2129	0.1630	0.1244	0.0946
1	0.9742	0.9114	0.8280	0.7358	0.6424	0.5527	0.4696	0.3947	0.3286
2	0.9980	0.9868	0.9620	0.9235	0.8729	0.8129	0.7466	0.6768	0.6063
3	0.9999	0.9986	0.9938	0.9835	0.9659	0.9402	0.9064	0.8649	0.8169
4	1.0000	0.9999	0.9992	0.9972	0.9928	0.9850	0.9726	0.9549	0.9314
5	1.0000	1.0000	0.9999	0.9996	0.9988	0.9969	0.9935	0.9877	0.9790
6	1.0000	1.0000	1.0000	1.0000	0.9998	0.9995	0.9987	0.9972	0.9946
7	1.0000	1.0000	1.0000	1.0000	1.0000	0.9999	0.9998	0.9995	0.9989
8	1.0000	1.0000	1.0000	1.0000	1.0000	1.0000	1.0000	0.9999	0.9998
9	1.0000	1.0000	1.0000	1.0000	1.0000	1.0000	1.0000	1.0000	1.0000
10	1.0000	1.0000	1.0000	1.0000	1.0000	1.0000	1.0000	1.0000	1.0000
11	1.0000	1.0000	1.0000	1.0000	1.0000	1.0000	1.0000	1.0000	1.0000
12	1.0000	1.0000	1.0000	1.0000	1.0000	1.0000	1.0000	1.0000	1.0000
13	1.0000	1.0000	1.0000	1.0000	1.0000	1.0000	1.0000	1.0000	1.0000
14	1.0000	1.0000	1.0000	1.0000	1.0000	1.0000	1.0000	1.0000	1.0000
15	1.0000	1.0000	1.0000	1.0000	1.0000	1.0000	1.0000	1.0000	1.0000
16	1.0000	1.0000	1.0000	1.0000	1.0000	1.0000	1.0000	1.0000	1.0000
17	1.0000	1.0000	1.0000	1.0000	1.0000	1.0000	1.0000	1.0000	1.0000
18	1.0000	1.0000	1.0000	1.0000	1.0000	1.0000	1.0000	1.0000	1.0000
19	1.0000	1.0000	1.0000	1.0000	1.0000	1.0000	1.0000	1.0000	1.0000
20	1.0000	1.0000	1.0000	1.0000	1.0000	1.0000	1.0000	1.0000	1.0000
21	1.0000	1.0000	1.0000	1.0000	1.0000	1.0000	1.0000	1.0000	1.0000
22	1.0000	1.0000	1.0000	1.0000	1.0000	1.0000	1.0000	1.0000	1.0000
23	1.0000	1.0000	1.0000	1.0000	1.0000	1.0000	1.0000	1.0000	1.0000
24	1.0000	1.0000	1.0000	1.0000	1.0000	1.0000	1.0000	1.0000	1.0000
25	1.0000	1.0000	1.0000	1.0000	1.0000	1.0000	1.0000	1.0000	1.0000

x	p = 0.10	p = 0.15	p = 0.20	p = 0.25	p = 0.30	p = 0.35	p = 0.40	p = 0.45	p = 0.50
0	0.0718	0.0172	0.0038	0.0008	0.0001	0.0000	0.0000	0.0000	0.0000
1	0.2712	0.0931	0.0274	0.0070	0.0016	0.0003	0.0001	0.0000	0.0000
2	0.5371	0.2537	0.0982	0.0321	0.0090	0.0021	0.0004	0.0001	0.0000
3	0.7636	0.4711	0.2340	0.0962	0.0332	0.0097	0.0024	0.0005	0.0001
4	0.9020	0.6821	0.4207	0.2137	0.0905	0.0320	0.0095	0.0023	0.0005
5	0.9666	0.8385	0.6167	0.3783	0.1935	0.0826	0.0294	0.0086	0.0020
6	0.9905	0.9305	0.7800	0.5611	0.3407	0.1734	0.0736	0.0258	0.0073
7	0.9977	0.9745	0.8909	0.7265	0.5118	0.3061	0.1536	0.0639	0.0216
8	0.9995	0.9920	0.9532	0.8506	0.6769	0.4668	0.2735	0.1340	0.0539
9	0.9999	0.9979	0.9827	0.9287	0.8106	0.6303	0.4246	0.2424	0.1148
10	1.0000	0.9995	0.9944	0.9703	0.9022	0.7712	0.5858	0.3843	0.2122
11	1.0000	0.9999	0.9985	0.9893	0.9558	0.8746	0.7323	0.5426	0.3450
12	1.0000	1.0000	0.9996	0.9966	0.9825	0.9396	0.8462	0.6937	0.5000

x									
13	1.0000	1.0000	0.9999	0.9991	0.9940	0.9745	0.9222	0.8173	0.6550
14	1.0000	1.0000	1.0000	0.9998	0.9982	0.9907	0.9656	0.9040	0.7878
15	1.0000	1.0000	1.0000	1.0000	0.9995	0.9971	0.9868	0.9560	0.8852
16	1.0000	1.0000	1.0000	1.0000	0.9999	0.9992	0.9957	0.9826	0.9461
17	1.0000	1.0000	1.0000	1.0000	1.0000	0.9998	0.9988	0.9942	0.9784
18	1.0000	1.0000	1.0000	1.0000	1.0000	1.0000	0.9997	0.9984	0.9927
19	1.0000	1.0000	1.0000	1.0000	1.0000	1.0000	0.9999	0.9996	0.9980
20	1.0000	1.0000	1.0000	1.0000	1.0000	1.0000	1.0000	0.9999	0.9995
21	1.0000	1.0000	1.0000	1.0000	1.0000	1.0000	1.0000	1.0000	0.9999
22	1.0000	1.0000	1.0000	1.0000	1.0000	1.0000	1.0000	1.0000	1.0000
23	1.0000	1.0000	1.0000	1.0000	1.0000	1.0000	1.0000	1.0000	1.0000
24	1.0000	1.0000	1.0000	1.0000	1.0000	1.0000	1.0000	1.0000	1.0000
25	1.0000	1.0000	1.0000	1.0000	1.0000	1.0000	1.0000	1.0000	1.0000

x	$p = 0.55$	$p = 0.60$	$p = 0.65$	$p = 0.70$	$p = 0.75$	$p = 0.80$	$p = 0.85$	$p = 0.90$	$p = 0.91$
0	0.0000	0.0000	0.0000	0.0000	0.0000	0.0000	0.0000	0.0000	0.0000
1	0.0000	0.0000	0.0000	0.0000	0.0000	0.0000	0.0000	0.0000	0.0000
2	0.0000	0.0000	0.0000	0.0000	0.0000	0.0000	0.0000	0.0000	0.0000
3	0.0000	0.0000	0.0000	0.0000	0.0000	0.0000	0.0000	0.0000	0.0000
4	0.0001	0.0000	0.0000	0.0000	0.0000	0.0000	0.0000	0.0000	0.0000
5	0.0004	0.0001	0.0000	0.0000	0.0000	0.0000	0.0000	0.0000	0.0000
6	0.0016	0.0003	0.0000	0.0000	0.0000	0.0000	0.0000	0.0000	0.0000
7	0.0058	0.0012	0.0002	0.0000	0.0000	0.0000	0.0000	0.0000	0.0000
8	0.0174	0.0043	0.0008	0.0001	0.0000	0.0000	0.0000	0.0000	0.0000
9	0.0440	0.0132	0.0029	0.0005	0.0000	0.0000	0.0000	0.0000	0.0000
10	0.0960	0.0344	0.0093	0.0018	0.0002	0.0000	0.0000	0.0000	0.0000
11	0.1827	0.0778	0.0255	0.0060	0.0009	0.0001	0.0000	0.0000	0.0000
12	0.3063	0.1538	0.0604	0.0175	0.0034	0.0004	0.0000	0.0000	0.0000
13	0.4574	0.2677	0.1254	0.0442	0.0107	0.0015	0.0001	0.0000	0.0000
14	0.6157	0.4142	0.2288	0.0978	0.0297	0.0056	0.0005	0.0000	0.0000
15	0.7576	0.5754	0.3697	0.1894	0.0713	0.0173	0.0021	0.0001	0.0000
16	0.8660	0.7265	0.5332	0.3231	0.1494	0.0468	0.0080	0.0005	0.0002
17	0.9361	0.8464	0.6939	0.4882	0.2735	0.1091	0.0255	0.0023	0.0011
18	0.9742	0.9264	0.8266	0.6593	0.4389	0.2200	0.0695	0.0095	0.0054
19	0.9914	0.9706	0.9174	0.8065	0.6217	0.3833	0.1615	0.0334	0.0210
20	0.9977	0.9905	0.9680	0.9095	0.7863	0.5793	0.3179	0.0980	0.0686
21	0.9995	0.9976	0.9903	0.9668	0.9038	0.7660	0.5289	0.2364	0.1831
22	0.9999	0.9996	0.9979	0.9910	0.9679	0.9018	0.7463	0.4629	0.3937
23	1.0000	0.9999	0.9997	0.9984	0.9930	0.9726	0.9069	0.7288	0.6714
24	1.0000	1.0000	1.0000	0.9999	0.9992	0.9962	0.9828	0.9282	0.9054
25	1.0000	1.0000	1.0000	1.0000	1.0000	1.0000	1.0000	1.0000	1.0000

x	$p = 0.92$	$p = 0.93$	$p = 0.94$	$p = 0.95$	$p = 0.96$	$p = 0.97$	$p = 0.98$	$p = 0.99$	$p = 1.00$
0	0.0000	0.0000	0.0000	0.0000	0.0000	0.0000	0.0000	0.0000	0.0000
1	0.0000	0.0000	0.0000	0.0000	0.0000	0.0000	0.0000	0.0000	0.0000
2	0.0000	0.0000	0.0000	0.0000	0.0000	0.0000	0.0000	0.0000	0.0000
3	0.0000	0.0000	0.0000	0.0000	0.0000	0.0000	0.0000	0.0000	0.0000
4	0.0000	0.0000	0.0000	0.0000	0.0000	0.0000	0.0000	0.0000	0.0000
5	0.0000	0.0000	0.0000	0.0000	0.0000	0.0000	0.0000	0.0000	0.0000
6	0.0000	0.0000	0.0000	0.0000	0.0000	0.0000	0.0000	0.0000	0.0000
7	0.0000	0.0000	0.0000	0.0000	0.0000	0.0000	0.0000	0.0000	0.0000
8	0.0000	0.0000	0.0000	0.0000	0.0000	0.0000	0.0000	0.0000	0.0000
9	0.0000	0.0000	0.0000	0.0000	0.0000	0.0000	0.0000	0.0000	0.0000
10	0.0000	0.0000	0.0000	0.0000	0.0000	0.0000	0.0000	0.0000	0.0000
11	0.0000	0.0000	0.0000	0.0000	0.0000	0.0000	0.0000	0.0000	0.0000
12	0.0000	0.0000	0.0000	0.0000	0.0000	0.0000	0.0000	0.0000	0.0000
13	0.0000	0.0000	0.0000	0.0000	0.0000	0.0000	0.0000	0.0000	0.0000
14	0.0000	0.0000	0.0000	0.0000	0.0000	0.0000	0.0000	0.0000	0.0000
15	0.0000	0.0000	0.0000	0.0000	0.0000	0.0000	0.0000	0.0000	0.0000
16	0.0001	0.0000	0.0000	0.0000	0.0000	0.0000	0.0000	0.0000	0.0000
17	0.0005	0.0002	0.0001	0.0000	0.0000	0.0000	0.0000	0.0000	0.0000
18	0.0028	0.0013	0.0005	0.0002	0.0000	0.0000	0.0000	0.0000	0.0000
19	0.0123	0.0065	0.0031	0.0012	0.0004	0.0001	0.0000	0.0000	0.0000
20	0.0451	0.0274	0.0150	0.0072	0.0028	0.0008	0.0001	0.0000	0.0000
21	0.1351	0.0936	0.0598	0.0341	0.0165	0.0062	0.0014	0.0001	0.0000
22	0.3232	0.2534	0.1871	0.1271	0.0765	0.0380	0.0132	0.0020	0.0000
23	0.6053	0.5304	0.4473	0.3576	0.2642	0.1720	0.0886	0.0258	0.0000
24	0.8756	0.8370	0.7871	0.7226	0.6396	0.5330	0.3965	0.2222	0.0000
25	1.0000	1.0000	1.0000	1.0000	1.0000	1.0000	1.0000	1.0000	1.0000

APPENDIX C

Cumulative Poisson Probability Distribution Table

$$P(x \le X) = \sum_{i=0}^{X} \frac{(\lambda t)^i e^{-\lambda t}}{i!}$$

λt

x	0.005	0.01	0.02	0.03	0.04	0.05	0.06	0.07	0.08	0.09
0	0.9950	0.9900	0.9802	0.9704	0.9608	0.9512	0.9418	0.9324	0.9231	0.9139
1	1.0000	1.0000	0.9998	0.9996	0.9992	0.9988	0.9983	0.9977	0.9970	0.9962
2	1.0000	1.0000	1.0000	1.0000	1.0000	1.0000	1.0000	0.9999	0.9999	0.9999
3	1.0000	1.0000	1.0000	1.0000	1.0000	1.0000	1.0000	1.0000	1.0000	1.0000

λt

x	0.10	0.20	0.30	0.40	0.50	0.60	0.70	0.80	0.90	1.00
0	0.9048	0.8187	0.7408	0.6703	0.6065	0.5488	0.4966	0.4493	0.4066	0.3679
1	0.9953	0.9825	0.9631	0.9384	0.9098	0.8781	0.8442	0.8088	0.7725	0.7358
2	0.9998	0.9989	0.9964	0.9921	0.9856	0.9769	0.9659	0.9526	0.9371	0.9197
3	1.0000	0.9999	0.9997	0.9992	0.9982	0.9966	0.9942	0.9909	0.9865	0.9810
4	1.0000	1.0000	1.0000	0.9999	0.9998	0.9996	0.9992	0.9986	0.9977	0.9963
5	1.0000	1.0000	1.0000	1.0000	1.0000	1.0000	0.9999	0.9998	0.9997	0.9994
6	1.0000	1.0000	1.0000	1.0000	1.0000	1.0000	1.0000	1.0000	1.0000	0.9999
7	1.0000	1.0000	1.0000	1.0000	1.0000	1.0000	1.0000	1.0000	1.0000	1.0000

λt

x	1.10	1.20	1.30	1.40	1.50	1.60	1.70	1.80	1.90	2.00
0	0.3329	0.3012	0.2725	0.2466	0.2231	0.2019	0.1827	0.1653	0.1496	0.1353
1	0.6990	0.6626	0.6268	0.5918	0.5578	0.5249	0.4932	0.4628	0.4337	0.4060
2	0.9004	0.8795	0.8571	0.8335	0.8088	0.7834	0.7572	0.7306	0.7037	0.6767
3	0.9743	0.9662	0.9569	0.9463	0.9344	0.9212	0.9068	0.8913	0.8747	0.8571
4	0.9946	0.9923	0.9893	0.9857	0.9814	0.9763	0.9704	0.9636	0.9559	0.9473
5	0.9990	0.9985	0.9978	0.9968	0.9955	0.9940	0.9920	0.9896	0.9868	0.9834
6	0.9999	0.9997	0.9996	0.9994	0.9991	0.9987	0.9981	0.9974	0.9966	0.9955
7	1.0000	1.0000	0.9999	0.9999	0.9998	0.9997	0.9996	0.9994	0.9992	0.9989
8	1.0000	1.0000	1.0000	1.0000	1.0000	1.0000	0.9999	0.9999	0.9998	0.9998
9	1.0000	1.0000	1.0000	1.0000	1.0000	1.0000	1.0000	1.0000	1.0000	1.0000

λt

x	2.10	2.20	2.30	2.40	2.50	2.60	2.70	2.80	2.90	3.00
0	0.1225	0.1108	0.1003	0.0907	0.0821	0.0743	0.0672	0.0608	0.0550	0.0498
1	0.3796	0.3546	0.3309	0.3084	0.2873	0.2674	0.2487	0.2311	0.2146	0.1991
2	0.6496	0.6227	0.5960	0.5697	0.5438	0.5184	0.4936	0.4695	0.4460	0.4232
3	0.8386	0.8194	0.7993	0.7787	0.7576	0.7360	0.7141	0.6919	0.6696	0.6472
4	0.9379	0.9275	0.9162	0.9041	0.8912	0.8774	0.8629	0.8477	0.8318	0.8153
5	0.9796	0.9751	0.9700	0.9643	0.9580	0.9510	0.9433	0.9349	0.9258	0.9161
6	0.9941	0.9925	0.9906	0.9884	0.9858	0.9828	0.9794	0.9756	0.9713	0.9665
7	0.9985	0.9980	0.9974	0.9967	0.9958	0.9947	0.9934	0.9919	0.9901	0.9881
8	0.9997	0.9995	0.9994	0.9991	0.9989	0.9985	0.9981	0.9976	0.9969	0.9962
9	0.9999	0.9999	0.9999	0.9998	0.9997	0.9996	0.9995	0.9993	0.9991	0.9989
10	1.0000	1.0000	1.0000	1.0000	0.9999	0.9999	0.9999	0.9998	0.9998	0.9997
11	1.0000	1.0000	1.0000	1.0000	1.0000	1.0000	1.0000	1.0000	0.9999	0.9999
12	1.0000	1.0000	1.0000	1.0000	1.0000	1.0000	1.0000	1.0000	1.0000	1.0000

λt

x	3.10	3.20	3.30	3.40	3.50	3.60	3.70	3.80	3.90	4.00
0	0.0450	0.0408	0.0369	0.0334	0.0302	0.0273	0.0247	0.0224	0.0202	0.0183
1	0.1847	0.1712	0.1586	0.1468	0.1359	0.1257	0.1162	0.1074	0.0992	0.0916
2	0.4012	0.3799	0.3594	0.3397	0.3208	0.3027	0.2854	0.2689	0.2531	0.2381
3	0.6248	0.6025	0.5803	0.5584	0.5366	0.5152	0.4942	0.4735	0.4532	0.4335
4	0.7982	0.7806	0.7626	0.7442	0.7254	0.7064	0.6872	0.6678	0.6484	0.6288
5	0.9057	0.8946	0.8829	0.8705	0.8576	0.8441	0.8301	0.8156	0.8006	0.7851
6	0.9612	0.9554	0.9490	0.9421	0.9347	0.9267	0.9182	0.9091	0.8995	0.8893
7	0.9858	0.9832	0.9802	0.9769	0.9733	0.9692	0.9648	0.9599	0.9546	0.9489
8	0.9953	0.9943	0.9931	0.9917	0.9901	0.9883	0.9863	0.9840	0.9815	0.9786
9	0.9986	0.9982	0.9978	0.9973	0.9967	0.9960	0.9952	0.9942	0.9931	0.9919
10	0.9996	0.9995	0.9994	0.9992	0.9990	0.9987	0.9984	0.9981	0.9977	0.9972
11	0.9999	0.9999	0.9998	0.9998	0.9997	0.9996	0.9995	0.9994	0.9993	0.9991
12	1.0000	1.0000	1.0000	0.9999	0.9999	0.9999	0.9999	0.9998	0.9998	0.9997
13	1.0000	1.0000	1.0000	1.0000	1.0000	1.0000	1.0000	1.0000	0.9999	0.9999
14	1.0000	1.0000	1.0000	1.0000	1.0000	1.0000	1.0000	1.0000	1.0000	1.0000

λt

x	4.10	4.20	4.30	4.40	4.50	4.60	4.70	4.80	4.90	5.00
0	0.0166	0.0150	0.0136	0.0123	0.0111	0.0101	0.0091	0.0082	0.0074	0.0067
1	0.0845	0.0780	0.0719	0.0663	0.0611	0.0563	0.0518	0.0477	0.0439	0.0404
2	0.2238	0.2102	0.1974	0.1851	0.1736	0.1626	0.1523	0.1425	0.1333	0.1247
3	0.4142	0.3954	0.3772	0.3594	0.3423	0.3257	0.3097	0.2942	0.2793	0.2650
4	0.6093	0.5898	0.5704	0.5512	0.5321	0.5132	0.4946	0.4763	0.4582	0.4405
5	0.7693	0.7531	0.7367	0.7199	0.7029	0.6858	0.6684	0.6510	0.6335	0.6160
6	0.8786	0.8675	0.8558	0.8436	0.8311	0.8180	0.8046	0.7908	0.7767	0.7622
7	0.9427	0.9361	0.9290	0.9214	0.9134	0.9049	0.8960	0.8867	0.8769	0.8666
8	0.9755	0.9721	0.9683	0.9642	0.9597	0.9549	0.9497	0.9442	0.9382	0.9319
9	0.9905	0.9889	0.9871	0.9851	0.9829	0.9805	0.9778	0.9749	0.9717	0.9682
10	0.9966	0.9959	0.9952	0.9943	0.9933	0.9922	0.9910	0.9896	0.9880	0.9863
11	0.9989	0.9986	0.9983	0.9980	0.9976	0.9971	0.9966	0.9960	0.9953	0.9945
12	0.9997	0.9996	0.9995	0.9993	0.9992	0.9990	0.9988	0.9986	0.9983	0.9980
13	0.9999	0.9999	0.9998	0.9998	0.9997	0.9997	0.9996	0.9995	0.9994	0.9993
14	1.0000	1.0000	1.0000	0.9999	0.9999	0.9999	0.9999	0.9999	0.9998	0.9998
15	1.0000	1.0000	1.0000	1.0000	1.0000	1.0000	1.0000	1.0000	0.9999	0.9999
16	1.0000	1.0000	1.0000	1.0000	1.0000	1.0000	1.0000	1.0000	1.0000	1.0000

λt

x	5.10	5.20	5.30	5.40	5.50	5.60	5.70	5.80	5.90	6.00
0	0.0061	0.0055	0.0050	0.0045	0.0041	0.0037	0.0033	0.0030	0.0027	0.0025
1	0.0372	0.0342	0.0314	0.0289	0.0266	0.0244	0.0224	0.0206	0.0189	0.0174
2	0.1165	0.1088	0.1016	0.0948	0.0884	0.0824	0.0768	0.0715	0.0666	0.0620
3	0.2513	0.2381	0.2254	0.2133	0.2017	0.1906	0.1800	0.1700	0.1604	0.1512
4	0.4231	0.4061	0.3895	0.3733	0.3575	0.3422	0.3272	0.3127	0.2987	0.2851
5	0.5984	0.5809	0.5635	0.5461	0.5289	0.5119	0.4950	0.4783	0.4619	0.4457
6	0.7474	0.7324	0.7171	0.7017	0.6860	0.6703	0.6544	0.6384	0.6224	0.6063
7	0.8560	0.8449	0.8335	0.8217	0.8095	0.7970	0.7841	0.7710	0.7576	0.7440
8	0.9252	0.9181	0.9106	0.9027	0.8944	0.8857	0.8766	0.8672	0.8574	0.8472
9	0.9644	0.9603	0.9559	0.9512	0.9462	0.9409	0.9352	0.9292	0.9228	0.9161
10	0.9844	0.9823	0.9800	0.9775	0.9747	0.9718	0.9686	0.9651	0.9614	0.9574
11	0.9937	0.9927	0.9916	0.9904	0.9890	0.9875	0.9859	0.9841	0.9821	0.9799
12	0.9976	0.9972	0.9967	0.9962	0.9955	0.9949	0.9941	0.9932	0.9922	0.9912
13	0.9992	0.9990	0.9988	0.9986	0.9983	0.9980	0.9977	0.9973	0.9969	0.9964
14	0.9997	0.9997	0.9996	0.9995	0.9994	0.9993	0.9991	0.9990	0.9988	0.9986
15	0.9999	0.9999	0.9999	0.9998	0.9998	0.9998	0.9997	0.9996	0.9996	0.9995
16	1.0000	1.0000	1.0000	0.9999	0.9999	0.9999	0.9999	0.9999	0.9999	0.9998
17	1.0000	1.0000	1.0000	1.0000	1.0000	1.0000	1.0000	1.0000	1.0000	0.9999
18	1.0000	1.0000	1.0000	1.0000	1.0000	1.0000	1.0000	1.0000	1.0000	1.0000

(continued)

λt

x	6.10	6.20	6.30	6.40	6.50	6.60	6.70	6.80	6.90	7.00
0	0.0022	0.0020	0.0018	0.0017	0.0015	0.0014	0.0012	0.0011	0.0010	0.0009
1	0.0159	0.0146	0.0134	0.0123	0.0113	0.0103	0.0095	0.0087	0.0080	0.0073
2	0.0577	0.0536	0.0498	0.0463	0.0430	0.0400	0.0371	0.0344	0.0320	0.0296
3	0.1425	0.1342	0.1264	0.1189	0.1118	0.1052	0.0988	0.0928	0.0871	0.0818
4	0.2719	0.2592	0.2469	0.2351	0.2237	0.2127	0.2022	0.1920	0.1823	0.1730
5	0.4298	0.4141	0.3988	0.3837	0.3690	0.3547	0.3406	0.3270	0.3137	0.3007
6	0.5902	0.5742	0.5582	0.5423	0.5265	0.5108	0.4953	0.4799	0.4647	0.4497
7	0.7301	0.7160	0.7017	0.6873	0.6728	0.6581	0.6433	0.6285	0.6136	0.5987
8	0.8367	0.8259	0.8148	0.8033	0.7916	0.7796	0.7673	0.7548	0.7420	0.7291
9	0.9090	0.9016	0.8939	0.8858	0.8774	0.8686	0.8596	0.8502	0.8405	0.8305
10	0.9531	0.9486	0.9437	0.9386	0.9332	0.9274	0.9214	0.9151	0.9084	0.9015
11	0.9776	0.9750	0.9723	0.9693	0.9661	0.9627	0.9591	0.9552	0.9510	0.9467
12	0.9900	0.9887	0.9873	0.9857	0.9840	0.9821	0.9801	0.9779	0.9755	0.9730
13	0.9958	0.9952	0.9945	0.9937	0.9929	0.9920	0.9909	0.9898	0.9885	0.9872
14	0.9984	0.9981	0.9978	0.9974	0.9970	0.9966	0.9961	0.9956	0.9950	0.9943
15	0.9994	0.9993	0.9992	0.9990	0.9988	0.9986	0.9984	0.9982	0.9979	0.9976
16	0.9998	0.9997	0.9997	0.9996	0.9996	0.9995	0.9994	0.9993	0.9992	0.9990
17	0.9999	0.9999	0.9999	0.9999	0.9998	0.9998	0.9998	0.9997	0.9997	0.9996
18	1.0000	1.0000	1.0000	1.0000	0.9999	0.9999	0.9999	0.9999	0.9999	0.9999
19	1.0000	1.0000	1.0000	1.0000	1.0000	1.0000	1.0000	1.0000	1.0000	1.0000
20	1.0000	1.0000	1.0000	1.0000	1.0000	1.0000	1.0000	1.0000	1.0000	1.0000

λt

x	7.10	7.20	7.30	7.40	7.50	7.60	7.70	7.80	7.90	8.00
0	0.0008	0.0007	0.0007	0.0006	0.0006	0.0005	0.0005	0.0004	0.0004	0.0003
1	0.0067	0.0061	0.0056	0.0051	0.0047	0.0043	0.0039	0.0036	0.0033	0.0030
2	0.0275	0.0255	0.0236	0.0219	0.0203	0.0188	0.0174	0.0161	0.0149	0.0138
3	0.0767	0.0719	0.0674	0.0632	0.0591	0.0554	0.0518	0.0485	0.0453	0.0424
4	0.1641	0.1555	0.1473	0.1395	0.1321	0.1249	0.1181	0.1117	0.1055	0.0996
5	0.2881	0.2759	0.2640	0.2526	0.2414	0.2307	0.2203	0.2103	0.2006	0.1912
6	0.4349	0.4204	0.4060	0.3920	0.3782	0.3646	0.3514	0.3384	0.3257	0.3134
7	0.5838	0.5689	0.5541	0.5393	0.5246	0.5100	0.4956	0.4812	0.4670	0.4530
8	0.7160	0.7027	0.6892	0.6757	0.6620	0.6482	0.6343	0.6204	0.6065	0.5925
9	0.8202	0.8096	0.7988	0.7877	0.7764	0.7649	0.7531	0.7411	0.7290	0.7166
10	0.8942	0.8867	0.8788	0.8707	0.8622	0.8535	0.8445	0.8352	0.8257	0.8159
11	0.9420	0.9371	0.9319	0.9265	0.9208	0.9148	0.9085	0.9020	0.8952	0.8881
12	0.9703	0.9673	0.9642	0.9609	0.9573	0.9536	0.9496	0.9454	0.9409	0.9362
13	0.9857	0.9841	0.9824	0.9805	0.9784	0.9762	0.9739	0.9714	0.9687	0.9658
14	0.9935	0.9927	0.9918	0.9908	0.9897	0.9886	0.9873	0.9859	0.9844	0.9827
15	0.9972	0.9969	0.9964	0.9959	0.9954	0.9948	0.9941	0.9934	0.9926	0.9918
16	0.9989	0.9987	0.9985	0.9983	0.9980	0.9978	0.9974	0.9971	0.9967	0.9963
17	0.9996	0.9995	0.9994	0.9993	0.9992	0.9991	0.9989	0.9988	0.9986	0.9984
18	0.9998	0.9998	0.9998	0.9997	0.9997	0.9996	0.9996	0.9995	0.9994	0.9993
19	0.9999	0.9999	0.9999	0.9999	0.9999	0.9999	0.9998	0.9998	0.9998	0.9997
20	1.0000	1.0000	1.0000	1.0000	1.0000	1.0000	0.9999	0.9999	0.9999	0.9999
21	1.0000	1.0000	1.0000	1.0000	1.0000	1.0000	1.0000	1.0000	1.0000	1.0000

λt

x	8.10	8.20	8.30	8.40	8.50	8.60	8.70	8.80	8.90	9.00
0	0.0003	0.0003	0.0002	0.0002	0.0002	0.0002	0.0002	0.0002	0.0001	0.0001
1	0.0028	0.0025	0.0023	0.0021	0.0019	0.0018	0.0016	0.0015	0.0014	0.0012
2	0.0127	0.0118	0.0109	0.0100	0.0093	0.0086	0.0079	0.0073	0.0068	0.0062
3	0.0396	0.0370	0.0346	0.0323	0.0301	0.0281	0.0262	0.0244	0.0228	0.0212
4	0.0940	0.0887	0.0837	0.0789	0.0744	0.0701	0.0660	0.0621	0.0584	0.0550
5	0.1822	0.1736	0.1653	0.1573	0.1496	0.1422	0.1352	0.1284	0.1219	0.1157
6	0.3013	0.2896	0.2781	0.2670	0.2562	0.2457	0.2355	0.2256	0.2160	0.2068
7	0.4391	0.4254	0.4119	0.3987	0.3856	0.3728	0.3602	0.3478	0.3357	0.3239
8	0.5786	0.5647	0.5507	0.5369	0.5231	0.5094	0.4958	0.4823	0.4689	0.4557
9	0.7041	0.6915	0.6788	0.6659	0.6530	0.6400	0.6269	0.6137	0.6006	0.5874
10	0.8058	0.7955	0.7850	0.7743	0.7634	0.7522	0.7409	0.7294	0.7178	0.7060
11	0.8807	0.8731	0.8652	0.8571	0.8487	0.8400	0.8311	0.8220	0.8126	0.8030
12	0.9313	0.9261	0.9207	0.9150	0.9091	0.9029	0.8965	0.8898	0.8829	0.8758
13	0.9628	0.9595	0.9561	0.9524	0.9486	0.9445	0.9403	0.9358	0.9311	0.9261
14	0.9810	0.9791	0.9771	0.9749	0.9726	0.9701	0.9675	0.9647	0.9617	0.9585
15	0.9908	0.9898	0.9887	0.9875	0.9862	0.9848	0.9832	0.9816	0.9798	0.9780
16	0.9958	0.9953	0.9947	0.9941	0.9934	0.9926	0.9918	0.9909	0.9899	0.9889
17	0.9982	0.9979	0.9977	0.9973	0.9970	0.9966	0.9962	0.9957	0.9952	0.9947
18	0.9992	0.9991	0.9990	0.9989	0.9987	0.9985	0.9983	0.9981	0.9978	0.9976
19	0.9997	0.9997	0.9996	0.9995	0.9995	0.9994	0.9993	0.9992	0.9991	0.9989
20	0.9999	0.9999	0.9998	0.9998	0.9998	0.9998	0.9997	0.9997	0.9996	0.9996
21	1.0000	1.0000	0.9999	0.9999	0.9999	0.9999	0.9999	0.9999	0.9998	0.9998
22	1.0000	1.0000	1.0000	1.0000	1.0000	1.0000	1.0000	1.0000	0.9999	0.9999
23	1.0000	1.0000	1.0000	1.0000	1.0000	1.0000	1.0000	1.0000	1.0000	1.0000

λt

x	9.10	9.20	9.30	9.40	9.50	9.60	9.70	9.80	9.90	10.00
0	0.0001	0.0001	0.0001	0.0001	0.0001	0.0001	0.0001	0.0001	0.0001	0.0000
1	0.0011	0.0010	0.0009	0.0009	0.0008	0.0007	0.0007	0.0006	0.0005	0.0005
2	0.0058	0.0053	0.0049	0.0045	0.0042	0.0038	0.0035	0.0033	0.0030	0.0028
3	0.0198	0.0184	0.0172	0.0160	0.0149	0.0138	0.0129	0.0120	0.0111	0.0103
4	0.0517	0.0486	0.0456	0.0429	0.0403	0.0378	0.0355	0.0333	0.0312	0.0293
5	0.1098	0.1041	0.0986	0.0935	0.0885	0.0838	0.0793	0.0750	0.0710	0.0671
6	0.1978	0.1892	0.1808	0.1727	0.1649	0.1574	0.1502	0.1433	0.1366	0.1301
7	0.3123	0.3010	0.2900	0.2792	0.2687	0.2584	0.2485	0.2388	0.2294	0.2202
8	0.4426	0.4296	0.4168	0.4042	0.3918	0.3796	0.3676	0.3558	0.3442	0.3328
9	0.5742	0.5611	0.5479	0.5349	0.5218	0.5089	0.4960	0.4832	0.4705	0.4579
10	0.6941	0.6820	0.6699	0.6576	0.6453	0.6329	0.6205	0.6080	0.5955	0.5830
11	0.7932	0.7832	0.7730	0.7626	0.7520	0.7412	0.7303	0.7193	0.7081	0.6968
12	0.8684	0.8607	0.8529	0.8448	0.8364	0.8279	0.8191	0.8101	0.8009	0.7916
13	0.9210	0.9156	0.9100	0.9042	0.8981	0.8919	0.8853	0.8786	0.8716	0.8645
14	0.9552	0.9517	0.9480	0.9441	0.9400	0.9357	0.9312	0.9265	0.9216	0.9165
15	0.9760	0.9738	0.9715	0.9691	0.9665	0.9638	0.9609	0.9579	0.9546	0.9513
16	0.9878	0.9865	0.9852	0.9838	0.9823	0.9806	0.9789	0.9770	0.9751	0.9730
17	0.9941	0.9934	0.9927	0.9919	0.9911	0.9902	0.9892	0.9881	0.9870	0.9857
18	0.9973	0.9969	0.9966	0.9962	0.9957	0.9952	0.9947	0.9941	0.9935	0.9928
19	0.9988	0.9986	0.9985	0.9983	0.9980	0.9978	0.9975	0.9972	0.9969	0.9965
20	0.9995	0.9994	0.9993	0.9992	0.9991	0.9990	0.9989	0.9987	0.9986	0.9984
21	0.9998	0.9998	0.9997	0.9997	0.9996	0.9996	0.9995	0.9995	0.9994	0.9993
22	0.9999	0.9999	0.9999	0.9999	0.9999	0.9998	0.9998	0.9998	0.9997	0.9997
23	1.0000	1.0000	1.0000	1.0000	0.9999	0.9999	0.9999	0.9999	0.9999	0.9999
24	1.0000	1.0000	1.0000	1.0000	1.0000	1.0000	1.0000	1.0000	1.0000	1.0000

(continued)

λt

x	11.00	12.00	13.00	14.00	15.00	16.00	17.00	18.00	19.00	20.00
0	0.0000	0.0000	0.0000	0.0000	0.0000	0.0000	0.0000	0.0000	0.0000	0.0000
1	0.0002	0.0001	0.0000	0.0000	0.0000	0.0000	0.0000	0.0000	0.0000	0.0000
2	0.0012	0.0005	0.0002	0.0001	0.0000	0.0000	0.0000	0.0000	0.0000	0.0000
3	0.0049	0.0023	0.0011	0.0005	0.0002	0.0001	0.0000	0.0000	0.0000	0.0000
4	0.0151	0.0076	0.0037	0.0018	0.0009	0.0004	0.0002	0.0001	0.0000	0.0000
5	0.0375	0.0203	0.0107	0.0055	0.0028	0.0014	0.0007	0.0003	0.0002	0.0001
6	0.0786	0.0458	0.0259	0.0142	0.0076	0.0040	0.0021	0.0010	0.0005	0.0003
7	0.1432	0.0895	0.0540	0.0316	0.0180	0.0100	0.0054	0.0029	0.0015	0.0008
8	0.2320	0.1550	0.0998	0.0621	0.0374	0.0220	0.0126	0.0071	0.0039	0.0021
9	0.3405	0.2424	0.1658	0.1094	0.0699	0.0433	0.0261	0.0154	0.0089	0.0050
10	0.4599	0.3472	0.2517	0.1757	0.1185	0.0774	0.0491	0.0304	0.0183	0.0108
11	0.5793	0.4616	0.3532	0.2600	0.1848	0.1270	0.0847	0.0549	0.0347	0.0214
12	0.6887	0.5760	0.4631	0.3585	0.2676	0.1931	0.1350	0.0917	0.0606	0.0390
13	0.7813	0.6815	0.5730	0.4644	0.3632	0.2745	0.2009	0.1426	0.0984	0.0661
14	0.8540	0.7720	0.6751	0.5704	0.4657	0.3675	0.2808	0.2081	0.1497	0.1049
15	0.9074	0.8444	0.7636	0.6694	0.5681	0.4667	0.3715	0.2867	0.2148	0.1565
16	0.9441	0.8987	0.8355	0.7559	0.6641	0.5660	0.4677	0.3751	0.2920	0.2211
17	0.9678	0.9370	0.8905	0.8272	0.7489	0.6593	0.5640	0.4686	0.3784	0.2970
18	0.9823	0.9626	0.9302	0.8826	0.8195	0.7423	0.6550	0.5622	0.4695	0.3814
19	0.9907	0.9787	0.9573	0.9235	0.8752	0.8122	0.7363	0.6509	0.5606	0.4703
20	0.9953	0.9884	0.9750	0.9521	0.9170	0.8682	0.8055	0.7307	0.6472	0.5591
21	0.9977	0.9939	0.9859	0.9712	0.9469	0.9108	0.8615	0.7991	0.7255	0.6437
22	0.9990	0.9970	0.9924	0.9833	0.9673	0.9418	0.9047	0.8551	0.7931	0.7206
23	0.9995	0.9985	0.9960	0.9907	0.9805	0.9633	0.9367	0.8989	0.8490	0.7875
24	0.9998	0.9993	0.9980	0.9950	0.9888	0.9777	0.9594	0.9317	0.8933	0.8432
25	0.9999	0.9997	0.9990	0.9974	0.9938	0.9869	0.9748	0.9554	0.9269	0.8878
26	1.0000	0.9999	0.9995	0.9987	0.9967	0.9925	0.9848	0.9718	0.9514	0.9221
27	1.0000	0.9999	0.9998	0.9994	0.9983	0.9959	0.9912	0.9827	0.9687	0.9475
28	1.0000	1.0000	0.9999	0.9997	0.9991	0.9978	0.9950	0.9897	0.9805	0.9657
29	1.0000	1.0000	1.0000	0.9999	0.9996	0.9989	0.9973	0.9941	0.9882	0.9782
30	1.0000	1.0000	1.0000	0.9999	0.9998	0.9994	0.9986	0.9967	0.9930	0.9865
31	1.0000	1.0000	1.0000	1.0000	0.9999	0.9997	0.9993	0.9982	0.9960	0.9919
32	1.0000	1.0000	1.0000	1.0000	1.0000	0.9999	0.9996	0.9990	0.9978	0.9953
33	1.0000	1.0000	1.0000	1.0000	1.0000	0.9999	0.9998	0.9995	0.9988	0.9973
34	1.0000	1.0000	1.0000	1.0000	1.0000	1.0000	0.9999	0.9998	0.9994	0.9985
35	1.0000	1.0000	1.0000	1.0000	1.0000	1.0000	1.0000	0.9999	0.9997	0.9992
36	1.0000	1.0000	1.0000	1.0000	1.0000	1.0000	1.0000	0.9999	0.9998	0.9996
37	1.0000	1.0000	1.0000	1.0000	1.0000	1.0000	1.0000	1.0000	0.9999	0.9998
38	1.0000	1.0000	1.0000	1.0000	1.0000	1.0000	1.0000	1.0000	1.0000	0.9999
39	1.0000	1.0000	1.0000	1.0000	1.0000	1.0000	1.0000	1.0000	1.0000	0.9999
40	1.0000	1.0000	1.0000	1.0000	1.0000	1.0000	1.0000	1.0000	1.0000	1.0000

APPENDIX D

Standard Normal Distribution Table

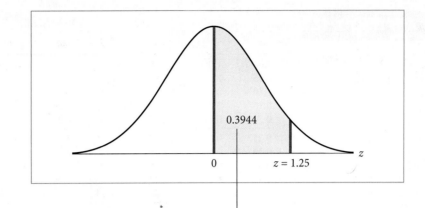

z	0	0.01	0.02	0.03	0.04	0.05	0.06	0.07	0.08	0.09
0.0	0.0000	0.0040	0.0080	0.0120	0.0160	0.0199	0.0239	0.0279	0.0319	0.0359
0.1	0.0398	0.0438	0.0478	0.0517	0.0557	0.0596	0.0636	0.0675	0.0714	0.0753
0.2	0.0793	0.0832	0.0871	0.0910	0.0948	0.0987	0.1026	0.1064	0.1103	0.1141
0.3	0.1179	0.1217	0.1255	0.1293	0.1331	0.1368	0.1406	0.1443	0.1480	0.1517
0.4	0.1554	0.1591	0.1628	0.1664	0.1700	0.1736	0.1772	0.1808	0.1844	0.1879
0.5	0.1915	0.1950	0.1985	0.2019	0.2054	0.2088	0.2123	0.2157	0.2190	0.2224
0.6	0.2257	0.2291	0.2324	0.2357	0.2389	0.2422	0.2454	0.2486	0.2517	0.2549
0.7	0.2580	0.2611	0.2642	0.2673	0.2704	0.2734	0.2764	0.2794	0.2823	0.2852
0.8	0.2881	0.2910	0.2939	0.2967	0.2995	0.3023	0.3051	0.3078	0.3106	0.3133
0.9	0.3159	0.3186	0.3212	0.3238	0.3264	0.3289	0.3315	0.3340	0.3365	0.3389
1.0	0.3413	0.3438	0.3461	0.3485	0.3508	0.3531	0.3554	0.3577	0.3599	0.3621
1.1	0.3643	0.3665	0.3686	0.3708	0.3729	0.3749	0.3770	0.3790	0.3810	0.3830
1.2	0.3849	0.3869	0.3888	0.3907	0.3925	0.3944	0.3962	0.3980	0.3997	0.4015
1.3	0.4032	0.4049	0.4066	0.4082	0.4099	0.4115	0.4131	0.4147	0.4162	0.4177
1.4	0.4192	0.4207	0.4222	0.4236	0.4251	0.4265	0.4279	0.4292	0.4306	0.4319
1.5	0.4332	0.4345	0.4357	0.4370	0.4382	0.4394	0.4406	0.4418	0.4429	0.4441
1.6	0.4452	0.4463	0.4474	0.4484	0.4495	0.4505	0.4515	0.4525	0.4535	0.4545
1.7	0.4554	0.4564	0.4573	0.4582	0.4591	0.4599	0.4608	0.4616	0.4625	0.4633
1.8	0.4641	0.4649	0.4656	0.4664	0.4671	0.4678	0.4686	0.4693	0.4699	0.4706
1.9	0.4713	0.4719	0.4726	0.4732	0.4738	0.4744	0.4750	0.4756	0.4761	0.4767
2.0	0.4772	0.4778	0.4783	0.4788	0.4793	0.4798	0.4803	0.4808	0.4812	0.4817
2.1	0.4821	0.4826	0.4830	0.4834	0.4838	0.4842	0.4846	0.4850	0.4854	0.4857
2.2	0.4861	0.4864	0.4868	0.4871	0.4875	0.4878	0.4881	0.4884	0.4887	0.4890
2.3	0.4893	0.4896	0.4898	0.4901	0.4904	0.4906	0.4909	0.4911	0.4913	0.4916
2.4	0.4918	0.4920	0.4922	0.4925	0.4927	0.4929	0.4931	0.4932	0.4934	0.4936
2.5	0.4938	0.4940	0.4941	0.4943	0.4945	0.4946	0.4948	0.4949	0.4951	0.4952
2.6	0.4953	0.4955	0.4956	0.4957	0.4959	0.4960	0.4961	0.4962	0.4963	0.4964
2.7	0.4965	0.4966	0.4967	0.4968	0.4969	0.4970	0.4971	0.4972	0.4973	0.4974
2.8	0.4974	0.4975	0.4976	0.4977	0.4977	0.4978	0.4979	0.4979	0.4980	0.4981
2.9	0.4981	0.4982	0.4982	0.4983	0.4984	0.4984	0.4985	0.4985	0.4986	0.4986
3.0	0.4987	0.4987	0.4987	0.4988	0.4988	0.4989	0.4989	0.4989	0.4990	0.4990

Exponential Distribution Table

Values of $e^{-\lambda a}$

λa	$e^{-\lambda a}$	λa	$e^{-\lambda a}$	λa	$e^{-\lambda a}$	λa	$e^{-\lambda a}$	λa	$e^{-\lambda a}$
0.00	1.0000	2.05	0.1287	4.05	0.0174	6.05	0.0024	8.05	0.0003
0.05	0.9512	2.10	0.1225	4.10	0.0166	6.10	0.0022	8.10	0.0003
0.10	0.9048	2.15	0.1165	4.15	0.0158	6.15	0.0021	8.15	0.0003
0.15	0.8607	2.20	0.1108	4.20	0.0150	6.20	0.0020	8.20	0.0003
0.20	0.8187	2.25	0.1054	4.25	0.0143	6.25	0.0019	8.25	0.0003
0.25	0.7788	2.30	0.1003	4.30	0.0136	6.30	0.0018	8.30	0.0002
0.30	0.7408	2.35	0.0954	4.35	0.0129	6.35	0.0017	8.35	0.0002
0.35	0.7047	2.40	0.0907	4.40	0.0123	6.40	0.0017	8.40	0.0002
0.40	0.6703	2.45	0.0863	4.45	0.0117	6.45	0.0016	8.45	0.0002
0.45	0.6376	2.50	0.0821	4.50	0.0111	6.50	0.0015	8.50	0.0002
0.50	0.6065	2.55	0.0781	4.55	0.0106	6.55	0.0014	8.55	0.0002
0.55	0.5769	2.60	0.0743	4.60	0.0101	6.60	0.0014	8.60	0.0002
0.60	0.5488	2.65	0.0707	4.65	0.0096	6.65	0.0013	8.65	0.0002
0.65	0.5220	2.70	0.0672	4.70	0.0091	6.70	0.0012	8.70	0.0002
0.70	0.4966	2.75	0.0639	4.75	0.0087	6.75	0.0012	8.75	0.0002
0.75	0.4724	2.80	0.0608	4.80	0.0082	6.80	0.0011	8.80	0.0002
0.80	0.4493	2.85	0.0578	4.85	0.0078	6.85	0.0011	8.85	0.0001
0.85	0.4274	2.90	0.0550	4.90	0.0074	6.90	0.0010	8.90	0.0001
0.90	0.4066	2.95	0.0523	4.95	0.0071	6.95	0.0010	8.95	0.0001
0.95	0.3867	3.00	0.0498	5.00	0.0067	7.00	0.0009	9.00	0.0001
1.00	0.3679	3.05	0.0474	5.05	0.0064	7.05	0.0009	9.05	0.0001
1.05	0.3499	3.10	0.0450	5.10	0.0061	7.10	0.0008	9.10	0.0001
1.10	0.3329	3.15	0.0429	5.15	0.0058	7.15	0.0008	9.15	0.0001
1.15	0.3166	3.20	0.0408	5.20	0.0055	7.20	0.0007	9.20	0.0001
1.20	0.3012	3.25	0.0388	5.25	0.0052	7.25	0.0007	9.25	0.0001
1.25	0.2865	3.30	0.0369	5.30	0.0050	7.30	0.0007	9.30	0.0001
1.30	0.2725	3.35	0.0351	5.35	0.0047	7.35	0.0006	9.35	0.0001
1.35	0.2592	3.40	0.0334	5.40	0.0045	7.40	0.0006	9.40	0.0001
1.40	0.2466	3.45	0.0317	5.45	0.0043	7.45	0.0006	9.45	0.0001
1.45	0.2346	3.50	0.0302	5.50	0.0041	7.50	0.0006	9.50	0.0001
1.50	0.2231	3.55	0.0287	5.55	0.0039	7.55	0.0005	9.55	0.0001
1.55	0.2122	3.60	0.0273	5.60	0.0037	7.60	0.0005	9.60	0.0001
1.60	0.2019	3.65	0.0260	5.65	0.0035	7.65	0.0005	9.65	0.0001
1.65	0.1920	3.70	0.0247	5.70	0.0033	7.70	0.0005	9.70	0.0001
1.70	0.1827	3.75	0.0235	5.75	0.0032	7.75	0.0004	9.75	0.0001
1.75	0.1738	3.80	0.0224	5.80	0.0030	7.80	0.0004	9.80	0.0001
1.80	0.1653	3.85	0.0213	5.85	0.0029	7.85	0.0004	9.85	0.0001
1.85	0.1572	3.90	0.0202	5.90	0.0027	7.90	0.0004	9.90	0.0001
1.90	0.1496	3.95	0.0193	5.95	0.0026	7.95	0.0004	9.95	0.0000
1.95	0.1423	4.00	0.0183	6.00	0.0025	8.00	0.0003	10.00	0.0000
2.00	0.1353								

Values of t for Selected Probabilities

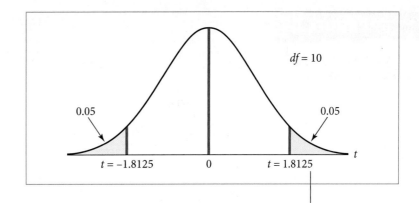

$df = 10$

0.05

0.05

$t = -1.8125$ 0 $t = 1.8125$

PROBABILITIES (OR AREAS UNDER t-DISTRIBUTION CURVE)

Conf. Level	0.1	0.3	0.5	0.7	0.8	0.9	0.95	0.98	0.99
One Tail	0.45	0.35	0.25	0.15	0.1	0.05	0.025	0.01	0.005
Two Tails	0.9	0.7	0.5	0.3	0.2	0.1	0.05	0.02	0.01
df					Values of t				
1	0.1584	0.5095	1.0000	1.9626	3.0777	6.3137	12.7062	31.8210	63.6559
2	0.1421	0.4447	0.8165	1.3862	1.8856	2.9200	4.3027	6.9645	9.9250
3	0.1366	0.4242	0.7649	1.2498	1.6377	2.3534	3.1824	4.5407	5.8408
4	0.1338	0.4142	0.7407	1.1896	1.5332	2.1318	2.7765	3.7469	4.6041
5	0.1322	0.4082	0.7267	1.1558	1.4759	2.0150	2.5706	3.3649	4.0321
6	0.1311	0.4043	0.7176	1.1342	1.4398	1.9432	2.4469	3.1427	3.7074
7	0.1303	0.4015	0.7111	1.1192	1.4149	1.8946	2.3646	2.9979	3.4995
8	0.1297	0.3995	0.7064	1.1081	1.3968	1.8595	2.3060	2.8965	3.3554
9	0.1293	0.3979	0.7027	1.0997	1.3830	1.8331	2.2622	2.8214	3.2498
10	0.1289	0.3966	0.6998	1.0931	1.3722	1.8125	2.2281	2.7638	3.1693
11	0.1286	0.3956	0.6974	1.0877	1.3634	1.7959	2.2010	2.7181	3.1058
12	0.1283	0.3947	0.6955	1.0832	1.3562	1.7823	2.1788	2.6810	3.0545
13	0.1281	0.3940	0.6938	1.0795	1.3502	1.7709	2.1604	2.6503	3.0123
14	0.1280	0.3933	0.6924	1.0763	1.3450	1.7613	2.1448	2.6245	2.9768
15	0.1278	0.3928	0.6912	1.0735	1.3406	1.7531	2.1315	2.6025	2.9467
16	0.1277	0.3923	0.6901	1.0711	1.3368	1.7459	2.1199	2.5835	2.9208
17	0.1276	0.3919	0.6892	1.0690	1.3334	1.7396	2.1098	2.5669	2.8982
18	0.1274	0.3915	0.6884	1.0672	1.3304	1.7341	2.1009	2.5524	2.8784
19	0.1274	0.3912	0.6876	1.0655	1.3277	1.7291	2.0930	2.5395	2.8609
20	0.1273	0.3909	0.6870	1.0640	1.3253	1.7247	2.0860	2.5280	2.8453
21	0.1272	0.3906	0.6864	1.0627	1.3232	1.7207	2.0796	2.5176	2.8314
22	0.1271	0.3904	0.6858	1.0614	1.3212	1.7171	2.0739	2.5083	2.8188
23	0.1271	0.3902	0.6853	1.0603	1.3195	1.7139	2.0687	2.4999	2.8073
24	0.1270	0.3900	0.6848	1.0593	1.3178	1.7109	2.0639	2.4922	2.7970
25	0.1269	0.3898	0.6844	1.0584	1.3163	1.7081	2.0595	2.4851	2.7874
26	0.1269	0.3896	0.6840	1.0575	1.3150	1.7056	2.0555	2.4786	2.7787
27	0.1268	0.3894	0.6837	1.0567	1.3137	1.7033	2.0518	2.4727	2.7707
28	0.1268	0.3893	0.6834	1.0560	1.3125	1.7011	2.0484	2.4671	2.7633
29	0.1268	0.3892	0.6830	1.0553	1.3114	1.6991	2.0452	2.4620	2.7564
30	0.1267	0.3890	0.6828	1.0547	1.3104	1.6973	2.0423	2.4573	2.7500
40	0.1265	0.3881	0.6807	1.0500	1.3031	1.6839	2.0211	2.4233	2.7045
50	0.1263	0.3875	0.6794	1.0473	1.2987	1.6759	2.0086	2.4033	2.6778
60	0.1262	0.3872	0.6786	1.0455	1.2958	1.6706	2.0003	2.3901	2.6603
70	0.1261	0.3869	0.6780	1.0442	1.2938	1.6669	1.9944	2.3808	2.6479
80	0.1261	0.3867	0.6776	1.0432	1.2922	1.6641	1.9901	2.3739	2.6387
90	0.1260	0.3866	0.6772	1.0424	1.2910	1.6620	1.9867	2.3685	2.6316
100	0.1260	0.3864	0.6770	1.0418	1.2901	1.6602	1.9840	2.3642	2.6259
250	0.1258	0.3858	0.6755	1.0386	1.2849	1.6510	1.9695	2.3414	2.5956
500	0.1257	0.3855	0.6750	1.0375	1.2832	1.6479	1.9647	2.3338	2.5857
∞	0.1257	0.3853	0.6745	1.0364	1.2816	1.6449	1.9600	2.3263	2.5758

APPENDIX G

Values of χ^2 for Selected Probabilities

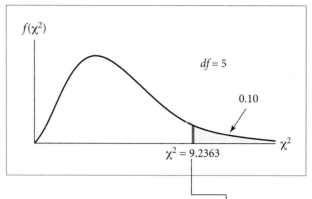

PROBABILITIES (OR AREAS UNDER CHI-SQUARE DISTRIBUTION CURVE ABOVE GIVEN CHI-SQUARE VALUES)

	0.995	0.99	0.975	0.95	0.90	0.10	0.05	0.025	0.01	0.005
df						Values of Chi-Squared				
1	0.0000	0.0002	0.0010	0.0039	0.0158	2.7055	3.8415	5.0239	6.6349	7.8794
2	0.0100	0.0201	0.0506	0.1026	0.2107	4.6052	5.9915	7.3778	9.2104	10.5965
3	0.0717	0.1148	0.2158	0.3518	0.5844	6.2514	7.8147	9.3484	11.3449	12.8381
4	0.2070	0.2971	0.4844	0.7107	1.0636	7.7794	9.4877	11.1433	13.2767	14.8602
5	0.4118	0.5543	0.8312	1.1455	1.6103	9.2363	11.0705	12.8325	15.0863	16.7496
6	0.6757	0.8721	1.2373	1.6354	2.2041	10.6446	12.5916	14.4494	16.8119	18.5475
7	0.9893	1.2390	1.6899	2.1673	2.8331	12.0170	14.0671	16.0128	18.4753	20.2777
8	1.3444	1.6465	2.1797	2.7326	3.4895	13.3616	15.5073	17.5345	20.0902	21.9549
9	1.7349	2.0879	2.7004	3.3251	4.1682	14.6837	16.9190	19.0228	21.6660	23.5893
10	2.1558	2.5582	3.2470	3.9403	4.8652	15.9872	18.3070	20.4832	23.2093	25.1881
11	2.6032	3.0535	3.8157	4.5748	5.5778	17.2750	19.6752	21.9200	24.7250	26.7569
12	3.0738	3.5706	4.4038	5.2260	6.3038	18.5493	21.0261	23.3367	26.2170	28.2997
13	3.5650	4.1069	5.0087	5.8919	7.0415	19.8119	22.3620	24.7356	27.6882	29.8193
14	4.0747	4.6604	5.6287	6.5706	7.7895	21.0641	23.6848	26.1189	29.1412	31.3194
15	4.6009	5.2294	6.2621	7.2609	8.5468	22.3071	24.9958	27.4884	30.5780	32.8015
16	5.1422	5.8122	6.9077	7.9616	9.3122	23.5418	26.2962	28.8453	31.9999	34.2671
17	5.6973	6.4077	7.5642	8.6718	10.0852	24.7690	27.5871	30.1910	33.4087	35.7184
18	6.2648	7.0149	8.2307	9.3904	10.8649	25.9894	28.8693	31.5264	34.8052	37.1564
19	6.8439	7.6327	8.9065	10.1170	11.6509	27.2036	30.1435	32.8523	36.1908	38.5821
20	7.4338	8.2604	9.5908	10.8508	12.4426	28.4120	31.4104	34.1696	37.5663	39.9969
21	8.0336	8.8972	10.2829	11.5913	13.2396	29.6151	32.6706	35.4789	38.9322	41.4009
22	8.6427	9.5425	10.9823	12.3380	14.0415	30.8133	33.9245	36.7807	40.2894	42.7957
23	9.2604	10.1957	11.6885	13.0905	14.8480	32.0069	35.1725	38.0756	41.6383	44.1814
24	9.8862	10.8563	12.4011	13.8484	15.6587	33.1962	36.4150	39.3641	42.9798	45.5584
25	10.5196	11.5240	13.1197	14.6114	16.4734	34.3816	37.6525	40.6465	44.3140	46.9280
26	11.1602	12.1982	13.8439	15.3792	17.2919	35.5632	38.8851	41.9231	45.6416	48.2898
27	11.8077	12.8785	14.5734	16.1514	18.1139	36.7412	40.1133	43.1945	46.9628	49.6450
28	12.4613	13.5647	15.3079	16.9279	18.9392	37.9159	41.3372	44.4608	48.2782	50.9936
29	13.1211	14.2564	16.0471	17.7084	19.7677	39.0875	42.5569	45.7223	49.5878	52.3355
30	13.7867	14.9535	16.7908	18.4927	20.5992	40.2560	43.7730	46.9792	50.8922	53.6719

APPENDIX H

F-Distribution Table: Upper 5% Probability (or 5% Area) under F-Distribution Curve

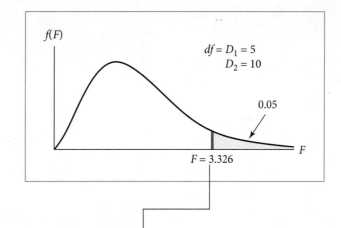

DENOMINATOR

$df = D_2$

NUMERATOR $df = D_1$

	1	2	3	4	5	6	7	8	9	10
1	161.446	199.499	215.707	224.583	230.160	233.988	236.767	238.884	240.543	241.882
2	18.513	19.000	19.164	19.247	19.296	19.329	19.353	19.371	19.385	19.396
3	10.128	9.552	9.277	9.117	9.013	8.941	8.887	8.845	8.812	8.785
4	7.709	6.944	6.591	6.388	6.256	6.163	6.094	6.041	5.999	5.964
5	6.608	5.786	5.409	5.192	5.050	4.950	4.876	4.818	4.772	4.735
6	5.987	5.143	4.757	4.534	4.387	4.284	4.207	4.147	4.099	4.060
7	5.591	4.737	4.347	4.120	3.972	3.866	3.787	3.726	3.677	3.637
8	5.318	4.459	4.066	3.838	3.688	3.581	3.500	3.438	3.388	3.347
9	5.117	4.256	3.863	3.633	3.482	3.374	3.293	3.230	3.179	3.137
10	4.965	4.103	3.708	3.478	3.326	3.217	3.135	3.072	3.020	2.978
11	4.844	3.982	3.587	3.357	3.204	3.095	3.012	2.948	2.896	2.854
12	4.747	3.885	3.490	3.259	3.106	2.996	2.913	2.849	2.796	2.753
13	4.667	3.806	3.411	3.179	3.025	2.915	2.832	2.767	2.714	2.671
14	4.600	3.739	3.344	3.112	2.958	2.848	2.764	2.699	2.646	2.602
15	4.543	3.682	3.287	3.056	2.901	2.790	2.707	2.641	2.588	2.544
16	4.494	3.634	3.239	3.007	2.852	2.741	2.657	2.591	2.538	2.494
17	4.451	3.592	3.197	2.965	2.810	2.699	2.614	2.548	2.494	2.450
18	4.414	3.555	3.160	2.928	2.773	2.661	2.577	2.510	2.456	2.412
19	4.381	3.522	3.127	2.895	2.740	2.628	2.544	2.477	2.423	2.378
20	4.351	3.493	3.098	2.866	2.711	2.599	2.514	2.447	2.393	2.348
24	4.260	3.403	3.009	2.776	2.621	2.508	2.423	2.355	2.300	2.255
30	4.171	3.316	2.922	2.690	2.534	2.421	2.334	2.266	2.211	2.165
40	4.085	3.232	2.839	2.606	2.449	2.336	2.249	2.180	2.124	2.077
50	4.034	3.183	2.790	2.557	2.400	2.286	2.199	2.130	2.073	2.026
100	3.936	3.087	2.696	2.463	2.305	2.191	2.103	2.032	1.975	1.927
200	3.888	3.041	2.650	2.417	2.259	2.144	2.056	1.985	1.927	1.878
300	3.873	3.026	2.635	2.402	2.244	2.129	2.040	1.969	1.911	1.862

DENOMINATOR

$df = D_2$

NUMERATOR $df = D_1$

	11	12	13	14	15	16	17	18	19	20
1	242.981	243.905	244.690	245.363	245.949	246.466	246.917	247.324	247.688	248.016
2	19.405	19.412	19.419	19.424	19.429	19.433	19.437	19.440	19.443	19.446
3	8.763	8.745	8.729	8.715	8.703	8.692	8.683	8.675	8.667	8.660
4	5.936	5.912	5.891	5.873	5.858	5.844	5.832	5.821	5.811	5.803
5	4.704	4.678	4.655	4.636	4.619	4.604	4.590	4.579	4.568	4.558
6	4.027	4.000	3.976	3.956	3.938	3.922	3.908	3.896	3.884	3.874
7	3.603	3.575	3.550	3.529	3.511	3.494	3.480	3.467	3.455	3.445
8	3.313	3.284	3.259	3.237	3.218	3.202	3.187	3.173	3.161	3.150
9	3.102	3.073	3.048	3.025	3.006	2.989	2.974	2.960	2.948	2.936
10	2.943	2.913	2.887	2.865	2.845	2.828	2.812	2.798	2.785	2.774
11	2.818	2.788	2.761	2.739	2.719	2.701	2.685	2.671	2.658	2.646
12	2.717	2.687	2.660	2.637	2.617	2.599	2.583	2.568	2.555	2.544
13	2.635	2.604	2.577	2.554	2.533	2.515	2.499	2.484	2.471	2.459
14	2.565	2.534	2.507	2.484	2.463	2.445	2.428	2.413	2.400	2.388
15	2.507	2.475	2.448	2.424	2.403	2.385	2.368	2.353	2.340	2.328
16	2.456	2.425	2.397	2.373	2.352	2.333	2.317	2.302	2.288	2.276

(continued)

DENOMINATOR

$df = D_2$	NUMERATOR $df = D_1$									
	11	**12**	**13**	**14**	**15**	**16**	**17**	**18**	**19**	**20**
17	2.413	2.381	2.353	2.329	2.308	2.289	2.272	2.257	2.243	2.230
18	2.374	2.342	2.314	2.290	2.269	2.250	2.233	2.217	2.203	2.191
19	2.340	2.308	2.280	2.256	2.234	2.215	2.198	2.182	2.168	2.155
20	2.310	2.278	2.250	2.225	2.203	2.184	2.167	2.151	2.137	2.124
24	2.216	2.183	2.155	2.130	2.108	2.088	2.070	2.054	2.040	2.027
30	2.126	2.092	2.063	2.037	2.015	1.995	1.976	1.960	1.945	1.932
40	2.038	2.003	1.974	1.948	1.924	1.904	1.885	1.868	1.853	1.839
50	1.986	1.952	1.921	1.895	1.871	1.850	1.831	1.814	1.798	1.784
100	1.886	1.850	1.819	1.792	1.768	1.746	1.726	1.708	1.691	1.676
200	1.837	1.801	1.769	1.742	1.717	1.694	1.674	1.656	1.639	1.623
300	1.821	1.785	1.753	1.725	1.700	1.677	1.657	1.638	1.621	1.606

DENOMINATOR

$df = D_2$	NUMERATOR $df = D_1$						
	24	**30**	**40**	**50**	**100**	**200**	**300**
1	249.052	250.096	251.144	251.774	253.043	253.676	253.887
2	19.454	19.463	19.471	19.476	19.486	19.491	19.492
3	8.638	8.617	8.594	8.581	8.554	8.540	8.536
4	5.774	5.746	5.717	5.699	5.664	5.646	5.640
5	4.527	4.496	4.464	4.444	4.405	4.385	4.378
6	3.841	3.808	3.774	3.754	3.712	3.690	3.683
7	3.410	3.376	3.340	3.319	3.275	3.252	3.245
8	3.115	3.079	3.043	3.020	2.975	2.951	2.943
9	2.900	2.864	2.826	2.803	2.756	2.731	2.723
10	2.737	2.700	2.661	2.637	2.588	2.563	2.555
11	2.609	2.570	2.531	2.507	2.457	2.431	2.422
12	2.505	2.466	2.426	2.401	2.350	2.323	2.314
13	2.420	2.380	2.339	2.314	2.261	2.234	2.225
14	2.349	2.308	2.266	2.241	2.187	2.159	2.150
15	2.288	2.247	2.204	2.178	2.123	2.095	2.085
16	2.235	2.194	2.151	2.124	2.068	2.039	2.030
17	2.190	2.148	2.104	2.077	2.020	1.991	1.981
18	2.150	2.107	2.063	2.035	1.978	1.948	1.938
19	2.114	2.071	2.026	1.999	1.940	1.910	1.899
20	2.082	2.039	1.994	1.966	1.907	1.875	1.865
24	1.984	1.939	1.892	1.863	1.800	1.768	1.756
30	1.887	1.841	1.792	1.761	1.695	1.660	1.647
40	1.793	1.744	1.693	1.660	1.589	1.551	1.537
50	1.737	1.687	1.634	1.599	1.525	1.484	1.469
100	1.627	1.573	1.515	1.477	1.392	1.342	1.323
200	1.572	1.516	1.455	1.415	1.321	1.263	1.240
300	1.554	1.497	1.435	1.393	1.296	1.234	1.210

APPENDIX H (continued)

F-Distribution Table: Upper 2.5% Probability (or 2.5% Area) under F-Distribution Curve

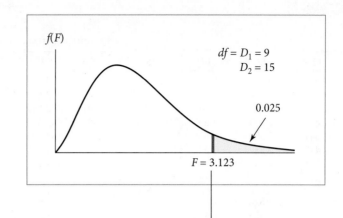

DENOMINATOR

$df = D_2$	NUMERATOR $df = D_1$										
	1	2	3	4	5	6	7	8	9	10	11
1	647.793	799.482	864.151	899.599	921.835	937.114	948.203	956.643	963.279	968.634	973.028
2	38.506	39.000	39.166	39.248	39.298	39.331	39.356	39.373	39.387	39.398	39.407
3	17.443	16.044	15.439	15.101	14.885	14.735	14.624	14.540	14.473	14.419	14.374
4	12.218	10.649	9.979	9.604	9.364	9.197	9.074	8.980	8.905	8.844	8.794
5	10.007	8.434	7.764	7.388	7.146	6.978	6.853	6.757	6.681	6.619	6.568
6	8.813	7.260	6.599	6.227	5.988	5.820	5.695	5.600	5.523	5.461	5.410
7	8.073	6.542	5.890	5.523	5.285	5.119	4.995	4.899	4.823	4.761	4.709
8	7.571	6.059	5.416	5.053	4.817	4.652	4.529	4.433	4.357	4.295	4.243
9	7.209	5.715	5.078	4.718	4.484	4.320	4.197	4.102	4.026	3.964	3.912
10	6.937	5.456	4.826	4.468	4.236	4.072	3.950	3.855	3.779	3.717	3.665
11	6.724	5.256	4.630	4.275	4.044	3.881	3.759	3.664	3.588	3.526	3.474
12	6.554	5.096	4.474	4.121	3.891	3.728	3.607	3.512	3.436	3.374	3.321
13	6.414	4.965	4.347	3.996	3.767	3.604	3.483	3.388	3.312	3.250	3.197
14	6.298	4.857	4.242	3.892	3.663	3.501	3.380	3.285	3.209	3.147	3.095
15	6.200	4.765	4.153	3.804	3.576	3.415	3.293	3.199	3.123	3.060	3.008
16	6.115	4.687	4.077	3.729	3.502	3.341	3.219	3.125	3.049	2.986	2.934
17	6.042	4.619	4.011	3.665	3.438	3.277	3.156	3.061	2.985	2.922	2.870
18	5.978	4.560	3.954	3.608	3.382	3.221	3.100	3.005	2.929	2.866	2.814
19	5.922	4.508	3.903	3.559	3.333	3.172	3.051	2.956	2.880	2.817	2.765
20	5.871	4.461	3.859	3.515	3.289	3.128	3.007	2.913	2.837	2.774	2.721
24	5.717	4.319	3.721	3.379	3.155	2.995	2.874	2.779	2.703	2.640	2.586
30	5.568	4.182	3.589	3.250	3.026	2.867	2.746	2.651	2.575	2.511	2.458
40	5.424	4.051	3.463	3.126	2.904	2.744	2.624	2.529	2.452	2.388	2.334
50	5.340	3.975	3.390	3.054	2.833	2.674	2.553	2.458	2.381	2.317	2.263
100	5.179	3.828	3.250	2.917	2.696	2.537	2.417	2.321	2.244	2.179	2.124
200	5.100	3.758	3.182	2.850	2.630	2.472	2.351	2.256	2.178	2.113	2.058
300	5.075	3.735	3.160	2.829	2.609	2.451	2.330	2.234	2.156	2.091	2.036

DENOMINATOR

$df = D_2$	NUMERATOR $df = D_1$										
	12	13	14	15	16	17	18	19	20	24	30
1	976.725	979.839	982.545	984.874	986.911	988.715	990.345	991.800	993.081	997.272	1001.405
2	39.415	39.421	39.427	39.431	39.436	39.439	39.442	39.446	39.448	39.457	39.465
3	14.337	14.305	14.277	14.253	14.232	14.213	14.196	14.181	14.167	14.124	14.081
4	8.751	8.715	8.684	8.657	8.633	8.611	8.592	8.575	8.560	8.511	8.461
5	6.525	6.488	6.456	6.428	6.403	6.381	6.362	6.344	6.329	6.278	6.227
6	5.366	5.329	5.297	5.269	5.244	5.222	5.202	5.184	5.168	5.117	5.065
7	4.666	4.628	4.596	4.568	4.543	4.521	4.501	4.483	4.467	4.415	4.362
8	4.200	4.162	4.130	4.101	4.076	4.054	4.034	4.016	3.999	3.947	3.894
9	3.868	3.831	3.798	3.769	3.744	3.722	3.701	3.683	3.667	3.614	3.560
10	3.621	3.583	3.550	3.522	3.496	3.474	3.453	3.435	3.419	3.365	3.311
11	3.430	3.392	3.359	3.330	3.304	3.282	3.261	3.243	3.226	3.173	3.118
12	3.277	3.239	3.206	3.177	3.152	3.129	3.108	3.090	3.073	3.019	2.963
13	3.153	3.115	3.082	3.053	3.027	3.004	2.983	2.965	2.948	2.893	2.837
14	3.050	3.012	2.979	2.949	2.923	2.900	2.879	2.861	2.844	2.789	2.732
15	2.963	2.925	2.891	2.862	2.836	2.813	2.792	2.773	2.756	2.701	2.644
16	2.889	2.851	2.817	2.788	2.761	2.738	2.717	2.698	2.681	2.625	2.568

(continued)

DENOMINATOR

$df = D_2$	NUMERATOR $df = D_1$										
	12	**13**	**14**	**15**	**16**	**17**	**18**	**19**	**20**	**24**	**30**
17	2.825	2.786	2.753	2.723	2.697	2.673	2.652	2.633	2.616	2.560	2.502
18	2.769	2.730	2.696	2.667	2.640	2.617	2.596	2.576	2.559	2.503	2.445
19	2.720	2.681	2.647	2.617	2.591	2.567	2.546	2.526	2.509	2.452	2.394
20	2.676	2.637	2.603	2.573	2.547	2.523	2.501	2.482	2.464	2.408	2.349
24	2.541	2.502	2.468	2.437	2.411	2.386	2.365	2.345	2.327	2.269	2.209
30	2.412	2.372	2.338	2.307	2.280	2.255	2.233	2.213	2.195	2.136	2.074
40	2.288	2.248	2.213	2.182	2.154	2.129	2.107	2.086	2.068	2.007	1.943
50	2.216	2.176	2.140	2.109	2.081	2.056	2.033	2.012	1.993	1.931	1.866
100	2.077	2.036	2.000	1.968	1.939	1.913	1.890	1.868	1.849	1.784	1.715
200	2.010	1.969	1.932	1.900	1.870	1.844	1.820	1.798	1.778	1.712	1.640
300	1.988	1.947	1.910	1.877	1.848	1.821	1.797	1.775	1.755	1.688	1.616

DENOMINATOR

$df = D_2$	NUMERATOR $df = D_1$				
	40	**50**	**100**	**200**	**300**
1	1005.596	1008.098	1013.163	1015.724	1016.539
2	39.473	39.478	39.488	39.493	39.495
3	14.036	14.010	13.956	13.929	13.920
4	8.411	8.381	8.319	8.288	8.278
5	6.175	6.144	6.080	6.048	6.037
6	5.012	4.980	4.915	4.882	4.871
7	4.309	4.276	4.210	4.176	4.165
8	3.840	3.807	3.739	3.705	3.693
9	3.505	3.472	3.403	3.368	3.357
10	3.255	3.221	3.152	3.116	3.104
11	3.061	3.027	2.956	2.920	2.908
12	2.906	2.871	2.800	2.763	2.750
13	2.780	2.744	2.671	2.634	2.621
14	2.674	2.638	2.565	2.526	2.513
15	2.585	2.549	2.474	2.435	2.422
16	2.509	2.472	2.396	2.357	2.343
17	2.442	2.405	2.329	2.289	2.275
18	2.384	2.347	2.269	2.229	2.215
19	2.333	2.295	2.217	2.176	2.162
20	2.287	2.249	2.170	2.128	2.114
24	2.146	2.107	2.024	1.981	1.966
30	2.009	1.968	1.882	1.835	1.819
40	1.875	1.832	1.741	1.691	1.673
50	1.796	1.752	1.656	1.603	1.584
100	1.640	1.592	1.483	1.420	1.397
200	1.562	1.511	1.393	1.320	1.293
300	1.536	1.484	1.361	1.285	1.255

APPENDIX H (continued)

F-Distribution Table: Upper 1% Probability (or 1% Area) under F-Distribution Curve

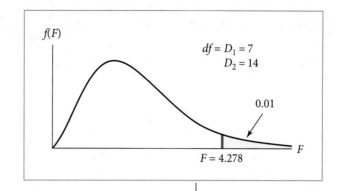

DENOMINATOR

$df = D_2$

NUMERATOR $df = D_1$

	1	2	3	4	5	6	7	8	9	10	11
1	4052.185	4999.340	5403.534	5624.257	5763.955	5858.950	5928.334	5980.954	6022.397	6055.925	6083.399
2	98.502	99.000	99.164	99.251	99.302	99.331	99.357	99.375	99.390	99.397	99.408
3	34.116	30.816	29.457	28.710	28.237	27.911	27.671	27.489	27.345	27.228	27.132
4	21.198	18.000	16.694	15.977	15.522	15.207	14.976	14.799	14.659	14.546	14.452
5	16.258	13.274	12.060	11.392	10.967	10.672	10.456	10.289	10.158	10.051	9.963
6	13.745	10.925	9.780	9.148	8.746	8.466	8.260	8.102	7.976	7.874	7.790
7	12.246	9.547	8.451	7.847	7.460	7.191	6.993	6.840	6.719	6.620	6.538
8	11.259	8.649	7.591	7.006	6.632	6.371	6.178	6.029	5.911	5.814	5.734
9	10.562	8.022	6.992	6.422	6.057	5.802	5.613	5.467	5.351	5.257	5.178
10	10.044	7.559	6.552	5.994	5.636	5.386	5.200	5.057	4.942	4.849	4.772
11	9.646	7.206	6.217	5.668	5.316	5.069	4.886	4.744	4.632	4.539	4.462
12	9.330	6.927	5.953	5.412	5.064	4.821	4.640	4.499	4.388	4.296	4.220
13	9.074	6.701	5.739	5.205	4.862	4.620	4.441	4.302	4.191	4.100	4.025
14	8.862	6.515	5.564	5.035	4.695	4.456	4.278	4.140	4.030	3.939	3.864
15	8.683	6.359	5.417	4.893	4.556	4.318	4.142	4.004	3.895	3.805	3.730
16	8.531	6.226	5.292	4.773	4.437	4.202	4.026	3.890	3.780	3.691	3.616
17	8.400	6.112	5.185	4.669	4.336	4.101	3.927	3.791	3.682	3.593	3.518
18	8.285	6.013	5.092	4.579	4.248	4.015	3.841	3.705	3.597	3.508	3.434
19	8.185	5.926	5.010	4.500	4.171	3.939	3.765	3.631	3.523	3.434	3.360
20	8.096	5.849	4.938	4.431	4.103	3.871	3.699	3.564	3.457	3.368	3.294
24	7.823	5.614	4.718	4.218	3.895	3.667	3.496	3.363	3.256	3.168	3.094
30	7.562	5.390	4.510	4.018	3.699	3.473	3.305	3.173	3.067	2.979	2.906
40	7.314	5.178	4.313	3.828	3.514	3.291	3.124	2.993	2.888	2.801	2.727
50	7.171	5.057	4.199	3.720	3.408	3.186	3.020	2.890	2.785	2.698	2.625
100	6.895	4.824	3.984	3.513	3.206	2.988	2.823	2.694	2.590	2.503	2.430
200	6.763	4.713	3.881	3.414	3.110	2.893	2.730	2.601	2.497	2.411	2.338
300	6.720	4.677	3.848	3.382	3.079	2.862	2.699	2.571	2.467	2.380	2.307

DENOMINATOR

$df = D_2$

NUMERATOR $df = D_1$

	12	13	14	15	16	17	18	19	20	24	30
1	6106.682	6125.774	6143.004	6156.974	6170.012	6181.188	6191.432	6200.746	6208.662	6234.273	6260.350
2	99.419	99.422	99.426	99.433	99.437	99.441	99.444	99.448	99.448	99.455	99.466
3	27.052	26.983	26.924	26.872	26.826	26.786	26.751	26.719	26.690	26.597	26.504
4	14.374	14.306	14.249	14.198	14.154	14.114	14.079	14.048	14.019	13.929	13.838
5	9.888	9.825	9.770	9.722	9.680	9.643	9.609	9.580	9.553	9.466	9.379
6	7.718	7.657	7.605	7.559	7.519	7.483	7.451	7.422	7.396	7.313	7.229
7	6.469	6.410	6.359	6.314	6.275	6.240	6.209	6.181	6.155	6.074	5.992
8	5.667	5.609	5.559	5.515	5.477	5.442	5.412	5.384	5.359	5.279	5.198
9	5.111	5.055	5.005	4.962	4.924	4.890	4.860	4.833	4.808	4.729	4.649
10	4.706	4.650	4.601	4.558	4.520	4.487	4.457	4.430	4.405	4.327	4.247
11	4.397	4.342	4.293	4.251	4.213	4.180	4.150	4.123	4.099	4.021	3.941
12	4.155	4.100	4.052	4.010	3.972	3.939	3.910	3.883	3.858	3.780	3.701
13	3.960	3.905	3.857	3.815	3.778	3.745	3.716	3.689	3.665	3.587	3.507
14	3.800	3.745	3.698	3.656	3.619	3.586	3.556	3.529	3.505	3.427	3.348
15	3.666	3.612	3.564	3.522	3.485	3.452	3.423	3.396	3.372	3.294	3.214
16	3.553	3.498	3.451	3.409	3.372	3.339	3.310	3.283	3.259	3.181	3.101

(continued)

DENOMINATOR

$df = D_2$	NUMERATOR $df = D_1$										
	12	**13**	**14**	**15**	**16**	**17**	**18**	**19**	**20**	**24**	**30**
17	3.455	3.401	3.353	3.312	3.275	3.242	3.212	3.186	3.162	3.083	3.003
18	3.371	3.316	3.269	3.227	3.190	3.158	3.128	3.101	3.077	2.999	2.919
19	3.297	3.242	3.195	3.153	3.116	3.084	3.054	3.027	3.003	2.925	2.844
20	3.231	3.177	3.130	3.088	3.051	3.018	2.989	2.962	2.938	2.859	2.778
24	3.032	2.977	2.930	2.889	2.852	2.819	2.789	2.762	2.738	2.659	2.577
30	2.843	2.789	2.742	2.700	2.663	2.630	2.600	2.573	2.549	2.469	2.386
40	2.665	2.611	2.563	2.522	2.484	2.451	2.421	2.394	2.369	2.288	2.203
50	2.563	2.508	2.461	2.419	2.382	2.348	2.318	2.290	2.265	2.183	2.098
100	2.368	2.313	2.265	2.223	2.185	2.151	2.120	2.092	2.067	1.983	1.893
200	2.275	2.220	2.172	2.129	2.091	2.057	2.026	1.997	1.971	1.886	1.794
300	2.244	2.190	2.142	2.099	2.061	2.026	1.995	1.966	1.940	1.854	1.761

DENOMINATOR

$df = D_2$	NUMERATOR $df = D_1$				
	40	**50**	**100**	**200**	**300**
1	6286.427	6302.260	6333.925	6349.757	6355.345
2	99.477	99.477	99.491	99.491	99.499
3	26.411	26.354	26.241	26.183	26.163
4	13.745	13.690	13.577	13.520	13.501
5	9.291	9.238	9.130	9.075	9.057
6	7.143	7.091	6.987	6.934	6.916
7	5.908	5.858	5.755	5.702	5.685
8	5.116	5.065	4.963	4.911	4.894
9	4.567	4.517	4.415	4.363	4.346
10	4.165	4.115	4.014	3.962	3.944
11	3.860	3.810	3.708	3.656	3.638
12	3.619	3.569	3.467	3.414	3.397
13	3.425	3.375	3.272	3.219	3.202
14	3.266	3.215	3.112	3.059	3.040
15	3.132	3.081	2.977	2.923	2.905
16	3.018	2.967	2.863	2.808	2.790
17	2.920	2.869	2.764	2.709	2.691
18	2.835	2.784	2.678	2.623	2.604
19	2.761	2.709	2.602	2.547	2.528
20	2.695	2.643	2.535	2.479	2.460
24	2.492	2.440	2.329	2.271	2.251
30	2.299	2.245	2.131	2.070	2.049
40	2.114	2.058	1.938	1.874	1.851
50	2.007	1.949	1.825	1.757	1.733
100	1.797	1.735	1.598	1.518	1.490
200	1.694	1.629	1.481	1.391	1.357
300	1.660	1.594	1.441	1.346	1.309

APPENDIX I

Distribution of the Studentized Range (*q*-values)

$p = 0.95$

D_2 \ D_1	2	3	4	5	6	7	8	9	10
1	17.97	26.98	32.82	37.08	40.41	43.12	45.40	47.36	49.07
2	6.08	8.33	9.80	10.88	11.74	12.44	13.03	13.54	13.99
3	4.50	5.91	6.82	7.50	8.04	8.48	8.85	9.18	9.46
4	3.93	5.04	5.76	6.29	6.71	7.05	7.35	7.60	7.83
5	3.64	4.60	5.22	5.67	6.03	6.33	6.58	6.80	6.99
6	3.46	4.34	4.90	5.30	5.63	5.90	6.12	6.32	6.49
7	3.34	4.16	4.68	5.06	5.36	5.61	5.82	6.00	6.16
8	3.26	4.04	4.53	4.89	5.17	5.40	5.60	5.77	5.92
9	3.20	3.95	4.41	4.76	5.02	5.24	5.43	5.59	5.74
10	3.15	3.88	4.33	4.65	4.91	5.12	5.30	5.46	5.60
11	3.11	3.82	4.26	4.57	4.82	5.03	5.20	5.35	5.49
12	3.08	3.77	4.20	4.51	4.75	4.95	5.12	5.27	5.39
13	3.06	3.73	4.15	4.45	4.69	4.88	5.05	5.19	5.32
14	3.03	3.70	4.11	4.41	4.64	4.83	4.99	5.13	5.25
15	3.01	3.67	4.08	4.37	4.59	4.78	4.94	5.08	5.20
16	3.00	3.65	4.05	4.33	4.56	4.74	4.90	5.03	5.15
17	2.98	3.63	4.02	4.30	4.52	4.70	4.86	4.99	5.11
18	2.97	3.61	4.00	4.28	4.49	4.67	4.82	4.96	5.07
19	2.96	3.59	3.98	4.25	4.47	4.65	4.79	4.92	5.04
20	2.95	3.58	3.96	4.23	4.45	4.62	4.77	4.90	5.01
24	2.92	3.53	3.90	4.17	4.37	4.54	4.68	4.81	4.92
30	2.89	3.49	3.85	4.10	4.30	4.46	4.60	4.72	4.82
40	2.86	3.44	3.79	4.04	4.23	4.39	4.52	4.63	4.73
60	2.83	3.40	3.74	3.98	4.16	4.31	4.44	4.55	4.65
120	2.80	3.36	3.68	3.92	4.10	4.24	4.36	4.47	4.56
∞	2.77	3.31	3.63	3.86	4.03	4.17	4.29	4.39	4.47

D_2 \ D_1	11	12	13	14	15	16	17	18	19	20
1	50.59	51.96	53.20	54.33	55.36	56.32	57.22	58.04	58.83	59.56
2	14.39	14.75	15.08	15.38	15.65	15.91	16.14	16.37	16.57	16.77
3	9.72	9.95	10.15	10.35	10.52	10.69	10.84	10.98	11.11	11.24
4	8.03	8.21	8.37	8.52	8.66	8.79	8.91	9.03	9.13	9.23
5	7.17	7.32	7.47	7.60	7.72	7.83	7.93	8.03	8.12	8.21
6	6.65	6.79	6.92	7.03	7.14	7.24	7.34	7.43	7.51	7.59
7	6.30	6.43	6.55	6.66	6.76	6.85	6.94	7.02	7.10	7.17
8	6.05	6.18	6.29	6.39	6.48	6.57	6.65	6.73	6.80	6.87
9	5.87	5.98	6.09	6.19	6.28	6.36	6.44	6.51	6.58	6.64
10	5.72	5.83	5.93	6.03	6.11	6.19	6.27	6.34	6.40	6.47
11	5.61	5.71	5.81	5.90	5.98	6.06	6.13	6.20	6.27	6.33
12	5.51	5.61	5.71	5.80	5.88	5.95	6.02	6.09	6.15	6.21
13	5.43	5.53	5.63	5.71	5.79	5.86	5.93	5.99	6.05	6.11
14	5.36	5.46	5.55	5.64	5.71	5.79	5.85	5.91	5.97	6.03
15	5.31	5.40	5.49	5.57	5.65	5.72	5.78	5.85	5.90	5.96
16	5.26	5.35	5.44	5.52	5.59	5.66	5.73	5.79	5.84	5.90
17	5.21	5.31	5.39	5.47	5.54	5.61	5.67	5.73	5.79	5.84
18	5.17	5.27	5.35	5.43	5.50	5.57	5.63	5.69	5.74	5.79
19	5.14	5.23	5.31	5.39	5.46	5.53	5.59	5.65	5.70	5.75
20	5.11	5.20	5.28	5.36	5.43	5.49	5.55	5.61	5.66	5.71
24	5.01	5.10	5.18	5.25	5.32	5.38	5.44	5.49	5.55	5.59
30	4.92	5.00	5.08	5.15	5.21	5.27	5.33	5.38	5.43	5.47
40	4.82	4.90	4.98	5.04	5.11	5.16	5.22	5.27	5.31	5.36
60	4.73	4.81	4.88	4.94	5.00	5.06	5.11	5.15	5.20	5.24
120	4.64	4.71	4.78	4.84	4.90	4.95	5.00	5.04	5.09	5.13
∞	4.55	4.62	4.68	4.74	4.80	4.85	4.89	4.93	4.97	5.01

Note: $D_1 = K$ populations and $D_2 = N - K$.

$$p = 0.99$$

D_2 \ D_1	2	3	4	5	6	7	8	9	10
1	90.03	135.0	164.3	185.6	202.2	215.8	227.2	237.0	245.6
2	14.04	19.02	22.29	24.72	26.63	28.20	29.53	30.68	31.69
3	8.26	10.62	12.17	13.33	14.24	15.00	15.64	16.20	16.69
4	6.51	8.12	9.17	9.96	10.58	11.10	11.55	11.93	12.27
5	5.70	6.98	7.80	8.42	8.91	9.32	9.67	9.97	10.24
6	5.24	6.33	7.03	7.56	7.97	8.32	8.61	8.87	9.10
7	4.95	5.92	6.54	7.01	7.37	7.68	7.94	8.17	8.37
8	4.75	5.64	6.20	6.62	6.96	7.24	7.47	7.68	7.86
9	4.60	5.43	5.96	6.35	6.66	6.91	7.13	7.33	7.49
10	4.48	5.27	5.77	6.14	6.43	6.67	6.87	7.05	7.21
11	4.39	5.15	5.62	5.97	6.25	6.48	6.67	6.84	6.99
12	4.32	5.05	5.50	5.84	6.10	6.32	6.51	6.67	6.81
13	4.26	4.96	5.40	5.73	5.98	6.19	6.37	6.53	6.67
14	4.21	4.89	5.32	5.63	5.88	6.08	6.26	6.41	6.54
15	4.17	4.84	5.25	5.56	5.80	5.99	6.16	6.31	6.44
16	4.13	4.79	5.19	5.49	5.72	5.92	6.08	6.22	6.35
17	4.10	4.74	5.14	5.43	5.66	5.85	6.01	6.15	6.27
18	4.07	4.70	5.09	5.38	5.60	5.79	5.94	6.08	6.20
19	4.05	4.67	5.05	5.33	5.55	5.73	5.89	6.02	6.14
20	4.02	4.64	5.02	5.29	5.51	5.69	5.84	5.97	6.09
24	3.96	4.55	4.91	5.17	5.37	5.54	5.69	5.81	5.92
30	3.89	4.45	4.80	5.05	5.24	5.40	5.54	5.65	5.76
40	3.82	4.37	4.70	4.93	5.11	5.26	5.39	5.50	5.60
60	3.76	4.28	4.59	4.82	4.99	5.13	5.25	5.36	5.45
120	3.70	4.20	4.50	4.71	4.87	5.01	5.12	5.21	5.30
∞	3.64	4.12	4.40	4.60	4.76	4.88	4.99	5.08	5.16

D_2 \ D_1	11	12	13	14	15	16	17	18	19	20
1	253.2	260.0	266.2	271.8	277.0	281.8	286.3	290.4	294.3	298.0
2	32.59	33.40	34.13	34.81	35.43	36.00	36.53	37.03	37.50	37.95
3	17.13	17.53	17.89	18.22	18.52	18.81	19.07	19.32	19.55	19.77
4	12.57	12.84	13.09	13.32	13.53	13.73	13.91	14.08	14.24	14.40
5	10.48	10.70	10.89	11.08	11.24	11.40	11.55	11.68	11.81	11.93
6	9.30	9.48	9.65	9.81	9.95	10.08	10.21	10.32	10.43	10.54
7	8.55	8.71	8.86	9.00	9.12	9.24	9.35	9.46	9.55	9.65
8	8.03	8.18	8.31	8.44	8.55	8.66	8.76	8.85	8.94	9.03
9	7.65	7.78	7.91	8.03	8.13	8.23	8.33	8.41	8.49	8.57
10	7.36	7.49	7.60	7.71	7.81	7.91	7.99	8.08	8.15	8.23
11	7.13	7.25	7.36	7.46	7.56	7.65	7.73	7.81	7.88	7.95
12	6.94	7.06	7.17	7.26	7.36	7.44	7.52	7.59	7.66	7.73
13	6.79	6.90	7.01	7.10	7.19	7.27	7.35	7.42	7.48	7.55
14	6.66	6.77	6.87	6.96	7.05	7.13	7.20	7.27	7.33	7.39
15	6.55	6.66	6.76	6.84	6.93	7.00	7.07	7.14	7.20	7.26
16	6.46	6.56	6.66	6.74	6.82	6.90	6.97	7.03	7.09	7.15
17	6.38	6.48	6.57	6.66	6.73	6.81	6.87	6.94	7.00	7.05
18	6.31	6.41	6.50	6.58	6.65	6.73	6.79	6.85	6.91	6.97
19	6.25	6.34	6.43	6.51	6.58	6.65	6.72	6.78	6.84	6.89
20	6.19	6.28	6.37	6.45	6.52	6.59	6.65	6.71	6.77	6.82
24	6.02	6.11	6.19	6.26	6.33	6.39	6.45	6.51	6.56	6.61
30	5.85	5.93	6.01	6.08	6.14	6.20	6.26	6.31	6.36	6.41
40	5.69	5.76	5.83	5.90	5.96	6.02	6.07	6.12	6.16	6.21
60	5.53	5.60	5.67	5.73	5.78	5.84	5.89	5.93	5.97	6.01
120	5.37	5.44	5.50	5.56	5.61	5.66	5.71	5.75	5.79	5.83
∞	5.23	5.28	5.35	5.40	5.45	5.49	5.54	5.57	5.61	5.65

Source: Extracted from H. L. Harter and D. S. Clemm, "The Probability Integrals of the Range and of the Studentized Range—Probability Integral, Percentage Points, and Moments of the Range," *Wright Air Development Technical Report 58–484,* Vol. 1, 1959.

APPENDIX J

Critical Values of r in the Runs Test

a. Lower Tail: Too Few Runs

n_1 \ n_2	2	3	4	5	6	7	8	9	10	11	12	13	14	15	16	17	18	19	20
2											2	2	2	2	2	2	2	2	2
3			2	2	2	2	2	2	2	2	2	2	2	3	3	3	3	3	3
4			2	2	2	3	3	3	3	3	3	3	3	3	4	4	4	4	4
5			2	2	3	3	3	3	3	4	4	4	4	4	4	4	5	5	5
6		2	2	3	3	3	3	4	4	4	4	5	5	5	5	5	5	6	6
7		2	2	3	3	3	4	4	5	5	5	5	5	6	6	6	6	6	6
8		2	3	3	3	4	4	5	5	5	6	6	6	6	6	7	7	7	7
9		2	3	3	4	4	5	5	5	6	6	6	7	7	7	7	8	8	8
10		2	3	3	4	5	5	5	6	6	7	7	7	7	8	8	8	8	9
11		2	3	4	4	5	5	6	6	7	7	7	8	8	8	9	9	9	9
12	2	2	3	4	4	5	6	6	7	7	7	8	8	8	9	9	9	10	10
13	2	2	3	4	5	5	6	6	7	7	8	8	9	9	9	10	10	10	10
14	2	2	3	4	5	5	6	7	7	8	8	9	9	9	10	10	10	11	11
15	2	3	3	4	5	6	6	7	7	8	8	9	9	10	10	11	11	11	12
16	2	3	4	4	5	6	6	7	8	8	9	9	10	10	11	11	11	12	12
17	2	3	4	4	5	6	7	7	8	9	9	10	10	11	11	11	12	12	13
18	2	3	4	5	5	6	7	8	8	9	9	10	10	11	11	12	12	13	13
19	2	3	4	5	6	6	7	8	8	9	10	10	11	11	12	12	13	13	13
20	2	3	4	5	6	6	7	8	9	9	010	10	11	12	12	13	13	13	14

b. Upper Tail: Too Many Runs

n_1 \ n_2	2	3	4	5	6	7	8	9	10	11	12	13	14	15	16	17	18	19	20
2																			
3																			
4				9	9														
5			9	10	10	11	11												
6			9	10	11	12	12	13	13	13	13								
7				11	12	13	13	14	14	14	14	15	15	15					
8				11	12	13	14	14	15	15	16	16	16	16	17	17	17	17	17
9					13	14	14	15	16	16	16	17	17	18	18	18	18	18	18
10					13	14	15	16	16	17	17	18	18	18	19	19	19	20	20
11					13	14	15	16	17	17	18	19	19	19	20	20	20	21	21
12					13	14	16	16	17	18	19	19	20	20	21	21	21	22	22
13						15	16	17	18	19	19	20	20	21	21	22	22	23	23
14						15	16	17	18	19	20	20	21	22	22	23	23	23	24
15						15	16	18	18	19	20	21	22	22	23	23	24	24	25
16							17	18	19	20	21	21	22	23	23	24	25	25	25
17							17	18	19	20	21	22	23	23	24	25	25	26	26
18							17	18	19	20	21	22	23	24	25	25	26	26	27
19							17	18	20	21	22	23	23	24	25	26	26	27	27
20							17	18	20	21	22	23	24	25	25	26	27	27	28

Source: Adapted from Frieda S. Swed and C. Eisenhart, "Tables for testing randomness of grouping in a sequence of alternatives," *Ann. Math. Statist.* 14 (1943): 83–86, with the permission of the publisher

Mann-Whitney U Test Probabilities ($n < 9$)

$n_2 = 3$

U \ n₁	1	2	3
0	.250	.100	.050
1	.500	.200	.100
2	.750	.400	.200
3		.600	.350
4			.500
5			.650

$n_2 = 4$

U \ n₁	1	2	3	4
0	.200	.067	.028	.014
1	.400	.133	.057	.029
2	.600	.267	.114	.057
3		.400	.200	.100
4		.600	.314	.171
5			.429	.243
6			.571	.343
7				.443
8				.557

$n_2 = 5$

U \ n₁	1	2	3	4	5
0	.167	.047	.018	.008	.004
1	.333	.095	.036	.016	.008
2	.500	.190	.071	.032	.016
3	.667	.286	.125	.056	.028
4		.429	.196	.095	.048
5		.571	.286	.143	.075
6			.393	.206	.111
7			.500	.278	.155
8			.607	.365	.210
9				.452	.274
10				.548	.345
11					.421
12					.500
13					.579

$n_2 = 6$

U \ n₁	1	2	3	4	5	6
0	.143	.036	.012	.005	.002	.001
1	.286	.071	.024	.010	.004	.002
2	.428	.143	.048	.019	.009	.004
3	.571	.214	.083	.033	.015	.008
4		.321	.131	.057	.026	.013
5		.429	.190	.086	.041	.021
6		.571	.274	.129	.063	.032
7			.357	.176	.089	.047
8			.452	.238	.123	.066
9			.548	.305	.165	.090
10				.381	.214	.120
11				.457	.268	.155
12				.545	.331	.197
13					.396	.242
14					.465	.294
15					.535	.350
16						.409
17						.469
18						.531

$n_2 = 7$

U \ n₁	1	2	3	4	5	6	7
0	.125	.028	.008	.003	.001	.001	.000
1	.250	.056	.017	.006	.003	.001	.001
2	.375	.111	.033	.012	.005	.002	.001
3	.500	.167	.058	.021	.009	.004	.002
4	.625	.250	.092	.036	.015	.007	.003
5		.333	.133	.055	.024	.011	.006
6		.444	.192	.082	.037	.017	.009
7		.556	.258	.115	.053	.026	.013
8			.333	.158	.074	.037	.019
9			.417	.206	.101	.051	.027
10			.500	.264	.134	.069	.036
11			.583	.324	.172	.090	.049
12				.394	.216	.117	.064
13				.464	.265	.147	.082
14				.538	.319	.183	.104
15					.378	.223	.130
16					.438	.267	.159
17					.500	.314	.191
18					.562	.365	.228
19						.418	.267
20						.473	.310
21						.527	.355
22							.402
23							.451
24							.500
25							.549

$$n_2 = 8$$

U \ n₁	1	2	3	4	5	6	7	8	t	Normal
0	.111	.022	.006	.002	.001	.000	.000	.000	3.308	.001
1	.222	.044	.012	.004	.002	.001	.000	.000	3.203	.001
2	.333	.089	.024	.008	.003	.001	.001	.000	3.098	.001
3	.444	.133	.042	.014	.005	.002	.001	.001	2.993	.001
4	.556	.200	.067	.024	.009	.004	.002	.001	2.888	.002
5		.267	.097	.036	.015	.006	.003	.001	2.783	.003
6		.356	.139	.055	.023	.010	.005	.002	2.678	.004
7		.444	.188	.077	.033	.015	.007	.003	2.573	.005
8		.556	.248	.107	.047	.021	.010	.005	2.468	.007
9			.315	.141	.064	.030	.014	.007	2.363	.009
10			.387	.184	.085	.041	.020	.010	2.258	.012
11			.461	.230	.111	.054	.027	.014	2.153	.016
12			.539	.285	.142	.071	.036	.019	2.048	.020
13				.341	.177	.091	.047	.025	1.943	.026
14				.404	.217	.114	.060	.032	1.838	.033
15				.467	.262	.141	.076	.041	1.733	.041
16				.533	.311	.172	.095	.052	1.628	.052
17					.362	.207	.116	.065	1.523	.064
18					.416	.245	.140	.080	1.418	.078
19					.472	.286	.168	.097	1.313	.094
20					.528	.331	.198	.117	1.208	.113
21						.377	.232	.139	1.102	.135
22						.426	.268	.164	.998	.159
23						.475	.306	.191	.893	.185
24						.525	.347	.221	.788	.215
25							.389	.253	.683	.247
26							.433	.287	.578	.282
27							.478	.323	.473	.318
28							.522	.360	.368	.356
29								.399	.263	.396
30								.439	.158	.437
31								.480	.052	.481
32								.520		

Source: Reproduced from H. B. Mann and D. R. Whitney, "On a test of whether one of two random variables is stochastically larger than the other," *Ann. Math. Statist.* 18 (1947): 52–54, with the permission of the publisher.

Mann-Whitney U Test Critical Values ($9 \leq n \leq 20$)

Critical Values of U for a One-Tailed Test at $\alpha = 0.001$ or for a Two-Tailed Test at $\alpha = 0.002$

n_1 \ n_2	9	10	11	12	13	14	15	16	17	18	19	20
1												
2												
3									0	0	0	0
4		0	0	0	1	1	1	2	2	3	3	3
5	1	1	2	2	3	3	4	5	5	6	7	7
6	2	3	4	4	5	6	7	8	9	10	11	12
7	3	5	6	7	8	9	10	11	13	14	15	16
8	5	6	8	9	11	12	14	15	17	18	20	21
9	7	8	10	12	14	15	17	19	21	23	25	26
10	8	10	12	14	17	19	21	23	25	27	29	32
11	10	12	15	17	20	22	24	27	29	32	34	37
12	12	14	17	20	23	25	28	31	34	37	40	42
13	14	17	20	23	26	29	32	35	38	42	45	48
14	15	19	22	25	29	32	36	39	43	46	50	54
15	17	21	24	28	32	36	40	43	47	51	55	59
16	19	23	27	31	35	39	43	48	52	56	60	65
17	21	25	29	34	38	43	47	52	57	61	66	70
18	23	27	32	37	42	46	51	56	61	66	71	76
19	25	29	34	40	45	50	55	60	66	71	77	82
20	26	32	37	42	48	54	59	65	70	76	82	88

Critical Values of U for a One-Tailed Test at $\alpha = 0.01$ or for a Two-Tailed Test at $\alpha = 0.02$

n_1 \ n_2	9	10	11	12	13	14	15	16	17	18	19	20
1												
2					0	0	0	0	0	0	1	1
3	1	1	1	2	2	2	3	3	4	4	4	5
4	3	3	4	5	5	6	7	7	8	9	9	10
5	5	6	7	8	9	10	11	12	13	14	15	16
6	7	8	9	11	12	13	15	16	18	19	20	22
7	9	11	12	14	16	17	19	21	23	24	26	28
8	11	13	15	17	20	22	24	26	28	30	32	34
9	14	16	18	21	23	26	28	31	33	36	38	40
10	16	19	22	24	27	30	33	36	38	41	44	47
11	18	22	25	28	31	34	37	41	44	47	50	53
12	21	24	28	31	35	38	42	46	49	53	56	60
13	23	27	31	35	39	43	47	51	55	59	63	67
14	26	30	34	38	43	47	51	56	60	65	69	73
15	28	33	37	42	47	51	56	61	66	70	75	80
16	31	36	41	46	51	56	61	66	71	76	82	87
17	33	38	44	49	55	60	66	71	77	82	88	93
18	36	41	47	53	59	65	70	76	82	88	94	100
19	38	44	50	56	63	69	75	82	88	94	101	107
20	40	47	53	60	67	73	80	87	93	100	107	114

Critical Values of U for a One-Tailed Test at $\alpha = 0.025$ or for a Two-Tailed Test at $\alpha = 0.05$

n_1 \\ n_2	9	10	11	12	13	14	15	16	17	18	19	20
1												
2	0	0	0	1	1	1	1	1	2	2	2	2
3	2	3	3	4	4	5	5	6	6	7	7	8
4	4	5	6	7	8	9	10	11	11	12	13	13
5	7	8	9	11	12	13	14	15	17	18	19	20
6	10	11	13	14	16	17	19	21	22	24	25	27
7	12	14	16	18	20	22	24	26	28	30	32	34
8	15	17	19	22	24	26	29	31	34	36	38	41
9	17	20	23	26	28	31	34	37	39	42	45	48
10	20	23	26	29	33	36	39	42	45	48	52	55
11	23	26	30	33	37	40	44	47	51	55	58	62
12	26	29	33	37	41	45	49	53	57	61	65	69
13	28	33	37	41	45	50	54	59	63	67	72	76
14	31	36	40	45	50	55	59	64	67	74	78	83
15	34	39	44	49	54	59	64	70	75	80	85	90
16	37	42	47	53	59	64	70	75	81	86	92	98
17	39	45	51	57	63	67	75	81	87	93	99	105
18	42	48	55	61	67	74	80	86	93	99	106	112
19	45	52	58	65	72	78	85	92	99	106	113	119
20	48	55	62	69	76	83	90	98	105	112	119	127

Critical Values of U for a One-Tailed Test at $\alpha = 0.05$ or for a Two-Tailed Test at $\alpha = 0.10$

n_1 \\ n_2	9	10	11	12	13	14	15	16	17	18	19	20
1											0	0
2	1	1	1	2	2	2	3	3	3	4	4	4
3	3	4	5	5	6	7	7	8	9	9	10	11
4	6	7	8	9	10	11	12	14	15	16	17	18
5	9	11	12	13	15	16	18	19	20	22	23	25
6	12	14	16	17	19	21	23	25	26	28	30	32
7	15	17	19	21	24	26	28	30	33	35	37	39
8	18	20	23	26	28	31	33	36	39	41	44	47
9	21	24	27	30	33	36	39	42	45	48	51	54
10	24	27	31	34	37	41	44	48	51	55	58	62
11	27	31	34	38	42	46	50	54	57	61	65	69
12	30	34	38	42	47	51	55	60	64	68	72	77
13	33	37	42	47	51	56	61	65	70	75	80	84
14	36	41	46	51	56	61	66	71	77	82	87	92
15	39	44	50	55	61	66	72	77	83	88	94	100
16	42	48	54	60	65	71	77	83	89	95	101	107
17	45	51	57	64	70	77	83	89	96	102	109	115
18	48	55	61	68	75	82	88	95	102	109	116	123
19	51	58	65	72	80	87	94	101	109	116	123	130
20	54	62	69	77	84	92	100	107	115	123	130	138

Source: Adapted and abridged from Tables 1, 3, 5, and 7 of D. Auble, "Extended tables for the Mann-Whitney statistic," *Bulletin of the Institute of Educational Research at Indiana University* 1, No. 2 (1953), with the permission of the publisher.

APPENDIX M

Critical Values of *T* in the Wilcoxon Matched-Pairs Signed-Ranks Test ($n \leq 25$)

n	LEVEL OF SIGNIFICANCE FOR ONE-TAILED TEST		
	0.025	0.01	0.005
	LEVEL OF SIGNIFICANCE FOR TWO-TAILED TEST		
	0.05	0.02	0.01
6	0	—	—
7	2	0	—
8	4	2	0
9	6	3	2
10	8	5	3
11	11	7	5
12	14	10	7
13	17	13	10
14	21	16	13
15	25	20	16
16	30	24	20
17	35	28	23
18	40	33	28
19	46	38	32
20	52	43	38
21	59	49	43
22	66	56	49
23	73	62	55
24	81	69	61
25	89	77	68

Source: Adapted from Table 1 of F. Wilcoxon, *Some Rapid Approximate Statistical Procedures* (New York: American Cyanamid Company, 1949), 13, with the permission of the publisher.

APPENDIX N

Critical Values d_L and d_U of the Durbin-Watson Statistic D (Critical Values Are One-Sided)

$\alpha = .05$

n	$P = 1$ d_L	d_U	$P = 2$ d_L	d_U	$P = 3$ d_L	d_U	$P = 4$ d_L	d_U	$P = 5$ d_L	d_U
15	1.08	1.36	.95	1.54	.82	1.75	.69	1.97	.56	2.21
16	1.10	1.37	.98	1.54	.86	1.73	.74	1.93	.62	2.15
17	1.13	1.38	1.02	1.54	.90	1.71	.78	1.90	.67	2.10
18	1.16	1.39	1.05	1.53	.93	1.69	.82	1.87	.71	2.06
19	1.18	1.40	1.08	1.53	.97	1.68	.86	1.85	.75	2.02
20	1.20	1.41	1.10	1.54	1.00	1.68	.90	1.83	.79	1.99
21	1.22	1.42	1.13	1.54	1.03	1.67	.93	1.81	.83	1.96
22	1.24	1.43	1.15	1.54	1.05	1.66	.96	1.80	.86	1.94
23	1.26	1.44	1.17	1.54	1.08	1.66	.99	1.79	.90	1.92
24	1.27	1.45	1.19	1.55	1.10	1.66	1.01	1.78	.93	1.90
25	1.29	1.45	1.21	1.55	1.12	1.66	1.04	1.77	.95	1.89
26	1.30	1.46	1.22	1.55	1.14	1.65	1.06	1.76	.98	1.88
27	1.32	1.47	1.24	1.56	1.16	1.65	1.08	1.76	1.01	1.86
28	1.33	1.48	1.26	1.56	1.18	1.65	1.10	1.75	1.03	1.85
29	1.34	1.48	1.27	1.56	1.20	1.65	1.12	1.74	1.05	1.84
30	1.35	1.49	1.28	1.57	1.21	1.65	1.14	1.74	1.07	1.83
31	1.36	1.50	1.30	1.57	1.23	1.65	1.16	1.74	1.09	1.83
32	1.37	1.50	1.31	1.57	1.24	1.65	1.18	1.73	1.11	1.82
33	1.38	1.51	1.32	1.58	1.26	1.65	1.19	1.73	1.13	1.81
34	1.39	1.51	1.33	1.58	1.27	1.65	1.21	1.73	1.15	1.81
35	1.40	1.52	1.34	1.58	1.28	1.65	1.22	1.73	1.16	1.80
36	1.41	1.52	1.35	1.59	1.29	1.65	1.24	1.73	1.18	1.80
37	1.42	1.53	1.36	1.59	1.31	1.66	1.25	1.72	1.19	1.80
38	1.43	1.54	1.37	1.59	1.32	1.66	1.26	1.72	1.21	1.79
39	1.43	1.54	1.38	1.60	1.33	1.66	1.27	1.72	1.22	1.79
40	1.44	1.54	1.39	1.60	1.34	1.66	1.29	1.72	1.23	1.79
45	1.48	1.57	1.43	1.62	1.38	1.67	1.34	1.72	1.29	1.78
50	1.50	1.59	1.46	1.63	1.42	1.67	1.38	1.72	1.34	1.77
55	1.53	1.60	1.49	1.64	1.45	1.68	1.41	1.72	1.38	1.77
60	1.55	1.62	1.51	1.65	1.48	1.69	1.44	1.73	1.41	1.77
65	1.57	1.63	1.54	1.66	1.50	1.70	1.47	1.73	1.44	1.77
70	1.58	1.64	1.55	1.67	1.52	1.70	1.49	1.74	1.46	1.77
75	1.60	1.65	1.57	1.68	1.54	1.71	1.51	1.74	1.49	1.77
80	1.61	1.66	1.59	1.69	1.56	1.72	1.53	1.74	1.51	1.77
85	1.62	1.67	1.60	1.70	1.57	1.72	1.55	1.75	1.52	1.77
90	1.63	1.68	1.61	1.70	1.59	1.73	1.57	1.75	1.54	1.78
95	1.64	1.69	1.62	1.71	1.60	1.73	1.58	1.75	1.56	1.78
100	1.65	1.69	1.63	1.72	1.61	1.74	1.59	1.76	1.57	1.78

$n = $ Number of observations; $P = $ Number of independent variables.
Source: Computed from TSP 4.5 based on R. W. Farebrother, "A Remark on Algorithms AS106, AS153, and AS155: The Distribution of a Linear Combination of Chi-Square Random Variables," *Journal of the Royal Statistical Society*, Series C (Applied Statistics), 1984, 29, pp. 323–333.

| | | $\alpha = .01$ | | | | | | | |
| | $P = 1$ | | $P = 2$ | | $P = 3$ | | $P = 4$ | | $P = 5$ |
n	d_L	d_U	d_L	d_U	d_L	d_U	d_L	d_U	d_L	d_U
15	.81	1.07	.70	1.25	.59	1.46	.49	1.70	.39	1.96
16	.84	1.09	.74	1.25	.63	1.44	.53	1.66	.44	1.90
17	.87	1.10	.77	1.25	.67	1.43	.57	1.63	.48	1.85
18	.90	1.12	.80	1.26	.71	1.42	.61	1.60	.52	1.80
19	.93	1.13	.83	1.26	.74	1.41	.65	1.58	.56	1.77
20	.95	1.15	.86	1.27	.77	1.41	.68	1.57	.60	1.74
21	.97	1.16	.89	1.27	.80	1.41	.72	1.55	.63	1.71
22	1.00	1.17	.91	1.28	.83	1.40	.75	1.54	.66	1.69
23	1.02	1.19	.94	1.29	.86	1.40	.77	1.53	.70	1.67
24	1.04	1.20	.96	1.30	.88	1.41	.80	1.53	.72	1.66
25	1.05	1.21	.98	1.30	.90	1.41	.83	1.52	.75	1.65
26	1.07	1.22	1.00	1.31	.93	1.41	.85	1.52	.78	1.64
27	1.09	1.23	1.02	1.32	.95	1.41	.88	1.51	.81	1.63
28	1.10	1.24	1.04	1.32	.97	1.41	.90	1.51	.83	1.62
29	1.12	1.25	1.05	1.33	.99	1.42	.92	1.51	.85	1.61
30	1.13	1.26	1.07	1.34	1.01	1.42	.94	1.51	.88	1.61
31	1.15	1.27	1.08	1.34	1.02	1.42	.96	1.51	.90	1.60
32	1.16	1.28	1.10	1.35	1.04	1.43	.98	1.51	.92	1.60
33	1.17	1.29	1.11	1.36	1.05	1.43	1.00	1.51	.94	1.59
34	1.18	1.30	1.13	1.36	1.07	1.43	1.01	1.51	.95	1.59
35	1.19	1.31	1.14	1.37	1.08	1.44	1.03	1.51	.97	1.59
36	1.21	1.32	1.15	1.38	1.10	1.44	1.04	1.51	.99	1.59
37	1.22	1.32	1.16	1.38	1.11	1.45	1.06	1.51	1.00	1.59
38	1.23	1.33	1.18	1.39	1.12	1.45	1.07	1.52	1.02	1.58
39	1.24	1.34	1.19	1.39	1.14	1.45	1.09	1.52	1.03	1.58
40	1.25	1.34	1.20	1.40	1.15	1.46	1.10	1.52	1.05	1.58
45	1.29	1.38	1.24	1.42	1.20	1.48	1.16	1.53	1.11	1.58
50	1.32	1.40	1.28	1.45	1.24	1.49	1.20	1.54	1.16	1.59
55	1.36	1.43	1.32	1.47	1.28	1.51	1.25	1.55	1.21	1.59
60	1.38	1.45	1.35	1.48	1.32	1.52	1.28	1.56	1.25	1.60
65	1.41	1.47	1.38	1.50	1.35	1.53	1.31	1.57	1.28	1.61
70	1.43	1.49	1.40	1.52	1.37	1.55	1.34	1.58	1.31	1.61
75	1.45	1.50	1.42	1.53	1.39	1.56	1.37	1.59	1.34	1.62
80	1.47	1.52	1.44	1.54	1.42	1.57	1.39	1.60	1.36	1.62
85	1.48	1.53	1.46	1.55	1.43	1.58	1.41	1.60	1.39	1.63
90	1.50	1.54	1.47	1.56	1.45	1.59	1.43	1.61	1.41	1.64
95	1.51	1.55	1.49	1.57	1.47	1.60	1.45	1.62	1.42	1.64
100	1.52	1.56	1.50	1.58	1.48	1.60	1.46	1.63	1.44	1.65

n = Number of observations; P = Number of independent variables.
Source: Computed from TSP 4.5 based on R. W. Farebrother, "A Remark on Algorithms AS106, AS153, and AS155: The Distribution of a Linear Combination of Chi-Square Random Variables," *Journal of the Royal Statistical Society*, Series C (Applied Statistics), 1984, 29, pp. 323–333.

APPENDIX O

Lower and Upper
Critical Values W
of Wilcoxon
Signed-Ranks Test

n	One-Tailed: $\alpha = .05$ Two-Tailed: $\alpha = .10$	$\alpha = .025$ $\alpha = .05$	$\alpha = .01$ $\alpha = .02$	$\alpha = .005$ $\alpha = .01$
	(Lower, Upper)			
5	0,15	—,—	—,—	—,—
6	2,19	0,21	—,—	—,—
7	3,25	2,26	0,28	—,—
8	5,31	3,33	1,35	0,36
9	8,37	5,40	3,42	1,44
10	10,45	8,47	5,50	3,52
11	13,53	10,56	7,59	5,61
12	17,61	13,65	10,68	7,71
13	21,70	17,74	12,79	10,81
14	25,80	21,84	16,89	13,92
15	30,90	25,95	19,101	16,104
16	35,101	29,107	23,113	19,117
17	41,112	34,119	27,126	23,130
18	47,124	40,131	32,139	27,144
19	53,137	46,144	37,153	32,158
20	60,150	52,158	43,167	37,173

Source: Adapted from Table 2 of F. Wilcoxon and R. A. Wilcox, *Some Rapid Approximate Statistical Procedures* (Pearl River, NY: Lederle Laboratories, 1964), with permission of the American Cyanamid Company.

APPENDIX P

Control Chart Factors

Number of Observations in Subgroup	d_2	d_3	D_3	D_4	A_2
2	1.128	0.853	0	3.267	1.880
3	1.693	0.888	0	2.575	1.023
4	2.059	0.880	0	2.282	0.729
5	2.326	0.864	0	2.114	0.577
6	2.534	0.848	0	2.004	0.483
7	2.704	0.833	0.076	1.924	0.419
8	2.847	0.820	0.136	1.864	0.373
9	2.970	0.808	0.184	1.816	0.337
10	3.078	0.797	0.223	1.777	0.308
11	3.173	0.787	0.256	1.744	0.285
12	3.258	0.778	0.283	1.717	0.266
13	3.336	0.770	0.307	1.693	0.249
14	3.407	0.763	0.328	1.672	0.235
15	3.472	0.756	0.347	1.653	0.223
16	3.532	0.750	0.363	1.637	0.212
17	3.588	0.744	0.378	1.622	0.203
18	3.640	0.739	0.391	1.609	0.194
19	3.689	0.733	0.404	1.596	0.187
20	3.735	0.729	0.415	1.585	0.180
21	3.778	0.724	0.425	1.575	0.173
22	3.819	0.720	0.435	1.565	0.167
23	3.858	0.716	0.443	1.557	0.162
24	3.895	0.712	0.452	1.548	0.157
25	3.931	0.708	0.459	1.541	0.153

Source: Reprinted from ASTM-STP 15D by kind permission of the American Society for Testing and Materials.

Answers to Selected Odd-Numbered Problems

This section contains summary answers to most of the odd-numbered problems in the text. The *Student Solutions Manual* contains fully developed solutions to all odd-numbered problems and shows clearly how each answer is determined.

Chapter 1

1-1. Descriptive; use charts, graphs, tables, and numerical measures.

1-3. A bar chart is used whenever you want to display data that have already been categorized, while a histogram is used to display data over a range of values for the factor under consideration.

1-5. Hypothesis testing uses statistical techniques to validate a claim.

1-13. statistical inference, particularly estimation

1-17. written survey or telephone survey

1-19. An experiment is any process that generates data as its outcome.

1-23. internal and external validity

1-27. Advantages—low cost, speed of delivery, instant updating of data analysis; disadvantages—low response and potential confusion about questions

1-29. personal observation data gathering

1-33. Part range $= \dfrac{Population\ size}{Sample\ size} = \dfrac{18,000}{100} = 180$

Thus, the first person selected will come from employees 1 through 180. Once that person is randomly selected, the second person will be the one numbered 100 higher than the first, and so on.

1-37. The census would consist of all items produced on the line in a defined period of time.

1-41. parameters, since it would include all U.S. colleges

1-43. a. stratified random sampling
    b. simple random sampling or possibly cluster random sampling
    c. systematic random sampling
    d. stratified random sampling

1-49. a. time-series
    b. cross-sectional
    c. time-series
    d. cross-sectional

1-51. a. ordinal—categories with defined order
    b. nominal—categories with no defined order
    c. ratio
    d. nominal—categories with no defined order

1-53. ordinal data

1-55. a. nominal data
    b. ratio data
    c. nominal data
    d. ratio data
    e. ratio data
    f. nominal data
    g. ratio data

1-61. interval or ratio data

1-67. a. Use a random sample or systematic random sample.
    b. The product is going to be ruined after testing it. You would not want to ruin the entire product that comes off the assembly line.

Chapter 2

2-3. a. $2^k \geq n$ or $2^{10} = 1,024 \geq 1,000$. Thus, use $k = 10$ classes.

    b. $w = \dfrac{High - Low}{Classes} = \dfrac{2,900 - 300}{10} = \dfrac{2,600}{10} = 260$ (round to 300)

2-5. a. 2.833, which is rounded to 3.
    b. Divide the number of occurrences (frequency) in each class by the total number of occurrences.
    c. Compute a running sum for each class by adding the frequency for that class to the frequencies for all classes above it.
    d. Classes form the horizontal axis, and the frequency forms the vertical axis. Bars corresponding to the frequency of each class are developed.

2-7. a. $1 - 0.24 = 0.76$
    b. $0.56 - 0.08 = 0.48$
    c. $0.96 - 0.08 = 0.86$

2-9. a.

Class	Frequency	Relative Frequency
2–3	2	0.0333
4–5	25	0.4167
6–7	26	0.4333
8–9	6	0.1000
10–11	1	0.0167

    b. cumulative frequencies: 2; 27; 53; 59; 60
    c. cumulative relative frequencies: 0.0333; 0.4500; 0.8833; 0.9833; 1.000
    d. ogive

2-13. a. The weights are sorted from smallest to largest to create the data array.

    b.

Weight (Classes)	Frequency
77–81	3
82–86	9
87–91	16
92–96	16
97–101	5
Total =	49

    c. The histogram can be created from the frequency distribution.
    d. 10.20%

2-15. a. $w = \dfrac{Largest - smallest}{number\ of\ classes} = \dfrac{214.4 - 105.0}{11} = 9.945 \rightarrow w = 10.$

    b. 8 of the 25, or 0.32 of the salaries are at least \$175,000
    c. 18 of the 25, or 0.72 having salaries that are at most \$205,000 but at least \$135,000

2-19. a. 9 classes
    b. $w = \dfrac{High - Low}{Classes} = \dfrac{32 - 10}{9} = \dfrac{22}{9} = 2.44$ (round up to 3.0)
    c. The frequency distribution with nine classes and a class width of 3.0 will depend on the starting point for the first class. This starting value must be at or below the minimum value of 10.
    d. The distribution is mound shaped and fairly symmetrical. It appears that the center is between 19 and 22 rounds

per year, but the rounds played are quite spread out around the center.

2-21. a. $2^5 = 32$ and $2^6 = 64$. Therefore, 6 classes are chosen.
b. The maximum value is 602,708 and the minimum value is 160 from the Total column. The difference is $602,708 - 160 = 602,548$. The class width would be $602,548/6 = 100,424.67$. Rounding up to the nearest 1,000 produces a class width of 101,000.

c.

Class	Frequency
$0 < 101,000$	33
$101,000 < 202,000$	2
$202,000 < 303,000$	2
$303,000 < 404,000$	1
$404,000 < 505,000$	2
$505,000 < 606,000$	1

d. The vast majority of airlines had fewer than 101,000 monthly passengers.

2-23. a. Order the observations (coffee consumption) from smallest to largest.
b. Using the $2^k > n$ guideline, the number of classes, k, would be 0.9 and $w = (10.1 - 3.5)/8 = 0.825$, which is rounded to 0.9. The class with the largest number is 6.2–7.0 kg of coffee.
c. The histogram can be created from the frequency distribution. The classes are shown on the horizontal axis and the frequency on the vertical axis.
d. 8.33% $(100 - 91.67)$ of the coffee drinkers sampled consume 8.0 kg or more annually.

2-29. a. The pie chart categories are the regions and the measure is the region's percentage of total income.
b. The bar chart categories are the regions and the measure for each category is the region's percentage of total income.
c. The bar chart, however, makes it easier to compare percentages across regions.

2-31. b. $= 1 - 0.0985 = 0.9015$

2-33. The bar chart is skewed, indicating that the number of $1 million houses is growing rapidly. The growth is exponential rather than linear.

2-35. A bar chart can be used to make the comparison.

2-37. a. The stem unit is 10 and the leaf unit is 1.
b. between 70 and 79 seconds

2-41. a. Leaf unit $= 1.0$
b. Slightly skewed to the left. The center is between 24 and 26.
c. $\bar{x} = \dfrac{2,428}{50} = 48.56$

2-43. a.

University Related	Religious Affiliated	Municipally Owned	Privately Held
$6,398	$3,591	$4,613	$5,191

b. The largest average charges occur at university-related hospitals and the lowest average appears to be in religious-affiliated hospitals.
c. A pie chart showing how that total is divided among the four hospital types would not be useful or appropriate.

2-47. The sales have trended upward over the past 12 months.

2-49. The line chart shows that year-end deposits have been increasing since 1997 but have increased more sharply since 2002 and have leveled off between 2006 and 2007 and recently become more volatile.

2-51. b. curvilinear
c. The largest difference in sales occurred between 2010 and 2011. That difference was almost 14 billions.

2-55. A slight positive linear relationship

2-61. b. Both relationships seem to be linear in nature.
c. This occurred in 1998, 1999, and 2001.

2-67. b. It appears that there is a positive linear relationship between the attendance and the year.

2-73. a. The independent variable is hours and the dependent variable is sales.
b. It appears that there is a positive linear relationship.

Chapter 3

3-1. $Q_1 = 4,423$; Median $= 5,002$; $Q_3 = 5,381$

3-3. $Q_1 = \dfrac{13.5 + 13.6}{2} = 13.55$

$Q_3 = \dfrac{15.5 + 15.9}{2} = 15.7$

3-7. a. $(31.2 + 32.2)/2 = 31.7$
b. $(26.7 + 31.2)/2 = 28.95$
c. $(20.8 + 22.8)/2 = 21.8$

3-9. a. Mean $= 19$; Median $= (19 + 19)/2 = 19$; Mode $= 19$
b. Symmetrical; Mean $=$ Median $=$ Mode

3-11. a. 11,213.48
b. Use weighted average.

3-13. a. Mean $= 114.21$; Median $= 107.50$; Mode $= 156$
b. skewed right

3-15. a. 562.99
b. 551.685
c. 562.90

3-17. a. 2008 Average $= \dfrac{\Sigma x_i}{n} = \dfrac{6826804000000}{8885} = 768351603.83$

2011 Average $= \dfrac{\Sigma x_i}{n} = \dfrac{7966700000000}{7436} = 10713690156$

b. Deposits went up and the number of institutions went down.
c. If, however, these data were considered "typical" and were to be used to describe past, current averages, they would be considered statistics.

3-19. a. Mean $= .33$
b. Median $= .31$
c. Mode $= .24$
d. The 800th percentile $= .40$ minutes.

3-21. a. $\bar{x} = \dfrac{1177.1}{13} = 90.55$ right-skewed
b. 0.392
c. 91.55
d. weighted average

3-25. a. Range $= 8 - 0 = 8$
b. 3.99
c. 1.998

3-27. a. 16.87
b. 4.11

3-29. Standard deviation $= 2.8$

3-31. a. Standard deviation $= 7.21$; IQR $= 24 - 12 = 12$
b. Range $=$ Largest $-$ Smallest $= 30 - 6 = 24$; Standard deviation $= 6.96$; IQR $= 12$
c. σ^2 is smaller than s^2 by a factor of $(N - 1)/N$. σ is smaller than s by a factor of $\sqrt{(N - 1)/N}$. The range and IQR are not affected.

3-33. a. The variance is 815.79 and the standard deviation is 28.56.
b. Interquartile range overcomes the susceptibility of the range to being highly influenced by extreme values.

3-35. a. Range $= 33 - 21 = 12$

$$\bar{x} = \frac{\sum_{i-1}^{n} x_i}{n} = 261/10 = 26.1$$

$$s^2 = \frac{\sum_{i=1}^{n}(x - \bar{x})^2}{n - 1} = 148.9/(10 - 1) = 16.5444;$$

$$s = \sqrt{s^2} = \sqrt{16.5444} = 4.0675$$

Interquartile range $= 28 - 23 = 5$

b. Ages are lower at Whitworth than for the U.S. colleges and universities as a group.

3-37. a. The range is 113.0, the IQR is 62.25, the variance is 1,217.14, and the standard deviation is 34.89.

b. No

c. Adding a constant to all the data values leaves the variance unchanged.

3-39. a. Mean $= -.125$ Standard Deviation $= 1.028$. IQR $= 1.1$

b. Prices have fallen slightly.

c. Variation in prices is greater than the average decrease.

3-41. a. Men spent an average of $117, whereas women spent an average of $98 for their phones. The standard deviation for men was nearly twice that for women.

b. Business users spent an average of $166.67 on their phones, whereas home users spent an average of $105.74. The variation in phone costs for the two groups was about equal.

3-43. a. The population mean is

$$\mu = \frac{\sum x}{N} = \$178,465$$

b. The population median is
$$\tilde{\mu} = \$173,000$$

c. The range is:
R = High $-$ Low
R $= \$361,100 - \$54,100$
$= \$307,000$

d. The population standard deviation is

$$\sigma = \sqrt{\frac{\sum(x - \mu)^2}{N}} = \$63,172$$

3-47. a. at least 75% in the range 2,600 to 3,400; $\mu \pm 2(\sigma)$.

b. The range 2,400 to 3,600 should contain at least 89% of the data values.

c. less than 11%

3-49. a. 25.008

b. $CV = 23.55\%$

c. The range from 31.19 to 181.24 should contain at least 89% of the data values.

3-51. For Distribution A: $CV = \frac{\sigma}{\mu}(100) = \frac{100}{500}(100) = 20\%$

For Distribution B: $CV = \frac{\sigma}{\mu}(100) = \frac{4.0}{10.0}(100) = 40\%$

3-53. a. $z = \frac{800 - \bar{x}}{s} = \frac{800 - 1,000}{250} = -0.80$

b. $z = 0.80$

c. $z = 0.00$

3-55. a. $\bar{x} = \frac{1,530}{30} = 51$; Variance $= 510.76$; Standard deviation $= 22.60$

b. $51 \pm 22.60, 51 \pm 2(22.60), 51 \pm 3(22.60)$, i.e., (28.4, 73.6), (5.8, 96.2), and (-16.8, 118.8). There are $(19/30)100\% = 63.3\%$ of the data within (28.4, 73.6),

$(30/30)100\% = 100\%$ of the data within (5.8, 96.2), $(30/30)100\% = 100\%$ of the data within (-16.8, 118.8).

c. bell-shaped population

3-57. a.

	Drug A	Drug B
Mean	234.75	270.92
Standard Deviation	13.92	19.90

b. Based on the sample means of the time each drug is effective, Drug B appears to be effective longer than Drug A.

c. Based on the standard deviation of effect time, Drug B exhibits a higher variability in effect time than Drug A.

d. Drug A, $CV = 5.93\%$; Drug B, $CV = 7.35\%$. Drug B has a higher coefficient of variation and the greater relative spread.

3-59. Existing supplier: $CV = \frac{0.078}{3.75}(100) = 2.08\%$

New supplier: $CV = \frac{0.135}{18.029}(100) = 0.75\%$

3-61. Anyone scoring below 61.86 (rounded to 62) will be rejected without an interview.
Anyone scoring higher than 91.98 (rounded to 92) will be sent directly to the company.

3-63. $CV = \frac{3,083.45}{11,144.48}(100) = 27.67\%$

At least 75% of CPA firms will compute a tax owed between $4,977.58——$17,311.38

3-65. a.

Variable	Mean	StDev	Variance	Q1	Median	Q3	IQR
Scores	94.780	4.130	17.056	93.000	96.000	98.000	5.000

b. Tchebysheff's Theorem would be preferable.

c. 99

3-73. The mode is a useful measure of location of a set of data if the data set is large and involves nominal or ordinal data.

3-75. a. 0.34

b. 0.34

c. 0.16

3-77. a. 364.42

b. Variance $= 16,662.63$; Standard deviation $= 129.08$

3-81. a. Comparing only the mean bushels/acre, you would say that Seed Type C produces the greatest average yield per acre.

b. CV of Seed Type A $= 25/88 = 0.2841$ or 28.41%
CV of Seed Type B $= 15/56 = 0.2679$ or 26.79%
CV of Seed Type C $= 16/100 = 0.1600$ or 16%
Seed Type C shows the least relative variability.

c. Seed Type A: 68% between 63 and 113
95% between 38 and 138
approximately 100% between 13 and 163
Seed Type B: 68% between 41 and 71
95% between 26 and 86
approximately 100% between 11 and 101
Seed Type C: 68% between 84 and 116
95% between 68 and 132
approximately 100% between 52 and 148

d. Seed Type A

e. Seed Type C

3-87. a. Mean $= 54.00$
Standard Deviation $= 3.813$

b. $\bar{x} \pm 1s = 54 \pm (3.813) = (50.187, 57.813)$
$\bar{x} \pm 2s = (46.374, 61.626)$
$\bar{x} \pm 3s = (42.561, 65.439)$

c. The Empirical Rule indicates that 95% of the data is contained within $\bar{x} \pm 2s$. This would mean that each tail has

$(1 - 0.95)/2 = 0.025$ of the data. Therefore, the costume should be priced at \$46.37.

3-89. a.

Variable	Mean	StDev	Median
Close-Open	−0.0354	0.2615	−0.0600

b. It means that the closing price for GE stock is an average of approximately four (\$0.0354) cents lower than the opening price.

c.

Variable	Mean	StDev	Median
Open	33.947	0.503	33.980
Close-Open	−0.0354	0.2615	−0.0600

Chapter 4

4-1. independent events

4-3. V, V V, C V, S C, V C, C C, S
S, V S, C S, S

4-5. a. subjective probability based on expert opinion
b. relative frequency based on previous customer return history
c. $1/5 = 0.20$

4-7. $1/3 = 0.333333$

4-9. a. $P(\text{Brown}) = \#\text{Brown}/\text{Total} = 310/982 = 0.3157$
b. $P(\text{YZ-99}) = \#\text{YZ-99}/\text{Total} = 375/982 = 0.3819$
c. $P(\text{YZ-99 and Brown}) = 205/982 = 0.2088$
d. not mutually exclusive since their joint probability is 0.1324

4-11. 0.375

4-15.

Type of Ad	Occurrences
Help-Wanted Ad	204
Real Estate Ad	520
Other Ad	306
Total	1,030

a. 0.1981
b. relative frequency
c. yes

4-17. a. relative frequency assessment method
b. $P(\#1) = \dfrac{4,000}{5,900} = 0.69$

4-19. a. $3,122/21,768 = 0.1434$
b. relative frequency assessment method

4-21. a. $P(Caesarean) = \dfrac{22}{50} = 0.44$

b. New births may not exactly match the 50 in this study.

4-23. The following joint frequency table (developed using Excel's pivot table feature) summarizes the data.

	Electrical	Mechanical	Total
Lincoln	28	39	67
Tyler	64	69	133
Total	92	108	200

a. $133/200 = 0.665$
b. $108/200 = 0.54$
c. $28/200 = 0.14$

4-25. a. $\dfrac{43}{100} = 0.43$

b. $\dfrac{5 + 6 + 6}{100} = 0.17$

c. For Pepsi, Probability $= \dfrac{5+6+6}{12+12+11} = \dfrac{17}{35} = 0.486$

For Coke, Probability $= \dfrac{6+6+6}{12+12+11} = \dfrac{18}{35} = 0.514$

d. For Pepsi, Probability $= \dfrac{7+6+8+5}{19+16+14+16} = \dfrac{26}{65} = 0.4$

For Coke, Probability $= \dfrac{12+10+6+11}{19+16+14+16} = \dfrac{39}{65} = 0.6$

4-27. a. $(0.9)(1 - 0.5) = 0.45$
b. $(0.6)(0.8) = 0.48$

4-29. $P(\text{senior 1 and senior 2}) = \left(\dfrac{5}{10}\right)\left(\dfrac{4}{9}\right) = \dfrac{20}{90} = 0.22$

4-31. a. $P(E_1 \text{ and } B) = P(E_1|B)P(B) = 0.25(0.30) = 0.075$
b. $P(E_1 \text{ or } B) = P(E_1) + P(B) - P(E_1 \text{ and } B)$
$= 0.35 + 0.30 - 0.075 = 0.575$
c. $P(E_1 \text{ and } E_2 \text{ and } E_3) = P(E_1)P(E_2)P(E_3)$
$= 0.35(0.15)(0.40) = 0.021$

4-33. a. $P(B) = \dfrac{\text{Number of drives from } B}{\text{Total drives}} = \dfrac{195}{700} = 0.2786$
b. $P(\text{Defect}) = \dfrac{\text{Number of defective drives}}{\text{Total drives}} = \dfrac{50}{700} = 0.0714$
c. $P(\text{Defect}|B) = \dfrac{P(\text{Defect and } B)}{P(B)} = \dfrac{0.0214}{0.2786} = 0.0769$

$P(\text{Defect}|B) = \dfrac{\text{Number of defective drives from } B}{\text{Number of drives from } B}$
$= \dfrac{15}{195} = 0.0769$

4-35. a. 0.61; 0.316
b. 0.42; 0.202; 0.518
c. 0.39

4-37. They cannot get to 99.9% on color copies.

4-39. $P(\text{Free gas}) = 0.00015 + 0.00585 + 0.0005 = 0.0065$

4-41. a. $P(\text{NFL}) = 105/200 = 0.5250$
b. $P(\text{College degree and NBA}) = 40/200 = 0.20$
c. $10/50 = 0.20$
d. The two events are not independent.

4-43. $P(\text{Line 1}|\text{Defective}) = (0.05)(0.4)/0.0725 = 0.2759$
$P(\text{Line 2}|\text{Defective}) = (0.10)(0.35)/0.0725 = 0.4828$
$P(\text{Line 3}|\text{Defective}) = (0.07)(0.25)/0.0725 = 0.2413$
The unsealed cans probably came from Line 2.

4-45. $P(\text{Supplier A}|\text{Defective}) = (0.15)(0.3)/0.115 = 0.3913$
$P(\text{Supplier B}|\text{Defective}) = (0.10)(0.7)/0.115 = 0.6087$
Supplier B is the most likely to have supplied the defective parts.

4-47. a. $P(E_1 \text{ and } E_2) = P(E_1|E_2)P(E_2) = 0.508(0.607)$
$= 0.308$
b. $P(E_1 \text{ and } E_3)/P(E_1|E_3) = 0.607/0.853 = 0.712$

4-49. a. 0.76
b. 0.988
c. 0.024
d. 0.9999

4-51. a. Probability first sampled device is defective $= 3/50 = 0.06$
b. $47/50*3/49 = 0.0576$
c. $47/50*46/49*45/48 = 0.8273$

4-53. a. 0.1856
b. 0.50
c. 0.0323
d. 0.3653

4-55. a. 0.119
    b. 0.4727
4-57. a. 0.50
    b. 0.755
    c. 0.269
4-63. a. 0.80; 0.40; 0.20; 0.60
    b. $A|\bar{B}$ and $\bar{A}|\bar{B}$ are complements.
4-65. a. 0.0156
    b. 0.1563
    c. 0.50
4-67. a. 0.149
    b. 0.997
    c. 0.449
4-69. a. the relative frequency assessment approach
    b. 0.028
    c. 0.349
    d. yes
4-71. Clerk 1 is most likely responsible for the boxes that raised the complaints.
4-73. a. $18/50 = 0.36$
    b. $4/50 = 0.08$
    c. $3/20 = 0.15$
    d. $10/18 = 0.556$
    e. There are a higher proportion of females whose functional background is marketing and a higher proportion of males whose functional background is operations.
4-75. a. $\dfrac{100}{300} = 0.33$
    b. $\dfrac{30}{300} = 0.10$
    c. $P(\text{East or } C) = P(\text{East}) + P(C) - P(\text{East and } C)$
        $= 0.25 + 0.333 - 0.103 = 0.48$
    d. $P(C|\text{East}) = P(C \text{ and East})/P(\text{East}) = 0.103/0.25$
        $= 0.41$
4-77. a. 0.3333
    b. Boise will get 70.91% of the cost, Salt Lake will get 21.82%, and Toronto will get 7.27% regardless of production volume.

Chapter 5

5-1. a. discrete random variable
    b. The possible values for x are $x = \{0, 1, 2, 3, 4, 5, 6\}$.
5-3. a. number of children under 22 living in a household
    b. discrete
5-5. 3.7 days
5-7. a. 130
    b. 412.50
    c. $\sqrt{412.50} = 20.31$
5-9. a. 15.75
    b. 20.75
    c. 78.75
    d. increases the expected value by an amount equal to the constant added
    e. the expected value being multiplied by that same constant
5-11. a. 3.51
    b. $\sigma^2 = 1.6499$; $\sigma = 1.2845$
5-13. a. 2.87 days
    b. $\sigma = \sqrt{1.4931} = 1.22$
    c. 1.65 days to 4.09 days
5-15. a. $58,300
    b. $57,480

5-17. a. Small firm profits = $135,000
    Mid-sized profits = $155,000
    Large firm profits = $160,000
    b. Small firm: $\sigma = \$30,000$
    Mid-sized firm: $\sigma = \$90,000$
    Large firm: $\sigma = \$156,604.60$
    c. The large firm has the largest expected profit.
5-21. a.

x	$P(x)$
14	0.008
15	0.024
16	0.064
17	0.048
18	0.184
19	0.216
20	0.240
21	0.128
22	0.072
23	0.016

    b. 19.168; $\sigma = \sqrt{\sigma^2} = \sqrt{3.1634} = 1.7787$
    c. Median is 19 and the quality control department is correct.
5-23. 0.2668
5-25. a. $P(x = 5) = 0.0746$
    b. $P(x \geq 7) = 0.2143$
    c. 4
    d. $\sigma = \sqrt{npq} = \sqrt{20(.20)(.80)} = 1.7889$
5-27. 0.1029
5-29. a. 0.1442
    b. 0.8002
    c. 4.55
5-31. a. 0.0688
    b. 0.0031
    c. 0.1467
    d. 0.8470
    e. 0.9987
5-33. a. 3.2
    b. 1.386
    c. 0.4060
    d. 0.9334
5-35. a. 3.46
    b. 0.012
    c. 0.004
    d. It is quite unlikely.
5-37. a. 0.5580
    b. 0.8784
    c. An increase in sample size would be required.
5-39. a. 2.96
    b. Variance = 1.8648; Standard deviation = 1.3656
    c. 0.3811
5-41. a. 0.3179
    b. 0.2174
    c. 0.25374
5-43. a. 0.051987
    b. 0.028989
5-45. a. 0.372
    b. 12 estimate may be too high.
    c. 0.0832
    d. 0.0003
    e. Redemption rate is lower than either Vericours or TCA Fulfillment estimate.

5-49. a. 9 corporations
   b. 0.414324
   c. 70th percentile is 12.
5-51. a. 0.0498
   b. 0.1512
5-53. 0.175
5-55. a. 0.4242
   b. 0.4242
   c. 0.4696
5-57. a. $P(x = 3) = 0.5$
   b. $P(x = 5) = 0$
   c. 0.6667
   d. Since $0.6667 > 0.25$, then $\bar{x} = 2$.
5-59. $P(x \geq 10) = 1 - 0.8305 = 0.1695$
5-61. 0.0015
5-63. a. $P(x = 4) = 0.4696$
   b. $P(x = 3) = 0.2167$
   c. 0.9680
5-65. a. 0.0355
   b. 0.0218
   c. 0.0709
5-67. a. 0.0632
   b. 120 Spicy Dogs
5-69. a. 0.0274
   b. 0.0000
   c. 0.0001
5-71. a. 8
   b. $\lambda t = 1(3) = 3$
   c. 0.0119
   d. It is very unlikely. Therefore, we believe that the goal has
      not been met.
5-75. a. This means the trials are dependent.
   b. does not imply that the trials are independent
5-77. a.

X	P(x)	xP(x)
0	0.56	0.00
1	0.21	0.21
2	0.13	0.26
3	0.07	0.21
4	0.03	0.12
		0.80

   b. Standard deviation = 1.0954; Variance = 1.20
5-79. 0.0020
5-81. 0.6244
5-83. a. 2.0
   b. 1.4142
   c. because outcomes equally likely
5-85. a. $E(x) = 750; E(y) = 100$
   b. $StDev(x) = 844.0972; StDev(y) = 717.635$
   c. $CV(x) = 844.0972/750 = 1.1255$
      $CV(y) = 717.635/100 = 7.1764$
5-87. a. 0.3501
   b. 0.3250
5-89. a. 0.02
   b. $E(X) = 0.6261$
   c. (0, 2.2783)
   d. $1 - 0.9929 = 0.0071$

Chapter 6

6-1. a. $\dfrac{225 - 200}{20} = \dfrac{25}{20} = 1.25$
   b. $\dfrac{190 - 200}{20} = \dfrac{-10}{20} = -0.50$
   c. $\dfrac{240 - 200}{20} = \dfrac{40}{20} = 2.00$
6-3. a. 0.4901
   b. 0.6826
   c. 0.0279
6-5. a. 0.4750
   b. 0.05
   c. 0.0904
   d. 0.97585
   e. 0.8513
6-7. a. 0.9270
   b. 0.6678
   c. 0.9260
   d. 0.8413
   e. 0.3707
6-9. a. $x = 1.29(0.50) + 5.5 = 6.145$
   b. $\mu = 6.145 - (1.65)(0.50) = 5.32$
6-11. a. 0.0027
   b. 0.2033
   c. 0.1085
6-13. a. 0.0668
   b. 0.228
   c. 0.7745
6-15. a. 0.3446
   b. 0.673
   c. 51.30
   d. 0.9732
6-17. a. 0.1762
   b. 0.3446
   c. 0.4401
   d. 0.0548
6-19. The mean and standard deviation of the random variable are
   15,000 and 1,250, respectively.
   a. 0.0548
   b. 0.0228
   c. $\mu = 15,912$ (approximately)
6-21. about $3,367.35
6-23. a. 0.1949
   b. 0.9544
   c. Mean = Median; symmetric distribution
6-25. $P(x < 1.0) = 0.5000 - 0.4761 = 0.0239$
6-27. a. $P(0.747 \leq x \leq 0.753) = 0.6915 - 0.1587 = 0.5328$
   b. $\sigma = \dfrac{0.753 - 0.75}{2.33} = 0.001$
6-31. a. skewed right
   b. approximate normal distribution
   c. 0.1230
   d. 2.034%
6-33. a. 0.75
   b. $Q_1 = 4.25/0.0625 = 8; Q_2 = 4.50/0.0625 = 12;$
      $Q_3 = 4.75/0.0625 = 16$
   c. 14.43
   d. 0.92

6-35. a. 0.9179
b. 0.0498
c. 0.0323
d. 0.9502
6-37. a. 0.3935
b. 0.2865
6-39. a. 0.7143
b. 0.1429
c. 0.0204
6-41. a. 0.4084; yes
b. 40,840
6-43. a. 0.2939
b. 0.4579
c. 0.1455
6-45. a. 0.0183
b. 0.3679
6-47. a. 0.0498
b. 0.4493
c. approximately, $\lambda = 0.08917$
6-49. a. positively skewed
b. Descriptive Statistics: ATM FEES

Variable	Mean	StDev
ATM FEES	2.907	2.555

c. $1 - 0.6433 = 0.3567$
6-55. a. 0.1353
b. 0.1353
6-57. a. 0.486583
b. 0.452934
c. 0.18888
6-59. 0.5507
6-61. Machine #1: 0.4236
Machine #2: 0.4772
6-63. 0.142778
6-65. Need an additional $11,500 - 400 = 11,100$ parking spaces.
$P(x < 60) = 0.7686$; shou
6-67. a. 0.3406
b. 0.5580
6-71. a. 0.3085
b. 0.3707
c. 93.36 minutes.
6-73. a. approximately normally distributed
b. Mean = 2.453; Standard deviation = 4.778
c. 0.0012
d. No
6-75. a. The histogram seems to be "bell shaped."
b. Mean = 396.36, Standard Deviation = 112.41
c. The 90th percentile is 540.419.
d. 376.71 is the 43rd percentile.
6-77. a. Uniform distribution. Sampling error could account for differences in this sample.
b. $f(x) = \dfrac{1}{b - a} = \dfrac{1}{35 - 24.8} = 0.098$
c. 0.451

Chapter 7

7-1. -18.50
7-3. $\bar{x} - \mu = 10.17 - 11.38 = -1.21$
7-5. a. -4.125
b. -13.458 to 11.042
c. -9.208 to 9.208

7-9. 0.64
7-11. a. $\mu = \dfrac{\sum x}{N} = \dfrac{864}{20} = 43.20$ days
b. $\bar{x} = \dfrac{\sum x}{n} = \dfrac{206}{5} = 41.20$ days;
Sampling error $= 41.20 - 43.20 = -2$
c. -28.4 days to 40.4 days
7-13. a. $3,445.30
b. $-$29.70
7-15. a. 1,432.08
b. 87.12
c. -175.937 to 178.634
7-17. a. Mean of sales = 2,764.83
b. Mean of sample = 2,797.16
c. $32.33 million
d. Smallest = $-$170.47; Largest = $218.41
7-21. a. Sampling error $= \bar{x} - \mu = \$15.84 - \$20.00 = -\$4.16$
b. Random and nonrandom samples can produce sampling error and the error is computed the same way.
7-23. $P(\bar{x} > 2,100) = 0.5000 - 0.3907 = 0.1093$
7-25. $\sigma_{\bar{x}} = \dfrac{\sigma}{\sqrt{n}} = \dfrac{40}{\sqrt{25}} = 8$
7-27. 0.0016
7-29. a. 0.3936
b. 0.2119
c. 0.1423
d. 0.0918
7-31. a. 0.8413
b. 0.1587
7-33. a. 0.3830
b. 0.9444
c. 0.9736
7-35. $P(\bar{x} \geq 4.2) = 0.5000 - 0.4989 = 0.0011$
7-37. $P(\bar{x} \leq 33.5) = 0.5000 - 0.2019 = 0.2981$
7-39. a. Descriptive Statistics: Video Price

Variable	Mean	StDev
Video Price	58.52	2.53

b. $P(\bar{x} \leq 58.52) = 0.00$
c. $P(\bar{x} \leq 58.52) = 0.0087$
d. Given the answers in parts b and c, it appears that the average retail price has declined.
7-43. 2010: Mean = 26720908, Standard Deviation = 1305395
2011: Mean = 31839619, Standard Deviation = 7298929
7-45. a. 0.8621
b. 0.0146
c. 0.8475
d. 0.7422
7-47. a. Sampling error $= \bar{p} - p = 0.65 - 0.70 = -0.05$
b. 0.1379
7-49. a. 0.8221
b. 0.6165
7-51. a. 0.9015
b. 0.0049
7-53. a. $p = \dfrac{x}{n} = \dfrac{27}{60} = 0.45$
b. $P(p \geq 0.45) = 0.5000 - 0.2852 = 0.2148$
7-55. $P(p \geq 0.09) = 0.5000 - 0.4838 = 0.0162$
7-57. a. 0.1020
b. 0.4522
c. ≈ 0.0

7-59. a. 0.0749
   b. 0.0359
   c. essentially 0
7-61. a. 58.86%
   b. 0.9472
   c. essentially zero
7-63. a. 131 over $100,000 and 70 of $100,000 or less
   b. 0.652
   c. 0.4761
7-67. Sample averages would be less variable than the population.
7-69. a. 405.55
   b. 159.83
7-71. A sample size of 1 would be sufficient.
7-73. a. 0.2643
   b. 0.3752
   c. 0.0951
7-75. a. Right skewed distribution; a normal distribution cannot be used.
   b. Sampling distribution of the sample means cannot be approximated by a normal distribution.
   c. 0.50
7-77. a. 0.8660
   b. 0.9783
7-79. a. $P(x > 16.10) = 0.5000 - 0.1554 = 0.3446$
   b. $P(\bar{x} > 16.10) = 0.5000 - 0.4177 = 0.0823$
7-81. Note, because of the small population, the finite correction factor is used.
   a. 0.1112
   b. Either the mean or the standard deviation or both may have changed.
   c. 0.2483
7-83. a. 0
   b. 0.4999
7-85. a. 0
   b. 0.117
7-89. a. 0.216
   b. 0.3275
   c. Reducing the warranty is a judgment call.

Chapter 8

8-1. 15.86————20.94
8-3. 293.18————306.82
8-5. 1180.10————1219.90
8-7. a. 1.69————4.31
   b. 1.38————4.62
8-9. 97.62————106.38
8-11. a. (11.6028, 15.1972)
   b. (29.9590, 32.4410)
   c. (2.9098, 6.0902)
   d. (18.3192, 25.0808)
8-13. a. $13.945————$14.515
   b. There is no reason to believe that this is out of line.
8-15. a. (4780.25, 5219.75)
   b. 219.75
   c. 109.875; $n = 716$
8-17. a. $5.29————$13.07
   b. These sample data do not dispute the American Express study.
8-19. a. 83.785
   b. (505.415, 567.985)

8-21. a. 163.5026————171.5374
   b. Increasing the sample size, decreasing the level of confidence, the standard deviation can be reduced.
8-23. a. 6.5368
   b. 6.3881————6.6855
8-25. a. 256.01, 80.68 (calculated using Excel's ST.DEV function)
   b. 242.01————270.01
   c. ± 14.00 seconds
8-27. 189
8-29. 918
8-31. 3,684.21
8-33. a. $n = 62$
   b. $n = 5726$
   c. $n = 2$
   d. $n = 306$
   e. $n = 35$
8-35. 249
8-37. a. 863
   b. 1. Reduce the confidence level to something less than 95 percent
      2. Increase the margin of error beyond 0.25 pounds.
      3. Some combination of decreasing the confidence level and increasing the margin of error.
8-39. $325 - 50 = 275$
8-41. a. 246
   b. 6147
   c. $0.44 to $0.51
8-43. a. 60
   b. 239
8-45. a. 292
   b. 165 additional households must be sampled.
8-47. a. 1,599
   b. Reduce the confidence level (lowers the z-value) or increase the margin of error or some combination of the two.
8-49. $1,698 - 75 = 1,623$
8-51. 0.224————0.336
8-53. a. The sampling distribution can be approximated by a normal distribution.
   b. (0.286, 0.414)
   c. 0.286 to 0.414
   d. 0.064
8-55. a. $\bar{p} = 0.175$
   b. (0.057, 0.293)
   c. $n = 888$
8-57. a. 0.324————0.436
   b. 9,604
8-59. $\bar{p} = 345/1000 = 0.345$
   a. Between 0.3155 and 0.3745
   b. 179.20————212.716
   c. $\bar{p} = (280/690) = 0.4058$. Between .3692 and .4424.
   d. 1,225
8-61. 0.895————0.925
8-63. a. 0.6627————0.7173
   b. 2401
   c. (2)(0.4791) = 0.9742
8-65. a. 0.1167
   b. 0.1131
   c. (0.0736, 0.1598)
8-67. a. 0.7444
   b. 0.6260————0.8628
   c. The sample size could be increased.

8-69. a.

```
Test and CI for One Proportion: Males

Test of p = 0.5 vs p not = 0.5

Event = yes


Variable   X    N   Sample p       99% CI          Z-Value  P-Value
Males      48  100  0.480000  (0.351312, 0.608688)  -0.40    0.689

Test and CI for One Proportion: Females

Test of p = 0.5 vs p not = 0.5

Event = yes


Variable   X    N   Sample p       99% CI          Z-Value  P-Value
Females    22  100  0.220000  (0.113297, 0.326703)  -5.60    0.000
```

    b. The largest ratio is 5.37 and the smallest would be $0.3513/0.3267 = 1.08$.

8-75. $0.2564 \le p \le 0.4936$

8-77. a. 0.7265————0.7935

    b. 25,427.50————27,772.50

8-79. a. 22 more

    b. $770

8-81. a. 5.21

    b. 390

    c. 2.00 work hours.

8-83. a. 0.7003————0.7741

    b. 32,279.4674————33,322.7227

8-85. a. 58.178 to 58.882. The entire confidence interval is above $56. It therefore seems very unlikely the average price has decreased.

    b. $n \approx 25$

Chapter 9

9-1. a. $z = 1.96$

    b. $t = -1.6991$

    c. $t = \pm 2.4033$

    d. $z = \pm 1.645$

9-3. a. $z_\alpha = -1.645$

    b. $t_{\alpha/2} = \pm 2.5083$

    c. $z_{\alpha/2} = \pm 2.575$

    d. $-t_\alpha = -1.5332$

    e. Invalid

9-5. a. Reject the null hypothesis if the calculated value of the test statistic, z, is greater than 2.575 or less than -2.575. Otherwise, do not reject.

    b. $z = -3.111$

    c. Reject the null hypothesis.

9-7. a. Reject the null hypothesis if the calculated value of the test statistic, t, is less than the critical value of -2.0639. Otherwise, do not reject.

    b. $t = -1.875$

    c. Do not reject the null hypothesis.

9-9. a. Reject the null hypothesis if the calculated value of the test statistic, t, is greater than 1.3277. Otherwise, do not reject.

    b. $t = 0.78$

    c. Do not reject the null hypothesis.

9-11. a. Type I error

    b. Type II error

    c. Type I error

    d. No error

    e. Type II error

    f. No error

9-13. a. $H_0: \mu \ge 30{,}000$

       $H_A: \mu < 30{,}000$

    b. $29{,}588.75

    c. Do not reject.

    d. Type II

9-15. a. $H_0: \mu \ge 3{,}600$

       $H_A: \mu < 3{,}600$

    b. Since $t = -0.85 > -1.8331$, the null hypothesis is not rejected.

9-17. a. $H_0: \mu \ge 55$

       $H_A: \mu < 55$

    b. Because $t = -0.93 > -2.4620$, the null hypothesis is not rejected.

9-19. The annual average consumer unit spending for food at home in Detroit is less than the national consumer unit average.

9-21. a. Since $t = -1.032.23 \ge -2.1604$, we do not reject the null hypothesis.

    b. Therefore, because we do not reject the null hypothesis, we did commit a Type I statistical error.

9-23. a. $z = 1.96$

    b. $z = -1.645$

    c. $z = \pm 2.33$

    d. $z = \pm 1.645$

9-25. Since $-2.17 > -2.33$, don't reject.

9-27. a. Reject the null hypothesis if the calculated value of the test statistic, z, is less than the critical value of the test statistic $z = -1.96$. Otherwise, do not reject.

    b. $z = -2.0785$

    c. reject

9-29. a. p-value $= 0.05$

    b. p-value $= 0.5892$

    c. p-value $= 0.1902$

    d. p-value $= 0.0292$

9-31. Because $z = -3.145$ is less than -2.055, reject H_0.

9-33. Since $z = 0.97 < 1.645$, we do not reject the null hypothesis.

9-35. Because $z = 1.543$ is less than 1.96, do not reject H_0. p-value $= 0.50 - 0.4382 = 0.0618$

9-37. a. $H_0: p \le 0.40$

       $H_A: p > 0.40$

    b. Since $z = 1.43 < 1.645$, we do not reject the null hypothesis.

9-39. a. $H_0: p \le 0.10$

       $H_A: p > 0.10$

    b. Since the p-value $= 0.1736$ is greater than 0.05, don't reject.

9-41. a. Since $z = 2.85 > 1.96$, reject H_0.

    b. p-value $= .5 - 0.4978 = 0.0022$

9-43. Because $z = 2.36$ is greater than 1.645, reject H_0.

9-45. a. $H_0: p \ge 0.50$

       $H_A: p < 0.50$

    b. Since $z = -6.08 < -2.05$, we reject the null hypothesis.

9-47. a. The appropriate null and alternative hypotheses are $H_0: p \ge 0.95$ $H_A: p < 0.95$

    b. Since $z = -4.85 < -1.645$, we reject the null hypothesis.

9-49. a. 0.80

    b. 0.20

    c. The power increases, and beta decreases.

    d. Since $\bar{x} = 1.23$, then $1.0398 < 1.23 < 1.3062$, do not reject H_0.

9-51. 0.8888

9-53. 0.3228

9-55. a. 0.0084

    b. 0.2236

    c. 0.9160

9-57. a. 0.1685

    b. 0.1446

    c. 0.1190

9-59. a. $H_0: \mu \geq 243$
$H_A: \mu < 243$
b. 0.0537
9-61. a. $H_0: \mu \geq 15$
$H_A: \mu < 15$
b. 0.0606
9-63. a. $H_0 = \mu \geq \$47{,}413$
$H_A: \mu < \$47{,}413$
b. 0.1446
9-65. 0.0495
9-67. a. Since $t = -3.97 < -1.6991$, we reject H_0.
b. 0.3557
9-77. a. If α is decreased, the rejection region is smaller, making it easier to accept H_0, so β is increased.
b. If n is increased, the test statistic is also increased, making it harder to accept H_0, so β is decreased.
c. If n is increased, the test statistic is also increased, making it harder to accept H_0, so β is decreased and power is increased.
d. If α is decreased, the rejection region is smaller, making it easier to accept H_0, so β is increased and power is decreased.
9-79. a. $z = \dfrac{\bar{x} - \mu}{\dfrac{\sigma}{\sqrt{n}}}$

b. $t = \dfrac{\bar{x} - \mu}{\dfrac{s}{\sqrt{n}}}$

c. $z = \dfrac{\bar{p} - p}{\sqrt{\dfrac{p(1 - p)}{n}}}$

9-81. a. $H_0: \mu \leq 4{,}000$
$H_A: \mu > 4{,}000$
b. Since $t = 1.2668 < 1.7959$, do not reject.
9-83. a. $H_0: p \geq 0.50$
$H_A: p < 0.50$
b. Since $z = -5.889 < -1.645$, reject the null hypothesis. Since $z = -5.889$, the p-value is approximately zero.
9-85. a. Since $z = -1.5275 > -1.645$, do not reject.
b. Type II error
9-87. a. yes
b. $p = $ value < 0.01; reject
9-89. a. yes
b. Since $z = -1.1547 > -1.96$, do not reject H_0.
9-91. a. $H_0: \mu = 6$ inches
$H_A: \mu \neq 6$ inches
b. Reject H_0 if $z > 2.58$ or $z < -2.58$; otherwise do not reject H_0. Also: If $\bar{x} < 5.9818$, reject the null hypothesis. If $\bar{x} > 6.0182$, reject the null hypothesis
c. Since $\bar{x} = 6.03 > 6.0182$, reject the null hypothesis.
9-93. a. Because $z = 1.18$, do not reject H_0.
b. The largest plausible average balance in the investors' accounts in which you could have 90% confidence = \$241,771.67.
9-95. p-value $= 0$, so reject H_0.
9-97. a. $H_0: \mu = 0.75$ inch
$H_A: \mu \neq 0.75$ inch
b. Since $t = 0.9496 < 2.6264$, do not reject H_0.
9-99. a. Since the p-value is less than α, we reject H_0.
b. 0.1170
9-101. a. Since the p-value is greater than α, we do not reject H_0.
b. 0.5476

Chapter 10

10-1. $-6.54 \leq (\mu_1 - \mu_2) \leq 0.54$
10-3. $-13.34 \leq \mu_1 - \mu_2 \leq -6.2$

10-5. $0.07 \leq (\mu_1 - \mu_2) \leq 50.61$
10-7. $-19.47 \leq \mu_1 - \mu_2 \leq -7.93$
10-9. a. -0.05
b. $-0.0974 \leq (\mu_1 - \mu_2) \leq -0.0026$
c. The managers can conclude the two lines do not fill bags with equal average amounts.
10-11. a. 2.1783
-0.1043————2.7043;
b. No difference in the setup time for the two additives.
10-13. a. The ratio between the two variances is 200.
b. (36.3551, 37.4449)
c. All values contained in the interval are plausible values for the difference in the means.
10-15. $-0.10 \leq \mu_1 - \mu_2 \leq 0.30$
10-17. a. 2.35%.
b. $-1{,}527.32$. 4,926.82
c. It is plausible there is no difference.
d. 3,227
10-19. Since $t = -4.80 < -2.1199$, reject.
10-21. Since $z = 5.26 > 1.645$, we reject the null hypothesis.
10-23. a. $H_0: \mu_1 = \mu_2$
$H_A: \mu_1 \neq \mu_2$
If $t > 1.9698$ or $t < -1.9698$, reject H_0.
b. Since $5.652 > 1.9698$, reject H_0.
10-25. $t = 0.896$; do not reject the null hypothesis.
10-27. a. $t = 0.9785 > -1.677$; do not reject.
b. Type II error
10-29. $t = -4.30 < -1.6510$; reject the null hypothesis.
10-31. a. $2084/2050 = 1.02$
b. p-value $= P(t \leq 5.36) \cong 1.00$, the null hypothesis is not rejected.
10-33. a. $9.60/1.40 = 6.857$. This is quite close to a ratio of 7. between the two population averages.
b. Since p-value $= 0.966 > 0.25$ do not reject the null.
10-35. a. $-13.76, -1.00$. Contains -10
b. p-value is greater than 0.025; do not reject the null hypothesis.
c. You should be able to reach the same conclusion using either a confidence interval estimate or a hypothesis test.
10-37. $-674.41 \leq \mu \leq -191.87$
10-39. a. $H_0: \mu_d \geq 0$
$H_A: \mu_d < 0$
b. Since $-3.64 < -1.3968$, reject H_0.
c. -2.1998————.7122
10-41. a. (7.6232, 13.4434)
b. $t = 0.37 < 1.459$
10-43. a. The samples were matched pairs.
b. $0.005 < p$-value < 0.01
10-45. a. $t = -7.35 < -1.98$; reject H_0.
b. -100.563————-57.86
10-47. a. Because $t = 35.5 > 2.5083$, reject the null hypothesis.
b. 0.511 compared to 0.011
10-49. $t = 1.068 < 2.136$; do not reject
10-51. a. The sampling distribution cannot be approximated with a normal distribution.
b. The sampling distribution cannot be approximated with a normal distribution.
c. The sampling distribution can be approximated with a normal distribution.
d. The sampling distribution cannot be approximated with a normal distribution.
10-53. p-value is greater than α; do not reject the null hypothesis.
10-55. a. Since $z = 2.538 > 1.96$, reject H_0.
b. Since $z = 2.538 > -1.645$, fail to reject H_0.
c. Since $z = 2.538 > 1.96$, reject H_0.
d. Since $z = 1.987 < 2.33$, fail to reject H_0.

10-57. $z = -0.4111 > -2.575$; do not reject.

10-59. a. p-value $= 0.025 < 0.05$; reject H_0.

    b. 0.00597

    c. The smallest difference equals the margin of error $= 0.00597$.

10-61. a. The sampling distribution can be approximated with a normal distribution.

    b. p-value $= 0.039 < 0.05$; reject.

10-63. a. The sampling distribution can be approximated with a normal distribution.

    b. p-value $= 0.095 > 0.01$; do not reject.

10-67. a. (2.1064, 7.8936).

    b. $t = -2.0687$

    c. $t = 2.0687$

10-69. $-120.8035 \text{——} 146.0761$

10-71. a. The normal distribution is appropriate.

    b. $z = 0.7745 < 2.17$; do not reject.

10-73. $-26.40 \le \mu_d \le -0.36$

10-75. $z = 1.9677 > 1.96$

10-77. a. Paired samples

    b. p-value $= 0.000 < 0.05$; reject.

    c. The plausible values are (0.5625, 0.8775).

10-79. a. $t = 5.25 > 2.3499$; reject.

    b. Type I

Chapter 11

11-1. $74,953.7 \le \sigma^2 \le 276,472.2$

11-3. Since $\chi^2 = 12.39 > 10.1170$, do not reject the null hypothesis.

11-5. a. Because $\chi^2 = 17.82 < \chi^2_{0.05} = 19.6752$ and because $\chi^2 = 17.82 > \chi^2_{0.95} = 4.5748$, do not reject.

    b. Because $\chi^2 = 12.96 < \chi^2_{0.025} = 31.5264$ and because $\chi^2 = 12.96 > \chi^2_{0.975} = 8.2307$, we do not reject the null hypothesis.

11-7. a. Since p-value $< \alpha$, reject H_0.

    b. Since the test statistic $= 1.591 <$ the χ^2 critical value $= 1.6899$, reject the null hypothesis.

    c. p-value $= 0.94$; do not reject.

11-9. $22.72 \le \sigma^2 \le 81.90$

11-11. $353.38 \le \sigma^2 \le 1,745.18$

11-13. a. $H_0: \mu \le 10$

      $H_A: \mu > 10$

    b. Since $1.2247 < 1.383$, do not reject H_0.

    c. Since $3.75 < 14.6837$, do not reject H_0.

11-15. a. $\sigma^2 = 4.203$

    b. Since the test statistic $= 12.05 <$ the χ^2 critical value $= 13.8484$, do not reject.

11-17. a. $\sigma^2 = 0.000278$

    b. Since p-value $= 0.004 < 0.01$, we reject.

11-19. a. If the calculated $F > 2.278$, reject H_0, otherwise do not reject H_0.

    b. Since $1.0985 < 2.278$, do not reject H_0.

11-21. a. $F = 3.619$

    b. $F = 3.106$

    c. $F = 3.051$

11-23. Since $F = 0.867 < 6.388 = F_{0.05}$, fail to reject H_0.

11-25. Since $3.4807 > 1.984$, reject H_0.

11-27. a. Since $2.0818 < 2.534$, do not reject.

    b. Type I error. Decrease the alpha or increase the sample sizes.

11-29. Since $F = 3.035 > 2.526 = F_{0.05}$, reject H_0.

11-31. Since $1.4833 < 3.027$, do not reject H_0.

11-33. a. The p-value $= 0$, reject the null of equal variances.

    b. More than 80% or the CEO salaries are greater than the previous salaries.

11-39. $0.753 \le \sigma^2 \le 2.819$

11-41. Since $1.2129 < 2.231$, do not reject.

11-43. a. Since $\chi^2 = 37.24 > \chi^2_U = 30.1435$, reject H_0.

    b. $P(x \ge 3) = 0.0230 + 0.0026 + 0.0002 = 0.0256$

11-45. a. Since $F = 2.263 > 1.752 = F_{0.025}$, reject H_0.

    b. Regardless of the test to be used in this situation, it would be necessary to determine if the populations' distributions had normal distributions.

11-47. Since $202.5424 < 224.9568$, do not reject.

11-49. Since $2.0609 > 1.4953$, reject the null hypothesis.

11-51. a. Since the p-value $= 0.496 > 0.05 = \alpha = 0.05$, do not reject.

    b. yes

Chapter 12

12-1. a. $SSW = SST - SSB = 9,271,678,090 - 2,949,085,157$
          $= 6,322,592,933$

      $MSB = 2,949,085,157/2 = 1,474,542,579$

      $MSW = 6,322,592,933/72 = 87,813,791$

      $F = 1,474,542,579/87,813,791 = 16.79$

    b. Because the F test statistic $= 16.79 > F_\alpha = 2.3778$, we reject.

12-3. a. The appropriate null and alternative hypotheses are

      $H_0: \mu_1 = \mu_2 = \mu_3$

      H_A: Not all μ_j are equal.

    b. Because $F = 9.84 >$ critical $F = 3.35$, we reject. Because p-value $= 0.0006 < \alpha = 0.05$, we reject.

    c. Critical range $= 6.0$; $\mu_1 > \mu_2$ and $\mu_3 > \mu_2$

12-5. a. $df_B = 3$

    b. $F = 11.1309$

    c. $H_0: \mu_1 = \mu_2 = \mu_3 = \mu_4$

      H_A: At least two population means are different.

    d. Since $11.1309 > 2.9467$, reject H_0.

12-7. a. Because $F = 5.03 > 3.885$, we reject H_0.

    b. Pop 1 and 2 means differ; no other differences.

12-9. a. Since $F = 7.131 > F_{\alpha=0.01} = 5.488$, reject.

    b. $CR = 1,226.88$; Venetti mean is greater than Edison mean.

12-11. a. Since $F = 1,459.78 > 3.885$, we reject H_0.

    b. Critical range $= 9.36$

12-13. a. Since $10.48326 > 5.9525$, reject H_0 and conclude that at least two population means are different.

    b. Critical range $= 222.02$; eliminate Type D and A.

12-15. a. Since $0.01 < 0.05$, reject H_0 and conclude that at least two population means are different.

    b.

	Absolute Differences	Critical Range	Significant?
Mini 1 – Mini 2	0.633	1.264	no
Mini 1 – Mini 3	1.175	1.161	yes
Mini 2 – Mini 3	1.808	1.322	yes

    Student reports will vary, but they should recommend either 1 or 2 since there is no statistically significant difference between them.

    c. $0.978 \text{——} 2.678$ cents per mile; $293.40 \text{——} 803.40$ annual savings

12-17. a. p-value $= 0.000 < \alpha = 0.05$

    b. Average length of life differs between Delphi and Exide and also between Delphi and Johnson. There is not enough evidence to indicate that the average lifetime for Exide and Johnson differ.

12-19. a. $H_0: \mu_1 = \mu_2 = \mu_3 = \mu_4$

      H_A: At least two population means are different.

      $H_0: \mu_{b1} = \mu_{b2} = \mu_{b3} = \mu_{b4} = \mu_{b5} = \mu_{b6} = \mu_{b7} = \mu_{b8}$

      H_A: Not all block means are equal.

b. $F_{Blocks} = 46.87669$; $F_{Groups} = 13.8906$

c. Since $46.876 > 2.487$, reject H_0.

d. Since p-value $0.0000326 < 0.05$, reject.

e. $LSD = 5.48$

12-21. Because $F = 14.3 >$ Critical $F = 3.326$, we reject and conclude that blocking is effective.
Because $F = 0.1515 <$ Critical $F = 4.103$, we do not reject.

12-23. a. Because $F = 32.12 > F_{\alpha=0.01} = 9.78$, reject the null hypothesis.

b. Because $F = 1.673 < F_{\alpha=0.01} = 10.925$, do not reject the null hypothesis.

12-25. a. Because $F = 22.32 > F_{\alpha=0.05} = 6.944$, reject the null hypothesis.

b. Because $F = 14.185 > F_{\alpha=0.05} = 6.944$, reject the null hypothesis.

c. $LSD = 8.957$

12-27. a. p-value $= 0.000 < \alpha = 0.05$

b. p-value $= 0.004 < \alpha = 0.05$

c. $LSD = 1.55$; $\mu_1 < \mu_3$ and $\mu_2 < \mu_3$

12-29. a. p-value $= 0.628 > 0.05$

b. p-value $= 0.000 < \alpha = 0.05$

c. $LSD = 372.304$; $\mu_1 > \mu_2 > \mu_3$

12-31. a. p-value $= 0.854 > \alpha = 0.05$. Therefore, fail to reject H_0.

b. Since $F = 47.10 > F_{0.05} = 5.143$, reject H_0.

c. p-value $= 0.039 < \alpha = 0.05$. Therefore, reject H_0.

12-33. a. Since $0.4617 < 3.8853$, do not reject H_0.

b. Since $2.3766 < 3.8853$, do not reject H_0.

c. Since $5.7532 > 4.7472$, reject H_0.

12-35. a. Since $F = 39.63 > F_{0.05} = 3.633$, reject H_0.

b. Since $F = 2.90 < F_{0.05} = 9.552$, fail to reject H_0.

c. Since $F = 3.49 < F_{0.05} = 9.552$, fail to reject H_0.
Since $F = 57.73 > F_{0.05} = 9.552$, reject H_0.

12-37. a. Because $F = 1.016 < F_{\alpha=0.05} = 2.728$, do not reject.

b. Because $F = 1.157 < F_{\alpha=0.05} = 3.354$, do not reject.

c. Because $F = 102.213 > F_{\alpha=0.05} = 3.354$, reject.

12-39. a. Since p-value $= 0.0570 > 0.01$, do not reject.

b. Since $2.9945 < 6.0129$, do not reject.

c. Since p-value $= 0.4829 > 0.1$, do not reject

12-41. a. $\alpha = 0.025 < p$-value $= 0.849$. Therefore, fail to reject.

b. Since $F = 15.61 > F_{0.025} = 3.353$, reject.

c. Since $F = 3.18 < F_{0.025} = 3.353$, do not reject.

d. Since $-2.0595 < t = -0.69 < 2.0595$, fail to reject.

12-49. a. $\alpha = 0.05 < p$-value $= 0.797$. Therefore, fail to reject.

b. Since $F = 25.55 > F_{0.05} = 3.855$, reject.

c. Since $F = 0.82 < F_{0.05} = 3.940$, do not reject.

12-51. a. Since $F = 3.752 > 2.657$, we reject.

b. Critical range $= 9.5099$; $\mu_1 > \mu_B$, $\mu_1 > \mu_{1F}$, and $\mu_1 > \mu_G$

12-53. a. Since $(F_{1,200,0.05} = 3.888 < F_{1,998,0.05} < F_{1,100,0.05} = 3.936) < F = 89.53$, reject.

b. Since $t = -9.46 < (t_{250,0.05} = -1.9695 < t_{998,0.05} < t_{100,0.05} = -1.9840)$, reject.

c. Note that $(t - value)^2 = (-9.46)^2 = 89.49 \approx 89.53$.

12-55. a. randomized block design

b. $H_0: \mu_1 = \mu_2 = \mu_3 = \mu_4$
H_A: At least two population means are different.

c. Since $3.3785 < 4.0150$, do not reject.

d. Since $20.39312 > 1.9358$, reject.

e. no difference

12-57. a. Since $F = 5.377 >$ Critical $F = 2.641$, reject.

b. Since $F = 142.97 > F_{0.05} = 5.192$ reject.

c. Since $F = 523.33 > F_{0.05} = 5.192$, reject.

Chapter 13

13-1. Because $\chi^2 = 6.4607 < 13.2767$, do not reject.

13-3. Because $\chi^2 = 227.83 > 18.3070$, we reject.

13-5. Because the calculated value of $595.657 > 13.2767$, we reject.

13-7. Because the calculated value of 4.48727 is less than 12.8345, do not reject.

13-9. a. Since chi-square statistic $= 3.379443 < 11.3449$, do not reject.

b. Based on the test, we have no reason to conclude that the company is not meeting its product specification.

13-11. Chi-square value $= 0.3647$; do not reject.

13-13. Since chi-square $= 3.6549 < 7.3778$, do not reject.

13-15. a. Because the calculated value of 1.97433 is less than the critical value of 14.0671, we do not reject.

b. Since $z = -16.12 < 1.645$, do not reject.

13-17. $\chi^2 = 50.3115 > 21.666$, reject the null hypothesis.

13-19. a. H_0: The row and column variables are independent.

b. H_A: The row and column variables are not independent.

c. The test statistic is 104.905.

d. $\chi^2 = 104.905 > 5.9915$

e. Since $\chi^2_{0.005} = 10.5965 < \chi^2 = 104.905$, then p-value < 0.005.

13-21. $\chi^2 = 300.531 > 16.8119$, reject the null hypothesis.

13-23. $\chi^2 = 86.9 > 12.5916$; reject.

13-25. Since $1.2987 < 9.4877$, do not reject.

13-27. $\chi^2 = 27.4510 > 13.2767$; reject.

13-29. a. $\chi^2 = 29.32 > 5.9915$; reject.

b. Since $-1.96 < z = 0.523 < 1.96$, do not reject H_0.

13-31. p-value $= 0.000 < \alpha = 0.05$

13-33. a. One option would be to combine Salt Lake City and Toronto into one group.

b. H_0: Type of warranty problem and manufacturing plant are independent.
H_A: The of warranty problem and manufacturing plant are not independent.
$6.7582 < 9.2104$; do not reject.

13-39. Since $59.464 > 7.81472$, reject H_0.

13-41. $25.2975 > 16.8118$; reject H_0.

13-43. $\chi^2 = 119.585 > 15.0863$; reject the null hypothesis.

13-45. $\chi^2 = 39.745 > 31.9999$; reject.

13-47. a. $\chi^2 = 125.1905 > 9.4877$; reject H_0 and conclude that blood pressure loss is not normally distributed with $\mu = 10$ and $\sigma = 4$.

b. Since $116.55 < 117.4069$; do not reject

c. Yes

d. $12.81——14.87$; no

13-49. $\chi^2 = 1.155 < 7.8147$; do not reject.

Chapter 14

14-1. $H_0: \rho \leq 0.0$
$H_A: \rho > 0.0$
$\alpha = 0.05$, $t = 2.50$, $2.50 > 1.7709$; reject.

14-3. a. $r = 0.206$

b. $H_0: \rho = 0$
$H_A: \rho \neq 0$
$\alpha = 0.10$, $-1.8595 < t = 0.59 < 1.8595$; do not reject H_0.

14-5. a. There appears to be a positive linear relationship.

b. $r = 0.9239$

c. $H_0: \rho \leq 0$
$H_A: \rho > 0$
$df = 10 - 2 = 8$
Since $6.8295 > 2.8965$, reject H_0.

14-7. a. fairly strong positive correlation
  b. $H_0: \rho \le 0$
    $H_A: \rho > 0$
    $\alpha = 0.01, t = 7.856 > 2.4066$; reject the null hypothesis.
14-9. a. The dependent variable is the average credit card balance. The independent variable is the income variable.
  b. does not appear to be a strong relationship
  c. $H_0: \rho = 0.0$
    $H_A: \rho \ne 0.0$
    $\alpha = 0.05, t = -1.56 > -2.1604$; do not reject.
14-11. a. $r = 0.979$
  b. $H_0: \rho \le 0$
    $H_A: \rho > 0$
    $\alpha = 0.05, 6.791 > t = 2.9200$ reject H_0.
14-13. a. -0.305
  b. $\alpha = 0.025 < p\text{-value} = 0.052$; do not reject H_0.
14-15. a. A positive linear relationship
  b. 0.51
  c. $t = 15.87 > 1.647$; reject the null hypothesis.
14-17. a. There appears to be a positive linear relationship.
  b. 1. $r = 0.7540$
    2. $H_0: p\text{-value} = 0.0073 < 0.05$; reject H_0.
    3. $\hat{y} = 58.7246 + 12.9410x$
  c. $t = 3.44$; reject.
14-19. a. $\hat{y} = 36.7 + 8.33x$
  b. $SE = 1,467$
    $SST = 7,050$
    $$R^2 = \frac{SSR}{SST} = 1 - \frac{SSE}{SST} = 1 - \frac{1,467}{7,050} = 0.79$$
  c. $S_e = \sqrt{\dfrac{SSE}{n-2}} = \sqrt{\dfrac{1,467}{8}} = 13.54$
  d. $s_{b_1} = \dfrac{s_e}{\sqrt{\sum x^2 - \dfrac{(\sum x)^2}{n}}} = \dfrac{13.54}{\sqrt{2,452 - \dfrac{154^2}{10}}} = 1.51$
  e. $t = 5.52 > 2.8965$; reject.
14-21. b. So $\sum(y - \hat{y})^2 = 7.60$
    So $\sum(y - \hat{y})^2 = 7.75$
    So $\sum(y - \hat{y})^2 = 7.65$
  c. The first equation
  d. $\hat{y} = 0.8 + 1.60x,$
14-23. a. A positive linear relationship
  b. $\hat{y} = 4.5 + 1.101(x)$
  c. $t = 7.7171 > 2.1009$; reject.
14-25. a. $\hat{y} = 171205.83 + 25.316x$
  b. $t = 7.08 > 2.0930$; reject.
  c. $R^2 = 0.725$
14-27. a. $\hat{y} = 95.7391 + 0.8649$ (minutes)
  b. $R^2 = 0.5722$
  c. $t = 8.095 > 2.68$; reject.
  d. $t = 8.0983 > 2.68$
14-29. b. no relationship $t = 0.46 < 1.9944$; do not reject.
14-31. a. A negative linear relationship
  b. Since $-5.8061 < -2.0484$, reject H_0 and conclude that there is a correlation between curb weight and highway mileage.
  c. $\hat{y} = 46.3298 + (-0.006)(4,012) = 22.2578$
14-33. b. Since $p\text{-value} = 0.0000 < \alpha < .1$, reject.
  c. 0.7925——$1.057314.34$
14-35. R-Square $= 0.0105$
14-37. a. $\hat{y} = 200 + 150(48) = 7400$
  b. 7399.37——7400.63
  c. 7397.26——7402.74

14-39. a. $(93.15, 99.87)$
  b. $(98.84, 105.76)$
  c. The margin of error for part a is 3.3687 and that of part b is 3.4647.
14-41. a. $\hat{y} = -4.7933 + 1.0488x$
  b. $\hat{y} = -4.7933 + 1.0488(100) = 100.09$
  c. 82.205——117.975
  d. 94.88——105.30
14-43. a. $y = 372 + 0.205x$
  b. $t = 5.16$; do not reject.
  c. 799.87 to 912.1
14-45. a. $\hat{y} = 513,915.25 + 1,093.989x$
  b. $917.807 < \beta_1 < 1,270.171$
  c. $4,200,154$ to $4,485,597$
  d. $3,684,809$ to $5,000,942$
14-47. a. $\hat{y} = 252.846 + (250.247)(x)$
  b. $\$250.25$
  c. $t = 28.61 > 2.6822$; reject H_0.
  d. $\hat{y} = 252.846 + (250.247)(30) = \$7,760.26$
  e. $\$7,601.12$——$\$7,919.41$
14-49. a. $\hat{y} = 14871 - 372x$
  b. $(9086, 9497)$
  c. $(10139, 12165)$
14-57. a. Since $4.7757 > 2.0484$, reject.
  b. $R^2 = (0.67)^2 = 0.4489$
14-59. a. A weak negative linear relationship
  b. -0.59974
  c. Since $-2.24845 < -1.3830$; reject H_0.
14-61. a. 0.01498——0.01502. Income is a significant variable since the interval does not contain 0.
14-63. a. Since $53.8462 > 1.649$, reject H_0.
  b. $\hat{y} = 1.0 + 0.028(80) = 3.24$
  c. GPS lower than expected.
  d. $\hat{y} = 1.0 + 0.028(65) = 2.82$
    2.491——3.149
14-65. a. A positive linear relationship.
  b. $\hat{y} = -19.3726 + 2.9026(x)$
14-67. a. Linear with a positive slope
  b. $p\text{-value} = 0.000 < \alpha = 0.05$; reject.
14-69. a. The independent variable would be advertising and the dependent variable would be sales.
  c. Since $-0.4173 < 2.1009$, do not reject.

Chapter 15

15-1. a. $\hat{y} = 87.7897 - 0.9705x_1 + 0.0023x_2 - 8.7233x_3$
  b. $F = 5.3276 > F_{0.05} = 3.0725$; also, $p\text{-value} = 0.00689 <$ any reasonable alpha. Therefore, reject $H_0: \beta_1 = \beta_2 = \beta_3 = 0$.
  c. $R_2 = \dfrac{SSR}{SST} = \dfrac{16,646.09124}{38,517.76} = 0.432$
  d. x_1 ($p\text{-value} = 0.1126 > \alpha = 0.05$; fail to reject $H_0: \beta_1 = 0$) and x_3 ($p\text{-value} = 0.2576 > \alpha = 0.05$; fail to reject $H_0: \beta_3 = 0$) are not significant.
  e. $b_2 = 0.0023$; $\hat{y}$ increases 0.0023 for each one-unit increase of x_2.
    $b_3 = -8.7233$; $\hat{y}$ decreases 8.7233 for each one-unit increase of x_3.
  f. The confidence intervals for β_1 and β_3 contain 0.
15-3. a. $b_1 = -412$; $b_2 = 818$; $b_3 = -93$; $b_4 = -71$
  b. $\hat{y} = 22,167 - 412(5.7) + 818(61) - 93(14) - 71(3.39) = 68,173.91$

15-5. a. $y_i = 5.05 - 0.051x_1 + 0.888x_2$

b.

	y_i	x_1
x_1	0.206	
x_2	0.919	0.257

$H_0: \rho = 0$
$H_A: \rho \neq 0$
$\alpha = 0.05, t = 0.5954, -2.306 < t = 0.5954 < 2.306$; we fail to reject H_0.

c. $H_0: \beta_1 = \beta_2 = 0$
H_A: at least one $\beta_i \neq 0$
$\alpha = 0.05, F = 19.07$
Since $F = 19.07 > 4.737$, reject H_0.

d.

Predictor	Coef	SE Coef	T	P	VIF
Constant	5.045	8.698	0.58	0.580	
x_1	−0.0513	0.2413	−0.21	0.838	1.1
x_2	0.8880	0.1475	6.02	0.001	1.1

15-7. a. $\hat{y} = -977.1 + 11.2\,(52\text{ WK HI}) + 117.72\,(\text{P-E})$

b. $H_0: \beta_1 = \beta_2 = 0$
H_A: at least one $\beta_i \neq 0$
$\alpha = 0.05, F = 39.80 > 3.592$; we reject.

c. $\hat{y} = 1,607$

15-9. a. $\hat{y} = 503 - 10.5x_1 + 2.4x_2 + 0.165x_3 + 1.90x_4$

b. $H_0: \beta_1 = \beta_2 = \beta_3 = \beta_4 = 0$
H_A: at least one $\beta_i \neq 0$
$\alpha = 0.05$
Since $F = 2.44 < 3.056$, fail to reject H_0.

c. $H_0: \beta_3 = 0$
$H_A: \beta_3 \neq 0$
$\alpha = 0.05, p\text{-value} = 0.051 > 0.05$; fail to reject H_0.

d. $\hat{y} = 344 - 0.186x_1$.
The p-value = 0.004. Since the p-value = 0.004 < 0.05, reject.

15-11. a. There is a positive linear relationship between team win/loss percentage and game attendance, opponent win/loss percentage and game attendance, and games played and game attendance. There is no relationship between temperature and game attendance.

b. There is a significant relationship between game attendance and team win/loss percentage and games played.

c. Attendance = 14,122.24 + 63.15 (Win/loss%) + 10.10 (Opponent win/loss) + 31.51 (Games played) − 55.46 (Temperature)

d. $R^2 = 0.7753$, so 77.53% is explained.

e. $H_0: \beta_1 = \beta_2 = \beta_3 = \beta_4 = 0$
H_A: at least one β_i does not equal 0.
Significance $F = 0.00143$; reject H_0.

f. For team win/loss %, the p-value = 0.0014 < 0.08.
For opponent win/loss %, the p-value = 0.4953 > 0.08.
For games played, the p-value = 0.8621 > 0.08.
For temperature, the p-value = 0.3909 > 0.08.

g. 1,184.1274; interval of $\pm 2(1,184.1274)$

h.

	VIF
Team win/loss percentage and all other X	1.569962033
Temperature and all other X	1.963520336
Games played and all other X	1.31428258
Opponent win/loss percentage and all other X	1.50934547

Multicollinearity is not a problem since no VIF is greater than 5.

15-15. a. $x_2 = 1, \hat{y} = 145 + 1.2(1,500) + 300(1) = 2,245$

b. $x_2 = 0, \hat{y} = 145 + 1.2(1,500) + 300(0) = 1,945$

c. b_2 indicates the average premium paid for living in the city's town center.

15-17. a. Decrease by 0.003.

b. Increase by 4.56, holding the weight constant.

c. $\hat{y} = 34.2 - 0.003x_1 + 4.56(1) = 38.76 - 0.003x_1$

d. $\hat{y} = 34.2 - 0.003(4,394) + 4.56(0) = 21.02$

e. Incorporating the dummy variable essentially gives two regression equations with the same slope but different intercepts.

15-19. a. $\hat{y} = 113.8 - 7.03x_1 - .13x_2$

b. $\beta_1 = $ The difference in the average PP100 between domestic and Asian vehicles.
$\beta_2 = $ The difference in the average PP100 between domestic and European vehicles.

c. $H_0: \beta_1 = \beta_2 = 0$
H_0: at least one $\beta_i \neq 0$
$F = .88314 > 3.3277$, so we do not reject H_0.

15-21. a. There appears to be a weak positive linear relationship between hours and net profit. There appears to be a weak negative linear relationship between client type and net profit.

b. $\hat{y} = -1,012.0542 + 69.1471(x_1)$

c. The p-value = 0.0531. The R^2 is only 0.3549.

15-23. a. $\hat{y} = 390 - 37.0x_1 + 0.263x_2$
$H_0: \beta_1 = 0$
$H_A: \beta_1 \neq 0$

c. $\alpha = 0.05$. Since $t = -20.45 < -1.9921$, we reject H_0.

d. $\hat{y} = 390 - 37.0x_1 + 0.263x_2 = 390 - 37.0(1) + 0.236(500) = 484.5 \approx 485$

15-25. a. A linear line is possible; nonlinear is more likely.

b. $\hat{y} = 4.937 + 1.2643x$; the p-value = 0.015 < α = 0.05, reject.

c. $\hat{y} = -25.155 + 18.983 \ln x$ Higher Adjusted R-Sq for nonlinear model.

15-27. b. two quadratic models; interaction between x_2 and the quadratic relationship between y and x_2
$\hat{y}_i = 4.9 - 3.58x_1 - 0.014x_1^2 + 1.42x_1x_2 + 0.528x_1^2x_2$

c. $\beta_3 x_1 x_2$ and $\beta_4 x_1^2 x_2$. So you must conduct two hypothesis tests:
i. $H_0: \beta_3 = 0$
$H_A: \beta_3 \neq 0$
$\alpha = 0.05, p\text{-value} = 0.488$; we fail to reject H_0.
ii. For $\beta_4 = 0$, the p-value = 0.001.

d. Conclude that there is interaction between x_2 and the quadratic relationship between x_1 and y.

15-29. a. The complete model is $y_i = \beta_0 + \beta_1 x_1 + \beta_2 x_2 + \beta_3 x_3 + \beta_4 x_4 + \varepsilon_i$. The reduced model is $y_i = \beta_0 + \beta_1 x_1 + \beta_2 x_2 + \varepsilon_i$. $H_0: \beta_3 = \beta_4 = 0, H_A$: at least one $\beta_i \neq 0$. $SSE_C = 201.72$. So $MSE_C = SSE_C/(n - c - 1) = 201.72/(10 - 4 - 1) = 40.344$ and $SSE_R = 1,343$. $\alpha = 0.05, F = 14.144; 14.144 > 5.786$; we reject H_0.

b. The complete model is $y_i = \beta_0 + \beta_1 x_1 + \beta_2 x_2 + \beta_3 x_3 + \beta_4 x_4 + \varepsilon_i$. The reduced model is $y_i = \beta_0 + \beta_1 x_3 + \beta_2 x_4 + \varepsilon_i$. $SSE_C = 201.72$. So $MSE_C = SSE_C/(n - c - 1) = 201.72/(10 - 4 - 1) = 40.344$ and $SSE_R = 494.6$. $H_0: \beta_1 = \beta_2 = 0; H_A$: at least one $\beta_i \neq 0; \alpha = 0.05, F = 3.63$ The numerator degrees of freedom are $c - r = 4 - 2 = 2$ and the denominator degrees of freedom are $n - c - 1 = 10 - 4 - 1 = 5$. The p-value = $P(F \geq 3.630) = 0.1062$. Fail to reject.

15-31. a. two dummy variables
$x_2 = 1$ if manufacturing, 0 otherwise
$x_3 = 1$ if service, 0 otherwise
Net profit = $-586.256 + 22.862x_1 + 2,302.267x_2 + 1,869.813x_3$

b. Net profit $= 5{,}828.692 - 334.406x_1 + 4.557139_1$ sq $+$
$2{,}694.801x_2 + 1287.495x_3$

15-33. a. Create scatter plot.

    b. Second-order polynomial seems to be the correct model.
$\hat{y} = 8{,}083 - 0.273x + 0.000002x^2$.

    c. $y = \beta_0 + \beta_1 x_1 + \beta_2 x_1^2 + \beta_3 x_2 + \beta_4 x_1 x_2 + \beta_5 x_1^2 x_2 + \varepsilon$

        i. The two interaction terms are $\beta_4 x_1 x_2$ and $\beta_5 x_1^2 x_2$. So you must conduct two hypothesis tests:

        ii. Test for $\beta_4 = 0$. Since the p-value $= 0.252 > 0.05$, we fail to reject H_0.

        Test for $\beta_5 = 0$. Since the p-value for $\beta_5 = 0.273 > 0.05$, we fail to reject H_0.

15-35. a. Create scatter plot.

    b. fifth-order polynomial

    c. The regression equation is $= 62.58 - 56.52x + 20.11\text{AP}2 - 3.46\text{AP}3 + .29\text{AP}4 - .0095\text{AP}5$.

    d. $\hat{y}_i = -1.30247 + .41x_1^2 - 0.08572x_1^3 + .004825x_1^4$

15-39. a. x_2 and x_4 only; x_1 and x_3 did not have high enough coefficients of partial determination to add significantly to the model.

    b. would be identical

    c. Stepwise regression cannot have a larger R^2 than the full model.

15-41. a. None are significant.

    b. Alpha-to-enter: 0.25; alpha-to-remove: 0.25
$\hat{y} = 26.19 + 0.42x_3, R^2 = 14.68$

    c. $\hat{y} = 27.9 - 0.035x_1 - 0.002x_2 + 0.42x_3, R^2 = 14.8$
The adjusted R^2 is 0% for the full model and 7.57% for the standard selection model. Neither model offers a good approach to fitting this data.

15-43. a. $\hat{y} = 32.08 + 0.76x_1 - 5x_3 + 0.95x_4$

    b. $\hat{y} = 32.08 + 0.76x_1 - 5x_3 + 0.95x_4$

    c. $\hat{y} = 32.08 + 0.76x_1 - 5x_3 + 0.95x_4$

    d. $\hat{y} = 32.08 + 0.76x_1 - 5x_3 + 0.95x_4$

15-45. a. $\hat{y} = -18.33 + 1.07x_2$

    b. one independent variable (x_2) and one dependent variable (y)

    c. x_1 was the first variable removed, p-value $(0.817) > 0.05$.
x_3 was the last variable removed, p-value $= 0.094 > 0.05$.

15-47. $\hat{y} = 1{,}110 + 1.60x_2^2$

15-49. a. There is multicollinearity among the predictor variables.

    b. Either crude oil or diesel prices should be removed.

    c. Removing crude oil prices.
$\hat{y} = 0.8741 + 0.00089x_2 - 0.00023x_3$

15-51. a. $\hat{y} = -16.02 + 2.1277x$

    b. p-value $= 0.000 < 0.05$

15-55. a. Calls $= -269.838 + 4.953(\text{Ads previous week}) + 0.834(\text{Calls previous week}) + 0.089(\text{Airline bookings})$
The overall model is not significant and none of the independent variables are significant.

    b. The assumption of constant variance has not been violated.

    c. It is inappropriate to test for randomness using a plot of the residuals over time since the weeks were randomly selected and are not in sequential, time-series order.

    d. Model meets the assumption of normally distributed error terms.

15-57. a. $\hat{y} = 0.874 + 0.000887x_1 - 0.000235x_2$

    b. The residual plot supports the choice of the linear model.

    c. The residuals do not have constant variances.

    d. The linear model appears to be insufficient.

    e. The error terms are normally distributed.

15-59. a. $\hat{y} = -6.81 + 5.29x_1 + 1.51x_2 - 0.000033x_3$

    b. Plot the residuals versus the independent variable (x) or the fitted value $(\hat{y}_i)$.

    c. $\hat{y} = 0.97 - 3.20x_1 + 0.285x_2 + 0.000029x_3 + 3.12x_1^2 + 0.103x_2^2 - 0.000000x_3^2$

    d. The residual plot does not display any nonrandom pattern.

    e. The error terms are normally distributed.

15-63. a. The relationship between the dependent and each independent variable is linear.

    b. The residuals are independent.

    c. The variances of the residuals are constant over the range of the independent variables.

    d. The residuals are normally distributed.

15-65. a. The average y increases by three units, holding x_2 constant.

    b. x_2, since x_2 only affects the y-intercept of this model.

    c. The coefficient of x_1 indicates that the average y increases by 7 units when $x_2 = 1$.

    d. The coefficient of x_1 indicates that the average y increases by 11 units when $x_2 = 1$.

    e. Those coefficients affected by the interaction terms have conditional interpretations.

15-69. a. The critical t for all pairs would be 2.1604, correlated pairs. Volumes sold (y) − Production expenditures
Volumes sold (y) − Number of reviewers
Volumes sold (y) − Pages
Volumes sold (y) − Advertising budget

    b. All p-values > 0.05

    c. Critical $F = 3.581$; since $F = 9.1258 > 3.581$, conclude that the overall model is significant.

    e. $\pm 2(24{,}165.9419) = \pm 48{,}331.8$

    f. Constant variance assumption is satisfied.

    g. The residuals appear to be approximately normally distributed.

    h. The model satisfies the normal distribution assumption.

15-71. The t-critical for all pairs would be ± 2.0687, correlated pairs are
For family size and age
For purchase volume and age
For purchase volume and family income

15-73. The significance $F = 0.0210$.

15-75. Age entered the model.
The R^2 at step 1 was 0.2108 and the standard error at step 1 was 36.3553. The R^2 at step 2 is 0.3955 and the standard error at step 2 is 32.5313.

15-77. Other variables that enter into the model partially overlap with the other included variables in their ability to explain the variation in the dependent variable.

15-79. a. Normal distribution of the residuals.

    b. The selected independent variables are not highly correlated with the dependent variable.

15-81. a. $\hat{y} = 2{,}857 - 26.4x_1 - 80.6x_2 + 0.115x_1^2 + 2.31x_2^2 + 0.542x_1x_2$

    b. The residual plot supports the choice of the linear model.

    c. The residuals do have constant variances.

    d. The linear model appears to be insufficient. The addition of an independent variable representing time is indicated.

    e. A transformation of the independent or dependent variables is required.

15-83. a. Quadratic relationship exists between cost and weight.

    b. $r = 0.963$
$H_0: \rho = 0$
$H_A: \rho \neq 0$
$\alpha = 0.05$;
Since the p-value $= 0.000 > 0.05$, we reject H_0.

    c. Cost $= -64.06 + 14.92(\text{Weight})$

    d. Cost $= 43.8 - 9.22(\text{Weight}) + 1.44(\text{Weight}^2)$
Comparing the R_{adj}^2 for the quadratic equation (97.6%) and the R^2 for the simple linear equation (92.8%), the quadratic equation appears to fit the data better.

15-85. Vehicle year $= 73.18 - 9.1(\text{Gender}) + 1.39(\text{Years education}) - 24(\text{Not seat belt})$ R-squared $= 14.959\%$

Chapter 16

16-3. Generally, quantitative forecasting techniques can be used whenever historical data related to the variable of interest exist and we believe that the historical patterns will continue into the future.

16-7. a. The forecasting horizon is 6 months.
b. a medium-term forecast
c. a month
d. 12 months

16-9. c.

Year	Radio	% radio	Newspaper	Laspeyres
1	300	0.3	400	100
2	310	0.42	420	104.59
3	330	0.42	460	113.78
4	346	0.4	520	126.43
5	362	0.38	580	139.08
6	380	0.37	640	151.89
7	496	0.43	660	165.08

d.

Year	Radio	% radio	Newspaper	Paasche
1	300	0.3	400	100
2	310	0.42	420	104.41
3	330	0.42	460	113.22
4	346	0.4	520	124.77
5	362	0.38	580	136.33
6	380	0.37	640	148.12
7	496	0.43	660	165.12

16-13.

Year	Labor Costs	Material Costs	% Materials	% Labor	Laspeyres Index
1999	44,333	66,500	60	40	100
2000	49,893	68,900	58	42	106.36
2001	57,764	70,600	55	45	113.59
2002	58,009	70,900	55	45	114.07
2003	55,943	71,200	56	44	112.95
2004	61,078	71,700	54	46	117.03
2005	67,015	72,500	52	48	122.09
2006	73,700	73,700	50	50	127.88
2007	67,754	73,400	52	48	123.44
2008	74,100	74,100	50	50	128.57
2009	83,447	74,000	47	53	134.95

16-15. a. The sum $= 1.07 + 6.16 + 8.32 + 15.55$.
b. 82.89%
c. 76.10%

16-17. a. 102.31
b. 15.41%
c. 14.43%

16-21. January $= 0.849$; July $= 0.966$

16-23. a. upward linear trend with seasonal component as a slight drop in the 3rd quarter
b. Normalize to get the following values:

Quarter	Seasonal Index
1	1.035013
2	1.020898
3	0.959934
4	0.984154

c. $MSE = 36.955$ and $MAD = 4.831$
d. and **e.**

Quarter	Period	Seasonally Unadjusted Forecast	Seasonal Index	Seasonally Adjusted Forecast
Quarter 1 2010	17	250.15	1.0350	258.91
Quarter 2 2010	18	256.17	1.0209	261.52
Quarter 3 2010	19	262.18	0.9599	251.68
Quarter 4 2010	20	268.20	0.9842	263.95

16-27. b. The seasonal indexes are:

Month	Index
1	1.02349
2	1.07969
3	1.16502
4	1.12147
5	0.98695
6	0.83324
7	0.86807
8	0.91287
9	0.97699
10	1.07311
11	1.01382
12	0.94529

c. $Forecast = 1.98 + 0.0459(Month)$
d. $F_{25} = 1.98 + 0.0459(25) = 3.12$. Adjusted $F_{25} = (1.02349)(3.12) = 3.19$.
$F_{73} = 1.98 + 0.0458589(73) = 5.32$. Adjusted $F_{73} = (1.02349)(5.32) = 5.44$.

16-29. a. seasonal component to the data
b. $MSE = 976.34$ and $MAD = 29.887$
c.

Quarter	Index
1	1.0290
2	0.9207
3	1.0789
4	0.9714

d.

2009	Period	Forecast
Qtr. 1	13	256.5620033
Qtr. 2	14	260.0884382
Qtr. 3	15	263.614873
Qtr. 4	16	267.1413079

e. $MSE = 926.1187$, $MAD = 29.5952$
f. The adjusted model has a lower MSE and MAD.

16-31. a. Forecast without transformation $= 36.0952 + 10.8714(16) = 210.0376$.
Forecast with transformation $= 65.2986 + 0.6988(16)^2 = 244.1914$.
Actual cash balance for Month 16 was 305. The transformed model had a smaller error than the model without the transformation.

b. Model without transformation:

For Individual Response y

Interval Half Width	48.27804189
Prediction Interval Lower Limit	161.7600534
Prediction Interval Upper Limit	258.3161371

Model with transformation:

For Individual Response y

Interval Half Width	23.89550188
Prediction Interval Lower Limit	220.29634337
Prediction Interval Upper Limit	268.08734713

The model without the transformation has the wider interval.

16-33. a. Linear trend evidenced by the slope from small to large values. Randomness is exhibited since not all of the data points would lie on a straight line.
  b. $H_0: \beta_1 = 0$
     $H_A: \beta_1 \neq 0$
     $\alpha = 0.10$, p-value $= 0.000$
  c. The fitted values are $F_{38} = 36,051$, $F_{39} = 36,955$, $F_{40} = 37,858$, and $F_{41} = 38,761$.
  d. The forecast bias is $-1,343.5$. On average, the model over forecasts the e-commerce retail sales an average of $1,343.5 million.
16-35. b. A trend is present.
  c. Forecast $= 136.78$, $MAD = 23.278$
  d. Forecast $= 163.69$, $MAD = 7.655$
  e. The double exponential smoothing forecast has a lower MAD.
16-37. a. The time series contains a strong upward trend, so a double exponential smoothing model is selected.
  b. The equation is $\hat{y}_t = 19.364 + 0.7517t$. Since $C_0 = b_0$, $C_0 = 19.364$. $T_0 = b_1 = 0.7517$.
  c. Forecasts

Period	Forecast	Lower	Upper
13	29.1052	23.9872	34.2231

  d.

Accuracy Measures	
MAPE	8.58150
MAD	2.08901
MSE	6.48044

16-39. a. The time series contains a strong upward trend, so a double exponential smoothing model is selected.
  b. $\hat{y}_t = 990 + 2,622.8t$. Since $C_0 = b_0$, $C_0 = 990$. $T_0 = b_1 = 2,622.8$.
  c. Forecast $= 58,852.1$
  d. $MAD = 3,384$
16-41. a. There does not appear to be any trend component in this time series.
     $MAD = 3.2652$
     $F_{14} = 0.25y_{13} + (1 - 0.25)F_{13} = 0.25(101.3) + 0.75(100.22) = 100.49$

16-43. a. Single exponential smoothing model is selected.
  b. The forecast is calculated as $F_1 = F_2 = 0.296$. Then $F_3 = 0.15y_2 + (1 - 0.15)F_2 = 0.15(0.413) + 0.85(0.296) = 0.3136$.
  c. $MAD = 15.765/71 = 0.222$
  d. $F_{73} = 0.15y_{72} + (1 - 0.15)F_{72} = 0.15(-0.051) + 0.85(0.259) = 0.212$
16-45. a. The double exponential smoothing model will incorporate the trend effect.
  b. From regression output, Initial constant $= 28,848$; Initial trend $= 2,488.96$. Forecast for period $17 = 72,450.17$. $MAD = 5,836.06$.
  c. The MAD produced by the double exponential smoothing model at the end of Month 16 is smaller than the MAD produced by the single exponential smoothing model.
  d. and e. Of the combinations considered, the minimum MAD at the end of Month 16 occurs when alpha $= 0.05$ and beta $= 0.05$. The forecast for Month 17 with alpha $= 0.05$ and beta $= 0.05$ is $71,128.45$.
16-47. a. a seasonal component
  b. The pattern is linear with a positive slope.
  c. a cyclical component
  d. a random component
  e. a cyclical component
16-51. a. There does appear to be an upward linear trend.
  b. Forecast $= -682,238,010.3 + 342,385.3(\text{Year})$ Since $F = 123.9719 > 4.6001$, conclude that there is a significant relationship.
  c. $MAD = 461,216.7279$
  d.

Year	Forecast
2010	4,929,275.00
2011	5,271,660.29
2012	5,614,045.59
2013	5,956,430.88
2014	6,298,816.18

  e. For Individual Response y

Interval Half Width	1,232,095.322
Prediction Interval Lower Limit	5,066,720.854
Prediction Interval Upper Limit	7,530,911.499

16-55. a. The time series contains a strong upward trend, so a double exponential smoothing model is selected.
  b. Since $C_0 = b_0$, $C_0 = -2,229.9$; $T_0 = b_1 = 1.12$.
  c. Forecast(2008) $= 740.073$
  d. $MAD = 89.975$
16-57. b. $y = 240.16 + 188.56$ (time period)
  c. $t = 17.85 > 2.2281$; reject.
  e. The $MAD = 80.91$ or 81.
  f. The forecast for 2011 $= 2503$ (rounded). The forecast for 2012 $= 2691$ (rounded).
16-59. b. The estimated linear trend line equation is $y = 823.12 + 7.032(x)$.
  e. Since $1.057 < 1.37$, reject H_0 and conclude that positive autocorrelation exists.

16-61. a. There appears to be a slight linear trend as well as a seasonal trend.

d.

Month	Period	Forecast
January	49	41907.4368
February	50	42247.4050
March	51	42587.3731
April	52	42927.3412
May	53	43267.3072
June	54	43607.2753
July	55	43947.2434
August	56	44287.2115
September	57	44627.1796
October	58	44967.1477
November	59	45307.1157
December	60	45647.0837

e. Deseasonalizing the data has increased the R^2 and decreased the MAD.

Month	Period	Unadjusted Forecast	Seasonal Index	Adjusted Forecast
January	49	41907.4368	0.8488	35572.333
February	50	42247.4050	0.8627	36445.963
March	51	42587.3731	0.7889	33595.260
April	52	42927.3412	0.8662	37182.217

16-63. a. Use Equations 16-18, 16-19, and 16-20 and follow Example 16-7. Beta = 0.2, Initial constant value = 23424.5567, Initial trend value = 420.89.
$MAD = 5181.12$

d.

	Beta			
Alpha	0.3	0.25	0.2	0.1
0.1	5190.35	5101.89	5013.90	4823.45
0.15	5397.24	5258.43	5130.99	4892.37
0.2	5538.02	5354.95	5181.12	4872.93
0.3	5374.41	5192.38	5019.96	4709.27

The values of alpha = 0.30 and beta = 0.10 provide the lowest MAD.

Chapter 17

17-1. The hypotheses are $H_0: \widetilde{\mu} \geq 14$
$\qquad\qquad\qquad\quad H_A: \widetilde{\mu} < 14$
$W = 36$
$n = 11, \alpha = .05$; reject if $W < 13$.

17-3. The hypotheses are $H_0: \widetilde{\mu} = 4$
$\qquad\qquad\qquad\quad H_A: \widetilde{\mu} \neq 4$
$W = 9, W = 19$:
Critical values for $n = 7$, assuming $\alpha = 0.1$ are 3 and 25. Cannot reject.

17-5. a. The hypotheses are $H_0: \widetilde{\mu} \leq 4$
$\qquad\qquad\qquad\quad H_A: \widetilde{\mu} > 4$

b. Using the Wilcoxon Signed Rank test, $W = 26$:
Upper tail test and $n = 12$, letting $\alpha = .05$,
reject if $W > 61$. So, cannot reject.

17-7. $H_0: \widetilde{\mu} \geq 11$
$H_A: \widetilde{\mu} < 11$
Using the Wilcoxon Signed Rank test, $W = 92$:
Reject if $W < 53$.

17-9. $H_0: \widetilde{\mu} = 30$
$H_A: \widetilde{\mu} \neq 30$
Using the Wilcoxon Signed Rank test, $W = 71.5, W = 81.5$:
Because some of the differences are 0, $n = 17$. The upper and lower values for the Wilcoxon test are 34 and 119 for $\alpha = 0.05$. Do not reject.

17-11. a. Using data classes one standard deviation wide, with the data mean of 7.6306 and a standard deviation of 0.2218:

e	o	$(o - e)^2/e$
14.9440	21	2.45417
32.4278	31	0.06287
32.4278	27	0.90851
14.9440	16	0.07462 Sum = 3.5002

Testing at the $\alpha = 0.05$ level, $\chi_\alpha^2 = 5.9915$.

b. Since we concluded the data come from a normal distribution, we test the following:
$H_0: \mu \geq 7.4$
$H_A: \mu < 7.4$
Decision rule: If $z < -1.645$, reject H_0; otherwise do not reject. $Z = 10.13$

17-13. a. Putting the claim in the alternate hypothesis:
$\qquad H_0: \widetilde{\mu}_1 - \widetilde{\mu}_2 \geq 0$
$\qquad H_A: \widetilde{\mu}_1 - \widetilde{\mu}_2 < 0$

b. Test using the Mann-Whitney U Test.
$U_1 = 40, U_2 = 24$
Use U_2 as the test statistic. For $n_1 = 8$ and $n_2 = 8$ and $U = 24$, p-value $= 0.221$.

17-15. a. $H_0: \widetilde{\mu}_1 - \widetilde{\mu}_2 \leq 0$
$\qquad\; H_A: \widetilde{\mu}_1 - \widetilde{\mu}_2 > 0$

b. Since the alternate hypothesis indicates Population 1 should have the larger median, $U_1 = 40$.
$n_1 = 12 \; and \; n_2 = 12$. Reject if $U \leq 31$.

17-17. $H_0: \widetilde{\mu}_1 - \widetilde{\mu}_2 = 0$
$H_A: \widetilde{\mu}_1 - \widetilde{\mu}_2 \neq 0$
Mann-Whitney Test and CI: C_1, C_2

C_1	$N = 40,$	Median = 481.50
C_2	$N = 35,$	Median = 505.00

Point estimate for $ETA_1 - ETA_2$ is -25.00
95.1% CI for $ETA_1 - ETA_2$ is $(-62.00, 9.00)$.
$W = 1,384.0$
Test of $ETA_1 = ETA_2$ vs. ETA_1 not $= ETA_2$ is significant at 0.1502.

17-19. a. $H_0: \widetilde{\mu}_1 - \widetilde{\mu}_2 = 0$
$\qquad\; H_A: \widetilde{\mu}_1 - \widetilde{\mu}_2 \neq 0$
With $n = 8$, reject if $T \leq 4$.
Since $T = 11.5$, we do not reject the null hypothesis.

b. Use the paired sample t test. p-value $= 0.699$.

17-21. $H_0: \widetilde{\mu}_1 - \widetilde{\mu}_2 = 0$
$H_A: \widetilde{\mu}_1 - \widetilde{\mu}_2 \neq 0$
With $n = 7$, reject if $T \leq 2, T = 13$.

17-23. $H_0: \widetilde{\mu}_2 = \widetilde{\mu}_1$
$H_A: \widetilde{\mu}_2 \neq \widetilde{\mu}_1$
If $T \leq 0$, reject H_0; $T = 8$.

17-25. $H_0: \widetilde{\mu}_W - \widetilde{\mu}_{WO} \leq 0$
$H_A: \widetilde{\mu}_W - \widetilde{\mu}_{WO} > 0$
$U_1 = (7)(5) + (7)(7 + 1)/2 - 42 = 21$
$U_2 = (7)(5) + (5)(5 + 1)/2 - 36 = 14$
Utest $= 21$
Since 21 is not in the table, you cannot determine the exact p-value, but you know that the p-value will be greater than 0.562.

17-27. a. $H_0: \widetilde{\mu}_1 \le \widetilde{\mu}_2$
$H_A: \widetilde{\mu}_1 > \widetilde{\mu}_2$
b. Since $T = 51$ is greater than 16, do not reject H_0.
c. Housing values are typically skewed.

17-29. $H_0: \widetilde{\mu}_1 = \widetilde{\mu}_2$
$H_A: \widetilde{\mu}_1 \ne \widetilde{\mu}_2$
$\mu = 40(40 + 1)/4 = 410$
$\sigma = \sqrt{40(40 + 1)(80 + 1)/24} = 74.3976$
$z = (480 - 410)/74.3976 = 0.94$
p-value $= (0.5 - 0.3264)2 = (0.1736)(2) = 0.3472$.
Do not reject H_0.

17-31. a. A paired-t test.
$H_0: \mu_d \ge 0$
$H_A: \mu_d < 0$
$t = (-1.7)/(3.011091/\sqrt{10}) = -1.785$
Since $-1.785 > t$ critical $= -2.2622$, do not reject H_0.
b. $H_0: \widetilde{\mu}_O \ge \widetilde{\mu}_N$
$H_A: \widetilde{\mu}_O < \widetilde{\mu}_N$
$T = 5.5$. Since $5.5 < 6$, reject H_0 and conclude that the medians are not the same.
c. Because you cannot assume the underlying populations are normal, you must use the technique from part b.

17-33. a. $H_0: \widetilde{\mu}_N \ge \widetilde{\mu}_C$
$H_A: \widetilde{\mu}_N < \widetilde{\mu}_C$
$U_1 = 4,297, U_2 = 6,203, \mu = 5,250, \sigma = 434.7413$
$z = -2.19$
p-value $= 0.0143$
b. a Type I error

17-35. a. The data are ordinal.
b. The median would be the best measure.
c. $H_0: \widetilde{\mu}_1 = \widetilde{\mu}_2$
$H_A: \widetilde{\mu}_1 \ne \widetilde{\mu}_2$
Using $\alpha = 0.01$, if $T \le 2$, reject H_0. Since $12.5 > 2$, do not reject H_0.
d. The decision could be made based on some other factor, such as cost.

17-37. a. $H_0: \widetilde{\mu}_1 = \widetilde{\mu}_2 = \widetilde{\mu}_3$
$H_A:$ Not all population medians are equal.
b. $H = 10.98$. Since, with $\alpha = 0.05, \chi_\alpha^2 = 5.9915$, and $H = 10.98$, we reject.

17-39. a. $H_0: \widetilde{\mu}_1 = \widetilde{\mu}_2 = \widetilde{\mu}_3 = \widetilde{\mu}_4$
$H_A:$ Not all population medians are equal.
b. Use Equation 17-10.
Selecting $\alpha = 0.05, \chi_\alpha^2 = 7.8147$, since $H = 42.11$, we reject the null hypothesis of equal medians.

17-41. a. Salaries in general are usually thought to be skewed.
b. The top-salaried players get extremely high salaries compared to the other players.
c. $H_0: \widetilde{\mu}_1 = \widetilde{\mu}_2 = \widetilde{\mu}_3$
$H_A:$ Not all population medians are equal.
$H = 52.531$. If $\alpha = 0.05, \chi_\alpha^2 = 5.9915$. Reject.

17-43. $H_0: \widetilde{\mu}_1 = \widetilde{\mu}_2 = \widetilde{\mu}_3 = \widetilde{\mu}_4$
$H_A:$ Not all population medians are equal.
Using PHStat, H test statistic $= 11.13971$. Adjusting for ties, the test statistic is 11.21, which is smaller than the critical value (11.34488). Do not reject.

17-45. $H_0: \widetilde{\mu}_1 = \widetilde{\mu}_2 = \widetilde{\mu}_3$
$H_A:$ Not all population medians are equal.
$H = 13.9818$, testing at $\alpha = 0.05, \chi_\alpha^2 = 5.9915$
Since $13.9818 > 5.9915$, reject H_0.

17-53. $H_0: \widetilde{\mu}_1 - \widetilde{\mu}_2 = 0$
$H_A: \widetilde{\mu}_1 - \widetilde{\mu}_2 \ne 0$
$U_1 = 107, U_2 = 14; U$ test $= 14$ with $\alpha = 0.05, U_\alpha = 30$.
Since $14 < 30$, reject H_0.

17-55. a. A nonparametric test.
b. $H_0: \widetilde{\mu}_O - \widetilde{\mu}_N \ge 0$
$H_A: \widetilde{\mu}_O - \widetilde{\mu}_N < 0$
$U_1 - 71, U_2 = 29; U$ test $= 29$
If $\alpha = 0.05, U_\alpha = 27$.
Since $29 > 27$, do not reject H_0.

17-57. The hypotheses being tested are
$H_0: \widetilde{\mu} = 1,989.32$
$H_A: \widetilde{\mu} \ne 1,989.32$
Find $W = 103, W = 68$.
With $\alpha = 0.05$, reject if $W \le 40$ or $W > 131$.

17-59. a. $H_0: \widetilde{\mu} = 8.03$
$H_A: \widetilde{\mu} \ne 8.03$
b. $W = 62.5, W = 57.5$
This is a two-tailed test with $n = 15$.
If $\alpha = 0.05$, reject if $W \le 25$ or $W > 95$.

17-61. $H_0: \widetilde{\mu}_1 = \widetilde{\mu}_2$
$H_A: \widetilde{\mu}_1 \ne \widetilde{\mu}_2$
Constructing the paired difference table, $T = 44.5$. With $\alpha = 0.05$, reject if $T \le 21$ or if $T \ge 84$.
b. a Type II error

17-63. a. They should use the Wilcoxon Matched-Pairs Signed Rank.
b. $H_0: \widetilde{\mu}_{w/oA} \ge \widetilde{\mu}_A$
$H_A: \widetilde{\mu}_{w/oA} < \widetilde{\mu}_A$
$T = 6$
Using $\alpha = 0.025, T_\alpha = 4$.
c. Do not reject H_0.

Chapter 18

18-1. a. c-chart
b. $\bar{c} = 8.98$
c. $UCL = 17.97, LCL = 0.0$

18-3. $\bar{p} = 270/(30*100) = 0.090$

$$UCL = 0.090 + 3*\sqrt{\frac{0.090*(1 - 0.090)}{100}} = 0.176$$

$$UCL = 0.090 - 3*\sqrt{\frac{0.090*(1 - 0.090)}{100}} = 0.004$$

18-5. a. x-bar chart centerline $= 6.217$
$UCL = 6.217 + 0.729(1.005) = 6.9496$
$LCL = 6.217 - 0.729(1.005) = 5.4844$
R chart centerline $= 1.005$
$UCL = 2.282(1.005) = 2.2934$
c. The process is in control.

18-7. a.

	Panel 1	Panel 2	Panel 3	Panel 4	Panel 5	X-Bar	Range
Hour 41	0.764	0.737	0.724	0.716	0.752	0.7386	0.048
Hour 42	0.766	0.785	0.777	0.79	0.799	0.7834	0.033
Hour 43	0.812	0.774	0.767	0.799	0.821	0.7946	0.054

b. Yes

18-9. a. p-chart
The 3-sigma upper control limit is $0.0793 + (3*0.0270) = 0.1603$. The 3-sigma lower control limit is $0.0793 - (3*0.0270) = -0.0017$, which is then set equal to 0.0000.
b. The process appears to be in control.
c. The process still appears to be in statistical control.

18-11. c. Based on the R-chart, it appears that the service time process is out of control.

18-13. a.

Week	Subgroup Mean	Subgroup Range
41	369.75	127
42	485.75	323
43	392.75	264
44	415.5	363
45	433.5	195

d. The control chart limits for the x-bar and R charts are calculated below:

$UCL = 415.761 + 0.729(117.489) = 501.41$

$CL = 415.761$

$LCL = 415.761 - 0.729(117.489) = 330.11$

$UCL = 2.282(117.489) = 268.11$

$CL = 117.489$

$LCL = 0(117.489) = 0$

18-15. a. The recomputed control chart limits are:

For x-bar chart

$UCL = 85.03 + 0.577(13.23) = 92.66$

$CL = 85.03$

$LCL = 85.03 - 0.577(13.23) = 77.40$

For R-chart

$UCL = 2.114(13.23) = 27.97$

$CL = 13.23$

$LCL = 0$

b.

Subgroup	33	34	35	36	37	38
Subgroup Mean	89	88.4	85.2	89.3	97.2	105.3

18-17. b. $UCL = 0.8246 + 3(0.038) = 0.9386$

$LCL = 0.8246 - 3(0.038) = 0.7106$

18-19. a. x-bar values

$UCL = 2.0855 + 0.308(2.9) = 2.9787$

$CL = 2.0855$

$LCL = 2.0855 - 0.308(2.9) = 1.1923$

R chart values

$UCL = 1.777*2.9 = 5.1533$

$CL = 2.9$

$LCL = 0.223*2.9 = 0.6467$

18-21. a. The Shewart factor for the x-bar chart, A2, with subgroup size of 4, is 0.729. For the R-chart, the Shewart factors are D3 = 0 and D4 = 2.282.

b. $UCL = 2.282*209.3 = 477.62304$

$LCL = 0*209.3 = 0.00$

c. $UCL = 1,345.4 + (0.729*209.3) = 1,497.98$

$LCL = 1,345.4 - (0.729*209.3) = 1,192.82$

18-23. $UCL = 0.140 + 3*\sqrt{\dfrac{0.140*(1 - 0.140)}{100}} = 0.244$

$LCL = 0.140 - 3*\sqrt{\dfrac{0.140*(1 - 0.140)}{100}} = 0.036$

18-25. Lower Control Limit = $0.9152 - 3*0.0279 = 0.8315$

Centerline = 0.9152

Upper Control Limit = $0.9152 + 3*0.0279 = 0.9989$

18-27. For the x-bar chart

$UCL = 76.7984 + 0.729(13.5974) = 86.7110$

$CL = 76.7984$

$LCL = 76.7984 - 0.729(13.5974) = 66.8859$

For the R-chart

$UCL = 2.282(13.5974) = 31.0294$

$CL = 13.5974$

$LCL = 0(13.5974) = 0$

References

Chapter 1

Berenson, Mark L., and David M. Levine, *Basic Business Statistics: Concepts and Applications*, 12th ed. (Upper Saddle River, NJ: Prentice Hall, 2012).

Cryer, Jonathan D., and Robert B. Miller, *Statistics for Business: Data Analysis and Modeling*, 2nd ed. (Belmont, CA: Duxbury Press, 1994).

DeVeaux, Richard D., Paul F. Velleman, and David E. Bock, *Stats Data and Models*, 3rd ed. (New York: Addison-Wesley, 2012).

Fowler, Floyd J., *Survey Research Methods*, 4th ed. (Thousand Oaks, CA: Sage Publications, 2009).

Hildebrand, David, and R. Lyman Ott, *Statistical Thinking for Managers*, 4th ed. (Belmont, CA: Duxbury Press, 1998).

John, J. A., D. Whitiker, and D. G. Johnson, *Statistical Thinking for Managers*, 2nd ed. (Boca Raton, FL: CRC Press, 2005).

Microsoft Excel 2010 (Redmond, WA: Microsoft Corp., 2010).

Scheaffer, Richard L., William Mendenhall, R. Lyman Ott, and Kenneth G. Gerow, *Elementary Survey Sampling*, 7th ed. (Brooks/Cole, 2012).

Siegel, Andrew F., *Practical Business Statistics*, 5th ed. (Burr Ridge, IL: Irwin, 2002).

Chapter 2

Berenson, Mark L., and David M. Levine, *Basic Business Statistics: Concepts and Applications*, 12th ed. (Upper Saddle River, NJ: Prentice Hall, 2012).

Cleveland, William S., "Graphs in Scientific Publications," *The American Statistician* 38 (November 1984), pp. 261–269.

Cleveland, William S., and R. McGill, "Graphical Perception: Theory, Experimentation, and Application to the Development of Graphical Methods," *Journal of the American Statistical Association* 79 (September 1984), pp. 531–554.

Cryer, Jonathan D., and Robert B. Miller, *Statistics for Business: Data Analysis and Modeling*, 2nd ed. (Belmont, CA: Duxbury Press, 1994).

DeVeaux, Richard D., Paul F. Velleman, and David E. Bock, *Stats Data and Models*, 3rd ed. (New York: Addison-Wesley, 2012).

Microsoft Excel 2010 (Redmond, WA: Microsoft Corp., 2010).

Siegel, Andrew F., *Practical Business Statistics*, 5th ed. (Burr Ridge, IL: Irwin, 2002).

Tufte, Edward R., *Envisioning Information* (Cheshire, CT: Graphics Press, 1990).

Tufte, Edward R., *The Visual Display of Quantitative Information*, 2nd ed. (Cheshire, CT: Graphics Press, 2001).

Tukey, John W., *Exploratory Data Analysis* (Reading, MA: Addison-Wesley, 1977).

Chapter 3

Berenson, Mark L., and David M. Levine, *Basic Business Statistics: Concepts and Applications*, 12th ed. (Upper Saddle River, NJ: Prentice Hall, 2012).

DeVeaux, Richard D., Paul F. Velleman, and David E. Bock, *Stats Data and Models*, 3rd ed. (New York: Addison-Wesley, 2012).

Microsoft Excel 2010 (Redmond, WA: Microsoft Corp., 2010).

Siegel, Andrew F., *Practical Business Statistics*, 5th ed. (Burr Ridge, IL: Irwin, 2002).

Tukey, John W., *Exploratory Data Analysis* (Reading, MA: Addison-Wesley, 1977).

Chapter 4

Blyth, C. R., "Subjective vs. Objective Methods in Statistics," *American Statistician,* 26 (June 1972), pp. 20–22.

DeVeaux, Richard D., Paul F. Velleman, and David E. Bock, *Stats Data and Models*, 3rd ed. (New York: Addison-Wesley, 2012).

Hogg, R. V., and Elliot A. Tanis, *Probability and Statistical Inference,* 8th ed. (Upper Saddle River, NJ: Prentice Hall, 2010).

Larsen, Richard J., and Morris L. Marx, *An Introduction to Mathematical Statistics and Its Applications,* 5th ed. (Upper Saddle River, NJ: Prentice Hall, 2012).

Microsoft Excel 2010 (Redmond, WA: Microsoft Corp., 2010).

Mlodinow, Leonard, *The Drunkard's Walk: How Randomness Rules Our Lives* (New York: Pantheon Books, 2008).

Raiffa, H., *Decision Analysis: Introductory Lectures on Choices Under Uncertainty* (Reading, MA: Addison-Wesley, 1968).

Siegel, Andrew F., *Practical Business Statistics*, 5th ed. (Burr Ridge, IL: Irwin, 2002).

Chapter 5

DeVeaux, Richard D., Paul F. Velleman, and David E. Bock, *Stats Data and Models*, 3rd ed. (New York: Addison-Wesley, 2012).

Hogg, R. V., and Elliot A. Tanis, *Probability and Statistical Inference,* 8th ed. (Upper Saddle River, NJ: Prentice Hall, 2010).

Larsen, Richard J., and Morris L. Marx, *An Introduction to Mathematical Statistics and Its Applications,* 5th ed. (Upper Saddle River, NJ: Prentice Hall, 2012).

Microsoft Excel 2010 (Redmond, WA: Microsoft Corp., 2010).

Siegel, Andrew F., *Practical Business Statistics*, 5th ed. (Burr Ridge, IL: Irwin, 2002).

Chapter 6

Albright, Christian S., Wayne L. Winston, and Christopher Zappe, *Data Analysis for Managers with Microsoft Excel* (Pacific Grove, CA: Duxbury, 2003).

DeVeaux, Richard D., Paul F. Velleman, and David E. Bock, *Stats Data and Models*, 3rd ed. (New York: Addison-Wesley, 2012).

Hogg, R. V., and Elliot A. Tanis, *Probability and Statistical Inference,* 8th ed. (Upper Saddle River, NJ: Prentice Hall, 2010).

Larsen, Richard J., and Morris L. Marx, *An Introduction to Mathematical Statistics and Its Applications,* 5th ed. (Upper Saddle River, NJ: Prentice Hall, 2012).

Microsoft Excel 2010 (Redmond, WA: Microsoft Corp., 2010).

Siegel, Andrew F., *Practical Business Statistics*, 5th ed. (Burr Ridge, IL: Irwin, 2002).

Chapter 7

Berenson, Mark L., and David M. Levine, *Basic Business Statistics: Concepts and Applications*, 12th ed. (Upper Saddle River, NJ: Prentice Hall, 2012).

Cochran, William G., *Sampling Techniques*, 3rd ed. (New York: Wiley, 1977).

DeVeaux, Richard D., Paul F. Velleman, and David E. Bock, *Stats Data and Models*, 3rd ed. (New York: Addison-Wesley, 2012).

Hogg, R. V., and Elliot A. Tanis, *Probability and Statistical Inference,* 8th ed. (Upper Saddle River, NJ: Prentice Hall, 2010).

Johnson, Richard A., and Dean W. Wichern, *Business Statistics: Decision Making with Data* (New York: Wiley, 1997).

Larsen, Richard J., and Morris L. Marx, *An Introduction to Mathematical Statistics and Its Applications,* 5th ed. (Upper Saddle River, NJ: Prentice Hall, 2012).

Microsoft Excel 2010 (Redmond, WA: Microsoft Corp., 2010).

Chapter 8

Berenson, Mark L., and David M. Levine, *Basic Business Statistics: Concepts and Applications*, 12th ed. (Upper Saddle River, NJ: Prentice Hall, 2012).

DeVeaux, Richard D., Paul F. Velleman, and David E. Bock, *Stats Data and Models*, 3rd ed. (New York: Addison-Wesley, 2012).

Hogg, R. V., and Elliot A. Tanis, *Probability and Statistical Inference,* 8th ed. (Upper Saddle River, NJ: Prentice Hall, 2010).

Larsen, Richard J., and Morris L. Marx, *An Introduction to Mathematical Statistics and Its Applications,* 5th ed. (Upper Saddle River, NJ: Prentice Hall, 2012).

Microsoft Excel 2010 (Redmond, WA: Microsoft Corp., 2010).

Siegel, Andrew F., *Practical Business Statistics*, 5th ed. (Burr Ridge, IL: Irwin, 2002).

Chapter 9

Berenson, Mark L., and David M. Levine, *Basic Business Statistics: Concepts and Applications*, 12th ed. (Upper Saddle River, NJ: Prentice Hall, 2012).

Brown, L., et al., "Interval Estimation for a Binomial Proportion," *Statistical Science*, 2001, pp. 101–133.

DeVeaux, Richard D., Paul F. Velleman, and David E. Bock, *Stats Data and Models*, 3rd ed. (New York: Addison-Wesley, 2012).

Hogg, R. V., and Elliot A. Tanis, *Probability and Statistical Inference,* 8th ed. (Upper Saddle River, NJ: Prentice Hall, 2010).

Larsen, Richard J., and Morris L. Marx, *An Introduction to Mathematical Statistics and Its Applications,* 5th ed. (Upper Saddle River, NJ: Prentice Hall, 2012).

Microsoft Excel 2010 (Redmond, WA: Microsoft Corp., 2010).

Siegel, Andrew F., *Practical Business Statistics*, 5th ed. (Burr Ridge, IL: Irwin, 2002).

Chapter 10

Berenson, Mark L., and David M. Levine, *Basic Business Statistics: Concepts and Applications*, 12th ed. (Upper Saddle River, NJ: Prentice Hall, 2012).

Cryer, Jonathan D., and Robert B. Miller, *Statistics for Business: Data Analysis and Modeling*, 2nd ed. (Belmont, CA: Duxbury Press, 1994).

DeVeaux, Richard D., Paul F. Velleman, and David E. Bock, *Stats Data and Models*, 3rd ed. (New York: Addison-Wesley, 2012).

Johnson, Richard A., and Dean W. Wichern, *Business Statistics: Decision Making with Data* (New York: Wiley, 1997).

Larsen, Richard J., Morris L. Marx, and Bruce Cooil, *Statistics for Applied Problem Solving and Decision Making* (Pacific Grove, CA: Duxbury Press, 1997).

Microsoft Excel 2010 (Redmond, WA: Microsoft Corp., 2010).

Siegel, Andrew F., *Practical Business Statistics*, 5th ed. (Burr Ridge, IL: Irwin, 2002).

Chapter 11

Berenson, Mark L., and David M. Levine, *Basic Business Statistics: Concepts and Applications*, 12th ed. (Upper Saddle River, NJ: Prentice Hall, 2012).

Cryer, Jonathan D., and Robert B. Miller, *Statistics for Business: Data Analysis and Modeling*, 2nd ed. (Belmont, CA: Duxbury Press, 1994).

DeVeaux, Richard D., Paul F. Velleman, and David E. Bock, *Stats Data and Models*, 3rd ed. (New York: Addison-Wesley, 2012).

Duncan, Acheson J., *Quality Control and Industrial Statistics*, 5th ed. (Burr Ridge, IL: Irwin, 1986).

Johnson, Richard A., and Dean W. Wichern, *Business Statistics: Decision Making with Data* (New York: Wiley, 1997).

Larsen, Richard J., Morris L. Marx, and Bruce Cooil, *Statistics for Applied Problem Solving and Decision Making* (Pacific Grove, CA: Duxbury Press, 1997).

Markowski, Carol, and Edmund Markowski, "Conditions for the Effectiveness of a Preliminary Test of Variance," *The American Statistician*, November 1990 (4), pp. 322–326.

Microsoft Excel 2010 (Redmond, WA: Microsoft Corp., 2010).

Siegel, Andrew F., *Practical Business Statistics*, 5th ed. (Burr Ridge, IL: Irwin, 2002).

Chapter 12

Berenson, Mark L., and David M. Levine, *Basic Business Statistics: Concepts and Applications*, 12th ed. (Upper Saddle River, NJ: Prentice Hall, 2012).

Bowerman, Bruce L., and Richard T. O'Connell, *Linear Statistical Models: An Applied Approach*, 2nd ed. (Belmont, CA: Duxbury Press, 1990).

Cox, D. R., *Planning of Experiments* (New York: John Wiley & Sons, 1992).

Cryer, Jonathan D., and Robert B. Miller, *Statistics for Business: Data Analysis and Modeling*, 2nd ed. (Belmont, CA: Duxbury Press, 1994).

DeVeaux, Richard D., Paul F. Velleman, and David E. Bock, *Stats Data and Models*, 3rd ed. (New York: Addison-Wesley, 2012).

Kutner, Michael H., Christopher J. Nachtsheim, John Neter, William Li, *Applied Linear Statistical Models*, 5th ed. (New York: McGraw-Hill Irwin, 2005).

Microsoft Excel 2010 (Redmond, WA: Microsoft Corp., 2010).

Montgomery, D. C., *Design and Analysis of Experiments*, 8th ed. (New York: John Wiley & Sons, 2012).

Searle, S. R., and R. F. Fawcett, "Expected Mean Squares in Variance Component Models Having Finite Populations," *Biometrics* 26 (197), pp. 243–254.

Chapter 13

Berenson, Mark L., and David M. Levine, *Basic Business Statistics: Concepts and Applications*, 12th ed. (Upper Saddle River, NJ: Prentice Hall, 2012).

Conover, W. J., *Practical Nonparametric Statistics*, 3rd ed. (New York: Wiley, 1999).

DeVeaux, Richard D., Paul F. Velleman, and David E. Bock, *Stats Data and Models*, 3rd ed. (New York: Addison-Wesley, 2012).

Higgins, James J., *Introduction to Modern Nonparametric Statistics*, 1st ed. (Pacific Grove, CA: Duxbury, 2004).

Marascuilo, Leonard, and M. McSweeney, *Nonparametric and Distribution Free Methods for the Social Sciences* (Monterey, CA: Brooks/Cole, 1977).

Microsoft Excel 2010 (Redmond, WA: Microsoft Corp., 2010).

Chapter 14

Berenson, Mark L., and David M. Levine, *Basic Business Statistics: Concepts and Applications*, 12th ed. (Upper Saddle River, NJ: Prentice Hall, 2012).

Cryer, Jonathan D., and Robert B. Miller, *Statistics for Business: Data Analysis and Modeling*, 2nd ed. (Belmont, CA: Duxbury Press, 1994).

DeVeaux, Richard D., Paul F. Velleman, and David E. Bock, *Stats Data and Models*, 3rd ed. (New York: Addison-Wesley, 2012).

Dielman, Terry E., *Applied Regression Analysis—A Second Course in Business and Economic Statistics*, 4th ed. (Belmont, CA: Duxbury Press, 2005).

Draper, Norman R., and Harry Smith, *Applied Regression Analysis*, 3rd ed. (New York: John Wiley and Sons, 1998).

Frees, Edward W., *Data Analysis Using Regression Models: The Business Perspective* (Upper Saddle River, NJ: Prentice Hall, 1996).

Kleinbaum, David G., Lawrence L. Kupper, Azhar Nizam, and Keith E. Muller, *Applied Regression Analysis and Multivariable Methods*, 4th ed. (Florence, KY: Cengage Learning, 2008).

Kutner, Michael H., Christopher J. Nachtsheim, John Neter, William Li, *Applied Linear Statistical Models*, 5th ed. (New York: McGraw-Hill Irwin, 2005).

Microsoft Excel 2010 (Redmond, WA: Microsoft Corp., 2010).

Chapter 15

Berenson, Mark L., and David M. Levine, *Basic Business Statistics: Concepts and Applications*, 12th ed. (Upper Saddle River, NJ: Prentice Hall, 2012).

Bowerman, Bruce L., and Richard T. O'Connell, *Linear Statistical Models: An Applied Approach*, 2nd ed. (Belmont, CA: Duxbury Press, 1990).

Cryer, Jonathan D., and Robert B. Miller, *Statistics for Business: Data Analysis and Modeling*, 2nd ed. (Belmont, CA: Duxbury Press, 1994).

Demmert, Henry, and Marshall Medoff, "Game-Specific Factors and Major League Baseball Attendance: An Econometric Study," *Santa Clara Business Review* (1977), pp. 49–56.

DeVeaux, Richard D., Paul F. Velleman, and David E. Bock, *Stats Data and Models*, 3rd ed. (New York: Addison-Wesley, 2012).

Dielman, Terry E., *Applied Regression Analysis—A Second Course in Business and Economic Statistics*, 4th ed. (Belmont, CA: Duxbury Press, 2005).

Draper, Norman R., and Harry Smith, *Applied Regression Analysis*, 3rd ed. (New York: John Wiley and Sons, 1998).

Frees, Edward W., *Data Analysis Using Regression Models: The Business Perspective* (Upper Saddle River, NJ: Prentice Hall, 1996).

Gloudemans, Robert J., and Dennis Miller, "Multiple Regression Analysis Applied to Residential Properties," *Decision Sciences* 7 (April 1976), pp. 294–304.

Kleinbaum, David G., Lawrence L. Kupper, Azhar Nizam, and Keith E. Muller, *Applied Regression Analysis and Multivariable Methods*, 4th ed. (Florence, KY: Cengage Learning, 2008).

Kutner, Michael H., Christopher J. Nachtsheim, John Neter, William Li, *Applied Linear Statistical Models*, 5th ed. (New York: McGraw-Hill Irwin, 2005).

Microsoft Excel 2010 (Redmond, WA: Microsoft Corp., 2010).

Chapter 16

Armstrong, J. Scott, "Forecasting by Extrapolation: Conclusions from 25 Years of Research," *Interfaces*, 14, no. 6 (1984).

Bails, Dale G., and Larry C. Peppers, *Business Fluctuations: Forecasting Techniques and Applications*, 2nd ed. (Englewood Cliffs, NJ: Prentice Hall, 1992).

Berenson, Mark L., and David M. Levine, *Basic Business Statistics: Concepts and Applications*, 12th ed. (Upper Saddle River, NJ: Prentice Hall, 2012).

Bowerman, Bruce L., and Richard T. O'Connell, *Linear Statistical Models: An Applied Approach*, 2nd ed. (Belmont, CA: Duxbury Press, 1990).

Brandon, Charles, R. Fritz, and J. Xander, "Econometric Forecasts: Evaluation and Revision," *Applied Economics*, 15, no. 2 (1983).

Cryer, Jonathan D., and Robert B. Miller, *Statistics for Business: Data Analysis and Modeling*, 2nd ed. (Belmont, CA: Duxbury Press, 1994).

DeVeaux, Richard D., Paul F. Velleman, and David E. Bock, *Stats Data and Models*, 3rd ed. (New York: Addison-Wesley, 2012).

Frees, Edward W., *Data Analysis Using Regression Models: The Business Perspective* (Upper Saddle River, NJ: Prentice Hall, 1996).

Granger, C. W. G., *Forecasting in Business and Economics*, 2nd ed. (New York: Academic Press, 1989).

Kutner, Michael H., Christopher J. Nachtsheim, John Neter, William Li, *Applied Linear Statistical Models*, 5th ed. (New York: McGraw-Hill Irwin, 2005).

Makridakis, Spyros, Steven C. Wheelwright, and Rob J. Hyndman, *Forecasting: Methods and Applications*, 3rd ed. (New York: John Wiley & Sons, 1998).

McLaughlin, Robert L., "Forecasting Models: Sophisticated or Naive?" *Journal of Forecasting*, 2, no. 3 (1983).

Microsoft Excel 2010 (Redmond, WA: Microsoft Corp., 2010).

Montgomery, Douglas C., and Lynwood A. Johnson, *Forecasting and Time Series Analysis*, 2nd ed. (New York: McGraw-Hill, 1990).

Nelson, C. R., *Applied Time Series Analysis for Managerial Forecasting* (San Francisco: Holdon-Day, 1983).

The Ombudsman: "Research on Forecasting—A Quarter-Century Review, 1960–1984," *Interfaces*, 16, no. 1 (1986).

Willis, R. E., *A Guide to Forecasting for Planners* (Englewood Cliffs, NJ: Prentice Hall, 1987).

Wonnacott, T. H., and R. J. Wonnacott, *Econometrics*, 2nd ed. (New York: John Wiley & Sons, 1979).

Chapter 17

Berenson, Mark L., and David M. Levine, *Basic Business Statistics: Concepts and Applications*, 12th ed. (Upper Saddle River, NJ: Prentice Hall, 2012).

Conover, W. J., *Practical Nonparametric Statistics*, 3rd ed. (New York: Wiley, 1999).

DeVeaux, Richard D., Paul F. Velleman, and David E. Bock, *Stats Data and Models*, 3rd ed. (New York: Addison-Wesley, 2012).

Dunn, O. J., "Multiple Comparisons Using Rank Sums," *Technometrics*, 6 (1964), pp. 241–252.

Marascuilo, Leonard, and M. McSweeney, *Nonparametric and Distribution Free Methods for the Social Sciences* (Monterey, CA: Brooks/Cole, 1977).

Microsoft Excel 2010 (Redmond, WA: Microsoft Corp., 2010).

Noether, G. E., *Elements of Nonparametric Statistics* (New York: John Wiley & Sons, 1967).

Chapter 18

Evans, James R., and William M. Lindsay, *Managing for Quality and Performance Excellence* (Cincinnati, OH: South-Western College Publishing, 2007).

Foster, S. Thomas, *Managing Quality: Integrating the Supply Chain and Student CD PKG*, 3rd ed. (Upper Saddle River, NJ: Prentice Hall, 2007).

Microsoft Excel 2010 (Redmond, WA: Microsoft Corp., 2010).

Mitra, Amitava, *Fundamentals of Quality Control and Improvement*, 2d ed. (Upper Saddle River, NJ: Prentice Hall, 1998).

Glossary

Adjusted *R*-squared A measure of the percentage of explained variation in the dependent variable in a multiple regression model that takes into account the relationship between the sample size and the number of independent variables in the regression model.

Aggregate Price Index An index that is used to measure the rate of change from a base period for a group of two or more items.

All-Inclusive Classes A set of classes that contains all the possible data values.

Alternative Hypothesis The hypothesis that includes all population values not included in the null hypothesis. The alternative hypothesis will be selected only if there is strong enough sample evidence to support it. The alternative hypothesis is deemed to be true if the null hypothesis is rejected.

Arithmetic Average or Mean The sum of all values divided by the number of values.

Autocorrelation Correlation of the error terms (residuals) occurs when the residuals at points in time are related.

Balanced Design An experiment has a balanced design if the factor levels have equal sample sizes.

Bar Chart A graphical representation of a categorical data set in which a rectangle or bar is drawn over each category or class. The length or height of each bar represents the frequency or percentage of observations or some other measure associated with the category. The bars may be vertical or horizontal. The bars may all be the same color or they may be different colors depicting different categories. Additionally, multiple variables can be graphed on the same bar chart.

Base Period Index The time-series value to which all other values in the time series are compared. The index number for the base period is defined as 100.

Between-Sample Variation Dispersion among the factor sample means is called the *between-sample variation*.

Bias An effect that alters a statistical result by systematically distorting it; different from a random error, which may distort on any one occasion but balances out on the average.

Binomial Probability Distribution Characteristics A distribution that gives the probability of x successes in n trials in a process that meets the following conditions:

1. A trial has only two possible outcomes: a success or a failure.
2. There is a fixed number, n, of identical trials.
3. The trials of the experiment are independent of each other. This means that if one outcome is a success, this does not influence the chance of another outcome being a success.
4. The process must be consistent in generating successes and failures. That is, the probability, p, associated with a success remains constant from trial to trial.
5. If p represents the probability of a success, then $1 - p = q$ is the probability of a failure.

Box and Whisker Plot A graph that is composed of two parts: a box and the whiskers. The box has a width that ranges from the first quartile (Q_1) to the third quartile (Q_3). A vertical line through the box is placed at the median. Limits are located at a value that is 1.5 times the difference between Q_1 and Q_3 below Q_1 and above Q_3. The whiskers extend to the left to the lowest value within the limits and to the right to the highest value within the limits.

Business Intelligence The application of tools and technologies for gathering, storing, retrieving, and analyzing data that businesses collect and use.

Business Statistics A collection of procedures and techniques that are used to convert data into meaningful information in a business environment.

Census An enumeration of the entire set of measurements taken from the whole population.

Central Limit Theorem For simple random samples of n observations taken from a population with mean μ and standard deviation σ, regardless of the population's distribution, provided the sample size is sufficiently large, the distribution of the sample means, $\bar{x}$, will be approximately normal with a mean equal to the population mean $(\mu_{\bar{x}} = \mu_x)$ and a standard deviation equal to the population standard deviation divided by the square root of the sample size $\sigma_{\bar{x}} = \sigma/\sqrt{n}$. The larger the sample size, the better the approximation to the normal distribution.

Class Boundaries The upper and lower values of each class.

Class Width The distance between the lowest possible value and the highest possible value for a frequency class.

Classical Probability Assessment The method of determining probability based on the ratio of the number of ways an outcome or event of interest can occur to the number of ways *any* outcome or event can occur when the individual outcomes are equally likely.

Closed-End Questions Questions that require the respondent to select from a short list of defined choices.

Cluster Sampling A method by which the population is divided into groups, or clusters, that are each intended to be mini-populations. A simple random sample of m clusters is selected. The items chosen from a cluster can be selected using any probability sampling technique.

Coefficient of Determination The portion of the total variation in the dependent variable that is explained by its relationship with the independent variable. The coefficient of determination is also called *R*-squared and is denoted as R^2.

Coefficient of Partial Determination The measure of the marginal contribution of each independent variable, given that other independent variables are in the model.

Coefficient of Variation The ratio of the standard deviation to the mean expressed as a percentage. The coefficient of variation is used to measure variation relative to the mean.

Complement The complement of an event E is the collection of all possible outcomes not contained in event E.

Completely Randomized Design An experiment is completely randomized if it consists of the independent random selection of observations representing each level of one factor.

Composite Model The model that contains both the basic terms and the interaction terms.

Conditional Probability The probability that an event will occur given that some other event has already happened.

Confidence Interval An interval developed from sample values such that if all possible intervals of a given width were constructed, a percentage of these intervals, known as the confidence level, would include the true population parameter.

Confidence Level The percentage of all possible confidence intervals that will contain the true population parameter.

Consistent Estimator An unbiased estimator is said to be a consistent estimator if the difference between the estimator and the parameter tends to become smaller as the sample size becomes larger.

Contingency Table A table used to classify sample observations according to two or more identifiable characteristics. It is also called a *crosstabulation table*.

Continuous Data Data whose possible values are uncountable and that may assume any value in an interval.

Continuous Random Variables Random variables that can assume an uncountably infinite number of values.

Convenience Sampling A sampling technique that selects the items from the population based on accessibility and ease of selection.

Correlation Coefficient A quantitative measure of the strength of the linear relationship between two variables. The correlation ranges from -1.0 to $+1.0$. A correlation of ± 1.0 indicates a perfect linear relationship, whereas a correlation of 0 indicates no linear relationship.

Correlation Matrix A table showing the pairwise correlations between all variables (dependent and independent).

Critical Value The value corresponding to a significance level that determines those test statistics that lead to rejecting the null hypothesis and those that lead to a decision not to reject the null hypothesis.

Cross-Sectional Data A set of data values observed at a fixed point in time.

Cumulative Frequency Distribution A summary of a set of data that displays the number of observations with values less than or equal to the upper limit of each of its classes.

Cumulative Relative Frequency Distribution A summary of a set of data that displays the proportion of observations with values less than or equal to the upper limit of each of its classes.

Cyclical Component A wavelike pattern within the time series that repeats itself throughout the time series and has a recurrence period of more than one year.

Data Array Data that have been arranged in numerical order.

Data Mining The application of statistical techniques and algorithms to the analysis of large data sets.

Degrees of Freedom The number of independent data values available to estimate the population's standard deviation. If k parameters must be estimated before the population's standard deviation can be calculated from a sample of size n, the degrees of freedom are equal to $n - k$.

Demographic Questions Questions relating to the respondents' characteristics, backgrounds, and attributes.

Dependent Events Two events are dependent if the occurrence of one event impacts the probability of the other event occurring.

Dependent Variable A variable whose values are thought to be a function of, or dependent on, the values of another variable called the *independent variable*. On a scatter plot, the dependent variable is placed on the y axis and is often called the response variable.

Discrete Data Data that can take on a countable number of possible values.

Discrete Random Variable A random variable that can only assume a finite number of values or an infinite sequence of values such as $[0, 1, 2, \ldots]$.

Dummy Variable A variable that is assigned a value equal to either 0 or 1, depending on whether the observation possesses a given characteristic.

Empirical Rule If the data distribution is bell shaped, then the interval

$\mu \pm 1\sigma$ contains approximately 68% of the values

$\mu \pm 2\sigma$ contains approximately 95% of the values

$\mu \pm 3\sigma$ contains virtually all of the data values

Equal-Width Classes The distance between the lowest possible value and the highest possible value in each class is equal for all classes.

Event A collection of experimental outcomes.

Expected Value The mean of a probability distribution. The average value when the experiment that generates values for the random variable is repeated over the long run.

Experiment A process that produces a single outcome whose result cannot be predicted with certainty.

Experimental Design A plan for performing an experiment in which the variable of interest is defined. One or more factors are identified to be manipulated, changed, or observed so that the impact (or influence) on the variable of interest can be measured or observed.

Experiment-Wide Error Rate The proportion of experiments in which at least one of the set of confidence intervals constructed does not contain the true value of the population parameter being estimated.

Exponential Smoothing A time-series and forecasting technique that produces an exponentially weighted moving average in which each smoothing calculation or forecast is dependent on all previous observed values.

External Validity A characteristic of an experiment whose results can be generalized beyond the test environment so that the outcomes can be replicated when the experiment is repeated.

Factor A quantity under examination in an experiment as a possible cause of variation in the response variable.

Forecasting Horizon The number of future periods covered by a forecast. It is sometimes referred to as *forecast lead time*.

Forecasting Interval The frequency with which new forecasts are prepared.

Forecasting Period The unit of time for which forecasts are to be made.

Frequency Distribution A summary of a set of data that displays the number of observations in each of the distribution's distinct categories or classes.

Frequency Histogram A graph of a frequency distribution with the horizontal axis showing the classes, the vertical axis showing the frequency count, and (for equal class widths) the rectangles having a height equal to the frequency in each class.

Hypergeometric Distribution The hypergeometric distribution is formed by the ratio of the number of ways an event of interest can occur over the total number of ways any event can occur.

Independent Events Two events are independent if the occurrence of one event in no way influences the probability of the occurrence of the other event.

Independent Samples Samples selected from two or more populations in such a way that the occurrence of values in one sample has no influence on the probability of the occurrence of values in the other sample(s).

Independent Variable A variable whose values are thought to impact the values of the *dependent variable*. The independent variable, or explanatory variable, is often within the direct control of the decision maker. On a scatter plot, the independent variable, or explanatory variable, is graphed on the x axis.

Interaction The case in which one independent variable (such as x_2) affects the relationship between another independent variable (x_1) and a dependent variable (y).

Internal Validity A characteristic of an experiment in which data are collected in such a way as to eliminate the effects of variables within the experimental environment that are not of interest to the researcher.

Interquartile Range The interquartile range is a measure of variation that is determined by computing the difference between the third and first quartiles.

Least Squares Criterion The criterion for determining a regression line that minimizes the sum of squared prediction errors.

Left-Skewed Data A data distribution is left skewed if the mean for the data is smaller than the median.

Levels The categories, measurements, or strata of a factor of interest in the current experiment.

Line Chart A two-dimensional chart showing time on the horizontal axis and the variable of interest on the vertical axis.

Linear Trend A long-term increase or decrease in a time series in which the rate of change is relatively constant.

Margin of Error The amount that is added to and subtracted from the point estimate to determine the endpoints of the confidence interval. Also, a measure of how close we expect the point estimate to be to the population parameter with the specified level of confidence.

Mean A numerical measure of the center of a set of quantitative measures computed by dividing the sum of the values by the number of values in the data.

Median The median is a center value that divides a data array into two halves. We use $\tilde{\mu}$ to denote the population median and M_d to denote the sample median.

Mode The mode is the value in a data set that occurs most frequently.

Model A representation of an actual system using either a physical or a mathematical portrayal.

Model Diagnosis The process of determining how well a model fits past data and how well the model's assumptions appear to be satisfied.

Model Fitting The process of estimating the specified model's parameters to achieve an adequate fit of the historical data.

Model Specification The process of selecting the forecasting technique to be used in a particular situation.

Moving Average The successive averages of n consecutive values in a time series.

Multicollinearity A high correlation between two independent variables such that the two variables contribute redundant information to the model. When highly correlated independent variables are included in the regression model, they can adversely affect the regression results.

Multiple Coefficient of Determination The proportion of the total variation of the dependent variable in a multiple regression model that is explained by its relationship to the independent variables. It is, as is the case in the simple linear model, called R-squared and is denoted as R^2.

Mutually Exclusive Classes Classes that do not overlap so that a data value can be placed in only one class.

Mutually Exclusive Events Two events are mutually exclusive if the occurrence of one event precludes the occurrence of the other event.

Nonstatistical Sampling Techniques Those methods of selecting samples using convenience, judgment, or other nonchance processes.

Normal Distribution The normal distribution is a bell-shaped distribution with the following properties:

1. It is *unimodal*; that is, the normal distribution peaks at a single value.
2. It is *symmetrical*; this means that the two areas under the curve between the mean and any two points equidistant on either side of the mean are identical. One side of the distribution is the mirror image of the other side.
3. The mean, median, and mode are equal.
4. The normal approaches the horizontal axis on either side of the mean toward plus and minus infinity (∞). In more formal terms, the normal distribution is *asymptotic* to the x axis.

5. The amount of variation in the random variable determines the height and spread of the normal distribution.

Null Hypothesis The statement about the population parameter that will be assumed to be true during the conduct of the hypothesis test. The null hypothesis will be rejected only if the sample data provide substantial contradictory evidence.

Ogive The graphical representation of the cumulative relative frequency. A line is connected to points plotted above the upper limit of each class at a height corresponding to the cumulative relative frequency.

One-Tailed Test A hypothesis test in which the entire rejection region is located in one tail of the sampling distribution. In a one-tailed test, the entire alpha level is located in one tail of the distribution.

One-Way Analysis of Variance An analysis of variance design in which independent samples are obtained from two or more levels of a single factor for the purpose of testing whether the levels have equal means.

Open-End Questions Questions that allow respondents the freedom to respond with any value, words, or statements of their own choosing.

Paired Samples Samples that are selected in such a way that values in one sample are matched with the values in the second sample for the purpose of controlling for extraneous factors. Another term for paired samples is *dependent samples*.

Parameter A measure computed from the entire population. As long as the population does not change, the value of the parameter will not change.

Pareto Principle 80% of the problems come from 20% of the causes.

Percentiles The pth percentile in a data array is a value that divides the data set into two parts. The lower segment contains at least $p\%$ and the upper segment contains at least $(100 - p)5$ of the data. The 50th percentile is the median.

Pie Chart A graph in the shape of a circle. The circle is divided into "slices" corresponding to the categories or classes to be displayed. The size of each slice is proportional to the magnitude of the displayed variable associated with each category or class.

Pilot Sample A sample taken from the population of interest of a size smaller than the anticipated sample size that is used to provide an estimate for the population standard deviation.

Point Estimate A single statistic, determined from a sample, that is used to estimate the corresponding population parameter.

Population Mean The average for all values in the population computed by dividing the sum of all values by the population size.

Population Proportion The fraction of values in a population that have a specific attribute.

Population The set of all objects or individuals of interest or the measurements obtained from all objects or individuals of interest.

Power The probability that the hypothesis test will correctly reject the null hypothesis when the null hypothesis is false.

Power Curve A graph showing the probability that the hypothesis test will correctly reject a false null hypothesis for a range of possible "true" values for the population parameter.

Probability The chance that a particular event will occur. The probability value will be in the range 0 to 1. A value of 0 means the event will not occur. A probability of 1 means the event will occur. Anything between 0 and 1 reflects the uncertainty of the event occurring. The definition given is for a countable number of events.

p-Value The probability (assuming the null hypothesis is true) of obtaining a test statistic at least as extreme as the test statistic we calculated from the sample. The p-value is also known as the *observed significance level*.

Qualitative Data Data whose measurement scale is inherently categorical.

Quantitative Data Measurements whose values are inherently numerical.

Quartiles Quartiles in a data array are those values that divide the data set into four equal-sized groups. The median corresponds to the second quartile.

Random Component Changes in time-series data that are unpredictable and cannot be associated with a trend, seasonal, or cyclical component.

Random Variable A variable that takes on different numerical values based on chance.

Range The range is a measure of variation that is computed by finding the difference between the maximum and minimum values in a data set.

Regression Hyperplane The multiple regression equivalent of the simple regression line. The plane typically has a different slope for each independent variable.

Regression Slope Coefficient The average change in the dependent variable for a unit change in the independent variable. The slope coefficient may be positive or negative, depending on the relationship between the two variables.

Relative Frequency The proportion of total observations that are in a given category. Relative frequency is computed by dividing the frequency in a category by the total number of observations. The relative frequencies can be converted to percentages by multiplying by 100.

Relative Frequency Assessment The method that defines probability as the number of times an event occurs divided by the total number of times an experiment is performed in a large number of trials.

Research Hypothesis The hypothesis the decision maker attempts to demonstrate to be true. Because this is the hypothesis deemed to be the most important to the decision maker, it will be declared true only if the sample data strongly indicate that it is true.

Residual The difference between the actual value of the dependent variable and the value predicted by the regression model.

Right-Skewed Data A data distribution is right skewed if the mean for the data is larger than the median.

Sample A subset of the population.

Sample Mean The average for all values in the sample computed by dividing the sum of all sample values by the sample size.

Sample Proportion The fraction of items in a sample that have the attribute of interest.

Sample Space The collection of all outcomes that can result from a selection, decision, or experiment.

Sampling Distribution The distribution of all possible values of a statistic for a given sample size that has been randomly selected from a population.

Sampling Error The difference between a measure computed from a sample (a statistic) and the corresponding measure computed from the population (a parameter).

Scatter Diagram, or Scatter Plot A two-dimensional graph of plotted points in which the vertical axis represents values of one quantitative variable and the horizontal axis represents values of the other quantitative variable. Each plotted point has coordinates whose values are obtained from the respective variables.

Scatter Plot A two-dimensional plot showing the values for the joint occurrence of two quantitative variables. The scatter plot may be used to graphically represent the relationship between two variables. It is also known as a *scatter diagram*.

Seasonal Component A wavelike pattern that is repeated throughout a time series and has a recurrence period of at most one year.

Seasonal Index A number used to quantify the effect of seasonality in time-series data.

Seasonally Unadjusted Forecast A forecast made for seasonal data that does not include an adjustment for the seasonal component in the time series.

Significance Level The maximum allowable probability of committing a Type I statistical error. The probability is denoted by the symbol α.

Simple Linear Regression The method of regression analysis in which a single independent variable is used to predict the dependent variable.

Simple Random Sample A sample selected in such a manner that each possible sample of a given size has an equal chance of being selected.

Simple Random Sampling A method of selecting items from a population such that every possible sample of a specified size has an equal chance of being selected.

Skewed Data Data sets that are not symmetric. For skewed data, the mean will be larger or smaller than the median.

Standard Deviation The standard deviation is the positive square root of the variance.

Standard Error A value that measures the spread of the sample means around the population mean. The standard error is reduced when the sample size is increased.

Standard Normal Distribution A normal distribution that has a mean = 0.0 and a standard deviation = 1.0. The horizontal axis is scaled in z-values that measure the number of standard deviations a point is from the mean. Values above the mean have positive z-values. Values below the mean have negative z-values.

Standardized Data Values The number of standard deviations a value is from the mean. Standardized data values are sometimes referred to as z scores.

Statistic A measure computed from a sample that has been selected from a population. The value of the statistic will depend on which sample is selected.

Statistical Inference Procedures Procedures that allow a decision maker to reach a conclusion about a set of data based on a subset of that data.

Statistical Sampling Techniques Those sampling methods that use selection techniques based on chance selection.

Stratified Random Sampling A statistical sampling method in which the population is divided into subgroups called *strata* so that each population item belongs to only one stratum. The objective is to form strata such that the population values of interest within each stratum are as much alike as possible. Sample items are selected from each stratum using the simple random sampling method.

Structured Interview Interviews in which the questions are scripted.

Student's *t*-Distributions A family of distributions that is bell shaped and symmetrical like the standard normal distribution but with greater area in the tails. Each distribution in the *t*-family is defined by its degrees of freedom. As the degrees of freedom increase, the *t*-distribution approaches the normal distribution.

Subjective Probability Assessment The method that defines probability of an event as reflecting a decision maker's state of mind regarding the chances that the particular event will occur.

Symmetric Data Data sets whose values are evenly spread around the center. For symmetric data, the mean and median are equal.

Systematic Random Sampling A statistical sampling technique that involves selecting every kth item in the population after a randomly selected starting point between 1 and k. The value of k is determined as the ratio of the population size over the desired sample size.

Tchebysheff's Theorem Regardless of how data are distributed, *at least* $(1 - 1/k^2)$ of the values will fall within k standard deviations of the mean. For example:

At least $\left(1 - \dfrac{1}{1^2}\right) = 0 = 0\%$ of the values will fall within $k = 1$ standard deviation of the mean.

At least $\left(1 - \dfrac{1}{2^2}\right) = \dfrac{3}{4} = 75\%$ of the values will lie within $k = 2$ standard deviations of the mean.

At least $\left(1 - \dfrac{1}{3^2}\right) = \dfrac{8}{9} = 89\%$ of the values will lie within $k = 3$ standard deviations of the mean.

Test Statistic A function of the sampled observations that provides a basis for testing a statistical hypothesis.

Time-Series Data A set of consecutive data values observed at successive points in time.

Total Quality Management A journey to excellence in which everyone in the organization is focused on continuous process improvement directed toward increased customer satisfaction.

Total Variation The aggregate dispersion of the individual data values across the various factor levels is called the *total variation* in the data.

Two-Tailed Test A hypothesis test in which the entire rejection region is split into the two tails of the sampling distribution. In a two-tailed test, the alpha level is split evenly between the two tails.

Type I Error *Rejecting* the null hypothesis when it is, in fact, true.

Type II Error *Failing to reject* the null hypothesis when it is, in fact, false.

Unbiased Estimator A characteristic of certain statistics in which the average of all possible values of the sample statistic equals a parameter, no matter the value of the parameter.

Unstructured Interview Interviews that begin with one or more broadly stated questions, with further questions being based on the responses.

Variance The population variance is the average of the squared distances of the data values from the mean.

Variance Inflation Factor A measure of how much the variance of an estimated regression coefficient increases if the independent variables are correlated. A *VIF* equal to 1.0 for a given independent variable indicates that this independent variable is not correlated with the remaining independent variables in the model. The greater the multicollinearity, the larger the *VIF*.

Variation A set of data exhibits variation if all the data are not the same value.

Weighted Mean The mean value of data values that have been weighted according to their relative importance.

Within-Sample Variation The dispersion that exists among the data values within a particular factor level is called the *within-sample variation*.

Index

A

Addition rule
  Individual outcomes, 153–156
  Mutually exclusive events, 160, 167
  Two events, 157–160
Adjusted R-square
  Equation, 622, 676
Aggregate price index
  Defined, 689
  Unweighted, 689–690, 735
All-inclusive classes, 38
Alpha, controlling, 367
Alternative hypothesis
  Defined, 337
  Formulating, 339–370
Analysis of variance
  Assumptions, 463, 465–467, 483, 497
  Between-sample variation, 464
  Experiment-wide error rate, 474
  Fisher's Least Significant Difference test,
    490–491, 506
  Fixed effects, 478–479
  Hartley's *F-max* test, 466n, 476n
  Kruskal-Wallis one-way, 761–765
  One-way ANOVA, 463–479
  One-way ANOVA table, 469
  Random effects, 478–479
  Randomized block ANOVA, 483–490
  Total variation, 464
  Tukey-Kramer, 473–478, 506
  Two-factor ANOVA, 494–501
  Within-sample variation, 464
Arithmetic mean, 4, 92
Autocorrelation
  Defined, 702
  Durbin-Watson statistic, 704–706, 735
Average, 4. *See also* Mean
  Equation, 4
  Moving average, 713
  Ratio-to-moving-average, 735
  Sample equation, 265
Average subgroup range, 779, 797

B

Backward elimination stepwise, 655–658
Balanced design, 463, 466
  Defined, 463
Bar Chart, 3
  Cluster, 58
  Column, 53
  Defined, 53
  Excel examples, 59
  Horizontal, 54–55
  Minitab instructions, 59
  Pie Chart versus, 58
  Summary steps, 557

Base period index
  Defined, 687
  Simple index number, 687–688, 735
Bayes' Theorem, 168–171
  Equation, 168
Best subsets regression, 659–661
Beta
  Calculating, 365–371, 367–371
  Controlling, 367–371
  Power, 372
  Proportion, 370–371
  Summary steps, 368
  Two-tailed test, 369–370
Between-sample variation
  Defined, 464
Bias
  Interviewer, 12
  Nonresponse, 12
  Observer, 12–13
  Selection, 12
Binomial distribution
  Characteristics, 190
  Defined, 190
  Excel example, 198
  Formula, 194–195
  Mean, 197–198
  Minitab instructions, 198
  Shapes, 199–200
  Standard deviation, 198–199
  Table, 195–196
Binomial formula, 194–195
Bivariate normal distribution, 565
Box and whisker plots
  ANOVA assumptions, 467
  Defined, 95
  Summary steps, 96
Brainstorming, 807
Business intelligence, 1
Business statistics
  Defined, 2

C

c-charts, 789–792, 798
  Control limits, 798
  Excel example, 791
  Minitab instructions, 791
  Standard deviation, 798
Census
  Defined, 15
Centered moving average, 713
Central limit theorem, 272–276
  Examples, 274–275
  Theorem 4, 274
Central tendency, applying measures, 90–92
Charts, 3
  Bar chart, 53–56, 58
  Box and whisker, 95–97
  c, 789–792

Charts (*continued*)
  Histogram, 41–46
  Line, 63–66
  p, 786–789
  Pie, 56–58
  R, 778–786
  Scatter diagram, 66–69, 561, 618
  Scatter plot, 560
  Stem and leaf diagrams, 59–60
  $\bar{x}$, 778–786
Chi-square
  Assumptions, 437
  Confidence interval, 454–455
  Contingency analysis, 544–545
  Contingency test statistic, 546
  Degrees of freedom, 437, 533, 537, 564
  Goodness-of-fit, 531–541
  Goodness-of-fit-test statistic, 533, 555
  Sample size, 533
  Single variance, 436–438, 471
  Summary steps, 439
  Test for single population variance,
    436–438, 458
  Test limitations, 569
Class boundaries, 39
Classes
  All-inclusive, 38
  Boundaries, 39
  Equal-width, 38
  Mutually exclusive, 38
Classical probability assessment
  Defined, 146
  Equation, 146
Class width
  Equation, 39
Closed-end questions, 8
Cluster sampling, 18–19
  Primary clusters, 19
Coefficient of determination
  Adjusted R-square, 622, 676
  Defined, 582
  Equation, 582, 605
  Hypothesis test, 583, 643–644
  Multiple regression, 620
  Regression analysis, 580–583
  Single independent variable case, 582
  Test statistic, 583
Coefficient of partial determination, 655
Coefficient of variation
  Defined, 113
  Population equation, 114
  Sample equation, 114
Combinations
  Counting rule equation, 193
Complement
  Defined, 156
  Rule, 156
Completely randomized design
  Defined, 463
Composite polynomial model
  Defined, 645
  Excel example, 645–646
  Minitab instructions, 647

Conditional probability
  Bayes' theorem, 168–171
  Defined, 161
  Independent events, 163–164
  Rule for any two events, 161
  Tree diagrams, 163–164
  Two events, 160–162
Confidence interval
  Average *y,* given *x,* 595–596
  Critical value, 299, 330
  Defined, 296
  Difference between means, 388–389
  Estimate, 307, 310, 390, 428, 458
  Estimation for regression coefficients, 626
  Excel example, 296–297, 307–308
  Flow diagram, 330
  General format, 299, 330, 387, 428
  Impact of sample size, 304
  Interpreting, 301
  Larger sample sizes, 310
  Margin of error, 301–302
  Minitab instructions, 297, 308
  Paired samples, 413–414
  Population mean, 297–304
  Population mean paired difference, 413
  Population mean unknown, 304
  Population proportion, 321–323
  Population variance, 441–442
  Regression slope, 594–595, 605, 627–628, 676
  Sample size requirements, 315–316
  Standard error of mean, 297–298
  Summary steps, 300, 309
  t-distribution, 304–310, 390–394
  two proportions, 420
  Unequal variances, 393–394
  Variance, 441
Consistent estimator
  Defined, 270
Consumer price index, 693–694
Contingency analysis, 544–550
  Chi-square limitations, 550
  Chi-square test statistic, 546
  Contingency table, 548–550
  Excel example, 548–550
  Expected cell frequencies, 549, 555
  Marginal frequencies, 544
  Minitab, 550
  $r \times c$ contingency analysis, 548–550
  2×2 contingency analysis, 544–548
Contingency table
  Defined, 544
Continuous data, 37
Continuous probability distributions
  Exponential distribution, 242–245
  Normal distribution, 225–236
  Uniform distribution, 240–241
Continuous random variables
  Defined, 183
Continuous variables
  Frequency distribution, 40–41
Convenience sampling, 15
Correlation coefficient
  Assumptions, 565

Cause-and-effect, 566
   Defined, 560, 617
   Equation, 560–561, 605, 617, 676
   Excel example, 561–563, 617
   Hypothesis test, 564
   Minitab instructions, 562, 617
   Test statistic, 564, 605
Correlation matrix, 617
Counting rule
   Combinations, 192–193
Critical value
   Calculating, 342–344
   Commonly used values, 299, 340
   Confidence interval estimate, 300
   Defined, 342
   Hypothesis testing, 341–342
Crosby, Philip B., 805–806
Cumulative frequency distribution
   Defined, 39
   Relative frequency, 39
Cyclical component
   Defined, 687

D

Data
   Categorizing, 23–24
   Classification, 28
   Cross-sectional, 21
   Discrete, 33
   Hierarchy, 21
   Interval, 22
   Issues with computing numerical measures, 97–98
   Measurement levels, 21–24
   Nominal, 21
   Ordinal, 22
   Qualitative, 20
   Quantitative, 20
   Ratio, 22
   Skewed, 88–89
   Symmetric, 88–89
   Time-series, 21
Data array, 37, 87
Data collection methods, 7, 28
   Array, 37
   Bar codes, 11–12
   Direct observation, 7, 11
   Experiments, 7, 8
   Issues, 12–13
   Personal interview, 11
   Telephone surveys, 7, 8–9
   Written questionnaires, 7, 9–11
Data frequency distribution. *See* Grouped data frequency
   distribution
Data mining, 1, 25–26
Decision rule
   Hypothesis testing, 344–347
Deflating time-series data, 694–695, 735
   Formula, 695, 735
Degrees of freedom
   Chi-square, 437
   One sample, 305
   Student's *t*-distribution, 304–305

   Unequal means, 393
   Unequal variances, 407, 429
Deming, W. Edwards
   Cycle, 806
   Fourteen points, 805
   Variation, 810
Demographic questions, 8
Dependent events
   Defined, 145
Dependent variable, 66, 613
Descriptive statistical techniques
   Data-level issues, 97–98
Descriptive statistics, 2–3, 69–70
Deseasonalization
   Equation, 717, 735
   Excel examples, 717
Direct Observation, 7, 11
Discrete data, 33
Discrete probability distributions, 182–187
   Binomial distribution, 190–198
   Hypergeometric distribution, 209–214
   Poisson distribution, 204–209
Discrete random variable
   Defined, 183
   Displaying graphically, 183–184
   Expected value equation, 184–187
   Mean, 184–186
   Standard deviation, 185–186
Dummy variables, 631–636
   Defined, 631
   Excel example, 633–636
   Seasonality, 718–720
Durbin-Watson statistic
   Equation, 703, 735
   Test for autocorrelation, 704–706

E

Empirical rule
   Defined, 115
Empty classes, 38
Equal-width classes, 38
Error. *See also* Standard error
   Experimental-wide error rate, 474
   Forecast, 701, 735
   Margin of error, 301–302, 330
   Mean absolute percent error, 758, 763
   Measurement, 13
   Standard error of mean, 297–298
   Sum of squares, 506, 580
   Type I, 340
   Type II, 340, 366–367
Estimate
   Confidence interval, 296, 388
   Difference between means, 387–394
   Difference between two population proportions,
      419–420
   Paired difference, 412–414
   Point, 296
   Testing flow diagram, 428
Estimation, 5, 296
   Sample size for population, 323–325
   Single population variance, 435–442

Event
  Defined, 143
  Dependent, 145
  Independent, 145
  Mutually exclusive, 144–145
  Sample space and, 141
Expected cell frequencies
  Equation, 549, 555
Expected value
  Binomial distribution, 196–198
  Defined, 184
  Discrete probability distribution, 185
  Equation, 185
Experimental design, 7
Experimental-wide error rate
  Defined, 474
Experiments, 7, 141
Exponential probability distribution
  Density function, 243
  Excel example, 244–245
  Minitab instructions, 244
  Probability, 242–243
Exponential smoothing
  Defined, 724
  Double smoothing, 728–731, 735
  Equation, 724
  Excel examples, 724–727
  Minitab instructions, 726, 727
  Single smoothing, 724–728
  Smoothing constant, 724
External validity, 13

F

Factor
  Defined, 463
Finite population correction factor, 271
Fishbone diagram, 807
Fisher's Least Significant Difference test,
    490–491, 506
Fixed effects analysis of variance test, 478–479
Flowcharts, 807
Forecast bias
  Equation, 707, 735
Forecasting
  Autocorrelation, 702–706
  Bias, 707, 735
  Cyclical component, 687
  Dummy variables, 718–720
  Durbin-Watson statistic, 703–706, 735
  Error, 701, 735
  Excel example, 708–711
  Exponential smoothing, 724–731
  Horizon, 684
  Interval, 684
  Linear trend, 685, 698, 735
  Mean absolute deviation, 701, 735
  Mean absolute percent error, 758, 763
  Mean squared error, 701, 735
  Minitab instructions, 708–710
  Model diagnosis, 684
  Model fitting, 684

  Model specification, 684
  Nonlinear trend, 708–712
  Period, 684
  Random component, 687
  Residual, 701–702
  Seasonal adjustment, 712–720
  Seasonal component, 685–687
  Seasonally unadjusted, 717–718
  Trend-base technique, 697–707
  True forecasts, 706–707
Forward selection stepwise, 655–658
Forward stepwise regression, 658
Frequency distribution, 32–41
  Classes, 38–39
  Continuous variables, 40
  Cumulative, 39
  Data array, 37
  Defined, 33
  Discrete data, 33
  Grouped data, 37–41
  Joint, 46–49
  Qualitative, 35–36
  Quantitative, 34
  Relative, 33–35
  Tables, 32–34
Frequency histogram
  Defined, 41
  Issues with Excel, 43
  Relative frequency, 45–46
  Summary steps, 44
F-test
  Assumptions, 446
  Coefficient of determination, 583
  Excel example, 451–452
  Minitab, 452
  Multiple regression, 621, 676
  Test statistic, 446
  Two variances, 445–453, 458

G

Goodness-of-fit tests, 530–541
  Chi-square test, 531–535
  Chi-square test statistic, 533, 555
  Degrees of freedom, 537
  Excel example, 535–537
  Minitab, 537
  Sample size, 533
Graphs, 3–4
Grouped data frequency distribution
  All-inclusive classes, 38
  Class boundaries, 39
  Classes, 38–39
  Class width, 38
  Continuous data, 37
  Cumulative frequency, 39
  Data array, 37
  Empty classes, 38
  Equal-width classes, 38
  Excel example, 37
  Minitab instructions, 37
  Mutually exclusive classes, 38

Number of classes, 38–39
Steps, 38–40

H

Hartley's F-test statistic, 466n, 476n
Histogram, 3, 41–46
  Empirical rule, 115–116
  Examples, 41–43
  Excel example, 43
  Issues with Excel, 43
  Minitab instructions, 43
  Quality, 807
  Relative frequency, 45–46
  Summary steps, 44
  Types of information, 41
Hypergeometric distribution, 209–214
  Multiple possible outcomes, 213–214
  Two possible outcomes, 211
Hypothesis
  Alternative, 337
  ANOVA, 464
  Null, 337
  Research, 338
  Summary steps, 339
Hypothesis testing, 5, 336–372
  Alternative hypothesis, 337
  Calculating beta, 365–371
  Chi-square test, 436–438
  Controlling alpha and beta, 367–371
  Correlation coefficient, 564, 617–618
  Critical value, 341–342
  Decision rule, 344–345, 344–347
  Difference between two population proportions, 420–424
  Excel example, 353–355, 403–405, 420–423
  Flow diagram, 428
  F-test, 445–453
  Means, 337–355
  Median, 743–769
  Minitab, 354, 404–405, 423
  Multiple regression analysis, 621–622
  Nonparametric tests, 743–769
  Null hypothesis, 337
  One-tailed test, 345–349
  Paired samples, 411–416
  Population mean, 351–355, 398–407
  Population proportion, 358–362
  Power, 371–372
  Power curve, 372
  Procedures, deciding among, 377
  p-value, 347–351, 400
  Significance level, 341–342
  Simple regression coefficient, 587
  Single population variance, 435–442
  Summary steps, 345, 352, 360, 399, 439
  t-test statistic, 351–352, 401, 415
  Two means, 398–407
  Two-tailed test, 349–351
  Two variances, 445–453
  Type I error, 340
  Type II error, 340, 365–372

Types of tests, 348–351
z-test statistic, 344–345

I

Imai, Masaaki, 806
Independent events
  Conditional probability rule, 163
  Defined, 145
Independent samples, 398
  Defined, 387, 446
  Hypothesis testing, 398–407
Independent variable, 66, 631
Index numbers, 687–695, 763
  Aggregate price index, 689–693
  Base period index, 687
  Consumer price, 693–694
  Deflating time-series data, 694–695, 735
  Laspeyres, 692–693, 735
  Paasche, 691–692, 735
  Producer price, 694
  Simple index number, 688–689, 735
  Stock market, 694
  Unweighted aggregate price, 689–690, 735
Inferences, 2
Interaction
  Cautions, 501
  Defined, 645
  Explained, 498–501
  Partial F-test, 647–651, 676
  Polynomial regression model, 643–647
Internal validity, 13
Interquartile Range
  Defined, 103
  Equation, 103
Interval data, 22
Interviewer bias, 12
Interviews
  Structured, 11
  Unstructured, 11
Ishikawa, Kauro, 806, 807

J

Joint frequency distribution, 46–49
  Excel example, 47–49
  Minitab instructions, 48
Judgment sampling, 15
Juran, Joseph, 805
  Ten steps, 806

K

kaizen, 806
Kruskal-Wallis one-way ANOVA
  Assumptions, 761
  Correction, 770
  Correction for ties, 765, 770
  Excel example, 763–765
  H-statistic, 469, 763, 765
  H-statistic corrected for tied rankings, 770
  Hypotheses, 790
  Limitations, 765
  Minitab instructions, 764
  Steps, 762–765

L

Laspeyres index, 692–693, 735
  Equation, 692, 735
Least squares criterion
  Defined, 572
  Equations, 573, 699, 735
  Regression properties, 576–579
Left-skewed data, 88
Levels
  Defined, 463
Linear trend
  Defined, 685
  Model, 697–700, 735
Line charts, 63–66
  Excel examples, 64–65
  Minitab instructions, 65
  Summary steps, 65
Location measures
  Percentiles, 93–95
  Quartiles, 95
  Weighted Mean, 92–93

M

MAD, 701–702
Mann-Whitney U-test, 749–754
  Assumptions, 749
  Critical value, 751–752
  Equations, 769
  Hypotheses, 749–750
  Large sample test, 752–754
  Minitab instructions, 780
  Steps, 749–752
  Test statistic, 752, 769
  U-statistics, 750, 752, 769
Margin of error
  Defined, 301, 323
  Equation, 301–302, 330
  Proportions, 330
Mean
  Advantages and disadvantages, 98
  Arithmetic, 4
  Binomial distribution, 196–198
  c-charts, 790, 798
  Defined, 82
  Discrete distributions, 184–186
  Discrete random variable, 184–187
  Excel example, 85, 90–91
  Expected value, 184–185
  Extreme values, 86–87
  Hypothesis test, 337–355
  Minitab instructions, 85
  Poisson distribution, 208, 223
  Population, determining required sample size, 315–316
  Population, estimating difference, 387–394
  Population equation, 82–84, 256
  Sample equation, 85–86, 256, 257
  Sampling distribution of a, 264–265
  Sampling distribution of a proportion, 282
  Summary steps, 84
  Uniform distribution, 242
  U-statistics, 752, 769
  Weighted, 92–93
  Wilcoxon, 756

Mean absolute deviation
  Equation, 701, 735
Mean absolute percent error
  Equation, 735, 758
Mean squared error
  Equation, 701, 735
Mean subgroup proportion, 786, 797
Measurement error, 13
Median
  Advantages and disadvantages, 98
  Data array, 87
  Defined, 87
  Excel example, 92, 95–96
  Hypothesis test, 743–769
  Index point, 87
  Issues with Excel, 91–92
Mode
  Advantages and disadvantages, 98
  Defined, 89
  Determining, 89–90
Model
  Building, 615–628, 684
  Correcting, 672
  Diagnosis, 620, 684, 709, 710–712
  Model fitting, 710
  Residuals, 664–671
  Significance, 621–622
  Specification, 615–616, 664, 684, 709–710
Model building concepts, 615–628
  Summary steps, 616
Moving average
  Centered, 713
  Defined, 713
Multicollearity
  Defined, 625
  Face validity, 625
  Variance inflation factor, 626, 676
Multiple coefficient of determination, 620, 676
  Equation, 620
Multiple regression analysis, 612–672
  Aptness of the model, 664–672
  Assumptions, 613, 664
  Best subsets method, 659–661
  Coefficient of determination, 620, 676
  Correlation coefficient, 617–618
  Dependent variable, 614
  Diagnosis, 616, 620
  Dummy variables, 631–636
  Estimated model, 613–614, 676
  Excel example, 633–636
  Hyperplane, 614
  Independent variable, 614
  Interaction effects, 643–647
  Interval estimate for slope, 627–628
  Minitab instructions, 619
  Model building, 615–628
  Multicollearity, 625–626
  Nonlinear relationships, 639–643
  Partial F-test, 647–651, 676
  Polynomial, 639–640, 676
  Population model, 613, 676
  Scatter plots, 618

Significance test, 621–622
Standard error of the estimate, 624, 676
Stepwise regression, 654–658
Summary steps, 616
Multiplication probability rule, 165
Independent events, 166–168
Tree diagram, 166
Two events, 165–166
Multiplicative time-series model
Equation, 713, 735
Seasonal indexes, 712–720
Summary steps, 718
Mutually exclusive classes, 38
Mutually exclusive events
Addition rule, 160
Defined, 144

N

Nominal data, 21
Nonlinear trend, 685–686
Nonlinear trend forecasting, 708–712
Nonparametric statistics, 743–769
Kruskal-Wallis one-way ANOVA, 761–765
Mann-Whitney U test, 749–754, 769
Wilcoxon matched pairs test, 754–757, 769
Wilcoxon signed rank test, 743–747, 769
Nonresponse bias, 12
Nonstatistical sampling, 15
Convenience sampling, 15
Judgment sampling, 15
Ratio sampling, 15
Normal distribution, 225–236
Approximate areas under normal curve, 236
Defined, 225
Empirical rule, 236
Excel example, 233–234
Function, 226
Minitab instructions, 233, 244
Standard normal, 226–236
Standard normal table, 228–230
Steps, 228
Summary steps, 237
Null hypothesis
Claim, 338–339
Defined, 337
Formulating, 339–370
Research hypothesis, 338
Status quo, 337–338
Two-tailed tests, 349–351
Numerical statistical measures
Summary, 129

O

Observer bias, 12–13
Ogive, 45–46
One-tailed hypothesis test
Defined, 348
Population variance, 439
One-way ANOVA
Assumptions, 463, 465–467
Balanced design, 463
Between-sample variation, 464

Completely randomized design, 463
Defined, 463
Excel example, 472–473, 476–477
Experimental-wide error rate, 474
Factor, 463
Fixed effects, 478–479
Hartley's F-test statistic, 466n, 476n
Levels, 463
Logic, 476
Minitab, 473, 477
Partitioning sums of squares, 464–465
Random effects, 478–479
Sum of squares between, 468, 506
Sum of squares within, 468, 506
Table, 467–470
Total sum of squares, 467, 506
Total variation, 464
Tukey-Kramer, 473–478, 506
Within-sample variation, 464
Open-end questions, 9
Ordinal data, 22

P

Paasche index
Equation, 691–692, 735
Paired difference, 412
Paired sample
Confidence interval estimation, 413–414
Defined, 411
Equation, 415
Hypothesis testing, 414–416
Point estimate, 412
Population mean, 412
Standard deviation, 412
t-test statistic, 415
Why use, 411–413
Parameters, 15
Defined, 82, 257
Unbiased estimator, 267
Pareto charts, 69–70
Pareto principle, 805
Partial F-test, 647–651, 676
Statistic formula, 648, 676
p-charts, 786–789
Control limits, 788, 798
Pearson product moment correlation, 561
Percentiles
Defined, 93
Location index, 94
Summary steps, 94
Personal interviews, 7, 11
Physical measurement, 12
Pie chart, 56–58
bar chart versus, 58
Defined, 56
Summary steps, 56
Pilot sample
Defined, 316
Proportions, 340
Point estimate
Defined, 296
Paired difference, 412

Poisson distribution, 204–209
  Assumptions, 205
  Equation, 205
  Excel example, 209
  Mean, 208
  Minitab instructions, 209
  Standard deviation, 208
  Summary steps, 207
  Table, 206–208
Polynomial regression model
  Composite model, 645
  Curvilinear relationships, 641–643
  Equation, 640, 676
  Excel example, 641–642, 645–646
  Interaction, 643–647
  Minitab instructions, 642, 643, 647
  Second order model, 640, 643–646
  Third order model, 641
Population
  Defined, 14–15
  Mean, 82–85, 256, 314–318, 399–407
  Proportion, 280, 321–325
  Testing a claim about, 338–340, 345–346
  Variance and standard deviation, 104–107
Population model, multiple regression analysis,
  613, 676
Power of the test
  Curve, 372
  Defined, 371
  Equation, 371, 377
Prediction interval for y given x, 596–598, 605
Probability
  Addition rule, 154–160
  Classical assessment, 146–147
  Complement rule, 156
  Conditional, 160–165
  Defined, 141
  Defining event of interest, 143–144
  Experiment, 141
  Independent and dependent events, 145
  Methods of assigning, 145–150
  Multiplication rule, 165–168
  Mutually exclusive events, 144–145
  Relative frequency assessment, 147–149
  Rules, 153–171
  Rules summary and equations, 176–177
  Sample space, 141–143
  Subjective assessment, 149–150
Probability sampling, 16
Producer price index, 694, 695
Proportions
  Confidence interval, 321–323
  Estimation, 321–325
  Hypothesis tests, 358–362, 370–371
  Pooled estimator, 421, 429
  Population, 280, 321–325
  Sample proportion, 321
  Sampling distribution, 279–285
  Sampling error, 282
  Standard error, 321
  z-test statistic equation, 377
p-value, 347–348

Q
Qualitative Data
  Defined, 20
  Dummy variables, 631–636
  Frequency distribution, 35–36
Qualitative forecasting, 684
Quality
  Basic tools, 806–807
  Brainstorming, 807
  Control charts, 807
  Deming, 805
  Fishbone diagram, 807
  Flowcharts, 807
  Juran, 805, 806
  Scatter plots, 807
  SPC, 807, 808–827
  Total quality management, 805
  Trend charts, 807
Quantitative Data
  Defined, 20
  Frequency distribution, 34
Quantitative forecasting, 684
Quartiles
  Defined, 95
  Issues with Excel, 95
Questions
  Closed-end, 8
  Demographic, 8
  Leading, 10
  Open-end, 9
  Poorly worded, 10–11

R
Random component
  Defined, 687
Random effects, 478–479
Randomized complete block ANOVA, 483–491
  Assumptions, 483
  Excel example, 486
  Fisher's Least Significant Difference test, 490–491, 506
  Minitab, 486
  Partitioning sums of squares, 484, 506
  Sum of squares blocking, 484, 506
  Sum of squares within, 485, 506
  Table, 485
  Type II error, 487
Random number table, 16–17
Random sample, 16
  Excel example, 17
Random variable
  Continuous, 183
  Defined, 183
  Discrete, 183
Range
  Defined, 103
  Equation, 103
  Interquartile, 103–104
Ratio data, 22–23
Ratio sampling, 15
Ratio-to-moving-average method, 714–716
  Equation, 714, 735

Regression analysis
Aptness, 664–671
Assumptions, 570
Coefficient of determination, 582, 605, 620, 676
Confidence interval estimate, 594–595, 605, 627–628, 676
Descriptive purposes, 592–595
Dummy variables, 631–636, 671
Equations, 605
Excel examples, 578, 579, 585–588, 593, 633–636
Exponential relationship, 661
Hyperplane, 614–615
Least squares criterion, 572
Least squares equations, 573, 605
Least squares regression properties, 576–579
Minitab instructions, 576, 578, 581, 593, 633–636
Multicollinearity, 625–626
Multiple regression, 613–672
Nonlinear relationships, 639–643
Partial F-test, 647–651, 676
Polynomial, 639–640
Prediction, 595–598, 605
Problems using, 598–599
Residual, 572, 576, 605, 701
R-squared, 582, 605, 620
Sample model, 572
Significance tests, 580–588
Simple linear model, 570, 605
Slope coefficients, 583–584
Standard error, 624, 676
Stepwise, 655–658
Summary steps, 587
Sum of squares error, 573
Sum of squares regression, 602
Test statistic for the slope, 587
Total sum of squares, 580, 605
Regression slope coefficient
Defined, 571
Excel example, 585
Intercept, 571
Interval estimate, 594–595, 605, 627–628
Minitab instructions, 585
Significance, 586–587, 622–623, 676
Slope, 571
Standard error, 584
Relative frequency, 33–35
Distributions, 33–41
Equation, 34
Histogram, 45–46
Relative frequency assessment
Defined, 147
Equation, 147
Issues, 148–149
Research hypothesis
Defined, 338
Residual
Analysis, 664–671
Assumptions, 664
Checking for linearity, 664–665
Corrective actions, 672
Defined, 572, 664
Equal variances, 667

Equation, 664, 676
Excel examples, 576–577
Forecasting error, 701
Independence, 667–668
Minitab instructions, 577, 669–671
Normality, 668–669, 671
Plots, 665–671
Standardized residual, 668–671, 676
Sum, 576
Sum of squared residuals, 576, 605
Review Sections
Chapters 1–3, 133–139
Chapters 8–12, 514–527
Right-skewed data, 88

S
Sample
Defined, 14
Mean, 85–86, 256, 257
Proportion, 280, 321
Size, 314–318
Sample size requirements
Equation, 315
Estimating population mean, 314–318
Estimating population proportion, 323–325
Estimating sample mean, 314–318
Estimating sample proportion, 330
Interval estimate, 304
Pilot sample, 316–318
Sample space, 141–142
Tree diagrams, 142–143
Sample variance, 107
Equation, 448, 458
Sampling distribution of a proportion, 279–285
Mean, 282
Standard error, 282
Summary steps, 284
Theorem 5, 282
Sampling distribution of the mean, 264–276
Central limit theorem, 272–276
Defined, 264
Excel example, 265–266
Minitab instructions, 266
Normal populations, 267–271
Proportions, 282–285
Steps, 276
Theorem 1, 267
Theorem 2, 267
Theorem 3, 268
Sampling error
Computing, 258–259
Defined, 256, 296
Role of sample size, 259–261
Single-proportion, 281
Sampling techniques, 15–19, 28
Cluster sampling, 18–19
Nonstatistical, 15
Statistical, 16
Stratified random sampling, 17–18
Systematic random sampling, 18

Scatter diagram/plot
Defined, 66, 560
Dependent variable, 66, 560
Examples, 560, 561, 618
Excel example, 67, 561–563
Independent variables, 66, 560
Minitab instructions, 67
Multiple regression, 640
Quality, 807
Summary steps, 68
Uses, 70
Seasonal component
Defined, 685–686
Seasonal index
Adjustment process steps, 712–720
Computing, 713–716
Defined, 713
Deseasonalization, 716–718, 735
Dummy variables, 718–720
Excel example, 686, 717–718
Minitab instructions, 717
Multiplicative model, 718
Normalize, 716
Ratio-to-moving-average, 714–716
Selection bias, 12
Selection bias, 12
Serial correlation, 702
Significance level
Critical values and, 341–342
Defined, 342
Significance tests, 580–588
Correlation, 562–564
Simple index number
Equation, 688–689
Simple linear regression
Assumptions, 570
Defined, 570
Equations, 570
Least squares criterion, 572, 573
Summary steps, 587
Simple random sample, 16
Defined, 257
Skewed data
Defined, 88
Left-skewed, 88
Right-skewed, 88
Standard deviation, 107–110
Binomial distribution, 198–199
c-charts, 798
Defined, 104
Discrete probability distribution, 185–186
Discrete random variable, 185–186
Excel example, 109–110, 121
Minitab instructions, 110, 121
Paired differences, 412
Poisson distribution, 208
Population standard deviation equation, 106
Population variance equation, 105
Regression model, 623–625
Sample equation, 107
Summary steps, 106
Uniform distribution, 242
U-statistics, 752, 769
Wilcoxon, 756

Standard error
Defined, 297
Difference between two means, 387, 428
Proportion, 321
Sampling distribution of a proportion, 282
Statistical process control, 788, 797
Standard error of regression slope
Equation, 584
Graphed, 586
Standard error of the estimate
Equation, 584
Multiple regression equation, 624
Standardized data values, 117–118
Population equation, 117
Sample data, 117
Summary steps, 118
Standardized residuals
Equation, 669, 676
Standard normal distribution, 226–236
Table, 228–230
States of nature, 340
Statistic, 82
Statistical inference procedures, 5
Statistical inference tools
Nonstatistical sampling, 15
Statistical sampling techniques, 16
Statistical process control, 774–792
Average subgroup means, 779, 797
Average subgroup range, 779, 797
c-charts, 789–792
Control limits, 780–783, 788, 790, 797
Excel examples, 778, 783
Mean subgroup proportion, 786, 787
Minitab instructions, 783
p-charts, 786–789
R-charts, 778–786
Signals, 783
Stability, 810
Standard deviation, 790
Standard error, 788, 797
Summary steps, 791
Variation, 775–776, 808–810
$\bar{x}$ charts, 778–786
Statistical sampling
Cluster sampling, 18–19
Simple random sampling, 16
Stratified random sampling, 17–18
Systematic random sampling, 18
Statistical sampling technique, 15
Statistics, 15
Defined, 82
Stem and leaf diagrams, 59–60
Summary steps, 59
Stepwise regression, 654–661
Backward elimination, 655–658
Best subsets, 659–661
Forward selection, 654–655
Standard, 658
Stratified random sampling, 17–18
Student's t-distribution, 304–310
Subjective probability assessment
Defined, 149

Sum of squares, partitioning, 464–465, 484
Sum of squares between
    Equation, 468, 506
Sum of squares blocking
    Equation, 484, 506
Sum of squares error
    Equation, 484–485, 574, 575, 580, 605
    Interaction, 649–650
Sum of squares regression
    Equation, 581
Sum of squares within
    Equation, 468, 484–485, 506
Symmetric Data, 88–89
Systematic random sampling, 18

T

Tchebysheff's Theorem, 116–117
t-distribution
    assumptions, 305, 401
    defined, 304
    degrees of freedom, 304–305
    equation, 305
    table, 306
    two means, 390–394
    unequal variances, 393–394
Telephone surveys, 7, 8–9
Test statistic
    Chi-square goodness-of-fit, 533
    Correlation coefficient, 564, 583
    Defined, 344
    Partial F-test, 648–649
    R-squared, 582
    t-test, 351–355, 401, 415
    Wilcoxon, 757
    z-test, 344, 398–400
Time-series data
    Aggregate price indexes, 689–690
    Components, 684–687
    Consumer price index, 693–694
    Defined, 21
    Deseasonalization, 717, 735
    Index numbers, 687–689, 693–695
    Laspeyres index, 692–693, 735
    Linear trend, 685
    Nonlinear trend, 708–712
    Paasche index, 691–692, 735
    Producer price index, 694
    Random component, 687
    Seasonal component, 712–720
    Trend, 697–712
Total quality management
    Defined, 805
Total sum of squares
    Equation, 464, 467, 580, 605
Total variation
    Defined, 464
Tree diagrams, 142–143, 163–164
Trend
    Defined, 685
    Excel example, 686, 697–698, 699–700, 701–702, 726
    Forecasting technique, 697–720
    Linear, 697–700, 698, 735
    Minitab instructions, 698, 699–700

    Nonlinear, 708–712
    Quality chart, 807
t-test statistic
    assumption, 351
    Correlation coefficient, 565, 638
    equation, 351, 377, 401, 415, 429
    paired samples, 415–416, 429
    Population variances unknown and not assumed equal, 407, 429
    Regression coefficient significance, 623, 676
Tukey-Kramer multiple comparisons, 473–478
    Critical range equation, 506
    Equation, 474
    Excel example, 476–478
    Minitab instructions, 477
Two-factor ANOVA, 494–501
    Assumptions, 497
    Equations, 497, 506
    Excel example, 495–501
    Interaction, 498–501
    Minitab, 500
    Partitioning sum of squares, 495–496, 506
    Replications, 494–501
    Table, 496
Two-tailed hypothesis test
    Calculating beta, 369–370
    Defined, 348
    Population variance, 440–441
    p-value, 349–351
    summary steps, 349
Type I error, 341
    Defined, 340
Type II error, 341
    Calculating beta, 365–367
    Defined, 340

U

Unbiased estimator, 267
Uniform probability distribution
    Density function, 240–241
    Mean, 242
    Standard deviation, 242
Unweighted aggregate price index
    Equation, 689–690, 735

V

Validity
    External, 13
    Internal, 13
Variable
    Dependent, 66
    Independent, 66
Variance
    Defined, 104
    F-test statistic, 446
    Population variance equation, 105
    Sample equation, 107, 446, 448
    Sample shortcut equation, 107
    Shortcut equation, 105
    Summary steps, 106
Variance inflation factor
    Equation, 626, 676
    Excel example, 626–627
    Minitab instructions, 627

Variation, 102–110, 808
  Components, 776
  Defined, 102
  Excel sample, 109–110
  Minitab sample, 110
  Normal Distribution, 776
  Sources, 775
  Types, 776

W

Weighted aggregate price index, 690–693
  Laspeyres index, 692–693, 735
  Paasche index, 691–692, 735
Weighted Mean
  Defined, 92
  Population equation, 92
  Sample equation, 93
Wilcoxon matched-pairs signed rank, 754–756
  Assumptions, 754
  Large sample test, 756–757
  Test statistic, 757, 769
  Ties, 756
Wilcoxon signed rank test, 744–747
  Equation, 769
  Hypotheses, 744
  Large sample test statistic, 745
  Minitab instructions, 773
  Steps, 744–745
Within-sample variation
  Defined, 464
Written questionnaires, 7, 9–11
  Steps, 9–11

Z

z-scores
  Finite population correction, 271
  Sampling distribution of mean, 271
  Sampling distribution of p, 283
  Standardized, 227
  Standard normal distribution, 237, 245
z-test statistic
  Defined, 344
  Equation, difference between population proportions, 421
  Equation, proportion, 360, 377
  Equation, sigma known, 344, 377
  Equation, two means, 398, 428
  Equation, two proportions, 421, 429
  Independent samples, 398

Values of t for Selected Probabilities

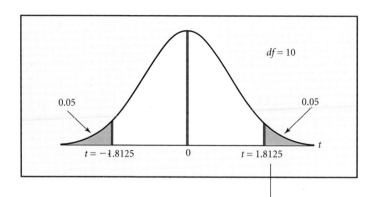

Probabilites (Or Areas Under t-Distribution Curve)

Conf. Level One Tail Two Tails	0.1 0.45 0.9	0.3 0.35 0.7	0.5 0.25 0.5	0.7 0.15 0.3	0.8 0.1 0.2	0.9 0.05 0.1	0.95 0.025 0.05	0.98 0.01 0.02	0.99 0.005 0.01
d. f.					Values of t				
1	0.1584	0.5095	1.0000	1.9626	3.0777	6.3137	12.7062	31.8210	63.6559
2	0.1421	0.4447	0.8165	1.3862	1.8856	2.9200	4.3027	6.9645	9.9250
3	0.1366	0.4242	0.7649	1.2498	1.6377	2.3534	3.1824	4.5407	5.8408
4	0.1338	0.4142	0.7407	1.1896	1.5332	2.1318	2.7765	3.7469	4.6041
5	0.1322	0.4082	0.7267	1.1558	1.4759	2.0150	2.5706	3.3649	4.0321
6	0.1311	0.4043	0.7176	1.1342	1.4398	1.9432	2.4469	3.1427	3.7074
7	0.1303	0.4015	0.7111	1.1192	1.4149	1.8946	2.3646	2.9979	3.4995
8	0.1297	0.3995	0.7064	1.1081	1.3968	1.8595	2.3060	2.8965	3.3554
9	0.1293	0.3979	0.7027	1.0997	1.3830	1.8331	2.2622	2.8214	3.2498
10	0.1289	0.3966	0.6998	1.0931	1.3722	1.8125 ◄	2.2281	2.7638	3.1693
11	0.1286	0.3956	0.6974	1.0877	1.3634	1.7959	2.2010	2.7181	3.1058
12	0.1283	0.3947	0.6955	1.0832	1.3562	1.7823	2.1788	2.6810	3.0545
13	0.1281	0.3940	0.6938	1.0795	1.3502	1.7709	2.1604	2.6503	3.0123
14	0.1280	0.3933	0.6924	1.0763	1.3450	1.7613	2.1448	2.6245	2.9768
15	0.1278	0.3928	0.6912	1.0735	1.3406	1.7531	2.1315	2.6025	2.9467
16	0.1277	0.3923	0.6901	1.0711	1.3368	1.7459	2.1199	2.5835	2.9208
17	0.1276	0.3919	0.6892	1.0690	1.3334	1.7396	2.1098	2.5669	2.8982
18	0.1274	0.3915	0.6884	1.0672	1.3304	1.7341	2.1009	2.5524	2.8784
19	0.1274	0.3912	0.6876	1.0655	1.3277	1.7291	2.0930	2.5395	2.8609
20	0.1273	0.3909	0.6870	1.0640	1.3253	1.7247	2.0860	2.5280	2.8453
21	0.1272	0.3906	0.6864	1.0627	1.3232	1.7207	2.0796	2.5176	2.8314
22	0.1271	0.3904	0.6858	1.0614	1.3212	1.7171	2.0739	2.5083	2.8188
23	0.1271	0.3902	0.6853	1.0603	1.3195	1.7139	2.0687	2.4999	2.8073
24	0.1270	0.3900	0.6848	1.0593	1.3178	1.7109	2.0639	2.4922	2.7970
25	0.1269	0.3898	0.6844	1.0584	1.3163	1.7081	2.0595	2.4851	2.7874
26	0.1269	0.3896	0.6840	1.0575	1.3150	1.7056	2.0555	2.4786	2.7787
27	0.1268	0.3894	0.6837	1.0567	1.3137	1.7033	2.0518	2.4727	2.7707
28	0.1268	0.3893	0.6834	1.0560	1.3125	1.7011	2.0484	2.4671	2.7633
29	0.1268	0.3892	0.6830	1.0553	1.3114	1.6991	2.0452	2.4620	2.7564
30	0.1267	0.3890	0.6828	1.0547	1.3104	1.6973	2.0423	2.4573	2.7500
40	0.1265	0.3881	0.6807	1.0500	1.3031	1.6839	2.0211	2.4233	2.7045
50	0.1263	0.3875	0.6794	1.0473	1.2987	1.6759	2.0086	2.4033	2.6778
60	0.1262	0.3872	0.6786	1.0455	1.2958	1.6706	2.0003	2.3901	2.6603
70	0.1261	0.3869	0.6780	1.0442	1.2938	1.6669	1.9944	2.3808	2.6479
80	0.1261	0.3867	0.6776	1.0432	1.2922	1.6641	1.9901	2.3739	2.6387
90	0.1260	0.3866	0.6772	1.0424	1.2910	1.6620	1.9867	2.3685	2.6316
100	0.1260	0.3864	0.6770	1.0418	1.2901	1.6602	1.9840	2.3642	2.6259
250	0.1258	0.3858	0.6755	1.0386	1.2849	1.6510	1.9695	2.3414	2.5956
500	0.1257	0.3855	0.6750	1.0375	1.2832	1.6479	1.9647	2.3338	2.5857
∞	0.1257	0.3853	0.6745	1.0364	1.2816	1.6449	1.9600	2.3263	2.5758